Jewish Writings
of the Second Temple Period

Compendia Rerum Iudaicarum ad Novum Testamentum

SECTION TWO

THE LITERATURE OF THE JEWISH PEOPLE
IN THE PERIOD OF THE SECOND TEMPLE AND THE TALMUD

IN THREE VOLUMES

I. MIQRA. Reading, Translation and Interpretation of the Hebrew Bible in
Ancient Judaism and Early Christianity
Editor: M. J. Mulder

II. JEWISH WRITINGS OF THE SECOND TEMPLE PERIOD. Apocrypha,
Pseudepigrapha, Qumran Sectarian Writings, Philo, Josephus
Editor: M. E. Stone

III. THE LITERATURE OF THE SAGES. Midrash, Mishnah, Talmud
Editor: S. Safrai

Advisory Editors:
Y. Aschkenasy, D. Flusser, J. Goldin, H. Kremers, Th. C. de Kruyf, R. Le
Déaut, G. W. MacRae, K. Stendahl, S. Talmon, E. Tov

Executive Editors:
W. J. Burgers, H. Sysling, P. J. Tomson

Published under the Auspices of the
Foundation Compendia Rerum Iudaicarum ad Novum Testamentum,
Amsterdam

Jewish Writings of the Second Temple Period

Apocrypha, Pseudepigrapha, Qumran Sectarian
Writings, Philo, Josephus

Edited by Michael E. Stone

1984
Van Gorcum, Assen
Fortress Press, Philadelphia

CIP-gegevens

Jewish

Jewish Writings of the Second Temple Period: Apocrypha, Pseudepigrapha, Qumran Sectarian Writings, Philo, Josephus / ed. by Michael E. Stone. — Assen : Van Gorcum — (Compendia Rerum Iudaicarum ad Novum Testamentum. Section Two: The Literature of the Jewish People in het Period of the Second Temple and the Talmud; vol. 2) Met bibliogr., index.
SISO 213 UDC 892.4(091):296.1
Trefw.: joodse godsdienst; literatuurgeschiedenis.

ISBN 90 232 2036 6 geb.
LC 83-48926

LIBRARY OF CONGRESS CATALOGING IN PUBLICATION DATA

Main entry under title:

Jewish Writings of the Second Temple Period.

(The Literature of the Jewish People in the Period of the Second Temple and the Talmud; 2) (Compendia Rerum Iudaicarum ad Novum Testamentum; section 2)
    Bibliography: p. 603
    Includes index.
    1. Religious literature, Jewish-History and criticism. I. Stone, Michael E., 1938—   . II.
    Series.
BM485.L57 vol. 2   296.1 s [296.1]   83—48926
ISBN 0—8006—0603—5 (U.S.)

Printed in The Netherlands by Van Gorcum, Assen

Foreword

The first section of *Compendia* was published in two volumes in 1974 and 1976. At that time it could not be foreseen that the preparation of the next section would take so many years, that only now a first part appears in print. The *Compendia* project is based on teamwork, which necessarily involves a great deal of consultation and discussion. At an advanced stage of preparation it became evident that the original plan was too narrow for an adequate treatment of the sources. In 1979 a new outline was prepared, providing for a three volume work instead of the original two, and a fresh team of editors was engaged to complete the work. The present volume is the first fruit of this undertaking and it is expected that the remaining two volumes will appear within two years.

It is an honourable duty for the *Compendia* Foundation to acknowledge all scholars who have given their contributions to the realization of the second section. First of all, we mention M. de Jonge, who very skilfully and energetically directed the editorial procedure in the first stage of the project and unselfishly cooperated in the move towards its final form. The basic outline of the section we owe to R. Le Déaut, whose great sensitivity to both the Jewish and Christian dimensions of the project substantially influenced the actual scope of the work. S. Sandmel was a full member of the editorial team of our section till 1970, when he resigned after his appointment as editor-in-chief of HUCA. His inspiring cooperation was very much appreciated and with deep sorrow we received the tidings of his sudden death in 1979. He was succeeded by G. Vermes, who resigned in 1974 because of other commitments, among them the heavy burden of the new edition of Schürer's *History of the Jewish People*. We also mention with gratitude the name of B. S. Jackson, who was a skilful and careful editor from 1972-1978.

The list of our acknowledgements is rather long, due to the extended editorial history of our section and we refrain from mentioning all the present members of the editorial board; their names appear on the title page of the present book. Some exceptions should, however, be allowed. We wish to mention with gratitude S. Safrai, who has guided the *Compendia* project from the beginning, was one of the chief editors of the

V

first section and signed for the volume in preparatation on the Literature of the Sages. We feel also much obliged to M. E. Stone, who was first engaged as an author and at a critical stage of the projected accepted full editorial responsibility for the present volume, taking an active part in the revision of its outline. Full and continuous assistance was provided in the preparation of the volume by the Foundation's executive editors W. J. Burgers and P. J. Tomson. We finally express our sincere thanks to the authors, who have shown a great deal of patience and understanding during the long history of the book.

We use this occasion to pay tribute to the memory of W. C. van Unnik, who died in March 1978. Van Unnik has shown great interest in the *Compendia* project from its start in 1967 and took part in many editorial meetings. He read all the contributions in the first section before printing and many of his comments found their way into the printed text. It is very regrettable that we had to miss him as reader in the preparation of the present volume. As early as 1947, in his inaugural lecture held at the University of Utrecht, Van Unnik expressed the view that early Christianity could be fully understood only in the context of Judaism: 'Jesus and Paul have after birth not been carried around the hearth, but they have been circumcised on the eight day and they lived accordingly.' It is this view which guided the *Compendia* project.

The *Compendia* Foundation deeply regrets the passing away of two of its members, C. A. Rijk and A. C. Ramselaar, who both fostered the Jewish-Christian dialogue in the Roman Catholic Church. Rijk was a member of the founding committee of the *Compendia* project, whereas Ramselaar was an active member of the Foundation from 1969 until his death in 1982. May their memory be a blessing for all who follow their steps on the road of brotherhood and peace between Jews and Christians. H. van Praag, who initiated the *Compendia* and has been president of the Foundation since its start in 1967, handed over the chairmanship to R. A. Levisson in Januari 1984.

J. van Goudoever,
Secretary of the Compendia Foundation.

Editor's Preface

The production of this volume has drawn upon the talents and energies of many. The Editor wishes to express his thanks in particular to those authors who so patiently bore with his new dicisions, who agreed to revise, sometimes to rewrite, articles and sections of articles, and to all the authors without whose writing and generous participation the volume could not have come into being.

A good deal of the intensive work of this volume was carried out while the Editor was Fellow-in-Residence of the Netherlands Institute for Advanced Study in the Humanities in 1980-81. His gratitude is expressed to the NIAS for the opportunities that year offered him.

M. E. Stone

Acknowledgements

The contribution by M. Gilbert was translated from the French by K. Smyth, who also did a stylistic revision of the articles by P. Borgen and D. Flusser. Much retyping has been done by Mss. C. A. Jaffe, I. M. C. Oey and M. A. Threlfall. The indices were prepared by H. Sysling.

The following translations have been used: *Revised Standard Version,* including the Apocrypha; *The Nag Hammadi Library in English,* ed. J. M. Robinson; *The Dead Sea Scrolls in English,* by G. Vermes; *The Pseudepigrapha of the O.T.,* ed. by R. H. Charles.

The Editors gratefully acknowledge the Loeb Classical Library (Harvard University Press: W. Heinemann Ltd.) for its permission to use its translations of Philo and Josephus. Fortress Press of Philadelphia is acknowledged for allowing use of parts of Nickelsburg, *Jewish Literature* for the preparation of chapters 2 and 3. Doubleday and Co, and J. H. Charlesworth graciously gave pre-publication access to *The Old Testament Pseudepigrapha* to some of the authors.

Contents

Introduction

Michael E. Stone

From its inception, *Compendia Rerum Iudaicarum ad Novum Testamentum* has been a joint Jewish and Christian endeavour. This is worth considering, for it is essential to the understanding of the project of which the present volume is part. It was not just to advance the cause of mutual understanding by general contacts and interchanges, essential as that aim is; the endeavour had to be jointly Jewish and Christian because learning about this period has developed essentially in two separate (and not always equal) streams.[1]

The implications are far-reaching for the study of history.[2] 'The understanding and view that we have of Jewish history of the age of the Second Temple are conditioned by these two main factors — the presuppositions of historiography and the character of the sources ... Clearly, the nature of the sourves which have been transmitted in both the Jewish and Christian traditions has been determined by the particular varieties of Judaism and Christianity which became "orthodox", or in other words, which became dominant and survived ... The material they preserved ... is that which was acceptable through the filter of orthodoxy.'[3] In other words, which material actually survived was determined by these two separate later traditions and their tendencies. Moreover, the influence of the later 'orthodoxies' was even more pervasive than this, for they determined not only what range of material survived, but also what parts of it were studied by scholars and what questions they posed to it. Jewish scholars tended on the whole to search for documents with resonances in classical rabbinic literarture or, at least, not contrary to it. Christian scholars sought material that illuminated the background of the New Testament, and what is more, some of them highlighted material that could be interpreted to justify their pejorative theological attitudes towards Judaism.

Recently, the distortions caused by theological *tendenz* have again been forcefully set forth by E. P. Sanders, echoing at many points the late George Foot Moore's strictures, half-a-century old. Sanders expounded

---

[1] Cf. *Compendia* I/1, p. x.
[2] Stone, *Scriptures, Sects and Visions*, p. 49-51.
[3] *Ibid.* 53.

the influence of theological prejudices of the most baseless kind on main streams of New Testament scholarship; they repeatedly led to acceptance of images of Judaism which responsible scholars had shown to be severely flawed and even false.[4] Apart from the fostering of anti-semitism, such distorted images of Judaism produced a distorted description of Christianity which issued from Judaism. The formulation of descriptions of Judaism, as indeed the evaluation of such descriptions, is a task within the historian's bailiwick, but naturally the description accepted by exegetes profoundly influences their interpretation of the New Testament.

The historical task should not be confused with the exegetical one, and the historical realities demand that the New Testament be viewed in the overall context of Judaism as well as in the light of the Church that sprang from it. It is to the former aspect of the historical task that the editor hopes that this volume will make a contribution,[5] for its aim is to present as balanced a picture as possible of the literary evidence for the description of Judaism. An honest rapprochement between Jewish and Christian scholarly traditions is an essential precondition of this. The desire to use as wide a range of evidence as possible and make it available to the reader also requires this cooperation, for Jewish and Christian scholarly traditions have developed diffedrent fields of expertise and different scholarly emphases.[6] Such a rapprochement will bear fruit first and foremost for the scholarly task. Moreover, in the final analysis it will also enhance the mutual respect and understanding of these two religious traditions.

Naturally, the general character of the *Compendia Rerum Iudaicarum ad Novum Testamentum* has determined the approach of the Editor in setting the policy for this volume. One sustained interest and concern which is expressed in all the articles, is that they should embody the results or critical, objective scholarship. Not only this, but they are written and edited with a consciousness of the scholarly discussion of the issues involved and its development. Furthermore, particular emphasis has been placed on showing the relationships between the various types of literature and themes included within the volume and other bodies of contemporary Jewish and Christian literature, as well as their biblical sources and rabbinic implications. These latter aspects are, of course, to form the subject matter of other volumes of this section (see below). Nonetheless, interlocking ideas, themes and literary forms have been highlighted even at the risk of some repetitiveness, since it is the basic perception of the volume that the literature it describes must be viewed in its broader context. Divisions had to be made between the various volumes of this literature

---

[4] Sanders, *Paul and Palestinian Judaism*, especially 1-58; Moore, 'Christian Writers'.
[5] See Stone *ibid.* 53-55 for detailed development of these views.
[6] By the preceding we do not intend to condemn, of course, all previous scholars and the complete tradition of learning developed over the past centuries. Nonetheless, the attitudes noted have been predominant enough to foster the most grave imbalances of presentation.

section of the *Compendia* and between the chapters of the present book themselves. To offset the impression created by this physical separation into chapters and volumes, a constant consciousness has been cultivated of relationships between the different documents and bodies of literature.

Since the literature is regarded as very much the product of groups and individuals within Jewish society of the time, it is our conviction that it cannot be properly understood without consideration of this aspect of its origins and of its purpose and function. Consequently, the volume has been provided with a historical introduction, not designed to replace the first section of *Compendia Rerum Iudaicarum ad Novum Testamentum,* which was devoted to the political and economic history of the period, but to set the stage for the chapters on literature that follow. A sustained interest in contexts of origin, in use and function has been maintained.[7]

The volume presents the literary production of Judaism in the period of the Second Temple, with the exclusion of the Bible on the one hand, and rabbinic literature on the other. In the text, the emphasis has been on producing a readable, balanced exposition which avoids the use of technical jargon, of untranslated ancient languages and of unnecessarily detailed catalogues of scholarly views and disputes. The aim is to produce a text which is available to the non-specialist, yet not tautological to the scholar. Access to the scholarly literature is provided by footnotes, by the annotated bibliography, and by the complete bibliographical list at the end of the volume. This provides both a key to abbreviations and an extended bibliography of the subject matter. Furthermore, this volume, like the others in this section of *Compendia,* is provided with its own indexes.

The volume is one of a projected three, and the two others of this section of *Compendia* will deal respectively with rabbinic literature and with the Bible as interpreted and understood in this period. The division into volumes is in a certain sense artificial like any other division, and so an impediment to understanding. The division that was finally accepted, after the most painful consideration, in part reflects the transmission of the documents. The volume on rabbinic literature comprises material relevant to the history of Jewish literature and thought transmitted within the Jewish tradition and in Semitic languages. The present volume includes material that was not transmitted by Jewish tradition. Part was preserved by the various Christian churches and part was uncovered by archaeological chance. The Bible volume, however, centres around the theme of how Sacred Scripture evolved, developed, and was used and regarded, draws on Jewish and Christian transmissions equally. This is, of

---

[7] Naturally, the extent to which the author of any particular chapter responded to this type of question or to other similar ones, depends in part on the nature of the literature and in part on his own predilections. The editor provided direction and orientation, but of course the authors wrote their own articles.

course, natural enough since the Bible is the common basis on which both traditions built.

Chronologically, the present volume comprises Jewish literature that was written after the Bible and is not rabbinic literature. Some of it, in fact, was written before the form of some of the biblical books we have preserved. So, parts of *1 Enoch* are certainly older than the visions of Daniel 7-12 and this is also true of Ben Sira. At the other end of the chronological spectrum, some of the books are later in date than parts of the Mishnah and other rabbinic traditions. Here the *Apocalypse of Abraham* may be mentioned as an example, a book probably written in the mid-second century C.E.

Most chapters of the book are organized by literary types; we hesitate to say simply 'genres' for, although that may be true of chapters on Apocalyptic Literature, Testaments or Prayers, it is surely not true of the chapters on historiography or on narrative literature. Dividing the literature by historical or social context was not consistently feasible. On the one hand, the Qumran sectarian writings do form a cohesive group as far as context of origin, date, character, theological and conceptual language and so forth are concerned. Consequently, it was possible to set them together in a single chapter and to pay due attention to their historical background. The same is true for the writings or Philo and Josephus. On the other hand, however, most of the Apocrypha and Pseudopigrapha exist in a sort of limbo in which our knowledge of their context of origin, the groups that wrote them, and the way in which they were used remains within the realm of imagination or at best of informed guess.

In this matter are implicit both the importance and the difficulty of the study of the Apocrypha, the Pseudepigrapha and the other literature dealt with in this volume. A great range of types of religious thought, cultural orientation, language of origin and apparently of context of origin are represented, yet, in spite of the plethora of documents, little is known of their actual socio-religious matrices or transmission.

The vast majority of the works handled in this volume are of literary types older than or different from those produced by the Rabbis. They all stem from the period between the Persian hegemony and the generation following the destruction of the Temple. They were all, with the exception of the Dead Sea scrolls and part of Ben Sira, transmitted to us only through the Christian churches. These features combine with the absence from rabbinic sources not just of these literary types, but even of basic aspects of the traditions contained in these writings, to indicate that they were most likely created and cultivated in circles or groups that were not 'proto-rabbinic'; or else that the sorts of literature and traditions that they preserved were later rejected (or at the very least neglected) by the Sages.[8]

_____

[8] One, fairly extreme approach to this is that of L. Ginzberg, 'The Attitude of the Synagogue to

In general, the explanations that seek to attribute this change in Jewish literary modes to rabbinic reaction against eschatological writing are not adequate in themselves, since they do not account for the lack of works of narrative or sapiential character from rabbinic tradition. Nor do theories highlighting the sectarian character of some works, such as *1 Enoch,* account for the neglect of other doctrinally unexceptional writings like Judith of the Epistle of Jeremiah. Nor does the language of composition play a major role, for most of the writings were written in Hebrew or Aramaic, not in Greek.

It is very likely the case, then, that there is no simple or single explanation of the non-transmission of much of this literature by the Sages. Certain of these factors may have led to the suppression of some of the works, but others, like Ben Sira, were known among the Sages (at least in a *florilegium*) and were positively regarded.

When the Apocrypha and Pseudepigrapha are compared with rabbinic literature, one is struck by the radical change in literary genres. None of the apocryphal and pseudepigraphical books written in Hebrew or Aramaic was composed as biblical exegesis citing and expounding verses. In contrast, the tie to the actual biblical text and its exposition lies very close to the heart of rabbinic creativity. On the whole, then, these writings show a different attitude to scriptural authority to that held by the Sages.

This too may be part of the explanation of the very complex phenomenon of pseudepigraphy. Not only are the books of the Apocrypha and Pseudepigrapha written without direct reference to the biblical text, they are mostly also attributed to figures from the time of the Bible. It seems likely that the two phenomena are interrelated and determined by a specific attitude to scriptural authority.[9] This is an essential factor for understanding the literature of the period.

Two further observations must be made on this point. The first is that the particular constellation of attitudes to authority and inspiration in the circles of the Qumran sect, and reflected therefore in their writings, differs from both of the above. The *peshers* and certain other Qumran documents are commentary on the Bible. Yet, the nature of the *pesher* which reveals, as the *Habakkuk Pesher* tels us, the meaning which even the prophets knew not when they spoke their words, indicates that the sect cultivated a particular sort of pneumatically inspired exegesis. The form of the *Temple Scroll* as a pseudepigraphon of God, paraphrasing and often changing the actual wording of the law of the Pentateuch, is another, striking indi-

---

Apocalyptic-Eschatological Writings,' *JBL* 41 (1922) 115-36; see further below, chap. 10. Wherever possible in this book, the relationship of the literature discussed with rabbinic traditions has been underlined.

[9] There is a sensitive analysis of aspects of this issue in Heinemann, *Darkei Ha-Aggada*, p. 177; see also below, chap. 10, pp. 427-33; chap. 3, pp. 100-101. This matter will be explored more fully in the volume on *Miqra.*

cator of a dominant, particular Essene self-understanding, different both from the Rabbis and from the vast body of the Apocrypha and Pseudepigrapha.

As far as Philo is concerned, he does present most of his writing in the form of biblical commentary. He had his forerunners in Jewish Hellenistic milieux, and the question of the *Sitz im Leben* of the various types of exegesis he uses is much discussed in scholarly circles. If it has a synagogal connection, it is to that extent like the midrashic homilies that were designed around the weekly Torah readings, although these can certainly not be traced back as far as Philo's time. Yet, with all that, the modes and style of his exegetical endeavour differ from those of the Rabbis and are obviously influenced by Hellenistic scholarship.

Indeed, there is no doubt about the influence of Hellenistic culture on the whole range of Jewish creativity in our period.[10] This is most evident in the writings produced in Greek by the Jews in the Diaspora. Philo's corpus has already been mentioned. Josephus too wrote his histories according to Greek historiographic norms rather than the biblical patterns used by, say, 1 Maccabees. Other Jewish Greek historians did the same, not to mention rhetors like the author of 4 Maccabees, or poets like Ezekiel the Tragedian and Pseudo-Phocylides. Sadly, much of this literature survives only in small fragments. In our treatment the fragments have generally been integrated into the chapters where they belong on grounds of content or general character.

The writings discussed in this volume indicate an extraordinary wealth and variety of Jewish religious and literary creativity in a very crucial period — that from which both rabbinic Judaism and Christianity issued. It is of intrinsic interest for the historian of Judaism to draw as full and detailed a picture he can of the varieties of Jewish life and creativity in that age. For it appears that, subsequently to it, many of these varieties disappeared or became subterranean. Moreover, in order truly to set the stage for the understanding of the New Testament, to compose a work *ad Novum Testamentum,* we need to enter the perspective of the age in which Christianity, and for that matter rabbinic Judaism, emerged. The primary means of entering into that perspective is the attentive study of the literary production of the era. That is done, we hope, in this volume. But not just the study of the literature is needed; it must be placed in context, both social and religious. This task has constantly been before the editor and the authors and if we have not always succeeded in it, it is for lack of information needed to make balanced judgements. Yet a perception of the

---

[10] The extent and character of this influence are, of course, much debated. Although not all of his conlusions are universally accepted, the magistral work of Martin Hengel states the case strongly for the period down to the Maccabean revolt: *Judaism and Hellenism.* The books by the late Saul Lieberman, *Greek in Jewish Palestine* and *Hellenism in Jewish Palestine* are rich contributions to a later period. The other literature is extensive.

variety, creativity, complexity and wealth of this era of Jewish religious life and of the literary production that issued from it, is the most striking result of the study undertaken here. It is our aspiration that it will exemplify a way of looking at *Res Iudaicae ad Novum Testamentum* that is organic, coherent and open.

Chapter One

The Historical Background

Isaiah Gafni

Introduction

The conquests of Alexander the Great ushered in a new era in the political and cultural history of the Near East.[1] In their wake, both the Jews of Judaea and their brethren in a rapidly expanding diaspora were subjected to radical forces of social and cultural change. These changes, effected by the introduction of Greek culture into the lands of the Near East that led to the emergence of the phenomenon commonly known as Hellenism,[1a] greatly transcended the purely political vicissitudes that were destined to envelop this part of the inhabited world.[2] Moreover, the perception of Alexander's military success as a major crossroads in the history of the region is not merely the product of modern historiographical hindsight, but apparently was already felt by Jews and non-Jews who experienced first-hand the far-reaching impact of the Greek conquest of, and assimilation into the East. Thus, for example, when the late second century B.C.E. author of 1 Maccabees set out to record the events leading up to the Hasmonean uprising, as well as that family's emergence as the central Judaean authority, he chose to introduce the events of 175-135 B.C.E. with a preamble describing — however erroneously — what came to pass 'after Alexander of Macedon, son of Philip . . . had completely defeated Darius, King of the Persians and the Medes'.[3]

The impact of Hellenism, and the reactions to that cultural phe-

---

[1] This article mainly covers Jewish history in Palestine. For the Diaspora see the first section of *Compendia*, especially chapters 3, 8, 9 and 13. For the use of Greek by Jewish authors see *ibid.*, chapter 22.

[1a] The earliest modern use of the term Hellenism is commonly attributed to Johann Gustav Droysen (1808-1884). It is noteworthy, however, that the term *Hellenismos* used to describe this particular manifestation of Greek culture and religion, was first employed by the author of 2 Maccabees (e.g. 4:13); similarly, he is the first known author to use the term *Ioudaismos* as signifying the religion of the Jewish people (e.g. 2 Macc 2:21). Cf. also Amir, 'Ioudaismos.'

[2] For a succinct overview of the period see Tarn-Griffith, *Hellenistic Civilization*; a highly readable account of Hellenistic culture is provided by Hadas, *Hellenistic Culture.*

[3] Such scene-setting preambles are commmon in biblical narrative, and the opening of 1 Maccabees is yet a further example of the author's conscious recourse to biblical style; cf. Goldstein, *I Maccabees*, 190-1. For the unsubstantiated claim that Alexander divided his kingdom among his officers while still alive (1 Macc 1:6) cf. Goldstein, 197.

nomenon, is one of the factors that left their mark on much of the literary activity of the Jewish people, during the period of the Second Temple as well as in the immediate aftermath of its destruction (70 C.E.). Indeed, this activity, which serves as the focus of the present volume, must be seen in the perspective of the ongoing interaction between political events, religious tendencies, and influences resulting from contacts between Jews and a variety of non-Jewish ethnic and social groups.[3a]

One of the striking features of Second Temple history is the fact that most Jews, not only in the Diaspora but in Palestine as well, never experienced complete Jewish sovereignty. The following chronological chart, listing the various rulers and regimes in Second Temple Palestine, clearly attests to this fact:

536-332 B.C.E. — The Persian Period
332-167 B.C.E. — The Hellenistic Period
167-141 B.C.E. — The Hasmonean Uprising
141- 63 B.C.E. — The Hasmonean State
63 B.C.E.-70 C.E. — Roman Rule (in varying stages and forms)

In a period of 600 years, only the approximately 80 years of Hasmonean statehood can be fairly categorized as a period of Jewish sovereignty, which even during this period was frequently of a very tenuous nature. This observation, however, reflects a modern value system, and one may ask whether the quest for national independence was uppermost in the minds of Jews throughout much of the Second Temple period. A closer look may reveal the dominant role religious interests played in this period.

Indeed, beginning with the edict of Cyrus itself (538 B.C.E.), the focus of Judaean restoration was around the Temple; the disappearance from the sources of any Davidic heir after Zerubbabel probably also reflects the dashing of any hopes for immediate restoration of the monarchy. If one perceives a national consolidation under Ezra and Nehemiah, this nevertheless was largely in the nature of a religious revival, and the reforms instituted by both leaders — cessation of intermarriage, enforcement of tithes and enhanced sanctification of the Sabbath — all place a stress on this revitalization of the Jewish religious community.

While the Hasmonean revolt was the first of a series of Jewish uprisings all linked to the establishment of Jewish hegemony in Jerusalem and throughout Judaea, it is equally true that all these uprisings were linked to some infraction of Jewish religious practice. Whether these took the form of outright religious persecution, as was the case under Antiochus IV Epiphanes, or whether the ideology of the rebels equated political subju-

---

[3a] In this article we do not touch on the question of languages used in Palestine. See for this matter *Compendia*, Section I, chapters 21 and 22.

gation with religious infidelity,[4] it was a real or perceived interference with Jewish religion and ritual that — more than any other single factor — could induce large numbers of Jews to take up arms, or not to defend themselves and sacrifice their lives. Religious commitment, while not always commensurate with the degree of practice maintained by all Jews throughout the period under discussion, nevertheless seems to emerge as a constant factor in Jewish society, regardless of the nature of political rule at any given time or place. This circumstance not only helps to explain the ongoing tensions between Jews and non-Jews, in Palestine as well as much of the diaspora, but also accounts for the passion displayed by various segments of the Jewish population in their disputes with other Jews.

The phenomenon of sectarianism might well be considered another outstanding feature of this particular stage of Jewish development. Much of the spiritual ferment and of the ensuing literary activity of the Second Temple period owes its proliferation to these divisions within Jewish society. This fact becomes all the more pronounced in light of subsequent rabbinic attempts at resolving certain internal disputes. While one might take issue with the appellation of 'normative' even for post-Temple Judaism, the existence of various religious and political movements and sects remains one of the dominant factors of Second Temple Judaism.[5] An appreciation of the origins and social significance of these groups, which are vital for the understanding of the literary documents treated in this volume, can best be served by establishing a chronological framework for the various periods of Second Temple history.

The Hellenistic Period

As defined by purely political criteria, the Hellenistic period in Palestine may be subdivided as follows: a) 332-301 B.C.E., the conquests of Alexander and wars of the *diadochi*; b) 301-200, Ptolemaic (Egyptian) rule over Palestine; c) 200-167, Seleucid (Syrian) rule over Palestine, up to the outbreak of the Hasmonean uprising.

Insofar as Jewish history is concerned, much of the Hellenistic period is marked by an extreme paucity of sources. One has only to glance through the relevant section of Josephus' *Antiquities* (Books 11-12) to realize that the best that historian could do was to weave together various legends and sources of a novelistic nature in an attempt to fill in the lacuna that exists. Thus we advance from the popular accounts of Alexander's encounter with the residents of Judaea and their high priest (*Ant.* 11:304-345), to the historian's rendition of the Epistle of Aristeas and the events surrounding

---

[4] This was the essence of the 'Fourth Philosophy', which served as the religous grounds for armed opposition to Rome by the *sicarii*; cf. Stern, 'Sicarii and Zealots'; *id.*, 'Zealots'.
[5] Cf. Simon, *Jewish Sects*, 1-16.

the appearance of the Septuagint (*Ant.* 12:11-118),[6] and conclude — if scholars are correct in placing the event in the late third century B.C.E.[7] — with the story of the Jewish tax collector Joseph son of Tobias (*Ant.* 12:158-222). To be sure, even these stories, however touched up or fictionalized they appear to be, nevertheless provide us with valuable insights into the atmosphere pervading Jewish-Greek relations in the early Hellenistic period. Thus the Alexander stories, whether in the version provided by Josephus or in the parallel rabbinic traditions,[8] attest not only to the impact of Alexander's conquests on the residents of Palestine, but *en passant* seem to reflect on an early positive relationship between Jews and Greeks. This relationship is borne out by the earliest statements on Jews and Judaism in the writings of Hellenistic authors, which for the most part were favourable and even laudatory,[9] frequently describing the Jewish people as 'philosophers by race',[10] from whom much can be learned.[11] Yet another statement in the Alexander stories, whereby the young general accedes to the request of the high-priest that the Jews be granted permission 'to observe their country's laws and in the seventh year to be exempt from tribute' (*Ant.* 11:338) seems to reflect the recognized status of Judaism as a *religio licita* during much of the Greek and Roman period, thereby illuminating the sensitivity displayed when this basic right was encroached upon.

In similar fashion, the story of Joseph, son of Tobias seems to contribute to our comprehension of the inroads made by the hellenizing process among certain strata of Jewish society. The background to the story, which must be sketched first, is Ptolemaic rule in Palestine. Here, information is equally scant, but the following is clear.[12] In Egyptian eyes Judaea seems to have been part of a larger territory called 'Syria and Phoenicia', encompassing Palestine, the Trans-Jordan, the cities of Tyre and Sidon as well as portions of southern Syria. At the head of all this territory stood a *strategos,* while the area itself was divided into *hyparchiai,* probably defined along ethnic lines. Thus Palestine incorporated the hyparchies of Idumea, Trans-Jordan, Samaria, with Judaea probably the hyparchy with the

---

[6] For Josephus' redaction of this work cf. Pelletier, *Flavius Josèphe.*

[7] Josephus inserts the story into the Seleucid reign over Palestine, but the narrative clearly reflects Ptolemaic rule; cf. Mazar, 'The Tobiads', 235; Tcherikover, *Hellenistic Civilization,* 128; Stern, 'Notes on the Story of Joseph the Tobiad'.

[8] *Megillat Taanit,* ed. Lichtenstein, 'Die Fastenrolle', 339; *Lev. Rabba* 13, 5 (p. 293); *B.T. Yoma* 69a; for a discussion of the numerous problems relating to the historicity of these traditions see Tcherikover, *Hellenistic Civilization,* 44ff. For literature on Alexander and the Jews cf. Marcus, 'Alexander the Great and the Jews'; Schürer, *History* 1, p. 138, n. 1.

[9] Cf. Stern, 'The Jews in Greek and Latin Literature', 1103-11.

[10] So Theophrastus (372-288/7 B.C.E.), cf. Stern, *Greek and Latin Authors* 1, 11.

[11] Aristotle, quoted by Clearchus of Soli; cf. Stern, *ibid.,* 50.

[12] Cf. Tcherikover, 'Palestine under the Ptolemies'; *id.,* in *WHJP* 6, 68-79. See also Hengel, *Hellenism* 1, 18-32.

highest concentration of Jews. Judaea closely resembles the Persian administrative unit of *Yehud*, and it appears that the borders of this area remained relatively fixed for centuries, until the changes introduced by the Hasmoneans. The northern boundary of Judaea was Bet-El (north of modern Ramallah), and the sourthern boundary, Bet Zur (just north of Hebron). To the east Judaea reached the Jordan river and Jericho, while the western border was situated approximately by the plain of Lydda. Certainly, Jews resided beyond these borders, such as in the Jewish enclave of Trans-Jordan known as the *Peraea,* as well as in the Galilee, albeit in smaller numbers.[13] In the eyes of the Ptolemaic administration, however, Judaea was the area of the Jewish *ethnos,* and its residents — Judaeans. The Hellenistic period served as the catalyst for the creation of two major Greek concentrations in Palestine. One of these was the stretch of coastal *poleis* from Ptolemais (Acre) in the north to Gaza in the south, while the other was the series of Greek cities in the Trans-Jordan, such as Pella, Dion, Gerasa and Philadelphia (Amman).[14] Here again, the demographic developments of the early Hellenistic period will have a lasting effect on the history of the land until the Destruction, in particular on the nature of relations with gentiles in Palestine throughout the Second Temple period. As more and more scholars have come to note, the social tensions encountered in the last century of Second Temple Palestine are not merely a reflection of animosity between conquered Jew and ruling Roman, but the result of a far more complex reality in which different ethnic and cultural societies lived in close proximity to each other, ruled over by yet a third party not always capable of maintaining a neutral position between the various groups.[15] It would appear then, that while sources for the Hellenistic period in Judaea are few, it is crucial for a precise understanding of much of the subsequent historical development of the Jewish people in the Greco-Roman world.

Given the scarcity of sources,[16] scholars are fortunate to have at their disposal a number of documents from the archive discovered in the Fayyum (Darb el Gerza) in 1915, and known as 'the Zenon papyri'. Named after an official serving under Apollonius, the Ptolemaic finance minister of the mid-third century B.C.E., the papyri provide information bearing primarily on the economic and administrative situation in Palestine at the

[13] The author takes issue with the commonly held view that only under Aristobulus I (104-103 B.C.E.) Galilee was 'Judaized', cf. e.g. Schürer, *History* 1, p. 217-8 n. 10. See below n. 70.

[14] To these one must add two internal centers of hellenized population: Samaria to the north, one of the mainstays of Greek (and Roman) rule in Palestine, and Marissa in Idumaea, a prime example of the hellenization of eastern elements of the local population — in this case the Phoenicians. For a comprehensive survey of the Greek cities cf. Schürer; *History* 2, 85-183.

[15] Cf. Rappaport, 'The Relations between Jews and Non-Jews'; for a study of one particular example, cf. Levine, 'The Jewish-Greek Conflict'.

[16] One exception to the scarcity of sources may be portions of *1 Enoch.* Cf. Stone, *Scriptures,* 27-35.

time.[17] One document stands out. It was written by (or for) Tobias, a prominent landowner in Trans-Jordan,[18] and most probably the father of Joseph, the hero of our story. It is addressed to Apollonius; and while dealing with mundane issues itself, it opens with the following preamble: 'Tobias to Apollonius greeting. If you and all your affairs are flourishing, and everything else is as you wish it, *many thanks to the Gods* (πολλὴ χάρις τοῖς ϑεοῖς).'[19]

Much has been argued to the effect that no intrinsic polytheistic overtones should be read into what was primarily a fixed and standard opening formula, possibly written by Tobias' scribe rather than by the Jewish landowner himself.[20] All this notwithstanding, if one takes into account the fact that Tobias was apparently married to the sister of the high priest Onias II, it becomes clear that certain new elements of a particular cultural and political orientation had begun to infiltrate portions of the Judaean establishment. Into this context the Joseph story, preserved by Josephus, finds its place. Approximately in the year 240 B.C.E. we encounter the highpriest refusing to fulfill his obligations as chief tax-collector on behalf of the Ptolemaic regime. A crisis looms, and in a major gathering on the Temple mount Joseph appears and saves the day, succeeding his uncle in the position of tax-farmer (*Ant.* 12:158ff.). His subsequent escapades in Alexandria, and in particular his passion for a local dancing-girl, point to a man who, while serving as representative of the Jewish people on the one hand, has nevertheless departed from traditional Jewish behaviour. Before us, in fact, emerges a typical example of the possibilities opened up by the Hellenistic world to certain ethnic leaders. This tension between fealty to ancient local traditions and the newly accessible and highly attractive cosmopolitan stage, serves as a major factor in the social ferment in Judaea, ultimately and inexorably leading to the clash between the two forces in the second century B.C.E. And so while novelistic in its present form, the Joseph story is nevertheless enlightening, particularly since the sons of this family were destined to serve as the vanguard of the hellenizing movement in Palestine. All but one of Joseph's sons, Hyrcanus, would ultimately throw in their lot with the successors to the Ptolemies in Palestine, the Seleucid Empire.

Politically, Palestine during much of the Hellenistic period served as a bone of contention between the two great Hellenistic monarchies in the east, and the third century B.C.E. was witness to at least five battles between the two powers, frequently referred to as 'the Syrian wars' due to the

[17] Cf. Tcherikover, 'Palestine'; *id., Corpus* 1, 115-30.

[18] The geographical location of the Tobiad estate has been conclusively fixed at Arak el Emir in Trans-Jordan, approximately 17 km. west of Amman; cf. McCown, 'The Araq el Emir and the Tobiads'.

[19] Tcherikover, *Corpus* 1, 126.

[20] Cf. *Ibid.,* 127 n. 2; Tcherikover, *Hellenistic Civilization,* 71.

Ptolemaic orientation of our sources. While the Ptolemies succeeded in withstanding Syrian pressure during most of the third century, the ascent to the throne of Antiochus III 'the Great' in 223 B.C.E. marks the beginning of a shift in power. Invading in 218 B.C.E., Antiochus succeeded in conquering almost all of Palestine, only to be defeated the following year by Ptolemy IV at Raphia, in one of the great battles of ancient history.[21] Syrian pressure, however, was maintained, and in 200 B.C.E., following the defeat of the Egyptian army at Paneas, Antiochus III became ruler in Palestine.

The effects of Seleucid rule in Palestine are at first glance enigmatic, for what appears in 200 B.C.E. to be a favourable relationship between the Jewish community and the new rulers of the land, deteriorated within three decades into turmoil and outright revolution, far exceeding anything of a similar nature under 100 years of Ptolemaic rule. Moreover, in the famous proclamation issued by Antiochus III upon his conquest of the land,[22] not only was provision made for the physical restoration and economic well-being of Jerusalem and the Jewish Temple, but the king explicitly proclaimed that 'all members of the nation shall have a form of government in accordance with the laws of the fathers' (κατὰ τοὺς πατρίους νόμους). All the more striking, then, is the fact that thirty-two years later the son of that same conqueror, Antiochus IV Epiphanes, inaugurated a systematic religious persecution in Judaea that was diametrically opposed to his father's decree. The change in Seleucid policy may be attributed at least in part to external events. Following the defeat of Antiochus III at the hands of Roman legions at Magnesia in 190 B.C.E., and the ensuing peace treaty of Apamea (188), the Seleucid Empire found itself in dire need of funds to pay the tributes forced upon it by Rome. Antiochus III himself was killed while attempting to sack a temple in Elymais (187), and under his successor Seleucus IV (187-175) the Jews of Palestine experienced a similar attempt to extract funds from the Temple of Jerusalem. The event, described in 2 Maccabees 3, reflects not only on the predicament of the Seleucids, but more importantly on the internal developments among the ruling class of Jerusalem. Apparently, elements within the priesthood and particularly the family of Bilga, had joined forces with the Tobiads in an attempt to usurp power from the high priest Onias. This new coalition seems to indicate not only a power struggle within the priestly oligarchy, but a cultural clash as well, for it is this element that ultimately carried out (if it did not instigate) the reforms initiated by Antiochus IV in Jerusalem, culminating with religious persecution.

Certainly, the exact part played by Jewish elements in the events leading up to the Hasmonean uprising is far from certain, and one must attribute at least part of the initiative to the king himself. The latter, who succeeded his

---

[21] Galili, 'Raphia 217 B.C.E. Revisited'.

[22] *Ant.* 12:138-44; cf. Bickermann, 'La charte séleucide'; *id.,* 'Une proclamation séleucide'.

brother in 175 B.C.E., was by all accounts a dynamic and original statesman, intent on reviving the glory of the Hellenistic East. To this end he devoted the first seven years of his reign to plans for the conquest of Ptolemaic Egypt. In this context one can understand the steps taken to ensure a loyal leadership in Judaea, which would necessarily serve as a staging area for the invasion of Egypt. Accordingly, a new highpriest — Jason, brother of Onias — was installed, and Jerusalem was effectively rendered a Greek *polis* (city-state) named Antioch.[23] This of course entailed the setting up of standard Greek civic institutions such as a gymnasium, and the author of 2 Maccabees (4:13-17) bemoans the sight of priests 'no longer interested in the services of the altar, despising the sanctuary, neglecting the sacrifices' and running to participate in Greek athletic games. The culmination of this reform was the appointment of yet another high priest, Menelaus (of the house of Bilga), a representative of the more extreme hellenizing forces.

The question of how far the hellenizing process had advanced within Jewish society by this time is still heatedly debated by historians. One school of thought, following in the steps of Schürer, contends that quite considerable progress had already been made, the Hellenists having the upper hand, and the only path open to the devout being 'to become a sect'.[24] The arguments adduced for this position all point to an obvious adoption of Greek language and phraseology, accompanied by various manifestations of Hellenistic art forms, systems of administration and diplomacy, public institutions, as well as the incorporation of basic Greek ideas and concepts into the literature of the period.[25] Thus, claimed Schürer, if the hellenization of the Jewish people ultimately failed, it was due to the over-zealous steps taken too hastily by Antiochus to advance this process, which lead in the end to the Hasmonean reaction. Ironically then, according to this line of thought Antiochus emerges as the one person responsible for saving Judaism.[26]

Countering this approach, one finds Tcherikover stressing two points: 1) much of the hellenizing process was confined to a particular class of Jews, namely the Jerusalem aristocracy and its peripheral elements; 2) the hellenization encountered and cited by scholars is frequently an external manifestation, serving political ends rather than reflecting deep-rooted cultural assimilation.[27]

These arguments were employed by Tcherikover in his attempt at solving the riddle posed by the very institution of religious persecution under Antiochus IV. As an exponent of Hellenistic polytheism, one might have

---

[23] Following the interpretation of Tcherikover, *Hellenistic Civilization*, 161, and 404-9.
[24] Schürer, *History* 1, 145.
[25] id. 2, 52-80; see especially Hengel, *Hellenism*.
[26] Schürer, *History* 1, 145.
[27] Tcherikover, *Hellenistic Civilization*, 118ff., 202f.; compare Hengel, *Hellenism* 1, 299.

expected Antiochus to reflect the tolerance characteristic of Greco-Roman culture. Various theories have been proposed on this issue,[28] one of the most noted being Bickermann's placing of the blame squarely on the shoulders of the Jewish leadership, i.e. Menelaus and the Jerusalem hierarchy.[29] Common to all theories was the assumption that religious persecution served as the catalyst for the Jewish uprising. If, however, Tcherikover is correct in his reconstruction of the chronological sequence of events leading up to the Hasmonean uprising, it would appear that popular opposition to the hellenizing process had been seething for some time, and that with Antiochus' retreat from Egypt in 168 this opposition broke out into open rebellion. After cruelly crushing this uprising, Antiochus followed through with the installation of gentile cults in Jerusalem, together with the placing of the Jewish religion outside of the law, and it was this that led to the rebellion of Mattathias and the Hasmonean family.[30] Whether or not we accept this approach in its entirety, one result is beyond argument. The Hasmonean uprising set in motion a process that not only succeeded in destroying the hellenizing party in Jerusalem and effectively placing a halt to all further assimilation of the Jewish community into the surrounding Greek environment, but ultimately led to the creation of a national political entity, the Hasmonean state, that changed radically the course of Second Temple history.[31]

The Hasmonean Uprising

The goals of the Hasmonean uprising were either never definitively stated by its leaders, or — as is more likely — underwent constant revisions in response to Seleucid reaction, and in light of the opportunities that presented themselves at various stages of the Jewish-Greek confrontation. At its inception under Mattathias (d. 166/5 B.C.E.) the revolt was primarily aimed at achieving religious freedom and the restoration of traditional Jewish worship in Jerusalem. These aims are the central theme of statements attributed to Mattathias (1 Macc 2:19-27), and were the immediate objectives of his son Judah (Maccabee),[32] at least until the re-dedication of

---

[28] Cf. Tcherikover's summary, *Hellenistic Civilization*, 175ff.
[29] Bickermann, *Der Gott der Makkabäer*; for a detailed refutation of this theory see Heinemann, 'Wer verlanlasste den Glaubenszwang'. Hengel concurs with much of Bickermann's approach, but see Millar, 'The Background'.
[30] Cf. Tcherikover 186f.; if accepted, this reconstruction would revolutionize our approach to the nature of the persecution, which now emerges far more as a *political* means for solving a state of unrest, rather than a *cultural-religious* act taken by the champion of hellenization. Compare, however, Schürer, *History* 1, 151ff. and note 37.
[31] Stern, 'The Hasmonean Revolt'.
[32] Only Judah goes by this title in the sources; for the various suggestions on etymology cf. Schürer, *History* 1, 158 n. 49.

the Temple in *Kislev* (December) 164 B.C.E.[33] This having been achieved,[34] there emerges a second stage of revolution, begun by Judah and carried forward by two of his brothers, Jonathan (160-142 B.C.E.) and Simon (142-135 B.C.E.).

In the immediate aftermath of the re-dedication of the Temple, Jews not only in Judaea but throughout Palestine (in particular in Galilee, Gilead, the Trans-Jordan and Idumea) found themselves confronting hostile neighbours bent on seizing the opportunity to attack these somewhat isolated Jewish communities. It is now for the first time that the Hasmonean brothers asserted themselves as defenders of the Jewish people at large, and not merely as local Judaean guerilla fighters. In a series of campaigns during the years 163-162, they clashed with various gentile populations outside of Judaea,[35] at times limiting themselves to inflicting military blows on their opponents (but with no intention of permanent conquest), and in certain cases warranted by the precarious state of the local Jewish population (such as in Western Galilee and the Gilead) accompanying military activity with the removal of Jewish communities to a safe haven in Judaea. The effect of this activity was to establish the Hasmonean brothers as national leaders over much of Jewish Palestine, a situation unacceptable to the Seleucids. Subsequent attempts by the monarchy to subdue Judah were either thwarted by unrest in the Syrian capital,[36] or met with defeat on the battlefield.[37] These defeats notwithstanding, it now became clear to Judah that the Seleucid Empire was not about to willingly relinquish its hold over Palestine, and thus the second stage of the Hasmonean revolution — the quest for national independence — was fully initated. The first step in this direction was the mutual defense treaty established between the Jews and the Roman Republic during the last year of Judah's life (161 B.C.E.).[38] The treaty served the interests of both parties; Rome had never recognized the legitimacy of the new Seleucid monarch, Demetrius I, and in any case was

---

[33] Official Syrian recognition of Jewish control over the Temple, as well as the abrogation of religious persecution, was proclaimed only in a letter from the child-king Antiochus V to Lysias (2 Macc 11:22-26) but was in essence achieved by Judah with the conquest of Jerusalem in 164 B.C.E.

[34] Judah's early military victories (166-164 B.C.E.) all follow a similar pattern: Seleucid forces from outside of Judaea attempt to link up with the Greek garrison at Jerusalem, and Judah succeeds in surprising these forces at various sites along their marches towards the city. With the citizens of the surrounding Judaean hills supportive of Judah's aims, there ensued a virtual Jewish siege of Jerusalem, ultimately enabling the Jewish leader to enter the city and reestablish traditional worship therein; cf. Avi-Yonah, 'The Hasmonean Revolt'.

[35] 1 Macc chap. 5; *Ant.* 12:327-53.

[36] 1 Macc 6:28-63; *Ant.* 12:367-81.

[37] 1 Macc 7:26-50; 2 Macc 15:1-39; *Ant.* 12:402-12; The defeat of Nikanor (13 *Adar* 161 B.C.E.) was established as a festival, with the event commemorated in *Megillat Taanit* as 'Nikanor's Day', Lichtenstein, 'Die Fastenrolle', 279-80, 346.

[38] 1 Macc 8:23-32; *Ant.* 12:417-19.

interested in weakening the Syrian hold on the Near East, as witnessed by the earlier ultimatum preventing the Seleucid conquest of Egypt.[39] As for Judah, the pact effectively served as the first official recognition of developing Jewish independence, and must have also served as a tremendous boost of morale for obviously battle-weary Jewish soldiers. In any case, the authenticity of the document has generally been accepted by modern scholars,[40] and Roman-Jewish friendship became a mainstay of Hasmonean policy almost until the conquest of the Hasmonean state itself by the Romans.[41]

The independence of Judaea was nevertheless far from established by the time of Judah's death in battle,[42] only a few months following the pact with Rome. It was left to the last of the Hasmonean brothers, Jonathan and Simon, to complete the process, and this was achieved not so much on the basis of military power, but rather thanks to keen political acumen that took maximum advantage of the growing decay within the Seleucid Empire. Constant dissension within the royal family created a situation of perpetual contenders and pretenders to the throne, and the Hasmonean brothers found themselves in a unique situation of being courted by the various sides for their support, with concomitant promises of Syrian recognition and support in return for Hasmonean allegiance. Thus on the Feast of Tabernacles, 152 B.C.E., the first Hasmonean high priest, Jonathan, was installed by a pretender to the Syrian throne, Alexander Balas,[43] and it was this recognition that convinced the King himself, Demetrius I, to make similar overtures. Against this background, the Hasmonean brothers were free to establish control over portions of Palestine beyond the borders of Judaea: Jonathan captured Jaffa for the first time, fought near Ashdod and received the city of Ekron from Alexander Balas. Some years later (following Balas' defeat in 145) portions of southern Samaria were added to the growing Jewish territory.[44] While Jonathan was executed by yet another Seleucid contender (Tryphon; 142 B.C.E.), Simon, the last of the Hasmonean brothers officially annexed Jaffa to the Judaean state,[45] and together with the conquest of Gezer,[46] a·fortress controlling the road from Jerusalem to the newly established Jewish port, rendered the Jewish state a

---

[39] Polybius 29: 27, 1-8; cf. Schürer, *History* 1, 151-2.
[40] Schürer, *History* 1, 171-13 and n. 33; Stern, *Greek and Latin Authors* 1, 342; Timpe, 'Der römische Vertrag'.
[41] Cf. Stern, 'The Relations between Judaea and Rome'.
[42] 1 Macc 9.
[43] 1 Macc 10:18-20; Balas claimed to be the real son of Antiochus IV Epiphanes.
[44] Cf. Tcherikover, *Hellenistic Civilization*, 235ff.; Schürer, *History* 1, 174-88 (Jonathan), 188-99 (Simon).
[45] 1 Macc 13: 11.
[46] 1 Macc 13:43ff.; the 'siege-engines' employed by Simon in this battle are evidence of the advances made by the Hasmonean army, slowly emerging as a major military force in the region.

viable economic as well as political entity. With the fall of the remaining Greek garrison (Hakra) in Jerusalem in 141 B.C.E.[47] as well as the foregoing that year of all Jewish taxation on behalf of the Seleucid Empire,[48] the Jewish state was an established reality. Diplomatic activity was enhanced,[49] and in 'a great assembly' on the Temple mount on the 18th of *Elul* 140 B.C.E., Simon and his sons were officially recognized by the Jewish people as high priests, political and military leaders 'until a faithful prophet should arise'.[50] This last clause, stressing the provisional appointment of the Hasmoneans, may allude to a certain opposition to Hasmonean rule or priesthood among some elements of Jewish society, and the appearance of certain political groups on the Judaean scene at this time is possibly an outgrowth of such opposition.

Beginning with the outbreak of the revolt at Modiin (1 Macc 2:15-28) the Hasmonean family played a central role in Jewish history for over one hundred and twenty years. While the prior history of the family is unclear,[51] the fact that it was descended from the priestly order of Joarib (1 Macc 2:1), listed first among the priestly families in 1 Chr 24:7,[52] must have rendered it a prominent family even before the uprising. Nevertheless, the ultimate establishment of the Hasmoneans as high priests was a departure from earlier Second Temple tradition, which linked the high priesthood with the 'sons of Zadok'.[53] This is frequently cited as the catalyst for the establishment of a 'Sadducean' party, stressing its own legitimacy as priests. In similar fashion, the Dead Sea sect placed great stress on the fact that within their ranks reside 'the sons of Zadok, the priests'.[54]

In general, the ferment caused both by the hellenizing movements of the early second century B.C.E., as well as by the Hasmonean uprising and subsequent concentration of power in that family's hands, seems to have supplied the major impetus for the formation of various groups and sects within the Jewish community. Already in Judah's day we encounter the *Hasidim*, a group willing to make do with the religious freedoms regained

---

[47] 1 Macc 13:49ff.; this day (23 Iyyar 141) was also established as a yearly festival, cf. Lichtenstein, 'Die Fastenrolle', 286-7, 319.

[48] 1 Macc 13:36-40.

[49] 1 Macc 14:20-23; 15:16-24.

[50] 1 Macc 14:27-49; for a detailed analysis of the proclamation recognizing the house of Simon, see Stern, *Documents*, 132-9; Goldstein, *I Maccabees*, 488-509.

[51] In *War* 1:36, Mattathias is described as a priest from Modiin, whereas *Ant.* 12:265 claims that he came from Jerusalem. 1 Macc 2:1 states that 'he moved away from Jerusalem and settled in Modiin'; cf. Schürer, *History* 1, p. 156 and n. 43.

[52] The different lists of priestly divisions from the early Second Temple period contain varying numbers of families as well as different orders; cf. Schürer, *History* 2, 246-7.

[53] Cf. Ezek 40:46, 44:15; Sir 51:12; Schürer, *History* 2, 407; Stern, 'Aspects of Jewish Society,' 567.

[54] 1QS*b* 3:22. For the Qumran use of 'sons of Zadok' cf. Vermes, *Qumran in Perspective,* 110. For another view see below, p. 545 n. 292.

in the early stages of the revolt, to the extent of embracing a Syrian-appointed high priest (Alkimos) ultimately responsible for their massacre.[55] While these *Hasidim* may or may not be the 'plant root' which God caused 'to spring from Israel and Aaron to inherit his land' according to the Dead Sea sect,[56] it is generally accepted that Qumran was settled by the time of John Hyrcanus I (135-104 B.C.E.),[57] and thus the origins of the sect probably date to the early Hasmonean period, with either Jonathan or Simon serving as 'the wicked priest called by the name of truth when he first arose'.[58] Similarly, Josephus makes his earliest references to Pharisees and Sadducees, as well as Essenes, within the context of Jonathan's rule.[59]

The Hasmonean State

From the days of Simon on, the ideological platform upon which the Hasmonean state was founded was clear. In reply to the demands of the last powerful Seleucid monarch, Antiochus VII Sidetes, to return conquered territories, Simon proclaims: 'We have neither taken other men's land, nor hold that which appertaineth to others, but the inheritance of our fathers which our enemies had wrongfully in possession a certain time. Wherefore we, having opportunity, hold the inheritance of our fathers' (1 Macc 15:33-34). To be sure, the conquests of Simon did not effect major ethnic changes in the settlement of Palestine, and the Hasmonean state still was comprised primarily of the historical district of Judaea (*Yehud*), with the addition of Jaffa and Gezer in the west, as well as portions of the Jewish Trans-Jordan (*Peraea*). Only following the death of Antiochus VII (129 B.C.E.), and during the reign of Simon's son John Hyrcanus I (135-104 B.C.E.) are we witness to the first stages of major territorial expansion. The brunt of Hyrcanus' attacks was felt by two ethnic groups in particular, the Samaritans and the Idumeans. The first community witnessed the destruction of its temple on Mount Gerizim,[60] together with the conquest of Shechem, whereas the Idumeans were permitted to remain in their land after agreeing to undergo conversion to Judaism.[61] Interestingly, this conversion had longlasting results, and with the subsequent conquest of Palestine by Pompey and removal of non-Jewish territory from the

---

[55] The precise identity of the Hasidim remains enigmatic; cf. Schürer, *History* 1, 157 n. 46; Hengel, *Hellenism* 1, 175-81.
[56] CD 1:7.
[57] Cf. De Vaux, *Archaeology,* 5; Vermes, *Qumran in Perspective,* 33.
[58] 1QpHab 8:8-9. For various identifications of this priest cf. Vermes, *ibid.* 151; Schürer, *History* 2, 586-7 and notes 50-55.
[59] *Ant.* 13:171-3. For an earlier dating of the sect's origins see below, pp. 544-7.
[60] *Ant.* 13:256-7; cf. Cross, 'Aspects'.
[61] *Ant.* 13:257-8.

remaining Jewish state,[62] Eastern Idumaea nevertheless remained part of Judaea. Needless to say, the most noteworthy consequence of the Idumean conversion was the subsequent introduction of the house of Antipater into the mainstream of Jewish affairs, but one might also take note of another prominent Idumean influence on later history, with the appearance of Idumean fighters among the most fanatical participants of the Great War against Rome.[63] Inasmuch as the territory of the Hasmonean state under Hyrcanus was almost three times that of earlier Judaea, one can appreciate the demographic constraints that required such steps as mass conversion,[64] and one might also assume that certain elements of society were further alienated by such political realities. In addition, Hyrcanus appears to be the first Hasmonean ruler to have employed a gentile mercenary army,[65] and a slow process of hellenization seems to have been introduced by this time into the new leadership of Judaea. Hints of this are apparent already in the proclamation appointing Simon and his sons,[66] whereas Hyrcanus' son Aristobulus I saw nothing wrong in attaching the title 'Philhellene' to his name.[67] The social unrest that resulted may serve to explain why Hyrcanus' rule serves as the first major stage for divisions between Pharisees and Sadducees,[68] with the Hasmonean ruler abandoning his traditional ties with the former party and joining forces with the latter. The Saducean party would henceforth remain a major force on the political scene, until the last days of Hasmonean independence and the Pharisaic ressurgence under Queen Alexandra Salome (76-67 B.C.E.)[69]

The fall of the cities of Scythopolis and Samaria in the last days of John Hyrcanus paved the way for the Hasmonean conquest of Galilee, which was achieved in the brief rule of Hyrcanus' son Aristobulus (104-103 B.C.E.).[70] With this conquest, all of the Jewish territories of Palestine were

---

[62] Cf. *War* 1:155-6; *Ant.* 14:74-5; whereas the area around Marissa was restored to its Greek character and inhabitants by Pompey, the area of eastern Idumea, surrounding Adourraim, was considered Jewish by that time and remained a portion of the vassal Jewish state; cf. *Macmillan Bible Atlas,* p. 136; Schürer, *History* 1, 268 n. 5.

[63] *Ant.* 17:254; *War* 4:22ff.; Rhoads, *Israel in Revolution,* 137-40.

[64] Cf. Tcherikover, *Hellenistic Civilization,* 247-9, who stresses that Judaization of certain gentile groups was a purely political act, with no religious missionary overtones.

[65] *Ant.* 13:249; Simon was praised for paying soldiers out of his own funds (1 Macc 14:32) but nowhere is it suggested that these soldiers were foreigners. Praise for personal contributions of rulers was common at the time, cf. Goldstein, *I Maccabees,* 504; Hyrcanus, however, probably angered the population by paying his soldiers out of funds taken from the Tomb of David.

[66] E.g. 1 Macc 14:43-45; cf. Tcherikover, *Hellenistic Civilization* 250-1.

[67] *Ant.* 13:318.

[68] *Ant.* 13:288-96; The Talmudic parallel to this story, *B.T. Kiddushin* 66a, refers to the Hasmonean ruler involved as 'Yannai', and much has been written on this discrepancy; cf. Schürer *History* 1, 214 n. 30; Alon, *Jews, Judaism and the Classical World,* 26-28 and n. 22; Levine, 'On the Political Involvement', 14, n. 8.

[69] Levine, 'The Political Struggle'.

[70] *War* 1:76 (Schürer, *History* 1, 217-8); Aristobulus converted the Iturean tribe (*Ant.* 13:319)

incorporated into the Hasmonean state, and the massive territorial expansion under Hyrcanus' successor Alexander Jannaeus (103-76 B.C.E.) [71] was primarily at the expense of the Greek population of the land. By the end of his rule, almost all of the Greek cities along the coast of Palestine (save Acre and Ashkelon), as well as most of the Hellenistic cities of the Trans-Jordan (with the exception of Philadelphia) were annexed to the Hasmonean kingdom. Jannaeus' successes were in no small part due not only to his military skills, but to the political constellation of the times, with a decaying Seleucid empire to the north,[72] and a still powerful Ptolemaic ally to the south.[73] The growing Nabatean encroachment into southern Palestine was another determining factor in Jannaeus' military policy, and the Hasmonean conquest of Gaza after a particularly cruel siege may partly have been motivated by the wish to prevent the Nabateans from using the city as a major port.[74]

If internal dissension existed in earlier Hasmonean times, it developed into outright rebellion during the days of Jannaeus. Josephus attributes numerous acts of cruelty to the Hasmonean monarch, including the execution of 50,000 Jews in a period of six years.[75] The 'furious young lion' reported in a Dead Sea scroll to have 'executed revenge on seekers of smooth things' and hung men alive,[76] may refer to Jannaeus and to that king's crucifixion of eight hundred Jews described by Josephus.[77] Opposition to the Hasmonean monarchy and priesthood is attested in various apocryphal works, where 'kings calling themselves priests of the

---

but there is no evidence to substantiate Schürer's claim that 'the population of Galilee was until this time more gentile than Jewish'. To the contrary: 1) as far back as the days of Judah the Maccabee, Jews fought the Seleucid army at Arbel (1 Macc 9:2); 2) Alexander Jannaeus was raised in Galilee, unthinkable if the population was primarily Greek and hostile to the Hasmoneans (*Ant.* 13:322); 3) in the first year of Jannaeus' reign (103 B.C.E.) the city of Asochis (Shihin) fell to Ptolemy Lathirus, who surprised the defenders by attacking on Sabbath (*Ant.* 13:337). If we add to this the fact that no major *polis* appears in central Galilee during the Hellenistic period, it becomes clear that Josephus' statement about Aristobulus is just what it says: a partial conversion of the Itureans, and not the Galilee at large.

[71] Sources are divided regarding the first Hasmonean king. Josephus (*Ant.* 13: 301; *War* 1:70) claims it was Aristobulus, while Strabo (*Geography* 16:2, 40) points to Alexander Jannaeus; cf. Stern, *Greek and Latin Authors* 1, 301-2, and 307, line 40. A similar debate involves the first stages of Hasmonean coinage, on which much has been written recently; cf. Rappaport, 'The Emergence of Hasmonean Coinage'.

[72] Cf. *Ant.* 13:365-71.

[73] Cleopatra's support of the Jewish kingdom was in part influenced by fear of her son and contender to the throne, Ptolemy Lathirus, as well as the pressure placed on her by her Jewish general Ananias, cf. *Ant.* 13: 349, 354-5; for the political background to Jannaeus' rule cf. Stern, 'Judaea and her Neighbours'.

[74] *Ant.* 13:360.

[75] *Ant.* 13:376.

[76] 1QpNah 1:6-8; cf. Schürer, *History* 1, 224-5, n. 22.

[77] *Ant.* 13:380; for the internal situation under Jannaeus see also: Rabin, 'Alexander Jannaeus'; Tcherikover, *Hellenistic Civilization*, 257-65.

most high God' are accused of 'working iniquity in the Holy of Holies',[78] and are guilty of 'laying waste the throne of David in tumultuous arrogance'.[79] To be sure, the negative picture of the late Hasmonean period is not a completely objective one. Almost all the literary sources for the period derive from the opposition to the Hasmonean family, and even Josephus, who prides himself on his Hasmonean lineage,[80] was forced by the paucity of sources to resort to a decidedly anti-Hasmonean historian, Nicolaus of Damascus,[81] for a description of the last stages of Hasmonean rule.

Moreover, even Josephus seems to allude to a certain rapprochement between the nation and Jannaeus towards the latter's final days.[82] To his wife Salome (76-67 B.C.E.) Jannaeus bequeathed a kingdom embracing almost all of the biblical Land of Israel, as well as imparting to her the good advice to restore Pharisaic influence to the royal court, as a means of re-establishing popular support for the monarchy.[83] Nothing, however, was capable of saving the Hasmonean state, whose days were numbered with the advance of Roman legions eastward. The civil war that erupted between Salome's two sons, Aristobulus II and Hyrcanus II, merely provided a pretext for subsequent Roman intervention into the affairs of Judaea,[84] and in any case the ultimate fall of Jerusalem in 63 B.C.E. to the army of Pompey must be considered a foregone conclusion.

Nevertheless, the impact of Hasmonean rule in Palestine transcends the brief period of Jewish independence, and its social, cultural and religious consequences were of primary importance. Under the Hasmoneans the hellenization that had swept through much of the Near East encountered an opposing cultural phenomenon, and in the ensuing battle between the Greco-Syrian elements in Palestine and the Jewish nation, the latter emerged victorious to a large extent.[85] While territorial conquests were torn away from Judaea by the Romans, the dominant ethnic and cultural community of the land remained the Jewish people, and this was destined to be the case for at least two more centuries, and in many ways through much of the late Roman and Byzantine periods as well.

---

[78] *Ass. Mos.* 6:1.
[79] *Pss. Sol.* 17:8. In both cases Herod, while himself cruel and 'alien to our race', nevertheless punishes his predecessors as they deserved.
[80] Josephus, *Life* 2.
[81] Cf. Stern, *Greek and Latin Authors* 1, 227ff. and in particular 230-1; *id.,* 'Nicolaus of Damascus'.
[82] *Ant.* 13:393-4; 398f.
[83] *Ant.* 13:400.
[84] *Ant.* 14:30f.
[85] On the seeming contradiction between this process and the above-noted 'hellenization' of the Hasmoneans themselves, cf. Tcherikover, *Hellenistic Civilization,* 264-5.

Roman Rule in Judaea

The fall of Jerusalem to the armies of Pompey in 63 B.C.E. signifies the end of the independent Jewish state, and the Roman conqueror was now required to choose a system of government for the newly acquired territory. Numerous options existed, from the outright annexation of the country to the province of Syria, to the setting up of a vassal state to be run by a member of the Hasmonean family. In fact, the former option was applied to the majority of Greek cities throughout Palestine,[86] but this system, it was felt, would be detrimental to the maintenance of peace within the Jewish portions of the land, given the unique nature of that population.[87] In general, Rome was not out to totally eradicate the Jewish nation, or even to abolish all existing Jewish political frameworks. The Jewish religion remained *religio licita* throughout almost all of Roman rule, and numerous attempts were made to grant the Jews of Palestine some semblance of self-rule. Certain principles of Roman rule in Palestine, however, begin to assert themselves almost immediately: a) whoever rules Judaea as a vassal king, prince or high priest — must bear total allegiance to Rome; b) any autonomous Jewish state will rule only over territory populated primarily by Jews (this principle was established by Pompey, but modified in later periods); c) the natural base of Roman rule throughout the East, and in Palestine as well, were to be the Greek cities, who were in Roman eyes the natural allies of Rome by virtue of their obvious cultural affinity. As noted above, this policy had far-reaching results in Judaea.

Based on the spirit of these principles, the arrangements under Pompey involved a total reorganization of the Jewish state.[88] Almost all of Jannaeus' conquests were torn from Judaea (as well as those non-Jewish territories annexed under his predecessors), and in Josephus' words 'the nation was confined within its own boundaries'.[89] These boundaries included primarily Judaea, Galilee, Eastern Idumaea and the Jewish Trans-Jordan, and at their head Pompey reinstated Hyrcanus II as high priest, apparently adding to this the title of 'Ethnarch' (*Ant.* 20:244), but abolishing the monarchy. The early history of this vassal state, however, makes it clear that the legacy of the Hasmoneans was not easily forgotten. Having succeeded in creating a unified Jewish state in much of Palestine, the Jewish population reacted violently to the attempt by Gabinius, a successor to Pompey and governor of Syria in 57-55 B.C.E., to divide the Jews of the land into five geographical and administrative units.[90] The lesson was not lost on subsequent Roman rulers, and from the days of

---

86 *War* 1:155-7; *Ant.* 14:75-76.
87 Cf. Schalit, in *WHJP* 7, 36; Smallwood, *The Jews*, 30.
88 Smallwood, *The Jews*, 27ff.
89 *War* 1:155; *Ant.* 14:74.
90 *War* 1:170; *Ant.* 14:91; cf. Schürer, *History* 1, 268 n. 5.

Julius Caesar[91] (48-44 B.C.E.) down to the destruction and beyond, the question of Jewish unity in the various territories of Palestine was never raised again.

Another and more pressing legacy of the Hasmonean period, however, was the unwillingness of major segments of the Jewish population to relinquish the political independence enjoyed during approximately eighty years of Hasmonean statehood. In this respect Josephus is justified in having a victorious Titus attack the Jews who 'ever since Pompey reduced you by force never ceased from revolution'.[92] Opposition to Rome, in fact, manifested itself in Judaea in one form or another from the earliest stages of Roman rule, and the various systems of government introduced by Rome into Palestine – from Pompey to the destruction of the Temple and the Bar-Kokhba war – all attest to the difficulties raised by the Roman-Jewish confrontation.

In general terms, Roman rule in late Second Temple Palestine may be divided into three major stages:[93] 1) vassal state under Hyrcanus II, 63-40 B.C.E.; 2) Herodian rule, 37 B.C.E. – 6 C.E.; 3) direct Roman rule, 6-66 C.E. (save for the brief reign of Agrippa I, 41-44 C.E.).

The first of these stages has been discussed briefly above, and what must be added here are two major phenomena. On the one hand, these years were constantly characterized by civil and political unrest, with the centre of dissent frequently focussing on the disenfranchised branch of the Hasmonean dynasty: Aristobulus II, the brother of Hyrcanus II; Aristobulus' son Alexander; and during the Parthian invasion of the Near East yet another of Aristobulus' sons, Antigonus. The latter was then briefly recognized by the Parthians – and enthusiastically by the Jews of Judaea – as the new Hasmonean monarch (40-38 B.C.E.).[94] It was this phenomenon that probably disqualified the Hasmonean family from serving as future Roman vassals in the land.

---

[91] Caesar's benevolent attitude towards the Jews is attested in the decrees granting privileges to Jews both of Judaea and the diaspora, cf. *Ant.* 14:190-222; the well known statement of Suetonius, *Jul.* 84:5, regarding the extent of Jewish mourning over Caesar's death, is just one of numerous allusions to this favourable relationship, cf. Schürer, *History* 1, 270-5.

[92] *War* 6:329.

[93] The following lines, far from being a detailed description of the period, are intended merely as an overview of certain central issues. For the vassal state in Judaea from Pompey to Herod cf. Schalit, in *WHJP* 7, 34-59; Schürer, *History* 1, 267-86; Smallwood, *The Jews*, 21-43. On the Herodian Period cf. Jones, *The Herods of Judaea*; Schalit, *König Herodes*; Schürer, *History* 1, 287-357; Smallwood, *The Jews*, 44-119; Stern, 'Herod'. For direct Roman rule, cf. Smallwood, *The Jews* 144-80, 256-92; Schürer, *History* 1, 357-98, 455-70; Stern, 'The Province of Judaea'.

[94] Beginning with this episode in Roman-Parthian affairs, and the short-lived Jewish independence reestablished by the Parthians, Jewish eyes in Palestine would henceforth turn eastwards, towards the Parthians in general and their brethren in that empire in particular, as a source for ultimate deliverance from Roman rule, cf. *War* 2:388-9, and compare *War* 6:343; cf. Ghirshman, *Iran*, 272; Debevoise, *A Political History of Parthia*, 93-95.

At the same time, the Idumean family of Antipater and his sons (Herod and Phasael) displayed unswerving loyalty to the various Roman rulers who successively laid claim to the eastern provinces (Pompey, Julius Caesar, Cassius, Mark Anthony, Octavian). It is therefore not surprising that with the Parthian retreat from Palestine and the fall of Antigonus, Herod — with the full backing of Anthony and the Roman legions, became the new vassal King of Judaea.

Herod's rule (37-4 B.C.E.) in Jerusalem brought about one of the most pronounced social upheavals in all of Second Temple history.[95] The elimination of the Hasmoneans as the dominant priestly family necessitated the creation of a new social aristocracy, one with no ties to the previous elite and that would also not pose a threat to the Herodian dynasty itself. The problem was particularly acute regarding the high priesthood, and here Herod solved the issue by turning to the diaspora. The high priesthood was first given to one Hananel of Babylon,[96] and then to a succession of priestly families from the Egyptian diaspora.[97] The latter were by all means legitimate priests, but probably closely attuned to the Hellenistic tendencies of Herod himself. Beyond the introduction of new families, the innovation here was also in the idea that the high priesthood was no longer the sole possession of one family, transmitted from father to son, but rather an appointment to be decided by the monarch. What ensued from Herod's reign was the creation of a priestly oligarchy,[98] from whose ranks high priests might be chosen, and in general a decline in the prestige of the office, at least in the eyes of certain popular elements of Jewish society.[99] It would be a mistake, however, to underestimate the power still wielded by the priests in the last generations of Second Temple history.[100]

In this context, Herod's cultivation of diaspora Jewry in general is noteworthy, and manifests itself both in the encouragement of immigration to Judaea[101] as well as Herod's defense of the religious and civic rights of Jews in the Greek diaspora.[102] That he was successful, for instance, in intervening on behalf of the Jews of Ionia, is primarily testimony to the

---

[95] Cf. Stern, 'Social and Political Realignments'.

[96] *Ant.* 15:22.

[97] Cf. Stern, 'Herod', 274; *id.* 'Aspects of Jewish Society', 570, 600ff.

[98] For a comprehensive discussion of the priestly nobility see: Jeremias, *Jerusalem*, 147-221; Schürer, *History* 2, 227-91; Stern, 'Aspects of Jewish Society', 561-612; on the appointment of high priests in late Second Temple history, see also Alon, *Jews, Judaism*, 48ff.

[99] *T. Menahot* 13:21; *B.T. Pesahim* 57a.

[100] Cf. Smallwood, 'High Priests'.

[101] Two significant examples of this phenomenon are the invitation addressed to a Babylonian-Jewish military leader, Zamaris, to settle with his countrymen in the north-eastern territories of Palestine (cf. *Ant.* 17:22-31), and the appearance of Hillel the Babylonian in Jerusalem.

[102] *Ant.* 16:27-65.

excellent relations maintained by Herod with the imperial court at Rome, whether Augustus himself or the commander of the Roman armies, Marcus Vipsanius Agrippa. This dual affinity of Herod's to the Greco-Roman world on the one hand, and nevertheless to Jewish interests — in Jerusalem as well as the diaspora — on the other hand, is certainly a major factor in the paradoxical behaviour of the Judaean monarch. The greatest contributor to Greek cities in Palestine, with his two major projects being the foundation of Caesarea and Sebaste, was nevertheless commemorated in Talmudic literature for building 'the Temple of Herod'.[103] In sum, however, the tyrannical nature of Herod's rule was its ultimate legacy; the same Talmudic text that praises him also stresses that he destroyed the Hasmonean family as well as the community of Sages (*B.T. Baba Bathra* 3b-4a), and his selling of Jews into slavery abroad[104] must have alienated the vast majority of Jews, with no appeasement capable of winning their hearts. The author of the *Assumption of Moses* leaves no doubt as to popular sentiment towards Herod:

> An insolent king will succeed them (the Hasmoneans), who will not be of the race of the priests, a man bold and shameless, and he will judge them as they shall deserve. And he will cut off their chief men with the sword, and will destroy them in secret places, so that no one may know where their bodies are. He will slay the young and the old, and he will not spare. The fear of him will be bitter unto them ... during thirty and four years. (*Ass. Mos.* 6:2-6)

Herod's success, in the long run, was in his capability of maintaining law and order, and thereby fulfilling the *sine qua non* required for Roman support. Upon his death in 4 B.C.E. it became abundantly clear that his chosen successor as king of Judaea, Archelaus,[105] was incapable of maintaining this order. After ten years of disturbances and Jewish exhortations[106] Judaea became a Roman province under direct Roman rule. What should not be overlooked, however, was that during this period of turbulence definite signs of eschatalogical expectations appear on the Judaean scene. Various popular uprisings seem to be led at this time by figures of a particular social stratum and physical bearing, i.e. men of low

---

[103] *B.T. Baba Bathra* 4a; for an analysis of Herodian building see: 'Herod's Building Projects: State Necessity or Personal Need? A Symposium', *Cathedra* 1 (1981), 48-80.

[104] *Ant.* 16:1-5; cf. Stern, 'Herod', 275-7.

[105] Archelaus was designated by Herod to succeed as King of Judaea, Idumea and Samaria, while two of his brothers were appointed tetrarchs over the northern territories of Palestine: Herod Antipas (4 B.C.E.-39 C.E.) over Galilee and Peraea, Philip (4 B.C.E.-33/34 C.E.) over Golan, Trachon and Batanaea. For the latter two rules cf. Schürer, *History* 1, 336-53. On Herod Antipas, commonly referred to in New Testament literature as Herod, see especially Hoehner, *Herod Antipas*.

[106] Ant. 17:299f.; *War* 2:80. The Jewish uprisings were not organized at the time, and what emerges from Josephus is a state of anarchy, cf. *Ant.* 17:269ff.; for the uprising put down by Varus, cf. *Ant.* 17:286f., *War* 2:66-79, *Seder Olam Rabba* ch. 30 ('Polemos of Asverus').

rank graced with impressive physical strength, who — placing crowns on their head and proclaiming themselves kings — begin to attack Roman forces. Three such cases (Judah son of Ezekias, Simon, Athronges)[107] all suggest a definite messianic zeal, and this phenomenon is not without parallel in the *sicarii* movement and its leadership in the last years of the Second Temple period.

With the introduction of direct Roman rule Judaea became a Roman province ruled by governors from 6-66 C.E. with the exception of the short reign of Agrippa I (41-44). Two major concentrations of Jewish population, however, remained beyond direct Roman rule for some time: Galilee and the Jewish Trans-Jordan remained part of the tetrarchy of Herod Antipas until 39 C.E., passing then into the hands of Agrippa I, and only upon the latter's death in 44 were joined to the Judaean province. In similar fashion the territories under Philip reverted upon his death in 34 to the Syrian province, in 37 to Agrippa, and finally to the province of Judaea.

In general, the status of Judaea in Roman eyes did not warrant its establishment as either a senatorial or imperial province, along the lines set up by Augustus.[108] Due to its proximity to Syria and the major concentration of forces there, no discernible need existed for the dispatch of a legion to Judaea. Frequently, in fact, the Syrian governor was considered responsible for Judaean affairs, beginning with the census carried out under Quirinius with the setting up of the province,[109] and up until the attempt by Cestius Gallus to quash the great Jewish rebellion in its early stages.[110] As a result of this policy, the governors of Judaea were not of the highest Roman rank, but rather of the *equites;* their official title at first was *praefectus,*[111] and from the rule of Claudius (41 C.E.) it became *procurator,* which indicates primarily an economic function.

The first stages of direct Roman rule in Judaea appear to have restored a measure of tranquillity to the land, and compared to Herodian times may have eased some tension. Before long, however, relations between the Jewish sector and the authorities deteriorated, beginning in the days of Pontius Pilate (26-36 C.E.) and getting progressively worse under the emperor Gaius Caligula (37-41 C.E.). The latter almost pushed the nation into outright rebellation with his demand that a statue be set up in the Jerusalem Temple,[112] the affair being resolved only by his assassination. By

---

[107] *Ant.* 17:271-85; *War* 2:56-65.

[108] Dio Cassius 53:12; cf. Stern, 'The Province of Judaea', 309-10.

[109] *Ant.* 17:355; 18:1-2; Luke 2:1-2; Acts 5:37; for the chronological problems regarding the census, cf. Schürer, *History* 1, 258-9, 399-427; Stern, 'The Province of Judaea', 372-4.

[110] *War* 2:499ff.

[111] As indicated by the inscription found in the theater of Caesarea relating to the governorship of Pontius Pilate; cf. Schürer, *History* 1, 358 n. 22; Stern, 'The Province of Judaea', 316, n. 4.

[112] Philo, *Legatio ad Gaium,* 188, 203ff.; *Ant.* 18:261; *War* 2: 185-7; Tacitus, *Hist.* 5:9.

the time of the last Roman governors, total anarchy seems to have prevailed in Judaea, and even Josephus who ordinarily refrains from blaming the Roman regime for the Jewish rebellion, makes no attempt to conceal his contempt for the last governors, in particular Gessius Florus.[113]

Institutions and Parties in Second Temple Judaea

The Roman conquest notwithstanding, considerable autonomy in local affairs as well as non-intervention in the religious life of the Jewish people was characteristic of much of the period under discussion.[114] Needless to say, much of this activity centered around the Temple and Jerusalem, which, beginning with the days of Persian rule over *Yehud*, remained a focal point of Jewish existence.[115] By early Hellenistic times the Jews were commonly identified with Jerusalem, to the extent that Polybius could refer to them as those 'living about the Temple of Jerusalem'.[116] As a result, the various components of Jewish leadership, and even those not of a strictly religious or ritualistic nature, nevertheless found themselves linked to Jerusalem. The most obvious of these elements was the high priesthood, which remained the central office within Jewish society throughout the Second Temple period. Not only was the high priest responsible for Temple ritual, but during much of the period he served as the political representative of the nation, and frequently as an economic functionary, responsible for the collection of taxes. Thus there emerged in the early Hellenistic period an impression of the Jewish people as a nation ruled by priests, spelled out in detail by Hecataeus of Abdera.[117] As we have noted, major changes in Jewish leadership ensued in later Second Temple times, and yet all are linked in one measure or another with the priesthood: the Hasmoneans served as high priests themselves; the Herodians married into the priesthood (as did the Tobiads before them) and appointed the high priests, and even in the midst of the Great War against Rome the priesthood played a major role.

Alongside the priesthood there apparently existed at different stages of Second Temple history various bodies or institutions representing other

---

[113] *War* 2:278; it is worth noting that during the reign of Claudius there was a marked change in the ethnic origin of officials in the Roman administration of Judaea. At least three of the last seven governors were of Greek or Eastern origin (as opposed to governors of Latin origin in the earlier period). This helps to explain the consistent support of Greek-Syrian elements displayed by the last governors, a phenomenon that contributed in no small measure to the strained relations between the authorities and the Jewish population.

[114] Cf. Safrai, 'Jewish Self-Government'.

[115] On the Temple and its place in Jewish life cf. Safrai, in *WHJP* 7, 284-337; see also Flusser, *WHJP* 8, 17-19; Schürer, *History* 2, 237-313.

[116] *Ant.* 12:136; for the inference here cf. Stern, *Greek and Latin Authors* 1, 114, note to line 136.

[117] Cf. Stern, *Greek and Latin Authors* 1, 28.

segments of society, and fulfilling different functions. The nature of one such institution, the Great Synagogue (כנסת הגדולה) remains enigmatic.[118] Certain scholars interpret this to refer to an early permanent institution in Jerusalem, a forerunner to the Sanhedrin, while others see it as a framework for the convening of representatives of the nation in times of crisis, or when fateful decisions had to be taken (e.g. the appointment of Simon, 1 Macc 14).[119]

By the Hellenistic period it is clear that alongside the priesthood there functioned a council of elders — gerousia — in Jerusalem. In fact, it was this body that seems to serve as the official representative institution of the Jewish people,[120] and until the Hasmonean uprising they commonly appear before the high priest in correspondence issued by the authorities.

By the late Second Temple period the existence of yet another institution is beyond doubt. An abundance of sources refer to the Sanhedrin from the first stages of Roman rule in Judaea,[121] with the first clear allusion to a trial before that body being the case of Herod, then a young governor of Galilee under Hyrcanus II and accused of murder.[122] Later trials appear in the New Testament, in relation to Jesus (Mark 14:53ff.), Peter (Acts 4) and Paul (Acts 22:30ff.).[123] Common to Josephus and the New Testament is the depiction of the Sanhedrin primarily as a tribunal and political body,[124] with the high priest serving in some major capacity. The rabbinic sources, on the other hand, frequently refer to the Sanhedrin (or 'The Great Court' and a variety of other names)[125] as a legislative body comprised of 70 or 71 elders, 'from whence halakhah goes out to Israel'.[126] Beyond those scholars who simply reject the historicity of one set of sources or another,[127] various theories have been proposed to reconcile the different descriptions. Some

---

[118] The 'Men of the Great Synagogue' appear in rabbinic sources as a link in the chain of Jewish tradition, spanning the period between the prophets and the sages (M. Aboth 1:1). Attributed to them in later rabbinic literature are the canonization of portions of the Scriptures, establishment of certain prayers and benedictions, as well as the division of the oral Law into various categories; cf. Mantel, 'The Nature of the Great Synagogue', 69ff.; id., in WHJP 8, 44-52.

[119] For further discussion see Kraus, 'The Great Synod'; Englander, 'The Men of the Great Synagogue'; Finkelstein, The Men of the Great Synagogue.

[120] E.g. Ant. 12:138; on the change in the status of the gerousia under the Hasmoneans cf. Stern, Documents, 34.

[121] The most comprehensive compilation of the material is Mantel, Studies in the History of the Sanhedrin; see also Schürer, History 2, 199ff.

[122] Ant. 14:168ff. The term appears first in Josephus in connection with the attempts by Gabinius to divide Judaea into five synhedria, cf. Ant. 14:91.

[123] For the trial of James see Ant. 20:200.

[124] See for example Josephus, Life 62, where the Sanhedrin serves as the governing body of Jews at the outset of the Great Revolt, instructing Josephus as commander of Galilee.

[125] Cf. Alon, The Jews in their Land, 187-8.

[126] T. Hagigah 2:9; T. Sanhedrin 7:1.

[127] Cf. Schürer, History 2, 210f.

have suggested concomitant bodies functioning alongside each other in Jerusalem;[128] while others have postulated a change in the nature and composition of the institution reflecting the political vicissitudes of the different periods.[129]

This last theory in particular takes into account the ongoing tension between the various sects and parties in Second Temple Judaea, a phenomenon discussed briefly above. As for the institutions in Jerusalem, the prolonged struggle between Pharisees and Sadducees could not help but make itself felt in almost all areas of religious and political activity. While the Pharisees never encouraged a total removal from Temple worship, their opposition to the Sadducean control of that Temple nothwithstanding, it is a fair guess to assume that the growing stress on the reading and preaching of the Torah in synagogues served as a major vehicle for enhancing the independent status of the Sages.[130] In the Temple itself numerous disputes erupted between proponents of the two groups, or more precisely between the priestly oligarchy given to Sadducean influence and the gathered masses supporting Pharisaic tradition. These disputes, needless to say, might have been rooted in the major distinction between the two groups, with the Pharisees 'passing on to the people certain regulations handed down by former generations and not recorded in the Laws of Moses' (i.e. Oral Tradition) while the Sadducees considered valid only those regulations written down.[131] Certain disputes, nevertheless, must have also reflected social and political tensions between the groups.[132]

Opposition to Rome and the Great Revolt

Pharisees and Sadducees chose to remain, and frequently clash, within the mainstream of Jewish life. At the same time, certain segments of society appear to have opted for a preparation towards the future, and a distinct

---

[128] In particular Büchler, *Das Synedrion;* Mantel, *Studies,* 61-101.

[129] Cf. Alon, *The Jews in their Land,* 185-205.

[130] For the Synagogue and its place in Second Temple history see Safrai, in *WHJP* 8, 65-98; *id.* 'Temple', 908-44.

[131] *Ant.* 13:297-8; one famous clash between representatives of the two groups in the *Sanhedrin* obviously reflects varying religious beliefs and traditions, cf. Acts 23:6-8.

[132] Cf. Marcus, 'The Pharisees'. However, this does not warrant the relegation of the Pharisees as a whole to the social class of 'urban Plebeians'; see Finkelstein, *The Pharisees,* 13. The literature on Pharisees and Sadducees is enormous, and to a degree reflects the source problem cited above regarding the Sanhedrin. In this case Josephus stresses the 'philosophical' differences between the groups (*War* 2: 162-6; *Ant.* 13:171-3; 297-8; 18:11-18); the New Testament is interested primarily in the groups as background for presenting the early Christian message (cf. Neusner, *From Politics to Piety,* 67-80); whereas the Rabbis were obviously interested in legal traditions over which differences existed, although it would be mistaken to overlook the numerous rabbinic references to disputes of a theological nature. For a bibliography on Pharisees and Sadducees cf. Schürer, *History* 2, 381-2.

apocalyptic fervour emerges towards the latter part of the Second Temple period.[133] This eschatological expectation of cataclysmic events and the 'end of days' need not, in and of itself, have required one to sever all ties with society. Most certainly such phenomena as the anticipation of a messianic deliverance had been widely accepted by a broad spectrum of Jews.[134] In this context, the Qumran community seems to have taken a more radical approach, believing that only those who prepare themselves totally for this event will ultimately share in its fruits; hence the well-known break of this group from the rest of society, their total separation 'from all perverse men who walk in the ways of wickedness' and their removal into the wilderness.[135] While the numerous components of apocalytic and ora- cular literature, as well as the particular theology of the Qumran sect, will be dealt with in subsequent chapters of this volume, the political aspect of these eschatological hopes must be stressed here, because it had an immediate impact on Jewish history in the last days of the Second Temple. As noted above, the Roman conquest in general, and in particular the turbulent days in Judaea following Herod's death, were an ideal setting for the propagation of beliefs regarding an imminent deliverance from the yoke of foreign conquest. Indeed, that messianic overtones are discernible within the anti-Roman movement appears beyond doubt. Josephus, who commonly refrained from alluding to messianic expectations, states openly that what aroused the rebels to take up arms 'was an ambiguous oracle, likewise found in their sacred scriptures, to the effect that at that time one from this country would become ruler of the world'.[136] These hopes hardly remained secret. Even Tacitus reports that in the priestly writings of the Jews there was a prophecy 'that this was the very time when the East would grow strong and that men starting from Judaea would possess the world'.[137]

In stressing this undercurrent of Jewish sentiment, however, one point must not be overlooked. Jewish opposition to Rome was far from united under one common banner or ideology. One of the striking aspects of the movement is the bitter fratricide that ensues almost until the fall of the Temple itself.[138] In describing the various groups, Josephus appears to

[133] The phenomenon itself, of course, is apparent throughout Second Temple history; cf. Charles, *Eschatology;* Russell, *The Message.*
[134] Cf. Schürer, *History* 2, 505-13; even one as moderate as Philo was party to such hopes, see Wolfson, *Philo* 2, 395-426.
[135] 1QS 8:13; 9:19-20.
[136] *War* 6:312.
[137] *Histories* 5:13,2. See also Suetonius, *Vespasian* 4:5, 'there had spread all over the orient an old and established belief that it was fated at that time for men coming from Judaea to rule the world.' On these prophecies cf. Stern, *Greek and Latin Authors* 2, 61-2.
[138] For various theories on the nature and identity of the different movements see: Farmer, *Maccabees;* Hengel, *Die Zeloten;* Smith, 'Zealots and Sicarii'; Appelbaum, 'The Zealots'; Stern, 'Zealots'; *id.,* in *WHJP* 8, 263-301, 374-7; Rhoads, *Israel in Revolution.*

distinguish between a Galilean element the roots of which go back to the early days of Roman rule, and the later rebels who appear on the Jerusalem scene with the outbreak of hostilities in 66 C.E., and are commonly referred to by Josephus as 'Zealots'.

The former group, Josephus claims, established a clearcut ideology of rebellion, as a reaction to the census of Quirinius: 'They said that the assessment carried with it a status amounting to downright slavery, and appealed to the nation to make a bid for independence'.[139] The implication of 'slavery' here has a decidedly religious overtone, and in this respect the ideology of the revolt assumed a religious motivation: 'They have a passion for liberty that is almost unconquerable since they are convinced that God alone is their leader and master'.[140] The proponents of this theology, which in effect raised the idea of political independence to a religious plane, are frequently designated as *sicarii* by Josephus. Rooted in Galilee, they were associated with a family of rebels, beginning with Ezekias in the days of young Herod's rule as governor of Galilee, through the leadership of Judah the Galilean (possibly the son of Ezekias), and down to the third and fourth generations of that family during the Great War. This attachment to a dynasty of sorts manifests itself with the appearance of yet another member of the family, Menahem, who appears in Jerusalem at the outset of the Great War as a sort of king,[141] and it is a reasonable assumption that messianic hopes were attached to his person. This party seems to have raised a radical social banner as well, and in the course of the early fighting in Jerusalem they set fire to the municipal archives 'eager to destroy the money-lender's bonds and to prevent the recovery of debts, in order to win over a host of grateful debtors, and to cause a rising of the poor against the rich'.[142] To be sure, the *sicarii* appear in Jerusalem at the very beginning of the war in 66, but were turned away by the local Zealot movement, with many of its members, among them Menahem, killed. Remants of the group retreated to Masada, where they were destined to live out the war until 74, when, having conquered the rest of the land, Roman forces finally confronted them, precipitating — if Josephus' account is to be trusted — one of the epic and tragic episodes of ancient Jewish history.[143]

In contrast to the *sicarii,* the Zealots appear in Josephus' account primarily as the Jerusalemite rebels, headed by several members of the priesthood, and with their major stronghold the Temple itself. During the war, however, these groups were joined by a variety of anti-Roman elements, initially the Idumeans, and after the fall of Galilee in autumn of 67,

---

[139] *Ant.* 18:4.
[140] *Ant.* 18:23.
[141] *War* 2:433-4.
[142] *War* 2:427.
[143] For two recent re-evaluations Josephus' account of the Masada suicide, cf. Cohen, 'Masada'; Stern, 'The Suicide of Eleazar ben Yair'.

by the most outstanding military figure of the war — John of Gischala.[144] Yet another leader — Simon bar Giora — joined these ranks somewhat later, with a religious and social platform not far from that of the *sicarii*. He too appears as a charismatic general with regal presence, and Josephus claims that each soldier under his command 'was quite prepared to take his very own life had he given the order'.[145] Given the variety of personal leaders, as well as the geographical, social and religious backgrounds of the various freedom-fighters, one can understand the tensions that existed within the Jewish camp, effectively precluding any real unified opposition to Rome.

The major part of the Great War itself lasted for four years, from the spring of 66 to the summer of 70. Josephus sees two events as responsible for igniting the conflagration: the clash between Jews and Greeks in Caesarea (*War* 2:284ff.) and the sacking of the Temple by Florus (*War* 2:293ff.). But obviously these were only the last overt expressions of an intolerable hostility that had taken hold of the country. Appointed by Nero to suppress the revolt was Titus Flavius Vespasian, one of Rome's leading generals;[146] the legions and various auxiliary forces placed at his disposal numbered some sixty thousand men. Vespasian cautiously proceeded in subduing the country bit by bit, conquering Galilee in 67 and most of Judaea in 68; from the Roman base in Jericho, at this stage, a contingent appears to have proceeded to Qumran and destroyed the Essene center there.[147] Nero's death on 9 June 68 brought a limited cessation to the hostilities, and after the abortive attempts at installing a new emperor, the legions of Egypt, Syria and Palestine proposed their own commander as candidate. One year later Vespasian was declared emperor, and the final phase of the war, culminating in the siege of Jerusalem, was left to his son Titus. The Temple itself went up in flames on the ninth and tenth of *Av*, 70 C.E. Josephus' attempts to exonerate Titus of all guilt for this event[148] have been convincingly set aside by modern historians.[149]

Between the Wars: From Jerusalem to Yavneh

The destruction of the Second Temple was most certainly a major turning point in Jewish history, but attempts at a precise definition of the ensuing processes have engendered lively debate among scholars. Naturally, the lack of one religious focal point, i.e. the Temple, facilitated an enhanced

---

[144] For recent studies on John of Gischala see Rappaport, 'John of Gischala'; *id.*, 'John of Gischala in Galilee.'

[145] *War* 4:510; 5:309; cf. Loftus, 'The Anti-Roman Revolts'.

[146] *War* 3:4f.

[147] Cf. *War* 2:152-3.

[148] *War* 6:238-41.

[149] Alon, *Jews, Judaism, and the Classical World,* 252-68. Cf. below, pp. 200-3.

role for the synagogue, and in similar fashion leadership passed to a great extent from priests to Sages.[150] These new elements of religious expression and authority, synagogue and Sages, ultimately served as geographically decentralizing factors within the Jewish community. The leadership framework set up at Yavneh following the destruction,[151] while taking care to stress continuity with Jerusalem, nevertheless served as a model for subsequent institutions, whether in other parts of Israel, particularly Galilee, or throughout the diaspora in a later stage. The argument for viewing the destruction as the beginning of Jewish *galut* (exile)[152] commonly stresses the mobility of these new institutions, which assured a slow but definite centrifugal process leading away from one recognized centre, be it the Land of Israel in general, or Jerusalem in particular.[153] Certainly, Jews living in the first centuries after the destruction tended to distinguish between two eras in Jewish history: 'the time of the Temple — and that of no Temple',[154] with the latter being referred to as 'this era' (הזמן הזה). Nevertheless, the very fact that no major mass exodus of Jews followed the destruction, coupled with an awareness that the major components of Jewish authority, the Patriarchate and the body of rabbis that functioned alongside that office, continued to be based in the Land of Israel for generations after the events of 70 C.E. — all this suggests that a distinction must be drawn between the creation of a potentially decentralized Judaism, and the outright commencement of *galut* itself.[155]

While the number of Jews who died during the Great War was by all accounts exceedingly high,[156] the spiritual devastation felt by the survivors was no less acute, and this emerges from a wide variety of sources. Among the last apocalyptic books written by Jews and included in the corpus of apocryphal and pseudepigraphal literature are works such as *2 Baruch* and *4 Ezra*, both written in the immediate aftermath of the destruction. The lamentation expressed in these works is accompanied by serious questions regarding the meaning of Jewish existence without a temple (e.g. *2 Baruch*

---

[150] See Neusner, *'A Life'*, pp. 196-199 for a summary of the advantages of Pharisaic leadership created by the destruction. On the nature of the transformation within rabbinic leadership following the destruction see Urbach, 'Class-Status'.

[151] For a description of Jewish autonomy and leadership after the destruction cf. Safrai, 'Jewish Self-Government', pp. 404-412.

[152] For an excellent exposition of this Hebrew term and its implications in Jewish history, see Ben-Sasson, *'Galut'*.

[153] See Urbach, 'The Jews in their Land'.

[154] E.g. *M. Hullin* 5:1.

[155] The main proponent of this approach is G. Alon, see his recently translated *The Jews in Their Land*, pp. 3-17.

[156] For a brief summary of the various figures in ancient historiography cf. Smallwood, *The Jews under Roman Rule*, p. 327 n. 152. For the political status and Roman administration of Provincia Judaea following the Great War cf. Schürer, *History* 1, pp. 514-520, and most recently Stern, 'The Roman Administration'.

chapter 10), and in certain respects is echoed by rabbinic descriptions of ascetics who abstained from aspects of normal life and undertook perpetual mourning.[157] These phenomena were met head-on by the leaders of the Yavneh generation, with the emerging philosophy attributed primarily to Rabban Yohanan ben Zakkai.[158] In response to his disciple's expressed fear that the lack of a temple precludes atonement for sin, Rabban Yohanan replies: 'We have another atonement as effective as this, and what is it? — Acts of loving kindness, as it is written: "For I desire mercy and not sacrifice" (Hos. 6:6)'.[159] The thrust of a number of regulations attributed to Rabban Yohanan ben Zakkai at Yavneh is the removal to Jewish communities at large of various customs once performed only in Jerusalem.[160] While these steps were justified as a means of 'remembering the Sanctuary', their ultimate effect was to induce large numbers of Jews into accepting the loss — albeit temporary — of the Temple, while at the same time maintaining part of the ancient ritual alongside the newly revised system of prayers.[161]

Rabban Yohanan ben Zakkai was followed at Yavneh by Rabban Gamaliel II.[162] Under Gamaliel, Yavnean institutions take on a measure of permanence. The patriarchate, with its particular blend of spiritual and political authority, begins only now to take shape,[163] and under Gamaliel II Palestinian hegemony over diaspora Jewry also reasserts itself. Great stress is placed on the functions of the new centre in all matters regarding the calendar, and contacts with various diaspora communities become more apparent.[164] One major consequence of this development (although possibly carried out after Gamaliel's death) may have been the decision to

---

[157] *T. Sotah* 15:11-15, ed. Lieberman p. 242-243; *B.T. Baba Bathra* 60b.

[158] For literature on Rabban Yohanan ben Zakkai cf. Schürer, *History* 2, p. 369 n. 55; see also Safrai, 'Rabban Yohanan ben Zakkai'.

[159] *Aboth de R. Nathan*, A ch. 4, p. 21 (transl. Goldin p. 34); cf. Neusner, *A Life*, pp. 188-192; Alon, *The Jews in their Land*, pp. 46-55.

[160] *M. Rosh ha-Shana* 4:1-4; *B.T. Rosh ha-Shana* 31b.

[161] No concrete evidence points to any serious resumption of sacrificial worship following the destruction (cf. Smallwood, *The Jews under Roman Rule*, p. 347 n. 62-63), although rabbinic law would seem to sanction such a development. Hence Safrai's contention that it was an active part of Rabban Yohanan's policy that prevented the renewal of sacrifices, cf. Safrai, 'Rabban Yohanan ben Zakkai', p. 211.

[162] The precise date of this succession, as well as the events surrounding Ben Zakkai's removal to Beror Hayil are unclear. Alon maintains that Gamaliel assumed leadership some 10-15 years after the destruction (cf. *The Jews in Their Land*, p. 119), and links Yohanan's retirement to opposition towards that sage among certain elements of the rabbinic movement; cf. Alon, pp. 337-343. Safrai maintains that it is untenable that a scion of a major Jewish family would have been allowed to acquire power and prestige under the Flavian dynasty; hence Gamaliel's appearance at Yavneh probably came upon the death of Diocletian in 96 C.E.; cf. Safrai, 'Restoration of the Jewish Community,' p. 30-31.

[163] For the degree of Roman involvement in this process see: Goodblatt, 'Roman Recognition'.

[164] Cf. Alon, *The Jews in Their Land*, pp. 232-252.

commission a new translation of the Bible into Greek, namely that of Aquila.[165] Clearly, those rabbis of Palestine who are mentioned in connection with this project — R. Eliezer b. Hyrcanus, R. Joshua b. Hananiah and R. Akiva — must have had the needs of Jews in the Hellenistic-Roman diaspora in mind. But this endeavour, which succeeded to a certain degree in replacing the Septuagint as the commonly accepted text among Greek-speaking Jews,[166] also reflects on another issue which Yavnean leadership seems to have taken up. If the Septuagint had fallen into disfavour in rabbinic eyes, one major reason was the fact that it had evolved into the widely accepted version of the growing Christian community.[167]

One of the major tasks taken up by the leadership of the Yavneh generation appears to be a redefinition of the boundaries of the Jewish community, slowly leading up to a negation of the very legitimacy of sectarian Judaism.[168] In this context one might view the period between the two great revolts in terms of Jewish-Christian relations as transitory.[169] In Palestine the issue was not yet one of confrontation between two distinct communities, but rather one of formulating a policy towards Jewish-Christians. While not all *minim* (heretics) in rabbinic literature are Judaeo-Christians, it is a fair assumption that the formulation of the *birkat ha-minim* and its insertion into the main prayer at the initiative of Gamaliel II, is part of a process of isolating and declaring against the legitimacy of Jewish-Christianity.[170]

While the term 'normativization' may be a bit extreme in defining the process of consolidation that Judaism underwent following the destruction,[171] there is an undeniable feeling that concerted efforts were being made to minimize further fragmentation of the Jewish community. This tendency is particularly manifest in the realm of rabbinic literature and the history of *halakhah*. The opening statement of *Tosefta Eduyot* (1:1) is frequently cited in this context: 'When the Sages entered the vineyard of Yavneh, they said: A time shall come when man shall seek a word of Torah and not find it, a word of the scribes and not find it . . . for one precept of the Torah shall not be like another. They declared: Let us begin with Hillel

---

[165] *P.T. Megillah* 1:2,71c; Jellicoe, *The Septuagint*, pp. 76-83.
[166] This is attested to by Church fathers such as Origen and Jerome, and as late as the 6th century there is evidence of Aquila being read in Jewish synagogues, in a *novella* of Justinian (Nr. 146; Feb. 13, 553).
[167] Cf. *Tanhuma, Tissa* 34 (127a): 'The Holy One Blessed be He foresaw that the nations of the world will translate the Torah and read it in Greek, and they say: We are Israel . . .'
[168] Cf. Baron, *History* 2, pp. 129ff.
[169] Cf. Avi-Yonah, *The Jews of Palestine*, pp. 137-145.
[170] Cf. Alon, *The Jews in their Land*, pp. 288-307. For the precise target and aims of this benediction see Kimelman, 'Birkat Ha-Minim'.
[171] Cf. Moore, *Judaism* 1, p. 3.

and Shammai'. Certain scholars consider this statement as alluding to the first stages of the redaction of the Mishnah, with tractate *Eduyot* being the first such collection.[172] Others, however, stress that what is reflected here is typical of the growing tendency at Yavneh, i.e. the need to arrive at decisions regarding those *halakhot* under dispute.[173] This development coincides with a whole series of traditions from Yavneh, all stressing the demand — voiced for the first time — that minority opinions acquiesce to the will of the majority,[174] and similarly that various Sages accept the ruling of the Patriarch.[175] Not insignificant in this context is the gathering concensus at Yavneh that the *halakhah* is to follow the teachings of the School of Hillel, one of the most central developments in the ultimate acceptance of the Mishnah as universally binding.[176]

It is, of course, difficult to appraise how successful all these efforts were at immediately effecting a more cohesive Jewish community. Two great Jewish revolts were to follow the destruction of the Second Temple by no more than one and a half generations: the Jewish uprising under Trajan (114-117 C.E.) which engulfed major segments of the Jewish community in Egypt, Nort Africa (Cyrene), Cyprus, Mesopotamia and possibly (albeit to a lesser degree) Judaea,[177] and the Bar-Kokhba uprising in Judaea itself (132-135). Whether the initial successes of these wars, particularly of the Bar-Kokhba uprising, attest to the degree of Jewish consolidation achieved by the sages of Yavneh is still a matter for scholarly debate.[178] What cannot be denied is the crucial role of the first generation of Sages following the destruction in overcoming the initial trauma, as well as redefining and passing on to subsequent generations much of what ultimately came to be recognized as historic post-Temple Judaism.

[172] Albeck, *Introduction to the Mishnah*, p. 82. Compare Epstein, *Introduction to Tannaic Litature*, p. 428, who limits the statement to an organization of the disputes between Hillel and Shammai, claiming that in fact earlier compilations of rabbinic law already existed.
[173] Cf. Urbach, *Sages*, p. 598.
[174] *M. Eduyot* 5:6; *B.T. Baba Metzia* 54 a-b.
[175] *M. Rosh ha-Shana* 2:8-9; *B.T. Bekhorot* 36a; *B.T. Berakhot* 27b-28a.
[176] See Safrai, 'The Decision According to the School of Hillel'.
[177] For a collection of articles on this war cf. D. Rokeah ed., *Jewish Rebellions in the Time of Traian 115-117 C.E.*, Jerusalem 1978.
[178] Cf. Oppenheimer, 'The Bar Kokhba Revolt', p. 40, who sees a direct link between national unity under Bar Kokhba and the achievement at Yavneh. For a debate on the nature of support for Bar Kokhba see: 'Bar Kokhba's Position as a Leader of the Nation', in *Cathedra* 29 (1983) 4-28 (a discussion, in Hebrew).

Chapter Two

Stories of Biblical
and Early Post-Biblical Times

George W. E. Nickelsburg

The post-exilic Jewish community produced a vast quantity of narrative literature. Common to this literature is its setting in Israelite history in relation to situations and characters known from this history. These narrative writings do not admit of easy classification, and some of them could, with good reason, have been grouped with texts treated elsewhere in this volume.

These problems notwithstanding, we have divided the narrative writings into two somewhat overlapping categories. In the next chapter we shall treat documents that are closely related to the biblical texts, often expanding, paraphrasing, and implicitly commenting on them. In the present chapter, we discuss an older type of narrative, which is only loosely connected with biblical traditions about Israel's past. Often this connection involves little more than the historical setting (e.g., the exile or diaspora) and some figure(s) from the past — a foreign king or a patriarch or prophet. The stories may also use biblical themes and may imitate biblical stories, but here the similarities cease.

Chronology presents one problem in determining the proper contents of this chapter. The book of Tobit and quite possibly an early stratum in Judith are older than the final form of the canonical book of Daniel. On the other hand, because the old stories in Daniel 1-6 were used in a document composed in the Maccabaean period and because these stories were imitated in writings from the post-biblical period, we shall treat Daniel 1-6 briefly here.

Another ambiguity relates to the stories that were incorporated into the Greek version of Daniel. In the form in which we know them, they function as expansions and imitations of a biblical text. However, it remains uncertain whether they were composed to be inserted into the biblical text or whether they were composed earlier, before their prototypes had become part of that text.

Finally, at the end of this chapter we discuss *Aristeas to Philocrates* and 3 Maccabees, two texts about events in the third century B.C.E. (post-biblical times). Because of their narrative form, we include them here. With equal justification they might have been grouped with Wisdom literature and historical writings respectively.

Daniel 1-6

Daniel 1-6 is a cycle of stories about Jewish courtiers in Babylon and their dealings with Mesopotamian kings.[1] Their common setting suggests that they originated and were collected in the Eastern diaspora.[2] Some of the stories are doubtless very old[3] and are part of a larger collection known and used ca. 165 B.C.E. by the Palestinian author of Daniel.[4]

The stories are basically of two types.[5] Chapters 2, 4, 5 pit Daniel, the Jewish sage, against his Chaldaean counterparts. The God of Israel is the giver of revelation, and he mediates the interpretation of this revelation through his sages alone. The content of this revelation, which comes to pass in the action in chapters 4 and 5, is that God delegates his authority to the kings of the earth, and he removes or punishes them when they rebel against this authority or fail to acknowledge it.[6] The second type of story, in chapters 3 and 6, employs an old literary genre about court rivalries and conspiracies known from the Joseph stories in Genesis 34ff., the book of Esther, and the story of Ahikar.[7] As in the other Danielic stories, the native courtiers are pitted against their Jewish rivals. Obedience to the God of Israel is challenged when his faithful servants are handed over to death because they choose to obey his law; but his mighty power is demonstrated when he delivers his servants, thus vindicating their trust in him and their obedience to his law.

The stories in Daniel 1-6 evince a common structure: the testing, the demonstration, and the acclamation of the power and sovereignty of the God of Israel, usually on the lips of the monarch. Consequently, the function of the stories is to sanction the presence of Jewish sages in foreign courts. When they remain faithful to their God, he protects them from

---

[1] For a more detailed discussion of the respective stories, see Humphreys, 'Life-Style,' 217-23; Collins, *Apocalyptic Vision,* 29-54; Nickelsburg, *Jewish Literature,* 19-25.

[2] See Humphreys, 'Life-Style,' 217-23; and Collins, *Apocalyptic Vision,* 54-59.

[3] Various dates around the end of the Persian period and the beginning of the Hellenistic period are suggested for the individual stories by Delcor, *Daniel,* 18-20, 85, 107, 123f., 132, 140. Some of the stories may reflect much earlier traditions; see Bickerman, *Four Strange Books,* 92-100. See also Collins, *Apocalyptic Vision,* 8-11. On the relationship between Dan 4 and the Qumran 'Prayer of Nabonidus,' see below, p. 36f.

[4] See Collins, *Apocalyptic Vision,* 57-59; and Bickerman, *Four Strange Books,* 92-100.

[5] Humphreys, 'Life-Style', 217-23; Collins, *Apocalyptic Vision,* 33-54.

[6] On Dan 2 as a special type of 'success story of the wise courtier,' see Niditch and Doran, 'Success Story.'

[7] On the general characteristics of this genre, see Nickelsburg, *Resurrection,* 49-52; and Nickelsburg, 'Genre,' 153-63. The Story of Ahikar (see below, p. 284) is at least as old as the fragmentary fifth century B.C.E. Elephantine papyrus on which the Aramaic text is found; see Cowley, *Aramaic Papyri,* 204-48. For a recent critical translation of the Aramaic, see Grelot, *Documents,* 427-52. For a translation of the various versions, see Harris, 'The Story of Ahikar'. On introductory matters, see Greenfield-Stone, 'Ahikar.'

danger and causes their activities to prosper (chaps. 1, 3, 6). Moreover, he enlightens them, so that they can be his spokesmen in this foreign environment (chaps. 2, 4, 5). A striking result of this witness is the veritable conversion of the monarchs and their unabashed confession of faith in the uniqueness and universal sovereignty of the God of Israel.

The Prayer of Nabonidus

This document is extant in one Qumran manuscript, three fragments of which preserve parts of twelve lines.[8] According to its superscription, it is 'The words of the pra[y]er that Nabonai prayed, the king of A[ssyria and Baby]lon, [the great] king, [when he was afflicted] with an evil ulcer in Teiman at the command of the [Most High] G[od].'[9]

The superscription was followed by a narrative in the first person singular, two paragraphs of which have been partly preserved. According to the first, Nabonidus was afflicted for seven years, until his sins were pardoned by a Jewish exorcist (very likely Daniel), who commanded him to write an account of the event in order to praise the name of the Most High God.[10] The second paragraph begins the account itself.[11] Nabonidus was afflicted in Teiman. 'For seven years [I] prayed to [all the gods of] silver and gold, [bronze and iron], wood (and) stone (and) clay, because[12] [I thou]ght that th[ey were] gods [. . .]'

A small fragment containing a few words from four lines appears to have come from a later part of the manuscript.[13] Here Nabonidus refers either to a dream he had or to his healing.[14] Then, speaking to an unknown figure, perhaps an angelic interpreter, he says, '. . . h]ow you resemble [Daniel . . .]'[15]

Because of the fragmented condition of the manuscript, any reconstruction of the whole of the document must remain uncertain.[16] That a

---

[8] 4QPrNab. See Milik, 'Prière', 407-11; Meyer, *Gebet,* 13-33.

[9] Translation follows Milik, 'Prière,' 408; Meyer, *Gebet,* 33.

[10] The name of Daniel does not appear in the extant fragments.

[11] According to Milik ('Prière,' 408-9) and Meyer (*Gebet,* 26), this paragraph was spoken by the exorcist to Nabonidus. The first person in the translation above follows Fitzmyer-Harrington, *Manual,* 3.

[12] Or 'from the time that,' *ibid.*

[13] Because this fragment is from a different piece of hide, Milik ('Prière,' 408) places it at least in column 4, and he is followed by Meyer, *Gebet,* 14.

[14] For alternative possibilities of translating אחלמת, see Milik, 'Prière,' 409; and Meyer, *Gebet,* 28 ('to dream'); and Fitzmyer-Harrington, *Manual,* 5 ('to make strong').

[15] On the possibility that Nabonidus is speaking to an angel, see Milik, 'Prière,' 410; and Meyer, *Gebet,* 52. The first letter of Daniel's name is seen by Milik, 'Prière,' 410; and Fitzmyer-Harrington, *Manual,* 3; Meyer (*Gebet,* 29) is sceptical. The published photograph indicates only a speck.

[16] Meyer's detailed reconstruction (*Gebet* 51-52), which is based on the extant fragments, as well as on a comparison with Daniel 4, is quite plausible but is unprovable in all its details.

dream was involved seems likely, regardless of one's interpretation of the last fragment. That Nabonidus saw an angel who resembled the Jewish sage he had previously seen is not at all impossible. A similar motif occurs in the story of the conversion of Aseneth, to whom the angel Michael appears, looking like a glorified form of Joseph.[17] Present evidence is too meager to support firm conclusions about the genre of the writing or about its supposed theology of suffering.[18]

Perhaps most remarkable about the document is its evident knowledge of the events and facts of the life of the historical Nabonidus: his sojourn in Teiman; his forsaking the gods of Babylon for the moon god, Sin; probably his interest in dreams.[19]

Nabu-na'id was the last king of the Neo-Babylonian empire and ruled from 555 until 539 B.C.E., when Cyrus captured Babylon. He was the father of Belshazzar, whom he placed in charge of Babylon and a large part of his armies during his long stay in Arabia, where he made his headquarters in the oasis city of Teiman (Tema).

Meyer may very well be right in arguing that the document originated in the Persian period in Babylonian Jewish circles that drew on historical sources and traditions about Nabonidus.[20] Even though the Qumran manuscript is to be dated ca. 50-1 B.C.E., the accuracy of its knowledge about Nabonidus — who is never mentioned in the Bible — strongly suggests that it is a copy of a much older writing. Its presence at Qumran may lend some support to hypotheses of a Babylonian immigration into that community or a related community.[21]

The similarities between this document and the story of Nebuchad-nezzar's illness in Daniel 4 (3:31-4:34 Aram.) have been universally recognized by commentators.[22] A Babylonian king, living away from Babylon, is ill for seven years (seven times, Dan 4:25 [4:22 Aram.]). A Jewish interpreter plays a prominent role. The king's illness, which is related to his failure to acknowledge the true God, is healed when he does acknowledge God. The king recounts the story in the first person.

---

[17] Cf. *Jos. As.* 14:9. As a parallel to the Aramaic formula, Milik ('Prière,' 410, n. 7) cites 4QTob aram^b, the Aramaic of Tob 7:2. Cf. *Barn.* 7:10, where Jesus' enemies compare the Glorified One with him whom they rejected.

[18] See Meyer, *Gebet,* 94-104.

[19] For details, see *ibid.,* 52-67. For a summary, see Oppenheim, 'Nabonidus.' For an English translation of the Babylonian texts on Nabonidus, to which Meyer refers, see Pritchard, *ANET,* 305-14, 560-3.

[20] Meyer, *Gebet,* 67-81, 105-12. The generalizations on which he excludes a date in Hellenistic times are, however, less than convincing (*ibid.,* 105-07).

[21] See Freedman, 'Prayer,' 31; and Meyer, *Gebet,* 107-08. On the opinions regarding such an immigration, see below, p. 546 n. 294.

[22] E.g., Milik, 'Prière,' 410-11; Freedman, 'Prayer,' 31-32; Cross, *Library,* 166-8; Meyer, *Gebet,* 42-52; Collins, *Apocalyptic Vision,* 47-49. It has also been suggested that this writing has influenced the story of the death of Antiochus Epiphanes in 2 Macc 9; see Mendels, 'A Note.'

Two factors indicate that the Prayer of Nabonidus represents a stage of the tradition that is earlier than the story in Daniel 4.[23] First, the document correctly states that Nabonidus spent a period of time in Teiman, away from Babylon. We know of no such period of absence during the reign of Nebuchadnezzar. Secondly, Daniel 5:18-23 makes reference back to chapter 4, contrasting Belshazzar with his father, who is wrongly identified as Nebuchadnezzar. The association indicates, however, that the story in chapter 5 is dependent on a form of the tradition in chapter 4 in which the protagonist was Nabonidus, the real father of Belshazzar.

Because of the fragmentary condition of the Prayer of Nabonidus, its precise relationship to the book of Daniel remains a matter of speculation. Nonetheless, several details in Daniel 5 suggest an acquaintance with something like the Prayer of Nabonidus and other traditions about Nabonidus. First, as has been noted, the author of chapter 5 knew that Belshazzar was the son of the protagonist in chapter 4. Secondly, Belshazzar's hybris is connected with the worship of 'gods of gold and silver [silver and gold in 5:23], bronze, iron, wood, and stone' (5:4,23). This list corresponds to the description of Nabonidus' idolatrous worship in 4QPrNab 1:7-8, but no such list appears in Daniel 4.[24] Finally, the allusion to the fall of Babylon in Daniel 5:30-31 recalls the historical fact that when the city was captured, Nabonidus was king and was on the scene.[25] It is not impossible, moreover, that the Prayer of Nabonidus stands in a more complex relationship also to the stories in Daniel 2 and 3. In chapter 2 the metals of which the colossus is composed correspond to the materials from which Nabonidus' idols were made. Chapter 3, moreover, speaks of Nebuchadnezzar's idolatry. All the stories relate how the Babylonian monarch acclaims the true God (see pp. 34-5, above). Noteworthy in chapters 3, 4, and 5 is the motif of hybris, which appears to have been lacking in the Prayer of Nabonidus,[26] where the king's conversion from idolatry is perhaps better paralleled to the story of Bel and the Dragon (see pp. 38-40, below).

Susanna

This story is one of several additions to the Book of Daniel, found only in the Greek translations of the book. Like the other Danielic stories, it is set in the diaspora. Its plot line follows that of Daniel 3 and 6. Susanna is cast

[23] See Cross, *Library,* 167.

[24] In Dan 2 the metals are mentioned as the components of the colossus, but not as materials from which idols are made.

[25] Cf. the Nabonidus Chronicle, iii rev., Pritchard, *ANET,* 306; the Cylinder of Cyrus *id., ANET,* 315-16.

[26] See Meyer, *Gebet,* 98; on the development of this motif in Daniel, see Collins, *Apocalyptic Vision,* 48-49.

in the role of the righteous one, and her trust in God and choice to obey his law leads to her condemnation. As she is being led to death, she is rescued by Daniel, her divinely sent deliverer, and she is vindicated of the charges against her. The story was placed at the beginning of the Greek book of Daniel to explain how young Daniel's wisdom led to his high esteem in Babylon (v. 64).[27] As in Daniel 3 and 6, the acclamation at the end of the story is directed to the God who saves (v. 60).

Susanna is introduced as a God-fearing woman (vv. 1-4). She makes a conscious and explicit choice in favour of obedience to God (vv. 22-23; cf. Dan 3:17). Protesting her innocence, she prays for deliverance (vv. 42-43). Throughout, her innocence and piety are contrasted with the wickedness and lechery of the elders.[28] Similarities to Genesis 39 suggest that the story has been influenced by the story of Joseph and Potiphar's wife, with the male and female roles here reversed.[29]

In this story, the old type of tale about court conspiracies has been democratized. The heroine is not a sage, but an ordinary, God-fearing person. Moreover, different from all the other Danielic stories, her enemies and persecutors are Jews. Thus, despite its diaspora setting, it focuses on the situation in the Jewish community, and it encourages obedience to God in the midst of the temptations and pressures that arise in the Israelite community.[30] The date and place of writing are uncertain.[31] The language of its composition is disputed.[32]

The story of the persecution and vindication of the wise or righteous one, attested in Genesis 34, Esther, Ahikar, and Susanna, is reflected also in Wisdom of Solomon 2-5. These texts, in turn, have shaped the story of Jesus' passion, as recounted in the four gospels.[33] In Acts 6-7 it is employed to recount the martyrdom of Stephen.

Bel and the Dragon

This double narrative is preserved among the Greek additions to Daniel. In the manuscripts it comes at the conclusion of the book. Its cast of characters and plot lines closely parallel those in Daniel 1-6.

The first narrative pits the Living God and his servant, Daniel, against the idol called Bel and his servants, the priests and the Persian king Cyrus. Daniel challenges the deity of the idol and enters into an ordeal that will

---

[27] See Moore, *Daniel*, 90, n. 23.

[28] Contrast vv. 1-3 with v. 5; vv. 20f. with vv. 22f.; v. 31 with v. 32; v. 56 with v. 57.

[29] Cf. v. 12 and Gen 39:10; v. 23 and 39:9; v. 26 and 39:14f.; v. 39 and 39:18.

[30] For the alternatives of interpretation, see Pfeiffer, *History*, 450-53, and Delcor, *Daniel*, 278.

[31] See Pfeiffer, *History*, 449f.; Delcor, *Daniel*, 273-7.

[32] See the discussion of Moore, *Daniel*, 81-84, who favours a Semitic original.

[33] On the Markan passion narrative, see Nickelsburg, 'Genre.' On Matthew, see Breech, *Testing*.

cost him his life if he loses (vv. 8-9; cf. Dan 3:15-18). The king acclaims Bel. The ordeal proves that Bel is only clay and brass, thus vindicating Daniel. The priests are killed, and Bel is destroyed. Nonetheless, Cyrus does not acknowledge the sovereignty of Daniel's God (vv. 23f.).

The second narrative pits the Living God and Daniel against the dragon and Cyrus. Again an ordeal vindicates Daniel, and the Babylonians complain that 'the king has become a Jew' (v. 28). Under pressure from the Babylonians, Cyrus has Daniel thrown in a lions' den. Daniel is sustained with food miraculously brought to him by Habakkuk the prophet, and he is delivered from the lions. The king acclaims Daniel's God, and his Babylonian opponents are thrown to the lions.

These two tales may have originated as separate stories,[34] but numerous motifs tie them together, especially the two parallel acclamations, the second superceding the first. Thus, in their present context, the two stories are inextricably interwoven into a single plot — the conversion of Cyrus — which is resolved only in the second half, when Cyrus acclaims Daniel's God.[35]

The similarities to Daniel 1-6 notwithstanding, the work has its own peculiar emphasis: an explicit and repeated polemic against idolatry. The term 'living God' is frequent in Jewish polemics against idols,[36] and our story is a demonstration of the impotence of the Babylonian gods in the face of the superior wisdom of Daniel, the servant of the living God (cf. also Dan 4:34; 6:26). Thus Cyrus' acclamation is a logical inference from the action and a fitting climax to the story.

A number of remarkable parallels to Isaiah 45-46 suggest that the double narrative in Bel and the Dragon may have developed as an exegesis on these chapters of Isaiah. The Lord addresses Cyrus (45:1), who does not know him (45:4), but who will come to know him (45:3). He is the Lord; besides him there is no other God (45:5, 6 etc. See Bel 41). He has created the heavens and the earth (45:18; see Bel 5; cf. also Isa 45:23). Isaiah 46:1-7 is an anti-idol polemic, which begins, 'Bel has fallen'.[37]

The stories in Bel and the Dragon make use of traditional motifs. Daniel's destruction of Bel's temple is reminiscent of the similar exploits of Abraham and Job.[38] The sarcastic touches throughout Bel and the Dragon

---

[34] Moore, *Daniel*, 121-5.
[35] Cf. also v. 3 (LXX) and v. 23; vv. 5 and 25; vv. 6 and 24; vv. 21 and 28. On the basis of these parallels, Fenz ('Ein Drache,' 12f.) argues that the author of the second story knew the first.
[36] Everding, *Living God*, 58-71, 224-79, 315-29.
[37] LXX reading. MT reads: 'Bel bows down; Nebo stoops' (RSV). For Nebo, some LXX mss. read *Dagon*. Curiously Cyprian (*Test.* 3:59) quotes Isa 46:1b, reading *Draco*, perhaps a reflection of our story's juxtaposition of Bel and the dragon. For a possible connection between the story of the dragon and Jer 51, see Moore, *Daniel*, 122-4. He also discusses attempts (by H. Gunkel and others) to see in this story an echo of the myth about the combat of Marduk and Tiamat, *ibid.*, 123-4.
[38] *Jub.* 12:1-14; *T. Job* 2-5. A more remote parallel is the story of Samson in Judg 16:23-30.

stand in a long tradition of polemics that make mockery of idols.[39] The story of Daniel and the dragon is obviously related to Daniel 6.

Bel and the Dragon shows many signs of being later than the stories in Daniel 1-6. The plot is more complex. It has lost its court setting in favour of idol-worshipping Babylonian paganism in general. Daniel's enemies are not rival sages, but pagan priests and 'Babylonians.' The uniqueness of Daniel's God as the 'living God' is central to the narrative. The king's conversion is explicit. 'The king has become a Jew' (v. 28). In almost all respects, the story of the lions' den looks secondary to the version in Daniel 6.[40] There seem to be additional legendary developments: Daniel is in the den six days rather than overnight; the number of lions is given; the lions have been made to go hungry, thus heightening the miracle (cf. Dan 3:19). Moreover, the incident about Habakkuk is an unnecessary intrusion. If the story in Daniel 6 is based on an exegesis of Psalm 91:11-13, the connection of the lions' den with the destruction of the dragon may reflect Psalm 91:13. Bel and the Dragon may already presuppose the collection in Daniel 1-6 and may have been composed to supply a story about the last of the kings under whom Daniel served according to Daniel 6:28. Its date and place of origin are uncertain,[41] as is the language of its composition.[42]

Tobit

Tobit is a rich and complex literary work. Central to the book is the story of Tobit himself: his piety, his suffering, and his healing. This basically simple plot is interwoven with two subplots about Sarah and about the recovery of Tobit's money. From these narrative materials, the author has composed a complex but well-integrated story that depicts real human beings and their emotions in life-like circumstances and that uses plots and characters to carry traditional themes from the Bible and ancient folklore.[43] As constituent parts of his story, he has also employed a number of contemporary literary forms: the testament (chaps. 4 and 14); wisdom *didache* (instruction), both in the testamentary contexts and from the mouth of an angel (4:3-21; 12:7-11; 14:10-11); prayers and a hymn of thanksgiving (3:2-6, 11-15; 8:5-6, 15-17; 13:1-18); and an extended angelophany (5:4-12:22). Our exposition will confine itself mainly to the present shape of Tobit as an integrated literary whole.[44]

---

[39] Cf., e.g., Isa 44:9-20; Wis 13-14; Ep Jer; *Apoc. Abr.* 1-8.

[40] See also Fenz, 'Drache,' 14.   [41] See Delcor, *Daniel,* 289-92.

[42] See the discussion of Moore, 119-20, who favours a Semitic original.

[43] On the parallels in folklore, see Pfeiffer, *History,* 268-71. On the biblical themes, see below. Reminiscent of the patriarchal narratives is the journey that results in the finding of a wife from one's own people.

[44] On the relationship of chaps. 13 and 14 to the rest of the book, see below, n. 55. Parts of all fourteen chapters have been found in one or more of the Qumran manuscripts of Tobit. See below, n. 66.

The belief that God rewards the righteous is basic to the book. The opening genealogy introduces Tobit[45] as a genuine Israelite (1:1-2). The narrative then commences with a description of his many acts of cultic devotion and kindness to others (1:3-18).

The main line of the plot leads righteous Tobit and innocent Sarah through suffering to healing. This healing and the blessings that ensue from it are to be interpreted in the light of the sections of the book which are formally teaching. Thus Tobit instructs his son, Tobias:

> Live uprightly . . . and do not walk in the ways of wrongdoing. For if you do what is true, your ways will prosper through your deeds.[46] Give alms from your possessions . . . Do not turn your face away from the face of any poor man, and the face of God will not be turned away from you. If you have many possessions, make your gift from them in proportion; if few, do not be afraid to give according to the little you have. So you will be laying up a good treasure for yourself against the day of necessity. For charity delivers from death . . . Do not hold over till the next day the wages of any man who works for you, but pay him at once; and if you serve God, you will receive payment.[47] (4:5-10, 14)

In his final testamentary parenesis, he makes similar observations, citing the positive and negative examples of Ahikar and his nephew Nadan (14:8-11).[48] In like fashion, the angel Raphael instructs Tobit and Tobias on the virtues of almsgiving and the righteous life (12:9-10). God rewards the righteous and punishes the wicked, a theme characteristic of Deutero-nomized wisdom (cf. Ben Sira, Baruch, and Wis 3-4).[49] The truth of this teaching is demonstrated in the narrative itself. Tobit recovers his money. His suffering is alleviated. His son marries the right kind of wife, and they present him with grandsons. He lives to a ripe old age.

This pattern of piety and reward notwithstanding, the major factor in the story is the suffering of Tobit (and Sarah), which intervenes between Tobit's piety and his reward and stands in evident contradiction to Tobit's claims that piety is blessed. Like the book of Job, the book of Tobit focuses on the problem of the suffering of the righteous person. Our author places his answer to this problem on Tobit's lips: 'For you have scourged me, but you have had mercy on me' (11:15 Grk. MSS. BA, Old Latin). The ex-

---

[45] In the Aramic, Tobit's name is *Tobi,* and his son's *Tobiyah;* Milik, 'Patrie,' 522, n. 2.

[46] Cf. *1 Enoch* 91:4; 94:1-4 for similar 'two ways' parenesis in a testamentary context.

[47] Translation from RSV. 'Alms' and 'charity' translate the Greek ἐλεημοσύνη, on which see below, n. 50.

[48] On the story of Ahikar, see above, n. 7 and below, p. 284. Here the wicked nephew Nadan is cited as a foil to Tobias, the obedient son. For other references to this tale, see Tob 1:21f.; 2:10; 11:18. On these and other parallels between Ahikar and Tobit, see Simpson, 'Tobit,' 189-92. In Tob 1:16-20, Tobit is described as a persecuted courtier, as is Ahikar in his own story.

[49] The literary forms in Tob 4; 12; 14 come from the wisdom tradition.

pression 'to have mercy' and its cognates are our author's most frequent descriptions of God's salvific activity,[50] and the formulation 'scourge-have mercy' is paradigmatic for this author, in the context of Israel's sin (see below). But what of the scourging of Tobit, the righteous man? The lengthy descriptions of God's salvific activity,[50] and the formulation 'scourge - have includes a confession of sin: 'Do not punish me for my sins and for my (transgressions committed in) ignorance (ἀγνοήματα)' (3:3). His harsh judgment of his wife (2:11-14)[51] and his lapses into unfaith (3:6; 10:1-3) are further indications that our author's righteous man is not a perfect man. He is in need of scourging.[52]

The fuller dimensions of God's activity are to be seen, however, in the manner in which the author weaves together plot and subplots, creating a chain of events leading from piety to blessing. Tobit's suffering is the result of his piety, for he is blinded while lying in the yard after burying a dead man.[53] In his blindness he mistakenly accuses his wife of theft, and her reproach of him leads him to pray for death. The subplot about Sarah is now introduced, paralleling the Tobit story in theme and structure.

Tobit's piety (2:1-7)	Sarah's innocence (presumed, e.g., 3:14)
Blindness (2:9-10)[54]	Asmodaeus (3:8a)
Reproach (2:11-14)	Reproach (3:7, 8b-9)
Prayer (3:1-6)	Prayer (3:10-15)

Two righteous people, the victims of senseless suffering and the objects of reproach, in a moment of despondency pray for death as a release from their suffering and reproach. The two plots are woven together by a common resolution. God responds to the prayers by sending his angel Raphael, who uses Tobias as his agent, providing him with the necessary theurgical equipment and information to drive off the demon and heal Tobit's blindness. Moreover, Tobias' marriage to Sarah solves the problem of her widowhood, and conversely her widowhood makes her available to

---

[50] For the verb ἐλεεῖν, and the related noun ἔλεος, and adjective ἐλεήμων, all applied to God, see 3:11 (S); 3:15 (BA, Old Latin); 6:18; 7:11; 8:4, 7, 16, 17; 11:15 (BA, Old Latin); 11:17; 13:2, 5, 9 (BA); 14:5. It is most probable, at least on the level of the Greek translation, that there is a relationship between the characterization of God as 'merciful' and 'doing mercy' and the frequent occurrence of the noun ἐλεημοσύνη ('alms,' 'charity,' etc). See Bultmann, 'ἔλεος', 485f.

[51] Cf. Abraham's self-righteous condemnation of sinners in *T. Abr.* 10 (Rec. A; chap. 12, Rec. B).

[52] For a similar description of 'the righteous man' and his 'chastening,' cf. *Ps. Sol.* 3:4-8; cf. also Jdt 8:27; 2 Macc 6:16; Ps 39 (38): 11; Prov 3:12.

[53] In 1:16-20, Tobit is described as a persecuted righteous man. In chap. 2, however, his suffering is not persecution, though the idea is perhaps inherent in the reproach of his neighbours and his wife (2:8, 14).

[54] Sarah's suffering is caused by the demon Asmodaeus, Tobit's blindness is caused by sparrows. For birds as the instruments of Satan, cf. *Jub.* 11:19-24.

be the kind of wife that Tobit had admonished Tobias to seek (4:12-13). Furthermore, the possibility of Tobias' finding Sarah was provided by the money that Tobit had deposited in Rages, by the circumstances which had made it impossible for him to collect it, and by his death-wish which had led him to remember the money and send Tobias off in search of it. Through the interweaving of these plots and the construction of this complex chain of events, our author expounds a view of a God who carefully orchestrates the events of history, working them to his own gracious ends. Such a view of divine sovereignty is also evident in Raphael's statement to Tobias that Sarah 'was destined for you before eternity' (6:18).

For the author of Tobit, God's dealings with the suffering righteous person are paradigmatic of his dealings with Israel. In his prayer (3:4-5), Tobit laments over Israel's sin and God's punishment of the nation through plunder, captivity, death and dispersion. He voices this sentiment in the midst of a complaint about his own suffering. In the last two chapters, Tobit speaks almost exclusively about the fate of the nation.[55] In the light of his new-found health, he utters a hymn of praise to the God who will also save Israel. Surely the captivity and dispersion are God's punishment for Israel's sins, but they are not ultimate punishment. Thus Tobit applies the formula 'scourge - have mercy' several times to Israel's present situation and future destiny (13:2, 5, 9; cf. 14:5). The fact that the formula occurs in parallel literature most frequently in connection with the nation[56] suggests that the author's application of it to Tobit's own suffering may be secondary, and that the problem of the captivity and dispersion and the hope for a re-gathering of the people are foremost in his mind. This return from dispersion will have as its focus proper pan-Israelite worship in a Jerusalem that will be rebuilt according to the glorious promises of Isaiah 54 and 60. In his testamentary forecast (14:4-7), Tobit envisages the Babylonian captivity, the return, the rebuilding of the temple, and then in a kind of consummation, the rebuilding of a glorious Jerusalem and the conversion of the Gentiles.

A key to our understanding of the author's situation and purpose is to be found in the structure of the book, the development of Tobit's character, and the unfolding of the events related to his life. Deeply stamped into the first part of the book is the senseless suffering of Tobit and Sarah and their families. In their prayers, which are spoken out of a sense of despair, they beg for release from a life that is effectively devoid of the gracious presence of God (cf. 13:2). God's response to these prayers takes a totally unex-

---

[55] For an argument against the originality of chaps. 13-14, see Zimmermann (*Tobit,* 24-27), who dates them after 70 c.e. The presence of chaps. 13-14 in the Qumran scrolls (see above, n. 44) argues, however, for an early date for the whole of chaps. 1-14.
[56] Cf. Ps 89(88):32-34; *Ps. Sol.* 7:8-10; 10:1-4; 18:4-7; Wis 12:22.

pected form. The function of the angelophany is to assert that indeed God 'is with' Tobit and Sarah.[57] When his purposes have become apparent, Tobit bursts into a hymn of unmitigated praise. The figure of Tobit is paradigmatic in his movement from despair (or rather a vacillation between despair and faith) to doxology.[58] The author addresses the Tobits of his own time, assuring them of God's gracious presence and activity, and calling them to doxology and to repentance and the pious life.

The book of Tobit is profoundly doxological in content and tone. In addition to the three hymns of praise, there are numerous references (especially exhortations) to the praise of God (3:11; 4:19; 11:1, 14, 16, 17; 12:6). Moreover, at the end of the angelophanic section, Raphael commissions Tobit to write a book which has an implicit doxological function: 'Praise God forever ... praise him forever ... And now give thanks to God, for I am ascending to him who sent me. Write in a book everything that has happened ... So they confessed the great and wonderful works of God, and acknowledged that the angel of the Lord had appeared to them' (12:17-22). The readers are to praise God because even now he is with them and because their future is in his hand. The dispersion of God's people, their absence from 'the good land' (14:4), and their inability to gather as a single worshipping community in Jerusalem are a problem of the first magnitude to our author. Yet he exhorts his readers to praise the God who will gather the scattered and bring the nations to worship at his temple.

Our author's second purpose is parenetic, as is evident from the several sections of formal *didache*. The gathering of the dispersion presupposes repentance (13:6) and the pious life. This piety involves prayer, fasting, and almsgiving (12:8),[59] and deeds of kindness to others, according to one's ability and station in life (4:7-11).[60] It also involves devotion to one's family

---

[57] For this particular insight and other helpful comments on Tobit, I am indebted to Prof. Norman Petersen. Typical of the angelophanic form are the following elements: appearance (5:4); 'being with' (5:16, 21; 12:12f.); self-revelation (12:15); reaction (12:16); reassurance, 'fear not' (12:17); commission (12:20); disappearance (12:21); confession (12:22). Cf. also 6:6ff., where Raphael functions as *angelus interpres*. Different from many angelophanies, where the angel is simply a messenger bringing news or a commission, here the presence of the angel going with Tobias is reminiscent of such passages as Exod 23:20; 32:34; 33:2. Similarly, the language of the angel's or God's being 'with' someone usually functions as reassurance to one who has been commissioned. Cf., however, Isa 7:14 and Matt 1:23. For a broader context for the helping angel, see Talbert, 'Myth,' 418-40.

[58] For a similar interpretation of the seer's progression in the visions in 4 Ezra, see Breech, 'Fragments,' 267-74.

[59] This particular collocation of pious acts is reflected in Matt 6:2-18, as also in the Yom Kippur liturgy (*Tefilah, Teshuvah, Tsedakah*).

[60] Both narrative and parenesis in Tobit say much about the use of wealth. Tobit is a rich and generous man, who exhorts his son to similar generosity.

and the maintenance of one's Israelite identity through endogamous marriage (4:12-13).[61]

The diaspora setting of Tobit is highly suggestive for a further delineation of the author's message and purpose. Although this literary setting need not prove that it was written outside Palestine, much in the book suggests that it was written in the diaspora:[62] Tobit's persecution by foreigners (1:16-20); the presence of neighbours not sympathetic to Tobit's pious concerns (2:8); the long exhortation to endogamy and the incorporation of this theme into the narrative; the continuous concern with the dispersion and the return. Within such a diaspora context, the author repeatedly affirms the universal sovereignty of Israel's God, and his presence and activity even among the dispersed, and in spite of their distress. He exhorts his people to maintain their identity in the land of their dispersion. The source of such identity is at the grass roots, in the family, in a respect for one's parents and in the preservation of one's tribal identity. Repentance and piety will lead to the gathering of the dispersion. Moreover, Israel is to acknowledge God among the nations (13:6), that they might join in the universal praise of him which constitutes the heart of Tobit's vision for the future.[63]

The time of writing is uncertain. It surely antedates the persecution of Antiochus. Since Tobit's reference to 'the prophets' (14:5) need not imply a fixed body of writings identical with those mentioned by Ben Sira, and since Tobit never speaks of the Law and the Prophets collectively as Scripture, a date before 200 B.C.E. is permissible.[64] The original language of Tobit was probably Aramaic.[65] Fragments of five manuscripts of Tobit have been identified among the Qumran Scrolls, four in Aramaic and one in Hebrew.[66] The Greek text of Tobit exists in a short form (represented by MSS. B and A, and followed by most of the versions) and a long form (represented by MS. S, and followed by the Old Latin), which appears to be closest to the Qumran Semitic MSS.[67]

The book of Tobit is remarkable for its incorporation of motifs, forms,

---

[61] Endogamy is spelled out as marriage within the tribe (4:12), and Tobias marries such a girl, but the whole of 4:12f. contrasts such endogamy with marriage to foreigners.

[62] For the many opinions on the place of writing, see Zimmermann (*Tobit*, 15-21), who suggests Antioch in Syria. For a provenance in Samaria, see Milik, 'Patrie,' 522-30. Lack of knowledge about the exact site of Nineveh need not exclude a location in the Eastern diaspora some distance from that site.

[63] Cf. the discussion of Dan 1-6, above, pp. 34-5.

[64] See Zimmermann, *Tobit*, 21-24; Simpson, 'Tobit,' 183-5; Lebram, 'Weltreiche, ' 329-31.

[65] Zimmermann, *Tobit*, 139-49; Thomas, 'Greek Text,' 470f. A final decision must await the publication of the Qumran evidence.

[66] For a list of the extant portions, see Milik, 'Patrie,' 522, n. 3.

[67] See Milik, 'Patrie,' 522; and Thomas, 'Greek Text,' 463-71. Two long lacunae in S (4:6-19; 13:7-10) can be filled in from MSS. BA and from the Old Latin. On the versions, see Zimmermann, *Tobit*, 127-38.

and formulae which occur with some frequency in apocalyptic literature: reference to a divine throne-room in which seven archangels mediate prayers in the presence of God (3:16; 12:12-15);[68] a duel between angel and demon with the binding of the latter (8:2-3);[69] an angelophany culminating in a commission to write a book (12:11-22);[70] divine names with universalistic connotations (13:6-11);[71] the description of a denouement with heavy universalistic overtones (13:11-18; 14:4-7).[72] This is not to say that Tobit is apocalyptic in its theology, but that the uniqueness of the apocalyptic phenomenon must be discussed with these parallels in mind.

Judith

For your power depends not upon numbers,
nor your might upon men of strength;
for you are God of the lowly,
helper of the oppressed,
upholder of the weak,
protector of the forlorn,
saviour of those without hope. (Jdt 9:11, RSV)

With these words Judith summarizes the central assertion of the book named after her. The plot of the story manifests the truth of this assertion.

Chapters 1-7 describe the developing crisis facing Israel. Nebuchadnezzar, the epitome of irresistible military might, breaches the impregnable defenses of his enemy to the east, 'Arphaxad', and dispatches Holofernes against the nations that have refused him aid.

Holofernes sweeps across Mesopotamia and down into Syria and Palestine (2:21-3:10). The Israelites prepare to resist and seek divine help through prayer, fasting and mourning rituals (chap. 4). Achior the Ammonite interprets their resistance in light of their history. Their strength is not in their armies, but in their God. When they are faithful to him, they are invincible. When they sin, they go down to defeat.

Holofernes retorts in a mock oracle:

Who is God except Nebuchadnezzar? He will send his forces and will destroy them from the face of the earth, and their God will not deliver them . . . So says King Nebuchadnezzar, the lord of the whole earth. For he has spoken; none of his words will be in vain. (6:2-4; cf. 2:5, 12)

---

[68] Cf. *1 Enoch* 9; 40; 99:3; and especially the formula in 104:1.
[69] Cf. *1 Enoch* 10:4f. On the angelic duel, see Nickelsburg, *Resurrection,* 11-15, 28-40.
[70] Cf., e.g., Dan 10-12 and the NT Book of Revelation, which take over the older form of the prophetic commissioning, substituting a lengthy historical apocalypse for the briefer message given the prophet; see Nickelsburg, *Jewish Literature,* 87.
[71] Cf. *1 Enoch* 9:4; 12:3; 25:3, 7; *T. Mos.* 1:12; cf. also 2 Macc 7:9.
[72] Cf. *1 Enoch* 10:17-22; 90:30-36; 91:14.

The fundamental tension in the story is now explicit. Who is God? YHWH or Nebuchadnezzar?[73] When Holofernes' army appears in full array, the people's courage melts (chap. 7). They conclude that God has sold them into the hand of the foreigner, and the exhortations of Uzziah, their ruler, are futile. The people 'are greatly depressed.'

Judith's appearance serves as a turning point in the narrative. Her address to the rulers and her prayer are crucial in several ways (chaps. 8-9). They depict Judith as a person of great faith and as a wise and eloquent spokeswoman of that faith. Moreover, it is Judith who presents a formal exposition of the view of God which the book as a whole dramatizes. Similarly, her censure of the people expresses the author's criticism of a lack of faith in this God. Finally, Judith's prayer wins the help of God. The triumph over Holofernes and the Assyrians is an answer to that prayer.

Judith's wisdom has its practical side, and her faith becomes operative in deed. A clever and resourceful assassin, she allows no detail to escape her preparations (10: 1-5). Once she is inside the Assyrian camp, deceit is her *modus operandi* (10:6-12:20). Her great beauty disarms the sentries and the rest of the army, leaving them wide-eyed with wonderment and hence blind to her treacherous intent. Playing up to Holofernes' arrogant pretensions, Judith addresses him as if he were the king himself (11:8, 19). Her conversation is a string of lies, half-truths, and double-entendres.[74] Dazzled by Judith's beauty, Holofernes 'loses his head before it has been cut off.'[75] His desire to possess Judith provides her with the opportunity she has been awaiting, and she parries his proposition with ambiguous answers (12:14, 18). Tossing caution to the winds, Holofernes drinks himself into a stupor. The time for ambiguities has ceased. Judith beheads the drunken general with his own sword and tumbles his body onto the floor. His humiliation 'at the hand of a woman' is complete.

The various themes in the story now resolve themselves. Judith returns to the city, proclaiming God's strength against Israel's enemies (13:11, 14). The Assyrian camp is the scene of chaos and terror. It is evident who alone is God. The God of Israel has fulfilled Achior's warning (5:21; cf. 14:18b). He has vindicated the faith of Uzziah (7:30; 13:14) and especially Judith (8:15-17; 9:11) and has shown the people's despair to have been groundless (7:24-28). He has met Holofernes' challenge (6:3). Nebuchadnezzar's pride has been turned to disgrace, and his attempt to be 'lord of the whole earth' (2:5; 6:4) has been foiled by the hand of a woman (9:10; 13:15; 16:6). His army is routed, and we hear no more of him in the book (16:25). Judith's song is a reprise of the central assertion in the book: the God of Israel is the champion of the weak and the oppressed; he destroys the power of the mighty and humbles the pride of the arrogant.

[73] Cf. Jdt 6:2 and Isa 45:5, etc.
[74] E.g., 11:5, 11-15, 16; 12:4. On irony in Judith, see Alonso-Schökel, 'Structures,' pp. 8-11.
[75] The word-play is that of Winter ('Judith,' 1024) and is worthy of our author's irony.

The book of Judith is patently fiction. It abounds in anachronisms and historical inaccuracies.[76] The setting of the story provides an obvious example. Nebuchadnezzar is introduced as king of the Assyrians (1:1), who makes war on Israel *after* their return from the Exile (5:18f.; 4:3). The unhistorical nature of the story is also reflected in the way in which it combines features of a number of biblical stories.[77] Judith herself appears to be a personification of several Israelite heroines: Miriam (Exod 15:20f.); Deborah and Jael (Judg 4-5); the woman of Thebez (Judg 9:53f.); and the woman of Abel Bethmaacah (2 Sam 20:14-22).

By conflating biblical characters and events, the author presents a condensation of Israelite history, which has a paradigmatic quality.[78] It demonstrates how the God of Israel has acted — and continues to act — in history, and it provides models for proper and improper human actions and reactions vis-à-vis this God. The God of Judith is the deliverer of his people, yet he remains sovereign and *not obligated* to act in their behalf (8:15-17). In moments of evident defeat, he tests the faith of his people (8:25-27). The citizens of Bethulia and Judith exemplify respectively those who fail and those who pass the test. Judith's activism is noteworthy. She does not passively await direct divine intervention. Her appeal to the activism of 'my father Simeon' is reminiscent of 1 Macc 2:24-26, which cites Phineas as a paradigm for Mattathias' activist zeal, and of the laudatory descriptions of Levi's participation in the slaughter at Shechem in the *Testament of Levi* and *Jubilees*.[79]

Although the precise *Sitz im Leben* of the book is uncertain, a didactic and exhortatory function is implied. This breaks through in Judith's speech, where the second person plurals in their literary setting are addressed to the rulers of Bethulia. As the speech is read, however, the reader is addressed. At one point in her song, Judith speaks like the mother of her people (16:5).[80]

Consonant with the book's didactic function is its attention to matters of piety and religious practice. While the author does not formally expound *halakhoth,* Judith is depicted as faithfully adhering to the commands of God, doubtless as they were construed in the author's time and religious circle.[81] As a widow, Judith lives in a state of extended mourning (8:4-6).

---

[76] See Pfeiffer, *History,* 292-95.

[77] See Dubarle, *Judith,* I, 137-56.

[78] The term *parabolisch* is used by Haag (*Judith*), who sees the book as a freely composed paradigmatic presentation of the forces inherent in and behind the empirical history of Israel. A similar view was espoused by Luther ('Prefaces,' 338-9), who cites the opinions of others.

[79] *T. Levi* 2-6; *Jub.* 30.

[80] Cf. also 2 Macc 7, where the mother of the seven brothers speaks in the idiom of Second Isaiah's Zion figure; see Nickelsburg, *Resurrection,* 106-08.

[81] For a discussion of the particulars, see Grintz (*Sefer Yehudith,* 47-51), who argues that the *halakhoth* are pre-Pharisaic.

48

She prays at the time of the burning of the evening incense (9:1). Like Daniel and his friends (Dan 1:5-16) and Tobit (Tob 1:10-12), she abstains from gentile food (10:5; 11:2).[82] Each evening she purifies herself by bathing in running water (12:7-9).[83]

Perhaps the most striking reference to religious practice is the conversion of Achior the Ammonite (14:10). Not only does this provide us with our earliest reference to a formal practice of accepting proselytes, the person in question belongs to one of the nations which the Torah forbade entrance into the Israelite nation (Deut 23:3). The inclusion of such a detail in a work of religious fiction is scarcely accidental. Perhaps the author found precedent in Isaiah 56:4-5 (contrast Deut 23:1 on the exclusion of eunuchs) or in the story of Ruth the Moabitess.[84] In any case, the viewpoint here espoused is altogether different from that of Ezra, for whom conversion was evidently not a possible solution for mixed marriages.[85]

The didactic character of the book suggests connections with the wisdom tradition. Judith is 'wise' (8:29; 11:8, 20f.). In the broad outlines of its plot and in certain particulars, Judith parallels some of the wisdom narratives in Daniel and Tobit (see above pp. 34f., 41ff.). The story is reminiscent of Daniel 3: the foreign ruler challenges God's power (6:3, cf. Dan 3:15), the heroine stands up to that challenge (8:15-17, cf. Dan 3:17f.), and in the end the ruler must acknowledge defeat (14:18, cf. Dan 3:28). In several respects, Judith is also reminiscent of Tobit. In both cases, the protagonist is depicted as a genuine Israelite (Tob 1:1; Jdt 8:1), whereas the people of Israel are brought from expressions of despair to the praise of the God who has delivered them. Both books end with a hymn and reference to the death of the protagonist.

The book of Judith is also noteworthy for what might be termed its feminism. In creating a protagonist, the author has chosen a woman, who calls to mind the Israelite heroines of the past — Judith, 'the Jewess.'[86] As the narrative unfolds, Judith is consistently depicted as superior to the men with whom she is associated. She is more eloquent than Uzziah and more

---

[82] Contrast the evident attitude of Esther (Esth 2:9) and the correction by the author of the Additions to Esther (14:17, on which, see below, 135-8). The issue of observing *kashrut* was especially acute during the persecution by Antiochus IV; cf. Dan 1; 2 Macc 6:18-7:41 and 1 Macc 1:47-48.

[83] Cf. also the reference to the laws of inheritance (8:7; 16:24) and of first fruits and tithes (11:11-14).

[84] See the discussion by Zeitlin, *Judith*, 24-25.

[85] Cf. Ezra 9:1, which mentions Ammonites, and see Myers, *Ezra-Nehemiah*, 76-79, 84. Cf. also n. 99, below.

[86] Judith also recalls certain Israelite heroes. Cf. her prayer in 13:7 with that of Samson in Judg 16:28; cf. also 13:6-8 and 1 Sam 17:51, where David beheads Goliath with his own sword. The author clearly parallels Judith's action with that of the patriarch Simeon; cf. 9:2-3; 9:8-10; 13:6-8. If one accepts a Hasmonaean date (see below), the name 'Judith' naturally suggests a comparison with Judas Maccabaeus.

courageous, faithful, and resourceful than any of the rulers of Bethulia. She deceives the Assyrian soldiers and humiliates and destroys Holofernes. Bagoas must admit that 'one Hebrew woman has brought disgrace on the house of Nebuchadnezzar.' At the end of the story, she gains the plaudits of Uzziah, Achior, and Joakim the high priest. In some passages, Judith's status as a woman appears to be synonymous with weakness (9:10; 14:18; 16:6f.). The author may be saying that God's power is operative through the weakest of human agents. Nonetheless, Judith is no weakling. Her courage, her trust in God, and her wisdom — all lacking in her male counterparts — save the day for Israel. Her use of deceit and specifically of her sexuality may seem offensive. For the author it is the opposite. She wisely chooses the weapon in her arsenal that is appropriate to her enemy's weakness. She plays his game, knowing that he will lose. In so doing, she makes fools out of a whole army of men and humiliates their general.

Because the book of Judith is fiction, attempts to date it are always tenuous, depending, as they do, upon the identification of the events in the book with other events in real history. These historical events are usually sought in the late Persian period or in the wars of Judas Maccabaeus.[87]

Persian elements in the story have long been recognized.[88] Earlier scholars identified Holofernes and Bagoas with a general of Artaxerxes III and his eunuch, who had these same names. The event in question was Artaxerxes' campaign against Phoenicia, Syria, and Egypt in 353 B.C.E.[89] More recently, Grintz has argued in detail for the book's composition c. 360 B.C.E., during the reign of Artaxerxes II.[90] The events in the book reflect the great Satraps' Revolt of that time, which spread across the western part of the Persian Empire.[91] The dating is supported by many items in Judith which reflect the socio-historical situation during the Persian, but not during the Hellenistic period.[92] Contrary to the claim that Judith contains much 'late' halakhic material, Grintz maintains that the *hala-khoth* in Judith are all non-Pharisaic, *i.e.*, pre-Pharisaic.[93]

An alternative identification of the events in Judith has suggested a post-Maccabaean date to many scholars.[94] Nebuchadnezzar may be understood as a figure for Antiochus IV.[95] This would explain why he is called an Assyrian, since the identification of the Assyria of biblical prophecies with Syria was commonplace in the biblical interpretation of

---

[87] For other, untenable suggestions, see Pfeiffer, *History*, 293-5.
[88] Dubarle, *Judith*, I, 131f.
[89] Pfeiffer, *History*, 294.
[90] Grintz, *Sefer Yehudith*, 15-55.
[91] *Ibid.*, 15-17. For an account, see Diodorus Siculus 15:90-92.
[92] Grintz, *Sefer Yehudith*, 18-55.
[93] *Ibid.*, 47-51.
[94] See Pfeiffer, *History*, 294f.; Eissfeldt, *Old Testament*, 586f.; Zeitlin, *Judith*, 26-31.
[95] In Dan 3, the final redactor of Daniel certainly intends Nebuchadnezzar to be a figure for Antiochus.

this period. The predominance of Holofernes tallies well with the presence of a number of Syrian generals in Palestine during the Maccabaean uprising. The defeat of a vastly superior invading army parallels Judas' defeat of the Syrians. Especially noteworthy are the similarities between this story and Judas' defeat of Nicanor.[96] Although Judith is set shortly after the return from Exile (4:3), the book does not speak of the rebuilding of the temple, but of the consecration of 'the vessels, the altar, and the temple after their profanation.' The similarity to Judas' consecration of the temple is striking (1 Macc 4:36-51). Three years later,[97] when Nicanor, a general of Demetrius I, threatened to burn the temple, Judas defeated his army. Nicanor was killed and decapitated, and his head was displayed outside Jerusalem (1 Macc 8:33-50; cf. Jdt 14:1). This event was celebrated annually, as both 1 and 2 Maccabees attest (cf. 1 Macc 7:49, 2 Macc 15:36).

One's choice between a Persian and a Hasmonaean date for Judith will depend upon the significance that one assigns to the various arguments. The non-Pharisaic nature of the halakhic materials is consonant with either a Persian or a Hasmonaean date. Pre-Pharisaic *halakhoth* could have continued to be observed in the author's community even after the beginning of the Pharisaic movement.[98] Persian influences in Judith are undeniable. In order to accept a Hasmonaean date, one must assume that a person at that time could have had detailed knowledge of the Persian period.

The events described in Judith evince similarities with both the Satraps' Revolt and the Maccabaean wars. The international character of the rebellion in Judith 1-3 suggests the Satraps' Revolt rather than the Maccabaean wars. On the other hand, some of the specific details in Judith tally closely with 1 and 2 Maccabees, whereas we have no certain and specific information that the Jews participated in the Satraps' Revolt.

Judith differs at a number of specific points from Diodorus' account of the Satraps' Revolt. The Revolt was more widespread than in Judith. For all his detail, Diodorus does not indicate that the revolt started in reaction to a request by Artaxerxes for military aid (Jdt 1:7-11). Conversely, Judith gives no hint of the mutual betrayals that took place among the satraps. Finally, in the Satraps' Revolt, Palestine was invaded by the Egyptians from the south and not by the Persians from the north, as Judith would suggest, if one accepts the identification.

Perhaps it is best to posit two stages of composition. A story originating in Persian times has been rewritten in Hasmonaean times.[99]

---

[96] See Zeitlin, *Judith*, 27-30. [97] For the chronology, see Goldstein, *1 Maccabees*, 166-8.
[98] In Grintz' argument, the pre-Pharisaic nature of the *halakhoth* does not prove, but supports the case for a Persian date.
[99] The reference to Achior's conversion presumes some considerable distance from the apparent impossibility in Ezra's time, that gentiles could enter the Israelite nation through conversion (thus necessitating the divorce of mixed marriages). Nonetheless, the reference could be part of the Hasmonean rewriting of the story.

It is generally agreed that Judith was composed in Hebrew.[100] Its setting in Bethulia may indicate the area near Dothan as the place of its composition.[101]

Although Judith was excluded from the canon of the Hebrew Bible, it remained a part of the Jewish haggadic tradition.[102] Moreover, in both Jewish and Christian circles, it has been an unusually fertile source of inspiration for the arts.[103]

The Martyrdom of Isaiah

The *Martyrdom of Isaiah* is the initial section of a Christian work, the *Ascension of Isaiah*. Allusions to this legend in the New Testament and the Babylonian and Palestinian Talmudim indicate that it is of Jewish origin.[104] This Jewish legend, which then served as a nucleus for the longer Christian writing,[105] probably included the following verses: *Ascension of Isaiah* 1:1-2a; 1:7-3:12; 5:1-14.[106] We shall confine our discussion to these verses.

The story begins in the twenty-sixth year of Hezekiah's reign, three years before his death. The king summons his son Manasseh and transmits certain commands to him (1:1-2, 7). Isaiah predicts that Manasseh will set aside these commands, that he will become an instrument of Beliar, and that he will put Isaiah to death. Hezekiah's protests are to no avail; Isaiah's martyrdom is determined and must come to pass (1:7-12).

When Manasseh succeeds his father, the prophecy begins to be fulfilled (2:1-6). Sammael[107] takes hold of Manasseh. The king disobeys Hezekiah's commands (2:1), forsakes the worship of the God of his father, and serves Satan and his angels (2:2). Moreover, he leads his father's house astray (2:3), and he turns Jerusalem into a center of apostasy, lawlessness, the occult arts, fornication, and the persecution of the righteous (2:4-6).

---

[100] See Zimmermann, 'Hebrew Original,' 67-74; Grintz, *Sefer Yehudith,* 56-63. Dubarle (*Judith,* 1, 67-74; 'L'authenticité,' 187-211) argues that the extant late Hebrew MSS. of Judith are not dependent on the versions, but reflect the original Hebrew.

[101] On the location of a Simeonite settlement in this area, see Grintz, *Sefer Yehudith,* 33; summarized in *id.,* 'Judith,' 452.

[102] See Dubarle, *Judith* I, 80-110.

[103] See *EJ* 10, 459-61.

[104] In Heb 11:37, the author alludes to the incident as to a familiar incident in the sequence of Jewish sacred history. Elements from the legend occur in *B.T. Yebamoth* 49a and *Sanhedrin* 103b; *P.T. Sanhedrin* 10, 28c and *Vita Isa.* 1. For targumic references, see Grelot, 'Deux Tosephtas,' 511-43.

[105] So Charles, *APOT* 2, 158; Tisserant, *Ascension,* 59; Flusser, 'Ascensio,' 30-47; Flemming – Duensing, 'Ascension,' 643; Philonenko, 'Martyre,' 1-10. Supporting a unitary Christian composition is Burch, 'Literary Unity,' 17-23; cf. also Torrey, *Apocryphal Literature,* 133-5.

[106] So Charles, *APOT* 2, 156-7.

[107] Perhaps 'Poison of God,' Blau, 'Samael,' 665, or 'the blind god' or 'the god of the blind,' Caquot, 'Commentaire,' 72; Pearson, 'Jewish Haggadic Traditions,' 467. The *Martyrdom* is notable for its many names for the chief demon or demons.

Isaiah withdraws from Jerusalem into the Judaean wilderness, where he is joined by a group of faithful prophets, who nourish themselves on wild herbs (2:7-11).

The false prophet Bechir-ra,[108] a descendant of Zedekiah ben Chenaanah, the opponent of Michaiah ben Imlah (2:12-16; cf. 1 Kgs 22:1-36), discovers the hiding place of Isaiah and his friends and brings a threefold accusation before Manasseh: the prophets predict the fall of Jerusalem and Judah and the captivity of king and people (3:6-7). Isaiah contradicts Moses by claiming to have seen God (Isa 6: 1ff.; cf. Exod 33:20).[109] He calls Jerusalem 'Sodom' and the princes, 'the people of Gomorrah.'

Because Beliar dwells in the hearts of Manasseh and his court, the king seizes Isaiah and has him sawn asunder (4:11-5:14). As Isaiah is being tortured, Bechir-ra, acting as the mouthpiece of Satan, attempts to get the prophet to recant. With the aid of the Holy Spirit, Isaiah refuses, curses Bechir-ra and the demonic powers he represents, and dies.

The biblical bases for our story are 2 Kings 20:16-21:18 and 2 Chronicles 32:32-33:20,[110] the accounts of the last years of Hezekiah and the reign of Manasseh. Detailed similarities are, however, very few in number — mainly the enumeration of Manasseh's sins. To the list of 2 Kings 21:2-6, the author adds in 2:4-6 only the stereotyped 'fornication.'[111] 'Persecution of the righteous' (2:5) appears to reflect 2 Kings 21:16 ('Moreover, Manasseh shed very much innocent blood . . .'), a passage that is doubtless the biblical justification for setting Isaiah's martyrdom in Manasseh's reign.[112] Beyond these similarities, the author 'footnotes' the Book of Kings (2:6) and moves on to create his own story.

The quasi-testamentary scene in chapter 1 has a twofold function. Isaiah's predictions introduce the scenario that follows. Hezekiah's commands are mentioned because Manasseh will disobey them. This contrast between pious father and wicked son, mentioned three times in 2:1-3, is explicit at only one point in each of the biblical accounts (2 Kgs 21:3; 2 Chron 33:3).

Isaiah's withdrawal to the wilderness is especially significant, because it is not required for the action of the story. The author could have had Isaiah apprehended in Jerusalem, following the model of the biblical accounts about Jeremiah. Similarly, there is no dramatic necessity for the presence of a group of prophets in Isaiah's company. Indeed they become a problem for the author, who must explain why they were not martyred along with Isaiah (5:13).

---

[108] For this name ('the elect one of evil'), see Flusser, 'Ascensio,' 35. The form does occur in some places in some manuscripts.

[109] This charge is mentioned in *B.T. Yebamoth* 49b.

[110] *Asc. Isa.* 2:6 suggests dependence only on the Book of Kings. Cf., however, *Asc. Isa.* 3:6 and 2 Chron 33:11.

[111] Cf. also *2 Bar.* 64:2.   [112] Cf. *B.T. Sanhedrin* 103b.

In contrast to Isaiah and his companions are the false prophet, Bechir-ra, and his entourage. They are at least as important as Manasseh in our author's view. The tracing of Bechir-ra's ancestry to Zedekiah ben Chenaanah reminds the reader of a similar situation in Israelite history. Michaiah opposed Zedekiah and his bevy of false prophets in the presence of wicked Ahab. At issue was true versus false prophecy. Michaiah claimed to have had a vision of God upon his throne. Zedekiah was possessed by a lying spirit. Michaiah, because of his opposition to both king and false prophet, was punished.

The Bible nowhere mentions Isaiah's death, much less his martyrdom at the hand of Manasseh. Chapter 5 is reminiscent of martyr stories from the time of Antiochus Epiphanes, specifically those in 2 Maccabees 6 and 7. Similarities include: torture in the presence of the king; the chance for salvation if the hero recants; a confessional speech which curses the enemy and makes light of mere physical death.[113] Nonetheless, the *Ascension of Isaiah* 5 has its own unique contours. The opponent of Isaiah here is not the king, but Bechir-ra, the false prophet. Moreover, there is a more basic polarity in the narrative between Satan, who dwells in Manasseh and supports Bechir-ra, and the Holy Spirit, who sustains Isaiah in his moment of trial. Here, as throughout the narrative, human personages are in reality the agents and instruments of supernatural powers, whether Satan or the Holy Spirit. The struggle between Isaiah and his opponents is essentially a battle between the forces of God and the powers of Satan.[114]

Any hypothesis about the date and provenance of this writing must account for these many points which define its peculiar character and constitute deviations from the biblical accounts. To begin with, this story is not a natural outgrowth from, or expansion of the biblical accounts of Manasseh's reign. Only one verse mentions a persecution, and there is no biblical evidence that Isaiah outlived Hezekiah. Our author used Manasseh's reign as a setting for Isaiah's martyrdom evidently because it paralleled the situation that he wished to reflect in his pseudepigraphic account. He appears to have lived in what he considered to be a time of great wickedness in Jerusalem, when the temple cult had been turned into the worship of Satan.

Two times suggest themselves as a setting for this story. The first is Antiochus' pollution of the temple and his persecution of the Jews in 168 B.C.E. The description of Isaiah's and his friends' retreat to the wilderness is reminiscent of similar accounts about Mattathias and Judah and his friends (see especially 1 Macc 2:6, 27ff.; 2 Macc 5: 27). We have already noted parallels to the martyr stories in 2 Maccabees 6-7. The difficulty with

---

[113] Cf. 2 Macc 7:7-11, 34-36.
[114] For a similar tendency in the narrative genre, cf. *Jub.* 17:15-18:16; 48:1-19. On the Gospel of Mark, see Robinson, *Problem,* 21-32.

this hypothesis resides in the figure of Manasseh. The archvillain ought not to be an Israelite king — or false prophet — but a foreign oppressor. In the idiom of the stories we have been investigating, we should expect a story about Nebuchadnezzar. Similarly, the polarity of true and false prophecy does not quite fit the Antiochan situation.

A second, more tenable setting has been suggested by Flusser, who sees the writing as a product of the Qumran community.[115] The following similarities are noteworthy. The angelic dualism that permeates the *Martyrdom* is characteristic of Qumran writings.[116] Especially close is the conception of two spirits resident in humanity and warring against one another.[117] The Qumranites' criticism of the Jerusalem cult and its wicked priest has a counterpart in this story about Manasseh and his Satan worship.[118] A retreat into the wilderness to escape the wickedness of the Jerusalem establishment is central to the Qumranic self-understanding.[119] The cast of characters in the *Martyrdom* parallels that in the scrolls:

Isaiah and his friends	The Teacher of Righteousness and his community
Manasseh	The Wicked Priest[120]
Bechir-ra	The False Oracle

The Teacher's claims to have special insights into the meaning of the Scriptures could have provided a basis for the kind of charge levelled against Isaiah in 3:8-9,[121] and the emphasis on the polarity of true and false prophecy is consonant with such texts as the *Pesharim* on Nahum and the Psalms.[122] The calling of Jerusalem and its princes 'Sodom' and 'the people of Gomorrah' is reminiscent of Qumranic typological exegesis.[123]

The similarities are very close. At the very least, we can attribute the writing to a religious group with a dualistic theology, which withdraws into the wilderness in order to escape from what it considers to be a satanic cult in Jerusalem. Our closest analogy is the Qumran community, but it is safer simply to attribute the work to a group within the wider orbit of Essene theology and self-understanding.[124]

---

[115] Flusser, 'Ascensio,' 30-37. The idea is developed in more detail by Philonenko, 'Martyre,' 1-10. See also Caquot, 'Commentaire,' 93.

[116] Cf. especially 1QS 3:13-4:26 and the documents in Milik, 'Milkî-ṣedeq,' 126-44. The closest parallel to the satanic name Melchî-ra (*Asc. Isa.* 1:8) Milkî-reša, and Isaiah's curse of Bechir-ra (5:9) closely parallels the curses in 4Q280 2:2 and 4Q287 4:4ff., see Milik, *ibid.*, 127, 130-31.

[117] Cf. 1QS 3:13-4:26.

[118] Cf. CD 4:12-18. Attribution of Satan worship to Manasseh may reflect the view that connects pagan deities with Satan and demons (*Jub.* 1:9-12; *Jos. As.* 12:9-10; 1 Cor 10:19-21).

[119] 1QS 8:12-16.

[120] The civil functions of the Hasmonaean princes facilitate a comparison with Manasseh.

[121] So Flusser, 'Ascensio,' 41-43. See 1QpHab. 7:1-5.

[122] 4QpNah; 4Q171 1:12-19.

[123] Cf. Flusser, 'Pharisäer, Sadduzäer.'

[124] The NT accounts about John the Baptist indicate that there were other apocalyptic prophets who retreated to the wilderness.

The occasion for the writing is less clear. Flusser compares the prophets' departure for Tyre and Sidon (*Asc. Isa.* 5:13) with the withdrawal to Damascus (CD 7:14ff.) and suggests that the *Martyrdom* was written in Damascus to justify the exile and to strengthen the faith of those who had entered the New Covenant there.[125] However, the incident in the *Martyrdom* seems to be mentioned as an *ad hoc* explanation for the fact that only Isaiah is martyred; the reference is all too brief and parenthetical to be the point of the document. Does the story imply the martyrdom of a saintly leader, indeed the Teacher of Righteousness, if one accepts a Qumranic identification? This is probably not demonstrable. The story surely implies persecution of some sort and sets up Isaiah as an example of how the present woes of the author's group were foreshadowed in sacred history. It exhorts the readers to stand fast, for in their battle with Satan – even if it be to death – they will be sustained by the power of the Holy Spirit. At a later time, the writer of the Epistle to the Hebrews would incorporate this legend into his recitation of sacred history, as he exhorted his readers to faith in the midst of (possible) persecution (Heb 10:32-12:13). There, however, Jesus is cited as the ultimate paradigm of faith and faithfulness (12:1-2).

The *Martyrdom* offers us an early example of the motif of the persecution of the prophets, which will emerge with some frequency in early Christian literature.[126] Moreover, as a story it is paralleled not only by such texts as 2 Maccabees 6 and 7 (see above), but also by such early Christian texts as the *Martyrdom of Polycarp*.

The Lives of the Prophets[127]

The *Lives of the Prophets* (*Vitae Prophetarum*) is a singular composition both in form and content comprising brief biographical sketches of the prophets of the Hebrew Bible. The work, attributed traditionally to Epiphanius, bishop of Salamis (315-403 C.E.), has been transmitted in an extravagant number of Greek recensions and Oriental languages.[128] Twenty-three 'lives' form the core of the book: Isaiah, Jeremiah, Ezekiel, Daniel, the twelve minor prophets, Nathan, Ahijah the Shilonite (1 Kgs 11:29), the 'man of God' who came to Jeroboam (1 Kgs 13), Azariah son of Oded (2 Chr 15:1), Elijah the Tishbite, Elisha his successor, and Zechariah son of Jehoiada (2 Chr 24:20-22). The life of Daniel fills nearly two pages of text and displays a fully-developed narrative artistry; the life of Joel merits but a short sentence. A number of the *Lives* provide little more than

---

125 Flusser, 'Ascensio,' 45-47.
126 Cf., e.g., Matt 5:12; 23:29-36; Luke 13:33-35; Acts 7:35-37, 52.
127 This section has been written by David Satran.
128 The standard edition of the Greek recensions remains Schermann, *Prophetarum Vitae Fabulosae*, 1-106. Translations of the text appear in Riessler, *Altjüdisches Schrifttum*, 871-80, 1321-2 (German) and Torrey, *The Lives of the Prophets*, 34-48 (English).

a convenient summary of details garnered from the Bible, while others provide a treasure-trove of (often unparalleled) extra-biblical material.

Common to all of the *Lives*, however, is a geographical framework including birth and burial notices of the prophets, and in several instances their tribal affiliation. These notices long have been regarded by researchers as a precious source of information regarding the geography of Palestine before the destruction of the Second Temple.[129] For alongside those sites familiar from the biblical *onomasticon* (Siloam, Anathoth, Tekoah, Shiloh, and others) the *Lives* offer a host of locations of either uncertain or completely unknown identity (Sabaratha, Sopha, Beth-Zouxar, Subatha, Kiriath-Maon). It has been suggested that these detailed birth and burial notices provide evidence of a *Megillat Yuhasin* (genealogical table) from the Second Temple period such as that discovered by R. Shimon b. Azzai in Jerusalem according to *B.T. Yebamoth* 49a.[130] Nevertheless, not all of the geographical traditions are to be taken at face value. The quintessentially brief *Life* of the prophet Joel consists of the following report: 'Joel was from the land of Reuben, in the field of Beth-Meon; he died in peace and was buried there.' This strange, and otherwise unattested, notice is best explained as an exceedingly creative exegesis of 1 Chr 5:1-8, where the same constellation of names is to be found. Likewise, the tribal attributions are notably idiosyncratic. Micah the Moreshtite, for example, is said to be from the tribe of Ephraim; this piece of geographical nonsense can only be understood as a result of the identification of the prophet with 'a man of the hill country of Ephraim, whose name was Micah' (Judg 17:1).

The bulk of the composition is given over to narratives of a decidedly legendary character. Some of these tales are purely extra-biblical and otherwise unattested: Isaiah's dying prayer and the miraculous issue of water from the fountain of Siloam; Jeremiah's extermination of the poisonous serpents of Egypt; the division of the waters of the river Chebar by Ezekiel in order to enable the Israelites to flee the Chaldeans; Jonah's return to the land of Israel subsequent to his prophecy in Nineveh. Other legends, equally unique, might best be described as amplifications of the biblical text: the vivid portrayal of Nebuchadnezzar's transformation into a beast and his repentance under Daniel's tutelage (Dan 4); Nathan's unsuccessful attempt to avert King David's sinful union with Bathsheba (2 Sam 11-12). Finally, a number of the *Lives* present interesting parallels to tales found in the *Apocrypha*. The legend of Jeremiah's concealment of the Ark prior to the destruction of the Temple, first recorded by Eupolemus

---

[129] Reland, a pioneer in the study of the historical geography of Palestine, made wide reference to the *Lives* in his *Palaestina.* The work also is cited repeatedly in Abel, *Palestine.* See especially Jeremias, *Heiligengräber* for a comprehensive attempt to employ the geographical notices of the *Lives.*

[130] Klein, 'Vitae Prophetarum,' 208-9.

(frg. 4), is narrated here in a form closely related to the account in 2 Macc 2:4-12.[131] Further details concerning the fate of the Temple vessels are contained in the *Life of Habakkuk*. There, too, the prophet's mysterious translation to Babylon in order to bring food to the captive Daniel appears in an abbreviated version quite distinct from that found in Bel and the Dragon (LXX Dan 14:33-39).

Much interest has been generated by the legends which preserve details regarding the violent deaths of the prophets. A number of these accounts are unparalleled in Jewish tradition: the death of Ezekiel, for example, is otherwise known only from Christian sources;[132] while the chastisement of the prophets Amos and Micah is a fully-developed theme in the Midrash,[133] only in the *Lives* do we actually learn of their martyrdom. Other legends, once again, are well-known from Jewish texts of the Second Temple period and from Rabbinic literature: Isaiah sawn asunder at the hands of Manasseh,[134] and the stoning of Jeremiah.[135] Finally, two reports are biblically based, involving little or no elaboration: the murder of Zechariah son of Jehoiada within the Temple (2 Chr 24:20-22); the death of the 'man of God' — known in our text as Joad — who prophesied before Jeroboam (1 Kgs 13:1-32).

The profound influence of Jewish traditions on early Christian attitudes toward martyrdom has received ample demonstration, yet the true nature and extent of Jewish martyrology prior to the destruction of the Second Temple remains a matter of some debate. It is hardly surprising, therefore, that in recent discussions of the issue evidence gleaned from the *Lives of the Prophets* figures prominently.[136] The legends concerning the prophets' deaths have been regarded as the background of Jesus' scourge: 'O Jerusalem, Jerusalem, killing the prophets and stoning those who are sent to you.'[137] Similarly, efforts have been made to parallel the accounts of the *Lives* with the enumeration in Heb 11: 32-38 of the (nameless) prophets who persevered by their faith. The question arises, however, whether this aspect of the composition has not been unduly emphasized.[138] As outlined above, less than one-third of the prophets (seven of twenty-three) meet unusual deaths, and of these reports two are derived solely from the

---

[131] Wacholder, *Eupolemus,* 237-42, discusses the earliest level of this tradition. The theme of the hidden Temple vessels appears as well in *Par. Jer.* 3:8-11, 18-20 and *2 Apoc. Bar.* 6:6-10; on the relationship between these sources and our text, see Nickelsburg, 'Narrative Traditions.'

[132] *Apocalypse of Paul* 49.

[133] E.g. *Pesikta de-Rav Kahana* 16, p. 269.

[134] Cf. *Martyrdom of Isaiah* 4:11-5:14; *B.T. Yebamoth* 49a and *Sanhedrin* 103b.

[135] Cf. *Paraleipomena of Jeremiah* 9:21-28; *Midrash Aggadah* on Num 30:15.

[136] See particularly Fischel, 'Martyr and Prophet,' 270-80 and Schoeps, 'Prophetenmorde,' 130-5. On the Jewish background of Christian martyrology, the following works are basic: Frend, *Martyrdom;* Klauser, 'Christlicher Märtyrerkult'; Flusser, 'Martyrdom'.

[137] Matt 23:37; Luke 13:34; cf. Matt 23: 29-36; Luke 11:47-51.

[138] As observed by Steck, *Israel,* 248-9.

biblical text. Further, where parallel legends exist in contemporary Jewish literature, one quickly appreciates the extreme brevity and understatement of the accounts in the *Lives*. Equal or greater emphasis, in fact, could be laid on the natural deaths and orderly burials of the prophets: Daniel is buried 'alone and with honour in the royal sepulchre' of the Persian kings; Haggai is laid to rest 'alongside the tomb of the priests, honoured as they are'; Hosea, Joel, and Nahum are all buried 'in peace' in their own land; both Nathan and Zechariah die having attained advanced age; Obadiah and Malachi are laid to rest with their fathers. Surely an author with a keen martyrological sense might have done better.

Our discussion thus far reflects to some degree the principal predilection (and weakness) of modern scholarship on the *Lives of the Prophets:* inordinate concern with the piquant details (geographical and narrative) of the composition, at the expense of a close analysis of the literary structure. The concerns and techniques developed during the last century of biblical research (including form- and redaction-criticism) have yet to be applied to the *Lives*. Do the birth and burial notices, for example, form an integral aspect of the text, or can they be identified as a literary framework introduced in a final stage of redaction? In like manner, far too little attention has been focused on those passages in the *Lives* which open with the recurrent phrase 'And he gave a sign ...' (e.g. Daniel, Hosea, Nahum, Jonah, Habakkuk, Zechariah son of Berachiah). These sections, characterized by elements of eschatological prophecy, bear a close thematic and linguistic relationship to the *Testaments of the Twelve Patriarchs*.[139] Finally, an issue too rarely raised (and still more rarely taken seriously) is that of audience — for whom was the work intended? It has been suggested that rather than an antiquarian catalogue of unusual place names and wondrous deeds, the *Lives of the Prophets* provides our earliest example of a 'pilgrim's guide' to the Holy Land. In short, questions of both literary structure and literary genre demand investigation.

This somewhat unbalanced approach to the study of the text has had its effect on almost all attempts to determine the date, provenance, and original language of the composition. A virtually exclusive interest in details relevant to the physical and spiritual landscape of first-century Palestine has encouraged similar conclusions regarding the origin of the work. Semiticisms perceived in the Greek recensions have been interpreted as certain evidence of an underlying Hebrew *Grundschrift*.[140] The general absence of overtly Christian passages has reinforced scholarly confidence

---

[139] Thus already Schermann, *Propheten- und Apostellegenden,* 120-2; for further observations regarding these sections (and possible connections with early Christian literature), see De Jonge, 'Christelijke Elementen.'

[140] The most extreme case for an original Hebrew composition predating the destruction of the Temple is Torrey, *Lives of the Prophets,* 1-17; his text and translation are frequently based upon a reconstructed *Vorlage*.

in the Jewish character of the *Lives* despite the text's reception and popularity in the Church. Christological references, however, are not an inevitable feature of Christian composition or redaction; equally revealing (if less obvious) details may yield to more subtle methods of analysis.[141] As with other texts of the Second Temple period, serious consideration must be given to the context of transmission. It would be ill-advised to forget that the *Lives of the Prophets* had only a presumed audience of first-century Jews; the work was of proven interest, however, to Byzantine Christians.[142]

The Testament of Abraham

This story about the events surrounding Abraham's death survives in two recensions, one long and the other short (see further below). Because the long recension is the more interesting and probably preserves a more original form of the narrative, we discuss it here.

When the time of Abraham's death arrives, God, out of special consideration for his 'friend,' dispatches Michael to bring the news and to command the patriarch to put his affairs in order, i.e., to make his testament. Abraham refuses to follow Michael and agrees only when God promises him a revelation of heaven and earth. During this chariot ride through the universe, Abraham calls down divine punishment on sinners whom he sees in the act of transgression. Fearing that sinless Abraham will annihilate the whole human race, God orders the patriarch up to heaven to see the judgment process and learn mercy. When Abraham successfully intercedes for a soul whose righteous deeds and sins are equally balanced in the judgment scale, he decides that he should also intercede for the sinners whom he previously condemned. They are brought back to life, and Abraham has learned about the compassion of a long-suffering God. Michael escorts him back to earth and, in the presence of his family, again orders him to make his testament. Once more he refuses, and then God sends Death, who relentlessly presses the patriarch, despite his protests, and finally takes his soul by a subterfuge.

The book is divided into two parallel and symmetrical sections (chaps. 1-15 and 16-20.[143] Each begins as God summons the messenger of death and ends with Abraham on his bed, surrounded by his household, i.e., the typical testamentary situation. Binding these two sections together is a double narrative thread: God's command that Abraham prepare for death and Abraham's refusal to do so. The plot line moves through the two

---

[141] Flusser, 'Paleae Historica,' 48-49 cautions against such facile assumptions. For an attempt to detect more elusive Christian elements in the *Lives*, see Satran, 'Daniel', 39-43.

[142] Kraft, 'Recensional Problem,' 131-7 argues persuasively the importance of a work's context of transmission. Especially relevant in this regard is Simon, 'Les Saints d'Israël.'

[143] For a comparison of the two parts, see Nickelsburg, 'Structure and Message,' 85f. The analysis that follows above is taken from *ibid.*, 86-88.

sections from God's initial command to its fulfillment with Abraham's death.

Each of the two parts has its own pace and tone, corresponding to its relative place in the development of the plot. Part I is lengthy and rambling, and it has more than its share of humorous touches: the double entendre in Michael's identification of himself (chap. 2); the picture of the disturbed patriarch, afraid to admit that he hears trees talking[144] and sees teardrops turning to pearls (chap. 3); Michael, unable to cope with Abraham's repeated refusals, making repeated trips to the divine throne-room for new orders (chaps. 4, 8, 9, 15). When Michael fails in his mission, we move to Part II, where a totally different pace and tone pervade. The divine messenger is 'merciless, rotten Death.' His identification of himself is quick and to the point. Abraham's continued refusals are met not by repeated trips to the throneroom, but by Death's pursuit of Abraham into the inner chambers of his house, right to his bed. This time Abraham's request for a revelation results in a fierce vision of the many faces of Death that strikes terror in the patriarch's heart. Again Abraham's family gathers around his bed, not to rejoice over his return, but to mourn over his imminent death. Now there is no command to make his testament, only the sudden, unexpected death about which he had inquired moments before. God's command is finally fulfilled. The plot is resolved.

The typical Jewish testaments employ the deathbed scenes as a setting for ethical and eschatological instruction that is not essentially connected with this setting.[145] The *Testament of Abraham,* on the other hand, focuses on the problem of death itself and right and wrong attitudes about its relationship to God's judgment.[146] By means of his plot line the author underscores the inevitability of death, while at the same time he deals sympathetically with the universal human fear of death and aversion to it. He employs the figure of Abraham to both ends. Abraham's exemplary righteousness could not save him from death: 'Even upon him there came the common, inexorable, bitter cup of death and the uncertain end of life' (chap. 1). In order to make his point, the author has composed a startling portrait of Abraham. Although he ascribes to the patriarch some of the virtues traditionally attributed to him (righteousness, hospitality), the author has glaringly omitted the most celebrated of these, viz., Abraham's obedient faith.[147] Indeed, he has created a veritable parody of the biblical and traditional Abraham. He fears God's summons to 'go forth' (cf. *T. Abr.* 1 and Gen 12:1), and his haggling with God takes on the character of

---

[144] On the legend of the speaking tree, see James, *Testament of Abraham,* 59-64.

[145] See below, pp. 325-6.

[146] For another possible example of a testament that dealt with the problem of death, see the discussion of the *Books of Adam and Eve,* below, pp. 111f.

[147] Cf., e.g., *Jub.* 17:15-18:16; 19:1-9; Sir 44:20; 1 Macc 2:52; 4 Macc 16:18-23; 18:2; Heb 11:8-9, 17-19; James 2:21-24; see Nickelsburg, 'Structure and Message,' 87, n. 1.

disobedience (contrast Gen 18:22-32). Seven times he refuses to go with God's messenger (chaps. 7, 9, 15, 17, 19, 20). The first line of the work leads us to expect a testament. What we get is a parody on the genre — a non-testament.

If the book as a whole presents a kind of parody on Abraham's much touted faith, a large segment of Part I — the chariot ride sequence (chaps. 10-14) — takes up another celebrated Abrahamic virtue, his righteousness, and depicts its dark reverse side — self-righteousness. The righteous patriarch cannot understand or tolerate sinners, and so he appeals to heaven for their destruction. Thus, the account of Abraham's heavenly journey functions primarily to further the author's parenetic purpose. Self-righteousness is always a danger for the righteous. More important, it is a sin to be repented of, because it fails to comprehend, and therefore it conflicts with the mercy of God, who desires not the death of the wicked, but that the wicked repent. By quoting Ezekiel 18:23 (*T. Abr.* 10), the author identifies as sin the oft-expressed cry of the righteous that sinners receive the just rewards of their deeds.[148]

Although the account of Abraham's heavenly journey serves primarily a parenetic purpose, it also reflects the author's eschatological views.[149] Abraham receives a double vision of the judgment process: the separation of the souls of the dead into the two gates leading to life and destruction (chap. 11) and the judgment before Abel (chaps. 12-14). Both scenes imply that the soul goes to its eternal destiny shortly after death. A bodily resurrection is never mentioned. References to a second judgment by the twelve tribes of Israel and a third judgment by God himself appear to be interpolations into the text.[150] The main judgment scene (chaps. 12-14) is derived in part from Jewish tradition. Its description of the two angelic scribes who function as advocate and accuser and the book of human deeds is paralleled in a number of other Jewish writings.[151] Abel is said to be judge because he is son of Adam, the father of all humanity. Parallel texts suggest, however, that the ascription to him of judicial powers may derive from his status as proto-martyr.[152] The balancing of righteous deeds and

---

[148] See Kolenkow, 'The Genre Testament,' 143-8; and Nickelsburg, *Testament of Abraham*, 293-5.

[149] For a detailed discussion of this section, see Nickelsburg, 'Eschatology.'

[150] *Ibid*, 41-47.

[151] *Ibid.*, 36-38. Because Michael is here the interpreting angel who accompanies Abraham on his cosmic tour, he does not assume his traditional role as advocate, on which, see Nickelsburg, *Resurrection*, 11-14. On Michael, see also Schmidt, *Testament* I, 79-92. On the two angels see also Kobelski, *Melchizedek*, 75-84.

[152] See Schmidt, *Testament* I, 64-65; Delcor, 'De l'origine,' 194-98; Nickelsburg, 'Eschatology,' 34-35. Noteworthy in the judgment scene in the short recension is the figure of Enoch the heavenly scribe (chap. 10-11); see Schmidt, *Testament* I, 65-67; and Pearson, 'The Pierpont Morgan Fragments.'

sins, on the other hand, appears to reflect Egyptian ideas attested in the Book of the Dead.[153] Also noteworthy in the judgment scene is the presence of Puruel, the angel 'who has power over fire and tests the deeds of men through fire' (chap. 13). A similar idea occurs in 1 Corinthians 3:13-14.[154] Whether Paul knew the *Testament of Abraham* or another form of the tradition cannot be determined with certainty.

Of special importance for the study of the *Testament* is the figure of *Thanatos,* or Death, whose activities are the subject of considerable speculation in chapters 16-20.[155] Similar in a way to the lying spirit in 1 Kings 22:21-23 and the satanic accuser in Job 1-2, Death is a negative figure who is, nevertheless, an inhabitant of the heavenly court and a servant of God. His ability to carry out his purpose through the death of any individual is subject to God's justice and mercy. Certain similarities to Jewish ideas notwithstanding, aspects of the figure of death in the long recension are best paralleled in Egyptian mythology,[156] and the presence of these ideas and of the weighing of the souls constitutes an interesting example of Jewish religious syncretism.

The theme of Abraham's refusal to accept death and other details in the *Testament* are paralleled in Jewish midrashim about the death of Moses, and it is quite likely the Moses traditions are earlier.[157] In any case, the parallels indicate a tendency of traditions about one figure in antiquity to become associated secondarily with another person.[158]

The precise relationship between the two recensions of the *Testament* is a matter of scholarly debate.[159] On the one hand, there is general agreement that the Greek of the long recension (A) represents, on the whole, a later period than that of the short recension (B).[160] However, scholars continue to debate which of the two forms of the story is more original. Considerations of structure and the logic of elements in the plot seem to suggest that,

---

[153] See Schmidt, *Testament* I, 71-76; and Nickelsburg, 'Eschatology,' 32-34.

[154] See Fishburne, 'I Corinthians.'

[155] See Kolenkow, 'The Genre Testament,' 143-48.

[156] See James, *Testament of Abraham,* 55-58; Schmidt, *Testament,* I, 101-10. However, cf. also 4QAmram[b] fg. 1:13-14 for a description of the satanic figure with a snake-like face, and cf. the commentary by Kobelski, *Melchizedek,* 30-32.

[157] See Loewenstamm, 'The Testament of Abraham.'

[158] Cf., e.g., the Job-like prologue to the story of the Akedah in *Jub.* 17:15ff. (see, below, pp. 98f.) and the similarities between the stories of Abraham's and Job's destruction of idolatrous temples in *Jub.* 12 and *T. Job* 2-5. See also Nickelsburg, *Jewish Literature,* 247-48. On the relationship of the *Testament of Abraham* and the *Testament of Job,* see Delcor, *Testament,* 47-51.

[159] On this question, see the articles by Nickelsburg, Schmidt, Martin, and Kraft, in Nickelsburg, *Testament of Abraham,* 23-137. See also the discussion by Sanders, 'Testament of Abraham.'

[160] James, *Testament of Abraham,* 34; Turner, *Testament, passim;* see also the vocabulary list in Delcor, *Testament,* 30f.

on the whole, the form of the story in the long recension is more original.[161] Nonetheless, there are narrative elements in the short recension that appear to be more primitive than their counterparts in the longer version. The two recensions are very likely the result of a complex history of (oral?) transmission, rather than of a simple dependence of A upon B or of B upon A.[162]

Opinions vary widely on the date of composition. Suggestions have ranged from the first century B.C.E. to the fifth or sixth century C.E. (the latter, for the final form of the long recension).[163] There are no historical allusions in the work, and arguments for the date are based largely on a comparison with the language and ideas in other works.

There is some consensus that the long recension originated in Egypt.[164] An argument for a Palestinian origin for the short recension is based mainly on the supposition that this recension is a translation of a Hebrew original.[165] That the *Testament* is written in a Semitizing Greek is indisputable.[166] Whether this indicates an origin in a Semitic language, or whether the Greek of the *Testament* imitates the style of translation Greek remains an open question.[167]

The *Testament* has been transmitted to us by Christian scribes. However, only the final words of the text can with certainty be said to be Christian: '... glorifying the Father and the Son and the Holy Spirit. To him be glory and power for ever. Amen' (chap. 20). Other expressions are reminiscent of phrases in the New Testament.[168] In most cases, they can be explained as reflecting a common Jewish milieu.[169] Others, which are peculiar to recension A may be the result of Christian scribal activity in the later revision of the language of this recension.[170] In any case, possible Christian phraseology does not appear to be frequent enough or sufficiently of the substance of the book to support an hypothesis of a Christian origin for the *Testament*.[171]

---

[161] See Nickelsburg, 'Structure and Message,' 47-64, 85-93. See also Sanders, 'Testament of Abraham.'

[162] On the variety of possible relationships, see Kraft, 'Recensional Problem,' 121-31.

[163] A good summary is provided by Schmidt, *Testament* I, 115-17. See also Delcor, *Testament*, 73-77, and Sanders, 'Testament of Abraham.'

[164] See James, *Testament of Abraham*, 76; Schmidt, *Testament* I, 71-76, 101-10; 119; Delcor, *Testament*, 67-69.

[165] Schmidt, *Testament* I, 119.

[166] See the data assembled by Martin, 'Syntax Criticism,' 95-120.

[167] See the critique of Martin by Kraft, 'Recensional Problem,' 133-35. See also Sanders, 'Testament of Abraham.'

[168] See James, *Testament of Abraham*, 50-51.

[169] This also seems to be the case with the parallel in 1 Cor 3; see above, n. 154.

[170] See above, n. 160.

[171] James (*Testament of Abraham*, 50-55) argued for a Christian origin, but he has generally not been followed. See, however, the cautious approach of Kraft, 'Recensional Problem,' 135-7.

Joseph and Aseneth

The patriarch Joseph is a prominent figure in Jewish literature. A large part of Genesis is devoted to his story, which becomes prototypical of later Jewish stories of the persecution and exaltation of the righteous person (see above, p. 34). His virtuous conduct is expounded at length in the *Testaments of the Twelve Patriarchs* (see p. 334). One item in the biblical account, however, was bound to create theological problems. Contrary to the partriarchal admonitions of Genesis as understood by post-exilic Judaism,[172] Joseph married a foreign woman — the daughter of an Egyptian priest (Gen 41:45). The story of *Joseph and Aseneth*[173] deals with this problem, describing Aseneth's conversion from idolatry and attributing to her the status of prototypical proselyte.[174]

Aseneth is introduced as a virgin of peerless beauty, whose hand in marriage is sought by suitors from far and near, among them the Pharaoh's son (chap. 1). She scorns them all and lives in virginal isolation in a great tower (chap.2). When Joseph announces his intention to dine with her father Pentepheres, the priest discloses to Aseneth his desire that she and Joseph, 'the mighty one of God,' should be married (chaps. 3-4). Aseneth scornfully refuses to have anything to do with this the adulterous 'alien and fugitive' (4:9f.).

When Joseph arrives, Aseneth retreats to her tower (chap. 5). As she peeks through her window, she is shocked by his divine, resplendent appearance and repents her rash words (chap. 6).

Assured that Aseneth is 'a virgin hating every man,' Joseph agrees to see her and to 'love her from today as my sister' (chap. 7). However, when Aseneth appears, Joseph refuses to kiss her, because she has polluted herself through idolatry (8:5). Aseneth is deeply chagrined at her rejection, and Joseph prays for her conversion, promising to return in a week (chaps. 8-9).

Aseneth retreats to her tower, where she mourns, fasts, and repents for seven days. She exchanges her royal robes for sack-cloth, destroys her idols, and casts them and her rich foods out the window (chaps. 9-10).

Aseneth is alone, forsaken by her parents and hated by all because of her repudiation of her idols. Gradually she comes to the decision to seek 'refuge' with the merciful God of Joseph (chap. 11). In her lengthy prayer (chaps. 12-13), she confesses her sin of idolatry and asks to be delivered from the devil, the 'father of the gods of the Egyptians,' who pursues her

---

[172] See Gen 24:3f., 37f.; 27:46; 28:1. The admonitions are expanded in *Jub.* 20:4; 22:20; and especially 30:7-16. See also Tob 4:12f.

[173] In the MT of Gen 41:45, Joseph's wife's name is *Asenath.* Here we are following the spelling of the LXX and the Greek text of *Joseph and Aseneth.*

[174] On the text of Joseph and Aseneth, see below, n. 207. Versification is that of Riessler, *Altjüdisches Schrifttum,* which follows the long text.

like a lion. She points to her acts of penitence and repudiation as signs of her true repentance and asks forgiveness for her idolatry and her blasphemy against God's 'son,' Joseph.

The archangel Michael appears, identifies himself, and commands Aseneth to replace her mourning garments with bridal array. He then conveys to her a threefold message: Joseph's God has heard her prayer; he will quicken her with immortality; she has been given to Joseph as a bride and will become a 'City of Refuge' for all the gentiles to turn to the living God (15:2-7). Michael commands Aseneth to bring a honeycomb which mysteriously appears in her storehouse. Placing his hand on her head, he transmits to her 'the ineffable mysteries of God' and bids her eat of the honeycomb, which is the spirit of life, made by the bees of paradise from the roses of life. Now she has eaten the bread of life and drunk the cup of immortality and been anointed with the unction of incorruption. Henceforth her flesh and bones will flower, and she will never die. When Aseneth turns her back momentarily, Michael vanishes.

The story now repeats the structure of the first part of the narrative with significant changes (chaps. 18-20; cf. chaps. 3-8).[175] The servant announces that Joseph will come to dine. Aseneth orders the meal prepared. She adorns herself with special bridal array, and her face is gloriously transfigured. Joseph arrives once again. Aseneth goes out to meet him. They embrace and kiss three times, and Aseneth receives 'the spirit of life,' 'the spirit of wisdom,' and 'the spirit of truth.' She is fit to be Joseph's bride. Her parents return, astonished at her beauty. Amid glorious ceremonies and feasting, Joseph and Aseneth are married by the Pharaoh (chap. 21).

Chapter 22 is an interlude, describing Aseneth's meeting with Jacob, whose angel-like appearance is described. Simeon and Levi are introduced as Aseneth's friends and protectors. This provides the transition to the last part of the story (chaps. 23-29). Pharaoh's son reappears as Joseph's rival, madly in love with Aseneth. He vainly seeks the help of Simeon and Levi in murdering Joseph. Finally, he enlists the help of the sons of Bilhah and Zilpah. Their attempted kidnapping of Aseneth and murder of Joseph are stymied, due to the help of Simeon, Levi, and Benjamin. The prince is mortally wounded. Later when the Pharaoh dies, Joseph becomes sole ruler of Egypt.

Integrated into the present literary work is a legend, known from other Jewish sources, which identified Aseneth as the daughter of Dinah and Shechem (cf. Gen 34).[176] Hints of the story are to be seen in the description of Aseneth (1:4f.), in the actions of the Egyptian prince (chaps. 1,23ff.), who is the counterpart of Shechem, and the major role played by Simeon

---

[175] Note the same use of double parallel structure in the *Testament of Abraham;* see above, pp. 60f.

[176] For the parallel sources, see Aptowitzer, 'Asenath,' 243-56; Philonenko, *Joseph,* 32-43.

and Levi, Aseneth's protectors (chaps. 22ff.).[177] This story dealt with the problem of Joseph's marriage to an Egyptian woman by maintaining that she was, in reality, an Israelite. The story replayed the events at Shechem, but the chastity of Dinah's daughter was preserved.[178]

The story of Aseneth's Israelite descent has been edited into a story that solves the problem of Genesis 41:45 in a different way. Aseneth is an Egyptian who is converted to the religion of Israel before she marries Joseph. This story controls the present form of *Joseph and Aseneth* and dominates the reader's attention. The story about Pharaoh's son (introduced in chap. 1) is employed mainly as a short second act (chaps. 23-29) that draws motifs from the main story[179] and serves the didactic purposes of the final author or editor. It demonstrates how God protects his new convert, and it exemplifies in the actions of Simeon, Levi, and Benjamin conduct that 'is proper for a man who worships God.'

Aseneth's conversion is twofold. Chapters 4-6 depict her change in attitude toward Joseph. At first she spurns 'the son of the shepherd from the land of Canaan,' saying she will marry the king's firstborn son (4:9-11). However, when she sees Joseph, she acknowledges him to be 'son of God' and likens his advent to a solar epiphany (chap. 6).[180] By describing Joseph in language appropriate to Pharaoh's son,[181] she is not only making a marital choice, she is also adumbrating her conversion from the gods of Egypt to the God of Joseph. This conversion and its implications are the main subject matter of chapters 2-23.

Aseneth's status as an idolatress constitutes a twofold problem for her. 1) Because she worships 'dead and deaf idols,' she is cut off from 'the living God.'[182]She exists in the realm of death and corruption, deprived of eternal life and incorruptibility (8:5, 9). Moreover, her idolatry has defiled her. Because she has blessed idols and partaken of the food and drink of their

---

[177] For a discussion of these and other elements from the older story, see Aptowitzer, 'Asenath,' 260-86.

[178] Cf. the book of Judith (above, n. 86) and the conscious typology between Judith and Simeon. Judith emerges undefiled.

[179] Cf. 23:10, 'son of God'; 27:10f., Aseneth's appeal to her conversion; the many references to ('what is proper for') one who worships God,' 22:13; 23:9, 10, 12; 28:7; 29:3; cf. 4:7; 8:5-7.

[180] Suggested by J. Z. Smith in correspondence. He comes from the east (5:2). The solar language is explicit in 6:5. As a parallel to Aseneth's recognition of Joseph and reaction to it, Burchard (*Dreizehnte Zeuge,* 69) correctly notes Psyche's discovery of Cupid in Apuleius, *Metamorphoses* 5:22. On the other hand, the contrast of Aseneth's former scorn of Joseph with her present acclamation of him as a 'son of God' is reminiscent of the wicked's change of mind in Wis 2 and 5. On the relationship of Wis 2, 4-5 and Gen 37ff., see Nickelsburg, *Resurrection,* 49, 58-62.

[181] For Egyptian texts describing the pharaoh as the son of Re, the sun god, see Pritchard, *ANET,* 234, 254, 370f. Cf. also the name Ramses.

[182] For the contrast, see 8:5; cf. also 11:8-10; 12:1, 5. The idea is traditional; cf. Bel and the Dragon, above, p. 39.

cult, her mouth is unclean.[183] For seven days, she does not dare to open her polluted mouth to address the living God (11:2f., 9; 12:5). 2) Her state of defilement imperils her relationship with Joseph. It is improper for a man who has blessed the living God and has partaken of the food and drink of immortality to kiss the polluted mouth of an idolatress (8:5).[184] The marriage of Joseph and Aseneth is forbidden.

Through her conversion, Aseneth passes from death to life (8:9).[185] After she has destroyed her gods and their sacrificial food and drink (10:12f.), she engages in a mourning ritual, evidently lamenting her sojourn in the realm of death (10:8-17).[186] Michael announces that Aseneth's name is now written in the book of life (15:2-4). The rituals that follow dramatize this fact and confer on her a new status that reverses her former deprivation. Michael confers on her the mysteries of God (16:13f.) in the place of the ignorance of her idolatry (12:4f.). She herself may now partake of the food and drink of immortality (16:13-16).[187] Her investiture in bridal array transfigures her appearance as a result of the eternal life that is now hers (chap. 18).[188] Her transfigured appearance so exceeds her previous beauty,[189] that Joseph does not recognize her (19:4f.). Joseph's kiss also bestows the spirit of life, wisdom, and truth (19:11). Their marriage is the final resolution of the plot of chapters 2-23.

Aseneth's is no ordinary conversion, for she does not marry an ordinary man. Joseph is the prototype of the persecuted and exalted righteous man.[190] Imbued with a special measure of God's spirit, he is mighty, wise, and clairvoyant (4:8f.; 6:1-7; 19:4). Glorious in appearance and resemb-

---

[183] Among the references to Aseneth's mouth are 8:5; 11:2, 9, 15; 12:4f; cf. 13:13. That the issue in Joseph and Aseneth is somehow related to the question of meat and idols was suggested by J. Z. Smith in correspondence.

[184] Although Joseph refuses to kiss Aseneth (for the reasons given), he makes the sexually explicit gesture of laying his hand on her breast, the function of which is unclear in the context. This is perhaps a remnant of the Dinah story. In the parallel tradition, Jacob placed around Dinah's neck an amulet on which was written the name of the God of Israel, Aptowitzer, 'Asenath,' 244. There may be a remnant of that motif in 3:6. Joseph's gesture here would be a move to take hold of the amulet. The recognition that followed is perhaps to be divined at precisely the same point in the second cycle of our story (19:10). The relatively rare verb in 19:10, ἀναζωοπύρησαν ('they lived again'), occurs in the LXX at Gen 45:27, where it describes Jacob's emotion when he hears that his long-lost son is alive.

[185] 8:9; cf. 15:4-5; 16:16. The language of 'realized' eschatology in these formulations finds its closest analogies in the hymns of Qumran (1QH 3:19-23; 11:3-14; cf. *Jos. As.* 15:12) and Philo's description of Therapeutic belief (*De Vita Contempl.* 13). See Nickelsburg, *Resurrection*, 152-6, 169.

[186] Suggested by J. Z. Smith in correspondence. It fits the author's death/life polarity.

[187] Aseneth does not receive either bread or a drink. Perhaps one should think of heavenly manna as the bread and honey from the honeycomb as the drink. The imagery of food and drink has probably been developed in polarity to the food and drink of idolatrous cult.

[188] For the imagery, cf. Sir 24:13-17; 50:8-12.

[189] Cf. especially 4:1, 'the bride of God.'

[190] See Nickelsburg, *Resurrection*, 49.

ling Michael,[191] he is called by the angelic title, 'son of God' and is set apart from mere mortals (6:5-7).[192] For such an one a special bride is required. Aseneth becomes a very special person. The angelophany has its typical commissioning function. Michael announces Aseneth's change of name. As in parallel biblical epiphanies, the name change denotes a change from individual to collective and matriarchal or foundational status.[193] Aseneth, who sought refuge, will be a city of refuge (13:12; 15:7). The first proselyte is the prototype of future proselytes. She is both woman and city, proselyte and congregation of proselytes. Her immortality is promised to all who follow her example and thereby become citizens of her city.

Although *Joseph and Aseneth* has more than its share of obscure passages, certain of its peculiar features and contours suggest a context and function. Different from other conversion stories (see above, pp. 34-7, 38-40), *Joseph and Aseneth* makes explicit reference to the author's own time. Aseneth of old is the prototype of proselytes now. What the author says about idolatry and about conversion applies to his own time. Immortality and eternal life are to be found only through the worship of the God of Israel, the living God, and idolators must completely forsake their idols and turn to him, if they would obtain it. Although both Pentepheres and Pharaoh acknowledge Joseph's God (4:6f.; 21:4), it is noteworthy that the author does not relate their conversion, though the analogy of the Danielic stories might lead us to expect it. It is Aseneth's conversion which is described, and specifically as it removes the impediment to her marriage to Joseph. The author may be forbidding any sort of contact between Jews and idolatrous gentiles on the grounds that it pollutes. In point of fact, however, he construes pollution from idols in a very specific and unusual way.[194] Marriage to an idol-worshipper is contaminating.

Was *Joseph and Aseneth* directed toward a Jewish or gentile audience? An answer is not easy. The message of the book has clear implications for Jews: abstain from idolatry; do not marry an idolater. Two considerations suggest, however, that the present writing was, in large part, intended for gentile readership. The first is the book's syncretism. Aspects of the story are clearly reminiscent of the tale of Cupid and Psyche.[195] The rituals of conversion — the laying on of hands and the conveying of mysteries, the sacred meal, investiture, a holy kiss — almost certainly betray the influence of non-Jewish initiatory rites.[196] Similarities between Aseneth and the

---

[191] Chaps. 5-6 are an epiphany scene. On the resemblance of Joseph and Michael, see 14:9.

[192] On Joseph's and Aseneth's supernatural beauty, see Betz, 'Geistliche Schönheit,' 76-79.

[193] See Burchard's discussion, *Untersuchungen,* 112-21. He cites such passages as Isa 62:4f.; Gen 17:5, 15; 32:28; Matt 16:17-19.

[194] Generalized references to the pollution of idols are too frequent to cite. A close parallel to 8:5 is 1 Cor 10:19-22, although there is no question of polluting the mouth.

[195] See Burchard, *Dreizehnte Zeuge,* 64-83; 'Joseph et Aséneth,' 84-96.

[196] *Ibid.* Burchard draws a comparison with Apuleius, *Metamorphoses* 11.

goddesses Isis and Neith have been noted.[197] Given the book's strong explicit and repeated polemic against idolatry, this blatant religious syncretism is strange to say the least. If it is directed to gentiles, however, it is understandable. Although the God of Israel alone is the living God — in whom alone is life — and idolatry is forbidden, Judaism is made attractive and understandable through the use of motifs and elements to which gentiles are accustomed. A second indication of an intended gentile audience is the fact that the story is written entirely from Aseneth's viewpoint. She is the central figure, and the author describes her thoughts and emotions: her suffering over the loss of Joseph; her distress at being abandoned by her family — an element that ill-befits the text (11:3-5; cf. 20:1f.); her uncertainty whether God will accept her repentance (11:7-15); her joy and relief when he does. The author has recounted a proselyte's progress from the viewpoint of the proselyte.

The author has written what is functionally a religious myth that explains the origins of proselytism. Its kerygmatic content is simple. Eternal life and immortality are to be found in the God of Israel alone, whose worship excludes idolatry. This God is, as he had revealed himself to Moses, 'a true God and living God, a merciful God and compassionate, and long-suffering and full of mercy and gentle, and not reckoning the sin of a humble man' (11:10; cf. Exod 34:6). Aseneth's marriage to a son of God reflects biblical imagery about the marriage of YHWH and Israel and may be parabolic of the covenantal relationship between the proselyte and God.[198] In accepting proselytes, God promises deliverance from the fury of the devil, who is piqued by the conversion (12:9-11). The second part of the story underscores this by demonstrating that God 'is with' his new convert, protecting her in mortal danger (26:2; 27:10f.).

In creating his myth, the author portrays both Joseph and Aseneth as larger than life figures, with special characteristics, as befits their archetypal status. The elaborate rituals may also function to underscore the special prototypical nature of Aseneth's conversion and need not imply that such rituals were employed in the author's community.[199] These ad hoc explanations raise some questions as to whether certain specific features in the story belong to the essence of the author's message or whether they are necessary trappings of the plot. In view of the YHWH-Israel language, is the author really making a statement about Jewish-gentile marriage? The specific construal of the nature of idolatrous pollution as an

---

[197] See Burchard, *Dreizehnte Zeuge,* 85; and Philonenko, *Joseph,* 61-79.

[198] See Isa 52:1f.; 54:1-13; 61:10f.; 62:1-2, where the imagery of remarriage and reinvestiture is prominent, and where the imagery fluctuates between woman and city. Jewish and Christian exegesis interpreted the Song of Songs allegorically of the relationship between God and his people. For a history of this exegesis, see Pope, *Song of Songs,* 89-192. Cf. also Eph 5:22f.; Rev 21:1f.

[199] Burchard, 'Joseph et Aséneth,' 96-100, whose notes cite ample literature in support of such rituals.

impediment to marriage, and the author's use of a popular erotic literary genre suggest that he is making such a statement.[200] On the other hand, Aseneth's marriage indicates that the author is not proposing permanent virginity as an ideal. The detailed description of Aseneth's virginal seclusion has a specific function in the story. There is a long tradition that idolatry and sexual immorality go hand in hand.[201] The author must show that Aseneth the idolatress remained the virgin that Joseph the son of God must needs marry.

The place of writing is disputed.[202] If it was written in Egypt, as has often been suggested,[203] its message would have a special bite. Pharaoh and an Egyptian priest acknowledged the God of Israel. Aseneth deserted her Egyptian gods and rejected Pharaoh's son in order to embrace the religion of Israel and marry an Israelite. What better precedents? The particular circle in which Joseph and Aseneth was written is uncertain.[204] The time of its composition is perhaps around the turn of the era.[205] It was composed in Greek.[206] Of the long and short forms of the Greek text, the former is most likely the original.[207]

Although there is no convincing evidence that *Joseph and Aseneth* is a Christian composition, it is easy to see why it was preserved and transmitted by Christian scribes. The rituals performed by Michael could be understood as foreshadowing the Christian Eucharist.[208] Moreover, the attention paid to Aseneth's rejection of Joseph and her subsequent acknowledgment of him as 'son of God,'[209] might also have been understood in terms of one's rejection and acceptance of Jesus as 'son of God.'[210]

---

[200] On the literary genre of *Joseph and Aseneth*, see Pervo, 'Joseph and Asenath,' who sees connections not only with the ancient erotic novel, but more with the Jewish sapiential novel. While wisdom teaching is not to be excluded (see above, n. 180), the eroticism of this work far exceeds anything else studied in this chapter.

[201] Cf., e.g., Num 25, Hos 1-3 and *passim* in the OT; Wis 14:24-26; Ep Jer 11, 43; Rom 1:24-27; Rev 2:14, 20.

[202] Burchard, *Untersuchungen,* 140-2.

[203] *Ibid.,* 140-3.

[204] See *ibid.,* 99-112. Burchard rejects a Christian origin, as well as Essene or Therapeutic origin; cf. however, above, n. 185.

[205] See Burchard, *Untersuchungen,* 143-51.

[206] *Ibid.,* 91-99.

[207] For a convincing argument supporting the originality of the longer text, see Burchard, *Untersuchungen,* 45-90. On the versions in Old Church Slavonic, Syriac, Armenian, and Latin, see Philonenko, *Joseph,* 11-15. See also Burchard, 'Joseph und Aseneth 25-29 Armenisch,' and 'Joseph und Aseneth Neugriechisch.'

[208] One interesting variant in the mss. of chap. 16 has Michael's finger trace the sign of a bloody cross on the honeycomb. Whatever the origins of the reading, it is indicative of the symbolic possibilities of the text; see Philonenko, *Joseph,* 188-9.

[209] Aseneth's concern about her blasphemy of Joseph is mentioned at length in both chaps. 6 and 13, and one has the impression that it is a sin of almost as great magnitude as her idolatry.

[210] For the polarity of rejection and confession of Jesus as son of God, cf. Mark 14:61-64;

Paraleipomena of Jeremiah

This writing is based on those parts of Jeremiah that describe the last days of Jerusalem. The action begins on the eve of Nebuchadnezzar's conquest.[211] The Lord addresses Jeremiah, commanding him and Baruch to leave the city, for he is about to deliver it to the Chaldaeans because of the sins of its inhabitants. At Jeremiah's request, God agrees to open the gates, lest the enemy boast over their ability to conquer 'the holy city of God' (1:4-11). As a divine sign confirming the impending destruction, angels descend from heaven with torches ready to set fire to the city. When Jeremiah asks that Abimelech be spared the sight of the city's destruction, God bids the prophet to send him into the vineyard of Agrippa, where he will be hidden 'until I cause the people to return to the city' (3:12-14) (cf. Jer 39:15-18, of Ebed-melech). At God's command, Jeremiah and Baruch consign the sacred vessels to the earth, where they will remain 'until the gathering of the beloved [people]' (3:18-20; cf. 3:4-11).[212] In the morning, Jeremiah sends Abimelech to Agrippa's property to gather figs. There the servant falls asleep for sixty-six years. Meanwhile the Chaldaean army surrounds Jerusalem. The city gates are found open. Jeremiah hurls the temple keys at the sun, exhorting it to take custody of them 'until the day that the Lord asks for them' (4:4f.).[213] Jeremiah is taken captive to Babylon, while Baruch is left behind in the environs of Jerusalem.

Abimelech awakes from his sleep, and finding the figs still fresh, he supposes that he has taken a brief siesta. A local inhabitant informs him that sixty-six years have passed since the people were taken captive. Abimelech shows him the fresh figs, and they conclude that a miracle has taken place because it is not the season for figs. An angel appears to Abimelech, in answer to his prayer, and leads him to Baruch, who interprets the miracle as proof that the time has come for the people to return to the city. (It is also a sign of the resurrection of the body, 6:6-10.) In response to Baruch's prayer, an angel appears and dictates a letter which Baruch is to send via eagle to Jeremiah in Babylon. '. . . Let the stranger . . . be set apart and let 15 days go by; and after this I will lead you into your city . . .

15:39; Matt 26:63-66; 27:40, 54. On the relationship of these passages to Wis 2 and 5 (see above, n. 180), see Nickelsburg, 'Genre,' 173-4, 183-84; and Breech, *Testing*.

[211] On the relationship between long and short forms of this writing, see É. Turdeanu, 'Légende,' 145-65. On the relationship of the three Armenian recensions to the Greek textual traditions, see Stone, 'Some Observations.' Chapter and verse numbering and translations here follow the edition of Kraft and Purintun.

[212] Cf. also 4:7. On the meaning of this expression, see Delling, *Jüdische Lehre*, 65-67.

[213] These themes are popular in rabbinic tradition, in part relating to the Second Temple. On the keys see, e.g., *B.T. Taanith* 29a; *Lev. R.* 19,6 (p.436) and *Aboth de R. Nathan* A, 4 and B, 7(p. 23f.). On the long sleep see the references given by Ginzberg, *Legends* 6, p. 409 n. 58.

He who is not separated from Babylon will not enter the city; and I will punish them by keeping them from being received back by the Babylonians' (6:16-17).

Moreover, Baruch writes, 'you will test them by means of the water of the Jordan; whoever does not listen will be exposed — this is the sign of the great seal.' (6:25) The divinely sent eagle carries the letter to Jeremiah, who reads it to the exiles and sends a reply to Baruch, describing the terrible plight of the exiles. In their despair, they even pray to a foreign god for deliverance (7:24-29).

Jeremiah exhorts the people to obey the commands in Baruch's letter (7:37-8:3). When the exiles arrive at the Jordan, those who refuse to 'forsake the works of Babylon' and abandon their foreign spouses are forbidden entrance into Jerusalem. Returning to Babylon, they are rejected there, and so they found the city of Samaria. Jeremiah once more calls on them to repent (8:7-12).

In the temple, after Jeremiah has offered special sacrifice and prayer, he appears to die; however, in three days he is revived, and he begins to describe a vision about 'the son of God, the Messiah, Jesus.' The people attempt to stone him for blasphemy, but he is miraculously protected until he has transmitted the entire contents of his vision to Baruch and Abimelech. Then he is stoned to death, [214] and Baruch and Abimelech bury him.

Scholarly opinion is divided on whether the writing is originally Jewish or Christian. In its present form it is clearly Christian, as is evident from Jeremiah's revelation (chap. 9). On this level, the ordeal at the Jordan may be interpreted as Christian baptism. Only the baptized can enter the holy city. Harris suggested that the writing was composed (after the Second Jewish Revolt) as an *Eirenicon,* or peace offer, from Christians to Jews, exhorting the latter to accept baptism and thus to renounce the Jewish faith that prevented them from returning to their home city.[215] This hypothesis has not found wide acceptance, although Bogaert modifies it slightly, suggesting that the writing was sent by Jewish-Christians to other Jewish-Christians.[216] Other commentators maintain a Jewish origin,[217] and there is much to commend this view. The sign of the great seal at the Jordan (6:25) could be circumcision.[218] The author likens the return from Babylon to the Exodus, and Jeremiah's role is analogous to those of Moses and

---

[214] Cf. *Vita Ieremiae* 1; cf. Heb 11:37. Cf. also Acts 7:54-60, where Stephen's stoning follows his claim to have a vision of the risen and exalted Christ.

[215] Harris, *Baruch,* 13-17.

[216] Bogaert, *Apocalypse,* 216-21.

[217] Delling, *Jüdische Lehre,* 68-74; Denis, *Introduction,* 74-75; Stone, 'Baruch,' 276-7.

[218] *Ibid.,* 276. On the use of 'seal' as a designation of circumcision, see Fitzer, 'σφραγίς,' 947; and Flusser — Safrai, 'Who Sanctified the Beloved in the Womb,' 51-55.

Joshua.[219] Perhaps also implied is a parallel with the circumcisions at Gilgal (Josh 5:2-9). More important for the question of authorship — none of the references to the eschaton in chapters 1-8 contains indubitable Christian allusions. The author awaits the gathering of Israel and the reconstitution of the Jerusalem cult, not the appearance of Jesus, the Messiah. This idea occurs only in chapter 9, which probably does not belong to the original form of the book. Thematically and structurally, the plot is resolved when Jeremiah leads the people back to Jerusalem. The story of his 'second death' appears to be influenced by other traditions, including the *Martyrdom of Isaiah*.[220] If we accept the hypothesis of a Jewish origin, the book appears to be an appeal to the Jews to prepare themselves for a return to Jerusalem by divesting themselves of gentile practices and associations: mixed marriages,[221] perhaps uncircumcision, perhaps some form of idolatry or participation in pagan cult.

Essential to this story are the problem of destruction and exile and the hope of return and restoration. The author takes up his narrative on the eve of destruction and exile, and he concludes it when the return has taken place and the problem with which the story began has been resolved. Moreover, at a number of points in the first part of the story, return and restoration are the last event in the author's purview (3:11, 14, 15). The literary function of the Abimelech incident is to provide a transition from exile to return.[222]

The focus and limits of the story are best explained if we suppose that the author is concerned with some similar problem in his own time. The apocalypses of 4 Ezra and 2 Baruch testify to the fact that Nebuchadnezzar's destruction of Jerusalem was viewed as a prototype of the destruction of 70 C.E.[223] A similar typology seems to be operative here.[224] If this is the case, it would appear that the author is using the Abimelech story to assert that there will be another return and restoration sixty-six years later, i.e., 136 C.E. Quite possibly he expects this return to be 'the gathering of the beloved' people of God, i.e. the return of the dispersion and the final restoration of Jerusalem.

In preparation for this return, *the readers* are exhorted to purify

---

[219] For parallels to the Exodus, cf. 6:23-25; 7:20. The crossing of the Jordan and entrance into the city are reminiscent of the book of Joshua. Other Exodus reminiscences occur in an earlier form of the tradition of the temple vessels in 2 Macc 2, on which see below, n. 229. Cf. also *Vita Ieremiae* 11-15.

[220] Delling, *Jüdische Lehre*, 14-16.

[221] *Ibid.*, 42-53. These concerns — explicit in the book — as well as the author's attitude about Samaritans, fit much better an hypothesis of Jewish rather than Christian composition.

[222] For a similar pattern in *1 Baruch*, see below, pp. 140-2.

[223] On the dating of *4 Ezra* and *2 Baruch*, see below, pp. 409f., 412.

[224] For a date early in the second century C.E., see Harris, *Baruch*, 1-25; Delling, *Jüdische Lehre*, 2-3; Bogaert, *Apocalypse*, 220-21.

themselves of the works of the places of their exile (here called Babylon).[225] They are to abstain from gentile defilement and to divorce foreign spouses, a requirement enforced by Ezra and Nehemiah after the first return.[226] Because Jerusalem is a holy city, and Israel, a holy people, defilement caused by contact with pagan spouses cannot be tolerated.[227] Samaria is thus identified as the home of a half-breed people, although the author's attitude is not wholly unconciliatory. Indeed he may be making an appeal to them.

The precise date of writing is uncertain. The year 136 C.E. is one year after Hadrian crushed the Second Jewish Revolt. Following that revolt, Hadrian issued an edict forbidding Jews to enter Jerusalem, and he reconstituted the city as a Roman colony. There is no explicit reference in this writing to the tragedy of 132-135, although it is possible that that author intends Nebuchadnezzar's destruction to be typical of the defeats of both 70 and 135. In such an event, the writing would have been composed between 135 and 136. It is also possible, however, that it was written a short time before the Second Revolt.

Nonetheless, our author has made use of earlier traditions. Parallels to *2 Baruch* are clear. Bogaert has argued for a dependence on *2 Baruch* itself.[228] There is, however, some evidence that our author used a source common to himself and *2 Baruch*, written in the name of Jeremiah, explaining the events leading up to the destruction of Jerusalem in 587.[229] Reference to such a written tradition is found in 2 Maccabees 2:1-8. It is noteworthy that the two stories in 2 Maccabees 1-2 are concerned with the cessation of the Jerusalem cult and its reinstitution. A rewritten account of the fall of Jerusalem could well have originated during the time of Antiochus Epiphanes, who appears in the literature as a type of Nebuchadnezzar. In any event, the stories are recounted in 2 Maccabees 1-2 in connection with the celebration of Judas' purification of the Jerusalem sanctuary after its defilement by Antiochus.

Epistle of Aristeas

This fictional account of the circumstances surrounding the Greek translation of the Torah was composed in the name of a certain Aristeas, who is alleged to have been an influential courtier of Ptolemy II Philadelphus (283-247 B.C.E.).[230] Purportedly, it was written for the edification of

[225] For the symbolic use of 'Babylon,' cf. Rev 18; cf. also 4 Ezra where 'Babylon' is the place of the author's exile.
[226] Ezra 9-10; Neh 13:23-27.
[227] On the problem of mixed marriages in our literature, see Delling, *Jüdische Lehre*, 42-44.
[228] Bogaert, *Apocalypse*, 177-221.
[229] Nickelsburg, 'Narrative Traditions,' 60-68.
[230] Eusebius (*Praeparatio Evangelica* 9:25) makes reference to a certain Aristeas, who wrote a book *Concerning the Jews;* see Hadas, *Aristeas*, 4.

Aristeas' brother Philocrates, whose interest in religious matters is noted in the proemium (1-8).

The first major section of the book recounts the events surrounding Ptolemy's request for a translation of the Law (9-82). Employing a device typical of Hellenistic fiction, the author supports his narrative with quotations from appropriate official documents.[231] The request for a translation originates with Demetrius of Phalerum, who is said to have been in charge of the king's library in Alexandria (9-11).[232] When Ptolemy agrees to the project, Aristeas convinces him that he should also free all the Jewish slaves in his realm (12-20). Aristeas then quotes the king's decree of emancipation (21-25), which may be a reworked version of a genuine decree of Ptolemy II calling for the registration of slaves in Egypt.[233] Demetrius draws up a memorandum recommending that the translation be made (28-32). In it he commends the Law as 'most philosophical'[234] and 'flawless' thanks to its divine origin, and he cites the alleged opinion of Hecataeus of Abdera in support of his viewpoint.[235] Aristeas then reproduces Ptolemy's letter to Eleazar the Jewish high priest, requesting the translation, and Eleazar's letter, acceding to the request (35-51). The section closes with a lengthy and detailed description of the gifts that Ptolemy sent to Jerusalem (51-82). The description is typical of the *ekphrasis*, a literary genre that flourished especially in Hellenistic times.[236] Here the description of the table of shewbread quotes the Septuagint version of Exodus 25:23-30; 37:10-15.[237]

The second major section is set in Judaea (83-171). Aristeas first describes Jerusalem, the temple, and its cult (83-106).[238] His idealized description of the country recalls utopian travelogues in classical and Hellenistic literature (107-20).[239] After these extensive digressions, Aristeas returns to the subject of the translation (120-29), and he praises the translators for their proficiency in both Jewish and Greek literature and their ability to discourse wisely about the Law. Aristeas then records Eleazar's lengthy speech on the Law (130-71), stressing the justice of the omniscient Law-giver and employing the allegorical method to explain the rationality of Jewish food laws (139-60).

---

[231] On this device, see *ibid.*, 52; cf. also 2 Maccabees and the Additions to Esther.

[232] For the historical problems relating to Demetrius, see Hadas, *Aristeas,* 7-8.

[233] *Ibid.,* 28-32.

[234] Cf. 4 Macc 4:1.

[235] A Hellenistic historian with connections with the court of Ptolemy I; see Hadas, *Aristeas,* 43-45, 111. For the extant fragments of Hecataeus' history, see Stern, *Greek and Latin Authors* I, 20-44.

[236] *Ibid.,* 47-48.

[237] *Ibid.,* 121.

[238] Note Aristeas' emotional response to the cult (96-99) and cf. Sir 50:1-21.

[239] Hadas, *Aristeas,* 48-50; and Tcherikover, 'Ideology,' 77-79.

The longest and chief section of the writing is again set in Alexandria; it recounts Ptolemy's reception of the seventy-two Jewish translators and the table talk during the banqueting that preceded the translation work (172-300). The sages are given immediate and unprecedented access to Ptolemy, who pays homage to them and the divine Law and orders a series of seven daily banquets (172-81). Following the literary model of the *symposium,* these banquets are the setting for learned answers to weighty questions posed by the king.[240] The topic of conversation is the theory and practice of kingship. Each of the seventy-two answers climaxes with a reference to 'God' or 'divine' activity.

There is little that is particularly Jewish in these answers. For the most part, their contents and themes — including the references to God and the imitation of God — are paralleled in pagan Hellenistic treatises on kingship.[241]

Aristeas' account of the actual translation work is very brief (301-7). Translations are compared and harmonized, and providentially the work is completed in seventy-two days. Thereafter the translation is ratified by the Jewish community, whose rulers anathematize revisions, additions, transpositions, or excisions (308-11). Then the entire translation is read to Ptolemy, who expresses his admiration for Moses' intellect (312). After promising that the books will be cared for with great reverence, the king dismisses the translators with great praise and lavish gifts (317-21). An epilogue addressed to Philocrates concludes the work.

Scholars universally agree that this work was written by a Jew rather than by an Egyptian courtier named Aristeas. The viewpoint, interests, and sympathies expressed by the author are clearly those of a Jew.[242] Moreover, archaizing statements, anachronisms, and historical inaccuracies indicate that the book was composed some time after the reign of Ptolemy Philadelphus.[243] Scholars do not agree, however, on the actual date of composition. Propals range from 250 B.C.E.[244] to 33 C.E.[245] Linguistic considerations suggest a date in the second half of the second century B.C.E.,[246]

---

[240] Hadas, *Aristeas,* 42-43; cf. 1 Esdras 3 —4:41, on which, see below, pp. 131-5.

[241] Hadas, *Aristeas,* 40-43. On the place of God and the imitation of God in such treatises, see Goodenough, 'Political Philosophy,' 65-78.

[242] Hadas, *Aristeas,* 5-6.

[243] *Ibid.,* 6-9.

[244] This early date is suggested by Sir Charles Wilson, quoted by Abrahams, 'Recent Criticism,' 330. More often a high date for a *terminus post quem* is set at 198 B.C.E., the Syrian conquest of Palestine, to which no allusion is made in the book; thus Abrahams *(Ibid.)* and others cited by Hadas, *Aristeas,* 9; and Pelletier, *Aristée,* 57-58.

[245] Graetz, 'Abfassungszeit'; for the range of dates and the problems relating to them, see Hadas, *Aristeas,* 9-17.

[246] Bickermann ('Datierung,' 284-93) argues for a date between 145-127 B.C.E. Meecham *(Aristeas,* 311-12) extends the date down to 100 B.C.E.

and cumulative external evidence supports such a date.[247] The author's 'accurate knowledge of the usages of the Ptolemaic court and chancellery' indicates Alexandria as the place of writing.[248]

Pseudo-Aristeas has written a thoroughly Greek book.[249] His language and style are literary *koine* Greek.[250] There are many indications that he was well versed in the literature of classical and Hellenistic antiquity: his references to such figures as Demetrius of Phalerum (9-11, etc.), Hecataeus of Abdera (31), Theopompus (314), and Theodectes (316);[251] his use of Greek philosophical terminology;[252] his indebtedness to such literary genres as the utopian description of a foreign land, the *ekphrasis,* the *symposium,* Hellenistic treatises on kingship, and the Cynic-Stoic *chreia* (homily);[253] and his celebration of the allegorical method of exegesis. Although the *Epistle of Aristeas* is often called such, it is not a letter. Quite likely, it is a written speech, which, due to its direct address, was confused with a letter.[254]

Nonetheless, Pseudo-Aristeas directs his writing to Jews.[255] This is especially evident when he explains and defends Jewish practices; for he ignores the more obvious and questioned practices such as circumcision, observance of the Sabbath, and the prohibition of pork, and deals with more detailed instances, such as the biblical chapters dealing with animals that chew the cud and part the hoof.[256]

The viewpoint of the author is marked by a tension between two attitudes. On the one hand, he has a profound admiration and respect for Greek culture and learning.[257] Not only does he speak in the style and idiom of cultured Greeks, he presents his much admired translators of the Law as adepts in Greek culture and philosophy. They are learned in the Jewish Law, but they are also able to express as their own viewpoint Hellenistic ideals of kingship. This same fusion is evident in the speech of Eleazar, whose allegorical interpretation derives similar ideals from the Law (148-51, 168). Even his criticism of pagan idolatry (134-38) does not erect a barrier between Jews and Greeks. As Aristeas points out to the king, 'the same God who has given them [the Jews] their law guides your kingdom also. . . . God, the overseer and creator of all things, whom they worship, is He whom all men worship, and we too . . . though we address

---

[247] Hadas, *Aristeas,* 18-54.
[248] *Ibid.,* 6.
[249] *Ibid.,* 54-59; Tcherikover, 'Ideology,' 63-69.
[250] *Ibid.,* 63; Hadas, *Aristeas,* 55; for details, see Meecham, *Aristeas,* 44-168.
[251] Hadas, *Aristeas,* 55.
[252] Tcherikover, 'Ideology,' 65.
[253] Hadas, *Aristeas,* 47-52.
[254] See below, p. 580 and note.
[255] *Ibid.,* 65-66; Tcherikover, 'Ideology,' 60-63.
[256] Hadas, *Aristeas,* 65-66; Tcherikover, 'Ideology,' 62.
[257] In the interpretation that follows, I am dependent on Tcherikover, 'Ideology.'

him differently, as Zeus and Dis' (15-16). Standing in tension with his positive appraisal of Hellenistic culture is the author's tenacious assertion, placed in the mouth of Eleazar, that in the Law God has fenced the Jews about 'with impregnable palisades and with walls of iron,' so that they 'should mingle in no way with any of the other nations' (139). Although they may, and should partake in Greek culture, the Jews are bound to obey the laws that are uniquely theirs and that differentiate them from the gentiles.

In this tension we may discern this author's purpose. He is counseling rapprochement without assimilation. 'The aim of Aristeas' propaganda was to bring up a generation of educated Jews, who would be able to live on equal terms with the Greek citizens of Alexandria and possibly to occupy high positions in the Ptolemaic army, at the court of the King and in the administration of the realm.'[258] At the same time, he argues that such productive interactivity does not negate the Jew's obligation to live according to the Law. His allegorical exegesis finds in the Law the same values that are idealized by the Greeks, and thus he validates it as binding on the Jews.

It is now evident why Pseudo-Aristeas has used the story of the translation of the Law[259] as the narrative plot in a writing that devotes much more space to matters other than the Law. The divinely revealed Law is one of the two strands of a cord that can bind Jews and Greeks together; it contains the prescriptions for the Jewish life style and a universal philosophy with ethical principles that guide both Jews and Greeks.[260] The second strand is the culture and learning of the Greeks, which provide the exegetical tools by which this commonality may be discovered and the conceptual framework by which it can be expressed. Thus it is not by accident that the author recounts the story of the Law's translation into Greek and the ratification of that translation as the authoritative Scripture of Alexandrian Judaism.[261]

Although the *Epistle of Aristeas* is concerned with substantial religio-cultural matters, Jews and Christians preserved the work and elaborated its contents primarily to undergird the authority of their Greek Scriptures,[262] and, indeed the name Septuagint ('the Seventy') is related to the number of

---

[258] *Ibid.*, 83-84.

[259] That Pseudo-Aristeas knew a tradition about the translation of the Law is clear; the shape and extent of that tradition is, however, uncertain. See the discussion by Hadas, *Aristeas*, 70-72.

[260] See Tcherikover, 'Ideology,' 71.

[261] These broader considerations seem a better explanation than an implied polemic against persons opposing a second century revision of the Greek Bible; on which see Hadas, *Aristeas*, 66-73.

[262] For details, see *ibid.*, 73-84; and Pelletier, *Aristée*, 78-98. Among Jewish writings, see especially Philo, *Moses* 2:25-44. Other Jewish sources do not speak of a miraculous translation. On the other hand, Christian writers after Justin Martyr emphasize the miraculous. Jerome, however, criticizes the idea.

translators.[263] Not surprisingly, these elaborations tended toward the miraculous. Philo and many of the early church fathers described how the various translators, isolated in their individual cells, produced independent translations that were in verbatim agreement. Under such conditions, the inspiration of the Septuagint was an obvious fact. Philo's meticulous allegorical interpretations had a firm foundation; Paul's admonition to Timothy ('All scripture is inspired by God and profitable for teaching, for reproof, for correction and for training in righteousness . . .' [2 Tim 3:16]) was provided with a narrative context.

These developments notwithstanding, the interpretation outlined above offers important materials for our understanding of the development of Hellenistic Judaism and early Christianity. This text reflects a remarkable attempt to synthesize Judaism and Hellenism, and it opens a window into Alexandrian Judaism before the development of anti-Semitic tendencies that would render such a synthesis difficult to say the least.[264] On the other hand, the *Epistle of Aristeas* provides us with a Jewish hermeneutical key to an understanding of the history-of-religions context of early Christian attitudes about the gentile Christians' obligations vis-à-vis the Law and their place in the economy of salvation.

3 Maccabees

Persecution, oppression, and miraculous deliverance are the subject matter of this little studied work. Its style is that of 'pathetic' history, in which the author 'strove to entertain his reader by playing strongly upon the emotions [Gk. *pathos*], with vivid portrayals of atrocities and heroism and divine manifestations and with copious use of sensational language and rhetoric, especially when presenting the feelings of the characters.'[265] Ptolemaic Palestine and Egypt provide the settings for the book's two separate parts, which are held together loosely by a common theme and plot.

The first part (chaps. 1-2), is itself comprised of two separate episodes. The original beginning of the book appears to have been lost,[266] and the story begins abruptly in the middle of a narrative that leads quickly to a brief but vivid account of the battle at Raphia in 217 B.C.E. between Ptolemy IV Philopator and Antiochus III ('the Great'). The accuracy of some of the details in 1:1-7 indicates dependence on a reliable historical

---

[263] On the problems relating to the number of translators (were there seventy, like the seventy elders who ascended Mount Sinai according to Exod 24:11, or were there seventy-two, six from each tribe, *Aristeas* 47-51?), see Hadas, *Aristeas,* 71-72.

[264] *Ibid.,* 63; Tcherikover, 'Ideology,' 84-85.

[265] Goldstein, *1 Maccabees,* 34, of the style of 2 Maccabees.

[266] In addition to the abrupt beginning, see 2:25, which presumes a part of the text now missing; see Hadas, *Maccabees,* 4-5.

source.[267] Dositheus' loyalty to the crown and his apostasy from Judaism (1:3) are motifs that foreshadow later developments in the book (3:3; 2:31-33).

Royal arrogance and divine judgment are the leitmotifs in the story of Ptolemy's visit to Jerusalem (1:8-2:24), and they will recur in the second part of the book. When Ptolemy expresses his intention to enter the holy of holies, he provokes a mass demonstration (described at length in the typical emotion-packed style of pathetic history) but is refused entrance to the holy of holies. Now his curiosity gives way to arrogance (1:25-26). However, in his prayer for deliverance Simon the high priest invokes the judgment of God, the sole King and Ruler, on Ptolemy's arrogance, citing precedents from the past (2:1-20) and confessing the nation's sins, which have led to the present disaster.[268] The divine scourge rescues the temple from defilement but this reinforces the king's arrogance (2:21-24; contrast 2 Macc 3:9-39 and the related story of Heliodorus, who learns his lesson).

Intent upon revenge Ptolemy returns to Egypt and orders a census of the Alexandrian Jews which will reduce them to the status of slaves (2:25-30), unless they accept initiation into the mysteries of Dionysus.[269] The scene highlights the king's arrogance and emphasizes the courage of the majority of Jews, who refuse to abandon their traditional religion.

For the second part of his book (chaps. 3-7) the author has reworked a legend originally set in the reign of Ptolemy VII (Euergetes II, 145-117 B.C.E.).[270] This legend is sketched by Josephus (*Ag. Ap.* 2:53-56) as follows: When Ptolemy VII sought to exterminate the Jews of Alexandria by loosing drunk elephants on them, the animals turned on Ptolemy's friends and killed many of them. The king then saw an apparition, and at the entreaty of his concubine, he repented of his deed. The Jews in their turn celebrated the event with an annual festival.

The author of 3 Maccabees has taken over this legend and identified its main character with the villain of chapters 1-2, Ptolemy IV. Although the thrust of the narrative in chapters 3-7 is clear, the conflation of sources and traditions has created more than a little confusion and contradiction.[271] The first contradiction relates to the cause of the persecution. When the Jews in Alexandria refuse to apostasize, Ptolemy determines to kill them (2:32-3:1), but his sentence includes all the Jews of Egypt. Furthermore, alongside Ptolemy's plan for genocide is a conspiracy against the Jews by certain other, unnamed people (3:2-7). Other contradictions follow. The people are brought from all over Egypt (4:1), yet they can fit into the

---

[267] Tcherikover ('Maccabees,' 2-3) suggests dependence on a Ptolemaic historian.

[268] Cf., e.g., 2 Macc 6:12-16; *Ps. Sol.* 2, 8.

[269] On the background of this detail, see Tcherikover, 'Maccabees,' 3-5.

[270] On the historical problems relating to this legend, see Hadas, *Maccabees*, 10-11; Tcherikover, 'Maccabees,' 6-8.

[271] *Ibid.*, 1-2.

confines of the hippodrome (4:11). Although they are marked for death, they are still subject to registration (4:14-21).

In theme and literary structure, the story in chapters 3-7 is generically a tale of the persecution and vindication of the righteous.[272] The conspiracy that commences the story is based on a perversion of the truth.[273] Although the Jews are loyal to the king (3:3), their adherence to their own special cultic and legal observances is construed as treason (3:4-7).[274] The loyalty and innocence of the Jews is attested, moreover, by certain 'Greeks' and friends and neighbours, who are unable to help them (3:8-10).[275] Nonetheless, Ptolemy's decree of extermination stresses the Jews' unique way of life, indicts them as traitors, and cites as evidence the incidents in 1:8-2:24 and 2:27-33. As the Jews face immediate and certain death in the hippodrome, Eleazar the priest offers an effective prayer for deliverance (6:1-15). The elephants trample the enemy soldiers (6:16-21).[276] The Jews are vindicated of the accusations against them and are set free (6:24-29). In this scene and the decree that follows (7:1-9), the king publicly acclaims the God he had opposed.[277] The Jews are authorized to execute the apostates (7:10-15).[278] Feasts of celebration follow, and the book ends on a note of jubilation and doxology.

Although the story in chapters 3-7 conforms to a known genre, it is characterized by motifs and literary devices already familiar to us from chapters 1-2, and these help to unify the two sections into a single work. As in the first part, the author narrates pathetic history (4:4-10; 5:25, 48-51). Three times, Hermon the keeper of the elephants tries to carry out his orders (5:1-22, 23-35, 36-6:21). This repetition builds up the suspense, but it also underscores the king's arrogance and stresses God's sovereign power and response to prayer (5:12-13, 25, 27, 30, 35). Eleazar's prayer parallels that of Simon the high priest in its recitation of previous examples of deliverance and judgment.

Third Maccabees accentuates the differences between Jews and gentiles and thus stands in marked contrast to the *Epistle of Aristeas,* a book with which it otherwise shares many literary and other features (see above p. 78f.). Whereas *Aristeas* asserts that the best in Greek culture has much in common with Judaism and that Jews and gentiles can coexist peacefully, 3 Maccabees recounts how exclusivistic attitudes about the sanctity of the

---

[272] On the genre, see above, n. 7. On 3 Maccabees, see Nickelsburg, *Resurrection,* 90-92.

[273] Stories of this genre normally begin with a conspiracy against the protagonist(s) and its cause. For a similar perversion of the truth, cf. Esth 3:8. For an inversion of the truth, cf. Sus 36-40.

[274] Treason is the issue in Esth 3:8, and civil disobedience, in Dan 3 and 6 and 2 Macc 7.

[275] The figure of the helper appears frequently in these stories; see Nickelsburg, 'Genre,' 160.

[276] On the punishment — often the death — of the antagonists, see ibid., 159, 162.

[277] Cf. also Dan 3:28; 6:25-27; Sus 60.

[278] An extension of the idea of the punishment of the antagonists.

temple, the worship of the one God, and the observance of God's Law have been the object of gentile derision and the cause of persecution. In contrast to Pseudo-Aristeas' glowing portrait of Ptolemy II as a model ruler and a patron of the Jews, the present author depicts Ptolemy IV — the main character of this work — as the epitome of the cruel, insolent, and unreasoning tyrant, who instigates serious troubles for the Jews and is brought to their side only through direct, repeated intervention by God. According to 3 Maccabees, Jerusalem suffers under gentile subjugation and Egypt is a place of exile, where the Jews live as strangers in a strange land (6:3, 10)[279] — even if they sometimes find friends and neighbours who admire and help them. The references to apostasy may indicate that the author perceives this as a real danger among his readers. In any event, he celebrates the courage of those who stand fast and promises them deliverance and vindication.

Two different kinds of considerations suggest two different dates for 3 Maccabees. According to one viewpoint the Greek word for census (*laographia*) indicates a date between 20 and 15 B.C.E.[280] This interpretation finds the closest analogy to our narrative in the seventh year of Augustus' reign (23/22 B.C.E.), when a census was taken in Egypt for the purpose of imposing a poll tax that discriminated between the citizens of the Greek cities and the people of the land, who were effectively reduced to a degraded and enslaved status. A second possible date for 3 Maccabees is derived from literary considerations. According to this interpretation a comparison of parallels in 3 Maccabees and the Greek additions to Esther indicates the priority of 3 Maccabees,[281] which must then be dated before 77 B.C.E., the *terminus ad quem* for the translation of Esther (see below, p. 138). It is possible that, along with the aforementioned contradictions, these conflicting indications of different dates reflect different stages in the literary history of 3 Maccabees.

Third Maccabees is related to a number of other Jewish writings. The differences notwithstanding, its style and language, the content of Ptolemy's second decree, and its division into scenes in Jerusalem and Alexandria resemble similar features in *Aristeas*.[282] Its style of pathetic history is akin to that of 2 Maccabees, and the stories in 3 Maccabees 2 and 2 Maccabees 3 are obviously variants of the same tradition.[283] Specific details in the plot of 3 Maccabees parallel the story of persecution and vindication in the canonical book of Esther.[284] Jews are cited for their

---

[279] Tcherikover, 'Maccabees,'' 25-26.
[280] See the detailed argument of Tcherikover, 'Maccabees,' 11-18.
[281] Motzo, 'Rifacimento.'
[282] See Emmet, 'Maccabees,' 157; Tracy, 'Maccabees'; Hadas, *Aristeas,* 32-38; *id., Maccabees,* 8-10.
[283] *Ibid.,* 11-12; see also Emmet, 'Maccabees,' 156-57.
[284] *Ibid.,* 6-7.

peculiar laws and accused of disobeying royal law. Their death is decreed, but they are rescued and celebrate the occasion with a special feast. Even closer to 3 Maccabees is the Greek translation and expansion of Esther, in which the two royal decrees and the prayers of Mordecai and Esther reveal verbatim parallels to their counterparts in 3 Maccabees (see below, p. 137).[285] Finally, as a story of the persecuted and vindicated righteous 3 Maccabees has important formal similarities with Wisdom 2:4-5 as well as a number of verbal parallels.[286]

Third Maccabees was composed in a florid, bombastic style of Greek.[287] Its concentration on the problems of Alexandrian Judaism strongly suggests that it was, in fact written in Egypt.[288]

BIBLIOGRAPHY

Daniel and the Prayer of Nabonidus
For critical edition of Greek texts of Susanna and Bel and the Dragon see ZIEGLER, *Susanna,* 80-91, 215-23. MEYER, *Das Gebet,* text, translation, and masterful study of the Prayer of Nabonidus, a necessary point of departure. For commentaries on Daniel, see MONTGOMERY, *Daniel;* CHARLES, *Daniel;* BENTZEN, *Daniel;* PLÖGER, *Daniel;* DELCOR, *Daniel,* which also includes a commentary on Bel and the Dragon and Susanna, and LACOCQUE, *Daniel.* COLLINS, *Apocalyptic Vision,* a seminal study of literary, theological and historical aspects of the canonical book and its sources. MOORE, *Daniel,* 23-149, translation, detailed notes on textual matters, introductory material, commentary, bibliography. An excellent point of departure for further study of Bel and the Dragon and Susanna.

Tobit
BROOKE et al., *The Old Testament in Greek* 3:1, pp. 35-144, critical edition of two Greek texts and of Old Latin. LEBRAM, 'Tobit', critical edition of Syriac text. SIMPSON, 'Tobit,' introduction, translation, detailed textual apparatus. ZIMMERMANN,*Tobit,* Greek Texts, annotated English translation, introduction. PFEIFFER, *History,* 258-84, introductory material. WIKGREN, 'Tobit.' MILIK, 'Patrie.' GAMBERONI, *Auslegung,* Christian interpretation of the book.

Judith
BROOKE et al., *The Old Testament in Greek* 3:1, pp. 43-84, critical edition of the Greek text. GRINTZ, *Sefer Yehudith,* introduction, commentary and

---

[285] *Ibid.,* 7-8; Motzo, 'Rifacimento.'
[286] Nickelsburg, *Resurrection,* 90-91, especially nn. 157-66.
[287] Emmet, 'Maccabees,' 156-58.
[288] So also Hadas, *Maccabees,* 22-23.

reconstruction of the Hebrew text. *Id.* 'Judith.' WINTER, 'Judith.' HAAG, *Studien*, discussion of biblical background, theology and literary character. DUBARLE, *Judith*, studies Greek and Latin texts in relation to Hebrew, traces the story through Midrashim and early Christian writers. ENSLIN-ZEITLIN, *Judith*, introduction, Greek text and translation, brief commentary, good bibliography. ALONSO-SCHÖKEL, *Structures*, uses tools of structural analysis. CRAVEN, 'Artistry and Faith,' a literary study.

Martyrdom of Isaiah

The entire *Ascension of Isaiah* is treated in four works: CHARLES, *Ascension*, an extensive introduction, annotated translation, critical edition of the Ethiopic texts, with a synoptic presentation of the Greek, Latin, and Slavonic (in Latin translation) texts; TISSERANT, *Ascension*, extensive introduction, translation, textual apparatus, notes; FLEMMING-DUENSING, 'Ascension,' brief introduction, and translation. For a briefly annotated translation with introduction, of only the *Martyrdom*, see CHARLES, 'Martyrdom.' A Qumran provenance for the *Martyrdom* is suggested by : FLUSSER, 'Ascensio'; PHILONENKO, 'Martyre'; CAQUOT, 'Commentaire' (translation and brief commentary on the *Ascension* 1-5, with special attention to the *Martyrdom*). STONE, 'Martyrdom,' introductory matters.

The Lives of the Prophets

The principal studies are NESTLE, *Marginalien und Materialien* 1-64 and SCHERMANN, *Propheten- und Apostellegenden* 1-133. See also the introductory material in Schermann's edition of the Greek text (*Prophetarum Vitae Fabulosae*, IX-XXXIII) for a survey of earlier scholarship. The most important M.S. of the *Lives* is the sixth-century Codex Marchalianus (Vat. Gr. 2125), a prime witness of Schermann's *recensio anonyma*. DENIS, *Introduction*, 85-90 provides a helpful summary of the researches of Nestle and Schermann, as well as updated information regarding the Greek recensions and Oriental versions. The most recent studies of the *Lives* have been dedicated to these versions: KNIBB, 'The Ethiopic Version'; LÖFGREN, 'An Arabic Recension'; STONE, 'Lives of the Prophets.'

The Testament of Abraham

JAMES, *Testament*, introduction, critical Greek text of the long and short recensions, summary of the Arabic version, translation of the related Coptic Testament of Isaac and Testament of Jacob. STONE, *Testament*, reprint of James's Greek texts with facing translation. SANDERS, 'Testament,' annotated introduction and translation of the two recensions. BOX, *Testament*, introduction, translation of the two recensions and of the Testament of Isaac and the Testament of Jacob. TURNER, *Testament*, supports the originality of the short recension. SCHMIDT, *Testament*, introduction, edition of the Greek of the short recension (considered to be the more original), including its best manuscript (E), translation of two recensions. DELCOR, *Testament,* introduction, commentary on long recension, translation of long recension and of the Greek, Coptic, Ethiopic and Arabic versions of the short recension, translation of the Testament of Isaac and Testament of Jacob. JANSSEN, *Testament,* introduction and annotated translation. NICKELSBURG, *Studies,* articles mainly on the recensional problem and parallel traditions, annotated bibliography, translation of Coptic and Slavonic versions of the short recension. TURDEANU, 'Testament', discussion of the Slavonic and Rumanian versions.

Joseph and Aseneth

BATIFFOL, 'Prière', long Greek text, introduction, supports Christian authorship. BROOKS, *Joseph and Asenath,* introduction, translation of the long text, with variants from the versions, Christian revision of Jewish work. APTOWITZER, 'Aseneth,' study of Joseph and Aseneth in light of parallel Jewish traditions. PHILONENKO, *Joseph,* introduction, short Greek text with facing translation, a Jewish novel with heavy allegorical content. BURCHARD, *Untersuchungen,* discussion of the texts, provenance, and date, a Jewish writing from around the turn of the era. *Id., Der dreizehnte Zeuge,* 59-88, discussion of Acts 9:1-19 in the light of Joseph and Aseneth, comparison with gentile literature. *Id.* 'Joseph et Aséneth,' state of the discussion regarding text, literary genre, and religious background. *Id.* 'Joseph und Aseneth Neugriechisch.' *Id.* 'Joseph und Aseneth 25-29 Armenisch.' SMITH, *Joseph and Asenath,* introduction, parallels to Joseph and Aseneth. PERVO, 'Joseph and Asenath,' relationship to the Greek novel. SÄNGER, *Antikes Judentum,* sees Joseph and Aseneth as a Hellenistic Jewish missionary writing that may reflect elements of a Jewish proselyte ritual (book was not available for consultation).

Paraleipomena of Jeremiah

HARRIS, *Baruch,* critical edition of the Greek text, introduction. KRAFT-PURINTUN, *Paraleipomena,* Greek text with selected apparatus (including versions), extensive annotated bibliography. STONE, 'Some Observations,' discussion of the Armenian version. TURDEANU, 'La Légende.' *Id.* 'Les Paralipomènes de Jérémie en Slave.' DELLING, *Jüdische Lehre,* discussion of the theology and other contents. BOGAERT, *Apocalypse,* 177-221, discussion of *Par. Jer.* and of its relationship to *2 Baruch.* STONE, 'Baruch.' NICKELSBURG, 'Narrative Traditions,' compares corresponding parts of the two writings and argues that both are dependent on a common source. GRY, 'La Ruine du Temple,' discussion of some parallel rabbinic traditions.

Epistle of Aristeas

THACKERAY, *Aristeas,* introduction, text, and apparatus. ANDREWS, 'Aristeas,' introduction and annotated English translation. MEECHAM, *Old-*

est Version, introduction and English translation. *Id. Aristeas,* reproduces Thackeray's text, detailed study of the Greek, linguistic commentary. For more recent translations see HADAS, *Aristeas,* extended introduction, text with facing English translation, a good starting point; PELLETIER, *Aristée,* introduction, text and critical apparatus with facing French translations and annotations, special atention to MSS. and textual matters. Two classical studies are: BICKERMANN, 'Datierung,' basic study on the date; TCHERIKOVER, 'Ideology,' the setting, message and purpose. See also JEL-LICOE, 'Occasion and Purpose.' On the relationship of the legend to the translation of the Septuagint, see ZUNTZ, 'Aristeas Studies 2'; GOODING, 'Aristeas.'

3 Maccabees

HANHART, *Maccabaeorum liber III,* critical edition of Greek text. EMMET, 'Maccabees,' introduction, annotated English translation. HADAS, *Maccabees,* introduction, Greek text with annotated English translation. MOTZO, 'Rifacimento,' relationship of 3 Maccabees and Greek Esther. TCHERIKOVER, 'Maccabees,' sources, literary and historical analysis, setting, ideology.

Chapter Three

The Bible Rewritten and Expanded

George W. E. Nickelsburg

In the previous chapter we discussed Jewish narrative literature set in biblical and early post-biblical times. Characteristic of the narratives about biblical times was their very loose connection with biblical traditions about Israel's past. The authors of these works used settings in biblical history and built stories around biblical characters, but, for the most part, their plots and the events recounted in them had no real counterparts in the biblical accounts. In the present chapter we shall treat literature that is very closely related to the biblical texts, expanding and paraphrasing them and implicitly commenting on them. This tendency to follow the ancient texts more closely may be seen as a reflection of their developing canonical status.

The order of our treatment reflects developing ways of retelling the events of biblical history. To judge from present evidence, this process of narration began with stories that recounted individual events or groups of episodes from relatively brief sections of the Bible. Our earliest text is the story of the fall of the watchers, preserved in *1 Enoch* 6-11. From it developed accounts of other episodes involving Enoch and Noah. Some of the earlier Enochic and Noachic traditions, as well as early narrative materials about other patriarchs, were subsequently alluded to, or reshaped and incorporated into such works as *Jubilees* and the Genesis Apocryphon, which are running paraphrases of extensive portions of the Pentateuch. The *Book of Biblical Antiquities* is a later paraphrase of much broader scope (Genesis to Samuel). Here the narrative elaborations are less traditional and more often the author's *ad hoc* creations. The Adamic literature is of uncertain date; like the Enochic and Noachic stories, it focuses on a brief portion of Scripture. The works of Philo the Elder, Theodotus, and Ezekiel the Tragedian are a special category and indicate relatively early attempts to recast the biblical narratives into forms that would appeal to the Hellenistic tastes of their audiences.

It is clear that these writings employ a variety of genres: running paraphrases of longer and shorter parts of the Bible, often with lengthy expansions (*Jubilees*, Genesis Apocryphon, *Biblical Antiquities*); narrative blocks in a non-narrative genre (stories about the flood in the apocalypse or testament known as *1 Enoch*); a narrative roughly shaped by a non-narrative genre (the quasi-testamentary *Apocalypse of Moses*); poetic presentations of biblical stories in epic and dramatic form (Philo the Elder, Theodotus, Ezekiel the Tragedian).

The last part of the chapter will discuss a different kind of expansion of the biblical text, viz., the introduction of new material into the texts themselves.

1 Enoch and the Book of the Giants

1 Enoch is a collection of apocalyptic traditions and writings of diverse genre and date, composed during the last three centuries B.C.E. and accumulated in stages.[1] Common to most of the components of the collection are three related apocalyptic myths: the fall of the watchers and the bloody deeds of their sons, the giants; the watchers' revelation of heavenly secrets to humankind; and Enoch's ascent to heaven (cf. Gen 5:24), where he is commissioned as a prophet of judgment and a scribe of esoteric traditions about the structure of the universe and the mysteries of the end-time. The stories that we consider here recount the events connected with these myths; most of them have been preserved in *1 Enoch*.[2]

1 ENOCH 6-11

These chapters conflate at least two mythic traditions about the angelic origins of sin and God's punishment of this rebellion.[3] The first of these traditions, in which Semihazah is the chief angelic rebel, is an expansion of parts of Genesis 6-9.[4] We may outline it as follows:[5]

1. *The origins of a devastated world:* a. the proposal, 6:1-8 (Gen 6:1-2a); b. the deed, 7:1a-c (Gen 6:2b); c. its results, 7:2-5 (Gen 6:4, 7)
2. *The turning point:* a. the pleas of the earth and humanity, 7:6; 8:4 (Gen 4:10f.); b. the angels see, hear, and intercede, 9:1-11 (Gen 6:5, 12)
3. *The divine resolution of the situation:* a Sariel is sent to Noah,[6] 10:1-3

---

[1] On the collection as a whole and its literary history, see below, pp. 395-408 and Nickelsburg, *Jewish Literature*, 46f., 150-51.
[2] For a broad survey of Noachic and flood traditions outside the Pseudepigrapha, see Lewis, *Study.*.
[3] For the various possibilities, see Hanson, 'Rebellion,' 197-202, 220-25; Nickelsburg, 'Apocalyptic and Myth,' 384-86; Collins, 'Methodological Issues,' 315-16; Nickelsburg, 'Reflections,' 311-12; Dimant, 'I Enoch 6-11'; Newsom, 'Development,' 313-14.
[4] Milik (*Enoch*, 30-31) argues that Genesis 6 is an abridgement of this part of *1 Enoch*. According to Barthelmus (*Heroentum*, 22-24, 198), Gen 6:3 is a secondary interpolation into Genesis, reflecting the tradition about Semihazah.
[5] For details, see Nickelsburg, 'Apocalyptic and Myth,' 386-9.
[6] For the angelic name, Sariel, see Milik, *Enoch*, 172-4.

(Gen 6:13-21); b. Michael is dispatched, 10:11-11:2 (Gen 8:17, 21f.; 9:1, 8-20).

Although the author quotes and alludes to the biblical text throughout his narrative, his final product differs significantly from Genesis. In section 1, he consistently identifies 'the sons of God' and the giants — rather than humankind — as the source of evil in the antediluvian world. The angels' intercourse with the daughters of men is explicitly an act of rebellion against God. The giants are not simply 'men of renown' (Gen 6:4); they are a race of malevolent halfbreeds, who devour the fruits of the earth, slaughter humankind and the animal world, and then turn on one another. The 'birds and beasts and creeping things' are their victims and not a part of 'all flesh' which God plans to annihilate (Gen 6:7).

In section 2, the author interpolates a lengthy intercessory prayer, in which the angels make a clear and pointed statement of the problem of evil, contrasting the repeated assertion that God knows and sees all things (Gen 6:5, 12) with the fact that he is not exercising his authority in support of justice.

In section 3, the author recasts the biblical material into two parts. God sends Sariel to instruct Noah how to save himself and his family from the coming deluge (10:3; cf. Gen 6:13). As in Genesis, he will be the patriarch of a new human race (10:3). Noah is viewed here as a righteous man (10:3; cf. 10:16), although we have not yet heard of a wicked humanity to which Noah would be an exception. The author's interest and emphasis are revealed in the second part of this section. God dispatches Michael against the angels and the giants and commands him to purify the earth. Since, in the author's interpretation of Genesis, the angels and the giants are responsible for the desolation and defilement of the earth, it is they who must be judged. Also significant is the manner in which the descriptions of the postdiluvian earth imply a veritable return to creation and paradisiacal conditions.

Our author utilizes an *Urzeit-Endzeit* typology; the judgment and new beginning in Noah's time are a prototype of the final judgment and new age. Thus, the description of the ancient judgment and the renewed earth is coloured by the author's expectations regarding the final judgment and the age to come.[7] This same typology is reflected in other parts of his elaboration of Genesis. The prayer of the angelic intercessors is in reality the bitter and desperate cry of the author's own people, who are querying about the problem of evil as they experience it at the hands of their enemies, the giants of the earth.

The narrative is implicitly exhortative. The author writes during a time

---

[7] See the questions raised by Collins ('Methodological Issues,' 317-19) and the response by Nickelsburg, 'Reflections,' 312.

of great violence and bloodshed. His people are experiencing a crisis of faith, expressed in the angelic prayer. Where is the justice of God, and why does he do nothing? The author answers his people in section 3. God has heard their prayers. He has issued his orders. The judgment is at hand! Therefore, stand fast.

The mythic imagery of the story is essential to the author's viewpoint. Section 1 presents his view of the nature of the present evil. Behind the brutal actions of violent men exists a world of malevolent and rebellious spirits. In the mighty of this world one confronts 'not flesh and blood, but principalities and powers.' Humanity's one hope is divine intervention.

The Semihazah story in *1 Enoch* 6-11 is an apocalypticized retelling of the Genesis story, and the author's restructuring of the biblical text and his mythical view of reality have counterparts in apocalyptic texts from the time of Antiochus Epiphanes.[8] The Semihazah story itself must be dated before the second century B.C.E. and perhaps as early as the wars of the Diadochi (323-302 B.C.E.).[9]

The second main strand of tradition in *1 Enoch* 6-11 depicts *Asael* as the chief rebel angel. The revolt is the revelation to humankind of forbidden information, mainly the arts of metallurgy and mining. Its principal result is man's ability to forge the implements of war. The tradition appears to reflect Gen 4:22; however, the idea that the metallurgical arts were revealed by a divine rebel suggests influence from Greek myths about Prometheus.[10] The revelation of other secrets is attributed to Semihazah and his companions; this motif may be secondary to the Semihazah story and due to the influence of the Asael material.[11]

Around this basic story of sin, judgment, and salvation, there has developed a cycle of stories about the various dramatis personae and their reactions to the impending disaster. In all these stories, Enoch figures prominently as the recipient and / or interpreter of revelation regarding the judgment.

1 ENOCH 12-16

An angel commands Enoch to announce judgment to the fallen watchers. At their request, he intercedes for them. In response to his prayer, Enoch is taken up to the heavenly temple, where God commissions him to announce the irrevocability of the sentence against the watchers and their progeny. Different from chaps. 6-11, the giants are not types of the violent in the

[8] Nickelsburg, 'Apocalyptic and Myth,' 391-5.
[9] *Ibid.*, 389-91; see also Barthelmus (*Heroentum*, 154-60, 175-83), who dates the book later, but sees allusions to Hellenistic royal ideology; see also Collins, 'Apocalyptic Technique,' 97-98.
[10] Barthelmus, *Heroentum*, 160-7; Nickelsburg, 'Apocalyptic and Myth,' 399-404. Hanson ('Rebellion,' 220-6) seeks a broader background in ancient Near Eastern mythology.
[11] See literature cited in n. 3 above.

author's time, but upon their deaths, their spirits are released as the host of demons that plague the world until the eschaton. The portrayal here of the watchers as disobedient priests from the heavenly temple suggests that this author has a complaint against the Jerusalem priesthood, and the setting of the story in upper Galilee near the ancient shrine of Dan may reflect the actual geographic place of origin of this tradition.[12]

1 ENOCH 106-107

These chapters recount the marvelous events surrounding Noah's birth. The child's resplendent appearance and precocious acts lead his father Lamech to suspect angelic conception.[13] His father Methuselah seeks an explanation from his father Enoch, since the latter dwells with the angels.

Enoch's oracle consists of two major parts. In the first part (106:13-18), he recounts the sin of the angels, summarizing briefly *1 Enoch* 6-7.[14] Then he announces the flood which will destroy the human race. Noah and his three sons will be saved, and Noah 'will cleanse the earth from corruption.' The climax of this part of the oracle is the command to assure Lamech that the child is his son and to 'call his name Noah, for he will be your remnant, from whom you will find relief.'[15] (106:18) The concluding line repeats the promise (106:18 ef).

The second part of the oracle deals with events after the flood (106:19-107:1). Iniquity will again increase for many generations until generations of righteousness arise and 'evil and wickedness come to an end, and violence ceases from the earth, and good things come to them upon the earth' (107:1). The story concludes with Methuselah's return and with the naming of the child, 'And his ..ame was called Noah — he who gladdens the earth from destruction.'[16] (107:2)

Noah's miraculous appearance and actions occupy the reader's attention for the first half of the story. However, they are important not in themselves, but as portents of Noah's significance and as the catalyst that

---

[12] Nickelsburg, 'Enoch, Levi, and Peter,' 582-7. See also Suter, 'Fallen Angel.'

[13] Not an unnatural conclusion, since a glorious appearance and the praise of God are both angelic characteristics. Presumed are the ideas in *1 Enoch* 6-7, although they are introduced in 106:13f. as a piece of new information. On the beauty of Noah and its parallels, see Betz, 'Geistliche Schönheit,' 71-86.

[14] The non-biblical words 'in the days of Jared' indicate dependence on *1 Enoch* 6:6. For other parallels, cf. 106:17c, 18 ef; 107:1def with 10:20.

[15] The author draws on the etymology in Gen 5:29. On the various explanations of the significance of Noah's name, see Milik, *Enoch*, 213-16. See also the next note.

[16] This second explanation of Noah's name is problematic. The Grk. verb εὐφραίηω means gladdens. The corresponding verb in the Eth. is *yāstafešeḥ* which may properly be translated 'will comfort'; see Charles, *APOT* 2, *ad loc.*; Knibb, *Enoch* 2, *ad loc.*, and cf. Dillmann, *Lexicon*, 1349. This corresponds with the occurrence of נחם (comfort) in Gen 5:29. However, since the Eth. root *faša* means rejoice, primarily, it may be best to suppose that the Eth. translator had the Grk. εὐφραίνω before him and used a form of the Eth. verb that is ambiguous.

leads Lamech to discover this. The story focuses on Noah's double role in God's redemptive activity. He is the saved one — the remnant that continues the human race after the destruction of the flood. He is also a saviour figure, who will cleanse the earth from corruption and bring joy to it after its destruction.[17] For the author, both of these functions are implicit in Noah's name, and hence he embodies his message in a naming story, which has its roots in Gen 5:28f. As such, it stands in the tradition of similar stories about the conception, birth, and naming of other important figures in biblical history: Isaac, Samson and Samuel.[18] In the details of its plot, however, it is closer to Matthew's story of the conception and birth of Jesus.[19] The version of the Noah story in the Genesis Apocryphon of Qumran and the related story about Melchizedek's miraculous conception in the appendix to *2 Enoch* are probably both secondary to the present story.[20]

The similarity between 106:18ef and 107:1def suggests a typology between the flood as an end to all evil and the eschaton, when evil will be obliterated completely and finally.[21] In its present location at the end of *1 Enoch,* this birth story offers the promise of a new beginning. Noah and the flood are symbols for the judgment and the new age announced throughout the book.

1 ENOCH 65-67 AND 83-84

Two other narratives in *1 Enoch* indicate significant parallels to the story of Noah's birth. In the first of these (chaps. 65-67), Noah is the main figure. Frightened at the sight of the earth having sunk down, he hurries to 'the ends of the earth,' seeking an explanation from Enoch. The patriarch reveals the coming end, but promises that Noah will be saved and will found a new race. In chapter 67, God informs Noah that the angels are

---

[17] In *1 Enoch* 10:20, Michael cleanses the earth. Cf., however, 1QGenAp 10-13 and *Jub.* 6:2.
[18] Gen 21; Judg 13; 1 Sam 1. All these births are miraculous in that God intervenes directly to overcome the mothers' barrenness. For similar ideas, cf. the oracles in Isa 7:1-17; 9:1-7.
[19] Fitzmyer, 'Contribution,' 399-400. See also Betz, 'Geistliche Schönheit,' 81. See also the next note. This story of Noah's birth is preserved in a Latin fragment (see Charles, *APOT* 2, 278-9), the precise provenance of which is unknown. It might reflect christological interest. Milik (*Enoch*, 30) suggests that it was taken from a world chronicle.
[20] Cols 2-5 of 1QGenAp are badly mutilated. Where they are intact, there are a number of close verbal parallels to *1 Enoch* 106-7. The main lines of the plot are the same as the latter except for the lengthy section describing Lamech's suspicion of, and conversation with his wife (2:3-18), on which see Doeve, 'Lamechs achterdocht,' 401-15. The story of Melchizedek's miraculous conception and birth also has this motif of the father's suspicion and is located at the end of *2 Enoch*. For translations see Morfill — Charles, *Secrets,* 85-93; and Vaillant, *Secrets,* 65-85. In some of its details this story is closer to Matt 1:18-25 than is the Noah story. For the fragments of yet another Noah story, the shape of which we cannot reconstruct with any certainty, see 1Q19, *DJD* 1, 84-86.
[21] Cf. also *1 Enoch* 91:5-9 for the same double pattern.

preparing an ark, and he promises that Noah's seed will continue, so that the earth will not be 'without inhabitant.'

The parallels between *1 Enoch* 83-84 and chapters 65-67 are especially close. Enoch sees in a vision that the earth has sunk down. He cries out to his grandfather Mahalalel, and describes the vision. Mahalalel predicts the destruction of the earth and tells Enoch to pray that a remnant may remain. Enoch's prayer is reminiscent of the prayers of the angels in chap. 9; however the petition is a request, 'to leave me a posterity on earth, and not destroy all the flesh of man, and make the earth without inhabitant' (84:5). We cannot here untangle the complicated history of the tradition represented by these three stories. Primitive elements may be present in each, indicating oral derivation from a common original.[22] All the stories have several elements in common. The sin of the angels is a major cause of the flood.[23] Of central concern is the continuation of the human race, and Noah is seen as its progenitor.[24] In the stories in chaps. 65-67 and 83-84 a typology between the flood and the final judgment is not explicit; however, like chaps. 106-107 and chaps. 6-11, they are set in *pre*diluvial times and describe the anxiety of the central figures. Concern about the extinction of the human race is common to 9:2 and 84:5, and the assurance of a remnant is present in all the stories. It is likely that all of these Noachic stories presume a typology between the flood and the final judgment. Moreover, they all reflect the uneasiness and anxiety inherent in times that spawn predictions of an imminent judgment. Conversely, they assure the reader that the righteous remnant will survive, even as they did at the time of the deluge. The typology of flood and final judgment also appears in sayings attributed to Jesus (Matt 24:37f.; Luke 17:26f.), but here the analogy functions as a warning. Perhaps Jesus is reversing a popular eschatological hope, as Amos did with the Day of the Lord (Amos 5:18-20).

THE BOOK OF GIANTS

The giants — the half-breed offspring of the rebel angels and the daughters of men — complete the cast of antediluvian characters who were the subject of extensive narrative treatment. The Book of Giants is extant, however,

---

[22] In 83:3, Enoch sees the earth sinking down *in a vision*, whereas in 65:1, before the waters are let loose (cf. chap. 66), Noah sees it sinking *in reality*. In 65:2, Noah seeks Enoch at the ends of the earth, as does Methuselah in 106:8. In 83:6, Enoch seeks his grandfather Mahalalel. In 106:18, the idea that Lamech will have a remnant in which he will find rest suggests the anxiety expressed by Enoch in 84:5. The evident word-play on Lamech in 106:1 Greek ('righteousness was made low,' from Aramaic מוך) may have been suggested by the idea of the sinking of the earth (65:2; 83:3).

[23] 65:6; 84:4; 106:13-17. This element is especially noteworthy, since different from chaps. 6-11, these stories stress the punishment of humankind and not of the angels.

[24] Only in chap. 84 is Noah not mentioned, but surely an answer to Enoch's prayer is implied (in the next vision?).

only in fraqments of six Qumran Aramaic manuscripts from the first century B.C.E.[25] and in fragments of a Manichaean version of the book preserved in a number of other oriental languages.[26] The fragmentary nature of the evidence makes any reconstruction uncertain, the more so until the Aramaic evidence has been published in full.[27] With these cautions in mind, we can, nevertheless, draw some conclusions on the basis of the painstaking work of Milik, who has sought to integrate the Qumran and Manichaean evidence.[28]

Central to the story are *Ohyah* and *Hahyah,* the sons of Semihazah, and *Mahawai,* the son of the rebel angel Baraqel. The names of the giants are causative forms of the verb 'to be' and are evident plays on the Tetragrammaton.[29] The angelic rebellion is exacerbated through blasphemy. Perhaps the names are intended to be ironic: the devastating giants are given names which imply creative activity. Ohyah and Hahyah are recipients of dreams that presage the coming judgment. According to the one dream, two hundred trees (the rebel angels; cf. *1 Enoch* 6:6) in a garden sprout branches (the giants) and are then inundated with water and destroyed by fire (the flood and their eternal destruction). Ohyah and Hahyah report their dreams to the rest of the giants, who commission Mahawai to seek an interpretation from Enoch, 'the distinguished scribe.' Mahawai flies to the outer reaches of the earth, where he obtains this explanation.

Similarities to the patterns in the other Enochic stories are evident, although the precise interrelationships between the traditions are not always discernible. The stories about the giants are surely secondary to *1 Enoch* 6-11 and presume the action in the latter.[30] They may have been composed as complements to *1 Enoch* 12-16: Enoch announces doom to the giants as he had done to their fathers. Mahawai's voyage to the ends of the earth in search of Enoch's interpretation is reminiscent of the similar quests by Methuselah (*1 Enoch* 106-107) and Noah (*1 Enoch* 65-67). However, the fragmentary nature of the stories about the giants does not permit a typological comparison with the Noah stories. Moreover, dating based on paleographic evidence is inconclusive.[31]

[25] Published in part by Milik, *Enoch,* 298-307. On the dates of the MSS., see below, n. 31.
[26] Published by Henning, 'Giants,' 52-74.
[27] Milik has presented in full 4QEnGiants[a] (*Enoch,* 310-17). F. has published parts of 4QEnGiants[bc] (*ibid.,* 303-8), to be published in full by Starky together with another MS. of the work (*ibid.,* 309). Milik (*ibid.,* 300-3, 309) identifies the already published 6Q8 and 1Q23 as copies of the Book of Giants.
[28] *Ibid.,* 298-317.
[29] *Ibid.,* 427, *sub Ahyâ.*
[30] Cf. 4QEnGiants[c] 5-7 with *1 Enoch* 9; and 4QEnGiants[a] 8:9-12 with *1 Enoch* 7:6; 10:1-3,4.
[31] Milik dates the MSS. as follows: 4QEnGiants[a] is contemporary with 4QEn[c] (ca. 30-1 B.C.E.), which contains chaps. 106-107 (*Enoch,* 310, 178). Actually Milik claims (*ibid.,* 310) that the Book of Giants was part of the same scroll as parts of *1 Enoch.* However, on the place of the Book of Giants in the Enochic corpus, see Greenfield and Stone, 'Pentateuch.' 4QEnGiants[b]

Stories about the rebel angels and the giants continued to influence Jewish and Christian tradition for many centuries,[32] and the dream about the trees may be reflected in *2 Baruch* 36 and *4 Ezra* 4:13-19.[33]

Jubilees

The *Book of Jubilees* is a rewritten version of Genesis 1 - Exodus 14, purportedly dictated to Moses on Mount Sinai by an angel of the presence.[34] The order of the book follows, with few exceptions, that of the Bible itself; however, the author's treatment of the wording of the biblical text varies widely. Often he reproduces that text verbatim. On occasion he deletes what he does not find useful.[35] Most typically, however, he recasts the narrative or makes additions to it in line with his interests and purpose. Especially noteworthy is the book's chronological framework, which divides history into weeks and jubilees of years, dating events in Israelite history to specific times in these cycles. The chronology culminates in the jubilee of jubilees, *Anno Mundi* 2451, with the entrance into the Land (or the giving of the Torah, according to one resolution of certain critical problems).[36]

The largest group of additions to the biblical text are halakhic. They appear in several forms. 1) The establishment of religious festivals are dated according to the solar calendar of 364 days that structures the book's chronology. 2) Additions within the narratives themselves depict the patriarchs properly observing the Torah. Most often these additions portray the celebration of a festival, again witnessing to the author's calendrical interest (e.g., 15:1f.; 16:20-31).[37] 3) The author places in the mouth of the patriarchs the commands and admonitions that he himself wishes to make to his readers. The most striking example of this occurs in Abraham's three testaments in chapters 20, 21, and 22. Similarly, in a long addition, Rebecca admonishes Jacob not to marry a Canaanite woman.[38] 4) The author adds to biblical stories halakhic commentaries, which often

---

was written ca. 100-50 B.C.E. (Milik, *Enoch,* 304, citing Cross). 6Q8 was written 50-1 B.C.E. (*ibid.,* 300, citing Cross). No manuscript of the book is early enough to indicate priority to *1 Enoch* 106-107, but this does not prove that the MSS. did not derive from much earlier archetypes.

[32] Milik, *Enoch,* 317-39. On the development in gnosticism see below, pp. 451-6.

[33] Ezek 17 and 31, Dan 4. Cf. Judg. 9:8-15.

[34] See 1:29; 2:1; cf. also 30:17-21; chap. 48, where his person is explicit. See also below, n. 62.

[35] E.g., Gen 12:11-15a, 18-19a at *Jub.* 13:12; Gen 13:5-10 at *Jub.* 13:17; Gen 20 at *Jub.* 16:10.

[36] See the discussion of Wiesenberg, 'The Jubilee of Jubilees,' of which VanderKam ('Author,' 209) promises a critique.

[37] On other matters, see, e.g., the mode of sacrifice in *Jub.* 15:1f. and the tithes to Levi in chap. 32.

[38] *Jub.* 25. In the biblical account (Gen. 28:1-4), Isaac admonishes Jacob; cf. *Jub.* 27:8-11, where he does so at Rebecca's behest.

begin with the expression, 'For this reason it is written (or ordained) in the heavenly tablets that . . .' In these commentaries the author utilizes some element in the biblical narrative as the springboard for his exposition on a point of law: nakedness is prohibited (3:31); feasts are to be observed according to the solar calendar (6:17-22); blood must not be consumed (7:28-33); circumcision must be performed, and only on the eighth day (15:25-34); one must not marry a foreign spouse (30:7-23); incest is forbidden (33:10-20; 41:23-27).

The non-halakhic revisions of the biblical texts vary in their content and function. The author frequently revises the biblical text in order to make a theological point. He interpolates Enochic traditions into the story of the flood and its aftermath (cf. *1 Enoch* 6-16). These additions explain the causes of the flood (chaps. 5 and 7) and the origins of the demonic world which is presupposed throughout the book.[39] References to the final judgment also drawn from the Enochic literature (cf. *Enoch* 10) are used in the narrative in *Jubilees* 5:10-16 and are expanded. Other eschatological additions occur from place to place (e.g., 16:6-9; 30:22).[40] The longest of these is 23:9-32. In context this apocalypse is an elaboration on the biblical reference to Abraham's age (Gen 25:7f.; *Jub.* 23:8). Because of sin, human life becomes increasingly shorter until, at the time of the end, infants will be like old men. Repentance will reverse the process, and there will be a return to primordial longevity. The time of the end is the author's own time, and in this passage he expresses his belief that the great reversal will take place imminently.[41]

Other non-halakhic additions and expansions are exhortative in function. We have already noted formal exhortations placed in the mouths of the ancients. While these may deal with specific points of law, they also contain more general ethical admonitions. Exhortations are also implied by narrative additions and commentaries on them. Most notable in this respect are the stories about Abraham, who is depicted as a model of a variety of virtues. He is a paragon of wisdom and insight. As such he sees through the folly of idolatry, teaches the Chaldaeans the science of agriculture, learns of the futility of astrological forecasting and studies 'the books of his fathers' (11:5-12:27). Moreover, his zeal leads him to burn the local idolatrous temple (12:12).[42]

The stories of the Sacrifice of Isaac and the purchase of the Cave of

---

[39] See, e.g., chap. 11; 17:16; 48:2-19. On the figure of Enoch in *Jubilees,* see VanderKam, 'Enoch Traditions.'

[40] See Davenport, *Eschatology, passim.*

[41] There is an interesting parallel between this passage and Mark 13. A predictive passage in a narrative setting makes reference to events in the real author's own time and implicitly recommends certain conduct. On Mark 13, see Petersen, *Literary Criticism,* 69-73.

[42] Cf. *Apoc. Abr.* 1-2 and *T. Job* 1-5. Cf. the other parallel to the Book of Job in the Sacrifice story mentioned below.

Machpelah are expanded to depict Abraham as a model of faithfulness and patient endurance under trial. The biblical story of the sacrifice states simply that 'God tested Abraham' (Gen 22:1). His celebrated faith is not mentioned in Genesis 22, but in Genesis 15:6 with reference to his belief in God's promise of a son. Taking the biblical motif of testing as his point of departure, the narrator transforms the biblical story (which is repeated almost verbatim) into a full-blown courtroom scene. He prefaces it with a confrontation between the angel(s) of the presence and the satanic accuser, the prince of *mastema,* clearly reminiscent of Job 1-2, (*Jub.* 17:15f.), and he concludes the story with reference to the defeat of the accuser (18:9-12). The story is but one example (though probably the example *par excellence*) of Abraham's lifetime of faithfulness to God and patient endurance (17:17f.). The author appears to have drawn on a tradition about the ten trials of Abraham, of which he names the bargaining over the Cave of Machpelah as the tenth (19:1-9).[43] In short, the author takes characteristics which the Bible explicitly attributes to Abraham in one situation and applies them to his behaviour in a variety of circumstances. The motif of faithfulness applied to the sacrifice becomes traditional in Jewish and Christian literature, and the motif of endurance under trial is applied to other patriarchs.[44]

Chapters 35-38 are a lengthy expansion on the list of Edomite kings in Genesis 36:31-39 (*Jub.* 38:15-24). The passage reflects contemporary Jewish-Idumaean hostility and explains its origin, stressing Jewish superiority. The point is made in a lengthy narrative describing relationships between Jacob and Esau that culminate in a war in which Jacob slays Esau. Other events contemporary to the author are alluded to in some of the commentaries in the form of predictions.

These many non-halakhic additions and revisions notwithstanding, our author's pervading interest and emphasis is halakhic. Unlike the above-cited material about Abraham, most of the stories about the patriarchs do not exemplify abstract vices or virtues, as in the *Testaments of the Twelve Patriarchs.* Good or bad behaviour involves, rather, obedience or disobedience of a specific law, and penalties are specified for such disobedience. The *halakhoth* propounded in *Jubilees,* touching on a wide variety of issues, differ at many points from Pharisaic and Sadducean *halakhoth,*[45] and like many of the Qumran *halakhoth,* they are noteworthy

---

[43] The author states that there were ten trials but does not tell us what they were. In addition to the Sacrifice and the Cave of Machpelah, he seems to enumerate six other trials in 17:17f. For the tradition, see *M. Aboth* 5:4 (Albeck, *Mishnah 4 ad loc.,* and p. 499); *Aboth de R. Nathan* A + B, p. 94f.; *Midr. Psalms* 18, 25 (77a-b). See also the next note.

[44] For Abraham's faithfulness exemplified in the sacrifice, cf. Sir 44:20; 1 Macc 2:52; Jdt 8:24-27; Heb 11:17; James 2:21-23. For Joseph's endurance in the face of ten trials, cf. *T. Joseph* 2:7. Cf. also Job's endurance in *T. Job.*

[45] Albeck, *Jubiläen,* 35-37. See also Safrai, 'Halakhic Literature', the typescript of which was graciously made available by the author.

for their severity.[46] To what extent these laws reflect early practice that was later relaxed and to what extent they represent sectarian innovation is a question in need of investigation. It does seem likely, however, that in some cases the author is protesting current practice in the Second Temple period.[47] The apocalypse in chapter 23 must be considered in this light. Israel is suffering for its disobedience to the Torah, i.e., the commandments and laws as this author expounds them.

Especially noteworthy is the attention given to calendrical matters. On the one hand, this interest is chronological, and the crucial dating of the entrance to the Land (or the giving of the Torah) reflects a belief in God's sovereignty over time and history.[48] On the other hand, the concern with calendar is halakhic in nature. The solar calendar has the force of law because it is rooted in the created structure of the universe,[49] and the chronological framework demonstrates the proper observance of the religious feasts in accordance with the solar calendar.[50] The 364 days of the year, according to this calendar, comprise exactly 52 weeks, which divide into four equal seasons (thirteen weeks), each of which begins on a Wednesday. All feasts begin not only on the same date, but also on the same day of the week, a Wednesday, a Friday, or a Sunday. In all cases, the Sabbath is avoided. This may be connected with the severity of the laws that govern the Sabbath, which are especially prominent in the book (2:1, 17-33; 50:6-13).[51] This emphasis on the Sabbath is perhaps to be connected with the author's interest in the cycles of seven and forty-nine years (note the juxtaposition of relevant laws in 50:1-5 and 6-13). Whether the author's solar calendar was ever in use in pre-exilic or Second Temple Judaism is a question that scholars continue to debate.[52]

Divine revelation is the ultimate authority for the *halakhoth* propounded in *Jubilees*. They were dictated to Moses by an angel of the presence. Details regarding the celestial structures on which the solar calendar is based were revealed first to Enoch (4:17). The source of all these laws are the immutable heavenly tablets. Alongside these claims to direct revelation, the author often indicates that there is an exegetical base for his laws. Specific laws derive from some detail or item in the biblical text that he is transmitting (and revising).

[46] *Ibid.* On the severity of the Sabbath laws, see Finkelstein, 'Jubilees,' 45; Albeck, *Jubiläen,* 36; Testuz, *Les idées,* 116; Schiffman, *Halakhah,* 78.
[47] Safrai, 'Halakhic Literature'.
[48] The chronology may also reflect eschatological speculation; see Testuz, *Les idées,* 164-77; and Davenport, *Eschatology,* 69-70, n. 3.
[49] This structure is described in *1 Enoch* 72-80, cited in *Jub.* 4:17.
[50] On the calendar, see the brief discussion by Herr ('Calendar,' 839-43) and other literature cited in the bibliography below.
[51] Albeck, *Jubiläen,* 7-12.
[52] On this issue, see most recently VanderKam, 'Origin'; and idem, '2 Maccabees 6,7A,' and the literature cited by him.

This process of transmitting and revising the biblical text reflects a remarkable view of Scripture and tradition. The pseudepigraphic ascription of the book to an angel of the presence and the attribution of laws to the heavenly tablets invest the author's interpretation of Scripture with absolute, divine authority.[52a] His understanding of biblical laws is God's, and his extraction of other laws from non-legal biblical texts is also of divine origin. Thus obedience to 'the laws' and 'the commandments' as he expounds them and a return to 'the paths of righteousness' as he reveals them are a *sine qua non* for the coming of the eschaton (23:26).[53]

This author's view of tradition differs formally from the familiar rabbinic view presented in *Mishnah Aboth* 1:1. This latter envisions an oral transmission from Sinai. According to *Jubilees*, *halakhoth* not found in the biblical text were already committed to writing on Mt. Sinai. On the other hand, the claim that these laws were inscribed on heavenly tablets parallels rabbinic views about the eternity of Torah.[54]

A variety of factors point to a time of writing in the second century B.C.E. Explicit citation of the book in the Qumran Damascus Document (CD 16:3f.) indicates a *terminus ad quem* ca. 100-75 B.C.E.[55] Paleographical evidence places the *terminus* close to 100 B.C.E.[56] A *terminus a quo* early in the second century is provided by the book's reflection of details of the Hellenistic reform. Two passages are noteworthy. The Jews 'should not uncover themselves as the gentiles uncover themselves' (3:31). Circumcision is the sign of the covenant (15:14), and uncircumcision is imitation of the gentiles (15:34).[57]

Charles, Testuz, and others have suggested that *Jubilees* was written in the reign of John Hyrcanus (ca. 110-105 B.C.E.) by a partisan of the Hasmonaean dynasty.[58] Two factors tell against this position. Supposed references to the Hasmonaeans are not all that clear or certain.[59] A pro-

---

[52a] Cf. below, pp. 427ff.

[53] A similarly exclusivistic view of Torah is well known from the Qumran Scrolls and seems to be assumed in *1 Enoch* 92-105. On the latter see Nickelsburg, 'The Epistle of Enoch.'

[54] See, e.g., *Gen. Rabba* 1:1, where Torah is identified with pre-existent Wisdom.

[55] On the citation, see VanderKam, *Studies*, 255-7.   [56] *Ibid.*, 254.

[57] Cf. 1 Macc 1:15, 2 Macc 4:12-14; Jos. *Ant.* 12:241. In view of these references to Jewish hellenization, Albright's arguments (*Stone Age*, 346) for a fourth to third century date must be rejected; similarly, the even earlier date of Zeitlin, 'Jubilees,' 1-31. See Testuz, *Les idées*, 35-39.

[58] See Charles, *Jubilees*, lviii-lxvi. On essential points he is followed by Testuz, *Les idées*, 34f. See also Eissfeldt, *The Old Testament*, 608.

[59] Charles (*Jubilees*, lix, 191) and Testuz (*Les idées*, 35) assert without evidence that the title 'Priest of the Most High God' (32:1) was borne only by the Hasmonaeans — an argument from silence. The title is implied in *T. Levi* 2-5, where the epithet 'Most High' occurs five times (3:10; 4:1-2; 5:1,7). That this testament was the product of Hasmonaean partisans (see Charles, *APOT* 2, 314, n. on 18:6) is problematic given the popularity at Qumran of the Aramaic testament (see Milik, 'Le Testament de Lévi'). The alleged reference to the dual civil and religious functions of the Hasmonaeans in 31:15 (Charles, *Jubilees*, lxii) is indemonstrable since the dual office was not new to the Hasmonaeans (VanderKam, *Studies*, 248-9). On the alleged references to the battles of Judas Maccabaeus (Charles, *Jubilees*, lxxii-lxxiii), see below, n. 67.

Hasmonaean bias is difficult to explain in a document that was obviously popular in the anti-Hasmonaean community at Qumran and that appears to have originated in circles closely related to Qumran (see below).

Davenport distinguishes three stages in the composition of *Jubilees*.[60] The basic document was composed ca. 200 B.C.E. to inspire obedience to the Torah in the face of encroaching hellenization.[61] The work was updated ca. 166-160 B.C.E. with references to the persecution under Antiochus, and again ca. 140-104 B.C.E., probably at Qumran. Davenport is correct in stressing the book's front against hellenization (see below). His literary analysis is, however, problematic.[62]

An alternative analysis of the dating of *Jubilees* is that of VanderKam.[63] His *terminus a quo* is Judas Maccabaeus' victory over Nicanor (161 B.C.E.), referred to in 34:2-9.[64] The *terminus ad quem* is determined by several factors. Although *Jubilees* has many close points of similarity with Qumran theology, the author belongs to a community that worships in Jerusalem (49:21). There is no hint of a wicked high priest or of an exodus to Qumran. Thus the terminus must be set before Simon's death (135 B.C.E.) and more likely before his acclamation as high priest (140 B.C.E.). The 'glowing terms' in which the priesthood is described suggests that the author does not know of the Hasmonaean high priesthood at all; thus a date before Jonathan's accession (152 B.C.E.) seems probable.[65]

VanderKam's dating of *Jubilees* is not without its difficulties. While it is true that he has made, to date, the strongest argument for the identification of *Jubilees* 34:2-9 and 37-38 as descriptions of the Maccabaean wars,[66] the identification is far from certain and depends on a number of textual emendations.[67] Two other factors must be considered. First, the apocalypse in 23:16ff. refers to events connected with the controversy over Hellenism.[68] Nonetheless, no reference is made to the person of Antiochus IV,

---

[60] Davenport, *Eschatology*, 10-18.

[61] According to Davenport (*ibid.*, 10-14), this document included 1:1-4a, 29a; 2:1-50:4 minus 4:26, 23:14-31, 31:14.

[62] His criteria for determining strata (*ibid.*, 80) are not always convincing. Specifically, on his hypothesis that the original book was an 'angelic discourse,' see VanderKam, 'Author.' Furthermore, the main points of this thesis are more presumed and asserted than proven in his book. On pp. 1-18 he presumes and never demonstrates the independent existence of the basic document. He never explicates his evidence for the later dating of 1:4b-26 (see p. 14, n. 2). Only in the case of chap. 23 does he provide a detailed analysis, pp. 32-46. In part his case appears to rest on the assumption that the parenetic and predictive character of 1:4bff. and 23:14ff. are inconsonant with the didactic function of the angelic discourse. However, cf. 15:34 with 23:23.

[63] VanderKam, *Studies*, 214-85.

[64] *Ibid.*, 217-29.

[65] *Ibid.*, 283-5.

[66] *Ibid.*, 217-38. The identification had already been made by Charles and Bousset, before him; see Charles, *Jubilees,* lxii-lxiii.

[67] See Nickelsburg's review of VanderKam, *Studies,* in *JAOS* 100 (1980), 83-84.

[68] See Nickelsburg, *Resurrection*, 46f.

his pollution of the temple, and his edict — an omission most unusual for a document of this period.[69] Secondly, many of *Jubilees'* additions to the biblical text of Genesis and Exodus have the Jew-gentile situation in focus. In addition to the strictures against nakedness and uncircumcision mentioned above (3:31; 15:34), are the following items. Observance of the lunar calendar is construed as following 'the feasts of the gentiles' (sic!) (6:35). Marriage to a gentile is strictly and repeatedly forbidden (20:4; 22:20; 25:1; 27:10; 30:1-15). Warnings are issued against idolatry (20:7-9; 22:16-18) and consuming blood (6:12-41; 7:30; 21:6). The author stresses Israel's unique covenantal relationship to God and qualitative difference from the gentiles (cf. also 2:31 on the Sabbath).[70] His stringent prohibitions against contact with the gentiles suggest that such contact was not infrequent in the Israel of his time.

These considerations suggest that *Jubilees* was written during the time of the Hellenistic reform close to 168 B.C.E. If one accepts VanderKam's dating, one must admit the strange omission in chapter 23. Moreover, the anti-gentile warnings must be read as post-factum reflections on the enormity of the deeds that brought on the disaster of the 160's[71] or as evidence for continued hellenization and Jew-gentile contact.

Connections between *Jubilees* and the Qumran community are especially close. The Damascus Document cites it as authoritative (CD 16:3-4). Twelve fragmentary manuscripts of *Jubilees* have been found at Qumran.[72] The religious ideas, theology, and laws in *Jubilees* closely parallel, and are often identical with those in writings unique to Qumran.[73] Either of the early dates suggested above precludes its actual composition at Qumran,[74] and there are some differences between *Jubilees* and the Qumran texts.[75] It issued from unnamed circles related to those responsible for the composition of Daniel 10-12, *1 Enoch* 72-82; 85-90; and 93:1-10; 91:12-17.[76] The historical relationship between these sects and the Qumran sect are now obscure, but the latter fell heir to their literature.

---

[69] *Ibid.* 47, n. 9.
[70] Testuz, *Les idées,* 59-74.
[71] This explanation was suggested to me by VanderKam in private correspondence, Feb. 20, 1977.
[72] For the publication and main discussions of these manuscripts, see the bibliography below.
[73] See VanderKam, 258-83. See also below, p. 530.
[74] Scholars accepting a later date for *Jubilees* are divided on the question of its relationship to Qumran. Milik (*Ten Years*, 32) and Grintz ('Jubilees,' 325f.) favor Essene provenance. Testuz (*Les idées*, 179-95) sees many similarities with Qumran, but also some differences.
[75] *Ibid.*; Schiffman (*Halakhah*, 78, 129) indicates some differences between the *halakhoth* of Qumran and those in *Jubilees*. See also VanderKam (*Studies*, 311-14) and Safrai, 'Halakhic Literature'.
[76] Manuscripts of Daniel and the relevant parts of *1 Enoch* have been found at Qumran. On the relationship between Dan 10-12 and *Jub.* 23, see Nickelsburg, *Resurrection*, 1-33. For parallels to *Jub.* 23:16, 26, cf. 1 Enoch 90:6f.; 93:10; CD 1:8-11. On the relationship between the calendars of *Jubilees* and Qumran, see the literature listed in the bibliography below.

Jubilees was composed in Hebrew, then translated into Greek, and from Greek into Ethiopic, in which language alone it is extant in its entirety.[77] Knowledge of the Hebrew original may be reflected in later Jewish midrashim.[78] The Greek version was well known among Byzantine Christian authors.[79] Some *halakhoth* of the Ethiopian Falashas are derived from *Jubilees,*[80] and the book continues to be printed in the Ethiopic Bible.

The Genesis Apocryphon

The Genesis Apocryphon from Qumran Cave I is a compilation of patriarchal narratives. The extant portion of the scroll covers the period from Lamech to Abraham,[81] but its badly deteriorated condition severely limits a reconstruction of its contents. Of the twenty-two extant columns, only five are legible in substantial portion (cols. 2, 19-22).[82] The narratives are versions of the biblical accounts, freely reworked in Aramaic and, largely, in the first person singular.[83] In places the actual wording of the Bible is reproduced, more often it is paraphrased, and not infrequently there are substantial additions, some of which parallel other contemporary written sources.[84]

Columns 2-5 related a version of the same story of Noah's birth that is preserved in *1 Enoch* 106-107 (cf. above pp. 93f.) The present version differs from *1 Enoch* in several ways: 1) Following the usual technique in this scroll, the narrator is the person immediately concerned, viz., Lamech, rather than Enoch. 2) Lamech's suspicion that Noah's conception was of angelic origin (cf. *1 Enoch* 106:6) leads to a lengthy and emotional scene-totally absent in *1 Enoch* — in which Lamech adjures his wife to reveal the truth of the matter (2:3-18). 3) *1 Enoch* stresses the child's miraculous appearance by a double repetition of the initial description (106:5f., 10-12). This appearance suggests to Lamech that the child is a portent of things to come (106:1b).[85] The Genesis Apocryphon eliminates Lamech's speech to

---

[77] Charles, *Jubilees,* xxvi-xxxiii; VanderKam, *Studies,* 1-18. Both also discuss the Latin and Syriac fragments of *Jubilees.* Brock ('Abraham') considers another Syriac text that parallels *Jub.* 11-12, but concludes it is based on a source common to *Jubilees* and not on the book itself.

[78] Charles, *Jubilees,* lxxv-lxxvii; *id., Ethiopic Jubilees,* 179-82.

[79] See Denis, *Introduction,* 150-62; and Milik, 'Recherches.'

[80] See Schiffman, *Halakhah,* 19, and the many parallels scattered throughout Albeck, *Jubiläen.*

[81] The first sheet of the scroll probably had other columns before the present column 1, and the fourth sheet (cols. 16-22) was attached to yet another, final sheet; Avigad — Yadin, *Genesis Apocryphon,* 14f.

[82] On the condition of the scroll, see *ibid.,* 12-15, and Fitzmyer, *Genesis Apocryphon,* 3f.

[83] In the badly preserved columns, see 5:3, 9, 26; 6:2, 6; 7:7; 10:13, 15; 12: 13-16. The narrative changes to third person at 21:23ff.

[84] On the genre of the scroll and its relationships to targum and midrash, see Fitzmyer, *Genesis Apocryphon,* 6-14, 30-39.

[85] Doeve, 'Lamechs achterdocht,' 409-10.

Methuselah (2:19; *1 Enoch* 106:5f.) and may or may not have contained the second repetition of the description.[86] The scene between Lamech and his wife is quite consonant with other emotionally oriented additions to the biblical accounts in this document[87] and may well be the work of its author. The present state of the text, however, permits no certain conclusions about the precise relationship between the two versions of the story. Columns 6-17 described the deluge and its aftermath. The legible parts of these columns reveal significant parallels (including chronological details) to non-biblical material in *Jubilees*.[88]

The story of Abram probably began in column 18. Columns 19-22 retell the events in Genesis 12:8-15:4. The fragmented beginning of column 19 (lines 7-10a) appears to parallel the slightly expanded version of Genesis 12:8-9 in *Jubilees* 13:8-10.[89] The story of Abram's sojourn in Egypt (Gen 12:10-20) is extensively elaborated in columns 19:10-20:32 but reveals only chronological parallels to *Jubilees* 13:11-15. Novelistic devices are employed, and independent forms (a dream and its interpretation, a description of Sarai's beauty, and a prayer) are introduced to create a story richer and more complex than its biblical counterpart. Abram's dream is likely intended as divine justification for his subsequent lie.[90] The lengthy description of Sarai's beauty follows a traditional genre,[91] but is suggested in Genesis 12:15, '. . . the princes of Pharaoh . . . praised her to Pharaoh.' A third addition is Abraham's prayer for judgment, which triggers the plague on Pharaoh and his household. Later Abram himself functions as the divinely empowered healer. Pharaoh's inability to consummate his marriage to Sarai has moral or apologetic overtones.[92] Through these additions, the biblical story is transformed so as to underscore the providence of God and his power over the Egyptian king. Abram is his agent — seer and interpreter of dreams, wise man, speaker of efficacious prayer, and a healer set in opposition to the magicians and physicians of Egypt. Thus he assumes characteristics associated with Joseph and Daniel.[93] The storyteller's art is evident in his development and resolution of the plot and in his portrayal of the relevant reactions and emotions of his characters. Columns 20:33-21:7 retell the story of Abram and Lot (Gen 13:1-13) in compressed

---

[86] The bottom of column 2 could have described again the confrontation between Lamech and his wife or the appearance of the child.

[87] Cf. 2:25; 7:7; 19:21; 20:8-9, 10, 12, 16; 21:7 (cf. *Jub.* 13:18); 22:5.

[88] See the citations in Fitzmyer, *Genesis Apocryphon*, 99-105.

[89] *Ibid.*, 105.

[90] See *ibid.*, 110. Cf. *T. Levi* 5 for a similar justification for Levi's participation in the slaughter in Shechem. On the dream see Dehandschutter, 'Le rêve,' 48-55. For a parallel to the dream, cf. *T. Abr.* 7.

[91] See Fitzmyer, *Genesis Apocryphon*, 119-20.

[92] *Ibid.*, 131-32.

[93] See Dehandschutter, 'La rêve,' 52-54.

form. God's promise and command to Abram (Gen 13:14-18) are reproduced almost in their entirety, with additions containing geographical information (21:10-12, 15-19). Genesis 14 is paraphrased in somewhat compressed form (21:23-22:26) with no striking additions to the Melchizedek incident. The scroll breaks off midway through an expanded version of Genesis 15:1-4 (22:27-34).

In retelling the biblical stories, the author of this work has employed techniques akin to those in *Jubilees,* parts of *1 Enoch,* and the *Testaments of the Twelve Patriarchs.* Similar to *Jubilees,* he has compiled a running narrative that parallels a sizable part of Genesis, and, indeed, he may have used *Jubilees* as a source.[94] His wording is a much freer paraphrase of Genesis than is generally the case in *Jubilees.* Different from *Jubilees* and the *Testaments,* the extant sections indicate little interest in halakhic matters or moral exhortation. Considerable notice is given to geographical details,[95] and there is some emphasis on prayer.[96] The author's treatment of his characters is marked by a sensitivity to the emotions and reactions that reflect their humanity.

The Genesis Apocryphon appears to have been actually composed in Aramaic[97] around the turn of the era.[98] Indications of Essene beliefs are not demonstrable.[99]

Portions of *1 Enoch, Jubilees,* and the Genesis Apocryphon comprise a related group of texts. They share related generic features. There is, moreover, some interdependence: the author of *Jubilees* has used material from stories that we know from *1 Enoch*; the writer of the Genesis Apocryphon appears to have known *Jubilees,* but has also used a story about Noah's birth found in *1 Enoch* but not in *Jubilees.* A common fascination with the figures of Noah and Enoch is evident. Quite possibly this is due to a common apocalyptic viewpoint, although this is not clear in the extant portions of the Genesis Apocryphon. Of significance is the presence of this

---

[94] See the discussion in Fitzmyer, *Genesis Apocryphon,* 16-17. Especially noteworthy is the chronological reference in 1QGenAp 22:27-28, which tallies with the chronology of *Jubilees.* Its placement here may well have been suggested by the typical introductory chronological reference in *Jub.* 14:1. The reverse relationship is highly unlikely. On the relationship between the biblical text used in *Jubilees* and in the Genesis Apocryphon, see VanderKam, 'Textual Affinities.'

[95] Cf. 2:23; 12:13; 16; 17; 19:11-12; 21:8, 10-12, 15-19.

[96] Cf. 12:17; 19:7; 20:12-16, 28; 21:2-3.

[97] Fitzmyer, *Genesis Apocryphon,* 25.

[98] See the discussion and opinions, *ibid.,* 16-19.

[99] *Ibid.,* 11-14. Doeve ('Lamechs achterdocht,' 411-14) sees a parallel between Lamech's suspicion of his wife and similar attitudes which Josephus attributes to the Essenes (*War* 2:121). However, the idea of angelic conception is present already in *1 Enoch* 106:6 (which Doeve, p. 415 does not think is dependent on the Genesis Apocryphon), and Lamech's questioning of his wife is natural and need not presume an Essene context.

literature in the Qumran library,[100] although we are not yet in a position to make well-informed conjectures about its specific religious and social provenances in relation to the Qumran community.[101]

The Book of Biblical Antiquities

This lengthy chronicle retells biblical history from Adam to the death of Saul.[102] The treatment of the ancient material varies widely. Lengthy portions of Scripture are briefly summarized or completely bypassed. Other sections are paraphrased, with occasional verbatim quotations. Still others are interpolated with prayers, speeches, or narrative expansions. In a few cases, whole new stories have been inserted, or old ones have been radically revised. Among the sections deleted are the following: Genesis 1-3; Genesis 12-50 (its contents are briefly summarized in *LAB* 8);[102a] Exodus 3-13; all the legal material in Exodus except chapter 20; almost the entire book of Leviticus; all the legal material in Numbers; Deuteronomy 1-30; the descriptions of the conquest in Joshua (chaps. 3-21); parts of 1 Samuel.

The Book of Judges is a notable exception to the author's techniques of excision and compression. Only chapters 1-3 have been deleted; however, they have been replaced by the lengthy story of Cenez (*LAB* 25-28). According to Judges 1:13, he was the father of Othniel; here he assumes Othniel's place as the first judge (Judg 3:7-14).[103] The stories of Deborah, Gideon, Abimelech, Jephthah, Samson, Micah, the Levite, and the war between Benjamin and Israel have all been retained, though with many revisions. The section corresponding to Judges comprises one-third of the entire work (*LAB* 25-49).

Two tendencies in the *Biblical Antiquities* are consonant with this concentration on the Book of Judges. The first relates to the historical pattern of Judges: sin; divine punishment by means of an enemy; repentance; salvation through a divinely appointed leader. The pattern and references to it appear in many of the (interpolated) speeches in the *Biblical Antiquities*.[104] In presenting this theme, the author often raises the question: Can

---

[100] Also noteworthy for their presence in the Qumran library are the Aramaic Testament of Levi (on its relationship to *1 Enoch* 12-16, see Nickelsburg, 'Enoch, Peter, and Levi') and, perhaps, Tobit (for parallels between Tobit and *1 Enoch*, see above p. 45f. n. 68-72.

[101] On this problem, see Nickelsburg, 'Social Aspects'; and *id.*, 'The Epistle of Enoch.' See also below, pp. 487-9.

[102] James (*Antiquities*, 60-65) and Strugnell ('Philo,' 408) believe that the ending of the *Antiquities* has been lost. Feldman ('Prolegomenon' lxxvii) and Perrot (*Les Antiquités*, 21-22) contest this hypothesis.

[102a] *LAB* indicates the Latin name of the book: *Liber Antiquitatum Biblicarum.*

[103] So also Josephus, *Ant.* 5:182, noted by James, *Antiquities,* 146.

[104] Cohn, 'An Apocryphal Work,' 322.

Israel survive the present onslaught of its enemies?[105] His affirmative answer is rooted in Israel's status as the chosen covenant people of God[106] and is sometimes spelled out in a recitation of Israelite history, including the partriarchal history he bypassed earlier in his narrative.[107]

A second tendency in the *Biblical Antiquities* relates to the manner in which the Book of Judges organizes history around great Israelite leaders.[108] The story of Abraham is radically revised: the patriarch was present at the building of the tower of Babel, but he and eleven others refused to participate in the idolatrous enterprise; from these twelve, Abraham is set apart as the only one who rejects the possibility of escape and confronts death in a fiery furnace (*LAB* 6).[109] The story of Moses' birth is prefaced by a lengthy episode involving his father, Amram, a leader of Israel, who convinces the elders of God's protection of the nation and leads a mass disobedience of the Pharaoh's decree (*LAB* 9). The other parts of the Pentateuch that are reproduced center mainly on the figure of Moses and his functions as mediator of the covenant, intercessor for his people, spokesman of God, and executor of his judgment (*LAB* 10-19); clearly he maintains his preeminent position in Israelite history (*LAB* 19:16). So too, the author's treatment of the book of Joshua centers on the figure of Moses' successor (*LAB* 20-24). Cenez is introduced and celebrated as a leader par excellence (*LAB* 25-28; cf. 49:1). The treatment of Judges makes specific moral judgments about Israel's leaders, often adding a motif of retribution lacking in the biblical text. Gideon, who dies unpunished for his idolatry (Judg 8:22-32), will be punished after death (*LAB* 36:4).[110] Jephthah's loss of his daugher is punishment for a wicked vow (*LAB* 39:11), and she is said to be wiser than her father (*LAB* 40:4). Samson is blinded because his eyes went astray (*LAB* 43:5). Judges 17-20 is unified around the theme of Micah and his idolatry (*LAB* 44-47); his punishment, not mentioned in Judges, is explicit (*LAB* 47:12), and Israel's initial defeat by Benjamin is punishment for those who did not oppose Micah's idolatry (*LAB* 47). The birth of Samuel is set against a vacuum of leadership in Israel, and he is designated as a leader like Cenez (*LAB* 49:1).Finally, the treatment of 1 Samuel centers mainly on the figures of Samuel, Saul, and David, which is quite consonant with the biblical book.

The message of the *Biblical Antiquities* is probably to be found in the two tendencies we have just described. The content of the many speeches put

---

[105] E.g., 9:3; 12:8; 18:10-11; 19:9; 30:4; 35:3; 49:3.
[106] See Perrot, *Les Antiquités*, 43-47.
[107] 18:5-6; 23; 32:1-10.
[108] See the detailed discussion by Nickelsburg, 'Good and Bad Leaders,' 50-62.
[109] Cf. Dan 3 and see Nickelsburg, 'Good and Bad Leaders,' 52. The legend of Abraham in the fiery furnace is found in rabbinic literature in various other forms. Cf. *Gen. R.* 38, p. 361-363, *Seder Eliahu Rabba* p. 27f., *Seder Eliahu Zutta* p. 47, *Midr. ha-Gadol Gen.* p. 206 and 252.
[110] For other references to *post-mortem* judgment, see 3:10; 16:3; 23:13; 25:7.

on the lips of the leaders of Israel functions as a kind of kerygma: Israel is God's people, chosen already before creation;[111] therefore, even when their very existence is threatened, God's covenant fidelity will deliver them. The embodiment of this 'kerygma' in speeches by Israelite heroes adds a particular dimension to the biblical portraits of these leaders and undergirds their significance in the present book. The author often contrasts them to the people, and his frequent use of the first person singular in their speeches underscores their individuality.[112] This literary technique as well as his portrayals of the leaders suggest that he is stressing good or bad leadership as an important constituent in the strong or weak religious and moral fiber of the nation.

The *Biblical Antiquities* has usually been dated shortly before or after the fall of Jerusalem in 70 C.E.[113] Similarities to *2 Baruch* and *4 Ezra* tend to support that contention,[114] and the book's many similarities with traditions in Josephus' *Antiquities* may also indicate a date late in the first century.[115] The message of the book, as we have profiled it, fits well into the post-70 period. A query about Israel's continued existence in the face of powerful gentile opposition and conquest would have been much to the point,[116] and it presents another facet of the problem raised by *2 Baruch* and *4 Ezra*.[117] The emphasis on the necessity of good leaders would have been especially appropriate after the chaos of the years 66-70 and their proliferation of would be Messiahs, prophets, and demagogues.[118] In such a context, the specific message and function of the book would be this. 'In the midst of oppression, disillusion, dissolution, and despair spawned by the events of 70, this author preaches a message of hope, appealing to God's promises to Abraham and Israel's status — even now — as God's chosen people. The day of Deborah stands as a promise (32:14). In God's right time, a ruler like Cenez will arise to deliver his people. The secret sins

---

[111] 60:2.

[112] E.g., 6:11; 9:3-6; 24:1 (cf. Josh 24:15).

[113] Cohn, 'An Apocryphal Work,' 327; James, *Antiquities*, 30-33; Strugnell, 'Philo,' 408; Harrington in Perrot — Bogaert, *Les Antiquités*, 78. Bogaert (*ibid.*, 66-74) suggests wider limits for the date. A date in the time of Pompey is proposed by Helot, 'La Datation.'

[114] For the parallels, see James, *Antiquities*, 46-58; Bogaert, *Apocalypse*, 247-52; and Feldman, 'Prolegomenon,' liv-lv.

[115] For the many parallels to Josephus, see *ibid.*, lviii-lxiv.

[116] Especially noteworthy is the frequent use of the negative form: God will *not forget* his promises (35:2-3). God will *not let* Israel *be totally destroyed* (9:3; 18:10; 30:4). He will *not cast off* his people forever, *nor hate* them to all generations (49:3). This negative formulation is spoken to people who suppose that they may have been totally rejected by God and permanently disenfranchised from the elect status.

[117] The two apocalypses ponder Israel's defeat at the hands of its enemies, and this relates to the question of God's justice. Pseudo-Philo raises, and rejects, the possibility that Israel's defeat may lead to its extinction. A similar query is made by Baruch (*2 Bar.*3:5-6).

[118] The chaos and crisis of leadership during these years are detailed by Rhoads, *Israel in Revolution*.

of the people will be found out, and the nation will be purged, and the precious stones of the twelve tribes will shine in the new Jerusalem (26:12-15).'[119]

The *Biblical Antiquities* is extant only in Latin, which is generally thought to be a translation of a Greek translation of a Hebrew original.[120] Its author is unknown, but the work came to be attributed to Philo of Alexandria because it was transmitted with genuine works of Philo.[121]

An exhaustive comparison of Pseudo-Philo's narrative technique with that in parallel writings would require extended treatment.[122] In general we may note the following. It differs from *Jubilees* in its highly selective reproduction of the text and its lack of halakhic interest. Indeed, whereas *Jubilees* makes many halakhic additions to the narratives, Pseudo-Philo deletes almost all of the legal material in the Pentateuch. Pseudo-Philo's selective reproduction of the text also differs from the Genesis Apocryphon; however, like the Apocryphon, the narrative is characterized by the addition of lengthy non-biblical incidents. The selective mixture of quotation, paraphrase, and expansion is similar to the Genesis Apocryphon and *1 Enoch* 6-11. As to contents, Pseudo-Philo almost completely ignores the Enochic-Noachic traditions that are so important to *1 Enoch, Jubilees,* and the Genesis Apocryphon.[123] The book's possible relationship to traditions attested in the rabbinic literature awaits detailed study.[124]

The Books of Adam and Eve

The story of Adam and Eve inspired a considerable volume of Jewish and early Christian literature. The *Vita Adae et Evae* and the *Apocalypse of Moses* are two major recensions of one such work.

THE APOCALYPSE OF MOSES

This Greek text is the shorter and simpler of the two recensions. It is primarily an account of the first father's death, its cause and its cure. Chapters 1-4 retell Genesis 4:1-25: the birth of Cain and Abel, the murder

---

[119] Nickelsburg, 'Good and Bad Leaders,' 63.

[120] James, *Antiquities,* 28-29; Strugnell, 'Philo,' 408; Harrington in Perrot — Bogaert, *Les Antiquités,* 75-77. See, however, Feldman, 'Prolegomenon,' xxv-xxvii.

[121] See James, *Antiquities,* 26-27; and Feldman, 'Prolegomenon,' xxii-xxiv.

[122] See James, *Antiquities,* 42-60; and Feldman, 'Prolegomenon,' li-lxxvi.

[123] The excursus on the final judgment and resurrection attached to the flood story at *LAB* 3:9-10 does suggest familiarity with the flood/final judgment typology so frequent in the Enochic texts (see above, pp. 90-5).

[124] See the many parallels in rabbinic literature cited in the index of Perrot —Bogaert, *Les Antiquités* 2, 294-9. On the problems of dating the possible common traditions, see Feldman, 'Prolegomenon,' xxxi.

of Abel, and the birth of Seth.[125] The function of this section is to introduce Seth, the recipient of important traditions and in other ways a central figure in the action that follows. Once Seth has appeared, the author moves quickly to Adam's terminal illness (5:1-2), and the remainder of the book deals with the events surrounding his death. Most of the elements of the testament genre (see below, chap. 8) occur in these chapters, although they are in the service of the author's special purposes and are part of a broader plot.[126]

When Adam sees that he is going to die, he summons his children (5:2). Since they do not understand what death is (5:4-6:3), he recounts his past — the Temptation, the Fall, and the expulsion from paradise (chaps. 7-8). Different from typical testamentary narratives, this recital does not exemplify good or bad conduct, but explains why Adam must die. Eve and Seth go in search of the oil of mercy that flows from a tree in paradise, so that Adam may find rest from his pain (chap. 9).[127] The story of the beast's attack on Seth (chaps. 10-12) is either an exegetical elaboration on Genesis 3:15 or an illustration of how, after the Fall, the beasts are no longer subject to humankind (cf 24:4).[128] When Seth and Eve pray for the oil of mercy (chap. 13), Michael responds by contrasting the present time and the future. Adam may not have the oil now, i.e., he must die. However, in 'the end of the times' there will be a resurrection. Then the delights of paradise will be given to 'the holy people,' and sin will be extirpated.

Eve now gathers her family and rehearses the events that brought death into the world (chap. 14). Like chapters 7-8, this longer account (chaps. 15-30) of the events in Genesis 3 explains Adam's death to his children.[129] The artful and imaginative elaboration of the biblical account describes the relationship between serpent and devil and the nature of the Fall, viz., Adam's and Eve's loss of their 'glory' and 'righteousness.' The author also expands the biblical list of consequences for Adam, Eve, and the serpent (chaps. 24-26). The detailed description of the expulsion from the garden repeats Adam's petition for mercy and God's response (chaps. 27-29). He asks for pardon, and God chides the angels for temporarily discontinuing the expulsion.[130] When Adam asks for the fruit of the tree of life, God responds, 'not now.' However, if Adam turns from sin, God will raise him up in the resurrection and give him of the tree of life. God does give Adam

---

[125] Elements in Eve's dream (*Apoc. Moses* 2:2-3 and especially the form in *Vita* 22:4) suggest an exegetical development from Gen 4:11.

[126] The author's purpose is often to be seen at precisely the point at which he diverges from the genre. For details see Nickelsburg, 'Related Traditions,' 516-19.

[127] On this motif and its development in later folklore, see Quinn, *Quest*.

[128] A connection with Gen 3:15 is more evident in *Vita* 37:3.

[129] See Nickelsburg, 'Related Traditions,' 518.

[130] The wording of this section is reminiscent of *1 Enoch* 63, especially 63:1, 5-6, 9. cf. also *1 Enoch* 63:11 and Gen 3:24.

permission to take herbs and seeds from paradise, so that he can offer incense to God and have food for his sustenance. The section closes with a stereotyped testamentary exhortation that the children not follow their parents' example (chap. 30).

The narration of the deathbed events now focuses on Adam's fate. We have the first indication of a concern with the disposal of Adam's body (31:3-4). Eve's prayer in behalf of Adam is typical of the book's emphasis on her primary responsibility for the Fall (32:1-2).[131] In confessing her sin, Eve implicitly lessens Adam's fault in the hope that he will obtain mercy. Eve's vision of the heavenly throne room (for which Seth acts as an 'angelus' interpres) provides the evidence that her prayer has been answered (chaps. 33-37). The angels intercede for Adam and then break into a hymn of praise because God has had mercy on him. The first father is purified in the Acherusian Lake[132] and is promised ultimate victory over Satan. Michael then conveys Adam's soul (37:6) to the heavenly paradise.

God gives the angels directions for the burial of Adam and Abel (38:1-41:2). His last word is: 'Adam, Adam . . . I told you that earth you are and to earth you will return. Again I promise you the resurrection; I shall raise you up on the last day in the resurrection with every man who is of your seed' (chap. 41). Again the author juxtaposes the necessity of Adam's death because of his sin (cf. Gen 3:19) with the promise of resurrection. Chapters 42-43 describe Eve's death and burial. Seth receives special instructions for her burial, together with the command to bury everyone in the same manner (43:2-3). Eve's death and burial close the narrative.

Speculation about the salvation of Adam and Eve is central to this book. Will God have mercy on the people responsible for the presence of sin and death in this world? The answer is twofold. Death is an inevitable consequence of Adam's (and Eve's) sin, and no amount of bargaining and praying can alter this fact.[133] Adam has been cut off from the tree of life; the most he can take from paradise are seeds to grow food and incense to accompany his prayer. In the latter is a bridge from condemnation to ultimate salvation, which is the author's second point. In spite of Adam's death, God does have mercy on the first father. He receives his soul and promises the resurrection of his body and access to the delights and eternal sustenance which he left behind in the garden.

The author's interest is not limited to speculation about Adam and Eve. The resurrection will be a general resurrection. The specifications for burial apply to 'every man who dies' (chaps. 38-43). If the death and trouble which Adam and Eve brought into the world are a universal malady, the resurrection provides a remedy for all 'the holy people' who

---

[131] Cf. 9:2; 10:1-2; 14:2; 21:6.
[132] An indication that the author was familiar with Hellenistic cosmology.
[133] For a similar theme, see the discussion of *T. Abr.*, above, pp. 60-4.

descend from him. Proper burial is performed in the hope of the resurrection and as a sign of it. Because of this hope, mourning must give way to joy. It must not extend beyond six days, since the seventh day is symbolic of the eternal rest.[134] In short, our author admits the inevitability of death for everyone, but he expresses his faith in the resurrection. As Adam was the creature of God and his image, so it is with all humanity; and the Creator will redeem his creature in the resurrection.[135]

THE LIFE OF ADAM AND EVE

Approximately one-half of the Latin *Vita Adae et Evae* overlaps with a similar proportion of the *Apocalypse of Moses*.

	Vita	*Apoc. Mos.*
Penitence, the devil's narrative, Cain's birth (section 1)	1:1-22:2	——
The birth of (Cain) Abel, Seth *et al.* (2)	22:3-24:2	1:1-5:1a
Adam's revelations to Seth (3)	chaps. 25-29	——
Adam's sickness, narrative (4)	chaps. 30-44	5:1b-14:3
Eve's narrative (5)	——	chaps. 15-30
Adam's death, Eve's vision, Adam's burial (6)	chaps. 45-48	31:1-42:2
Eve's testament (7)	49:1-50:2	——
Eve's death and burial (8)	50:3-51:3	42:3-43:4

The overlapping parts of the *Apocalypse* and the *Vita* parallel one another closely in order and wording. The material found in the *Vita,* but not in the *Apocalypse of Moses,* occurs in three blocks (*Vita* 1:1-22:2; 25 - 29; 49:1-50:2).

The narrative thread that binds together *Vita* 1-22 is Adam's and Eve's quest for food, although other episodes and themes are interspersed. When Adam and Eve are driven from paradise, they find the earth devoid of food (1:1-4:2). They hope that acts of penitence will obtain divine favour and result in the gift of food (4:3—6:2). Adam will fast forty days and then spend forty days in the Jordan River. Eve is to stand in the waters of the Tigris for thirty-seven days. Satan appears to Eve in the guise of an angel (cf. *Apoc. Moses* 17) and once again deceives her (7:1-10:4). He then explains his treachery in an account of his expulsion from heaven (11-17; cf. Isa 14). After Cain's birth, which is narrated as a separate incident (18:1-21:3), God sends Adam seeds to grow the food for which he has been searching (22:2).

[134] This idea is clearer in *Vita* 51:2.
[135] On the soteriology of the work, see Sharpe, 'The Second Adam.' For the relationship between creation and redemption with reference to resurrection, cf. 2 Macc 7:11, 22-23, 27-29.

In chapters 25-29, Adam transmits secret knowledge to Seth. In the first part of this instruction (25:1-29:1), he relates his vision of God after his expulsion from the garden.[136] Its theme (God's threat of death, Adam's petition, God's promise of mercy) parallels the last part of Eve's narrative in the *Apocalypse of Moses* 27-29.[137] The second half of Adam's instruction is an historical apocalypse revealed to Adam after he had eaten of the tree of knowledge (29:2-9).

In the *Apocalypse of Moses* 14, Adams bids Eve to recount the story of the Fall, and Eve's narrative follows. In *Vita* 44 Adam tells Eve to recount the story *after his death.* At that time and immediately before her own death, Eve gathers her children. However, she does not tell the story of the Fall. Rather she repeats Michael's instructions that the children should write on clay and stone tablets the lives of Adam and Eve (chaps 49-50). The book ends with Seth fulfilling this command.

There are two major structural differences between the *Apocalypse of Moses* and the *Vita.* Eve's narrative is missing in the *Vita,* and three blocks of material in the *Vita* are missing in the *Apocalypse of Moses.*

An explanation of these differences is very possibly to be found in Slavonic and Armenian versions of this work. The Slavonic version follows the order of the *Apocalypse of Moses,* and lacks none of the latter's major sections, although it compresses some of them. The end of Eve's narrative differs in three major respects, however. The dialogue between God and Adam is shortened. Adam leaves paradise without any seeds. The narrative then continues with a section that parallels *Vita* 1-22 and describes how Adam looks for food.[138]

The situation is somewhat different in the Armenian *Penitence of Adam.*[139] The book begins with the account of the penitence of Adam and Eve, the devil's narrative, and the birth of Cain which corresponds with *Vita* 1-22. Thereafter, the *Penitence* agrees in its structure with the *Apo-*

---

[136] Scholem (*Jewish Gnosticism*, 17, n. 10) mentions this text in his discussion of Merkabah texts. Terminological similarities to Merkabah texts are evident. The parallels between this text and *1 Enoch* 12-16 (see below, n. 142) also point toward a connection with Jewish mystical texts; see Nickelsburg, 'Enoch, Levi and Peter,' 576-82.

[137] The end of the passage (*Vita* 28:3-29:1) suggests that in fact the incident took place before the expulsion from the garden. To what waters does the author have reference: the water-like appearance in throne visions (Scholem, *Jewish Gnosticism*, 14-15); or the rivers around the earthly paradise (Gen 2:10-14)? For God's heavenly palace of ice, cf. *1 Enoch* 14:8-14, on which see Nickelsburg, 'Related Traditions,' 526-27; and *id.,* 'Enoch, Levi, and Peter,' 578-80.

[138] This section is shorter than *Vita* 1-22 and shows some evidence of confused compression. It omits the account of Cain's birth. More important, Adam and Eve receive food early in the account (chap. 31) and not at the end as in the *Vita.* Thus the penitence does not serve the same function as in the *Vita.* See also the next note.

[139] For a translation, see Stone, *Penitence of Adam.* Lüdtke ('Georgische Adam-Bücher') has published an account of the Georgian version, which appears to correspond very closely in order and content to the Armenian *Penitence*; see *ibid.,* 155-6.

calypse of Moses against the *Vita.* That is, it lacks Adam's revelation to Seth and Eve's testament (sections 3 and 7 in the above plan) and it contains Eve's narrative (section 5). The account of the expulsion, however, omits mention of the seeds for food (chap. 29).[140]

In both the Slavonic version and the *Penitence,* the story of the quest for food and the penitence is the counterpart of the request for seeds in the *Apocalypse of Moses* 29:4-6. A comparison of all the texts raises two questions. 1) Is the longer story in *Vita* 1-22 and *Penitence* 1-22 an expansion of the incident in the *Apocalypse of Moses* 29, or are the relevant elements in the latter a compression of the longer story? 2) Is the original placement of the story of the quest and penitence to be found in the Slavonic *Adam and Eve* or in the Armenian *Penitence* and the *Vita?*

A final and certain solution to these problems is not possible on the basis of presently published texts and analyses. Clearly all the texts are witnesses to a long and complex history of literary and possibly oral transmission, and each of them represents a different stage in the development of this transmission.

The present author's hypothesis is, however, as follows.[141] Section 1 (*Vita* 1-22; *Penitence* 1-22) is largely an expansion of its counterparts in the *Apocalypse of Moses.* The story and description of the penitence of Adam and Eve is religiously motivated (see below). The role played by the devil in this section (chaps. 7-10) dramatizes the fact that temptation is a continuing fact of life. The devil's narrative reflects theological speculation (chaps. 11-17) that may be hinted at in *Apocalypse of Moses* 16:3. The story of the birth of Cain (chaps. 18-21) is more ambiguous. It may be an elaboration of the *Apocalypse of Moses* 25:3, although the latter could well be a fleeting allusion to the longer story. In section 2 the account of Adam's ascent to the heavenly paradise (*Vita* 25-29:1) is a revision of the heart of Eve's narrative (*Apoc. Moses* 24-29). The transformation of the account was probably due to a theology of a transcendent God, which preferred a theophany in the heavenly paradise to God's descent to earth as depicted in Genesis 3. The account reflects traditional ascent texts such as *1 Enoch* 12-16.[142] Adam's second revelation to Seth about the future of the world (*Vita* 29:2-10) and Eve's testament (section 3, chaps. 49-50) comprise the kind of apocalyptic material that is at home in testamentary literature. These may have been drawn from an Adamic testament, also alluded to in Josephus (*Ant.* 1:70-71).[143] If the account of Adam's and Eve's penitence is, in fact, an expansion of Eve's narrative, the account may very likely have been placed

---

[140] As in the *Vita,* Adam and Eve decide on acts of penitence in order to obtain food (chap. 4). However, by the end of the section (chap. 22), this motivation has been forgotten, different from *Vita* 22:2, where the receipt of the seeds brings the section to a logical conclusion.

[141] For details, see Nickelsburg, 'Related Traditions,' 516-25, especially 524-5.

[142] *Ibid.,* 526-28.

[143] *Ibid.,* 525, 532.

originally after that narrative, as it is in the Slavonic version. The episode would have later been moved to its present position in the *Vita* and the *Penitence* because it belonged there chronologically, i.e., before the story of Adam's death.

In short, the *Apocalypse of Moses* is a more original form of the work. The *Vita* is an expansion of the earlier work — although it may contain some original elements that have dropped out of the *Apocalypse* and some original wording now revised in the *Apocalypse*. The Slavonic and Armenian versions are related and intermediate steps in the recensional process.[144]

Introductory questions about these Adamic works are not easily answered. The date of composition of the *Apocalypse of Moses* and the *Vita* cannot be determined with any certainty.[145] Although the author of the *Vita* may well have known the Adamic tradition referred to by Josephus around the end of the first century,[146] the date of that putative work is itself unknown.

The *Apocalypse of Moses* is extant in Greek,[147] and the Latin *Vita* and the Slavonic and Armenian versions doubtlessly derive from Greek originals.[148] Scholars have suggested that alleged mistranslations, Semitic constructions, and Semitic word-plays indicate that such Greek texts were based on Hebrew originals[149] or on Hebrew or Aramaic sources.[150] While the non-biblical word-play in *Vita* 21:3 (Cain = קין; reed = קנה/קני) clearly reflects Hebrew or Aramaic midrashic activity,[151] derivation of the whole work from a Semitic original (rather than composition in Semiticizing Greek) has not been demonstrated.

An important point of dispute is whether the *Apocalypse* and the *Vita* are Jewish or Christian compositions.[152] Although all the extant versions have been transmitted in Christian circles and contain occasional Christian allusions, this does not exclude the possibility that the original work was

---

[144] The priority of the *Apocalypse of Moses* is argued by Wells, 'Adam and Eve,' 128. According to Meyer ('Vita,' 205-07), both the *Apocalypse* and the *Vita* preserve elements from a Hebrew original.

[145] After a lengthy discussion, Kabisch ('Die Entstehungszeit') identifies the *Apocalypse of Moses* as a Jewish writing of the second centurey C.E. Wells ('Adam and Eve,' 126-27) inclines toward the first century C.E. Denis, (*Introduction,* 6-7) suggests first or early second century. None of the criteria are totally convincing.

[146] See above, n. 143.

[147] For the texts see Tischendorf, *Apocalypses,* 1-23.

[148] On the Latin, see Meyer, 'Vita,' 207. On the Slavonic, see Jagić, 'Slavische Beiträge,' 3. On the Armenian, see Conybeare, 'Apocalypse of Moses,' 217; and Preuschen, *Adamschriften,* cited by Kabisch, 'Die Entstehungszeit,' 110.

[149] Fuchs, 'Das Leben,' 511; Meyer, 'Vita,' 207.

[150] Wells, 'Adam and Eve,' 129-30.

[151] See Fuchs, 'Das Leben,' 515, n. h; Wells, 'Adam and Eve,' 138.

[152] For the variety of opinions, see Denis, *Introduction,* 6.

composed by a Jew or that the secondary recensions were Jewish. Christian allusions could be interpolations. On the other hand, dependence on Jewish sources does not exclude Christian composition from such sources. A crucial text in this respect occurs in the *Apocalypse of Moses* 13:3-5 and its parallels in *Vita* 42 and *Penitence* 42, viz., Michael's answer to the request for the oil of mercy. According to the *Apocalypse of Moses,* Michael announces the resurrection of all flesh from Adam to that day and their receipt of the delights of paradise. According to the *Penitence,* Christ will resurrect Adam's body and baptize him in the Jordan, and Michael will anoint 'the new Adam' with the oil of joy. In the *Vita,* an interpolated passage from the Gospel of Nicodemus[153] describes how Christ will come and raise the body of Adam and all the dead, and he (Jesus) will be baptized in the Jordan and will anoint all believers with the oil of mercy. This interpolation appears to have replaced a reading similar to that in he *Penitence.* Whether such a reading was original to a work that was then, by definition, a Christian composition,[154] or whether the reading was a Christian revision of an originally Jewish reading (such as *Apoc. Moses* 13:2-5) is a matter to be debated.

Although the Jewish or Christian origins of these works cannot yet be determined with certainty, there is a series of allusions that suggest one aspect of the books' provenance, viz., the references to ablutions and immersion in water. In her vision, Eve sees Adam washed in the Acherusian Lake (*Apoc. Moses* 37:3). The apocalypse in *Vita* 29:9 makes reference to water purification, and in *Vita* 1ff., both Adam and Eve carry out an act of penitence by standing at length in the rivers Jordan and Tigris. Moreover, the Christian passages in *Penitence* 42 and *Vita* 42 speak of Adam's and Jesus' baptism in the Jordan. All of this suggests that the book was composed and transmitted in Jewish and/or Christian baptist circles.[155] Moreover, a careful comparison of the penitential and other ritual acts described in the book with parallel materials in Jewish and Christian sources may indicate a feasible context for the composition and transmission of the books in Jewish and/or early Christian circles.[156]

The figures of Adam and Eve were the subject of endless speculation in Jewish and early Christian circles, as is evident from the commentaries of Philo of Alexandria, the writings of Paul the Apostle (Rom 5:12-21; 1 Cor 15:42-50),[157] and the late first century apocalypses (*2 Bar.* 54:15; *4 Ezra*

---

[153] Meyer, 'Vita,' 204-05.

[154] That the Christian reading in the *Penitence* is the more original is the opinion of M.E. Stone, expressed in conversation.

[155] Briefly suggested in Nickelsburg ('Related Traditions, 538) following the suggestions of G.W. MacRae and A. Böhlig regarding the Gnostic *Apocalypse of Adam.*

[156] For an example of such an analysis of Jewish and early Christian Daniel traditions, see Satran, 'Daniel.'

[157] On Paul's Adam/Christ typology, and its Jewish background, see Brandenburger, *Adam und Christus.*

3:20-27; 4:30-32; 7:116ff.; cf. *3 Bar.* 4).[158] Moreover, works such as the *Hypostasis of the Archons* and the *Apocryphon of John* offer the peculiarly Gnostic interpretations of the acts of the first parents and their consequences. The figure of Seth is also crucial in Gnostic literature.[159]

The works that we have considered here are only a small part of a vast Adamic literature generated in Jewish, Christian, and Gnostic circles. The *Apocalypse of Moses* and the *Vita* may themselves be based on an earlier Adamic testament or testaments (see above, p. 111). In turn, the Gnostic *Apocalypse of Adam* is a testament with important affinities to the present texts (not the least an interest in water ablutions) and possibly roots in other Jewish tradition.[160] The many other Christian Adamic works are still in need of careful study.[161]

Hellenistic Jewish Poets

The pseudonymous or anonymous texts discussed thus far in this chapter have tended to follow the prose form employed in their biblical prototypes. In this section we discuss three named authors who used the Greek poetic genres of the epic and the drama as their narrative media. These authors are known to us only through fragments of their works, which were collected by Alexander Polyhistor, a Greek writer of the mid-first century B.C.E. Parts of his work, *On the Jews,* were preserved, in turn, in book 9 of Eusebius' *Praeparatio evangelica.*[162] These poets are noteworthy examples of Hellenistic Jews who sought to bring the resources of Greek culture into a creative interaction with Jewish religion and culture.

PHILO THE EPIC POET

The veneration of the Homeric epic and the composition of new epic works were important and typical features of the Hellenistic age.[163] Following this literary and cultural trend, and writing in flowery, bombastic, and often obscure Greek,[164] Philo the epic poet composed a work of uncertain length entitled *On Jerusalem.* Eusebius has preserved from Alexander

---

[158] On the Adam speculation in *4 Ezra* and *2 Baruch,* see *ibid.,* 27-42. On 3 Bar. 4, see Nickelsburg, *Jewish Literature,* 300-1.

[159] See below, pp. 446ff., 453. For a broad perspective, see the papers gathered in Layton, *Rediscovery* 2: *Sethian Gnosticism.*

[160] See above, n. 154. On the work itself, see below, pp. 470-4.

[161] For a summary description of the other Adamic works, see Denis, *Introduction,* 7-14. For more detailed descriptions of some of these works, see Frey, 'Adam.' For a briefly annotated translation of the Armenian *Death of Adam,* see Stone, 'Death.'

[162] For other Jewish works preserved by Polyhistor, see below, pp. 160ff.

[163] See Gutman, 'Philo,' 59-63.

[164] *Ibid.,* 37; Wacholder, *Eupolemus,* 283.

Polyhistor six short fragments drawn from three contexts in the poem — a total of twenty-four hexameter verses.

These fragments were arranged by Polyhistor in chronological order, beginning with Abraham (*Praepar. evang.* 9:17,1-19,3). After Polyhistor's brief summary of the story of the sacrifice of Isaac (9:19,4) Eusebius gives the first two fragments of Philo's epic, assigned by Polyhistor to the first book of *On Jerusalem* (9:20,1). Its subject matter is Abraham and especially the sacrifice. Philo very likely included the event in his epic because of the traditional identification of Mt. Moriah with the temple mountain in Jerusalem.[165] The first fragment, in typical epic style, is addressed directly to Abraham; its language is obscure.[166] God is referred to as 'the thunderer,' a Homeric epithet for the god Ares.[167] The end of the passage interprets the event as the confirmation of God's promise of offspring, now realized in the existence of Israel.[168] The second fragment, also drawn from the account of the sacrifice, is phrased in the third person and anticipates God's intervention at the climactic moment in the story.

Polyhistor's third fragment from Philo is the second of two passages that he quotes about the patriarch Joseph (*Praepar. evang.* 9:23-24). He attributes it to the fourteenth book of Philo's *On Jerusalem.*

> For them the great leader of all, the Most High, created a most blessed dwelling place (ἕδος), even of old, from (the time of) Abraham and Isaac (and) Jacob, blessed with children, whence came Joseph, who as an interpreter of dreams, bearing the sceptre on Egypt's throne, whirling about time's secrets in the flood-time of fate.

Although the thrust of this passage is clear enough, a number of particulars remain obscure. These in turn affect our understanding of the shape of Philo's epic. 'For them' appears to refer to the Israelites, but what is the blessed dwelling place? Is it the promised land,[169] or, given the subject of the poem, is it Jerusalem, the dwelling place of God?[170] Also problematic is the space that the author devotes to this 'dwelling place' and to Abraham, Isaac, and Jacob. Joseph appears to be mentioned almost as an afterthought. Did the context say more about Joseph? If so, why would Polyhistor — who quotes the passage for what it says about Joseph — have

---

[165] See 2 Chr 3:1; and explicitly *Jub.* 18:13; Jos. *Ant.* 1:224, 226; 7:333.

[166] Compare the translations by Gutman ('Philo,' 40) and Attridge ('Philo').

[167] For this use of βριήπυος, see Homer, *Iliad* 13: 521, cited by Attridge, 'Philo.'

[168] In the biblical account itself (Gen 22:1) God tests Abraham by asking him to give up the tangible evidence of the fulfilment of the promise of a multitude of progeny made earlier (Gen 12:3; 13:14-17; 15:5-6, etc.). On Abraham's faith as the subject of the test, see above, pp. 98-9.

[169] So also Attridge, 'Philo.'

[170] For this meaning, see Liddell-Scott, *Lexicon*, sub ἕδος. The meaning would be that God has established his dwelling place in Jerusalem *for their benefit.*

dropped such material while retaining the first half of the passage? These questions bear on attempts to emend 'fourteenth' to read 'fourth,' on the grounds that Philo would not have taken fourteen books to describe the patriarchal history up to Joseph.[171] In fact, we know nothing about the order of Philo's epic or about the context in that epic in which the present passage occurred. The chronological ordering of Polyhistor's excerpts provides no certain index of the order of any of the works that he quotes.

The final three fragments from Philo's poem describe the water system of Jerusalem (*Praepar. evang.* 9:37). They are quoted as from one section of *On Jerusalem*, but its location in the poem is not specified. Among the extracts, these three fragments appear at the end of a section on Solomon (19:30-34) and are the third of four passages on the topography and hydraulic system of Jerusalem (9:35-38). The fragments stress the abundance of the city's water, as do the passages from Timochares (*History of Antiochus*) and *Aristeas to Philocrates,* which are also quoted by Polyhistor.[172]

The fragments from Philo's epic provide a tantalizing glimpse of a Jewish author who employed a Hellenistic literary genre to sing the praises of his capital city and of the history of the people who inhabited it and worshipped there.[173] Such contents were consonant with other, non-Jewish epics of the period.[174] Beyond this and the epic form that Philo employs and some occasional linguistic parallels to the Greek epics, it is difficult to determine the manner and the extent of Greek influence on the poem.[175]

The date of the epic is debated. If one identifies the author with Philo (the elder) mentioned by Josephus (*Ag. Apion* 1:218) and Clement of Alexandria (*Strom.* 1:141,3), he should probably be dated between the historians Demetrius (221-204 B.C.E.) and Eupolemus (161-157 B.C.E.). Both Josephus and Clement give the sequence: Demetrius, Philo, Eupolemus.[176] The identification, however, is far from certain.[177] The *floruit* of Alexander Polyhistor in the mid-first century B.C.E. provides a *terminus ante quem,* and a date as early as the late second century seems quite possible. The poem reflects detailed knowledge of Jerusalem but

---

[171] See Gutman, 'Philo,' 38; Wacholder, *Eupolemus*, 282-3; Attridge, 'Philo.'

[172] For a translation of Timochares, see Stern, *Authors* 1, 135. See also the discussion and translation of *Schoinometresis Syriae*, which also is quoted by Polyhistor, Stern, *Authors* 1, 137-8. Common to *Aristeas* 88-90, Philo, fg. 6, and Sir 50:3 is reference to the water system of the temple, as well as a panegyrical tone.

[173] Fg. 6, with its reference to the temple, indicates that this institution and its functions were an important part of Philo's poem.

[174] See the discussion of Gutman, 'Philo,' 59-63.

[175] Gutman ('Philo,' 40-57) draws some far-reaching conclusions about the nature of Greek influence in the first fragment, but Wacholder ('Philo,' 407) does not agree. See also the different translation by Attridge, 'Philo.'

[176] For this identification, see Schürer, *Literature,* 223-24; and Denis, *Introduction,* 270-71.

[177] The identification is questioned by Wacholder, 'Philo,' 407; and Attridge, 'Philo.'

need not point to a Palestinian origin. The author's knowledge of Jerusalem could have come from a written source or an extended stay in the city.[178] Egyptian writings such as the *Sibylline Oracles,* the *Epistle of Aristeas,* and 3 Maccabees, indicate sufficient interest in Jerusalem to justify the Alexandrian provenance to which other Hellenistic aspects of the poem may point.[180]

THEODOTUS THE EPIC POET

Eusebius' extracts from Alexander Polyhistor which preserve fragments attributed to Theodotus' epic poem *On the Jews* differ in significant ways from the preserved fragments of Philo's *On Jerusalem.* As to length, the forty-seven hexameter lines and additional prose summary are well over twice the amount preserved from Philo. The fragments, moreover, are gathered in one place (*Praepar. evang.* 9:22, under the heading of Jacob), and the editorial comments indicate that they were drawn from a single context. Together they retell a single incident in the Bible, whose general narrative shape we can reconstruct. The subject matter is the rape of Dinah and the sack of Shechem (cf. Gen 33:18-34:31).

Because the summaries and fragments reproduce most of the essentials of the biblical account and comprise, in themselves, a unified and understandable whole, it is probable that they faithfully reproduce most, if not all, of the relevant part of Polyhistor's text. His technique here was to present a prose summary followed by a fragment of the poem, drawn either from the part summarized or from the material immediately following it. There are eight such fragments with prose introductions and a brief concluding prose summary.

The first summary and fragment introduce the story by providing its setting (9:22,1). In *On the Jews,* Theodotus explained the name and origin of Shechem (summary) and described features of its geographical setting and physical appearance (nine lines of description are quoted). Fragment 2 and its prose introduction (9:22,2) anticipate the outcome of the story (Shechem was conquered by the Hebrews when Hamor was its ruler) and introduce the characters (Jacob, Hamor, and his son Shechem). The third segment is a flashback (9:22,3), briefly describing Jacob's arrival in Mesopotamia and his activities there. The prose introduction summarizes the fifteen line fragment that follows. Jacob fled to Mesopotamia after a dispute with his brother. He was received by Laban and married his two

---

[178] On Philo's possible connections with Jerusalem, see Wacholder, *Eupolemus,* 282-83. However, his conjecture that Philo was a member of 'the highest echelons of the priestly class' is scarcely justified on the basis of the fragments. Interest in temple and cult is hardly evidence of priestly status.

[180] Alexandria is suggested as a possibility by Attridge, 'Philo.'

daughters. They bore him eleven sons, who were very wise, and a daughter, Dinah, who was beautiful and of noble spirit.

The introduction of these characters prepares us for the action in the first major scene,[181] which is depicted in a lengthy prose summary (9:22,4-5) and two quotations (9:22,6-7). When Jacob arrived in Shechem,[182] Hamor received him and provided him with land (Gen 33:18-19), where he worked with his eleven sons and his daughter Dinah. The story of Dinah's visit to Shechem, her rape, and Hamor's and Shechem's visit to Jacob are briefly recounted (cf. Gen 34:1-17). This lengthy summary is followed by two poetic fragments of three or four lines (probably taken from the part of the poem summarized in prose)[183] which provide the rationale for circumcision. Fragment 4 (9:22,6) corresponds roughly to Genesis 34:14-16: Hebrews may marry only persons of their own race. Fragment 5, which appeared in the poem 'a little below' the previous one, makes reference to the divine institution of the Abrahamic covenant of circumcision (9:22,7; cf. Gen 17:1-14).

Fragments 6 and 7, which comprise scene two of the story, are an addition to the biblical account which provides a rationale for Simeon's and Levi's attack on Shechem (9:22,8-9) that is paralleled in contemporary Jewish writings. The action is initiated by Simeon, who co-opts his brother,[184] and it is based on a divine oracle that God would give ten peoples to the children of Abraham (frag. 6).[185] God prompted the brothers to attack the city because its inhabitants were 'impious' (ἀσεβεῖς) and did evil to whoever came to them' (frag. 7).[186]

A third scene completes the story. Two prose lines summarize the attack on Shechem (cf. Gen 34:25-26a): Levi and Simeon enter the city fully armed (καθωπλισμένους),[187] kill whomever they meet and then dispatch Hamor and Shechem.[188] A poetic fragment of seven lines describes the

---

[181] Not only are Jacob and his eleven sons and daughters mentioned at the beginning of the next scene, but Dinah's beauty will be the cause of the incident.

[182] This item at the beginning of this summary (9:22,4) recalls the last item in the previous summary (9:22,3).

[183] The last line of 9:22,5 (Hamor agrees to the circumcision) presumes Jacob's speeches here recorded and links with opening line in 9:22,8, which begins the second scene.

[184] The order, Simeon and Levi, follows the biblical account (Gen 34:25), but the prominence of Simeon is asserted in Jdt 9:2. See also the next note.

[185] Cf. T. Levi 5:3, where Levi receives an angelic commission to avenge the deed; 6:1, where he finds a shield; and 6:8, where he 'saw' God's sentence against Shechem. For Levi as a visionary and prophet, cf. also Jos. As. 22:13; 23:8, and on the typology between this story and that of Shechem, see above, pp. 66-7. In view of the tradition of Levi as a prophet, the ascription of the oracle to Simeon here is odd and may reflect some confusion or manipulation of the tradition.

[186] Cf. T. Levi 6:8-10.

[187] Cf. T. Levi 5:3, where Levi receives a sword and shield from the angel, and 6:1, where he finds a shield.

[188] The order Simeon/Levi and Hamor/Shechem follows Gen 34:25-26. T. Levi 6:4 reverses the order but attributes the deaths of the two men to Levi and Simeon respectively.

murderous act in detail. Three prose lines about the pillaging of the city and the rescue of Dinah (cf. Gen 34:26b-29) conclude the account and the extracts from Theodotus.

The story as recounted by Polyhistor is remarkable for its unity and narrative flow. The scene is set. The characters are introduced. The action follows with due explanation of the characters' motivations. These motivations and other hints of the author's point of view — particularly as these are evident in his manipulation of the biblical material — provide some clues as to the book's provenance and author's purpose.

Our discussion will look at two competing claims about the provenance of the work. Conventional wisdom since Freudenthal (1875) has argued for a Samaritan origin.[189] According to this view, the title, *On the Jews*, given by Polyhistor is simply wrong. Rather the epic described the history of 'the holy city' (ἱερὸν ἄστυ) Shechem, and may even have been entitled *On the Foundation of Shechem*.[190] Most recently Collins has offered a detailed refutation of this view and argued that Theodotus was 'a militant and exclusivistic Jew,' who here defends and glorifies Hyrcanus' conquest of Shechem.[191]

As we have observed, fragment 1, which is an addition to the biblical account, serves as an introduction to the story. The lush description of the landscape is paralleled by similar passages in Homer, which introduce such unhappy events as Odysseus' sojourn with Calypso (*Od.* 5:55-75) and his encounter with the Cyclops (*Od.* 9:105-142). These parallels neutralize claims that the poem was written in praise of Shechem.[192] That the epic itself spoke in detail about the foundation of Shechem or glorified the city cannot be determined from present evidence.[193] Of Shechem itself we hear no more in the preserved fragments.

Once Jacob and the two Shechemite princes are introduced, the story immediately focuses on Jacob. His arrival is told against the background of his exploits in Mesopotamia. His reception and subsequent deception by Laban appears to be an artistically contrived foil for his reception by Hamor and the subsequent violation of hospitality by his son.[194]

---

[189] Freudenthal, *Studien*, 99-100; Denis, *Introduction*, 272; Hengel, *Hellenism*, 1, 59, 89, 266; Wacholder, *Eupolemus*, 283-5.

[190] Jacoby, *Fragmente*, 3C, 2, no. 732.

[191] Collins, 'Theodotus.' The hypothesis of a Samaritan origin was previously challenged by Kippenberg, *Garizim*, 84; and Charlesworth, *Modern Research*, 210. See also now, Fallon, 'Theodotus.'

[192] Even less can it be shown that the description was intended as a counterpart of Philo's glorification of Jerusalem, as is suggested by Wacholder, *Eupolemus*, 283-4.

[193] Furthermore, the Homeric expression, 'the holy city,' need only reflect the biblical view that Shechem was a sacred site. See Collins, 'Theodotus,' 94.

[194] The verb, ὑποδέχομαι ('receive'), occurs 9:22,3 of Laban and 9:22,4 of Hamor. On the Shechemites' violations of hospitality, cf. also *T. Levi* 6:8-10.

Two factors in the first scene (frags. 4-5) argue for a Jewish provenance and against a Samaritan origin. The requirement of circumcision is set by Jacob and is explained as a divine ordinance. There is no hint that this demand is a deceitful ploy (contrast Gen 34:13). A similar tendency is evident in the second scene (frags. 6-7). We are not told that the Shechemites did in fact undergo circumcision. Thus the treachery of the brothers' attacking the helpless men is bypassed in silence.[195] This feature is more easily attributed to a Jewish than to a Samaritan author. More important, the slaughter of the Shechemites is described as a divinely sanctioned act of judgment on the impious Shechemites,[196] of whose lawless character and deeds the rape of Dinah was simply an example.[197] The viewpoint is hardly that of a Samaritan. The gory description of the murder of Hamor and Shechem has many parallels in the accounts of the Trojan war[198] and helps to arouse the emotions of the reader, who happily sees divine vengeance enacted.

In short, both in its own right and in comparison to the biblical account, the present story is easily explicable as a Jewish product and is completely mystifying in the context of a Samaritan hypothesis. Moreover, a number of the details which set this story off from its biblical counterparts are paralleled in such Jewish documents as the *Testament of Levi* 5-7, *Jubilees* 30, and Judith 9.[199]

This story appears to have a typological dimension that reflects contemporary Jewish-Samaritan hostility.[200] The Hebrews, the children of Abraham, are characterized by the rite of circumcision and are contrasted with the uncircumcized inhabitants of Shechem — who in the author's time would have been the Samaritans. Moreover, a divine oracle justifies the Hebrews' domination over 'ten people' — i.e., the land of the North.[201]

A determination of the precise nature of the hostility between Jews and Samaritans in the author's time depends upon the dating of the poem. This, however, is uncertain. In the light of archeological evidence, the description of the great wall in fragment 1 appears to point to a date before the middle of the second century B.C.E., when the great cyclopean wall fell into disuse.[202] Collins argues, on the other hand, that the story may well reflect Hyrcanus' conquest of Shechem (between 129 and 107 B.C.E.) and

---

[195] While an argument from this silence is not decisive, the circumcision is also not mentioned in *Jubilees* 30 and in the account by Josephus, *Ant.* 1:337-41. This suggests a common apologetic tendency; see Collins, 'Theodotus,' 97; and Fallon, 'Theodotus.'

[196] See also *T. Levi* 5-7; *Jub.*. 30:5-7; Jdt 9:2-4, all cited by Collins, 'Theodotus,' 96-97.

[197] Cf. *T. Levi* 6:8-11; 7:2-3 and Sir 50:26.

[198] As a single example that could be multiplied many times, cf. *Iliad* 17:617-19.

[199] See above, nn. 185-8, 194-7. The texts are part of the anti-Samaritan hypothesis of Collins, 'Theodotus,' and are also cited by Fallon, 'Theodotus.'

[200] Collins, 'Theodotus,' 98.

[201] *Ibid.*, 100.

[202] Bull, 'A Note,' 227.

that the author could have described an architectural feature known to him, even if it was no longer functional or in good repair.[203] The point is moot. The violent description in fragment 8 can be explained by epic style and anti-Samaritan invective. Other Jewish documents certainly written before Hyrcanus' attack retell or allude to the story of Shechem with an equallyu bitter tone.[204] Thus it remains unclear whether the present work describes or prescribes such an attack.

The extent of the original poem cannot be determined with any certainty. The title, *On the Jews,* suggests a scope considerably broader than the single incident now preserved. Whether the flashback technique in fragments 3 and 5 indicates that the poem did or did not include these incidents cannot be determined on the basis of present evidence.[205] In any case, the given title of the work and the content of the present story suggest that the poem was intended to serve as nationalistic propaganda, a function consonant with the epic form.[206] The poet's familiarity with the environs of Shechem suggests that the poem may have been written by a Palestinian, perhaps for a Diaspora Jewish audience.[207]

As its hexametric prosody indicates, the poem was composed in Greek, of condiserably higher quality than that of Philo the epic poet.[208] The literary considerations mentioned above also reflect the quality of Theodotus' artistry.

EZEKIEL THE TRAGEDIAN

'The Leading Out' (ἡ ἐξαγωγή) was the title of a drama composed in iambic trimeters — the usual tragic verse — by a certain 'Ezekiel the Poet of Tragedies.'[209] Two hundred sixty-nine verses of the drama have been preserved for us in the extracts of Alexander Polyhistor in Eusebius' *Praeparatio evangelica* 9:28-29.[210] The preserved fragments follow quite closely the biblical account, and specifically the text of the Septuagint,[211]

---

[203] Collins, 'Theodotus,' 101.

[204] On the dates of these documents, see above pp. 50f., 101-3.

[205] One can argue that the presence of the flashback implies that the incident has not been previously treated. However, see Collins, 'Theodotus,' 94.

[206] *Ibid.,* 102.

[207] *Ibid.,* 102-3.

[208] Thus uniformly, Schürer, *Geschichte* 3, 500; Gutman, 'Philo,' 36-37; Wacholder, *Eupolemus* 283-4; Collins, 'Theodotus,' 102.

[209] For this title, see Eusebius, *Praepar. evang.* 9:28.1. Clement of Alexandria refers to him as 'Ezekiel, the Poet of Jewish Tragedies' (*Strom.* 1:23).

[210] Two selections from the first fragment (lines 7-39, 50-54) are also preserved by Clement (*ibid.*), and lines 256-69, describing the phoenix bird, are reproduced without attribution in Pseudo-Eustathius' *Commentary on the Hexaemeron* (*PG* 18:729D, cited by Mras, 537). Line numbers given here are those of Robertson and follow the sequence of quoted text in Eusebius.

[211] For details, see Robertson, 'Ezekiel.'

with some concessions to dramatic convention and necessity and some additions reflecting Jewish exegetical tradition.

Polyhistor's fragments begin with a lengthy monologue by Moses, which functioned as the prologue to the drama (58 lines; *Praepar. evang.* 9:28, 2-3). Moses has just arrived in Midian (line 58).[212] Typical of the tragic prologue, the speech summarizes the past circumstances and events that provide a setting for the drama. These include Jacob's departure from Canaan and his arrival in Egypt, the oppression by the Egyptians, Moses' birth and his discovery by Pharaoh's daughter, his upbringing in the royal palace, and his slaying of the Egyptian and flight from Egypt — a pithy summary of Genesis 46 and Exodus 1:1-2:15. The comment after line 31 indicates that some material has been omitted, perhaps some extra-biblical details about Moses' infancy.[213]

The first Episode (or Act) described how Moses met and helped the daughters of the Midianite priest (Exod 2:16-17). Only seven lines are preserved, including a fragment of a speech in which Zipporah identified herself and her father (9:28, 4).

From Polyhistor's summary comment, it appears that the next Episode elaborated greatly on Exodus 2:18-21 and described Moses' marriage to Zipporah. In two lines of preserved dialogue, Zipporah discusses her (forthcoming?) marriage with a certain *Chous,* either her brother or a suitor.[214]

After interrupting his account of Ezekiel to include some material pertaining to Zipporah's genealogy drawn from the Jewish historian Demetrius (9:29, 1-3), Polyhistor returns to his account of the drama. Here he reproduces twenty-two lines of a dialogue in which Moses recounts a dream and his father-in-law interprets it (9:29, 4-6). The material is without counterpart in the biblical account. Structurally the scene was probably linked to the description of Moses' marriage.[215]

In his dream Moses is conveyed to Sinai's peak, where he sees a gigantic throne and upon it, God himself in human semblence. God bids him approach the throne, gives him the sceptre, seats him on the throne and crowns him. From the throne, Moses beholds the whole universe. According to the interpretation, Moses 'will cause a great throne to arise,' (line 95), and he himself will rule over mortals. His vision of the universe is inter-

---

[212] Cf. the wording of Exod 2:22.

[213] This comment is problematic because lines 30-31 reflect Exod 2:10b and lines 32-33 correspond to Exod 2:10a, while lines 34-35 suggest in brief retrospect what logically might have been the content of the section omitted by Polyhistor, viz., Moses' education by his mother.

[214] On the problem of this section, see Robertson, *ad loc.*

[215] If one wishes to limit Ezekiel's drama to a traditional five episodes, this scene must be tied to either the previous or succeeding fragment. A change of location to Mt. Horeb in the next fragment and the connection: Zipporah/Zipporah's father suggests that it should be linked with what precedes. For an analysis of this fragment, see Starobinski-Safran, 'Un poète'.

preted not cosmologically, but historically; he will see all things present, past, and future.

The use of a dream to foretell the future is a relatively common device in Greek drama.[216] In the present scene, however, a number of features indicate this author's indebtedness to Jewish tradition, as well. The description of God is reminiscent of the throne visions in Isaiah 6 and Ezekiel 1-2.[217] That the deity invites Moses to sit upon the throne can be related to the commissioning function of those visions. More important, it recalls the enthronement of the one like a son of man in Daniel 7 and, indeed, the first person account of Enoch's appointment as Son of Man in *1 Enoch* 71. Other features are paralleled in the account of Enoch's ascent in *1 Enoch* 14 and of Abraham's ascent in the *Apocalypse of Abraham* 19.[218] In general, the idea of the exaltation of a mortal has many parallels in Jewish tradition,[219] and the image of the stars prostrating themselves before Moses is probably drawn from the story of Joseph and his dream of exaltation.[220] Parallels between this passage and other Moses traditions are also evident. The tradition of Moses' vision of God's throne on Mount Sinai is rooted in Exodus 24:9-11. His vision of heaven and the cosmos is mentioned in *2 Baruch* 59:4-12, and Pseudo-Philo connects a similar vision with Moses' viewing of the land before his death (*LAB* 19:10).[221] Moses' knowledge of past, present, and future has its biblical base in Deuteronomy 32, but the idea is expanded in the *Testament of Moses*.[222] Moses' enthronement draws on the idea that the prophet was also king, an idea attested in Philo of Alexandria and the Rabbis and based on Deuteronomy 33:5.[223] His being seated upon God's throne may reflect Exodus 7:1 ('See, I make you as God to Pharaoh'). Whether line 85 implies a messianic hope as the fruition of royal functions of God, Moses, and the kings of Israel is uncertain.[224]

This evidence indicates that Ezekiel here reflects significant Jewish traditions about Moses and about enthronement. The twofold division of

[216] Cf. Aeschylus, *Persians* 181-214; *Choephori* 526-39; Sophocles, *Elektra* 417-30; Euripides, *Hecuba* 68-97; all cited by Snell, 'Ezechiels Moses-Drama,' 155; and Starobinski-Safran, 'Un poète,' 220.

[217] *Ibid.*

[218] Especially noteworthy in the *Apocalypse of Abraham* is the patriarch's view down through the spheres.

[219] See Nickelsburg, *Resurrection*, especially chapter 2.

[220] Starobinski-Safran, 'Un poète,' 220. On the Joseph story and the motif of exaltation, see Nickelsburg, *Resurrection*, 49.

[221] *2 Bar* 59 is cited by Starobinski-Safran, 'Un poète,' 221-2. For another Mosaic ascent text dated to the day of his death, see the texts from *Bereshit Rabbati*, translated by Attridge, 'The Ascension.'

[222] On the *Testament of Moses* as an expansion of the last chapters of Deuteronomy, see Harrington, 'Interpreting Israel's History.'

[223] Starobinski-Safran, 'Un poète,' 221. For a detailed discussion, see Meeks, 'The Prophet-King,' 107-17, 177-97. Cf. also below, pp. 267-8.

[224] This is suggested by Starobinski-Safran, 'Un poète,' 223-4.

the material into dream and interpretation, while it is not foreign to analogous scenes in Greek drama, may well indicate that Ezekiel has made use of an apocalyptic account of vision and interpretation.[225] The disparity between the content of the vision and that of the interpretation (here cosmology becomes history) is also a well known feature of such apocalyptic accounts.[226] That Ezekiel may have drawn on a Mosaic tradition seems quite possible. In any case, his insertion of the material provides a framework for his interpretation of Moses' activities in the remainder of the drama. According to lines 36-38, the young Moses was given a royal upbringing.[227] Here Ezekiel anticipates Moses' functions as ruler of Israel. The functions will, of course, include a confrontation with the Egyptian king.

The third Episode in the drama is Moses' encounter with God at the burning bush (*Praepar. evang.* 9:29, 7-13). Eusebius has preserved 103 lines of dialogue from Polyhistor's extracts. First Ezekiel describes the encounter and conversation at the bush, reproducing the substance of Exodus 3:1-4:17 with some rearrangement and additions (9:29,7-11; lines 90-131), which serve his dramatic purposes. By placing the material about Moses' staff (Exod 4:2-7) after the discussion about Moses' speech defect — Exod 4:10-16), he provides a link with the account of the ten plagues. Reference to the Nile turning to blood (Exod 4:9) leads to the actual account of the first plague, which is accomplished by means of Aaron's staff (Exod 7:17ff.). Thus still speaking in the future tense, but with no shift in scene, God moves into a description of the ten plagues (lines 131-51; cf. Exod 8-11) and from there into his commands for the Passover (lines 152-92; cf. Exod 12-13). This conflation and manipulation of the biblical material avoided an extra change in scene and presented the content of the dramatic events in Egypt while avoiding the difficulty of depicting them on stage.[228] While it is inappropriate to speak here of haggadic and halakhic material, it is noteworthy, nonetheless, that Ezekiel considers the celebration of Passover sufficiently significant for him to repeat in detail the divine commandments regarding its observance.

The fourth Episode of the drama recounted the Egyptians' pursuit of Israel and their destruction in the Sea (*Praepar. evang.* 9:29,14; cf. Exod 14). The event itself is not depicted, but the story is told in a fifty-line speech by a messenger, evidently the sole Egyptian survivor of the disaster. This scene would have been set in Egypt among the Egyptians. The device of a messenger narrating action that taste or the limits of the theater prevented from being depicted on stage is a well known convention of

---

[225] For examples of such accounts, cf. Dan 7 and *1 Enoch* 17-32; 40; 46; 52-56.

[226] See, e.g., the discussion of *4 Ezra* in Stone, 'The Concept.'

[227] See Meeks, *The Prophet-King*, 153.

[228] Thus Robertson, 'Ezekiel.'

Greek drama. An unmistakable parallel and probably the model for this scene is the messenger's description of the Persian defeat in Aeschylus' *The Persians* 353-514.[229]

The fifth and final Episode was set among the palms of Elim (*Praepar. evang.* 9:29,16; cf. Exod 15:27). A person unidentified by Polyhistor speaks to Moses, commenting on the lush beauty of the place (lines 243-53). Among the creatures inhabiting the oasis with its palm trees (φοῖνιχες) was the phoenix bird (φοῖνιξ)[230] whose beauty is described in the sixteen lines that conclude the fragments from Ezekiel's drama. The descriptions of the place and the bird are consonant with one another and suggest that Ezekiel is depicting Elim as a kind of paradise.

In *The Exodus*, Ezekiel has employed a major Greek literary genre to interpret Israelite history. His combination of content and form was a good one. The scriptural material and its development in the Jewish tradition offered a rich potential for the development of character and plot and the presentation of dramatic action. That the story had the status of a national epic made it all the more a prime candidate for dramatic presentation. Although Ezekiel may not have been a great and significant poet, the surviving fragments indicate that this work did have its moments of beauty and dramatic effect.[231] His 'metrics are competent,'[232] and his knowledge and use of dramatic technique and tradition are readily evident.[233] Although his focus on an historical event differs from dramatic practice of the classical period,[234] the fragments suggest that the figure of Moses was central and crucial to the action.

Two features of the fragments are best explained by the hypothesis that the drama was created for actual representation on the stage [235]: the avoidance of scenes that were unpresentable; God's explicit statement that he could be heard but not seen. The occasion for such a presentation is uncertain; however, the detailed recounting of commands regarding Passover suggest that the play would have been of special interest in the passover season. The precise function of such a presentation cannot be ascertained on the basis of the fragments. Nonetheless, it would have offered a Jewish audience a drama from their own rather than from gentile religious tradition, and that in itself would certainly have been a motivat-

---

229 Snell, 'Ezechiels Moses-Drama,' 154.
230 For the association of the phoenix and the palm tree, see Ovid, *Metamorphoses* 15, 391-400, cited by Robertson, 'Ezekiel.' On the myth of the phoenix, see van der Broek, *The Myth*.
231 Snell, 'Ezechiels Moses-Drama,' 151, 164, 153.
232 Strugnell, 'Ezekiel,' 453.
233 See Snell, 'Ezechiels Moses-Drama,' 154-7.
234 Robertson, 'Ezekiel.'
235 See Schürer, *Geschichte* 3, 502; Snell, 'Ezechiels Moses-Drama,' 153-4; Robertson, 'Ezekiel.'

ing factor for an author writing in a center of Hellenistic culture and learning.[236]

Whether that center of culture was Alexandria is debatable.[237] Knowledge and use of the legend of the phoenix may support such a conclusion.[238] In such a case, the play would have served to maintain one's Jewish identity over against those gentiles in one's immediate environs.[239]

The date of writing is uncertain. A *terminus post quem* is the third century B.C.E., when the Greek translation of the Torah — which Ezekiel quotes — was first made. A *terminus ad quem* is the mid-first century B.C.E., when Polyhistor excerpted his fragments.[240]

Concerning Ezekiel himself we have no external evidence except the title 'The poet of (Jewish) Tragedies,' which indicates that *The Exodus* was not his only dramatic work.

Supplements to Biblical Books

In the previous part of this chapter we discussed works that interpreted biblical stories by retelling and paraphrasing them, often adding new material. Here we shall discuss supplements to biblical books, i.e., blocks of text interpolated into, or added to the form of the biblical books that is known to us in the canonical Hebrew Bible. In the case of 1 Esdras, Esther, Jeremiah, and Daniel, these supplements have been transmitted in the Septuagint. However, the brief narrative entitled 'the Songs of David' has been preserved only in the Hebrew Qumran Psalter (11QPs^a). Some of these additions, supplements, and interpolations surely existed independently of the biblical texts with which they are now associated. In their present context, however, they interpret the earlier forms of the texts. In this respect their function is akin to that of the texts discussed in the first part of this chapter.

In this section there is a problem of classification; some of the present texts could have been grouped with works treated elsewhere in this volume. For example, Baruch could have been placed with the wisdom literature, and the additions to Daniel, with Psalms, Hymns, and Prayers. They are discussed here because of their function as interpretations of Scripture.

The biblical interpretation in these supplements is of two sorts. At many

---

[236] See Holladay, 'Portrait.'

[237] An Alexandrian provenance is generally accepted; see Wacholder, *Eupolemus*, 286; Snell, 'Ezechiels Moses-Drama,' 151. Robertson ('Ezekiel') argues that the evidence is indecisive.

[238] On the connections between Egypt and the phoenix, see Rush, 'Phoinix: Der Wundervogel,' 416-19.

[239] Other works of likely Egyptian provenance which take a rather dim view of the Egyptians include Wisdom of Solomon and 3 Maccabees. On *Joseph and Aseneth*, see above, pp. 69f.

[240] Attempts to date the work to the time of the supposed appearance of the phoenix are speculative, Robertson, 'Ezekiel.'

points, the contents of the supplements interpret a wide variety of biblical material. For example, the Song of the Three Young Men in the Greek Daniel is a variation on a number of biblical psalms, and the last part of Baruch paraphrases Second Isaiah. More immediately, however, all these supplements interpret the biblical books in or alongside of which they have been placed.

Since all but one of these texts have been preserved only in the Greek Bible,[241] it is convenient to discuss all of them — including the Hebrew addition to the Psalter — in the order of the books' occurrence in the Septuagint.

THE STORY OF DARIUS' BODYGUARDS
(1 Esdras 3-4)

1 Esdras is extant only in the Greek Bible and the versions dependent on it.[242] Its contents parallel 2 Cronicles 35-36, the book of Ezra, and Nehemiah 7:73-8:13. The order of some of the material from Ezra has been rearranged, and there are some additions from other sources. The most significant of these is the story we discuss here.

In its present context in 1 Esdras the story relates the incident responsible for the completion of the Second Temple.[243] King Darius has summoned all his rulers and feted them to a great banquet (3:1-3). Afterwards, when he has retired, his three bodyguards devise a contest. Each of them will propose the one thing that he considers 'the strongest.' The king will then bestow great honours on the one whose proposal seems the wisest (3:4-7). The three proposals are: 'Wine is the strongest'; 'The king is the strongest'; 'Women are the strongest, but truth is victorious over all' (3:8-12). The next day the king summons his rulers to his council chamber and commands the three bodyguards to defend their proposals (3:12-17a).

The speeches parallel one another in form and rhetoric.[244] They begin and close with similar formulae. Throughout, the three speakers appeal to the audience to agree with them, employing the negative form of the rhetorical question: 'Is not . . .? Does not . . .?' The author's ingenuity lies not simply in the cleverness and humour of their assertions and in their ability to support the respective propositions, but, more important, in the manner in which each speaker oversteps the previous arguments.[245]

For the first bodyguard, wine is the strongest (3:17b-24). Its power over men can be seen in its capacity to transform and lead their minds astray,

---

[241] The story of the three bodyguards in 1 Esdras 3-4 is also recounted by Josephus in *Ant.* 11:33-58, but this is dependent on a form of 1 Esdras.

[242] On 1 Esdras see below, pp. 157-60.

[243] On the relationship of the story to its context, see below, n. 265.

[244] For further details, see Crenshaw, 'The Contest,' 80.

[245] *Ibid.,* 81.

and to erase all social distinctions. According to the second bodyguard, the king is the strongest (4:1-12). As the king's rulers here present can attest, men are strong, for they rule over land and seas and all that is in them. The king, however, is stronger, because he is lord over all these rulers. The point is illustrated by a series of examples, all formulated in a stereotyped way. The third bodyguard — now identified as Zerubbabel — discourses on women and truth (4:13-32, 33-40). He agrees that the king is great, men are many, and wine is strong. But it is women who rule and lord it over all of these. They give birth to the king, the people who rule over sea and land (cf. 4:2), and those who plant the vineyards that produce the wine. In that sense women are superior to all that the previous speeches have acclaimed as strongest. Furthermore, women receive the same attention, obedience, and benefits that kings receive. If wine leads men's minds astray, women cause men to *lose* their minds (4:26). For women, men perish and stumble and sin (4:27). Surely the king is mighty and feared by all, but even he is not exempt from the power of women. With a touch of ironic humour, Zerubbabel depicts Darius as a captive to the whims and antics of his concubine, Apamē (4:29-31).

The king and his nobles look at one another, probably less in agreement with his wisdom than in astonishment at his outspokenness.[246] However, before they can respond, Zerubbabel outdoes himself by launching into a second speech (4:33-41), this one on the unsurpassed power of truth. It is a brilliant stroke. While the speech is interesting and important in its own right and as a refutation of all the previous speeches, its immediate function is to disarm any objections to Zerubbabel's irreverent observations about the king's conduct. If these were true, they cannot be objected to. This is, in effect, admitted at the end, when truth is acclaimed.

In this speech Zerubbabel follows the technique employed in the previous speeches, arguing or asserting the superiority of the object of his praise over those previously discussed. Here, however, it is not simply a matter of superiority. Rather, the absoluteness of truth relativizes all that has been previously mentioned. 'Truth' is here a polyvalent term. It has connotations not only of truth, but also of rightness, steadfastness, and uprightness.[247] As a quality of God, it excludes its opposite, unrighteousness, which characterizes everything that has been previously praised: wine, the king, women, all the sons of men and their deeds (4:36b-37). Moreover

---

[246]Laqueur ('Ephoros,' 170) sees the natural continuation of 4:33 in 4:41, with 4:34-40 as an interpolation (see below). This does not exclude our interpretation of 4:33 in the present form of the story.

[247] ἀλήθεια may here reflect the Aramaic קושטא . See Torrey, 'Nature and Origin,' 25. קושטא in the Aramaic Targum translates both צדק and אמת in Hebrew. Likewise, preserved fragments of the Aramaic of *1 Enoch* 91ff. indicate that קושטא stands behind both ṣedeq and *rete* in the Ethiopic of that work, indicating that the single Aramaic term was rendered both as 'uprightness' and 'truth' by the Greek translator.

truth exacts righteous judgment from all who are unjust and wicked and shows no partiality (a further defense of Zerubbabel's asserting the truth about the king). Thus, to truth belong all the qualities that would seem to belong to wine, the king, and women, viz., strength, kingship, authority, and greatness, and they are hers forever. Therefore 'Blessed is the God of Truth' (4:40).

The people acclaim truth as great and strongest of all (4:41), and the king offers Zerubbabel the great honours that the bodyguards had anticipated (4:42). When he requests, instead, that the temple be rebuilt and its vessels returned to Jerusalem, Darius agrees (4:42-57). Zerubbabel's prayer makes clear that it was God who gave him the wisdom that was victorious in this contest (4:58-60; cf. 3:4).

Although the story makes good sense in its present form and context, careful analysis indicates a number of literary problems that suggest that the story has been altered or revised in the course of its transmission. A difficulty is immediately evident in the opening verses.[248] According to 3:3, King Darius awoke before the guards devised their contest, although the subsequent action suggests that the king was still asleep (see especially v. 13). Moreover, it is unclear, under these circumstances, how the guards could be certain that the king would reward the winner of the contest. The version of the story in Josephus (*Ant.* 11:34—36) solves the problem by having Darius propose the contest and promise the rewards.[249] Further-more, a number of literary considerations suggest that the speech about truth is an intrusion into a story describing three guards giving three speeches,[250] and that the original story placed the speech about the king before the one about wine.[251] A natural (and naive) beginning is that the king is the strongest. The second bodyguard refutes this by showing how wine neutralizes the power of the king. The third shows how both of these are subject to the power of women. How the story might have ended and dealt with the affront to the king's dignity is uncertain.[252]

In its present form and context, the tale of the bodyguards is a Jewish story. Its hero is the builder of the Second Temple, and the story explains how he came to accomplish this feat. In doing so, it employs a tradition known to us in the stories in Daniel 1-6 (see above, pp. 34-35). The

---

[248] On these problems, Zimmermann, 'Story,' 181-2.

[249] Zimmermann, *ibid.*, 194-7, posits that Josephus knew an earlier version of the story. For another view, see below p. 158f.

[250] Laqueur, 'Ephoros,' 170-71. In particular he notes that in 3:3 the three bodyguards agree to speak of *one* thing, but that Zerubbabel breaks the rules by speaking about two. He also sees 4:34-40 as an intrusion between 4:33 and 4:41, and he makes reference to other problems. He is followed by Pohlmann, *Studien*, 39-40.

[251] Laqueur, 'Ephoros,' 171. Crenshaw ('The Contest,' 82) disagrees.

[252] Since the story is clearly unhistorical, ideas as to what could or could not have happened in such circumstances cannot govern a reconstruction of the story.

Jewish youth pits his divinely given wisdom (4:58-60) against that of his gentile colleagues in the Mesopotamian court, and he wins both the contest and the king's favour.[253] The story climaxes with an acclamation of God and a doxology of his truth. Other features in the story — the various observations about wine and women and kings — have many parallels in Jewish wisdom literature, and the Jewish audience of 1 Esdras would have read them in such a context.[254] Especially close to the Bible are statements about a man forsaking his parents for his wife (4:20-21; cf. Gen 2:24) and claims about the power and eternity of truth (4:38; cf. Ps 117:2; 146:6).[255]

Nonetheless, a majority of scholars have rightly argued that the story is most likely of non-Jewish origin.[256] Parallels to Jewish wisdom literature do not prove Jewish origin, since this wisdom literature itself reflects a broader, international tradition.[257] Even the formulation about the eternity of truth — though it may have been drawn from the Bible — has close parallels in Egyptian wisdom sayings.[258] When the story is read apart from its present context, there is little in it that is unambiguously Jewish. The identification of the third bodyguard as Zerubbabel is a secondary intrusion.[259] The parallels to the Danielic stories, which provide a broad literary analogy to the tale, are themselves based on non-Jewish models.[260] Taken as a whole, the story has many parallels in the folklore of many nations.[261] In short, the Jewish author of 1 Esdras has revised a gentile story and reused it as a catalyst for a crucial event in Israelite history. God endows Zerubbabel with the wisdom that enables him to win the contest and secure the king's permission to rebuild the temple.

Although scholars have debated the original language of the story, there is some consensus that it was composed in Aramaic rather than in semiticizing Greek.[262] The story's time and place of origin are uncertain. Torrey identified the concubine Apamē with the Persian wife of Ptolemy I

[253] Parallels with the story of Esther have also been noted; see Torrey ('Story,' 47-48), who also discusses parallels with Daniel.

[254] See Myers, *I and II Esdras,* 54-56, and Crenshaw, 'The Contest,' 77-79. Especially noteworthy is the similarity between 1 Esdras 4:6-9 and the series in Eccl 3:1-9, cited in *ibid.,* 85-86.

[255] See Pohlmann, *Studien,* 44.

[256] See Torrey, 'Story,' 45-46; Laqueur, 'Ephoros,' 172; Rudolf, 'Der Wettstreit,' 179; Zimmermann, 'Story,' 185, 197-98; Pfeiffer, *History,* 251-57; Pohlmann, *Studien,* 40-47.

[257] Cf. below pp. 283-4.

[258] Humbert, 'Magna est veritas.'

[259] Torrey, 'Story', 57; Pohlmann, *Studien,* 38. The identification occurs very late in the story and breaks into the context.

[260] This is evident from the similarities between these stories and the originally non-Jewish story of Ahikar. Cf. below, p. 284.

[261] See Laqueur, 'Ephoros,' 172; Pfeiffer, *History,* 252-54; Crenshaw, 'The Contest,' 74-76.

[262] See Torrey, 'Nature and Origin,' 23-25; Zimmermann, 'Story,' 183-94 — even if one does not agree with all the alleged mistranslations from Aramaic; and Pohlmann, *Studien,* 48-49. Rudolf ('Der Wettstreit,' 182-85) argues for a Greek origin.

and suggested that the story originated either in Egypt or Palestine ca. 300 B.C.E.[263] However, the identification of Apamē is uncertain, as are any conclusions about date and place of origin based on it.[264]

The circumstances and manner in which the story was incorporated into 1 Esdras and the literary origins of 1 Esdras itself are matters that continue to be discussed.[265]

ADDITIONS TO THE BOOK OF ESTHER

The Greek translation of Esther includes six passages not found in the Hebrew version of the book, and they are universally recognized to be additions to the Hebrew version.[266] Alongside these additions, certain passages in the Hebrew have been changed. When Saint Jerome revised the Old Latin version of the Bible, he removed all but the last of the additions and appended them as a collection at the end of the canonical book. In this position they received the chapter and verse numbers found in modern editions. Here is the order of the Greek translation:

Hebrew Text	Additions
	A. 11:2-12:6, introduction, Mordecai's dream, transition
1:1-3:13	
	B. 13:1-7, Artaxerxes' decree of extermination
3:14-4:17	
	C. 13:8-14:19, Mordecai's, Esther's prayers
5:1-2 (omitted)	D. 15:1-16, Esther before the King
5:3-8:12	
	E. 16:1-24, Artaxerxes' decree
8:13-10:3	
	F. 10:1-11:1, interpretation of dream, conclusion, colophon

Some of the alterations in the Greek are paralleled in other of the old court tales (see above, pp. 34-35) and especially in 3 Maccabees (se above, pp. 83-84).

Additions A and F. The book is framed by Mordecai's dream and its interpretation. The battle of the dragons (representing Mordecai and

---

[263] Torrey, 'Story,' 39-42.

[264] Myers, *I and II Esdras,* 55.

[265] On this very difficult problem, see below, pp. 159-60, Torrey, 'Nature and Origin'; Pfeiffer, *History,* 233-50; Pohlmann, *Studien,* 32-73. On the relationship between the text of 1 Esdras and the canonical material, see Klein, *Studies.*

[266] See Moore, *Additions,* 153-54.

Haman), the phenomena in heaven and earth, and the gentiles' preparation for war against the Jews add a cosmic dimension to the tale. In the midst of this tumult appears Esther, depicted as a tiny spring become a river, God's appointed deliverer sent in answer to the people's prayer. Chapter 12 (Gk A:12-17) expands on 2:21-23, which is then altered at that place in the Greek translation to indicate that Mordecai's promotion was the cause of the conspiracy against the king (cf. Dan 6:3-4).

Addition B. The 'copy' of Artaxerxes' decree adds a note of authenticity to the narrative. [267] The charges against the Jews (13:3-5) elaborate on 3:8, stressing the Jews' peculiarity and alleged disobedience by adding the motifs of hostility and strangeness. This hostility and other wording unique to 13:4-7 are paralleled in 3 Maccabees 3:7, 24-26.[268]

Addition C. The prayers of Mordecai and Esther add an important religious dimension that is not explicit in the Hebrew book. The deliverance of the Jews comes in response to prayer. Mordecai's prayer is roughly paralleled by the prayers of Simon and Eleazar in 3 Maccabees 2 and 6. Mordecai's 'remembrance' of all the works of the Lord (13:8, Gk. C:1) may indicate the priority of 3 Maccabees, where God's deeds are enumerated. In 14:2, Gk. C:13, Esther's acts of self-abasement constitute a foil for her self-adornment in 15:1, Gk. D:1.[269] Her prayer climaxes in a petition that God use her speech as an instrument of deliverance (14:13-14, Gk. C:24-25; cf. Jdt 9). Verses 15-18, Gk. C:26-29 answer questions about the propriety and problems of Esther's Jewish-gentile marriage.[270] The attack on the temple which Esther anticipates (14:9, Gk. C:20) is not mentioned earlier in the book. This may indicate the priority of 3 Maccabees, where the king attempts to enter the temple and then contemplates its destruction (chaps. 1-2; 5:42-43; cf. also Esth 14:8, 10; 2 Macc 4:16).[271]

Addition D. This expansion and replacement of 5:1-2 adds a strong dramatic and emotive element to the story. Esther's audience with the king is depicted with language at home in biblical epiphanies.[272] Verses 2 and 8 interpret the king's response to Esther as an answer to her prayer, made the more dramatic and miraculous by the king's sudden change of disposition.

---

[267] For a similar use of documents, see above, p. 76, the *Letter of Aristeas.*

[268] Comparisons with 3 Maccabees are based on Motzo, 'Rifacimento,' 275-80.

[269] For a metaphorical use of this double imagery, cf. Bar 4:20; 5:1-2.

[270] Cf. the Greek revision of 2:20.

[271] It is also possible that there is some connection with Artaxerxes' decree that the building of the temple cease; cf. Ezra 4:6-24.

[272] Cf. the language and imagery in Gk. Esther 15:1-7 with *1 Enoch* 14:19-15:1, which doubtless reflects contemporary court protocol, but intensifies the imagery in a way that is also evident in Gk. Esther 15:1-7.

Addition E. This decree adds a note of authenticity. More important, it resolves tensions created in the first part of the story. God has judged the arrogant enemy who accused his people (16:2-6). Thereby he vindicates their innocence, which is acclaimed by the king (16:15-16), who also publicly acclaims the universal sovereignty of this God (16:21). These elements are all typical of the tales about the persecuted righteous (see above, pp. 34f., 37f.). Verbatim parallels indicate a close relationship between 16:3-6, 10-16 and 3 Maccabees 6:23-28; 7:2; 3:18; and 5:20.

In the Hebrew book of Esther, a tale about a persecuted and exalted courtier (Mordecai) is the nucleus of a story about the persecution and rescue of the Jewish people.[273] The additions and changes in the Greek version underscore some tendencies in the Hebrew book and serve a number of literary, religious, and theological purposes.

From a literary point of view, the additions and changes embellish and reinforce the genre and sharpen the focus on the fate of the people, here 'the righteous nation' (11:9). They also enhance the book's dramatic appeal and add a note of authenticity.[274]

More important to the reviser's purpose, the additions and changes add an explicitly religious dimension to the original form of the book, which never mentions God. The nation is God's people (10:9), and their deliverance is from him and in answer to prayer. The temple is of concern. Also in focus from time to time is the propriety of Esther's marriage to a gentile and her life-style in his court (14:15-18; 2:20).

The additions to Esther may have accreted in stages. Sections A, C, D, F give some indications of having been composed in Hebrew and added to a Hebrew form of the book, while sections B and E appear to have been composed in Greek.[275] The precise relationship between the Greek Esther and 3 Maccabees is uncertain. Parallels between 3 Maccabees and the parts of the Greek Esther that were possibly translated from Hebrew might suggest that 3 Maccabees is dependent on the whole of the Greek Esther. However, if the prayers and decrees were added to Esther in Greek, the Greek version as a whole may well be dependent on 3 Maccabees.[276] The purpose of such a revision might have been to introduce into Egyptian Jewry the celebration of the feast of Purim in the place of the festival that commemorated the Jews' deliverance from death in the hippodrome.[277]

---

[273] Nickelsburg, *Resurrection*, 50-51.
[274] Moore, *Additions*, 153.
[275] On the issue of the original language, see *ibid.*, 155 and the literature cited there.
[276] Motzo ('Rifacimento') argues the dependence of the Greek Esther upon 3 Maccabees. Moore *(Additions,* 197-99), who does not cite Motzo, compares 3 Maccabees with both the Hebrew and Greek Esther. 3 Maccabees is dependent on the Hebrew book, but the Greek version may be dependent in some places on 3 Maccabees.
[277] Motzo, 'Rifacimento,' 287-90.

The Greek Esther is preserved in two forms.[278] The first of these, attested in almost all manuscripts of the Septuagint, follows the content of the Masoretic text quite closely, but is often free and paraphrastic in its translation. The second form is preserved in only four minuscules.[279] It is shorter than the Septuagint at many points and contains many Hebraisms not found in the Septuagint. The very small incidence of verbatim agreement between the two versions may well indicate that they are separate translations, based on somewhat different Hebrew texts, rather than recensions of a single translation. If there were two separate translations, the additions would have been borrowed by one translation from the other.[280]

The colophon in the Septuagint (11:1) attributes the translation to 'Lysimachus the son of Ptolemy, one of the residents of Jerusalem,' and indicates that it was brought to Egypt during the fourth year of the reign of Ptolemy and Cleopatra, that is in 77 B.C.E. (Ptolemy XII)[281] or, less likely, 114 B.C.E. (Ptolemy VIII).[282]

DAVID'S COMPOSITIONS

This prose passage of ten lines is extant only in the Qumran *Psalms Scroll,* where it has been inserted between 2 Samuel 23:1-7 and Psalm 140 (11QPs^a 27:2-11).[283] Two statements about David's inspiration frame an enumeration of his poetic compositions.

Wisdom language fills the opening lines (2-4). David was a sage (חכם) and a learned man, or scribe (סופר), enlightened by God and enlightening others. According to line 11, he was the recipient of words of prophecy from the Most High. The obvious source of these ideas is 2 Samuel 23:1-4, the psalm that precedes this passage.[284]

The combination of wisdom and prophetic attributes is not the fortuitous result of this author's dependence on passages about David which mention such attributes. In Sir 24:30-34, the sage likens wisdom to prophecy, as he speaks of his own activity, also employing the light metaphor.[285] Thus the author of the present passage describes David's activities in categories current in Palestinian Judaism of the Greco-Roman

---

[278] For a discussion of the text and relevant bibliography, see Moore, *Additions,* 162-65.

[279] See Hanhart, *Esther,* 15.

[280] Moore (*Additions,* 165) thinks it likely that the additions originated in the Septuagint text.

[281] See Bickerman, 'The Colophon.'

[282] This dating is accepted by Moore, *Additions,* 250.

[283] On the non-canonical contents and order of tha Scroll, see Sanders, *Dead Sea,* 10-14. For the text of this passage, a translation, and some commentary, see *ibid.,* 134-37; and the *editio princeps, id., Psalms Scroll,* 91-93. For the passage in context, see *ibid.,* 48. The title here given is drawn from these publications.

[284] Sanders (*Psalms Scroll,* 92) cites this passage, as well as 2 Sam 14:20 and 1 Sam 16:12b-23.

[285] See Hengel, *Hellenism* 2, 134-6.

period. Wisdom, like prophecy, is 'given' by God (lines 3, 11). The emphasis on David's wisdom is also consonant with the presence of several non-canonical sapiential psalms in the Qumran *Psalms Scroll*.[286]

David's inspired wisdom is embodied in his poetic compositions, which the central part of this passage enumerates in categories (lines 4-10). These compositions — a total of 4,050 — include 3,600 psalms (תהלים) and 450 songs (שיר). Among the latter are: 364 to be sung over the *tamid* offering, one each day of the year; 52 for the *korban* offering on the sabbaths; thirty for various festivals, and four for making music over the stricken.[287]

The place of its insertion into the *Psalms Scroll* indicates that this passage is primarily an interpretation of the psalm known to us from 2 Samuel 23. It draws upon and emphasizes the psalm's description of David as an inspired psalmist and prophet, and it elaborates on this by an enumeration of his compositions.

The categories in this enumeration indicate the author's special interest in the cult and in the cultic function of the psalter. The specifying of 364 psalms for the daily offering presumes the solar calendar known in *Jubilees* and in Qumranic calendrical texts and indicates that this passage was penned by a member of the Qumran community or someone with similar views on the calendar.[288] If it is Qumranic, it is important as a testimony to a continuing interest in the temple cult in a group that had cut itself off from that cult.

There is an evident connection between this passage and 1 Kings 4:29-34 (Heb. 5:9-14), which describes Solomon's wisdom and his literary output. In such a case, it is probably not by accident that the total of David's compositions exceeds Solomon's 3,000 proverbs and 1,005 songs.[289] A comparison with Solomon's wisdom — also 'given' by God (1 Kgs 4:29, Heb. 5:9) — would also be implicit, although mention of David's wisdom here was generated by the factors mentioned above.

The insertion of this passage into the psalter and the inclusion of 2 Samuel 23 and the apocryphal Psalm 151 (termed by Sanders 'a poetic midrash on I Sam 16:1-13')[290] reflect a developing tendency to associate the psalter with David.[291] Traditional interpretations of first century Jewish religious thought have stressed David's role as patriarch of the royal

---

[286] Sanders, *Psalms Scroll*, 92.
[287] On the identification of psalms belonging to these various categories, see Sanders, *Psalms Scroll*, 93, and the bibliography cited in *ibid.*, 92, n. 1.
[288] *Ibid.* On *Jubilees*, see above, p. 100. On Qumran, see below, p. 530.
[289] Sanders, *Psalms Scroll*, 92. For the Masoretic text's 1005 songs, the Septuagint reads 5000.
[290] *Ibid.*, 56. It is noteworthy that this scroll contains two interpretations of biblical passages about David.
[291] *Ibid.*, 92; Sanders, *Dead Sea*, 157-8.

messianic line. The present passage, with its portrait of David as sage, prophet, and the composer of cultic songs par excellence, offers us a glimpse of a broader range of Davidic speculation, which may set some of the old texts in new perspectives. Noteworthy in this respect is Acts 2:25-36, which interprets the Davidic Psalm 16 to refer to Jesus, mentioning that David was a prophet (2:30-31).[292] In a more general framework, 'David's Compositions' provides further testimony to the diversity of early Judaism.

BARUCH

This is the first of several works attributed to Baruch, the secretary of Jeremiah. It stands after the book of Jeremiah in many manuscripts of the Greek Bible. The work divides into four sections of diverse origins: narrative introduction (1:1-14); prayer (1:15-3:8); wisdom poem (3:9—4:4); and Zion poem (4:5-5:9). These sections are bound together by the common theme of Exile and Return, which is often expressed in biblical idiom.

The introduction (1:1-14) describes the alleged purpose of the book and the circumstances of its origin. In the fifth year after the destruction of Jerusalem (i.e., in 582 B.C.E.), Baruch assembled the Jewish leaders in Babylon for a formal hearing of the book.[293] After rituals of repentance, they contributed money to be sent to Jerusalem together with the temple vessels that Nebuchadnezzar had taken as booty. The high priest was to offer sacrifice, pray for Nebuchadnezzar and his son Belshazzar, and intercede for the exiles in the words of the prayer that constitutes the second section of the book.

The prayer (1:15-3:8) is comprised of a corporate confession of sins and a petition that God will withdraw his wrath and return the exiles to their homeland.[294] Its logic follows the scheme of Deuteronomy 28-32, and the language of both Deuteronomy and Jeremiah has heavily influenced its wording.[295] Verbal parallels to Daniel 9:4-19 indicate a very close relationship also to that prayer.[296]

The inhabitants of Jerusalem are first to confess their own sins[297] and

---

[292] Although this passage may imply that David uses the first person because he is speaking of his descendent, it speaks only of his function as prophet and not as messianic forebear.

[293] For this meaning of 'to read in one's hearing,' see Orlinsky, 'The Septuagint,' 94-96.

[294] Moore (*Additions*, 291) suggests that 2:5-3:8 may originally have been three independent prayers; his divisions are unconvincing, however. 'And now . . .' (2:11) would hardly begin a prayer. 2:31-35 and 3:6-8 are logically related (see above) and represent similar clusters of motifs that are hardly coincidental.

[295] On Deuteronomy, see the notes in Whitehouse, 'Baruch,' 583ff; on Jeremiah, see Tov, *Baruch*, 13-27.

[296] See Moore, 'Dating,' 312-17; idem, *Additions*, 291-3.

[297] See 1:15 and 2:1-2 and note the contrast between 'we' in Jerusalem and 'they' in dispersion in 2:3-5.

140

admit that they are now suffering the curses of the covenant which Moses predicted in Deuteronomy (1:15-2:5). In a second, parallel confession they are to speak in the name of the exiles (2:6-10).

The petitionary part of the prayer (2:11-18) begins with the formulaic 'And now . . .' Here, as throughout the prayer (and the introduction), God is addressed by his proper name (translated κύριος), and the covenantal relationship is indicated by the title 'God of Israel' (cf. 3:1,4; and 'our God,' *passim*). The exiles pray that God's wrath will turn from them, that he will deliver his people and grant them favour with their captors, and that he will look down and consider his people. The language of Exodus 3:7-8, 20-21 is reflected throughout this passage, for the author, like Second Isaiah, construes return from Exile as a second Exodus.

In 2:19-26 the people again confess their sins and acknowledge God's just punishment. Then in 2:27-35 they return to Deuteronomy for a word of hope: God's promise that when they repent in the land of their Exile, he will return them to their own land, increase their numbers, and then make an everlasting covenant with them.[298] In 3:1-8 they raise the prayer that God anticipated (cf. 2:31-33 and 3:7-8). The prayer breaks off without an explicit request for return, but the implications are clear.

Chapters 3:9-4:4 contain a wisdom poem in the tradition of Sir 24.[299] It differs from the previous section of Baruch in several significant respects: its poetic (as opposed to prose) form; its concentration on Torah as Wisdom; its dependence on the language of Job; and its use of 'God' rather than 'Lord.' These differences notwithstanding, it has been made an integral part of Baruch.

The poem is connected to the previous section by 3:9-13.[300] Israel is 'dead' in the land of their enemies (3:10-11; cf. 3:4) because they have forsaken the fountain of wisdom (3:12; cf. Jer 2:13), that is, the Torah, the commandments of life (3:9; cf. Deut 30:15-19).

The finding of wisdom is the topic of the poem, which is beholden to Job 28:12-28. The opening strophe admonishes the readers to learn where there is wisdom and strength and life (3:14). The next three strophes enumerate those who have *not* found wisdom (3:15-19, 20-23, 24-28). By contrast God alone found the way to wisdom, and he has given it to Israel alone (3:29-37). The last strophe (4:1-4) make explicit the identification of Wisdom and Torah hinted at in 3:29-30 (cf. Deut 30:11-13). Like Sir 24, this poem asserts that Wisdom is embodied in the Torah and grants life to

---

[298] Cf. Deut 30:1-5 but also 1 Kgs 8:47; cf. also Tob 13:7.

[299] There are important differences between the poems. The personification of Wisdom in Baruch 3:9-4:4 is less clear than it is in Sirach 24. This poem is *about* her rather than *by* her. She is the object of a search rather than the one who searches the universe. Only in 4:1 is she the subject of a verb of action.

[300] The passage may be redactional; the reference to the dead recalls 3:4. However, the direct address to Israel and the appellative 'God' (rather than Lord) are at home in the poem.

those who hold her fast.[301] Conversely it threatens with death those who forsake her, which explains why Israel is now 'dead' in the land of her captivity. The author appeals to the readers to repent (4:2) and find life, which here implies Return, and he concludes with a blessing (4:4) that paraphrases Deut 33:29.

Although this poem paraphrases Job 28, its explicit nationalism is foreign to its prototype (cf. 3:36-37 with Job 28:23-28), while it parallels Sir 24 and fits well with the rest of Baruch. Explicit references to Israel (3:9, 24, 36; 4:2, 4) and 'our God' (3:35) are complemented by the Wisdom/Torah identification and the consequent distinction between Israel and the gentiles.

Having appealed for the obedience that can change Israel's fortunes, the author begins his last major section (4:5-5:9), issuing the first of several exhortations to 'take courage.' God's punishment is not final (4:6). Although this section is again stamped with the language of Deuteronomy,[302] the controlling metaphor is Second Isaiah's image of Mother Zion and her children.[303]

Before the author turns to his hope of the future, he again rehearses the past: the nation's sin and their punishment through exile (4:6-20). The main speaker in this passage is Mother Zion, who recounts her sorrows to her neighbours. She then addresses her children in a pair of strophes that also begin with 'take courage' (4:21-26, 27-29), and she appeals to them to offer the prayer for deliverance that stands at the beginning of the book. The individual units of these strophes are generally marked by a contrast between past calamity and future salvation.

In view of this prospect for salvation, the author then addresses four strophes to Jerusalem herself, each beginning with an imperative to act out a stage of the unfolding drama of salvation (4:30-35; 4:36-37;[304] 5:1-4;[305] 5:5-9).[306]

Having now expressed his hope for salvation and return, the author has solved the dilemma with which the book began. Prayer has been answered. Exile and Dispersion have ended. Sorrow has turned to joy.

A proper literary and historical analysis of Baruch requires a careful comparison of the book with parallel materials in Jeremiah. To date this has not been done, and it is possible here only to sketch out the issues and their implications for our understanding of the work.

---

[301] Cf. especially 3:37-4:2 with Sir 24:8-11, 24.

[302] Cf. 4:7-8 with Deut 32:17-18 and 4:25 with Deut 33:29 (LXX).

[303] See the many parallels cited by Kneucker, *Baruch, ad loc.* Specifically, the author reflects a tradition paralleled in 2 Macc 7 (see Nickelsburg, *Resurrection*, 106-8) and *Ps. Sol.* 11 (see Moore, *Additions*, 314-16).

[304] Cf. Isa 49:14-23; 54:1-13; 60:4-9.

[305] Cf. Isa 52:1-2.

[306] See the discussion of Moore, *Additions*, 314-16.

Obvious from the outset is a connection between the book's ascription to Baruch, the companion and secretary of Jeremiah (cf. Jer 32:12-16; 36:4-32), and its setting in the wake of the destruction of Jerusalem and its message of Return from Exile. Closer inspection indicates a large number of verbal parallels between the book and a variety of passages in Jeremiah.[307] A comparison of the prayer (1:15-3:8) with its counterpart in Daniel 9:4-19 indicates the following: 1) Baruch's prayer is 47% longer than Daniel's.[308] 2) Almost all of the Jeremianic phrases in Baruch's prayer are in passages not found in Daniel's prayer.[309] Daniel's prayer, on the other hand, contains very few Jeremianic expressions not found in Baruch 1:15-3:8.[310] 3) All but one of Daniel's references to the desolation of Jerusalem have as their counterparts in Baruch references to the exiles in Babylon.[311] 4) The most extensive of the passages found in Baruch, but not in Daniel, are additional confessions of sin[312] and expressions of hope that God will rescue his people from Exile.[313]

These data suggest the following hypothesis about the origin of 1:1-3:8. The author has taken up a traditional prayer of confession (attested also in Daniel 9)[314] which was structured on the scheme of Deuteronomy 28-32, but also employed some cliches from Jeremiah. He has greatly expanded it with other Jeremianic material[315] and made it the heart of a work attributed to Jeremiah's scribe. Thus, the borrowings from Jeremiah in both the introduction and Baruch's version of the prayer are the work of a single author.

Although we cannot be certain whether the prayer behind Baruch 1:15-3:8 and Daniel 9:4-19 focused on the problems of Jerusalem or the exile, or both,[316] from a compositional point of view, Baruch differs from

---

[307] The parallels are quoted in Hebrew in Tov, *Baruch*, 13-27. They are found almost exclusively in the first two sections (Tov, *Translation*, 126). The narrative introduction (1:1-14) has drawn many details from Jeremiah, especially from its narrative passages.

[308] Moore, *Additions*, 292.

[309] See the comparison in Wambacq, 'Les prières.' An exception is the cliche in Bar 2:11/Dan 9:15.

[310] An exception is Dan 9:7; cf. Jer 29:14.

[311] Cf. Dan 9:12 and Bar 2:2; Dan 9:16 and Bar 2:13-17.

[312] Bar 1:19, 20-21; 2:24.

[313] Bar 2:27ff.

[314] See Moore, 'Dating,' 312-17. For another prayer in the same tradition, see 'The Words of the Heavenly Lights,' a Qumran text published by Baillet, 'Un receuil.' For an English translation, see Vermes, *Dead Sea Scrolls*, 202-05.

[315] Often he takes words from Jeremiah's oracles of indictment and incorporates them into confessions of sins committed. Elsewhere details in Jeremiah's threats of punishment are described as having taken place.

[316] Some of the confusing data are these: Daniel's is a prayer of confession relating to the desolation of Jerusalem, a matter of central concern for the author of that book. The author of Baruch, because of the particular fiction of his book includes a double confession, for those in Jerusalem and those in exile. However, 'The Words of the Heavenly Lights' also has this double focus.

Daniel 9 in its almost exclusive focus on Exile and Return. This is the case in the prayer, both in passages that have Danielic counterparts that refer to the desolation of Jerusalem and in passages without Danielic parallels. More important, the author sets his story in Babylon and writes his book as a kind of letter calling on the Jerusalemites to pray for the return of the exiles. This last point is especially striking if we compare 1:1, 9 with Jeremiah 29:1-2; 24:1.[317] Jeremiah 29 is the prophet's letter written from Jerusalem to the exiles in Babylon. In it he counsels them to make themselves at home in their new city, because it will be 70 years before they will return. Jeremiah's words are in opposition to false prophets who have counselled rebellion against Babylon and have opposed Jeremiah's prediction of a long exile, and he predicts doom on those who have remained in Jerusalem. Here Baruch writes from Babylon to Jerusalem, asking the Jerusalemites to expedite the exiles' return. Finally, it should be noted, the repeated expressions of confession, not found in Daniel 9,[318] lend to this work — in spite of its pseudepigraphic character — a sense of earnestness in the face of real guilt.

The precise compositional relationship between 1:1-3:8 and the last two sections of the present book of Baruch (3:9-4:4 and 4:5-5:9) remains something of a problem.[319] Although there is virtual unanimity that 1:1-3:8 was composed in Hebrew, scholars have reached no such consensus on 3:9ff.[320] If either or both of the last two sections were composed in Greek, it would follow that they were added to 1:1-3:8 only after it was translated into Greek. Also noteworthy is the difference in idiom between the first two and the last two sections. Given the propensity of the author of 1:1-3:8 to use the Jeremianic idiom, the lack of any number of clear allusions to Jeremiah in 3:9-5:9 is striking.[321] Another possible indicator is 1:14, which states that the function of 'this book' is to enable the people in Jerusalem to make confession. Does this suggest that the exhortations and promises in 3:9-5:9 were not part of 1:1-3:8 when it was first composed?

---

[317] Bar 1:1 employs a formula paralleled in Jer 29:1. Bar 1:9 is most closely paralleled in Jer 24:1, but the formulation is close enough to Jer 29:2 to indicate that that chapter may well have suggested the association of the two passages in one context here.

[318] This emphasis on confession is noted by Goldstein, 'Baruch,' 98.

[319] For a summary of suggested solutions, see Burke, Baruch, 32, 63, n. 321. See also Moore, Additions, 314-16, and Goldstein, 'Baruch,' 187-89.

[320] On the Hebrew origin of 1:1-3:8, see Pfeiffer, History, 416-17; Moore, Additions, 259-60; and especially Tov, Translation, 111-33; id. Baruch, 5-27, who provides a retroversion of these chapters into Hebrew. On the difficulties of positing a Hebrew text of 3:9-5:9, see Pfeiffer, History, 419-21; Moore, Daniel, 260; R. A. Martin, 'Criteria,' 297-306, 309-10 (who thinks that 3:9-4:4 may derive from a Hebrew Vorlage); and Tov, Translation, 126. Supporting a Hebrew original for 3:9-5:9 are Kneucker (Baruch, 354-61), who provides a retroversion; Goldstein, 'Baruch', 187-89; and Burke (Baruch), who argues the position in great detail and offers 'a systematic and scientific reconstruction of the original Hebrew text' (p. xxi).

[321] The only certain allusion to Jeremiah in these sections is 3:12, which draws on Jer 2:13.

These difficulties notwithstanding, all of the book's four diverse parts are united by the common theme of Exile and Return. Unless compelling evidence can be mustered to demonstrate that either of the last two parts was composed in Greek, it is probably a safe hypothesis that the author of 1:1-3:8 was, in fact, responsible for the composition of the book more or less as we have it.

Since the book makes no reference to historical events after the sixth century, its date is uncertain. The book as a whole and its parts have been dated variously between the fourth century B.C.E. and the second century C.E.[322] Reasonable certainty concerning the date of the translation of the book of Jeremiah establishes 116 B.C.E. as a *terminus ante quem* for the composition of 1:1-3:8, since this part was translated by the translator of Jeremiah.[323] Even if 1:15-3:8 is dependent on Daniel 9:4-19,[324] that prayer itself is almost certainly traditional,[325] and thus the date of Daniel provides no *terminus post quem* for Baruch 1:1-3:8.[326] Similarly, parallels between Baruch 4:37-5:9 and *Psalms of Solomon* 11 are of no real help, since we cannot be certain about the date of that psalm.[327]

The fictional date in Baruch 1:2 may provide a clue to the date of composition. If Nebuchadnezzar is a stand-in for Antiochus IV the book is possibly to be dated to 164 B.C.E., five years after Antiochus's sack of Jerusalem and after Judas's purification of the Temple. The high priest Jehoiakim would be none other than Alcimus. The book would be an appeal both to accept the authority of Antiochus V, the son of Antiochus IV (i.e., Belshazzar, son of Nebuchadnezzar; cf. 1:11-13 and the emphasis in 2:21-23), and to seek that obedience to the Torah that would facilitate the return of the Dispersion, especially, perhaps, those sold into slavery by Antiochus IV and his lieutenant, Apollonius (2 Macc 5:14; 1 Macc 1:32; 2 Macc 5:24). Dating the book in this time would explain the fictional setting and would also fit well with the strong consciousness of sin, guilt, and punishment that pervades chaps. 1-3.[328] On the other hand, if one is

---

[322] For a summary of the possibilities and issues, see Pfeiffer, *History*, 415-23. See also Kneucker (*Baruch*, 32-37), who dates the book between 167 B.C.E. and 135 C.E.!

[323] Tov, *Translation*, 111-33, 165.

[324] This is argued by Wambacq, 'Les prières.'

[325] See Moore, 'Dating,' 312-17.

[326] The problem is further complicated by the fact, agreed upon by most critics, that the prayer in Dan 9 is a secondary insertion in that book; see Moore, *Daniel*, 292.

[327] For the parallels, see Ryle — James, *Psalms*, lxxii-lxxvii. Since the *Psalms of Solomon* as a collection are generally dated to the mid-first century B.C.E. and Baruch is most likely dependent on the psalm (see Moore, *Additions*, 314-16), the decade after the conquest of Pompey is often given as a *terminus post quem* for Baruch or this part of it; see, e.g., Wambacq, 'L'unité,' 575. Moore (*Additions*, 314-16) confines the parallels to Bar 5:5-9 (see, however, Nickelsburg, *Jewish Literature*, 153, n. 41), which he sees as a late addition to Bar 1:1-5:4. The difficulty with the argument from comparison is that *Ps. Sol.* 11 is one of the least typical psalms in the collection and could be a traditional piece reused in the first century collection.

[328] This dating is proposed by Goldstein in 'Baruch'.

inclined to play down the importance of the fictional setting and to emphasize the discrepancies between the narrative and the circumstances of 164, then a date higher in the second century, or perhaps earlier, may be more plausible.[329]

Present evidence offers some hints regarding the status of Baruch (or Baruch 1:1-3:8) in relationship to the book of Jeremiah. According to Tov, at least Baruch 1:1-3:8 was translated into Greek by the same person who translated Jeremiah.[330] This suggests that at least Baruch 1:1-3-8 was once joined to Jeremiah in a Hebrew scroll.[331] In major manuscripts of the Greek Bible, Baruch appears between Jeremiah and Lamentations. The fact that some of the church fathers cite the work as Jeremianic ('Jeremiah says') suggests that they considered it to be either an appendix to Jeremiah or a part of it.[332]

Other, later works associated with the figure of Baruch are also set in the aftermath of the Babylonian destruction of Jerusalem and deal with the problems of destruction and dispersion and the hope of restoration. Both *2 Baruch* and *3 Baruch* (see below, pp. 408-12) were written after the fall of Jerusalem in 70 C.E. They anticipate eschatological restoration and heavenly salvation respectively. The *Paraleipomena of Jeremiah* was probably composed after the Second Revolt (see above, p. 75). Like the present work, its theme is Exile and Return. Quite possibly it is based on a Jeremianic work that dated from the time of Antiochus Epiphanes, the period suggested above for the composition of Baruch 1:1-3:8.[333]

THE EPISTLE OF JEREMIAH

Satirical polemics against idols and idolatry are a developing mode of expression in exilic and postexilic literature.[334] Taking his cue from one such text in Jeremiah 10:2-15[335] and from the prophet's letter in Jeremiah 29, this author has composed a tractate which he alleges to be the copy of

---

[329] For a date before 168 B.C.E., see Moore, *Additions,* 260. His arguments are met, at least in part, by Goldstein, 'Baruch.' Nonetheless, at least two elements in Baruch fit the time of the Exile better than 164 B.C.E. In the fifth year, Nebuchadnezzar was alive, but Antiochus IV was not. Unlike 582, the principal problem in 164 was not captivity.

[330] See above, n. 323.

[331] Tov, *Translation,* 169.

[332] *Ibid.*

[333] Nickelsburg, 'Narrative Traditions.'

[334] See Roth ('For Life, He Appeals to Death,' 21-47), who discusses Isa 40:18-41:7; 44:9-20; 46:5-8; Jer 10:3-8; Hab 2:18-19; Ps 115:4-8; 135:15-18; Wis 13:10-19; 15:7-13; the Epistle of Jeremiah; Bel and the Dragon; *Jub.* 12:2-5; 20:8-9. In rabbinic literature, one famous example is Abraham's ironical polemic against idolatry, preceding his martyrdom. See the sources cited in n. 109.

[335] Cf. vv. 67-70 with Jer 10:2-5. For details see Moore (*Additions,* 357-58), who also notes the influence of Isa 44 and 46; Ps 115 and 135; Deut 4:27-28 (*ibid.,* 319-323).

another letter Jeremiah wrote to the exiles in Babylon.[336] Beyond this claim in the superscription (v. 1), however, there are no indicators in the text that it is either Jeremianic or a letter.[337]

In the introduction (vv. 2-7) the author tells his readers that they will see gods of silver, gold, and wood carried in procession and worshipped and feared by the gentiles. Such fear should not possess the Jews. In their hearts they should determine to worship the Lord, whose angel is with them to witness their thoughts and requite them.[338]

Following this introduction are ten sections of unequal length (vv. 8-16; 17-23; 24-29; 30-40a; 40b-44; 45-52; 53-56; 57-65; 66-69; 70-73) in which the author heaps up arguments and evidences that demonstrate that idols are not what the gentiles suppose or claim they are.

The author's message is explicit in a refrainlike, slightly varying formula that punctuates and concludes each of the ten sections and recalls vv. 4-5 in the introduction.[339] Typical is v. 23: 'Thence you will know that they are not gods. Therefore do not fear them'.

The claim that idols are not gods is negative in form and antithetical in function. It is a conclusion drawn from a multitude of observations about the things that idols do not and, more strongly, 'cannot' (vv. 8, 19, 34, 35) do. Idols do not and cannot do all the things that gods do (vv. 34-38, 53, 64, 66f.). In a parallel argument that remains implicit the author recounts without comment practices in the idol cult or by its priests which he considers inappropriate: e.g., cultic prostitution (v. 43); the priests' theft of gold and silver and robes from the idols (v. 10, 33), etc.

Carrying his argument one step further the author points out that these false gods cannot even do the things that humans do: speak, see, and breathe (vv. 8, 19, 25). Put in the strongest way possible, they cannot even help themselves (vv. 12-14, 18, 24, 27, 55). This last point is also implied by describing how the idols are the object of a number of human actions: they are decked out with crowns and robes (vv. 9-12), carried in procession (v. 26), hidden in time of war or calamity (v. 48). But most fundamentally, the fabrication process itself is a parable of their falseness: gold and silver on the outside but wood underneath; they are not what they appear or are claimed to be (vv. 50, 44).

The ironic use of simile provides the author with yet another means of

---

[336] For yet another pseudepigraphic Jeremianic letter see *Par. Jer.* 7. See also the letters ascribed to Baruch: 1 Baruch and *2 Baruch* 78-87. The latter, like the present work, is sent to tribes in Exile, albeit in Assyria.

[337] Cf. below, p. 584 n. 26.

[338] I interpret vv. 6-7 to be referring to a common topic. For the idea cf. Wis 1:6-10. The Greek verb ἐκζητεῖν frequently has connotations of judgment and refers to searching out for the purpose of requiting. Cf. *1 Enoch* 104: 7-8.

[339] The formulas occur in vv. 16, 23, 29, 40, 44, 49, 52, 56, 64, 69, 72.

mocking the false gods. He likens them to things that are useless and altogether inappropriate as images of the deity (vv. 12, 17f., 20, 70-73).

The uniqueness of the Epistle of Jeremiah lies not in the types of arguments presented. Many of these have parallels elsewhere, both in biblical and post-biblical Jewish literature[340] and in the writings of pagan philosophers.[341] The special character of the Epistle is in the persistence with which the author pursues his point by means of repetition and rhetorical devices.

The Epistle of Jeremiah is extant only in the Greek Bible and the versions dependent on it. One small fragment of the Greek has been identified among the scrolls of Qumran Cave 7.[342] There is, however, substantial evidence in the text that the work was composed in Hebrew. A fair number of difficult or incoherent expressions in the Greek can be explained as mistranslations from Hebrew, and a similar hypothesis explains some of the variants in the Greek manuscripts.[343]

The precise date of composition cannot be determined with any certainty. Two data indicate a *terminus ad quem* ca. 100 B.C.E. The Epistle is cited in 2 Maccabees 2:2,[344] which is to be dated early in the first century B.C.E.[345] The Qumran Greek fragment of the Epistle is dated ca. 100 B.C.E.[346] This suggests that the Hebrew original was written some time before the turn of the century. Verse 3 of the Epistle may indicate a date of composition a full two centuries earlier. Here the author predicts that the exilic period will last up to seven generations. If one presumes that the author would not create a false prophecy, one can posit a *terminus ad quem* ca. 317-307 B.C.E., seven generations of forty years after the first or second deportation in 597 or 587 B.C.E.[347]

The place of writing is uncertain. The author's evident familiarity with aspects of Babylonian religion[348] may indicate composition in Mesopotamia, although an author so informed could have written the book any place where idolatry presented a threat.[349]

---

[340] See above, n. 334.

[341] See the fourth epistle of the Cynic, Ps. Heraclitus; Heinemann, 'Pseudo-Herakleitos'; Attridge, *First Century Cynicism,* 58-61; Malherbe, *The Cynic Epistles,* 190-3; and the parallels cited by Attridge, *First Century Cynicism,* 13-23.

[342] See Baillet, *DJD* 3, 143.

[343] See the list in Ball, 'Epistle,' 597-98, and the discussion in his notes; see also Naumann, *Untersuchungen,* 47; and Moore, *Additions,* 326-7, and his notes.

[344] See Moore, *Additions,* 327; but see Naumann, *Untersuchungen,* 52-53.

[345] See Goldstein, *1 Maccabees,* 36.

[346] See Baillet, *DJD* 3, 143.

[347] See Moore, *Additions,* 334-5; see also Naumann (*Untersuchungen,* 53), who is cautious on the use of v. 3, but still dates the work in the late fourth century B.C.E.

[348] See the detailed discussion in *ibid.,* 3-31.

[349] Cf., e.g., *1 Enoch* 99:7, 9, in a Palestinian document.

The book's evident composition in Hebrew suggests that the intended audience was Jewish; this is further supported by vv. 29-30, 43, which assume that the audience shares the Jewish presuppositions of the author's critique of Babylonian religion.

The placement of the Epistle varies in biblical manuscripts. In the Codices Vaticanus and Alexandrinus, in the Milan manuscript of the Syriac Hexapla, and in the Arabic version, it stands immediately after Lamentations. In other Greek and Syriac manuscripts and in the Old Latin version, the Epistle is appended to the book of Baruch. As a result, modern editions often count it as chapter 6 of that work.

THE PRAYER OF AZARIAH AND THE SONG OF THE THREE YOUNG MEN

In the previous chapter we discussed Susanna and Bel and the Dragon, the two stories that frame the book of Daniel in its Greek versions (pp. 37-40). The present addition was inserted into the Greek Daniel between 3:23 and 3:24. It consists of a prayer of confession attributed to Azariah (Abednego) and a hymn of praise placed on the lips of the three young men. These two poetic pieces are joined to each other and to verses 23 and 24 by some brief narrative prose.[350]

Azariah's prayer stands in the tradition of the national laments of the canonical Psalter (e.g., Pss 74, 79, 80).[351] It differs from these psalms in its explicit use of the pattern of traditional Israelite covenant theology and its occasional allusions to the language of Deuteronomy 28-32.[352] In these respects, it parallels most closely the prayers of confession in Baruch 1:15-3:8 and Daniel 9:4-19, although the latter make more frequent and explicit reference to Deuteronomy 28-32.[353] Also noteworthy in the Prayer of Azariah is its prologue (vv. 3-5), in which God is 'blessed' for his righteous judgments, that is, his present punishment of the nation's sins. Although the motif of God's righteous judgment does occur in the canonical psalter with some frequency, it is also noteworthy in Daniel 9:7 and Baruch 1:15 and 2:6, and it is a frequently repeated motif in the *Psalms of Solomon*.[354] Thus it is a characteristic of the Jewish theologies of the Greco-Roman period which are wrestling with disparity between Israel's covenantal status and its present misfortune.

Azariah's prayer appears to have been a previously existent composition reused for its present purpose. Its insertion here conforms to a typical

---

[350] The versification used here follows that of standard translations of the Apocrypha. Editions of the Greek Daniel begin versification with v. 24 (i.e., English v. 1 is Greek v. 24, etc.).

[351] Kuhl, *Die drei Männer*, 100. On this *Gattung*, see Kraus, *Psalmen* 1, LI-LII.

[352] For details, see Nickelsburg, *Jewish Literature*, 28.

[353] On these prayers, see above, pp. 140-1.

[354] Cf., e.g., *Ps. Sol.* 2:16-18 and 8:30-40.

Jewish literary pattern: deliverance comes in response to prayer.[355] In point of fact, however, the contents of this prayer hardly fit the young men's present predicament. No mention is made of the mortal danger in which they find themselves. Rather they confess the nation's sins, which have led to desolation and defeat, and it is from these that they pray for deliverance. Thus the prayer is more appropriate to the general circumstances of the Babylonian Exile or to the time of Antiochus' persecution of the Jews, that is, to the supposed or the real setting of the book of Daniel. Reference to the cessation of the cult and lack of leadership (v. 15) and to the unjust and wicked king (v. 9) may indicate that the prayer was actually composed during the persecution.[356] In any case, it is, together with Daniel 9:4-19, Baruch 1:15-3:8, and the Qumran 'Words of the Heavenly Luminaries,'[357] part of the penitential liturgical tradition of post-biblical Judaism.

The prose insertion following the prayer forms a transition to the second half of the addition. Verses 23-25 emphasize the ferocity of the fire, thus heightening the miracle, although v. 25 may be an answer to the prayer in vv. 20c-21.[358] Verses 26-27 describe the miraculous deliverance for the curious reader and provide cause for the three young men to sing their hymn of praise.[359]

The hymn divides into four major sections. Verses 29-34 are a doxology to the God who is enthroned in his temple (vv. 31-33), perhaps his heavenly temple (v. 34). Stylistic considerations may indicate that this section was composed separately from the rest of the hymn.[360] Verses 35-66 are a threefold appeal for the whole creation to join in the praise of God. Verses 35-51 are addressed to heaven, its inhabitants and its elements. Verses 52-60 extend the appeal to the earth, its components and its inhabitants, following in general the order of creation in Genesis 1. Having mentioned the last-created beings, 'the sons of men,' the author now addresses Israel in particular (vv. 61-65). Finally, as a climax v. 66 makes reference to the three

---

[355] Cf. 1 Macc 4:30-34; 2 Macc 3:15-24; 3 Macc 2; and Esth 14-15, as well as the addition in the Greek translation of Esther placed after 4:17 in the canonical book with the same effect.

[356] Moore, *Additions*, 46. See, however, Kuhl (*Die drei Männer*, 103-04), who suggests a date much earlier in the post-exilic period. Reference to the lack of a prophet could have been made at *any* time that *the author* believed there was no prophet.

[357] See below pp. 567, 570ff.

[358] Verse 25 has been taken over from v. 22 in the original, which has dropped out of some manuscripts of the Greek. Perhaps the author of the addition displaced it so that it could function as an answer to the prayer.

[359] The original story does not actually describe the deliverance but only the king's discovery of the miracle. In order to insert the prayer before that discovery, the author of the addition must mention the deliverance here.

[360] See Kuhl, *Die drei Männer*, 99-100; Moore, *Additions*, 75-76. The change from direct address of God to speech about God need not be determinative, however. Cf., e.g., Pss 104, 106, 116, 118, 135, and 144, where such fluctuation can be found. On Moore's conclusions about the relationship of the hymn to Tobit 8:5 (*Additions*, 76), see below, n. 365.

young men and the reason for singing the hymn. The brevity of this reference in the context of such a long hymn suggests that here too the author of the addition has employed an extant liturgical work, inserting this verse to make the hymn relevant to its new context.

The genre of this composition is that of a Hymn.[361] Its closest counterpart in the canonical Psalter is Psalm 148, although the relationship between the two hymns is uncertain.[362] The structure of the present hymn, with identical refrain after each line, recalls Psalm 136 and suggests that the hymn may originally have had an antiphonal liturgical function. The wording of vv. 67-68 closely parallels Psalm 136:1-3. As with the Prayer of Azariah, we have an example of Jewish liturgical tradition preserved now in a secondary setting.

The hymn cannot be dated with any certainty. Its theme is perennial. The two brief songs of praise in Tobit 8:5-6 and 15-17 very possibly reflect knowledge of this hymn, including its introduction.[363] This suggests a date at least well back into the third century.[364]

These two poetic compositions were probably written in Hebrew.[365] If this is the case, they and their narrative framework may have been inserted into the Semitic manuscript of Daniel from which the Greek translation was made. Alternatively, they could have been translated and inserted into Daniel by the Greek translator of that book.

This long addition has the effect of breaking up the continuity of the story in Daniel 3. On the other hand the sharp contrast between the tone and genres of the two poems serves to underscore the change in the action from disaster to salvation.[366] The poems convert the story from mere narrative to quasi-liturgical drama, eliciting the involvement of an audience attuned to such liturgical tradition and, perhaps, familiar with the compositions themselves.

The liturgical function of these compositions was not lost on the early

---

[361] Kuhl, *Die drei Männer*, 90-99. On the Gattung, Hymn, see Kraus, *Psalmen* 1, XLI-XLV.

[362] Kuhl, *Die drei Männer*, 97-98; Pfeiffer, *History*, 448; Kraus, *Psalmen* 2, 961. For a comparison of the two compositions, see *ibid.* and Moore, *Additions*, 42-43.

[363] Moore (*Additions*, 76) notes that 'the first two cola of Tobit 8:5 correspond fairly accurately to the general theme and opening lines of the Ode (vv. 29-34), and that its third colon is a capsule statement of our Psalm.' He suggests that this combination may have inspired a scribe to add the Ode to vv. 35ff. However, Moore takes no note of further parallels between Tob 8 and this hymn: the reference to creation in Tob 8:6; the references to God's saints and all his creatures, and to his angels and his chosen ones in the prayer in 8:15. Nor does he note that both prayers in Tobit change from direct address to God ('Blessed are you') to the third person *imperative* ('let the heavens . . . your creatures, etc., bless you'). Thus on the basis of both style and content, it is equally likely that the author of Tobit has used our hymn, including its introduction, but without its present conclusion.

[364] See above, p. 45.

[365] Pfeiffer, *History*, 445; Moore, *Additions*, 4-49. For a retroversion of the entire addition into Hebrew, see Kuhl, *Die drei Männer*, 128-33, 150-55, 158, 161.

[366] See the discussion of Tobit, above, pp. 43-44.

church. They were included in the collection of 'Odes' which was appended to the book of Psalms in Greek manuscripts of the Bible written in the fifth century and thereafter.[367] They continue to be used in the liturgies of the Greek Orthodox Church,[368] and the Song of the Three Young Men is still found in many Christian hymnals, often under its Latin name, *Benedicite opera omnia.*

BIBLIOGRAPHY

1 Enoch and the Book of Giants

The stories about Noah and Enoch, the fallen angels and the giants have been the subject of a considerable number of related articles: HANSON, 'Rebellion'; NICKELSBURG, 'Apocalyptic and Myth'; COLLINS, 'Methodological Issues'; HANSON, 'Response'; NICKELSBURG, 'Reflections'; DIMANT, '1 Enoch 6-11'. SUTER, Fallen Angel'; NEWSOM 'Development'; NICKELSBURG, 'Enoch, Levi, and Peter'; COLLINS, 'Apocalyptic Technique'. Treatments written independently of these include: DIMANT, 'Fallen Angels'; DELCOR, 'Le Mythe'; BARTHELMUS, 'Heroentum'. For the Qumran texts of the Book of Giants, see MILIK, *Enoch*, 298-317. For the Manichaean texts, see HENNING, 'Book of Giants'. On the relationship of the book to *1 Enoch*, see GREENFIELD — STONE, 'Pentateuch'.

Jubilees

On the Qumran Hebrew manuscripts of *Jubilees*, see VANDERKAM, *Studies* 18-101, comparison of all published Hebrew fragments with the Ethiopic manuscripts. For a critical edition of the Ethiopic text and for the Greek, Syriac, and Latin fragments, see CHARLES' *Ethiopic Jubilees*. Five or six other Ethiopic manuscripts are mentioned in BAARS—ZUURMOND, 'Project'. On the Greek version, see Milik, 'Recherches'. For a concordance of the Latin Fragments, see DENIS, *Concordance*. For an annotated English translation with introduction, see CHARLES, 'Jubilees'. For a somewhat more detailed introduction and commentary, see CHARLES, *Jubilees*. A helpful introduction to the thought of the book is provided by TESTUZ, *Les idées*. The text of the Hebrew fragments, the biblical text employed in *Jubilees*, and the date of the book are discussed by VANDERKAM, *Studies*. On *halakhah* in *Jubilees*, see FINKELSTEIN, 'The Book of Jubilees'; ALBECK, *Das Buch der Jubiläen*. On eschatology, see DAVENPORT, *Eschatology*. A vast

---

[367] Rahlfs, *Psalmi cum Odis,* 78.
[368] Swete, *Introduction,* 254.

literature has developed on the calendar of *Jubilees*, in part as it relates to the Qumran calendar. JAUBERT, 'Le calendrier des Jubilés et de la secte de Qumrân'; *id.*, 'Le calendrier des Jubilés et les jours liturgiques de la semaine'; *id.*, *La date de la Cène*; LEACH, 'Method'; TALMON, 'Calendar Reckoning'; MILIK, *Ten Years*, 107-13; WIESENBERG, 'The Jubilee of Jubilees'; KUTSCH, 'Der Kalendar'; *id.*, 'Die Solstitien'; CAZELLES, 'Sur les origines'; BAUMGARTEN, 'The Calendar'; WIRGIN, *Jubilees*; ZEITLIN, 'Judaean Calendar'; HERR, 'The Calendar'; VANDERKAM, 'Origin'; *id.*, '2 Maccabees 6, 7A'.

The Genesis Apocryphon

AVIGAD — YADIN, *A Genesis Apocryphon, editio princeps,* introduction, text, translation, plates. FITZMYER, *The Genesis Apocryphon*, introduction, text, translation, and detailed commentary, bibliography.

The Book of Biblical Antiquities

COHN, 'An Apocryphal Work', the first major treatment of the work with many insights that are still valid. JAMES, *Antiquities*, extensive introduction, translation; reprinted in 1971 with a lengthy 'Prolegomenon' by FELDMAN, who comments on James' edition, provides many corrections, and carries on a dialogue with subsequent scholarship. BOGAERT, *Apocalypse*, 242-58, the relationship of Pseudo-Philo to *2 Baruch*. STRUGNELL, 'Philo', a summary article. HARRINGTON, *Hebrew Fragments*, text and translation of the parts of the Hebrew *Chronicles of Jerahmeel* which correspond to Pseudo-Philo, a retroversion from the Latin. DIETZFELBINGER, *Pseudo-Philo*, introduction, annotated German translation. For the most recent major work, see HARRINTON — CAZEAUX, *Les Antiquites* 1, a text-critical introduction, critical text of the Latin with facing French translation; volume 2 by PERROT — BOGAERT, contains an introduction, commentary, and extensive bibliography. On the message and setting of the work, see NICKELSBURG, 'Good and Bad Leaders'.

The Books of Adam and Eve

For a critical edition of the Greek texts of the *Apocalypse of Moses*, see TISCHENDORF, *Apocalypses*, 1-23. For an analysis of the manuscripts, textual history of the Books of Adam and Eve, transcription of the Greek texts, and concordance, see NAGEL, *La Vie*. The Latin text of the *Vita*, together with an extensive introduction, was published by MEYER, *Vita*, and a critical edition was published by MOZLEY, 'Documents'. For a text and translation, with discussion, of the Slavonic version, see JAGIĆ, 'Slavische Beiträge'. For a translation of the Armenian *Repentance*, see ISSAVERDENS, 'Penitence'

153

and of the *Penitence*, STONE, 'Penitence'. The Georgian version is discussed by LÜDTKE, 'Georgische Adam-Bücher'. For an English translation, with introduction, of the *Apocalypse,* the *Vita,* and the Slavonic version, see WELLS, 'Adam and Eve'. For an important early discussion of the *Apocalypse of Moses,* see KABISCH, 'Die Entstehungszeit'. On the theology of the Apocalypse, see SHARPE, 'The Second Adam'. On the *Apocalypse* and the *Vita,* and their relationship to one another and to the Gnostic *Apocalypse of Adam,* see NICKELSBURG, 'Related Traditions'. For an English translation of the *Apocalypse of Adam,* see MACRAE — PARROTT, 'Apocalypse'. On the wide spate of Adam literature, see the extensive article by FREY, 'Adam'. On the Armenian literature about Seth and Adam, see STONE, 'Armenian Seth Traditions'.

Philo the Epic Poet

MRAS, *Eusebius,* 506-07, 517-18, 546-47, critical text of Greek. JACOBY, *Fragmente,* 3c 2, 689-90, critical text of collected Greek fragments. DENIS, *Fragmenta,* 203-04, Greek text. ATTRIDGE, 'Philo' (forthcoming), introduction with bibliography, annotated English translation. WALTER, *Fragmente,* annotated German translation. Studies include: Schürer, *Literature,* 222-4, older bibliography; DALBERT, *Theologie,* 33-35; GUTMAN, 'Philo', an extensive discussion; DENIS, *Introduction,* 270-71, discussion with bibliography; WACHOLDER, 'Philo'; *Id., Eupolemus,* 282-3.

Theodotus the Epic Poet

MRAS, *Eusebius,* 212-16, critical text of Greek. JACOBY, *Fragmente,* 3 c 2, 692-94, critical text of Greek. DENIS, *Fragmenta,* 204-7, Greek text. WALTER, *Fragmente,* annotated German translation. FALLON, 'Theodotus' (forthcoming), introduction, annotated English translation. Studies include, FREUDENTHAL, *Studien,* 99-100, argument for Samaritan origin; SCHÜRER, *Literature,* 224-5; BULL, 'A Note', a discussion of relevant archeological evidence at Shechem; DENIS, *Introduction,* 272-3; WACHOLDER, *Eupolemus,* 283-5; COLLINS, 'Theodotus', detailed critique of hypothesis of Samaritan origin.

Ezekiel the Tragedian

MRAS, *Eusebius,* 524-38, critical text of Greek. DENIS, *Fragmenta,* 207-16, Greek text. ROBERTSON, 'Ezekiel' (forthcoming), introduction, annotated translation. SCHÜRER, *Literature,* 225-8, brief comments, older bibliography. KUIPER, 'Le poète juif Ezechiel'. WIENEKE, *Ezechielis,* detailed study in Latin. DALBERT, *Theologie,* 52-65. DENIS, *Introduction,* 273-7. SNELL, 'Ezechiels Moses-Drama', special attention to relationship to classical drama. STRUGNELL, 'Notes', on the text and metre of the fragments. STAROBINSKI-SAFRAN, 'Un poète', analysis of the enthronement scene and its antecedents. HOLLADAY, 'The Portrait of Moses in Ezekiel the Tragedian.' DELLING-MASER, *Bibliographie*, 55, additional bibliography.

The Story of Darius' Bodyguards
(1 Esdras 3-4)

HANHART, *Esdrae liber I*, critical edition of the Greek text. COOK, 'I Esdras', introduction, annotated translation. TORREY, 'Story', historical questions, relationship to context. LAQUEUR, 'Ephoros', 168-72, brief, but perceptive early analysis of literary problems. SCHALIT, 'The Date and Place'. RUDOLF, 'Der Wettstreit', general discussion; ZIMMERMANN, 'Story', alleged mistranslations from Aramaic, literary problems and reconstruction. PFEIFFER, *History*, 250-7, special attention to historical matters and extra-Israelite parallels. POHLMANN, *Studien*, important discussion of many aspects in the context of a treatment of 1 Esdras as a whole. MYERS, *I and II Esdras*, translation with brief commentary. CRENSHAW, 'The Contest', literary and rhetorical features, context within Israelite wisdom tradition.

Additions to the Book of Esther

HANHART, *Esther*, critical edition of the Greek texts. BICKERMAN, 'Colophon', an important discussion of the date of the translation. *Id.*, 'Notes', a good introduction to major issues. BROWNLEE, 'Le livre grec d'Esther', the additions are an orthodox correction of the Hebrew book. MOORE, *Additions*, annotated translation of the Hebrew book, interwoven with a translation of the additions and a commentary on them. MOTZO, 'Rifacimento', Greek translation was made on the basis of 3 Maccabees.

David's Compositions

SANDERS, *Psalms Scroll*, 91-93, text, translation, and some commentary. *Id.*, *Dead Sea*, 134-6, a more popular version of the *editio princeps*.

Baruch

ZIEGLER, *Ieremias, Baruch*, 450-67, critical edition of Greek text. TOV, *Baruch*, Greek text, English translation, Hebrew retroversion of 1:1-3:8 and Hebrew parallels from Jeremiah. WHITEHOUSE, 'Baruch', introduction and annotated translation, dates the work ca. 78 C.E. KNEUCKER, *Baruch*, extensive introduction, German translation and commentary, retroversion of entire book into pointed Hebrew; it remains a learned and indispensable tool. PFEIFFER, *History*, a good discussion of major introductory issues.

MOORE, *Additions*, 255-316, translation and commentary. TOV, *Translation*, 111-33, comparison of translation techniques in Jeremiah and Baruch 1:1-3:8, concluding that the two were translated by the same person and that the translation was revised by the same person. GOLDSTEIN, 'Baruch', the historical setting of the book, in 163 B.C.E. BURKE, *The Poetry of Baruch*, philological study and analysis of the poetry in 3:9-5:9.

The Epistle of Jeremiah

ZIEGLER, *Ieremias, Baruch, Threni, Epistula Ieremiae*, 494-504, critical edition of Greek text. BALL, 'Epistle', introduction, annotated translation, emphasis on Hebrew *Vorlage*. NAUMANN, *Untersuchungen*, background in Babylonian religion, philological details, historical setting. MOORE *Additions*, 317-58, introduction, translation, commentary.

Additions to Daniel

ZIEGLER, *Susanna, Daniel, Bel et Draco*, 119-32, critical edition of the Greek text. KUHL, *Die drie Männer*, detailed philological, form-critical, and historical discussion of Daniel 3 including the addition; retroversion of the addition into Hebrew. MOORE, *Additions*, introduction, translation, commentary.

Chapter Four

Historiography

Harold W. Attridge

Jews of the Hellenistic and early imperial periods evidenced a lively interest in their past, and the narrative literature of the period which rehearsed
one or another aspect of that past was enormous, as the preceding chapters
have shown. Certain works stand out from that large narrative corpus as
attempts to tell all or part of that past in some systematic, chronologically
founded fashion and these works may usefully be treated separately as
historiographical narratives. The category remains a rather broad one,
including, on the one hand, works which stand in one way or another
within the tradition of biblical historiography developed in the books of
Samuel, Kings and Chronicles. Such a work would certainly be 1
Maccabees, which, in its original language, style and theological outlook,
continues the biblical tradition. The historical genre also includes a large
number of works written in the traditions of Greek historiography, such as
2 Maccabees or the *War* and *Antiquities* of Josephus. Here also stand many
works which survive only in fragmentary form and which reflect various
types of Hellenistic historical literature, not only the political and military
history exemplified by the Maccabean books, but also ethnographic and
antiquarian history which was often cultivated in this period for various
apologetic, polemical or propagandistic ends. Although it is important to
recognize the diversity in Hellenistic historical literature, one may still ask
in some cases whether a particular work, especially if it survives only in
fragmentary form, is really historiographical in the sense described above.
Some of the works treated here might be equally well considered as
scriptural paraphrases (1 Esdras), exegetical treatises (Demetrius), or even
popular romances (Artapanus).

1 Esdras

1 Esdras, which bears this title in the Septuagint, but is designated 3 Esdras
in the Vulgate,[1] is one work which is not easily classified. It continues

---

[1] The titles of the Ezra literature vary in different traditions. The title 2 Esdras is particularly
problematic, since it is used in the English Apocrypha as the title of the Christian redaction of

traditions of biblical historiography, but it does so primarily as a translation into Greek of material paralleled in 2 Chronicles (35:1-36:21), all of Ezra and a small part of Nehemiah (7:72-8:13). The work thus describes the last years of the first temple, from the Passover celebration of Josiah to the destruction of the temple (1:1-55). It goes on to record the edict of Cyrus and the first return of Jews to Jerusalem, their work on the new temple, and the opposition to that work on the part of the Samaritans (2:1-25). Then follows a lengthy account (3:1-4:63), unparalleled in Hebrew Ezra or its more literal Greek equivalent, 2 Esdras, of a banquet of the Persian king Darius, at which three of his bodyguards engage in a contest to name the strongest thing imaginable.[2] The winner happens to be Zerubbabel, who asks the king to honour his commitment to rebuild Jerusalem and to restore the temple vessels, and Darius graciously grants the request. After a brief preface (5:1-6) not found in Ezra, the narrative resumes its parallel with earlier biblical materials and records the preparations for the return of the Babylonian exiles, their arrival in Jerusalem, the reconstruction of the temple and the further resistance to that work on the part of neighbours and royal officials (5:7-7:15). Then 1 Esdras gives an account of the activity of Ezra himself (8:1-9:55), all but the last verses of which are paralleled in Hebrew Ezra. The concluding scene (9:37-55), with Ezra's reading of the Law to the assembly in Jerusalem, is paralleled by Neh 7:72-8:13. The work ends abruptly with an incomplete sentence, 'And there were gathered together,' which is probably a secondary addition indicating where in 2 Esdras the sequel is to be found.

The date of 1 Esdras cannot be precisely determined. It was certainly written before the middle of the first century C.E., since it was used by Josephus as the basis for his account of the post-exilic period.[3] Allusions to Daniel (4:40 = Dan 2:37; 4:59 = Dan 2:22-23) indicate that the work was

---

the Ezra Apocalypse, 4 Esdras of the Vulgate, a work not preserved in Greek. The following chart illustrates the basic relationships among the various Ezra texts:

Hebrew Bible	Septuagint	Vulgate	English Apocrypha
Ezra	2 Esdras	1 Esdras	
Nehemiah	3 Esdras	2 Esdras	
	1 Esdras	3 Esdras	1 Esdras
		4 Esdras	2 Esdras

Further adding to the possible confusion surrounding the nomenclature for these texts is the practice of distinguishing the Christian framework (chapters 1-2, 15-16) within which the Ezra Apocalypse is set. The following designations are also encountered:

1 Ezra	Ezra-Nehemiah of the Hebrew Bible
2 Ezra	4 Esdras (Vulgate) = 2 Esdras (Eng. Apoc.) Chapters 1-2
3 Ezra	1 Esdras (Septuagint) = 3 Esdras (Vulgate) = 1 Esdras (Eng. Apoc.)
4 Ezra	4 Esdras (Vulgate) = 2 Esdras (Eng. Apoc.) Chapters 3-14
5 Ezra	4 Esdras (Vulgate) = 2 Esdras (Eng. Apoc.) Chapters 15-16

[2] See above, pp. 131-5.

[3] *Ant.* 11:1-158. For discussion of the relationship between 1 Esdras and Josephus, see Bloch, *Quellen*, 69-77; Cohen, *Josephus*, 42-43; Myers, *I and II Esdras*, 8-15.

written after 165 B.C.E. The Greek vocabulary and translation style, which, compared to 2 Esdras (LXX), is freer, suggest a second-century B.C.E. date of composition. The provenance is quite unknown.

The immediate sources of the material in 1 Esdras and the aims of the work have both been matters of dispute. The fact that 1 Esdras totally ignores the work of Nehemiah has suggested to some that this work is based on a source which gave an account of Zerubbabel and Ezra alone, a source which was combined with the memoires of Nehemiah into the canonical books of Ezra-Nehemiah. It seems more likely, however, that 1 Esdras, where parallel to the Biblical texts, is simply a translation of selected portions of Ezra-Nehemiah, perhaps in a textual form slightly different from, and more original than, that of the Masoretic text.[3a] That text may have provided some of the smaller bits of additional material found in 1 Esdras but not in Ezra (1 Esdras 1:21-22, 5:55, 6:8c) and the Hebrew may account for the omission of 2 Chron 36:22-23. The account of the contest of the bodyguards is a bit of legendary material which was probably not Jewish in origin. It bears similarities to the court-tales in the first half of Daniel and its addition to the translation of the Zerubbabel-Ezra story parallels other additions to the Greek translations of Daniel and Esther.[4]

Historical difficulties plague this brief narrative, as they do the Ezra literature in general. The most glaring problem arises from the transposition of the material of Ezra 4:7-23 to a position before the material of Ezra 2. This has the effect of placing the reign of Artaxerxes I (464-423 B.C.E.) prior to the reign of Darius I (522-485 B.C.E.). This difficulty was recognized by Josephus, who corrects the chronology of the Persian kings in his paraphrase of 1 Esdras (*Ant.* 11:21, 30, 120, 184). In addition to the errors in Achaemenid chronology, the story of Persian authorization to rebuild the temple manifests internal inconsistencies. Permission is initially granted by Cyrus (2:1-11), but this grant is ignored in the account of Zerubbabel and the banquet of Darius (4:42-46). There Darius is reminded that *he* had made a vow to rebuild the temple and of Cyrus it is said only that he set apart the sacred vessels from the Jerusalem temple when he destroyed Babylon. This latter inconsistency probably was caused by the combination of the story of the bodyguards at the banquet, which had already been Judaized and adapted to Zerubbabel, and the basic acount of

---

[3a] While some scholars have argued that 1 Esdras is based on an earlier Greek translation of Ezra-Nehemiah, it seems more likely that the work is an original translation from its Semitic sources. For discussion of the issue, see Eissfeldt, *The Old Testament,* 575; Myers, *I and II Esdras,* 5-6; and Pohlmann, *3. Esra-Buch,* 377-8. On the relationship between 1 Esdras and the more literal translation of Ezra in 2 Esdras (LXX), see Pohlmann, *3. Esra-Buch,* 378-9.

[4] For discussion of the story of the contest of the bodyguards, see Torrey, 'The Story' and *Ezra Studies,* 23-24; Schalit, 'The Date and Place'; Rudolph, 'Der Wettstreit' and Pohlmann, *3. Esra-Buch,* 380-3.

the postexilic period from Ezra. Both difficulties indicate how little 1 Esdras is a work of critical historiography.

It is unclear precisely what functions this work was initially meant to serve. The selective retelling of a particular portion of past history can, as in the case of 2 Maccabees, have discernible tendencies, although in the case of that work the tendencies are more apparent. Little indication is given by programmatic remarks or tendentious additions in the text of 1 Esdras about the purpose to be served by this retelling. The fact that the work presents a picture of the continuity between the old and the new temples may indicate that it was designed to play some role in the polemics of the second century between the Jerusalem temple and it rivals, the Oniad temple at Leontopolis in Egypt, and the Tobiad temple at 'Araq-el-Amir in the Transjordan.[5] Similarly, the omission of any mention of Nehemiah may be the result of a conscious attempt by pious circles who felt themselves to be the successors of Ezra to suppress any memory of Nehemiah's work. Such hypotheses, based as they often are on arguments from silence, remain quite speculative. It may be that 1 Esdras simply served didactic purposes, purposes enhanced by the account of the banquet of Darius. The work, in other words, conveys to a Greek reading audience, in a succinct and entertaining form, the theological lesson of Ezra-Nehemiah, that God watches over those who piously serve him, as well as the moralistic message that truth is most powerful.[6]

Fragments of Hellenistic Historians

1 Esdras may be the earliest fully preserved Jewish work from the Hellenistic period which might be considered historiographical in some loose sense. There were, however, works which have a more secure claim to be histories which antedate 1 Esdras. These works, along with the remains of other early Greco-Jewish literature, survive only in fragments which were ultimately preserved by Josephus or the Church Fathers. These excerpts from Greco-Jewish texts were not made directly by Josephus, Clement of Alexandria or Eusebius, but derive from the work of earlier compilers, the most important of whom was the grammarian L. Cornelius Alexander, surnamed Polyhistor.[7] He was a native of Miletus, who was born in 105

---

[5] For other possible evidence of this polemic, see Collins, *Sibylline Oracles*, 44-55; Goldstein, 'Tales of the Tobiads'. Note also the letters prefaced to 2 Maccabees, on which see Momigliano, 'Second Book'; Goldstein, *I Maccabees*, 545-50; and Bunge, 'Unersuchungen', 530-1, 600-1. All of these probably deal with the Oniad temple at Leontopolis. For evidence of a Tobiad temple at 'Araq el-Emir, see Lapp, 'Second and Third Campaigns.' For further discussion of this archaeological evidence, see Hengel, *Hellenism* 1, 273-5.

[6] For discussion of various hypotheses about the purpose of the work, see Myers, *I and II Esdras*, 8-9 and Pohlmann, *3. Esra-Buch*, 382.

[7] The classical study of Alexander is Freudenthal, *Alexander Polyhistor*. For recent discussions of the significance of his compilation, see Denis, *Introduction*, 241-8; Wacholder, *Eupolemus*,

B.C.E., deported to Rome as a slave during the Mithradatic wars and freed by the dictator Sulla around 82 B.C.E. He composed at least twenty-five works, many of them dealing with the oriental nations which had come under Roman domination by the middle of the first century. These works, one of which was *On the Jews,* presented selections from earlier Hellenistic literature by or about the oriental nations in an attempt to inform the educated Roman public about their new subjects. The most important Jewish authors of narrative works transmitted through Alexander were Demetrius, a chronographer of the third century B.C.E.; Eupolemus, a Judaean historian of the mid-second century; an anonymous Samaritan of the second century whose work was erroneously transmitted under the name of Eupolemus; and Artapanus, a novelistic author of the third or second century. Brief fragments survive from three other probably Jewish historians, Aristeas, Cleodemus Malchus, and Theophilus. A fourth figure, Philo the Elder, is mentioned by Josephus, though he may be identical with an epic poet excerpted by Alexander.

DEMETRIUS

Eusebius preserves five fragments of Demetrius treating aspects of Pentateuchal history: the Akedah, patriarchal history from Jacob through Moses, the ancestry of Moses, the bitter waters of Elim, and the arming of the Israelites after the Exodus.[8] Clement of Alexandria preserves yet another fragment which contains a chronological reckoning from the fall of the northern kingdom to the fall of Jerusalem and from that time until the reign of Ptolemy IV Philopator.[9] The last fragment provides a means of dating the work of Demetrius to the third century, since Philopator reigned from 221-204 B.C.E. Clement also preserves a title for Demetrius' work, 'On the Kings in Judaea.' It is not certain that all the fragments derive from that work, although it is quite possible that the schematic Pentateuchal history served as a preface to an account of the Judaean monarchy.

From these brief fragments it would appear that Demetrius attempted to retell Jewish history in a sober, even 'scientific' way, paying careful attention to the chronological data in his biblical source, which was clearly the Septuagint. Whether his work served apologetic aims directed at gentiles is unclear. Demetrius was, however, clearly concerned to reconcile apparent contradictions and difficulties within the biblical text. This concern is explicit in the fragment dealing with the arming of the Israelites which

---

44-52 and Walter, *Fragmente,* 91-92. The fragmentary texts of the authors preserved by Alexander are available in Denis, *Fragmenta,* 175-202 and Jacoby, *Fragmente* III C, 722-3.
[8] The fragments in Eusebius, *Praeparatio evangelica* are: 9:21,1-19, on patriarchal history; 9:29,1-3 on Moses; 9:29,15 on the waters of Elim; and 9:29,16 on the arming of the Israelites.
[9] This fragment is in Clement of Alexandria, *Stromata* 1:21,141, 1-2.

begins, 'Someone asks how the Israelites, who went out unarmed, obtained weapons.' Demetrius answers that after crossing the Red Sea the Israelites travelled for three days, sacrificed and then returned and picked up the arms of the drowned Egyptians. The form of this fragment suggests that at least part of this work was modeled on 'question and answer' literature. This form, along with the careful chronological calculation especially apparent in the fragment on history from Jacob to Moses, suggests that Demetrius' work is the product of an exegetical school, possibly at Alexandria. Here, in any case, we find a Jew clearly operating within a thoroughly hellenized literary environment, exploring his traditions within the framework provided him by Greek historiography.[10]

EUPOLEMUS

Five fragments of Eupolemus survive, primarily in Eusebius. The first gives a brief description of Moses. The second is a lengthy selection which summarizes the succession of the prophets from Moses through Samuel and then gives an account of the reigns of David and Solomon with a focus on the building of the Jerusalem temple. A third brief fragment, which may have been part of the preceding account, provides a further detail about the decoration of the temple with golden shields by Solomon and then mentions his death. A fourth fragment records an apocryphal prophecy of Jeremiah about the Babylonian captivity and describes the beginning of that period.[11] A final fragment found only in Clement of Alexandria contains a chronological reckoning from Adam to the 'fifth year of Demetrius and the twelfth year of Ptolemy,' which was 120 years before the Roman consulships of Gnaius Domitius and Asinius.[12]

The last fragment provides useful information about the date of Eupolemus. The reference to the Roman consuls, which no doubt stems from the source used by Clement in which Eupolemus was excerpted, is certainly to 40 B.C.E., when Gn. Domitius Calvinus and C. Asinius Pollio were consuls. The two Hellenistic monarchs mentioned by Eupolemus himself were Demetrius I Soter of Syria (162-151 B.C.E.) and Ptolemy VII Euergetes II (Physcon). The latter ruled Egypt, after a fashion, from 145 to 116. He had, however, been proclaimed king by the Alexandrians in 169

---

[10] For discussion of Demetrius' work, see Gutman, *Beginnings* 1, 132-9; Denis, *Introduction*, 248-51; Hengel, *Hellenism* 1, 69; Wacholder, *Eupolemus*, 98-104; Walter, *Aristobulos, Demetrios, Aristeas*, 280-3 and Bickerman, 'The Jewish Historian'. For rabbinic interest in reconciling biblical chronological data, see the *Seder Olam* and *B.T. Sanhedrin*, 69b.
[11] The fragments in Eusebius, *Praeparatio evangelica* are: 9:26,1 on Moses; 9:30,1-34,18 on the prophets and the temple; 9:34,20 on Solomon's shields; 9:39,2-5 on the prophecy of Jeremiah.
[12] Clement of Alexandria, *Stromata* 1:21,141, 4-5. The fragments, as well as the testimonia to Eupolemus, are translated in Wacholder, *Eupolemus*, 307-12.

and, after being displaced by the Romans in favor of his brother, Ptolemy VI Philometor, had ruled in Cyrenaica until 145. Thus, Eupolemus, possibly because he recognized Physcon as the legitimate Egyptian king, used 169 as his initial regnal year. The fifth year of Demetrius and the twelfth of Ptolemy thus was 157 B.C.E., a little less than 120 years before the consular year of Domitius and Asinius. Eupolemus' work is thus probably to be dated several years prior to the middle of the second century B.C.E.

Although Eusebius gives 'On the Prophecy of Elijah' as the title of the work from which the fragment on David and Solomon derives, that title is probably an error by Alexander Polyhistor. Clement records the fragment about Moses, under the title of 'On the Kings in Judaea,' the same title which Clement ascribes to the work of Demetrius. This was probably the designation for the work from which all the fragments come. Eupolemus does, however, indicate an interest in prophecy, not only in the fragment on Jeremiah and the end of the monarchy, but also in his designation for all the pre-monarchical leaders of the Jewish people. He may thus have written a separate work on the subject.

Eupolemus is, in one regard, unique among the fragmentary Greco-Jewish historians, in that there is a probable reference to him apart from his literary remains. 1 Macc 8:17 mentions Eupolemus, son of John, who served as an envoy from Judas Maccabeus to Rome in or shortly before 160 B.C.E. His father, John, also served in a diplomatic capacity in the time of Antiochus III, according to 2 Macc 4:11. The emphases of the remaining fragments of Eupolemus are certainly compatible with the identification of their author as an educated Palestinian, associated with the leadership of the Maccabean revolt and in intimate contact with the wider Hellenistic world. The existence of Eupolemus' Greek history indicates the continuing impact of Hellenistic culture in Palestine even after the Maccabean revolt.

Much more than in the case of Demetrius, the work of Eupolemus displays definite encomiastic and apologetic tendencies. The initial fragment on Moses, which claims that he was the 'first sage,' who provided an alphabet to the Jews from whom it passed to the Phoenicians and the Greeks, represents a common concern of the cultural polemics of the Hellenistic age. In this period 'barbarian' historians, such as Manetho in Egypt, Berossus in Babylon, and Philo of Byblos (or possibly his alleged source, Sanchuniathon), wrote in Greek to extoll their national traditions. In such literature the claim was regularly made that the oriental traditions were chronologically and qualitatively superior to Greek culture. Such apologetics, of course, had precedents in Greek tradition itself, in particular in ethnographic literature of the sort composed by Hecataeus of Abdera. The cultural polemics of the Hellenistic period were taken up in the explicitly apologetic work of Josephus. Later, Church Fathers such as Eusebius, used the tradition to demonstrate the priority of biblical revelation to pagan philosophy and culture. The brief fragment of

163

Eupolemus on Moses represents an early attestation of this venerable apologetic tradition.[13]

In the lengthy fragment on David and Solomon, political tendencies are particularly evident. David is said to have campaigned victoriously against 'the Syrians beyond the Euphrates, Commagene, the Assyrians in Galadene and the Phoenicians . . . the Idumaeans, Ammanites, Moabites, Ituraeans, Nabataeans, Nabdaeans, Suron the King of Tyre and Phoenicia.' Furthermore, it is claimed that David made a treaty of friendship with Vaphres, the King of Egypt. Solomon, on his accession to the throne, corresponds, on a basis of equality and mutual respect, with Suron and Vaphres about the temple which he is about to build. Much of this account is, of course, fanciful, although the royal correspondence has a biblical model in the account in 1 Kgs 5:2-9 and 2 Chron 2:3-16 of the correspondence between Solomon and Hiram of Tyre. The letters, like the report of David's military success, serve to display the ancient and honourable political position of the Jewish nation, a status which it was in the interest of Judas and his supporters to claim in their struggle against Seleucid hegemony.[14]

Another prominent feature of the fragments of Eupolemus is their concentration on the temple of Solomon. The passage on the subject may have been simply a descriptive excursus, the like of which appear later in Josephus. Nonetheless, the enthusiasm for the temple which Eupolemus displays probably reflects general Jewish sentiment at the temple's restoration in 164 by Judas Maccabeus.

Eupolemus follows his biblical sources, both Greek and Hebrew, quite loosely, as can be seen already from the use of the fictitious Vaphres. It is, however, surprising to find the assertions that David was Saul's son, or that David turned over to Solomon the materials for building the temple, 'in the presence of Eli and the leaders of the twelve tribes.' Some details of this sort may be errors on the part of Alexander Polyhistor. Other nonscriptural data, such as the remark that Jeremiah kept the ark of the covenant and the tablets of the Law when the first temple was destroyed, probably reflect traditional legend.[15] Nonetheless, it is clear that Eupolemus was not content simply to repeat earlier historical works, and he hardly feels himself bound to a scriptural canon of history

The work of Eupolemus may be understood as apologetic in a broad sense. It does not offer a defense of the Jews against anti-Jewish calumnies in the specific ways that the *Antiquities* or *Against Apion* of Josephus later

---

[13] For the Greek literary and cultural traditions which Eupolemus reflects, see Gutman, *Beginnings* 1, 15-35; Wacholder, *Eupolemus,* 71-96 and Hengel, *Hellenism* 1, 92-95.

[14] Josephus (*Ant.* 8:55-56) comments on the evidential value of the correspondence between Hiram and Solomon found in his biblical source, indicating the apologetic potential of such material.

[15] For similar legendary material, cf. 2 Macc 1:19-2:15.

would do. Eupolemus' work does serve as a piece of political and cultural propaganda for the Jews of the second century who had come into such violent conflict with an important part of the Hellenistic world.[16]

PSEUDO-EUPOLEMUS

One further fragment is preserved by Eusebius under the name of Eupolemus, but this assignment is certainly an error, probably committed by Alexander Polyhistor. The fragment has affinities with another notice transmitted anonymously.[17] Both are probably the work of a single author who was probably a Samaritan. In the first and longer fragment there is an account of Abraham as the person who discovered astrology and the 'Chaldaean science' and transmitted these to the Phoenicians and later to the Egyptians. Suggestive of a Samaritan origin is the remark that Abraham, after his victory over the eastern (here Armenian) kings of Genesis 14, was entertained at the temple of the city of Argarizin (i.e., Har Garizim), 'which is translated Mountain of the Most High' where the priest-king Melchizedek gave him gifts. The fragment ends with the report of Abraham's teaching the Egyptians astrology, which, it now appears, Abraham did not himself invent. Instead, the discovery is attributed to Enoch, who is loosely connected with a euhemeristic genealogy tracing the descendents of Kronos, in which Enoch is syncretized with the Greek Titan Atlas. The second and briefer fragment mentions that Abraham had traced his descent back to the giants, that the tower of Babel was named after its founder Belos, and that Abraham brought astrology to the Phoenicians and Egyptians.

These fragments of the anonymous Samaritan, although apparently dependent on the Septuagint, display a higher degree of openness to the Hellenistic environment than was evident either in Demetrius or Eupolemus, and that openness seems to be attested in other reports about the Samaritans during this period.[18] The euhemeristic account of early history again reflects an important tendency of Hellenistic ethnographic historiography, especially the works of such figures as Hecataeus, Manetho, and the later Philo of Byblos.[19]

---

[16] For discussions of the general significance of Eupolemus, see Gutman, *Beginnings* 2, 73-99; Denis, *Introduction,* 252-5; Walter, *Fragmente,* 93-98; Charlesworth, *The Pseudepigrapha* 107-8; and Wacholder, *Eupolemus.*

[17] The fragments are found in Eusebius, *Praeparatio evangelica* 9:17,2-9 and 18,2. For a translation, see Wacholder, *Eupolemus,* 311-12.

[18] Syncretism was by no means the exclusive property of Samaritans in this period. Freudenthal initially suggested that several of the fragments of Greco-Jewish literature were Samaritan products. Most of his suggestions have been rejected. On this issue, see Collins, 'The Epic of Theodotus.'

[19] On the latter figure, see Attridge — Oden, *Philo of Byblos.*

Date and provenance of the anonymous Samaritan are uncertain. The silence of the text on the destruction of the temple on Mt. Garizim by John Hyrcanus in 129 B.C.E. might provide a *terminus ante*. The relative denigration of the Egyptians, who are the last to receive the esoteric knowledge of the east, may indicate a pro-Seleucid bias, which would not be unexpected in a Samaritan of the early second century. Although Palestinian provenance is likely, the possibility cannot be excluded that the author wrote somewhere in the Diaspora, where Samaritan communities were also to be found.[20]

ARTAPANUS

Eusebius preserves three fragments of the work of Artapanus, one of which has a partial parallel in Clement of Alexandria.[21] The first fragment claims that the Jews were originally called 'Hermiouth,' which is translated into Greek as 'Judaeans,' but were later called 'Hebrews' after Abraham, who travelled to Egypt and taught the locals astrology. The second fragment records the history of Joseph and attributes to him the first systematic division of Egyptian land. The third fragment is a lengthy account of Moses, elaborately embellished in the fashion of an adventure novel. The saga begins with the deaths of Abraham, his son Mempsasenoth, and the king of Egypt, named Pharethothes in the first fragment. Under the new king, Palmanothes, the Jews are treated harshly, but the king's daughter, Merris, who is sterile, adopts a Jewish child, Moses by name. Merris is the bride of Chenephres, the ruler of Memphis and 'of a good part of Egypt.' When he comes of age, Moses, whom the Greeks call Musaios, teacher of Orpheus, provides numerous benefits for his stepfather, by inventing boats, architectural devices, military equipment, water works and, last but not least, philosophy. He also devises the Egyptian system of nomes and assigns to each the deity to be worshipped there. He further provides for the priests by giving them hieroglyphics and assigning them special territories, in return for which they honour him as a god, under the name of Hermes (the Greek equivalent of the Egyptian Thoth).[22] Chenephres is ungrateful and envious of Moses and he plots against his step-son. He first sends him on a campaign against the Ethiopians with an inadequate

[20] For discussion of Pseudo-Eupolemus, see Gutman, *Beginnings* 2, 95-108; Denis, *Introduction,* 261-2; Hengel *Hellenism,* 1, 88-92; Walter, *Fragmente,* 137-40; Wacholder, 'Pseudo-Eupolemus' and *Eupolemus,* 287-93.

[21] The fragments are to be found in Eusebius, *Praeparatio evangelica* 9:18,1 on the original name of the Jews; 9:23,1-4 on the story of Joseph; 9:27,1-37 on the story of Moses. Sections 22-25 of Eusebius' account are paralleled in Clement of Alexandria, *Stromata* 1:23,154, 2-3.

[22] Thus, Moses here takes on some of the features often attributed to Osiris as the founder of Egyptian culture. Cf. Diodorus Siculus, *Bibl. Hist.* 1:14-15, and Plutarch, *De Iside et Osiride,* 13. Furthermore, Moses has certain features associated with Hermes-Thoth in Diodorus 1:16, with whom he is explicitly identified by Artapanus.

peasant force. Nonetheless, Moses is spectacularly successful. In the course of the campaign he founds a new city, named after himself, Hermopolis. The Ethiopians so love him that they undertake circumcision.[23] When Moses returns from the campaign, he teaches further useful arts of civilization, including the use of the plough. Chenephres, acting in spite, orders the Apis bull and the other animals sanctified by Moses to be buried in order to hide the inventions of Moses. He then tries to have Moses slain while on an expedition to bury Merris who has just died. Moses avoids the plot and founds the city of Meroe. When he returns, Moses kills Chenephres' chief henchman in self-defense and then flees to Arabia, where he marries the daughter of Raguel. Raguel wants to invade Egypt and put Moses on the throne, but Moses will not hear of it. Meanwhile, Chenephres contracts elephantiasis because he had ordered the Jews to distinguish themselves by wearing linen clothing. Moses, after the burning bush encounter, returns to Egypt where he is imprisoned. He miraculously escapes when, during the night, the doors of the prison automatically open. (It was the parallel between this account and the report of the escape of Peter in Acts 12:3-17 which caught the attention of Clement of Alexandria.) When Moses is brought to Chenephres he is asked for the name of his God. Moses whispers it into the king's ear and the latter is struck dumb until he is revived by Moses. Then there follows an account of the plagues which provides the occasion for further aetiologies. The annual Nile flood, for example, begins as one of the plagues. Similarly, the magic staff of Moses is the prototype of the staves which appear in every Egyptian temple. Finally, Moses is successful in securing the release of the Jews, although no Egyptian firstborn dies in the process. Different rationalistic explanations of the crossing of the Red Sea are offered on behalf of the Memphites and the Heliopolitans, but the miraculous passage is recounted in all its splendour. The account closes with a physical description of its hero, and the notice that he led the Exodus in his eighty-ninth year.

Artapanus, like Eupolemus and Pseudo-Eupolemus, displays many of the characteristic motifs of the often apologetic cultural and ethnographic historiography of the Hellenistic period. Here, as in Pseudo-Eupolemus, Abraham appears as the inventor of astrology and Moses is in many ways the culture-bringing 'first sage' described by Eupolemus. Furthermore, the euhemerism which surfaced in the genealogy of Enoch in Pseudo-Eupolemus appears massively here in the syncretization of Moses with Musaios and Hermes. Also like Pseudo-Eupolemus, Artapanus displays a remarkable tolerance of non-Jewish — specifically Egyptian — culture (e.g., Moses establishes Egyptian religion). That culture, however, is seen to be derivative, and in some cases amusingly so (e.g., mummified sacred

---

[23] On this legend of Moses' Ethiopian campaign, which also appears in Josephus *Ant.* 2:238-53, see most recently, Rajak, 'Moses in Ethiopia.'

animals are the result of a plot against Moses). Through the exaltation of Moses, Artapanus asserts Jewish superiority. It is a claim made with gentle disdain but without stridency or rancour.

Although the title of Artapanus' work is given as 'On the Jews' and 'Judaica,' it is unclear how much, if any, beyond Moses he extended his story. While the account has its affinities with important strands of Hellenistic historiography, the elaborate embellishment and dramatization of the life of Moses suggest that the work had closer ties to popular romance than to serious historiography, and that its aim was as much to entertain as to instruct. Dating precisely the work of Artapanus is impossible. He certainly wrote before Alexander Polyhistor and thus not later than 100 B.C.E. and he could have been active in either the second or third centuries. Alexandria was probably his home.[24]

Other Fragmentary Historians

The remaining fragments of Jewish historical works are much more limited in scope. Eusebius preserves from Alexander Polyhistor a fragment of a work 'On the Jews' by Aristeas, who is not to be confused with the fictive author of the letter to Philocrates. The fragment summarizes the story of Job who was 'originally called Jobab.' The passage may have been part of a historical work or possibly of some exegetical tract. It follows the general outline of the biblical account, with some legendary additions, a few of which are reflected in the Theodotianic additions to Job and in the *Testament of Job*.[25]

Cleodemus, 'the prophet, also called Malchus,' appears in Josephus, who is in turn cited by Eusebius.[26] Josephus claims Alexander Polyhistor as his source, but it is not clear that he here drew from Alexander's work on the Jews.[27] The passage gives a brief report on three sons of Abraham by Katura: Sures, who gave his name to Syria, and Japhras and Apheras, who gave their names to the city of Aphra and to the country of Africa. These two are said to have campaigned in Africa with Heracles and one of them gave his daughter in marriage to the Greek hero who begot Diodorus, who begot Sophon. This brief text recalls Artapanus and Pseudo-Eupolemus in its attempt to harmonize pagan and Jewish traditions. There is no indication that Cleodemus was, like Pseudo-Eupolemus, a Samaritan. His interest in Africa and in an African version of the Heracles saga, paralleled

---

[24] For discussion of the work of Artapanus, see Braun, *History and Romance*, 26-31, 99-102; Gutman, *Beginnings* 2, 109-35; Denis, *Introduction*, 255-7; and Walter, *Fragmente*, 121-6.

[25] The fragment is in Eusebius, *Praeparatio evangelica* 9:25,1-4. For discussion, see Denis, *Introduction*, 258-9; and Walter, *Aristobulos, Demetrios, Aristeas*, 293-6.

[26] The fragment is found in Josephus, *Ant.* 1:239-41 and Eusebius, *Praeparatio evangelica* 9:20, 2-4.

[27] On this issue, see Walter, 'Zur Überlieferung.'

in the court chronicles of Juba II of Mauretania, suggests that Cleodemus was a Jew of that region, possibly of Carthage. Beyond the fact that he wrote before Alexander Polyhistor, nothing can be said of his date.[28]

Eusebius, between two fragments of Eupolemus, mentions a writer, Theophilus, who relates that Solomon sent to the king of Tyre the gold left over from the decoration of the Jerusalem temple. The king of Tyre then used this gold in connection with a statue of his daughter. It is unclear whether this fragment is from a Jewish author. The name Theophilus appears in a list in Josephus of Greeks who wrote on Judaism and this Theophilus is probably the author of the fragment in Eusebius. Josephus (*Ag. Ap.* 1:217-18) may have been mistaken about the ethnic affiliation of this writer, as he was about Demetrius, Eupolemus and Philo the elder, but the fragment is much too small to give any indication of the nature of Theophilus' work.[29]

It is remotely possible that the elder Philo just mentioned is also to be included among Greco-Jewish historians. However, portions of an epic poem attributed to a Philo survive through Alexander Polyhistor in Eusebius, while there are no narrative fragments.[30] It is most likely, then, that the Philo mentioned by Josephus was a poet and not a historian.

PSEUDO-HECATAEUS

In addition to the various historical narratives written by Jews, and occasionally by Samaritans, under their own names during the Hellenistic period, there was at least one pseudepigraphical historical work written by a Jew which circulated during this period. This was hardly an isolated phenomenon, and there are numerous apologetic and propagandistic pseudepigrapha in other genres written by Jews during this period. The historical work in question was entitled 'On Abraham and the Egyptians' and was attributed to Hecataeus, the Greek ethnographer of the late fourth and early third century B.C.E., whose genuine work may well have influenced many of the Greco-Jewish authors of the second century.[31] The work 'On Abraham' is cited by Clement of Alexandria, who quotes a poetic fragment, also pseudepigraphical, attributed to Sophocles, which

---

[28] For discussion of Cleodemus, see Gutman, *Beginnings* 1, 136-43; and Denis, *Introduction*, 259-61.

[29] The fragment is found in Eusebius, *Praeparatio evangelica* 9:34,19. For discussion, see Walter, *Fragmente*, 109-110.

[30] Cf. Eusebius, *Praeparatio evangelica* 9:20,1; 24,1; 37,1-3. On Philo the Epic Poet see pp. 118-21.

[31] The certainly genuine fragment of Hecataeus which mentions the Jews is preserved in Diodorus Siculus, *Bibl. Hist.* 40:3. For a text, translation and notes, see Jacoby, *Fragmente*, III A #264, fr. 6, with commentary; *Fragmente*, III a, pp. 34-52; and Stern, *Greek and Latin Authors* 1, 20-35. For discussion, see Gutman, *Beginnings* 1, 39-73 and Wacholder, *Eupolemus*, 85-96. See also Stern, 'The Jews', 1105-9.

'Hecataeus' is said to have cited.[32] Josephus, in recounting the story of Abraham in the first book of his *Antiquities* also mentions a work of 'Hecataeus,' along with works by Berossus and Nicolaus of Damascus pertinent to Abraham and his times. It is likely that this is the same pseudepigraphical work mentioned by Clement, and some of the non-biblical details about Abraham in Josephus may ultimately derive from this source.[33]

It has also been suspected that citations in Josephus' *Against Apion* of a work 'On the Jews' by Hecataeus derive from a pseudepigraphon. The longest of these is a series of citations dealing with Jews under Alexander the Great and his immediate successors.[34] Connected with these may be a brief reference in *Ag. Ap.* 2:43 to the granting of Samaria to the Jews by Alexander. The tone of these fragments is generally favourable to the Jews, even when they are said to have 'razed to the ground' 'the temples and altars erected in the country by its invaders.' Although Greek attitudes toward Jews in the early Hellenistic period were generally positive,[35] such approbation would be unexpected in the genuine Hectaeus. Other arguments have been advanced to support the theory that these fragments in the *Against Apion* are pseudepigraphical, but these are inconclusive.[36] Nonetheless, the tenor of these remarks suggests either that another pseudepigraphon is involved here, or that an authentic work of Hecataeus has been slightly revised by Josephus or an intermediate Jewish source.[37]

[32] Clement of Alexandria, *Stromata* 5:113,1-2.

[33] Josephus, *Ant.* 1:154-68.

[34] Josephus, *Ag. Ap.* 1:183-205, 213b-214a.

[35] Early Greek attitudes to Moses have been usefully illuminated by Gager, *Moses*. For his skeptical position on the question of Pseudo-Hecataeus, see 'Pseudo-Hecataeus Again.' For a survey of early Greek literature on the Jews, see Stern, *Greek and Latin Authors* 1.

[36] For discussion of such an anachronism in the matter of Jewish taxes, see Schaller, 'Hekataios.' These arguments have been discussed and rejected by Stern, *Greek and Latin Authors* 1, 41.

[37] Among scholars who have recently argued that both the fragments on Abraham from Eusebius and Josephus, *Antiquities* and the fragments on Moses from Josephus, *Against Apion* are pseudepigraphical, there is considerable difference of opinion about the relationship of the fragments. Wacholder (*Eupolemus*, 259-87) finds three pseudepigrapha. The first, consisting of the fragments from *Ag. Ap.* 1:183-205 and 213-14, and attested in the *Letter of Aristeas* 83-120, is assigned to the early Hellenistic period, c. 300 B.C.E. The second, consisting of *Ag. Ap.* 2:43-47, to which there is an allusion in *Ant.* 12:3-8, is assigned to the Hellenistic period, i.e., between the composition of the *Letter of Aristeas* in the mid-second century B.C.E. and the work of Josephus. The third, consisting of Clement, *Stromata* 5:113,1-2 and Josephus, *Ant.* 1:159, is assigned to the second century B.C.E., before Aristobulus. Wacholder further claims that this is the text about whose authenticity the second-century grammarian Philo of Byblos expressed doubts. Cf. Origen, *Contra Celsum* 1:15b. Walter (*Fragmente*, 144-53), on the other hand, sees only two pseudepigrapha. The first, consisting of Josephus, *Ag. Ap.* 1:183b-205a, 213b-214a, and 2:43, is assigned to a Jew of the diaspora in the late second century B.C.E. The second, consisting of Josephus, *Ant.* 1:154-68 and Clement, *Stromata* 5:113, 1-2, is assigned to an Alexandrian Jew of the first century B.C.E. or the first century C.E.

The fragments of Greco-Jewish histories from the first two centuries of the Hellenistic period offer a tantalizing glimpse into the processes of of assimilation and cultural polemics which were at work among Jews during the period,[38] but they make little or no contribution to the understanding of contemporary political developments. Such is the concern of the two major Jewish histories of the period, 1 and 2 Maccabees.

1 Maccabees

1 Maccabees[39] is the principal source for the history of the Hasmonean family from the outbreak of the revolt against the religious persecution by Antiochus IV (167 B.C.E.) to the end of the reign of Simon (134 B.C.E.). The work also notes the accession of Simon's son, John Hyrcanus (134-104 B.C.E.), and it refers to accomplishments of his reign recorded in the 'chronicles of his high priesthood' (16:24). This allusion suggests that the history was composed late in the reign of Hyrcanus or possibly shortly after his death.[40] In any case, it could not have been written after 63 B.C.E., since it displays a favourable attitude toward the Romans which would be highly unlikely after Pompey's desecration of the temple in that year. The original language of 1 Maccabees was almost certainly Hebrew and the Semitic style of the original shows clearly through the Greek translation.[41] Although it has occasionally been argued that the last two chapters are a secondary addition to the work, since they are ignored in the paraphrase of 1 Maccabees by Josephus, the work is best understood as an integral unity and the absence of the last two chapters in Josephus is probably to be explained by his reliance on other Hellenistic sources.[42]

While 1 Maccabees records events of the second century in a generally

---

[38] It is possible that other fragments attributed to Greek authors of the Hellenistic period are also pseudepigraphical Jewish works written for apologetic purposes. The well-known passage on the Jews in Strabo, for example, (*Geog.* 16:2,34-46, on which see Stern, *Greek and Latin Authors* 1, 294-311), may contain or be based on such a text. For that possibility, see Schürer, *Geschichte* 3, 156; Nock, 'Posidonius;' Gager, *Moses*, 44-47; and Lebram, 'Idealstaat.'

[39] The original Hebrew title of the work, *Sarbethsabaniel,* is preserved by Origen, whose canon-list is cited by Eusebius, *Ecclesiastical History* 6:25,2. The precise interpretation of that title is debated. It may represent a corruption of a Hebrew *sar beth el,* as proposed by Schunck (*1. Makkabäerbuch,* 289), or *sphar beth sabanai'el,* as argued by Goldstein (*I Maccabees,* 16).

[40] Most treatments of 1 Maccabees date the work late in the second century B.C.E. Goldstein (*I Maccabees,* 63) dates it slightly later, in the reign of Alexander Jannaeus, but before 90 B.C.E.

[41] In addition to the manuscript witnesses to the text of 1 Maccabees, the old Latin and Syriac translations, as well as the paraphrase of the work by Josephus in *Antiquities* 12 and 13, are of textual importance. On this issue, see Goldstein, *I Maccabees,* 175-9 and Schunck, *1. Makkabäerbuch,* 290.

[42] Among more recent commentators, only Zeitlin (*First Book of Maccabees,* 27-33) argues for the addition of the last two chapters after the destruction of the temple in 70 C.E. For discussion of the issue, see Abel — Starcky, *Maccabées,* 9, 16; Schunk, *Quellen,* 7-15; Arenhoevel, *Theokratie, 94-96;* and Goldstein, *I Maccabees, 25-26.*

sober and straightforward fashion, it clearly does so from a perspective favourable to the Hasmonean dynasty, who are presented as pious biblical heroes, God's chosen instruments for the deliverance of his people. Mattathias, the head of the clan, in striking the first blow of rebellion, 'burned with zeal for the law, as Phinehas did against Zimri the son of Salu'.[43] Before he dies, Mattathias addresses his sons and leaves them a testament of devotion to the Torah.[44] He proposes that they emulate various biblical examples of zeal and fidelity to tradition, including Abraham, Joseph, Phinehas, Joshua, Caleb, David, Elijah, and the companions of Daniel (2:51-60). The author of the work thus implicitly places Mattathias and his sons in that tradition which is held up as the ideal. Later Jonathan's position will be described in terms of the biblical judges (9:73). Here, as in many of the comparisons with biblical proto-types, there is an implicit defense of the legitimacy of the irregular, char-ismatic leadership exercized by the Hasmoneans.[45]

The piety of Judas Maccabeus is emphasized in a series of speeches and prayers uttered during his campaigns. Before engaging the Seleucid general Seron at Beth-horon, Judas exhorts his troops to be of good courage since 'It is not on the size of the army that victory in battle depends, but strength comes from heaven' (3:19). Similarly, before doing battle with the general Gorgias, Judas encourages his men, 'Do not fear their numbers or be afraid when they charge. Remember how our fathers were saved at the Red Sea, when Pharaoh with his forces pursued them. And now let us cry to Heaven, to see whether he will favour us and remember his covenant with our fathers and crush this army before us today. Then all the Gentiles will know that there is one who redeems and saves Israel' (4:9-11). Likewise, before engaging Lysias and his forces Judas prays that God will deliver the Greeks to him and his troops as he delivered the Philistines to David and Jonathan. Such speeches and prayers are more than rhetorical exercises. Rather, the sentiments which the author of this work has his protagonists express provide a theological evaluation of the events which are narrated, events in which God's delivering hand is seen to be at work as it was of old.

The importance of the Hasmonean family as the instruments of that deliverance is made clear in the presentation of an episode in which an unauthorized expedition meets with disaster (5:55-62). The author here editorializes. 'Thus the people suffered a great rout because, thinking to do a brave deed, they did not listen to Judas and his brothers. But they did not belong to the family of those men through whom deliverance was given to Israel' (5:61-62).

[43] 2:26. Cf. Num 25:6-11.
[44] On this passage, see Adinolfi, 'Il testamento' and Nickelsburg, *Resurrection,* 97-102.
[45] On the traditional models used to portray the Maccabean heroes, see Arenhoevel, *Theokratie,* 40.

172

While the legitimacy of the leadership of the Hasmonean house is thus seen to rest on the divine selection of a family conspicuous for its piety and devotion to traditional laws, the opponents of the family are frequently described as 'lawless ones.' It is 'lawless man' who initially want to make a covenant with surrounding gentiles (1:11). The 'lawless and ungodly men of Israel' support Alcimus for the high priesthood (7:8). After the death of Judas the 'lawless emerged in all parts of Israel, all the doers of injustice appeared' (9:23). The same lawless villains regularly plot against Jonathan (9:58; 10:61; 11:21, 25). In treating the opposition to the Hasmoneans under this single opprobrious rubric, the author has obscured some of the real tensions within Israelite society during the second century, in the interests of his pro-Hasmonean program. The only indication that some opposition to the Hasmoneans might have had a specifically religious basis comes in the notice that after the appointment of Alcimus as high priest certain 'Hasideans' sought peace with him as a 'priest from the line of Aaron' (7:12-14). The fact that their trust was misplaced and that sixty of their number were treacherously slain by Alcimus and his Greek supporters, indicates the justice of the author's initial judgement on the wickedness of the opponents of the Hasmoneans.

Another significant distortion occurs in the author's description of the state of affairs in Jerusalem prior to the Maccabean revolt. Although the author suggests that the program of hellenization had significant local support (1:1-15, 43) he places on Antiochus IV most of the blame for the events leading up to the persecution (1:21-53). The king is later made to recognize the sinfulness of his actions in attempting to suppress traditional Jewish practices. On his death-bed, sick from grief at the news of the defeat of his general, Lysias, he laments, 'To what distress I have come! And into what a great flood I am now plunged! For I was kind and beloved in my power. But now I remember the evils I did in Jerusalem. I seized all her vessels of silver and gold; and I sent to destroy the inhabitants of Judah without good reason. I know that it is because of this that these evils have come upon me; and behold, I am perishing of deep grief in a strange land' (6:11-13). Here again the theological dimension of the evaluation of history in 1 Maccabees is evident. Just as the successes of the Hasmoneans were due to divine care for pious Israel, so the defeat of their enemies was a sign of God's righteous retribution.

While the author of 1 Maccabees establishes the legitimacy of the Hasmonean line on religious grounds, he does not neglect to show that the dynasty had a generally recognized political legitimacy in the eyes of the major powers of the second century. To this end he includes a number of documents, prominently including letters in which various Seleucid monarchs or pretenders appoint or confirm Jonathan or Simon as high priests (Alexander Balas to Jonathan, 10:18-20; Demetrius I to Jonathan, 10:25-45; Demetrius II to Jonathan, 11:30-37; Demetrius II to Simon,

13:31-40; Antiochus VII to Simon, 15:2-9). Relations with states outside the Seleucid empire also receive attention. The embassy to Rome dispatched by Judas and the resultant treaty of alliance, recorded on bronze tablets in Jerusalem, is recounted in 1 Maccabees 8. That alliance is confirmed under Jonathan (12:1-4) and Simon (14:16-19), in whose reign Rome again intervenes in Seleucid affairs on behalf of the Jews (15:15-24). Furthermore, the author records on several occasions the relations between the Jews and the Spartans.[46] The first occasion is a letter of Jonathan, which is based on and which reflects a letter of the pre-Hasmonean high priests (12:5-23). The relationship is continued under Simon (14:16-23).

Perhaps the most significant evidence for the author's pro-Hasmonean stance is a bit of documentary evidence, consisting of a proclamation (14:27-45) of the 'great assembly of the priests and the people and the rulers of the nation and the elders of the country' (14:28), proclaiming their gratitude to Simon for the liberty and prosperity which he had brought to Israel and recording their decision to have him as 'their leader and high priest for ever, until a trustworthy prophet should arise' (14:41). In this decree, the Jewish people themselves definitively acknowledge what charisma, divine guidance, and external powers have produced, a period of virtual messianic bliss under Hasmonean political and religious leadership.[47]

Another important dimension of 1 Maccabees is the celebration of that Hasmonean leadership in a series of poetic reflections on the events related.[48] These poetic reflections begin on a mournful note as the author laments the desecration of the temple during the persecution by Antiochus:

> Her (Jerusalem's) sanctuary became desolate as a desert;
>> her feasts were turned into mourning,
> her sabbaths into a reproach
>> her honour into contempt.
> Her dishonour now grew great as her glory;
>> her exaltation was turned into mourning (1:39-40).

Similar sentiments appear on the lips of Mattathias:

---

[46] On ancient attitudes toward Sparta in general, see Tigerstedt, *The Legend of Sparta.* For the alleged kinship of Jews and Spartans, which represents a common form of cultural propaganda in the Hellenistic world, see Hengel, *Hellenism* 1, 72; Schüller, 'Some Problems;' and Cardauns, 'Juden und Spartaner.' In his apologetics for Judaism, Josephus will also exploit certain Jewish-Spartan parallels. Cf. *Ag. Ap.* 2:130, 172, 225-31, 259, 271.

[47] On the the Messianic overtones of the portrayal of Simon's reign, see especially Arenhoevel, 'Eschatologie' and *Theokratie,* 58-69. For the possible political purposes of 1 Maccabees' portrayal of the Hasmoneans, see Goldstein, *I Maccabees,* 62-89. For discussion of the 'great assembly' mentioned in 1 Macc 14:28, see Schürer, *History* 2, 199-226 and Safrai, 'Jewish Self-Government'.

[48] On the poetic pieces in 1 Maccabees, see especially Neuhaus, *Studien.*

Alas! Why was I born to see this,
  the ruin of my people, the ruin of the holy city,
and to dwell there when it was given over to the enemy,
  the sanctuary given over to aliens?
Her temple has become like a man without honour;
  her glorious vessels have been carried into captivity.
Her babes have been killed in her streets,
  her youths by the sword of the foe.[49]

The leadership of Judas receives hymnic praise:

He extended the glory of his people.
  like a giant he put on his breastplate;
he girded on his armour of war and waged battles,
  protecting the host by his sword.
He was like a lion in his deeds,
  like a lion's cub roaring for prey.[50]
He searched out and pursued the lawless;
  he burned those who troubled his people.
Lawless men shrank back for fear of him;
  all the evildoers were confounded;
  and deliverance prospered by his hand (3:3-6).

Although Judas thus receives due recognition, it is Simon to whom is given the longest and most fulsome praise:

The land had rest all the days of Simon.
  He sought the good of his nation;
his rule was pleasing to them,
  as was the honour shown him, all his days . . .
They tilled their land in peace;
  the ground gave its increase,
  and the trees of the plains their fruit.
Old men sat in the streets;
  they all talked together of good things;
  and the youths donned the glories and garments of war.
He supplied the cities with food
  and furnished them with the means of defense,
  till his renown spread to the ends of the earth.
He established peace in the land,
  and Israel rejoiced with great joy.
Each man sat under his vine and his fig tree,
  and there was none to make them afraid.[51]

[49] 2:7-9. The language of this and the preceding hymnic piece is paralleled in Pss 44, 74, 79 and the book of Lamentations. Cf. also 4 Ezra 10:21-22.
[50] Note the imagery in Hos 5:14.
[51] Thus conditions under Simon parallel those under Solomon, as described in 1 Kgs 4:25, and as predicted for 'the latter days' in Mic 4:4. Cf. Zech 3:10.

No one was left in the land to fight them,
 and the kings were crushed in those days.
He strengthened all the humble of his people;
 he sought out the law,
 and did away with every lawless and wicked man.
He made the sanctuary glorious
 and added to the vessels of the sanctuary (14:4-15).

The idyllic picture painted in these verses summarizes succinctly the positive attitude toward the Hasmonean house which characterizes 1 Maccabees.

The record of second-century history contained in 1 Maccabees certainly depended on earlier sources, although the precise delineation of those sources remains problematic.[52] The fact that there are two calendrical systems used in the work, one relying on the official Macedonian Seleucid era for dating events of general history, the other relying on the Babylonian version of the Seleucid era for dating internal events of Jewish history, suggests the use of two major sources.[53] One of these was probably a history of the Seleucids, the other either a chronicle or possibly several separate chronicles of the Hasmoneans. The documentary materials may have been taken from such earlier works or directly from the official archives. While the author of 1 Maccabees may have used still other sources, there is little solid evidence for them.

2 Maccabees

The second Maccabean history is, from a literary point of view, a much more complex document than 1 Maccabees and that complexity has led to a broad diversity of opinion about the nature and aims of the work. 2 Maccabees is introduced with two letters (1:1-9, 1:10-2:18), containing a citation of a third (1:7-8), which call upon Egyptian Jews to celebrate the festival of the rededication of the temple. The bulk of the work is a history of the Maccabean revolt from the inception of the Hellenistic reform until the defeat of the Seleucid general, Nicanor, by Judas Maccabeus. This history is not an original composition, but rather, as a preface (2:19-32) indicates, it is an epitome of a lost, five-volume work by one Jason of Cyrene. Major problems arise in attempting to understand the relationship between the prefaced letters and the epitome of Jason's history.

---

[52] The sources of 1 Maccabees have been extensively analyzed by Schunck, *Quellen,* summarized in his *1. Makkabäerbuch,* 291-2. His results have been criticized by Neuhaus, 'Quellen.' Independently Goldstein (*I Macabees,* 37-54 and 90-103) offers a different, and more speculative, source analysis. For a partial criticism, see Cohen, *Josephus,* 44, n. 77. For further discussion of possible sources for 1 Maccabees, see Wacholder, *Eupolemus,* 27-38.
[53] For the complex problems of chronology in the Maccabean histories, see Abel — Starcky, *Maccabées,* 35-38; Schaumberger, 'Seleukidenliste'; Hanhart, 'Zur Zeitrechnung;' Lebram, 'Zur Chronologie;' and Goldstein, *I Maccabees,* 21-26 and 161-74.

Dating of 2 Maccabees and of its components is one such problem. The underlying history by Jason of Cyrene must have been written after the victory over Nicanor, the last event recorded, and before the work of the epitomator. Since the history is familiar with many details of Seleucid administration and possibly refers to Eupolemus as a contemporary (4:11), Jason may well have been a witness of the events which he describes.[54] The epitomator certainly worked before the destruction of Jerusalem by the Romans in 70 c.e. and most likely before the seizure of the city by Pompey in 63 b.c.e. Otherwise, the statement of 15:37 that, since the victory over Nicanor, the city had remained in Jewish hands would make little sense. The tendency of the epitome to idealize the piety of Judas and ignore the other Hasmoneans also fits well in the situation of tension between the Hasmonean rulers and their more pious subjects which characterized the latter portion of the reign of John Hyrcanus and the reigns of his successors, especially Alexander Jannaeus. Thus, the years 125-63 b.c.e. may serve as the general time span within which the epitome was written.

Further precision about the epitomator's date depends on his relationship to the prefixed letters. It is hardly likely that he added to this work the second letter (1:10-2:18), which contains an account of the death of Antiochus IV (2:11-17) quite at variance with the account in the body of the work (9:1-18). The presence of two such contradictory reports would hardly be compatible with the epitomator's expressed aim of simplifying the narrative to make it more easily remembered (2:25).[55] It is, however, possible that the epitomator is responsible for the placement of the first letter (1:1-9) at the beginning of his work.[56] Since that letter is dated to year 188 of the Seleucid era, i.e., 124-23 on the Jewish reckoning of that era,[57] it is possible that the epitome itself was written in that year. In any case, the presence of the second letter (1:10-2:18) makes it clear that there was a third stage in the production of 2 Maccabees, an adaptation and perhaps further reworking of the epitomator's work.[58] The final redactor may have

---

[54] On Jason, see Schürer, *History* 1, 19-20; Abel — Starcky, *Maccabées* 34; Hengel, *Hellenism* 1, 95-99 and Habicht, *2. Makkabäerbuch,* 170. Goldstein (*I Maccabees,* 62-89) adopts a significantly different position, arguing that Jason's work was a response to 1 Maccabees, written in the first decades of the first century b.c.e.

[55] For this position, see Goldstein, *I Maccabees,* 36 and Habicht, *2. Makkabäerbuch,* 175 and 199-200. For the opposing view that the second letter was added by the epitomator himself, see Momigliano, *Prime linee,* 84-92 and Bunge, 'Untersuchungen' 157-8.

[56] See Momigliano, 'The Second Book;' Bunge, 'Untersuchungen', 195; and Habicht, *2. Makkabäerbuch,* 174-5.

[57] The basic work on the first letter is Bickerman, 'Ein jüdischer Festbrief.' See also Goldstein, *I Maccabees,* 34-36, who argues that this letter may not have been added by the epitomator.

[58] Although some scholars, most notably Momigliano, 'The Second Book' and Bunge, 'Untersuchungen,' argue for only two stages in the development of 2 Maccabees, the hypothesis of at least a three stage development has of late gained wide support. See Schunck, *Quellen,* 99; Hanhart, 'Zur Zeitrechnung', 74; Habicht, *2. Makkabäerbuch,* 175; Goldstein, *I Maccabees,* 36, 545-57; and Doran, 'Studies', 16.

been responsible for the addition of the first letter as well. When he did his work is quite unclear. Dates between 77 B.C.E. and the reign of Nero have been proposed without any decisive evidence.[59]

The historical portion of 2 Maccabees has a much more limited scope than 1 Maccabees and very different stylistic and ideological tendencies. It is written in a highly literary Greek, with much greater attention to the emotional impact and to the didactic value of the events which it relates.[60] Whether these literary and theological tendencies are characteristics of Jason of Cyrene or his epitomator is unclear. The latter claims to be engaged primarily in reducing the scope and complexity of Jason's work (2:24-26), but he also compares himself to an artist who decorates what a master builder has constructed (2:29). His epitomizing may well have involved more than mere abbreviation, and there are certainly sections of the work which are unlikely to be the work of Jason.[61]

The epitome is concerned to illustrate a fundamental theological theme,[62] that the events of Jewish history show God at work caring for his people, rewarding the faithful and punishing the impious. The impious in this case are primarily those villains, Antiochus IV and Nicanor, who set themselves in opposition to God's law and temple. Both are portrayed in almost mythical terms as adversaries who presume to resist the cosmic sovereignty of God. Antiochus, when he hears of the initial victories of Judas, resolves to 'make Jerusalem a cemetery of Jews' (9:4). He is brought low by a mysterious intestinal disease which is a fitting punishment for his arrogance: 'Thus, he who had just been thinking that he could command the waves of the sea, in his superhuman arrogance, and imagining that he could weigh the heights in a balance, was brought down to earth in a litter, making the power of God manifest to all' (9:8). He dies in worm-eaten

---

[59] Thus, Schunck (*Quellen*, 127) places the final redactor at the turn of the Christian era; Levy ('Les deux livres', 33) under Claudius or Nero; Goldstein (*I Maccabees,* 551-7) shortly after 78-77 B.C.E. Habicht (*2. Makkabäerbuch*) is properly sceptical of any precise dating.
[60] It is often claimed that Jason and/or the epitomator wrote in the style of 'tragic' or 'pathetic' historiography. See, e.g., Goldstein, *I Maccabees,* 34 and Habicht, *2. Makkabäerbuch,* 189. The existence of such a distinct historical genre has been called into question by Doran ('2 Maccabees'), although the rhetorical effects of the work cannot be denied.
[61] In addition to the prefixed letters and epitomator's preface, which are certainly not the work of Jason, the following passages in the body of the work are probably to be assigned to the epitomator: 3:24-25, 27-28, 30; 4:17, 5:17-20; 6:12-17; 7:1-42; 9:18-27; 12:43-45; 14:37-46; and 15:36-39. Zambelli ('La composizione', 286-7) has also argued that chapters 12-15 are not from the work of Jason, but this position is unlikely. On the whole issue, see Habicht, *2. Makkabäerbuch,* 171-2. On the other hand, Momigliano, *Prime linee,* 98-100 and Goldstein (*I Maccabees,* 33, 80) maintain that the epitomator omitted Jason's account of the death of Judas. For criticism of this position, see Habicht, *2. Makkabäerbuch,* 173-4.
[62] On the theological program of 1 Maccabees, see Bickerman, 'Makkabäerbücher', 794 and Habicht, *2. Makkabäerbuch,* 185-91. Goldstein (*I Maccabees,* 62-89) connects the theology with anti-Hasmonean polemics and sees Jason's work as, among other things, a defense of earlier pietistic literature, such as the book of Daniel.

agony, he 'who a little while before had thought that he could touch the stars of heaven' (9:10). The king's painful death is, furthermore, a particularly fitting requital for the sufferings which he had inflicted on the Jews: 'So the murderer and blasphemer, having endured the most intense suffering, such as he had inflicted on others, came to the end of his life by a most pitiable fate' (9:28). Nicanor, like Antiochus, utters a dire threat against God's holy place, 'If you do not hand Judas over to me as a prisoner, I will level this precinct of God to the ground and tear down the altar, and I will build here a splendid temple to Dionysus' (14:33). Like Antiochus, he sets himself in direct opposition to God, by ordering Jews compelled to follow him to attack Judas on the sabbath. They respond, 'It is the living Lord himself, the Sovereign in heaven, who ordered us to observe the seventh day.' Nicanor replies, 'And I am a sovereign also, on earth, and I command you to take up arms and finish the king's business' (15:4-5). Nicanor's head and hands, 'which had been boastfully stretched out against the holy house of the Almighty' eventually hang on the citadel in Jerusalem (15:35).

Numerous other villains receive fitting punishment for their crimes. The Greek official who treacherously murdered the virtuous high priest Onias is killed by the Lord (4:38). Jason, who had bribed his way into the office of Onias and who later attacked Jerusalem after he in turn had been removed from the high-priesthood, meets a miserable end and lies unburied in exile (5:1-10). Those who set fire to the sacred gates are themselves burned to death (8:33). Finally, the hellenizing high priest Menelaus, who had succeeded Jason, succumbs to the *lex talionis*. He attempts to accompany Antiochus V and Lysias on their campaign against Judea, but instead is blamed for the whole calamitous situation. He is sent for execution to Beroea where there is a lofty tower full of ashes into which persons guilty of sacrilege are thrown. 'By such a fate it came about that Menelaus the lawbreaker died, without even burial in the earth. And this was eminently just; because he had committed many sins against the altar whose fire and ashes were holy, he met his death in ashes' (13:7-8).

If history is a catalogue of just divine retribution, then the desecration of the temple and the persecution of God's people must have been due to their sins. The theological concern to demonstrate this proposition no doubt led either Jason or his epitomator to include much valuable information not found in 1 Maccabees about the events leading up to the revolt. Chapter 4 and the beginning of chapter 5 detail the process of hellenization and the attendant intrigues among members of the priestly aristocracy in Jerusalem.[63] The theological significance of those events is brought out in

---

[63] The fundamental work on the subject is Bickerman, *God of the Maccabees,* which has been further developed by Tcherikover, *Hellenistic Civilization;* Hengel, *Hellenism* 1, 277-309; and Goldstein, *I Maccabees,* 104-74. See also Momigliano, *Alien Wisdom,* 97-122.

several subsequent remarks. Antiochus, after the revolt of Jason, takes the city, not realizing 'that the Lord was angered for a little while because of the sins of those who dwelt in the city, and that therefore he was disregarding the holy place' (5:17). The same point is made by one of the seven children cruelly martyred in the presence of Antiochus (7:18). The belief that suffering of any sort is the result of sin also is applied to a case of Jews who died in battle against Gorgias. When their bodies were recovered, it was discovered that they had all taken 'sacred tokens of the idols of Jamnia, which the law forbids the Jews to wear' (12:40).

The suffering of the Jews, then, is portrayed as a result of their own sins, but it is also seen as a token of God's love. Suffering is, in proverbial terms, a form of education, and the desecration of the temple is not an indication that God had abandoned his chosen people, but only that he was leading them to reconciliation (5:19-20). The clearest statement of this theodicy is the editorial comment inserted before the well-known dramatic description of the martyrdoms of the old man Eleazar and the woman and her seven sons (6:18-7:42).[64] Either Jason or his epitomator reflects that 'these punishments were designed not to destroy but to discipline our people. In fact, not to let the impious alone for long, but to punish them immediately, is a sign of great kindness. For, in the case of the other nations, the Lord waits patiently to punish them until they have reached the full measure of their sins; but he does not deal in this way with us, in order that he may not take vengeance on us afterward when our sins have reached their height. Therefore, he never withdraws his mercy from us. Though he disciplines us with calamities, he does not forsake his own people' (6:12-16).

The chastisement of the chosen nation does, it is recognized, lead to the suffering of innocent and pious people. What gives such sufferers courage to accept their lot is the belief in a future resurrection. This belief is found on the lips of several of the child martyrs. The second boy thus replies to the threats of Antiochus, 'You accursed wretch, you dismiss us from this present life, but the King of the universe will raise us up to an everlasting renewal of life, because we have died for his laws' (7:9). The third son willingly offers his tongue and hands for amputation, saying, 'I got these from Heaven, and because of his laws, I disdain them, and from him I hope to get them back again' (7:11). Similarly, an old man, Razis, dies of self-inflicted wounds rather than be taken by soldiers of Nicanor. Before he dies, he hurls his own entrails at the hostile crowd 'calling upon the Lord of life and spirit to give them back to him again' (14:46). The martyrs, whose pathetic deaths are so dramatically recounted, serve not only as models of

[64] For analysis of this chapter and discussion of its parallels in contemporary and traditional Jewish literature, see Nickelsburg, *Resurrection,* 93-109. For rabbinic sentiments similar to those of 2 Maccabees, cf. *Sifre Deut.* 32 (ed. Friedman, f. 73b); *Mekhilta, Bahodesh* 10 (pp. 239-241), and *B.T. Berakhoth* 5a-b. On the whole issue, see Büchler, *Studies,* and Moore, *Judaism* 2, 248-56.

'nobility and ... courage' (6:31), but also of the beliefs which can instill such courage, while those beliefs answer a possible objection to the theodicy developed in the text.

The converse of the belief that suffering is due to sin, so amply illustrated in 2 Maccabees, is that piety ultimately produces success and divine vindication. The paradigm case of such vindication is the defense of the temple against Heliodorus, agent of the Seleucid monarch Seleucus V, who tries to plunder the temple treasury while Onias is high priest. In response to the prayers of this pious (3:1) man, Heliodorus is repulsed by the apparition of a heavenly horseman (3:22-30). Thrown to the ground and struck dumb, he is revived through the intercession of Onias (3:31-34). The paradigmatic significance of this event is later made clear when the success of Antiochus is contrasted with the failure of Heliodorus to enter the temple (5:18).

As the epitomator indicated in his preface (2:21), the history which he relates contains a series of such epiphanies. One is an omen of ill before the persecution (5:2), but the rest are manifestations by which the pious Jews receive divine aid in battle (10:29) or encouragement before a battle (11:8). Perhaps the most dramatic of these epiphanies is the dream which Judas has before his decisive victory over Nicanor. There he has a vision of the pious Onias and of the prophet Jeremiah who bestow on him a golden sword with which to strike down his adversaries (15:12-16). These manifestations of divine power, so conspicuously lacking in 1 Maccabees, indicate quite clearly that God was directly responsible for the deliverance of his people.

Judas, frequently called simply the Maccabean, is certainly God's agent of deliverance, but there is no indication that the special divine favour shown him extends to his family. Neither his father nor his brothers are mentioned and the striking belief of 1 Maccabees that deliverance of Israel could only be given through the Hasmonean family (1 Macc 5:61-62) is totally lacking. Furthermore, the Judas whom we meet in 2 Maccabees is a far more pious leader than even the hero of 1 Maccabees. There is, for example, no indication that the Sabbath was ever infringed by Jewish rebels, as is clear from 1 Macc 2:39-41. On the contrary, Judas is described as observing the Sabbath (12:38), and that he would have done so even in the event of an attack seems to be implied by Nicanor's strategy (15:1). The pious Judas is not only portrayed on numerous occasions as praying for divine aid (e.g., 8:2, 10:16, 11:6, 12:15, 14:15, 15:21-24), but he also provides another example of belief in the resurrection, when he makes an offering for the sins of his dead soldiers (12:43-45), a passage which became important for Christian theologians.

2 Maccabees is thus a work in which the theological lessons drawn from history dominate the presentation of events. Nonetheless, this didactic work preserves important historical information. The details about the

process of hellenization prior to the persecution have already been mentioned. Of equal importance is a series of letters included in chapters 9-11 which throw light on the closing stages of the revolt.[65] The attribution and sequence of these have been misunderstood either by Jason or his epitomator. The letter in chapter 9, purporting to be from Antiochus IV to 'his worthy Jewish citizens' (9:19) announcing the appointment of his son Antiochus V as king, may well be spurious. The letters in chapter 11 are almost certainly authentic, although the implication that they all involve Antiochus V during the Judaean campaign of 163 B.C.E. is incorrect. The earliest of these letters (11:27-33), proposing an amnesty to Jews who lay down their arms, is, in fact, a letter of Antiochus IV written before the campaign of his general, Lysias, in 164 B.C.E. The second letter (11:16-21) is from Lysias to the partisans of Judas during negotions connected with that campaign. The letter from Roman envoys to the Jews (11:34-38) is also connected with those negotiations. The latest letter (11:22-26) is the only one actually from the reign of Antiochus V, and it probably dates to 163 B.C.E. In it, the measures taken against the Jews under Antiochus IV are finally and definitively repealed.

While the epitome of Jason's work is thus primarily a didactic reflection on history which preserves some valuable data, 2 Maccabees in its final form may well have been designed for a specific cultic purpose. The two introductory letters, as already noted, call upon Egyptian Jews to observe the festival of the rededication of the temple. The first of these (1:1-9), dating from 124 and containing a fragment of a letter dating from 143-142 B.C.E., is a relatively simple appeal to celebrate the feast of 'booths in the month of Chislev' (1:9). The second letter is more elaborate. It purports to be from those in Judaea and Judas to Aristobulus, teacher of king Ptolemy (1:10). Although the authenticity of the letter has often been questioned, it may, at least in part, be genuine.[66] The letter announces the death of Antiochus IV (1:10-17), appeals for the celebration of the 'feast of booths and the feast of the fire given when Nehemiah . . . offered sacrifices' at the same time as Judas and his partisans are to celebrate the purification of the temple (1:18). The letter then goes on to describe the legend of Nehemiah's fire (1:19-36); it records the story that Jeremiah hid the temple vessels (2:1-8); then alludes to the initial dedication of the temple by Solomon (2:9-12). The books from which such legends are derived are briefly mentioned (2:13-15) and the letter closes with a final appeal to celebrate the eight-day feast (2:16-18). The appeals in these letters were probably

[65] The problems surrounding these letters have been largely resolved through the work of Habicht, 'Royal Documents.'

[66] For the inauthenticity of the letter, see Bickerman, 'Ein jüdischer Festbrief', 234, where the composition is dated to *c.* 60 B.C.E. See also Hengel, *Hellenism* 1, 100 and Habicht, *2. Makkabäerbuch,* 199. For defense of the authenticity of at least part of the letter, see Momigliano, *Prime linee,* 84-94; Bunge, 'Untersuchungen', 32-152; and Wacholder, 'The Letter.'

directed specifically toward Jews who were attracted to the temple constructed at Leontopolis by Onias IV, son of the last legitimate high priest.[67] In any case, the combination of the letters and the epitome may have been designed to make the latter into a sort of festal scroll for Hanukkah, as Esther was for Purim.[68]

Other Historical Works

2 Maccabees is the last substantial surviving historical work written by a Jew during the Hellenistic period. Two other Maccabean books survive, but these sould hardly be classified as histories. 3 Maccabees is an edifying legendary account of the unsuccessful persecution of Egyptian Jews and 4 Maccabees is an elaborate rhetorical reflection on the deaths of the Maccabean martyrs illustrating the power of 'pious reason.'

Philo, the Jewish philosopher and exegete, was little concerned with contemporary history. However, in two apologetic tracts, the *In Flaccum* and the *Legatio ad Gaium*[69] he records the tumultuous events in Alexandria during the 30's of the first century C.E., and the subsequent embassies to the emperor sent to settle the question of Jewish rights in the city. Neither work is a history in any strict sense. Rather, history is used here as in the *narratio* of a forensic speech. Nonetheless, Philo's two works provide valuable historical data. The major historian of the first century, Josephus, deserves special treatment.

BIBLIOGRAPHY

Bibliographies for the texts treated in this article, as well as for other Jewish literature from the Hellenistic period have been prepared by CHARLESWORTH, *Pseudepigrapha* and DELLING, *Bibliographie.* No single secondary work treats all of the texts, but HENGEL, *Hellenism,* offers a comprehensive survey of the period and of the cultural and literary forces at work.

1 Esdras
The Greek text has been most recently edited by HANHART, *Esdrae Liber 1.* For recent studies, see MYERS, *I and II Esdras* and POHLMANN, *Studien zum dritten Esra* and *3. Esra-Buch.*

---

[67] See above, n. 5.

[68] Goldstein (*I Maccabees,* 551-7) suggests that the final form of 2 Maccabees was in fact modeled on Esther, used as a festal scroll for Purim in Egypt after 78-77 B.C.E.

[69] See below, pp. 250-2. For the texts, see Box, *In Flaccum* and Smallwood, *Legatio.*

Fragmentary Historians

The Greek text is available in JACOBY, *Fragmente;* DENIS, *Fragmenta* and HOLLADAY, *Fragments.* Introductory surveys may be found in DENIS, *Introduction;* WALTER, *Fragmente; id. Aristobulos, Demetrios, Aristeas.* The classical study of these texts is FREUDENTHAL, *Alexander Polyhistor.* For a survey of the theological dimension of these texts, see DALBERT, *Die Theologie.* An important recent study focusing on Eupolemus, but discussing several of the fragmentary historians is WACHOLDER, *Eupolemus.*

1 and 2 Maccabees

The most recent editions of the Greek texts are KAPPLER, *Maccabaeorum liber I* and HANHART, *Maccabaeorum liber II.* For discussion of the textual problems, especially of 2 Maccabees, see HANHART, 'Zum Text' and KILPATRICK, 'Besprechung.' The most important studies of the many problems connected with these texts are MOMIGLIANO, *Prime linee;* ABEL, *Les livres;* ABEL-STARCKY, *Maccabées;* SCHUNCK, *Die Quellen;* ZAMBELLI, 'La composizione;' ARENHOEVEL, *Die Theokratie;* BUNGE, 'Untersuchungen'; GOLDSTEIN, *I Maccabees;* DORAN, 'Studies'; *Propaganda;* HABICHT, *2. Makkabäerbuch;* and SCHUNCK, *1. Makkabäerbuch.* All of these commentaries and studies contain further bibliography.

Chapter Five

Josephus and His Works

Harold W. Attridge

Never may I live to become so abject a captive as to abjure my race or to forget the traditions of my forefathers (*War* 6:107)

Flavius Josephus, or Joseph ben Matthias, is certainly the single most important source for the history of the Jewish people during the first century C.E. His lifetime spanned the turbulent years leading up to the revolt of the Jews against Rome, the period of the war itself, and the years immediately following, when Judaism was in the process of reconstituting itself on a new basis. His literary remains consist of three major works, the *Jewish War* in seven books; the *Jewish Antiquities* in twenty books; and the apologetic tract, *Against Apion,* in two books. He also composed an autobiographical work, the *Life,* as an appendix to the *Antiquities.*

Each of these works relied in one way or another on earlier sources which Josephus recast to serve several apologetic purposes. Any use of his writings must take account of these various tendencies and they will constitute the primary focus of this survey.

The Career of Josephus and his Autobiography

At the beginning and end of his autobiographical work and in scattered references throughout his writings, Josephus provides us with the basic facts about his life. The bulk of his autobiography, as well as a substantial portion of the *War,* is devoted to the brief period of time, from the fall of 66 to the summer of 67, when he served as a leader of the Jewish revolutionary forces in Galilee.

Josephus was born of a distinguished priestly family in Jerusalem (*Life* 2; *War* 1:3) in the first year of the reign of the emperor Gaius, 37-38 C.E. (*Life* 5). He also claimed to be descended through his mother from the Hasmoneans (*Life* 2), a claim on which the *War,* with its relatively pro-Herodian stance, is silent. Josephus portrays his youth as that of a child prodigy, who 'made great progress in my education, gaining a reputation for an excellent memory and understanding' (*Life* 8), to such an extent that, at the age of fourteen, he was consulted by the chief priests and leading men of the city on particular points of the laws (*Life* 9). Although there is, no doubt, exaggeration in this flattering portrait, it probably reflects the fact that Josephus, as a member of the Jerusalem aristocracy, did receive a sound education in Jewish traditions and at least the rudiments of Greek learning.

The historian relates that at the age of sixteen he completed his formation by making the rounds of the various schools of Jewish thought and practice, the Pharisees, Sadducees and Essenes (*Life* 10). Not content with such scholastic experience, he then spent a period of three years with a desert hermit, Banus (*Life* 11). At the completion of his ascetical training, he returned to Jerusalem in his nineteenth year (55-56 C.E.) and determined to follow the ways of the Pharisees, 'a sect having points of resemblance to that which the Greeks call the Stoic school' (*Life* 12). This account of Josephus' adolescence appears rather artificial. One has to wonder how much of an exposure Josephus received to the three 'schools' during a period the bulk of which was devoted to desert asceticism. The account, which has its parallels in other stories of philosophers' quests, serves to indicate that Josephus made an informed choice in opting for the Pharisees.[1] The claim to close association with that sect, as well as the particularly favourable picture of it, is a characteristic of Josephus' later writing. In contrast, the earlier account of the sects in the *War* (2:119-66) paints a glowing picture of the Essenes, as the most attractive representatives of Jewish traditions. Perhaps that portrait in the *War* represents the earlier predelictions of the historian, who had spent such a lengthy period with his desert hermit, although it also serves well the apologetic tendency of the *War* to portray authentic Judaism as distinct from that of the revolutionaries.

Josephus goes on to relate how, in his twenty-sixth year (*c*. 63-64 C.E.), he was chosen to serve as a member of an embassy to Rome, dispatched to secure the release of certain priests who had been imprisoned and sent to the capital by the procurator Felix (*Life* 13). Although he does not record the outcome of the embassy, Josephus indicates that it gave him the opportunity to move in the highest Roman circles, including Poppaea, Nero's consort (*Life* 16). At that point in his autobiography, Josephus begins the account of his activity during the war years, an account with special problems because of its parallel in the *War*. That period of the historian's career and the problems with its sources will be discussed separately.

After the war Josephus received from Titus and Vespasian grants of land in the coastal plain and in Judaea (*Life* 422, 425). Josephus held this land *in absentia,* since he was taken to Rome, granted citizenship, lodged in the Flavians' private household, and provided with a pension (*Life* 423). It was in this position, as a client of the Flavians, that he wrote his first major

---

[1] The apologetic description of the Jewish sects as philosophical schools is a common element in several of Josephus' works. Cf. *War* 2:119-66, *Ant.* 13:171-3, 18: 116-19. On these passages, see Moore, 'Fate'; Smith, 'Description'; Wächter, 'Haltung.'

historical work, the *War*. At this time, Josephus also enjoyed at least correct relations with Agripa II, who expressed qualified approval of the *War* (*Life* 363-66). During this period, the historian was subject to accusations that he continued to support revolutionary activities (*Life* 424-26, *War* 7:447-50), but he was vindicated by his imperial patrons. It is not entirely clear how long Josephus enjoyed a special position after the death of his major benefactor, Titus, in 81 C.E. He claims that Domitian continued to favour him with a grant of immunity from taxes on his land in Judaea (*Life* 429). It may, however, be significant that the patron of his later works, the *Antiquities* (1:8), the *Life* (430), and the *Against Apion* (1:1, 2:1, 296), was not the emperor, but a certain Epaphroditus, probably Marcus Mettius Epaphroditus, a learned grammarian and *littérateur* active in Rome in the last third of the first century C.E.[2]

Josephus provides a few details of his domestic life. His first wife was left in the besieged city of Jerusalem (*War* 5:419). He married again while a captive of the Romans, at the behest of Vespasian. His second wife was a woman taken captive at Caesarea who soon left him (*Life* 414-15). While in the company of Vespasian at Alexandria, he married again and his third wife bore him three children, of whom a son, Hyrcanus, survived. Josephus divorced this woman and married once again. By his fourth wife, a native of Crete, he fathered two more sons, Justus and Simonides Agrippa (*Life* 5, 427). The date of the historian's death is unknown, but it was probably not much later than 100 C.E. and may have been several years earlier.

As already noted, describing Josephus' activity during the war years presents certain knotty problems, due to the two conflicting accounts preserved in the *War* and the *Life*.[3] Both accounts focus on the activity of Josephus in Galilee (*Life* 28-413, *War* 2:568-646). For this period, both works report the same events, although in a different order and with quite different perspectives. The *War* also provides information not found in the *Life* about the defense by Josephus of Jotapata and his capture by the Romans (*War* 3:141-408) and about his subsequent service to the Romans during the siege of Jerusalem (*War* 5:362-419, 541-7).

---

[2] There are in fact two individuals named Epaphroditus who may have been Josephus' patron. One was Nero's freedman and secretary, who was banished and then executed by Domitian in 95 C.E. Cf. Cassius Dio 67:14.4. If this Epaphroditus was the historian's patron, then the apologetic tract *Against Apion* was completed in less than two years after the publication the *Antiquities* and *Life*. This is probably too brief a period for completion of that work. It thus seems more likely that the patron is to be identified with grammarian Epaphroditus, known from the Suda lexicon.

[3] The problems of the *Life* have been most recently and thoroughly treated by Cohen, *Josephus*. For previous attempts to deal with the difficulties presented by the two accounts, see Cohen's survey, pp. 8-23. Uncritical harmonizations still appear, such as Zeitlin, 'Josephus Flavius.'

In the *War,* the earlier of the two accounts,[4] Josephus presents himself as an ideal general (*stratēgos*), elected by the people of Jerusalem at the outset of the revolt (*War* 2:568). On his arrival in Galilee in the fall of 66, he fortifies the leading cities (*War* 2:572-76) and trains an army of 100,000 men (*War* 2:577-84), an activity totally omitted from the *Life.* He overcomes opposition from such figures as John of Gischala (*War* 2:589-94, 624-31), who later plays a leading role in besieged Jerusalem, and from factions in Tiberias (*War* 2:614-23, 632-46). He maintains his position until the final confrontation with Vespasian in the summer of 67. His preeminence as a general is recognized by the Roman commander, who, when informed that Josephus is surrounded at Jotapata, is told that he should attack the city, 'because its fall, could he but secure Josephus, would amount to the capture of all Judaea' (*War* 3:143). Vespasian himself regards it as an act of divine providence that 'the man reputed to be the most sagacious of his enemies' was within his grasp (*War* 3:144). Josephus, the resourceful general, conducts a vigorous defense[5] of Jotapata against the Roman siege and displays ingenuity and perseverance (*War* 3:175). By 'divine providence' he escapes death and, when brought before Vespasian, he takes on a new role as a messenger of God and prophesies Vespasian's imminent elevation to imperial dignity.[6] Vespasian spares him, and two years later, when the prophecy is fulfilled, frees him (*War* 4:622-9). A false report of Josephus' death reaches Jerusalem and it fills the city with 'profoundest grief.' Indeed, the 'lamentation for the commander was national' (*War* 3:435-36). Later, of course, Josephus' popularity plummets when his defection to Rome becomes known (*War* 3:438), and, while serving the Romans during the siege of Jerusalem, he is subject to assaults from his countrymen (*War* 5:541-7). The picture of Josephus here, with all of its self-importance and vanity, is a consistent one of a noble warrior and worthy adversary to the Romans, who ultimately bows to necessity and to the will of God.

The self-portrait of the *Life* has very different tones. Composed as an appendix to the *Antiquities,* and thus probably written in or shortly after 94 C.E., this work serves primarily as an *apologia* for the historian against the attacks of as rival, Justus of Tiberias.[7] Although Josephus twice vilifies

---

[4] The *War* in its final form was probably published in the early 80's. The *Life* was published as an appendix to the *Antiquities* in 93 C.E. For discussion of these dates, see below, pp. 192f. and 210f.

[5] For a discussion of the typical features of this account, see Cohen, *Josephus,* 95-96. The account of the siege is perhaps the most dramatic example of the tendency to portray Josephus as the ideal general, but it is hardly unique.

[6] The prophecy of Josephus recorded in *War* 3:400-2 is also mentioned in Suetonius, *Vesp.* 5:6 and Cassius Dio 66:1,4. The self-portrayal of Josephus as a prophet, possibly modelled after Jeremiah, has been frequently discussed. See, e.g., Lindner, *Geschichtsauffassung,* 49-68, and Daube, 'Typology', 18-36. Cf. also Michel, 'Ich komme.'

[7] For discussion of the work of Justus, see especially Rajak, 'Justus' and Cohen, *Josephus,* 114-43, with references to further literature. Note, in particular, Cohen's critique (*Josephus,*

Justus (*Life* 36-41, 335-367), he does not explicitly describe his rival's accusations. We gain some idea of what these probably were from the obvious tendencies of the account.

Josephus now presents himself as, at most, a very reluctant participant in the revolt. Upon his return from his embassy to Rome, he finds the nation in turmoil and endeavours to dampen the revolutionary fervour (*Life* 17-19). He consorts with the chief priests and leading Pharisees and, following their program, 'professes to concur' with the revolutionaries, hoping that the revolt would soon be suppressed by Cestius (*Life* 22-23). When Cestius is defeated, Josephus is sent to Galilee, not as a general, but as a member of a panel of three priests, whose mission is 'to induce the disaffected to lay down their arms.' Those arms were to be reserved for the 'picked men' of the nation, who would wait and see what the Romans would do (*Life* 29). Josephus seeks peace by buying off the 'brigands' who torment the countryside (*Life* 77-78) and, as he privately confides to Justus and his father Pistus when he has taken them prisoner, he is a realist about Roman power (*Life* 175). He was not the cause of the revolt of such centers as Tiberias, which, torn by factional strife and at the instigation of Justus himself, was already seditious before Josephus arrived (*Life* 32-42, cf. 340).

Throughout his activity in Galilee, Josephus does not act tyrannically, but conducts himself with moderation. He restrains the 'Galileans' in their wrath against the city of Tiberias (*Life* 97-100), defends refugees from forcible circumcision (*Life* 112, 149), puts down opposition without bloodshed (*Life* 174), and preserves the property of King Agrippa and his supporters for its rightful owners (*Life* 68, 128-30). His honesty and chivalry are above reproach, as he vehemently protests, 'I preserved every woman's honour; I scorned all presents offered to me as having no use for them; I even declined to accept from those who brought them the tithes which were due to me as a priest' (*Life* 80). His kindliness and moderation make him generally beloved (*Life* 84, 122, 206, 231, 251).

Josephus particularly insists on the legitimacy of his position. He claims, for instance, that his action in retaining grain from Roman stores at Gischala was justified because of the 'authority entrusted to me by the Jerusalem authorities' (*Life* 72, cf. 393). He describes in great detail the episode of John of Gischala's attempt to supplant him by appealing to those Jerusalem authorities (*Life* 189-322), an episode barely touched upon in the parallel account (*War* 2:626-31). Although he does not deny that the Jerusalem leadership wanted to remove him, he argues that key figures such as Ananus the high priest were initially opposed to such action and were only brought to it by bribery (*Life* 194-6). Josephus claims that he nevertheless maintained his position of leadership in Galilee because of the

128-32) of the view of Laqueur that issue between Justus and Josephus was primarily an historiographical one.

189

general esteem of the Galilean population, who prevailed upon him, despite his reluctance, not to yield to the Jerusalem authorities (*Life* 204-7) and who, in the presence of an embassy from Jerusalem, hailed him as their 'benefactor and saviour' (*Life* 259).

It seems likely, then, that Justus of Tiberias had accused Josephus of being a tyrannical revolutionary who had brought about the ruin of his family and his city, who caused Tiberias to revolt, who opportunistically usurped authority in Galilee and exploited that authority for personal gain, and who was repudiated as a leader not only by the general populace but also by the chief authorities of the nation. Josephus, already stung by accusations of continued revolutionary sentiments during his years in Rome (*Life* 424-6, *War* 7:447-50), attempts in response to paint a picture of his activity in the crucial months before the siege of Jotapata in a way that differs not only from that of his accuser, but also from his own earlier version.

Sorting out the 'historical Josephus' from these two conflicting accounts is no easy task, and any reconstruction of his leadership in Galilee must be tentative. Nonetheless, in each account, and especially in the *Life*, there are details which conflict with the overall tendency of the work and these can form the basis for a balanced assessment of the historian's activity. For example, in the *War,* Josephus indicates that he governed Galilee with the aid of a council of seventy elders (*War* 2:571). In the *Life,* where we expect to find an emphasis on the legitimacy of Josephus' authority, we instead hear that the Galilean grandees accompanied Josephus as 'hostages for the loyalty of the district' (*Life* 79). In a work which emphasizes Josephus' moderation, it is jarring to hear of his assaults on various cities (*Life* 81-82, 373). In a work highlighting Josephus' peaceful intentions, it is striking that Josephus has to admit, and significant that he rapidly glosses over, his fortifying activities (*Life* 187-88).

That such seemingly historical data are preserved in the *Life* is, on the one hand, evidence that Josephus composed this apologetic tract hastily. At the same time, they suggest that the immediate source of the account in the *Life* was not the *War's* story of Josephus the great general, but a *memoire* of his Galilean activity, written by Josephus shortly after the events and originally used as the basis for his thematic treatment in the *War*.[8]

The Josephus who emerges from a sifting of the two accounts is some-

---

[8] The theory that the *Life* is not simply a redaction of the account of Josephus' activity presented in the *War,* but rather an independent reworking of a common source was initially proposed by Laqueur, *Der jüdische Historiker*. Although the hypothesis has been criticized, especially by Schalit ('Josephus and Justus'), it has been ably defended in a modified form by Cohen (*Josephus*, 67-83), who bases his case not only on a detailed comparison of the parallel passages in the *Life* and the *War,* but also on a general discussion of Josephus' manner of handling his sources (*Josephus*, 24-66).

thing between the epic hero of the *War* and the moderate aristocrat of the *Life*. He probably came to Galilee initially as a member of a commission of three appointed by the revolutionary government in Jerusalem largely directed at that time by priests like himself. That commission probably had a limited, but by no means pacifistic, mandate.[9] Josephus, possibly exceeding the initial terms of that commission,[10] established himself as a military leader, perhaps with the aid of a small group of mercenaries (*Life* 77) or with the support of some of the Galilean peasantry (*Life* 98). His motives in taking this course of action are the least clear element in the whole picture, and they were probably mixed.[11] Like other Jerusalem priests who initiated the revolt (*War* 2:409), he may well have supported many of its aims, and desired to make resistance to Rome effective in Galilee. At the same time, there may well have been in Josephus' action an element of opportunism and a desire for personal advancement. His membership in the priestly aristocracy, which he exploits as a justification for his 'prophetic' role in the *War* (3:400-2), could well have given him the sense that he was divinely authorized to play a leading political and military role. At the same time, his integrity in handling resources which came into his hands is hardly above question, despite, or rather because of, the frequent protestations of innocence in the *Life*. Another of the significantly jarring elements of the *Life* is the admission by the historian that he kept the grain stores of Gischala 'either for the Romans or *for my own use*' (*Life* 72). Similarly, the assertions that Josephus intended to return to their rightful owners properties which had been confiscated (*Life* 128; *War* 2:597) could reflect the sentiments of an aristocrat dealing with his peers, but more likely are simply self-serving rationalizations. That

[9] Significant for determining the initial purpose of the commission may be the remark that Josephus' associates wanted to return to Jerusalem 'having amassed a large sum of money from the tithes which they accepted as their priestly due' (*Life* 63). Perhaps the collection of such revenues was a primary purpose of the triumvirate. Another significant detail, unless it is a part of Josephus' later pro-Pharisaic tendency, is the remark (*Life* 65) that the commission had been urged to press for the demolition of Herod's palace in Tiberias. This may have been a symbolic move designed to assert the authority of Jerusalem over Herodian territory.

[10] If the portrait of the *Life* is not wholly tendentious at this point, — and it is hardly clear what the tendency would be, — the admission of Josephus that, at the departure of his fellow commissioners, he requested further instructions from Jerusalem (*Life* 62), at least indicates a discontinuity between the aims of the commission and Josephus' later activity in Galilee. The reference to vague instructions which Josephus claims to have received may be part of this attempt to defend the legitimacy of his position.

[11] The discussion by Freyne (*Galilee*, 78-91 and 241-45), while heavily indebted to Cohen, properly questions whether Josephus' action was motivated primarily by revolutionary conviction. Other examples of individuals opportunistically jockeying for political and military position at the outbreak of the revolt may be found in the pages of Josephus. Note, e.g., account of the intrigues of Varus/Noarus (*Life* 48-61 and *War* 2:481-3). The discussion by Freyne (*Galilee*, 234-41) of other leading Galilean figures illustrates well the probable complexity of their motivations.

Josephus intended to betray Galilee to the Romans was an accusation which apparently circulated during his activity there (*War* 2:594, *Life* 132). Josephus himself fosters the impression that there was some basis to the rumour with the obvious tendencies of the *Life*. Nonetheless, this rumour seems to have little foundation. The 'revelatory' experiences at Jotapata which led Josephus to assume his prophetic role (*War* 3:351) probably represented a decisive turning-point in his understanding of his relationship with Rome as well.

The flattering and apologetic descriptions of the historian's activities in ther *Life* and the *War* conceal as much as they disclose, but they do indicate something of the complexity of the man and of those qualities of character which prompted him to become involved as he did in the revolt against Rome. Similar ambition and vanity are manifest in Josephus' later role as an apologetic historian, who defended himself and his people not with the sword but with the pen.

The Jewish War

The first work of Josephus the historian was his account of the Jewish revolt against Rome and its suppression by the forces of Vespasian and Titus between 66 and 73 C.E. The work in seven books was composed while he was a dependent of the Flavians in Rome and that relationship influenced many of its tendencies.

DATE

The *War* is normally dated between 75, the date of the dedication of the Flavian Temple of Peace[12] mentioned in *War* 7:158, and 79, the year of Vespasian's death. The latter date is normally taken to be a *terminus ante*, because Josephus reports having presented Vespasian copies of his work (*Life* 359-61, *Ag. Ap.* 1:50-51). It seems likely, however, that the final version of at least Books 1-6 was published in the reign of Titus (June 79 to Sept. 81).[13] A *terminus post quem* of 79 seems to be provided by the disparaging treatment accorded by Josephus to Aulus Caecina Alienus in *War* 4:634-44. Alienus[14] initially supported Vitellius but defected to Vespasian and remained in imperial favour until being executed by Titus shortly before the death of Vespasian. This fact may be reconciled with Josephus' own comments by assuming either that he revised his completed

---

[12] Cf. Cassius Dio 66:15,1.

[13] For fuller discussion of the position of dating the *War* adopted here, see Cohen, *Josephus*, 84-90, with references to further literature.

[14] Cf. Cassius Dio 66:16,3 and Suetonius, *Titus* 6.

work after 79, for which there is little good evidence,[15] or, more likely, that he presented to Vespasian only portions of his work, as he did also to Agrippa (*Life* 365). Whatever Josephus gave to Vespasian, several facts support the suggestion that he published his completed edition of at least Books 1-6 under Titus. It is Titus to whom Josephus devotes most of his attention in the *War*. Only he is mentioned in the preface (*War* 1:10) and only he is given credit for endorsing the whole work (*Life* 363). The prominence accorded to Domitian in Book 7, as well as stylistic differences between that book and the preceding six, suggest that it may be a Domitianic addition.

SOURCES

In composing the *War* Josephus drew upon a number of sources. The first of these was his own Aramaic account of the fall of Jerusalem composed for Jewish readers in Mesopotamia to discourage them from sedition (*War* 1:3,6).[16] He claims elsewhere that his accounts were based on his own eyewitness experience of the siege and the careful notes he took during that time (*Ag. Ap.* 1:48-49). The account of Jewish history which precedes the story of the war itself probably relies on Nicolaus of Damascus, a Greek member of the court of Herod the Great who composed, among other things, a universal history. This work, only fragments of which survive, was also a source for part of the *Antiquities,* where Josephus acknowledges his debt by severely criticizing the tendencies of the earlier historian. There is no such explicit acknowledgement of the importance of Nicolaus in the *War*, but it is probable that Josephus made use of his work and the quality and detail of his account of Jewish history from the end of the Herodian to the pre-war years witnessed by Josephus himself is clearly inferior to that part of his work which probably depends on Nicolaus.[17]

In addition to the historical sources which Josephus used, he possibly drew upon certain Roman materials such as commentaries on the campaign by Vespasian and Titus or on a Roman historical work utilizing such commentaries. Such sources, mentioned in *Life* 342, 358 and *Ag. Ap.* 1:56, may lie behind the detailed accounts of Roman military operations in Galilee, Judaea and Jerusalem, and behind the important survey of the

---

[15] The suggestion that the *War* underwent several editions has been made on various grounds by different scholars, including Laqueur, *Der jüdischer Historiker,* 57-59; Eisler, *Jesous Basileus*; Thackeray, *Jewish War,* vii-ix; and Michel, 'Zur Arbeit', 101.

[16] On the Aramaic version, see most recently Hata, 'First Version.' The suggestion developed by Eisler, in *Jesous Basileus,* that the Slavonic version of Josephus is ultimately dependent on the Aramaic version, perhaps in a Greek translation independent of the *War* and entitled the *Halosis* or 'Capture' of Jerusalem, has won little acceptance. For criticism, see especially Zeitlin, *Josephus on Jesus*; and more recently Rubinstein, 'Observations.'

[17] On the life and work of Nicolaus, see especially Wacholder, *Nicolaus.*

Roman army and the disposition of its legions in Book 3. Finally, as noted above, there may have been a written source for the two different accounts by Josephus of his activity in Galilee.[18]

CONTENT

On the basis of these various sources, Josephus, probably with the aid of literary assistants (*Ag. Ap.* 1:50), composed a dramatic and integrated account of the revolt and the history which preceded it. Book 1 begins with a lengthy preface (1-30) and then gives an account of Jewish history from the Maccabean revolt to the death of Herod (31-673). Book 2 describes the successors of Herod and the first procurators (1-270), the last procurators and the outbreak of the revolt (271-565), and the initial activity of Josephus in Galilee (566-646). Book 3 describes the Roman campaign in Galilee in 67, with a focus on the siege and capture of Jotapata, the town defended by Josephus (110-408). Book 4 records the final stages of the Galilee campaign of 67 (1-120), the internal situation of revolutionary Jerusalem (121-409), important events in Roman history for the years 68-69, including the fall of Nero, the turbulence of the year of the four emperors, and the final victory of Vespasian's forces, alternating with various episodes of Jewish revolutionary activity in Judaea and environs (410-663). Book 5 is devoted to a description of the siege of Jerusalem. Book 6 describes the fall of Jerusalem and the burning of the Temple. Book 7 records the triumphal return of Vespasian and Titus to Rome (1-62), the fall of the Jewish strongholds of Machaerus (163-215) and Masada (252-406), further revolutionary activity in North Africa (407-453) and it concludes with a brief epilogue (454-5).

This historical account is interspersed with a number of excursus providing background information on geographical or institutional matters. The most important geographical sections treat Herod's building projects (1:401-30), Ptolemais (2:188-191), Galilee (3:35-58), Gennesareth (3:506-21), Jericho and the Dead Sea (4:451-85), Hebron (4:530-3), Egypt (4:607-15), Jerusalem and the Temple (5:136-247), Machaerus (7:164-89) and Masada (7:280-303). In addition, Josephus describes the Roman army (3:70-109) and the Jewish sects (2:119-66) or 'philosophical schools,' a topic which appears in the *Antiquities* with different emphases.

The historical narrative is also enlivened and illuminated, as was customary in ancient historiography in general, with a number of speeches by the leading figures.[19] The most important of these are: the speech of

---

[18] For source criticism of the *War,* see especially Lindner, *Geschichtsauffassung,* 3-16, where the earlier source-critical discussions especially by Weber (*Josephus und Vespasian*) and Schlatter (*Zur Topographie*) are reviewed. See also Schürer, *History* 132-33 and 47, n. 6. On the issue of the possible written source for Josephus' own activity in Galilee, see note 8 above.

[19] For a complete list of the rhetorical pieces in the *War,* see Hata, 'First Version', 102-4. The most significant speeches are analyzed in detail in Lindner, *Geschichtsauffassung,* 21-48. Cf. also Michel and Bauernfeind, 'Eleazarreden.'

Agrippa II attempting to stop the revolt at its outset (2:345-407); the speech of Josephus on suicide at Jotapata (3:362-82); the speeches of the priests Ananus (4:162-92) and Jesus (4:239-69) in their opposition to the Zealots and Idumeans, whose leader Simon replies (4:272-282); the speeches of Josephus during the siege of Jerusalem (5:363-419) and outside the beleaguered Temple (6:96-110); two speeches on suicide by Eleazar, leader of the Sicarii at Masada (7:320-36, 341-88); and, finally, a series of speeches by the Roman protagonist, Titus (3:472-84; 6:34-53, 328-50). These speeches are particularly important for illustrating the tendencies of Josephus' work.

TENDENCIES

In the preface to the *War* Josephus tries to describe the sort of history which he claims to be writing. His remarks, which echo many of the commonplaces of the programmatic remarks of Greek historians, suggest that the *War* is the same sort of history as that written by the fifth-centry Athenian Thucydides in describing the Peloponnesian war or by the second-century Greek historian Polybius, who chronicled the rise of Rome. Both classical historians wrote objective and critical accounts of political and military affairs to which they had been, in large part, eyewitnesses. Polybius, in particular, may have served a a model for Josephus. Both the Greek and the Jewish historian wrote as exiles in Rome and both attempted to make sense for their countrymen of Rome's relationships with them, while offering to the Romans a favourable account of their peoples. In addition, Polybius may have directly inspired Josephus to include such material as his excursus on the Roman army, which the Greek historian had discussed in his *Hist.* 6:19-42. Even some of the tendentiousness in the lament by Josephus for his people could find its historiographical precedent in Polybius, who lamented the demise of his own people's political independence (*Hist.* 38:4).[20]

Despite its claims to sobriety and objectivity, Josephus' account of the Jewish revolt has several clearly defined tendencies. (1) In addition to its flattering portrayal of Josephus himself, it lays the blame for the revolt and the destruction of Jerusalem and its Temple on the revolutionary leaders whom Josephus regularly describes as brigands (λῃσταί) and tyrants. (2) While it generally absolves Roman leadership from blame for the catastrophe, it paints a particularly flattering portrait of Titus, who appears as the hero of the siege. (3) While casting blame and praise on the human actors in the drama of Jerusalem's fall, it suggests that the outcome was

---

[20] For discussion of the historiographical commonplaces of the preface, see Attridge, *Interpretation*, 43-51, 57-60. For futher discussion of Josephus and Polybius, see Shutt, *Studies*, 102-6.

195

determined by God's will. (4) While isolating responsibility for the revolt, it arouses sympathy for the Jewish people as a whole, who suffered so severely and lost so much. Josephus alludes to several of these themes in his preface (*War* 1:10-11); their development in the course of the narrative merits more detailed comment.

RESPONSIBILITY FOR THE DESTRUCTION OF JERUSALEM

While Josephus is willing to lay some of the blame for the war at the feet of the last procurators, especially Albinus and Florus (2:223-78), it is the Jewish revolutionaries and their leaders who bear the major portion of the blame. The theme of Jewish responsibility for the catastrophe begins in Book 2. The major speech attributed to Agrippa II[21] warns the insurgents after the cessation of sacrifices for Rome of what the consequences of their actions will be. He contrasts the futility of making war on a power which controls such a vast empire (2:348-90) and goes on to warn that war will force the Jews to violate their religious principles and alienate God, to whom alone they can look for aid against the Romans (390-4). He argues that by their madness in revolting from Rome they will be as responsible for their own destruction as if they had taken their own lives (394-6).

Josephus highlights certain events in the following period which illustrate the Jewish responsibility for the ultimate catastrophe and bear out the predictions of Agrippa. The first of these is the treacherous slaying of the Roman garrison of Jerusalem after its surrender to the partisans of Eleazar, the priest and captain of the temple guard who took the initiative in putting an end to the sacrifice for Rome. Josephus expresses his evaluation of the event in terms of the contrasting attitudes of Romans and Jews to the massacre: 'To the Romans this injury — the loss of a handful of men out of a boundless army — was slight; but to the Jews it looked like the prelude to their ruin. Seeing . . . the city polluted by such a stain of guilt as could not but arouse a dread of some visitation from heaven . . . To add to its heinousness, the massacre took place on the sabbath, a day on which, from religious scruples, Jews abstain even from the most innocent acts' (2:454-6).

The theme of the revolutionaries' responsibility, based upon their violation of the Law and desecration of the Temple, continues in the course of Josephus' description of the situation in revolutionary Jerusalem in Book 4. Here again, evaluations of certain central events and several speeches are used to indicate the significance of the developing action. After describing the anarchy and factional strife which followed the en-

---

[21] Agrippa is portrayed in a favourable way in the *War*, a factor which, no doubt, elicited his generally favourable response to the work (*Ag. Ap.* 1:51). Contrast the portrayal of Agrippa in *Antiquities* 20.

trance into Jerusalem of the various bands of 'brigands' (4:121-46), who now make up the 'Zealots' (4:161),[22] Josephus describes what he considers their most serious offenses, the abrogation of the rights of the traditional high-priestly families through a process of electing the high-priests by lot, and the conversion of the Temple into a fortress (4:147-54). In remarks that reflect his aristocratic, priestly biases, Josephus comments that the rebels 'glutted with the wrongs which they had done men, transferred their insolence to the Deity and with polluted feet invaded the sanctuary' (4:150).

The Zealots meet resistance from the former high-priest Ananus and other members of the Jerusalem aristocracy who had assumed positions of leadership at the beginning of the revolt in the preceding year (2:563). In his speech to the people of Jerusalem, in which he incites them against the Zealot 'tyrants,' Ananus is made to dwell on the profanation of the Temple, 'laden with such abominations and its unapproachable and hallowed places crowded with the feet of murderers' (4:163). He goes on to contrast the behaviour of the insurgents with that of the Romans, 'who never violated one of our sacred usages, but beheld with awe from afar the walls that enclose our sanctuary' while 'persons born in this very country, nurtured under our institutions and calling themselves Jews freely per-ambulate our holy places with hands yet hot with the blood of their countrymen' (4:182-3).[23]

Ananus, a 'man of profound sanity, who might have saved the city, had he escaped the conspirators' hands' (4:151) ultimately falls when the Idumaeans enter the city to aid the Zealots (4:314-16). Like the massacre of the Roman garrison, Josephus views this action as significant for the fate of the city; 'I should not be wrong in saying that the capture of the city began

---

[22] The identity of the Zealots and their relationship to other groups in the Jewish revolt is a hotly contested issue. The thesis that they represented a unified, continuous opposition to Roman rule throughout the first century has been defended by Hengel (*Die Zeloten* and 'Zeloten und Sikarier'). The more likely situation, that the Zealots only emerged as a distinct group at the start of the revolut, is argued by Smith, 'Zealots and Sicarii;' Rhoads, *Israel in Revolution*, 97-110; and Horsley, 'Sicarii.'

[23] Later, Josephus himself (5:362-3) and Titus (6:124-8) are portrayed as making similar accusations against the Jewish revolutionaries. Although Josephus' judgement here is harsh and tendentious, it is paralleled in various rabbinic sources which declare that the city and the temple were destroyed because of the people's sins. Note, e.g., the famous sermon of Yohanan ben Zakkai, the earliest version of which is found in *Mekhilta, Bahodesh* 1, 203-4. Note, too, the opinion (voiced by R. Yohanan ben Torta, floruit first half of second cent. c.e.) that the Temple was destroyed because of greed and groundless hatred (*P. T. Yoma* 1, 38c; cf. *T. Menahot* 13:22; *B.T. Yoma* 9a-b). For similar reflections on the fall of Jerusalem contemporary with Josephus, see 2 Bar 1:4 and 4 Ezra 3:26.

The claim that the Romans had never before violated Jewish religious observances is, of course, tendentious. In a well-known episode, Pompey had entered, and thus defiled, the sanctuary, though, according to Josephus, he immediately ordered it cleansed. Cf. *War* 1:152-3, *Ant.* 14:72-3.

with the death of Ananus, and that the overthrow of the walls and the downfall of the Jewish state dated from the day on which the Jews beheld their high priest, the captain of their salvation, butchered in the heart of Jerusalem' (4:318).

The theme of the revolutionaries' responsibility for the catastrophe is also developed through evaluations of the character, aims, and methods of exercising power of the various revolutionary leaders. This polemical strain begins in Book 2, with special attention being devoted to John of Gischala, the rival of Josephus from Galilee, who later became a leading figure in besieged Jerusalem. The historian describes him as 'the most unscrupulous and crafty of all who have ever gained notoriety by such infamous means. Poor at the opening of his career, his penury had for long thwarted his malicious designs; a ready liar and clever in obtaining credit for his lies, he made a merit of deceit . . . his hopes fed on the basest of knaveries. For, he was a brigand' (2:585-7). At the end of the same book, Josephus briefly mentions another of the figures who is later to play a prominent role in Jerusalem, Simon son of Gioras, who begins a 'career of tyranny' by mustering a large band of rebels who plunder and maltreat the wealthy (2:652).

After the death of Ananus, first John (4:389) and later Simon (4:577) come to power within the city and exercise control over different areas until the city's fall to Rome. On numerous occasions Josephus characterizes their rule as tyrannical and catalogues what he considers the outrages perpetrated by their partisans (4:382-8, 559-65). The internal strife growing out of the rivalry between them is exacerbated when a third faction forms around Eleazar who holds the inner sanctuary of the Temple (5:1-20). According to Josephus, this factional strife contributed in a very material way to the fall of the city. In attempting to overcome their rivals, both John and Simon burned provisions of the other party, 'as though they were purposely serving the Romans by destroying what the city had provided against a siege and severing the sinews of their own strength.' Josephus maintains that 'the city certainly fell through famine, a fate which would have been practically impossible, had they not prepared the way for it themselves' (5:24-26). Thus, the destruction of the city and the Temple was the responsibility of the tyrannical revolutionaries in several senses. They suppressed or intimidated those more 'moderate' elements in the city, such as the high-priestly aristocrats, who might ultimately have made terms with Rome; they polluted the sanctuary and incurred divine wrath; and they ultimately weakened the strength of the defenders of the city and thus made it easy prey for Rome.

Josephus continues to sound these themes as the siege progresses. He lets Titus on his arrival at the city recognize that 'the people were longing for peace, but were overawed by the insurgents and brigands and remained quiet merely from inability to resist' (5:53). As the siege operations begin,

Josephus notes, 'They suffered nothing worse at the hands of the Romans than what they inflicted upon each other . . . For I maintain that it was the sedition that subdued the city, and the Romans the sedition, a foe far more stubborn than her walls; and that all the tragedy of it may properly be ascribed to her own people, all the justice to the Romans' (5:256-7). After further descriptions of internal strife between Simon and John, Josephus expostulates, 'To narrate their enormities in detail is impossible; but, to put it briefly, no other city ever endured such miseries, nor since the world began has there been a generation more prolific in crime . . . It was they who overthrew the city, and compelled the reluctant Romans to register so melancholy a triumph, and all but attracted to the Temple the tardy flames' (5:442-4). In the last stages of the siege Josephus records what he regards as John's sacrilegious plundering of the Temple on the principle that 'those who fought for the Temple should be supported by it' (5:564). This prompts the historian to one of his more vituperative outbursts, 'Nor can I here refrain from uttering what my emotion bids me say. I believe that, had the Romans delayed to punish these reprobates, either the earth would have opened and swallowed up the city, or it would have been swept away by a flood, or have tasted anew the thunderbolts of the land of Sodom. For it produced a generation far more godless than the victims of those visitations, seeing that these men's frenzy involved the whole people in their ruin' (5:566). In one of his speeches to the defenders of the city Josephus himself sounds similar notes. In addressing John of Gischala he charges him with defiling the sanctuary while the Romans attempt to preserve it; 'Pure indeed have you kept (the Temple) for God! . . . And do you impute your sins to the Romans, who, to this day, are concerned for our laws and are trying to force you to restore to God those sacrifices which *you* have interrupted? Who would not bewail and lament for the city at this amazing inversion, when aliens and enemies rectify your impiety, while you, a Jew, nurtured in her laws, treat them more harshly even than your foes?' (6:99-102).

In one last sense, responsibility for the destruction of the Temple is laid at the feet of the insurgents. Josephus claims that it was they who initiated the burning of the Temple, a claim alluded to in the passage from *War* 5:444 cited above. According to Josphus, the conflagration begins with the firing, in self-defenxe, of one of the Temple's outer porticoes (6:164-5). The fire in the porticoes did not affect the sanctuary, which was subsequently put to the torch by Roman troops, yet even that action Josephus sees as the responsibility of the Jewish defenders, on the grounds that the Roman soldiers were acting without the approval of their superiors and in response to a Jewish attack (6:351-3). This description of the events leading up to the burning of the Temple also serves to exonerate Titus of any responsibility.

The case made by Josephus against the revolutionaries is summarized in a catalogue of the rebels and their crimes which prefaces the account of the fall of Masada and the Sicarii who were defending it (7:254-74). This case is, as it were, ratified by the confession placed on the lips of Eleazar, leader of the Sicarii, who asks, in his exhortation to his comrades to commit suicide, 'But did we hope that we alone of all the Jewish nation would survive and preserve our freedom, as persons guiltless toward God and without a hand in crime — we who had even been the instructors of the rest?' Eleazar goes on to argue that the deprivation of all hope of deliverance 'betokens (God's) wrath at the many wrongs which we madly dared to inflict upon our countrymen. The penalty for those crimes let us pay not to our bitterest foes, the Romans, but to God through the act of our own hands' (7:332-3).

PRO-FLAVIAN ELEMENTS

For Josephus, then, the destruction of Jerusalem and the Temple is the fault of one particular segment of the Jewish people. In suppressing the revolt, the Romans were acting properly, and the Flavian patrons of Josephus are depicted as men of outstanding virtue who richly deserve to share in Rome's good fortune. Josephus, in fact, spends little time on Vespasian, briefly characterizing him, through the eyes of Nero, as 'a man with the steadiness resulting from years and experience, with sons who would be a sure hostage for his fidelity, and whose ripe manhood would act as the arm of their father's brain' (3:6). Josephus does describe the personal valour of the Roman commander at the siege of Gamala (4:31), but the historian is primarily concerned with Vespasian's sons. Domitian is treated briefly in Book 7, where his military exploits are described in glowing, and certainly exaggerated, terms (7:85-88).[24] Titus, who succeeded to his father's command after the latter's departure for Rome in 69 and who directed the siege of Jerusalem, is the main focus of Josephus' attention.

Two major themes dominate Josephus' portrait of Titus, his valour as a general and his compassion as a man. He appears on the scene at *War* 3:64 when, after an unusually swift passage from Achaea to Alexandria, he takes command of the legions there and brings them on a forced march to Ptolemais. He sees action at the fall of Jotapata, where he is the first to mount the walls in the assault that ends the siege (3:324). Later, at Tarichaeae, Titus finds himself confronted by a large Jewish force (3:471). While waiting for reinforcements, which no doubt made a significant contribution to the eventual outcome (3:485), Titus inspires his troops with a stirring speech (3:472-84). He then defeats the Jewish forces outside the walls, and personally leads his troops into the town (3:497), while its defenders, 'terror-struck at his audacity,' flee in disarray.

---

[24] Tacitus (*Hist.* 4:85-86) gives a rather different, and less flattering, version of Domitian's military exploits.

Josephus finds numerous occasions to comment on his hero's bravery at the siege of Jerusalem. During a reconnaisance ride around the city when he first arrives, Titus, with a small escort, is cut off from the main body of his cavalry force by a party of Jews. 'Perceiving that his safety depended solely on his personal prowess,' he leads his companions through the enemy ranks (5:59). As the tenth legion takes up its position on the Mount of Olives, Jewish sallies take the legionaries by surprise and throw them into disorder. Titus twice saves the day by his personal intervention. Ignoring the warnings of his staff (5:88), he rallies his troops and himself leads the attack on the Jews. The same pattern appears later when a Jewish assault on Roman siege engines is repulsed (5:284-8) and when, after the second wall had been breached, a Jewish counter-attack threatens the Roman troops (5:339-40). Throughout the battle the Romans owe their success to 'above all, Titus, ever and everywhere present beside all' (5:310).

While Titus is depicted as a man of extraordinary courage, he also is seen to display those virtues of compassion and humaneness which mark true nobility. This compassion is directed first at his own troops and he 'cared as much for his soldiers' safety as for success' (5:316). When some of his men are cut off in the assault on the temple, his deep grief at their plight consoles them in their deaths (6:184-5). More significant for Josephus is the compassion which he attributes to Titus in his attitudes toward conquered Jews. He is particularly moved at the sight of the youthful Josephus in his chains after the capture of Jotapata (3:396) and later requests that the future historian be severed from his bonds (4:628). When he advances on Gischala, he hesitates before ordering an assault and gives the population an opportunity to surrender. He does this not as standard military practice, but because he 'was already satiated with slaughter and pitied the masses doomed along with the guilty to indiscriminate destruction' (4:92).

During the siege of Jerusalem, where evidence for the compassion of Titus is not abundant, Josephus nonetheless finds it. During the Roman assault on the north wall a group of Jews implore Titus for mercy. 'In the simplicity of his heart' he believes their entreaty (5:319), although it turns out to be a ruse. Because of such treachery, Titus decides that 'in warfare compassion is mischievous' (5:329) and proceeds with vigorous siege actions. Yet, apparently, Titus did not completely learn his lesson. While he displays little mercy, he still pities the Jews. He is moved, for instance, by the sight of the results of famine in the besieged city, the 'valleys choked with dead and the thick matter oozing from under the clammy carcasses.' Then 'he groaned and, raising his hands to heaven, called God to witness that this was not his doing' (5:519).

The innocence which Titus protests in the face of Jewish suffering forms a recurrent theme during the account of the latter stages of the siege. It reinforces the image of Titus the compassionate by showing his unwillingness to inflict suffering. At the same time, of course, it heightens the blameworthiness of the revolutionaries. Thus, Titus addresses John of Gischala and his forces within the Temple and, echoing themes prominent in the speeches of Agrippa, Ananus and Josephus,[25] accuses them of polluting the holy place. At the same time he affirms his own innocence with an oath, 'I call the gods of my fathers to witness and any deity that once watched over this place — for now I believe that there is none — I call my army, the Jews within my lines, and you yourselves to witness that it is not I who force you to pollute these precincts. Exchange the arena of conflict for another and not a Roman shall approach or insult your holy places; nay, I will preserve the Temple for you, even against your will' (6:124-8). Titus reacts with horror and protestations of innocence at reports of cannibalism in the famine-racked city (6:214-19), but Josephus is particularly concerned to prortray his attitude toward the Temple. The reluctance to destroy the sacred place, which appears in the general's address to the revolutionaries, emerges again in a council with his staff prior to the final assault on the Temple. There he declares that 'he would not wreak vengeance on inanimate objects instead of men, nor under any circumstances burn down so magnificent a work; for the loss would affect the Romans, inasmuch as it would be an ornament to the empire if it stood' (6:241). This version of Titus' attitude during the siege, contradicted by a later source,[26] clearly serves to enhance Josephus' portrait of his compassionate hero. That portrait receives its finishing touches in the account of the parley between Titus and the leading rebels after the burning of the Temple. Titus engages in this exchange with Simon and John, 'anxious, with his innate humanity, at all events to save the town' (6:324). During the negotiations he addresses a long speech to his opponents describing his approach to his task, 'I came to this city, the bearer of gloomy injunctions from my reluctant father. The news that the townsfolk were disposed to peace rejoiced my heart. As for you, before hostilities began I urged you to pause; for a long while after you had begun them I spared you: I gave pledges of protection to deserters, I kept faith with them when they fled to me; many were the prisoners whom I compassionated, forbidding their oppressors to torture them; with reluctance I brought up my engines against your walls; my soldiers, thirsting for your blood, I invariably restrained; after every victory, as if defeated myself, I invited you to peace. On approaching the Temple, again in deliberate forgetfulness of the laws of war, I besought you to spare your own shrines and to preserve the Temple for yourselves, offering you unmolested egress and

---

[25] Cf. *War* 2:390-4, 4:182-3, 5:362-3, 6:99-102.

[26] The fourth-century Christian Sulpicius Severus, probably dependent on a lost portion of Tacitus, reports (*Chron.* 2:30), *At contra alii et Titus ipse evertendum in primis templum censebant.* On this passage, see Thackeray, *Jewish War* xxiv-xxv, and Schürer, *History* 1, 506-7. See also Alon, *Jews,* 252-68, where the classical and Talmudic evidence is fully discussed.

assurance of safety, or, if you so wished, an opportunity for battle on some other arena. All offers you scorned and with your own hands set fire to the Temple' (6:344-6). Once again the innocence of Titus is correlated with the guilt of the Jewish revolutionaries.

The portrait of Titus as the reluctant and compassionate destroyer of Jerusalem is briefly sketched for the last time when he revisits the site of the campaign on a journey from Antioch to Alexandria before departing for his triumph in Rome. He 'commiserated its destruction, not boasting, as another might have done, of having carried so glorious and great a city by storm, but heaping curses upon the criminal authors of the revolt, who had brought this chastisement upon it: plainly did he show that he could never have wished that the calamities attending their punishment should enhance his own deserts' (7:112-13).

The whole picture of Titus stands in striking contrast to reports in Roman sources about perceptions of his character prior to his accession to the principate. Suetonius (*Tit.* 7:1) reports that Titus was suspected of cruelty, unchastity, greed and extravagance. Cassius Dio (*Hist.* 66:18, 1) notes that Titus, as emperor, committed no act of murder or amatory passion, either because his character had changed for the better when he became emperor, or because he simply did not live long enough to show his true colours. It may be that the flattering portrait in Josephus was deliberately designed to counter adverse public opinion and create a favourable image of the new emperor.[27]

THEOLOGICAL REFLECTIONS

Since the Jewish revolutionaries were wicked and the Roman conquerors were not only brave but blameless in their conquest of the city, then, according to Josephus, the fall of Jerusalem was not an adventitious event, but a necessity dictated by God himself. This is a theme which permeates the *War* in various forms. At several of the important turning points in the history of the revolt, Josephus notes that other possible outcomes did not occur because God was in control, guiding events to their inexorable conclusion. Thus, after recounting the surprising defeat of Cestius late in 66, Josephus remarks, 'Had he but persisted for a while with the siege, he would have forthwith taken the city; but God, I suppose, because of those miscreants, had already turned away even from His sanctuary and ordained that that day should not see the end of the war' (2:539). Thus Cestius, perhaps by divine guidance, failed in his potentially successful expedition against Jerusalem. Later, John of Gischala is similarly

---

[27] As suggested by Yavetz, 'Reflections.' For earlier analyses of the the pro-Flavian tendencies of the *War,* see Weber, *Josephus und Vespasian*; and Briessmann, *Tacitus,* and Alon, *Jews,* 252-68.

preserved by God for a purpose. John managed by a ruse to escape Titus who had laid siege to Gischala and Josephus remarks, 'But after all, it was by the act of God, who was preserving John to bring ruin upon Jerusalem, that Titus was not only influenced by this pretext for delay, but even pitched his camp farther from the city' (4:104).

As we have already seen, the deaths of the priests Ananus and Jesus during their struggle against the Zealots and Idumaeans were seen by Josephus as a major turning point in the revolt. The priests' party was overcome due to an oversight on the part of Ananus who did not carefully inspect his sentries. While they slept, the Zealots let the Idumaeans into the city and they gained control. Josephus comments that the failure of Ananus to inspect his sentries occurred 'not through any remissness on his part, but by the overruling decree of Destiny (εἱμαρμένη) that he and all his guards should perish' (4:297). The impersonal term, 'Destiny,' here reflects vocabulary common in some Hellenistic historians, but Josephus, in the context of the *War,* often uses this and related terms not for some impersonal force, but for the inexorable will of the God worshiped in the Temple at Jerusalem.[28] This is clear from a passage later in the same context. After recording the deaths of Ananus and Jesus, Josephus praises their virtues and remarks, 'It was, I suppose, because God had, for its pollutions, condemned the city to destruction and desired to purge the sanctuary by fire, that He thus cut off those who clung to them with such tender affection' (4:323). Once the Zealots are in power after this turning point, they tyrannize the city, thus setting the stage for fulfillment of an 'ancient prophecy' that the sanctuary would be burnt when it was visited by sedition (4:388).[29]

The destruction of the Temple itself naturally provides Josephus with an occasion for similar reflections. Before reporting how the Jews themselves had begun the burning of the porticoes, Josephus notes 'God, indeed long since, had sentenced (the Temple) to the flames; but now in the revolution of the years had arrived the fated day (εἱμαρμένη ἡμέρα), the tenth of the month of Lous, the day on which of old it had been burnt by the king of Babylon' (6:250).[30] The alleged coincidence in the dates of the destruction

[28] The nature and function of the Hellenistic historical and philosophical terminology (τύχη, εἱμαρμένη, etc.) in Josephus has frequently been discussed. See especially Schlatter, *Wie sprach,* 53-54, and *Theologie,* 32-34; Michel — Bauernfeind, *De Bello Judaico* (2:212-14); Lindner, *Geschichtsauffassung,* 85-94; and Stählin, 'Schicksal.' As Lindner in particular shows, the terminology is not used throughout Josephus' works in a uniform way, and some of his usages are probably attributable to his non-Jewish sources.

[29] It is unclear what the prophecy is to which Josephus alludes. Thackeray (*Jewish War,* 114-15) cites a similar *vaticinium post eventum* in *Sib. Or.* 4:115-18.

[30] Cf. Jer 52:12, where the tenth of Ab (= Syrian Lous) is given as the date of the destruction of the first temple. Contrast 2 Kgs 25:8, which gives the seventh of Ab. The traditional date on which the destructions are remembered, is, of course, the ninth of Ab. Cf. *M. Taanith* 4:6, which records the same coincidence of dates, among a longer list of such phenomena.

of the two temples provides Josephus with further matter for reflection on God's will: 'Deeply as one must mourn for the most marvellous edifice . . . yet may we draw very great consolation form the thought that there is no escape from Fate (εἱμαρμένη) for works of art and places any more than for living beings. And one may well marvel at the exactness of the cycle of Destiny (περίοδος); for, as I said, she waited until the very month and the very day on which, in bygone times, the Temple had been burnt by the Babylonians' (6:268). The historical coincidence is taken by Josephus as a clear sign of divine control of history.[31] The deity's hand in the destruction of the Temple is further revealed by a series of spectacular omens, portents, and prophecies (6:288-315).[32]

While God has abandoned his Temple and consigned it to the purifying flames, he definitely watches over the Romans. The divine guidance of Rome forms one of the main themes in the speech by Agrippa at the opening of the revolt. Agrippa is made to speak of this divine guidance in a thoroughly Hellenistic way by speaking of the favours which Fortune (τύχη) has bestowed on Rome (2:360, 373, 387). Once again, this language of Hellenistic historiography, like the language of Destiny (εἱμαρμένη), does not ultimately refer to some power beside or above God, but is a way of expressing His control over the whole historical process. This is made clear in the speech of Agrippa, who finally says 'for, without God's aid so vast an empire could never have been built up' (2:391). Both the basic theological theme and the specific language used to present it recur, like other *Leitmotifs* of the *War*, in one of the speeches of Josephus to the defenders of Jerusalem. He argues that it is illegitimate to scorn as masters those to whom the universe was subject, for 'Fortune, indeed, had from all quarters passed over to them, and God, who went the round of the nations, bringing to each in turn the rod of empire, now rested over Italy' (5:366-7).

Josephus affirms that the effects of God's providential care are particularly evident in the lives of the leading figures of his history. Nero sends Vespasian to suppress the revolt, 'moved, may be, also by God, who was already shaping the destinies of empire' (3:6). After the prophecy of Josephus that Vespasian would become emperor has been fulfilled, and 'fortune was everywhere furthering his wishes,' Vespasian himself realizes that 'divine providence (πρόνοια) had assisted him to grasp the empire and that some just destiny placed the sovereignty of the world in his hands' (4:622). Josephus too, notes that it is God who had committed the empire

[31] A similar argument for indicating the influence of divine providence is advanced by Josephus in connection with the start of the war. At *War* 2:457, it is alleged that the Jews of Caesarea were massacred by their gentile neighbours 'on the same day and at the same hour' at which the Roman garrison was treacherously slain in Jerusalem.

[32] On these prophecies and portents, as well as other apocalyptic elements in the *War*, see Michel, 'Studien zur Josephus;' Böcher, 'Heilige Stadt;' Hahn, 'Josephus;' De Jonge, 'Josephus;' and Thoma, 'Weltanschauung.'

to the hands of the Flavians (5:2). Later, the salvation of Titus, after being cut off with a small contingent of cavalry before the walls of Jerusalem, leads the historian to remark, 'Then, more than ever, might the reflection arise that the hazards of war and the perils of princes are under God's care' (5:60).

Josephus counts himself among those who were specially favoured by divine providence. Just before his capture in a cave at Jotapata, he remembers the 'nightly dreams, in which God had foretold to him the impending fate of the Jews and the destinies of the Roman sovereigns' (3:351). So inspired, and recognizing that 'Fortune has passed to the Romans,' Josephus decides to surrender, 'not as a traitor, but as God's servant' (3:354).[33] Then, when his companions draw lots in a suicide pact, Josephus finds himself left alone with a single companion whom he convinces to surrender. This occurs, 'should one say by fortune or by the providence of God' (3:391). It is clear from the subsequent portrayal of Josephus as a messenger of God to Vespasian (3:400-2) how he would answer his rhetorical question.

The history of the revolt thus has a clear theological dimension rooted in Biblical historiography, although it is not without precedent in Hellenistic historiography.[34] In one other respect Josephus' description of the revolt conforms to tendencies current in much Greek historiography of the Hellenistic period, tendencies severely criticized by such critical historians as Polybius, whom Josephus so closely parallels in his programmatic preface. While it is not necessary to posit a clearly-defined school of 'tragic' or 'pathetic' historiography,[35] it is important to note the prevalence among many Hellenistic historians of rhetorical tendencies to highlight the dramatic impact of the actions being described, and to play upon the emotions of the readers.[36] Josephus, perhaps aided by his literary assistants, clearly follows such tendencies in his portrayal of the sufferings of the Jewish people during the course of the revolt.

---

[33] On this passage, see especially Lindner, *Geschichtsauffassung,* 49-68.

[34] For biblical precedents for Josephus' theology of history, cf. e.g., 2 Kgs 17:7-20, 23:26-27, 24:3-4; 2 Chr 36:15-21. Among Greek historians, note, for example, the description by the historian of the Augustan age, Diodorus Siculus, of historians as 'ministers of divine providence' (*Bibl. Hist.* 1:1,3). There, providence is understood primarily as the divine activity which rewards the righteous and punishes the wicked. On this topic, see Attridge, *Interpretation,* 159-65.

[35] The category has been justly criticized by Doran, '2 Maccabees.' The *locus classicus* for the theory of a genre of tragic history is Polybius' critique of Phylarchus in *Hist.* 2:56,11-12. Cf. Attridge, *Interpretation,* 48, n. 1.

[36] For discussion of this rhetorical historiography, see Cohen, *Josephus,* 90-91 and Attridge, *Interpretation,* 41-56.

JEWISH SUFFERING

The vignettes of Jewish suffering begin, as they end, with a suicide scene. The first such incident occurs in connection with the treachery against the Jews of Scythopolis, who had been fighting alongside their gentile neighbours against the Jewish revolutionaries. When they are betrayed by their gentile fellow citizens, one of their number, Simon, who had been conspicuous as a warrior, decides to slay himself and his family rather than let them fall into the hands of the gentiles. He then puts to the sword his hoary-headed father, his mother, his wife and children, and finally himself (2:476). At about the same time, riots break out in Alexandria and the prefect Tiberius Alexander, the apostate Jew who had been procurator of Judaea and who was later to serve as Titus' aide during the siege of Jerusalem, orders his troops to quell the disturbances. The Jews resist, but once they gave way, 'wholesale carnage ensued. Death in every form was theirs ... there was no pity for infancy, no respect for years: all ages fell before their murderous charge, until the whole district was deluged with blood and the heaps of corpses numbered fifty thousand' (2:496-7). Later, the defenders of Jotapata exhibit a pathetic valour during a nocturnal engagement, 'fearful shrieks from the women within the town mingled with the moans of the dying victims without. The whole surrounding area in front of the fighting line ran with blood, and the piles of corpses formed a path to the summit of the wall. The echo from the mountains around added to the horrible din; in short, nothing that can terrify ear or eye was wanting on that dreadful night' (3:248-50).[37] Similar pathetic scenes of carnage accompany the accounts of the fall of the Galilean town of Japha (3:293-7), of the destruction of the Jewish fleet at Joppa (3:422-7), and of the rebel force on Lake Genessareth. After the Romans on that occasion had done their work, 'one could see the whole lake red with blood and covered with corpses, for not a man escaped. During the following days the district reeked with a dreadful stench and presented a spectacle equally horrible. The beaches were strewn with wrecks and swollen carcases: these corpses, scorched and clammy in decay, so polluted the atmosphere that the catastrophe which plunged the Jews in mourning inspired even its authors with disgust' (3:529-30).[38]

After further short sketches of the suffering of the defenders of Gamala (4:70-83) and of John of Gischala's partisans in their flight from Galilee to Jerusalem (4:109-10), Josephus turns his attention to Jerusalem and proceeds to describe the effects of the siege and the internal strife in lurid tones. In the words of the priest Jesus to the Idumaeans, they would find in the city 'houses desolated by (*scil.* the revolutionaries') rapine, poor widows

---

[37] A similar remark is made about the siege of Jerusalem at *War* 6:274.
[38] Some of the imagery in such scenes of carnage and gore may be biblical; cf., e.g., Deut 28:25-26.

and orphans of the murdered in black attire, wailing and lamentation throughout the city' (4:260). As a result of the Zealots' tyranny, the dead lay piled in heaps and the revolutionaries, 'as though they had covenanted to annul the laws of nature along with those of their country, and to their outrages upon humanity to add pollution of Heaven itself, they left the dead putrefying in the sun.' In this situation 'none of the nobler emotions was so utterly lost amid the miseries of those days as pity' and, as a result, 'such terror prevailed that the survivors deemed blessed the lot of the earlier victims, while the tortured wretches in the prisons pronounced even the unburied happy in comparison with themselves. Every human ordinance was trampled under foot, every dictate of religion ridiculed by these men' (4:382-5). The tyranny of the Zealots seems mild in comparison with that of Simon. After his wife has been captured by the Zealots, he advances to the walls of Jerusalem, 'like some wounded beast, when it has failed to catch its tormentors.' Anyone who ventures outside the city is seized, tortured, and killed, and in the 'extravagance of his rage he almost gnaws their very corpses' (4:540-1). In the face of the slaughter wrought by internecine strife, Josephus, perhaps again assuming a prophet's mantle,[39] utters an apostrophe to the doomed city, 'What misery to equal that, most wretched city, hast thou suffered at the hands of the Romans, who entered to purge with fire the internal pollutions? For thou wert no longer God's place, nor couldest thou survive, after becoming a sepulchre for the bodies of thine own children and converting the sanctuary into a charnel-house of war. Yet, might there be hopes for an amelioration of thy lot, if ever thou wouldst propitiate the God who devastated thee!' (5:19-20).

As the siege progresses and famine within the city takes its toll, Josephus strives to paint an ever more graphic and moving picture of the sufferings of his people. The city, beset by strife, is torn in pieces 'like some huge carcass' (5:27). Famine 'overpowers all the emotions, but of nothing is it so destructive as of shame: what at other times would claim respect is then treated with contempt. Thus, wives would snatch the food from husbands, children from fathers, and — most pitiable sight of all — mothers from the very mouths of their infants, and while their dearest ones were pining in their arms they scrupled not to rob them of the life-giving drops' (5:429-30). Josephus describes several such piteous scenes caused by the famine, which, like a bird of prey, 'enlarging its maw, devoured the people by households and families' (5:512). These scenes climax in an act 'unparalleled in the history whether of Greeks or barbarians, and as horrible to relate as it is incredible to hear' (6:199).[40] This act was the cooking and eating by a mother of her own child and Josephus gives a detailed

[39] On the Jeremianic elements in Josephus' lament, see Lindner, *Geschichtsauffassung,* 132-41.
[40] Despite Josephus' disclaimer, a similar scene of cannibalism in a siege is depicted in 2 Kgs 6:28-29 and 'prophesied' in Lev 26:28 and Deut 28:53. Cf. also Bar 2:2-3.

description of the dramatic scene, the physical and emotional agony which prompted the woman to commit such a deed, the anguished words addressed to the baby before its death, the confrontation with the rebels who appear on the stage when they smell roasted meat, and the fact that this deed alone seems to have instilled in them horror and stupefaction (6:201-13). This is certainly 'tragic' history at its worst.

While the woman devouring her own child symbolically epitomizes the situation of the inhabitants of Jerusalem, the suicide of the Sicarii at Masada provides Josephus with a final opportunity for arousing sympathy for his people. The account of the fall of Masada, in fact, serves an important literary function. As we have already noted, the speeches of Eleazar provide a culminating affirmation of the theme of the revolutionaries' responsibility for the revolt. At the same time, the suicide bears out the prediction put on the lips of Agrippa that revolt would be an act of self-destruction (2:394-6), a prediction that was first fulfilled in the initial pathetic scene of Simon's suicide.[41]

As a device for eliciting sympathy for the Jewish people as a whole, the story of the suicide of the Sicarii is, however, problematic. Here, by their own admission, it is not the innocent bystanders who suffer, but those who instigated the revolt. Hence, while Josephus addresses an apostrophe to the Sicarii as 'Wretched victims of necessity, to whom to slay with their own hands their own wives and children seemed the lightest of evils!' (7:393), he relies primarily on the final speech of Eleazar to convey the sense of desolation which the destruction of Jerusalem must have inspired in many a pious Jew. In his second and final speech the rebel leader exclaims 'And where now is that great city, the mother-city of the whole Jewish race, intrenched behind all those lines of ramparts? . . . What has become of her that was believed to have God for her founder? Uprooted from her base she has been swept away, and the sole memorial of her remaining is that of the slain still quartered in her ruins! Hapless old men sit beside the ashes of the shrine and a few women, reserved by the enemy for the basest outrage? Which of us, taking these things to heart, could bear to behold the sun, even could he live secure from peril?' (7:375-8). Although Josephus at Jotapata (3:361-82) himself rejected the option of self-destruction and although he polemicizes against the revolutionaries, who, in his opinion, were responsible for the destruction of Jerusalem, the sentiment attributed to Eleazar expresses something of his own attitude, and concludes that 'lament' which was an acknowledged part of his work (1:11).

The *Jewish War* then is a complex historical work, providing invaluable historical data as well as various tendentious reflections on and interpretations of those data. In the work, Josephus is obviously concerned to

---

[41] The suicide of the Jews of Scythopolis is, in fact, alluded to by Eleazar, leader of the Sicarii at Masada in his speech at 7:365.

portray his own involvement in the revolt against Rome in a favourable light, by indicating that he was first a worthy adversary for Roman arms, then a divinely inspired prophet. At the same time, he is concerned to make plain what were the causes of the revolt. Throughout the action of the war, the Romans, and particularly Josephus' imperial patrons, are shown to be men of honour and compassion, while the full responsibility for the catastrophe is laid at the feet of the Jews. Josephus, however, is careful to indicate that it was not the entire Jewish nation which was to blame. Rather, responsibility rests primarily on the revolutionary leaders, whose revolt was not only against Roman political power, but against God and his Temple as well. The pathetic plight of the Jewish people in the midst of the war's devastation and carnage thus offsets to some extent the theme of the revolutionaries' guilt, and while the apologetic tendencies of Josephus' later works are not as apparent, the appeal for sympathy for the victims of the war foreshadows the more explicit appeals for understanding and accommodation which emerge in the *Antiquities* and the *Against Apion.*

The Antiquities

The second and longest work of Josephus was his twenty-volume *Jewish Antiquities,* which carries the story of his people from the creation to the administration of the last procurators before the war with Rome. This is a much more unwieldy and uneven work than the *War,* which it supplements in many respects. It continues and makes even more explicit various apologetic tendencies evident in the earlier work, while it corrects some of the critical tendencies of the *War* and lays the basis for accommodation between rabbinic Judaism and the Roman authorities.

DATE

The *Antiquities* can be dated with precision due to Josephus' own reference in the conclusion (20:267) to the thirteenth year of Domitian and the fifty-sixth year of his own life, i.e., 93-94 C.E. It has occasionally been suggested that the work underwent two editions, with the second edition containing the *Life* as an appendix written after the death of Agrippa II in 100 C.E. However, that date for Agrippa's death, provided by the ninth-century Byzantine excerptor Photius, is not supported by numismatic and epigraphical evidence for Agrippa's reign, which ends in 94. It also seems unlikely that Agrippa was still alive when Josephus wrote Book 20, which displays a disparaging attitude toward the king. There, Josephus records the rumour of Agrippa's incest with his sister Berenice (20:145), mentions the general hatred toward him of his subjects (20:212) and notes his abrogation of ancestral custom (20:218). While there are some redundancies at various points in the work, they are to be attributed to the historian's relative carelessness in composing this lengthy work and not to the effects of a second edition. Hence, the entire work, with its autobiographical appendix, was most probably issued in a single edition in 93-94 C.E.[42]

SOURCES AND CONTENTS

In this work, Josephus used a much broader range of sources than in the *War* with its relatively narrow focus. It will be most convenient to indicate these sources as part of a survey of the work's contents. The *Antiquities* falls into two halves, the first of which records Jewish history until the time of the first destruction of Jerusalem, and which concludes with the prophecy of Daniel. Throughout these first ten books, Josephus basically provides an interpretative paraphrase of Scripture, embellished with diverse legendary materials. The text of Scripture used throughout is a Greek version. Josephus may, in some instances, have consulted a Hebrew text or Aramaic *targum*, but the evidence for such Semitic sources, and particularly for the use of *targum*, is slender at best.[43] The occasional Semitic idioms in Josephus' Greek may reflect his own native language and not a written source, or they may be evidence of recensional activity in the Greek biblical text. It is, for instance, clear that for some portions of his narrative Josephus used a Greek text not of the LXX variety, but in a form closer to the later Lucianic revision.[44]

The non-scriptural details which appear throughout the first ten books, and more abundantly in Books 1-5, are paralleled in various sources. Josephus indicates that he had access in some form to earlier hellenized Jewish historians such as Cleodemus Malchus, mentioned in *Ant.* 1:240. Parallels to the romance of Artapanus appear in the legends about Moses (*Ant.* 1:161-8, 2:232-53), and scattered chronological details recall the works of Demetrius and Eupolemus. The fact that Josephus elsewhere refers (*Ag. Ap.* 1:218) to several of these figures as Greek indicates that he probably did not have direct access to them, but knew them through a secondary source such as Alexander Polyhistor, mentioned in connection with Cleodemus. Whether Josephus drew on Alexander's compilation on the Jews or on some other intermediary source remains unclear. Dependence on Philo, though often suggested, is quite unlikely.[45]

---

[42] On the questions of the death of Agrippa II, the dating of the *Life* and its relationship to the *Antiquities*, see especially Schürer, *History* 1, 481-2 and Barish, 'Autobiography.' For the hypothesis of a second edition of the *Antiquities*, cf. Laqueur, *Der jüdische Historiker*, 1-6 and Schürer, *History* 1, 54.

[43] For general discussion of the sources of the first half of the *Antiquities*, see Schalit, *Qadmoniot*, xxvii-xxxi and Attridge, *Interpretation*, 29-38, with references to further literature.

[44] For a detailed study of the biblical text underlying the paraphrase of the books of Samuel, see Ulrich, *Qumran Text*.

[45] On Josephus' use of Hellenistic Jewish literature, see Walter, 'Zur Überlieferung;' on his alleged dependence on Philo see Attridge, *Interpretation*, 36.

Many of the non-scriptural details in Josephus' paraphrase are paralleled in various re-writings of Scripture from the Second Temple period, such as *Jubilees* and the *Liber antiquitatum biblicarum* erroneously attributed to Philo. Josephus may have used such materials or may have relied on oral traditions familiar from his youth in Jerusalem or from diaspora exegetical traditions. It is clear in any case that he was not a slave to any particular exegetical tradition, but used a variety of sources with a good deal of flexibility.[46]

Besides using various sources for non-biblical details, Josephus cites a number of non-Jewish works, especially in his paraphrase of the early chapters of Genesis (1:94, 108, 118-19, 159). These sources, which serve to bolster the reliability of his account of Jewish origins, were probably not used by Josephus directly, but were taken from a secondary source such as the universal history of Nicolaus of Damascus, who is mentioned on several occasions in connection with the earlier figures (1:94, 108, 159).

Josephus elaborates his sources in various ways.[47] He condenses and systematizes non-narrative material, such as the legal sections of the Pentateuch (3:224-86, 4:199-301), promising a fuller treatment of such matters in a planned, but never published, work, 'On Customs and Causes' (3:223, 4:198, cf. 1:25, 20:268). Similarly, prophetic books generally receive very summary treatment.[48] Narrative material, suitable as it is for Josephus' historical aims, receives more of his attention, and he expands it in several regular ways. For his *koine* sources he is concerned to improve vocabulary and style, a concern which appears through the *Antiquities* and which should not be attributed to literary assistants.[49] More significantly, Josephus endeavours to make biblical history more comprehensible to the Hellenistic world generally by hellenizing 'barbaric' names and by using common literary and philosophical themes. He also makes the narratives more dramatic, by focusing explicitly on the psychological dimensions of the leading characters, by heightening the emotional impact of important scenes, by introducing rhetorical set-pieces, and by highlighting the erotic

---

[46] Note the general collection of parallels from haggadic sources to the non-biblical details in Josephus assembled by Rappaport, *Agada.* Some further parallels are provided by Franxman, *Genesis* and Feldman, *Biblical Antiquities.*

[47] For general discussions of Josephus' techniques in his biblical paraphrase, see Heinemann, 'Josephus' Method;' Attridge, *Interpretation,* 38-41; Franxman, *Genesis,* 9-27; Cohen, *Josephus,* 34-43; and Downing, 'Redaction Criticism.'

[48] On Josephus' treatment of biblical prophets, see especially Delling, 'Die biblische Prophetie' and Van Unnik, *Flavius Josephus,* 41-54.

[49] The theory that Josephus relied heavily on literary assistants with discernible predilections for various classical authors was advanced by Thackeray, *Josephus,* 100-24, but it has been frequently criticized. Cf. Richards — Shutt, 'The Composition;' Shutt, *Studies* and Justus, 'Zur Erzählkunst.' Josephus' concern for language and literary style is also evident in his paraphrase of the *Letter of Aristeas* in *Antiquities* 12, which has been carefully studied by Pelletier, *Flavius Josèphe.*

possibilities of several episodes.[50] Such literary devices serve not simply to make a more colourful and appealing story, aims later admitted by Josephus (14:2), but to provide a foundation for the theological and ethical messages which he wishes to extract from biblical history. Since these lessons stand in continuity with the tendencies of the whole work, they will be discussed after this review of the contents of the *Antiquities.*

The second half of the work falls into three main sections. Books 11 through 13 deal with Jewish history in the post-exilic and Hellenistic periods through the reign of Alexandra Salome. Books 14 through 17 deal with the rise and fall of the Herodian kingdom, from the activity of Antipater, father of Herod and supporter of Hyrcanus II, to the deposition of Herod's son, Archelaus, in 6 C.E. The last segment, Books 18 through 20, does not have a single clear focus, but includes various accounts of Jewish history in the land of Israel and in the eastern and western diasporas, as well as accounts of Roman imperial history loosely bearing on Jewish affairs prior to the revolt against Rome.

In Book 11 Josephus still relies on biblical sources, quite clearly in their Greek form. His account of post-exilic history depends primarily on 1 Esdras (*Ant.* 11:1-158), 2 Esdras (11:159-83, 197-303) and Esther, with its apocryphal Greek additions (11:184-296). Josephus here follows his sources fairly closely, but is concerned to correct them on such matters as Achaemenid royal history. At the end of this book Josephus records the conquest of Palestine by Alexander the Great and the relationship between Jews and Samaritans and of each group with Alexander. This largely legendary material is based on unknown sources.

In Book 12 Josephus offers his paraphrase of two known sources, *The Epistle of Aristeas* (*Ant.* 12:11-118) and 1 Maccabees 1:1-9:22 (*Ant.* 12:237-434). Within and around this material Josephus incorporates accounts of the immediate successors of Alexander (*Ant.* 12:1-10), of the Seleucids (12:129-37), and of the pre-Maccabean high-priests (12:43-44, 156-7, 387); documentary evidence for Jewish rights accorded by various rulers (12:119-28, 138-53); information, including official documents, on the Samaritans (12:257-64); and a lengthy legendary account of the Tobiad family who served as tax collectors for the Ptolemies in the third century B.C.E. (12:154-236). The sources for this non-biblical material are uncertain. The Hellenistic political history may derive in part from Polybius, who is explicitly criticized at *Ant.* 12:259. Much of the material on internal Jewish history may derive from Nicolaus of Damascus, who is explicitly acknowledged to be the source of the information about the privileges accorded to the Jews of Asia by Marcus Agrippa (12:127).

[50] Numerous recent studies have highlighted aspects of Josephus' methods of hellenizing Jewish history. See, e.g., Feldman, 'Abraham,' 'Man's Decline,' 'Esther;' Spródowsky, *Hellenisierung;* Moehring, 'Novelistic Elements;' Van Unnik, 'Josephus' Account;' and Attridge, *Interpretation.*

213

In Book 13 Josephus continues his paraphrase of 1 Maccabees (13:1-61, 80-170, 174-214), once again interspersing material from his Hellenistic and Jewish sources dealing with the Oniads and other Jews in Egypt (13:106-21, 135-44), the Jewish sects (13:171-3), the later Hasmoneans (13:215-432), and further documentary evidence for Jewish rights (13:259-64). The parallels with 1 Maccabees end at *Ant.* 13:214 in the reign of Simon, and the last three chapters of 1 Maccabees have no parallel in this paraphrase. This fact has led to speculation that Josephus' text of the earlier work ended abruptly at 13:42. It seems more likely, however, that Josephus simply chose to follow his other sources, which had played an increasingly important role throughout the later Maccabean material.[51] These sources, which are used also in the following books, certainly included Nicolaus of Damascus, cited or mentioned at *Ant.* 13:250-1, 347; 14:9, 68, 104; and 16:183, and Strabo, cited explicitly or mentioned at 13:287, 319, 347; 14:35, 68, 104, 112-18, 138-9; 15:9-10. Josephus refers to other figures, such as Timagenes (13:344) and Livy (14:68), but these were probably known to him only through his major sources. In this and the preceding book, Josephus has a large number of cross-reference formulas which have no referent in the works of Josephus. Some of these may have been copied blindly from one of Josephus' Hellenistic sources, although most are probably merely a stylistic device for closing discussion on a topic.[52]

Book 14, which begins with a new programmatic introduction (14:1-3), records the activity of Antipater and his son Herod until the death of Antigonus, the last Hasmonean ruler. Although the narrative is somewhat fuller, it parallels fairly closely the account of the period in the *War.* The major difference from the earlier work is the incorporation of large blocks of documentary evidence for the status of Jews (14:112-18, 145-55, 185-267, 306-23).

Books 15 and 16 give an account of Herod's reign, from the death of Antigonus until the execution of Herod's two sons by Mariamme, Alexander and Aristobulus. This account, which diverges substantially from the parallel in the *War,* is significantly more detailed and dramatic. The tendencies which were prominent in the biblical paraphrase are again apparent and the narrative is replete with descriptions of the motives and emotional states of the leading characters, with speeches which reveal the significance of the action and with various moralizing comments. Much of this is probably the work of Josephus himself, although some may derive from his sources. Here, as throughout the material parallel to the *War,* Josephus does not seem to be reworking his own earlier account, but

[51] The relationship of Josephus to 1 Maccabees has been much discussed. Most recently, see Cohen, *Josephus,* 44-47 and the literature cited there.
[52] See Niese, 'Der jüdische Historiker' and Cohen, *Josephus,* 45.

rewriting his major source, Nicolaus of Damascus. This is indicated, for example, by the appearance of brief allusions in the *War* to events more fully described in the *Antiquities*.[53] In addition to the work of the pro-Herodian Nicolaus, Josephus probably used an additional, anti-Herodian source or sources, possibly mentioned at 15:174 under the rubric of sources 'other than' the *Memoirs* of Herod. It is unclear whether Josephus knew those *Memoirs* in their original form, or only through the work of Nicolaus, but it is clear that the 'other sources' are hostile to Herod. These sources are particularly apparent in the lengthy negative assessment of Herod at 15.267-98, a section of the book unparalleled in the *War* and both formally and contentually distinct from its surroundings. Their influence may be felt in other passages, critical of Herod and unparalleled in the *War* (e.g., 15:9-67, on the death of Antigonus and Herod's domestic problems; 174-87, on the death of Hyrcanus; 16:1-11, on Herod's tyranny). Once again, in the midst of the Herodian history, there is a short passage containing Roman decrees on the status of Jews, with some important comments about their significance (16:160-78).

Book 17, which recounts the rise and fall from favour of Herod's son Antipater, Herod's death and the rule of Archelaus, once again parallels fairly closely the account in the *War* with some elaborations, some changes of order and a few additional evaluative comments.

The materials in Book 18 are quite disparate, with few parallels in the *War,* and they are of unknown origin. Josephus records various events of the history of the land of Israel in the period following the demise of Archelaus. These include the revolt of Judas and Saddok (18:1-10); the administration of the first procurators (18:26-38) and of Pilate (18:55-64, 85-95); the death of Philip and the reign of Herod Antipas (18:106-42, 240-56), a section which includes a survey of the whole Herodian family (18:127-42); and the affair of Gaius' statue (18:261-309). A lengthy section is devoted to the early history of Herod Agrippa I (18:143-239), which includes much information on Tiberius and the imperial family (18:168-94, 205-23). Josephus discusses various events of diaspora history including the expulsion of Jews from Rome under Tiberius (18:81-84), an account preceded by the colourful story of a scandal in the contemporary Roman worship of Isis (18:65-80). Troubles in Alexandria receive brief treatment (18:257-60). Events in Parthia are discussed on several occasions (18:39-54, 96-105), leading up to the detailed account of two Babylonian Jewish guerrila leaders, Asinaeus and Anilaeus (18:310-79).

Three passages in Book 18 are of special interest. Early in the book, in a position corresponding to the parallel discussion in the *War* (2:119-66), Josephus again discusses the sects or schools within Judaism, here begin-

---

[53] For discussion of Josephus' methods of using his sources here, see especially Cohen, *Josephus,* 52-58, with references to earlier treatments.

ning with the Pharisees, and devoting roughly equal attention to each group (*Ant.* 18:11-25). Later, in the account of Pilate's administration, appears the *Testimonium Flavianum* (18:63-64), a brief report on Jesus, the authenticity of which has long been open to question. It seems likely that the passage is at basis genuine, although it has probably been altered in some details by Christian transmitters of the text.[54] A similar brief report on John the Baptist appears in the account of the reign of Antipas (18:116-19), and this passage is generally accepted as genuine.

Book 19 contains a lengthy account of the assassination of Gaius and the accession of Claudius (19:1-277), doubtlessly based on a Roman source. That source has most frequently been identified as an historical work by the senator Cluvius Rufus, mentioned by Tacitus and Pliny. The major reason for this identification is the fact that Cluvius appears in Josephus' account in a brief conversation with another senator, in which he cleverly quotes Homer (19:91-92). Nonetheless, it is possible that this anecdote was transmitted in some other source.[55] Whatever the origin of this material, Josephus has included it primarily because of the prominent role played in the accession of Claudius by Herod Agrippa I (19:236-77), and much of the rest of the book gives an account of Agrippa's reign (19:292-366). The only other significant block of material in this book is devoted to an account of the relations between Jews and Greeks in Alexandria and to Claudius' edict on the subject of Jewish rights (19:278-91). One further bit of documentary evidence on Jewish rights appears in the account of Agrippa's reign, in the form of a letter from Petronius, the Roman governor of Syria, to the city of Dora (19:303-11).

In the last book of the *Antiquities* Josephus describes the administration of the procurators who governed Judaea after the death of Agrippa (20:1-16, 97-147, 160-223, 252-8), paralleling the account in the *War* (2:223-83), although with many divergences in detail. One characteristic difference is the incorporation of a letter of Claudius allowing the high-priestly vestments to be kept by the Jews (20:10-14). Within the account of Palestinian history Josephus inserts a further report on Mesopotamian Jewry, now recording the conversion to Judaism of the royal family of Adiabene (20:17-96). He also includes an account of the death of Claudius and the accession of Nero (20: 148-59), more detailed than the parallel in the *War* (2:249-51), a report on the death of James, the brother of Jesus (20:200-3), and a brief history of the high priests of Jerusalem (20:224-51). Josephus concludes the book, and the *Antiquities,* with an epilogue reviewing the contents, rehearsing his qualifications to write such a work, and discussing projected volumes (20:259-68).

---

[54] For a review of the extensive earlier literature on the passages on Jesus, see Schürer, *History* 1, 428-41, and Feldman, *Bibliography,* 42-43. For the more recent discussion, see Dubarle, 'Témoignage;' Pines, *Arabic Version*; Pötscher, 'Josephus;' Bammel, 'Zum Testimonium Flavianum;' and Bell, 'Josephus the Satirist.'

[55] For doubts about the use of Cluvius Rufus, see Feldman, 'The Sources.'

TENDENCIES

Just as in the *War*, Josephus models his general account of Jewish history on clearly recognizable Greek works. While Polybius and the tradition of political and military historiography served as the primary model for the *War,* it was the antiquarian history represented by Dionysius of Halicarnassus which supplied the model for Josephus' next work. Dionysius, active under Augustus, composed a general history of Rome, also in twenty books and also styled an 'Antiquities,' which had the explicit aims of dispelling ignorance of Roman history and institutions among the Greeks and of providing a suitably inspiring account of virtuous individuals.[56] This explicitly didactic, rhetorical historiography is represented by other figures such as the compiler Diodorus of Sicily, a contemporary of Dionysius, for whom the historian is a 'minister of divine providence' (*Bibl. Hist.* 1:1,3).

Using such precedents Josephus, after some remarks on the various motives for writing history (*Ant.* 1:1-4), presents a comprehensive work, comprising 'our entire ancient history and political constitution' (1:5), which, like the Septuagint (1:10-13), would provide for the Greek-speaking world not only information, but also religious and moral instruction. Josephus summarizes this instruction: 'But speaking generally, the main lesson to be learnt from this history by any who care to peruse it is that men who conform to the will of God, and do not venture to transgress laws that have been laid down, prosper in all things beyond belief, and for their reward are offered by God felicity; whereas, in proportion as they depart from the strict observance of these laws, things (else) practicable become impracticable, and whatever imaginary good thing they strive to do ends in irretrievable disasters' (*Ant.* 1:14).

Immediately following this summary of the lesson of Jewish history, Josephus suggests another dimension to his work. He requests his readers to 'fix their thoughts on God and to test whether our lawgiver has had a worthy conception of His nature and has always assigned to Him such actions as befit His power, keeping his words concerning Him pure of that unseemly mythology current among others' (1:15). This contrast between Moses and other legislators is then continued in the last segment of the preface (1:18-26). While these remarks are particularly appropriate to the biblical paraphrase which immediately follows, they constitute an explicitly apologetic appeal, which, with the moralizing portrayal of divine providence, runs through the whole work and serves to unite, at least in a superficial way, its rather disparate contents.

---

[56] The overall similarity in structure and title between Josephus and Dionysius of Halicarnassus has often been noted. For discussion of the detailed resemblances in the programmatic prefaces, see Attridge, *Interpretation,* 43-59 and Van Unnik, *Flavius Josephus,* 26-40.

DIVINE PROVIDENCE

The fundamental theological theme of the *Antiquities,* that history is a record of divine providence at work rewarding the good and punishing the wicked, indicates the roots of Josephus in the biblical historiography of the Deuteronomist and the Chronicler, but it is worked out in a distinctive way. To express this divine governance of affairs Josephus relies primarily on the Greek term *pronoia,* which, for the most part, replaces the more deterministic language of fate and destiny used prominently in the *War.*[57] This terminology for divine providence becomes, in the biblical paraphrase, the dominant interpretative motif, replacing such important themes in Josephus' sources as election and covenant. This adaptation of biblical theology, which makes the lessons of the Jewish past immediately accessible and generally applicable to the gentile world, is developed in various ways.

Josephus sees divine providence at work principally in those singular, or even miraculous, events where the righteous are spectacularly rewarded and the wicked decisively punished. It is on these events that Josephus lavishes his dramatizing skills. In the biblical paraphrase Josephus pays special attention, for example, to the Akedah and Exodus events. In both there are pathetic scenes, of Abraham's plight when called upon to sacrifice his only son (1:222-3) and of the Israelites pitifully caught between the Egyptians and the sea (2:325-8). In both there are rhetorical flourishes, on the part of Abraham (1:228-31) and of Moses (2:330-3). Both events manifest God's care for those who trust in him and act righteously.

In the biblical paraphrase Josephus is as much concerned with examples of punishment of the wicked as with rescues of the righteous. Two events exemplify important aspects of this theme. In Book 4 Josephus recounts at length the revolts against the authority of Moses by the priests Korah, Dathan and Abiram (4:14-66) and by Zambrias (biblical Zimri), leader of the Hebrew youths who have been corrupted by the daughters of Midian (4:131-55). Both are taken by Josephus to be cases of rebellion against the 'ancestral laws,' based on personal ambition (Korah) or sexual passion (Zambrias). In both cases Moses is opposed as tyrannical (4:22, 145-50), but the outcome shows that tyranny and disaster result rather from the abandonment of his laws. A similar abandonment of ancestral law and the Mosaic 'constitution', now caused by excessive luxury, occurs after the invasion of Canaan (5:132-5).[58]

The theology of history which is developed in connection with those highly dramatic scenes is reinforced through the sentiments of leading

[57] For the language here, see note 28 above and Attridge, *Interpretation* 71-108, 145-65.
[58] On the Midianite episode, see Van Unnik, 'Josephus' Account' and Attridge, *Interpretation,* 119-140.

characters. Moses, for instance, in his farewell speech to the Israelites (4:180-193), which is loosely modelled on Deuteronomy, reminds his people that 'God, who heretofore has governed you, and by whose will I too have been of service to you, will not at this point set a term to His providence, but so long as ye yourselves desire to have His protection, by continuing in the paths of virtue, so long will ye enjoy His watchful care' (4:185).

The themes which emerge in such passages of the biblical paraphrase reappear in the later historical accounts, in a rather muted way in the accounts of post-exilic and Maccabean times, but massively in connection with Herodian history. In the Books 11 through 13, the similar fates of Haman and Antiochus IV are, predictably, taken to exemplify divine retributive justice at work (11:247, 268; 12:358) and Nehemiah is made to deliver a speech linking human righteousness and divine providence (11:169-71). In addition to such archvillains as Haman and Antiochus, the Samaritans are painted with particularly unfavourable colours. Here they are the primary examples of those who have rejected or tried to suppress 'ancestral traditions.' They are 'apostates from the Jewish nation' (11:340), who profess themselves to be Jews when things are going well, but, when things go ill for the Jews, they claim other ancestry and repudiate Jewish religious practice, as they do at the time of the Maccabean uprising (12:259-61). Divine providence is also reflected in the example of the *lex talionis* when the blood of Aristobulus is spilled on the spot where his brother was murdered at his behest (13:314).

TREATMENT OF HEROD

The account of Herod in the *Antiquities* is a prime example of the combination of literary and theological interests of the historian. This account is generally recognized to be less favourable to the king than the parallel in the *War,* and Josephus himself indicates that he has a 'pro-Hasmonean' bias, when he criticizes the treatment of Herod in Nicolaus of Damascus, his major source. Of him he says, 'since he lived in Herod's realm and was one of the associates, he wrote to please him and to be of service to him, dwelling only on those things that redounded to his glory, and transforming his obviously unjust acts into the opposite. We, however, being of a family closely related to the kings descended from Asamonaios and therefore having the priesthood together with (other) honours, have considered it unfitting to tell any falsehoods about them, and for this reason we relate their deeds with sincerity and fairness' (16:184-7). The reasons for Josephus' critical attitude toward Herod may thus simply reflect his *amour propre* as a descendent of the Hasmoneans,[59] or it may

---

[59] As noted above, the claim is also advanced in *Life* 2, but is passed over in silence in the *War.*

have resulted from strained relations between himself and Agrippa II, suggested in 16:187[60] and reflected in Book 20. Whatever the reason, Josephus now takes the career of Herod and his immediate successors to be both in itself a prime example of divine providence at work and also an essential component in the providentially directed chain of events leading up to the destruction of Jerusalem by the Romans.

Josephus gives numerous indications that he has found in the history of the Herodian family the lessons which he adumbrated in his programmatic preface. Occasionally these indications are imbedded in the narrative. Thus, after Herod has executed his wife Mariamme, he is filled with remorse, and at the same time, 'there arose a pestilential disease which destroyed the greater part of the people and also the most honoured of his friends, and this caused all to suspect that their misfortune had been brought upon them by God in His anger at what had lawlessly been done to Mariamme' (15:243). More frequently, the lesson is presented in editorial comments such as those on the drought and plague which broke out in the thirteenth year of Herod's reign, 'whether from God's being angry or because misfortune occurs in such cycles' (15:299). A similar comment appears in connection with the story of Herod's opening of the tomb of David, which in itself manifested providence at work through the miraculous destruction of two of Herod's soldiers (16:182). It was this story which prompted the critical remarks by Josephus on Nicolaus cited above. It also leads him to the reflection that 'it seemed as if it was because of the attempt which Herod had made upon the tomb that the state of affairs in his household became worse, whether it was the wrath (of God) that caused just those ills from which he was suffering to grow even worse and to develop into incurable misfortunes, or whether Fortune attacked him at a time so appropriate to the occasion as to provoke no little suspicion that these misfortunes had come upon him because of his impiety' (16:188). The diffidence about his theological judgement which Josephus expresses in these remarks, reminiscent of the 'rationalistic' comments on the miraculous in the biblical paraphrase, is surely as disingenuous as they are.[61]

The final lengthy reflections on the domestic strife between Herod and his sons by Mariamme continue in the same vein (16:395-404). After asking whether the outcome should be blamed on Herod, his sons or on fortune,

---

[60] Josephus there claims to 'have respect for many of his descendants who are still reigning.' The possessive pronoun is wrongly referred to 'Asamonaios' by Marcus and Wikgren, *Jewish Antiquities* 283. It must, rather, refer to Herod. Josephus goes on to note that his desire to honour the truth 'provoked those very persons to anger.' Agrippa II may well have been among the descendants of Herod so provoked.

[61] Comments such as 'on these matters let everyone decide according to his fancy' (*Ant.* 1:108) appear frequently, e.g., 2:348, 3:81. They reflect a formula found frequently in Dionysius of Halicarnassus, e.g., *Ant. Rom.* 1:248. They hardly indicate that Josephus himself discounted or disregarded the 'miraculous' elements of his tradition. For Josephus' attitude toward the miraculous, see Delling, 'Wunderbare' and MacRae, 'Miracle.'

Josephus assigns a share of the blame to each. Here, once again, Josephus uses Hellenistic language to express a biblical theology of history, with the same concern for the issue of the freedom of the will later used to describe Pharisaic doctrine (18:12-15). Here the basic aim of Josephus is to indicate the human moral failings, especially on the part of Herod, which led to the tragedy: 'For (Herod) to kill (his sons) so quickly and to gratify the passion that overpowered him was a sign of an irreligious spirit that is beyond assessment ... to do so after deliberating a long time and after frequent starts and as frequent hesitations, and finally to take a stand and accomplish the deed — this is the act of a murderous mind that cannot be turned from evil' (16:402-3).

Later editorial comments sounding the theme of a righteous providence are simpler and more straightforward. Before discussing the fall from grace and execution of Herod's eldest son, Antipater, Josephus remarks, 'I shall relate the whole story of this in order that it may be an example and warning to mankind to practice virtue in all circumstances' (17:60). Herod's final illness 'became more and more acute, for God was inflicting just punishment upon him for his lawless deeds' (17:168).

The lawless deeds on which Josephus focuses are important for the development of his basic theme. The executions of leading figures such as Hyrcanus ('neither just nor an act of piety' 15:182), Mariamme, and Herod's sons certainly play an important role in the assessment of his reign. Equally significant for what Josephus considers to have been the long-term implications of that reign are some less dramatic events. Josephus introduces his account of the pagan games inaugurated by Herod with the comment that 'Herod went still farther in departing from the native customs, and through foreign practices he gradually corrupted the ancient way of life, which had hitherto been inviolable. As a result of this we suffered considerable harm at a later time as well, because those things were neglected which had formerly induced piety in the masses' (15:267). Although these remarks, along with the section which follows, may derive from an anti-Herodian source, they certainly fit the characteristically Josephan themes enunciated in the biblical paraphrase. Divine providence is seen to favour the Jews only when they preserve the authentic Mosaic 'constitution.' Insofar as the reign of Herod marked a departure from that ancient and honourable way of life, it spelled disaster for the people. The same note that Herod violated ancestral laws introduces Book 16, where his decision to sell thieves into foreign slavery is recorded, another relatively minor incident which takes on special significance due to its prominent placement at the beginning of the new book (16:1-5). Later, Archelaus, the son of Herod, continues the tradition of 'transgressing ancestral law' by marrying Glaphyra (17:341).

If the reigns of Herod and his son are seen as a contributing factor in the decay of the ancestral laws which ultimately provoked divine wrath,

Josephus suggests that those reigns themselves were in part due to the earlier failings of Jewish leadership. The subjection of the people to the Romans and the transference of royal power from priests to commoners (such as Herod) is blamed on the dissension between Hyrcanus and Aristobulus, the sons of Alexander Jannaeus (14:77-78). Later, the Pharisee Samaias, who rebuked the Sanhedrin when it acquitted Herod of the charge of murdering Hezekiah in Galilee, advised the people to submit to Herod, saying, 'that on account of their sins they would not be able to escape him' (14:176).

The theological lessons are drawn in similar, if less dramatic, ways in the final segment of the *Antiquities*. The subsequent history of the Herodian line is rehearsed because 'it affords a proof of Divine Providence, showing how neither numbers nor any other wordly advantage can avail aught without acts of piety toward the Divine power. For, within a century of Herod's decease it came about that all but a few of Herod's issue, and there were many, had perished. It may contribute to the moral instruction of mankind to learn what their misfortunes were' (18:127-8). Success attends those who are pious and righteous and who preserve the ancestral laws, such as the Jews who peacefully protest the Roman standards brought to Jerusalem by Pilate (18:99), and the Jews and the Roman governor, Petronius, who resist the order of Gaius to establish his statue in the Temple (18:267, 284, 288, 305); Herod Agrippa I who is careful to observe all the traditional laws (19:293); and Izates, the convert from Adiabene (20:48, 72, 84, 91). On the other hand, those who abandon or suppress the ancestral laws, and thus show themselves to be impious and injust, are duly punished. These include the Jewish embezzlers who pretend to be interpreters of the law and whose wickedness causes the expulsion from Rome under Tiberius (18:84); Herod Antipas, the destruction of whose army by the Nabataeans resulted from his unjust execution of John the Baptist (18:119); the Babylonian Jewish warlord Anilaeus, whose decline begins when he takes a Parthian wife and violates ancestral law (18:340); and the emperor Gaius, the story of whose assassination 'provides evidence of God's power' while teaching that good fortune 'ends in catastrophe unless it goes hand in hand with virtue' (19:16). Above all, the lesson of the *Antiquities* is taught by the various Jewish revolutionaries, such as the followers of the 'fourth philosophy,' allegedly begun by Judas and Saddok after the demise of Archelaus. The sedition based on their novel 'philosophy' provides 'a lesson that an innovation and reform in ancestral traditions weighs heavily in the scale in leading to the destruction of those who engage in them' (18:9). Josephus similarly declares, echoing a major theme of the *War*, that 'God himself, for loathing the impiety (*scil.* of the Sicarii), turned away from our city and, because He deemed the Temple to be no longer a clean dwelling place for Him, brought the Romans upon us and purification by fire upon the city' (20:166).

222

PROPHECY

In addition to the various touches which attempt to show providence at work in the rewards of the righteous and punishments for the wicked, the general theme of divine providence is also developed both in the biblical paraphrase and through the reign of Herod by attention to the phenomenon of prophecy. Although Josephus' treatment of biblical prophets is generally limited, he does note the fulfillment of prophecies by David (8:109-10), Elijah (8: 418-20), Isaiah (11:5-6, 13:64, 68) and Jeremiah (10:142, 11:1) and he devotes a considerable part of Book 10 to a paraphrase of Daniel. Fulfillment of the 'prophecies' of Daniel about events of the Maccabean era is later noted (12:322), but at the end of the paraphrase of Daniel, Josephus records his most significant observation on prophecy. Fulfillment of Daniel's predictions should enable one to 'learn ... how mistaken are the Epicureans, who exclude Providence from human lives and refuse to believe that God governs its affairs or that the universe is directed by a blessed and immortal Being to the end that the whole of it may endure, but say that the world runs by its own movement without knowing a guide or another's care ... It therefore seems to me, in view of the things foretold by Daniel, that they are very far from holding a true opinion who declare that God takes no thought for human affairs. For, if it were the case that the world goes on by some automatism, we should not have seen all these things happen in accordance with this prophecy' (10:278-81).[62]

Josephus maintains that the 'exact succession of the prophets', which guarantees the historical reliability of the records which they composed, ended in the Persian period (*Ag. Ap.* 1:41), but he is equally convinced that the phenomenon of prophecy continues and bears constant testimony to divine providence. From the post-exilic and Hasmonean periods he cites the evidence of the prophetic dreams of Alexander the Great and the high priest Jaddus (*Ant.* 11:327, 333). Later he discusses the prophetic gifts of John Hyrcanus (13:282, 300, 322) and of the Essenes (13:311). In the Herodian period prophecy continues, and, not surprisingly, bears out the evaluation of Herod expressed in Josephus' editorial comments. Perhaps the most important example is the prophecy of the Essene Manaemus (Menaḥem) to the boy Herod. The prophet predicts Herod's elevation to royalty and advises the lad 'to love justice and piety toward God and mildness toward your citizens,' but he predicts that Herod will not do so: 'you will forget piety and justice. This, however, cannot escape the notice of God, and at the close of your life His wrath will show you that he is mindful of these things' (15:375-6).

---

[62] On this passage critical of the 'Epicureans' see Van Unnik, 'An Attack' and Attridge, *Interpretation*, 102-4.

Among subsequent Herodians, Archelaus and his wife Glaphyra both have prophetic dreams (17:345, 352). These dreams, and the interpretation of the first by an Essene named Simon, had been mentioned in the *War* (2:112-13). Here Josephus appends a comment which makes explicit their relevance to the moral to be derived from his whole history: 'I do not consider such stories extraneous to my history, since they concern these royal persons, and, in addition, they provide instances of something bearing on the immortality of the soul and of the way in which God's providence embraces the affairs of man' (17:354).

MORALIZING

The didactic dimension of the *Antiquities* is not exhausted by its various developments of the major theological theme of divine providence. Josephus fulfills his promise to write the history of the Jews who were 'trained in piety and the other virtues' (1:6) by paying particular attention to the whole spectrum of virtues exemplified by leading figures of his history. In the biblical paraphrase he regularly composes little encomia, praising Saul, for example, as 'just, courageous and wise' (6:346) or David as 'courageous, prudent, mild, kind, just and humane' (7:390-1). Naturally, the character of Moses receives special comment. He was a man of courage (3:13, 65, 4:42), who worked for the good of his people (3:212, 313), accepting toil and tribulation on their behalf (2:229, 290, 4:42). At his death, he is given a fitting eulogy by the historian as one who 'surpasses in understanding all men that ever live' who 'found favour in every way, but chiefly through his thorough command of his passions' (4:329-31). This picture of a man of Stoic self-mastery and surpassing virtue who stands at the source of Jewish tradition serves an obvious apologetic function, continuing a theme inaugurated in the remarks on Moses in the preface.[63]

The moralizing in the biblical paraphrase is also served by portrayals of activities to be avoided, the pride of Nimrod (1:113) or Samson (5:301), or the greed of Cain (1:61). Josephus also suggests some of the factors which lead to moral corruption and the abandonment of the ancestral law, sensuality (4:130), ambition (7:37-38) and presumption (9:222-3).

Subsequent history also provides suitable occasions for moralizing reflection. Some of this is certainly taken over from Josephus' sources, such as the remarks on the way envy and calumny sever the bonds of friendship (13:310), made in connection with the slaying of Antigonus at the instigation of Aristobulus, and paralleled in the *War* (1:77). Similarly, many of the remarks on the character of Herod, on his intense passion (15:82, 209-12, 218), or his ambition and love of glory (16:150-9) may derive from

[63] For discussion of the figure of Moses here and in other Jewish literature of the Hellenistic and Roman periods, see Tiede, *Charismatic Fiugure*, 207-40 and Holladay, *Theios Aner*, 47-102.

one or another of Josephus' sources, but he gladly incorporates them into his explicitly moralistic work.

The didactic features of the *Antiquities* serve to express Josephus' biblically based, but hellenistically conceived, theology of history. The whole work can be viewed as an attempt to paint a picture of the meaning of history already sketched in the *War*, but on a much broader canvas. At the same time, these didactic features serve indirectly an apologetic function, by indicating that Jewish tradition is marked by high ethical and religious ideals. Jews came into conflict with Rome only when they abandoned their traditions, and the result of their actions could have been predicted by anyone who understood their past.

DEFENSE OF JEWISH RIGHTS

This implicit, but fairly obvious, apologetic dimension of the *Antiquities* is accompanied by the explicit and concrete defense of Jewish rights in the Greco-Roman world conducted through the second half of the work. As noted above, these books are punctuated by collections of documentary evidence of various types relevant to the status and rights of Jews in the Hellenistic kingdoms, and particularly the Roman empire. Josephus makes quite clear his motives in presenting this material. Before citing decrees of Julius Caesar, he indicates that he introduces this material, 'in order that the other nations may not fail to recognize that both the kings of Asia and of Europe have held us in esteem and have admired our bravery and loyalty' (14:186). At the end of this major collection in Book 14, Josephus again comments that the various decrees 'have furnished clear and visible proofs of our friendship with the Romans' (14:266). Later, letters of Mark Anthony are cited to show the 'thoughtfulness which the Romans showed for our nation' (14:323). The most detailed statement on the part of Josephus about the intended effects of citing the documentary evidence appears after the citation of several decrees attributed to the Augustan period (16:162-73). They are provided 'since this account of our history is chiefly meant to reach the Greeks in order to show them that in former times we were treated with all respect and were not prevented by our rulers from practising any of our ancestral customs, but, on the contrary, even had their cooperation in preserving our religion and our way of honouring God. And if I frequently mention these decrees, it is to reconcile the other nations to us and to remove the causes for hatred which have taken root in thoughtless persons among us as well as among them' (16:174-5). Particularly noteworthy in this comment is the theme of 'preserving the ancestral laws' which plays so prominent a role in the theological thematic of the *Antiquities*. Immediately afterwards there appears another comment which makes explicit what appeared to be the implicit apologetic element in that theology of history. Josephus makes an appeal to his gentile readers: 'And it is most profitable for all men, Greeks and barbarians alike, to practice justice, about which our laws are most concerned and, if we sincerely abide by them, they make us well disposed and friendly to all men' (16:177).

Although Josephus' purpose in citing the various decrees and letters is clear, the source from which Josephus obtained his information and the historical value of the materials cited are uncertain. Much of the documentary evidence probably came to Josephus from his major source for the Herodian period, Nicolaus of Damascus, to whose history Josephus refers the interested reader after citing the confirmation of Jewish rights in Asia by Marcus Agrippa (12:127). Nicolaus, in the company of Herod, had spoken before Agrippa on behalf of Ionian Jews, and Josephus later describes the episode, including Nicolaus' speech on the occasion, which is perhaps the longest piece of formal rhetoric in the *Antiquities* (16:31-57). It is likely that either in preparation for the occasion or in writing his own account of it later, Nicolaus did collect documentary materials bearing on the issue of Jewish rights. Such evidence is referred to, but not cited, in the speech attributed to Nicolaus at 16:48. Later documents, such as the materials from the reign of Claudius (19:278-91, 303-11, 20:10-14), could not, of course, have come from this source. Josephus may have collected them himself, or have derived them from some other, unknown source. Although most of the documents accurately use the proper legal forms and their authenticity is generally accepted, they contain numerous historical anomalies. These may be due to accidents of transmission or they may be an indication that some of the documents are apologetic forgeries.[64]

THE PHARISEES AND THE FUTURE OF JEWISH-ROMAN RELATIONS

The various apologetic strands of the *Antiquities* are admittedly aimed at influencing gentile public opinion in favour of the Jews, and most particularly in favour of Jews who strictly observe the 'ancestral laws.' This apologetic tendency may well have been designed to serve the interests of the rabbinic circles at Jamnia, although the case is not unambiguously clear.[65] Josephus does devote special attention to the Pharisees, of whom the rabbis at Jamnia were the successors. The reviews of the three Jewish sects (13:171-3, 18:11-25) certainly give greater prominence to the Pharisees than is accorded them in the parallel passage in the *War* (2:119-66), although in both it is recognized that they are the 'premier school' (*War* 2:162, *Ant.* 18:15). Moreover, many of Josephus' editorial comments reflect the theological positions attributed to the Pharisees

---

[64] For discussion of the sources for Josephus' documentary evidence, see Smallwood, *The Jews*, 558-60, with the earlier literature cited there. Doubts about the authenticity of some of the documents have recently been raised by Moehring, '*Acta pro Judaeis.*'

[65] For discussion of Josephus' pro-Pharisaic attitudes in the *Antiquities* see Smith, 'Palestinian Judaism;' Neusner, *From Politics*, 45-66; and Cohen, *Josephus*, 237-41.

(16:398, 17:384). Nonetheless, the *Antiquities* is not a consistent piece of pro-Pharisaic propaganda. The rather disparaging remarks on the sect in the account of Herod's reign, possibly deriving from Nicolaus, are allowed to stand (17:41). Furthermore, while Josephus may have disguised the possible Pharisaic affiliations of the 'doctors of the Law' who incite youths of Jerusalem to remove Herod's eagle from the temple (17:149), he does admit that one of the founders of the despised 'fourth philosophy,' was Saddok the Pharisee (18:4).

Along with the, somewhat inconsistent, pro-Pharisaic tendency of the *Antiquities,* the relatively anti-monarchical elements of the work may have been aimed at influencing a shift in Roman policy after the death of Agrippa II away from its traditional support of the Herodian family. Such an antimonarchical tendency was evident in the attitudes taken toward Herod and Agrippa II, although here again Josephus, in his generally favourable attitude toward Agrippa I, is inconsistent. The anti-monarchical tendency may also be reflected in the scattered remarks on the nature of the traditional form of the Mosaic 'constitution'. In his summary of the Law in Book 4, he has Moses say, 'Aristocracy, with the life that is lived thereunder, is indeed the best: let no craving possess you for another polity, but be content with this, having the laws for your masters and governing all your actions by them' (4:223). An 'aristocracy' is the form of government in the happy period of Persian rule (11:111),[66] before the Hasmoneans re-introduce kingship. Later, when Aristobulus and Hyrcanus quarrel and the people appeal to Pompey to relieve them of kingship, they argue that the authentic ancestral tradition is to be ruled by priests, not kings (14:41), and Pompey's agent Gabinius restores an 'aristocratic' form of government (14:91). Josephus ends his survey of the history of the high-priests near the conclusion of his work with the note that after the demise of Archelaus the government again became an 'aristocracy' (20:351). Thus, Josephus may have intended his apologetics for 'traditional' Judaism to have a practical political effect, although this is only implicit in his work.

Against Apion or On the Antiquity of the Jews

The last work of Josephus is not a history but a polemical and apologetic tract, which continues, in a much more explicit fashion, some of the major tendencies of his historical works. The two-volume tract was written after the *Antiquities,* to which it refers on several occasions (*Ag. Ap.* 1:1, 54; 2:136, 287). A more precise date cannot be ascertained with any certainty.

---

[66] Once again, Josephus is hardly consistent. In his survey of the history of the high priests (20:234) he describes the constitution of the Jews in the post-excilic period until the Maccabean revolt as a 'democracy.' Like some of the inconsistencies in his work, this note may be due to his source.

The work probably appeared in the last years of Domitian or in the reign of Nerva, but there is no reference to a contemporary Roman emperor.

Josephus begins Book 1 by defending the antiquity of the Jewish people, which had apparently been challenged by critics on the grounds that Jews are not mentioned in early Greek sources. This accusation leads Josephus to a critical comparison of Greek and oriental historiographical traditions (1:1-68). He employs many commonplaces of the cultural polemics of the Hellenistic period, criticizing the Greeks for their inaccuracy as historians resulting from their inattention to ancient public records, their concern for literary style over accuracy and their incessant rivalries. He, on the other hand, claims to stand at the end of a lengthy tradition of self-consistent, priestly historiography, which relies on carefully preserved records and scriptures (1:35-36).[67] Following these critical remarks on Greek historians, Josephus demonstrates the antiquity of the Jews by adducing testimonies from various oriental and Greek sources (1:69-218). This section of his work provides a valuable collection of citations from earlier sources.

Josephus next turns to a refutation of various charges made against the Jews by Hellenistic authors. The remainder of Book 1 is concerned with the accounts of the Exodus presented by the third-century Egyptian author Manetho (1:228-87), the first-century Stoic philosopher and Alexandrian librarian Chaeremon (2:288-303), and the late-Hellenistic Alexandrian writer Lysimachus (2:304-20). According to Manetho's account, for example, the Exodus was primarily the work of a rebel priest of Heliopolis, Osarsiph, who organized a group of lepers confined to the eastern stone quarries by a Pharaoh Amenophis. Osarsiph, who changed his name to Moses, also appealed for outside assistance to the Solymites, descendents of the Hyksos who has been previously expelled from Egypt. This coalition initially was victorious over the Egyptians and brutally pillaged Egypt, but it was eventually expelled by Amenophis. Then Osarsiph/Moses led his followers to the land of the Solymites (1:228-50). Josephus has little difficulty in criticizing this account, although he is happy to find in it a testimony to the antiquity of the Jewish people, through their identification with the Hyksos (1:103-5).

In Book 2 Josephus turns to his refutation of the anti-Jewish slanders of Apion, an Alexandrian rhetorician of the first century C.E., who has given his name to the whole work. Apion had served as a member of the delegation sent to Gaius by the Greeks of Alexandria to contest the civil rights of the Alexandrian Jews (*Ant.* 18:257). His critical remarks on the Jews were

---

[67] A particularly clear example of such polemics against Greek historiography is found in Philo of Byblos, a Phoenician mythographer of the late first and early second century, fragments of whose *Phoenician History* are preserved by Eusebius. See Attridge — Oden, *Philo of Byblos.*

apparently contained in a five-volume history of Egypt, mentioned in *Ag. Ap.* 2:10. Josephus treats Apion's accusations in four general categories: his account of the Exodus (2:8-32); his accusations against the Jews of Alexandria (2:33-78); and various stories about the temple worship, including the allegations that the head of an ass was venerated there (2:79-88, 112-20) and that a Greek was ritually slain each year (2:89-111). A final section contains miscellaneous accusations: that Jews swore an oath of hostility against Gentiles (2:121-4), that their misfortunes indicated their inferiority (2:125-34) and that the Jewish nation had not produced any eminent individuals who had made significant contributions to human welfare (2:135-42).

In refuting these accusations, Josphus uses a variety of polemical techniques. Various *ad hominem* invectives punctuate Josephus' defense. Thus, Apion was basically a mendacious character (2:12), who even lied about his own birthplace (2:29). His slanders involve impudence and ignorance (2:26, 37). Indeed, he is characterized by the 'impudence of dog or the mind of an ass' (2:85). Josephus also regularly uses sarcasm to undermine the credibility of Apion's claims, characterizing, for example, Apion as an 'accurate grammarian' (2:15), while demonstrating the inaccuracies of his factual statements. Josephus also frequently uses a *reductio ad absurdum*. He thus asks how a mob of lame and leprous Jews exiting from Egypt could have survived even a day's march (2:23). Similarly, Josephus asks how a single human victim could have sufficed to feed the thousand of participants in the Jewish feasts (2:100). Josephus also indulges in counter-polemic, criticizing Egyptian religion (2:65-67, 85-88, 138-42), the seditious character of the Egyptians (2:68-70) and the lack of the Egyptians' citizen status in Alexandria (2:71-72). Finally, Josephus adduces counter-evidence to show the falsity of Apion's claims, alluding to the privileges accorded to Jews by various Hellenistic and Roman rulers (2:42-47) and noting the purity and sanctity of Jewish religious practices (2:102-10). The refutation of Apion's accusations ends with a report of his death, a fitting example of poetic justice. For, according to Josephus, the polemicist died from complications resulting from a medically required circumcision (2:143-4).

Josephus continues his apologetic work with an encomium on the Jewish law, or the Mosaic 'constitution' (2:145-220). Moses, the most ancient lawgiver, established a 'theocracy' (2:164), which surpasses the constitutions of the Greeks because it makes piety the central virtue (2:170), and inculcates other virtues through both theory and practice (2:169, 171-3).[68] Those who live under this constitution, which is guided by priests

---

[68] The account of Jewish law here bears some resemblance to other Jewish apologetic literature of the period. Note, e.g., Philo's *Hypothetica* preserved in Eusebius, *Praeparatio evangelica* 8:5,11. For discussion of some of the parallels, see Belkin, *Alexandrian Halacha*. It should be noted that Josephus makes some similar apologetic moves in his brief thematic summaries of Jewish laws in the *Antiquities* 3:224-86, 4:196-301.

and conducted as an elaborate ritual (τελετή 2:187-8), exhibit a unity of belief (2:168-79) and an endurance in the face of persecution, based on hope in a better life (2:218). After a critical contrast of this Mosaic constitution with the political, philosophical, and religious traditions of the Greeks (2:220-286), Josephus recapitulates his argument (2:287-90) and delivers a final encomium on the Jewish laws (2:291-6).

That final passage gives some sense of the apologetic fervour which marks the whole of the work:

> Upon the laws it was unnecessary to expatiate. A glance at them showed that they teach not impiety, but the most genuine piety; that they invite men not to hate their fellows, but to share their possessions; that they are the foes of injustice and scrupulous for justice, banish sloth and extravagance, and teach men to be self-dependent and to work with a will; that they deter them from war for the sake of conquest, but render them valiant defenders of the laws themselves; inexorable in punishment, not to be duped by studied words, always supported by actions. For actions are our invariable testimonials, plainer than any documents. I would therefore boldly maintain that we have introduced to the rest of the world a very large number of very beautiful ideas. What higher justice than obedience to the laws? What more beneficial than to be in harmony with one another, to be a prey neither to disunion in adversity, nor to arrogance and faction in prosperity; in war to despise death, in peace to devote oneself to crafts or agriculture; and to be convinced that everything in the whole universe is under the eye and direction of God? (2:291-4)

With that encomium Josephus concludes his literary output. Like much of his work, it exhibits the attempt to make comprehensible in Greek terms, here the terms of Greek political theory,[69] the nature and excellence of Jewish tradition. In the process, the Greek categories themselves undergo a redefinition, or refocusing. In the *War* the language for determinism or chance had been used to convey a notion of divine providence guiding the fate of the Jewish nation. Thus, 'fate' and 'chance' become not blind forces, but aspects of the moral will which guides history. Similarly here, the Torah is a political arrangement, a not inappropriate equivalent, but a political arrangement with a unique form ('theocracy')[70] and focus

[69] The tactic of presenting an apology for Judaism through an analysis of its 'lawgiver's' activity was not inaugurated with Josephus. For discussion of the technique in earlier Jewish apologetics, see Wacholder, *Eupolemus*, 76-85. Josephus may have drawn some inspiration from such Greek sources as Diodorus' discussion of the Pythagorean lawgiver Zaleucus (*Bibl. Hist.* 12:20,13) and Dionysius of Halicarnassus' presentation of the work of Numa (*Ant. Rom.* 2:18,1) and Romulus (*Ant. Rom.* 2:20,1-3).

[70] The term appears here for the first time in Greek literature and it may well be a neologism coined by Josephus himself.

('piety'). If there is any originality in the apologetic program of Josephus, it lies in this subtle redefinition of the interpretative categories used to make Jewish tradition comprehensible.

Conclusion

Whether or not Josephus had any effect on Roman opinion about Jews and Judaism is unclear. He was read widely in Christian circles and his works were translated into Latin by the sixth century.[71] The *War* also circulated in free paraphrase under the name of Hegesippus.[72] During the medieval period a rather free Slavonic version of the *War* was composed.[73] This version probably does not contain any material more authentic than the Greek tradition. Another product of the medieval period was a Hebrew work, the *Josippon,* based upon the *War, Antiquities* and *Against Apion,* as well as the Latin Hegesippus and other traditions. This work in turn generated Arabic, Ethiopic and Latin translations.[74]

Apart from the *Josippon,* the works of Josephus do not seem to have had a significant impact on Jewish tradition. Josephus in fact marks the end of a literary era. The biblical historiographical traditions had been further developed during the Hellenistic period under the added impetus of Hellenistic historical models. In the world dominated by Greek culture this literary tradition had provided one of the best avenues for the apologetic attempt to make Jewish traditions understood and respected in the world at large. As the leaders of post-70 Judaism became less concerned with that enterprise and more intent on reconstruction of Judaism in defiance of the harsh realities of history, historiography in general lost its appeal and relevance.[75] If there are any 'disciples' of Josephus, they are to be found in

[71] The Latin translations of at least the *Antiquities* and the *Against Apion* appear to have been made at the instigation of Cassiodorus in the sixth century. Cf. *Institutiones* 1:71,1 and Schürer, *History* 1, 58. For the text see now Blatt, *Latin Josephus* and Boysen, *Contra Apionem.*

[72] For the text see Ussani, *Hegesippi.* For discussion, see Mras, 'Hegesippus-Frage.'

[73] For the text, see Istrin, *La prise* and Meshcherskii, *Istoriga.*

[74] For earlier literature on the Josippon, see Schürer, *History* 1, 117-18. A critical edition of the text, with an introduction and a commentary, has been prepared by Flusser, *Josippon.* See also his 'Der lateinische Josephus.'

[75] For the few quasi-historical works composed by Jews of the rabbinic period, the *Megillath Taanith,* the *Seder Olam* and the *Megillath Antiochus,* see Schürer, *History* 1, 114-16. Perhaps *5 Maccabees* should also be included in this category. The work is as yet unedited, and its relationships to such works as the Josippon are unclear. For information, see Charlesworth, *Pseudepigrapha,* 153-6.

The traditions of Jewish historiography from the Hellenistic and early Roman periods may also have been continued in the corpus of Samaritan Chronicles. In particular, it has been claimed that portions of the *Book of Joshua,* containing a version of the biblical text with various midrashic additions, is of remote antiquity. However, the present Arabic text dates to the fourteenth century, and it is uncertain how much earlier its traditions are. For the text, see Gaster, 'Das Buch' and for a general survey of the Samaritan chronicles, see Macdonald, *Theology,* 44-49. Note also Macdonald's edition of the Samaritan *Sepher ha-Yamim* (*Samaritan Chronicle* No. II).

Christian ecclesiastical historians of the fourth and subsequent centuries.[76]

BIBLIOGRAPHY

General bibliographies with detailed surveys: FELDMAN, *Scholarship (1937-1962);* SCHRECKENBERG, *Bibliographie.* See now FELDMAN, *Josephus and Modern Scholarship 1937-1980.* The standard critical texts are by NIESE, *Flavii Josephi Opera* and NABER, *Flavii Josephi Opera Omnia.* There are texts and translations by THACKERAY, *The Life, Against Apion, The Jewish War, Antiquities I-IV, Antiquities V-VIII;* MARCUS, *Antiquities IX-XI; Antiquities XII-XIV;* MARCUS — WIKGREN, *Antiquities XV-XVII* and FELDMAN, *Antiquities XVIII-XX;* REINACH — BLUM, *Contre Apion;* PELLETIER, *Autobiographie;* and MICHEL — BAUERNFEIND, *De Bello Judaico.* An important research tool for Josephus' studies has been provided by RENGSTORF, *A Complete Concordance.* The most influential accounts of the work of the historian as a whole are NIESE, 'Josephus;' HÖLSCHER, 'Josephus;' and SCHÜRER, *History,* pp. 43-63; and THACKERAY, *Josephus.*

The vitality of current research on Josephus is evidenced by the recent collection of essays edited by BETZ *et al., Josephus-Studien.* Several recent studies have contributed significantly to the study of the individual works of the historian. These are ATTRIDGE, *The Interpretation,* which treats primarily the historiographical and apologetic techniques in the first half of the *Antiquities;* COHEN, *Josephus,* which focuses on the *Life,* but makes important observations about the general development of the historian, his use of sources and the tendencies of his various works; LINDNER, *Geschichtsauffassung,* which explores the sources and the literary structure of the *War;* and SCHALIT, *Qadmoniot,* a Hebrew translation of the *Antiquities* with a detailed introduction. Each of these works provides detailed reviews of scholarship on the problems with which they are concerned. Text-critical work on the Josephan corpus has been advanced in recent years with the work of SCHRECKENBERG, *Flavius-Josephus Tradition* and *Untersuchungen.*

---

[76] Note the citations of Josephus in Eusebius, *Ecclesiastical History* 1:1-3:10, where the Jewish historian serves as Eusebius' main source for his tendentious, anti-Jewish, account of the political history of the first century. Eusebius relies heavily on the lurid, accounts of Jewish suffering from the *Jewish War* in his discussion of the fall of Jerusalem (*Hist. Eccl.* 3:5,7-3:8-9), in order to illustrate 'how the punishment of God followed close after them (*scil.* the Jews) for their crime against the Christ of God' (*Hist. Eccl.* 3:5,7; cf. 3:7,1-9).

Chapter Six

Philo of Alexandria

Peder Borgen

One of the main aims of this study is to show that Philo (c. 10 B.C.E. to 45 C.E.) was basically following Jewish exegetical principles when commenting on the Pentateuch, the Law of Moses, for the benefit of Jewish and Hellenistic readers. As a Hellenistic Jew, he wrote in Greek and was also familiar with the popular philosophies of his day. These Greek approaches he incorporated into his exegesis, but he claimed that the true wisdom of the Greeks was derived from the Bible.

The proportion of influence to be ascribed to Judaism and to Hellenistic philosophy respectively in the writings of Philo has been much debated. Some scholars hold that the Greek language and culture of his writings are only a veneer on a thoroughly Jewish mentality.[1] Others find that Philo was the complete Hellenist, using Greek culture on the Jewish religion while defending and propagating it.[2] What is not sufficiently regarded in either view is that Philo's aim was definitely practical — to bring his readers to follow the revealed Law of the Pentateuch. Here, as elsewhere, no sharp distinction should be drawn between Hellenistic and Palestinian Judaism.[3]

The first part of this study will be an account of Philo's writings, summed up under three heads — 'Exposition of the Laws of Moses'; allegorical interpretations; thematic writings, including the philosophical ones. A systematic treatment of aspects of Philo's background and thought follows. Finally, there is a short study of the surviving fragments of Aristobulus, a predecessor of Philo.[3a]

The Exposition of the Laws of Moses

Some works of Philo follow in general the chronology of the Pentateuch. They are parts of one comprehensive work, which may be designated as the

---

[1] See Bentwich, *Philo Judaeus,* 8.
[2] Bousset, *Religion des Judentums,* 449-52; Windisch, *Frömmigkeit*; Leisegang, 'Philo', 1-50; *id. Der heilige Geist*; Reitzenstein, *Mysterienreligionen,* 223ff.; Bréhier, *Les Idées*; Pascher, *Königsweg*; Goodenough, *Light*; Jonas, *Gnosis* 2/1, 38.
[3] See Lieberman, *Hellenism*; *id. Greek*; Meyer, *Hellenistisches*; Hengel, *Hellenism*; Cf. Safrai, 'Relations'; Sandmel, *Philo's Place,* XX and XXIII.
[3a] Quotations and English titles of works are according to Colson, *Philo Works,* as also abbreviations of Latin titles (see *ibid.* vol. 1, pp. xxiii-xxiv).

'Exposition of the Laws of Moses.'[4] It comprises: *On the Creation, On Abraham, On Isaac, On Jacob, On Joseph, On the Decalogue, On the Special Laws, On the Virtues* and *On Rewards and Punishments.* All have survived except *On Isaac* and *On Jacob.* On the basis of Philo's own terminology and outline, the 'Exposition' can be divided in three parts:[5] the story of creation, the historical part and the legislative part. The *Life of Moses* was formerly classed in a group of miscellaneous writings, but Goodenough has shown that this and the 'Exposition' were companion works.[6] In these exegetical works Philo paraphrases and expands the biblical text and so gives his own views. A similar method may be found in the *Book of Jubilees,* the *Genesis Apocryphon* and the *Biblical Antiquities* of the Pseudo-Philo.[7] They are sometimes called 'rewritten Bible', a term which also suits Philo's 'Exposition' and the *Life of Moses.*

THE LIFE OF MOSES 1 AND 2

These two works[8] cover most of the story of Moses given in the Pentateuch, the most important omission being that of the theophany on Sinai which is dealt with in *On the Decalogue* (32ff.).[9] The first work covers the early life and education of Moses and his main activities as king and leader of the Israelites in their escape from Egypt and their adventures in the wilderness. The second deals with Moses as law-giver (12-65), high priest (66-186) and prophet (187-292).

Moses was the king of a nation destined to be consecrated above all others to offer prayers for the human race, for its deliverance from evil and participation in the good (1-149). He was the best of all law-givers, and his laws will endure as long as the universe. All other peoples honour the laws of the Jews, such as the Sabbath and the Day of Atonement. The supreme

---

[4] Cf. Goodenough, 'Exposition of the Law.'

[5] In *Praem.* 1-3, Philo divides the 'Exposition of the Law' into three main parts: the story of creation, the historical part and the legislative part. In *Mos.* 2:45ff., two parts are mentioned, the historical and the legislative. But here the historical part is divided into the creation story and the genealogical part, as in the first two points of the outline given in *Praem.* 1-3.

[6] *Ibid.* Goodenough points to *Virt.* 52 and *Praem.* 53ff., where Philo refers to the *Life of Moses.* Moreover, Philo envisages in *Mos.* 2:45ff. the 'Exposition' and its scheme.

[7] Cf. above, pp. 89f. See Rost, *Einleitung,* 98-101; 136-9; 146-8. Philo covers the biblical story from creation to Joshua's succession to Moses; *Jubilees* narrates the story from creation to the giving of the Law on mount Sinai; the *Genesis Apocryphon* is only preserved in parts, covering Genesis from the birth of Noah to 15:4; finally the *Biblical Antiquities* contain an abstract of the biblical story from Gen 5 to the death of Saul.

[8] The *Life of Moses* is treated as three works in all manuscripts and editions before Cohn. The second treatise ended at para. 65. This can hardly be correct, since Philo himself speaks of two books in *Virt.* 52. Cohn's division of the *Life of Moses* into two works is therefore followed by Colson and Arnaldez in their editions. See Cohn, *Philonis Opera* 4, XXX; Colson, *Philo Works* 6, VII and 274; Arnaldez, *Oeuvres de Philon* 22, 11-12.

[9] See Colson, *Philo Works* 6, 274-5.

proof of the universal acceptance of the laws of Moses is their translation into Greek, ordered by the king Ptolemy Philadelphus himself, an occasion celebrated annually on the island of Pharos in which Jews and Gentiles participate (2:186). Moses as high priest established the priesthood in Israel, and the priestly tribe was the nucleus of all mankind as regards the blessed eschatological life to come (2:12-186). As prophet he defended the Jewish religion and foretold the future of the nation (2:187-291).

Philo's purpose in writing the *Life of Moses* is to show the divine calling of Moses and the Jewish people to worship God, keep the Sabbath and serve the whole world. Philo expects that the new (eschatological) era will come when all nations cast aside their ancestral customs and honour the laws of Moses alone (2:43-44). Thus the book was written to tell Gentile readers about the supreme law-giver whose laws they are to accept and honour. It was also to strengthen the Jews for their universal role.[10] This dual purpose fits well the situation of the Jewish community of Alexandria in the period before Gaius Caligula, when Jews were actively penetrating the Greek community. Philo's work offers an ideological basis for pursuing this goal as Jews.

The form of this work is determined by the four offices of Moses. In Judaism the three offices of king, priest and prophet could be united in one person. In addition, the office of lawgiver was also ascribed to Moses.[11] To these Jewish elements Philo has added features which resemble a Greek *bios,* a biographical novel. His presentation of Moses thus abandons the Pentateuchal structure, and becomes a life of Moses from birth to death.[12]

---

[10] Scholars used to take the *Life of Moses* as an apologetic presentation of Judaism to the Gentiles. See Cohn, 'Einteilung und Chronologie', 415f. Goodenough, 'Exposition,' 110f. regards it as an introduction to Judaism, written for Gentiles. Arnaldez, *Oeuvres* 22, 19-20, thinks that the purpose is to give a justification of the Jewish faith on the basis of God's action towards his people through Moses. At the same time the book gives the basic justification for Philo's own expository enterprise. B. Badt, in Cohn *Werke Philos* 1, 218, has seen the importance which Judaism's universal calling has for the background and the purpose of the book.

[11] See Delling, 'Wunder-Allegorie-Mythus', 73-74. Josephus, *Ant.* 13:299f. says that John Hyrcanus held the three offices of king, priest, and prophet. Since the *Life of Moses* recounts the foundation of the Jewish religion and its message to the world, the proclamation of the message of Jesus to the world in the Gospels of the New Testament may be compared with this missionary purpose of Philo's books on Moses.

[12] Priessning, 'Die literarische Form', points out the similarity to Suetonius' imperial biographies, and the Alexandrian scholarly biographies as found in Plutarch. Like the *Life of Moses* these biographies consist of a chronological life history from the person's birth to the main period of his life. Then follows his public work, organized by topics, as also is the case in the *Life of Moses.* The next point in such a biography, a presentation of the person's private life, is, however, lacking in the *Life of Moses.* Instead, Philo characterizes the Jewish people, whose founder Moses was. Finally, as in the biographies, Philo tells the death of Moses. Elements of panegyric, of aretalogies, and of edificatory biography are also present. Cf. also Wendland, *Hellenistisch-römische Kultur*, 205, n. 2; Schmid-Stählin, *Geschichte der griechischen Literatur*, 654.; Leisegang, 'Philon', 30-1; Arnaldez, *Les Oeuvres,* 14ff., 22. (Historical novel); Delling, 'Wunder', 73-74.

ON THE CREATION

On the Creation is the first treatise in the 'Exposition'. It deals with Gen 1-3, creation and the sin of Adam and Eve. After an introductory section (1-12), Philo tells the story of creation following the scheme of the six work-days and the Sabbath of Gen 1:1-2:3, and using Gen 2:4-5 as a concluding summary (13-130). Subsequent points from Gen 2 and 3 are then elaborated upon (131-170a), including the sin of Adam and Eve and their punishment. The conclusion of the treatise (170a-172) makes explicit the teaching of the creation story. The scheme of the *hexaemeron* (six days) is paraphrased and expanded, as in other Jewish writings.[13] Philo considers that the story of creation is the necessary background to the laws of Moses given at Mount Sinai (3).[14] Moreover, the story of creation points to a corresponding eschatological possibility: the first father of the race lived without toil or trouble, in lavish abundance. These glorious times will return — in spite of the punishment of Adam and Eve for their disobedience — if the religious and ethical conditions are met (79ff.).

On the Creation deals also with philosophical issues. These are particularly evident in para. 170-1, where Philo concludes his story of creation with criticism of the Pyrrhonic (sceptical) doubt about God's existence, the Aristotelian view that the world had no beginning, the Epicurean plurality of worlds and denial of Providence.[15] Philo here has much in common with Plato's *Timaeus* and Stoicism. Some of the concepts held in common with the *Timaeus* are: an intelligible world (of 'forms') transcending the visible world (16, etc.; *Timaeus* 30C; 33B); the Goodness of the Father and Maker of all things (21; *Timaeus* 29E); the simultaneity of time and the world (26; *Timaeus* 38B). Some of the Stoic ideas are: the world as a city (3 and 19); time as measured space (26); the fourfold hierarchical order of creatures (66-68). Since he thinks that the Greek philosophers have borrowed these ideas from the writings of Moses, he regards them as originally Jewish, thus expressing the high self-regard of the Jews as the chief nation in the world. The Jew who observes the laws of Moses is a cosmopolitan ('citizen of the world'), since these laws are universal (3). In this situation, as Goodenough has rightly argued, Philo had not only Jews but also Gentiles in mind and thus brought the Jewish story of creation into the general philosophical debate on the origin of the world.

[13] See 4 Ezra 6:38-59; *Jubilees* 2:1-21; *2 Enoch* 24-30, etc.
[14] Cf. *Mos.* 2:45-52. The connection between the work of creation and the revelation on Sinai appears also in rabbinic literature. Cf. *M. Aboth* 5:1; *Aboth de Rabbi Nathan* A, 31 (p. 90f).
[15] See Colson, *Philo Works* I, 476. Polemic against Epicurean denial of providence also occurs in Rabbinic writings. See Urbach, *Sages* I, 28-31. A similar polemic is found as early as Ben Sira. See Hengel, *Hellenism,* 141f.

ON ABRAHAM

The historical part of the 'Exposition' covers the biblical story from the events after Adam and Eve to the death of Joseph. The title of the first work, *On Abraham,* is somewhat inadequate, since it also contains the stories of Enos, Enoch and Noah, drawing on parts of Gen 4-26. After placing the work within the framework of his 'Exposition' (1-6), Philo interprets Enos as 'hope'[16], Enoch as 'repentance'[17] and Noah as 'justice'[18]. Their yearnings for virtue resemble 'the studies of children', whereas the direct ancestors of Israel, Abraham, Isaac and Jacob, may be compared to full-grown athletes (48).

The outline of Abraham's life follows in part the chronology of the biblical narrative. However, the main principle of organization is systematic, so that the events illustrate the subject matter concerned, piety, hospitality, tact and kindness, courage and self-control. In every case, except the last (which describes Abraham's resignation at the death of Sarah) the narrative of particular events in Abraham's life is followed by an allegorical interpretation.[19]

Although the works on Isaac and Jacob are lost, Philo's basic interpretation of the three Patriarchs is summed up in *On Joseph* 1: Abraham means wisdom or virtue from study, Isaac from nature, and Jacob from practice.[20] Here Philo is drawing on a broad Greek tradition about education, in which instruction, nature and practice are discussed in relation to virtue. Plutarch associates the triad with Pythagoras, Socrates and Plato.[21] To Philo, these aspects of virtue and wisdom characterize the Jewish people and its religion; *On Abraham* 56 states that the triad Abraham/study, Isaac/nature and Jacob/practice engenders the 'royal' people also called a 'priesthood' and 'holy nation' (Exod 19:6).[22] Philo interprets the Patriarchs in relation to creation and the giving of the Law on Mount Sinai. The

[16] *Abr.* 7-16, see Gen 4:26 according to the Septuagint.
[17] *Abr.* 17-26, see Gen 5:24.
[18] *Abr.* 27-46, see Gen 6:9. See the similar exposition in *Praem.* 11-7.
[19] Literal exposition of parts of Gen 11:31-12:9 in 60-7 and allegorical in 68-89; so too Gen 12:10-20 in 90-8 and in 99-106; Gen 18 in 107-18 and in 119-32; Gen 19 in 133-46 and in 147-66; Gen 22 in 167-77 and in 200-7; Gen 13:5-11 in 208-16 and in 217-24; Gen 14 in 225-35 and in 236-44; and finally literal exposition of Gen 16:1-6, Gen 23, etc. in 245-61. Philo sums up Abraham's life in his faith (Gen 15:6) and in his characterization as presbyter (Gen 26:5) in 262-76.
[20] See also *Mos.* 1:76, etc.
[21] See Hadot, 'Etre, Vie, Pensée', 125-6; Borgen, *Bread,* 103ff; Plutarch, *De liberis educandis* 2A-C.
[22] This is explicitly stated in *Abr.* 98. Philo writes of the marriage of Abraham and Sarah: 'That marriage from which was to issue not a family of few sons and daughters, but a whole nation, and that the nation dearest of all to God, which, as I hold, has received the gift of priesthood and prophecy on behalf of all mankind.' The same view of the patriarchs is also expressed in *Decal.* 1, where Philo characterizes them as 'founders of our nation'.

Patriarchs are living laws (ἔμψυχοι νόμοι), that is, they are an embodiment of the divine cosmic laws. Conversely, the specific laws given on Mount Sinai are memorials of the life of the ancients, and commentaries on it (5). Jewish and Platonizing motifs are woven together here. The Jewish motif is the correspondence between the practices of the Patriarchs and the Mosaic Law. For example, according to the *Book of Jubilees*, Noah, Abraham and others observed and enjoined the laws inscribed on heavenly tables which were later given to Moses.[23] A similar correlation is found in Philo, but here the Platonizing element makes the lives and words of the Patriarchs archetypes, and the Mosaic laws copies.[24]

On Abraham shows some influence of the literary forms of Hellenistic biographies. It contains certain topics of the panegyric, and its allegorical section show affinities with religious and philosophical biography written to edify.[24a]

ON JOSEPH

The outline of this work further illustrates the tension observed in *On Abraham,* and especially in the *Life of Moses,* between a chronological organization founded on the biblical narrative and a systematic and subject-centered presentation. In the first section (2-156) the exposition of Gen 37:2-41:46 is systematic, but in 157-270 the story follows Gen 41:47-50:26 with omissions and amplifications. In the systematic part (2-156) the exposition is on two levels, literal and allegorical, as is also the case in *On Abraham* 60-244.[25]

On Joseph reflects the relationship between Jews and the Gentiles of Philo's time. One difference between them is in sexual ethics and marriage laws (42ff., 56f.). The Hebrews are strict on such matters, while licentiousness has shattered the youth of Greeks and barbarians alike. In Egypt it is easy for Jewish youth to leave the ancestral way of life for alien ways,

---

[23] *Jubilees* 6:17; 15:1; 16:28, etc.; See Bousset, *Religion des Judentums,* 125, n. 3 and 126, n. 1. The idea that the Patriarchs kept the commandments of the Torah is familiar in rabbinic dicta as well. See Urbach, *Sages,* 335f.

[24] Sandmel, *Philo's Place,* 49. Cf. p. 108: 'The rabbis say that Abraham observed the Law; Philo says that the Law sets forth as legislation those things which Abraham did.' Sandmel emphasizes the contrast between Philo and the Rabbis. Philo indicates himself, however, that he merely modifies the view that Abraham obeyed the Law: 'Such was the life of the first, the founder of the nation, one who obeyed the Law, some will say, but rather, as our discourse has shown, himself a law and unwritten statute.' (*Abr.* 276)

[24a] See Priessning, 'Die literarische Form,' 145-50. A brief summary in English is given in Hamerton-Kelly, 'Sources', 11-13. See also Marcus, 'Recent Literature,' 473-4. For *topoi* of the rhetorical panegyric, see: *Abr.* 115, *eudaimonismos*; 178-199, *synkrisis*; it omits anything pejorative about Abraham (Sarah and Hagar, Gen 16 and 21; Abimelech, Gen 20 and 21:22-23).

[25] Literal exposition of Gen 37:2-36 is given in 2-27, followed by allegorical in 28-36; so too Gen 39:1-20 in 37-53, and 54-79; literal exposition of Gen 39:21-41:46 is found in 80-124, and two allegorical interpretations in 125-50, and in 151-6.

because the Egyptians deify things created and mortal, and are blind to the true God (254). Another difference is in table fellowship. When Joseph gave a feast for his own family and the Egyptians, he feasted each party according to its ancestral practice. Surprisingly, the Egyptians followed the same seating order as the Hebrews, which indicates that in older times, before Joseph introduced good order, their style of life was less civilized (202-6).

Joseph's free and noble birth anticipates his future role (69 and 106); his authority as governor, indeed as king of Egypt, was from God, the Creator, who had the Jewish nation as his own loyal people (107 and 119).[26] Indeed, Goodenough thinks the purpose of *On Joseph* is to 'suggest that the real source for the highest political idea of the East, the ideal of a divinely appointed and guided ruler, had had its truest presentation in Jewish literature, and highest exemplification at a time when a Jew was, in contemporary language, prefect of Egypt.'[27]

On Joseph combines narrative elements with the standard topics of eulogy[28] and so resembles edifying Hellenistic biography. This is to a lesser degree the case in its allegorical sections.

ON THE DECALOGUE AND ON THE SPECIAL LAWS

The legislative part of the 'Exposition of the Laws of Moses' starts with *On the Decalogue*. It serves as a summary of the laws to be explained in detail in *On the Special Laws*. Chronological order and systematic presentation are again combined. The biblical order is sometimes followed, as for the giving of the Law at Mount Sinai, which comes after the story of creation and the patriarchs. But on the whole systematic interests predominate. In these treatises on the written laws, Philo is mainly concerned with the legal parts of Exodus, Leviticus, Numbers and Deuteronomy. At times, relevant elements from Genesis are included.

In *On the Special Laws* the usual procedure is to begin with an elaboration on a given commandment, similar to though fuller than that in *On the Decalogue*, and then to go on to discuss particular enactments which Philo thinks may be set under it. Book 1 interprets the first and second commandments, against polytheism and idols, and gives details on knowledge and worship of God.[29] Book 2 covers laws which can be assigned to the next three commandments: not taking God's name in vain (regulations on oaths and vows), keeping the Sabbath (special laws on

---

[26] For a full discussion of Philo's political theology, and in this connection also of *On Joseph*, see Goodenough, *Politics*, especially 43-63.

[27] *Ibid.* 62.

[28] See above n. 24a.

[29] The first and second commandments here are in the usual rabbinic counting held as the second 'word'.

various feasts), and honouring parents (duties of parents and children to each other). In Book 3, Philo interprets the commandment against adultery (special laws on sexual irregularities), and murder. Book 4 treats the last three commandments, against stealing (various forms of dishonesty), false witness and covetousness.

Philo's idea was that the Decalogue served to establish the general categories of law, which were then applied in detail by various precepts. Philo here seems to develop systematically a notion also found in Palestinian tradition, that the Decalogue contained *in nuce* all the commandments of the Mosaic law.[30]

ON THE VIRTUES AND REWARDS AND PUNISHMENTS

These two works form the final section of the 'Exposition'. *On the Virtues* is connected with *On the Special Laws* 4:133-5, where Philo says that the virtues ared needed for all commandments, and are not confined to any particular one. Justice is presented in *Special Laws* 4:136-238, while courage, philanthropy, repentance and magnanimity, are treated of in *On the Virtues*. Subjects are not treated in an abstract or analytical way. Courage (1-50), philanthropy or kindness (51-174), repentance (175-186) and magnanimity (187-227) serve rather as key words and are illustrated from the Pentateuch.[31]

The virtues of courage and magnanimity, as well as the virtue of justice treated in the *Special Laws* 4:136-238, reflect Greek (Platonic and Stoic) terminology and ideas. To Philo however, these virtues are biblical and characterize the Jewish nation. So their source is God and his laws. Philo makes repentance a virtue in a way in which the Greeks did not, and it is in particular applied to conversion from atheism and polytheism.

In the opening paragraph of *Rewards and Punishments,* Philo reviews the scheme of the Pentateuch (creation, history, legislation), which he employs for the 'Exposition'. Then he defines the relationship between the virtues and the rewards and punishments: those who are schooled in the laws and exhortations are called into the sacred arena to be tested; the true athletes of virtue will gain victory and rewards while the unmanly will suffer defeat and punishments (1-6).[32] The treatise falls into two main parts; the first

[30] See *Targum Ps.-Jonathan* on Exod 24:12. For the debate between Wolfson (Rabbis and Philo understood the Decalogue in a similar manner) and Urbach (no parallel can be drawn), see Hecht, 'Preliminary Issues.' Hecht points out that Urbach does not consider the evidence of the Targums.

[31] Courage, from parts of Num 25 and 30, and of Deut 20, 22 and 28; philanthropy, from Num 27 and various laws in Exod, Lev and Deut; repentance, from parts of Deut 26 and 30 and Pentateuchal ideas about proselytes; magnanimity, from passages about Adam and Cain, Noah and Ham, sons of Abraham, Tamar, etc. in Genesis.

[32] This understanding of rewards and punishments is anticipated in *Mos.* 52-65. See Goodenough, 'Exposition of the Law' 112.

deals with rewards and punishments (7-78) and the second with blessings and curses (79-172).[33] The work is largely based on Genesis, and seems to re-use, in briefer form, the earlier *On Abraham* and *Life of Moses,* and possibly the lost *On Jacob* and *On Isaac* (see 7-66). In the rewards assigned to the children of Jacob, interest mainly focuses on the Jews as a nation (65-66). The second part of the treatise continues the main sequence of the 'Exposition'. While *On the Decalogue* and *Special Laws* give an exposition of laws in Exodus, Leviticus, Numbers and Deuteronomy, the blessings and curses cover other sections in these books, with main emphasis on Lev 26 and 28, and Deut 28.[34] Victory over human and natural enemies, wealth, long life and happiness are the blessings (79-126); famine, cannibalism, slavery, business failures, diseases and wars are the curses (127-151). The Jewish nation, of which the others are satellites, has the blessings of peaceful alliances (93, 114, 125; cf. *Mos.* 2:44), and successful defensive war. If the nation is for a while rejected, proselytes take over the role of the Jews. Philo's treatment of the blessings and curses follow the line of Jewish tradition.[35] But, as usual, Greek philosophy, especially Platonic and Stoic, colours the work.[36]

Allegorical Interpretations

Besides the 'Exposition of the Laws of Moses', Philo wrote another type of biblical commentary, on passages mainly selected from the Pentateuch. The commentary often expands into short essays on a subject. Allegorical interpretation is frequently used.

QUESTIONS AND ANSWERS ON GENESIS AND EXODUS

This work is a commentary on Genesis and Exodus, in the form of questions and answers. Most of the Greek original has been lost and we mainly depend on the ancient Armenian version.[37] The original work may have taken in other books of the Pentateuch, but Eusebius knew only the section of Genesis and Exodus.[38] Greek fragments preserved by Byzantine

[33] Between the two parts a transitional passage is missing, to conclude the discussion of rewards and punishment and to introduce blessings and curses. See Colson, *Philo Works* 8, 455.
[34] These observations tell against Goodenough's attempt to separate the section on blessings and curses from Philo's larger work, the Exposition of the Laws of Moses. See Goodenough, 'Exposition of the Law' 118ff.
[35] See Ps 78; 105; 106; 135; 136; .Ezek 20; Sir 44-50; Wis 10; I Macc 2:52-61; Hebr. 10; cf. Acts 7.
[36] See A. Beckaert in Arnaldez, *Les Oeuvres* 26, especially p. 16.
[37] R. Marcus, in Colson, *Philo Works* Suppl. 1-2 (1953). See the Armenian and the Latin translations in Aucher, *Philonis Iudaei Paralipomena Armena.*
[38] *Hist. eccl.* 2:18, 1 and 5.

writers deal only with Genesis or Exodus with two doubtful exceptions. Therefore we probably have the whole of the work.[39]

The commentary is mostly on two levels, the literal and the allegorical, as in the 'Exposition of the Laws of Moses'. It is not, however, a verse by verse commentary, like the 'Exposition'. The relationship between *Questions and Answers* and the *Allegorical Interpretation of Genesis 2-3,* will be discussed later. Both works have the form of a commentary on verses or passages from the Pentateuch. Some scholars have suggested that *Questions* is catechetical, while *Allegorical Interpretation* is more scholarly.[40] Against this is the fact that in general, where *Questions* overlaps with *Allegorical Interpretation,* there is no substantial difference. Moreover, the question and answer form also occurs in the 'Exposition of the Laws of Moses', where it does not serve a catechetical aim.[41] Scholars have observed that the question and answer form is also found in Greek commentaries on Homer.[42] But it equally occurs in Palestinian exegetical tradition[43] and Philo may therefore share this influence from Greek exegetical forms with Jewish tradition.[44]

[39] See Marcus, in Colson, *Philo Works,* Suppl. 1, pp. X-XII. The Armenian version of *Questions and Answers on Genesis* (Q.G.) divides the work into 4 books, covering the complete original Greek text, which was, however, divided into 6 books. The first 3 books of the Greek original correspond to the first 3 books of the Armenian version. Greek book 4 corresponds to Armenian 4, 1-70, Greek 5 to Armenian 4, 71-153 and Greek 6 to Armenian 154-245. The Armenian version of *Questions and Answers on Exodus* (Q.E.), contains two books of unequal size. Book 1 covers Exod 12:2-23 (25 pages in Aucher's edition), while book 2 (aside from the first section on Exod 20:25) covers Exod 22:21-28:34 omitting several verses (80 pages in Aucher's edition). If we suppose that *Q.E.* was divided into books of about the same length as those of *Q.G.,* we must conclude that the present book 1 is less than half of the original and that the present book 2 is either a complete book or else contains parts of several of the original books.

[40] Schürer, *Geschichte* 3, 644 and 648; Colpe, 'Philo', 342.

[41] Cf. *Op.* 72-75, 77-88, and *Decal.* 36-43. Questions of etymology *Op.* 77 (cf. *Q.G.* 1:43); *Op.* 72 and *Decal* 36 (cf. *Q.G.* 1:15). Use of question and answer form in *L.A.* 1:101-4 (cf. *Q.G.* 1:15) and *L.A.* 1:85-87 (cf. *Q.G.* 1:13). See Borgen-Skarsten, 'Quaestiones et Solutiones'; cf. Sandmel, 'Philo's Environment,' 249, who thinks that the verse by verse exposition in *Q.G.* and *Q.E.* were preliminary notes on the basis of which Philo eventually composed some continuous treatises.

[42] Cohn, *Einteilung;* R. Marcus in Colson, *Philo Works Suppl.* 1, p. IX. See examples of Homeric commentary in H. Schrader, *Porphyrii Quaestionum Homericarum ad Iliadem Pertinentium reliquias,* Fasc. I, Leipzig 1880. The form of questions and answers was frequently used in Christian exegesis. Early on, it reflected controversies between orthodox and heretic. From the 4th century on, the commentaries rather treat traditional problems than live issues. The form was also used for personal counselling and pedagogics. See Schäublin, *Untersuchungen,* 49-51; Dörries, 'Erotopokriseis, B.'

[43] Cf. Hallewy, 'Biblical Midrash.'

[44] For example, a close parallel both in form and in content exists in *Op.* 77-78 and *T. Sanhedrin* 8:7-9. The issue discussed in both passages is why Adam was created last, and the answers are partly the same: God is compared to a human host, who invites the guest when the meal is ready. Philo and the *Tosefta* clearly render two versions of the same tradition. In this passage Philo explicitly states that he has received the tradition from 'those, who have studied more deeply than others the laws of Moses, and who examine their contents with all possible minuteness . . .'

ALLEGORICAL INTERPRETATIONS OF GENESIS

Several treatises of Philo have the form of a verse by verse commentary on biblical texts taken from Gen 2:1-41:24.[45] These commentaries vary in length and are more complex in form than *Questions and Answers,* though the question and answer form is also used.[46] In this they are closer to the Midrashim than to the commentaries found at Qumran.[47] Originally the title of all these commentaries seems to have been 'Allegorical Interpretations of the Laws'. This name is now given only to the first work, on Gen 2:1-3:19. The others have different titles.

The first work, *Allegorical Interpretation of Genesis 2-3,* consists of three treatises, the first two of which are combined in the manuscripts.[48] In the third treatise, more than in the others, extensive elaborations on related Pentateuchal passages are inserted into the commentary on texts from Genesis.[49] *Allegorical Interpretation* has a practical aim. Allegory is used to deduce, from the story of creation and paradise, principles to fortify the Jews of Alexandria in their religious and moral life. They were, it seems, exposed to the temptations of wealth and luxury, with rich banqueting a special occasion of sin; and education was used as a step towards political careers incompatible with Jewish ideals.[50]

In the treatises following *Allegorical Interpretation on Genesis 2-3,* essays occasioned by biblical texts predominate.[51] We distinguish three groups. The first group comprises: *On the Cherubim, On the Sacrifices of Abel and Cain, The Worse Attack the Better, On the Posterity and Exile of Cain, On the Giants* and *On the Unchangeableness of God.* They provide elaborate allegorical explanations of expulsion from paradise, the cherubim, Adam and Eve, Cain and Abel and the giants (Gen 3:24-6:4).[52]

---

[45] Philo may have written other treatises of this nature. In *Her.* 1, Philo refers to a treatise on Gen 15:1, now lost. For the lost treatise *On Dreams,* see below p. 245. Other lost treatises may have interpreted parts of Genesis not covered by the extant writings. See e.g. Cohn, *Einleitung,* 393, 402.

[46] Questions and answers are found in: *L.A.* 1:33-41; 48-52; 70-71; 85-87; 90; 91-92a; 101-104; 105-108; 2:19-21; 42-43; 44-45; 68-70; 80-81; 3:18-19; 49ff; 65-68; 77-78; 184-185; 188. See especially the close agreements between *L.A.* 1:85 and *Q.G.* 1:13; *L.A.* 1:101 and *Q.G.* 1:15; *Cher.* 21f. and 55ff.; *Sac.* 11ff and 128ff; *Det.* 57ff. and 80ff.; *Post.* 33ff., 40ff. and 153; *Gig.* 55ff.; *Deus* 11f., 60ff., 70ff., 86ff., 104 and 122. See further *Som.* 1:5ff.; 12f.; 14ff.; 41f. and *Som.* 2:300ff.

[47] See the Qumran commentary on Habakkuk (1QpH) and *Mekhilta de Rabbi Ishmael* and *Genesis Rabba* etc. Cf. Dahl, *Studies in Paul,* 165-6.

[48] See Cohn, *Philonis Opera* 1, p. LXXXVI and p. 113, note.

[49] See for instance Philo on Gen 2:8 and Gen 3:14. The second treatise holds a middle position. Cf. Adler, *Studien,* 8-24.

[50] *L.A.* 1:75f.; 86; 2:17; 29; 2:107; 3:155-6; 167; 220-1.

[51] Cf. Adler, *Studien,* 8 and 66-67.

[52] Some of the topics are: banishment (*Cher.* 1ff.), the mistaken idea that what we have is our own and not God's (40ff.), the contrasting ideas of man's mind as master and God as master (*Sac.* 1ff.), the precedence of virtue (11ff.) the danger of tardiness and postponement (52ff.), the

The second group consists of the treatises: *On Husbandry, Concerning Noah's Work as a Planter, On Drunkenness* and *On the Prayers and Curses Uttered by Noah when he Becamer Sober.* They are parts of one single composition, as can be seen from the transitional statements.[53] The first three works are based on Gen 9:20-21 and the last is a commentary on Gen 9:24-27. They are well-organized lectures on themes suggested by words in the text. The biblical story of Noah's cultivation of the vine, his drunkenness and recovery, leads to a discussion of the contrast between civilization and barbarism (*On Husbandry*); God as husbandman, with examples of his work (*Planter* 1-139); a survey of the philosophical schools on drunkenness (incompletely preserved in *Planter* 140-77); wine and drunkenness as symbols of folly, stupor and greediness (*On Drunkenness*); God's goodness, the curse on evil and the virtues of moral excellence and physical well-being (*On Sobriety*).

The third group consists of *On the Confusion of Tongues, On the Migration of Abraham, Who is the Heir, On the Preliminary Studies, On Flight and Finding, On the Change of Names* and *On God.* They are a miscellaneous group though some are on closely related topics. They continue the verse by verse commentary on Genesis now taking in Gen 11-18, but bring in other parts of the Bible when systematic and topical interests vary the structure. *Confusion* and *Change of Names* defend the laws of Moses and Jewish institutions against apostates of the Jewish community who are inclined to mock. *Preliminary Studies* is on general Greek education (*Encyclia*) and touches also the relationship of Jewish and Greek culture. The last part of this work (158-80) treats of wisdom's (Sarah's) rebuke and the rejection of Hagar, that is, elementary education. *On Flight and Finding* takes up this idea (2) and moves on to Hagar and the subject of fugitives (Gen 16:9 ff.), a subject which is linked with various attitudes in worldly life and the service of God. *Migration of Abraham* and *Who is the Heir* treat of Jewish religious life and ideals in contrast to pagan life in Egypt and its temptations. The fragment of *On God*, extant only in Armenian, concerns the revelation to Abraham at the oak of Mamre, Gen 18, mainly seen as affirming God's control over the world. This treatise is perhaps to be included in Philo's allegorical interpretations.[54]

---

stable and firm life of virtue (88ff.) the opposing principles of love of self and love of God, with only the apparent victory of the false view of self-love (*Det.* 1ff.) further characterizations of the impious who do not recognise God and His gifts, and of the pious (*Post.* 1ff.), (sensual) pleasure and, by contrast, the God-born life (*Gig.* 1ff.), God's constancy and unchangeableness (*Deus*).
[53] *Plant* 1 is linked with *Agr.* by: 'We have said in the former book ... In this book ...'. *Ebr.* 1 says: 'The views ... have been stated by me ... in the preceding book. Let us now consider ...' *Sobr.* 1 reads: 'having in the foregoing pages dealt fully with the words of the lawgiver on ..., let us proceed to carry on the thread of our discussion.'
[54] See Aucher, *Philonis Paralipomena Armena*, 613-19; Schürer, *Geschichte* 3, 658. Siegert, *Drei Predigte* thinks this fragment is not authentic.

ON DREAMS

This work treats of the dreams mentioned in the Pentateuch. Since the thematic exposition predominates, it can hardly be called a commentary and therefore rather resembles that of *On Virtues and Rewards*.

Only two treatises *On Dreams* survive. However, in the opening section Philo refers to three kinds of dreams and to an earlier treatise on the first kind; apparently it went lost. The first extant treatise deals with the two dreams of Jacob in Gen 28:10-22 and Gen 31:10-13 (1:3-188 and 189-256). They reveal that man's understanding and the soul of the universe interlock, which enables man to foresee the future. These dreams which are of the second kind, are caused by angels (1:157, 230 and 189-190). In this context Philo explains the basis of man's (i.e. the Jew's) communication with God, especially his confidence in God. This basis is a 'prophecy' which explains moral and social life, and criticizes the luxury and gluttony of those whose days are spent in law courts, council chambers and theatres; 'none such is a disciple of the Holy Word' (120-4). The biblical dreams reveal that the sophists, ventriloquists and soothsayers of Egypt are political evils (220ff.); that the Jewish nation has a universal role in the world (175-6, 215); and how the various elements of education combine (205). Turning to the future, Philo exhorts the followers of Jacob: 'For so shalt thou be able also to return to they father's house, and be quit of that long endless distress which besets thee in a foreign land' (255-6).

The second extant treatise is on the dreams of Joseph (Gen 37:8-11), the chief butler and baker (Gen 40:9-11 and 40:16-17) and Pharaoh (Gen 41:17-24). They are of the third type, caused by man's soul when asleep. Joseph's dream of the sun, moon and eleven stars bowing to him is used to denounce the vanity of those who set themselves above other men and nature itself.[55] Some are foolish enough to feel aggrieved if the whole world does not fall in with their wishes — people like the Persian king, Xerxes, and the Germans.

The three types of dream correspond to the description given by the Stoic Posidonius: 'There are three ways in which men dream as a result of divine impulse: first, the soul is clairvoyant of itself because of its kinship with the gods; second, the air is full of immortal souls (i.e. the daemons) already stamped, as it were, with the marks of truth; and third, the gods in person converse with men when they are asleep.'[56]

---

[55] See *Som.* 2:110-38; Goodenough, *Politics,* 29-30. Goodenough rightly doubts that *Som.* 2:123ff. refers to Flaccus.

[56] Cicero, *De divinatione* 1:30, 64. Translation taken from Wolfson, *Philo* 2, 57. See also Colson, *Philo Works* 5, 593 and Cohn, *Werke Philos* 6, 177, n. 2.

PSEUDO-PHILO, ON JONAH AND ON SAMSON

These two works are included as authentic in the Armenian corpus of Philo's writings.[56a] They are in fact Hellenistic Jewish writings, with many features in common with Philo,[56b] but they are not from his pen. They embroider pleasantly the biblical stories of Samson, up to Judg 13-14, and Jonah. In both sermons there are deviations from the biblical story, some midrashic interpretations as well as short theological and moral observations. Some of these interpretations are quite common, others unusual or even unique. *On Samson* also contains comparisons with other biblical passages i.e. the annunctiation of Isaac's birth and the entertaining of the angels by Abraham. But the literal meaning is preserved, with each book making its own point. *On Jonah* brings out the divine benevolence, exhibited towards Jonah and the sinful city of Nineveh. *On Samson* depicts how a truly good man can be discerned under an apparently dubious personality like Samson. One may note that both works comment on texts outside the Pentateuch, going beyond the usual range of Philo's exegesis.

The Armenian translations of *On Jonah* and *On Samson* are valuable witnesses to the originals, as they were done by the 'Philo-hellene' school of translators in the sixth century.[56c] They stay very close to the Greek, with Graecized vocabulary and syntax, so that valid efforts can be made to reconstruct the originals. The same can be seen in authentic works of Philo in the Armenian version.

Thematic Works

The other writings of Philo deal mainly with social and religious elements in the Jewish community, philosophical debate and historical and political events. Discussion is carried on in terms of the principles laid down in exegesis of the Bible. Indeed it seems that the thematic works in general presuppose the exegetical works, and that some were written in the last period of Philo's life. Some scholars question a late dating for Philo's philosophical works (*Every Good Man is Free, On the Eternity of the World,* and *On Providence*). However their argument is based on the doubtful assumption that Philo took less interest in philosophy after he began to interpret the Pentateuch. At least one philosophical work, *Alexander or Whether the Animals Have Reason* is late, since it refers (para. 27) to the year when Germanicus was consul, 12 C.E. It may be even later, if the embassy to Rome (para. 54) is the one to Gaius Caligula in 39/40 C.E. But

---

[56a] Both *On Jonah* and *On Samson* were translated together with Philo and are transmitted in various MSS, among his works. They were also interpreted with other works of Philo by ancient Armenian commentaries; see Grigorian, 'The Armenian Commentaries', 94ff.

[56b] Lewy, *De Jona*; cf. Siegert, *Drei Predigte.*

[56c] Lewy, *De Jona*, 9-17. See his bibliography.

why divide Philo's life into a philosophical youth and an exegetical maturity? The presence of the Jewish and the Greek communities of Alexandria affected his whole life, which made exegesis and philosophy important to him all the time.[57]

HYPOTHETICA

Eusebius quotes two fragments from two works of Philo, known to him as *Hypothetica* and *Apology of the Jews*.[58] He also includes *On the Jews* in a list of Philo's works.[59] These three titles probably indicate one and the same treatise.[60] The fragments deal with parts of the Pentateuch, from Jacob (Gen 25) to the conquest of the Land in Joshua and Judges. Biblical exegesis mostly gives way to descriptions of Judaism in Philo's time: the nation has existed since Jacob's day and is very numerous (6:1); for more than two thousand years it has not changed a word of what Moses wrote but would die rather than accept anything contrary to the laws and customs he laid down (6:9). Where Gentiles are lax, Jews are strict, in law and morals (7:1-9);[61] the Sabbath is central, since it provides opportunity for studying the Law, and influences all mankind and the rest of nature (7:10-20); finally, the Essenes learned from Moses the life of fellowship (11:9-18). All this is a defence against those who might wish to see the Jews as no better than others.[62]

Certain differences between the *Hypothetica* and other writings of Philo have raised doubts about its authenticity. However, basic agreements do exist, for example in the description of the Sabbath in the fragments and elsewhere.[63] Moreover, similar differences occur in the admittedly authentic writings of Philo.[64] All they need mean is that different traditions are employed; and Philo's exegetical method can find several meanings in one text.

ON THE CONTEMPLATIVE LIFE

The opening part of this treatise shows that it is the second section of a larger work. A reference to the Essenes (cf. *Every Man is Free* 75-91; *Hypothetica* 8:11,1-8) probably presupposes a lost treatise on the practical

---

[57] Cohn, *Einteilung,* 389ff. Cf. Colson, *Philo Works* 9, 2; Sandmel, *Philo,* 32; Terian, *De animalibus,* 28-31.

[58] *Praep. Evang.* 8:6, 1-7 and 8:11, 1-18.

[59] *Hist. Eccl.* 2:18, 6.

[60] See Colson, *Philo Works* 9, 407.

[61] Cf. *P.T. Abodah Zarah* 1, 39a bottom: 'Idolatrous religion is lax.'

[62] Cf. *Hypothetica* 6, 2; 7, 1; 11; 14, etc.

[63] Cfr. *Mos.* 2:215; *Som.* 2:127; *Prob.* 80ff.; *Spec.* 2:61-62.

[64] See Heinemann, *Bildung,* 353 and 516ff.

life, which the Essenes illustrate; just as the contemplative life is exemplified by the Therapeutae.[65]

Essenes and Therapeutae are important to Philo because they are models of Judaism according to his ideals.[66] They keep the Law and are destined for heaven. They justify his interpretation of Abraham as wise through study, Jacob by nature and Isaac through practice.[67] The Therapeutae are citizens of heaven, even in this world (90), as are all true Jews; proselytes are assigned places in heaven.[68] As noted already, the Essenes exemplify the practical good life, which in Philo is often linked with knowledge.[69]

Then, these communities point on to the universal community of 'the end of days', with evil overcome and all men serving God according to the Law of Moses. Their universal relevance comes out when their way of life is contrasted with the pagan (40ff.; cf. *Every Man is Free* 76ff.), and their superiority to such legendary figures as Anaxagoras and Democritus demonstrated (14-16; cf. *Every Man is Free* 91) and when they are seen as the representation of perfect goodness for Greek and barbarian alike. The site of the Therapeutae community near Alexandria is the goal and fatherland of all future good men (22), while the Essenes are admired by kings and commoners alike.[70]

EVERY GOOD MAN IS FREE

In the opening section of this work, the author refers to a lost companion treatise called *Every Bad Man is a Slave*.[71] The present treatise deals with the Stoic theme that only the wise man is truly free.[72] This is confirmed from the Pentateuch. Thus in 42ff. Philo argues that supreme freedom belonged to 'him who was possessed by love of the divine and worshipped

---

[65] So also Cohn, *Philonis Opera* 6, p. IX; K. Bormann in Cohn, *Werke Philos* 7, 44, n. 1, and apparently Colson, *Philo Works,* 9, 104. Geoltrain, *La Vie Contemplative,* 14-15 (*Prob.*), Goodenough, *Introduction,* 36 (*Apol. Iud.*) and F. Daumas in Arnaldez, *Les Oeuvres* 29, 11-12 (*Apol. Iud.*) differ.

[66] This interest might seem surprising since these communities did not belong, as Philo did, to mainstream Judaism. See Josephus, *Ant.* 18:1, 5; cf. *Prob.* 75, on the Essenes. The Therapeutae seem to follow liturgical practices also found in the Book of Jubilees. See K. Bormann, in Cohn, *Werke Philos* 7, 44, 46.

[67] See the discussion of agreements between the Essenes and the Therapeutae and between Jacob and Abraham, in Sandmel, *Philo's Place,* 194-6.

[68] Cf. e.g. *Praem.* 152.

[69] Cf. *L.A.* 1:58: 'The theory of virtue is perfect in beauty and the practice and exercise of it is a prize to be striven for.' See futher Wolfson, *Philo* 2, 264ff.

[70] See *Hypothetica* 11, 18; *Prob.* 88-91.

[71] On the various introductory questions, such as authenticity, etc., see K. Bormann in Cohn, *Werke Philos* 7, 1-2 and references given there.

[72] See especially Colson, *Philo Works* 9, 1ff. for *Prob.* 66ff., where Philo seems to refer to the views of others, without stating this explicitly, see *ibid.* 13, note e.

the Self-existent only, as having passed from a man into a god, though, indeed, a god to men . . .' He quotes in this context Exod 7:1, 'And the Lord said to Moses: See I make you as god to Pharaoh,' a text often used elsewhere.[73] The exposition indicates one important aspect of Philo's method of argument: the various levels of freedom of the good man receive their full dimension in Moses and those who follow him in worshipping the Self-existent only.

Among the Jews, the Essenes are exemplary: morally excellent and free (75-91). They love God, virtue and men, and they base their understanding of God and their way of life on study of the laws of their fathers, being particularly observant of the Seventh Day.

The treatise seems to serve as an exhortation to the Jews and as an attack on those who ascribe citizenship or freedom to the possessors of civil rights, and slavery to others. According to Philo, the full citizens and state officials of Alexandria are slaves and exiles, not free men. Rather the good man, even if not on the burgess rolls, is to be called citizen (6-7, 158). This was very relevant in Alexandria, where Jews were struggling for citizenship against the Greek citizens who wished to classify them as slaves on the same level as the native Egyptians.

ON THE ETERNITY OF THE WORLD

In this work[74] Philo defends the doctrine of the indestructibility of the world. He mentions three other views. 'Democritus with Epicurus and the Greek mass of Stoic philosophers maintain the creation and destruction of the world' (8). Aristotle and before him certain Pythagoreans held that the world is uncreated and indestructible (10-12). But Plato saw the world as created and indestructible (13-16). Some attributed this view to Hesiod (17-18). But 'long before Hesiod, Moses, the Lawgiver of the Jews, said in the Holy Books, that it (the world) was created and imperishable' (19).[75] The rest of the work (20-149) argues in favour of this, ending with the statement, 'in what follows we have to expound the answers given in opposition to each point' (150). This shows that the treatise is incomplete, with the end probably lost.[76]

ON PROVIDENCE

This treatise is preserved in an Armenian translation, with Greek fragments in Eusebius. It is in two books, in the form of a dialogue beween

---

[73] *L.A.* 1:140; *Sac.* 9; *Det.* 39f., 161f.; *Mig.* 84, 169; *Mut.* 19, 125, 128f.; *Som.* 2:189.
[74] For a discussion of authenticity, etc., see the introductions by K. Bormann in Cohn, *Werke Philos* 7, 71ff. and 166ff., with references.
[75] On the creation of the world see *Op.* 7, 171; *Conf.* 114; *Som.* 2:283, and on its indestructibility see *Decal.* 58.
[76] See Schmid-Stählin, *Geschichte*, 627f.

Philo, maintaining that the world is governed by providence, and Alexander, raising doubts and difficulties. This Alexander is probably Philo's nephew Tiberius Julius Alexander, who afterwards apostatized. The first book has been worked over by someone who eliminated the dialogue form and made interpolations.[77]

The notion of providence was important in Greek philosophy, especially in Stoic polemic against Epicurean views. Philo maintains that the doctrine comes from the laws of Moses, as presented in Philo's expositions, where God is the good Creator, Father and Sustainer of the World, and Judge (1:35). He rejects astrology and horoscopes. The same terminology is used as in his exegetical works (1:48).[78] As Philo saw it, he used biblical principles to criticize false philosophy.

ALEXANDER OR WHETHER THE ANIMALS HAVE REASON

This treatise is preserved in an Armenian translation.[79] It takes the form of a dialogue between Philo and Lysimachus, a relative of his, about a dissertation written by Philo's nephew, Julius Tiberius Alexander. According to Leisegang, nothing in the dialogue itself shows that the persons taking part were Jews. The views expressed by Philo here are selected according to Jewish criteria, however, and are consistent with ideas he puts forward in other writings. Animals know nothing of God, cosmos, law, ancestral customs, state and political life. This knowledge is exclusive to man. These ideas are Stoic, but are selected by Philo, because they are central in his interpretation of the Pentateuch. Then, animals have none of man's conscious and purposeful art ($\tau\acute{\epsilon}\chi\nu\eta$). Philo gives the full Stoic definition of art in *On the Preliminary Studies* 141, à propos of Gen 16:5. The views expressed in *Alexander* must therefore be seen in the context of Philo's exegetical works.[80]

FLACCUS AND ON THE EMBASSY TO GAIUS

In his exegetical works (*On Abraham*, etc.) Philo occasionally applies principles he derives from the Bible to contemporary events.[81] So too in his *Flaccus* and *Embassy to Gaius*,[82] though here no texts are quoted, and the

---

[77] For introductory questions, see L. Früchtel in Cohn, *Werke Philos* 7, 267-71 and Colson, *Philo Works* 9, 447ff.

[78] See the footnotes of L. Früchtel in Cohn, *Werke Philos* 7, 280-316.

[79] See Terian, *De animalibus*, and Leisegang, 'Philo'.

[80] In contrast to Leisegang ('Philo', 8), Terian (*De animalibus*, 46) states that 'the Mosaic treatment of animals must be considered as the determining factor in moulding his thought.'

[81] See *Som.* 2:123ff., on a governor of Egypt who attempted to disturb the ancestral customs of the Jews. Cf. 3 Maccabees, which tells of these conflicts between Ptolemy Philopator and Judaism, two of them in Alexandria.

[82] For introductory questions, especially whether the two treatises were parts of a larger number of writings, see for example Smallwood, *Legatio ad Gaium*; Colson, *Philo Works* 9, 295-301 and Box, *In Flaccum*.

main interest is historical. Therefore the works are important historical sources, related and interpreted by an eye-witness. The Jewish nation, and not just an individual, is envisaged in *Flaccus*. This bears out our view that relations between Jew and Gentile are the context of Philo's writings.

He explains that worship in the Temple of Jerusalem (*Flaccus* 44-46; *Gaius* 231), assembly in synagogues (*Flaccus* 13; *Gaius* 132) and observance of the Law of Moses (*Flaccus* 74, 83, 96; *Gaius* 361 etc.) are characteristics of the Jewish people, to maintain which they are ready to die (*Flaccus* 48 etc.). In *Gaius* 3-7, summing up his view of Judaism, Philo affirms, as elsewhere, God's creative and kingly powers, his providence and his power of rewarding or punishing.[83] The Jewish people, whose God is the creator, acts as suppliant for mankind (*Gaius* 3), thus linking God and man. In a sense, God's universal providence is the outcome of his care for the Jews.[84]

Flaccus and Gaius Caligula may have proved to be enemies of the Jews (*Flaccus* 24 etc.; *Gaius* 373) but were in reality enemies of God himself, Flaccus by his proud arrogance (*Flaccus* 124; 132), Gaius by his claim to be a god (*Gaius* 75; 367f. etc.). The part of *Gaius* telling of his fate is lost, but the punishment and death of Flaccus, as interpreted through Philo's biblical principles, remain (*Flaccus* 107-191). The two works provide therefore significant parallels to his explanation of Num 15:30 (*On Virtues* 171-174), where the high-handed sinner provokes God.[85] In the end, according to Philo, Flaccus recognized the truth of the Jewish Bible. 'King of gods and men', he cried,' so then thou dost not disregard the nation of the Jews, nor do they misreport thy providence, but all who say they do not find in thee a champion and defender go astray from the true creed. I am clear proof of this, for all the acts which I madly committed against the Jews I have suffered myself . .' (*Flaccus* 170).

Flaccus and *Gaius* bear out a point we make elsewhere, that the gymnasium, with the clubs and religious associations, fomented hostility against the Jews of Alexandria. Philo saw the Greeks around him as licentious, gluttonous and given to political intrigues. But in the matter of civil rights, they were privileged beyond the Jews, though the Jews in turn were here better off than the native Egyptians (*Flaccus* 78-80).

The two works are theologically interpreted history,[86] and in this they resemble traditional Jewish historiography.[87] But contemporary literary forms have also had their influence. The story of Flaccus' journey into exile on the island of Andros is in the pattern of Greek historical essay-writing.

[83] See *Deus* 77-78 and *Plant.* 50. Cf. Smallwood, *Legatio ad Gaium,* 156-7.
[84] See Goodenough, *Politics,* 13 and Smallwood, *Legatio ad Gaium,* 152. On biblical background for the phrase, see *Praem.* 44.
[85] *Virt.* 171: men of windy pride (cf. *Flacc.* 124; 152) overstep the limits of human nature (*Virt.* 172; cf. also *Gaius* 75).
[86] Cf. F. W. Kohnke in Cohn, *Werke Philos* 7, 168.
[87] Cf. Josephus, *Ant.* 19:20-23; Acts 12:20-23, continuing biblical traditions.

So it may be largely imaginative, since Philo gives many details of which, in Alexandria, he could have had only very vague knowledge. Elements such as the lament of the central figure, his recall of past misfortunes, his despair, repentance, and fear of approaching death are common topics in such literature, especially where it takes in travels. According to *Gaius* 373, the story reveals Gaius' character, a standard motif in moral tales which hold out examples.[88]

The ending of *Gaius*, 'One must tell the palinode,' raises problems. This indicates a recantation to follow. Presumably it told of Gaius' death and his successor Claudius' new policy, which was more favourable to the Jews. But if, as is more probable, Philo means that history itself brought about the change, no additional writing need be supposed.[89]

Philo's cultural, social and religious background

THE SOCIAL AND POLITICAL SITUATION

Philo belonged to one of the wealthiest and most prominent Jewish families in Alexandria.[90] His brother, Alexander Lysimachus, was probably chief inspector of customs on the Eastern border of Egypt and guardian of the Emperor Tiberius' mother.[91] Alexander was rich enough to lend money to the Jewish King, Agrippa I, and to plate the gates of the Temple of Jerusalem in gold and silver. His apostate son Alexander had a public career which took him to the highest post of a Roman official in Egypt, that of prefect.[92] Philo himself was chosen in his old age[93] to head a delegation of five,[93a] sent by the Jewish community of Alexandria to the Emperor Gaius Caligula[94] in 39-40 This is the one certain date in his life; so he may have been born between 15 and 10 B.C.E. and have died about 45-50 C.E.[95]

Philo gives glimpses of his public social life. He took part in banquets,[96]

---

[88] See K. H. Gerschmann and F. W. Kohnke in Cohn, *Werke Philos* 7, 125-6 and 168-9.

[89] See Colson, *Philo Works* 10, 187 note a, and F. W. Kohnke in Cohn, *Werke Philos* 7, 169.

[90] On Philo's family and life see especially Schwartz, 'La Famille de Philon'; *id.* 'L'Egypte de Philon.'

[91] Tcherikover, *Corpus* 1, 49 (esp. n. 4), 67; Schalit, 'Alexander Lysimachus.'

[92] *Praem,.* 152. On Tiberius Alexander, see Tcherikover, *Corpus* 1, 53, 75, 78-79. Goodenough, *The Politics*, 65; Lepape, 'Préfet d'Alexandrie'; Turner, 'Tiberius Iulius Alexander'; Schürer, *History* I, 456-8.

[93] *Gaius* 182.

[93a] *Gaius* 370. According to Josephus, *Ant.* 18:257, the Jewish and the Greek embassies each consisted of three men.

[94] *Gaius* 178-79.

[95] For the dating of this mission see Schürer, *History* I, 388-98.

[96] *L.A.* 3:155f.

frequented the theatre, and heard concerts;[97] he watched boxing, wrestling[98] and horse-racing.[99] Relations between Jews and Gentiles in Alexandria were strained, the sore point being the participation of the Jews in Hellenistic cultural institutions and their request for full citizen rights. Philo speaks of both points.[100] Speaking of fees paid to join clubs, he says: '... when the object is to share in the best of possessions, prudence, such payments are praiseworthy and profitable; but when they are paid to obtain that supreme evil, folly, the practice is unprofitable,'[101] and can lead to Egyptian animal worship.[102] Another issue was participation in the triennial festivals of wrestling, boxing etc. organized by the cities. To Philo, these festivals occasion rivalry, anger and licentiousness. A Jew should try to avoid taking part, but if compelled to do so, should not hesitate to be defeated.[103]

By joining in cultural life, the Jews of Alexandria aimed at full citizenship of the Greek *polis*. The letter from the Emperor Claudius to the Alexandrians gives evidence of such a strong movement among the Jews: 'The Jews ... I order ... not to intrude themselves into the games presided over by the *gymnasiarchoi* and the *kosmetai* (producers and directors) ...'[104] General education and the Gymnasium were therefore matters of concern to Jews, since they were conditions for full civil rights.[105] Full Greek citizens were exempted from the Roman poll tax, the provincial Hellenes paid a lower rate, and native Egyptians paid the tax in full. The Jews in Alexandria pressed for equal status with the Greeks there. The Greeks in turn, tried to deprive the Jews of the privileges granted by the Emperor

[97] *Ebr.* 177; *Prob.* 141.
[98] *Prob.* 26.
[99] See *hypothetica* in Eusebius, *Praep. ev.* 7:14, 58.
[100] See *Spec.* 1:21f., 331ff.; *Cher.* 90 ff.; *Sac.* 130; *Post.* 2ff., etc.
[101] *Ebr.* 20ff.
[102] *Ebr.* 95.
[103] See *Agr.* 110-21. Both Philo and the rabbinic tradition rejected idolatry. But the Rabbis were mostly stricter in their view of Jews who participated in non-Jewish cultural and social life; theatres, circuses and gymnasia were regarded as the very antithesis of 'synagogue and school'. Nevertheless, rabbinic writings, Philo, and archeology show that Jews attended, and to some extent shared such activities, *B.T. Gittin* 47a confirms Philo's statement, *Agr.* 110-21, that Jews might be compelled to take part in pagan athletic games. R. Simeon ben Lakish is said to have once been a professional gladiator, which he justified on the ground of grim necessity (See the article 'Sports' in *EJ* 5, 291; Billerbeck, *Kommentar* 4/1, pp. 353-414; Baer, 'Israel', 89-90, 112 etc.; Tcherikover, *Corpus* 1, p. 39, n. 99; Levine, *Caesarea,* 70-72; Borgen, *Pluralism,* 106-15.) Other issues are also reflected, such as war and its theological implications, *Agr.* 86ff. (cf. 90; horse-rearing in its literal meaning), debates with sophists, who seem here to mean pagan intellectuals, since they are called impure pigs, *Agr.* 136-44 (cf. *Gaius* 361).
[104] See Tcherikover, *Corpus* 2, 43 and 53; on discussion of this passage, see Stern, 'Jewish Diaspora,' 131.
[105] See Tcherikover, *Corpus* 1, 37-41; Stern, 'Jewish Diaspora,' 124-31; Borgen, *Bread,* 111. On general education see below.

Augustus, and have them classified with the native Egyptians.[106] After Gaius Caligula became Emperor in 37 C.E. these quarrels in the religious, cultural and juridical field led to anti-Jewish riots which grew into a pogrom. A military uprising by Jews against Greeks followed in 41 C.E. on the death of Gaius Caligula and the accession of Claudius.[107] Many Jews from Palestine and the Egyptian hinterland took part in the revolt, as can be seen from the fact that Claudius forbade Alexandrian Jews to permit Jews from Syria and Egypt to enter the city.[108] As already noted, Claudius excluded the Jews from the gymnasium and its attendant activities.

There are indications in Philo's writings of his involvement in politics before the embassy to Rome. How precisely, we do not know. He says that 'envy' had plunged him in the ocean of civil cares.[109] This may mean conflicts arising from the ancient envy which Egyptians had of Jews.[110] Philo's engagement in politics was clearly very reluctant. He advises his fellow-Jews to be cautious in their dealings with the non-Jewish political authorities.[111]

GREEK EDUCATION AND PHILOSOPHY

Philo's writings show that he had a wide Greek education. He has an excellent command of Greek, a good literary style and knows many Greek philosophers and writers. In his youth he received the Greek general education at school, the *Enkyklios paideia,* which he treats of extensively in *On the Preliminary Studies.* He describes this education:

> For instance when I first was incited by the goads of Philosophy to desire her I consorted in early youth with one of her handmaids, Grammar, and all that I begat by her, writing, reading and study of the writings of the poets, I dedicated to her mistress. And again I kept the company with another, namely Geometry, and was charmed with her beauty, for she shewed symmetry and proportion in every part. Yet I took none of her children for my private use, but brought them

---

[106] The situation of the Alexandrian Jews has been discussed by Stern, 'Philo of Alexandria,' 18-19; *id.,* 'Jewish Diaspora', 122-33; Safrai, 'Relations,' 184ff; Applebaum, 'Legal Status,' 434-40.

[107] Josephus, *Ant.* 19:278ff.

[108] See 'The letter of Claudius to the Alexandrians,' in Tcherikover, *Corpus* 2, 41 and 43: 'Nor are they to bring in or invite Jews coming from Syria or Egypt, or I shall be forced to conceive graver suspicions.'

[109] *Spec.* 3:3.

[110] *Flaccus* 29.

[111] Cf. the whole of *Som.* 2:78-92; Goodenough, *Politics,* 5-7. For similar views among some Pharisees, see Alon, *Jews, Judaism,* 18-47.

as a gift to the lawful wife. Again my ardour moved me to keep company with a third; rich in rythm, harmony and melody was she, and her name was Music, and from her I begat diatonics, chromatics and enharmonics, conjunct and disjunct melodies, conforming with the consonance of the fourth, fifth or octave intervals. And again none of these did I make a secret hoard, wishing to see the lawful wife, a lady of wealth with a host of servants ministering to her. (74-76)

Philo thought all general education should prepare for philosophy, the 'lawful wife' who has handmaids. In this he follows an allegorical interpretation of Homer's Penelope, such as is found in Plutarch: those wear themselves out in general studies and fail to master philosophy, are like the suitors who could not win Penelope and contented themselves with her maids.[112] Philo adapts this, however, to his interpretation of Sarah and Hagar (Gen 16:1-6). When Abraham failed at first to have a child by Sarah (philosophy), he took the maid Hagar (general studies) in her place. *On the Preliminary Studies* starts with Genesis 16:1-2 and the allegorical interpretation of Sarah and Hagar is the scriptural basis of Philo's theory of general education.

These schools had for the Jews of Alexandria crucial political significance. Abraham's double relationship, to Hagar and to Sarah, points to Alexandrian Judaism's external and internal relations.[113] Philo often stresses that Hagar was Egyptian[114] and Ishmael, son of Abraham and Hagar, is naturally 'a bastard' (*On Sobriety* 8). But Sarah represents the true spirit of Judaism and is therefore called the mother of the Jews, 'the most populous of nations.'[115] Accordingly, Abraham, representing the Jewish nation, receives education from two schools: the general education which the Jews share with their pagan neighbours, and then, that of the genuine, Jewish philosophy. Thus, ... 'the virtue that comes through teaching, which Abraham pursues, needs the fruits of several studies, both those born in wedlock, which deal with wisdom, and the baseborn, those of the preliminary lore of the schools' (*Preliminary Studies* 35). General education is thus on the borderline between Judaism and paganism, an *adiaphoron*, therefore in itself neither good nor bad. Or again, Philo

---

[112] Plutarch *De Liberis Educandis*, 7D. Other versions of this allegory are referred to in von Arnim, *Fragmenta* I, 78. See Colson, 'Philo on Education', 153-4; Cohn, *Werke* 5, p. 24, n. 7 and 6, p. 7, n. 2; Wolfson, *Philo* 1, 145 ff. Borgen, *Bread*, 108-9.

[113] In his introduction to *De Congressu*, Heinemann recognized that the situation of Judaism is reflected in this allegory. He says that Philo here follows the methods of the interpreters of Homer. (See Cohn, *Werke* 6, p. 4).

[114] Cf. *Q.G.* 3:19, 21; *Abr.* 251 and especially *Cong.* 20ff.

[115] *Cong.* 2-3. See Heinemann, *De Congressu*, p. 4, n. 3 for this understanding of the passage.

describes general education as the 'well between Kadesh and Bered', that is, 'on the borderland (μεθόριος) between the holy and the profane.'[116]

Some conclusions about Philo's knowledge of Greek philosophy may be drawn from explicit quotations, and the philosophical ideas he uses. Stoicism and the Pythagorean and Platonic traditions predominate. Philo's view that general education prepares for philosophy and his definition of philosophy as 'the practice or study of wisdom, which is the knowledge of things divine and human and their causes' (Preliminary Studies 79) are Stoic,[117] as is also his division of philosophy into logic, ethics and physics.[118] From the Platonic tradition he takes over the distinction between the 'forms' or ideas and the visible world, and between soul and body. From the Pythagoreans come speculations on numbers.[119] Philo also shows familiarity with other philosophical schools[120] and with Greek literature in general.[121]

Non-Jewish sources have been incorporated in such a way that little identification of authors seems possible. But from allusions, terminology and forms of thought, some trends have been identified with a fair degree of certainty.[122] Platonic elements,[123] mystical speculation on numbers with emphasis on Pythagorean traditions,[124] and Stoic terms and fragments[125] have been identified.

---

[116] Fug. 212-3. See Siegfried, Philo, 261, who ignores the background of Judaism versus paganism in the passage. The term ἡ μέση παιδεία, which Philo used in Mut. 255, etc., expresses the same view of general education which therefore means 'middle ground' or 'neutral education'. Colson, 'Philo on Education,' 153, n. 1, refers rightly to the Stoic μεσά ἀδιάφορα, but cannot explain Philo's use, not having seen it in its context, the relationship between Judaism and paganism.

[117] See von Arnim, Fragmenta 2, 36.

[118] See L.A. 1:57; Spec. 1:336; cf. Agr. 14f.

[119] Op. 13, 89-102 etc.

[120] Cf. Wolfson, Philo I, 107-14.

[121] Among Greek authors mentioned are: Aeschylus, Aristotle, Boethus, Chrysippus, Cleanthes, Democritus, Diogenes, Euripides, Heraclitus, Hesiod, Hippocrates, Homer, Ion, Ocellus, Panaetius, Philolaus, Pindar, Plato, Solon, Sophocles, Xenophon, Zeno. See Earp, 'Index of Names.' Cf. Alexandre, 'La culture profane chez Philon.'

[122] For example, it has been demonstrated that in Ebr. 164-205 Philo depends on the Ten Tropes of the Phyrronic philosopher Aenesidemus. See von Arnim, Quellenstudien. Fragments in Som. 1:21-23 (a doxography of the four elements) and Som. 1:53 (on meteorological matters) have been traced back to the lost Vetusta Placita. See Wendland, 'Doxographische Quelle'; Hamerton-Kelly, 'Sources,' 6; Borgen, Bread, 4. Goodenough, 'Neo-Pythagorean Source,' suggests that Philo in Heres 130ff. draws on a text of Heraclitus which had been reworked by Neopythagoreans.

[123] See Theiler, Forschungen; id. 'Philo und der Beginn des Kaiserzeitlichen Platonismus'; id. 'Philo und der hellenistisierte Timaeus'; Whittaker, God-Time-Being, 33-57; Früchtel, Kosmolog. Vorstellungen; Dillon, Middle Platonists, 139-83.

[124] See Staehle, Zahlenmystik; Boyancé, 'Muses.'

[125] See index in Von Arnim, Fragmenta, for fragments from Philo; id., Quellenstudien; Apelt, De rationibus; cf. Wendland, Philo.

PHILO AND THE JEWISH COMMUNITY

Philo identifies himself as a Jew of Alexandria, living according to Jewish laws and customs: 'our ancestral customs . . . and especially the law of the Seventh Day which we regard with most reverence and awe.'[126] He has been to Jerusalem and worshipped in the Temple.[127] He distinguishes sharply Jews and non-Jews and bitterly condemns apostate Jews. He criticizes prosperous Jews, who 'look down on their relations and friends and set at naught the laws under which they were born and bred, and subvert the ancestral customs.'[128]

Philo speaks of Jewish institutions in Alexandria. There were many synagogues in each section of the town, and one synagogue was very large and notable.[129] He often describes how the synagogues function, stressing the reading and explanation of the Bible: 'And will you sit in your conventicles and assemble your regular company and read in security your holy books, expounding any obscure point and in leisurely comfort discussing at length your ancestral philosophy.'[130] Unfortunately, he does not provide any definite information about Jewish education or his own part in it. Whether he knew Hebrew or not has been much discussed, but no general consensus has been reached.[131]

Philo uses the Septuagint, in his view an exact and inspired translation of the Hebrew original. It reveals the sacred writings to the Greek-speaking world,[132] including most Jews of Alexandria, where the Septuagint was the usual Bible. Philo refers to an old custom, 'to hold every year a feast and general assembly in the island of Pharos, whither not only Jews but multitudes of others cross the water, to do honour to the place in which the light of that version shone out.'[133] To what extent Philo's quotations agree with the Septuagint used by the Jewish community of Alexandria is uncertain, as in the process of transmission Philo's quotations may have been adapted to other recensions of the Septuagint.[134]

---

[126] *Som.* 2:123.

[127] *Prov.* 2:64: 'There is a city on the sea coast of Syria called Ascalon. While I was there at a time when I was on my way to our ancestral Temple to offer up prayers and sacrifices . . .'

[128] *Mos.* 1:31.

[129] *Gaius* 132-4. This synagogue may have been the 'double colonnade' of Alexandria mentioned in *B.T. Sukkah* 51b; *T. Sukkah* 4:6.

[130] *Som.* 2:127. See survey of texts and literature in Borgen, *Bread*, 56, n. 1. Philo's texts on synagogue assemblies have been examined by my student, Hegstad, *Synagogen.*

[131] Philo knew Hebrew: Siegfried, *Philo*, 142-5; Wolfson, *Philo* 1, 88; did not: Heinemann, *Bildung*, 524ff.; Stein, *Allegorische Exegese*, 20ff.; Nikiprowetzky, *Commentaire*, 50-81; Sandmel, *Philo's Place*, 11-13 and 49. Hanson, 'Philo's Etymologies,' thinks that Philo knew a little Hebrew, but probably drew most of his etymologies from an etymological list or dictionary.

[132] *Mos.* 2:26-44.

[133] *Mos.* 2:41-42.

[134] See the discussion in Katz, *Philo's Bible*, 3-4, 103; Howard, 'The aberrant text'; Borgen, *Bread*, 19-20; 41 n. 5.

Philo's exegesis is mainly based on the Pentateuch. This may reflect Alexandrian custom,[135] as only the Pentateuch was used in the regular community reading.[136] The Pentateuch would be of special interest to Jews in Egypt, where Moses lived and the Exodus began.

Philo often indicates that he uses other Jewish sources as well as the Bible. He refers to these sources in the *Life of Moses:* 'But I will . . . tell the story of Moses as I have learned it, both from the sacred books . . . and from some of the elders of the nation (παρά τινῶν ἀπὸ τοῦ ἔθνους πρεσβυτέρων); for I always interwove what I was told with what I read.'[137] The question arises here whether Philo depended only on local Jewish tradition,[137a] or also on wider ones, including Palestinian *Haggadah* and *Halakhah*.[138] Philo's own visit to Jerusalem, his knowledge of conditions and events in Palestine, the frequent contacts between Alexandrian and Palestinian Jews and the fact that both groups recognized the Temple of Jerusalem as their center, at least strongly indicate that Philo knew and followed Palestinian traditions.[138a] This conclusion is confirmed by a comparison of Philo with the rabbinic writings.[139]

Philo practiced the common *Halakhah* with regards to worship in the Temple of Jerusalem, the Temple tax[139a] and pictures and statues in Temple and synagogues.[140] His visit to the Temple may indicate that he recognized its rules about calendar and sacrifices. Philo knew of the conflicts between Pilate and the Jewish authorities in Palestine arising from the *Halakhah*.[141] In some cases where Philo's views are in conflict with the

---

[135] Thyen, *Homilie,* 74. Palestinian synagogues probably read pericopes from the Prophets (and the Writings) as well as from the Pentateuch. See Jacobs, 'Torah', 1248; and cf. Luke 4:17.

[136] This explanation seems more plausible than Knox's ('A Note on Philo's Use of the Old Testament') that Philo knew only the Pentateuch, apart from 'testimonies' containing a few passages from other biblical books, or Colson's ('Philo's Quotations from the O.T.'), that Philo concentrated on the Pentateuch because of its higher authority and of his own preferences. Cf. Borgen, *Bread* 55, esp. n. 3.

[137] *Mos.* 1:4.

[137a] Cf. Delling, 'Perspektiven', 139-41.

[138] Philo's dependence on oral traditions is evident, regardless of whether he knew or used the Jewish technical terms of 'Oral Law', or 'Unwritten Law'. Hirzel, 'Agraphos Nomos,' and Heinemann, 'Die Lehre', do not think that Philo knew the Jewish concept of an authoritative oral Law. Wolfson, *Philo* I, 188f., thinks that he does.

[138a] See Heinemann, *Bildung,* 16-43.

[139] The fact that the redaction of the rabbinic writings is of a much later date does not exclude such a comparison. In recent years there has been a growing interest in examining rabbinic traditions through literary criticism, history of tradition and form criticism, to try to date various developments in rabbinic literature. Josephus, Philo and the New Testament are used as aid for such analyses. See for example Neusner, *Early Rabbinic Judaism,* 100-36; *id. The Rabbinic Traditions* 3, 143-79, with discussion of Gerhardsson, *Memory and Manuscript,* and others. For a comparison of Philo and rabbinic literature see especially Alon, *Jews,* 89-137.

[139a] *Spec.* 1:78; *Gaius* 156. Cf. also *Flaccus* 45-56.

[140] See *Gaius* and *Flaccus,* especially the reactions of both Alexandrian and Palestinian Jews against statues of the Emperor.

[141] See *Gaius,* 299-305. Cf. Smallwood, *Legatio ad Gaium,* 300-7.

rabbinic *Halakhah,* it can be proved that they represent an earlier stage of common practice.[142] Examples of haggadic views in Philo which have parallels in the rabbinic writings are: the rivalry among the stars as to precedence[143]; the angel who appeared to Moses in the burning bush being the image of God[144]; Moses growing extraordinarily fast[145]; why Adam was last to be created[146]; the manna and the well simultaneously, not conforming to the regular sequence of rain from heaven and bread from earth.[147]

Philo as Biblical Exegete

With regard to Philo's exegetical aims and methods, some scholars see him as the main representative of Hellenistic Judaism, in contrast to Palestinian Judaism as representented in the rabbinic sources.[148] This distinction does not do justice to Philo's own view of the situation. While he is involved in debates with fellow Jews in Alexandria, their views may, from his perspective, reflect corresponding debates in Judaism in general, Palestine included. Philo is primarily an exegete. Sometimes he agrees with other exegetes, sometimes he supplements them, and often he repudiates them;[149] but he does not reveal the identity, whereabouts or social status of his partners in debate. Indeed, more research is needed, to examine whether they represent specific schools.[150] Tentatively, the following observations can be made.

---

[142] For examples see Alon, *Jews:* priestly dues to be brought to the Temple, *Spec.* 1:152 (pp. 89-102); capital cases to be brought before the High Court in Jerusalem according to Philo, and before the small Sanhedrins in the various towns according to rabbinic tradition (pp. 102-12); the death penalty for an idolator or a sorcerer to be executed by zealots (Philo) and their trial by a court like other transgressors in rabbinic tradition (pp. 112-24); the *shofar* to be blown on New Year only in connection with sacrifices in the Temple (Philo); the *shofar* to be sounded outside Jerusalem also in rabbinic tradition (pp. 124-32).

[143] *Som.* 2:14 and *Gen. Rabba* 6, 3 (p. 42); *B.T. Hullin* 60b. See Frankel, *Paläst. Exegese,* 43.

[144] *Mos.* 1:66 and *Exod. Rabba* 2, 5. See Siegried, *Philo,* 145-7.

[145] *Mos.* 1:18 and *Exod. Rabba* 1, 26. See Stein, *Philo und der Midrasch,* 45.

[146] *Op.* 77-78 and *T. Sanhedrin* 8:7-9.

[147] *Mos.* 1:201-2; 2:267 and *Exod. Rabba* 25, 2. 6 etc. See Borgen, *Bread,* 7-14.

[148] See for example Sandmel, *Philo of Alexandria;* Goodenough, *Introduction.* Moore, *Judaism,* mostly ignores Philo in his presentation of 'normative' Judaism. Cf. note 3 above.

[149] See Schroyer, 'Jewish Literalists.' See also Bréhier, *Idées philosophiques,* 55, n. 1-2 and 56, n. 1; Bousset, *Schulbetrieb,* 4. More research is needed to see whether Philo's opponents do represent specific schools.

[150] In his analysis of Philo's allegorical commentaries Bousset (*Schulbetrieb*) attempts to distinguish between Jewish sources which were open to Hellenistic culture, and Philo's own contributions which were more Jewish and religious in their emphasis. This criterion seems arbitrary, and does not do justice to the complexity of Philo's situation and sources. Bousset's suggestion that various exegetical schools are reflected in Philo's writings is still pertinent, however; cf. Borgen, *Bread,* 4.

Philo seems to refer to two differents groups of exegetes who championed literal exegesis. One was faithful to Judaism, while another used literal exegesis to attack and ridicule the Pentateuch and Judaism. Some of the views of the 'faithful literalists' are:[151] in Deut 34:4 God humiliates Moses by not permitting him to enter the promised land;[152] in Gen 11:7-8 the confusion of tongues refers to the origin of the Greek and barbarian languages;[153] Gen 26:19-32 tells about actual digging of wells;[154] in Exod 22:26f. material return of garment is meant;[155] the consistency of the rules about leprosy in Lev 14:34-36 is a matter of discussion.[156] In arguing with the other group, Philo reflects disputes between non-Jews or Jewish apostates and Jews. The treatise *On the Change of Names* serves as defence against the literalism of a jester whom Philo himself had heard, and who committed suicide as a punishment from God (60-62). The change of one letter in Abram/Abraham and Sara/Sarrai is ridiculed,[157] as is the story of Jacob and Esau and their food;[158] some maintain that the Bible contains myths (such as the story about the tower of Babel) similar to those which Jews ridicule when recited by others.[159] *On the Confusion of Tongues* serves also as defence against such mockery.[160]

Philo also tells of Jews who used allegory to such an extent that valid Jewish custom was undermined. The central passage is *Migration* 89-93:

> There are some who, regarding laws in their literal sense in the light of symbols of matters belonging to the intellect, are overpunctilious about the latter, while treating the former with easygoing neglect. Such men I for my part should blame for handling the matter in too easy and off-hand a manner: they ought to have given careful attention to both aims, to a more full and exact investigation of what is not seen and what is seen, to be stewards without reproach. As it is as though they were living alone by themselves in a wilderness, or as though they had become disembodied souls, and knew neither city

---

[151] Philo often refers to such exegetes without calling them literalists. Some of their other views: in Gen 1:1 'beginning' has a chronological sense (*Op.* 26: *L.A.* I:2); in Gen 2:8 Paradise is a real garden (*Q.G.* I:8); in Gen 2:19 animals are seen as helpmeets for man since they were used for food (*Q.G.* I:18); the first couple had acute eyes and ears to perceive heavenly beings and sounds of every kind (*Q.G.* 1:32, commenting Gen 3:1); according to Gen 6:6 God repented (*Q.G.* 1:93 and *Deus* 21); in Gen 8:1 real wind dried up the waters of the flood (*Q.G.* 2:28).

[152] *Mig.* 44-45.

[153] *Conf.* 190.

[154] *Som.* 1:39.

[155] *Som.* 1:92-102.

[156] *Deus* 133.

[157] *Mut.* 60-62 and *Q.G.* 3:43 and 53.

[158] *Q.G.* 4:168.

[159] *Conf.* 2-3

[160] Pearson, 'Friedländer Revisited,' 30-31; cf. also *Heres* 81.

nor village nor household nor any company of human beings at all, overlooking all that the mass of men regard, they explore reality in its naked absoluteness. These men are taught by the sacred word to have thought for good repute, and to let go nothing that is part of the customs fixed by divinely empowered men greater than those of our time. It is quite true that the Seventh Day is meant to teach the power of the Unoriginate and the non-action of created beings. But let us not for this reason abrogate the laws laid down for its observance, and light fires or till the ground or carry loads or institute proceedings in court or act as jurors or demand the restoration of deposits or recover loans, or do all else that we are permitted to do as well on days that are not festival seasons. It is true also that the Feast is a symbol of gladness of soul and of thankfulness to God, but we should not for this reason turn our backs on the general gatherings of the year's seasons. It is true that receiving circumcision does indeed portray the excision of pleasure and all passions, and the putting away of the impious conceit, under which the mind supposed that it was capable of begetting by its own power: but let us not on this account repeal the law laid down for circumcising. Why, we shall be ignoring the sanctity of the Temple and a thousand other things, if we are going to pay heed to nothing except what is shown us by the inner meaning of things. Nay we should look on all these outward observances as resembling the body, and their inner meanings as resembling the soul. It follows that, exactly as we have to take thought for the body, because it is the abode of the soul, so we must pay heed to the letter of the laws. If we keep and observe these, we shall gain a clearer conception of those things of which these are symbols; and besides that we shall not incur the censure of the many and the charges they are sure to bring against us.

In this crucial passage, Philo as it were summarizes his attitude as an exegete. The symbolical, though higher and more important, practically never invalidates the literal.[161] (Exceptionally, Philo discards the literal meaning altogether[162] or allows it only a limited role). Philo combines literal and symbolical methods of exegesis, stressing symbolism against literalists[163] and the literal sense against over-spiritualization.[164]

---

[161] See the discussion of *Migr.* 89-93 in Borgen, 'Observations.' On literal and symbolic exegesis in rabbinic Judaism, see Belkin, *Oral Law*, 11ff., 97; Sandmel, *Philo of Alexandria*, 21-22, 174; Dan, 'Allegory'; Mansoor, 'Sadducees'; Vermes, *Post-Biblical Jewish Studies*, 59-91. Cf. Urbach, *Sages* 1, 286-314, where reference is made also to Jesus' (eschatological) exegesis in Matt. 5:21-48 (p. 294).
[162] *Det.* 95 (taken literally the sentence is contrary to reason); 167 (the literal meaning unknown); *Post.* 7 and *Deus* 21 (rejection of anthropomorphic view of God).
[163] *Som.* 1:39.   [164] *Plant.* 70f.

261

At times Philo discusses other views which do not readily fall into the classification of literal and symbolic exegesis, although they may be combined with such an approach. As an example, we quote the following: 'There are some whose definition of reverence is that it consists in saying that all things were made by God, both beautiful things and their opposites. We would say to these, one part of your opinion is praiseworthy, the other part on the contrary is faulty . . .'[165]

The sources of Philo's allegorical method have been much discussed. Did he draw on Greek allegorical methods (especially as employed by the Stoics on Homer) or on Jewish traditions?[166] He undoubtedly followed the Stoics, who read natural phenomena and ethical norms into Homer, though Philo emphasized the ethical, which he based on his concept of God. But other parallels are found in the *Haggadah*, especially as regards the idealization of the Patriarchs and other biblical persons, often by means of etymologies.

It may be maintained that Philo attempts to make the allegorical method serve his aims as a Jewish exegete. In this respect, his allegorical interpretation shows affinities with the hermeneutical concept of prophecy and fulfillment.[167] He spells out abstract principles which he sees in the biblical text, and these in turn can be applied to individuals and the Jewish community, serving to interpret specific events. Philo also adapts allegorical interpretation to the Jewish notion of election, which he uses to claim for the Jews and their sacred writings elements from Greek philosophy, education, ethics and religion. Conversely, to Philo allegorical interpretation is a way in which the wisdom of the laws of Moses and Jewish religious institutions can be disclosed to the world.

In order to understand the background of Philo's exegesis, it is important to analyse the way in which he use his sources, whether written or oral. The starting point of this analysis must be the fact that most of his writings take the form of an exposition, and consist of explanatory paraphrases of words, phrases and sentences of the biblical texts. Thus, Philo (along with other exegetes in Alexandria) interweaves biblical texts and Jewish and non-Jewish (Greek) traditions. The exegesis of Exod 16:4 may be quoted:[168]

> That the *food* of the soul is not earthly but *heavenly,* we shall find abundant evidence in the sacred Word: *Behold I rain upon you bread out of heaven, and the people shall go out and they shall gather the day's*

---

[165] *Agr.* 128-9. Cf. *L.A.* 1:35, 59; 3:204ff. The Jewish sceptics, discussed by Heinemann, *Bildung,* 104, are relevant.

[166] See Heinemann, *Allegoristik;* Grant, *Letter and Spirit;* Stein, *Allegorische Exegese.*

[167] See Sandmel, 'Environment,' 249-50; *id., Philo of Alexandria,* 24-28; cf. Borgen, *Bread,* 108-11; 133-6; Stone, 'Judaism,' 4-5. On the Jewish concept of prophecy and fulfillment and Stoic allegory, see Bultmann, 'Weissagung,' 162-3.

[168] *L.A.* 3:162-8. See Borgen, *Bread,* 1-20, 122-46.

portion for a day, that I may prove them whether they will walk by my Law or not. You see that the soul is fed not with things of earth that decay, but with such words as God shall have poured like rain *out of* that lofty and pure region of life which the prophet has given the title of *heaven* . . . And this is why he goes on with the words: *that I may prove them whether they will walk in My Law or not;* for this is the divine *law,* to value excellence for its own sake . . .

The words from Exodus are italicized. In the last sentence they are parapharased with the Stoic phrase 'to value excellence for its own sake' being added, which has parallels in Palestinian Judaism.[169] In the first part of the quotation they are paraphrased to include terms from natural science, such as the 'lofty' (μετάρσιος) and 'pure' (καθαρός) sky.[170] The combination of heavenly manna and bread from earth resembles a fragment from the *Haggadah* on the same theme.[171] Finally, the contrast between the heavenly food of the soul and the earthly food of the body reflects Platonism.[172]

Jewish haggadic traditions are often woven into Philo's paraphrase, e.g. that man is to imitate God;[173] the question why the serpent was not allowed to defend himself;[174] the grass that man had to eat (Gen 3:18) as the food of animals.[175] In his etymologies he resembles midrashic exegesis.[176]

Besides direct exegesis ('this is', 'this means', etc.) there is exegesis in the form of questions and answers. In this Philo uses standard formulas, sometimes flexibly.[177] Questions can be introduced by 'why' or by longer phrases, such as 'it is to be inquired why' and 'it is worth discussing why'.[178] Answers may be given without introductory formulas. But often set phrases occur, such as 'it is then to be said, that . . .'[179] Set phrases are also found in Philo's direct exegesis. Some examples are: a) 'He says not merely "shall

---

[169] Von Arnim, *Fragmenta* 3, 11. For a Palestinian parallel, see *Sifre Deut.* 306 (p. 338). See Wolfson, *Philo,* 279-303; Borgen, *Bread,* 122, 126-7.

[170] Borgen, *Bread,* 130-1.

[171] *Ibid.* 16, 127ff. See *Exod. Rabba* 25,2; *Mekhilta, Wayassa* 2 (p. 161); *Mos.* I:201-202 and 2:267.

[172] See Plato, *Phaedrus* 247 CD; 248 BC; 246 DE; *Protagoras* 313 C; *Phaedo* 84 AB.

[173] In *L.A.* 2:65. Cf. *Exod. Rabba* 26,2; *Mekhilta, etc.* See Billerbeck, *Kommentar* 1, 372.

[174] In *L.A.* 2:65. Cf. *Gen. Rabba* 20,2 (p. 182-3); *Num. Rabba* 19,11 and *B.T. Sanhedrin,* 29a.

[175] In *L.A.* 3:251. Cf. *Targum Ps.-Jonathan* on Gen 3:17 and *Vita Adae et Evae* chs. 1-9.

[176] See for instance *Mig.* 43 and *Mekhilta* on Exod 15:11. See Borgen, *Bread,* 64. Another example is *Det.* 47, where Philo opts for one reading against another: 'It must be read in this way (οὕτως ἀναγνωστέον).' This resembles the rabbinic expression אל תקרי ... אלא. See Borgen, *Bread,* 63 and Siegfried, *Philo,* 176.

[177] See Borgen-Skarsten, 'Quaestiones et Solutiones.'

[178] See for example *Q.G.* 1:1, etc. *Op.* 77-78 and *L.A.* I:91-92; *Op.* 72-5; *L.A.* I:85-87, 101-4 and *Decal.* 36-43.

[179] In the *Questions and Answers on Gen. and Exod.* there is often no introductory formula. Examples of set phrases are found in *L.A.* 1:85-7, 91-2, 101-4 and *Decal.* 36-43.

eat", but also "feedingly", *that is,* chewing and masticating the nourish-ment . . .'[180] b) "'Is separated" *is equivalent to* "has boundaries to define it'".[181] c) 'The words "and there was not a man to work the ground", *mean this*: the original idea of the mind did not work the original idea of sense-perception . . .'[182]

With these remarks in mind, we may now summarize Philo's method of composition.[183] 1. His intention being to interpret a given passage of Scripture, he interweaves words from the text into his explanatory paraphrase, and uses various types of etymology, etc. 2. He fuses Jewish traditions of exegesis with terms and views from Greek philosophy so that his exegesis expresses his philosophical interests. 3. He selects and recasts elements from philosophical and exegetical traditions, using set phrases to link them to the scriptural text.

Philo's Thought

In Philo, biblical exegesis and philosophy are inseparable: he is a philo-sophically minded exegete, and a philosopher imbued with the Bible. True philosophy, which is the full understanding of the Law of Moses, can only be developed in the context of Jewish religion. Since he subordinates his Greek philosophy to his aims as exegete of the Pentateuch, his thought cannot be presented as a system. It will be well, however, to take up some central topics which display his mind.

THE ARCHITECT

In *On the Creation* 15-25, the exposition is mainly devoted to the parable of an architect building a city, used to illustrate how God created the world. The image of the Creator as architect also occurs in rabbinic writings.[184] Without discussing the dating of this material, we shall use it for compar-ison with Philo, noting common features and Philo's own philosophical exegesis.

Philo speaks of an architect who made a model of the city he was to build; so too a late rabbinic *midrash* portrays a king who made a model of the foundations, entrances and exits of a future palace. According to Philo, the architect first thought out his plan. Similarly, in an anonymous *midrash,* the builder first planned the desired building.[185] To Philo, the Word (*Logos*) of God in the act of creation is important. The parable of the

---

[180] *L.A.* 1:98, commenting on Gen 2:16. Cf. *L.A.* I:29, 54, 65; 2:45, 62, 77, 92, etc.
[181] *L.A.* I:65, commenting on Gen 2:10-14. Cf. *L.A.* 3:219, 246, 247, 253, etc.
[182] *L.A.* I:27, commenting on Gen 2:5. Cf. *L.A.* I:22; 3:78.
[183] Cf. similar emphasis on Philo as an exegete in Nikiprowetzky, *Commentaire,* 236-42, etc.
[184] *Gen. Rabba* 1, 1 (p. 2) and other sources referred to below.
[185] Both versions are quoted by Urbach, *Sages* 2, 777 n. 74; 1, 200-1 respectively.

architect in the same anonymous *midrash* appeals to Psalm 33:6, 'By the word of the Lord the heavens were made.'

Thus Philo's parable of the architect resembles rabbinic exegesis of the creation story. But his philosophical interests make him focus attention on the intellectual activity of the architect: the model of the city is not material, but an image in the mind. The parable then expresses the idea that the model of this world is the intelligible world conceived by God before He created the sensible world.

Here Jewish traditions about God as architect fuse with Platonism. But Philo identifies these Platonic ideas with the Torah revealed through Moses; then, the Platonism is modified by the affirmation that God alone is at work. While the model (*paradeigma*) in Plato's *Timaeus* was independent of the Demiurge, in Philo it becomes God's creation. There were similar trends in Middle Platonism, as for example in Antiochus of Ascalon (born 130 B.C.E.), who identified the Demiurge with the Stoic *Pneuma* or *Logos*, placing the paradigm in the *Timaeus* within the intellect of the *Logos*, on the pattern of which the physical world was constructed. However, Philo is the first known to state explicitly that the model, the intelligible world, is God's creation.[186]

A corresponding philosophical exegesis is found in Philo's understanding of God's *Logos*. Philo's phrase 'the *Logos* of God who brings creation about', may echo Psalm 33:6, 'By the Word of the Lord the heavens were made', and can in itself be understood as God's creative, spoken word.[187] However, Philo blends this concept of God's *Logos* with Platonic and Stoic terminology, as in Middle Platonism. He identifies *Logos*, a technical term of Stoicism, with the Platonic world of 'forms'.[188] The *Logos* is not primarily God's spoken word, but his mental activity in the act of creation. On the other hand, Philo stresses the Jewish view that the *Logos* is God's, the Creator's. Philo also discerns a double creation in Gen 1-2: first that of the intelligible world, and then that of the sensible world.

How could Philo interpret Gen 1:1-5 as the creation of the intelligible world? In *On the Posterity of Cain* 65, Philo cites Gen 2:4 'the day in which God created heaven and earth'. He understands that 'day' to mean the first day. But if the creation was on the first day, how could it last another five days? The solution was that on the first day the world of 'forms' was

---

186 See Dillon, *Middle Platonists*, 93-95; 158-9. It is debated whether the Sages also depend on Platonic ideas in their use of the parable. Even if they did, Philo' exegesis is more clearly philosophical. See the discussion in *Sages* 1, 199-201.

187 θεοῦ λόγον . . . κοσμοποιοῦντος (*Op.* 24), following the Hebrew text. The Septuagint reads: 'were made firm.'

188 Dillon, *Middle Platonists*, 95, 159-60. Cf. the Septuagint rendering of the second half of the same verse (32:6), 'and all of their power (*dunamis*) by the breath (*pneuma*) of his mouth.' The *Logos-pneuma* here may have been used for the *Pneuma-Logos* concept of Antiochus of Ascalon mentioned above.

created, and the visible world on the remaining days. This harmonization of Gen 1:1-5 and Gen 2:4 corresponds to the discussion by the Rabbis of the same verses.[189]

THE HEAVENLY NOURISHMENT

In *Allegorical Interpretation* 3:162, manna is understood as 'the food of the soul', in contrast to earthly, perishable food. This implies that the soul belongs to heaven, as in the *Timaeus* 90, where Plato describes man as a plant rooted in heaven, through the soul which distinguishes him from animals. Following Plato, a widespread Greek tradition understands man as a 'being between heaven and earth.'[190] This view, which Philo adopts not only here but in many other places,[191] is paralleled in rabbinic tradition. There too, the place of man is between heaven represented by the angels and earth represented by animals. This view of man may be influenced by Platonism but the dualism of soul and body is radically modified by the belief in God as creator of both. Actually, anthropological ideas in Persian religion come closer to the Jewish than do Platonic views.[192]

The main point here is not to identify the soul and heaven, but that the soul feeds on heavenly nourishment, manna. Again, Philo reflects the thought of Plato, who speaks frequently of the nourishment of the soul.[193] There are less striking parallels to this in rabbinic writings, for instance, the notion of the Torah as bread and manna.[194] In Philo, manna as food of the soul, seems to fit into an individualistic kind of philosophy, based on a dualism of heaven and earth, soul and body. But in Philo 'the soul' does not in fact have primarily an individualistic sense. It refers to the Jewish nation collectively. The passage goes on: 'The people, and all that goes to make the soul, is to go out and gather and make a beginning of knowledge . . .' Compare *On Drunkenness* 37: 'He (Moses) in his wisdom was recalling the whole people of the soul to piety and to honouring God and was teaching them commandments and holy laws.' Thus 'the soul' is associated with piety, the honouring of God, the commandments and holy laws, the very characteristics of the Jewish people which contrast with 'a city or commonwealth peopled by a promiscuous horde, who swing to and fro as their idle opinions carry them' (*On Drunkenness* 36). The Jewish people

---

[189] Urbach, *Sages* I, 185-7.
[190] For the following discussion, see Borgen, *Bread,* 127-41.
[191] Borgen, *Bread,* 129; Jaeger, *Nemesios von Emesa,* 98ff.
[192] *L.A.* 3:161; *Op.* 135; *Det.* 84-5, etc. *B.T. Hagigah* 16a; *Pesikta Rabbati* 43 (179b); *Tanhuma* (ed. Buber), *Bereshit* 17 (6b); *Sifre Deut.* 306 (p. 340-1); *Gen. Rabba* 8,11 (p. 65); 12,8 (p. 106f.) etc. See Meyer, *Hellenistisches,* 88ff. For Persian ideas see Urbach, *Sages* I,250-1.
[193] *Phaedrus* 247 CD; 248 BC; 246 DE; *Protagoras* 313 C; *Phaedo* 84 AB.
[194] *Mekhilta, Wayehi* 1 (p. 76); cf. *Exod. Rabba* 25,7.

represents the organization in which the heavenly quality, 'the soul' is realized, according to Philo.

Finally, *Allegorical Interpretation* 3:162 identifies the heavenly food as 'words' (*logoi*). The plural *logoi* has many different shades of meaning in Philo and must in each case be defined according to its context. In our case, it is associated with the heavenly nourishment of the Jewish nation, the 'soul'. An important parallel is found in *Decalogue* 13: 'Naturally therefore, he first led them away from the highly mischievous souls, and then began to set the nourishment before their minds — and what should the nourishment be but laws and divine words (*logoi*)?' Here also, the laws and words of God are described as food for the minds in the desert, associated with the manna. This interpretation implies that the Jewish laws and statutes are in harmony with the heavenly laws and principles. The '*logoi*' here represent the order of things set by God, known to the nation which is 'soul'. The heavenly order is in fact revealed in the law of Moses.

Thus the Stoic *Logos* is modified by a platonizing distinction between heaven and earth and represents the Jewish Law, not God as in Stoicism;[195] and since the Law was made up of many precepts, Philo uses the plural *logoi*. At the same time, the parallel with rabbinic thought continues. There too, the conception of man as a creature between animals and heavenly beings is applied to Israel, seen as a people of heavenly quality;[196] the traces of the identification of manna with the Torah also correspond.

Having given an example of Philo's philosophical exegesis with respect to cosmology, and another which interpreted the Jewish nation as the people of heavenly quality, we should now exemplify how figures of the Pentateuch serve as authoritative ideals for the nations. See *Moses* 1:158:

> Again, did he not enjoy the greater partnership with the Father and Maker of all, having been deemed worthy of the same title? For he was named god and king of the whole nation, and entered, we are told, into the darkness where God was, that is into the formless, invisible, incorporeal, and archetypal essence of existing things, beholding what is hidden from the sight of mortal nature. And making himself and his own life public like a well-wrought picture, he set up a beautiful and godlike piece of work, a model for those willing to copy it.

Here Philo interprets Moses' ascent of Mount Sinai, using the Septuagint rendering of Exod 20:21, which in English reads: 'Moses went into the

---

[195] Von Arnim, *Fragmenta* 2, 269; 1, 24. See Kleinknecht, 'λέγω, B.'.
[196] See Jervell, *Imago Dei,* 86f. especially 86, n. 65.

darkness where God was' (Hebrew text 20:18, 'approached'). And 'the darkness' is the 'formless, invisible, incorporeal, paradigmatic essence of existing things,'[197] which means that Moses ascended from the mountain into God's realm. In rabbinic writings Moses also enters heaven.[198] Moreover, Moses' ascent makes him 'god and king'. Meeks has shown that Philo here draws on exegetical traditions also known from rabbinic writings.[199] In one tradition, Moses was made 'god' after having ascended on high from Mount Sinai.[200] In another, he shared God's kingship, and God, who apportions some of his glory to those who fear Him, gave him his heavenly *corona* as His earthly vice-regent.[201] As in *Moses* 1:158, Moses as 'god' goes back on Exod 7:1, 'See, I have made you a god to Pharaoh.'

In Philo, these ideas are given a philosophical interpretation. The good man partakes of the precious things of God so far as he is capable. Moses in particular has the divine titles of God and king. Philo interprets this as Moses' partnership with God. Partnership (κοινωνία), means 'participation' and in Greek religion characterizes liturgical communion between worhippers and the gods. Plato's philosophy saw men's partnership with the gods as the highest form of happiness, and the Stoics defined the cosmos as a commonwealth of gods and men in partnership.[202]

Again, Philo combines Platonic and Stoic notions. From Stoicism comes the idea that the good man is a citizen of the world,[203] and as such partakes of the precious things of God. Platonic thought is reflected in the concept that Moses had a special partnership with God in the intelligible world of 'forms'. Philo's monotheism made him suppress any polytheistic aspects.

Moses' kingship made him an intermediary between God and men. His life imitates the visionary world and his subjects imitate him. This double imitation is a commonplace in descriptions of Hellenistic kingship.[204] In Philo however, Moses' kingship is linked with his quality as lawgiver (*Moses* 1:162). Thus, Philo employs midrashic tradition about Moses' ascent of Sinai and interprets it on the basis of Hellenistic kingship theory, while drawing on Platonism and Stoicism. These were his ideals for the Jewish nation and its universal role in the world.[205]

---

[197] Exod 20:21 is interpreted in a similar way also in *Gig.* 54; *Post.* 14 and *Mut.* 7.

[198] *Num. Rabba* 12,11; *Midrash Psalms* 24,5 (102b); 68,11 (160a). In *Mekhilta, Bahodesh* 4, p. 217 and 238, the idea is explicitly rejected by R. Yose and R. Yishmael, but R. Akiba accepts it dialectically on the basis of Exod 20:19 (*ibid.*, pp. 216f.; 238). See further Borgen, 'Exegetical Traditions,' 243-4.

[199] Meeks, *Prophet-King.*

[200] *Pesikta de R. Kahana, Berakha* (p. 443).

[201] *Tanhuma* (ed. Buber) *Behaalotkha* 15 (26a-b).

[202] Hauck, 'κοινός κτλ'.

[203] Von Arnim, *Fragmenta* 1, 262.

[204] Meeks, *Prophet-King*, 111; Goodenough, *Light,* 186, n. 34; *id.,* 'Political Philosphy', 88-91.

[205] The Jewish traditions which Philo utilizes here and in many other places may be classified as early stages of Merkabah-mysticism, with its emphasis on the ascent into heaven and on God's kingship. See especially Scholem, *Major Trends,* 54-57. Cf. Ginzberg, *Legends* 5, 416-18.

THE COSMIC SIGNIFICANCE OF JEWISH EXISTENCE

Looking for a dominant feature in Philo's thought, some scholars have pointed to the tendence to bridge the gap between the transcendent God and man by intermediaries.[206] This is not enough. To Philo, it is specifically the Jewish people which intermediates between God and man. The notion of the universal significance of Israel dominates in this tought.

Central here is Philo's interpretation of the name 'Israel', which is based on his etymological reading איש ראה אל (the man who sees God) or שור אל (seeing God).[207] Among many others, Goodenough believes that Philo in general uses this etymology as a spiritual concept only, not meaning the Jewish nation, but first the Patriarchs, and then those who were granted the vision of God, whether Jew or Gentile.[208] Other scholars maintain that Philo applies this concept to the Jewish nation. Others try to reconcile these views by bringing them under the one concept of ascent from earth to heaven.[209] But *Gaius* 4 shows that the Jewish nation is meant.

The center of Jewish existence is Jerusalem and its Temple. All Jews see Jerusalem as mother city, their 'metropolis'.[210] Its earthly buildings are not its all, but essentially represent God's cosmos.[211] Its name Jerusalem reveals the main attribute of God, and man's relation to him, for etymologically, Philo says, Jerusalem means 'vision of peace'; this means vision of God, since peace is the chief of the powers of God.[212] Surprisingly, the *Logos*, a central concept to Philo, is equally charaterized as a 'metropolis', and he regards Jerusalem as a manifestation of the divine *Logos* spoken by God when he created the world. Indeed the chief, surest and best mother city, 'metropolis,' which is more than just a city, is the Divine *Logos,* and to take refuge in it is supremely advantageous.[213] Furthermore, he seems to expect that all Jews of the Diaspora would be brought back to Jerusalem and the Holy Land in the eschatological age.[213a]

Equally, the Temple in Jerusalem is an earthly counterpart of the cosmic heavenly Temple:

> The highest, and in the truest sense the holy, temple of God is, as we must believe, the whole cosmos, having for its sanctuary the most

---

[206] Sandmel, *Philo of Alexandria,* 90; Cohn, *Lehre vom Logos,* 330-1; Jonas, *Gnosis* II/1, 74f.

[207] See Borgen, *Bread,* 115-18.

[208] Goodenough, *Light,* 136.

[209] Dahl, *Das Volk Gottes,* 108-13.

[210] *Flaccus* 46.

[211] Philo draws here on Stoic ideas of the cosmos as a city. See Wolfson, *Philo* 1, 328. Cf. *Som.* 2:250.

[212] Cf. *Som.* 2:250-4.

[213] Cf. *Fug.* 94-95.

[213a] *Praem.* 165; cf. *Mos.* 2:44.

sacred part of all existence, even heaven, for its votive ornaments the stars, for its priests the angels who are servitors to His powers... There is also the temple made by hands; for it was right that no check should be given to the forwardness of those who pay their tribute to piety and desire by means of sacrifices either to give thanks for the blessings that befall them or to ask for pardon and forgiveness for their sins. But he provided that there should not be temples built either in many places or many in the same place, for he judged that since God is one, there should be also only one temple.[214]

Of the Levitic priests Philo says that their perfection of body and soul makes them the image of God. This requisite pefection of body is a token of the perfection of the immortal soul, fashioned after the image of God, i.e. of the *Logos* through whom the whole universe was created.[215] So, the high priest in the Jerusalem Temple is the true portrait of man.[216]

Again, the biblical picture of Aaron as a mediator and as Moses' interpreter is developed into the high priest as the sacred *Logos* who separates and walls off holy thoughts from the unholy.[217] Aaron was *Logos* in utterance,[218] and the perfect interpreter.[219] Along the lines of Jewish tradition, Philo attributes cosmic significance to the high priest. His vestments symbolize the whole cosmos, he is consecrated to the Father of the world, and thus is invested with universal meaning for the service of the Creator.[220] The worship of the One God is seen in contrast to the erroneous polytheism of other nations. Therefore, it is worship on behalf of all mankind: through the Levites, the Jewish nation is the priesthood of all nations.[221]

Illuminating is Philo's explanation of the feasts, of which only the Sabbath can be mentioned here. Jews, he says, regard the Sabbath with great reverence and will not yield to political authorities who want to abolish it.[222] Already in the Pentateuch, the celebration of the Sabbath is founded on creation (Gen 2:2-3) and Philo is fertile in his interpretation of the Sabbath and its cosmic role. For instance, he elaborates in Pythagorean

---

[214] *Spec.* 1:66f. Cf. the biblical ideas of the heavenly model of the tabernacle (Ex 25:9-40; cf. 1 Chr 28:19) and generally the Jewish idea of a heavenly temple (Bietenhard, *Die himmlische Welt*). Cf. also Stoic ideas on the cosmos as a temple, Cohn, *Werke* 2, 29 n. 2 and Platonism on the world of forms (Sowers, *Hermeneutics,* 105-12); Heinemann, *Bildung,* 45-58.

[215] Cf. *Spec.* 1:80-81.

[216] Cf. *Som.* 1:215.

[217] *Heres* 201-202, cf. *L.A.* 3:45 and 118.

[218] *Migr.* 78; *Det.* 39, 126.

[219] *Det. 132;* cf. *Cher.* 17; *Post.* 132; *Gig.* 52; *Fug.* 108, 117. See Heinemann, *Bildung,* 59-62 on Platonic and Stoic elements.

[220] *Spec.* 1:84-97.

[221] *Spec.* 2:166-7; *Mos.* 2:196; *Spec.* 1:97.

[222] *Som.* 2:123-4.

fashion on the number seven, as did Aristobulus. One example out of many may be given: Moses recognized in the seventh day the birth of the world, celebrated in heaven and on earth, as all things rejoice in the full harmony of the sacred number seven. Hence, the Hebrew people, who follow the laws of nature, must celebrate this festival too.[223] Basically, feasts and joy belong to God alone, for God alone is entirely blessed, exempt from all evil. But from this joy of God the joy of man flows, as a mixed stream.[224]

The above illustrates how Philo gives a cosmic and universal relevance to Jerusalem, the Temple and the Sabbath, as also to the laws of the Jewish nation and the role of Moses. By introducing his laws into the story of creation, Moses implies that the universe is in harmony with the Law and the Law with the world. Thus the man who observes the Law is constituted a loyal citizen of the world.[225] Primarily, this is Moses, a true cosmopolitan,[226] in accordance with the development of that idea. In the second place, the people of Israel is meant. Moses' action when he 'smote the Egyptian and hid him in the sand' (Exod 2:12), reveals a double dualism, in Philo's view: the dualism between body and soul, and between Gentiles and Jews. The Egyptians and their way of life are the evil body of passions, and those who worship the real God, the Jews, belong to the realm of the soul.[227] Thus the terms applying to individuals, such as soul, reason, body etc. acquire collective connotations with Philo.[228]

Like Aaron the high priest, Moses is a messenger and mediator between God and man. As such, he is identified with an archangel, or with the *Logos* and in this capacity says: '"and I stood between the Lord and you" (Deut 5:5), that is neither uncreated as God, nor created as you, but midway between the two extremes, a surety to both sides, ... For I am the harbinger of peace to creation from that God whose will is to bring wars to an end, who is ever the guardian of peace.'[229] Similarly, Moses was one among the many angels when he mediated at Sinai and spoke on God's behalf to the people. He served as one of the *logoi*.[230] Philo can even say that God sent Moses as a loan to the earthly sphere.[231] This explains Moses' authority: though a figure of the past, he still determines the lives of Jews in the time after him. They are to imitate him[232] and they are his disciples.[233]

---

[223] *Mos.* 2:210-11.
[224] *Spec.* 2:53-55; *Cher.* 86. See Wolfson, *Philo* 1, 79-80; 95-96; 2, 265-6. Heinemann, *Bildung,* 110-18; 140-2.
[225] *Op.* 3. For Philo's use of Stoic ideas here, see Colson, *Philo Works* 1, 475.
[226] *Mos.* 1:157; cf. *Conf.* 106.
[227] *L.A.* 3:37-39; *Fug.* 148.
[228] See Borgen, *Bread,* 133-6; 143.
[229] *Heres* 205-6; cf. *Som.* 1:143.
[230] *Som.* 1:143.
[231] *Sac.* 9.   [232] *Mos.* 1:159.
[233] *Det.* 86; *Post.* 12; *Conf.* 39; *Heres* 81; *Spec.* 1:59, 345; 2:256. See especially Mack, 'Imitatio Mosis.'

It was Moses who communicated the basic self-revelation of God as 'I am He that is'.[234] This means that 'God alone has veritable being',[235] and that God's nature is to be, not to be spoken. Yet, so that the human race should not lack a title to give to the supreme goodness, he allows them to use the title of 'Lord God.'[236]

Abraham, the ancestor of the Jewish race, is at the same time the prototype of proselytes, since he left his native country and its polytheism to discover the One God. In doing so he gained all the other virtues.[237] Philo distinguishes three types of men: the earth-born, the heaven-born and the true men of God. Abraham began as a man born of heaven, searching into the nature of the ethereal region. Later, he became a man of God, and the God of the Universe was his god in a special sense and by a special grace. The sons of earth are those who follow the pleasures of the body.[238] By combining these notions, which are given in two separate passages, we see that the sons of earth are in fact pagans or apostates. The men of heaven are pagans who, like young Abram, seek heaven and the Creator. The men of God then are the Jews, who like the older Abraham are wholly owned by God.[239]

Philo's concept of revelation can now be better understood. According to some scholars, he distinguishes in a general way between the lesser mystery of knowing God through creation and the greater mystery in which man experiences the vision of God himself.[240] This distinction should be understood more specifically on the basis of the difference between Jews and other men: the chosen people have received the revelation of God. And although other men share in a certain knowledge of God through creation and reason, it is only through the revelation received by the Jews that man is truly known by God.[241]

---

[234] ὁ ὤν, Exod 3:14.

[235] *Det.* 160.

[236] *Mut.* 11-12; cf. *Som.* 1:231-4. Cf. Wolfson, *Philo* 1, 210; 2, 119-21. Elsewhere, Philo interprets the name 'God' (Theos) to mean God's creative and gracious power, while 'Lord' (Kyrios) is taken to indicate God's authority and ruling power (*Mut.* 29; *Abr.* 121; *Conf.* 137; *Mos.* 99; *Som.* I:162f. etc.) See Wolfson, *Philo* I, 223-5; 2, 136. Philo's view resembles one tradition preserved in rabbinic writings, while the more widespread rabbinic tradition associates God's beneficent/creative power with 'YHWH' (cf. *Kyrios*), and his governing activity with 'Elohim' (cf. *Theos*).

[237] *Virt.* 212-19.

[238] *Gig.* 60-67.

[239] On Philo's views on proselytism see Borgen, 'Observations,' 87-88 and *id.*, 'The Early Church.'

[240] See Früchtel, *Die kosmologische Vorstellungen,* 107-10; 144-71; Mühlenberg, 'Das Problem der Offenbarung.'

[241] *Post.* 11; *Abr.* 79f.; *Som.* 1:68; *Gaius* 6.

THE LOGOS

We come finally to another central concept of Philo, the *Logos,* which has already been mentioned several times in the preceding sections.[242] At times Philo maintains that God is unknowable,[243] transcending virtue and the good and the beautiful.[244] He is 'that which exists' (τὸ ὄν), or 'he who exists' (ὁ ὤν). But, although God himself is unknowable, his activities, which are called his powers (*dynameis*) can be known. Central powers are: God's activity in creating the world, represented by the name 'God' (*Theos*), and his continued activity in governing the world, indicated by the name 'Lord' (*Kyrios*). The universe consists of the intelligible and the sensible world, both created and governed by God. God's powers are in the intelligible sphere, but reach into this world and are knowable by man.

Philo's technical use of the term *Logos* connotes God's mental activity during the act of creating. The *Logos,* one of the powers of the intelligible world, reaches into our world, mainly through the mediators Moses and Aaron, both called *Logos.* The plural *logoi* can indicate the heavenly principles which are embodied in the laws and precepts given to the Jews through Moses.

In another sense, the *Logos* and the *logoi* may be conceived as heavenly figures such as angels and archangels. The *Logos* is also called a 'second god',[245] or God's first-born. This *Logos* has many names: 'the beginning', 'the name of God', 'the man after his image', and 'he that sees' (Israel).[246]

The meaning of Philo's *Logos* is therefore complex: it embraces the scriptural 'word', biblical figures, heavenly beings, the laws of Moses, and Platonic and Stoic elements. In some places Philo uses the related concept of wisdom, *Sophia.* When Sarah is a cosmic and heavenly figure she can be named *Sophia,* following Jewish Wisdom tradition.[248]

Philo sometimes uses sexual imagery to describe the relationship bet-

---

[242] In so far as this survey draws on material from the preceding sections, no references are given here.

[243] On Platonic-Pythagorean influence in Philo's transcendentalism, see Dillon, 'Transcendence of God.'

[244] *Op.* 8.

[245] *Som.* 1:229.

[246] *Conf.* 146. Some scholars point to similarities between Philo and Gnosticism for such personifications. Käsemann, *Gottesvolk,* 54ff., thinks that Philo's concept of Logos has been coloured by the Gnostic 'Urmensch.' Borgen, 'God's Agent,' 147-8, points to similarities between personified ideas in Philo and in Gnosticism, but concludes that both Philo and some Gnostic traditions draw on Jewish Merkabah traditions. See also below, p. 466f. For a critical appraisal of gnostic interpretations of Philo, see Sandmel, *Philo's Place* p. xvi; Simon, 'Eléments gnostiques', 359-76; Pearson, 'Philo and the Gnostics'; McL. Wilson, 'Philo of Alexandria.'

[248] *L.A.* 2:82; *Cong.* 9:13; 22; 79f. *Mut.* 15-153, etc. On the varied uses of the concept of wisdom (Sophia) in Philo see Dillon, *Middle Platonists,* 163-4; Mack, *Logos und Sophia.*

ween God and the world. The contrast between male and female symbolizes the contrast between the spiritual and the irrational or between the eternal and the transitory. Matter is 'female', while form or *logos* is 'male'. But the highest *Logos* and of course God himself, are essentially asexual.[249]

Philo and His Predecessor Aristobulus

Five large fragments of Aristobulus are found in Eusebius' *Historia Ecclesiastica* and *Praeparatio Evangelica*.[250] Clement of Alexandria has parallels to parts of Fragments 2-5. References to Aristobulus are also found elsewhere in the writings of Clement and Eusebius, as well as in Origen (*Contra Celsum* 4:51) and 2 Maccabees. According to 2 Macc 1:10, Aristobulus came from a high-priestly family, and (as also stated by Clement and Eusebius) lived in the time of Ptolemy VI Philometor (ca. 181-145 B.C.E.).[251] There has been much debate on the authenticity of these fragments and their date, to which we will return later.

Aristobulus wrote in the form of a dialogue, where he answered questions raised by the Ptolemaic king. A similar form is used in Philo's *Questions and Answers on Genesis and Exodus*.[252] Clement and Eusebius describe Aristobulus as a Peripatetic. But the fragments show more affinities with Platonic and Pythagorean thinking. In fact, Aristobulus was a Jew who drew on Greek ideas eclectically. Two concerns of Aristobulus can be seen: 1) that Jewish philosophy, found in the Law of Moses, has many points of agreement with the Greeks who learned from Moses; 2) to solve the problem created by anthropomorphisms used of God, he largely uses the allegorical method.

---

[249] Baer, *Male and Female.*

[250] The fragments are found in *Hist. Eccl.* 7:32,17-18 (Fragment 1, taken from the writings of Anatolius) and *Praep. Evang.* 8:10,1-17 (Fragment 2); 13:12,1-2 (Fragment 3); 13:12,3-8 (Fragment 4); 13:12,9-16 (Fragment 5, partly found also in 7:14,1). See Walter, *Der Thoraausleger,* 7-8.

[251] 2Macc 1:10 is probably an editorial addition from about 50 B.C.E. It testifies to the general knowledge of Aristobulus' writings in Alexandria at that time. See further Clement *Strom.* 1:150, 1-3; Eusebius, *Praep. Evang.* 9:6,6; 8:9,38. Elsewhere (*Hist. Eccl.* 7:32,16) Eusebius says that Aristobulus lived at the time of Ptolemy II Philadelphos (285 B.C.E.) The latter dating is not reliable; the dating to the time of Ptolemy VI Philometor is probable. See Walter, *Der Thoraausleger,* 13-26; 35-40.

[252] Walter, *Der Thoraausleger,* 29-31, overemphasizes the difference between the dialogue form of Aristobulus and the question and answer form. He suggests that Aristobulus' work was probably a thematic treatise on the correct principle of interpretation for the law of Moses, and some of the valuable philosophical insights gained from such an approach. On the question and answer form in various parts of Philo's works, see Borgen-Skarsten, 'Quaestiones et Solutiones.'

In *Fragment 3* Aristobulus states that Plato and Pythagoras derived ideas from the Law of Moses allegedly known to them from pre-Alexandrian translations. Philo entertained similar theories. He says that Heraclitus derived his theory of opposites from Moses, or 'snatched them from him like a thief';[253] and Greek legislators copied from the laws of Moses.[254] More cautiously, he says that the Greek philosopher Zeno seemed to have learned from the laws of Moses.[255] Philo here draws on a tradition already found in Aristobulus. Aristobulus was even more specific than Philo, since he presents a particular theory of pre-Alexandrian translations.[256]

Fragment 4 develops two related topics. The first is how to understand 'the divine voice'. Contemplating the construction of the world, Pythagoras, Socrates and Plato were led to recognition of the truth of the creation story in the book of Moses. At the same time Aristobulus tells what in his opinion is the proper understanding of the 'divine voice'. It was not a real spoken word, but the preparation for the works of creation (ἔργων κατασκευάς). He finds the scriptural basis of this interpretation in Gen 1, which says of each thing: 'and God said, — and it was done.' It cannot be said that Aristobulus here develops an allegorical interpretation in the strict sense of the term. He does not bring out the inner, spiritual meaning of 'the divine voice', but only modifies the phrase to mean God's creative activity in general.[257] A similar interpretation of God's *Logos* is given by Philo: God spoke and at the same time acted, setting no interval between the two; or a truer view might be that His very word was deed.[258]

The second topic is another aspect of the doctrine of God: the existence of one invisible God, one creation and God's rule over the universe. Aristobulus adduces the 'Sacred Book of Orpheus' (an imaginary book) and verses of the Stoic Aratus as witnesses. Orpheus and Aratus were inferior to Moses, however, because they had no 'holy concepts of God'. They were therefore to be corrected. The passages quoted contained originally the polytheistic names Dis and Zeus. Aristobulus replaces these names by *Theos,* God: 'We have interpreted the passage as is necessary by removing the names Dis and Zeus which occur in the poems, since their meaning relates to God . . . For all philosophers agree that one must have holy concepts of God, and this is something with which our school is most concerned.'[259] For Aristobulus, the Jews are basically a

---

[253] *Q.G.* 3:5; 4:152; cf. *Her.* 214.

[254] *Spec.* 4:61.

[255] *Prob.* 51-53.

[256] Cf. Stein, *Die allegorische Exegese*, 10,11; Hengel, *Hellenism* I, 165-6; Wolfson, *Philo* 1, 141-2.

[257] Cf. Stein, *Die allegorische Exegese*, 10; Walter, *Der Thoraausleger*, 141-9.

[258] ὁ λόγος ἔργον ἦν αὐτοῦ, *Sac.* 65.

[259] *Praep. Evang.* 13:12,7-8.

nation of philosophers. Although other philosophers have some value, true philosophy is found among the Jews.[260]

In *Fragment 5*, Aristobulus discusses the Sabbath on the basis of the creation story in Gen 1:1-2:4a and the words on Wisdom and creation in Prov 8:22f. We may note the following points.

a) Aristobulus modifies the concept of time found in the creation story. The enumeration of six days was for the purpose of establishing the course of time within the created world. In this way Aristobulus attempts to bring the biblical conception of creation in time into agreement with Greek idea of the timeless activity of God. Only God's creation is subject to the category of time, not God himself.[261] This idea is further developed by Philo, who stresses that time was formed as part of creation and did not exist prior to it,[262] and that the enumeration of six days indicates that in creation there was need of order.[263]

b) Wisdom is said to be created before heaven and earth. However, in a 'midrashic' elaboration Aristobulus goes beyond Proverbs and says that all light comes from Wisdom. This conjunction of Wisdom and primal light is further developed in Wisdom 7:22-26. Correspondingly, Philo associates light and *Logos*: the invisible light, perceptible only by the mind, has come into being as an image of the divine *Logos*.[264] Thus Aristobulus, Philo and Wisdom each offer philosophical formulations of the concept of primal light which was current in Judaism. Aristobulus also refers to the view of some Peripatetic philosophers, who likewise say that wisdom has the role of a lamplighter, because those who persevere in following her find that their life continues long in a state of rest (ἀταράξοι).[265]

c) In interpreting the Sabbath, Aristobulus makes the number seven the principle of cosmic order. Those who see, find here proof of the divine ordering of the world, an order which the Jewish feast of the Sabbath makes manifest. The Sabbath and the number seven also structure human knowledge. The seventh day is to be kept holy 'as a symbol of our "sevenfold *logos*", to which we owe our knowledge of human and divine things.'[266] Here the Stoic definition of philosophy is applied to Jewish

---

[260] Cf. Hengel, *Hellenism* 1, 164. The Orphic poem exists in various forms in Clement of Alexandria and in writings attributed to Justin Martyr. The verses taken from the Stoic Aratus are taken from his *Phaenomena* 1-9, also quoted in Acts 17:28 (*Phaenomena* 5). See Walter, *Der Thoraausleger*, 103-23.

[261] *Praep. Evang.* 13:12,12.

[262] *L.A.* 1:2; *Op.* 26; *Sac.* 68.

[263] *Op.* 13, 27-28, 67; *L.A.* 1:3f. See Hengel, *Hellenism* I, 166; Wolfson, *Philo* 1, 311-12; Walter, *Der Thoraausleger*, 65-66.

[264] *Op.* 31.

[265] See Hengel, *Hellenism* 1, 166-9; Aalen, *'Licht' und 'Finsternis'*, 175f.; Billerbeck, *Kommentar* 4, 960ff.

[266] *Praep. Evang.* 13:12,12-13.

religion and the Sabbath, and attributed to Jewish philosophy. Again, the Law of Moses is basic for gaining knowledge of human and divine things. In these Stoic terms 4 Macc 1:16f. also describes wisdom as 'knowledge of divine and human things' and as the training of the Law, a description Philo also uses to characterize the Jewish philosophy and way of life.[267]

d) Verses attributed to Hesiod, Homer and the legendary poet Linus are quoted in order to show how non-Jewish writers glorify the Sabbath, confirming the cosmic and spiritual significance of the number seven.[268] Two quotations are listed for Hesiod, three for Homer, and four for Linus. Walter finds Hesiod 1 (from *Works and Days* 770) authentic, and Homer 2, taken from the *Odyssey* 5:262. But Homer's 'The fourth day came, and he had finished all,' reads in Aristobulus: 'The seventh day came, and he had finished all.' Homer 3 is apocryphal: 'On the morning of the seventh day, we left the flood of Acheron.' Aristobulus adds allegorical comment to the verse. It means liberation from the forgetfulness which afflicts the soul, and from evil, through the sevenfold *Logos* from which we receive knowledge of the truth.[269] Since seven is the key term in the quotation, the comment most probably refers to the Sabbath as central in the Jewish religion. Only the cosmic force of seven can repress the evil forces of the soul. This liberation comes through the contemplation done on the seventh day, the Sabbath.[270] Aristobulus' emphasis on the theological significance of the Sabbath is founded on the cosmic interpretation of the seventh day in Gen 2:1-4a. More developed speculations on the Sabbath appear in Philo[271] and in Josephus.[272]

In *Fragment 1* Aristobulus discusses the Passover in connection with the calendar. Passover is to be celebrated after the vernal equinox, in the middle of the first month. But the lunar calendar is not neglected since sun and moon both should pass through the same equinoctial sign. While Aristobulus remains here within the context of debates on the calendar in Judaism, he shows knowledge of a Hellenistic Egyptian solar calendar.[274]

---

[267] *Cong.* 79. See Hengel, *Hellenism* 1, 166-7; Walter, *Der Thoraausleger,* 68-75. On 4 Macc, see below pp. 316-9.

[268] *Praep. Evang.* 13:12,13-16.

[269] *Praep. Evang.* 13:12,15.

[270] The other verses cited can only be mentioned in a summary fashion. Hesiod 2, probably Homer I, and Linus 2-5, come from a non-Jewish Pythagorean source. A Jewish editor seems to have produced Linus I (which Clement, *Strom.* 5:107, assigns to Callimachus) and to have modified Homer I and 2, and Linus, 4-5. Walter, *Der Thoraausleger,* 150-71.

[271] *Mos.* 2:21ff.; *Op.* 89; *Decal.* 96-101, etc.

[272] *Ag. Ap.* 2:282. God's resting on the seventh day (Gen 2:1-3), is often discussed, here in Aristobulus, in Philo and in rabbinic writings; compare John 5:17. Cf. Walter, *Der Thoraausleger,* 170-171; Barrett, *The Gospel according to St. John,* 255-6.

[274] The calendar given by the Essenes is solar. See Herr, 'The Calendar', 839-43. Cf. above, p. 100 on the calendar in *Jubilees.*

Eusebius' report on Aristobulus' view of the date of Passover is brief, but we gain the impression that it is connected with the cosmic significance of the feast.[275]

The problem of anthropomorphism is treated in *Fragment 2,* where King Ptolemy objects that the Law of Moses ascribed bodily organs and human passions to God. Aristobulus begins his answer with a statement of principle: if men are to understand the real meaning of the Law of Moses, they should not fall victim to mythological and human conceptions. For literalists, Moses has no great message; the anthropomorphisms are to be interpreted in line with the appropriate conception of God.[276] Aristobulus' formulations indicate that he is not only attacking Greek critics of the Law of Moses, but also its conservative Jewish defenders. His own view is that when the Pentateuch speaks of the 'hands of God', it means his powers, as is seen from Exod 3:20; 9:3; 13:19, 16. When the phrase 'God stood' is used, it means the existence and immutability of the created world. Heaven never becomes earth, nor the sun the moon, nor the moon the sun; things are not interchangeable. Furthermore, the descent of God on Mount Sinai, Exod 19:17-20, was not local, for God is everywhere. The appearance of fire and the sound of trumpet were wrought miraculously as a display of God's energy, Deut 4:11; 5:23; 9:15.

Greek interpretation modified or removed the anthromorphisms in Homer. The same occurs in many Jewish writings interpreting the Bible; apart from Aristobulus, we find it in Philo, the Septuagint, the Targumim and the Midrash. Thus *Targum Onkelos* interprets 'God's hand' (Exod 3:20) in the same way as Aristobulus: it means God's power. The *Mekhilta* says that God did not descend on Mount Sinai, but that Moses heard the call from God as if it came from the top of the mountain.[277] Anthropomorphisms are also excluded by Philo, on the principle that '. . . to say that God uses hands or feet or any created part at all is not the true account.'[278] He interprets Exod 24:10 like Aristobulus: 'they saw the place where the God of Israel stood, for by standing or establishment he indicates his immutability.'[279] Finally, on the phrase 'the Lord came down', Gen 11:5, Philo states the following principle: 'To suppose that the Deity approaches or departs, goes down or goes up . . . is an impiety.'[280]

---

[275] Hengel, *Hellenism* I, 235; 2, 157-8, n. 813; See especially Strobel, 'Der Termin'; *id.* 'Zur Funktionsfähigkeit', 410; cf. Limbeck, *Die Ordnung des Heils,* 134-75, on the Essene calendar.

[276] *Praep. Evang.* 8:10,1-6.

[277] *Mekhilta, Bahodesh* 4, p. 216-7.

[278] *Conf.* 98.

[279] *Som.* 2:222.

[280] *Conf.* 134-40. See Maybaum, *Die Anthropomorphien;* Lauterbach. 'The Ancient Jewish Allegorists'; Heinemann, *Altjüdische Allegoristik;* Werblowsky, 'Anthropomorphism'; Fritsch, *The Anti-Anthropomorphisms;* Van der Leeuw, 'Anthropomorphismus'; Wolfson, *Philo* 1, 56-60; 2, 127-8.

Some scholars have held that the above fragments presuppose Philo's writings.[281] Stein and especially Walter, have convincingly shown otherwise.[282] Philo represents a developed allegorical exposition and often draws a distinction of principle between the literal and the allegorical or spiritual meanings. Aristobulus, with less developed allegories, remains within the ambit of the Septuagint, the Targumim and the Midrashim. Nevertheless, his use of Greek philosophy and quotations makes him representative of an Alexandrian Jewish trend towards Philo's developed expositions. Like Philo, he stresses the cosmic significance of Judaism, and shows that Philo's philosophical exegesis was not an isolated case.

Within his own historical context Aristobulus builds a bridge between traditional Judaism and Hellenism. His exegesis of the Law of Moses must be understood as a positive effort to adapt the concepts of Jewish tradition to the demands of a new situation, that of a Jewish community trying to assert itself *vis à vis* Hellenism. This Jewish Alexandrian concern was inherited by the early Church. Clement of Alexandria and Eusebius of Caesarea use the fragments from Aristobulus in order to document their thesis that Greek wisdom depends on Jewish wisdom as revealed in the Law of Moses.

The Significance of Philo[283]

The translation of the Bible into Greek is not only an indication of the numerical strength of Alexandrian Jewry early in the Hellenistic period, but also of its integration into the Greek-speaking world. Along with the Septuagint, Alexandrian Jews produced their own Greek literature, of which the historian Demetrius and the tragedian Ezekiel, both from the 3rd century B.C.E., are the earliest representatives. This production continued with the *Letter of Aristeas,* Aristobulus in the 2nd century B.C.E. and the Wisdom of Solomon in the first century B.C.E.; it reached its peak in Philo.

Philo reflects more firsthand knowledge of Hellenistic culture in general and Greek philosophy in particular than earlier Alexandrian Jewish writers, though direct historical lines can be drawn from Aristobulus' allegorical and philosophical exegesis and the philosophical language of the Wisdom of Solomon to Philo. Philo was not only the culmination point of a

---

[281] Amongs the scholars who do not accept the authenticity are: Wendland, 'Aristobulus,' and Bréhier, *Les Idées.*

[282] Stein, *Die allegorische Exegese,* 7-11; Walter, *Der Thoraausleger,* esp. 58-86; 141-9. Others in favour of authenticity are: Schürer, *Geschichte;* Hanson, *Allegory and Event;* Walter, 'Anfänge'; Fraser, *Ptolemaic Alexandria;* Hengel, *Hellenism.*

[283] See Fraser, *Ptolemaic Alexandria* I, 687-716; Sandmel *Philo,* 148-63; Amir, 'Philo Judaeus,' 415; Chadwick, 'St. Paul and Philo of Alexandria'; Borgen, *Bread; id.* 'The Place of the O.T.'; *id.* 'Observations'; Urbach, *Sages* (index s.v. Paul, Philo).

literary tradition within Alexandrian Judaism, he was also the end of it. Apparently, no significant works were produced after him.

Philo remained almost unknown in Jewish tradition until the sixteenth century. It was the Christian Church which preserved and adopted Philo; Byzantine anthologies even cite excerpts of Philo under the heading 'of Philo the Bishop'. Clement of Alexandria, Origen and Ambrose were influenced by Philo in their allegorical exegesis and in their use of such concepts as wisdom, *logos* and faith.[284]

In modern historical research, Philo is studied as a source for Greek philosophy, as a representative of Second Temple Judaism and as a forerunner of early Christian thought. As for the latter, Philo has especially been studied to throw light on the concept of *Logos* in the Gospel of John, on Platonisms in the Epistle to the Hebrews and exegetical techniques and forms used in the New Testament.[285] Finally, Philo's writings reflect a variety of movements within Judaism in the time of the beginnings of Christianity and this observation has thrown light on some of its conflicts and debates, particularly in relation to Judaism and the Hellenistic world.[286]

BIBLIOGRAPHY

The basic edition of the Greek text is the *editio maior* of COHN-WENDLAND. Text and translations are found in COLSON *et al., Philo, Works* (Loeb); ARNALDEZ *et al., Les Oeuvres de Philo d'Alexandrie,* and COHN *et al., Die Werke Philos.* BORGEN and SKARSTEN have produced the machine-readable Greek text of Philo, on the basis of Cohn-Wendland's *editio maior,* supplemented by the Loeb edition. The Armenian text of *De Animalibus,* with a translation and commentary, has been published by TERIAN.

Important tools for the study of Philo are offered by MAYER, *Index Philoneus.* This index does not cover all texts and fragments extant in Greek. All Greek texts are included in BORGEN-SKARSTEN, *KWIC-Concordance.* The basic bibliography of Philo studies is that of GOODHART-GOODENOUGH, 'A Bibliography of Philo', in Goodenough, *The Politics,* which covers work through 1936. For the subsequent period see: FELDMAN, *Scholarship;* HILGERT, 'Bibliography'; *id.,* 'Bibliographia Philoniana 1935-1981', and NAZZARO, *Recenti Studi.* Feldman's bibliography often includes points of evaluation. Nazzaro summarizes the works listed, often

---

[284] See Chadwick, 'Philo'; Bousset, *Schulbetrieb;* Heinisch, *Der Einfluss Philos;* Siegfried, *Philo,* 303-99.

[285] Williamson, *Philo and the Epistle to the Hebrews;* Dodd, *The Interpretation of the Fourth Gospel,* especially 54-73; Borgen, *Bread.* Philo also throws light on other New Testament writings, such as Paul's letters. See especially Chadwick, 'St. Paul and Philo of Alexandria.'

[286] This concerns, e.g., the issue of feasts and circumcision in Jewish Alexandria. See Borgen, 'Observations'; *id.,* 'Paul preaches circumcision'.

rendering comments made by others in reviews etc. See also BORGEN, 'Critical Survey'.

A strong tradition in Philonic research sees anthropological dualism as a key to his thinking. BOUSSET, *Religion,* regarded Philo as a representative of ecstatic mystical piety. WINDISCH, *Frömmigkeit,* laid emphasis on the Platonic form of dualism in Philo's theology and piety. LEISEGANG ('Philon', and *Der Heilige Geist*), interpreted Philo on the basis of Greek mysticism and the mystery religions. With various approaches and emphases, REITZENSTEIN, *Mysterienreligionen*; BRÉHIER, *Idées philosophiques* and PASCHER, *Königsweg,* use Egyptian mystery religion in their interpretation. GOODENOUGH (*Light; Introduction* and *Jewish Symbols*) also interprets Philo against a background of mystery religions. He thought that Philo represented a broad movement within Hellenistic Judaism, in which the Biblical story and Jewish rites were transformed into a mystery religion of its own kind. SANDMEL (*Philo's Place; Philo of Alexandria*), modified Goodenough's view, maintaining that Philo and his associates reflected a marginal, aberrant version of Judaism. MACK, *Logos und Sophia,* interprets Philo largely against the background of Isis-Osiris mythology and Jewish Wisdom traditions.

FRÜCHTEL, *Die kosmologischen Vorstellungen,* interpreted Philo on the basis of Middle Platonism, and regarded Philo's mystical cosmology as a philosophical product developed at the desk. DILLON, *The Middle Platonists,* suggests that Philo essentially adapted contemporary Alexandrian Platonism to his exegetical purposes. WOLFSON's study (*Philo 1-2*), is part of a comprehensive project under the general title 'Structure and Growth of Philosophic Systems from Plato to Spinoza.' For Wolfson Philo's thought is a philosophical derivative of Pharisaic Judaism. VÖLKER, *Fortschritt,* thinks that Philo's writings are primarily expressions of the piety of a devoted Jew. Interpretation of Philo against the background of Gnosticism has been suggested by JONAS, *Gnosis*; KLEIN, *Die Lichtterminologie* and BAER, *Male and Female.*

Among more specialized studies, we may mention: SIEGFRIED, *Philo von Alexandria* and NIKIPROWETZKY, *Le commentaire,* who analyses Philo's exposition of the Scriptures. They pay attention to Jewish as well as Greek elements. So also STEIN, *Die allegorische Exegese* and *Philo und der Midrasch.* More one-sided emphasis on the Greek background of Philo's allegories is placed by HEINEMANN, *Allegoristik*; FRÜCHTEL, *Die kosmologischen Vorstellungen*; CHRISTIANSEN, *Die Technik.*

These different views of Philo's allegory also imply a corresponding difference in understanding Philo's use of Palestinian haggadah and halakhah, and his possible use of common Jewish traditions which were even more widely known. Among scholars who have examined in detail Philo's use of Palestinian traditions are BELKIN, *Philo and the Oral Law* and

RITTER, *Philo und die Halacha.* ALON, *Jews, Judaism and the Classical World,* shows that Philo at times represents a pre-rabbinic halakhah which also existed in Palestine. On the other hand, HEINEMANN, *Philons Bildung* and GOODENOUGH, *Jewish Jurisprudence,* deny that Philo was dependent on common Jewish traditions.

Among the more specific issues taken up by scholars in recent years are GOODENOUGH, *The Politics;* MENDELSON, *Secular Education* and OTTE, *Sprachverständnis.* Among the several studies which illuminate the social and political situation of Alexandrian Jewry are: BLUDAU, *Judenverfolgungen;* WILCKEN, *Antisemitismus;* BELL, *Juden und Griechen;* TCHERIKOVER-FUKS, *Corpus;* TCHERIKOVER, *Hellenistic Civilization* and SMALLWOOD, *The Jews under Roman Rule.*

Sporadic use of Philo is found in New Testament scholarship. More extensive discussion is given by MEEKS, *The Prophet King;* CHADWICK, 'St. Paul and Philo'; *id.* 'Philo and the Beginnings of Christian Thought'; WILLIAMSON, *Philo and the Epistle to the Hebrews;* PEARSON, *Philo and the Gnostics;* BORGEN, *Bread; id.,* 'Observations'; BOUSSET, *Jüdisch-christlicher Schulbetrieb;* HEINISCH, *Der Einfluss Philos* and SIEGFRIED, *Philo von Alexandria,* pp. 303-99.

An important collection of Philo studies, with survey articles, bibliography, and articles on specific issues has been published recently: *Philon und Josephus* (ANRW II, 21/1).

Aristobulus

The texts of the fragments of Aristobulus are found in Eusebius, *Kirchengeschichte,* ed. SCHWARTZ; *Die Praeparatio Evangelica,* ed. MRAS; *Clemens Alexandrinus I: Protrepticus and Paedagogus,* ed. STÄHLIN. The main studies on Aristobulus are the two published by WALTER, 'Anfänge' and *Der Thoraausleger.* He gives a thorough discussion of the authenticity of the fragments and the many problems raised by their quotations from Greek literature. Walter also offers important insights for the understanding of Aristobulus, and his place within (Alexandrian) Judaism.

Chapter Seven

Wisdom Literature

M. Gilbert

Introduction

Wisdom thinking is to be found in all ages and among all peoples. In the complicated experiences of everyday life and all the problems it poses, gifted people who have often remained anonymous, have tried to sift out principles which would lead men to success in existence and to a balanced and harmonious way of life. Further, having found such principles or made such judicious observations, they formulated them in well-turned sayings, easy to memorize and agreeable to hear.

The Bible did not escape this trend. Jer 31:29 and Ezek 18:2, for instance, quoted the popular proverb, 'The fathers have eaten sour grapes, and the children's teeth are set on edge.' Wisdom thinking was everywhere couched in a variety of forms. Along with proverbs, one finds fables, parables, riddles and so on. The Bible too recounts the parable of Nathan (2 Sam 12:1-4), the fables of Jotham (Judg 9:7-15) and of Jehoash (2 Kgs 14:9), the riddle of Samson, 'Out of the eater came something to eat. Out of the strong came something sweet,' (Judg 14:14). Some people had more ability than others. Joseph was able to interpret dreams, Gen 41, and the woman of Tekoa pleaded successfully with David for the return of Absalom, 2 Sam 14:2ff. There was folk wisdom and family lore, as in Tobit 4:5ff. Wisdom was to be the appanage of princes, and in the Bible it is principally Solomon's, the paragon of wise men. A large number of sayings are attributed to him, and perhaps also the composition of onomasticons, lists of plants and animals, 1 Kgs 5:12-13. He is said to have solved the riddles put to him by the queen of Sheba, 1 Kgs 10:1ff.

Solomon played a still more important part in the development of wisdom in Israel. As organizer of the new state, he had to have capable administrators around him, and it is possible that schools or academies were set up for this purpose, to train the flower of the youth adequately, since they were called to take on responsibilities in the city or state. The need for international contacts must also, it seems, have led to Israel's profiting by the wisdom of neighbouring peoples.[1]

---

[1] Contrast the abuse of court wisdom, see Isa 5:21; 29:14; Jer 8:8-9; 9:22-23.

It was also characteristic of the ancient Near East, from the third millenium on, to have assembled sayings and maxims into collections, such as the Instructions of Shuruppak in Sumerian,[2] or those of Ptah-hotep, Meri-ka-Re or Ani in Egypt, or later, towards 1000 B.C.E., Amen-en-Opet there. The influence of this last collection is seen in Prov 22:17-24:22. Other booklets use a structured discourse to develop a more general line of reflection on life, death, suffering and so on. This sometimes occurs within a story. One may note in particular the monologue *Ludlul bel nemeqi,* the Babylonian Job, or the *Pessimistic Dialogue between Master and Servant,* both from Mesopotamia, or, in Egypt, the *Dispute over Suicide* (between a despairing man and his soul) and the *Protests of the Eloquent Peasant* — to mention only some of the more striking.[3]

In this connection, special mention must be made of the *Wisdom of Ahikar.* This court story of pagan origin, containing also a collection of wisdom sayings, was found in an Aramaic papyrus among the writings of the Jewish community of Elephantine (5th century B.C.E.).[4] The story, telling of a conspiracy against the hero by his nephew, and the beginning of its failure (here the Aramaic text stops), may have some historical basis.[5] It had wide repercussions in antiquitiy, especially marked in Tobit,[6] and was translated and adapted in Greek, Syriac and other languages.[7] The original may have been in Akkadian or more probably Aramaic. The wisdom sayings which follow, a hundred and ten in number, are like those found in all ancient collections of the type: they speak of children's education, which should be strict; of the obedience due to the king; the difficulty of personal relationships; of prudence in speech. Some fables are included. The sayings are of pagan origin: the gods Shamash and El being mentioned several times. It is notable that, though the story of Ahikar was of pagan origin, it also circulated among the Jews of Elephantine, and that in the Book of Tobit, Ahikar appears as a Jew.[8]

WISDOM LITERATURE IN THE HEBREW BIBLE

Israel likewise made collections of its traditional wisdom and produced works of very great quality. We shall follow the story of these books down to the period with which we are concerned in these pages.

The Book of Proverbs contains many collections of sayings, mostly in the form of couplets or quatrains, coming from various periods and various

---

[2] Alster, *Instructions of Šuruppak;* Cazelles, 'Nouvelles études.'
[3] Pritchard, *ANET,* 405-40; Lambert, *Babylonian Wisdom;* Fox, 'Two Decades.'
[4] Cowley, *Aramaic Papyri,* 204-48; Grelot, *Documents araméens,* 429-52.
[5] See Van Dijk, 'Tontafelfunde', 217.
[6] See below, n. 134 and Greenfield, 'Ahiqar in the Book of Tobit.'
[7] See Denis, *Introduction,* 210-14.
[8] In Tob 1:22, Ahikar becomes Tobit's own nephew.

backgrounds. The first collection, 10:1-22:16, assembles proverbs attributed directly to Solomon. Their authenticity is doubtful. The second, 25-29, contains 'proverbs of Solomon' said to have been collected by 'the men of Hezekiah'. Other collections come from wise men, 22:17-24:22, which are said to be influenced by the wisdom of Amen-en-Opet; 24:23-34.[9] Two other collections are not of Israelite origin, the words of Agur, 30:1-14 and the words of Lemuel 'which his mother taught him' 31:1-9. In addition, there is a group of numerical proverbs, 30:15-31. All these sayings are concerned with everyday life, the family, life in society, work, the court and relations with God. The final redaction of all these collections, however, probably took place soon after the Babylonian exile. The editors added an introduction, 1-9, where the disciple is strongly urged to listen carefully to the wisdom teacher, who warns him in particular to avoid bad companions and 'the strange woman.' The same editors are probably responsible for the final poem on the mistress of the house, 31:10-31. Proverbs seems to have been used by the wise men of later times. Its influence on Ben Sira can be felt[10] and, less clearly, on Wisdom.[11] Prov 8 in particular reappears in modified form in Sir 24 and Wis 7-9, with certain perspectives enlarged.[12] The Greek version of Proverbs seems to be a rather free translation, adding about a hundred and thirty lines, either from a paraenetic perspective or in an effort to show the Greek reader the meaning or the moral application of the text.[13]

Unlike Proverbs, the Book of Job, which is said to date from the middle of the fifth century B.C.E., is the work of one single genius, even though it is agreed that important additions have been made to his work. The main theme is that of the just man suffering. Job, conscious of his innocence, goes so far as to accuse God, whom he blames for his unjust sufferings. Finally, 'out of the whirlwind' 38:1, God intervenes, to remind Job of the limits of man's knowledge and power. Shaken, Job bows and remains silent.[14] This masterly work is one of the loftiest literary achievements of mankind. It gives Israel's view of a universal problem and

---

[9] Marzal, *Enseñanza de Amenemope*, 42-67.

[10] Duesberg, *Scribes inspirés*, 706-11.

[11] Larcher, *Etudes*, 97-9.

[12] Sir 24:9 depends on Prov 8:23, but in Wis 7:21; 8:6, the term τεχνῖτις, artisan, chooses to interpret the Hebrew word אמון of Prov 8:30 in a way which attributes an active part to Wisdom in creation.

[13] Gerleman, 'Septuagint Proverbs' and *Studies*, maintains that the translator had some Stoic influences; see McKane, *Proverbs*, 33-5.

[14] The plan of the book as it stands is as follows: Prologue, in prose. Once happy, Job falls into misery (1-2); Job's initial lament (3); first cycle: the three friends speak out one after another and Job answers each in turn (4-14); second cycle: the same (15-21); third cycle (incomplete and corrupt; 22-27); interpolation: hymn on the inaccessible nature of Wisdom (28); Job's final apologia (29-31); interpolation: Elihu's discourse (32-37); two-fold theophanic discourse of the Lord and two-fold answer of Job (38:1-42:6); prose epilogue: Job is restored to his prosperity (42:7-17).

preserves its universal character, since Job is not an Israelite. The Septuagint Greek version, made probably before 100 B.C.E.,[15] is a very free rendering of the original Hebrew. The translator seems to have aimed at a circle of cultivated readers and not the official reading of the synagogue.[16] Fragments of a *targum* on Job were found at Qumran.[17] The text follows rather closely the original Hebrew. Finally, the *Testament of Job* (see pp. 349ff.) looks like a *midrash* on the biblical book. It recounts the life and death of Job.[18]

The short book of Qohelet (Ecclesiastes), which is most often dated to the third century B.C.E., is one of the most modern of the Bible in the tone it takes, and the existential questions it raises. Its general thesis is that 'all is vanity.' In spite of what the wise men said, the order and meaning of things, and of life itself, are beyond the limits of human reason. There is no agreement about plan, language, unity of authorship. As to foreign influences, some scholars refer to Mesopotamian[19] and others to Greek sources.[20] Qohelet has left few traces in the period we are concerned with, apart from the discussion of its status at Jamnia. Some fragments of the Hebrew text were found at Qumran,[21] but it is never quoted in the documents of the community. Likewise, it is not quoted in Ben Sira, Wisdom, by Philo or in the New Testament. The dating and nature of the Greek version found in the Septuagint have been subject to debate.[22] The book is also quoted by the Tannaim,[23] who generally interpret it in terms of morality

---

[15] Alexander Polyhistor (80-40 B.C.E.) quotes the Septuagint addition after Job 42:17.

[16] Notably, many passages, coming to about six hundred lines, are not translated, increasingly, so as the book goes on. In Job 22-31 there are gaps of twenty-five percent; in Job 32-38, thirty-five percent; see Dhorme, *Job*, CLVII-CLXII. These gaps were filled by Origen on the basis of Theodotion's version.

[17] Van der Ploeg-Van der Woude, *Targum de Job;* Sokoloff, *Targum to Job;* Jongeling *et al., Aramaic Texts.*

[18] See Denis, *Introduction*, 100-4; Brock, *Testamentum Iobi;* Schaller, *Testament Hiobs;* Nicholls, *Structure and Purpose.*

[19] Loretz, *Qohelet.*

[20] Braun, *Kohelet.*

[21] 4QQoh^a-d: Qoh 5:13-17; 6:3-8; 7:1-9, 19-20.

[22] Barthélemy, *Devanciers d'Aquila*, 21-33, 158f, attributes it to Aquila, at the request of the Jamnia assembly or of Akiba himself. This view is questioned by Grabbe, 'Aquila's Translation'. Di Fonzo, *Ecclesiaste*, 95, dates the Greek version to the years 150-130 B.C.E. According to Bertram, 'Hebräischer und griechischer Qohelet', the vanity and futility of human effort, according to the Hebrew, becomes in this version the frivolity and capriciousness of the human spirit and its consequent estrangement from God.

[23] Hillel the Elder (*T. Berakhoth* 2:21 — Qoh 3:4a, 5b), Akabya ben Mahalaleel (*P.T. Sotah* 2, 18a — Qoh 12:1), R. Eliezer (*B.T. Shabbath* 153a — Qoh 9:8; *B.T. Erubin* 40b — Qoh 11:2), R. Ishmael (*Sifre Deut.* 129 (p. 262) — Qoh 9:12; *P.T. Shabbath* 14, 14d — Qoh 10:8); R. Meir (*P.T. Ketuboth* 7, 31b — Qoh 7:2; *P.T. Nedarim* 1, 36d, *B.T. Nedarim* 9a, *T. Hullin* 2:17 — Qoh 5:4), R. Judah ha-Nasi (*B.T. Nedarim* 9a, *T. Hullin* 2:17 — Qoh 5:4), R. Nathan (*Mekhilta Kaspa* 20, p. 327 — Qoh 7:26).

and ascetism, not history.[24] Authorship is attributed to Solomon by some second century Tannaim.[25] Melito is the first Christian, at about 170 C.E., to mention Qohelet among the canonical books. He had found a list of them in Palestine.[26]

Some psalms, called 'wisdom' or 'didactic' psalms, may be added to these three books of the wisdom literature of the Hebrew Bible. Just which psalms they are is disputed, because of the great difficulty of determining the literary genre.[27] The psalms which celebrate the Torah may be included, (Pss 1; 19b; 119), like those which simply give instruction (Pss 37; 91; 112; 127), or those which reflect on humanity's lot, (Pss 49; 73, which has been likened to Job,[28] and 90). They confirm that wisdom thinking in the Bible is not confined to the three books of wisdom literature.

THE CONCEPT OF WISDOM

In the course of time, and under various influences, the notion of wisdom took on diverse shades of meaning. A gradual evolution is already perceptible in the Hebrew Bible, even if it is difficult to determine the exact chronological order of the changes. Ancient proverbs were already aware of the limits of all human wisdom (Prov 16:1, 2, 9; 19:14, 21), while God appears more and more clearly as the supremely Wise, in his work of creation (Ps 104:24; Jer 10:12) as in his guidance of history (Isa 31:1-2; Job 12:13). It is he who bestows wisdom on man (Gen 41:16, 39; Exod 31:1-11; 35:30-35; Dan 1:7; 5:14), and primarily on the king (Isa 11:2), in the wake of Solomon (1 Kgs 3:4-15; 2 Chr 1:7-12). For only 'God understands the way to it, . . . he saw it . . . and searched it out' (Job 28:23, 27).[29]

Wisdom is also personified: see Prov 1:20-33; 8; 9:1-6, and particularly Prov 8.[30] Wisdom, addressing the crowd, praises the honesty of her words, her role in the just social order and her presence beside the Lord, from whom she came forth, while he was organizing the world. She is the eldest daughter of God, and her delight is to be with men. How is this personification of wisdom to be understood? This is related to the broader question of intermediaries between God and the world. This figure of Wisdom is a

---

[24] There is only one messianic interpretation which appears at the end of the second century, dealing with Qoh 12:1b (*B.T. Shabbath* 151b: Simeon ben Eleazar).

[25] R. Simeon ben Menasya (*T. Yadaim* 2:14; *B.T. Megillah* 7a), R. Eliezer (*B.T. Shabbath* 152b), R. Simeon ben Eleazar (*B.T. Shabbath* 151b).

[26] See Eusebius, *Hist. Eccles.* 4:26,14. After 192 C.E., Clement of Alexandria gives the first two quotations from it, which he does from the Greek version contained in the Septuagint. He also considered it an inspired book. See *Stromata,* 1:13,58 — Qoh 1:16b, 17b, 18a; 12b.

[27] See Luyten, 'Psalm 73 and Wisdom', 59-64, who also discussed the relation to worship of these psalms.

[28] Luyten, 'Psalm 73 and Wisdom', 73-80.

[29] Zerafa, *Wisdom of God.*

[30] Gilbert, *La Sagesse de l'Ancien Testament,* 202-18.

purely literary personificaton according to some, which is a minimalistic view. Others have spoken of hypostasis, a vague notion,[31] while yet others speak of a personification of the order of the world, the source of which is in God.[32] Finally, others speak of the presence of God in the world and among men. At the origin of this personification, traces of certain myths can be detected. The Egyptian goddess Maat is similar in some respects,[33] and perhaps also the myth of the *Urmensch* (Primordial Man) of which Ezek 28:1-19 preserves traces. Alternatively, the personification could go back also to an ancient form of myth to be found in *Ethiopian Enoch* 42, where Wisdom is said to have descended from heaven, to dwell among men. Finding no welcome, she returns to God's side.[34]

In various forms, from the end of the biblical era on, there are texts pointing out that for Israel the Torah is authentic wisdom, Israel's wisdom (Deut 4:6; Jer 8:8; Ezra 7:14 compared to 7:25). Later, from Sir 24:23 and Bar 4:1-4 on, the Torah definitely appears as the Wisdom entrusted by God to Israel; it is the privileged expression of God's own Wisdom. In rabbinical writings, the close similarity has become standard. The master interpreters of the Torah and guides of the people are henceforth known as the Sages (*Hakhamim*).

Consequently, the scope of the investigations of the teachers of wisdom was gradually widened in the post-bliblical period. Their interest was no longer confined to the universal. It also took in all that went to make up Israel's own inheritance including its religious history. Thus similarities between Prov 1-9 and Deuteronomy or the prophets Isaiah and Jeremiah have been noted.[35] Sir 44-50 explicitly praises the men of old and Wis 10-19 is mainly concerned with re-interpreting the events of the exodus, as also Wis 7-9 the exploits of Solomon.

Indeed, the figure of Solomon, based on 1 Kgs 3:4-15 (the dream at Gibeon), 5:9-14 (his culture), 10:1-13 (his meeting with the queen of Sheba), always remained a vivid memory in the types of wisdom current in the period after the Hebrew Bible, where Proverbs, Canticles and Qohelet are already attributed to him. He is and remains the wise man *par excellence*. The book of Wisdom takes him explicitly as its patron and three chapters, chs. 7-9, are inspired by the older tradition concerning him. The same elements of 1 Kings were also given other interpretations. Flavius Josephus recounts traditions from Phoenicia and elsewhere which tell of Solomon's skill in solving riddles.[36] He even notes the fame of Solomon as

---

[31] See von Rad, *Weisheit,* 189, 192-3; Wilckens, 'Sophia', 508; Larcher, *Etudes,* 338-9, 399.

[32] Von Rad, *Weisheit,* 193-4, 204-5.

[33] Kayatz, *Studien zu Proverbien;* von Rad, *Weisheit,* 199-200, 218, 226.

[34] See Schlüsser-Fiorenza, 'Wisdom Mythology,' 26-33; Wilcken, 'Sophia,' 508-9.

[35] Robert, 'Attaches littéraires.'

[36] *Ag. Ap.* 1:111-20; *Ant.* 8:144-9.

an exorcist.[37] The name of Solomon also figures in the Graeco-Roman magical papyri, and even at Qumran.[38]

ENCOUNTER WITH GREEK WISDOM

The meeting of Judaism with Greek culture was to enrich wisdom even more.[39] In the Seven Sages of ancient Greece, wisdom already appears as above all a design for living marked by poise and an ability to pronounce judiciously on the problems of politics as well as on those of everyday life. Socrates claims nobility for wisdom against the Sophists, on account of its being divine. But he also affirms man's need to become its friend through the practice of virtue. With Plato, wisdom is reduced to the domain of the intellectual, since it leads through contemplation to intuitive knowledge of the divine Forms, in particular the Form of the Good and of the Beautiful. Aristotle for his part distinguishes wisdom (σοφία), which, as knowledge of first causes and principles, is to be identified with philosophy, from practical wisdom or prudence (φρόνησις), which recalls the characteristics of ancient wisdom. After Aristotle, it was the Stoics mainly who were interested in wisdom. For them, it was 'the science of things human and divine'.[39a] It is identified with the all-pervading *Logos* and for man it is an ideal which he can attain by the practice of philosophy and virtues. This ideal wisdom, the one and only virtue in fact, is realized, according to the Stoics, in the person of the wise man, whose famous paradoxes they enunciate. But the difficulty of attaining this perfect wisdom led the Stoics to devote themselves more and more to *phronesis,* the practical wisdom which is the fruit of virtue.

Wisdom, as defined in Greek philosophy, had an influence on Hellenistic Judaism, mainly seen in the Wisdom of Solomon[40] and in Philo's reflections on wisdom. In addition, Hellenism had also made a mythical figure of wisdom. *Sophia* was identified with the goddess Athena, regarded as a universal principle. Other speculations saw in it the mother of the gods, the soul of the world and so on. It seems very likely that Philo's reflections draw their inspiration in part from such speculations.[41]

Finally, Greek wisdom was also expressed in gnomic form, as early as the Seven Sages.[42] This literary form is found in Hellenistic Judaism, in the

---

[37] *Ant.* 8: 44-48.
[38] See Preisendanz, *Papyri graecae magicae* I, 102, 170; 2, 198, 206, etc.; Van der Ploeg, 'Petit rouleau', 130f.; Denis, *Introduction,* 64-6; Lohse, 'Solomon,' 463. One would be slow to see in Wis 7:17-21 allusions to occult sciences; see Larcher, *Etudes,* 193-201.
[39] See Wilcken, 'Sophia,' 467-74; Larcher, *Etudes,* 350-4.
[39a] Von Arnim, *Fragmenta* 2, p. 15, n. 35-36. See also 4 Macc 1:16.
[40] See Larcher, *Etudes,* 356-61.
[41] See Leisengang, 'Sophia,' 1026-31; Larcher, *Etudes,* 354-6.
[42] See Küchler, *Frühjüdische Weisheitstraditionen,* 236-61.

Sayings of Phocylides, and even in the collection of originally pagan *Sentences of Sextus* which was taken up by early Christianity.

Wisdom of Ben Sira

The work of Ben Sira has reached us in a state of disorder which scholars have not yet fully cleared up. He wrote in Hebrew, but his work was mainly preserved in Greek, Latin and Syriac translations. The Hebrew text has been recovered bit by bit, and we now have about two thirds of it.

The Hebrew fragments are in three groups:

1. Some were found at Qumran, and therefore date from before 69 C.E.[43] and some at Masada, from before 73 C.E.[44]

2. Fragments of five manuscripts from about the 11th century were found in 1896 in the Genizah of the Karaite synagogue in Cairo. They came into various hands, and were published one after another with the sigla A, B, C, D, E.[45] Some commentators thought they were merely a re-translation back into Hebrew from some Greek or Syriac versions, but this is now generally ruled out. The following episode may throw light on their history. Timothy I, Patriarch of Seleucia, tells in a letter dated about 800 C.E. that a group of manuscripts had been found some ten years earlier in a cave near Jericho, containing some Old Testament books and other Hebrew works. Could they have included a Hebrew text of Ben Sira, the archetype of the manuscripts found at Cairo in 1896? The idea is no more than plausible.[46]

3. There are quotations in the works of the Tannaim, the Amoraim and other later Jewish autorities. More recent quotations are in Saadya, 10th century C.E.[47]

The Greek translation is in two forms.[48]

1. There is a shorter text in the great uncials, Sinaiticus, Vaticanus and Alexandrinus.[49]

2. There is a longer text mainly preserved through minuscule 248.[50]

---

[43] 2Q18 (*DJD* 3, 75) — Sir 1:19-20; 6:14-15, 19-31; 11QPs^a (Sanders, *Psalms Scroll,* 79-85) — Sir 51:13, 20b, 30b; see below p. 559.

[44] Sir 39:27-32; 40:10-19, 26-30; 41:1-44:71; ed. Yadin, *Ben Sira Scroll.*

[45] See Levi, *Hebrew Text;* Di Lella, 'Recently Identified Leaves.'

[46] See Di Lella, *Hebrew Text,* 81-91.

[47] See Schechter, 'Quotations'; Cowley-Neubauer, *Original Hebrew,* XIX-XXX; Segal, *Sefer ben Sira,* 45.

[48] All MSS. of the Greek translation change the order of the following chapters: 30:25-33:13a in the Hebrew become 33:16b-36:10a in the Greek; 33:13b-36:16a in the Hebrew become 30:25-33:16a in the Greek. The Hebrew sequence, which is confirmed by the Vetus Latina and the Syriac versions, is the right one.

[49] In Ziegler's edition of *Sapientia Iesu filii,* which is followed here, the numbering of the verses includes the additions of the longer Greek text; see below. The Vetus Latina, see below, which adds still more to the text, numbers the verses differently.

[50] See the edition of MS 248 by Hart, *Ecclesiasticus.*

The version called the Vetus Latina seems to have been made in Africa, by Christians, the second half of the second century C.E. It contained only chapters 1-43 and 51. Other translators completed it later with the prologue and the 'Praise of Famous Men' 44-50. This version, which is close to the longer Greek text, was adopted into the Vulgate in the fifth century.[51]

The Syriac Peshitta version, finally, seems to have been based on a Hebrew text, and also made by a second century Christian.[52]

Studies of these witnesses have not yet produced a clear and complete idea of the history of the text. But agreement seems to have been reached about the following points:

1. Ben Sira wrote in Hebrew, at Jerusalem (Sir 50:27), 190 B.C.E. For it is probable that Sir 50:1-24 was written in praise of the high priest Simon II, who held office when Antiochus III entered Jerusalem in 198 B.C.E. And there is no hint in the work that the great crisis of the years 167-64 had taken place. This text, called Hebrew I, is supposed to be the archetype of the Qumran and Masada manuscripts.

2. In 132 B.C.E. Ben Sira's grandson, living in Egypt, undertook a Greek translation, which is given in the great uncials. This follows from the fact that the prologue with which the text begins in these manuscripts says, v. 27, that the translation was begun in the thirty-eighth year of the late King Euergetes.[53]

3. Between 50 B.C.E. and 150 C.E.[54] the Hebrew text underwent changes, some deliberate and some not, which included additions here and there. The Cairo manuscripts, especially A, contain numerous doublets which could to some extent reflect this new stage of the text, called Hebrew II. The Peshitta seems to have been based on it.

4. A second Greek translation, 'Greek II', made between 150 and 200 C.E., seems to have been based on the new Hebrew text. It is quoted by Clement of Alexandria some time before 215.[55] But it does not seem that this new translation was preserved intact. The Greek manuscripts with the long text, especially 248, really give, many think, Greek text I, with passages added from Greek II.[56] In fact the Vetus Latina seems to be the best witness for this new Greek II. When Cyprian quotes Ben Sira he follows the Vetus Latina.[57] Finally this last version itself adds in here and there some pieces which show Christian influence.

---

[51] See the edition *Sapientia Salomonis/Liber Hiesu Filii Sirach* (Biblia Sacra iuxta latinam Vulgatam versionem ad codicum fidem 12) Roma 1964. Following his principle of the *veritas hebraica,* Jerome did not himself translate Ben Sira into Latin, though he had in his possession a Hebrew text of the book (*PL* 28, 1242).

[52] Edition Lagarde, *Libri VT apocryphi syriace.*

[53] This is generally taken to mean Ptolemy VIII, 170-116 B.C.E.

[54] Maybe even earlier; see Skehan, Review of Rüger, *Text und Textform,* p. 274.

[55] He quotes, for instance, Sir 1:21a, 22a; 19:5b; 26:22.

[56] So Ziegler's edition.

[57] See below, p. 301.

One concludes, therefore, that great prudence is needed when speaking of the text of Ben Sira. One can really only rely on Hebrew text I and Greek text I. Hebrew text II, Greek text II and the Vetus Latina have to be read in their original perspective, which will have to be defined (see pp. 298-300 below).

AUTHOR

Ben Sira's name is Yeshua, Jesus (Prologue 7; 50:27; 51:30), whose father was Eleazar, a Jerusalemite (50:27); he was married and had children and grandchildren, one of the latter being the translator of his work into Greek. He was eminent in Jerusalem society, a counsellor of the government (39:4) who travelled abroad frequently (34:12; 39:4). These travels sometimes brought him into danger, but his fear of the Lord always proved his salvation (34:13-17). And he learned much about men from these travels (34:9-11; 39:4). He was a scribe, and proud of his profession (39:1). Much of his time was given over to reading and meditating on the Torah, the Prophets and the Writings (Prologue 7-11; 39:1-3). He probably took up teaching in his concern to transmit his experiences and later (Prologue 7, 12) started to write or assemble his notes. He was aware that he was the last to represent a great tradition (33:16), and even considered himself a successor of the prophets (24:33). His one aim was to hand on what he had himself learned to future generations at home and abroad.

COMPOSITION AND STRUCTURE

Following the classical tradition of Hebrew poetry, Ben Sira often makes use of parallelism in a verse. And he seems only to have written in couplets.[58] Treatment of subjects varies in length, sometimes only one couplet (11:1-3), sometimes two (11:4, 5-6; 43:9-10, 11-12; 50:25-26). Mostly, however, paragraphs are lengthened to meet the needs of the subject and reflections on it. Paragraphs sometimes link up: a two-fold prayer for prudence in speaking and for avoidance of sensuality is followed by instruction on the right use of words and the wrong use of the body by men and by women (22:27-23:27). Judgment is needed in choosing a wife, a friend and an adviser (36:23-37:15). Trades using manual labour cannot be combined with the craft of the scribe (38:24-39:11). Two clearly marked units stand out at the end of the book: one on the works of God in the world (42:15-43:33), the other the 'Praise of Famous Men' (44:1-49:16), to which is added the description of the high priest Simon (50:1-21).

Did Ben Sira follow a plan? There is nothing to suggest this, so far. There are no doubt several passages on wisdom (1:1-10; 4:11-19; 6:18-37;

---

[58] Rickenbacher, *Weisheitsperikopen*, 130-1.

292

14:20-15:10; 24:1-34), which seem to mark stresses in the first part of the collection. But they have no perceptible influence on the passages which precede or follow them. Then, at 24:30-34, the author seems to be about to end by speaking about himself, while at 33:16-18 he speaks again of himself in a similar fashion. This has led some to think that Ben Sira's work came in stages. The first might have been when he put together chs. 1 to 24 in an order which escapes us. He might then have added in successive stages 25:1-33:18, then 33:19-42:14; 42:15-49:16, and finally ch. 50. But this is only a hypothesis.[59]

SUBJECTS

The book, usually called Ecclesiasticus or 'The Wisdom of Jesus the Son of Sirach' after its title and the inscription at the end, begins with the words, 'All wisdom comes from the Lord and is with him for ever' (1:1). This is a key text. It indicates that the term 'wisdom' is ambivalent. Man's wisdom comes from God and not from man himself. But wisdom, which is not a purely human quality, abides in God. So Ben Sira, along with Prov 8 and Job 28 (and later Bar 3:9-4:4), considers that wisdom cannot be mentioned without its being referred to God. This he does to begin with (1:1-10) and again further on, in the middle of the book (24). Other passages tell how wisdom is acquired (especially 4:11-19; 6:18-37; 14:20-15:10) or describe the wise man (24:30-34; 37:16-26; 39:1-11).

More clearly than previous writers in the Bible (Isa 31:1; Job 12:13), Ben Sira affirms that the Lord is wise, that he is indeed the only wise being (1:8-9). While Job 28:27 said that the Lord had seen and assessed the value of wisdom when he created the world, Ben Sira insists that wisdom was created by the Lord before all things (1:4, 9; 24:8-9). He affirms (1:9-10), more definitely than Prov 8:27-30a, Jer 10:12 and Ps 104:24, that the Lord poured it out on all his works and even on all flesh, like the Spirit according to Joel 3:1. Wisdom, as the Word, came from the mouth of God (24:3). Having governed the world and all humanity (24:4-6), it settled in Israel at the Creator's command (24:7-8; see Bar 3:37-38). Implanted in the sanctuary of Zion, it gradually grew, like the tree of life, to the size of the people of God itself, to which it gives itself as food and drink (24:10-22). Ben Sira sees the Torah, God's revelation to his people, coming through his deeds as much as his words, as the supreme expression of wisdom (24:23). It is like the glorious terebinth and the fruitful vine (24:16-17), which are elsewhere figures of Israel (Isa 5:1-7; 6:13).

How does the wise man acquire wisdom? Wisdom rears its children like a mother (4:11). Its method is severe and demanding, since it tries out the

---

[59] See Segal, *Sefer Ben Sira,* who finds quite a regular structure; Roth, 'Gnomic-Discursive Wisdom'; Beentjes, 'Recent Publications.'

docility of its people (4:17-18). Anyone who abandons it will find himself abandoned by it (4:19). The fool will find it too demanding and will not adhere to it (6:20-22). It has to be sought the way the hunter waits for and pursues his prey or as the lover watches and approaches the beloved till he possesses her (6:26-28; 14:22-25). Men must live under its shadow (14:26) and accept its yoke (16:24-25), which will become as splendid an ornament as that of the high priest (6:29-31).

These symbols are mainly to show the relation between wisdom and the one who seeks it, which is love. But for Ben Sira, one enters gradually into possession of wisdom. Perseverance and tenacity are required. This means in point of fact listening to the wise men and long meditation on the Torah and its precepts, to appreciate their value and make them one's own (6:37). This is the work and achievement of the wise man (39:1-3).

He must also be a man of prayer. From morning on, he turns to the Lord and entreats him (39:5; see Isa 50:4-5; Wis 16:28). This will make him pleasing to God. He will acquire wisdom and be capable of communicating it (39:6-8), which is anyway his duty (37:23). But then he must be more than just an orator or a teacher who does not match deeds to words (37:19-22).[60] When giving his teaching, the wise man knows that he is only a channel for the water which leads to paradise (24:31). His work is a service, but when he is writing down his doctrine, he is working for future generations and other lands (24:32-34; 33:18). His reward is to be honoured during his life and after his death (37:24-26; 39:9-11).

FEAR OF THE LORD. Ben Sira often speaks of this, and even devotes one of his first paragraphs to it (1:11-2:18)[61] and the tailpiece of the Hebrew, 50:29, sums up by saying, 'For the fear of the Lord is life.' The subject is so important that some have thought it was the key to the book.[62] But the central theme is indeed wisdom. The older wisdom teachers said that the fear of the Lord was the beginning of wisdom (Prov 1:7; 9:10). This is repeated by Ben Sira (1:14), but he adds that it is the fullness of wisdom (1:16) and its crown (1:18). There is no wisdom, then, without fear of the Lord, which means that for Ben Sira wisdom is in the religious and not in the merely secular order. Wisdom and fear of the Lord are in a way identified (1:27) but this involves accepting and fulfilling the Torah (19:20; 21:11), since fear of the Lord is shown and practised by welcoming the Torah (1:15-16; 23:27), so that all wisdom implies doing the Torah (19:20; 33:2). Such is the life of the wise (1:26; 6:37). Understood in this way, fear of the Lord is the greatest good (25:10-11; 40:26-27). No doubt one who fears the Lord must expect trials (2:1-18), but he will live serenely

---

[60] Ben Sira asks God to purify his tongue and the desires of his heart (22:27-23:6), before giving his doctrine on the faults of the tongue and sensuality.
[61] The fear of the Lord is no longer mentioned in 42:15-50:26.
[62] Haspecker, *Gottesfurcht.*

(34:9-20). Ben Sira is sure that he who fears the Lord deserves to be honoured (10:19-25), finds life joyful (1:12) and enjoys the affection of his friends (6:15-17). He also insists on the interior values of fear of the Lord. It is marked by confidence (2:6-11), love (2:15-16) in the Lord, abandonment to his will and flight from sin (1:27-30; 32:14-16). In short, man before God is characterized by fear of the Lord.

TORAH. Ben Sira often invites his disciples to observe the Torah and carry out its precepts, which is the way true fear of the Lord is shown and true wisdom gained or preserved. But he shows little interest in the details of the precepts or in specifying them. When he comments on the precept of showing respect to parents, he does not mention the Torah (3:1-16). But he does so when he urges his listeners to give the priest his due share (7:31), to avoid rancour (28:7), to help the poor (29:9), or not to come empty-handed before the Lord (35:6-7). Still, it cannot be said that all his teaching is based on the Torah. It would be more correct to say that he reads the Torah with the eyes of the wise man. Here Sir 24 is fundamental. Ben Sira recognizes the Torah, now in book form (24:23), as expressing God's wisdom. As the efficacious word of God, it governs the universe, is implanted in Jacob and radiates from the temple all over the land. It grows like a luxuriant plantation, giving itself to its own, who find in it their food. The Torah seems to be precisely the privileged expression of God's work in creation and history. The precepts which it bids men make their own are their means of entering this great current and of responding by their works to the work of God. In this sense, the Torah is God's wisdom offered to his people. Hence the wise man meditates on the Torah (Prologue 8; Sir 39:1). The great events brought about by God in human history go to enrich the wise man's reflections, in a sort of philosophy of history (see especially 44-49, but also 16:7-10; 16:26-17:14). As to the precepts, on which Ben Sira has little to say, it is wise to observe them. This is even to give God his due worship (35:1). He thus carries on a tradition seen as early as Deut 4:6-8; Ezra 7:14, 24; and which was to be maintained later in Judaism: the Torah — that is wisdom (cf. above, pp. 287f.).

WORSHIP. Ben Sira takes great interest in this. One has only to read again the description of the high priest Simon (50) to see how much our bourgeois sage admires the liturgy. When he reviews the heroes of the past, he stays longest with Aaron, describing with relish the magnificence of his liturgical trappings, and the eternal covenant made with his descendants (45:6-22). But Ben Sira's reflections take in more than praise. He insists on the need of making the moral life, even on the social plane, correspond to the liturgical act of sacrifice (34:21-35:26). It is mockery to use ill-acquired goods in sacrifices (34:21). No one should 'offer the Lord a bribe' (35:14). But to keep the Torah and be charitable is the same as making an offering

(35:1, 4). Going still further, Ben Sira explains in ch. 24 that God's wisdom, which he identifies with the Torah, is itself performing a liturgical action. It rises up like incense to God and penetrates its disciples, consecrating them as do the sacred oils (24:15). To serve wisdom is therefore to serve in the sanctuary (4:14).

NATURE. Ben Sira often speaks of the world, but more often of history and humanity. The 'Praise of Famous Men' (44-49) is preceded by a passage on nature (42:15-43:33), where Ben Sira praises the Lord for his created works. These are enumerated on the ancient catalogue system (Gen 2:19-20; 1 Kgs 5:13; Job 38-39), but he uses it to disclose in them the glory of their creator, which their mystery cannot hide from the wise. As works of God, they remain impenetrable. When Ben Sira tries to show the dimensions of man's liberty, so that God is not made responsible for evil or man a slave to determinism, he appeals to the work of God in the beginning, the creation of the world and of man (16:26-17:14). But he has more to add. From the start of his book, he insists that the Lord, the only one who is wise, has poured out in his generosity wisdom on all his works and on all flesh (1:9-10). He shows more explicitly, ch. 24, that wisdom governs all creation before being commanded by God to settle in Israel. Now, according to Ben Sira, the fullness of wisdom's activity is what one finds expressed in the Torah, and this is then the perfect expression of the order of the cosmos (chap. 24; Prov 8:22-31 laid the groundwork for this assertion). Finally, in 39:12-35, Ben Sira notes the ambivalence of the cosmic works of the Lord. There is no trace of dualism in the elements of the world, but they end up differently. Some bring deliverance, others punishment. The real split is on the human level, man being responsible for the evil he does. In themselves 'the works of the Lord are all good' (39:33). From all these passages, as also from 33:7-15, it is clear that when Ben Sira has recourse to the cosmic work of God it is to throw light on the questions which man puts to himself about himself and about God.[63]

HISTORY. When Ben Sira takes up events in Israel's own traditions, the first wisdom teacher to do so, it is from the wise man's viewpoint. The whole development of Israel's religious history, seen under the aspect of God's gracious offer, is above all the work of wisdom, which was extended to take in the whole people among whom the Lord had commanded it to settle (24). Then, Ben Sira argues firmly from certain episodes taken from the Pentateuch (see 16:6-10). He does not shrink from re-interpreting (17:11-14) the events of Sinai and the gift of the Torah[64] in the light of creation, in order to remind his disciples of man's moral responsibility. It is

[63] See Prato, *Problema della teodicea.*
[64] The Greek, however, mentions an 'eternal covenant', 17:12; see also 45:5.

in chs. 44-49, however, that Ben Sira appears as the most ancient representative in Israel of a type of literature found later to some extent in 1 Macc 2:51-64 and Wis 10. This is the 'Praise of Famous Men', which gives a survey of the great heroes of the Bible. The main thing which strikes one in these chapters is that Ben Sira while following the chronological order of these persons (down to Nehemiah, though with Adam to close the series), seems to rely on the Bible as an established canon. Thus the twelve prophets are mentioned at 49:10. Further, he does not praise so much God's action in them and through them as the men themselves, whom he sees as giants, examples often worth propounding and imitating by the wise man. There are no doubt depraved characters among them, of whom he speaks frankly, like the Bible itself. Some examples are not to be followed, like that of Solomon. No other thread can be seen to run through this historical retrospect. The covenant is not used to justify the choice of the persons spoken of. At most, one could note some insistence on Aaron and Phinehas, that is, on the sacerdotal tradition; but Ezra is not mentioned. In fact, the survey simply follows the historical sequence of patriarchs, prophets, kings and so on. This is because, except for some special cases, all are worthy of the admiration of the wise.

SOCIETY. Ben Sira, in magisterial command of wisdom, writes down what he thinks will be of help to young people from well-off and cultured families, to prepare them to take their place in society. Indeed, social relations take up much of the book. He dwells first on the family. With the decalogue, he teaches that parents must be respected (3:1-16). Women are spoken of mainly in terms of marriage. Ben Sira sees only the wife, rarely the mother, and says nothing about the husband's having to love and respect his wife. At the most, he sincerely admires harmony between wife and husband (25:1). He only speaks about marriage from the man's point of view. He is addressing young men, no doubt, but his attitude seems to have been conditioned to some extent by the pattern of family life in his time, where the husband was always the master. He insists that the wife should be carefully chosen. She must be sensible (25:8), educated and reserved (26:14-15), especially when speaking (36:28), but Ben Sira has nothing to say about her religious virtues. A good wife is important (26:1-4; 36:26-31) because the husband runs risks from other women, even other wives (9:1-9; 26:9-12; 42:12-14). The husband is therefore regarded as a frail creature, and if his marriage turns out badly, he is miserable. But it seems as though the main cause of breakdown is the bad choice of a wife (25:13-26; 26:5-8). Ben Sira's teaching shows a man jealous of his independence and authority (33:20-24). He is keen on education and reserve. He is for a strict upbringing of children, such as was then usual (7:23; 30:1-13). It is a much greater risk to have a daughter than a son (7:24-25; 22:3-6; 42:9-11). With household slaves one must be severe but just

(33:25-33). He is strongly in favour of friendship (6:5-17), but friends must be well chosen (12:8-18; 37:1-6) and then treasured loyally (22:19-26). The poor and the unhappy must be treated with kindness (3:30-4:10; 7:32-36; 29:8-13), and generosity is called for towards all. One must be ready to make a loan or go guarantee (29:1-7; 14-20).

Ben Sira recommends self-discipline, prudence and reserve, especially in speech: see 3:17-29; 4:20-6:4.

THE FUTURE. What is in store for the nation and the individual? Ben Sira does not look forward to the day when a Messiah comes to set up a new order of things. There is, then, no trace in his work of a firm messianic expectation.[65] In his doctrine of the last things, he simply takes traditional notions for granted, and these have a very limited range:[66] man's life does not go on in a hereafter, only Sheol awaits mortal man, and 'the expectation of man is worms' (7:17b Hebrew MS.A). In fact it seems that Ben Sira has not given much thought to these questions about the future. He simply stresses his confidence in the priesthood, which will take care of the nation's future (45:24-26; 50:22-24). And when he speaks of death it is in a the tone of a man who has no illusions (14:11-19; 40:1-11; 41:1-4). Posthumous fame is the only afterlife the wise or just man can hope for (41:11-13).

ADDITIONS

Some texts attributed to Ben Sira give rise to doubts as to their authenticity. But specialist opinion is divided.
1. The prayer at 36:1-22, for the deliverance and restoration of an Israel now under foreign oppression, contrasts sharply in its harshness with the ordinarily peaceable tone of Ben Sira.[67] Some critics hold that this psalm could have had its origin at Qumran. Further, it is possible to see in it resemblances to the Jewish prayer called the Eighteen Benedictions.[67a]
2. After the signing-off at 50:27-29, the Greek, Latin and Syriac Peshitta versions add a ch. 51, in two paragraphs. The first is a thanksgiving prayer (51:1-12), in which the psalmist explains why he is praising God. Having been falsely accused and persecuted on all sides, he was near death, with no one to sustain him. Then he turned to the Lord, and the Lord heard his prayer and delivered him.
3. The second paragraph of this appendix (51:13-30) is a poem on the

---

[65] See Caquot, 'Ben Sira et le messianisme.'
[66] Hamp, 'Zukunft'.
[67] Middendorp, *Stellung Jesus Ben Sira,* 125-32, is against its authenticity, which Marböck, 'Gebet um die Rettung Zions', defends.
[67a] On this and the two following hymnic additions see below, pp. 557, 559.

passionate search for wisdom. Part of the Hebrew text has been found at Qumran among a collection of psalms (11QPs^a), which seems to suggest that this poem existed independently of Ben Sira's work, in the first century B.C.E. It is an alphabetic poem in the Hebrew, and the images are rather definitely sensual. But the Greek translation, which was made from a Hebrew text, tones them down:[68] since his youth, the poet has ardently desired wisdom and asked it of God in prayer (like Solomon, 1 Kgs 3:4-15; Wis 7:7; 8:21; 9). Having obtained it, he invites the disciple to learn from him.

Specialists have not yet reached agreement about the origin of the additions in the second recension (Greek II).[69] These additions emphasize, sometimes even to the point of misconception (see 16:10), some doctrinal elements which are in sharp contrast to the original text of Ben Sira:

1. There is emphasis on divine providence and its role in human affairs. 'The Lord hardened Pharaoh so that he did not know him; in order that his works might be known under heaven. His mercy is manifest to the whole of creation, and he divided his light and darkness among men' (16:15-16; see also 16:18; 17:21). 'And there is no other beside him; he steers the world with the span of his hand, and all things obey his will; for he is king of all things, by his power separating among them the holy things from the profane' (18:2-3).

2. There is emphasis on the salvation bestowed by the Lord. 'When you hear these things in your sleep, wake up! During all your life love the Lord, and call on him for your salvation' (13:14; see also 17:26). 'Do not cease to be strong in the Lord, cleave to him so that he may strengthen you; the Lord Almighty alone is God, and besides him there is no saviour' (24:24).

3. The Last Things are emphasized: 'The fear of the Lord is the beginning of acceptance, and wisdom obtains his love. The knowledge of the Lord's commandments is life-giving discipline; and those who do what is pleasing to him enjoy the fruit of the tree of immortality' (19:18-19). As for the way of sinners, 'at its end is hell, darkness and torment' (21:10 Vg).[70]

4. Like 19:18-19 quoted above, the additions emphasize that fear and love of God go together: 'The fear of the Lord is a gift from the Lord, for it sets [men] upon paths of love' (1:12cd); 'I am the mother of beautiful love, of fear, of knowledge and of holy hope' (24:18); 'The fear of the Lord is the

---

[68] See Delcor, 'Texte hébreu du Cantique,' 162.
[69] Schlatter, *Neugefundene hebräische Stück*, 163-76, 190f, attributes them to Aristobulus, a hypothesis recently taken up again by Prato, 'Lumière interprète de la Sagesse,' with reference to 17:5 in particular. Hart, *Ecclesiasticus*, 272-320, underlines what he saw as the Pharisee tendency of the Greek additions. But Kearns, 'Ecclesiasticus', 549f., thinks the text called Hebrew II is by the Essenes and has a connection with Qumran.
[70] See further the additions of the Vetus Latina at 6:16, 22; 18:22; 24:22.

beginning of love for him, and faith is the beginning of clinging to him' (25:12).[71]

RECEPTION IN JUDAISM AND EARLY CHRISTIANITY

The Wisdom of Ben Sira was accepted by Palestinian Judaism by the first century B.C.E. This is indicated by the manuscript found at Masada, which dates from the beginning of the century, in combination with *P.T. Berakhot* 7, 11b (see also *Ber. Rabbati* 91), where Simeon ben Shetah, about 90 B.C.E., is reported to justify his sitting between King Alexander Jannaeus and the queen by quoting Ben Sira by name: 'Praise wisdom and she will exalt you (cf. Prov 4:8a) and will seat you among the princes' (cf. Sir 11:1). In the first century C.E. the book continued to circulate, as at Masada and Qumran. But nothing is known about the use made of it or the interpretation it was given in Judaism. There is no trace of its canonicity being debated at the synod of Jamnia (Yavneh) at the end of the century. One even has the impression that no objections were raised to its not being made part of the Jewish canon of scripture. The opinion of Rabbi Akiba (d. after 135 C.E.) is of great importance. According to *P.T. Sanhedrin* 10, 28a, Akiba held that the Book of Ben Sira was one of the 'exterior books the reading of which excludes from the world to come.' According to Moore,[72] the 'exterior books' would be the equivalent of 'the books of the *minim*', meaning those of heretics, as can be seen from *B.T. Sanhedrin* 100b, and probably, according to *T. Yadaim* 2:13, Christian books. But Ginsberg has shown that 'exterior books' are simply 'books which are not part of the canon of scripture'.[73] According to Rabbi Akiba, they could not be used for public reading or for school instruction. But Ben Sira could be read in private. And the many quotations from it given by the Tannaim and the Amoraim show that it was highly esteemed.

The name of Ben Sira appears nowhere in the New Testament, and he is nowhere explicitly quoted. Heb 12:12a seems to be an effort to reproduce Isa 35:3, but is in fact much closer to Sir 25:23. But does similarity mean dependence? The same is true of the other writings of the New Testament, especially James.[74] Sometimes the similarities seem to imply an influence, which is as hard to define as to deny. So too in the prologue of John (John 1).[75] Sir 4:31 seems to have been the literary source for *Didache* 4:6 (c. 70

[71] The Vetus Latina also adds some passages which seem to be by a Christian, at 2:9 (mention of charity, as in 1 Cor 13:13), 24:18 (see John 14:6) and so on.
[72] Moore, 'Definition of the Jewish Canon.'
[73] Ginsberg, 'Attitude of the Synagogue,' 120-32; see also Haran, 'Problems of the Canonization', 245-59.
[74] See Mayor, *James*, LXXIV-LXXVI; Chaine, *Jacques*, LI-LVII; contacts between Sir and the NT are listed in Sundberg, *Old Testament*, 54-55.
[75] See Spicq, 'Le Siracide.'

C.E.) and for *Barnabas* 19:9 (beginning of the second century C.E.). *Didache* 1:6 has been compared with Sir 12:1, though the similarity has been contested.[76] In any case, none of these Christian texts names Ben Sira as the source of a quotation. Melito of Sardis, about 170 C.E., omits Ben Sira from his list of the canonical books accepted in Palestine. But some time before 200 probably, Clement of Alexandria quotes Ben Sira sixty times, and provides about eighty verses of the longer Greek text. The quotations, all taken from the first thirty-nine chapters, are often introduced by the formula, 'Scripture says.' The book is called 'The Wisdom of Jesus the Son of Sirach' and its author Solomon or the Pedagogue. Quotations are in fact most numerous in the work of Clement entitled *Paedagogus,* from which one may deduce the use made of Ben Sira at Alexandria. A little later, in the Latin Church of Africa, Cyprian provides some twenty-five exact quotations taken from the Old Latin version, but none from the 'Praise of Famous Men' (chs 44-50). His quotations are introduced by such formulas as, *Scriptura divina dicens* (*Ep.* 71, 2; Sir 31:30) or again, *Sicut locutus est Dominus per prophetam dicens (Ep.* 59:15; Sir 16:1-2). – It follows that during the first half of the third century C.E., the Wisdom of Ben Sira seems to have been accepted unhesitatingly as sacred scripture by Christians, and that the long text was used. The triumph of the short recension came later.

The Wisdom of Solomon

Most specialists now admit that this book was written in Greek from the start. The few authors who tried to reconstruct an original Hebrew or Aramaic behind the Greek text could only do so at the cost of modifications which affected the very meaning of the text.[77] The rhythmic prose of the Wisdom of Solomon (or: Book of Wisdom, as it was called in the Latin tradition) seems to have been well preserved in the great uncials.[78] One can therefore rely on the Greek text when taking up the main question posed by the book, its unity.[79] To do so, we shall first examine its literary structure in the light of its contents.

CONTENTS AND LITERARY STRUCTURE

The first part, chs. 1-6, is addressed directly to 'the rulers of the earth' (1:1), who are urged to love justice and avoid perverse thoughts, words and acts, since nothing escapes the wisdom of God, and punishment awaits the

---

[76] See Audet, *Didachè,* 275-80; Skehan, 'Didachè 1:6', and for another view Bogaert, 'Bulletin V,' 95.

[77] Purinton, 'Translation,' envisaged a Hebrew original; Zimmermann, 'Book of Wisdom,' an Aramaic.

[78] The Vetus Latina can be used to restore some passages, such as 2:9, but not 1:15.

[79] Ziegler's edition of *Sapientia Solomonis.*

ungodly (1:1-12). To show what happens, the author at once lets the ungodly speak. Life seems to them to lead nowhere, so they decide to enjoy to the full the time they have. But the sight of the just man, the example of his fidelity to the ancestral traditions and the reproaches he addresses them, impel them to persecute him, a man who entrusts himself to the Lord (2:1-20). This speech by the ungodly is set in a framework of fundamental truths: the ungodly are wrong, because God created human beings for immortality, incorruptibility, and the creatures of the world are vehicles of salvation (1:13-16; 2:21-24). The author then applies these affirmations to three types of the just whose paradoxical life seems to be a disaster: the suffering just, the sterile woman and the eunuch — both, however, loyal believers — and finally the just man who dies in the prime of life. All will receive their reward at the time of God's 'visitation', that is, beyond the grave, while the ungodly, contrasted with them group by group, will be punished (3-4). Then the author, to give an echo of the speech where the ungodly set out their programme, puts a new speech on their lips — one which they make in the afterlife, when they discover the bliss of the just and the futility of their own lives (5:1-13). Yes, God will fight for the just by arming all creation on their behalf (5:14-23). The author finally returns once more to his address to the rulers, inviting them to listen to the instruction he is to give, because a severe judgment awaits them. Then he gives a short description of wisdom, confining himself now to its beneficial aspects. Wisdom confers incorruptibility and eternal kingship, and the author concludes by defining his purpose: 'I will tell you what wisdom is and how she came to be,' 6:22. Such is the theme of this second address to rulers, echoing the opening one and announcing what follows (6).

The structure, therefore, of the first part of Wisdom is concentric, as several authors have clearly seen:[80]

A   Address to rulers and description of wisdom as avenger
B   Speech of the ungodly — 'enjoy life, persecute the just man'
C   Three types of the just life, and three types of the ungodly life
B' Second speech of the ungodly, in the afterlife
A' New address to rulers, description of the benefits of wisdom; plan of the rest of the discourse.

The second part of the book, chs. 7-9, shows how the sage, who presents the characteristics of Solomon, has obtained wisdom, what it brought him, what it is, where it comes from and what it achieves. The author, speaking in the first person singular in this part of the book, starts by explaining that he was born in the same state as the rest of mankind, meaning that no one has wisdom by heredity (7:1-6). If he obtained wisdom, it was because he

[80] Wright, 'Structure,' 168-73; Reese, 'Plan', 394-6; Perrenchio, 'Struttura di Sap 1:1-15.' 291-307 and 'Struttura di Sap 1:16-2:24 e 5:1-23'; Nickelsburg, *Resurrection,* 48 n. 1; 67.

asked it of God rather than the other advantages of royalty. And he recognizes that these other advantages were conferred on him along with and through the wisdom he had asked for (7:7-12). The author then returns to his aim of speaking of wisdom, and, asking God for grace to do justice to his theme, insists that it was from God that he got the wide culture of which he can boast. He is thoroughly proficient in all the sciences of his day, but it is in fact wisdom which has taught him (7:13-21). He then tries to give a description of wisdom, by attributing to it, a spiritual being, a series of twenty-one attributes or qualities. Wisdom's purity is abolute, it penetrates all things and only seeks to do good. To justify these attributions, the author shows how wisdom is a reflection, a mirror, a perfect image of God. This explains what it does: it governs the universe and makes men friends of God and prophets (7:22-8:1). Since wisdom is the intimate of God since the beginning of creation, the author wishes to have it as spouse, since it is superior to all possessions and all virtues (8:2-8). Furthermore, says the pseudo-Solomon, if wisdom is my bride I shall be seen to possess the qualities of a king, in council as in war (8:9-16). This is why, knowing that it is not enough to be well-born and that wisdom is to be had only by begging it of God, he decides to compose his prayer (8:17-21). This (9) is in three strophes.[81] The first, (9:1-6) speaks of mankind in general, as does the third (9:13-18), while the second treats of Solomon (9:7-12). The prayer as a whole has a concentric structure. The third section corresponds to the first, but with the themes in the reverse order: human frailty, the gift of wisdom, the achievement of man's end (9:13-18). In the middle section (9:7-12) again a concentric pattern: Solomon's call, wisdom with God, the gift of wisdom, wisdom with Solomon, Solomon's success in his call.

The concentric pattern to be seen in this prayer, and in the first part of the book, is there again in the second part:[82]

A   Solomon is born like everyone else
B   But he asks wisdom of God and gets all royal attributes
C   He has even been given all the achievements of culture
D   Description of wisdom: nature, origin, function
C' Wisdom brings all good things and surpasses the virtues
B' With wisdom, Solomon will be a great king
A' Wisdom, even for the well-born, is only had by prayer.

The prayer of which the structure has been explained above, does not form part of this concentric pattern. It forms the high point in the plan and is put at the centre of the book.

The third part, chs 10-19, is mainly a recollection of the story of man's and Israel's origins as told in the first pages of the Bible, from Adam to the

---

[81] See Gilbert, 'Structure de la prière.'
[82] See Wright, 'Structure,' 168, 173-4.

events of the exodus. It begins by recalling briefly the principal heroes of the book of Genesis. They owed their deliverance to wisdom, while those who abandoned it perished (10). This page links up with the last verse of the preceding prayer and ends with a succinct reminder of the main events of Israel's exodus under Moses' leadership, alluding in 10:20-21 to the canticle of Exodus 15.

From ch. 11 on, the book is complicated in structure. In the main, the author, without following literally the story of Exodus, contrasts the plagues which struck the Egyptians with the blessings granted to Israel. But these comparisons are interrupted by two long digressions (11:15-12:27; 13-15). Pharaoh had ordered the newly born infants of the Israelites to be thrown into the Nile (Exod 1:22; Wis 11:6). The water of the river was turned into blood and became undrinkable, while Israel got water from the rock in the desert (11:1-14). The plagues of insects are first noted briefly (11:15). Before explaining what they were at greater length (16:1-14), the author inserts two digressions. The first (11:15-12:27) seems to answer a tacit question: why does God use such ridiculous means of punishing? The author compares these plagues of insects with the punishment of the Canaanites through hornets, to show that God imposes moderate punishment because he loves his creatures and only seeks the conversion of the guilty. But if these remain obstinate, he will go further and futher and exact the ultimate penalty. The second digression (13-15) also seems to answer to a tacit question: why does God use animals to punish the Egyptians? The author explains that of the three main types of religion practised by the pagans of his day, worship of the world and its elements (13:1-9), worship of idols (13:10-15:13) and worship of living animals (15:14-19); this last, secular in Egypt, is the worst and most blameworthy deviation. So God uses what the Egyptians adore in order to punish them. Once he has demonstrated this, the author returns to the exodus and describes what happened to both parties and compares their lot. Briefly, he contrasts the frogs which infested Egypt so badly that everyone lost appetite, with the quails which Israel fed on in the desert (16:1-4). The flies and locusts which attacked and bit the Egyptians are contrasted with the bronze serpent which God used to heal the Israelites when they themselves were bitten by poisonous serpents in the desert (16:5-14). The plague which is placed in the middle of the description is that of the hail and lightning by which the Egyptians' harvest was destroyed. But God sent manna to feed Israel in the desert. In these last events, the author's main point is that the world is transformed and becomes an ally of the just (16:15-29). The plague of darkness fills the Egyptians with fear, while Israel has light to cheer it both in Egypt and during its flight to the sea (the pillar of fire) (17:1-18:4). Like the plagues of insects, the two descriptions with which the story ends are introduced together, and the decree by which Pharaoh ordered the newly born infants of the Israelites to be killed is again noted (18:5). The author contrasts the death of the first-born of the Egyptians with Aaron's inter-cession at the time of Korah's revolt in the desert (Num 17:6ff.; Wis 18:6-25). Finally, the Red Sea swallows up Pharaoh and his army but opens to deliver Israel (19:1-9), and the story ends with another allusion to Exod 15 (Wis 19:9). In conclusion, the author takes up again briefly the essential element of the main events of the exodus: the world is changed so that it can fight harder for the just (19:10-12, 18-21) against ungodly enemies who are even worse than the inhabitants of Sodom (19:13-17). The last verse of the book reminds the Lord that in countless ways, always and everywhere, he glorified, that is, delivered, his people.

This lengthy recital of the events of the exodus (leaving aside the two digressions, 11:15-12:27; 13-15, and the conclusion, 19:10-22) can be grouped in two ways. One separates all the parallel descriptions of plagues and blessings, which gives seven items; the other joins, with the author of Wisdom, the two types of insect plague and the two last:[83]

Water of the Nile — water from the rock (11:1-14)
Noxious insects — quails (16:1-4)
   Flies and locusts — bronze serpent (16:5-14)
Harvest ruined by hail — manna (16:15-29)
Darkness — light (17:1-18:4)
Fate of the first-born of the Egyptians — Israel spared (18:6-25)
   Engulfed by the Red Sea — freed through the Red Sea (19:1-9).

Some more observations may be made. As has been mentioned above, Wis 10:20 and 19:9 contain allusions to Exod 15, which form an inclusion to the whole. Then, Pharaoh's decree to have the infants killed is mentioned at the beginning (11:6), and again at 18:5, which gives another *inclusio*. Finally, the story begins and ends with events where water is paramount. Then again, in both patterns the plague of hail and lightning which destroys the crops and the contrasting manna (16:15-29) are at the centre. And this in fact provides the author with the solution to his analyses: all creation fights for the just. At the end of the book, also the end of the third part, this fundamental notion is taken up again (19:10-12, 18-21), and is brought to a conclusion by another allusion to the manna, now seen as nourishment for immortality (19:21). So this third part also shows elements of a concentric pattern.

The structural relationship of these elements may be indicated by the following schema:

Allusion to Exod 15 (10:20)
Plague of water (11:1-14)
Pharaoh's decree (11:6)
. . . .

---

[83] Compare Reese 'Plan,' 398f and Wright, 'Structure,' 169, 176-84.

    Role of creation (16:24-25)

    . . . .

    Pharaoh's decree (18:5)

    Plague of water (19:1-9)

    Allusion to Exod 15 (19:9)

       Conclusion: Role of creation (19:10-12, 18-21).

In the two digressions, the first (11:15-12:27) shows the similarity of what happened with the Egyptians (11:15-12:2) and what happened with the Canaanites (12:3-18). There is a lesson for Israel here (12:19-22), which the author draws before going back to the story of the plagues (12:23-27). The second digression has the following content: worship of the world and its elements (13:1-9); worship of idols (13:10-15:13); worship of living animals (15:14-19). A concentric pattern can be seen in the discussion of worship of idols:[84]

A   Idols of gold, silver, stone and especially wood; role of the woodman (13:10-19)

B   Invocation of God; reference to history; bridging piece (14:1-10)

C   Punishment of idols; invention of idolatry, and its consequences; punishment of idolators (14:11-31)

B'   Invocation of God; reference to history; bridging piece (15:1-6)

A'   Idols of clay; role of the potter (15:7-13).

As to the general pattern of the book, it can be seen that some special features crop up everywhere. Diptychs appear in the contrasting events of the exodus, but also in the earliest part of the book, when the just and the ungodly are contrasted (esp. 3-4), or again in the first major digression, which contrasts Egyptians and Canaanites (11:15-12:27) and then again in the second, where the contrast between idolators and Noah or Israel is emphasized. On the other hand, the concentric pattern can be observed in all parts of the book, even in the third part according to our analysis or in the second major digression (13-15).

One must also bear clearly in mind how well the various parts are linked to each other. The second, where wisdom is treated of explicitly, is heralded already at the end of the first (6:22). The third links up with the last verse of the closing prayer of the second (9:18), while the long look back on the events of the exodus is signaled by the short summary with which ch. 10 ends. Furthermore, the prayer of Wis 9 continues in hymn form till the last verse of the book.

LITERARY GENRE

Can the whole book, with its actual pattern, be assigned to any particular

[84] See Wright, 'Structure,' 180; Gilbert, *Critique des dieux*, 252-6.

type (genre) of literature? Since Focke and especially since Reese,[85] the Book of Wisdom has been regarded as a *Logos protreptikos* (exhortation or initiation). But there are two objections to this classification. For one thing, very little is really known about the *Protreptikos* of Aristotle as a whole, which is taken to be the main example of this type of writing. And then, the third part of the book, chs. 10-19, does not correspond to this particular type. But the hypothesis has at least the advantage of indicating a type of writing which was in fact Greek. There is no type of literature in the Bible into which Wisdom as a whole fits.

It seems better to follow Beauchamp[86] and treat Wisdom as in the genre of encomium. Aristotle, followed by Cicero and Quintilian, classes discourses as deliberative, judgmental and epideictic. This last does not aim at passing judgment or at urging a decision with a bearing on the future. It tries to impel the hearer either to admire somebody or to practise a virtue or develop a quality. This last type of discourse is called the encomium. The descriptions of this type of writing given by Aristotle and his successors correspond to what we find in Wisdom.[87]

There is an introduction which is addressed directly to the audience and tries to arouse its attention and interest. The theme is summed up briefly and readers are urged to put it into practice. To show what is at stake in the discourse, those who refuse to practise what is to be praised are heard. What they say is criticized and some difficult or paradoxical situations are described to show how necessary it is to agree with the encomium. The exordium ends with a brief description of the object of the encomium, and the plan of the rest of the discourse is set out. The first part of Wisdom corresponds exactly to this procedure.

The encomium itself should show three things: the origin, nature and activity or function of what is to be praised. This is the hardest part, both for speaker or writer, and for audience or reader from whom special effort is demanded. In Wisdom, the second part, announced 6:22 at the end of the exordium, corresponds to this programme. But the subject in this case makes it necessary to distinguish two aspects of the origin. There is the origin of wisdom itself, and its origin in Solomon. The author begins with the second aspect. Solomon's wisdom was not hereditary, but came through prayer, and only prayer can occasion wisdom in man (7:1-7; 8:17-21; 9). The origin of wisdom itself is to be found in God, of whom it is the image, mirror and reflection, because it shares his intimacy (7:25-26; 8:3). The nature of wisdom is described through its twenty-one attributes.

---

[85] Focke, *Entstehung*, 85 (on Wisdom 1-5); Reese, *Hellenistic Influence*, 117-21; Winston, *Wisdom*, 18-20.

[86] 'Epouser la Sagesse,' 358-60.

[87] See Aristotle, *Rhetoric*, 1358b, 17-29; 1367b, 26-30; 1392a, 4-7; 1393b, 23-29; 1394a, 12-13; 1414b-1420a. Cicero, *Orator*, 12:37; 13:42; *De Oratore*, 84:342-8; Quintilian, *Instit. Orat.*, 3:4, 12-14 and 3:7.

It is essentially absolute purity, penetrating all things and working for good (7:22-24). This leads the author to speak of its activity, which is inherent in its nature. It animates the universe and makes men friends of God and prophets (7:27-8:1). Indeed, it is 'fashioner of all that exists' (7:21; 8:4-6), mother of all good things, which it then brings to the soul who receives it (7:12). Hence its action stems from its nature and origin. It affects the whole world and all who welcome it. Characteristic, however, of the Book of Wisdom is that this encomium sees prayer as the first requisite. Nothing else can bring man wisdom. This is why the encomium as such ends with a prayer (9).

To fortify hearer or reader and make them really desirous of practising what has been held out as praiseworthy, Aristotle and his successors pre-scribed a development of the theme by means of well-known examples. This part is less demanding and can be longer or shorter as the author wishes. One good way of driving home the lesson of these examples, while still speaking implicitly of the activity or works of the thing praised, is to contrast the opposite line of action. Contrasts throw light. The case of those who practise what is praised is contrasted with the case of those who are against it. This was termed the *syncrisis* i.e. comparison. Further, care is taken to draw a moral for the audience from the contrasts thus brought out. The author is also free to introduce digressions, again to fortify the reso-lution of the reader. The discourse ends with a brief summary of the lesson to be drawn from the examples. A final attack on the opponents leads in the conclusion, which is kept as short as possible. The hearer or reader is left to decide. Wis 10-19 again corresponds perfectly to the rules laid down by the masters of Greek rhetoric. The examples set out are so well known to the readers that no names have to be mentioned. All are basic elements in the tradition known to the readers. The comparisons are worked out in detail and the two digressions are well placed. The ending corresponds to the principles of Greek rhetoric as well. The only difference — and this is along the lines of the special feature of the encomium itself — is that the developments based on the examples are given in the form of a hymn. The author constantly addresses God, not the reader or hearer, as he did in the prayer of ch. 9; and so even in the last verse of the book.

Once this is recognized, there seems to be no difficulty in seeing the book as a unity, and this can be confirmed by some other instances. One of the most a striking is the use of what Reese called flashbacks.[88] A number of widely separated passages chime with one another in theme and vocabu-lary. And then, important parts of the book consist of *midrash*. Such are the stories about the exodus (11-19) and also the fundamental texts where Solomon is spoken of (1 Kgs 3:4-15; 5:9-14; 2 Chr 1), which are used to

---

[88] *Hellenistic Influence,* 123-40.

build up to the praise of wisdom (7-9). Some critics have even seen in the introductory chapters a sort of *midrash* on Isa 52:13-15.[89]

MESSAGE

Once the unity of the book has been accepted, as is done by most contemporary commentators, the question arises as to the main theses of the author. One must try to answer by showing how the author links up his various themes.

The community for which the book is written is in a situation of conflict and paradox. So the author states that after the death of the body there is a hereafter, to which wisdom leads. The main problem in the Jewish community where the author lives is the meaning of this earthly life. Complaints against God are heard, as during the exodus (1:10-11). The community has split. Some people have abandoned the Jewish tradition in which they were born and brought up (2:12), to opt for a world view of the Epicurean type.[90] As they do not believe in an afterlife, all that remains is to make the best of this. But since the believer is a burden by the very fact that he is true to his faith, the apostates go so far as to envisage persecuting and killing him (2). And then, the life of the faithful is itself a paradox. Good men are suffering, they are childless instead of being blessed with children, dying in the prime of youth instead of aging with dignity — such paradoxes! Confronted with this sort of situation — which perpetually recurs — the author affirms that God created the world for life, that man was made as an incorruptible being and that the just will enjoy immortality in God, while the ungodly, by refusing all thought of an afterlife, make a pact with death, spiritual death, a pact which will come into effect at the time of God's 'visitation', at the end of this earthly life. And this visitation will take the form of a great battle. God himself, using the elemental forces as weapons, will give battle for the just against the ungodly. The reader will ask himself how the author can be sure this cosmic struggle will take place. An explanation is offered in the two following parts of the book.

The author has in fact special teaching on wisdom. Beginning with the first page of his book, he asserts that wisdom is universally present (1:7), being none other than the Spirit of the Lord which fills the universe and holds all things together. Taking up the Stoic notion of *pneuma*,[91] the author echoes it when he praises wisdom. 'Because of her pureness she pervades and penetrates all things' (7:24). 'She reaches mightily from one end of the earth to the other, and she orders all things well' (8:1). More active than in Prov 8, wisdom is even the 'fashioner of all things' (7:22;

---

[89] Suggs, 'Wisdom 2:10-5'; Nickelsburg, *Resurrection*, 58-68.
[90] See Larcher, *Etudes*, 213-6.
[91] See Larcher, *Etudes*, 374-6.

8:4-6). It is God's presence in the world. Anyone who desires it, more than a man desires a spouse,[92] must ask God for it. It will not be refused him, because it is found if searched for (6:12), and anyone who desires it and receives it, gets all the good things of this world and has immortality in store for him (6:18-19; 8:17). Thus wisdom is the pledge of immortality and its active presence in the world can do nothing but good for the people of whom it makes God's friends. But man still has to ask God for it. To obtain it is to fulfil mankind's vocation, as it is to fulfil one's personal call (9). Finally, this was the experience of Solomon, idealized here, and more probably that of the author himself. But the author is sure of it, because he sees in his ancestors people who were purified by wisdom, enlightened about the will of the Lord and, in a word, saved (9:18).

The third part of the book (10-19) uses examples to prove that the sage is right in asking for wisdom and that God uses elemental forces when he gives battle for the just against their enemies. So the three parts of the book hang together. Linking up directly with the end of the prayer, ch. 10 shows that wisdom saved Adam after his sin or preserved Joseph from sin, that it guided Noah, Abraham, Lot, Jacob and finally the whole people of Israel through Moses, and brought them all deliverance. Thus the exodus was the work of wisdom. Then, in the parallel accounts of the events of the exodus (11-19), the author shows that the elements of the world fought against the enemies of Israel, as is stated explicitly when the destructive hail on the Egyptians' crops is contrasted with the manna (16:17, 24). This comes up again at the end (19:18-21), and when properly understood, can be seen to be nothing other than the work of wisdom in the world. It follows that when the author affirms in the introduction that God will use the forces of the universe as weapons at his 'visitation' (5:17-23), his faith can be justified by pointing to the fact that this happened already in the events by which Israel was founded. The last verse of the book (19:22) is there to say that what has happened will always be happening again, no matter where and no matter how. The events of the exodus confirm the author's hope and view of the last things, as they also strengthen the wish for wisdom he evokes in his readers.

ORIGINALITY

Wisdom is a well-planned and homogeneous exposition, much different from Prov 10-31, Qohelet and Ben Sira, where texts seem to have been strung together with no such order. It also has very different thoughts to offer on everyday life. Wisdom is closer to Prov 1-9 and to Job, which take up equally large and complicated questions, and also treat of them in well

---

[92] See Beauchamp, Epouser la Sagesse.'

constructed discourses. But Wisdom uses the history of Israel as the basis of its reflections, and builds its vision of history much more organically than Sir 44-49 into its exposition.

The originality of the Book of Wisdom can also be seen in its notion of wisdom. As has been said above, the author goes beyond Prov 8 and even Sir 24 in attributing an active role to wisdom in creation. It is the craftsman of all things (7:22; 8:6) and 'by its choice decides on the works of God' (8:4). It governs the universe, as is also said in Sir 24:6, but does so now by its presence at the heart of things, totally penetrating and animating the world (1:7; 7:24; 8:1). This last characteristic seems to have been taken over from Stoicism, where the *pneuma* had a similarly cosmic role. But the author takes good care not to divinize wisdom. It is of God, his mirror, reflection, image (7:26) but it is not God. On the other hand, the author approximates Wisdom to the Spirit of God (1:6-7; 7:22; 9:17). It contains God's Holy Spirit, to which the author assimilates it at 9:17. Here he echoes the prophecies of Ezekiel (Ezek 36:27 etc.), by attributing to wisdom an active role in men's moral life — 'thus the paths of those on earth were set right' (9:18).[93] In this way the author has succeeded in leaving behind the materialism of the Stoic *pneuma*. Wisdom is also assimilated to the divine Logos through which God created the world (9:1-2) and through which all wounds are healed (16:12). And when on the night of the Passover, the destroyer of the first-born of the Egyptians is said to be the Logos, the Logos should probably be understood as an aspect of wisdom. There is, however, a doctrine given by Sir 24 (and Bar 3:9-4:4) which the author does not assert. He never assimilates wisdom and the Torah. He says that wisdom makes known what is pleasing to the Lord, that is, the Torah, but he goes no further.

Another special feature of Wisdom is the doctrine of immortality, the incorruptibility of the human being.[94] Man is the image of God himself and was therefore created incorruptible by God (2:23), who 'created all things that they might exist' (1:14). The means of obtaining this incorruptibility or immortality is the practice of justice (1:15), the recognition of the sovereignty of the Lord (15:3). Hence the just, who were sustained in their trials by the hope of immortality (3:4), will subsist with God in love (3:9). Wisdom confers immortality on man, because love of wisdom impels man to obey its laws (6:17-19). To obtain wisdom is therefore to be assured of immortality (8:17). The author is certainly envisaging the incorruptibility of the whole of man's being. He does not speak of resurrection, but it may be admitted that he envisages the body's existing after physical death,[95] since he does not confine himself to speaking of incorruptibility but goes

---

[93] See Gilbert, 'Volonté de Dieu'.
[94] See Larcher, *Etudes,* 263-300.
[95] See Beauchamp, 'Salut corporel'; Larcher, *Etudes,* 321-7.

on, at 19:21, the end of his book, to say that manna is an ambrosial food, meaning that its assures the eater of immortality.

Finally, the originality of Wisdom may be seen from the way it assimilates Hellenistic culture. Not only does the author write in Greek, use a Greek literary genre and take over, with due modifications, the Stoic doctrine of *pneuma,* but closely akin to the bible though he is, he adopts the imagery, vocabulary and theories of contemporary Stoicism, a component of Middle Platonism. But he shows no mastery of these philosophies. His knowledge, indirect, seems to derive only from his general education.[96] This may be illustrated by two points. In Wis 13:1-9, the author seems clearly to be discussing a doctrine coming from the lost works of Aristotle, according to which the nature of the divine can be known from the world as a starting-point.[97] But he eliminates the pantheistic tendencies of this doctrine by stating that recourse must also be made to the analogy of proportionality. Then, he adopts the Hellenistic doctrine of 'philanthropia'. This virtue, composed of goodness, kindness and mercy, is found, he says, in God (12:8) and in wisdom (1:6; 7:23). And Israel should imitate its God by practising it towards its enemies (12:19). The universalism of the author of Wisdom goes beyond that of his predecessors in the Bible.[98]

From all that has been said, the origin and aim of Wisdom emerges. The work is exclusively Jewish, the work of a believing and cultured sage who reflects on Israel's heritage and wishes to speak of it to a divided community, where perhaps doubt holds sway. It is in Egypt, probably at Alexandria, where Hellenistic culture flourished, that one should think of the book being written. The study of the vocabulary, along with certain allusions, such as to the *pax romana* in 14:22,[99] suggests that it should be dated to the reign of Augustus at the earliest, that is, not before 30 B.C.E. It could even be from the first decades of the first century C.E. The book aims in particular at young Jews who will have the task of being leaders of the community once their education is over. This would give even more relevance to the example of Solomon as a young man, and his prayer.

CIRCULATION

Curiously enough, no Jewish writer of the first centuries C.E. mentions or quotes Wisdom. The survival of the book was due to Christianity. It cannot be proved that any New Testament writer knew it, but certain similarities can be shown to exist between Wisdom and some passages of the New

---

[96] See Larcher, *Etudes.* 181-236; Reese, *Hellenistic Influence.*

[97] See Gilbert, *Critique des dieux,* 1-52; Dubarle, *Manifestation naturelle,* 125-54; Gilbert, 'Connaissance de Dieu,' 204-6.

[98] See Gilbert, 'Conjecture', 552-3.

[99] See Gilbert, *Critique des dieux,* 172.

Testament.[100] The same is true of the writings of the Apostolic Fathers and the Apologists. Similarity does not betoken dependence. The existence of the same type of religious environment would explain both the similarities and the acceptance of Wisdom in Christianity.[101]

The first mentions of Wisdom, as in the *Muratorian Canon,* and the first explicit quotations, come at the end of the second century.[102] The Vetus Latina version was probably made in Christian Africa, between 150 and 200.[103] So about 200, Wisdom was known in Egypt, Africa and Rome. Origen makes use of it, and, to stop at about 200, the *Teachings of Silvanus,* a non-Gnostic piece of Christian writing from Nag Hammadi, shows dependence in at least one instance on Wisdom.[104]

The Sentences of Phocylides

The Sentences of Phocylides are a collection of 230 hexameters, in dactyls, in the Ionic dialect of Greek.[105] The work seems to have had little impact in antiquity. The first known quotations from it are found in the miscellany compiled by Stobaeus in the fifth century C.E.[106] No quotations are found in the Church Fathers.

But even before Suidas, c. 1000, verses 5-79 were inserted, with some additions, in the *Sibylline Oracles,* Book 2. This was probably done by a Christian writer.[107] Phocylides had a wide vogue in the Middle Ages. There is a large number of manuscripts, five of which are important. The text is satisfactory, though eleven verses are spurious.[108] The *Sentences* had their greatest success during the Renaissance, having been published for the first time at Venice in 1495, and going through frequent reprints. The book was used in schools. Doubts were raised as to the authorship of the work first by Friedrich Sylburg in 1591[109] and then by Joseph Scaliger in 1606,[110] who

[100] See Larcher, *Etudes,* 11-30; Matt 27:43, 54 and Wis 2:18; Rom 1:18-23 and Wis 13:1-9; Rom 5:12 and Wis 2:24; Rom 9 and Wis 11-12; Col 1:15-17 and Wis 7:24-26; 1 Pet 1:6-7 and Wis 3:5-6.

[101] See Clement of Rome, *Ep. Cor.* 3:4 and Wis 2:24; *Ep. Cor.* 27:5 and Wis 11:21b; 12:12; *Herm.* 26:1 and Wis 7:28; Melito of Sardis, *Homily on Easter,* 24-34 and Wis 17-18; Larcher, *Etudes,* 36-38.

[102] See Larcher, *Etudes,* 38-41; Grant, 'Book of Wisdom.' The explicit quotations are in Clement of Alexandria, *Paedagogus,* 2:1,7; *Stromata,* 2:2,6; 6:14,110; 6:15,120 and fragment 23, edited by Staehlin, *Clemens Alexandrinus* 3, p. 202; Tertullian, *Adversus Valentinianos,* 2:2.

[103] See De Bruyne, 'Etude sur le texte latin.'

[104] *Silvanus* 113, 1-7 and Wis 7:25-26; see Winston, *Wisdom,* 69.

[105] Here we follow Van der Horst, *Sentences.*

[106] Stobaeus, 3:3,28 quotes vv. 125-128, 130.

[107] Between vv. 55 and 149; see Denis, *Introduction,* 216-17.

[108] See Young's edition, *Theognis;* vv. 31, 37, 87 are found in the secondary MSS.; v. 36 is a doublet of v. 69b; v. 129 is missing in two important MSS. of the 10th century, namely, M (Paris) and B (Oxford); vv. 116-117, 144-146, 155, 218 are in MS. V (Vienna), 13-14th century.

[109] *Epicae.*

[110] *Animadversiones.*

regarded the *Sentences* as the work of a Christian. Less and less interest was then taken in the work, till Jacob Bernays' demonstration of its Jewish authorship, 1856, revived interest.[111]

The *Sentences* cannot in fact be attributed to the Ionian poet of Miletus of the middle of the 6th century B.C.E., who was rated highly in antiquity for his wisdom and practical advice,[112] and ranked with Hesiod, Theognis and other celebrated Greek classics. The author of the *Sentences* succeeded no doubt in rendering faithfully enough the Ionic of the author whose name he borrowed, and several passages can be more or less paralleled in classical Greek authors.[113] But the language of the *Sentences* is clearly Hellenistic in parts,[114] and as had already been noted by Scaliger, there are definite echoes of the Bible, and indeed of the Septuagint, which are of course entirely absent in the real Phocylides.[115] These similarities concern characteristic elements of the Bible. Concern for the poor appears vv. 10, 19, 22-23, 28-29. V. 59 contains an allusion to Jer 9:22. Vv. 84-85 draw on Deut 22:6-7. Vv. 103–104 suggest the resurrection of the body. Vv. 164-174 may well be explained by Prov 6:6-8 of the Septuagint; and so on.

If the *Sentences* were written by a Jew, as is now generally admitted, why was a pseudonym used? Three explanations at least have been offered.

1. According to Alon, the writer was aiming at fellow-Jews, to show them that they were missing no Greek culture by remaining Jews, since Phocylides, so highly esteemed by pagans, coincides with the precepts of the Torah.[116]

2. Other authors see the *Sentences* as Jewish propaganda, aimed at pagans in the hope of refining their morals.[117]

3. Others think the book was written by a 'God-fearer', a pagan accepting a certain number of Jewish precepts without actually becoming a Jew. The aim would be to show his pagan friends that the precepts he accepts were already taught by the celebrated Phocylides.[118] No convincing arguments have been offered in favour of any of these three explanations.

One can agree with Van der Horst in dating the *Sentences* to the reigns of

---

[111] *Phokylideische Gedicht.*

[112] Van der Horst, *Sentences,* 60-62, reproduces the ancient witnesses.

[113] Vv. 124-128 are said to depend, directly or indirectly on Protagoras; v. 143 on Theognis, 1133ff.; vv. 159-160 evoke Hesiod, *Works and Days,* 383-694; vv. 199-204 could depend on Theognis 183-190; etc.

[114] Van der Horst, *Sentences,* 55-57, noted at least thirty forms, words or usages which had been unknown before the Hellenistic period, fifteen of which occur only from the first century B.C.E. onwards.

[115] H. Herter's review of F. Dornseiff, *Echtheitsfragen antik-griechischer Literatur,* in *TLZ* 66 (1941), 17-19.

[116] 'Halakhah in the Teaching of the Twelve Apostles,' 279.

[117] Van der Horst, *Sentences,* 73-74, objects to this hypothesis.

[118] Van der Horst, *Sentences,* 76, note 21, points out that the Wisdom of Menander of Egypt, 3-4th century C.E. might also be the work of a 'God-fearer.'

Augustus and Tiberius, that is, between 30 B.C.E. and 37 C.E.[119] Some features of the Greek do not appear in fact earlier than the first century B.C.E. and then, peaceful relations between Jews and pagans were possible during the period indicated, especially if the book was written in Alexandria, as is suggested by v. 102.[120]

The author used hexameters, in dactyls, in the tradition of Greek and gnomic poetry,[121] giving a rule of life in brief sayings, often linked by no more than the fact that they deal with the same subject or various aspects of a subject. Sometimes, however, the author offers proof of the rule of life which he lays down, and these proofs are sometimes given short developments. To show, for instance, that envy is wrong, he takes examples from the universe, vv. 70-75. He uses the example of the ant and the bee to encourage people to work, 164-74. Speaking of the harm done by love of riches, he questions the use of gold, 44-47. But the writing remains well within the canons of Greek style. There is no such parallelism as is found in classical Hebrew poetry.

Subjects succeed each other abruptly and provide the reader with no clear view of the arrangement.

Two introductory verses attribute these 'counsels' to 'the most wise' Phocylides. The text then runs on with no definite indication of any divisions. Vv. 3-8 give a summary of the Decalogue, but omit any reference to the rejection of idolatry or to the sabbath. Vv. 9-41 first urge justice, 9-21, then mercy towards the poor, 22-41, and are based, as already noted by Bernays, on Lev 19, which at the time of writing could have seemed the central chapter of the Torah.[122] Then come some verses on the harm done by love of riches, 42-47. Returning to warnings addressed directly to the reader, the author dwells on the traditional virtues of the sage — honesty, modesty, self-mastery, 48-58 and especially moderation in all things, 59-69. Then he speaks of avoiding envy and other vices, 70-96. A section where the ideas are more coherently developed treats of death and the afterlife, 97-115. He continues with the uncertainties of life, urging the reader to adapt to circumstances, 116-21. He praises wisdom, especially prudence in speech, 122-31, and advises his readers to avoid vice and practice virtue, 132-52. The last two sections are more homogeneous, especially in the praise of work, 153-74. The longer, at the end, lists counsels for family life, wife, children, old people and slaves, 175-227. Vv. 228-30 serve as a conclusion.

This sequence of sayings (here we follow Van der Horst)[123] is loosely

---

[119] *Sentences*, 81-82.
[120] Dissection of the human body (v. 102) is said to have been practised only at Alexandria; see Van der Horst, *Sentences*, 82-83.
[121] See Küchler, *Frühjüdische Weisheitstraditionen*, 236-302.
[122] Van der Horst, *Sentences*, 66-7.
[123] Van der Horst, *Sentences*, 80, 89-103.

arranged, like the collections of Greek maxims. The work of pseudo-Phocylides differs a good deal from Proverbs, Ben Sira and Wisdom. Proverbs, especially 10:1-31:9, does not collect its teachings by subject-matter. Wisdom provides a well-constructed discourse. But Ben Sira sometimes collects sayings on the same theme into a sequence.

There are few strictly biblical features in the *Sentences*. Its teachings are on the whole much the same as can be found in proverbs in any part of the world. Van der Horst has noted that more than half the verses have their equivalent in Greek maxims.[124] Though the first groups of sayings are inspired by the Decalogue and Leviticus 19, the strictly religious significance of the latter has almost disappeared in the *Sentences*. There is a constant invitation to practise the fundamental virtues, but without a similarly constant appeal to religious motives.

Nonetheless, the writer recognizes that man is the image of God, by his *pneuma* or spirit, his *psyche* or soul, 105-106. The soul is immortal (115) and even the body, it would seem, is destined to rise again (103-104), something Wisdom did not say outright. What he says about God could have been acceptable to others than Jews. But he says little about God. He does not say, for instance, that God grants pardon. Only, God is rich in blessing and the only truly wise (54).[125] The writer recognizes implicitly that God is creator of all (125-128). Wisdom is a purely human attribute, and there is nothing like Prov 8, Sir 24 or Wis 7-9 in the *Sentences*. Even when they read, 'Wisdom directs the course of lands and cities and ships' (131), this is no more than the lesson of purely human experience; compare Wis 6:24; 14:3.

The meagre doctrinal content of the *Sentences* is probably why the Church Fathers did not refer to them, in spite of the fine moral teaching they contain. But even such teaching is not what makes the *Sentences* interesting. Their interest lies in the fact that the ethics and wisdom of Israel here encounter those of pagan Hellenism.

4 Maccabees

The Fourth Book of Maccabees, written in Greek, and not strictly speaking of the Wisdom type, is nevertheless akin to it in some ways. It treats the mastery which reason should exercise over the passions.

The author introduces his theme in an exordium, explaining that he will give as an example the martyrdom of Eleazar, seven brothers and their mother (1:1-12). The first section of the discourse gives definitions, in philosophical terms, of the relations between reason and the passions, and says that the former rules the latter by being the intellect judging arightly

---

[124] Van der Horst, *Sentences*, 79.
[125] See Sir 1:6 but also Heraclides Ponticus, quoted by Van der Horst, *Sentences*, 151.

and choosing the life of wisdom. This is illustrated by some examples, briefly put: Joseph resisting Potiphar's wife, Moses moderating his anger against Dathan and Abiram, Jacob reproving his sons for their indignation against the people of Shechem, and David refusing the water fetched for him by his warriors at the risk of their lives (1:13-3:18). Then, as a historical prelude, there is the story of how Apollonius tried to seize the temple treasures, and how he was failed; this is followed by a description of how Antiochus Epiphanes tried to force the Jews to eat pork, contrary to their law, and to apostatize (3:19-4:26). After this introduction, the martyrdom of Eleazar (5-7) is described at length, with the old man speaking fluently and his merits highly praised at the end: 'only the wise and courageous man is lord of his emotions' (7:23). Then comes the main development, on the martyrdom of the seven brothers and their mother (8:1-18:9). The tyrant urges the brothers to take up Greek customs and so gain his friendship. But far from yielding to fear, they have decided to remain faithful to the law and confident in God: 'we shall be with God for whom we suffer' (9:8). One after another, beginning with the eldest, they then suffer martyrdom, proclaiming their fidelity to God and his law (9:10-12:19). Their courage and virtue are then praised, seen as proof that reason rules the passions (13-14:10). Then the heroism of their mother is praised, as she encourages each of them to face death for fidelity to religion (14:11-16:25). When she too is condemned to death, she throws herself into the fire, preferring not to be touched by the executioners (17:1-6). The eulogy ends with the blessings accorded by God to the nation by reason of the martyrdom of his faithful. 'The tyrant was punished and the homeland purified — they having become, as it were, a ransom for the sin of our nation' (17:21). Finally, we hear how the mother exhorted her sons to remain faithful to the teaching of the Bible which they had received from their father (18:6-19). A short epilogue and a doxology terminate the discourse (18:20-24).

This remarkable piece of Greek rhetoric, written in the Asiatic style, is intended to be an eulogy of the martyrs. It achieves its aim by explaining their courage in the light of Greek philosophy, one of the principles of which is that reason rules the emotions. Using all the resources of oratory, this eulogy is presented as a speech really given on some unknown occasion, and not as a book to read; see 1:10, 12; 3:19; 14:9. There are clear indications of Platonic and Stoic influences, as may be seen already in the main thesis as also in the naming of the four cardinal virtues; see for instance 1:18 and Wis 8:7. But the author can hardly be said to have belonged to one or other of these schools.[126] All he knows of Greek philosophy was what came in his general knowledge. Any philosophical veneer merely covers the most basic tents of Jewish faith.

---

[126] See Breitenstein, *Beobachtungen*, 132-75.

The speech is like 2 Macc 6-7 in content, and only the aim of the author of 4 Maccabees, rather than unknown sources such as the lost work of Jason of Cyrene (2 Macc 2:23), explain the differences. One of these is the length of the description of the martyrdom of the mother. Oratorical licence is perhaps a better explanation of the speech than the obscurity of its sources.

The basic statement of the work is that total fidelity to the Lord and his Law, even to death, is something possible and beneficial. Steeped in the Bible, the author is convinced that God looks after his own. He takes up the Greek term 'providence' and adds to it the nuance, as do Philo and other Jewish teachers, that divine providence is directly interested in human beings (9:24; 13:19; 17:22). To die a martyr is not to disappear but to gain eternal life (15:2; 17:18), to live for God (7:19; 16:25), to be with him (9:8), to gain incorruptibility (9:22; 17:12), and immortality (16:13) of the soul (18:23). Unlike 2 Macc 7:9, 23; and 14:46, 4 Maccabees does not speak of the resurrection of the body. To die a martyr also means serving as a ransom through suffering, expiating the faults of the community, purifying the fatherland, gaining peace for the nation and chastisement for the tyrants, whose arrogance is already conquered by the martyr's endurance (1:11; 6:29; 9:24; 12:17; 17:20-22; 18:4). These affirmations go further than 2 Macc 6:12-17; 7:37-38. Some occur again in the New Testament; see Matt 20:28. They may also have been influenced by Isa 53:8-12.

Eusebius (*Hist. eccl.* 3:10,6) and Jerome (*De viris illustribus,* 13) wrongly attribute 4 Maccabees to Flavius Josephus, and give it the title 'Of the Sovereignty of Reason'. The author is in fact unknown. He wrote the work at Alexandria, or, more probably, at Antioch, where later tradition placed the martyrdom of the seven brothers.[127] The date of composition is still matter for discussion. While some think of the reign of Caligula,[128] about 40 C.E., others put it as late as Trajan or Hadrian, the first part of the second century.[129] Rabbinic tradition does in fact speak of the martyrdom of a mother and her seven sons under Hadrian.[129a] The discourse may have been occasioned by the feast of Hanukkah or even by commemoration of the seven brothers at the place of their martyrdom, as some have suggested.[130] Proofs are not easy to find.

In any case, 4 Maccabees was known to Christians. Some Fathers drew inspiration from it.[131] The text was in the main transmitted by Christians, as were translations. Among others, the *Passio SS. Machabaeorum,*[132] a

[127] See Rampolla del Tindaro, 'Martyre et sépulture.'
[128] Hades, *Fourth Book,* 95-99.
[129] Dupont-Sommer, *Quatrième Livre;* Breitenstein, *Beobachtungen,* 173-5.
[129a] *Seder Eliahu Rabba* 30 (pp. 151-3); *Pesikta Rabbati* 43 (180 b).
[130] Hadas, *Fourth Book,* 103-9.
[131] Gregory of Nazianzus, *PG* 35, 911-954; John Chrysostom, *PG* 50, 617-628; 64, 525-550; Ambrose, *PL* 14, 627ff., 662f.; see Freudenthal, *Flavius Josephus,* 29-34.
[132] Edited by Dörrie.

Latin adaptation of 4 Maccabees, seems to go back to the fourth century. Further, even without affirming a relation of influence,[133] certain analogies must be recognized between 4 Maccabees and the ancient Christian theology of Martyrdom.

Texts Related to Wisdom Literature

Besides the works which are expressly and wholly concerned with wisdom, some other Jewish and early Christian writings which are related to the wisdom literature should be mentioned. From Jewish literature the following works belong to this category. *Pirke Aboth* is a collection, mostly in chronological order, of the characteristic sayings of the principal Tannaim, working back through their predecessors to Moses. The main subject matter is the behaviour of the Sage and the study of the Torah (chs. 1-2), the afterlife and judgement (chs. 3-4, chapters associated with Akiba and his school). Ch. 5 deals mainly with events narrated in the Bible and draws a portrait of the disciple. These sayings, which often touch on practical details of everyday life, are not without their nobility and religious depth. The invitation to study Torah, which is the fundamental thesis, inspired by respect for God's plan for the world and man, of which Israel is the witness. Tobit seems to link up, through its references to Ahikar, to the wisdom tradition.[134] Ch. 4 gives Tobit's testament in the form of a counsel or maxims, some of which are taken exactly from Ahikar.[135] Baruch 3:9-4:4 is an invitation to Israel to remain faithful to the Torah, which is the path of knowledge or wisdom which God has revealed only to Israel. This poem, similar in subject matter to Job 28 and Sir 24, may have been written in the second century B.C.E.[136] 1 Esdras 3:1-5:6 is a story of wisdom character. This text has a certain resemblance to Egyptian and Greek stories. It seems to be later than the Book of Daniel and earlier than Flavius Josephus.[137]

Wisdom texts of early Christianity are to be found in the New Testament and in some early patristic works. The synoptic gospels often report Jesus' teaching in sapiential form. The Sermon on the Mount (Matt 5-7) is a good example. His parables are like the *meshalim* of the rabbis. Some texts explicitly attribute wisdom to Jesus (Luke 2:40, 52; Matt 13:54 and parallels). There are four texts which affirm that Jesus is the sage par

---

[133] Surkau, *Martyrien*, maintains that a Jewish literary genre was the source for Christian stories of martyrdom. This is going too far; see the reviews by P. Devos in *Analecta Bollandiana* 67 (1939) 136-8 and by F. M. Abel in *RB* 53 (1946) 306-8.
[134] On the book of Tobit, see above, pp. 40-6.
[135] Ahikar is mentioned Tob 1:21-22; 2:10; 11:19, and in 14:10 where the narrative is resumed. Tob 4:10, 15, 17, 19 seem to have taken these sayings from those of Ahikar — though not according to the Aramaic text.
[136] On Baruch see above, pp. 141-2.
[137] On 1 Esdras see above, pp. 133f.

excellence or even wisdom itself (Matt 11:19 and Luke 7:35; Matt 11:25-30 and Luke 10:20-22; Matt 12:42 and Luke 11:31; Matt 23:34-36 and Luke 11:49-51). The prologue of the Gospel of John (1:1-18), attributes to the Logos, Jesus, qualities affirmed of wisdom in Jewish writings. The discourse on the bread of life in John 6 is to be explained in part by biblical and other Jewish texts dealing with the banquet offered by wisdom (Prov 9:1-6; Sir 24:19-21). There are some major texts in the epistles of Paul where Jesus is seen as the embodiment of God's wisdom, especially 1 Corinthians 1-2 and Colossians 1:15-20. Finally, the Epistle of James has the appearance of a sapiential book, staying close to everyday life, and mainly addressed to Christians coming from the Jewish diaspora. The *Two Ways*, the way of life or light and the way of death or darkness, seems to be a short work of moral teaching, written by a Palestinian Jew before 70 C.E. It is known only through three Christian works, which depend on it: *The Doctrine of the Twelve Apostles* preserved only in Latin; the *Didache* 2:2-6:1, which prefaces the *Two Ways* with some Christian doctrine (1:3-2) from befvore 70; and the *Epistle of Barnabas,* 18-20, which seems to be from between 130 and 150.[138]

The *Sentences of Sextus* are an originally pagan work, re-written by a second century Christian. It contains 451 religious and moral aphorisms, in Greek.

The *Teachings of Silvanus,* a piece of wisdom writing found at Nag Hammadi in 1948. It is Christian, not gnostic, and seems to have been written at the end of the second century or the beginning of the third, at Alexandria. The inspiration is Jewish, though it shows Stoic tendencies in ethics and Platonic in speaking of God.[139]

BIBLIOGRAPHY

Wisdom Texts from the Ancient Near East
The principal texts of Mesopotamian and Egyptian wisdom have been translated in PRITCHARD, *ANET,* 405-40, See also LAMBERT, *Babylonian Wisdom;* ALSTER, *Instructions of Šuruppak;* VAN DIJK, *Sagesse suméro-accadienne;* NOUGAYROL, 'Sagesses babyloniennes'; BUCCELLATI, 'Wisdom and Not'; LICHTHEIM, *Ancient Egyptian Literature* 1, 58-80, 134-92; 2, 135-78; 3, 159-217; LECLANT, 'Documents nouveaux', and 'Sagesses de l'Egypte'; FOX, 'Two decades'; WILLIAMS, 'Sages of Ancient Egypt.' For Greek Wisdom see the systematic presentation by LEISENGANG, 'Sophia', and the general studies by HENGEL, *Hellenism,* and Küchler, *Frühjüdische Weisheitstraditionen.*

[138] See Kraft-Prigent, *Epitre de Barnabé,* 12-20; Rordorf-Tuilier, *Doctrine des Douze Apôtres,* 22-34.
[139] See Zandee, 'Morale des 'enseignements''.

Wisdom of Ahikar. The Aramaic text has been edited by COWLEY, *Aramaic Papyri*, 204-48, and translated and annotated by GRELOT, *Documents araméens*, 429-52.

Biblical Wisdom Literature

General. A survey by MURPHY, 'Hebrew Wisdom.' General works: DUESBERG, *Scribes inspirés;* especially VON RAD, *Weisheit in Israel.* Collected studies: NOTH-THOMAS (eds.), *Wisdom in Israel;* GAMMIE (ed.), *Israelite Wisdom;* especially CRENSHAW (ed.), *Studies,* and GILBERT (ed.), *Sagesse de l'Ancien Testament.* General issues: MCKANE, *Prophets and Wise Men;* WHYBRAY, *Intellectual Tradition.* Connections with non-biblical wisdom: HUMBERT, *Recherches;* RINGGREN, *Word and Wisdom* (on hypostasis); SCHMID, *Wesen und Geschichte;* PERDUE, *Wisdom and Cult.*

The Book of Proverbs. Bibliography up to 1970 by VATTIONI, 'Studi'. Major commentaries: TOY (1899), GEMSER (1963^2), BARUCH (1964), MCKANE (1970). Studies on Prov 1-9: ROBERT, 'Attaches littéraires'; KAYATZ, *Studien;* WHYBRAY, *Wisdom in Proverbs;* LANG, *Weisheitliche Lehrrede* and *Frau Weisheit.* On Prov 10-29: SKLADNY, *Ältesten Spruchsammlungen;* HERMISSON, *Studien.* On Prov 22,17-24,22 and Amenemope: MARZAL, *Enseñanza;* BRYCE, *Legacy.* On Prov 30: SAUER, *Sprüche Agurs.* Thematic Studies: RICHTER, *Recht und Ethos;* BÜHLMANN, *Rechten Reden.* Linguistic connections with Ugaritic: DAHOOD, *Proverbs,* and VAN DER WEIDEN, *Proverbes.* On the Septuagint: MEZZACASA, *Studio critico;* GERLEMAN, 'Septuagint Proverbs' and *Studies.* On the Vetus Latina: SCHILDENBERGER, *Altlateinischen Texte.*

The Book of Job. Major commentaries: DRIVER-GRAY (1921), DHORME (1926), FOHRER (1963), GORDIS (1978), ALONSO SCHÖKEL (1983). Some studies: JUNG, *Answer to Job,* from a psychoanalytical perspective; WESTERMANN, *Aufbau;* GESE, *Lehre;* SNAITH, *Book of Job;* LÉVÊQUE, *Job et son Dieu;* NEMO, *Job et l'excès du mal.* Connections with Ugaritic: BLOMMERDE, *Northwest Semitic;* CERESKO, *Job 29-31.* The targum found at Qumran (11Q): VAN DER PLOEG-VAN DER WOUDE, *Targum de Job;* SOKOLOFF, *Targum of Job;* JONGELING-LABUSCHAGNE, *Aramaic Texts.* The Testament of Job: BROCK, *Testamentum Iobi;* SCHALLER, *Testament Hiobs.*

Qohelet. Survey: BRETON, 'Qoheleth Studies.' Major commentaries: PODECHARD (1912), ZIMMERLI (1962), HERTZBERG (1963), DI FONZO (1967), LYS (1977: on Qoh 1-4), LAUHA (1979), LOHFINK (1980). Major studies: GORDIS, *Koheleth* (with commentary); LORETZ, *Qohelet* (connections with Egyptian and especially Mesopotamian wisdom); BRAUN, *Koheleth* (connections with Greek thought); ELLERMEIER, *Qohelet* (structure, composition and meaning of the text); DAHOOD, 'Influence in Qohelet' (linguistic connections with Ugaritic). The text found at Qumran: MUILENBURG, 'Qoheleth Scroll'; VOGT, 'Fragmentum Qohelet'. On the Septuagint version, BERTRAM, 'Hebräischer und griechischer Qohelet';

BARTHÉLEMY, *Devanciers,* 21-33, 158-9; HOLM-NIELSEN, 'Interpretation'; GRABBE, 'Aquila's Translation'. The targum which contains traditions related to those of the Palestinian Targum, has been translated by GINSBURG, *Coheleth,* 502-19, and analysed by KOMLOSH, 'PSHAT and DRASH'. The midrash (7th-8th cent. C.E., but with Tannaic traditions) has been translated by WÜNSCHE, *Midrasch Kohelet,* and by COHEN, in FREEDMAN-SIMON, *Midrash Rabbah* 8.

Ben Sira

Bibliography: DELLING, *Bibliographie,* 131-6. Concordances: *Ben Sira* (Hebrew text and concordance); BARTHÉLEMY-RICKENBACHER, *Konkordanz* (Hebrew); WINTER, *Concordance to the Peshitta.* The better commentaries are those of SMEND (1906) and PETERS (1913). Studies on the history of the text: DI LELLA, *Hebrew Text,* and RÜGER, *Text und Textform.* On the texts found at Qumran: on 2Q18 see *DJD* 3, 75, nr 18; Segal, 'Ben Sira in Qumran'. On 11QPs^a, col XXI-XXII, see *DJD* 4, 79-85; DELCOR, 'Siracide LI'; RABINOWITZ, 'Qumran Hebrew'; SKEHAN, 'Acrostic Poem'. On the text found at Masada, see YADIN, *Ben Sira Scroll;* MILIK, 'Fragment mal placé'; BAUMGARTEN, 'Some Notes'; STRUGNELL, 'Notes and Queries'. A list of the Hebrew fragments found in the Cairo Genizah, with indications of their editions, is given in DUESBERG-FRANSEN, *Ecclesiastico,* 335-6, and VATTIONI, *Ecclesiastico,* XIX-XXIII. For a study of these Hebrew texts, cf. LEVI, *Ecclésiastique;* SEGAL, *Sefer Ben Sira* (commentary in Hebrew); LEVI, *Hebrew Text;* DI LELLA, 'Recently Identified'. On the origin of the Hebrew fragments found at Cairo, see LAMBERT, 'Manuscrits, IV'; DI LELLA, 'Qumrân'. A list of Ben Sira quotations in rabbinic literature is given by SCHECHTER, 'Quotations', and COWLEY-NEUBAUER, *Original Hebrew,* XIX-XXX. The best critical edition of the Greek text which also enables to distinguish the additions to the shorter text, is that of ZIEGLER, *Sapientia Iesu filii Sirach;* the longer recension of MS. 248 is edited by HART, *Ecclesiasticus.* The Latin version is edited in *Sapientia-Sirach;* it is studied in DE BRUYNE, 'Ecclésiastique'. The Syriac text is edited by LAGARDE, *Libri Veteris Testamenti apocryphi syriace,* and reproduced by VATTIONI, *Ecclesiastico.* On the evolution of the text of Ben Sira, see, apart from the article by DE BRUYNE just mentioned, SEGAL, 'Evolution'; ZIEGLER, 'Hexaplarische Bearbeitung'; and the two studies mentioned above by DI LELLA and RÜGER. On Ben Sira quotations by the first Christians see, apart from the studies by Hart and De Bruyne just mentioned, EBERHARTER, 'Ecclesiasticuszitate' and 'Text of Ecclesiasticus'; VACCARI, 'Dove sta scritto'; ZIEGLER, 'Zu ἐνεφυσίωσεν'. Articles on the thought of Ben Sira: HASPECKER, *Gottesfurcht;* HADOT, *Penchant mauvais;* MARBÖCK, *Weisheit im Wandel;* RICKENBACHER, *Weisheitsperikopen;* MIDDENDORP, *Stellung;* PRATO, *Problema della teodicea;* STADELMANN, *Ben Sira als Schriftgelehrter;* REITERER, *'Urtext' und Uebersetzungen* (on Sir 44:16-45:26). Principal shorter studies:

BAUMGARTNER, 'Literarischen Gattungen'; BÜCHLER, 'Conception of Sin'; SPICQ, 'Siracide et structure' (connection with John 1); HAMP, 'Zukunft'; MOWINCKEL, 'Metrik'; KAISER, 'Begründung der Sittlichkeit'; PAUTREL, 'Ben Sira et le stoïcisme'; CONZELMANN, 'Mutter der Weisheit' (on Sir 24:3-4); CAQUOT, 'Ben Sira et le messianisme'; DELCOR, 'Siracide LI'; GILBERT, 'Eloge de la Sagesse' (on Sir 24), and 'Ben Sira et la femme'; MARBÖCK, 'Sir. 38, 24-39, 11'; PRATO, 'Lumière'; MACKENZIE, 'Ben Sira as historian' (on Sir 44-49); JACOB, 'Sagesse et religion'.

Wisdom of Solomon

GILBERT, 'Bibliographie'. Greek text: the best critical edition is that of ZIEGLER, *Sapientia Salomonis*. On the Vetus Latina: THIELE, *Sapientia*. On the text of the Vulgate: see the Roman critical edition, *Sapientia*. On the Syriac version: EMERTON-LANE, *Wisdom*. Major commentaries: GRIMM, (1860), DEANE (1881), CORNELY (1910), HEINISCH (1912), GOODRICK (1913), WINSTON (1979), LARCHER (appeared from 1983). Some earlier studies: HEINISCH, *Griechische Philosophie;* GÄRTNER, *Komposition;* FOCKE, *Entstehung;* SCHÜTZ, *Idées eschatologiques;* BÜCKERS, *Unsterblichkeitslehre;* SKEHAN, *Studies* (especially on the connections between Wisdom and the older biblical books). Some recent studies: ZIENER, *Theologische Begriffssprache;* LARCHER, *Etudes* (on the impact of Wisdom on the N.T. and its reception in Christianity; Hellenistic influence; eschatology; conception of Wisdom and of the Spirit); REESE, *Hellenistic Influence;* GILBERT, *Critique des dieux* (Wis 13-15); OFFERHAUS, *Komposition und Intention*. Some short studies: WEISENGOFF, 'Impious' (on Wis 2); COLOMBO, 'Πνεῦμα σοφίας'; DUBARLE, 'Source'; DELCOR, 'Immortalité' (the latter two studies on the connections with Qumran); BEAUCHAMP, 'Salut Corporel'; TAYLOR, 'Eschatological Meaning'; WRIGHT, 'Structure'; GILBERT, 'Structure de la prière' (Wis 9); NICKELSBURG, *Resurrection*, 48-92; MACK, *Logos und Sophia*, 63-107; BEAUCHAMP, 'Epouser la Sagesse'.

Phocylides and 4 Maccabees

VAN DER HORST, *Sentences;* HADAS, *Fourth Book* (text and commentary); DUPONT-SOMMER, *Quatrième Livre*. Studies: RAMPOLLA, 'Martyre et sépulture'; SURKAU, *Martyrien;* BREITENSTEIN, *Beobachtungen*. DÖRRIE has edited the *Passio SS. Machabaeorum*.

Texts Related to Wisdom Literature

Tobit. On the unpublished texts found at Qumran, see MILIK, 'Patrie de Tobie', 522, n. 3. The Greek and Latin versions have been edited by BROOKE-MCLEAN-THACKERAY, *Old Testament* 3:1, 85-144. On Tobit and Ahikar, GREENFIELD, 'Ahiqar in Tobit'; DESELAERS, *Buch Tobit*, 438-48.

New Testament. On the parables: FIEBIG, *Altjüdische Gleichnisse;* BUZY, *Introduction aux Paraboles;* HERMANIUK, *Parabole;* PAUTREL, 'Canons du mashal'. On the synoptic gospels: BULTMANN, *Geschichte der synoptischen Tradition*, 73-113; BEARDSLEE, 'Uses of Proverbs'. On the sapiential aspects which can be ascribed to the Quelle: ROBINSON, 'ΛΟΓΟΙ ΣΟΦΩΝ'; EDWARDS, *Theology of Q*, 58-79. On Jesus as Wisdom: CHRIST, *Jesus Sophia;* SUGGS, *Wisdom, Christology;* and the criticism by JOHNSON, 'Reflections'. On the analogies between Matt 11:25-30 and Sir 51: FEUILLET, 'Jésus et la Sagesse'; CERFAUX, 'Sources scripturaires'; LAMBERT, 'Mon joug'. On the Gospel of John: DODD, *Historical Tradition*, 315-405; BRAUN, 'Saint Jean, la Sagesse', and *Jean le Théologien* 2, 115-50. On John 1 and the wisdom books: HARRIS, *Origin of the Prologue;* SPICQ, 'Siracide et la structure'; DODD, *Interpretation*, 273-5; on John and Wisdom: ZIENER, 'Weisheitsbuch and Johannesevangelium'. On Paul: WINDISCH, 'Göttliche Weisheit'; DAVIES, *Paul and Rabbinic Judaism*, 147-76; FEUILLET, *Christ Sagesse;* for a different view: CERFAUX, *Christ*, 189-208; VAN ROON, 'Relation'. On Col 1; 15-20: BURNEY, 'Christ as the APXH'; FEUILLET, 'Premiers-nés'; ALETTI, *Colossiens 1, 15-20*.

Patristic texts: AUDET, *Didachè;* RORDORF-TUILIER, *Doctrine*, 22-34, 140-69, 203-10 (Latin text of the 'Doctrina Apostolorum'); PRIGENT-KRAFT, *Barnabé*, 12-20, 194-219; CHADWICK, *Sentences of Sextus*. For the *Teachings of Silvanus* see the English translation by PEEL-ZANDEE; their essay 'The Teachings of Silvanus' and ZANDEE, 'Morale des enseignements.'

Chapter Eight

Testaments

J. J. Collins

The Genre Testament

Every tradition-oriented society has attached great importance to the last words of famous men. Farewell discourses abound in the biblical tradition from the earliest stages, e.g. Gen 49 (Jacob), Deut 33 (Moses), Joshua 23-24 (Joshua), 1 Sam 12 (Samuel), 1 Kgs 2:1-9, 1 Chr 28-29 (David). Yet the independent genre testament only emerges in the Hellenistic age, and is poorly attested even then apart from the *Testaments of the Twelve Patriarchs.*

The most fundamental defining characteristic of a testament is that it is a discourse delivered in anticipation of imminent death. Typically the speaker is a father addressing his sons, or a leader addressing his people, or his successor. The testament begins by describing in the third person the situation in which the discourse is delivered, and ends with an account of the speaker's death. The actual discourse, however, is delivered in the first person.

It is questionable whether the pattern of the content can be built in to the definition of the genre.[1] The *Test. 12 Patr.* display a consistent pattern which involves three basic elements: a) historical retrospective, in the form of a narrative about the patriarch's life (the *Testament of Asher* is the only exception); b) ethical exhortation; and c) prediction of the future. These predictions often display the so-called 'Sin-Exile-Return' pattern which is typical of the Deuteronomic history.[2] The *Testament (Assumption) of*

---

[1] The most thorough attempt to defend a definition of the genre which includes a set pattern of content, is that of von Nordheim, *Das Testament als Literaturgattung.* His outline is most fully exemplified in the *Test. 12 Patr.,* but he admits that major elements of this outline may be absent in a given testament. M. de Jonge in his review of this work (*JSJ* 12, 1981, pp. 112-17), has even questioned whether there is enough evidence to speak of a genre at all. The broader genre of farewell discourse is discussed by Cortès, *Los discursos.*

[2] A detailed outline of the *Test. 12 Patr.* is given by von Nordheim, *Das Testament,* 90 and Hultgård, *L'eschatologie* 2, 136-164. A simpler outline is given by Nickelsburg, *Jewish Literature,* 232. The 'Sin-Exile-Return' pattern was identified by M. de Jonge, *The Testaments,* 83-86. The affinity of the Testaments with the Deuteronomic 'covenant form' has been pursued by Baltzer, *The Covenant Formulary.* Kolenkow, 'The Genre Testament and Forecasts of the Future' distinguishes between 'ethical' testaments (*Test. 12 Patr.*) and 'blessing-revelation' testaments and emphasizes future predictions as a key element in the genre.

Moses consists almost entirely of prediction. As in the *Test. 12 Patr.*, much of the prediction is an *ex eventu* account of the history of Israel. There is very little direct exhortation and no historical retrospective. The *Testament of Job*, by contrast, is predominantly retrospective and is a re-telling of the life of Job. While the conduct of the patriarch is evidently exemplary, direct exhortation is found in only two brief passages. There is also no future prediction. In each case the testament may be said to have a hortatory purpose,[3] but the exhortation is much more direct and explicit in the *Test. 12 Patr.* than in the *Testament of Moses.* In short, the form of a testament is constituted by the narrative framework; the contents can not be said to follow a fixed pattern.

The Corpus

Test. 12 Patr., Test. Moses and *Test. Job* are the only clear examples of testaments from the area under consideration here which are independent works. (The conclusion of *Test. Moses* is lost, so we can only assume that it ended with some account of the death of Moses). To these might arguably be added the fragmentary 4Q Visions of Amram from Qumran, which is presented as the book of the words of the vision of Amram , son of Kohat, son of Levi, which he transmitted to his sons on the day of his death.[4] However, the conclusion of the work is missing, and even the introduction differs from the usual format of a testament since it is a summary heading rather than a direct narrative. The content of the testament concerns the vision of the demonic Melchiresha and his angelic counterpart (presumably Melchisedek). In so far as the words of Amram constitute a vision report they are significantly different from the *Test. 12 Patr., Test. Moses* or *Test. Job* (although vision reports are found as a subordinate element in *Test. Levi, Test. Naphtali* and *Test. Joseph*).

A number of other works which are known as testaments either do not conform to the genre or fall outside the scope of this review for other reasons. It is now well-known that the *Testament of Abraham* is not a testament at all, since it contains no farewell discourse by Abraham.[5] The work is a narrative which contains an apocalypse in Abraham's chariot ride (Rec. A, 10-15; Rec. B, 8-12). Since this apocalypse is an integral and crucial element in the story, *Test. Abraham* can be viewed either as a narrative or as an apocalypse,[6] but it is clearly not a testament.

---

[3] Harrelson, 'The significance of Last Words.'
[4] Von Nordheim, *Das Testament*, 115-18. He also cites a frament which Milik attributes to a testament of Kohat. See further Kobelski, *Melchizedek*, 3-48.
[5] Kolenkow, 'The Genre Testament and the Testament of Abraham'; von Nordheim, *Das Testament*, 136-50.
[6] Collins, *Apocalypse*, 42; *id.,* 'The Genre Apocalypse.'

The *Testament of Solomon* bears only a superficial resemblance to the genre.[7] In 15:14 Solomon says that he wrote this testament before his death so that the Israelites might know the power of the demons and their shapes, and the names of the angels by which the demons are defeated. Again in the final chapter (26:8) Solomon declares that he wrote this testament (ταύτην μου διαθήκην) so that those who hear it might pray, attend to the last things and find grace forever. However, the usual testamentary framework, describing the occasion and concluding with the death, is missing. The narrative begins in the third person and slides into the first person without formal notice. The content consists mainly of demonological lore. There is only a very small hortatory component, in the negative example of Solomon's lust and idolatry. In its present form the work is clearly Christian and dates from about the third century C.E. Some of the narrative sections may be Jewish in origin and date from the first century C.E., but the presentation of the work as a testament is a later development.

The *Testament of Adam* consists of three parts.[8] The first is the *Horarium* which concerns 'the hours of the day and of the night and the times at which various creatures offer worship'. Adam is the implied speaker, but there is no narrative framework. The second part is a prophecy by Adam of the coming of Christ, his own (Adam's) death and future restoration through Christ, and the Flood. This section ends with the burial of Adam, and the placing of his testament in the Cave of the Treasures. The third section is a treatise on the heavenly powers. While these three sections were apparently intended to form a unity by the final redactor, they are only loosely related to each other. The *Horarium* is found independently in Greek.[9] Only the second section bears any formal resemblance to a testament, in so far as it is an address of Adam to his son Seth and describes his burial. Even here the narrative introduction describing the occasion of the testament is missing. *Test. Adam* is clearly Christian in its present form and the Christian elements are most obvious in the prophecy.[10] The recon-

---

[7] McCown, *The Testament of Solomon;* von Nordheim, *Das Testament,* 185-93. For a new translation and introduction by Duling, 'The Testament of Solomon', which updates McCown's work, see Charlesworth, *Pseudepigrapha.* Duling emphasizes the evidence that Solomon was associated with magic in first century Palestine, but leaves the provenance of the Testament open.

[8] Robinson, *The Testament of Adam.* The Testament also exists in Arabic, Karshuni, Ethiopic, Old Georgian and Armenian. See also Bezold, 'Das arabisch-äthiopische Testamentum Adami.'

[9] See further Stone, *Armenian Apocrypha.* The authorship of the *Horarium* is attributed to Adam in some writings and to Apollonius of Tyana in others.

[10] Robinson, *The Testament of Adam,* concludes that the *Horarium* is an originally Jewish composition, the prophecy is either a Christian composition or a heavily interpolated Jewish work and the treatise on the angels may be Jewish with slight interpolation. He dates the prophecy to the third century C.E. The *Horarium* may be older but the date of the treatise on the angels is quite uncertain. Robinson holds that the original language was Syriac.

struction of an earlier Jewish testament is complex and inevitably hypothetical.[11]

The *Testaments of Isaac and Jacob* illustrate a later, Christian, development of the genre.[12] Both are closely related to *Test. Abraham,* each describes the circumstances of the death of the patriarch and include a heavenly journey. Unlike Abraham, however, both Isaac and Jacob give their final exhortations in anticipation of death, and so each of these works can be regarded as a testament although they have extensive narrative frameworks and include apocalyptic heavenly journeys. Both are clearly Christian in their present form.

Recently von Nordheim has argued that both these testaments are substantially Jewish, and that the Christian elements are superficial.[13] His main argument is that they belong together with the *Testament of Abraham* and constitute *The Testaments of the Three Patriarchs.*[14] Yet it seems unlikely that the three were composed together. *Test. Abraham* is a highly ironic work, in which Abraham resists death (and so the will of God) to the end, and where excessive zeal for the punishment of sinners is shown to be itself sinful. There is no such irony in *Test. Isaac* and *Test. Jacob,* which are far more conventionally edifying. Further, if *Test. Abraham* had been part of a Jewish trilogy we should expect that it would have undergone Christian revisions analogous to those in *Test. Isaac* and *Test. Jacob,* but this not the case. The main Jewish influence in these books comes from the *Test. Abraham,* and, in the case of *Test. Jacob,* the text of Genesis. A Christian author who undertook to complete the *Testaments of the Three Patriarchs* could easily have drawn on these sources. Accordingly, the hypothesis that

---

[11] Von Nordheim, *Das Testament,* 171-84. We may note that a formally complete *Testament of Adam* is found (without the title) in the *Cave of the Treasures* 6:6-21 (Budge, *The Book of the Cave of the Treasures,* 71-74), in which Adam gives instructions for his burial, tells Seth to be ruler of the people and warns against contact with the sons of Cain. Von Nordheim supposes that this passage reflects an early strand of the *Testament of Adam.* Already in the *Life of Adam and Eve* 30:1, we read that when Adam was 930 years old and knew that his days were coming to an end he summoned his sons to speak with them. The following chapters contain a brief dialogue with Seth in which Adam recounts the story of the Fall, but Adam does not give an extended testament. Instead a narrative describes the attempt of Eve and Seth to get the oil of life. Then after six days Adam dies. These chapters do not amount to a testament of Adam but they attest an early interest in his death and last words. On the *Life of Adam and Eve* see Nickelsburg, above pp. 110-18.

[12] *Test. Isaac* survives in Bohairic, Sahidic, Arabic and Ethiopic; *Test. Jacob* in Bohairic, Arabic and Ethiopic. See Kuhn, 'The Sahidic Version of the Testament of Isaac'; *id.* 'An English Translation'; Gaselee, 'Appendix'; Delcor, *Le Testament d'Abraham,* 186-267; Stone, 'The Testament of Jacob' (1968); *id.,* 'Two Additional Notes'; Charlesworth, *Modern Research,* 123-5; 130-3.

[13] Von Nordheim, *Das Testament,* 136-70.

[14] This title is found in the *Apostolic Constitutions* 6:16. It presumably refers to the *Testaments of Abraham, Isaac and Jacob,* but we have no guarantee that the collective title was Jewish in origin.

there were Jewish testaments of Isaac and Jacob remains unproven.[15]

There are, however, a number of testaments embedded in other Jewish works of the period before Bar Kokhba. Tobit 14 contains a testament of Tobit which is largely predictive but includes a brief exhortation to 'keep the law and the commandments, and be merciful and just, so that it may be well with you.' 1 Macc 2:49-70 contains a testament of Mattathias, which recalls the great deeds of the fathers and concludes with an exhortation to 'be courageous and grow strong in the law' (1 Macc 2:64). The book of *Jubilees* contains testaments of Abraham (chap. 21) and Isaac (chap. 36). Both are primarily exhortations to practise righteousness. The *Book of Biblical Antiquities* contains testaments of Moses (chap. 19, cf. Deut 31-34), Joshua (chaps. 23-24, cf. Joshua 23-24) and Deborah (chap. 33). *2 Enoch* is presented as a discourse of Enoch before his death. Specifically, chaps. 14-18 contain Enoch's parting testament and conclude with the assumption of Enoch to heaven.[16] In *2 Apoc. Bar.* 43-47 Baruch gives his last instruction to his people, but the passage does not conclude with his death.

These testaments embedded in other works show that the literary form was widely known despite the paucity of testaments as free-standing works. They also remind us that there is only a thin line between the genre 'testament' and the broader category of 'last words' where the distinctive testamentary framework is lacking.

Relation to Other Literature

Literary testaments occur in Greek literature but they are poorly attested and late.[17] Menippus of Gadara (approx. 300 B.C.E.) is said to have written διαθῆκαι, but they have not survived. Presumably his use of the form was ironic, as were his *Nekyia* and epistles. The parodies of Menippus do not necessarily presuppose literary testaments, as he may have adapted the juridical form of testament or will. Later, testaments are ascribed to Apollonius of Tyana and Peregrinus Proteus. More broadly, Greek literature

---

[15] Two other alleged Jewish testaments may be mentioned briefly. *A Testament of Hezekiah* is quoted by Cedrenus about 1100 C.E. and the citation corresponds to verses in the *Ascension of Isaiah* (3:13b-4:18); as identified by Charles (see *Ascension of Isaiah*). However, that passage is neither called a testament nor bears the form of a testament and is clearly Christian in its present form. The so-called *Testament of Orpheus* is indeed a Jewish poem, which is said to come from a book entitled *Diathēkai* (Ps. Justin, *De Monarchia* 2). The poem is also preserved in other recensions without reference to the *Diathēkai*. In its present form it is not a testament. See Denis, *Introduction*, 230-8; *id.*, *Fragmenta Pseudepigraphorum*, 163-7.

[16] Vaillant, *Le Livre des Sécrets d'Hénoch*, 55-65. *1 Enoch* also concludes with instructions of Enoch to his children. Nickelsburg has suggested that 'At an early stage in the literary history of 1 Enoch chaps. 1-36 and 92-105 may have formed the major parts of an Enochic testament, with chaps. 81-82 and 91 serving as a narrative bridge between the two parts' (*Jewish Literature*, 150).

[17] Küchler, *Frühjüdische Weisheitstraditionen*, 415-19; Lohmeyer, *Diatheke*, 32-35; Hultgård, *L'eschatologie* 2, 87-91.

has plentiful examples of 'last words' or farewell discourses which are not distinguished from their contexts as testaments.[18]

The Jewish genre testament does not appear to have been modelled on Hellenistic literature but can be most readily traced to the Bible. The blessing of Jacob in Genesis 49 is already in the form of a testament, and is in fact called the Testament of Jacob in some manuscripts.[19] Here we find already the testamentary framework in the third person, which begins with the occasion (49:1) and concludes with the death of the patriarch. Deut 31-34 is a less clearcut example, but one which had obvious influence on the later tradition.[20]

Recently von Nordheim has sought the origins of the genre in the wisdom instructions of the ancient near east.[21] Undoubtedly there is an affinity between testaments and other traditional discourses of fathers to sons, but the wisdom instructions lack the specific death-bed setting. Besides, the moral exhortation typical of wisdom is only one element in the composition of the testaments, and in some testaments narrative and prediction take a dominant role.

The Jewish testaments are often associated with apocalypses. The association is usually based on the *ex eventu* prophecies of history and eschatological sections in *Test. Moses* and the *Test. 12 Patr.* We should note, however, that prophecies of history are not a necessary element in testaments and are lacking in *Test. Job.* A more significant point of affinity lies in the common use of pseudepigraphy. Both the apocalypses and the testaments augment their authority by using the names of ancient, revered figures. The testaments differ from the apocalypses, however, in the role assigned to these figures. In the testaments, the patriarchs are the givers of revelation and instruction and speak from their own experience. The apocalyptic visionaries are cast as recipients of revelation which is mediated to them by supernatural beings (usually angels) although they may then pass it on to their sons in the manner of testaments.[22]

The *Test. 12 Patr.* and *Test. Moses* exhibit a Deuteronomic view of history which sees a pattern of sin and punishment in the history of Israel. This pattern, however, is not a necessary feature of the genre testament. We will discuss it in relation to the individual testaments.

The survival of the genre in early Christianity is shown by the Christian adaptation of *Test. 12 Patr.* and the complicated history of *Test. Isaac, Test.*

---

[18] Stauffer, 'Abschiedsreden,' gives examples from Homer, Plato, Sophocles, Herodotus and Xenophon.

[19] Wevers, *Genesis*, 28; Stone, 'The Testament of Jacob' (*EJ*); Charlesworth, *Modern Research*, 131-2.

[20] See further von Nordheim, *Die Lehre der Alten* 2.

[21] *Ibid.* The main texts are the Egyptian instructions of Ptahhotep, Onksheshonqy, Merikare and Amenemhet.

[22] Collins, *Apocalypse*, 44-45.

Jacob and *Test. Adam.*[23]   In the New Testament, we do not find any fully developed testament. The most significant analogies to testaments are found in the farewell discourses in John 13-17 and Acts 20:17-37.[24] Farewell discourses also remained important in the rabbinic tradition.[25]

The Testaments of the Twelve Patriarchs

TEXT AND PARALLEL TRADITIONS

The *Test. 12 Patr.* are preserved in Greek, Armenian and Slavonic. Charles, in his 1908 edition, used 9 Greek MSS., 12 Armenian and a Slavonic translation.[26] He distinguished two families in the Greek MSS., α and β, and regarded both as translations from Hebrew. The MS. *c* of the family α was regarded as the best MS. The Armenian text (A) is somewhat shorter than the Greek. Since some of the passages omitted by A are Christian, Charles sought to use this shorter text to remove the Christian influence on the *Test. 12 Patr.*, at least in part.

Charles' position has been rendered obsolete by futher discoveries of manuscripts.[27] More significantly his critical decisions have been challenged. The Hebrew originals of α and β are now widely rejected. M. de Jonge argued that the α text is a late inferior recension of the β text, and that *b* is the best MS. of the β family.[28] Accordingly, De Jonge used the *b* MS. in his *editio minor.*[29] More recently, in the new *editio maior,* he has completely discarded Charles' classification of α and β.[30] Instead, the textual tradition is divided into two branches or families: family I, consisting of the witnesses *b* and *k*, and family II, comprising all other witnesses — i.e. the split is located within Charles' family β, while α is only a late recension within family II.

De Jonge also argued against Charles that the Armenian version had been greatly overrated and that its omissions 'disfigure the text in many places.'[31] It is of little value for the removal of Christian interpolations. Subsequent studies have generally supported De Jonge's view that 'many variants noted in Charles' edition are inner-Armenian variants and do not

---

[23] The fifth century *Testament of the Lord* is an exceptional adaptation of the genre, since it is a discourse of the risen Lord. See Yarbro Collins, 'The Early Christian Apocalypses,' 77-78.

[24] Munck, 'Discourses d'adieu'; Michel, *Die Abschiedsrede des Paulus.*

[25] Saldarini, 'Last Words.'

[26] Charles, *Testaments of the Twelve Patriarchs.*

[27] H. J. de Jonge, 'Die Textüberlieferung.'

[28] M. de Jonge, *The Testaments* (1953) 13-22, in part following Hunkin, 'The Testaments.'

[29] De Jonge, *Testamenta XII Patriarcharum.*

[30] De Jonge, *The Testaments. A Critical Edition,* XXXIII-XLI. Compare *Studies,* 174-9 and H. J. de Jonge, 'Die Textüberlieferung.'

[31] De Jonge, *The Testaments,* 30-31.

represent differences between the prototype of the Armenian version and the Greek. The Greek text from which A derives will not have been so very different from the Greek manuscripts in our possession'.[32] The reappraisal of the textual tradition by De Jonge and his students has not gone unchallenged.[33] However, even De Jonge's critics now reject Charles' views on the text. It seems safe to say that the attempt to remove Christian interpolations by means of text criticism has been thoroughly undermined.

The textual history is further complicated by the existence of materials which are closely but only partially related to individual testaments. *Test. Judah* 3-7 relates the exploits of Judah. Parallel narrations of the same material can be found in *Jub.* 34:1-9 and in *Midrash Wayissau*.[34] The relations between these documents are very complex. They apparently depend on a common oral tradition, but use it in somewhat different ways.

Semitic parallels to *Test. Naphtali* and *Test. Levi* have been known since the turn of the century.[35] The Hebrew *Testament of Naphtali*[36] is now generally recognized as late, but its relation to the Greek is disputed.[37] A further parallel to *Test. Naphtali* 1:6-12 has been discovered in a Qumran fragment (Cave 4) written in Hebrew, which contains the genealogy of Bilhah.[38] In the third appendix to his edition (1908) Charles printed two Aramaic fragments of the same manuscript from the Cairo geniza, which had been discoverd at Oxford and Cambridge. These fragments provide a partial parallel to *Test. Levi* 8-13 and a remote parallel to *Test. Levi* 6. Charles also published in the same appendix a Greek fragment which was inserted in *Test. Levi* 18:2 in a manuscript from Mt. Athos (denoted *e*). This fragment provides a close parallel to the Aramaic. The Mt. Athos manuscript has another important addition at *Test. Levi* 2:3. Further fragmentary Aramaic parallels have now been found at Qumran. Milik has published fragments from Cave 1 and 'some more important pieces' from Cave 4 which parallel the texts from the Geniza and the two inserted

---

[32] De Jonge, *Studies*, 123. Burchard, 'Zur Armenischen Überlieferung'; Stone, *The Testament of Levi; id. The Armenian Version of the Testament of Joseph; id.* 'New Evidence for the Armenian Version of the Testaments of the *Twelve Patriarchs.'* Hultgård, *L'eschatologie* 2, 11-52 regards the Armenian as one of four independent branches of the textual tradition. On the Slavonic, see Turdeanu, *Apocryphes Slaves*, 239-75.

[33] Becker, *Die Testamente der Zwölf Patriarchen*, 17-21, follows an eclectic method and avoids the selection of the best text. So also Hultgård, *Croyances Messianiques.*

[34] The Midrash is printed in Charles, *The Greek Versions*, 235-8.

[35] *Ibid.* 239-56.

[36] Gaster, 'The Hebrew Text of One of the Testaments of the Twelve Patriarchs,' thought that it was the original of the Greek Testament.

[37] De Jonge, *The Testaments*, 52-60; Korteweg, 'The Meaning of Naphtali's Visions,' argue that both the Hebrew and the Greek depend on a common source and that the Hebrew is in some respects closer to the original. In contrast Becker, *Die Testamente*, 22, sees the Hebrew Testament as a late, loose adaptation of the Greek.

[38] Milik, *Ten Years of Discovery*, 34; *id., The Books of Enoch*, 198.

passages in the Mt. Athos MS.[39] The relationship between these Qumran fragments and the Greek *Test. Levi* is also disputed.[40] Small Aramaic fragments of *Test. Judah, Test. Joseph*[41] and *Test. Benjamin*,[42] and Hebrew fragments of *Test. Judah*[43] are reported to have been identified at Qumran. The identification of these smaller fragments, however, is quite uncertain and no weight can be placed upon them as yet.

CONTENTS

a) The *narrative sections* typically recount some episode from the patriarch's life to illustrate some vice or virtue, which is then the subject of the hortatory section. So for example in *Test. Reuben,* the story of Reuben's intercourse with Bilhah (Gen 35:22) serves as the point of departure for an exhortation against fornication. In *Test. Simeon,* Simeon's envy of Joseph becomes the basis for the exhortation. In *Test. Issachar,* the simplicity of the patriarch becomes the topic of a positive exhortation. Zebulun is also a positive model of compassion. *Test. Judah* interweaves the story of Judah's military exploits and that of his fornication. *Test. Joseph* contains two well-developed stories.[44] The first concerns Joseph's chastity in face of the seduction of the Egyptian woman (chaps. 3-9). The second story is episodic in nature and describes how Joseph's self-effacing love restrained him from bringing shame on others, especially the brothers who sold him into slavery. *Test. Levi* differs from the other testaments in so far as the narrative does not exemplify a virtue or vice but establishes the priesthood of Levi. In *Test. Asher* the narrative is replaced by a discourse on the two ways.

In most cases the narratives have a point of departure in the biblical text, but the story is developed to bring out the characteristic emphases of the testaments. So, for example, Judah's sin with Tamar is due to drunkenness, and Bilhah's drunkenness was the occasion of Reuben's sin. Joseph refuses to reveal the deed of his brothers, although this reticence is not mentioned in the biblical text. In cases such as these the development of the text is determined by the hortatory purpose. In view of the Qumran fragments we must assume that the Greek testaments also drew on older sources.

[39] Milik, 'Le Testament de Lévi en araméen'; *id., Ten Years,* 34; *id.,* 'Testament de Lévi' in *DJD* 1, 88-89; *id., The Books of Enoch,* 23-25; Grelot, 'Notes sur le Testament Araméen de Lévi'; Greenfield — Stone, 'Remarks on the Aramaic Testament of Levi from the Cairo Geniza.'

[40] De Jonge, *Studies,* 247-60; Haupt, *Das Testament Levi,* regards the Aramaic Levi as a source for *Test. Levi.* Becker, *Untersuchungen,* 69-105, argues for a more remote relationship.

[41] Milik, 'Ecrits préesseniens de Qumrân.'

[42] Fitzmyer, 'The Contribution of Qumran Aramaic to the Study of the New Testament', 405.

[43] Baillet, 'Le volume VII de *Discoveries in the Judaean Desert,*' 78

[44] See the essays in Nickelsburg, *Studies on the Testament of Joseph;* Hollander, *Joseph as an Ethical Model,* 16-49.

A feature of the narratives which requires special note is the prominence of Joseph. He is lauded as a man of exemplary virtue (*Test. Reuben* 4:8-10, *Test. Benjamin* 3) and he is third, after Levi and Judah, in the resurrection (*Test. Judah* 25:1). *Test. Naphtali* lacks the unfavourable remarks on Joseph found in the Hebrew testament.[45] In the testaments of Simeon, Zebulun, Dan and Gad the theme is illustrated by the attitude of the patriarchs towards Joseph. There is no doubt that in the final form of the *Test. 12 Patr.* Joseph is regarded as a type of Christ. This idea is explicit in *Test. Benjamin* 3:8 and is highly compatible with the emphasis on the selling of Joseph and on his forgiving love, while these emphases are not necessarily Christian in origin.[46]

b) We may distinguish three types of *hortatory material* in the *Test. 12 Patr.*, all of them interrelated: First, there is the exposition of a particular vice or virtue, with the aid of biblical examples; second are lists of vices and/or virtues, and third are passages which put such lists in a dualistic context, e.g. by elaborating the contrast of the two ways.

The exposition of a particular virtue may be illustrated from *Test. Reuben*. First, the patriarch declares his theme: 'Pay no heed to the face of a woman . . .' (3:10). He then provides as an illustration his misdemeanor with Bilhah (3:11-15) and concludes with the exhortation to 'pay no heed to the beauty of women . . .' (4:1-5). This exhortation is complete in itself but is supplemented in 4:6-6:5 with another, similarly structured sermon. Again, the patriarch begins by enunciating his theme: 'For a pit unto the soul is the sin of fornication.' This time the example adduced is that of Joseph: 'how he guarded himself from a woman and purged his thoughts from all fornication' (4:8). The evil of women is further illustrated by the story of the Fall of the Watchers before the Flood (5:1-7). Finally the exhortation concludes 'beware therefore of fornication' (6:1).

The biblical incidents are included here specifically as illustrations of a vice or virtue and its effects. The passages begin with the declaration of a theme, illustrate it by examples from biblical history and conclude with an exhortation. They constitute a rounded self-contained homily within the testament.[47] We may compare the list of examples of faith and the exhor-

---

[45] De Jonge, *The Testaments*, 97.

[46] *Ibid.*, 98-100. De Jonge sees christological references in *Test. Zebulun* 4:4, where Joseph spent three days and three nights in the pit (cf. Matt 12:40) and in *Test. Gad* 2:3-4, where Joseph is sold for 30 pieces of gold. For a defence of the Jewish origin of this portrait of Joseph, see Harrelson, 'Patient Love in the Testament of Joseph.' Compare also Flusser, 'A New Sensitivity.'

[47] On the structure of homilies in the Hellenistic synagogue see especially Borgen, *Bread from Heaven*, 28-58; Thyen, *Der Stil der jüdisch-hellenistischen Homilie*. The structure of the homiletic passages in the *Test. 12 Patr.* has been analysed by Aschermann, *Die paränetische Formen;* cf. *TLZ* 81 (1956), 479-80.

tation to perseverance in Hebrews 11-12. Similarly in *Test. Joseph* 2:4-10:3 we have a self-contained piece of exhortation. The patriarch begins by announcing his theme of ὑπομονή or endurance (2:7). He illustrates this at length from his adventures with the Egyptian woman (chaps. 3-9).[48] The discourse concludes with the repetition of the moral: 'Ye see therefore my children how great things patience worketh' (10:1) and an exhortation 'So ye too if ye follow after chastity and purity with patience and prayer . . . the Lord will dwell among you . . .' (10:2-3). Similar homiletic passages are found in *Test. Simeon* 2:5-5:3, *Test. Judah* 13-17. It should be noted that the theme of chastity and fornication enjoys special prominence in the *Test. 12 Patr.* [49]

The second type of hortatory material in the *Test. 12 Patr.* consists of lists of vices and virtues.[50] These lists are of various kinds. In *Test. Reuben* 2-3 we find a list of seven spirits which are appointed against man: the spirits of fornication, insatiability, fighting, obsequiousness, pride, lying and injustice. We may compare the evil spirit from God which fell upon king Saul (1 Sam 18:10), the spirit (or spirits) which will rest on the Messiah according to Isa 11:2 and the role of the two spirits in the *Community Rule* of Qumran (cf. below pp. 533-6).

Other passages in the *Test. 12 Patr.* catalogue the consequences of a particular virtue or vice. *Test. Gad* 4-5 elaborates the consequences of hatred and contrasts the effect of righteousness. *Test. Benjamin* 6 provides a list of things which the inclination of the good man does not do. Similarly *Test. Issachar* 4:2-6 lists the things which the simple-minded man does not do: covet gold, overreach his neighbour, etc.

Precedents for these negative lists can be found in the 'confessional' passages of the Bible such as Deut 26:13b-14: 'I have not transgressed any of the commandments, neither have I forgotten them. I have not eaten of the tithe while I was mourning or removed any of it while I was unclean or offered any of it to the dead; I have obeyed the voice of the Lord my God.' Further examples can be found in 1 Sam 12:3, Job 31:16-18 or in the Egyptian *Book of the Dead.* The analogy with the *Test. 12 Patr.* is obvious, but also limited.[51] Here the speaker is no longer simply a man, but a man who embodies a particular virtue. The sharply increased interest in the

---

[48] This section of *Test. Joseph* is apparently influenced by the Hellenistic Romance literature. See M. Braun, *History and Romance;* Pervo, 'The Testament of Joseph and Greek Romance.' Pervo regards the passage as a homily rather than a romance.

[49] Eppel, *Le Piétisme juif,* 154-7. For this theme in later Jewish literature see Safrai, 'The Teaching of Pietists in the Mishnaic Literature.'

[50] On the phenomenon in Hellenistic, Jewish and Christian literature, see Vögle, *Die Tugend- und Lasterkataloge im Neuen Testament;* Wibbing, *Die Tugend- und Lasterkataloge im Neuen Testament;* Kamlah, *Die Form der katalogischen Paränese im Neuen Testament.*

[51] Von Rad, 'Die Vorgeschichte der Gattung vom 1 Kor. 13:4-7'. See further Ps. 24; Ezek 18:5-9; Jer 17:5-8.

virtues as such is a characteristic of the Hellenistic age. We may recall Philo's use of the patriarchs as allegories of virtues (above, p. 237f.) Philo also makes frequent use of lists of vices and virtues.[52] The influence of Greek popular philosophy is very probable in the catalogues of vices and virtues in Paul and Philo, and cannot be discounted in the *Test. 12 Patr.,* but again we may also compare the lists of virtues and vices associated with the two spirits at Qumran (1QS 4).[53]

The third type of hortatory material involves the contrast of the two ways. It is typical of the *Test. 12 Patr.* that virtues and vices are contrasted in pairs — e.g. the fornication of Reuben with the chastity of Joseph or the envy of Simeon with the forgiving love of Joseph. Consequently the catalogues of vices and virtues imply an ethical dualism in which two contrasting ways of life are set forth. This is most fully developed in the doctrine of the two ways in *Test. Asher:* 'Two ways hath God given to the sons of men, and two inclinations and two kinds of action and two modes (of action) and two issues. Therefore all things are by twos, one over against the other. For there are two ways of good and evil and with these are the two inclinations in our breasts discriminating them . . .' (1:3-5).

The doctrine of the two ways has its roots in the ethics of the Bible, especially in the Wisdom tradition.[54] Prov 4:10-14 contrasts the way of wisdom with the path of the wicked. Ps 1:6 says that 'the Lord knows the way of the righteous, but the way of the wicked will perish.' However there is no implication of metaphysical dualism in these texts. They simply clarify basic options by formulating them in terms of binary oppositions. Such contrasts are probably universal. In Hesiod's *Works and Days* 287-92 we read: 'Badness can be got easily and in shoals: the road to her is smooth, and she lives very near us. But between us and Goodness the gods have placed the sweat of our brows: long and steep is the path that leads to her, and it is rough at the first.'[55]

Test. Asher goes beyond this purely ethical dualism. There we read that if the soul inclines to the evil inclination it is ruled by Beliar (1:8). Further: 'the latter ends of men do show their righteousness (or unrighteousness) when they meet the angels of the Lord and of Satan. For when the soul departs troubled, it is tormented by the evil spirit . . . which also it served in lusts and evil works. But if he is peaceful with joy he meets the angel of peace, and he leads him into eternal life' (6:4-6). The opposition of the angel of peace and the evil spirit or Beliar is fundamental to the *Test. 12*

[52] For references see Conzelmann, *1 Corinthians,* 100.
[53] Wibbing, *Die Tugend- und Lasterkataloge,* 45-61; Kamlah, *Die Form der katalogischen Paränese,* 53-103, argues for Persian influence on the scrolls at this point.
[54] Michaelis, 'Ὁδός,' rejects Harnack's theory that there was a course for proselytes under the title 'Two Ways.'
[55] See also Heracles' choice between the ways of vice and virtue in Xenophon, *Memorabilia* 2:1,21-34.

Patr. Beliar is mentioned in 11 of the 12 Books (he is missing only in *Test. Gad,* and Satan is mentioned there). Especially in this respect, there is an obvious analogy with the doctrine of the two spirits at Qumran.[56] Yet the language of *Test. Asher* emphasizes the options with which humanity is confronted, rather than the metaphysical conflict of the two Spirits, and it makes quite clear that the sons of Asher must choose to cleave to goodness and destroy the evil inclination by good works (chap. 3).[57] On the other hand, 1QS 3:13-4:26 suggests that humanity is already divided between the lots of Light and Darkness, even though the very fact that so much space is given to exhortation and rules would seem to imply that some choice is possible (cf. below, pp. 533-6). However, the introduction of the angelic figures in the *Testament* does mark a significant development beyond the ethical dualism of the Wisdom literature towards a metaphysical dualism.

The doctrine of the two ways is also widespread in early Christianity. The best known examples are *Did.* 1-6 and *Barn.* 18-21.[58] According to the *Didache* 'there are two ways, one of life and one of death.' The way of life is the love of God and neighbour. The way of death is illustrated by a catalogue of sins: cursing, murder, adultery etc. The formulation of *Barnabas* is closer to that of Qumran: the ways are Light and Darkness. Over the one are the angels of God and over the other the angels of Satan. Again, each way is illustrated by a list of vices and virtues.

The ethics of *Test. 12 Patr.* are presented in broad moral terms.[59] Despite numerous references to the law (νομος and ἐντολη are used 60-70 times) there are few references to specific laws. There is no reference to the sabbath. Circumcision is mentioned only in *Test. Levi* in connection with the destruction of Shechem, not in the context of positive teaching. The Jewish cult is only discussed in connection with the eschatological priest. Purity laws are cited in *Test. Asher* 2:9 and 4:5 but are applied metaphorically to characterize types of sinners.[60] The emphasis is on virtues rather than on specific commandments. The sin most often singled out for condemnation is fornication.

c) Three motifs stand out in the *future predictions* of the patriarchs: first is the pattern of sin, punishment and restoration, or sin-exile-return; second is the special position of Levi and Judah; third is the coming of the Messiah(s) and the eschatological scenario. These predictions are sometimes simply asserted. At other times they are based on the authority

---

[56] Nickelsburg, *Resurrection,* 156-65. Cf. also *Test. Judah* 20:1.

[57] On the 'evil inclination' and its good counterpart in later Jewish writings see Moore, *Judaism* 1, 474-96; Porter, 'The Yeçer Hara.'

[58] Also *Doctrina Apostolorum* 1-5 and the *Mandates* in the *Shepherd of Hermas.* See further Audet, 'Affinités littéraires et doctrinales du Manuel de Discipline.'

[59] Kee, 'The Ethical Dimensions.'

[60] Contrast the emphasis on ritual and cultic matters in Aramaic *T. Levi.*

of the fathers, especially Enoch. The allusions to Enoch, in particular, serve to associate the *Test. 12 Patr.* with apocalyptic tradition.

The sin-exile-return pattern may be illustrated from *Test. Issachar* 6: 'I know, my children that in the last times your sons will abandon simplicity and cleave to insatiableness . . . and abandoning the commandments of the Lord, they will cleave to Beliar . . . You therefore tell your children, so that if they sin they may turn the more quickly to the Lord, for he is merciful and will deliver them to bring them to their land.' This pattern is rooted in the Deuteronomic theology of history which was widespread in post-exilic Judaism. The pattern is found in *Test. Levi* 10; 14-15; 16; *Test. Judah* 23; *Test. Zebulun* 9:5-7; *Test. Dan* 5:4, 8-9; *Test. Naphtali* 4; *Test. Asher* 7; *Test. Benjamin* 9:1-2.[61]

The Levi-Judah passages are related both to the sin-exile-return pattern and to the messianic expectation.[62] In *Test. Reuben* 6:5, *Test. Simeon* 5:4 and *Test. Gad* 8:2 the patriarch warns his sons that they will rebel against Levi and Judah and incur punishment. Levi is usually mentioned before Judah and evidently takes precedence over him. Levi is explicitly ranked first in *Test. Judah* 25:1. These passages are not messianic, but affirm Levi's priesthood and Judah's kingship.[62a]

Other passages go further, and speak of the salvation which is to come from Levi and Judah. In *Test Dan* 5:10 the salvation of the Lord will arise from Judah and Levi. The passage goes on to describe how the Lord will defeat Beliar and bring about salvation. In *Test. Naphtali* 8:2 the patriarch tells his sons to follow Levi and Judah for through Judah salvation will arise for Israel, for through his sceptre God will be seen dwelling among men, to save the race of Israel.

The most striking characteristic of the expectation of the *Test. 12 Patr.* is the association of the Messiah with both Levi and Judah. According to *Test. Simeon* 7 'the Lord will raise up from Levi, as it were a high priest and from Judah as it were a king, God and man. He will save all the nations and the race of Israel.' Similarly in *Test. Joseph* 19:6 the children of Joseph are to honour Levi and Judah because from them will arise the Lamb of God who will save all the nations and Israel by grace. In *Test. Levi* the focus is on the Levitical Messiah. He will be 'a new priest' but his star will arise in heaven as a king.[63] He will open the gates of Paradise and remove the

---

[61] De Jonge, *The Testaments*, 83-86.

[62] *Ibid.*, 86-89. The theory of Charles that the *Testaments* were writen in support of the Hasmonean priest kings is mainly based on these passages. For an extensive study of the roles of Levi and Judah and an attempt to reconstruct the historical development of the *Testaments*, see Hultgård, *L'Eschatologie* 1.

[62a] Also *Test. Issachar* 5:7, *Test. Judah* 2:1-5.

[63] For an extended discussion of this figure see Hultgård, *L'eschatologie* 1, 268-381; *id.*, 'The Ideal Levite.' On the Levitical Messiah in Aramaic *T. Levi*, see Greenfield — Stone, 'Remarks on the Aramaic Testament of Levi.'

threatening sword from Adam, and give the holy ones to eat from the tree of life. Beliar will be bound by him and he will give his children authority to trample the evil spirits (*Test. Levi* 18:10-12). *Test. Judah* 24, on the other hand, speaks of a man from the seed of Judah, who will arise like the sun of righteousness, walking with the sons of men. No sin will be found in him, and the heavens will be opened over him. He will judge and save all who call upon the Lord among the Gentiles.

In their final form the *Test. 12 Patr.* envisage one Messiah, who is associated with both Levi and Judah and is evidently identified as Christ. Since the Messiah is associated with both these tribes, and they are both singled out for leadersip, it is probable that the *Test. 12 Patr.* adapt an earlier Jewish expectation of two Messiahs. The main parallel for such a conception is found in the expectation of the messiahs of Aaron and Israel in the Qumran scrolls. The roots of this dual messiahship should be sought in the organization of the post-exilic community under Zerubbabel and the high priest Joshua, the two 'sons of oil' of Zech 4:14, and its revival may be seen as a reaction against the monopolization of power by the Hasmonean priest kings.[64]

A number of the Testaments conclude with a prediction of resurrection: *Test. Judah* 25, *Test. Benjamin* 10:6-10, *Test. Zebulun* 10:1-4, *Test. Simeon* 6:7. Afterlife is also implied in *Test. Levi* 18:10-14.

RELATION TO OTHER LITERATURE

The pattern of the contents of the *Test. 12 Patr.* has often been associated with the so-called 'covenant form' of the Bible.[65] This form is characterized by the sequence of history, stipulations, and consequences (curses and blessings in the older literature). It is attested especially in the Deuteronomic literature but also in a wide spectrum of prayers and liturgical poems in the post-exilic period.[66] We have already noted the pattern of historical retrospective, exhortation and future prediction in the *Test. 12 Patr.* and this pattern resembles the covenant form in a general way. However, in the biblical covenant the review of history served to remind the people of God's saving acts and therefore of their obligation to him. In the *Test. 12 Patr.* the historical element consists of stories from the lives of the patriarchs which illustrate a virtue or a vice. History is used as a source of moral example. In short, the *Test. 12 Patr.* can not be regarded as

---

[64] Cf. below, pp. 538-42. See further Collins, 'Patterns of Eschatology at Qumran'; Hultgård, *L'eschatologie* 1, 65-66.

[65] So especially Baltzer, *The Covenant Formulary;* Küchler, *Frühjüdische Weisheitstraditionen*, 415-545.

[66] Neh 9; Dan 9:4b-19; Bar 1:15-3:8; Pr. Azariah; LXX Pr. Esther; 3 Macc 2:2-20; Tobit 3:1-6; 4Q Words of the Luminaries 1:8-7:2; 1QS 1:24b-2.1; CD 20:28-30. See Steck, *Israel und das gewaltsame Geschick der Propheten.*

examples of the covenant form. [67] A closer parallel to the Deuteronomic theology lies in the sin-exile -return passages, such as *Test. Issachar* 6.

The *Test. 12 Patr.* have obvious affinities with the apocalyptic literature, both in the pseudonymous attribution to ancient figures and in the historical 'predictions' which often conclude with references to messianic expectation and to resurrection. However, the *Test. 12 Patr.* differ from the apocalypses precisely by reason of their adherence to the Deuteronomic pattern of sin and punishment. In the apocalyptic books the course of events is, typically, irreversible and humans can only choose which side they wish to be on. In the Deuteronomic tradition, however, God can change the course of events in response to repentance and prayer.[68] The *Test. 12 Patr.* usually presuppose that the course of history can be changed, and this assumption is implicit in the sin-exile-return passages. Only in a few passages do we find a suggestion of apocalyptic determinism.[69]

The hortatory sections of the *Test. 12 Patr.* have a general affinity to the wisdom tradition.[70] The re-telling of the biblical stories is loosely related to the phenomenon of midrash, more especially to the so-called 're-written Bible' as we find it in such works as *Jubilees* and the *Book of Biblical Antiquities.*[71]

Three other clusters of parallels are more controversial. Within a few years of the discovery of the Qumran scrolls scholars began to note a number of significant resemblances.[72] The figure of of Beliar looms large in the *Test. 12 Patr.* and stands in binary opposition to the angel of peace. Also in *Test. Judah* 20:1 two spirits lie in wait for man, the spirits of truth and deceit. The *Community Rule* from Qumran contrasts the Spirit of Light and the Spirit of Darkness, and the *War Scroll* speaks of an eschatological battle between Belial, leading the Sons of Darkness, and Michael leading the Sons of Light. Yet it must be said that the dualism of the *Test. 12 Patr.* falls far short of that of the Scrolls since it lacks the note of predeterminism.

Another noteworthy point of contact between the Scrolls and the *Test. 12 Patr.* lies in the dual role of Levi and Judah in the *Test. 12 Patr.* and of the Messiahs of Aaron and Israel in the Scrolls. The correspondence here is far

---

[67] So also Hollander, *Joseph as an Ethical Model*, 3.

[68] Collins, *The Apocalyptic Vision of the Book of Daniel*, 185-7.

[69] In *Test. Levi* 4:1-6 the Lord hears the prayer of Levi not to avert the coming catastrophe but to remove the individual from evil, while judgment takes its course.

[70] These affinities are stressed by von Nordheim and Küchler.

[71] So Nickelsburg, *Jewish Literature*, categorizes the *Testaments* under 'The Exposition of Israel's Scriptures.'

[72] Slingerland, *The Testaments of the Twelve Patriarchs*, 45-47. See especially Dupont-Sommer, *Nouveaux Aperçus;* Otzen, 'Die neugefundenen hebräischen Sektenschriften'; Kuhn, 'Die beiden Messias Aarons und Israels.' Flusser, 'The Testaments of the Twelve Patriarchs,' finds in the *Testaments* a fusion between the Dead Sea Sect and similar groups and the Pharisaic outlook.

from exact. The titles are different, and the *Test. 12 Patr.* fuse the heirs of Levi and Judah into a single messianic figure, at least in the final redaction. Moreover, the messianic passages in the *Test. 12 Patr.* have a strong Christian colouring. The significance of the parallel here is that the scrolls have shown that the expectation of a double messiahship with the priest in the predominant role was at home in Judaism in the pre-Christian period and so have helped to explain why the Messiah should be associated with both Levi and Judah.

Apart from these noteworthy parallels the *Test. 12 Patr.* lack the most distinctive features of the Scrolls, which deal with the organization and history of the sectarian community,[73] and can not be regarded as a product of the Qumran community. It is likely, however, that some of the traditions incorporated in them were originally developed in the second century B.C.E. in circles which shared some of the ideas of the Qumran sect.[73a]

There are numerous parallels with the New Testament. These are most obvious in the messianic passages. *Test. Joseph* 19 speaks of a virgin from Judah, from whom will be born a lamb without fault. *Test. Simeon* 7 foretells a figure from Levi and Judah who will be God and man. According to *Test. Judah* 24:1 no sin will be found in the Messiah from Judah, and the heavens will open over him. In *Test. Naphtali* 8:2 God will appear dwelling among men through the sceptre of Judah.[74]

Further parallels abound in the hortatory sections of the *Test. 12 Patr.*, although these are less obvious.[75] Most noteworthy is the attitude of forgiving love associated with Joseph, who is cast in some passages as a type of Christ. The double commandment to love God and neighbour is found in *Test. Dan* 5:3. There are numerous parallels in phraseology between the *Test. 12 Patr.* and the Pauline epistles.[75a] The direction of the influence has been disputed. We cannot assume priority of the New Testament in all cases, but the Christological passages show that there was extensive Christian influence on the final form of the *Test. 12 Patr.*

Finally, De Jonge argued that the *Test. 12 Patr.* should be reckoned to the same group of writings as the *Didache, Epistle of Barnabas* and the *Shepherd of Hermas.*[76] We have already noted that the motif of the 'Two Ways' occurs in the *Didache* and *Barnabas. Hermas, Mand.* 6:2,1 mentions two angels, one of righteousness and one of wickedness, which may be compared to the two spirits of *Test. Judah* 20:1 or to the antithesis of Belial and the angel of peace. The idea that the Lord dwells in the hearts of

---

[73] Becker, *Untersuchungen*, 149-51.
[73a] Cf. below p. 546.
[74] See further De Jonge, *The Testaments*, 89-94.
[75] Charles, *APOT* 2, 291-2, speaks of 'influence on the NT.'
[75a] *Test. Levi* 6:11 ἔφθασε δὲ ἡ ὀργὴ κυρίου ἐπ᾿ αὐτοὺς εἰς τέλος; cf. 1 Thess 2:16 ἔφθασεν δὲ ἐπ᾿ αὐτοὺς ἡ ὀργὴ εἰς τέλος.
[76] De Jonge, *The Testaments*, 119-20.

believers and the devil flees from them is found in the *Test. 12 Patr.* and in the *Mandates of Hermas.*[77] None of these points, however, is peculiar to these early Christian writings. The argument that 'the general tone of these writings is often reminiscent of the ethical teaching of the *Test. 12 Patr.* even where no verbal parallels exist,' only testifies to the widespread common ethic which Hellenistic Judaism shared with the Gentile world and which was taken over by Christianity.[78]

COMPOSITION

Few questions in the area of the Pseudepigrapha have given rise to such diverse opinions as the composition of the *Testaments of the Twelve Patriarchs.*[79] Current opinion is divided between three main views:

1. The *Test. 12 Patr.* are Jewish documents interpolated by a Christian. This view was formulated at the end of the 17th century and commanded a consensus in the period 1900-1950. The greater number of recent studies still subscribe to some form of this view.[80]

2. A more specific variant of the interpolation theory regards the *Test. 12 Patr.* as Essene writings with very few Christian interpolations.[81] This view has won few adherents in recent years. Despite the noteworthy parallels to the Qumran scrolls, the *Test. 12 Patr.* lack references to the history of the sect and do not show a sectarian ideology.[82] Moreover, much of the *Test. 12 Patr.* seems to have been written in Greek and cannot be easily retroverted into a Semitic language.

3. The *Test. 12 Patr.* are Christian documents which drew on Jewish sources. This is the traditional view, which has also been energetically defended in recent years.[83]

There is no doubt that the *Test. 12 Patr.* are Christian in their final form, and so constitute evidence for Christianity in the second or early third

---

[77] *Ibid.,*93-94.

[78] See Collins, *Between Athens and Jerusalem,* chap. 4. Hollander, *Joseph as an Ethical Model,* also finds a lack of specifically Christian elements in the parenetic section. Kee, 'The Ethical Dimensions,' finds the ethics of the *Testaments* akin to Stoicism.

[79] For the history of research see H. J. de Jonge, 'Die Patriarchentestamente von Roger Bacon bis Richard Simon'; Slingerland, *The Testaments;* Becker, *Untersuchungen,* 129-58.

[80] This view was endorsed in the influential collections of the *Pseudepigrapha* edited by Kautzsch and Charles. Recent proponents include Becker, Hultgård, Kee; Burchard-Jervell-Thomas, *Studien;* Rengstorff, 'Herkunft und Sinn der Patriarchen-Reden,'

[81] Dupont-Sommer, *The Essene Writings from Qumran,* 301-5; Philonenko, *Les Interpolations chrétiennes.*

[82] Philonenko's arguments that the apparently Christological passages should be applied to the Teacher of the Righteousness have been widely rejected (see Slingerland, *The Testaments,* 60-65).

[83] This view was revived by M. de Jonge, *The Testaments* (1953) and has been defended by him and his students in several publications, with a few modifications. See *Studies,* 183-316. So also Milik, *Ten Years,* 34-35. For further references see Becker, *Untersuchungen,* 146.

century.[84] Yet the distinctively Christian elements are less than we usually find in Christian works, such as *Hermas,* with which the *Test. 12 Patr.* are often compared. There is also no doubt that the *Test. 12 Patr.* draw extensively on Jewish sources. The fragments of *Test. Levi* and *Test. Naphtali* (and possible fragments of other testaments) which have been found at Qumran have thrown some light on this matter. These fragments show significant differences from the Greek text of the *Test. 12 Patr.* If they represent an earlier stage of the *Test. 12 Patr.* there must have been a considerable process of development. The crucial question however is whether the Jewish documents were already in the form of *Testaments of the Twelve Patriarchs.* Unfortunately, the Qumran fragments are not extensive enough to allow us to grasp their overall structure. We cannot be sure that there was a *Testament of Levi* at Qumran, only traditions about Levi which were eventually taken up in a Testament. The presence of traditions relating to the relatively obscure figure of Naphtali might be taken as evidence that there was a collection relating to all twelve patriarchs, but the evidence is simply inconclusive.[85] Much of the material in the Greek *Test. 12 Patr.* is compatible with either Jewish or Christian authorship.[86]

PROVENANCE AND DATE

The question of composition is inseparable from that of provenance. The final Christian form is usually dated to the second half of the second century, or the beginning of the third.[87] A few passages show evidence of a much earlier date. In *Test. Levi* 17:11 the sinful priests of the seventh week, who immediately precede the 'new priest' of the eschatological age can be identified plausibly with the hellenizers, on the eve of the Maccabean revolt. *Test. Naphtali* 5:8, which says that 'Assyrians, Medes, Persians, Chaldeans and Syrians' will hold Israel captive, fails to include the Romans in the list. This passage was presumably written before the expulsion of the Syrians in 141 B.C.E.[88] Some of the parallels with the Qumran scrolls,

---

[84] There have been few studies of the *Testaments* as a Christian document, despite the urgings of M. de Jonge. A noteworthy exception is Jervell, 'Ein Interpolator interpretiert.' Jervell still assumed the theory of Jewish authorship with Christian interpolations.

[85] Becker, *Untersuchungen,* has attempted to reconstruct the history of composition by form-critical methods. He argues that the testament form belonged to the earliest stage. The individual *Testaments* were then expanded by the incorporation of traditional, usually hortatory, material. Finally a Christian editor made minor adaptations. Formally distinct units are usually assumed to have different origins. This correlation has no logical necessity. See the critique of Becker by Slingerland, 'The Testament of Joseph', who argues that the framework is the work of the redactor.

[86] See e.g. Amstutz, *Aplotes;* Berger, *Die Gesetzauslegung Jesu.*

[87] De Jonge, *Studies,* 184.

[88] Bickermann, 'The Date of the Testaments.'

especially in the matter of the dual messiahship, may reflect traditions from the Hasmonean period.[89] Much of the parenetic material, however, is virtually timeless and could have been composed by either Jew or Christian anywhere in the Hellenistic and Roman eras.

The parallels from Qumran show that the *Test. 12 Patr.* drew on some traditions which were current in Judea. Much recent scholarship however, has emphasized the affinities of the *Test. 12 Patr.* with Hellenistic, and specifically Egyptian Judaism.[90] There is now a virtual consensus that the *Test. 12 Patr.* were written in Greek, although some passages were translated from Semitic sources.[91] The ethics of the *Test. 12 Patr.* with their emphasis on specific virtues, find their closest Jewish parallels in the Diaspora.[92] The prominence of Joseph, not only in *Test. Joseph* but also in *Test. Reuben, Simeon, Dan, Gad* and *Benjamin,* may have been a Jewish Egyptian development, since Joseph was obviously associated with Egypt. Diaspora provenance appears most likely for the parenetic material (though not necessarily all of it). There is no evidence to tie the framework of the *Test. 12 Patr.* to any specific location.

In view of the uncertainty of provenance, little can be said on the *Sitz-im-Leben.* The homiletic style of the hortatory sections suggests that some of the material was developed in the synagogue, or conceivably the church services of Jewish Christianity. The testament as such is a literary (rather than an oral) form. The major purpose of the *Test. 12 Patr.* would seem to be to convey ethical teaching and they may have been used in an educational or instructional setting.[93]

The Testament of Moses

THE TEXT AND ITS IDENTIFICATION

In 1861 Antonio Ceriani published a fragmentary Latin manuscript which he had found in the Ambrosian Library in Milan and which he identified as the *Assumption of Moses.*[94] The identification was based on chap. 1 verse

---

[89] Hultgård, *L'eschatologie* 1, 68. Hultgård locates the composition of the *Testaments* in northern Israel in the early first century B.C.E. (*L'eschatologie* 2, 223-7), but allows for a Hellenistic Jewish redaction, which did not alter the basic structure, and for Christian additions.
[90] So Becker, Thomas, Rengstorff.
[91] R. A. Martin has argued that *T. Joseph* is in part translation Greek ('Syntactical Evidence'). Charles held that the original language was Hebrew (*APOT* 2, 287-8). See now the arguments of Hultgård, *L'eschatologie* 2, 168-87. Hultgård regards the present form of the *Testaments* as a Hellenizing translation of a Semitic original (probably Aramaic).
[92] Hollander, *Joseph as an Ethical Model,* 92, 94-97.
[93] Hollander, *ibid.,* 96, proposes a setting in a Hellenistic school.
[94] The basic edition, translation and commentary is still that of Charles, *The Assumption of Moses.* See also his treatment in *APOT* 2, 407-24, A new translation by J. Priest is found in Charlesworth, *Pseudepigrapha* 1, 919-934.

14, which corresponds to a quotation from the *Assumption of Moses* by Gelasius (*Hist. eccl.* 2:17,17). Gelasius elsewhere (2:21,7) refers to the dispute between Michael and the Devil in the *Assumption of Moses*. This episode is not found in the manuscript published by Ceriani, but is often referred to in patristic sources and even already in the New Testament in Jude, verse 9. (The allusion is not identified in Jude but is specified in Clement, Origen and other patristic sources). The Latin manuscript does not refer to the death of Moses or his subsequent assumption at all and, since it is primarily a prophecy delivered before death, it is more properly described as a testament.[95] In fact the *Stichometry* of Nicephorus and other lists mention a *Testament of Moses* immediately before the Assumption, and the dominant opinion of scholars is that Ceriani's text corresponds to the *Testament* rather than the *Assumption*. In view of the citations in Gelasius, some have suggested that the *Testament* and the *Assumption* were combined in a single book.[95a] The surviving Latin text is incomplete, and may have concluded with an account of the assumption of Moses. The manuscript published by Ceriani is still the only text of this work. It is a palimpsest from the sixth century and is illegible in places. The consensus of scholarship is that the Latin was translated from Greek, but the original was in a semitic language, most probably Hebrew.

RELATION TO OTHER LITERATURE

The work published by Ceriani may be viewed as a re-writing of the last words and demise of Moses in Deut 31-34.[96] The first chapter contains the announcement of Moses' forthcoming death, the commissioning of Joshua as his successor and instructions to preserve the books which were being transmitted (cf. Deut 31). Then in chaps. 2-9 there is an extensive review of the history of Israel, indicating a pattern of sin and punishment (somewhat like Deut 32). Chap. 10 brings the denouement of history and the exaltation of Israel (cf. Deut 33, the blessing of Moses). Finally, the death and burial of Moses in Deut 34 was presumably adapted in the lost conclusion of the Latin manuscript. The apocryphal book was not following Deuteronomy rigorously and its essential debt to the biblical book lies in the use of Moses' last words as a context and in the pattern of sin and punishment in the history of Israel.

The testamentary character of the apocryphal book is clear; it is the

---

[95] Laperrousaz, *Le Testament de Moïse;* Nickelsburg, *Studies on the Testament of Moses;* von Nordheim, *Das Testament*, 194-207.

[95a] See Charles, *ibid.* on this problem. See Jude 9 and James, *Testament of Abraham*, 16-20. The opinion has recently been expressed that the material in the Greek *Palaea* dealing with the death of Moses was drawn from the lost Assumption; see Flusser, 'Palaea Historica,' 72-4 and references there.

[96] Harrington, 'Interpreting Israel's History; Nickelsburg, *Jewish Literature*, 83-83.

farewell discourse of Moses, framed by the introductory explanation of the circumstances, and, presumably, by Moses' departure at the end. *The Testament of Moses* is simpler in form than the *Testaments of the Twelve Patriarchs,* which typically include a narrative about the patriarch's life, to exemplify a vice or virtue, and a hortatory section. These elements are not found here, but the review of history with an eschatological conclusion is typical of the *Test. 12 Patr.*, as is the Sin-Exile-Return pattern, which derives from the Deuteronomic view of history. The *Testament of Moses* has many affinities with apocalyptic literature but is not an apocalypse in form.[97] The decisive difference lies in the manner of revelation. An apocalypse always involves a mediating angel (or other supernatural figure) who interprets symbolic visions or guides the visionary on a heavenly tour. Here Moses is the giver of revelation, not the recipient. The affinities of the *Testament of Moses* with the apocalyptic writings lie in the *ex eventu* (after the fact) prophecy of history and the transcendent eschatology in chap. 10. There was an extensive literature dealing with the death of Moses in antiquity, in the later Jewish and Samaritan traditions and in Slavonic, Ethiopic and Armenian Church traditions.[98] The present work should be distinguished from the so-called *Apocalypse of Moses,* which is really a recension of the *Life of Adam and Eve,* and from the *Prayer of Moses* which is part of the *Book of Biblical Antiquities* (19:14-16).[99] Origen (*De principiis* 3:2,1) uses the title *Ascension of Moses* for the document which contains the dispute between Michael and the Devil.

CONTENTS: A THEOLOGY OF HISTORY

The *Testament of Moses* seeks to demonstrate a theology of history, according to which God created the world on account of his people, although this design is hidden from the Gentiles (1:12-13). The history itself falls into two cycles. The first, in chaps. 2-4, covers the period down to the Babylonian exile. What is remarkable here is that the southern tribes view their exile as punishment for the sin of the northern tribes, even though it is admitted that some southern kings broke the covenant. The sin of the northern tribes lies in their breach with the Jerusalem temple. The second cycle begins with the restoration after the exile and concludes with another time of wrath and persecution. This time a man named Taxo[100]

---

[97] Collins, *Apocalypse*, 45-46.
[98] For references see Charlesworth, *Modern Research*, 160-6. For rabbinic material see Ginzberg, *Legends of the Jews* 3, 439-81; 6, 151-68.
[99] There are several medieval Jewish documents in Hebrew which deal with the ascension of Moses.
[100] The name Taxo (Greek ταξῶν), has been correlated with the Hebrew מחקק (Mowinckel, 'The Hebrew equivalent of Taxo in Ass. Mos. IX.'). Taxo has been identified by some with the Eleazar of 2 Macc 6:18 by *gematria,* but other solutions of this mysterious name have been suggested too. Cf. Delcor, 'La législation des sectaires,' 60-66.

from the tribe of Levi takes his seven sons and resolves to die rather than transgress the law. Then the kingdom of God is ushered in and Israel is exalted to the stars. In chap. 12 Moses adds some explanatory comments to console Joshua. The departure of Moses should not cause great anxiety because God has foreseen and provided for the entire course of history. Those who transgress the commandments will suffer at the hands of the Gentiles, but those who observe them will prosper.

The theology of the *Testament* may be categorized as a thorough-going 'covenantal nomism'.[101] Salvation comes through membership of the Jewish people, and this membership requires observance of the commandments. It is remarkable that the Deuteronomic theology of reward and punishment is maintained even in the light of the persecution of the righteous in chaps. 7-9. The strong emphasis on the solidarity of all the people in the first cycle of history gives way to a distinction between those who observe the law and those who do not in chap. 12. The most significant variation on the basic covenantal nomism is found, however, in the story of Taxo. In the time of persecution, a righteous man can turn the tide of history by purifying himself and submitting to death rather than break the law. The reason is that God will 'avenge the blood of his sons' as promised in Deut 32:43. The paradigm of Deut 32 is invoked explicitly in the story of the martyrs in 2 Macc 7:6 and implicitly in 1 Macc 2:37. Taxo is exceptional in so far as he deliberately sets out to provoke the divine vengeance by innocent death.[102]

DATE, PURPOSE AND PROVENANCE

In its present form the *Testament of Moses* must be dated around the turn of the era, since there is a clear allusion to the partial destruction of the temple in the campaign of Varus in 4 B.C.E. (see 6:8-9).[103] The document shows no awareness of the final destruction of 70 C.E. Scholarly opinion is divided as to whether chaps. 5-6, which develop the course of history through the first century B.C.E. were part of the original document or a later insertion. These chapters clearly refer to the Hasmoneans, Herod and the campaign of Varus. Yet the final persecution, in chap. 8, is strongly reminiscent of the persecution under Antiochus Epiphanes. Charles attempted to resolve this anomaly by re-arranging the chapters so that 8-9 stood before 5-6.[104] This proposal is unacceptable since the logic of the

---

[101] For the phrase: Sanders, *Paul and Palestinian Judaism.*
[102] Licht, 'Taxo, or the Apocalyptic Doctrine of Vengeance.'
[103] This date is accepted for the whole document by Brandenburger, *Himmelfahrt Moses,* 59-60.
[104] Charles, *The Assumption,* 28-30. A variant of Charles' theory is offered by Lattey, 'Messianic Expectation.'

book demands that the divine intervention in chap. 10 follow directly on the most severe persecution and especially on the episode of Taxo and his sons.[105] The specificity of the account of the persecution in chap. 8 suggests that this is an account of the author's time, rather than a stereotyped eschatological scenario.[106] In this case we must assume that chaps. 5-6 were inserted to update the book. The account of the persecution then becomes an eschatological scenario in the revised document.[107] Support for the theory of a second redaction can be found in 10:8 where the phrase 'the wings of the eagle' is an addition, and may allude to the pulling down of the golden eagle over the temple gate shortly before the campaign of Varus (*Ant.* 17:6,3).[108]

The *Testament of Moses* serves a two-fold purpose. On the one hand, it assures the law-abiding Jews that the world is created for them, even though this design may be hidden in the present. On the other hand it encourages non-violent resistance. The way to usher in the kingdom of God is not through militant action, but through purification, scrupulous observance of the law, and martyrdom. The latter point is reinforced through the implicit contrast between Taxo and Mattathias, father of the Maccabees.[109] Both Taxo and Mattathias (in 1 Macc 2) come from priestly families, invoke the law and their fathers and urge their sons to die for the law. Significantly, however, Taxo has seven sons, the perfect number, while Mattathias has only five. Mattathias looks to Judas for vengeance, but Taxo looks to God. The style of action represented by Taxo is in evident contrast to that of Mattathias, and is rather reminiscent of the martyrs in the cave in 1 Macc 2:31-38. The contrast with Mattathias would surely have been obvious at the turn of the era when 1 Maccabees was in circulation, and when the militant factions in Judaism remembered the Maccabees as heroes.[110] (It is significant that two of the rebel leaders in the time of Varus were named Judas and Simon). However, the contrast may have been apparent already at the time of the Maccabean rebellion.

Despite occasional attempts to ascribe the *Testament of Moses* to the Essenes or some other party, we have no adequate basis for such an attribution.[111] The only hint of sectarian provenance is the statement in 4:8 that after the restoration the 'two tribes' will be sad and lament because

[105] Licht, 'Taxo', 95-103; Nickelsburg, *Resurrection*, 43-45.
[106] Nickelsburg, *Studies on the Testament of Moses*, 34.
[107] Collins, 'The Date and Provenance of the Testament of Moses.'
[108] Yarbro Collins, 'Composition and Redaction of the Testament of Moses 10.'
[109] Collins, 'The Date and Provenance,' 28.
[110] See Farmer, *Maccabees, Zealots and Josephus*, 125-58; *id.*, 'Judas, Simon and Athronges'. Two of the rebel leaders in the time of Varus were named Judas and Simon.
[111] Collins, 'The Date and Provenance,' 30-31. Essene authorship was first proposed by M. Schmidt-A. Merx in 1868. It has been recently espoused by Laperrousaz.
[112] So Schürer, *Geschichte* 3, 295-6; Charles, *The Assumption*, 15.

they cannot offer sacrifices to the God of their fathers. This verse may imply a rejection of the Second Temple,[112] but it is possible that it refers to those of the southern tribes who remained in exile, and so could not offer sacrifices with any frequency.[113]

The Testament of Job

TEXT AND STRUCTURE

The *Testament of Job* is preserved in four medieval Greek manuscripts, a medieval Slavonic translation and a partial Coptic translation from the fifth century which is as yet unpublished.[114] There is little doubt that it was composed in Greek, in view of its dependence on the Septuagint.[115]

Two factors bear on the generic character of the work. First, the *Testament* is a re-writing of the canonical book of Job and so is frequently, though imprecisely, called a midrash.[116] The *Testament* picks up a few points from the Septuagint which are not in the Hebrew: Job's friends are kings and Job will share in the resurrection. In contrast to the canonical book, Job understands and accepts his suffering.[117] The *Testament* supplies a new motivation for Satan's hostility to Job by having Job destroy one of his temples. So the story is no longer one of passive suffering but of an active conflict between Satan and Job. Much of the text goes freely beyond the biblical prototype, to describe a direct struggle between Job and Satan. There are also episodes involving women and a number of hymnic passages which have no biblical foundation.

Second, the story is cast as a testament.[118] The narrative begins in the third person. Job, before his death, summons his children. The main body of the work is in the first person, and concerns the story of Job's life. This falls into two main sections: the struggle of Job and Satan and the confrontation of Job with his friends. At the end of each section, a moral is drawn (27:7 and 45:2). While there is far less direct exhortation than in *Test. 12 Patr.*, the narrative is clearly meant to carry a moral. There are no eschatological predictions, but there is a curse on Elihu (chap. 43) and the

---

[113] So Schwartz, 'The Tribes of As. Mos. 4:7-9'.

[114] Schaller, *Das Testament Hiobs*, 316-18. For the Greek text see Kraft, *The Testament of Job*; Brock, *Testamentum Iobi*.

[115] Schaller, 'Das Testament Hiobs und die Septuaginta-übersetzung des Buches Hiobs.' Schaller argues for the priority of the LXX throughout. Torrey, *History of New Testament Times*, 70-71, held that it was composed in Aramaic. James, *Apocrypha Anecdota* 2, xciv, suggested that it was a Christian translation of a Hebrew midrash.

[116] Kohler, 'The Testament of Job'; Denis, *Introduction*, 100; Rahnenführer, 'Das Testament Hiobs und das NT.'

[117] Compare James 5:11.

[118] Von Nordheim, *Das Testament*, 119-35.

daughters of Job will live in heaven (chap. 47). After Job's final exhortation in chap. 45 there is a third person account of the distribution of his property, including the cords with which he had girded himself, which he leaves to his daughters.[119] This is a natural element in a testament, since it is the focal point of legal wills,[120] although it is omitted in the *Test. 12 Patr.* At the end Job's soul is taken up to heaven on a chariot and his body is buried.

In part, the differences from *Test. 12 Patr.* may be explained from the character of Job. He is presented as a king of Egypt (28:7) not as an ancestor of the Jewish people. Hence there are no predictions about the history of the people. The author who chose Job as his model was less interested in the future of the Jewish nation than in individual piety.

CONTENTS

At the beginning of *Test. Job,* Job, called Iobab, lives near a venerated idol, but has come to question whether this is the God who made heaven and earth.[121] One night 'a voice in a great light' informed him that the idol was not God but the 'power of the devil by which human nature is deceived.' Job immediately asks for authority to raze the shrine, but he is warned:

> If you attempt to destroy and you purge the place of Satan
> he will angrily rise up against you for battle
> except that he will not be able to bring death upon you . . .
> But if you endure, I shall make your name renowned
> in all earthly generations until the consummation of the age . . .
> And you will be raised up in the resurrection
> and you will be like an athlete who spars and endures hard
> labours and wins the crown.[121a]

Job proceeds to raze the temple anyhow, and so the drama of Job's suffering is set in motion.

The introductory story of Job's conversion in chaps. 2-5 provides the framework for the rest of the book, and points clearly to one aspect of the book's message. Job is an exemplary athlete of virtue who wins a crown by endurance. This motif is a common one in Hellenistic Judaism.[122] We have

---

[119] This passage is widely thought to be an addition. See James, *Apocrypha Anecdota* 2, xciv-xcvi; Spittler, *The Testament of Job.* Spittler regards the passage as a Montanist addition. For a defence of its authenticity see Collins, 'Structure and Meaning in the Testament of Job,' 48.

[120] See Lohmeyer, *Diatheke,* chap. 1.

[121] Compare the conversion of Abraham in *Jub.* 12 and *Apoc. Abraham.* See Ginzberg, *Legends* 1, 209-17.

[121a] *Test. Job* 4:4-9. The English translation is according to Kraft, *The Testament of Job.*

[122] Pfitzner, *Paul and the Agon Motif,* 38-72; Jacobs, 'Literary Motifs in the Testament of Job,' 1-3.

350

seen above that the *Testamens of the Twelve Patriarchs* typically inculcate specific virtues (pp. 334-7). The virtue of endurance is highlighted in the first part of the book (chaps. 2-27) where Job is directly involved in conflict with Satan. In 1:3 Job introduced himself as one who exhibits complete endurance and again in chap. 27 Satan repeats the athletic image in acknowledging his defeat by Job. Job draws the moral in 27:10 by exhorting his children to patience.

However, endurance is not an end in itself. Job describes himself in 18:6-7 as a merchant at sea who is prepared to lose all he has if only he can reach a certain city and share in its riches. So, says Job, 'I also now considered my possessions as nothing compared to approaching the city about which the angel had spoken to me.' In fact, the angel had not told Job of a city, but had promised retribution, fame and a share in the resurrection, all of which were given to Job in the Septuagint. The author of *Test. Job* feels free to substitute the heavenly Jerusalem for these more traditional rewards.

It is clear from *Test. Job* 18 that Job's endurance is based on the knowledge imparted to him by the angel of the future hope and the heavenly reality of the 'city.' The athletic metaphor for the conflict between Job and Satan refers then on a deeper level to the conflict between revealed knowledge and Satanic deception which was already implied in the initial situation. So Satan repeatedly takes on disguises in an effort to deceive Job, first as a beggar (chap. 7), then as king of the Persians (chap. 17), then as a great storm (20:5) and finally as a seller of bread (chap. 23). Job is able to penetrate the disguises. His knowledge gives rise to endurance and so he triumphs.

The second part of *Test. Job* (28-44) describes Job's confrontation with his friends (which makes up nearly all the biblical book). The (non-biblical) lament of the kings for Job (chap. 32) introduces the major motif of the second half of the book by its refrain: 'where now is the glory of your throne?' Job replies that his throne and his glory are in heaven and that earthly kings and their glory will pass away. We have, then, a two-fold contrast. First, there is a contrast between Job's misery and his former prosperity; second between the fragility of the earthly kingdom and the heavenly throne.

The real issue between Job and his friends is awareness of heavenly reality. Job has insight into heavenly things while the friends have not. This point is well illustrated by the extraordinary exchange between Baldad and Job in 35-38. Job's assertion that he has a throne in heaven raises a very natural problem for Baldad: Has Job, as a result of his prolonged suffering, gone mad? The response to his first question must have increased his doubt — Job says that his heart (mind) is not on earth but in heaven. This prompts Baldad to ask him about heavenly realities: Why does this God in whom

Job trusts allow a faithful servant to suffer? And how does the sun which sets in the West proceed to rise in the east again?

The correlation between the two questions is not immediately evident. Baldad might be thought to have answered his own first question. However, in both questions Baldad is challenging Job's claim to know heavenly realities. His remarks on the impossibility of judging the ways of God indicate his own belief that heavenly knowledge is impossible. Job's reply seems to agree with Baldad, but is ironic. He by no means retracts his claim to heavenly knowledge, but that knowledge is not natural to man. It requires special revelation and is certainly not accessible to one so earthly-minded as Baldad. Job proceeds to reaffirm his knowledge of heavenly realities with another vision in chap. 40.

Elihu, in chap. 41, goes beyond the others in seeking to expose Job's 'non-existent portion.' He is said to be 'filled with Satan.' The struggle is still between Job and Satan and the issue is faith in the heavenly reward of Job.

Job's confrontation with his friends is resolved by the theophany, which is dealt with very briefly here. The three friends are reconciled to God through the mediation of Job. This is in accordance with the biblical story, but it now carries the implication that those who lack heavenly revelation depend on the intercession of those who enjoy it.

Elihu, however, as the representative of Satan, is condemned to permanent destruction. His fate is spelt out in a hymn on the lips of Eliphaz in chap. 43. Elihu now becomes the counterpart to Job. Even as Job is restored, Elihu's 'kingdom has passed away, his throne has decayed, and the honour of his pretense is in Hades' (43:5).

Job's insight into heavenly realities is also shown through a series of contrasts with *women*. In chap. 7, Job's servant fails to recognize Satan and thereby highlights Job's ability to recognize him. In chaps 24-26, Job's wife, who has given the hair of her head to buy food for Job, fails to see the devil standing behind her until Job calls him forth. In chap. 39, Job's wife again shows her lack of insight by asking the kings to recover the bones of her children. Job opposes her, saying that the children have been taken up to heaven, and both his wife and the kings then see the children in heaven. The women are not evil. Like the three kings, but not Elihu, they are victims rather than agents of deception. Neither Job's wife nor his servant definitively transcends the state of deception (although Job's wife sees her children in heaven and then dies in peace). After the theophany, however, we find a remarkable account of the inheritance of Job's daughters (46-50). The daughters are given the bands which God gave to Job when he bade him gird up his loins like a man. When they gird themselves, their hearts are changed so that they no longer think earthly thoughts but speak the language of the angels. Further, their inheritance causes them to 'live in heaven' (47:3). Womankind in *Test. Job* symbolizes, like the three kings, the human state of ignorance,[123] which is transformed at the end through the mediation of Job into heavenly knowledge and heavenly life.

The story of Job's conversion is reminiscent of that of Abraham in *Jub.* 12 and *Apoc. Abraham*. Abraham's faithful endurance through ten trials is stressed in *Jubilees*,[124] and Joseph is similarly patient in *Test. Joseph*. The importance of belief in heavenly reality is reminiscent of the Wisdom of Solomon.[125] The story has various points of similarity with the *Testament of Abraham*.[126] Perhaps the most noteworthy is the manner in which the soul is taken to heaven in a chariot. Affinities with the tradition of *merkabah* mysticism have often been noted[127] and these also apply to apocalypses of the diaspora such as *3 Baruch* and *2 Enoch*,[128] Despite the prohibition of marriage with foreigners (45:4) the view of Judaism presented is not an exclusive one and accords well with the literature of the diaspora in the first century.[129]

In the New Testament, the most obvious parallel is with the Epistle of James, which may possibly have the *Testament* in mind when it refers to the patience of Job.[130] Hebrews 10-12 views life as a struggle to be endured and lists the heroes of faith who triumphed by endurance. The importance of revealed knowledge from heaven is fundamental to the Gospel of John.[131]

Since Job is said to be king of Egypt (28:7), Egypt is the most likely place of composition, and nothing in the Testament contradicts this view. The date is more difficult to establish. In view of the dependence on the Septuagint, it cannot be earlier than 100 B.C.E. The affinities with Hellenistic Jewish literature, such as *Test. Abraham*, make a date in the period 100 B.C.E.-150 C.E. probable, but it is not possible to be more precise.[132]

---

[123] The portrayal of women in *Test. Job* as lacking heavenly insight is in accordance with Philo's use of female imagery for the irrational soul. See Baer, *Philo's use of the Categories Male and Female*, 40-53.

[124] *Jub.* 19:8. Nickelsburg, above p. 99.

[125] Nickelsburg, *Jewish Literature*, 248.

[126] Delcor, *Le Testament d'Abraham*, 47-51.

[127] Kee, 'Satan, Magic and Salvation in the Testament of Job.'

[128] Collins, 'The Genre Apocalypse in Hellenistic Judaism.'

[129] Collins, *Between Athens and Jerusalem*, chap. 6. Compare the attitude to inter-marriage in Joseph and Aseneth.

[130] James 5:11. See Spitta, *Zur Geschichte und Literatur des Urchristentums*, 170-8. Of course the motif of the patience of Job may have been independent of the *Testament*.

[131] Nickelsburg, *Jewish Literature*, 248. See further Rahnenführer, 'Das Testament,' 83-88.

[132] Delcor, 'Le Testament de Job,' 72-73, argues for a date about 40 B.C.E. by seeing in the 'King of Persians' a reference to Pacorus. However, kings of Persia were traditional enemies of Egypt. See Collins, 'Structure and Meaning,' 50.

Philonenko has suggested that *Test. Job* originated in a community of Therapeutae.[133] The prominence of hymns might be thought to accord with the singing of the Therapeutae and the ecstatic speech of Job's daughters with the inclusion of women in the choirs (Philo, *Cont.* 80). Neither of these points is unambiguous, however, and there is no parallel in *Test. Job* for the meal of the Therapeutae or their contemplative life. Given the paucity of information on the Therapeutae, there is not enough evidence to attribute *Test. Job* to that, or to any, sectarian group.[134]

BIBLIOGRAPHY

The first systematic study of the genre testament is VON NORDHEIM, *Das Testament.*

Testaments of the Twelve Patriarchs

CHARLES, *The Greek Versions,* standard edition for more than 50 years; DE JONGE, *Testamenta XII Patriarcharum, editio minor* of a single manuscript; *id., The Testaments, editio maior,* should now be regarded as the standard edition.

For the history of scholarship see SLINGERLAND, *The Testaments* and H. J. DE JONGE, 'Die Patriarchentestamente von Roger Bacon bis Richard Simon,'; CHARLES, *The Testaments of the Twelve Patriarchs,* classic formulation of the theory that the *Testaments* are Jewish with Christian redactional additions; DE JONGE, *The Testaments,* first major challenge to the consensus represented by Charles, revived the theory of Christian authorship; PHILONENKO, *Les Interpolations chrétiennes,* extreme formulation of the Qumran hypothesis, which would interpret the christological pasages in the *Testaments* as references to the Teacher of Righteousness; FLUSSER, 'The Testaments,' locates the *Testaments* between the Essenism of the Scrolls and Pharisaism; BECKER, *Untersuchungen,* most elaborate redaction-critical study of the *Testaments* to date; views the *Testaments* as a Jewish composition which passed through at least two stages prior to the Christian redaction. Part of the history of composition is located in the Diaspora; DE JONGE, *Studies,* reformulation, with some modification, of the theory of Christian authorship; HULTGÅRD, *L'Eschatologie,* lengthy study of the *Testaments* as a Jewish document, from a 'history of religions' perspective; KEE, 'The Testaments of the Twelve Patriarchs,' variant of the theory of Jewish authorship with Christian redaction.

---

[133] Philonenko, 'Le Testament de Job et les Thérapeutes'; *id., Le testament de Job.* So also Spittler, *The Testament,* 53-83. On the mystical hymns see below p. 563f.
[134] For a sharp critique of the Therapeutae hypothesis see Schaller, *Das Testament,* 309-11. Schaller regards the provenance of *Test. Job* as an open question.

Testament of Moses

CHARLES, *The Assumption,* still the standard edition.

LICHT, 'Taxo,' seminal article on the logic of the *Testament;* LAPERROUSAZ, *Le Testament,* substantial commentary, regards the *Testament* as Essene; NICKELSBURG, *Studies,* collection of essays which debate the major issues of date, provenance and structure; BRANDENBURGER, *Himmelfahrt,* introduction, translation and notes; PRIEST, 'The Assumption,' introduction, translation and notes.

Testament of Job

BROCK, *Testamentum Iobi;* KRAFT, *The Testament of Job* (with translation). COLLINS, 'Structure and Meaning,' analysis of coherence of the *Testament;* SCHALLER, *Das Testament Hiobs,* introduction, translation and notes; SPITTLER, 'The Testament of Job,' introduction, translation and notes. See now NICHOLLS, *Testament of Job,* which appeared after the present article had been written.

Chapter Nine

The Sibylline Oracles

J. J. Collins

Oracles, or inspired utterances, are a very widespread form of religious speech. Much of the Hebrew Bible is taken up with the oracles of the prophets. Prophecy declined in the post-exilic period, but we know from Josephus that there were prophets who uttered oracles throughout the Hellenistic period.[1] These oracles have only been preserved in summary form or are very short. We do have, however, a lenghty corpus of Jewish oracles, attributed to the Sibyl.

The standard collection of Sibylline oracles consists of twelve books, numbered 1-8 and 11-14. The anomalous omission of the numbers 9 and 10 from the sequence of books is due to the nature of the manuscript tradition.[2] There are, in fact, two distinct collections. The first contains books 1-8,[3] and was published in Basel in 1545. The second collection begins with a ninth book, which is made up of material found also in the first collection: Book 6, a single verse which has been placed at the beginning of Book 7 and Bk. 8:218-428. Then follows Bk. 10, which is identical with *Sib. Or.* 4. Books 11-14 follow in sequence. The first two books of the collection should be numbered 9 and 10, but since they only repeat material found in Books 1-8, they are omitted in the editions. The numbering of Books 11-14 is retained. Books 11-14 were first published by Angelo Mai in 1817 and 1828.[4]

The twelve books of the *Oracula Sibyllina* were written over a span of more than 700 years. Books 3, 4 and 5 are generally recognized as Jewish works from the period before Bar Kokhba. It is also probable that Bk. 11 was composed by a Jew about the turn of the era, and that Books 1-2

---

[1] Meyer, 'Prophecy and Prophets'; Michel, 'Spätjüdisches Prophetentum.'
[2] The two major editions of the *Sibylline Oracles* are those of Geffcken, *Die Oracula Sibyllina* and Rzach, *Oracula Sibyllina*. For a complete English translation, with introductions and notes by Collins see Charlesworth, *Pseudepigrapha*. For full discussion of the text of the Sibyllina see Geffcken, *Die Oracula Sibyllina*, XII-LIII, and Rzach, 'Sibyllinische Orakel,' 2119-22. Rzach gives the more complete listing of the manuscripts which make up each group.
[3] This collection consists of 2 manuscript groups, φ and ψ. The anonymous prologue is found only in group φ. There, *Sib. Or.* 8:486-500 is lacking. *Sib. Or.* 8 is placed first.
[4] The first complete edition was that of Alexandre, *Oracula Sibyllina.*

preserve substantial portions of an underlying Jewish oracle from about the same time. Books 12-14 are Jewish, but much later. Book 8 preserves substantial Jewish material from the late second century C.E. Books 1-2, 6, 7 and 8 are Christian in their final form.[5]

The Phenomenon of Sibylline Oracles

The twelve books of the standard collection are all, in their final shape, either Jewish or Christian. Sibylline prophecy was, however, originally a pagan phenomenon. The Sibyl herself is always depicted as an aged woman, uttering ecstatic prophecies. In the earliest attestations, from the fifth and fourth centuries B.C.E., the word Sibyl refers to a single individual,[6] but if there ever was a historical Sibyl she was lost in the mists of legend by that time. As from the fourth century B.C.E. we read of a number of Sibyls.[7] The most famous were those of Erythrea in Asia Minor and of Cumae in Italy. Varro listed ten Sibyls — Persian, Libyan, Delphic, Cimmerian, Erythrean, Samian, Cumean, Hellespontian, Phrygian and Tiburtine.[8] The *Suda* (a tenth century lexicon) and the anonymous preface to the standard collection repeat this list but identify the Persian Sibyl with the Hebrew. Pausanias (10:12,1-9) lists four: the Libyan Sibyl, Herophile of Marpessus (whom he identifies with the Delphic, Erythrean and Samian Sibyls), Demo of Cumae and Sabbe of the Hebrews (also called Babylonian or Egyptian by some).

The most famous collection of Sibylline oracles in antiquity was the official one at Rome. According to popular legend these oracles originated in the time of Tarquinius Priscus.[9] It is quite probable that Rome had acquired a collection of oracles in Greek hexameters before the fall of the monarchy.[10] These oracles were entrusted to special keepers, first two men, then ten, finally fifteen. Consultation had to be authorized by a decree of the senate. No other body of literature was granted such prestige in the Greco-Roman world.

When the temple of Jupiter was burnt down in 83 B.C.E. the Sibylline books were destroyed. When the temple was rebuilt seven years later, oracles were gathered from various places, especially Erythrea.[11] In view of

---

[5] Geffcken, *Komposition;* Rzach, 'Sibyllinische Orakel'; Collins, 'The Sibylline Oracles.'

[6] So Heraclitus, in Plutarch, *De Pythiae Oraculis* 6 (397a), Aristophanes, *Peace,* 1095ff.; Plato, *Phaedrus,* 244b.

[7] So Aristotle, *Problemata,* 954a; Heracleides Ponticus in Clement, *Stromata* 1:108,1.

[8] See Lactantius, *Divinae Institutiones,* 1:6.

[9] The legend is recounted in the anonymous preface to the Sibyllina. See also Dionysius of Halicarnassus, *Roman Antiquities* 4:62.

[10] On the Roman oracles see Diels, *Sibyllinische Blätter;* Rzach, 'Sibyllinische Orakel,' 2103-2116 and Bloch, 'L'origine des Livres Sibyllins Rome.' See also Cancik, 'Libri Fatales.'

[11] Dionysius of Halicarnassus 4:62,5-6.

the diverse origins of these oracles it is probable that the collection was made up of short oracles rather than long continuous ones. Two oracles have survived which were allegedly part of the Roman Sibylline corpus.[12] The first runs to seventy verses and deals with the birth of an androgyne. The second is related to the founding of the Ludi Saeculares and consists of prescriptions of rituals. It contains 37 verses. While these oracles are substantial in length they are far from the developed continuous oracles which are typical of the standard collection. The interest in prodigies and rituals evidenced here seems typical of the Roman Sibyllina (cf. Tibullus 2:5, 71-78). The Roman oracles were consulted in serious crises of any kind.

The fragments of other pagan Sibylline oracles which have survived are relatively brief and describe either the Sibyl herself and her relationship with the gods (usually Apollo) or woes to come upon specific places.[13] The characteristic tone of the oracles is expressed by the Erythrean Sibyl as 'foreseeing on behalf of men hardships difficult to bear.' The persistent prophecies of doom recall the 'oracles against the nations' of the Old Testament prophets. None of the extant pagan Sibylline oracles however contains the attempted prophecy of the entire course of history which we find in some of the Jewish and Christian books. However we should note that Virgil in the *Fourth Eclogue* refers to the 'ultima aetas' of the Cumaean Sibyl, which may, then, have divided all history into periods.[14]

In view of the brevity and limited scope of the extant pagan Sibyllina some scholars distinguish sharply between these oracles and the longer continuous oracles found in our collection, and see the prototype of the latter in the long poem attributed to Lycophron, called the *Alexandra*.[15] This is an allegorical *ex eventu* prophecy, put in the mouth of Alexandra or Cassandra, daughter of Priam, which deals with the fate of the heroes after the Trojan war and also with Greek and Roman history in the Hellenistic age (vss. 1412-50).[16] The poem shares some important features with the Jewish Sibyllina which are not found in the extant pagan fragments. The

[12] These oracles are found in Phlegon, *Mirabilia* 10 and *De Longaevis* 4. They are discussed by Alexandre, *Oracula Sibyllina* 2, Excursus III; Rzach, 'Sibyllinische Orakel,' 2111-13 and Jacoby, *Fragmente* 2 D, 846-8.

[13] The fragments of the pagan Sibyls are conveniently collected in Alexandre, *Oracula Sibyllina* 2, 118-47. To these should be added the fragment published by Crönert, 'Fragmentum Osloense.'

[14] The commentary of Servius on the *Fourth Eclogue* renders the periodization and eschatology of the Cumean Sibyl more explicit: 'saecula per metalla divisit, dixit etiam qui quo saeculo imperatet, et Solem ultimum, id est decimum, voluit' (*Servii Grammatici qui feruntur in Vergilii Bucolica Georgica Commentarii*, ed. G. Thilo, Leipzig 1887, 44-45). See Flusser, 'The Four Empires in the Fourth Sibyl.'

[15]So especially Wolff, 'Sibyllen und Sibyllinen.' Cf. Kurfess, *Sibyllinische Weissagungen*, 19-20.

[16] See Ziegler, 'Lykophron (8)'; Josifovic, 'Lykophron'; Barber, 'Lycophron (2).' Lycophron lived in the 3rd century B.C.E. but the poem is often dated to the second century.

most important of these characteristics is the extended *ex eventu* prophecy, which might be taken as an attempt to cover the entire span of world history. The veiled allegorical allusions are typical of the Sibyllina, as of all *ex eventu* prophecy. The *Alexandra* also emphasizes the conflict between East and West, a favourite Sibylline theme.[17]

Yet it is by no means clear that the *Alexandra* was a prototype of the Sibylline form. *Ex eventu* prophecy was a common device in Greek drama — Cassandra herself figured in the *Oresteia* of Aeschylus. Further the Erythrean (or Marpessan) Sibyl was said to have prophesied about Helen, the war between Asia and Europe, and the fall of Troy.[18] It is possible that the *Alexandra* was modelled on Sibylline oracles rather than vice versa.

Another possible source of influence on the Sibylline form has been found in the writings of Berossus. Pausanias reports that some people identified Sabbe (the Hebrew Sibyl) as a Babylonian Sibyl and said that she was the daughter of Berossus.[19] Berossus was a Chaldean priest who lived in the first quarter of the third century B.C.E. He was said to be an astrologer, and he wrote a history of Babylonia which began with the myths of the creation and ended with a prediction of cosmic destruction.[20] Since such a recent historical figure could not possibly be the father of the Sibyl, various theories have been advanced to explain the alleged relationship.

In *Sib. Or.* 3:809-10 the Sibyl says that she has come from Babylon. The same book, *Sib. Or.* 3:97-161, includes an account of the fall of the tower of Babel and a euhemeristic adaptation of Greek mythology. Since the work of Bousset and Geffcken this passage has been widely accepted as a fragment of the Babylonian Sibyl.[21] The relation of that Sibyl to Berossus is then explained by postulating that Berossus derived material from the Sibyl or vice versa. However there is no real evidence that any passage in *Sib. Or.* 3 derives from a Babylonian Sibyl. The fall of the tower can be explained as an expansion of the biblical narrative.[22] The euhemeristic

---

[17] *Alexandra* 1283-1450. See Kocsis, 'Ost-West Gegensatz in den jüdischen Sibyllinen.'
[18] Pausanias 10:12,1-9.
[19] *Ibid.*
[20] See Schnabel, *Berossos;* Burstein, *The Babyloniaca of Berossus.* The authenticity of the passage which refers to cosmic destruction (Seneca *Nat. Quaest.* 3:29,1) has been questioned by Jacoby, *Fragmente* 3 C, 395-7 and others because it is the first such reference in Babylonian Literature. However, this is not an adequate reason to reject the passage. Berossus may have derived the idea from a non-Babylonian source.
[21] Bousset, 'Die Beziehungen der ältesten jüdischen Sibylle zur Chaldäischen.' Geffcken, 'Die babylonische Sibylle.'
[22] The account of the tower in Josephus, *Ant.* 1:118, uses the plural 'gods.' This has often been taken to reflect a pagan source, probably Berossus. Josephus explicitly claims to be citing the Sibyl at this point. However, the plural 'gods' is not found in our text. Even if Josephus had access to a Babylonian source we cannot infer that the Sibyl also did. See Nikiprowetzky, *La troisième Sibylle,* 15-36.

passage on Greek mythology has nothing to indicate Babylonian origin.[23] The existence of a Babylonian Sibyl cannot be clearly established. The alleged relationship between the Sibyl and Berossus may be due to the analogous interest in universal history or to some less specific reason, such as their common reputation for wisdom.

Other Related Literature

More light is thrown on the genre of the Sibyllina by the political oracles of the Hellenistic age.[24] Phlegon, in his *Mirabilia,* preserved a group of oracles which were said to have been uttered after the battle of Magnesia and were attributed to Antisthenes of Rhodes.[25] One oracle was allegedly uttered by a Syrian officer who rose from the dead and prophesied in verse that Zeus would take vengeance on Rome. In another, the Roman consul Publius became ecstatic and prophesied that Rome would be destroyed by an eastern horde led by an Asiatic king. While these oracles have been preserved in a highly legendary framework, they illustrate the use of oracles for political propaganda in the Hellenistic Near East.

Opposition to Rome is also the theme of the *Oracle of Hystaspes,* a document of Persian origin which is preserved in the *Divine Institutions* of Lactantius (7:14-21).[26] This is 'a wonderful dream interpreted by a boy who uttered divinations' which predicted 'that the Roman empire and name would be taken from the world.' The original oracle has been dated to the second century B.C.E. An older Persian work, in the form of an apocalypse, is widely thought to underlie the *Zand-i Vohuman yasn,* or *Bahman Yasht.*[27] Zarathustra sees a vision of a tree with either four (chap. 1) or seven (chap. 3) branches. The vision is interpreted by Ahura Mazda to refer to kingdoms. The last kingdom is ruled by '*divs* with dishevelled hair,' who have been interpreted as the Greeks.[28] Then the millennium of Zarathustra will end. While the *Zand* contains much later material, it attests an anti-Greek oracle from the Hellenistic age.

In Egypt there was a tradition of political prophecy which is attested in such early documents as the *Admonitions of Ipuwer* and the *Vision of*

---

[23] One other passage, *Sib. Or.* 3:381-387, is ascribed to a Babylonian Sibyl by Eddy, *The King is Dead,* 127. The same passage is ascribed to a Persian Sibyl by Geffcken. It refers to the destruction of Babylon.

[24] See in general Eddy, *The King is Dead;* Fuchs, *Der geistige Widerstand.*

[25] Jacoby, *Fragmente* 2 B, 1174-7; Collins, *The Sibylline Oracles,* 7.

[26] Hinnels, 'The Zoroastrian Doctrine'; Windisch, *Die Orakel des Gystaspes.* Cf. below p. 422 and n. 217 there.

[27] Anklesaria, *Zand-i Vohuman Yasn;* Collins, *Apocalypse,* 208-10; Flusser, 'The Four Empires.'

[28] Eddy, *The King is Dead,* 19.

Neferrohu.[29] From the Hellenistic period we find the *Demotic Chronicle,* a fragmentary papyrus in the form of a commentary on an ancient text.[30] It looks forward to 'a man from Heracleopolis who will rule after the Ionians' and says that the prophet of Harsaphis will rejoice at his coming. Another Demotic papyrus contains *The Oracle of the Lamb to Bocchoris.*[31] This document was composed in late Persian or early Hellenistic times and updated in the Roman era. It predicts an invasion of Egypt from Syria followed by 900 years of oppression, which will finally be brought to an end by the god. The *Potter's Oracle* survives in three papyri of the second and third century C.E. and was composed in Greek.[32] The original oracle most probably dates to the second century B.C.E. The prophecy predicts Greek rule, followed by a state of chaos. There will be war with a king from Syria. Finally a 'king from the sun' will be sent by the 'great goddess' (Isis) and will restore Egypt.

The main Jewish counterpart to the Hellenistic political oracles is found in the apocalyptic literature.[33] The Judeo-Christian *Sibyllina* have obvious similarities with the 'historical' apocalypses:[34] pseudepigraphy, eschatology, review of a broad sweep of history with frequent use of periodization and *ex eventu* prophecy. However, the oracles lack the distinctive apocalyptic form of mediated revelation. They are uttered by the Sibyl, without recourse to visions and interpreting angels. The Jewish *Sibyllina* also lack the apocalyptic interest in the angelic world and, except for Bk. 4, in the judgment beyond death.[35] It is also noteworthy that the Sibyl was a pagan figure, while the apocalypses are attributed to biblical figures.

The main analogies with the New Testament are found between *Sib. Or.* 5 and the Book of Revelation. Both contain bitter attacks against Rome, prompted in part by the destruction of Jerusalem. Both refer to Rome as Babylon and make extensive use of the Nero legend.[36] The eschatological role of baptism in *Sib. Or.* 4 is significant as background to John the Baptist and to early Christian baptism.[37]

---

[29] Lanczkowski, *Altägyptischer Prophetismus;* Assmann, 'Königsdogma und Heilserwartung.' For overviews of the Hellenistic material see Griffiths, 'Apocalyptic in the Hellenistic Era'; Attridge, 'Greek and Latin Apocalypses,' 168-70; Collins, *The Sibylline Oracles,* 12-15.
[30] Daumas, 'Littérature prophétique.'
[31] Krall, 'Vom König Bokchoris.'
[32] Koenen, 'Die Prophezeiungen des Töpfers'; *id.* 'The Prophecies of the Potter.' Dunand, 'L'Oracle du Potier.'
[33] See Collins, 'Jewish Apocalyptic against its Hellenistic Near Eastern Environment.'
[34] Collins, *Apocalypse,* 30, 36, 46-47.
[35] The Christian Sibyllina show an increased interest in these matters.
[36] See Yarbro Collins, *The Combat Myth in the Book of Revelation,* 176-84.
[37] Collins, 'The Place of the Fourth Sibyl.'

The Jewish Adaptation of the Form: Book Four

The clearest example of Jewish adaptation of an older Sibylline oracle is provided by *Sib. Or.* 4. In its present form the book dates from the late first century C.E.[38] However, it contains a substantial older oracle in vss. 49-401.[39] This oracle is structured by a twofold division of history into ten generations and four kingdoms. The Assyrians are said to rule for six generations, the Medes for two and the Persians for one. Then the tenth generation and fourth kingdom coincide in the Macedonian empire. We should expect that this climactic kingdom would be followed by some event of a definitive nature. Instead there follows a passage on Rome and its eventual downfall (145-48). Since Rome is not integrated into the numerical sequence we must assume that vss. 102-151 are a later addition, and that the original oracle referred to no historical empire after Macedonia. Since only one generation is allotted to the Macedonians, the oracle should be dated to the early Hellenistic period, probably to the early third century B.C.E. This oracle then is probably the oldest passage in the present Sibylline corpus.

It is probable that the original oracle contained an eschatological conclusion after the Macedonian empire. It is possible, but not, of course, certain, that the eschatological passage in *Sib. Or.* 4:173-92 also formed the conclusion to the older oracle. This passage refers to a conflagration, followed by a resurrection of the dead and a judgment. Even if this passage was part of the original oracle, that oracle was not necessarily Jewish. The ideas of conflagration and resurrection could be derived from Persian religion.[40] The reference to Gehenna in vs. 186 betrays the hand of a Jewish redactor, but he may have only modified the eschatology of the Hellenistic oracle. Even the reference to the Flood in vs. 53 is not necessarily Jewish, since both the Greeks and Babylonians had traditions of a great Deluge. The description of the four empires itself contains nothing which is specifically Jewish. The oracle evidently looks forward to the fall of Macedonia, but it is not motivated by any specifically Jewish grievance.

The possibility that the older oracle in vss. 49-101 was written by a Jew cannot be definitely excluded. However, the lack of specifically Jewish characteristics is significant, even if the author was in fact a Jew. The older oracle is primarily a specimen of anti-Macedonian resistance literature from the Near East.[41] The schema of four kingdoms is found in the Persian

---

[38] The date of *Sib. Or.* 4 is not disputed. The main discussions of the book are those of Geffcken, *Komposition*, 18-21; Thomas, *Le Mouvement Baptiste*, 46-60; Nikiprowetzky, 'Réflexions'; Peretti, 'Echi di dottrine esseniche'; Flusser, 'The Four Empires,' 148-75 and Collins, 'The Place of the Fourth Sibyl.'

[39] This has long been recognized. See Geffcken, *Komposition*, 18.

[40] Flusser, 'The Four Empires,' 162-74. The reference in Servius (above note 14) to the rule of the sun in the last generation may reflect an expectation of conflagration in the Cumean Sibyl.

[41] See Collins, *The Sibylline Oracles*, chap. 1; Eddy, *The King is Dead.*

363

Zand and in Daniel (chs. 2 and 7).[42] The schema of ten generations is attributed to the Cumean Sibyl by Servius.[43] The oracle in *Sib. Or.* 4 is exceptionally lacking in indications of its provenance and of the grievance from which it arose. However, it clearly fits in the context of the well-known use of Sibylline oracles as political propaganda throughout the Hellenistic world.[44]

This political oracle from the Hellenistic age was adapted by a clearly Jewish author in the late first century C.E. The additions by the redactor are found in vss. 1-48, 102-72 (and possibly 173-92). Vss. 102-51 are a collection of oracles which bring the older oracle up to date by referring to the destruction of the Jerusalem temple (126), the eruption of Vesuvius (130-32) and the legend of Nero's return (138-39).[45] The chief importance of this passage is that it preserves the political interest of the original oracle. The threat of destruction which hung over Macedonia in the earlier oracle is here transferred to Rome (145-48).

Sib. Or. 4 in its present form is a political oracle directed against Rome, but it is not content to simply announce its message of destruction. The political polemic is combined with moral and religious exhortation. In vss. 1-48 the Sibyl condemns idolatry (6-7), sexual offences (33-34), injustice and violence, and emphasizes monotheism and God's power as creator. The distinctive doctrine of these verses, however, is the rejection of temple worship. According to vss. 8-11 God does not have a temple of stone but one not made by hands. In vss. 27-30 the pious reject all temples and sacrificial cult. These passages are not an attack on the Jewish temple (which no longer existed) but they undermine the very idea of temple worship, and make no allowance for the possibility of an acceptable temple. In this respect Book 4 contrasts sharply with the Egyptian Sibylline tradition represented by Books 3 and 5.[46]

In vss. 161-77 we find another hortatory passage which is more directly related to the eschatology of the book. These verses say what people must do to avert the final conflagration: refrain from violence, 'wash your bodies in perennial rivers' and supplicate God. The pivotal role assigned to baptism here, as an immediate way of averting the eschatological disaster, is strikingly reminiscent of John the Baptist and quite different from the ritual washings of *Sib. Or.* 3:592-93, which are not presented in an eschatological context.[47]

[42] The schema of the four kingdoms is also found in a number of Roman authors. See Swain, 'The Theory of the Four Monarchies'; Flusser, 'The Four Empires,' 153-62.

[43] It is of course also found in Jewish writings: the Apocalypse of Weeks in *1 Enoch*, 11Q Melchizedek and *Sib. Or.* 1/2. Cf. also *M. Aboth* 5:2. References to the 'tenth generation' recur frequently throughout the Sibylline corpus.

[44] See Collins, *The Sibylline Oracles*, 2.

[45] The Nero legend was a favourite Sibylline theme. See Collins, *The Sibylline Oracles*, 80-87.

[46] See further Collins, 'The Place of the Fourth Sibyl,' 365-69.

[47] This baptism is also quite different from the ritual washings of the Essenes despite the efforts

The combination of baptism, rejection of temple-cult and a lively eschatological expectation finds its closest parallels in the beliefs of the Christian Ebionites and Elchasaites.[48] There is nothing in Book 4 to suggest Christian authorship, but the book was presumably written in Jewish baptist circles, of a similar kind to these Christian sectarian movements. Syria, or the Jordan valley, remain the most likely geographical milieux for the first century redaction,[49] although the evidence is less than conclusive.

The significance of Book 4 for the development of the Sibylline tradition lies in its adaptation of an older political oracle which was either gentile or, at least, lacked distinctively Jewish traits. The book retained the political interest of the older oracle, but associated political events with divine retribution for moral and ritual performance. The periodization of history found in the older oracle lent urgency to the present since the eschatological judgment was now imminent. Accordingly, eschatology served to frame the moral and ritual exhortation and give it urgency. This combination of eschatology and exhortation is typical of the Jewish use of Sibylline oracles.

Book Three

The third book of Sibylline oracles is the oldest complete book of the collection. The composite nature of the book has been recognized by virtually all scholars.[50] In fact we may distinguish three stages:[51] 1) the main corpus: vss. 97-349 and 489-829; 2) oracles against various nations: 350-488; 3) vss. 1-96 which probably constitute part of a different book. One verse, 776 ('for mortals will invoke the son of the great God') must be regarded as a Christian interpolation.[52]

THE MAIN CORPUS

The main corpus consists of five oracles which are juxtaposed so as to

---

of scholars to identify them — e.g. most recently Peretti, 'Echi di dottrine esseniche' and Noack, 'Are the Essenes Referred to in the Sibylline Oracles.' See the critique by Nikiprowetzky, 'Réflexions,' 29-57.

[48] See Collins, 'The Place of the Fourth Sibyl,' 379.

[49] See Thomas, Le Mouvement Baptiste, 48-49; Collins, 'The Place of the Fourth Sibyl,' 379; Nikiprowetzky, La troisième Sibylle, 232-3 and 'Réflexions' 59 has argued for Egyptian provenance. However, there is no positive evidence for Egyptian origin, and the contrasts we have noted with Sib. Or. 3 and 5 (especially the rejection of temple-worship) argue against it.

[50] Geffcken, Komposition, 1-17; Peretti, La Sibilla Babilonese nella Propaganda Ellenistica; Collins, The Sibylline Oracles, 21-71. Nikiprowetzky, La Troisième Sibylle, defends the essential unity of the book, but even he allows for some exceptions.

[51] See Collins, The Sibylline Oracles, 28.

[52] Nikiprowetzky, La Troisième Sibylle, 329, apparently takes the verse as Jewish and understands 'son of God' as the temple.

complement each other: vss. 97-161; vss. 162-95; vss. 196-294; vss. 545 — 656; vss. 657-808.

The first of these stands apart from the rest of the book. It describes the fall of the tower of Babylon (97-104); the war of the Titans against Cronos and his sons (105-55) and gives a list of world empires (156-61). As we have seen above, the fall of the tower has often been thought to be a fragment of a Babylonian Sibyl, possibly influenced by Berossus, but this theory is unfounded. The euhemeristic account of Cronos and the Titans is exceptional in the Sibylline corpus and may well be borrowed from some non-Jewish source. The list in vss. 156-61 mentions eight kingdoms, but we should add the first kingdom, that of Cronos, and the anticipated eschatological kingdom. This section serves as an introduction to the rest of the book. It also roots the third Sibyl in universal rather than Jewish history. Irrespective of the possibility that some parts of this section were borrowed from a pagan source, there is nothing here that is distinctively Jewish. Rather, the Sibyl draws on myths and legends which were familiar to the gentiles to introduce her message. The list of ten kingdoms is added as the trademark of Sibylline prophecy.[53]

The other four sections present a recurring sequence of (1) sin (usually idolatry) which leads to (2) disaster and tribulation, which is terminated by (3) the advent of a king or kingdom. The third section of the book (196-294) describes the Babylonian exile and restoration.[54] In the other sections the king is expected in the future. In vss. 162-95 the king who brings the period of disasters to an end is identified as the seventh king of Egypt from the Greek dynasty, and in vss. 545-656 as a king 'from the sun,' which should be interpreted as 'an Egyptian king.'[55] In the final section the reference is to a kingdom raised up by God (767).

The date of the main corpus is fixed by three references to the seventh king of Egypt in vss. 193, 318 and 608. While the enumeration of the Ptolemies is confused by the question whether one should include Alexander and by the overlapping reigns of Philometor and Physcon, the most probable solution is that the oracles were written under Ptolemy VI Philometor and the seventh king was either Philometor himself, or, more

---

[53] Cf. the ten generations in the Hellenistic oracle in *Sib. Or.* 4 and the reference to the tenth generation in Servius' explication of the Cumean Sibyl.

[54] Nolland, 'Sib Or III', argues that verses 282-94, which ostensibly refer to the restoration under Cyrus, refer typologically to the author's own day, which is identified as the time of Antiochus Epiphanes. Since Nolland takes the oracle to refer to a Davidic Messiah and since it does not refer to the Maccabees, he dates it 'prior to significant Maccabean success.' However, even if we accept the typological interpretation, which is not certain, the only individual king mentioned is Cyrus, a gentile. This suggests typologically that the Messiah would be a gentile king. Silence on the Maccabees may be due to lack of support for them.

[55] The phrase also occurs in the *Potter's Oracle* where the reference is clearly to an Egyptian king. See Collins, *The Sibylline Oracles*, 40-41.

probably, his anticipated successor.[56] The main corpus, then, should be dated in the period 163-45 B.C.E.[57]

Philometor was noted for his good relations with the Jews. During his reign two Jews, Onias and Dositheus, rose to be prominent generals in the army,[58] and this Onias is presumably identical with the priest who founded the temple at Leontopolis. The enthusiasm for the Egyptian king in *Sib. Or.* 3 would seem particularly appropriate if the oracles were written by a follower of Onias. The emphasis on warfare and politics throughout the book is very different from the spiritualizing tendencies usually associated with Alexandrian Judaism. Further the third Sibyl shows an interest in the Jewish temple which is unparalleled in any document from Egyptian Judaism (cf. vss. 286-94; 564-67; 657-59 715-18). Such an interest is obviously highly compatible with a follower of the priest Onias. The temple referred to by the Sibyl is the Jerusalem temple. It is highly probable that the oracles were written before the temple at Leontopolis was built.[59] Accordingly, we may hypothesize that the oracles were written in circles associated with Onias, though not necessarily located, as yet, at Leontopolis.[60]

While the earliest stage of the book cannot be definitely shown to have incorporated gentile Sibyllina, it certainly drew on the hopes and expectations of the gentile world. The hope for an ideal king or kingdom was widespread in the Near East in the Hellenistic age.[61] By endorsing a Ptolemaic king as virtual Messiah the Sibyl could hope to lay a substantial common basis for relations between Jews and gentiles. The use of the Sibylline form further emphasized the theme that the gentiles and Jews shared one humanity with common interests.

---

[56] For detailed argument see Collins, 'The Provenance of the Third Sibylline Oracle,' 1-5; *The Sibylline Oracles*, 28-33.

[57] Nikiprowetzky, *La Troisième Sibylle*, 209-12 argues for a first century date, mainly because of the prominence of Rome in vss. 175-90. However, that passage makes special note of Roman outrages in Macedonia (190). This reference makes far better sense in the context of the Macedonian wars of the second century B.C.E. than in the first century. Nikiprowetzky implausibly identifies the seventh *king* as Queen Cleopatra VII.

[58] Josephus, *Ag. Apion* 2:49, claimed that Philometor entrusted his whole realm to the Jews.

[59] The land for the temple was probably given in recognition of services over a number of years. Therefore the temple was not built for several years after Onias arrived in Egypt. See Collins, 'Provenance,' 14-15.

[60] See more fully Collins, 'Provenance,' 5-17; *The Sibylline Oracles*, 38-53. Momigliano, 'La Portata Storica' argues that *Sib. Or.* 3 was written to assert the unity of Egyptian and Palestinian Judaism after the Maccabean revolt. He sees a reference to the revolt in verses 194-195: 'And then the people of the great God will again be strong.' This allusion is far too vague and should be understood as future hope, not as a prophecy after the fact. There is nothing in *Sib. Or.* 3 which indicates sympathy with the Maccabees. The emphasis on a king of Egypt is quite alien to the nationalism of the Maccabees, but is strikingly compatible with the politics of the Oniads both before and after the revolt.

[61] See Collins, *The Sibylline Oracles*, ch. 1.

As in Book 4, the eschatology of *Sib. Or.* 3 served as a supporting frame for moral exhortation. Certain types of action lead to destruction, certain others to deliverance. In the second section, vss. 162-95, the main cause of destruction is the misconduct of the Romans, especially homosexuality (185-86) and covetousness (189). In the third section (196-294) the Babylonian exile is a direct punishment for idolatry (275-85). In the fourth section (545-656) the Greeks are endangered because of idolatry (545-55) but can avoid disaster by sending sacrifices to the Jewish temple. They are contrasted with the Jews, who honour the temple with sacrifices and avoid idolatry (575-90), adultery and homosexuality (595-600). Again in 601-607 the gentiles are said to be in danger because of homosexuality and idolatry. Finally in the last section (675-808) the Sibyl again appeals to the Greeks to refrain from idolatry, adultery and homosexuality (762-66) and prophesies that people from all countries will send gifts to the temple (715-19; 772-73). The main message of *Sib. Or.* 3 then would seem to lie in the denunciation of idolatry and sexual abuses, and the advocacy of the Jewish temple.[62]

This is not, of course, to suggest that the eschatology of the book is ornamental. Rather, as in Book 4, eschatology and ethics are interdependent. The Sibyl is preaching that respect for the Jewish temple and ethical behaviour are essential prerequisites for the ideal kingdom.

There is no reason to posit a literary relationship between Books 3 and 4. As we shall see, various Jewish writers in various places used the Sibylline form, for basically similar motives. The Egyptian origin of *Sib. Or.* 3 is rarely disputed, and the book may be seen as initiating a tradition of Sibylline prophecy in Egyptian Judaism.

AGAINST THE NATIONS, 3:350-488

The next stage of *Sib. Or.* 3 consists of four diverse oracles which lack any ethical exhortation and are included because of the general Sibylline interest in political oracles. The four oracles are vss. 350-80; 381-87; 388-400; and 401-88.

Vss. 350-380 predict the vengeance of Asia on Rome, which will be exacted by a lady, a *despoina*. The lady in question should be identified as Cleopatra, who also represented Egypt, as its queen, and Isis, whom she claimed to incarnate.[63] The oracle must have been written shortly before the battle of Actium (30 B.C.E.) and, presumably, in Egypt. There is nothing specifically Jewish in these verses, but whether they were composed by a

---

[62] *Sib. Or.* 3:591-595 gives a brief description of some of the more specific practices of this branch of Judaism. They raise their arms in prayer to God and practise ritual washings. Despite occasional attempts to relate these practices to the Essenes or Pythagoreans, the evidence is not sufficient to permit the identification of a sect. See Nikiprowetzky, *La troisième Sibylle*, 238-59.
[63] For detailed argument see Collins, *The Sibylline Oracles*, 57-71. The identification was proposed by Tarn, 'Alexander Helios and the Golden Age.'

Jew or only taken over, we must note that they are quite in harmony with the enthusiasm of the earlier Sibyl for the Ptolemaic house. The oracle is significant for its lack of ethical or religious exhortation and it shows that Jewish Sibyllists could also engage in purely political propaganda. The oracle continues a vein of anti-Roman polemic which was present already in 3:175-90 and came to play an increasingly prominent role in the Jewish Sibyllina.

Vss. 381-87 predict the fall of the Macedonian kingdom after the conquest of Babylon. They are ascribed to a Persian Sibyl by Geffcken and to a Babylonian Sibyl by Eddy.[64] However, the evidence for either attribution is entirely insufficient. These verses constitute an old fragment incorporated here simply because it was a Sibylline oracle. We have no clue as to its provenance.

Vss. 388-400, again, are directed against the Macedonians. The man, clad in purple, who will come to Asia, is certainly Alexander.[65] This oracle was updated by a Jewish Sibyllist who added references to the root with ten horns and the horn growing on the side, clearly with reference to Daniel 7. This passage also stands as an isolated piece of anti-Hellenistic propaganda.

Vss. 401-488 have been plausibly attributed by Geffcken to the Erythrean Sibyl.[66] According to Varro, the Sibyl of Erythrea prophesied that Troy would fall and that Homer would write falsehoods.[67] Pausanias (10:12,2) says that she sang of Helen and the Trojan war. These are precisely the themes which we find in 3:401-32. The place-names in this section are predominantly in Asia Minor. In vss. 464-69 there is a reference to the Roman civil war and vs. 470 speaks of a man from Italy who goes to Asia. Lanchester has plausibly identified the latter as Sulla.[68] If he is right this oracle should be associated with the Mithridatic wars and was probably incorporated in *Sib. Or.* 3 together with vss. 350-80.

The oracles in vss. 350-480 contain no ethical teachings. With the possible exception of vss. 350-80 they are gentile oracles, incorporated to bring *Sib. Or.* 3 up to date and add to its Sibylline flavour.

VARIOUS ORACLES, 3:1-96

The opening ninety-six verses of *Sib. Or.* 3 are made up of four oracles: vss. 1-45 are direct hortatory material and have their closest parallels in the Sibylline Fragments preserved in Theophilus. They attest a highly spiritual

---

[64] See above, note 23.
[65] Eddy, *The King is Dead,* 12, following Bousset, 'Beziehungen'; Rowley, 'The Interpretation' suggests Antiochus Epiphanes.
[66] Geffcken, *Komposition,* 13.
[67] Lactantius, *Div. Inst.* 1:6.
[68] Lanchester, 'The Sibylline Oracles,' 387.

idea of God, similar to that found in the Orphic fragments and Philo. God is eternal (3:15) self-begotten and invisible (3:11). Idolatry is the supreme sin because it is not in accordance with truth. Despite the spiritual emphasis these oracles are not adverse to sacrificial cult, but only insist that it be offered to the true God (Fragment 1:20-22). In themselves, vss. 1-45 and the Fragments could have been written at any time in the late Hellenistic or early Roman periods. If we can assume that they originally formed a unit with any part of vss. 46-92 we can fix their date more precisely.

Vss. 46-62 must be dated shortly after the battle of Actium. Vs. 52 ('Three will destroy Rome with piteous fate') refers to the second triumvirate.[69] Vss. 46-47 presuppose that Rome had already gained control over Egypt. Vss. 75-92 were also written after the battle of Actium. These verses are dominated by the figure of Cleopatra, the 'widow' of vs. 77. Both oracles reflect the disillusionment of Cleopatra's supporters after her defeat. The hope for a glorious kindom which dominates the earlier oracles is replaced by the expectation of a day of destruction, marked by brimstone from heaven in vss. 60-61 and the collapse of the heavens and a stream of fire from heaven in vss. 80-85. The *despoina* Cleopatra, from whom so much was expected, is here the widow who brings desolation to the universe. Like Babylon in Isa 47:8-9, her claim to universal rule leads only to her widowhood.

It is not clear what relationship there is between vss. 1-45 and these eschatological oracles. Kurfess has suggested that they belong together and constitute the original second book of the collection,[70] and this theory is supported by some evidence from the manuscripts.[71] If he is correct these oracles present the usual combination of eschatology and ethics, although the relation between the two is not made explicit.

The main significance of these oracles lies in the transformation of the attitudes towards Cleopatra after Actium. Never again would a Jewish Sibyllist place messianic hopes in an Egyptian leader. Instead, we read in vs. 49 of a 'holy prince' who will rule the whole earth forever. Since he will manifest 'the great kingdom of the immortal king' (48) the prince in question may be God himself. At least he is not said to come from any specific human dynasty or nation. The Sibyl here seems to despair of help through any human agency and look for a direct supernatural intervention. This tendency becomes more pronounced in *Sib. Or.* 5.

---

[69] See Collins, *The Sibylline Oracles*, 65.
[70] *Sib. Or.* 1/2 were originally a single book. See below.
[71] Kurfess, 'Christian Sibyllines,' 707. In most MSS. the present *Sib. Or.* 3 is introduced as an extract 'from the second book, about God.' Before vs. 93 three MSS. in the class ψ insert the note 'seek here the remnants of the second book and the beginning of the third.' Vss. 93-96 form a distinct but fragmentary oracle.

There is one other oracle in Book 3: vss. 63-74. These verses relate the coming of Beliar, the signs he will perform and his eventual destruction. He is said to come ἐκ Σεβαστηνων, a phrase which can be most plausibly understood as 'from the line of the Augusti.'[72] Beliar should then be identified as Nero, returning either from the dead or from the east. The return of Nero plays a prominent part in *Sib. Or.* 4 and 5 and in the development of the Antichrist traditions.[73] This oracle is a late addition here, since it could not have been written before 70 C.E. By invoking the figure of Belial it shows a further progression towards the expectation of direct supernatural intervention in history, which we have noted in 3:46-62 and 75-92.

In *Sib. Or.* 3, then, we find at least three stages of an ongoing tradition, marked by eschatological expectations centred on the Ptolemaic house and, in the earliest stage, a strong interest in the Jerusalem temple. The later oracles show a changing attitude towards Egypt and an emphasis on eschatological destruction rather than salvation. This change resulted from historical circumstances, especially the conquest of Egypt by the Romans. It becomes more pronounced in the oracles of *Sib. Or.* 5.

Book Five

The fifth Sibylline book consists of six oracles (or, in some cases, collections).[74] Vss. 1-51 form an introduction to the book, which reviews history from Alexander to Hadrian (or, if vs. 51 is original, Marcus Aurelius). Then follow four oracles, vss. 52-110; 111-178; 179-285 and 286-434. These share a common pattern: 1) oracles against various nations; 2) the return of Nero as an eschatological adversary; 3) the coming of a saviour figure; 4) a destruction, usually by fire. Finally there is a concluding oracle, vss. 435-530, which ends with an elaborate battle of the stars in vss. 512-53. One brief passage, vss. 256-59, reflects Christian redaction. Even here it is probable that an original Jewish reference has only been modified by an allusion to the crucifixion.[75]

Not all sections of the book were necessarily written at the same time. In view of the bitterness of complaint about the destruction of the temple (e.g. 398-413) and the prominence of the Nero legend, we might suggest a date towards the end of the first century C.E. for the four central oracles.

[72] See Collins, *The Sibylline Oracles,* 86.
[73] Collins, *The Sibylline Oracles,* 80-87. In the *Ascension of Isaiah* 4:1 Beliar is said to come in the likeness of Nero ('a lawless king, the slayer of this mother.')
[74] See Collins, *The Sibylline Oracles,* 73-95. *Sib. Or.* 5 is discussed by Geffcken, *Komposition,* 22-30, Rzach, 'Sibyllinische Orakel,' 2134-40 and Nikiprowetzky, 'Réflexions,' 30-33.
[75] Vs. 257: 'who stretched out His Hands on the fruitful wood.' See Collins, *The Sibylline Oracles,'* 402. See also Noack, 'Der hervorragende Mann.'

The Egyptian origin of the book is not disputed. The major themes of Book 3 are continued here — interest in the temple, expectation of a saviour figure, portrayal of an eschatological adversary.[76] In *Sib. Or.* 5:501-13 we read that there will be a temple of the true God in the land of Egypt,[77] which will be destroyed by an invasion of Ethiopians. This enigmatic passage is further confused by the statement that the Ethiopians will leave the Triballi, who were properly a people in Thrace. We are forced to ask whether the author is thinking of Ethiopians in a geographical sense at all. In *Sib. Or.* 3:319-20 the Ethiopians are identified with Gog and Magog, and so may be understood as a general name for eschatological adversaries. It is possible then that the Sibyl is speaking allegorically in this passage. If so, the most obvious reference would be to the destruction of Leontopolis by the Romans. If this is so we find in Book 5 a striking indication of continuity with the earliest, Oniad, oracles of Book 3. Even if the temple and its destruction in Book 5 are purely eschatological events with no historical reference, the idea is more intelligible if the Sibyllist stood in a tradition which was once associated with the founder of Leontopolis.

By contrast with Book 3, Book 5 is openly hostile to its gentile neighbours. Relations between Jews and gentiles in Egypt deteriorated in the first century C.E.[78] Two sections of Book 5 (vss. 52-110 and 179-285) are dominated by oracles of doom against Egypt. The Sibyl is even more bitter against Rome. In a powerful invective in vss. 162-78 Rome is denounced because of immorality, adultery and homosexuality (166) and because she destroyed Jerusalem (160-61). The eschatological adversary who appears in the four central oracles of the book is the returning Nero, personification of the evil of Rome.[79]

The saviour figure in Book 5 differs from the earlier oracles by the striking fact that he is said to come from heaven. This is most explicit in vs. 414, where he is said to come 'from the expanses of heaven.' In vs. 256 the saviour comes 'from the sky' but since vs. 257 is clearly Christian the authenticity of 256 is open to question. In vs. 108 the saviour figure is a king 'from God,' which is not necessarily heavenly, but obviously could be. In 158-59 the function of the saviour figure is exercised by a 'great star' which comes from heaven and burns the sea and Babylon (158-59).[80] The

---

[76] I.e. Nero in *Sib. Or.* 5 Cf. the 'king from Asia' in *Sib. Or.* 3:611, Cleopatra in 3:75-92 and Belial in 3:63-74.

[77] This idea had a biblical basis in Isa 19:19 but is nevertheless highly unorthodox.

[78] See Collins, *The Sibylline Oracles*, 76-77. On the relevance of *Sib. Or.* 5 as background to the Diaspora revolt see further *id. Between Athens and Jerusalem*, chap. 3 and Hengel, 'Der politische Messianismus.'

[79] Nero was expected to return from Parthia, not, at least explicitly, from the dead. See Yarbro Collins. *The Combat Myth*, chap. 4.

[80] Stars were frequently associated with saviour figures in the Hellenistic world, and were often identified with the angelic host in the Old Testament and apocalyptic writings. See Collins, *The Sibylline Oracles*, 90-92.

heavenly character of the saviour figure reflects the Sibyl's despair of salvation through human agency. Only a direct supernatural intervention could offer any hope.

Sib. Or. 5 still stops short of the otherworldly (angelic) form of salvation envisaged by some apocalyptic Jewish texts, and, in fact, of any belief in afterlife or resurrection. When the Sibyl envisages any restoration, it is earthly in nature — there are two prophecies of a glorious Jerusalem in 249-55 and 420-27. However, the main emphasis in Book 5 falls not on restoration but on destruction. The book ends with a conflagration and a starless heaven without any sign of future hope.

As in the earlier Sibyllina, Book 5 joins its pronouncement of destruction to the denunciation of ethical transgressions. Here again we find polemic against idolatry (vss. 75-85; 278-80; 353-56; 403-05; 495-96) and sexual offences, especially homosexuality (386-93; 430). Most striking is the interest in the temple (vss. 268, 407, 433, 501-2) since the temple had been destroyed for several years. This persistence of cultic piety shows the gulf which separates Book 5 from Book 4.

Sib. Or 5 marks the end of the stream of Sibylline tradition attested in Book 3. The positive and optimistic relations between Jews and gentiles which originally prompted the use of the Sibylline form as a common medium, had now given way to outright hostility.[81]

Book Eleven

One other Sibylline book, Book 11, was most probably written in Egypt before the Jewish revolts, but it stands apart from the tradition represented by Books 3 and 5. It has received little scholarly attention since its date is disputed and it is at best an enigmatic piece.[82]

Sib. Or. 11 reviews history from the Flood to the death of Cleopatra. Historical figures are represented by the numerical equivalent of their initials. The list of kingdoms appears to be basically derived from the list in 3:159-61.[83] The first kingdom is that of Egypt (11:19-32). Then we find the unhistorical sequence of Persia (47-50), Media (51-60), Ethiopia (61-79), Assyria (80-105), Macedonia (186-223), Egypt (232-60) and Rome (261-314). Within the framework provided by this list *Sib. Or.* 11 has made some modifications. A Hebrew kingdom, ruled by Moses, is inserted between the first rule of Egypt and that of Persia (33-41). The kingdom of

---

[81] Of course the Sibylline Oracles had long been used to express hostility to Rome. On the phenomenon of anti-Roman prophecy in general see Fuchs, *Der geistige Widerstand* and McMullen, *Enemies of the Roman Order,* 128-62.

[82] The main discussions of *Sib. Or.* 11 are those of Dechent, *Sibyllinische Weissagungen,* 49-88; Geffcken, *Komposition,* 64-66; Rzach, 'Sibyllinische Orakel,' 2152-5; Bousset, 'Sibyllen und Sybillinische Buecher,' 278; Kurfess, *Sibyllinische Weissagungen,* 333-41; *id.* 'Oracula Sibyllina XI (IX)-XIV (XII), nicht christlich sondern jüdisch.'

[83] Kurfess, *Sibyllinische Weissagungen,* 333.

Assyria contains no reference to Babylon (unlike 3:160) and is described in remarkably positive terms. The Assyrian king is a champion of the law of God (81-82) and will build the temple of God (87). In fact we must understand the Assyrians here as name for the Jews and the king as Solomon.[84]

Vss. 109-61 are a digression on Romulus and Remus (109-117), the Trojan War (122-43), Aeneas (144-62) and Virgil (163-71).[85] Then a confused passage which includes a reference to the Persian invasion of Greece (179-82) intervenes before the rise of Macedonia. The second kingdom of Egypt is focused primarily on the time of Cleopatra (243-60) and the book concludes with an oracle on the conquest of Egypt by Rome.

Two scholarly hypotheses on the date of the book have been proposed. Geffcken and Rzach date it to the third century C.E. on the assumption that the reference to the Roman conquest of Mesopotamia and the Parthians is a *vaticinium ex eventu*.[86] Both scholars support this date with stylistic considerations and the similarity of Book 11 to Books 12-14. Over against this position Bousset has argued that the oracle would not have stopped with Cleopatra if it were written much later, and therefore should be dated to the turn of the era.[87] Kurfess has supported this position with further considerations.[88] There is no reference in the book to peoples with whom Rome came into conflict in the second century, no reference to the fall of the Temple and little real hostility to Rome.

The assumption of Geffcken and Rzach that the conquest of Mesopotamia could only be prophesied after the fact is not justified. The Parthians were a menance to Roman power in the East in the first century B.C.E. and their subjection might well be prophesied by any one sympathetic to Rome.[89] The argument of Bousset, that an oracle which concludes with Cleopatra must be presumed to have been written shortly after her death, would be conclusive if it were certain that *Sib. Or.* 11 was composed as an independent unit. However, the possibility arises that Books 11 and 12 belong together.[90]

Sib. Or. 12:1-11 may be considered as a summary of Book 11, since it singles out the 'citizen of Pella' (cf. 11:219, 'Pellaean Ares'), who falsely

---

[84] Geffcken, *Komposition*, 66.

[85] This passage is modelled on the figure of Homer in *Sib. Or.* 3:419-25. See Kurfess, *Sibyllinische Weissagungen*, 336.

[86] Geffcken, *Komposition*, 66; Rzach, 'Sibyllinische Orakel,' 2154.

[87] Bousset, 'Sibyllen,' 278.

[88] Kurfess, *Sibyllinische Weissagungen*, 339. Dechent, *Ueber das erste, zweite und elfte Buch*, 49-88, also argued for an early date on less substantial grounds.

[89] The exact reference to the Parthians is disputed. The verb in vs. 161 is μηχυνεϑ which Geffcken understands as μηχυνετο (tarried) but Kurfess takes as μηχυνεται (tarries). However, even if we read a past tense, the use of tenses in the Sibyllina is too fluid to permit any inference that the event in question was already past.

[90] This was suggested in a private communication by John Strugnell.

claimed descent from Zeus Ammon (11:197), Aeneas, the descendent of Assaracus (11:144) and the 'children of the flock-devouring beast,' Romulus and Remus (11:110-17). Further, Book 12 picks up where Book 11 leaves off and has a similarly favourable attitude to the Romans.

However, the question is further complicated by the fact that the verses 12:1-11, which provide the summary of Book 11, are taken directly from Book 5. Two possibilities therefore emerge:

a. *Sib. Or.* 11 may have drawn on Book 5. We have seen that much of Book 11 is built on the list of kingdoms in 3:159-61. The passage on Virgil is based on 3:419-25. Even the passages on Cleopatra in 250-53 and the conquest of Egypt in 285-90 may be based on 3:397-400 and 350-60. On this hypothesis Book 11 would be almost completely derived from earlier Sibyls.

b. Alternatively *Sib. Or.* 5:1-11 may already have been a summary of Book 11. Both Books 5 and 12 are primarily interested in the period after Actium. Vss. 1-11 (common to both books) are distinctly a summary. However, some of the details in that summary, such as the references to the 'son of Assaracus' and the 'children of the beast' do not occur in any Sibyl before *Sib. Or.* 5 unless we assume an early date for Book 11. The references to Roman origins in Book 11 could be supplied from popular tradition, or, at least in part, from Virgil.

While neither of these hypotheses can be established with certainty, the second seems the more probable of the two. The choice of details in 5:1-11 is most easily explained if that passage is summarizing an earlier Sibyl. Further support for an early dating can be found in 11:171 which says that Virgil will conceal the Sibyl's writings until after his death. This reference makes most sense if the book was written shortly after Virgil's death in 19 B.C.E. The fact that Book 12 picks up where Book 11 leaves off may be somewhat coincidental, since that point marks the beginning of the Roman empire. Book 12 is not conspicuously dependent on Book 11 and draws much more directly on Book 5. In view of these considerations we accept *Sib. Or.* 11 as an independent oracle, culminating in the conquest of Egypt, and written about the turn of the era.

Book 11 then stands in a literary relationship to both Books 3 and 5. It drew heavily on Book 3 for its main outline and for many details. Book 5 began with a summary of Book 11. Nevertheless, Book 11 does not belong to the same tradition as the other Egyptian Sibyllina. It lacks most of the concerns of Book 3 and 5 — interest in the temple, expectation of a saviour figure and eschatological judgment, polemic against idolatry and sexual abuses. In fact it is remarkably void of the theological and hortatory concerns of the other books.

The relation of *Sib. Or.* 11 to the other Egyptian Sibyllina is best seen in its treatment of Cleopatra. The dirge in vss. 285-97 refers to her as an 'ill-wed maiden' who 'will make amends for all you formerly did in wars of men.' This passage is a direct reversal of the taunts against Rome in 3:357-58: 'virgin, often drunken with your weddings of many suitors, as a slave will you be wed, without decorum,' and vss. 350-52: 'However much wealth Rome received from tribute-bearing Asia, Asia will receive three times that much again from Rome, and will repay her deadly arrogance to her.' *Sib. Or.* 11 may be understood as a rebuttal of the earlier Sibyl. It lacks any criticism of Rome: on the contrary, its explicit interest in Aeneas and his progeny and the prophecy of Roman victory over the Parthians (vs. 161) reflect a pro-Roman attitude. By contrast, even the earliest stage of Book 3 is sharply critical of Rome (175-95) and even the anti-Cleopatran oracle in 3:75-92 contains no hint of an endorsement of her conqueror.

Sib. *Or.* 11 is also the only early Sibylline oracle that clearly originated in Alexandria.[91] While it was familiar with the earlier pro-Ptolemaic oracles of the Oniad tradition it did not share their politics. It is therefore an important reflection of the diverse political attitudes in Egyptian Judaism, and even within the Sibylline corpus.

The Jewish Stratum in Books One and Two

One other Jewish Sibylline oracle should be dated about the turn of the era: the Jewish stratum in *Sib. Or.* 1-2. As is well-known, the first two books of the Sibylline oracles are not separated in the MSS. and in fact constitute a unit.[92] Study of this oracle is complicated by the fact that the original Jewish oracle has been disrupted by extensive Christian interpolations. The original oracle was built on the familiar Sibylline pattern of ten generations. The first seven are preserved without interpolation in 1:1-323.[93] Then follows a Christian passage on the incarnation and career of Christ in 1:324-400. Book 2 begins with a transitional passage in vss 1-5 and resumes the original sequence in vss. 6-33. However, the eighth and ninth generations have been lost and we arrive directly at the tenth and ultimate period in vs. 15.

In the remainder of Book 2 (vss. 34-347) Jewish and Christian elements are intertwined, and are sometimes difficult to distinguish. Vss. 154-76 is clearly Jewish, since it culminates in the universal rule of the Hebrews (175). A number of passages are clearly Christian: 2:45-55 has Christ preside over the final judgment, and since 2:34-44 and 2:149-53 belong

---

[91] This is shown by the reference to the founding of Alexandria in vss. 219-20 and the eulogy of the city in 232-35.

[92] See Geffcken, *Komposition,* 47-53; Rzach, 'Sibyllinische Orakel,' 2146-52 and Kurfess, 'Oracula Sibyllina I-II.'

[93] Geffcken, *Komposition,* 48 argued that *Sib. Or.* 1:175-79 and 193-96 were Christian interpolations derived from 8:184-87 and 7:7, 9-12, but he has been convincingly refuted b Kurfess, 'Oracula Sibyllina I-II,' 151-60.

with this passage they are probably Christian too. 2:177-86 is based on the parable of the watchful servant (Matt 24:46-51; Luke 12:36-40). 2:190-92 ('Alas for as many as are found bearing in the womb') is paralleled in Mark 13:17, but could arguably be derived independently from Jewish tradition. 2:238-51 refers to the coming of Christ with his angels and the condemnation of the Hebrews. 2:311-12 refers to the intercession of the virgin.

The extract from Ps. Phocylides found in 2:56-148 is in itself Jewish but is inserted here in the Christian passage on the contest for entry into heaven. This interpolated passage has itself in turn undergone Christian interpolation; about 20 lines were added. Hence it forms part of the Christian redaction.[94]

The remaining verses of Book 2 could have been written by either a Jew or a Christian. Most scholars take such passages as more probably Jewish. Accordingly 1:1-323 and 2:6-33, 154-76 can be definitely assigned to the Jewish stage, while vss. 187-89, 193-237, 252-310 and 313-47 are possibly Jewish but could also possibly be Christian. Geffcken dated the Jewish stage to the third century C.E.[95] The Sibyl and Noah are depicted on coins from Asia Minor in the third century. Since Noah figures prominently in Book 1 and the oracle was most probably written in Asia Minor, Geffcken saw here evidence for a third century date. In fact, however, this evidence cannot preclude an earlier dating for Book 1. The Sibyl and Noah were associated already in the second century B.C.E. in 3:827. Geffcken's other arguments for a late date are the author's poor style and irregular metres. Such aberrations in Sibylline literature were not peculiar to any one period and cannot serve as criteria for dating.[96]

The *terminus post quem* for the Jewish stage of Books 1 and 2 is supplied by the fact that Rome is the only power singled out for destruction in the tenth generation (2:18). Rome was prominent in Asia Minor from the beginning of the second century B.C.E. but the fact that it is the only power mentioned suggests a date after Actium, when Roman power in the East was consolidated. Since there is no reference to the destruction of Jerusalem in the Jewish sections of the book and the favourite Sibylline theme of Nero's return is missing, the original oracle was probably composed before 70 C.E. There is a reference to the fall of Jerusalem in 1:393-96, but it is not accompanied by any recriminations against Rome. That reference comes at the end of the long Christian insert on Christ. There is no reference to the fall of Jerusalem in the tenth generation. The only offence mentioned in connection with the destruction of Rome is idolatry (2:17). It is highly unlikely that a Jew writing after 70 and hostile to Rome would fail

---

[94] See Kurfess, 'Das Mahngedicht.' On Ps Phocylides see Van der Horst, *The Sentences of Pseudo-Phocyclides*, on the interpolation pp. 84f.
[95] Geffcken, *Komposition*, 49.
[96] See Rzach, *Metrische Studien zu den Sibyllinischen Orakel;* Bousset, 'Sibyllen,' 274.

to emphasize the destruction of Jerusalem. It is most probable then that the original Jewish oracle was composed around the turn of the era, within the outer limits of 30 B.C.E. and 70 C.E.[97]

The Jewish oracle is usually thought to have been written in Phrygia, since Phrygia is the first land which emerges after the Flood (1:196-98) and Ararat is located there (1:261-62).[98] There is no other indication of local provenance. If this ascription is correct Books 1 and 2 are among the very few documents which have survived from the Jews of Asia Minor in this period.

Books 1 and 2 show certain structural similarities to Book 4. The ten generations of Books 1 and 2 extend from creation to the final judgment, and are punctuated by the Flood in the fifth generation. In Book 4 the ten generations (and four kingdoms) extend from the Flood to the final conflagration — i.e. they are compressed into the second half of the schema of Book 1. Book 4 also refers to resurrection and the punishment of the damned in Gehenna (4:186). These subjects are treated at length in Book 2. Despite these similarities it is not possible to demonstrate literary dependence between the two Sibyls. We have noted already that the periodization in Book 4 belongs to an older Hellenistic oracle, and that similar periodization is attributed to the Cumean Sibyl. It is more probable then that both Books 1/2 in Asia Minor and Book 4 in Syria independently drew on the same, or similar, Sibylline models. The division of history into two cycles which end respectively with a Flood and a conflagration may also be influenced by the idea of the Great Year.[99]

As usual in the Sibyllina, eschatology provides a framework for exhortation. The impending destruction of the world provides an occasion for preaching the crucial ethical values on which the judgment is based. So in 1:50-70 and 174-98 Noah warns his contemporaries of the sins which lead to destruction and the ways to avoid it. The sins in question are commonplace: violence (155-57, 176), deceit (177), adultery and slander (178) and lack of reverence for God (179). The remedy prescribed is simply repentance and supplication (167-69). Because of the Christian redaction we do not know whether there were similar admonitions in the final generation.

We cannot be sure just how much of the eschatology in *Sib. Or.* 2 derives from the Jewish Sibyl. At least 2:154-76 is Jewish. This passage looks for an eschatological kingdom of the Hebrews 'as of old,' — presumably an earthly utopia. Such an earthly eschatology would certainly be in keeping with the usual Sibylline expectations. However, the description of the resurrection in 2:214-37 is quite possibly Jewish. The reference to the giants

[97] This is the position of Kurfess. 'Oracula Sibyllina, I-II,' 165.
[98] Geffcken, *Komposition,* 50. Ararat was usually located in Armenia.
[99] See Collins, *The Sibylline Oracles,* 101-2. The idea is found in Heraclitus and Plato and is implicit in Hesiod. See also Josephus, *Ant.* 1:70-71; *Adam and Eve* 49; 2 Peter 3:6-7.

(2:231-32) is an explicit point of contact with Book 1, and the account of resurrection is reminiscent of Ezekiel 37. The natural sequel to such a resurrection is not a heavenly state but rather a transformation of the earth, which we find in 2:317-29. The punishment of the wicked by fire (2:285-310) is found as early as Isa 66:24 and was common in intertestamental Judaism.[100] Many features of the infernal punishment of the damned were also available in Hesiod's description of the punishment of the Titans in the *Theogony* and Plato's myth of Er in the *Republic* book 10 and *Gorgias* (523). There is no reason why the eschatological punishments in Book 2 should not be Jewish in origin.

We have no evidence as to what situation gave rise to this Jewish oracle. The book shares the anti-Roman tendency of much Sibylline literature. However, if the eschatological passages in Book 2 are substantially Jewish the Sibyl was even more strongly concerned with the judgment of individuals after death. In that case the work is largely hortatory in function, designed to discourage the sins which lead to condemnation. Like most of the Sibylline books this one has also an apologetic dimension. The use of the Sibylline form emphasizes the common ground of Jew and gentile. The appeal to Greek readers is broadened by the Sibyl's extensive use of Hesiod, especially the *Works and Days*. In Book 1 each half of world history is divided into four declining ages, followed by a fifth in which the world is destroyed. The sixth generation, the first after the Flood, is said to be golden (1:284). This schema, and several verbal parallels reflect direct use of Hesiod by the Sibyl.[101]

The Later Jewish and Christian Sibyllina

The Jewish section of *Sib. Or.* 8 (1-216) continues the tradition of anti-Roman polemic which we found in Books 3 and 5. It can be dated to the late second century C.E., but the place of origin is uncertain. The polemic against Rome is not motivated by specific Roman acts against any particular people, but by imperial greed and social injustice.[102]

Sib. Or. 12-14 by contrast are Alexandrian in origin and continue the pro-Roman tradition initiated in Book 11.[103] They are virtually void of ethical and religious material, but provide brief comments on the Roman emperors from Augustus to the Arab conquest of Egypt. Each book picks up where the previous one left off. Presumably they represent an ongoing

---

[100] E.g. 1QS 2:8; *1 Enoch* 21. See Collins, *The Sibylline Oracles,* 109.
[101] See further Kurfess, 'Homer und Hesiod im 1 Buch der Oracula Sibyllina'; and especially Gatz, *Weltalter,* 79-83.
[102] The main discussions of *Sib. Or.* 8 are those of Geffcken, *Komposition,* 38-46; Rzach, 'Sibyllinische Orakel,' 2142-46 and Kurfess, *Sibyllinische Weissagungen,* 316-23.
[103] Geffcken, 'Römische Kaiser im Volksmunde der Provinz'; Scott, 'The Last Sibylline Oracle of Alexandria.'

tradition which was repeatedly updated. There is a short eschatological conclusion at the end of Bk. 14. The significance of these books lies in their evidence of the ways in which the Roman emperors were perceived in the eastern provinces.

The Christian adaptations of the Sibylline oracles are mainly concerned to show that even the pagan Sibyl prophesied of Christ. The Christian redactor of Books 1 and 2 does not greatly alter the impact of the Jewish oracle. His main contribution was to identify Christ as saviour figure and eschatological judge. 1:324-86 is a proclamation of Christ and recounting of his life. The eschatology of Book 2 was already closer to early Christian eschatology than most of the other Jewish oracles. The redactor accentuated the emphasis on individual morality by adding a contest for entry to heaven and a list of vices.

The Christian redaction of Book 8 consists of a collection of oracles which may be diverse in orgin. The themes of the oracles are: Christ and the incarnation (251-336 and 456-79), eschatology (337-58 and 217-50), a hymn in praise of God (429-55), denunciation of idolatry (359-428) and ethical and ritual exhortation (480-500). The major theme is, again, the proclamation of Christ. The eschatological passage in 217-50 is presented as an acrostic poem which spells out with the initials of each line the words Ιησους Χριστος Θεου Ὑιος Σωτηρ Σταυρος.[104] The Christian redaction of Book 8 was known to Lactantius, and therefore written before the end of the third century.

Only two books in the present Sibylline corpus, Books 6 and 7, were composed *de novo* by Christians. Book 6 is a mere 28 verses and is a hymn to Christ. It is written in epic hexameters, but makes no reference to the Sibyl, and was not necessarily composed as a Sibylline oracle.

Book 7 is almost as enigmatic as Bk. 6. It is poorly preserved and consists of a loose collection of oracles, framed by a reference to the Flood (7-15) and an extended eschatological conclusion. The most distinctive passage in the book concerns a strange rite commemorating the baptism of Christ (76-84). Water is sprinkled on fire and a dove is released to heaven. This is said to commemorate the begetting of the Logos by the Father. Book 7 has often been characterized as Gnostic, but without adequate reason.[105]

The Christian books and segments in the present corpus date from the second and third centuries, but the tradition flourished on into the Middle Ages.[106] The Tiburtine Sibyl, which was composed in Greek towards the end of the fourth century and soon translated into Latin, was reworked, again in Latin, in the tenth or early eleventh century. Lactantius (early

---

[104] This is the only acrostic poem in the *Oracula Sibyllina*, although acrostics were considered criteria for the authenticity of pagan Sibylline oracles.
[105] Kurfess, 'Christian Sibyllines,' 707-8. See Gasger, 'Some Attempts to label the Oracula Sybillina, Book 7.'
[106] See further McGinn. *Visions of the End,* 18-21, 43-50.

fourth century) cited the Sibyls extensively and even Augustine quoted the Sibyl and included her among the members of the City of God. Sibylline prophecy served various functions over the centuries, but one of the most basic was undoubtedly that formulated by Lactantius: 'Since all these things are true and certain, foretold by the harmonious prediction of all the prophets; since Trismegistus, Hystaspes and the Sibyl all uttered the same things, it is impossible to doubt that hope of all life and salvation resides in the one religion of God' (*Epitome Institutionum* 68 [73]).

BIBLIOGRAPHY

Text: GEFFCKEN, *Die Oracula Sibyllina*, notable collection of religio-historical parallels; RZACH, *Oracula Sibyllina*, text, apparatus and parallels to Homer and Hesiod.

Studies: GEFFCKEN, *Komposition und Enstehungszeit*, date and provenance of each of the 12 books; RZACH, 'Sibyllinische Orakel,' extensive review of the phenomenon of Sibylline prophecy and of the individual Sibylline books; LANCHESTER, 'The Sibylline Oracles,' introduction, translation and notes; KURFESS, *Sibyllinische Weissagungen*, text, translation and notes to *Sib. Or.* 1-11; COLLINS, *The Sibylline Oracles*, date, provenance and themes of books 3 and 5; *id.* 'The Sibylline Oracles,' introduction, translation and notes to all 12 books; NIKIPROWETZKY, *La troisème Sibylle*, detailed study of book 3.

Chapter Ten

Apocalyptic literature

Michael E. Stone

General

The apocalypse emerged, from the third century B.C.E. at least, as a major literary genre and one which was to have a lasting influence on Judaism and Christianity. The apocalypses, as the title indicates, are primarily books of revelations typified by the vision form.[1] The visions experienced by the seer are usually symbolic, particularly when they bear the character of political prediction.[2] In any case, the vision typically bears a mystifying veneer and most often an *angelus interpres* appears to explicate to the seer the interpretation of the symbols or the meaning and implication of the vision. The vision is not published under its writer's name, but is attributed to a famous figure drawn from the past.[3] This pseudepigraphy is typical of the apocalypses and the reasons usually suggested for it are discussed below. They include, most plausibly, the association of a particular tradition of teaching with the name of some ancient seer. Moreover, the cessation of the prophetic office is often emphasized and the consequent attribution of later visions to figures from the period in which prophecy was still active.

The apocalyptic writings embrace a great variety of contents. Two general categories seem, however, to be particularly prominent. The first is eschatology. Apocalyptic eschatology is permeated by the expectation of the imminent end and, for it, the advent of the end does not depend upon human action.[4] The second type of material, here called the speculative, is the revelation of heavenly or similar secrets. The secrets revealed may include matters of cosmography and uranography, angelology and

---

[1] Greek ἀποκάλυψις. On the use of the term cf. Kaufmann, 'Apokalyptik', 1143.

[2] On the nature of this symbolism, see Collins, 'Symbolism of Transcendence', and previous bibliography there.

[3] Except for the Apocalypse of John (whether John of the Apocalypse is to be distinguished from the Evangelist or not). The lack of pseudepigraphy in this case is doubtless due to the different eschatological self-understanding of the Christian community from which the Apocalypse of John stemmed. Contrast Rev 22:10 with Dan 12:4 for a clear illustration of this. See Yarbro Collins, 'Early Christian Apocalypses', 71.

[4] Man's repentance may affect his own fate, but not usually that of the world.

meteorology, calendar and cosmogony, and more.[5] A third, less prominent subject appears in a number of cases, a pietistic, moral preaching.

The apocalypses have been transmitted almost exclusively by the various Christian churches. Thus they survive today in numerous languages: Greek, Latin, Ethiopic, Syriac, Church Slavonic, Armenian, Georgian and others. Some fragments of certain of these books have turned up among the Dead Sea scrolls, and these serve to highlight the fact that there were apocalypses written in each of the chief literary languages of the Jews in the period of the Second Temple — Hebrew, Aramaic, and Greek.

Although the present chapter is devoted to the apocalypses as a literary genre, some general observations about their worldview may be made. The apocalypses tend to break the nexus of a directly operative causal relationship between human action and political events which lay at the basis of the Deuteronomistic literature and of the view of classical prophecy.[6] They often delineate the expected future as meta-historical, frankly cosmic in character. The progress and fate of the world are largely determined by superhuman forces; history is viewed as an overall process, with the vindication of God's righteousness only to be made evident at its termination. Action takes place in the heavenly as well as the earthly sphere and secrets of history and eschaton, of the upper world and the lower are all objects of the seer's intense interest.

Apocalypses and the Bible

APOCALYPSES AND PROPHECY

The roots of the apocalypse should be sought in biblical literature, first and foremost in prophecy.[7] It is impossible today to document in detail the development of apocalypse from prophecy because of the paucity of source materials stemming from the fourth and third centuries B.C.E. in which this process might be traced.[8]

---

[5] This is a most ancient element of the apocalypses: see Stone, 'Third Century'; id., Scriptures, 32-47. Material about the heavenly world has been assembled by Bietenhard, Himmlische Welt. On some aspects of speculative learning in apocalypses, see Gruenwald, Apocalyptic, 7-10 and passim.

[6] This is true even where destruction (e.g. Isa 34) or salvation (e.g. Isa 51) is described in cosmic, supernatural terms.

[7] See in general Collins, Apocalypse, 29-30; Gruenwald, 'Apocalyptic Literature', 92-94.

[8] See Kaufmann, Toledot 8, 394-5; Milik, 'Fragments araméens', 347-8; id., Books of Enoch, 25-36 claims that 1 Enoch 1-36 were composed towards the middle of the third century B.C.E., utilizing an earlier source which is embedded in present chaps. 6-19. This earlier source, he suggests, lay before the final redactors of Gen 6:1-4. This latter observation is not soundly based, although both 1 Enoch 1-36 and The Book of the Luminaries which underlies 1 Enoch 72-82 should be dated to the third century. Gruenwald, 'Dissertation', 13-36 and Apocalyptic,

Nonetheless, certain features of later prophecy, both formal and substantial, clearly indicate the incipient development of the apocalypse. These are the roots from which the apocalypse sprang. Formally, the following features should be observed. First, the development by Ezekiel of the use of extended metaphors; these presage the extensive and complex sustained symbolic visions of the apocalypses. Such are chaps. 16 (Jerusalem the harlot), 17:1-10 (interpreted in vv. 11-19), 19, etc.[9] Second, in proto-Zechariah occur a number of night visions composed of symbols and their subsequent interpretations by an angelic intermediary. This structure strongly resembles that found in the apocalypses. Particularly striking in this respect is the vision of the golden candelabrum and its interpretation, an involved symbolic structure with a sustained interpretation.[10] A third passage showing a remarkable systematic formal relationship to the apocalypses is Ezekiel, chaps. 40-48, the vision of the ideal Jerusalem. In this part of the book, the prophet through the mediation of an angel, is taken on an extensive tour of the new Jerusalem.[11] This section of Ezekiel resembles not only writings such as *The Description of the New Jerusalem* from Qumran, but also such passages as Enoch's guided tour of secret places of heaven and earth (*1 Enoch,* chaps. 17-36) and many other sections of the apocalypses.

Some aspects of the substance of the apocalypses also find extensive precursors in the prophetic literature. The most evident of these is eschatology. Certain basic stances of the apocalypses distinguish between their eschatology and that of the prophetic writings,[12] but this does not gainsay

16-19 also implies an early date. He claims that Sir 3:21-22 and 49:8 presuppose an existing esoteric tradition which is substantially identical with that of the apocalyptic literature. With his views, contrast von Rad's observations on the attitude of the wisdom tradition to those areas of knowledge lying beyond its realm of discourse (*Wisdom,* 97-110). Gruenwald's case as regards Ben Sira and the consequent early dating of the apocalyptic tradition is strengthened by the early date of the first and third parts of *1 Enoch.*

[9] Kaufmann, *Toledot* 7, 504-5 also treats the relationship between Ezekiel's imagery and apocalyptic symbols. In 'Apokalyptik', 1147-8 he deals in some detail with other biblical antecedents of apocalyptic visions. See also Hanson, 'Apocalypse', 28.

[10] On the origin of the vision structure, see Kaufmann, *Toledot* 8, 232. There are considerable difficulties in the text of Zech 3-4, see *ibid.,* 248-9. The importance of proto-Zechariah for the study of apocalyptic visions has been stressed by Uffenheimer, *Visions of Zechariah.* The differences between prophetic and apocalyptic uses of symbols are stressed by Kaufmann, 'Apokalyptik', 1144. He noted the movement towards the 'mystifying' style in prediction, particularly eschatological, which is typical of apocalyptic writing. The article by North ('Prophecy to Apocalypse') deals with the relationship between both parts of Zechariah and apocalypses. Confusion of the type referred to on pp. 392-4 below besets this article.

[11] On the speculative tradition of the heavenly or ideal Jerusalem, see Stone, 'Lists', 445-6 and notes 3-4 and references there. With the angelic figure, compare Ezek 8:2; see also Kaufmann, *Toledot* 8, 254.

[12] See above, p. 383 and below, pp. 392-3. Collins, 'Apocalyptic Eschatology' recently tried to identify the distinguishing element of apocalyptic eschatology as the transcendence of death. See also North, 'Prophecy to Apocalypse', 5-58. A useful discussion of the term and its meaning is that of Müller, *Ursprünge,* 1-9.

the relationship that exists between them. Recently it has been suggested that the shift from prophetic to apocalyptic eschatology was fundamentally the result of the transfer of the realm in which eschatological hopes were expected to be fulfilled from the on-going process of history to the end of history or beyond, and that this transfer was largely the result of the political situation in post-exilic Judea.[13] Other views would propose that this movement in religious thought was basically the result of foreign influence, Iranian[14] or Greek.[15] The presence of such influences is not to be denied but they were probably not decisive in bringing about the shift from prophetic to apocalyptic eschatology, although they doubtless had subsidiary influence on this shift. Chief texts in the prophetic books showing development in the direction of apocalyptic eschatology are Isaiah, chaps. 24-27, Ezekiel, chaps. 38-39,[16] Deutero-Isaiah and Deutero-Zechariah, particularly chapter 14.[17] Isa 24-27 contains prophecies of God's terrible

[13] Hanson, 'OT Apocalyptic', 454-79; *Dawn,* passim; 'Apocalypticism', 29-30. Compare also Collins, 'Apocalyptic Eschatology'. On the recent debate over apocalyptic eschatology, see Koch, *Rediscovery, passim.* A thoughtful critique of Hanson's position which, however, does not greatly affect our statement is Carroll, 'Twilight of Prophecy'.
[14] The question of Iranian influence is much debated. A convenient summary of views is that of Duchesne-Guillemin, *Religion de l'Iran,* 257-64. The information there and in the article by Winston ('Iranian Component') seems basically inconclusive for our period. The considerations urged by Shaked, ('Qumran and Iran') strengthen the parallels. Shaked is conscious of the chronological stumbling block. This is that the relevant Iranian sources are centuries later than the Jewish ones (pp. 443-4). Nonetheless, he argues that Iranian ideas influenced Judaism since 'the motifs in Zoroastrianism form a coherent unity with other aspects of the Zoroastrian religion, and may be seen to have emerged in an organic manner, while in Israel the same themes cannot be claimed to be "natural" to the same extent' (p. 443). On Iranian eschatology, see Shaked, '*Menog* and *gētig'.* The most recent study which proposed extensive Iranian influence is by Hultgård, 'Das Judentum und die iranische Religion'. The issues he raises are not literary ones. On the general problem, see also Widengren, 'Iran and Israel', 144ff., Lambert, *Background,* 8-9, and Schmithals, *Apocalyptic Movement,* 117-20. Hanson's work has gone a long way towards blunting the point of Shaked's argument (see articles cited in previous note). At another level of discussion, some Persian works of admittedly later date than the Jewish apocalypses, have many of the characteristics of the genre 'apocalypse'; see Collins, *Apocalypse,* 207-17.
[15] Direct Greek influence has been urged by Glasson, *Greek Influence,* and a major re-evaluation of it was made by Martin Hengel, *Hellenism* I, 107ff. However, even in the section dealing with 'Higher Wisdom through Revelation as a Characteristic of Religion in Late Antiquity' (Vol. I, pp. 210-18), Hengel does not succeed in finding close parallels to apocalyptic views of speculative 'wisdom'. On the *Potter's Oracle* and other such Hellenistic Egyptian works closely parallel to the political apocalypses see above p. 361f. On Greek works of 'apocalyptic genre', see the essay by Attridge, 'Greek and Latin Apocalypses.' The complexity of the relationship between the apocalypses and the Hellenistic Near East has been stressed by Collins, 'Jewish Apocalyptic'. On possible Akkadian origins, see n. 220, below.
[16] On this pericope, see in detail Zimmerli, *Ezechiel* 2, 921-75, particularly 945ff. and 973ff.
[17] The chief biblical texts having relationship to the apocalypses were dealt with by Frost, *Old Testament Apocalyptic.* He would add Joel and certain other Isaianic material to the texts mentioned here. Hanson sees the range of relevant biblical passages as still broader: see *Dawn,* passim; 'Zechariah 9'.

vengeance which will lead to a desolation of human society and of the world. These are counterpointed with prophecies of future joy or the coming reward of Israel. Both these themes are presented in terms harking back to older mythological or semi-mythological conceptions transferred into the eschatological realm.[18] From the view-point of form, these chapters are prophecy and not an apocalypse; in content they are close to apocalyptic eschatology. A similar development is the way the ancient idea of the divine warrior shifts from primordial to historical and then to eschatological. Such shifts are particularly typical of Deutero-Isaiah.[19]

The description of the enemies and their leader Gog (Ezek 38-39) formed a fertile source for many descriptions of the eschatological war. Indeed, already for Ezekiel himself, it seems, the enemy took on a non-historical dimension.[20] A third passage standing clearly on the way leading to the apocalypse is Zech 14, the prime example from Deutero-Zechariah, which is relevant in nearly all its parts.[21] In this chapter the eschatological war has taken on a fully cosmic dimension.

It follows that major features may be discerned in the later prophetic literature which point towards extensive developments in apocalyptic literature; these are features both of form and content. Interestingly, the formal features do not occur in passages in which the content is analogous to that of the apocalypses. The one exception to this is Ezek 40-48 which, in form, resembles the heavenly journeys of the apocalypses and in content is not too remote from them. In this passage, however, a particular tradition of very antique origin is reflected,[22] the tradition of the heavenly temple and its measurements, cf. Exod 25:9, 40 and 1 Chr 28:19.[23] This tradition is contained in *The Description of the New Jerusalem* from Qumran,[24] Rev 21:9-27, 2 Apoc. Bar. 59:4, and other sources.[25] Again, it has been rightly stressed that there is no biblical prophecy which exhibits the particular historical perspective typical of the apocalypses.[26]

It should be noted, of course, that an interest in eschatology stands in no

---

[18] Such is e.g. the eschatological feast (28:2-8) and compare the formulation by Cross, *Canaanite Myth*, 99-111. Other aspects of this are discussed by Hanson, 'Prolegomena to Apocalyptic'.

[19] Cross, *Canaanite Myth*, 99-111 and earlier bibliography there. See also Hanson, 'Jewish Apocalyptic', 48-53. In *Die Apokalyptik*, 18ff., von der Osten-Sacken discusses various dimensions of the relationship between Deutero-Isaiah and the apocalypses.

[20] Kaufmann, *Toledot* 7, 578-82 treats this vision. He emphasizes its peculiar characteristics.

[21] Hanson, *Dawn*, 369ff.

[22] Cf. Hamerton-Kelly, 'Temple', 6ff.

[23] Perhaps also Zech 2:5-9; see Kaufmann, *Toledot* 8, 236f. Contrast, however, Uffenheimer, *Visions of Zechariah*, 91f. and compare Hamerton-Kelly, 'Temple', 5ff.; Jongeling, 'Publication provisoire'.

[24] *DJD* 1, 134; 3, 84, 184.

[25] For detailed analysis, see Stone, 'Lists', 445-6, notes 3-4.

[26] See Kaufmann, *Toledot* 8, 401 and further references there.

contradiction to a strong concern for history. Indeed, many apocalypses treat the past history of Israel or of the world in one way or another. This interest, combined with developed views of periodization (see below, pp. 436-7 and note 286) and remythologization gives the understanding of history in the apocalypses its particular perspective.[26a] The way that the recital of past history functions within the overall framework of the apocalypses has yet to be explicated in full. Its role as *vaticinium ex eventu* to lend authority to future prediction is not an exclusive, perhaps not even a primary one. Moreover, the part that biblical historiography plays in the formation of apocalyptic literature, with its own particular historiographic approach, has still to be studied.

APOCALYPSE AND THE WISDOM LITERATURE

Some lines of connection may be discerned between the apocalypses and the wisdom literature. The sapiental character of the stories in Daniel has been emphasized and implications drawn from the utilization of a wisdom figure like Daniel as the pseudepigraphic author of an apocalypse.[27] Von Rad's claim that the origin of apocalyptic is in Wisdom alone, however, seems extreme.[28] The recent emphasis upon the speculative material in the apocalypses serves to highlight certain points of contact and connection between them and biblical wisdom literature; it still does not demonstrate von Rad's claim.[29] These points of contact, it eventuates, are almost exclusively limited to formal and structural features. The central text in which a relationship between the the content and ideas of apocalyptic speculation and the wisdom books may be discerned is Wis 7:17-21. In this

von Rad

[26a] Davis, 'Apocalyptic and Historiography' is too general and a bit polemical, He rightly stresses the interest of the apocalypses in past history, but says nothing of their particular perspective. A number of interesting observations relevant to this matter are made by Collins, 'Pseudonymity', 333-8.

[27] Von Rad, *Theologie* 2, 317f.; *id.*, *Wisdom*, 16. Kaufmann, *Toledot* 8, 402f. has a most interesting discussion of the wisdom, mantic and 'prophetic' features of the Daniel figure as presented in Dan 1-6. The supposed central role of the Book of Daniel in the original development of apocalyptic literature was most strongly urged by Rowley, *Relevance of Apocalyptic*, 39f. The early date now accepted for parts of the Enochic literature must modify this position. Hengel, *Hellenism* I, 180f., still regards Daniel as the oldest apocalypse and associates this earliest stage of development with the Hasidim; cf. von der Osten-Sacken, *Apokalyptik*, 46ff. and Delcor, 'Développement de l'apocalyptique'. See also Collins, 'Court-Tales', 231-4.

[28] See von Rad, *Theologie* 2, 319ff.; *id.*, *Wisdom*, 272-83. For a critique see Vielhauer, 'Apocalyptic', 597; Koch, *Rediscovery*, 36-48; von der Osten-Sacken, *Apokalyptik*, 9-12 and *passim;* Schmithals, *Apocalyptic Movement*, 129-30. Interesting comments on the role of wisdom in apocalyptic origins are made by Carroll, 'Twilight of Prophecy', 29-30.

[29] Compare particularly Job 38; *2 Apoc. Bar.* 59; *4 Ezra* 4:5-9, 5:36-7. See von Rad, *Gesammelte Studien* I, 262-72; *id. Wisdom*, 18-9. Contrast the evaluation of the role of the speculative material by von der Osten-Sacken, *Apokalyptik*, 60-1.

passage, too, the overlap is only partial and there is no indication of such interests in the wisdom literature before Wisdom of Solomon.[30] It has recently been suggested that the mantic wisdom of ancient Israel, and not the school-wisdom, is the context in which many features of apocalyptic literature can be seen to originate. This certainly may have been a contributing factor; if so, the question of Mesopotamian influences must be weighed.[31]

[margin note: mantic wisdom not school wisdom]

Finally, the great spread of wisdom terminology in all the literature of the Second Temple period should be noted. Thus, 1QS 4:1-3, 22, 24; 4 Ezra 14:47 and many other sources may be observed. This terminology is divorced, in texts like these, from the particular meaning it has in older wisdom writing and serves to denote whatever teaching or doctrine the writer using it considered to be highest 'wisdom' or 'understanding'. This seems to indicate that here a merely superficial relationship is involved. After the time of Ben Sira (see Sir 51:23) there is no evidence for a unique sociological matrix in which wisdom traditions were transmitted, and it seems likely that this wisdom terminology has become very general in its significance. Meaningful contacts should be sought where there is common ground in conceptual or at least formal structure.[33]

Points of contact may also be sought between certain Psalms hymning God as creator by listing his creations and the range of natural phenomena which were a subject of apocalyptic curiosity. Such points lie in the list of natural phenomena rather than in how these different elements of nature were understood or discussed.[34]

---

[30] See Stone, 'Lists', 436-8 (*pace* von Rad, *Wisdom*, 16); see also North, 'Prophecy to Apocalyptic', 58-62. Reese suggests that this range of interests is related to the curricular spread of Alexandrian learning; see *Hellenistic Influence*, 8 etc.

[31] On the role of Israelite mantic wisdom, see Müller, *Ursprünge*, 268-73. Collins, 'Cosmos and Salvation' takes up this point once again, urging Mesopotamian or Chaldean influences. J.Z. Smith also attempts to argue that apocalyptic originated in Babylonian scribal wisdom; see 'Wisdom and Apocalyptic'. The question of Mesopotamian elements now must be reassessed, see Stone, 'Third Century B.C.E.', 485ff.; *id.*, *Scriptures*, 39-47.

[32] See von der Osten-Sacken, *Apokalyptik*, 29ff.

[33] A standard piece of evidence in this connection is the small fragment reflecting the 'myth' of hypostasized wisdom in *1 Enoch* 42. Yet this is out of context in *1 Enoch* and not typical of it or of the other apocalypses. It is probably best regarded as part of wisdom literature. Compare, e.g., from the point of view of N.T. studies the observations by Koester in Robinson — Koester, *Trajectories*, 219-22, particularly 220. Clearly, Jewish wisdom ideas and terminology played a role in the later development of Gnostic myth and terminology. See, e.g., the analysis by MacRae, 'Sophia Myth'. On schools in ancient Israel, see von Rad, *Wisdom*, 17-8.

[34] The early strata of this relationship were dealt with by von Rad, *Gesammelte Studien* 1, 262-72; on the later stages of it, see Stone, 'Lists', 426ff. It is not clear that the use of the term 'wisdom' to describe aspects of the activities of the apocalyptic seers is helpful: see, e.g., the discussion in Hengel, *Hellenism* 1, 202-10; cf. Stone, 'Lists', 435-9.

APOCALYPSE AND THE FULFILLMENT OF PROPHECY

It could very well be expected that the apocalypses would set forth the ways in which biblical prophecies were to be fulfilled. After all, the Bible was seen as the central divine revelation and its prophecies were regarded by many as having eschatological application. Moreover, it is abundantly clear from the literature of Qumran that certain texts in the Bible were interpreted eschatologically or messianically in the period of the Second Temple and were quoted to verify eschatological predictions.[35] This is also true for early Christianity which sought in the New Testament and in the writings of the apostolic age to show that biblical prophecies were fulfilled.[36] Or again, the quotation of Scripture and its exegesis is, of course, constitutive of rabbinic midrash. Thus the function of the Bible in literature of the Second Temple period and allied writings as a source of authority whose message is to be discovered by exegesis seems indubitable.

Recent scholarship has tried systematically to show that eschatological discourse in some apocalypses is also informed by biblical prophecies.[37] Yet this use of biblical prophecy differs from that of, say, the early Christian sources. What is absent from the apocalypses is the invoking and exegesis of scriptural quotations, the use of 'proof texts'. The apocalypses often predict the eschatological events, sometimes at considerable length and in considerable detail. Yet the events so predicted are not structured so as patently to fulfil expectations aroused by the then current eschatological exegesis of texts drawn from the biblical prophecies. There is, of course, the perpetual reinterpretation of Jeremiah's seventy years,[38] and 4 Ezra 13 is explicitly dependent on Daniel 7. Ezek 1 played a special and rather different role. Yet these are rare exceptions and, even if a few more examples are added, they do not affect the observation made here.

---

[35] Certain of the *pesharim*, 4 Q Testimonia, 11 Q Melchizedek and other documents show this clearly. On the other hand, some Qumran texts, like the *War Scroll*, resemble the apocalypses in this respect. See Bruce, *Biblical Exegesis*, 7-11, 16-17.

[36] See, e.g., the use of πληρόω of prophecies in many cases in the New Testament, such as Matt 1:22, 2:15, 4:14, 8:17, etc. On formulae and character of quotation in the Dead Sea scrolls and the New Testament, see Stendahl, *School of St. Matthew*, 39-213 and Fitzmyer, *Semitic Background*, 3-58. The existence of *Testimonia*, collections of biblical citations, in the early Church witnesses to the same view of Scripture; see Fitzmyer, *ibid.*, 59-89.

[37] That biblical prophecy served as a source for many elements of apocalyptic eschatology is obvious and the effects of biblical language on all the literature of the age of the Second Temple need no demonstration in detail. This is, in fact, what Russell shows in *Method and Message*, 178-95, and see the pertinent observations of Hartmann, *Prophecy Interpreted*, 108-9, 137-9. More recently he has developed his method in *Asking for a Meaning*, especially pp. 7-12.

[38] So Jer 25:12, 29:10; 2 Chr 36:20-27; Zech 1:18, 7:5; Dan 9:2, 24; *T. Levi* 17:1 *et al.;* see also Russell, *Method and Message*, and particularly Wolff, *Jeremia*, 113-6, 200ff. Koch, 'Die mysteriösen Zahlen', discerns a relationship between the Judean regnal chronology and the reinterpretations of the 70 years. See further note 286, below.

It follows that this different treatment of Scripture is due to the fact that the apocalypses had a different attitude to Scripture from that of the Qumran sectaries, the Sages or the early Church. This stemmed, doubtless, from a different self-understanding and view of inspiration.[39]

OTHER FEATURES OF APOCALYPTIC ORIGINS

Speculative interests: the publication of the Qumran manuscripts of *1 Enoch* has shown clearly that the first and third parts of that composition, *The Book of the Watchers* (chaps. 1-36) and *The Book of the Luminaries* (the source of *1 Enoch* 72-82) were composed by the third century B.C.E.[40] The content and character of these oldest fragments of apocalyptic literature are far from exclusively or even predominantly eschatological. Indeed, their range of contents shows that there existed in Judaism of the third century B.C.E. a developed 'scientific' lore about astronomy, astrology, calendar and angelology. At this time, the cosmos and all its parts were the object of learned speculation. Yet, it seems clear that the 'scientific' or speculative interests were beyond the pale for the tradents of biblical literature, in which they find almost no expression.

In addition, from *1 Enoch* 14 it is patent that a tradition (and apparently the practice) of ascent to the environs of the Deity was also well established very early. This chapter shows, even more surprisingly, that by the third

---

[39] Indeed, there is very little overt quotation of Scripture in the apocalypses and almost none in eschatological contexts. On the different attitudes to Scripture of the apocalyptic and midrashic writings, see Heinemann, *Darkei ha-Aggadah*, 174-5. The view of Hengel, *Hellenism* 1, 206-7 seems difficult to accept holus-bolus, as the observations of the last paragraph make evident. On the *Testament of Moses* and its relation to Deuteronomy, see above p. 345-7. On the influence of Jeremiah on *2 Apocalypse of Baruch*, see Wolff, *Jeremiah*, 147-9. It is not extensive. It would be futile and unrealistic to deny the influence of the Bible on the language and concepts of apocalyptic authors; cf., e.g., Steck, 'Die Aufnahme von Genesis'. All that is being discussed here is the attitude to the Bible, and particularly to biblical prophecy. Schmithals, while noting the problem, nonetheless offers no satisfactory solution (*Apocalyptic Movement*, 69-71). It can be questioned, for example, whether 'the apocalyptic writings in fact replace the Old Testament as the final revelation' (*ibid.*, 71); a sensitive analysis of 4 Ezra 14 leads us in a different direction, see p. 414 below. Gruenwald claims that at the heart of apocalyptic literature is an esoteric interpretation of Scripture. He fails to bring examples, however, from the literary apocalypses (*Apocalyptic*, 19-25).

[40] See Milik, *Books of Enoch*, 104 and 273 for the dates of the oldest manuscripts. On the matters discussed in this section, see in greater detail: Stone, 'Third Century B.C.E.', 486-92; *idem*, *Scriptures*, 27-47. Schmithals, *Apocalyptic Movement* denies that the 'apocalyptic' has an 'independent cosmological interest' (p. 31ff.). His argument is not compelling on this point and, in general, his book confuses categories of ancient thought and literature by making them subservient to present theological concerns; compare also *ibid*, pp. 130-1. Sacchi, 'Libro de Vigilanti' draws certain implications of the early date of this document for the study of apocalyptic literature. See note on Sacchi in *JSJ* 10 (1979), pp. 122-3.

century B.C.E. Ezek 1 already served as the basis of such contemplation.[41] The existence of such visions shows a deep change in the view of man and of the norms of religious experience, when they are compared with the Hebrew Bible.

Mesopotamian elements: A number of studies have indicated, over the years, that the figure of Enoch was heavily influenced by Mesopotamian models.[42] The influence of the Hellenistic Chaldean astrologers, who became so prominent in that age, has been particularly emphasized by some scholars.[43] Others have highlighted the Mesopotamian character of the astronomical theories propounded by *The Book of the Luminaries* and of the map of the world presumed by the various parts of *1 Enoch.*[44] Milik reports that Mesopotamian names and mythical personages figure in *The Book of the Giants,* a book belonging to the Qumran Enochic corpus.[45]

Thus, certain of the streams flowing into Jewish apocalyptic literature seem to have come to no expression in the Bible. This does not necessarily mean that they were due to foreign influences, although a body of evidence has been assembled that points towards Mesopotamian influence particularly upon the scientific aspects of some of the speculative lore. Other aspects of this oldest apocalyptic literature, such as the ascent vision material, show none such.

Definition and Description

The problem of definition and characterization has proved consistently intractable. Clarity is to be achieved only if a clear distinction is drawn between 'apocalypticism' and 'apocalypse'. This somewhat paradoxical pronouncement is a result of the situation existing in scholarship.[46] The term 'apocalypticism' is used by many scholars to designate a specific pattern of ideas, and scholars' interest has centered chiefly upon the relationship between this pattern of ideas and New Testament thought.

---

[41] See Scholem, *Major Trends,* 40-63; *id., Jewish Gnosticism, passim,* but particularly 14-19; cf. Stone, 'Third Century B.C.E.,' 488; *id., Scriptures,* 32-4. See also Rowland, 'Visions of God,' who studies the development of this aspect of the apocalypses and the role of Ezekiel chap. 1 in its growth. He does not deal, however, with the full range of the 'speculative' elements. This is also the subject of Gruenwald, *Apocalyptic,* 29-72. The ascent of the soul is, of course, a much broader phenomenon. The classic study remains that of Bousset, 'Himmelsreise der Seele'; compare also Colpe, 'Himmelsreise der Seele'.

[42] Jansen, *Henochgestalt* and Grelot, 'Légende d'Henoch' are particularly important.

[43] Jansen, *Henochgestalt,* 1-4; Collins, 'Cosmos and Salvation', 131-2.

[44] For the former see, e.g., Hengel, *Hellenism* 1, 209; for the latter Grelot, 'Géographie mythique'.

[45] Milik, *Books of Enoch,* 311-13.

[46] The matter is analysed at length in the 'Post-Script' to Stone, 'Lists'. So also Koch, *Rediscovery,* 15ff. Schmithals, *Apocalyptic Movement, passim,* fluctuates between genre, thought structure and socio-religious entity.

This 'apocalypticism' is also called 'apocalyptic' by many. 'Apocalypse' on the other hand is a literary genre with certain distinctive characteristics which can be listed. The genre itself and its relationship to allied literary types are not yet adequately understood in all their details, but it is usually possible to decide whether a given work is an apocalypse. A recent study, based on a systematic survey of a broad range of Jewish, Christian and pagan writings from late antiquity, reached the following, tentative, genre definition:

> 'Apocalypse' is a genre of revelatory literature with a narrative framework, in which a revelation is mediated by an otherworldly being to a human recipient, disclosing a transcendent reality which is both temporal, insofar as it envisages eschatological salvation, and spatial insofar as it involves another, supernatural world.[47]

collins

'Apocalypticism' is characterized by a recent scholar in terms of the following features: the acute expectation of the fulfillment of divine promises; cosmic catastrophe; a relationship between the time of the end and preceding human and cosmic history; angelology and demonology; salvation beyond catastrophe; salvation proceeding from God; a future saviour figure with royal characteristics; a future state characterized by the catchword 'glory'.[48] All these features bear upon eschatology.

KOCH

The problem arising from this definition is that many works which belong to the genre 'apocalypse' contain much that is not covered or rendered comprehensible by the above description, while many works not formally apocalypses are imbued with this apocalypticism. This contradiction can be resolved in various ways. Some scholars employing this definition, stringently delimit the number of apocalypses, admitting only Daniel, *1 Enoch, 2 Enoch,* 4 Ezra, *2 Apocalypse of Baruch, Apocalypse of Abraham* and Revelation as prime witnesses.[49] There seems no good reason to exclude *3 Apocalypse of Baruch* and other works from the discussion because they do not fit the description. Even if this is done, *1 Enoch* in

---

[47] So Collins, *Apocalypse,* 9; that volume sets forth the genre analysis in detail. See further views of Collins, in 'Apocalyptic Genre'. See also Vielhauer, 'Apocalyptic', 582-6; Koch, *Rediscovery,* 19-30 already attempted, on the whole successfully, to characterize apocalypticism and the apocalypses separately. See, following him, Barr, 'Jewish Apocalyptic', 15-16, 18-19.

[48] Koch, *Rediscovery,* 28-33. This list is more helpful than that given by Russell, *Method and Message,* 105. He does not differentiate between conceptual features appropriate to 'apocalypticism' and literary features relevant to the apocalypses. See also Hanson, *Dawn,* 11. Hanson's attempt at a definition is better, but it does not really apply to the apocalypses. See in detail Stone, 'Lists', 440-42, and the comments by MacRae, 'Apocalyptic in Gnosticism', 1. Hanson, 'Apocalypticism', 29-31 approaches the problem of definition starting from the position taken by Stone; see in detail note 273 below. Schmithals' observation that apocalyptic is an attempt to deal with pessimism about reality should be evaluated as phenomenological rather than historical. Even then, it is not in accord with the structure, content and evident sources of the oldest apocalypses (*Apocalyptic Movement,* 40-45).

[49] Koch, *Rediscovery,* 19-20.

particular, as well as *2 Apocalypse of Baruch* and *Apocalypse of Abraham* have much unexplained 'speculative' material. Other scholars, observing the fact that much material in the apocalypses is not explained by, or even included in, such definitions, suggest broadening the definition.[50] In principle, this suggestion is a very proper one, yet it seems unlikely that in practice it will be accepted widely. The usage of scholarship is too deeply ingrained. Instead, the better part of wisdom is to maintain a clear distinction beteen 'apocalyptic' and the apocalypses.[51]

Consequently, 'apocalyptic' or 'apocalypticism' should be regarded as a pattern of thought, primarily eschatological in character, typifying some apocalypses and also a number of works belonging to other genres of literature of the period of the Second Temple, such as some of the Qumran *pesharim, The Testament (Assumption) of Moses,* or *The Testaments of the Twelve Patriarchs.* It does not supply a key to the understanding of the particular literary forms of the apocalypses, for example, or of the combination of ideas or of diverse material in them.[52] An illusion persists, because of the terminological confusion, that by defining apocalypticism something has been said about the apocalypses. A result of this is that the religious phenomenon or phenomena which the apocalypses represent have been obscured. Yet, in fact, each of these two phenomena, both 'apocalypses' and 'apocalypticism' must be dealt with in its own right. The present chapter deals with the literary genre 'apocalypse'.

The Apocalypses

GENERAL

Before proceeding to a detailed discussion of the characteristics of the genre and of the conceptual patterns informing it, the chief extra-canonical apocalypses are introduced, viz. *1 Enoch, 2 Enoch, 2 Apocalypse of Baruch, 3 Apocalypse of Baruch,* 4 Ezra and *Apocalypse of Abraham.*[53] There are other Jewish apocalypses of the period. Some are known by name only,

---

[50] Betz, 'Religio-Historical Understanding', 134-5. See also Vielhauer, 'Apocalyptic', 587-8 who simply disclaims the importance of the 'speculative element'.

[51] Stone, 'Lists', 443.

[52] The discussions by Cross, Hanson and others really bear upon apocalypticism. See, e.g., Cross, *Canaanite Myth,* 332-3.

[53] It should be observed that in this section the bibliography cited is indicative of the chief directions scholarship has taken and not exhaustive of either views or of their supporters. Fairly detailed bibliographies may be found in Eissfeldt, *Introduction* and Charlesworth, *Modern Research.* For the older scholarly writing, Schürer, *Geschichte* 3 is usually fairly exhaustive.

mentioned in ancient lists or by early writers.[54] Others are extant in fragments, either uncovered at Qumran, such as *Visions of Amram*[55] and the pseudo-Ezekiel work from Cave 4 being edited by Strugnell,[56] or preserved through quotations in patristic literature.[57] Thus it seems likely that ancient documents lie behind citations attributed to an apocalypse of Elijah[58] or Ezekiel[59] or others. A good deal of early Jewish literature may still be recovered by a careful sifting of quotations preserved in patristic sources. There are, moreover, a number of smaller apocalypses, or fragments close to apocalypses in character, embedded in more extensive works of different genre. Such are, e.g., *T. Levi* 2-5, 18; *Jub.* 23; *T. Abr.* 10-12.

1 ENOCH

Enoch appears in the literature of the Second Temple period primarily as a recipient and teacher of divine knowledge; as a scribe, inventor of writing and of the calendar.[60] This picture of Enoch may be formed following Mesopotamian precedents.[61] Outside the Enoch books themselves, it is apparently referred to by Sir 44:6 and certainly mentioned by 1QGenAp 2:2, *Jub.* 4:16-23, Heb 11:5-6. The *Genesis Apocryphon* and *Jubilees* show clear affinity with the Enoch literature; by way of contrast, however, note that Enoch also looms large in the (probably Samaritan) pseudo-Eupolemus (in Eusebius, *Hist. Eccl.* 17) and in *T. Abr.* B 9. These latter

---

[54] The chief texts are conveniently found in James, *Lost Apocrypha*, xii-xiv. A considerable amount of unpublished material exists in manuscripts.

[55] Milik, '4 Q Visions'.

[56] Pseudo-Ezekiel apparently belongs to this category. Perhaps *The Description of the New Jerusalem* and 4QpsDan (Milik, 'Prière de Nabonide') should be included here. The proportion of previously unknown apocalypses among the manuscripts from Qumran is significantly small, see pp. 423-7, below.

[57] Many of the citations preserved in patristic and other ancient and mediaeval sources may be found assembled in Fabricius, *Codex Pseudepigraphus* and James, *Lost Apocrypha*.

[58] James, *Lost Apocrypha*, 53-61; Stone — Strugnell, *Elijah* is an exhaustive collection of Elijah *testimonia*. It is difficult to accept Rosenstiehl's view of the Coptic Elijah apocalypse as basically Jewish in its present form (*Apocalypse d'Elie*). A new copy of the Coptic Elijah apocalypse was published recently by Pietersma *et al.*, *Elijah*.

[59] James, *Lost Apocrypha*, 64-70; Stone, 'Ezekiel'; Denis, *Fragmenta*, 121-8. Compare also Bonner, *Apocryphal Ezekiel*, which fragment may be related to 4Qpseudo-Ezekiel being edited by J. Strugnell, as well as to certain quotations attributed to this prophet.

[60] A tradition exists, primarily in Hellenistic Jewish sources, that makes him the type of the one who repents. This is found in the grandson's translation of Ben Sira's Hebrew אות דעת as ὑπόδειγμα μετανοίας (Sir 44:16). Yadin, *Ben Sira Scroll, ad loc.* also admits that this phrase in the Hebrew text is genuine. The same idea also occurs in Philo's writings, e.g. *Abr.* 17, *Q. G.* 1:82 and may perhaps also occur, in a polemical application, in *Gen. Rabba* 25,1 (pp. 238-9). All of these except Ben Sira are based on the exegesis of 'after the birth of . . .' (Gen 5:22). Compare also Wis 4:10-11. For a possible alternative interpretation of this tradition, see Dimant, *Fallen Angels*, 120-21.

[61] See above, p. 391.

show no particular connection with the Enochic literature and they are examples of the spread of traditions about Enoch into sources of varied types.[62]

The idea of Enoch's elevated status, his identification with the 'Man' (*1 Enoch* 71) or his transformation into an angel (*2 Enoch* A 22:1-10 = Vaillant, p. 27) lives on into Jewish sources of a mystical character and in late midrashim.[63] Its origins are unclear as also is the relationship of this idea to that of his translation; *2 Enoch* certainly puts the heavenly ascent of Enoch for visionary purposes into the last year of his life.[64] Nor is the source of the idea of Enoch as heavenly scribe or wise man evident from the biblical passages dealing with him; it appears in the Jewish literature full-grown.[65] Enoch, then, is a figure with whom very rich traditions were associated and the growth of an extensive literature around him is not surprising.

The *First Book of Enoch* or *Ethiopic Enoch* is in fact a compilation of five books, each of which appears with its own title and usually its own conclusion. These five books are combined into a single work in the Ethiopic version in which, alone, the whole is preserved.[66] In addition to the Ethiopic text, extensive parts of the book have survived in Greek. Two papyri have come to light, the so-called Gizeh papyrus which was uncovered in 1886-7 and contains much of the first part of the book,[67] and the Chester Beatty papyrus containing part of the last section of it.[68] Extended quotations in the *Chronicle* by George the Syncellus run largely parallel to

---

[62] On the spread of the Enoch traditions, see Greenfield – Stone, 'Enochic Pentateuch', 56, 61-3.

[63] Most notable is his identification with Metatron in *3 Enoch*. See the valuable observations of Greenfield, 'Prolegomena' xxxi-xxxii. The tradition of Enoch's heavenly journeys and his subsequent return to the earth may be related to the exegesis of 'and Enoch walked with God' in Gen 5:22. This could have been understood to refer to a walking with God, that is a heavenly ascent, after the birth of Methusaleh and before his translation which is related in Gen 5:24. See particularly Sjöberg, *Menschensohn*, 47-189.

[64] Gen 5:24 was often interpreted of his translation. The Septuagint rendering of Gen 5:24 is not completely unambiguous; it was understood to refer to translation by Heb 11:5. So too the verse was understood by *Targum Onkelos* Gen 5:24 (one reading); Josephus, *Ant.* 1:85 and the Enoch books. This view is strongly opposed in *Gen. Rabba* 25,1 (pp. 238-9), but is taught in *Midrash ha-Gadol Gen.*, p. 132. See also Urbach, *The Sages* 1, 335.

[65] See pp. 391-2, above.

[66] The most recent edition is that of Knibb, *Ethiopic Enoch*. Work remains to be done on the relationship between the Ethiopic and Greek versions. Nickelsburg has made a thorough comparison of the two versions for chaps. 97-104, see 'Enoch 97-104'. Knibb has made many observations on the relationship between the Ethiopic, Greek and Aramaic texts, as has Nickelsburg. A survey of recent scholarship on *1 Enoch* may be found in Nickelsburg, 'Enoch in Recent Research'; see also Harrington, 'Research', 151-2. In general, see Nickelsburg, *Jewish Literature*, 47-55, 90-4, 145-51, 224-5.

[67] The text is printed in Charles, *Ethiopic Enoch* and most conveniently in Fleming – Rademacher, *Das Buch Henoch*.

[68] Bonner, *Last Chapters*.

the text in the Gizeh papyrus, with many variations.[69] There is also a small Greek fragment in the Vatican library, as well as a large number of quotations by ancient authorities. The earliest of these is Jude 14b-15 (= *1 Enoch* 1:9). There are also some small fragments in Syriac and Latin,[70] and fragments in a Greek papyrus of the fourth century C.E. have recently been identified.[71]

In recent decades the chief advance in the study of the text of the book has been the discovery of fragments from eleven manuscripts of parts of it at Qumran,[72] which contain parts of all the sections of the book except *The Similitudes* (*1 Enoch* 37-71).[73] The discovery of these manuscripts permits the resolution of a series of debated issues in the criticism of the book, such as the original language of its parts (all the manuscripts are in Aramaic), or the ordering of such displaced chapters as the latter part of the *Apocalypse of Weeks*. Moreover their editor has drawn a number of major conclusions from them, viz. the antiquity of the five-fold or pentateuchal structure of the Ethiopic book; the late origins of *The Similitudes* and the original position of *The Book of the Giants* in its stead in the 'Enochic Pentateuch'; and the primitive character of chaps. 6-19.[73a]

The existence of *The Book of Giants* at Qumran was demonstrated by Milik.[74] This forms the fifth work attributed to the Enoch cycle identified by him at Qumran. From this Milik infers that: 1) There was an Enochic Pentateuch; and 2) the Enochic Pentateuch was copied on two scrolls, since

---

[69] Most conveniently in Fleming — Rademacher, *Das Buch Henoch*.

[70] See Denis, *Introduction* for list of citations and editions of the fragments, and other introductory information. Much such information and bibliography may be found in Charlesworth, *Modern Research*, 98-103. The Greek fragments were published anew by Black in *Apocalypsis Henochi*.

[71] Milik, 'Fragments grecs d'Henoch' from *The Book of the Luminaries* and from *The Dream Visions*.

[72] Most of these fragments are now available in Milik, *Books of Enoch*.

[73] They are distributed as follows:

Chapters	Sigla of MSS containing parts of these chaps.							
1-36	4QHen	a	b	c	d	e		
72-82	4QHen^{astr}					a	b	c	d
83-90	4QHen			c	d	e	f		
91-107	4QHen			c			g		

Milik, *Books of Enoch 6*, sets forth the exact contents of each MS. and publishes fragments of many of them. They date from between the late third cent. B.C.E. to early first cent. C.E.

[73a] For further elaboration of these arguments, see Greenfield — Stone, 'Enochic Pentateuch'.

[74] Milik, 'Turfan et Qumran'. The work had been recovered in a fragmentary fashion from Manichean sources by Henning, 'Book of Giants'. Another, apparently Enochic work was known among the Manichees, see Henning, 'Ein manichäisches Henochbuch'. Some of the Qumran texts are now published by Milik, *Books of Enoch*, 298-317.

together with the full form of the *Book of the Luminaries* it could not have been fitted onto one single scroll. He states that manuscript 4QHen[c] probably contained *The Book of Giants* as well[75] and that manuscript 4QHen[d] and manuscript 4QHen[e] probably contained this Enochic Tetrateuch too.[76] He further suggests that about 400 C.E. a Greek Enochic Pentateuch existed in which *The Book of the Luminaries* had been drastically reduced in scope and placed in third position, *The Book of Giants* had been replaced by *The Similitudes* and chap. 108 had been added.[77] This is, however, all by way of hypothesis, unsupported by any solid evidence except the following: 1) three Enochic works do exist at Qumran in one manuscript (4QHen[c]) and two of them in two further manuscripts; 2) fragments of five or more Enochic works turned up at Qumran; and 3) a different collection of five works exists in the Ethiopic form of *1 Enoch*.

It is by no means self-evident that, even if five works were combined into one book in the Ethiopic manuscripts, they were conceived of (presumably on the basis of analogy with the Mosaic Pentateuch) as an 'Enochic Pentateuch'. Even if this were true for the Ethiopic manuscripts (and it has not been demonstrated to be so) nothing in points 1) and 2) in the foregoing paragraph shows that this was so at Qumran. The occurrence of five works at Qumran may be mere chance — a sixth did not survive the damage of time or has not yet been identified (1Q19 perhaps might be regarded as such).[78] Furthermore, more significantly, neither the number of Enochic works found at Qumran, we submit, nor the number copied into the same roll of parchment shows whether the books were conceived of as a 'Pentateuch' or not, as an examination of the Qumran manuscripts of the Mosaic Pentateuch and of the Mosaic apocrypha confirms.[79] Evidence for this would have to be sought in statements in ancient sources, either in the books themselves or in external authorities, that the *Books of Enoch* were a Pentateuch. To the best of our knowledge none such exists.

Milik's late date for the composition of *The Similitudes* has been contested by other scholars.[80] They would consider *1 Enoch* 56:5-7 to refer to

---

[75] 4QHenGean[a] was copied by the same scribe as 4QHen[c]; Milik says that it is a different manuscript, see 'Turfan et Qumran', 124. Compare however *Books of Enoch*, 310, cf. 58 and 76 where he claims that it is the same manuscript.

[76] 'Fragments araméens', 334-5; *Books of Enoch*, 15. There seems to be no evidence of this beyond Milik's assertion.

[77] 'Fragments araméens', 373ff.; *Books of Enoch*, 89-107.

[78] Grelot has recently suggested that 4QMess aram, the so-called 'Elect of God text' also belongs to the Enochic literature; see 'Ecritures' 488-500.

[79] The books of the Mosaic Pentateuch usually occur on their own. No more than two books of the Mosaic Pentateuch occur in the same manuscript and this is true only in a small minority of cases. *The Book of Jubilees* and perhaps *The Temple Scroll* are Mosaic pseudepigrapha found at Qumran, bringing to six or seven the number of works found there which are attributed to Moses.

[80] See Greenfield—Stone, 'Enochic Pentateuch'; Greenfield, 'Prolegomena', xvi-xviii. Hindley, 'Date for the Similitudes' suggests a date early in the second century C.E. and an

the Parthian invasion of 40 B.C.E.[81] This date, together with the references to Herod's attempted cure in the waters of Callirhoe and his loss of mental stability (67:7-9) soon before his death[82] seem to speak convincingly for an early date, a view strengthened by the terminological arguments that have been adduced.[83] One might add that an ancient date is implied by the use of 'Son of Man', an old Jewish title, although strangely, for Milik this is a sign of dependance on the New Testament.[84] Moreover, it is difficult to conceive of a late, Christian work largely devoted to the prediction of the coming of a super-human Son of Man, existent in the thought of God before creation, which does not make the slightest hint at his (from Enoch's view-point) future incarnation, earthly life and preaching, or crucifixion and their cosmic implications.[85] Further, in chapter 71, admittedly an appendix to *The Similitudes,* the Son of Man is specifically identified as Enoch. This is rather unlikely in an appendix to a Christian composition, which itself would undoubtedly be Christian.[86] In view of these considerations, then, there seems no reason to exclude *The Similitudes* from the discussion of the Jewish Enoch literature. It is most probable, however,

---

Antiochean provenance. A lucid review of the issues is Knibb, 'Date of the Parables'. Milik's position is also challenged by Mearns, 'Parables' and by VanderKam, 'Contemporary Study of 1 Enoch'.

[81] Milik suggests, since he dates *The Similitudes* late on other grounds, that 'Parthians and Medes' refers to Palmyreans. This strange view is put forth on the basis of the use of the words *mdy* and *md* for the Palmyreans in Safaitic inscriptions. One fails to see why 'Parthians' does not simply mean 'Parthians'. See Sjöberg, *Menschensohn,* 37-8; Greenfield — Stone, 'Enochic Pentateuch', 59-60.

[82] Josephus, *Ant.* 17:171-3; *War* 1:656-60.

[83] Greenfield, 'Prolegomenon', xviif.; Greenfield — Stone, 'Enochic Pentateuch', 56-7.

[84] See Stone, 'Messiah in IV Ezra', 307-8, showing that it was supressed as a title in Jewish sources by the end of the first century C.E.; Greenfield — Stone, 'Enochic Pentateuch', 57.

[85] This cannot be attributed to a concern for pseudepigraphical consistency, for there are numerous examples which can be adduced to show that no such concern inhibited Christian authors and scribes in the course of composing or copying works of this character.

[86] See already Sjöberg, *Menschensohn,* 4-5 and sources quoted there. Milik's statement is quite astounding: 'Il me semble *tout à fait* certain qu'il n'existait pas à l'époque pré-chrétienne, dans un texte araméen, hébreu ou grec, *puisqu'* aucun fragment sémitique ou grec n'en a été répéré dans les très riches lots manuscrits des grottes de Qumran. C'est *donc* une composition grecque chrétienne' (my italics, M.E.S.). It just does not follow that the absence of a book from those manuscripts which survived at Qumran implies more than just that about their existence. The Book of Esther is not found there, nor the Book of Baruch, nor the *Assumption of Moses,* nor the *Books of Adam and Eve,* nor many other incontrovertibly Jewish and early apocrypha. To say these are in doctrinal conflict with the Qumran sect and were consequently excluded from their library is just to open up one way of explaining the absence of *The Similitudes.* The Enochic tradition was shown above to have been known in circles far broader than the Qumran sect. Milik's arguments about the *Sibylline Oracles* and the Sibyl seem to us to have no weight for dating *The Similitudes of Enoch:* they do show his considerable erudition. The quotation above is drawn from 'Fragments araméens', 375. Other observations on Milik's views may be found in Greenfield — Stone, 'Enochic Pentateuch'; *id.* 'Books and Traditions of Enoch'.

that *The Similitudes* comes from circles other than those close to the Qumran sectaries.

The *Book of Enoch* reflected in these textual witnesses and first and foremost in the Ethiopic version, is composed of five independent works. The first, chaps. 1-36 may be entitled, following Milik, *The Book of the Watchers*. In this, three literary units have usually been discerned: chaps. 1-5, introduction; chaps. 6-11 (or according to other analyses 6-16) story of the Watchers; and chaps. 17-36, Enoch's journeys to remote parts of the earth. Charles claimed that chaps. 1-5 show contact, in their use of terminology, with all parts of the book except chaps. 72-82. This, he claimed, implied their composition (in Hebrew) as an introduction to the whole of the book. Their occurrence in 4QHen[a] and 4QHen[b] which apparently only ever contained chaps. 1-36 makes this less certain. In those manuscripts, too, they are found in Aramaic. Chap. 1 contains an epiphany described in language recalling biblical prophecy,[87] followed by a call for the righteousness of man (chaps. 2-5). This summons is based on the notion that the regularity of the natural phenomena is founded upon morality, thus providing a paradigm for human action.[88] There follows the section dealing with the fall of the Watchers and its results and with Enoch's activities in heaven on their behalf. These chapters are clearly marked off from chaps. 1-5 by a superscription and they form an independent literary unit. Moreover, they are not a simple unity in themselves but apparently combine two traditions in a ˅omplex fashion. The first describes the fall of Shemhazai,[89] chief of the fallen angels, and his angelic band, while the other is concerned with Azael and his sins.[90] The results of the fall of Shemhazai and his angels were the corruption of mankind, the destruction wrought by the giants, their offspring and the spirits which issued from them, and the Flood.[91] Azael's sin was the corruption of mankind by the teaching of the secret and forbidden arts (chap. 8) which led to moral evil and corruption (10:15f.) and the Flood.[92] The combined story, as it now

---

[87] The introductory verses are based upon Num 24:3-4, Deut 33:1 and perhaps Ezek 1:1, implying great prophetic authority for Enoch: see Stone, 'Lists', 444-5. See Hartmann, *Prophecy Interpreted*, 113-4 for a somewhat differing view. The *crux interpretationis* in v. 4 is difficult, but see now VanderKam, 'Theophany of Enoch', particularly pp. 132-3.

[88] See Stone, 'Lists', 428-30 for another dimension of this. A book-length treatment of *1 Enoch* 1-5 is Hartmann, *Asking for a Meaning*. This raises many interesting points.

[89] The form of the name in the Qumran manuscripts is שמיחזה.

[90] The form of the name varies in the different sources. See in detail Dimant, *Fallen Angels*, 58. She has convincingly isolated the tradition of this angel from that of Shemhazai and his band and shown its unique characteristics; see *ibid.*, 23-72.

[91] Chap. 7; *Jub.* 10:1-15 makes the evil spirits that sprang from the giants after their destruction in the flood the cause of disease. These matters are the subject of *The Book of the Giants*. One possible thesis dealing with this material in relationship with family purity is advanced by Suter, 'Family Purity'.

[92] For an important analysis of the structure and function of these traditions, see Dimant,

occurs, serves to explain the origins of evil upon earth.[93] Enoch's role in these events is one of (unsuccessful) intercession on behalf of the Watchers and then the pronouncement of judgement upon them (chaps. 12-16).

It should be observed that in chap. 14, the description of Enoch's ascent before the Throne of God for intercession, Scholem has detected terminological usages clearly appertaining to the mystic tradition.[94] Chapters 17-36 relate two journeys by Enoch through the distant and wondrous places of the earth. The first is connected with the preceding chapters by chap. 19,[95] the second, not very naturally, by chap. 21. Most of the material in these chapters is 'speculative' — not totally subordinated to major eschatological themes (although such are present) and not explained by the Watchers legend. This element of speculation is also connected with the figure of Enoch by the books of *Jubilees* and Ben Sira.[96]

In chapters 37-70, to which chap. 71 is an appendix, are found three *Parables* or *Similitudes*,[97] chaps. 38-44, 45-57, and 58-70. They are marked by common terminology and interests and are primarily of eschatological import. In addition, significant elements of astronomical, cosmological, and other such material are found in them.[98] The first parable reveals eschatological reward and punishment, the Elect One, and cosmic secrets. The second parable is more complex in character. It centers first and foremost on the revelation of the Son of Man or the Elect One. He is a

---

Fallen Angels, passim. It is impossible here to set forth her analysis in detail because of its complexity, but it throws new and important light on their formation and the way they functioned. See also next note.

[93] Hanson, 'Rebellion', has urged the influence of ancient, Near Eastern mythical patterns in these chapters. Nickelsburg, 'Apocalyptic and Myth', with a different emphasis, sees some influence from the myth of the Titans and envisages the wars of the Diadochi as a possible *Sitz im Leben* for the formation of these chapters. For an evaluation of the methodological assumptions of these two articles, see Collins, 'Methodological Issues'. A more recent attempt to analyze *1 Enoch* 6-19 is Newsome, '1 Enoch 6-19'.

[94] Scholem, *Major Trends,* 44. See also Maier, *Von Kultus zur Gnosis,* 125ff.; Stone, 'Third Century B.C.E.', 488; Gruenwald, *Apocalyptic,* 32-37.

[95] This is considered by Milik to derive from the same source as chaps. 6-16. Dimant's work has made this improbable.

[96] *Jub.* 4:17-25 and Sir 44:16. *Jubilees* differs at various points from the traditions presented by *1 Enoch,* but the basic views as to the range, character, and variety of interests which are attributed to Enoch are the same. Milik, *Books of Enoch,* attempts to date this section to the third or fourth century and suggests various origins for the cosmographic concepts. An attempt at an overall view of function and purpose, with many interesting insights is Collins, 'Apocalyptic Technique'.

[97] The term is used by the Ethiopic text, but its precise meaning is difficult to ascertain as it relates to these literary units. No parallels occur. A recent study of the *Similitudes of Enoch* is Suter, *Parables of Enoch.* Caquot, 'Chapitres 70 et 71' argues that these chapters form a single unit, all of it an appendix to *The Similitudes* designed to identify Enoch with the Son of Man. See further note 106, below.

[98] See, e.g., 41:1-9, 43. Compare the comments in Stone, 'Lists'. *The Similitudes of Enoch* present themselves as primordial wisdom, revealed uniquely to Enoch (chap. 37).

pre-created redeemer figure who is to be an eschatological judge.[99] The title 'Son of Man' by which he is designated in some places has, naturally, aroused a good deal of interest, particularly among students of the New Testament. The transcendental characteristics of this figure, his pre-creation or pre-selection, his enthronement and his judging have served to sharpen this.[100]

The origins of the figure doubtless lie largely in exegesis of Dan 7, as well as in existing traditions of expectation of a cosmic redeemer.[101] The characteristic functions of such a figure extend beyond those normally attributed to the Davidic Messiah.[102] In chaps. 52-56 the theme of the punishment of the Watchers recurs and Enoch receives revelations about this. In chap. 56 the eschatological war is described.

The third parable, chaps. 57-70, deals chiefly with the cosmic eschatological judgement to be executed by the Elect One. In this parable are embedded some sections in which Noah speaks in the first person. In these Noah, not Enoch is the one addressed.[103] It seems very likely that these sections derive from an independent source document here preserved.[104]

---

[99] Attempts have been made, most notably by Charles, *The Ethiopic Version,* dependent upon Beer, 'Das Buch Henoch', to isolate two sources in the *Similitudes of Enoch.* One would be characterized by the title 'Son of Man' and the other by the title 'Elect One'. The Elect One is associated with 'the angel of peace' and the Son of Man with 'the angel who went with me'. The chief literary arguments were assembled by Beer. The analysis is not convincing and differences in titles of the saviour figure should perhaps be explained on different grounds. In 46:3 the election of the Son of Man is related! See Sjöberg, *Menschensohn,* 31-34 for a critical discussion of such theories. The two titles, their contexts and relationship are investigated by Theisohn, *Richter.*

[100] So *1 Enoch* 45:3, 46:4-8, 48:3-6, 62:2, etc. The best analysis of this material remains that of Sjöberg. He rejects the older view that the Son of Man is simply to be identified with the *Urmensch,* which figure probably influenced Adam speculations: see *Der Menschensohn,* 190-8 and bibliography there. A recent analysis, seeking to set the Son of Man figure in its 'tradition-historical' context is Theisohn, *Richter.* See also Altmann, 'Adam Legends' where, likewise, no such hints can be found. A recent collection of material relating to the cosmic man figure is Schenke, *Der Gott 'Mensch'.* See also Stone, 'Messiah in IV Ezra' and Russell, *Method and Message,* 342-52. The bibliography on the Son of Man figure is enormous, and no attempt is made here to present even a summary of it. Much of it does not relate to issues involved in *The Similitudes of Enoch.* Nickelsburg, *Resurrection,* 70ff. has dealt with aspects of the Son of Man as servant; cf. also Sjöberg, *Menschensohn,* 46-7. See most recently Collins, 'Heavenly Representative'; see also note 106, below.

[101] Another striking example of this type of redeemer figure is Melchizedek in 11QMelchizedek and *2 Enoch.* Compare the recent publication of Qumran material by Milik, 'Milkî-sedeq'.

[102] See, e.g., Stone, 'Messiah in IV Ezra,' 303-12.

[103] *1 Enoch* 60:7-10 with which must be associated at least 60:24, 65:1-12 and 67-68.

[104] See Stone, 'Noah'; James, *Lost Apocrypha,* 11-12. Dimant, *Fallen Angels,* 122-40 re-assesses the evidence, questioning whether all the fragments customarily attributed to the 'Book of Noah' actually come from such a work, or whether various works of differing character are involved. The Qumran 'Book of Noah' (1Q19) contains material which is closely related to one source of *1 Enoch* but was not itself the direct literary source of *1 Enoch.*

This parable exhibits clear contacts with the legends associated with Enoch in the first part of the book, *The Book of the Watchers.* Such contacts can be discerned both in the 'Noah' material (65:6ff., 67) and in the other chapters, e.g. 69.[105] Chapter 71 tells of Enoch's assumption to heaven and transformation into the Son of Man.[106] In general, *The Similitudes* does not seem to be created upon a clear, unified literary structure or a systematic development of ideas. It is a composite and complex writing, characterized throughout by a distinctive terminology and style. In it, an intense interest in eschatology is exhibited, typified by a cosmic redeemer who will be enthroned as eschatological judge. This teaching is combined with a lively interest in various aspects of speculative knowledge.

The Qumran fragments of *The Book of the Luminaries* or the *Astronomical Treatise* as some call it (chaps. 72-82) have proved very significant. They clearly show that the text of this section which has been transmitted in the Ethiopic tradition is the result of radical abbreviation of a much longer original.[107] From this document it is clear that the heavenly mechanics, according to its author's views, dictated a solar cycle of 364 days, implying a calendar year of the same length, a view also found in the Essene writings and *The Book of Jubilees.*[108] The association of Enoch with calendar and astronomy is ancient indeed. Further, a knowledge of such information is thought to be a proper part of apocalyptic revelation and is included in many catalogues of the contents of such revelations.[110] Another dimension of this is that a relationship was thought to exist between the order of nature and morality. For this author, the observance of correct calendar was directly related to moral rectitude.[111] Indeed, human evil will be connected profoundly with a perversion not merely of the computation of

---

[105] This chapter is apparently an independent piece or pieces not fully integrated into the larger work.

[106] This seems to contradict chap. 70. Chap. 71 is generally thought to be an appendix and the end of chap. 70 is certainly the conclusion of the major literary unit. See on the content and structure of these two chapters, Sjöberg, *Menschensohn,* 147-89, particularly 159f. and Caquot, 'Chapitres 70 et 71'. See also note 97, above. On the vision of chap. 71, see Gruenwald, *Apocalyptic,* 42-45. There has been a lively debate in recent years on the term 'Son of Man' in *1 Enoch;* see, e.g., Casey, 'The Term 'Son of Man' and Vermes, 'Debate'.

[107] Milik, *Books of Enoch,* 19.

[108] Milik, *ibid.,* is of the view that the lost parts of this work dealt with the intercalations necessary to adjust this solar calendar and the lunar year. On the solar year of 364 days at Qumran and in other sources see Milik, *Ten Years of Discovery,* 107-13 and references there. Beckwith, 'Enoch Literature and Calendar' is of the view that the *Book of the Luminaries* is of Jewish, pre-Essene origin, from a period of 251-200 B.C.E. He proposes that the pseudonymic character is designed to strengthen 'pre-Essene' claims against rival groups.

[110] See, e.g., *2 Enoch* 23:1 (Vaillant, 27), 40:1-3 (Vaillant, 41); *1 Enoch* 60:11-13, 14-22, 41:1-7, 43:1-2; cf. Stone, 'Lists', *passim.*

[111] Evil brings about a confusion of the natural and astronomical order, an idea already to be observed in descriptions of the Day of the Lord in the prophetic books. Cf. von Rad, 'Day of Yahweh'. The idea also occurs in the predictions of the messianic woes.

the calendar, but of the very astronomical cycles themselves (see chaps. 80-81).[112] This idea is most clearly expressed in the notion of the perversion of the order of the stars and that it was concealed from the sinners (80:4-7). The idea is analogous to that expressed in chaps. 2-5 referred to above. This moral aspect of calendar and astronomy serves to highlight the importance attributed to the revelation made to Enoch. This comprised the correct calendar and therefore revealed the true cosmic order. Hence, it is clear that for *The Book of the Luminaries,* calendar and astronomy are not part of secular science. They appertain to secret knowledge, sacred in character.[113]

In chapters 83-90, *The Dream Visions,* two dreams which Enoch received are described. The first foretells the Flood (chaps. 83-84), while the second relates the course of history down to the time of Judas Maccabeus. Both dream visions are related by Enoch as part of his instruction of his son Methusaleh. The second has been of particular interest. It is typified by the presentation of the persons and nations of human history under the form of animals, according to a carefully constructed hierarchy. Those figures most highly regarded, like angels, are given human form.[114] The vision shows an intimate knowledge of the traditions relating to Enoch; it exhibits a particular theory of seventy shepherds (angelic rulers) of post-exilic Israel,[115] as well as clear eschatological expectations, including the establishment of the Temple at the end of days and the punishment of the fallen angels.

> And I saw till the Lord of the sheep brought a new house greater and loftier than the first, and set it up in the place of the first which had been folded up . . . and all the sheep were within it . . . And I saw till they laid down that sword, which had been given to the sheep and it was sealed before the presence of the Lord and all the sheep were invited into that house, but it held them not. And the eyes of them all were opened, and they saw the good and there was not one among them that did not see. And I saw that that house was large and broad and very full. (90:29-35)

[112] The idea that the regularity of the relationship between the luminaries exhibits the moral order to which they submit is widespread in the literature of the age. See *1 Enoch* 43:2, 41:5 and in general chaps. 2-5; *T. Napht.* 3:2 and already Sir 16:26:8. Further sources exist, see Stone, 'Lists', 428-30; compare also Gruenwald, *Apocalyptic,* 10-11.

[113] This is the probable explanation of the fact that by the standards of contemporary Hellenistic astronomy, that of Enoch is archaic. See the observations of Hengel, *Hellenism* 1, 209 drawing upon older authorities.

[114] Angels, e.g., *1 Enoch* 87:2, 90:14, etc.; Noah, 1 *Enoch* 89:1; Moses, 1 *Enoch* 89:3. Although one should beware of attributing excessive weight to the intrinsic meaning of apocalyptic symbol structures (as distinct from their interpretations — see also the remarks of Breech, 'Function of 4 Ezra', 273) it is notable that in Ezekiel, Daniel, etc. angels are presented as men, while 'man' also serves as the title of an eschatological figure in the *Similitudes of Enoch.* Klijn, 'From Creation to Noah' discusses the aggadic traditions embodied in this symbolism, as well as seeking rabbinic parallels.

[115] See Flusser, 'Seventy Shepherds'; Milik, 'Fragments araméens', 357.

It is noteworthy that no interpretation of the symbols was offered.

The Epistle of Enoch (chaps. 91-108), thus entitled in the superscription, is extant in the Chester Beatty papyrus (except for chap. 108). The chief import of this writing is moral teaching which has an eschatological emphasis. Forms of exhortation, such as the 'woe' pronouncements, are found in this section which is also formulated as Enoch's teaching of Methusaleh.[116] The hortatory forms as well as the moral stances implied by them are of great interest when compared with those of the Qumran sect and the New Testament. This material is also parallel to Enoch's instruction in *2 Enoch* in which too 'blessed' and 'woe' forms are found.

The Qumran manuscripts also confirm the hypothesis that *The Apocalypse of Weeks,* separated into two sections in the Ethiopic version, was originally a single work. In the Ethiopic text, Weeks 1-7 occur in chap. 93, following Weeks 8-10 which are found in 91:12-17. This displacement occurred within the Greek version from which the Ethiopic was translated or in an archetype of all surviving Ethiopic manuscripts.[117] It was propsed that this little apocalypse reflects the views of the Qumran sect,[118] with the events described at the end of the seventh week (93:10) referring to the foundation of the sect. It may better refer, however, to another, apparently earlier group. The exact criteria used in periodization are not clear, but the structural symmetry between pre-history (Weeks 1-3) and meta-history (Weeks 7-10), with four intervening weeks of history proper, has been stressed. The central point of the four weeks of history is the building of the Temple.[119] The apocalypse concludes with the judgement of the fallen angels and the establishment of a new heaven and a new earth in the tenth Week (91:15-17).[120] It seems likely that this was an originally independent piece of writing which was inserted into the last part of *1 Enoch.*

In the Ethiopic and Greek versions two chapters are found (105-6) which relate the story of the birth of Noah. These do not occur in the Qumran manuscripts of *The Epistle of Enoch,* but the story, together with some other material not paralleled in *1 Enoch,* is preserved in a Hebrew document from Cave 1, 1Q19. This section of *1 Enoch* also circulated independently in Latin. The text is very similar to the story of the birth of Noah in 1QGenAp and to the narrative of the miraculous birth of

---

[116] Woes: 94:6-8, 95:4-6, etc. On the forms and character of this section of *1 Enoch* see Nickelsburg, '1 Enoch 92-105'.

[117] Milik, 'Fragments araméens', 360. On possible reasons for this displacement, see Stone, 'Lists', 424-5. A recent detailed study of this part of *1 Enoch* is Dexinger, *Zehnwochenapokalypse.* He argues that it derived from Hasidean circles and is the first real apocalypse; see in his summary, 182-9.

[118] Thorndike, 'Apocalypse of Weeks'. Others would urge the Hasidean origins from a pre-Qumran period; e.g. Hengel, *Hellenism;* Milik, *Books of Enoch,* 253ff. See preceding note.

[119] See particularly Licht, 'Theory of Ages'.

[120] 93:11-14 are found in an expanded form in the Qumran manuscripts of Enoch, see Milik, *Books of Enoch,* 269ff. Much there is reconstructed.

Melchizedek in *2 Enoch.* As observed above, certain passages of *The Similitudes* (60:7-10 and, at least, 60:24, 65:1-2, 67-68) also seem to derive from a work of which Noah was the hero.[121] A work or works attributed to Noah doubtlessly existed,[122] and 1Q19, as has already been observed, contains some sections not found in the Noachic fragments of *1 Enoch.* This all makes it probable that chapters 105-106 derive from a source other than *The Epistle of Enoch.*[123] There is, moreover, great proximity between certain aspects of the Noachic and Enochic traditions[124] which may help explain their combination in surviving sources.

The Book of Giants, mentioned above (note 74), although apparently not an apocalypse in the strict sense of the term, is intimately connected with the Enoch literature. It deals with the giants, offspring of the Watchers, that which befell them, and their subjugation by the four archangels. Milik has published some fragments of it in Aramaic.

2 ENOCH

This work, also entitled *Slavonic Enoch* or *Book of the Secrets of Enoch* survives only in old Church Slavonic and some other Slavic languages. The manuscript tradition in which it has transmitted is very complex.[125] The Slavonic is clearly a translation of a Greek text,[126] but the question of the original language remains a subject of conjecture.[127] Similar are the matters of its composition and date, but there seems to be no good reason to doubt its early date.[128] It has rightly been observed that the shorter

---

[121] See *Jub.* 10:13-4 and the introduction to *Sefer Asaf ha-Rofe,* that text based on the passage in *Jubilees.* See also *Jub.* 21:10, Greek expansion to *T. Levi* 53-56, *Sefer ha-Razim,* Introduction, *et al.*

[122] Dimant, *Fallen Angels,* 122-40 gives a detailed evaluation.

[123] Comparative material to such traditions of miraculous births is fairly plentiful. A selection may be found in Cartlidge – Dungan, *Documents,* 129-36. Compare also Petzke, *Apollonius von Tyana,* 161-2 and references there.

[124] See the observations of Dimant, *Fallen Angels,* 108-21, particularly 117-19.

[125] The most recent edition, with a detailed text-critical introduction is Vaillant, *Sécrets d'Hénoch.* The form of text he selects as most original is neither the long nor the short form given in Charles' edition, but an intermediate type close to that of Kahana *Ha-Sefarim ha-Hitsonim).* F. Andersen of Brisbane, Queensland, Australia is engaged on the preparation of a new edition. See for further bibliography Charlesworth, *Modern Research,* 103-7. See also Nickelsburg, *Jewish Literature,* 185-8.

[126] Vaillant, *Sécrets d'Hénoch,* viii assumes but does not demonstrate this. See, however, his notes 14 (p. 3), 9 (p. 5), 13 (p. 7) which constitute sufficient proof.

[127] The famous Greek acrostic interpretation of the name Adam does not occur in the best recension, cf. Vaillant, *Sécrets d'Hénoch,* 33; Pines, 'Concept of Time', 73 pointed out one seemingly undeniable Hebrew expression.

[128] Milik dates it to the ninth century C.E., chiefly because it knows all the documents of *1 Enoch,* see *Books of Enoch,* 109-10. Above, however, it has been demonstrated that there is no reason to date the latest of these as late as Milik would. His views are contested by F. Andersen on a variety of grounds, see Charlesworth, 'Seminars on Enoch', 316-8. See also Greenfield,

recension, the one without editorial expansions, contains no Christian elements.[129]

Although apparently familiar with the Enochic writings that were incorporated in *1 Enoch*, *2 Enoch* differs from them in religious atmosphere and contents. Such variety within the Enochic literature is not surprising, for it is attested elsewhere. Thus, 1) *The Similitudes* differ from the other parts of *1 Enoch;* and 2) pseudo-Eupolemus and Ben Sira, *inter alia,* indicate that various Enochic traditions were known outside Qumran, in a variety of other circles. Certain parallels to Zoroastrianism have been suggested to exist in the part of the book relating the story of creation and in certain of its eschatological views, but this serves merely to highlight the complexity of the book's origins without opening the way to a decisive conclusion about their character.[130] Sacrificial practice apparently identical with that forbidden as sectarian by rabbinic sources has been detected in the book,[131] and clear connections with the terminology and views of the *Shiur Komah* speculations have also been discerned in it.[132] These considerations do not, at the present stage of our knowledge, aid in establishing the circles in which the work originated.

2 Enoch deals with three chief subjects. First, Enoch ascends through the heavens, achieves a vision of God, is transfigured into an angel, and receives God's revelation of the secrets of the process of creation (chaps. 1-34).[133] Next he descends upon earth, reveals the heavenly mysteries to his children and gives them his moral instruction (chaps 35-68). From this point until the end of the book, the story of the antediluvian priesthood is found. This narrative commences with Adam and reaches its climax in the narrative of the miraculous birth of Melchizedek who is Noah's nephew by his apocryphal brother Nir. Melchizedek is eventually assumed to heaven where he is guarded safely until after the Flood.

Each of these sections of *2 Enoch* presents views and traditions which are unparalleled. The recital of the events and process of creation (chaps. 25-26) and the cosmogonic figures Adoil and Aruchaz mentioned there are unlike any other preserved form of cosmogony.[134] Or, another example of such unique traditions is the completely preserved series of benedictions

---

'Prolegomena', xviii. The basis for the late date suggested by A.S.D. Maunder, supported by Lake, 'The Date' has been adequately disproved by Rubinstein, 'Slavonic Book of Enoch', 1ff. It is based upon parts of the long recension considered secondary by Vaillant.

[129] Scholem, *Ursprung*, 64-5.

[130] Pines, 'Concept of Time', 72-87; Philonenko, 'Cosmogonie', 112-13. See further suggestions by Widengren, 'Iran and Israel', 158ff., 162ff.

[131] Pines, 'Concept of Time', 72-87.

[132] Scholem, *Kabbalah,* 17 citing *2 Enoch* 39:6 (Vaillant, p. 39).

[133] On the creation, and the character of the cosmogonic description, see Scholem, *Ursprung,* 64-65.

[134] Concerning these names, see Rubinstein, 'Slavonic Book of Enoch', 16-7; Scholem, *Urspring,* 64.

and curses which are part of Enoch's teaching of his children. Of particular note is the section dealing with Melchizedek's wondrous birth. Son of Noah's brother Nir, he was endowed with super-human characteristics. This part of the book was reckoned until recent years to be a Christian addition, inspired by Heb 7:1-10. Two considerations now weigh against this. First, the Melchizedek story in the recension considered most original by Vaillant, contains no Christian elements. Secondly, the discovery and publication of 11QMelchizedek shows that the attribution of a special role to Melchizedek occurs in undisputably Jewish texts. It should be observed, moreover, that the presentation of Melchizedek in *2 Enoch* differs in many of its characteristics from the figure presented in Heb 7:1-10 and that the figure presented there in turn differs from that in 11QMelchizedek. This indicates the existence of a variety of views about Melchizedek in Jewish circles.[135]

2 Enoch, therefore, is clearly part of the Enoch literature. Yet it presents a considerable number of traditions which cannot be paralleled elsewhere in extant literature. Moreover, the atmostphere of the book differs from that of the other Enoch writings.

THE SYRIAC APOCALYPSE OF BARUCH

This work belongs to a rather extensive literature attributed to Baruch[136] whose name was also known in the theurgical and oracular literature.[137] Works related to this Baruch literature have also turned up among the Dead Sea scrolls.[138] This indicates that Baruch's pseudepigraphic role did not start in the period following the destruction of the Second Temple, a view that might otherwise have been entertained.

---

[135] Concerning Melchizedek, see Milik, 'Milkî-sedeq', 96-126 and further bibliography cited there. See also Fitzmyer, *Semitic Background,* 221-7; Delcor, 'Melchizedek'. On the rabbinic tradition of Melchizedek, see Aptowitzer, 'Malkizedek'. Gnostic speculation also centered around him and he figures as the chief protagonist in an (unfortunately fragmentary) Nag Hammadi treatise (CG IX 1). On this see Pearson, 'Introduction to Melchizedek'.

[136] This includes, in addition the Book of Baruch, *3 Apocalypse of Baruch* and *Paralipomena of Jeremiah.* There were also Gnostic books attributed to him, see Violet, *Apokalypsen,* xcii-xcv and Bogaert, *L'Apocalypse de Baruch,* 258-60. The Ethiopic Baruch apocalypse, apparently a later work, has been most recently translated in its Falasha version by Leslau, *Falasha Anthology,* 57-78. It contains a good deal of interesting material. Bogaert studied the pseudepigraphic use of the name 'Baruch' and concluded that *2 Apocalypse Baruch* is the oldest true Baruch pseudepigraphon ('Nom de Baruch'). Further introductrory material may be found in Charlesworth, *Modern Research,* 83-91; Wolff, *Jeremia,* 30-59. See also Nickelsburg, *Jewish Literature,* 281-7.

[137] Bidez – Cumont, *Mages hellénisés* I, 49, 2. 129, 131, 135. It is not clear that βαρουχ in *PGM* 5, 480; 45, 3, etc. is a proper name. On the Baruch figure, see Bogaert, *L'Apocalypse de Baruch,* 103ff.

[138] Baillet, 'Le travail d'édition', 65f. Compare the observations of Wolff, *Jeremia,* 34-5.

The *Syriac Apocalypse of Baruch (2 Apoc. Baruch)* is extant in Syriac; most of it only in one manuscript, the famous Codex Ambrosianus.[139] There also exists an Arabic translation made from Syriac.[140] A Greek papyrus fragment of the fifth or sixth century has been identified,[141] and in addition, quotations of the work or from a common source are preserved in Greek in *Paraleipomena Ieremiou*.[142] Moreover, graecisms, errors originating in Greek, as well as transliterations detected in the Syriac text confirm the view that the Syriac was translated from Greek.[143] Scholars have also isolated possible indications that the original was Hebrew.

The book falls into seven distinct sections, each separated from its neighbour by a fast. This structure, it is obvious, implies at least a single editorial hand.[144] The chief issue in the criticism for the book has been that of its composition. A complex source theory was accepted at the end of the last century and the beginning of this century.[145] This theory should be re-examined, for the source analysis proposed is so complicated that it is quite suspect. That the book was composed using identifiable sources is evident from its many points of contact and similarity with 4 Ezra, although it differs from that book in some of its points of view and emphases.[146] It also seems not unlikely that both works are related to the *Biblical Antiquities*, later falsely attributed to Philo.[147] Thus, it is difficult to

---

[139] Chaps. 57-86 occur in quite numerous copies of a textual type differing from Codex Ambrosianus. See also for details of textual transmission Violet, *Apokalypsen*, lvi-lxii and Bogaert, *L'Apocalypse de Baruch*, 33-56. The most recent edition is by Bidawid (1973).

[140] Van Koningsveld, 'An Arabic Manuscript'.

[141] P. Oxy. III, No. 403, pp. 4ff.

[142] For text, see Kraft — Purintun, *Paraleipomena Ieremiou*. Chief citations were assembled by Violet, *Apokalypsen*, lxiv-lxvi; Bogaert, *L'Apocalypse de Baruch*, 177-221 has a more complex analysis of the relationship. On pp. 222-41 he has also analysed the relations between *Pesikta Rabbati* and *2 Apoc. Bar.* Nickelsburg, 'Narrative Traditions' has argued against Bogaert that *Para. Ier.* and *2 Apoc. Bar.* depend upon a common source. Hadot, 'L'apocalypse syriaque de Baruch' has written a critical review of Bogaert's chief thesis.

[143] Violet, *Apokalypsen*, lxiv-lxvi; Bogaert, *L'Apocalypse de Baruch*, 353-80 declares himself unsure whether there was a Hebrew original or whether the work was written in Greek; see also *id.*, 'Nom de Baruch', 59-60.

[144] New divisions commence at 5:7, 9, 12:5, 21, 35, 47. Following chap. 35 a fast is not mentioned.

[145] So, e.g., Charles, *Apocalypse of Baruch*, liii-lxv following earlier authorities. The problem has been addressed most recently by Klijn, 'Baruch', 65-76. There a summary of older, as well as of more recent discussions can be found. Klijn asserts the importance of the recognition that sources exist, without proposing any major new analysis of the work. The issue is ignored by Grintz, 'Syriac Apocalypse of Baruch', by Rist in *IDB* 1, 361f. and by Eissfeldt, *Introduction*. Note, however, the comments by Violet, *Apokalypsen*, lxxiiiff. on this issue.

[146] See also Eissfeldt, *Introduction*, 629; the parallels are discussed by Violet, *Apokalypsen*, lxxxi-lxxxviii, cf. Bogaert, *L'Apocalypse de Baruch* 1, *passim*. Views on the date of these books and the relationship between them implied by the dating may be found summarized in Harnisch, *Verhängnis*, 11-12.

[147] See Bogaert, *Apocalypse de Baruch*, 242-57; parallels are set out in detail by Violet, *Apokalypsen*, lxxvii-lxxxi.

deny the complex character of *2 Apocalypse of Baruch*. Nonetheless, the relations between these sources, those isolated by the critics, and the present form of the work remain unclear.[148] The book was probably composed in its present form at the very end of the first century or at the beginning of the second century C.E.

The chief issues of concern to the book are the problems of theodicy arising out the situation of Israel after the destruction of the Temple, and out of the condition of man in general.

> For I was mourning regarding Zion, and I prayed for mercy from the Most High, and I said: 'How long will these things endure for us? and will these evils come upon us always?' And the Mighty One did according to the multitude of his mercies, . . . and he showed me visions that I should not again endure anguish, and he made known to me the mystery of the times . . . (81:2-4)
>
> The end of time is close, the messianic woes at hand, for the youth of the world is past, and the strength of creation already exhausted, and the advent of the times is very short. (85:10)

The views of the author, however, seem to be much less controversial and polemical than those expressed by the writer of 4 Ezra. Thus, by way of example, one may contrast the attitude to sin and God in *2 Apoc. Bar.* 48:44-47 and that evinced in 4 Ezra, chap. 3, particularly vv. 20-22. The main weight of the author's interest is eschatological and the book contains no explicit visions of speculative content. In this respect, too, it resembles 4 Ezra, but in contrast to that writing, it does admit material relevant to speculative themes in other contexts.[149]

THE GREEK APOCALYPSE OF BARUCH

This apocalypse is preserved in two Greek manuscripts and in some Slavonic recensions, the latter so-far inadequately edited.[150] It is, perhaps, first attested by Origen (*De princip.* 2:37).[151] The relationship of the Slavonic texts to the Greek manuscripts is not sufficiently understood and they may prove important for the restoration of the original.

---

[148] Note also that the 'Letter to Babylon' mentioned in 77:17 is missing,

[149] See, e.g., 4:2-7, 59, 76 (cf. *Bib. Ant.* 19:10). On these subjects see Stone, 'Lists', 419-23, etc. The revelation to Baruch is clearly structured on that to Moses, and compare Deut 34:1-3.

[150] Picard, *Apocalypsis Baruchi*, 67-79. On the Slavonic, see references in Denis, *Introduction*, 80-81. A new edition of the Slavonic text is being prepared by H. E. Gaylord. The extensive introduction by James, *Apocrypha Anecdota 2*, li-lxxi has not yet been superseded and it contains many valuable observations. More recent information may be found in Charlesworth, *Modern Research;* Wolff, *Jeremia*, 35-36, 86-87; see also Nickelsburg, *Jewish Literature*, 299-303. A concordance has been made by Denis — Janssens, *Concordance*.

[151] But if he refers to the work, it is to a variant and perhaps earlier form: see the comment by Picard, quoted by Denis, *Introduction*, 79.

The *Greek Apocalypse of Baruch (3 Apoc. Baruch)* is a sustained vision which relates an assumption. Baruch is taken to heaven by an angel and to him are revealed matters of cosmology and uranography: Hades, the sun, the moon and the modes of their progression, together with other features of the heavens. Moreover, Baruch sees those responsible for the building of the Tower of Babel, the souls of the righteous in the form of birds singing praise of God, and the archangel Michael and his actions relating to the good and evil deeds of men and human prayers. The book, therefore, although reflecting a distinct interest in reward and punishment, shows no explicit concern with the eschaton and its coming.

The framework is the destruction of the Temple and Baruch's mourning over this event (chap. 1). Yet none of the acute anguish and deep questioning which pervade 4 Ezra and *2 Apocalypse of Baruch* and *Apocalypse of Abraham* can be discerned in *3 Apocalypse of Baruch*. Nor is concern for reward and punishment permeated by any tension about questions of theodicy or the desire to resolve them.[152]

The traditions reflected in *3 Apocalypse of Baruch* are in some respects unique or rare in Jewish literature. The number five for the heavens is most noteworthy and has no fellow. Yet there are clear indications that the book is incomplete and moveover, there are strong hints in it that further heavens exist in addition to the five. The angel Michael, after all, goes to and comes from somewhere and the gates (11:1-2) lead somewhere (chaps. 11-15). It is difficult to determine whether the repeated promises that Baruch will see 'the glory of God' (6:12, 7:2, 11:2) imply a lost final section or not. That there were seven heavens in the author's view is thus not impossible, although it is unprovable.[153]

Others notable features include the relationship between this book and traditions occurring in other Baruch writings.[154] Moreover, the description of the phoenix and the chariot of the sun resembles that in *2 Enoch (3 Apoc. Bar.* 11 = *2 Enoch* A 12).[155] Many parallels to features of the book have been found in midrashic and talmudic sources.[156]

The Jewish authorship of the work has been defended recently, but it cannot be doubted that at least 4:15, 13:4, and 15:4 are Christian interpo-

---

[152] But see the observations of Picard, 'Observations', especially pp. 87 ff.

[153] Picard, *Apocalypsis Baruchi*, 77 denies that the book originally contained a description of the seven heavens and Baruch's journey through them. If he is correct, then Origen, *De princip.* 2:3,6 is not quoting *2 Apoc. Bar.*

[154] On *2 Apoc. Baruch* see Denis, *Introduction*, 81 with little substantial evidence, and see Hughes, '3 Baruch', 527; Ginzberg, 'Baruch'. The book clearly knows traditions found in *Paralipomena Ieremiou*, viz. the archangel Michael (chap. 11, cf. *Para. Ier.* 9) and Abimelek and the vineyard of Agrippa (Title, v. 2, cf. *Para. Ier. passim*).

[155] This material on the phoenix does not occur, however, in the text of *2 Enoch* translated by Kahana, *Ha-Sefarim ha-Hitsonim*.

[156] Ginzberg, 'Baruch'; Grintz, 'Greek Apocalypse of Baruch'; Ginzberg, *Legends* 6, 443.

lations.[157] In particular the structure of chap. 4 is complicated, containing an interpolation (v. 15) which, in Christian terms, praises the vine which the preceding and following verses condemn. It was, they say, planted by Sammael in Eden as the Tree of Knowledge, dislodged from there by the Flood, and replanted by Noah whose shame it caused (vv. 8-14, 16-17). The original language of *3 Apoc. Bar.* is generally admitted to have been Greek and the work might have been composed in the second century C.E.[158]

4 EZRA

This work, also known as *Second Esdras* or the *Apocalypse of Ezra* is the most widely known and translated of the extra-canonical apocalypses.[158a] The book was normally included in the Vulgate, and so in the Protestant Apocrypha, but not in the Septuagint. So the Greek version has perished, except for a few quotations in ancient authorities,[159] and in two later Greek apocalypses, the *Apocalypse of Esdras* and the *Apocalypse of Sedrach,* as well as in the Latin *Vision of Ezra.*[160] The work is preserved in various ancient versions, Latin, Syriac, Ethiopic, Georgian, Arabic and Armenian. Some Coptic fragments have also been uncovered. Of these, the two groups: Latin and Syriac, Ethiopic and Georgian are considered best to preserve the text. The book was probably written between 95 and 100 C.E. The date is established upon the identification of the three heads of the eagle in chap. 13 with the Flavian emperors.[161] In the Latin version two additional chapters precede and two follow the text of the apocalypse itself. They are of different origin from it.

Like *2 Apocalypse Baruch,* the book is made up of seven visions. The first three are dialogues between the seer and the angel; the next three are symbolic visions; and the last one (chap. 14) is a narrative of the revelation of the sacred books to Ezra.[162] There is no doubt of the unifying overall

---

[157] See Picard, *Apocalypsis Baruchi,* 75-79; Denis, *Introduction,* 82 and already Ginzberg, 'Baruch'.

[158] Denis, *Introduction,* 82. The existential stance referred to above in this section seems to speak for a certain remoteness from the destruction of the Temple.

[158a] On the titles of Ezra works, see above, p. 157-8.

[159] Such are Clem. Alex., *Stromat.* 3:16,100,3; *Const. Ap.* 2:14,9 etc. See Denis, *Introduction,* 195-7; Myers, *Esdras,* 131-4; Violet, *Ezra-Apokalypse,* xlxff.

[160] The parallels are set forth by Violet. *ibid.,* li-lix; see on this literature, Stone, 'Metamorphosis of Ezra'.

[161] So already Schürer, 3, 236-9; see Stone, *Eschatology,* 1-11; Myers, *Esdras,* 129. A recent expression of a dissenting view is by Schwartz, 'Date de IV Esdras'. The bibliography for the versions will be found in the Introductions to Violet, *Esra-Apokalypse* and *Apokalypsen* and in Stone, 'Textual Criticism', 107-15. To these add Bidawid's edition of the Syriac; Stone, 'New Manuscript'; Rubinkiewicz, 'Un fragment grec'; Stone, *Armenian IV Ezra.* See in general on 4 Ezra, Nickelsburg, *Jewish Literature,* 287-394.

[162] On the literary form and structure, see Breech, 'Function of 4 Ezra'. He has emphasized the importance of form as bearing meaning central to the teaching of the book.

literary form of the book, in spite of various source analyses that have been proposed.[163] The dialogues raise certain basic issues which stem from the contemplation of the meaning of the destruction of the Temple. Questions about the justice of God's management of the world are to the fore, focusing on the fate of Israel ('Are their deeds any better that inhabit Babylon? Has he for this rejected Zion?' 3:28); on God's purpose in and responsibility for the creation of sinful humanity ('If then with a light word thou shalt destroy him who with such infinite labour has been fashioned by the command, to what purpose was he made?' 8:14); and on other similar issues all centered about the dual problems of God's relationship to man and to Israel.[164] Notable is the exclusive concentration of the author on theological issues of this sort and on their eschatological correlatives. He consistently ignores, or indeed polemically opposes all the aspects of speculative knowledge.[165]

The three symbolic visions which follow these dialogues are very different from them. Yet they are, in the final analysis, the answers to the questions raised in the dialogues. This corresponds to the way that the short revelation found at the end of each dialogue opens the path to the resolution of the issues raised in it. It follows from this, and it is notable, that the questions asked, apparently in the form of learned dialogue, are answered by the revelatory symbolic visions.[166] The first of the visions is of the mourning woman who was transformed into a builded city, symbolizing the rebuilt Jerusalem. This vision is central in the conceptual structure of the book, as it marks the shift from mourning and agony to consolation.[167] The second is the dream of the eagle, 'the fourth kingdom which appeared in a vision to your brother Daniel' (12:11). Its heads, wings and underwings in bewildering proliferation stand for the rulers of the Roman empire in the first century. The third vision is also a dream. Ezra sees 'as it were a man' who rises from the sea and flies with the clouds of heaven (13:3). He destroyed attacking multitudes and led back joyous crowds. He is interpreted to be the Davidic Messiah, judging the wicked and assembling all the scattered tribes of Israel in his kingdom. The reinterpretation of the

---

[163] So already Gunkel in *TLZ* (1891), 5-11; *id.*, 'Das vierte Buch Ezra', 343; Keulers, *Eschatologische Lehre*, 36-54; Stone, *Eschatology*, 13-17; Myers, *Esdras*, 120.

[164] Myers, *Esdras*, 120. An extensive study is Thompson, *Responsibility for Evil.* Harnisch, *Verhängnis*, 60-67 maintains that the views of the author are expressed in the angelic responses to Ezra's questioning. The views expressed in Ezra's questions are representative of a point of view against which the author of 4 Ezra is polemicizing. This position has been questioned, justly, by Breech, 'Function of 4 Ezra', 270; Hayman, 'Problem of Pseudonymity'. On the central issues of the book, see now Stone, 'Reactions to Destructions'.

[165] See Stone, 'Paradise' and *id.* 'Lists', 419-26.

[166] A major objection to Harnisch's contention is that the angel's answers are so often pat or evasive.

[167] See Stone, 'Reactions to Destructions', 183-4.

cosmic language of the symbolic vision into the Davidic Messiah judging the wicked is notable.[168]

The final vision describes Ezra's activity as a revealer, through the typology of Moses. Both to Moses on Sinai and to Ezra were revealed esoteric and exoteric books. As Moses gave the Torah, Ezra restored it. To him were revealed, in addition to the twenty-four biblical books, seventy books. These contained the true, inner teaching, for in them is 'the spring of understanding, the fountain of wisdom, and the stream of knowledge' (14:47).[169]

The chief critical issue has been that of the composition of the book. One school of opinion distinguished five separate sources in the book, held together by the work of a redactor.[170] Others emphasize the structural unity and the terminological commonality of the composition. They maintain the substantial unity of the present form of the work without denying the possible utilization of various sources by the author.[171] This view has predominated in recent scholarship without a really satisfactory explanation being found for the inconsistencies of style and thought which led the source critics to their conclusions.

No impression of Essene or associated sectarian ideas can be found in 4 Ezra and the book often conforms to traditional rabbinic exegesis and views.[172] It also has features in common with the *Biblical Antiquities* of pseudo-Philo and with *2 Apocalypse of Baruch*.[173] *Biblical Antiquities* is probably a source of 4 Ezra, while *2 Apocalypse Baruch* probably depends on it. There has been considerable debate about the original language of the book, but Hebrew seems to be the strongest contender.[174]

---

[168] See above, note 84; also Stone, 'Messiah in IV Ezra'.

[169] This is the oldest source for the number twenty four for the biblical books.

[170] Kabisch, Box, de Faye and others have held this view. The sources are usually identified as follows: S (Salathiel Apocalypse, cf. 3:2) comprises most of Visions I-IV; A (Eagle Vision); M (Son of Man Vision); E¹ (Ezra Vision, chap. 14); E² (the short revelatory passages in Visions i-IV). R, i.e. the redactor, is responsible according to this theory for the combination of these sources and their partial reconciliation with one another by the addition of editorial phrases or verses.

[171] So Clemen, Gunkel, Sanday, Violet, Keulers and Breech, 'Function of 4 Ezra'. A summary of views for and against with appropriate bibliographical references may be found in Breech's article. See also Stone, 'Messiah in IV Ezra'.

[172] Cf. 6:7-10 and *Gen. Rabba* 63, 8 (p. 692); *Midrash ha-Gadol Gen.* p. 440-1. Fragments of a midrash on the thirteen *middot* are also preserved in 4 Ezra 7:123ff. See Simonsen, 'Ein Midrasch'. Boyarin ('Penitential Liturgy'), discerned in 7:102-8:36 a reflection of an ancient *Selihot* (penitential) liturgy.

[173] In general on 4 Ezra, see Stone, 'Ezra'.

[174] Stone, 'Textual Criticism', 109ff.; Denis, *Introduction*, 199-200; Myers, *Esdras*, 115-18 adds nothing new.

THE APOCALYPSE OF ABRAHAM

This writing is one of the least known of the Jewish apocalypses, probably for the simple reason that it was not included in the collections edited by Kautzsch and Charles. Like the Book of Daniel it is composed of two distinct parts, narratives concerning the seer and apocalyptic revelation. The narratives tell the story of Abraham's discovery of God, a tale which was widespread in differing forms in Jewish apocryphal and midrashic literature.[175] The form of the story as it occurs in The *Apocalypse of Abraham* is unparalled in the ancient sources, and it has been attributed to a different author from the one who wrote the visions.[176] There seems to be no compelling reason to accept this view and the stories suit well in their present place. They form a fitting preamble to the extensive vision which follows, since they culminate in Abraham's remarkable prayer in which he asks for knowledge of God (chap. 7).[177]

The existence of parallel stories elsewhere in contemporary literature indicates that the writer was not creating *de novo,* but drawing upon current traditions, in the first part of the work at least. The vision is tied exegetically to Gen 15 of which it is an enormously expanded retelling. When he finishes his prayer, Abraham is immediately promised descendants and then he is granted a vision of history and of the eschaton. In this revelation of 'the ages' and 'what is reserved', Abraham sees God, the heavens and their secrets, and the reward and punishment of men.

The chief critical problem in the latter part of the book is the composition of chapter 29. It is generally admitted that a considerable part of this chapter is a Christian interpolation. Yet the actual teaching of this passage is strange indeed, whether it is regarded from a Christian view-point or from a Jewish one. The passage speaks of an man arising from the side of the heathen and worshipped by the heathen, by some of Israel, and by Azazel. This is an unusual description of Christ. Still, pending further insights, it does seem most reasonable to identify this figure as Christ and view the passage as a Christian interpolation. A Jewish interpretation

---

[175] Chief references are cited by Ginzberg; Box, *Apocalypse of Abraham,* 88.; see also Nickelsburg, *Jewish Literature,* 294-9.

[176] Ginzberg, *ibid.,* considers the form of the story in *Apocalypse of Abraham* to be earlier than that which is found in the *Book of Jubilees,* but he would date *Jubilees* later than is acceptable today. He is followed by Frey, 'Abraham', 30 and others. In fact, the Dead Sea scrolls confirm that *Jubilees* is to be considered much earlier than Ginzberg thought. Thus his observation, if it is true, refers to the form of the stories but not to the dates of the documents.

[177] Reference is made back to the stories from the vision, in chaps. 9, 10, 19, and 26. The stories contain no references forward to the vision, except of course for the prayer in chap. 7 to which, in fact, the rest of the book containing the vision is the response. Indeed, the nature of the plot and the material in the first chapters does not readily offer contexts in which such references forward might have been made.

would be even more difficult.[178] Perhaps it is of an unidentified sectarian character.

The *Apocalypse of Abraham* is preserved in a number of Slavonic recensions and a Romanian version.[179] The Slavonic version was made from Greek[180] and that Greek probably from a Hebrew or Aramaic original.[181] Some possible references or allusions to this work in patristic sources have been assembled.[182]

The vision is related in the context of Genesis, chap. 15, which vision was commonly regarded as being a revelation of heavenly or eschatological secrets.[183] The *Apocalypse of Abraham* has certain features in common with another pseudo-Abrahamic work, the *Testament of Abraham*. In particular, both works describe extensive revelations of the heavenly realm and of aspects of eschatology. The *Apocalypse of Abraham* is, however, characterized by the greater sense of urgency that pervades its eschatological aspirations. This is caused by a concern for theodicy, a pondering of the ways of God and his justice, which in turn is aroused by the reactions of the writer to the destruction of the Second Temple (chaps. 27-31). This dynamic is very like that to be discerned in 4 Ezra and *2 Apocalypse of Baruch*, to which works the *Apocalypse of Abraham* bears a similarity. Some scholars have gone so far as to suggest the existence of literary relationship between 4 Ezra and the *Apocalypse of Abraham*.[184]

In the past the book has been said to have 'gnostic features'.[185] It certainly is in some ways unique among the Jewish apocalypses and it is well to examine some of its unique aspects. These relate to cosmology and the vision of the heavens and are similar to ideas found in Jewish mystical literature and tradition. The angel Jaoel appears as the chief angel in the *Apocalypse of Abraham*. He is related to Metatron in function. Indeed, a famous rabbinic dictum about Metatron is only comprehensible if in that

---

[178] Bonwetsch, *Apokalypse Abrahams*, 63ff. recognized the Christian character of this section, but the interpolation was first identified as such by Box, *Apocalypse of Abraham*, 78ff. Licht, 'Abraham' has stressed the singularity of this figure.

[179] For details of the Slavonic transmission as known until early this century, see J. Landman in Box, *Apocalypse of Abraham*, x-xv and for a summary of new material that has appeared since and for much information about different Slavonic Abrahamic works, see Turdeanu, 'Apocalypse d'Abraham'.

[180] So, e.g., Box, *Apocalypse of Abraham*, 15 and other critics.

[181] Box, *ibid.*, xv-xvi; Rubinstein, 'Hebraisms'. For references to further literature, see Denis, *Introduction*, 37f.

[182] Denis, *ibid.*

[183] So, e.g., 4 Ezra 3:13; *Mekhilta*, *Yitro* 9 (p. 236); *Gen. Rabba* 44, 14f. (p. 437), 44, 21 (pp. 443f.) and Targums to Gen 15:9. Cf. *2 Apoc. Bar.* 4:3-4; Ginzberg, *Legends* 5, 229-30 who describes chaps. 11-32 as 'a Midrash on Gen 15:9-14 with pronounced gnostic features.' This seems somewhat extreme.

[184] Thus Licht, 'Abraham'. *Non liquet.*

[185] See, e.g., Ginzberg, 'Abraham'; Denis, *Introduction*, 38. On a possibly gnostic 'Apocalypse of Abraham's see below p. 446f.

case the name Metatron is seen as a surrogate for Jaoel, for of Metatron it says 'his name is like his Master's'.[186] This angelic figure is also known from certain gnostic texts.[187] The role of Jaoel as the highest celestial power below God is a very notable feature of the *Apocalypse of Abraham*. This is, however, not a particularly gnostic view.

Abraham's vision experience is described in terms known from other mystical writings.[188] Moreover, the celestial song which Abraham is instructed to sing by the angels when he receives the vision of God is unlike any song found elsewhere in the apocalypses (cf. *1 Enoch* 71:11-12). Its closest analogies seem to lie in the idea of the unceasing celestial songs recorded in the *Merkabah* books. [189] The revelation consists first of a vision of God, his Throne and attendants (chaps. 17-18). As has been remarked, this section is particularly close to the early mystical texts. Next, Abraham sees the firmaments from the highest to the lowest (chaps. 19-20), the earth and the abyss (chaps. 20-21). This form of vision, a looking down from the highest heaven to the depth is of unusual character. In it the revelation of the secrets is a result of the illumination gained by the vision of God. The vision changes to the sight of a picture relating all the events which have happened or which will befall humanity (chaps. 21-end).[190]

The latter part of this revelation centers on the sin of Adam and its implications for mankind, as well as on the destruction of the Temple and its aftermath (cf. 4 Ezra).[191] The adversary who attempts to foil Abraham and mankind is called Azazel, a name known from *1 Enoch* and from certain Qumran documents, most notable being 4Q180, 1:7-10. The role played by him here is fully Satanic: he is moreover a fallen angel, like in *1*

---

[186] So *B.T. Sanhedrin* 38b. Metatron is also mentioned in *B.T. Hagigah* 15a, *B.T. Abodah Zarah* 3b. 'Jaoel' is formed of the tetragrammaton and the theophoric element 'el'. See Scholem, *Kabbalah*, 377-81 and cf. *id.*, *Major Trends*, 68f. and note, where further evidence concerning this angel is adduced. Box, *Apocalypse of Abraham*, xvf. had already observed the similarities between Jaoel and Metatron. Contrast Ginzberg, 'Abraham'. See in detail, Scholem, *Jewish Gnosticism*, 43-55.

[187] Scholem, *Major Trends*, 68-69.

[188] *Ibid.*

[189] Scholem, *Jewish Gnosticism*, 20-30 and particularly p. 23 and the texts cited there.

[190] Scholem, *Major Trends*, 72; *id.*, *Kabbalah*, 18 pointed out the concept of the veil seen by the mystics of the *Merkabah* school in which are woven all the deeds of men and their ends. (See also Hofius, *Thron Gottes*, but his observations are not particularly relevant at this point). The mystics' curtain is very similar to the picture revealed to Abraham in chaps. 21f. of *Apocalypse of Abraham*. The same function is played earlier by the heavenly tablets which are revealed to the seer. So, e.g., *1 Enoch* 81:2, 4Q180 1:3, *et al.* On the heavenly books of the deeds of the righteous and the wicked, see the sources adduced by Hengel, *Hellenism* 1, 200-1, and notes. *Apocalypse of Abraham* further characterizes this wondrous picture as follows: 'whatever I (God) had determined to be was already planned beforehand in this (picture), and it stood before me ere it was created.' With this aspect of the picture, compare *Gen. Rabba* 1,1 (pp. 1-2), Philo, *Op.* 16-23 and *passim*.

[191] See Rubinstein, 'Problematic Passage'. Above, the similarities between this range of interests and that of 4 Ezra were observed.

Enoch and in 4Q180. His garments will be given to Adam.[192] In chaps. 20, 22, and 29 the idea of Azazel's rule jointly with God over this world is to be found, together with the idea that God granted him authority over the wicked. These ideas are clearly dualistic in character.[192a] The idea of the joint rule of Azazel and God in this world resembles the doctrine of the *Rule of the Community,* according to which there are two powers whom God appointed to rule in the world (cf. 1 QS 3:20-1).

The apocalyptic part of the work, then, shows analogies with other apocalypses of eschatological interest on the one hand, and with the mystical writings and their cosmology on the other. It is an important representative of the genre, particularly significant as providing a link between the apocalypses and the *Merkabah* mystical books.

Apocalypses and Other Genres

APOCALYPSE AND TESTAMENT

The views and concepts of apocalyptic eschatology, as was observed above, are of rather broad distribution in the period of the Second Temple. In this section, however, interest will center on certain literary genres which show closer or remoter relationship with the apocalypses, and not on the spread of the ideas of apocalyptic eschatology.

A particularly close relationship exists between the apocalypses and certain of the pseudepigraphical testaments. Of special note in this connection are *The Testaments of the Twelve Patriarchs,* and *The Testament of Moses.*[193] Other works, apparently belonging to the genre 'testament', notably *The Testament of Solomon* also show clear points of contact with the apocalypses. These common features comprise, among others, pseudepigraphy,[194] and the presence (not dominant in the testaments) of visions and subject matter concerned with eschatological revelations and cosmological secrets.[195] The testament is a death-bed address, usually by some ancient seer or patriarch. It is a genre which was considered particularly apt for the passing on of eschatological or cosmic secrets.[196]

---

[192] Cf. *Vita Adam* 17 where Adam prays *et da mihi gloriam eius (i.e. diaboli) quam ipse perdidit.*

[192a] Azazel's worship of the man in the interpolation in chap. 29 remains difficult.

[193] This is often entitled *The Assumption of Moses.* Ancient references were assembled by Clemen in Kautzsch, *Apokryphen* 2, 311-12. On its genre, see Charles, *APOT* 2, 407-8; Kolenkow, 'Testament'. The boundaries of 'the apocalypse' in contrast with other genres are indicated by Collins, *Apocalypse,* 10-11.

[194] But since this is typical of much of the literature of the age, it perhaps should not be assigned too much weight in the context.

[195] *T. Solomon* is a special case in this respect.

[196] See, e.g., *Jub.* 45:14, *Gen. Rabba* 62, 2 (pp. 670-4). A new, major study of the genre 'Testament' is underway and the first part of it has been published by von Nordheim, *Das Testament.* See review of this by M. de Jonge, *JSJ* 12 (1981) 112-17.

The testament of Jacob in Genesis 49, was interpreted eschatologically and may have formed a sort of prototype of such revelatory testaments,[197] and the revelation to Moses before his death was similarly viewed.[198] Such contexts, furthermore, were thought suitable for reviewing one's life and drawing moral or ethical conclusions from it. So paraenesis of a moral character is also an integral part of the testaments. The moral teaching of *The Epistle of Enoch* and of *2 Enoch,* for example, bears this testamentary character and much of the exhortation of the other apocalypses may also derive from testamentary contexts. In the *Testaments of the Twelve Patriarchs,* which is in its present form probably a Christian recension of Jewish sources of diverse character,[199] many of these features are preserved. Pseudepigraphic, it presents deathbed exhortations of a moral character delivered by the twelve sons of Jacob. Into these are introduced certain eschatological and even cosmological visions, some symbolical in character, as well as much eschatological prediction.[200]

THE TESTAMENT OF MOSES

The Testament of Moses is also sometimes called *The Assumption of Moses.* Of the extant testaments, this is closest to an apocalyptic vision of the historical type. Nonetheless the title *Testament of Moses* seems quite justified by the framework in which the vision is presented.[201] It is preserved in a single, sixth-century, Latin manuscript apparently copied from a fifth-century examplar. The Latin was translated from Greek,[204] which is generally admitted to be a translation from Hebrew.[205]

The historical prediction placed in Moses' mouth continues from his own days with fair accuracy down to the death of king Herod and the rule of his sons.[206] This recital is followed by a prophecy of the terrible suffer-

---

[197] So Gen 49:1, and *Targum Onkelos* there; *Gen. Rabba* 98, 2 (p. 251).

[198] See, e.g., *Bib. Ant.* 19:10-13, cf. Deut 32:49, 34:1-3.

[199] See De Jonge, 'Christian Interpolations' on the general problem of the composition of the *Testaments of the Twelve Patriarchs.* See also his summary in 'Recent Studies'. The most recent research is well reflected in De Jonge, *Studies on the Testaments,* while a history of research is given by Slingerland, *Patriarchs Research.*

[200] A few examples drawn from numerous occurrences are: cosmological vision (*T. Levi* 3); eschatological prediction (*T. Levi* 4, *T. Judah* 25); prediction of history periodized schematically (*T. Levi* 17-18).

[201] The book is incomplete in its present form, and if it is the *Testament of Moses* referred to in the *Stichometry* of Nicephorus, then about half of the book is lost. That eighth-century list of apocryphal writings attributes 1,100 *stichoi* to it, which is about twice as many as have survived. See Charles, *APOT* 2, 407-8. On p. 408, note 1 Charles speculates as to the possible contents of these lost chapters.

[204] Charles, *Assumption of Moses,* xxxvi-xxxviii; Laperrousaz, 'Testament de Moïse', re-evaluates the critical issues, as well as offering a new edition of the Latin text with a French translation and notes.

[205] Charles, *Assumption of Moses,* xxxviii-xlv.

[206] 6:6-7, see Charles, *ibid.,* lv-lviii.

ings which would ensue (chaps. 7-8). Into the midst of this, the story of Taxo of the tribe of Levi and his seven sons who died martyrs' deaths rather than transgress the commandments of the Lord is introduced. They purify themselves through prayer and fasting and withdraw to a cave where they meet their end. These events are eschatological and are designed to hasten the end by summoning divine vengeance. This view is an interesting one when the book's determinism is also taken into account.[207]

This story has its closest parallels in the stories of the martyrs reported from the Maccabean period. Indeed a recent study suggested, instead, that the historical revelation originally referred to the Maccabean period and that it was later updated at the time of Herod's sons, by an editor.[210] On the Taxo episode follows a description of God's eschatological coming in vengeance, the uproar and disturbance this causes in the whole cosmos, and the eschatological elevation of Israel to the stars of heaven.[211]

The *Testament of Moses,* as far as it is preserved, is purely historical-eschatological in interest. No hint is found of those other subjects which were of concern to the apocalyptic authors, subjects related to the revelation of the heavens and their secrets or of the hidden parts of the earth. The eschatological views of the book show no expectation of any redeemer other than God himself and the vindication which is described in chap. 10 is that of Israel against her enemies.

THE TESTAMENT OF ABRAHAM

The question whether *The Testament of Abraham* is Jewish or Christian in origin has been debated in the past, but recent studies seem to indicate that it is a predominantly Jewish work. As distinct from the other testaments it is not merely Abraham's deathbed address, but contains narratives of events surrounding his death.[211a]

The book presents a combination of two elements, narrative and revelatory vision. In this respect it is similar to Daniel and *Apocalypse of Abraham.* Unlike them, however, the narrative and revelatory vision are here fully integrated in the literary structure, whereas in both those works the narrative elements precede the visions. The highpoint of Abraham's vision of the heavens is the judgement of the souls and the fate of the righteous and wicked. There is a detailed vision of the heavenly court and the various functionaries there. Issues of divine justice and mercy thus play

---

[207] So in the important article of Licht, 'Taxo'. A dissenting view is that of Priest, 'Reflections'.

[210] Licht, 'Taxo', 95-103; Nickelsburg, *Testament of Moses,* 33-37 suggests further support for this view, and the writer is convinced by this and by the critique by Collins, 'Some Remaining Problems'. Collin's article, 'Date and Provenance' makes comprehensible the context of the later redaction of the work. See also Yarbro Collins, 'Composition'.

[211] See Collins, 'Apocalyptic Eschatology' 34-5; Nickelsburg, *Resurrection,* 29-31.

[211a] See above, pp. 60ff.

a central role in the book. Yet it is notable that its descriptions of these matters lack any heightened tension or intense expectation of the vindication of God's justice. They have the character, rather, of legend or story bearing a strong moral point and message. Most remarkable in this connection is the moral point made by contrasting Abraham's indignation over the sins of the wicked with God's mercy towards them (A8, 14). In the description of the heavenly judgement of the individual souls, the weighing of the deeds of men takes center stage (A 12-13). Abel is judge over the souls of men. Apocalyptic eschatology is evident in the rather obscure prediction of the three judgements which together constitute cosmic judgement (A 13).[212] A certain interest in angelology and other features of the upper world is to be detected, but these subjects are not of primary concern to the book.

ORACLES AND APOCALYPSES

There are certain obvious similarities between the Jewish Hellenistic oracular literature and the apocalypses. The Jews, and later the Christians, wrote oracles which were attributed to various oracles or inspired men and women famous in Hellenistic antiquity. The best known of these are the *Sibylline Oracles,* a substantial part of which (almost all of Books 3 and 5 and parts of Book 4) have good claims to Jewish authorship. These collections of oracles have certain points in common with the apocalypses.

The form, the Sibylline oracle, is naturally much older than these Jewish oracles, and it is pagan in origin.[213] In their pagan, pre-Jewish form and from this stage on, the Sibylline oracles have a strongly political character of prediction which also bears a largely eschatological dimension. So the Jewish Sibyl presents examples of political prediction of eschatological character, as do many pagan compositions, particularly in Egypt in the period preceding and contemporary with the Sibylline books.[214] Yet their eschatological hope is, on the whole, set forth in terms drawn unmistakably from contemporary and earlier Jewish eschatology.[215]

---

[212] See particularly Nickelsburg, *Testament of Abraham,* 23-64 and also other papers in the same volume. Milik, '4Q Visions' published a work entitled *Visions of Amram* which, so he claims, is that referred to by Origen, *Comm. xxxv* on Luke 12:58f. This reference has, in the past, always been taken to refer to *Testament of Abraham. Testament of Abraham* or something very similar seems to lie behind pseudo-Clement, *Recog.* 1:32-33. Delcor, 'Testament d'Abraham' sets forth the background of certain traditions in the work.

[213] See general bibliography collected by Denis, *Introduction,* 111ff. The theories of literary analysis vary and the oracles are undoubtedly complex literary works.

[214] On the supposed Persian eschatological expectations, see Swain, 'Four Monarchies'. In general, on the oriental opposition to Rome, see Fuchs, 'Geistige Widerstand' and the extensive bibliography there. See also Flusser, 'Four Empires'; M. Smith, 'Common Theology', 145-6 has commented on this type of oracle in ancient Near Eastern sources.

[215] On this whole issue, see particularly Collins, *Sibylline Oracles,* 97-115 where many of these matters are set out in detail.

[margin handwriting: ① oriental discontent]

[margin handwriting: ② predict political future]

From this it is immediately evident that the *Sibylline Oracles* share certain features with the apocalypses. First, to some measure, it seems that the same springs of oriental discontent with Hellenistic Greek rule fed some apocalyptic political formulations and those of the *Sibylline Oracles*. Second, both genres predict the future and claim supernatural sanction for their political eschatology. Moreover, in some extended political prophecies, the Sibylline books show an apprehension of the overall structure of history resembling that which can be detected in the political apocalyptic visions.[216]

Yet it should be stressed, in spite of such analogies, the two genres are quite different. In the *Sibylline Oracles* there is far less sustained development of ideas than in the apocalypses. The *Sibylline Oracles* are written as political and religious propaganda, directed outward at the pagan world; a function difficult to attribute to the apocalypses. Moreover, the apocalypses place great emphasis upon the process of revelation as it is expressed in them, and on the esoteric character of the information thus revealed. Even if the esotericism is assumed, this stance involves quite different presuppositions than do the *Sibylline Oracles*. Further, the sort of interest in the secrets of creation and the heavenly realm which is so important in some apocalypses is completely missing from the Sibylline literature.

There has been considerable debate as to whether another Hellenistic political oracle, that attributed to Hystaspes, a more or less legendary Persian sage and king, is a Jewish work or not. This document is found embedded in certain ancient writings, chiefly the *Divine Institutes* by Lactantius. It teaches, apparently, an eschatology very close to that of the apocalypses. The formal and structural features, as far as they can be uncovered, are like those of other political oracles. Thus, even if Hystaspes is not another example of Jewish utilization of an established pagan oracle tradition for polemical purposes, it is important evidence for the sort of prophecies that were current under the names of ancient oriental seers,[217] and their similarities to Jewish oracles.

The resemblance obtaining between certain pagan Egyptian oracles of political and eschatological character and the apocalypses has been observed above. There are a number of such works which have generally been compared with political apocalyptic literature. The chief ones are: *The Demotic Chronicle* (Ptolemaic in date), *The Potters Oracle* (written after 311 B.C.E.) and *The Apocalypse of the Lamb to Bocchoris*. Perhaps the

---

[216] Note, e.g., the fourth kingdom oracle in *Sib. Or.* book 4 and see Fluser, 'Four Empires'.

[217] The classic monograph of Windisch, *Orakel,* argues against the Jewish authorship; cf. above, p. 361. For further discussion see Collins, *Sibylline Oracles,* 9-12. See now Flusser, 'Hystaspes and John of Patmos', defending Jewish authorship. There may be more basis for seeing in Hystaspes a revealer of divine secrets (cf. Windisch, *Orakel,* 14-5) than there is for the Sibyl, but the general close relation of the two is well established. See also Widengren, 'Iran and Israel', 172-7.

'Asclepius', a treatise found in the *Corpus Hermeticum* should also be included in this category. It shows the persistence of these eschatological oracles, although the eschatology in it varies from the earlier forms.[218] These Hellenistic Egyptian oracles are typified by a survey of preceding history in a fairly clear form and then this is followed by more or less obscure predictions of the arrival of the reign of a new king. He was expected to re-establish the rule of righteousness and order in the country, to drive out the hated foreign rulers and to re-establish the ancient structure of things.

It is easy to see in such oracles, even if written in the Greek language, the expression of oriental sentiments of opposition to Hellenistic rule. As such, similar oracles can be found elsewhere in the Greek East.[219] The parallels with the apocalypses are clear and some dimensions of the expression of political hope in the apocalypses are analogous to similar expressions in the political oracles.[220] Yet, the hope of restoration of the Davidic kingdom or of the rule of God goes back to biblical sources, and the lines of connection between biblical literature and the apocalypses noted above seem much more significant than the similarities with the Hellenistic political oracles. Once more, it should be observed that the 'speculative' features of the apocalypses have no parallels in the Hellenistic oracular literature. Thus, although the political aspect of the apocalypses should be related to the common aspirations of the oriental peoples, the form and content of such aspirations is peculiarly Jewish in the apocalypses.

APOCALYPSES AND THE QUMRAN WRITINGS

Quite different to the situation observed with the political oracles of the Hellenistic age is that which obtains when one tries to characterize the relationship between the apocalypses and the sectarian writings from Qumran. The tensely eschatological features of the self-understating of the Qumran covenanters have been stressed by historians and other scholars.[221] These features, which were to a great extent constitutive of the

---

[218] See Hengel, *Hellenism* 1, 184ff. and notes, where extensive bibliography is cited. See also Collins, *Sibylline Oracles,* 12-15 and full bibliography there. McCown, 'Egyptian Apocalyptic' has dealt in some detail with this literature in comparison with the Jewish sources.

[219] See Hengel, *Hellenism* 1, 185-6.

[220] See also von Gall, *Basileia,* 48-82. There are certain analogies to the apocalyptic historical recitals in the Akkadian texts discussed by Hallo, 'Akkadian Apocalypses'; See also the comments of and the sources cited by Lambert, 'History and the Gods', 175-7; *id. Background,* 10-17. In this latter work, he explores possible channels of transmission of Mesopotamian material to the Jews. These are remoter than those of the Egyptian texts. Hengel, *Hellenism* 1, 185f., points to some such oracles from Asia Minor and Syria. He emphasizes differences between the political oracles and the apocalypses (1, 186).

[221] The literature is quite extensive, see, e.g., Cross, *Ancient Library of Qumran,* 76ff. and note the modification of his position in 'New Directions', 157ff.

being of the sect, were expressed in many aspects of their life, including their writings. It thus follows that there are fairly numerous documents of sectarian cast which are eschatological in their emphasis and interest.[222]

PESHER

Indeed, the *pesher,* that form of biblical commentary which, as far as is known, is peculiar to the Qumran sect, is very often eschatological in import.[223] The importance of the *pesharim* in relationship to the apocalypses, however, extends beyond their eschatological teaching. Like the apocalypses, they too claim to be the embodiment of a special knowledge

אל 'רזי

of heavenly secrets. These secrets, the רזי אל ('the mysteries of God') are not revealed, it is true, in an ecstatic vision as are the mysteries unveiled to the apocalyptic seers. Rather, they seem to be uncovered by a special way of reading the biblical text, by a special mode of exegesis; even though this mode of exegesis itself may have been revealed to the Righteous Teacher (1QpHab 7:3-6). Furthermore, these secrets were primarily eschatological in character. Thus the parallel between the apocalypses and the Qumran writings also relates to a consciousness of divine inspiration expressed in different modes, as well as to the material of common interest.

Now it is undeniable that the Qumran sect also wrote and speculated about secret heavenly knowledge which was of non-eschatological character. Such interests of theirs included calendar, physiognomy, angelology, and so forth.[224] If all of these interests and subjects were regarded by them as part of the same body of revealed information then the results would be of considerable interest, for they would form a complex of material and a range of interests very much like those of the apocalypses. What remains unknown, however, is how the different types of knowledge contained in different documents from varied dates relate to each other and how they were regarded by the sect. This is impossible to ascertain from the documents published, but on the whole the sectarian documents differ from the apocalypses by virtue of the very fact that these subjects were not found combined in the same literary framework. The role in the sectarian life of the Enochic documents, in which many of these elements are found combined, is not completely clear.

---

[222] Works of eschatological character abound, such as 4Q174, 4Q177, 4Q182. 1Q27 is an eschatological prophecy; 4QMessAram also apparently belongs to this category. Cross' use of 'apocalyptic' on pp. 198ff. refers not only to the literary type, but also to the cast of thought. See further pp. 392-4 above.

[223] See 1QpHab, 3QpIsa (3Q4), 4QpIsa*a* (4Q61), 4QPs*a* (4Q71) and others. Cf. below pp. 507f., 538f. on the importance of eschatology in the *pesharim.*

[224] See 1QpHab 6:12-7:8 on the understanding of the *pesher.* See also Gruenwald, *Apocalyptic* (Dissertation). 45ff.; Bruce, *Biblical Exegesis,* 7-9. The question of what additional subject matter was considered by the sect to be revealed secrets is an interesting one. Was calendar included in this? Certainly so, if the Enochic *Book of the Luminaries* is taken into account. Does the cryptic writing of 4Q186 indicate that this physiognomic material was regarded as revealed secrets? This does not seem unlikely. Were texts such as the *Angelic Liturgy* from Cave 4 in this category? If so, then the range of Qumran revealed information would approximate that of the apocalypses.

It is possible that the view of continued revelation through the activity of *pesher* which was doubtless part (even a central part) of that study of Scripture to which the Essenes devoted a third of their time (1QS 6:6-8) is the reason for the notable paucity of works which are presented as revelations to ancient seers.[225] The function of this particular feature of the apocalypses may have been fulfilled by different means.

This observation remains tentative, of course, until the publication of all the Qumran documents is completed. Among the texts known to date a few documents should be mentioned as having a particularly close likeness to the apocalypses. These are, it should be emphasized, a rather small proportion of those published. They include the *Description of the New Jerusalem* which has been found in a number of manuscripts.[226] This is a vision of the heavenly city which the anonymous seer visits, guided, led and instructed by an angel.[227] This work belongs within the speculative tradition of the heavenly Jerusalem and is formally similar to the heavenly journey of the apocalyptic seer.[228] Second, 4Qpseudo-Daniel is a work belonging to the same genre as the canonical Daniel apocalypse. The published fragments are very small, but as far as can be judged from them, it contains narratives of events in which Daniel and a king took part and at least one extensive historical vision. It is possible that two different works are involved in the three manuscripts which have been published.[229] The literary form of 4Qpseudo-Ezekiel is not clear yet, but it seems likely that it too is an apocalypse. 4Q Visions of Amram also belongs to this class of writing.[230] *The Angelic Liturgy* (4QSerek Shira) is a text crucial for the development of Jewish esotericism and understanding of the heavenly sphere. Whether it has an encompassing literary framework or is simply a collection of angelic hymns is unknown.[231]

---

[225] See pp. 390-1, above.

[226] See in particular *DJD* 3, 184-193 and 1Q32, 2Q24, and 5Q15.

[227] Note expressions like מחזי אני (2:2, 6, etc.), cf. Dan 4:7.

[228] See Stone, 'Lists'.

[229] Milik, 'Prière de Nabonide', 411-15.

[230] Milik, '4Q Visions'.

[231] Strugnell, 'Angelic Liturgy'. Note that, although many of the texts counted by Eissfeldt as Qumran apocalypses have points of connection with the apocalypses, texts such as 1Q19 'The Book of Noah'; 1Q21 Aramaic Testament of Levi; 1Q22 Words of Moses; 1Q24 'Meteorological Fragment' are not apocalypses. 1Q27 is an eschatological prophecy which is not formally an apocalypse. 6Q14 is called 'Texte apocalyptique' by the editors of *DJD* 3 for no evident reason. Some of the other surviving fragments may have come from apocalypses, even though no distinctive signs of this are preserved in the extant morsels of text. Carmignac, 'Qumran', 28-33 accepts *Description of the New Jerusalem, Angelic Liturgy, Prayer of Nabonidus,* and *Visions of Amram* as apocalypses, as well as *1 Enoch* and *Jubilees.* We would contest the place of *Prayer of Nabonidus* in this list, and query that of *Angelic Liturgy.* On the texts mentioned in this note, see Fitzmyer, *Tools.* The character of the 'visions cosmologiques . .' noted by J. Starcky in Baillet, 'Le travail d'édition', 66 remains unclear.

Perhaps more enigmatic than any of the works mentioned is the work entitled _The War of the Sons of Light against the Sons of Darkness_ (the _War Scroll_). This is a document of unparalleled character. The book is presented as a narrative prediction and prescription of laws and orders for the wars which will precede and lead up to the great eschatological battle, as well as of that battle itself.

The interest of the scroll for the study of the apocalypses is manifold. First, it is an extensive development of the theme of the eschatological war. Starting from pre-biblical origins, this eventually becomes one of the salient features of the eschatological scheme in the apocalypses.[234] The length of time assigned to the war in the scroll is unparalleled in any other source. Even more remarkable is the extraordinary detail of this sustained description: little like this precise prediction and prescription of the future events is to be found in the apocalypses. Second, it is of considerable note that in the final battle the divine and the human, heavenly and earthly come together. The battle is that of the forces of the righteous against the wicked and of the heavenly hosts against the Satanic.[235] The Qumran community is organized like Israel in the desert and like the host of the Children of Light.[236] The foreshadowing of the realization of eschatological events in the life of the community adds a dimension to the _War Scroll_ which cannot be traced for the apocalypses. It may explain why there was such an intense interest in the war and in all the particulars of the organization of the hosts and the expected battle. The community producing the scroll itself expected to participate in the battles.[237] This mythological aspect of the understanding of reality is an important common feature of the _War Scroll_ and the apocalypses; for the apocalypses, however, the sociological matrix in which this was realized in the life of the community remains shrouded in darkness.

Third, incidentally, the scroll provides a good deal of information in

---

[234] Notes 17 and 18, above. The sources in the apocalypses and other contemporary literature are numerous. See, by way of example, 4 Ezra chap. 13; cf. Box, _Ezra-Apocalypse,_ ad loc. and sources cited there.

[235] The _religionsgeschichtliche_ background of these views is clear. See sources quoted in notes 17 and 18 above. Collins contrasts this conflict with that in Daniel, and sees Persian influence in it ('Holy War'); on mythical elements in Danielic descriptions, see Clifford, 'History and Myth'.

[236] Collins, 'Apocalyptic Eschatology', 31ff. has suggested that 'the community believed that it had already transcended death by passing over into the community of the angels' (p. 35). The formulation of this point bz Licht tends in the same direction, but is more cautious (_Thanksgiving Scroll,_ 35). See also the extensive discussion by Kuhn, _Enderwartung, passim_ and particularly pp. 113ff. and 176ff.

[237] On the relationship between the actual Qumran community and the eschatological community of the righteous, see Cross, _Ancient Library of Qumran,_ 203ff.; Licht, _Thanksgiving Scroll,_ 50, 131f. gives an important formulation of this concept.

angelology ②

areas like <u>angelology</u> which are important for the understanding of the apocalypses.[238]

In summary two points should be stressed. First, the scroll shows certain connections with the apocalypses: prediction of the future, details of cosmology, the eschatological war, and the implied predestination of eschatological events. Second, the *War Scroll* differs from the apocalypses: in genre, as a sort of predictive prescription it is unlike them. Its painstakingly detailed prediction of events is qualitatively different from that of the apocalypses and its legislation of their every feature is similarly unparalleled. This difference may be comprehensible in light of the function the scroll could have performed in a sect with the self-understanding of the Qumran covenanters. Such dimensions of the apocalypses are at least unknown and so unverifiable.

Features of the Apocalypses

PSEUDEPIGRAPHY, INSPIRATION AND ESOTERICISM

The apocalypses are presented as visions or revelations of sec cosmos and heavens, of history or of the eschaton. These consistently pseudepigraphical in character. Pseudepigraphy a common feature of very much of the literature, Jewish and pag the Hellenistic-Roman age.[239] In Jewish literature it is particu spread in this period, very few of the Apocrypha and Pseud being other than pseudepigraphic in attribution.[240] Yet, maintained that the pseudepigraphy of the apocalypses form class in the Jewish writings because of the nature of the claim their contents and teaching;[241] and various suggestions have bee

---

[238] Yadin, *Scroll of the War*, 229-42. The overall development of angelology in the period of the Second Temple is far from limited to the apocalypses. On it compare the sources and studies cited by Kaufmann, 'Apokalyptik', 1151-2; Hengel, *Hellenism* 1, 231ff.; Russell, *Method and Message*, 235-62.

[239] For a general survey of pseudepigraphical literature in the Hellenistic world, see Speyer, *Die literarische Fälschung*. See also the material assembled by Hengel, *Hellenism* 1, 205f. Speyer deliberately excludes Jewish 'echte (sic!) religiöse Pseudepigraphie' from consideration. Some of the issues of Jewish pseudepigraphy are reviewed by Metzger, 'Literary Forgeries'.

[240] There is an unfortunate terminological overlap between 'Pseudepigrapha', the name of a more or less fixed body of writings and 'pseudepigraphy', the literary practice of attributing one's writings to someone else, usually an ancient seer, worthy or other dignitary.

[241] It may be contrasted, it seems, with the pseudepigraphy say of the Prayer of Manasseh which fills a lacuna in 2 Chr 33:18-9, or that of the Book of Baruch, which writing, both commonplace and unexceptional in its ideas, is a natural extension of the Book of Jeremiah. Analogous to the apocalypses in pagan literature are among others, the Hermetic writings, both in the range and the character of their interests.

to explain apocalyptic pseudepigraphy.[242] It does seem that it cannot be explained merely as the result of adherence to a literary convention or as a convenient formal feature. At the least it appears to reflect the relationship of the writing to a common received tradition of teaching related to the name of a specific ancient sage or saint.

Such a view finds *prima facie* support in the shared character of material associated with the same ancient figure in sources between which no literary dependence exists.[243] In order fully to appreciate the nature of pseudepigraphic claims in the apocalypses, however, others of their features must be considered.

The boldness and gravity of the claim to inspiration made by these works is the first factor to be evaluated. It has already been remarked that the opening words of *1 Enoch* bring together prophetic claims of Moses, Balaam, and perhaps of Ezekiel.[244] By clear implication, Enoch's claim is considerable indeed. But apocalypses also make explicit claim to general inspiration (*1 Enoch* 93:1). Furthermore they purport to transmit knowledge recorded upon the heavenly tablets seen by the seer on high,[245] learned by eating the fruit of the tree of knowledge (*Vita Adam* 29), unveiled as part of the revelation at Sinai (*Jub.* 1; *2 Apoc. Bar.* 59; 4 Ezra 14), or revealed to the transfigured seer by an angel at God's command, or even by God himself (*2 Enoch* 22:4-12 = Vaillant, 25-27; 24:1ff. = Vaillant, 29; 33:3ff. = Vaillant, 33).

Classic in this connection is 4 Ezra 14 claiming Mosaic authority, indeed authority beyond that of Moses, for the apocalyptic revelations.[246] These claims are serious enough in their own right. They achieve special solemnity when the crucial nature of what is revealed is borne in mind. It is true wisdom, saving knowledge, in 4 Ezra's words 'the spring of understanding, the fountain of wisdom and the stream of knowledge' (14:47).[247]

---

[242] Russell, *Method and Message,* 127-39 has summarized various approaches to this issue. They are not repeated here. He does not take account of Kaufmann's view, *Toledot* 8, 398f. He maintains that what is surprising is that *all* the apocalypses are pseudepigraphical. He regards this pseudepigraphy as a function of the messianic arousal of the Maccabean period when prophecy arose anew. Since it was believed that commissioned prophecy had ceased, this prophetic arousal found its expression (Kaufmann does not quite explain how) in the pseudepigraphic apocalypses. This view must now be modified by the early date of parts of Enoch and by the need to account for the 'speculative' dimension of the apocalypses. Collins, 'Pseudonymity', 331f. isolates the search for authority and *ex eventu* prophecy as chief motives in the use of pseudepigraphy. For a variation of the view that pseudepigraphy is a claim to particular authority, see Beckwith, 'Enoch Literature and Calendar' and also note 108, above.

[243] Enoch is a fine example of this; cf. Hengel, *Hellenism* 1, 204-5 who draws no conclusions from the evidence.

[244] Above, p. 400. See Hengel, *Hellenism* 1, 205-6; Stone, 'Lists', 444.

[245] *1 Enoch,* 93:1, cf. 81:1-2, 106:9, *T. Asher* 7:5; *Prayer of Joseph (apud* Origen, *Philocal.* 23:15). For a variant on this theme, see above, note 190.

[246] So the seventy books of secret, esoteric knowledge are to be understood.

[247] Cf. *1 Enoch* 82:2f. and other places.

Above, certain of the implications of the fact that the apocalypses do not set out to fulfill biblical prophecy were mentioned. They point to a view of independent authority on the part of the apocalyptic writer. It has also been claimed persuasively that the methods of exegesis in the apocryphal literature in general and *a fortiori* in the apocalypses, show that the possibility of inspiration and the results of independent individual cogitation were accorded more weight than in rabbinic literature, this also leading to a less intimate tie to the biblical text.[248]

When these factors are brought into account it becomes clear that pseudepigraphy is basically more than a literary form. Its origins must reflect at least the existence of a common body of apocalyptic lore associated with the name of the supposed author to which the particular book could be seen as belonging.[249] This cannot be urged for each and every apocalypse, of course, for in some cases pseudepigraphy may have become a matter of literary convention. Yet it seems likely to be true of most of them.

With such considerations as these may be associated the question whether behind the traditional form of pseudepigraphic vision there lies actual ecstatic experience and practice of the authors. The broad diffusion of visions in the religious life of the Hellenistic age is well known.[250] The use of the vision as the form of pseudepigraphic writing in the apocalypses presupposed, for its plausibility, the prevalence of actual visionary activities within the society.[251] The occurrence of visions and other pneumatic phenomena is also witnessed by the historical sources relating to Judaism of that era.[252] The resemblance between the experience attributed to Abraham in *Apocalypse of Abraham* and those of mystics has been observed.[253]

---

[248] Heinemann, *Darkei ha-Aggadah*, 174-5. Contrast the remarks of Hengel, *Hellenism* 1, 171ff.

[249] See Russell, *Method and Message* on this problem. One wonders about the weight of his arguments based on a supposed sense of 'contemporaneity' of events of different periods of history and on theories of corporate personality, but the other considerations that he adduces are weighty. See also Vielhauer, 'Apocalyptic', 584; Volz, *Der Geist Gottes*, 119-20. Collins observes, with a different emphasis: 'the attribution of a work to an ancient author, such as Enoch or Shem effectively removes it from the time and place of the present. In this way the impression of the inadequacy of the present world and the need to derive revelation from elsewhere is confirmed' (*Apocalypse*, 12). For yet a different approach see Gruenwald, 'Apocalyptic Literature', 104-6.

[250] Dodds, *Greeks and the Irrational*, 102-34, 236-69. The phenomenon is common.

[251] Russell, *Method and Message*, 158-77 has a broad discussion of this issue.

[252] Cf. Zech 13, Josephus, *Ant.* 13:282, 299, 311-13; 14:22; 15:373-9; 13:345f., *War*, 1:68f., 78-80; 2:112-17; Vielhauer, 'Apocalyptic', 601-4, but he contrasts prophecy and apocalyptic too strongly, see pp. 596-7. The cases cited here all vary in character but they are clear evidence of pneumatic and visionary activities. On Philo's view of ecstaticism, see Lewy, *Sobria Ebrietas*.

[253] Scholem, *Major Trends*, 52.

State
of
mind

The types and character of the various visions have been catalogued conveniently in a recent work and one is struck, in certain cases, by the vividness and detail of the description of the seer's state of mind before his experience and his physical and spiritual reactions to it.[254] It is, of course, impossible to know whether in any given case this is merely a literary description or whether it reflects actual praxis and experience of the authors. One might try to find descriptions of the discipline and techniques used to induce the trance and vision. Even in literary expression, such descriptions might serve as an indication of the real basis of the ecstatic practice ascribed to the ancient seer. Sadly, in the apocalypses there seems to be no information which might reflect actual features of any discipline or techniques beyond the widespread mention of prayer, solitude, fasting and penitence as preludes to the vision.[255] The only exception may be the description of the ascetic way of life of Isaiah and his disciples (*Mart. Isa.* 2:11) in which something of the way of life of some apocalyptic group may be reflected.[256]

Again, the introduction of a form of visionary experience which has no precursor in the Bible argues for innovation based on contemporary practice and views. This is, of course, the assumption to heaven and revelation of heavenly reality to the assumed.[257] This type of experience is not reported by any of the pre-exilic sources. Its appearance in later times also implies, it seems, a new view of 'psychology' and it was to prove of lasting significance.[258]

[254] For a categorization, see Russell, *Method and Message*, 159-73. Good examples of the vividness of the description of the reaction may be found in 4 Ezra 6:36-7, 10:30, etc. On the subject matter of this Section, see in particular the incisive remarks of Gunkel in Kautzsch, *Apokryphen* 2, 340-3. See also Russell, *Method and Message*, 164-5. The point was already made by Bousset, *Religion des Judentums*, 369-70.

[255] Russell, *Method and Message*, 169-73 has assembled a number of sources, but many of these are not to be seen as reflecting actual practice. No clear patterns emerge beyond that noted here. Breech, 'Function of 4 Ezra', 272 has explained the eating of flowers and grass in 4 Ezra 9:24f. on literary grounds. This may be accurate and the lack of any corroborative evidence makes it unlikely that this is part of an ascetic discipline. The cup Ezra is given to drink symbolizes the Holy Spirit (4 Ezra 14:39-40). The symbol is widespread, see Lewy, *Sobria Ebrietas*, 55-56.

[256] Flusser and Philonenko have suggested seeing the story of *Mart. Isa.* as an allegory for the Righteous Teacher and his disciples; see on this Stone, 'Martyrdom of Isaiah'.

[257] *1 Enoch* 14:8, etc., *2 Enoch* 3:1, 36, *Vita Adam* 25:3, *T. Levi* 2:6, *Apoc. Abr.* 12, 15, etc., 2 Cor 12:2-4 and other sources. See Russell, *Method and Message*, 167-8, who lists further references and makes some suggestions about psychological presuppositions; cf. pp. 391-2 above. On the vision of ascent, see Gruenwald, 'Jewish Apocalyptic', 94-97. He has suggested that the recurrent feature of sitting by water at the time of receipt of visions may reflect some technique analogous to leukanomancy, see 'The Mirror'.

[258] Thus, of course, Tannaitic sources such as that preserved in *B.T. Hagigah* 14b: see Scholem, *Major Trends*, 52. So also *Merkabah* mystical sources, see *ibid.*, 40-57; *Jewish Gnosticism*, 14-19. On the purpose or function of the ascent, see Stone, *Scriptures*, 32-34; Collins, *Apocalypse*, 26-27. Hengel, *Hellenism* 1, 204-5 recognizes the possibility raised here without drawing any far-reaching conclusions from it.

These considerations make it conceivable that, in some cases, behind the visionary experiences which are attributed to the seers lay actual ecstatic practice of the apocalyptic authors. Such experience would then be mediated in a pseudepigraphic form, which phenomenon may be compared with the pseudepigraphic form of the visions in the writings of early Jewish mysticism. Indeed a relationship between the seer in his ecstatic state and the pseudepigraphic author is a possibility which might be entertained as a partial explanation of pseudepigraphy.[259] Decisive internal or external evidence for such ecstatic practices has not been forthcoming so far. Yet this possibility should be borne in mind and its significance for the understanding of pseudepigraphy and the apocalyptic view of inspiration considered.[260]

A third feature which must be brought into account is the claimed esotericism of the apocalypses. They certainly claim to be the disclosure of divine secrets made to the seer by special revelation.[261] Moreover, such revelations were thought to have been transmitted from ancient times,[262] and stress is usually laid upon the secrecy of transmission.[263] These writings were to be hidden until the end, 'the words are shut up and sealed until the time of the end' (Dan 12:9). That they are now publicly revealed is a sign that the end is at hand.

One dimension of the esotericism of the apocalypses, then, is their own claim to embody a tradition secretly transmitted from old. Another dimension of the esotericism of the apocalypses has been stressed, their providing the real, inner meaning of scriptural revelation.[264] This view is true only to a limited extent for it has already been observed above that the apocalypses only partly tie themselves to Scripture.[265] 'The twenty four books that thou hast written publish, that the worthy and unworthy may read (therein): but the seventy last thou shalt keep to deliver them to the wise among the people' (4 Ezra 14:45-46, cf. 3-6). Here a central characteristic of esoteric writing is clearly set forth: it is to be transmitted secretly

---

[259] See Stone, 'Vision or Hallucination?'.

[260] This view was already urged, in a somewhat different form by Kaufmann, 'Apokalyptik', 1145-6. Whether, as suggested above, the apocalyptic writer experienced some revelation of the seer to whom the book was attributed, or even identified with him, is unknown. Such experience would, naturally, affect the view of inspiration held by the author.

[261] See Russell, *Method and Message,* 107-8 Hengel, *Hellenism* 1, 210-18 particularly emphasizes this feature as shared with other Hellenistic writings. See also Collins, 'Pseudonymity', 340-1.

[262] *1 Enoch* 82, 108:1ff., *2 Enoch* 33:9-10.

[263] Russell, *Method and Message,* 109-18 isolates two, or perhaps three lines of secret tradition 'associated with the names of Enoch (with Noah), Moses (with Ezra) and possibly Daniel' (p. 109).

[264] Gruenwald, *Apocalyptic* (Dissert.) 1-4. See now his article 'Esoteric Literature'.

[265] See pp. 390-1. This view is admirably suited to a discussion of some of the Qumran writings. writings.

only to initiates or select worthies. The *Rule of the Community* states that after a man has become accepted as a member of the sect, 'the Interpreter shall not conceal from them ... any of those things hidden from Israel which have been discovered by him' (1QS 8:11-12).[266] It may be asked whether the apocalypses were esoteric in this sense. Were they actually the secret teachings of conventicles of apocalypticists revealed only to initiates? This is certainly what would normally be meant by saying that they were esoteric.

The sectarian documents from Qumran apparently were esoteric in this sense. Like the Nag Hammadi gnostic texts, only archeological chance delivered them into our hands and in ancient times they were indeed kept secret. The apocalypses, it seems, were not esoteric in this sense. *4 Ezra*, from which the above quoted statement was drawn was very widely known and translated. *1 Enoch*, for example, was quoted by the Epistle of Jude, and such cases could be multiplied manyfold. The apocalypses were not esoteric in the sense of being the inner or secret teaching of a clearly defined group. It might be suggested that this non-esoteric character was itself a result of the self-understanding of the writers. The teachings had indeed been transmitted in secret, but now the end was near, the times had come to publish them. Yet in fact, this point of view is rather difficult to sustain consistently for the apocalypses.[267]

Thus when esotericism of the apocalypses is spoken of it refers at the most to the writers' view of how the material that they are now publishing was transmitted. It is not possible to show that the books functioned as vessels of esoteric teaching within clearly organized socio-religious groups in the Second Temple period. The comparison with the writings known to have been esoteric in this latter sense tends to indicate that the apocalypses were not such. In some cases, even the emphasis upon the esotericism of the transmission from antique times is absent. Texts like *2 Enoch* 54 (= Vaillant, 55) state: 'Et les livres que je vous ai donnés, *ne les cachez pas*, expliquez-les à tous ceux qui le veulent'.

Finally, it should be observed that a crucial difference between the apocalypses and much of biblical literature is that the apocalypses, like most contemporary documents, were composed as books. The complexity of literary composition and of symbolic structures, together with the pseudepigraphical form, witness to this. That there was a great deal of traditional material behind them is doubtless; units of it can often be isolated within them. Yet the apocalypses were composed as works of

---

[266] That the Essene doctrines were secret is well known, compare the observations of M. Smith, *Clement of Alexandria*, 197-8 on 'Secrecy in Ancient Judaism'. Similarly, we have nothing of the writings of esoteric, Hellenistic sects.

[267] It might be held for the Apocalypse of John, see note 3, above. Some other works were not interested in eschatology. *1 Enoch* 92 regards its teaching as comfort and encouragement for the future righteous. Hengel, *Hellenism* 1, 209 dismisses this as a stylistic feature.

WORKS
of
Literature

literature and this fact must affect the considerations urged above as well as issues of form and literary criticism.[268]

PURPOSE AND FUNCTION OF THE APOCALYPSES

It seems to be most likely that there is no single answer to the question why and to serve what end the apocalypses were written. Some books are violently anti-Seleucid or anti-Roman and they were probably designed to play a role in political events.[269] Those such as Daniel, 4 Ezra and *2 Apocalypse of Baruch* whose primary concern lay upon the axis theodicy-eschatology usually bear within themselves part of the answers to these questions. For the other works, and for the non-eschatological materials in general, the answers are diverse. Thus, as noted above, astronomy and some calendaric materials are important to those involved in polemic about the calendar, but the function of certain types of cosmological and cosmogonic material is quite inscrutable.[270] Continuities pointed out with the *Merkabah* books serve to highlight this difficulty in the apocalypses.[271] One can only point to a certain common interest in revealed secrets: to the seer is made known that which even the angels did not know (*2 Enoch* 40:2-3 = Vaillant, 41). Of course, at the early stages, this 'scientific' knowledge may have been part of the intellectual culture of the day, with roots in priestly or certain wisdom concerns.[272] Nonetheless questions of its function in the apocalypses remain unsolved.

It might be possible to resolve some of these difficulties if more were known about the sort of socio-religious matrix in which these works were formed. Yet this remains obscure. It is clear that 4 Ezra, to select a simple example, was written after the destruction of the Temple in response to the acute problems arising from that destruction. Yet, how exactly this work functioned and to whom it was directed are questions the answers to which remain beyond our ken.[273] Most of the Enoch books were transmitted by

---

[268] See Russell, *Method and Message,* 118-19. See the observations of Reicke, 'Da'at'.

[269] This view is commonplace, see recently Russell, *Method and Message,* 17.

[270] See Stone, 'Lists', 443.

[271] Scholem, *Kabbalah,* 67-8; Hamerton-Kelly, 'Temple', 12-13 tries to explain these interests as deriving from a concern at the time of the Restoration for speculation about the heavenly Temple. This seems too slender a thread, and see on this tradition above, notes 23-24.

[272] See Stone, 'Third Century B.C.E.'

[273] Hartmann, *Prophecy Reinterpreted,* 51-52 in order to justify treatment of apocalypses by individual pericopes rather than by broader units, suggests that apocalypses may have been read portion by portion at meetings of apocalyptic groups. This is sheer speculation and not particularly persuasive. It may be possible to isolate such pericopes, but not on these grounds, cf. *ibid.,* 53-54 in practice. See also Picard, 'Observations' for some different speculations, equally unproven. Hanson, 'Apocalypticism', 31-33 attempts a 'historical-sociological sketch of apocalypticism'. This is a sociological ideology, distinct from the literary genre 'apocalypse' and from 'apocalyptic eschatology'. The proof of its existence is, alas, largely a matter of inference; see also Collins, *Apocalypse,* 4. Lebram, 'The Piety' attempts to use the character of paraenesis, implied or explicit, in certain apocalypses to infer something about the groups from which they originated. This attempt, in parts, is rather fanciful.

433

the Qumran covenanters (among others) but at least the earliest of them ante-date the foundation of the sect. They were not necessarily written by the Essenes. Again, it does not seem to be justified to extrapolate from the Qumran community to hypothesize *Sitze im Leben* for non-Essene writings. This is the more so because of the comparative dearth of apocalypses at Qumran.

The underlying problem of all the apocalypses, a recent study has urged, is that this world is disordered. The solution is expected from beyond it. The disorder is explicit in those works referring to the eschatological breakdown of social and cosmic order. Revelation that must come from outside to a pseudonymous sage of old, an eschatological solution of a radical character — these factors combine to suggest that 'this world is out of joint, one must look beyond it for a solution.' This, even if it is accepted in full, provides only a most general indication of purpose and function.[273a] The lack of specific knowledge still plagues us. A nuancing of this approach is the suggestion that the typical apocalyptic technique is the 'transposition of the frame of reference from the historical' and its setting in the perspective of a transcendent reality 'which is both spatial and temporal.'[273b] This leads to a possible resolution of the seer's problems.

From the above it follows that only with considerable difficulty can anything systematic be discerned about development within the genre. Given the antiquity of most of the parts of *1 Enoch* and of Daniel, and the definitely later date of 4 Ezra, *2 Apocalypse of Baruch* and *Apocalypse of Abraham*, certain observations can be made. The *Dream Visions of Enoch* and Daniel show reactions to the events surrounding the Maccabean revolt, with their strong emphasis upon the historical and political vision and almost exclusive interest in eschatology.[274] That the apocalypses did not originate with the Maccabean revolt is now clear from the date of the earliest Enoch manuscripts from Qumran. These third century writings show a much greater interest in speculative or 'scientific' matters than those of the time of the Maccabean revolt. Over against all these earliest books, perhaps in the later ones a greater penchant for fairly abstract formulations of problems of religious concern can be found. The former are more exclusively preoccupied with mythological or symbolic structures.[275] These observations, however, scarcely constitute an analysis of development, and

---

[273a] Collins, *Apocalypse,* 27; see also preceding note. Schmithals, *Apocalyptic Movement* speaks blithely of 'believers in apocalyptic' and 'the apocalyptic movement' (pp. 13 and 14-18), assuming their existence without any discussion of whether such was actually the case. See also *ibid.,* 46ff.

[273b] Collins, 'Apocalyptic Technique', 111.

[274] See Hengel, *Hellenism* 1, 181ff. for a characterization of the historical views of these early writings.

[275] The contrasts drawn by Hengel, *ibid.,* 346-7 seem to us not to penetrate to the heart of the differences.

the position of *2 Enoch, 2 Apocalypse of Baruch,* and the *Similitudes of Enoch,* to mention a few, remains obscure.

There exist certain halakhic references and other associated materials which serve to identify works which stem from circles which were close to, or different from what may be called 'proto-rabbinic' Judaism. Fairly obviously, the calendar serves as a clear indicator and thus *1 Enoch* is stamped as sectarian in particular by the *Book of the Luminaries* (chaps. 72-82, especially the self-consciousness expressed in ch. 82). Similarly the sectarian sacrificial practice referred to in *2 Enoch* has been noted above and witnesses to its origins. But these seem likely to be in different circles to those of *1 Enoch,* for its calendar differs from that book's. 4 Ezra is commonly regarded as particularly close to rabbinic Judaism. A similar relationship may be observed between *2 Apocalypse of Baruch* 10:19 (the virgins who weave the Temple veil) and the regulation in *M.Shekalim* 8:5.[276]

Indications such as these can help in the difficult task of placing these works in their social or religious setting within contemporary Judaism. Yet it is notable that, just as the apocalypses reflect the broad range of languages in which the Jews spoke and wrote — Hebrew, Aramaic and Greek — so too halakhic and ritual practices mentioned by them are indicative of different groups within and types of Judaism, even though all of these cannot be clearly identified. The broad spread of these works particularly highlights the importance of this type of literature in its age.

Concluding Comments

It is thus clear that the apocalypse was a chief literary expression in its time of the ecstatic, visionary, indeed mystical dimension of Judaism. It was one of the most typical of the forms of literature of the period of the Second Temple, which indicates the importance of this dimension of religious experience at the time. The special emphases of the apocalypses led to certain developments which were to prove most influential for subsequent Judaism and Christianity. The heightening of the eschatological element, typical of the apocalypses, has long been emphasized as central to the development of Christianity and the eschatological has remained one of the most persistent modes of the Christian religion.[277] Many of the apoca-

---

[276] See Lieberman, *Greek,* 104f.; and *id., Hellenism,* 167f.

[277] The literature on the Christian apocalypses is quite extensive. Much of it is to be found in Yarbro Collins, 'Early Christian Apocalypses'. A study of the interrelation of Jewish and Christian apocalypses of the Byzantine period is to be found in Himmelfarb, *Tours of Hell.* Some approaches to the dynamic of the shift from the earlier Jewish to the later Christian apocalypses is to be found in Geoltrain — Schmidt, 'De l'apocalyptique juive'. A learned study of one such development is Berger, *Daniel-Diegese.* It is not yet possibly finally to formulate the role of apocalyptic literature in gnostic origins. A number of the Nag Hammadi documents are apocalypses. See Robinson, *Nag Hammadi Library* and on gnostic apocalypses, Fallon,

lypses were actually preserved by the various Churches and Christianity produced abundant writings of this genre attributed to figures drawn alike from the New and Old Testaments.[278]

REJECT. BY RABBIS

In Judaism too, the apocalypses left a significant mark. Future hopes and expectations first so impressively formulated in some of the apocalypses became the normal way of expressing such aspirations.[279] The dynamic of Messianism became a part of the religious structure of Judaism and was to prove repeatedly influential in its development.[280] Structural and terminological links tie this literature to the *Merkabah* and *Hechalot* mystical books.[281] There are also Jewish apocalypses from the Byzantine and later periods.[282] The apocalypses of the Second Temple period, however, do not seem to have any vogue in Jewish circles in later ages for reasons which are not altogether clear.[283] The sectarian features of certain works doubtless put them in ill-favour, while anti-eschatological reactions to disastrous revolts and wars may also have been a factor in this.[284] Yet the almost total rejection of all the apocryphal and pseudepigraphical books in rabbinic circles may hint at a broader explanation.

BROADER CONCEPT, OF HISTOR. PROCESS

The apocalypses, by virtue of their grasp of history as a whole were able to operate with a far broader notion of the historical process than their predecessors.[285] They could thus engage in periodization, in the division into sections of what had earlier been conceived as an on-going dynamic.[286] The division of history into eras or periods made possible the

'Gnostic Apocalypses', and further bibliography there, Apocalyptic elements have been discerned in gnostic texts; such are the eschatological elements that are discussed by MacRae, 'Apocalyptic in Gnosticism', 5ff. See also Attridge, 'Gnosticism and Eschatology'. For Graeco-Roman and Persian examples, see Collins, *Apocalypse,* 12-13; 207-18 and Attridge, 'Latin Apocalypses'.

[278] Hennecke—Schneemelcher, *New Testament Apocrypha;* Tischendorf, *Apocalypses Apocryphae.*

[279] Bloch, *The Apocalyptic in Judaism,* traces some of these developments, perhaps too enthusiastically.

[280] Scholem's remarks in *Messianic Idea,* 1-36 are particularly important.

[281] There have been a number of articles on the relationship of messianism and mysticism in Judaism, particularly in the debate between Scholem and Tishby. On this, see most recently Werblowsky, 'Mysticism'. On other aspects of the relationship between apocalypticism and the *Merkabah* books, see Gruenwald, *Apocalyptic,* 12-13.

[282] Even-Shmuel, *Midreshei Ge'ulah* conveniently collects this material. For a survey of some rabbinic works, apocalypses by genre, see Saldarini, 'Rabbinic Literature'.

[283] Ginzberg, 'Attitude of the Synagogue' expresses an extreme view. Other suggestions are made by Gruenwald, 'Jewish Apocalyptic'. See also, for a more synthetic attempt to resolve this issue, Saldarini, 'Apocalyptic and Rabbinic'.

[284] Changing attitudes to Scripture and inspiration do not seem to have prevented the composition of the *Merkabah* books or the later Jewish apocalypses.

[285] Compare discussion and bibliography in Russell, *Method and Message,* 217ff.

[286] Contrast von Rad's view, *Wisdom,* 267ff. These observations remain true whether or not periodization ultimately went back to non-Jewish sources, see bibliography in Hengel, *Hellenism* 1, 182f. On some possible biblical foreshadowing of such calculations, see Russell,

formulation of this process in terms of an encompassing theory of history. It follows, of course, that the periodization of history was a function of the search for its meaning. Knotty theological issues — divine justice, providence, reward and punishment, the nature of man and the function of Israel — proved amenable to solution for their day in these terms. In the historical apocalypses meaning was found in history viewed as a totality and not sought in its discrete events.

When events, typically the destruction of the Temple, were such as to demand immediate response and therefore could not be satisfactorily answered in terms of the overall understanding of the historical process, various responses could be made. The event could be viewed as a cosmic one (*2 Apoc. Bar.* 3:5ff); it could be claimed to be, in fact, less important than it seemed by transferring its true meaning to the metahistorical realm (*ibid.* 4:2-7) or, finally, the question could be removed to more abstract conceptual levels, thus becoming theological in character (4 Ezra *passim*).

The apocalypses, therefore, beyond their importance as illustrating a stage in the historical development of certain streams of religiosity in Judaism, also show a bold attempt to reach a view encompassing the whole historical process, from creation to eschaton. This is made possible in part by the greater willingness they evince to talk of the supra-human and to emphasize the roles of the heavenly protagonists in the cosmic drama. There is, therefore, in this a partial re-mythologization of Judaism, in which the historical as the arena of divine action remains, but remains removed to a different level of comprehensiveness. The re-mythologization is in part due to a surfacing of older religious ideas not evident in biblical literature. The new religious atmosphere of the Hellenistic age also contributed to it, and the apocalypses are truly children of their age.

NB

BIBLIOGRAPHY

Apocalypse and the Bible

On biblical antecedents see KAUFMANN, 'Apokalyptik'; FROST, *Old Testament Apocalyptic;* cf. also KAUFMANN, *Toledot* 7, 504-5; 8, 232. The role of Zechariah is stressed by UFFENHEIMER, *Visions of Zechariah* and HANSON, 'Zechariah 9.' The function of speculations about a heavenly Jerusalem is

Method and Message, 207 and on the periodization in Cross, *Canaanite Myth,* 295-6, 305. An important article on periodization is that of Licht, 'Theory of Ages' and see also his 'Time and Eschatology'. Schmithals (*Apocalyptic Movement, passim*) would, with clear theological *Tendenz,* make all elements of the apocalypses subservient to the category of 'history'. This, we submit, does not cohere with the realities to be observed in the apocalypses. See above, note 38. An important analysis in terms of type and function of apocalyptic timetables is Hartmann, 'Timetables'.

discussed, with further bibliography, by STONE, 'Lists,' 445-6. On the position of Deutero-Isaiah, see CROSS, *Canaanite Myth,* 99-111; VON DER OSTEN-SACKEN, *Die Apokalyptik,* 18ff.; COLLINS, 'Apocalyptic Eschatology,' attempted to characterize the distinguishing element of apocalyptic eschatology, while HANSON, *Dawn,* stressed its development out of late prophetic eschatology. The debate is reviewed by KOCH, *Rediscovery.* The implication of the existence in *1 Enoch* 14 of a speculative tradition rooted in Ezekiel 1, was noted by SCHOLEM, *Major Trends,* 40-63; see also GRUENWALD, *Apocalyptic,* 32-37. Some implications of the early date of this are drawn in STONE, 'Third Century B.C.E.,' 488; *id., Scriptures,* 32-4.

On Wisdom and Apocalyptic: VON RAD pressed the view that apocalyptic arose out of wisdom, see *Theologie* 2, 317-21; *id., Wisdom,* 272-83. Critiques of this are Vielhauer, 'Apocalyptic', 597; KOCH, *Rediscovery,* 36-48; VON DER OSTEN-SACKEN, *Die Apokalyptik,* 9-12. Recently emphasis has been laid on the role of Israelite mantic wisdom in apocalyptic origins by MÜLLER, *Ursprünge;* cf. COLLINS, 'Cosmos and Salvation.'

On apocalyptic as fulfilment of prophecy, see RUSSELL, *Method and Message,* 178-85; HARTMANN, *Prophecy Interpreted; id., Asking for a Meaning,* 7-12. GRUENWALD, *Apocalyptic,* 19-25, sees an esoteric interpretation of Scripture as lying at the heart of apocalyptic.

On foreign influences in apocalyptic origins: the Iranian influence on the origins of apocalyptic literature and thought is an old theory. Summary statements and bibliography are to be found in DUCHESNE-GUILLEMIN, *Religion de l'Iran,* 257-64; WINSTON, 'Iranian Component' and most recently HULTGÅRD, 'Das Judentum und die iranische Religion.' Greek influence is urged by GLASSON, *Greek Influence,* and is thoroughly reassessed by HENGEL, *Hellenism.* Near Eastern elements have been stressed by HANSON, *Dawn;* COLLINS, 'Hellenistic Near Eastern Environment.' Akkadian influences have been suggested by HALLO, 'Akkadian Apocalypses'; LAMBERT, 'History and the Gods,' 175-7; *id., Background;* while MCCOWN has noted Egyptian influences in 'Egyptian Apocalyptic.' Mesopotamian features of the early speculative tradition in the Enoch literature have also been discussed: See JANSEN, *Henochgestalt;* GRELOT, 'Légende d'Henoch'; *id.,* 'Géographie mythique'; STONE, 'Third Century B.C.E.'; *id.,* Scriptures, 39-49. The antiquity of this material and its importance for apocalyptic origins is stressed in STONE, 'Lists.'

Definition and Description

On the problematic, with a discussion of past views, see STONE, 'Lists,' 439-43; KOCH, *Rediscovery,* particularly pp. 15ff., 19-30. COLLINS, *Apoca-*

lypse, is a systematic attempt to reach a genre definition. See also BETZ, 'Religio-Historical Understanding,' 134-5.

The Apocalypses

English translations are to be found in CHARLES, *APOT;* introductory material in CHARLESWORTH, *Modern Research;* DENIS, *Introduction;* articles in *IDB, DBS* and *EJ;* NICKELSBURG, *Jewish Literature.* These are not cited in the following sections, nor are translations into other languages. A new English translation apeared in Charlesworth, *Pseudepigrapha.* Among histories of research, note SCHMIDT, *Die jüdische Apokalyptik;* KOCH, *Rediscovery;* others also exist.

Fragments in ancient sources are assembled in Fabricius, *Codex Pseudepigraphus;* JAMES, *Lost Apocrypha;* STONE-STRUGNELL, *Elijah.* Qumran fragments are listed by FITZMYER, *Tools;* compare CARMIGNAC, 'Apocalyptique'. EISSFELDT, *Introduction.*

1 Enoch: Ethiopic text most recently in KNIBB, *Ethiopic Enoch;* Greek texts in FLEMING-RADEMACHER, *Das Buch Henoch;* BONNER, *Last Chapters;* Aramaic texts from Qumran in MILIK, *Books of Enoch.* Bibliographical survey in NICKELSBURG, 'Enoch in Recent Research.' Book of Giants in MILIK, 'Turfan et Qumran', Critical studies are very numerous, particularly in recent years, during which many critiques of Milik's views have been published. See GREENFIELD-STONE, 'Enochic Pentateuch,' and 'Books and Traditions of Enoch'; KNIBB, 'Date of the Parables.' On the figure of Enoch, see GRELOT, 'Légende d'Henoch'; JANSEN, *Henochgestalt;* STONE, 'Lists,' 444-5; GREENFIELD, 'Prolegomena.' On chapters 1-5 see HARTMANN, *Asking for a Meaning;* on chapters 6-19 see DIMANT, *Fallen Angels;* HANSON, 'Rebellion'; NICKELSBURG, 'Apocalyptic and Myth.' On Similitudes see SJÖBERG, *Menschensohn;* SUTER, *Parables of Enoch;* on Luminaries, MILIK, *Ten Years of Discovery,* 107-13; on Dream-visions see KLIJN, 'Creation to Noah'; FLUSSER, 'Seventy Sheperds'; on Epistle see NICKELSBURG, '1 Enoch 92-105'; on Apocalypse of Weeks see DEXINGER, *Zehnwochenapokalypse.*

2 Enoch: edition and translation VAILLANT, *Sécrets d'Hénoch.*Studies are: PINES, 'Concept of Time'; RUBINSTEIN, 'Slavonic Book of Enoch'; SCHOLEM, *Ursprung,* 64-5. On the Melchizedek fragment see MILIK, 'Milki-sedeq,' 96-126; FITZMYER, *Semitic Background,* 221-67.

2 Apocalypse of Baruch: text in BIDAWID, *Peshitta* IV,3; translation and extensive commentary BOGAERT, *L'Apocalypse de Baruch.* On text see VIOLET, *Apokalypsen,* LVI-LXII, See also CHARLES, *Apocalypse of Baruch;* KLIJN, 'Baruch'; NICKELSBURG, 'Narrative Traditions.'

3 Apocalypse of Baruch: Greek text most recently in PICARD, *Apocalypsis Baruchi;* concordance by DENIS-JANSSENS. Studies by JAMES, *Apocrypha Anecdota* 2, LI-LXXI; PICARD, 'Observations'; GINZBERG, 'Baruch.'

4 Ezra: texts in VIOLET, *Esra-Apokalypse;* see STONE, 'Textual Criticism'; BIDAWID, *Peshitta* VI,3; STONE, 'New Manuscript'; *id., Armenian IV Ezra;* RUBINKIEWICZ, 'Un fragment.' Translations and commentaries abound; note the following: BOX, *Ezra-Apocalypse;* VIOLET, *Apokalypsen;* MYERS, *Esdras.* Particular points are examined in KEULERS, *Eschatologische Lehre;* THOMPSON, *Responsibility for Evil;* HARNISCH, *Verhängnis.* Literary and other issues are examined by BREECH, 'Function of 4 Ezra'; HAYMAN, 'Problem of Pseudonomity': STONE, 'Reactions to Destructions'; *id.,* 'Messiah in IV Ezra.'

Apocalypse of Abraham: for texts, translations and commentary see BONWETSCH, *Apokalypse Abrahams;* BOX, *Apocalypse of Abraham.* Studies include: GINZBERG, *Apocalypse of Abraham;* TURDEANU, 'L'Apocalypse d'Abraham'; RUBINSTEIN, 'Hebraisms'; *id.,* 'Problematic Passage.'

Apocalypses and Other Genres

On Apocalypse and Testament see COLLINS, *Apocalypse,* 1-20; KOLENKOW, 'The Assumption of Moses as a Testament'; VON NORDHEIM, *Das Testament.*

On the Testaments of the Twelve Patriarchs: summaries of recent research may be found in DE JONGE, 'Recent Studies'; *id., Studies on the Testaments.* For a history of scholarship, see SLINGERLAND, 'Patriarchs Research.' See in this volume, chap. 8.

On the Testament of Moses see CHARLES, *Assumption of Moses;* LAPERROUSAZ, 'Testament de Moïse'; LICHT, 'Taxo'; NICKELSBURG, *Testament of Moses.* See also in this volume chap. 8.

On Oracles see COLLINS, *Sibylline Oracles;* WINDISCH, 'Orakel'; WIDENGREN, 'Iran and Israel,' 172-7; HENGEL, *Hellenism* 1, 184-6. See also this volume, chap. 9.

Features of Apocalypses

Pseudepigraphy: Hellenistic pseudepigraphy in general is discussed by SPEYER, *Die Literarische Falschung.* See also HENGEL, *Hellenism* 1, 205-6; on Jewish pseudepigraphy see METZGER, 'Literary Forgeries'; RUSSELL, *Method and Message,* 127-39; KAUFMANN, *Toledot* 8, 398-9; COLLINS, 'Pseudonymity,' 331-2; *id.,* 'Introduction,' 12.

Inspiration: on Hellenistic inspiration experience, see DODDS, *Greeks and the Irrational;* for Jewish material, see RUSSELL, *Method and Message,* 158-77; GUNKEL in KAUTZSCH, *Apokryphen* 2, 340-3; STONE, 'Vision or Hallucination?'

Esotericism: RUSSELL, *Method and Message,* 107-18, discusses various aspects of this; HENGEL, *Hellenism* 1, 210 also emphasizes its occurrence in Hellenistic writings. Other aspects are stressed by GRUENWALD, 'Esoteric Writings'; SMITH, *Clement of Alexandria,* 197-8.

On periodization of history, see VON RAD, *Wisdom,* 267ff; HENGEL, *Hellenism* 1, 182-3. On its biblical origins see CROSS, *Canaanite Myth,* 295-6, 305. In general see the important papers of LICHT, 'Theory of Ages' and 'Time and Eschatology'. On the purpose and function of periodization, see HARTMANN, 'Timetables.'

Concluding Comments

On early Christian and gnostic apocalypses see YARBRO COLLINS, 'Early Christian Apocalypses' and sources cited there; HIMMELFARB, *Tours of Hell;* MACRAE, 'Apocalyptic in Gnosticism.'

On later Jewish apocalypses see BLOCH, *The Apocalyptic in Judaism;* SCHOLEM, *Messianic Idea,* 1-36; texts in EVEN-SHMUEL, *Midreshei Geulah.* On rabbinic attitudes to apocalyptic see GINZBERG, 'Attitude of the Synagogue'; SALDARINI, 'Apocalyptic and Rabbinic.'

The proceedings of the Uppsala Colloquium on Apocalypticism (Hellholm, *Apocalypticism*) were graciously made available to the writer in proof by the editor. Unfortunately they arrived too late to be integrated fully into the text and notes. The volume as a whole represents an extraordinary resource and stimulus for future students of the subject and will be of great import for the development of scholarship. It presents a wealth of information about apocalypticism in Judaism and Christianity, and also in other Mediterranean and Near Eastern cultures, as well as essays on theological, phenomenological and other second-order problems. Many of the problems and issues raised in the course of the present chapter are illuminated by papers in that volume, although in the final analysis the issues both of origin and definition remained unsolved.

Chapter Eleven

Jewish Sources in Gnostic Literature

Birger A. Pearson

Introduction: The Problem of Jewish Gnosticism

It is widely acknowledged that Gnosticism, especially in its earliest forms, displays a fundamental indebtedness to Jewish concepts and traditions. This fact has been made all the more evident as a result of the discovery and publication of the Coptic texts from Nag Hammadi.[1] Indeed, some scholars, the present author included, have argued that Gnosticism takes its origin from within Judaism.[2] Other scholars argue with considerable force that such a thing is improbable, if not impossible.[3] Still others, for very good reasons, take a broader view of Gnosticism, and speak of various forms of the Gnostic religion: Jewish, Christian, and pagan. In this view one can legitimately speak of a Jewish Gnosticism,[4] as well as Christian and other forms of Gnosticism. The Jewish forms of Gnosticism should, in any case, be differentiated from the kind of Jewish Gnosticism described

---

[1] References to the Nag Hammadi texts are according to the *Facsimile Edition* edited by Robinson (*NHC*), by codex (Roman numeral), manuscript page and line. For an English translation of all of the tractates in the Nag Hammadi corpus, plus those in the Berlin Gnostic Codex (*BG* 8502), with brief introductions, see Robinson, *Nag Hammadi Library.* Quotations from Nag Hammadi texts in this article have been taken from that volume, except where otherwise noted. For a full bibliography on the Nag Hammadi Codices, and on Gnosticism in general, see Scholer, *Nag Hammadi Bibliography.*

[2] An early proponent of this view was Friedländer, *Der vorchristliche Gnosticismus;* cf. Pearson, 'Friedländer Revisited.' For discussion of more recent studies, until 1970, see Rudolph, 'Forschungsbericht,' *TR* 36 (1971) 89-119. See also e.g. Rudolph, *Gnosis,* 275-82; Quispel, 'Origins,' and 'Gnosis,' 416-25; MacRae, 'Jewish Background,' esp. 97-101; Dahl, 'Arrogant Archon'; Pearson, 'Jewish Haggadic Traditions,' esp. 469-70, and 'Jewish Elements in Gnosticism,' esp. 159-60. Stroumsa's important dissertation should also be mentioned here: *Another Seed.* Stroumsa traces the key notions in Sethian Gnosticism to Jewish sources.

[3] See esp. Jonas, *Philosophical Essays,* 274, 277-90; Van Unnik, 'Die jüdischen Komponente.' More recent studies in which the Jewish factor is downplayed are nevertheless also more ambiguous on the question. See e.g. Maier, 'Jüdische Faktoren'; Yamauchi, 'Jewish Gnosticism?'; Gruenwald, 'Jewish-Gnostic Controversy,' and 'Jewish Merkavah Mysticism.' In the last-named article, for example, Gruenwald takes issue with my contention that Gnosticism 'originates *in a Jewish environment*' (p. 44, italics his), yet eight pages later expresses his agreement with Rudolph that 'Gnosticism emerged from a Jewish matrix' (p. 52).

[4] See e.g. Stone, *Scriptures,* 99-103.

by Scholem in one of his famous books,[5] which can more conveniently be described as Jewish mysticism.[6]

The relationship between the Gnostic religion of late antiquity and Judaism is especially difficult to assess. Gnosticism is, in any case, a religion in its own right,[7] and there are good reasons for using such a designation as the Gnostic religion instead of Gnosticism or Gnosis, terms which are susceptible of imprecise usage in scholarly discourse.[8] The basic reason for the difficulty in assessing the relationship between the Gnostic religion and Judaism is that the former is essentially anti-Jewish in its intentionality. The Gnostic spirit is radically anti-cosmic and revolutionary in all of its modes of expression.[9] Judaism, on the other hand, is the clearest expression in late antiquity of the religious affirmation of the cosmos, with its doctrine of the one and only God, Creator of heaven and earth. Thus, it seems hardly possible to speak of a Gnostic Judaism; this would imply a contradiction in terms.[10] And if one can speak of Jewish forms of Gnosticism, as I think it is quite appropriate to do, it is still necessary to bear in mind that such a thing implies a revolutionary protest, on the part of the actual Jews involved, against their own traditions, indeed an apostasy from Judaism.

It is one of the curiosities of the religious history of late antiquity that certain Jewish intellectuals apparently could and did utilize the materials of their ancient religion — Bible and extra-biblical sources and traditions of various kinds — in order to give expression to a new, anti-cosmic religion of transcendental *gnosis*. To be sure, it is the Christian forms of the Gnostic religion which are the most well-known and whose materials are the most abundant. It was in the second century C.E. — wherein most of out extant Gnostic sources can be situated historically — that the essential decisions were made in ecclesiastical circles regarding the basic forms the Christian religion would take. There is some irony, too, in the fact that Christianity, which had made its own moves away from its Jewish roots, was compelled to reaffirm the basic pro-cosmicism inherent in Jewish monotheism,[11] with

[5] *Jewish Gnosticism.*

[6] See e.g. Jonas, *Philosophical Essays,* 288; Gruenwald, 'Jewish Merkavah Mysticism,' 41-42. Cf. also Gruenwald's monograph, *Apocalyptic,* 110.

[7] The best full-length studies on the Gnostic religion as a whole are Jonas, *Gnostic Religion,* and Rudolph, *Gnosis.*

[8] Cf. the attempt at defining Gnosticism put forward at the Messina Colloquium on the Origins of Gnosticism, in Bianchi, *Le origini dello gnosticismo,* xxvi-xxix. Cf. Rudolph's criticisms in 'Forschungsbericht,' *TR* 36 (1971) 13-22.

[9] See esp. Jonas, *Philosophical Essays,* 272-4. Dahl rightly calls attention to the fact that the Gnostic revolt is directed above all against the Creator of the cosmos. See 'Arrogant Archon,' esp. p. 689.

[10] These issues are treated with considerable perspicacity by Tröger, 'Attitude towards Judaism,' and 'Frühjudentum und Gnosis,' esp. p. 318.

[11] See Bauer's remarks on the retention of the Old Testament in ecclesiastical Christianity over against Gnostics and other heretics: *Orthodoxy and Heresy,* 195-202.

the concomitant result that the anti-Jewish thrust in Christian Gnostic texts can frequently be taken as directed against the growing Christian ecclesiastical establishment rather than against Judaism *per se*.[12] One of the problems involved in attempting to identify Jewish or Jewish Gnostic sources in Gnostic literature, therefore, is that the basic texts available frequently (though not always!) appear in Christian dress.[13]

In what follows, I shall begin simply by listing the titles of books found in association with Gnostic groups, or referred to in Gnostic texts, titles of known Jewish books or of unknown books arguably of Jewish or Jewish Gnostic origin. I shall then give examples of how Jewish texts are utilized in Gnostic literature, with special attention to the Enoch literature. Moving to more controversial ground, I shall give examples of Jewish or Jewish Gnostic sources which seem to be imbedded in Christian Gnostic documents. I shall also take up the problem of the christianization of Gnostic texts. Finally, I shall focus our attention on some extant Gnostic documents which can, in their entirety, be designated as Jewish Gnostic texts, rather than Christian Gnostic or pagan Gnostic. From all of this some conclusions can then be drawn on the entire question of the utilization of Jewish sources in Gnostic literature.

Jewish Sources Cited by Name

The Gnostics' use of the Old Testament — not only Genesis but other books as well — is too well-known to come under consideration here.[14] We shall restrict ourselves, therefore, to extracanonical literature, first with reference to the heresiologists' accounts of the various Gnostic groups known to them. Epiphanius (fourth century) happens to be our richest source for this purpose. To be sure, Irenaeus (second century) had already indicated that the Gnostic make use of 'an unspeakable number of apocryphal and spurious writings,'[15] but Epiphanius supplies us with actual names.

'Apocalypses of Adam' are said to have been in use among the Nicolaitan Gnostics (*Haer.* 26:8,1), and we may surmise that the Gnostic *Apocalypse of Adam* now known from the Nag Hammadi discovery was one of these,[16] as well (perhaps) as the other *Apocalypse of Adam,* presumably a

---

[12] Tröger, 'Attitude towards Judaism,' 89-90.

[13] It is for this reason, in fact, that some scholars have denied the existence of a pre-Christian, Jewish Gnosticism. See e.g. Yamauchi, 'Pre-Christian Gnosticism?' and *Pre-Christian Gnosticism.*

[14] See e.g. Wilson, 'Gnostics and the OT,' and several of the essays in Tröger, *Altes Testament.* See also the article on the Gnostic use of the Bible in *Compendia* II/1 (forthcoming).

[15] *Inerrabilem multitudinem aprocryphorum et perperum scripturarum* (*Adv. Haer.* 1:20,1, with reference to the Marcosians).

[16] On *Apoc. Adam* see discussion below. See also, below, discussion of the Cologne Mani Codex.

Jewish apocryphon, known from various patristic sources.[17] The same group used a 'Gospel of Eve' and 'many books in the name of Seth' (*Haer.* 26:8, 1). The latter would certainly have included strictly Gnostic material ('Ialdabaoth' is mentioned in connection with them, *ibid.*) and a number of books in the name of Seth are now to be found in the Nag Hammadi Corpus.[18] Non-Gnostic Jewish books in the name of Seth also circulated in late antiquity,[19] though we have no way of knowing whether such were included in the Nicolaitan library.[20] A book of 'Noria' is said to have been used among these same Gnostics (*Haer.* 26:1, 4-9), consisting of a fanciful retelling of the story of Noah's ark, 'Noria' in this instance being Noah's wife.[21]

Epiphanius records that books in the name of Seth and Allogenes (= Seth) were in use among the Sethians and the closely-related Archontics (*Haer.* 39:5, 1; 40:2, 2; 40:7, 4).[22] These books were probably, in the main, Gnostic compositions, but it cannot be excluded that non-Gnostic Jewish Seth books were also in use.[23] Books in the name of Moses were also to be found in these Gnostics' libraries (*Haer.* 39:5,1), and these may have included such Jewish apocryphal writings as the *Testament of Moses,* the *Assumption of Moses,* and the Adam-book now known as the *Apocalypse of Moses,* as well as others.[24] The *Ascension of Isaiah* is listed by Epiphanius among the book used by the Archontics (*Haer.* 40:2, 2), and it is to be noted that this is not a Gnostic book.[25]

One other book cited by name by Epiphanius as in use among the Sethian Gnostics (*Haer.* 39:5,1) is an *Apocalypse of Abraham.* This document may have been the same apocryphon as the non-Gnostic Jewish

---

[17] Cf. James, *Lost Apocrypha,* 7-8; Denis, *Introduction,* 11-12; Stone, *Armenian Apocrypha,* 44-45.

[18] The *Gospel of the Egyptians* (III, 68, 1-3); the *Second Treatise of the Great Seth;* the *Three Steles of Seth* and *Allogenes.* Cf. Pearson, 'The Figure of Seth,' 491-6; and Tardieu, 'Les Livres de Seth.'

[19] Cf. *2 Enoch* 33:10, and Klijn, *Seth,* 112. Cf. also below, on the apocalypses of Seth cited in the Cologne Mani Codex.

[20] The 'Gospel of Eve' sounds like a purely Gnostic work, whose title reflects the appropriation by the Gnostics of the Christian use of the term 'gospel' as a literary designation. Cf. James, *Lost Apocrypha,* 8; Denis, *Introduction,* 302.

[21] On Norea and the various books related to this figure see below, pp. 464-9. Cf. also Denis, *Introduction,* 301.

[22] Cf. Pearson, 'The Figure of Seth,' 495.

[23] Cf. n. 19, above.

[24] On the *Testament of Moses* and the *Assumption of Moses* see the articles in Nickelsburg, *Studies on the Testament of Moses,* and Denis, *Introduction,* 128-41; cf. also above pp. 344-9. On the *Apocalypse of Moses* see e.g. Denis, *Introduction,* 3-7. For another Moses book cited in a Gnostic source, of a sort which may also have been in use among the Sethians, see below, on the 'Archangelikē of Moses the Prophet,' cited in *Orig. World.*

[25] See e.g. Denis, *Introduction,* 170-6; Hennecke-Schneemelcher, *Apocrypha* 2, 642-63; cf. Nickelsburg, above p. 52-56 (on the *Martyrdom of Isaiah,* of which the *Ascension of Isaiah* is now a part).

apocryphon under that name now extant in Slavonic.[26] It is more likely, however, that the Sethian *Apocalypse of Abraham* was a Gnostic work, in view of the very interesting (though late) information supplied by Theodore Bar Konai (8th century) regarding the Audians, a Gnostic sect which seems to have been closely related to the Sethian Gnostics, and who used 'an apocalypse under the name of Abraham'. This apocryphal work, in typically Gnostic fashion, attributed the creation of the world to 'Darkness' and six other 'powers'.[27]

The church father Hippolytus does not provide much information of use to us in the present connection, but his notices about the *Paraphrase of Seth* (*Ref.* 5:19, 1-22, 1) in use among the Sethian Gnostics should be mentioned here, as well as his discussion of the Gnostic book entitled *Baruch* (*Ref.* 5:26, 1-27, 5). These items are discussed elsewhere in this article.[28]

Clement of Alexandria provides some information of possible relevance. He informs us that Isidore, the son and disciple of Basilides, wrote a book called *Expositions of the Prophet Parchor,* in which he refers to the views of Pherecydes, who in turn was dependent upon 'the prophecy of Ham.'[29] While both Parchor and Ham have been placed in the company of Jewish apocrypha,[30] it might be better to accept the view of James and others that the 'prophecy of Ham' was some sort of alchemical writing. Who the prophet Parchor was is anybody's guess.[31]

In our primary sources, i.e. the extant Gnostic literature, it is rather rare to find specific references to sources utilized, or the names of books to which the reader might turn for further information. One such example can be found, however, in the *Apocryphon of John* (*NHC* II, 19,6-10): 'Now there are other ones (i.e. angels) over the remaining passions whom I did not mention to you. But if you wish to know them, it is written in the Book of Zoroaster.' Which 'Book of Zoroaster' is referred to here (there were

---

[26] See e.g. Denis, *Introduction,* 37-38; Collins, *Apocalypses,* 36-37; cf. above pp. 415-8.

[27] See esp. Puech, 'Fragments retrouvés,' 273. The Audians also had a work called the Apocalypse (*gelyōneh*) or Book (*kᵉtābā*) of the Strangers (*dᵉnukrāyē*), which told of the seduction of Eve by the archons (Puech *ibid.,* 274); see now the discussion by Stroumsa, *Another Seed,* 58-60. This book may, indeed, have been identical to one of the Allogenes books used by the Archontic (Sethian) Gnostics, according to Epiphanius, who uses the plural form *Allogeneis* in his discussion: *Haer.* 40:2, 2 (Archontics); 39:5, 1 (Sethians). Allogenes ('stranger') is a Gnostic name for Seth. Cf. Pearson, 'The Figure of Seth,' 486. It should be noted that Epiphanius' discussion of the Audians (*Haer.* 70) is clearly deficient; for example, one could not guess, from the information given by him, that the Audians were Gnostics.

[28] On the *Paraphrase of Seth* see the discussion of the *Paraphrase of Shem,* below, p. 475. On *Baruch* see below, p. 470, and n. 177.

[29] *Strom.* 6:6, 53, 5. Cf. Foerster, *Gnosis 2,* 82.

[30] Cf. Oepke, 'Βίβλοι ἀπόκρυφοι in Christianity', 994.

[31] Cf. James, *Lost Apocrypha,* 16, on Ham. Parchor may be the same as Barkōph, who with Barkabbas is named as a Basilidian prophet by Eusebius (*Hist. eccl.* 4: 7, 7). Barkabbas is named as a prophet of the Nicolaitan Gnostics by Epiphanius (*Haer.* 26:2, 2).

apparently many in circulation in Gnostic groups in late antiquity)[32] we have no way of knowing. That it might have had a Jewish colouration is not to be excluded as a possibility.[33]

One Nag Hammadi tractate has a number of references to other books, some of which may be of Jewish origin or colouration. I refer to the treatise *On the Origin of the World,* wherein reference is made to the following titles: 1. 'The Archangelikē of Moses the Prophet' (II, 102, 8-9); 2. 'The First Book of Noraia' (102, 10-11) = 'The First Logos of Noraia' (102, 24-25); 3. 'The Book of Solomon' (107, 3); 4. 'The Seventh Cosmos of Hieralaias the Prophet' (112, 23-25); 5. 'The Schēmata of the Heimarmenē of the Heaven Which is Beneath the Twelve' (107, 16-16); and 6. 'The Holy Book' (110, 20; 122, 12-13).

The first-named book may have some connection with a magical text edited by Reitzenstein, an 'archangelic hymn which God gave to Moses on Mt. Sinai.'[34] The second one recalls the 'Book of Noria' already cited in connection with the Nicolaitan Gnostics known to Epiphanius.[35] It has also been suggested that a Noraia book may have been used as one of the sources for the *Hypostasis of the Archons,*[36] a document which not only displays a considerable Jewish colouration, but also stands in close relationship to *Orig. World.* The *Thought of Norea* may also be cited in this connection, for this short tractate may be based upon a previously-existing Noraia book; it also stands in a close relationship with *Hyp. Arch.*[37]

The third in our list has as its subject 'forty-nine androgynous demons' with their names and functions (IX, 106, 27-107, 3), and appears to have been one of a number of Solomon books associated with magic, astrology, and demonology circulating in late antiquity.[38] The *Testament of Solomon* comes readily to mind in this connection.[39] As for the other books men-

---

[32] See e.g. Porphyry, *Vit. Plot.* 16; Clem. Alex., *Strom.* 1:15, 69, 6. Cf. Giversen, *Apocryphon Johannis,* 253. The colophon to *Zostrianos* (*NHC* VIII, 1:132, 9) concludes with the phrase, 'Words of Zoroaster.'

[33] The suggested content of the book referred to, i.e. the role of the angels in creating man, and the various passions ruled by the angels, is surely compatible with a Jewish provenience. Cf. e.g. Philo *Fug.* 78-70 and *T. Reuben* 2-3. Zoroaster was sometimes identified with the biblical Seth. Cf. Bousset, *Hauptprobleme,* 378-82. For further discussion of *Ap. John,* see below.

[34] ὕμνος ἀρχαγγελικός, ὃν ἔδωκεν ὁ θεὸς τῷ Μωυσῇ ἐν τῷ ὄρει Σινᾷ (Reitzenstein, *Poimandres,* 292). Cf. Böhlig, *Schrift ohne Titel,* 32.

[35] Above, p. 446.

[36] On *Hyp. Arch.* see discussion below. Cf. also Böhlig, *Schrift ohne Titel,* 32.

[37] See Pearson, *Nag Hammadi Codices IX and X,* 87-99, esp. 89.

[38] Böhlig, *Schrift ohne Titel,* 32. Cf. Doresse, *Secret Books,* 170, 172; Reitzenstein, *Poimandres,* 295.

[39] See McCown, *The Testament of Solomon,* and Conybeare, 'Testament of Solomon'. On Solomonic books of magic in antiquity see e.g. McCown, *Testament of Solomon,* 90-104; cf. also the list of pseudo-Solomonic works in *J.E.* 11, 446-8. See now also D. C. Duling in Charlesworth, *Pseudopigrapha* 1, 935-87.

tioned, we are pretty much in the dark.[40] 'Hieralaias the prophet' is otherwise unknown. The subject of his book is apparently cosmology (cf. 112, 10-25), as is that of the 'Schēmata,' which also refers to the various 'good powers' which inhabit the various levels of the cosmos (cf. 107, 4-17). 'The Holy Book' is a Gnostic document of Jewish colouration.[41]

In *Pistis Sophia*, a Coptic Gnostic manuscript (the Askew Codex) discovered in the 18th century, Jesus is quoted as follows:[42]

> Because even for the righteous themselves who have never done evil
> (= the Gnostics), and have not committed sins at all, it is necessary
> that they should find the mysteries which are in the Books of Jeu,
> which I caused Enoch to write in Paradise when I spoke with him
> from the Tree of Knowledge and from the Tree of Life. And I caused
> him to place them in the rock of Ararad, and I placed the archon
> Kalapatauroth, which is over Gemmut, upon whose head are the feet
> of Jeu, and who goes round all the aeons and the *Heimarmene* (i.e.
> Fate). I placed that archon to watch over the Books of Jeu because of
> the Flood, so that none of the archons should envy them and destroy
> them. (Book 3, ch. 134)

This information is not easy to untangle. We know of two Gnostic 'Books of Jeu,' extant in the Bruce Codex,[43] but these are not expressly attributed to Enoch. On the other hand, there may be a possible allusion here to various traditions circulating under the name of Enoch, presumably in Egypt,[44] related to the Jewish Enoch literature. The Qumran fragments of the Enochic *Book of Giants* refer to Enoch sending from Paradise two tablets containing ante-diluvian wisdom and warning of the flood to come.[45] And the figure of the divine 'Jeu' referred to here may be derived from the traditions known to us from the mystical Enoch literature

---

[40] Cf. Doresse's interesting but speculative discussion, *Secret Books,* 171-4.

[41] The quotation from it in *Orig. World* (II,110,31-111,1) presents a typically Gnostic interpretation of the tree of knowledge in Paradise. The context of the second reference to this book (121,35-123,1) refers to three phoenixes of Paradise, and 'the hydria in Egypt.' Böhlig rightly emends the text at 122,18-19 to read *nnhydr[i]a*, translating the word as *Wasserschlangen* (*Schrift ohne Titel*, 94-95). The translation of Robinson, *Nag Hammadi* has 'crocodiles.' Cf. also Tardieu, *Trois mythes gnostiques,* 262-9. A possible allusion here to *2 Enoch* 12:1 has been noticed by Doresse, *Secret Books,* 172-4. See below, for discussion of the possible use of *2 Enoch* in other Gnostic texts.

[42] Schmidt-MacDermot, *Pistis Sophia,* 349-50. Cf. also *Pistis Sophia* ch. 99 (Schmidt-MacDermot, 247); and Milik, *Books of Enoch,* 99-100.

[43] See Schmidt-MacDermot, *Books of Jeu.*

[44] See Pearson, 'Pierpont Morgan Fragments,' 228-9; cf. Perkins, *Gnostic Dialogue,* 139-40.

[45] 4QEnGiants*a* 7ii and 8; Milik, *Books of Enoch,* 314-16. For discussion see Stroumsa, *Another Seed,* 166-7. On the Manichaean *Book of Giants,* an adaptation of the Enochic book of the same name, see below.

449

preserved in Hebrew (*3 Enoch*), revolving around the figure of 'the Lesser YWHW', i.e. Metatron.[46]

We turn now to the Manichaean literature. As is well-known, Manichaeism is a form of Gnosticism which is programmatically syncretistic, Mani presenting himself as the last of a series of heavenly emissaries going back to Adam, including other Old Testament patriarchs, Zoroaster, Buddha, Jesus, and Paul.[47] It has recently been established, as a result of the discovery and publication ofthe Cologne Mani Codex,[48] that Mani's formative period was spent in a Jewish-Christian baptiet sect with Gnostic proclivities, viz. that of Elchasai.[49] Moreover it is becoming increasingly clear that Mani's Gnostic system shows massive influences from Sethian Gnosticism.[50] That Jewish and Jewish Gnostic books were utilized by Mani should not be surprising.

Indeed Manichaean sources do refer to such source material, circulating under the name of key Old Testament patriarchs. We read in a Coptic Manichaean homily that 'all of the apostles have ... proclaimed this struggle in every one of their books, from Adam until now.'[51] A Middle Persian fragment (M299) tells us that Vahman, a Holy Spirit figure, 'proclaimed his greatness through the mouths of the primeval prophets, who are: Shem, Sem, Enosh, Nikotheos ... and Enoch.'[52] Seth (called Sethel in Greek and Coptic sources) is an especially important figure for the Manichaeans,[53] and a book called the 'Prayer of Sethel' is referred to in the

---

[46] See e.g. *3 Enoch* 12 *et passim* in Odeberg's edition, and his remarks, pp. 188-91. Cf. Gruenwald, *Apocalyptic*, 191-208; Scholem, *Jewish Gnosticism*, 43-44, and *Major Trends*, 68-69. On *3 Enoch* see now also Alexander, 'Historical Setting,' and *id.* in Charlesworth, *Pseudepigrapha* 1, 223-315.

[47] See e.g. Widengren, *Mani and Manichaeism*, esp. 139-44.

[48] See Henrichs-Koenen, 'Mani Codex.' Greek text and English translation: Cameron-Dewey, *Mani Codex;* cf. their bibliography, p. 6.

[49] On Elchasai and the *Book of Elchasai* see Hennecke-Schneemelcher, *Apocrypha* 2, 745-50; and Klijn-Reinink, *Jewish-Christian Sects*, 54-67.

[50] This point was already made by Widengren (*Mani and Manichaeism*, 22) and has been greatly elaborated by Stroumsa. See *Another Seed*, 226-78.

[51] Polotsky, *Manichäische Homilien* 14, lines 29-31, my translation. The text is fragmentary. On the OT patriarchs in Manichaean literature, and the use of Jewish apocrypha attributed to them, see Henrichs-Koenen, 'Mani Codex,' 107-108.

[52] Asmussen, *Manichaean Literature*, 12. For Shem or Sem in this text we should read Seth. An apocalypse of Nikotheos was in use by the (Sethian) Gnostics known to Plotinus' circle in Rome: Porph. *Vit. Plot.* 16. Nikotheos is named as a Gnostic prophet in the untitled text of the Bruce Codex (ch. 7); see Schmidt-MacDermot, *Books of Jeu*, p. 235. He is also a highly regarded figure in Zosimus' treatise on the letter *Omega*. See e.g. Festugière, *Revelation* 1, 263-74; Scott, *Hermetica*, vol. 4, 104-44; Stroumsa, *Another Seed*, 217-26. The lore supposedly derived by Zosimus from this Nikotheos includes the interpretation of the letters of the name Adam, meaning the four cardinal directions (E.W.N.S.). Cf. *2 Enoch* 30:13.

[53] Stroumsa, *Another Seed*, 226-39. The form of the name Sethel, found not only in Manichaean but also in Mandaean material (*Šitil*), is probably based upon a Hebrew etymology attested in rabbinic, as well as Gnostic, sources: *štl*, 'to plant.' See Stroumsa, 113-15.

Coptic *Kephalaia* (ch. 10). This book apparently treated 'the fourteen great aeons,' and was probably a Gnostic composition of some sort.[54] The patriarch Enoch, too, is credited with 'songs,' presumably in literary form, in a Middle Persian text (M22).[55] Another Middle Persian text (M625c) refers to Enoch interpreting someone's dream, and is probably based on a lost Enoch apocryphon.[56]

The most interesting testimony, for our purposes, is contained in the Cologne Mani Codex, which contains a Greek biography of Mani's early life. It is stated in this document that 'each one of the forefathers showed his own revelation to his elect, which he chose and brought together in that generation in which he appeared, and ... wrote (it) and bequeathed it to posterity' (47, 3-13).[57] There follow in the text (48, 16-60, 12) references to, and quotations from, an apocalypse of Adam, of Sethel, of Enosh, of Shem, and of Enoch. Moreover for each of these patriarchs references are made to other writings, implying that other books are attributable to these patriarchs in addition to the apocalypses cited. There is nothing specifically Gnostic about the material quoted; these apocalypses could easily be lost Jewish apocryphal works.[58] In the case of Adam it is stated that 'he became mightier than all the powers and the angels of creation' (50, 1-4), clearly a Gnostic doctrine, found expressly in the *Apocalypse of Adam* from Nag Hammadi (*NHC* V, 64, 14-19). It is possible, therefore, that Mani not only knew a non-Gnostic Jewish 'apocalypse of Adam,' quoted in the Mani Codex, but also a Gnostic 'apocalypse of Adam,' identical with, or similar to, the Nag Hammadi document of that name.[59]

Enoch Literature in Gnostic Texts

Enoch traditions[60] played a very important role in the elaboration of Gnostic mythology and in the production of Gnostic literature. We have already noted the function of the patriarch Enoch in Manichaeism and in other Gnostic contexts, and begin this section with Mani's use of the Enochic *Books of Giants,* fragments of which have turned up at Qumran in

---

[54] Böhlig, *Kephalaia* 42, lines 25-26. Böhlig regards the Manichaean 'fourteen aeons' as a parallel to the 'thirteen kingdoms' plus 'kingless generation' in *Apoc. Adam* (*NHC* V, 77, 27-83, 4). See 'Jüdisches und Iranisches,' 152, n. 3; and see below, on *Apoc. Adam*.

[55] Asmussen, *Manichaean Literature,* 37.

[56] See Henning, 'Ein manichäisches Henochbuch.' Milik (*Books of Enoch,* 303) thinks that this apocryphon is identical with the *Book of Giants* found at Qumran. Greenfield — Stone ('The Enoch Pentateuch,' p. 63) surmise that it is the same apocryphon that is quoted in the Mani Codex (on which see below).

[57] Cameron-Dewey translation.

[58] So e.g. Henrichs, 'Literary Criticism,' 725; Stroumsa, *Another Seed,* 228; Greenfield-Stone, 'The Enoch Pentateuch, ' 62-63; cf. n. 56 above.

[59] Cf. discussion below of *Apoc. Adam*.

[60] Cf. above, pp. 90-97.

the original Aramaic.[61] The *Book of Giants* is an elaboration of the myth of the giants born to the 'sons of God' and the 'daughters of men,' according to Gen 6:4. Mani's own *Book of Giants* was written in Syriac, and fragments of this work are extant in Middle Persian, Sogdian, and Uygur versions.[62] It seems to have been simply a gnosticizing adaptation of the Jewish book now attested from Qumran.[63] The Jewish *Book of Giants* circulated along with other Enoch literature, and is datable, in its original Aramaic version, to the second century B.C.E. The Aramaic fragments have not all as yet been published, but Milik has produced a preliminary edition, with translation, and in that work discusses the relationship between the Qumran fragments and the Manichaean *Book of Giants.*[64]

That Mani also knew the Enochic 'Book of Watchers' (= *1 Enoch* 1-36), which together with the astronomical Enoch document (*1 Enoch* 72-82) may constitute the oldest extra-biblical religious Jewish literature known,[65] is also quite probable. The Coptic *Kephalaia* contains passages,[66] which, even if they reflect specifically Gnostic and Manichaean features,[67] seem clearly to be based on *1 Enoch* 6-10. This passage tells of the descent of the angels (Watchers) and their liaison with the daughters of men, resulting in the birth of the giants (cf. Gen 6:1-4).[68]

---

[61] 4QEnGiants, edited, translated, and discussed by Milik, *Books of Enoch*, 298-339. Cf. also his 'Turfan et Qumrân'.

[62] See esp. Henning, 'The Book of Giants'; cf. Milik, *Books of Enoch*, 310, 317-21. This book is cited in the Gelasian Decree as the 'Book of Ogias'; cf. Milik, 321, and James, *Lost Apocrypha*, xiii, 40-42.

[63] So Milik, *Books of Enoch*, 310; Stroumsa, *Another Seed*, 255-64.

[64] Milik, *Books of Enoch*, 58, 298-339; 'Turfan et Qumân'.

[65] Stone, *Scriptures*, 31; cf. Milik, *Books of Enoch*, 7, 28.

[66] The following passages (from *Kephalaion* 33) are especially noteworthy in this connection: 'Behold again how the Great King of Honour, who is Thought, exists in the third firmament. He is [. . .] with wrath, and a great rebellion [occurred], when malice and anger occurred in his camp, namely the Watchers (*negrēgoros*; Greek: ἐγρήγοροs) of heaven, who came down to the earth in his watch. They did all (sorts of) works of malice; they revealed the arts in the world, (and) they revealed to men the mysteries of heaven . . . And malice occurred in his camp, when the abortions fell to the earth.' (On the word-play *nepīlīm-nepalīm* see below, p. 463, and n. 127.) '. . . On account of the malice and the rebellion which took place in the camp of the Great King of Honour, namely the Watchers who came down to the earth from heaven, on their account the four angels were commanded, and they bound the Watchers with an eternal fetter in the prison of darkness. Their sons were destroyed on the earth.' (Böhlig, *Kephalaia*, 92, 24-31; 93, 1-2; 93, 23-27, my translation.) The first of these passages is cited by Henning as an allusion to the Book of Giants; see 'The Book of Giants,' 71. The meaning of the word translated here as 'darkness' (*netkmkamt*), is not certain, but the context in *1 Enoch* provides a good control of the meaning.

[67] The context puts the events here narrated before the creation of Adam, as in some of the Sethian Gnostic material. Cf. Stroumsa, *Another Seed*, 43-111.

[68] The 'four angels' referred to here are mentioned by name in *1 Enoch* 9:1, and 10:1-11: Michael, Sariel, Raphael, and Gabriel. The command to bind in a prison of darkness Asael, one of the Watchers, is narrated in *1 Enoch* 10, as is the command to destroy the sons of the Watchers. The names vary from one MS. to another, even within the Ethiopic MS. tradition.

The myth of the descent of the angels (*1 Enoch* 6-10; cf. Gen 6:1-4) was widely elaborated in Jewish literature of the Second Temple period, and served to answer the question of the origin of evil on the earth.[69] This myth plays an important role, too, in Gnostic literature.[70] In the particular case just now treated, we can see evidence of a direct reliance by the Manichaean author on the Enochic 'Book of Watchers,' as well as influences of already gnosticized versions of this myth, circulating presumably among Sethian Gnostics.[71]

We turn now to a particularly important text of Sethian Gnosticism, the *Apocryphon of John.*[72] This is one of many Gnostic texts which contain the myth of the creation of the world and men by the archons, a myth which, in turn, is ultimately derived in part from the Jewish myth of the fallen angels.[73] One passage shows direct literary dependence upon *1 Enoch,* as illustrated in the following table:[74]

1 Enoch	*Ap. John*
The angels desire the daughters of men, and resolve to take wives and beget offspring (6:2).	The Chief Archon makes a decision and sends his angels to the daughters of men in order to produce offspring (26, 16-20).
Šemiḥazah demurs. Then they all bind themselves with an oath (6:3-5).	At first they do not succeed; then they gather and make a plan (29, 20-23).
Two hundred of them come down to Mt. Hermon. The names of their leaders are given (6:6-8).	

See the *apparatus criticus* in Knibb's edition of *1 Enoch.* I have used here the forms of the names as they appear in the Aramaic fragments edited by Milik. On these four angels see also Yadin, *Scroll of the War,* 237-40.

[69] Cf. e.g. Nickelsburg, 'Apocalyptic and Myth.' The other biblical myth serving this purpose, the Fall of Adam, is combined with the myth of the angels already in *Adam and Eve.* This is a pattern which has undoubtedly influenced the Gnostic interpretation. See Stroumsa, *Another Seed,* 32, and especially Delcor, 'Le mythe de la chûte des anges,' 48.

[70] Fully elaborated by Strouma, *Another Seed,* 43-111.

[71] Cf. n. 50, above.

[72] For an important discussion of the Sethian Gnostic system, and the Gnostic texts which should be labelled as Sethian, see Schenke, 'Gnostic Sethianism.' The following Nag Hammadi tractates fall into the Sethian category, according to Schenke (p. 588): *Ap. John; Hyp. Arch. ; Gos. Eg.; Apoc. Adam; Steles Seth; Zost.; Melch.; Norea; Marsanes; Allogenes; Trim. Prot.*

[73] Stroumsa, *Another Seed,* 43-111. See below, for additional discussion of the Gnostic mythology of *Ap. John.*

[74] The long version of *Ap. John* from *NHC* II is cited; the parallel passage in the *BG* version is 73, 18-75, 10. For Coptic text of Codex II (+ III and IV) see Krause, *Drei Versionen;* cf. Giversen, *Apocryphon Johannis.* For Coptic text of *BG* see Till-Schenke, *Gnostische Schriften.* For an English translation of the *BG* version see Foerster, *Gnosis* 1, 105-120. For *1 Enoch* I have used Knibb's edition.

	They create an Imitation Spirit (29, 23-26).
The angels take wives, and teach them charms and spells. The women bear giants, who become predators on earth (7:1-6).	The angels take the likenesses of the husbands of the daughters of men, filling them with the Spirit of Darkness.
'Aśa'el teaches people metallurgy and other technological skills, and the people go astray (8:1-2).	The angels teach people metallurgy and lead them astray (29, 30-30, 2).
Magic and astrology are introduced (8:3).	
People cry out in their misery and destruction (8:4).	People languish in mortality and ignorance, and the whole creation is enslaved (30, 2-7). They take wives and beget children, and hardness of heart prevails until now, under the influence of the Imitation Spirit (30, 7-11).

The context in *Ap. John* is essentially a running commentary on Gen 1-6, organized as a dialogue between Jesus ('the saviour') and his disciple John, who serves as Jesus' interlocutor.[75] The passage before us is part of a response given by Jesus to a question (misplaced in the document as it stands) concerning the origin of the Imitation Spirit (27,31-32; cf. 26, 20.27.36). It is the introduction of this Imitation Spirit in our text which represents the most substantial deviation from the passage in *1 Enoch* 6-8.[76] Otherwise *Ap. John* follows *1 Enoch* quite closely, and clearly is literarily dependent upon it.

One other deviation from *1 Enoch* is of interest here: In contrast to *1 Enoch* 7, *Ap. John* has the angels assume the likeness of the *husbands* of the daughters of men in order to accomplish their purpose. This idea may derive from *T. Reuben* 5:5-7 or one of its sources.[77] Thus, whereas *1 Enoch* 6-8 is utilized in *Ap. John,* we note also the influence of other non-biblical Jewish material (including a two-spirits doctrine)[78] in the elaboration of the

---

[75] An especially useful discussion of the structure of *Ap. John* (unfortunately in Norwegian) is Kragerud, 'Formanalyse.' Cf. also Giversen, 'Apocryphon of John,' and Schenke, 'literarische Problem.'

[76] See below, p. 460, for discussion of the 'Imitation Spirit' in *Ap. John.*

[77] Cf. Stroumsa, *Another Seed,* 53. The date of *Test. 12 Patr.* is, of course, a matter of controversy. See e.g. Becker, *Untersuchungen;* Collins, above pp. 343-4, and 'Jewish Apocalypses,' 46 and bibliography pp. 57-58.

[78] The Two Spirits' doctrine found in 1 QS 3:13 ff. comes readily to mind in this connection.

myth. This passage stands as a well-defined unit in which no obvious Christian features are found, in spite of the Christian literary framework of *Ap. John,* which we shall discuss below.[79]

Another Gnostic text text from Nag Hammadi contains a possible use of the same material from *1 Enoch,* viz. *Orig. World (NHC* II, 123, 4-15).[80] While the motif of the seduction of the 'daughters of men' by the angels is absent from this passage, the descent of these angels is reflected, and their role in teaching men magic and other godlessness is stressed, as in *1 Enoch* 7-8.[81] One more example is found in *Pistis Sophia,* ch. 15.[82] There one can easily see reflected *1 Enoch* 7:1 and possibly 8:3, specifically in the clause, 'those [mysteries] which the transgressing angels brought down, namely their magic.'[83]

We have already noted, in passing, a possible connection between *Orig. World* and *2 Enoch.*[84] Another Nag Hammadi document, *Zostrianos,* shows some remarkable parallels with *2 Enoch,* a Jewish apocalypse originating in the Egyptian diaspora, probably in the first century C.E.[85] Indeed, Scopello[86] has recently made the claim that *Zost.* is literarily dependent upon *2 Enoch.* She shows this with special reference to two passages, both of which describe the heavenly ascent of the prophet Zostrianos in a manner similar to that of Enoch.[87]

---

[79] I try to show that the basic content of *Ap. John* as a whole is a product of Jewish Gnosticism and that its Christian features are the result of christianizing redaction.

[80] 'For when the seven rulers were cast out of their heavens down upon the earth, they created for themselves angels, i.e. many demons, in order to serve them. But these (demons) taught men many errors with magic and potions and idolatry, and shedding of blood, and altars, and temples, and sacrifices, and libations to all the demons of the earth, having as their co-worker Fate, who came into being according to the agreement by the gods of injustice and justice.'

[81] Cf. Stroumsa, *Another Seed,* 52.

[82] 'Now it happened when they waged war against the light, they were all exhausted together, and they were cast down into the aeons, and they became like the earth-dwellers who are dead and have no breath in them. And I took a third part of all their power so that they should not work their wicked actions, and in order that when men who are in the world call upon them in their mysteries — those which the transgressing angels brought down, namely their magic — that when now they call upon them in their wicked actions, they are not able to complete them' (Schmidt-MacDermot, 25).

[83] Cf. Milik, *Books of Enoch,* 99. The use of the verb παραβαίνειν here (Coptic *entauparaba*) may also reflect *1 Enoch* 106:13, παρέβησαν τὸν λόγον κυρίου. Cf. the discussion, above, on Enoch and the 'Books of Jeu' in *Pistis Sophia.*

[84] See above, p. 449, on the possible connection bezween the quotation from the 'Holy Book' (*NHC* II, 110, 31-111, 1) and *2 Enoch* 12:1.

[85] *Pace* Milik, *Books of Enoch,* 107-116. See also Greenfield-Stone, 'Books of Enoch,' 98-99; F. I. Andersen, in Charlesworth, *Pseudepigrapha* 1, esp. 94-97.

[86] 'Apocalypse of Zostrianos.'

[87] Scopello arranges these parallels as follows (*ibid.,* 377, 379):

Zostrianos	2 Enoch
I received the image of the Glories there. I became like one of them. (5, 15-17)	I looked at myself and I was as one of his Glorious Ones and there was no difference of aspect. (ch. 9)

Scopello points to other correspondences between *Zost.* and *2 Enoch* in the course of her argument,[88] and makes a good case for the dependence of the former upon the latter. She also demonstrates that *Zost.* — a text which shows no Christian influence[89] — has utilized a number of Jewish traditions, and concludes that attention to such influences in texts like *Zost.* 'can cast a new light upon the controversial problem of the existence of a Jewish gnosticism.'[90]

Another example of the possible use of *2 Enoch* by a Gnostic author can be cited, viz. the first tractate of the *Corpus Hermeticum: Poimandres. Poimandres* has numerous features in common with *2 Enoch,* both in structure and in specific content, and, timidly stated, 'it is not out of the question that the author of the *Poimandres* was familiar with one or more apocalypses in the Enoch tradition of the sort represented by *2 Enoch*.'[91] In fact, Scopello's arguments regarding *Zost.* strengthens the case for a direct dependence of *Poimandres* upon *2 Enoch.*[92]

We have seen that actual literary dependence upon *1 Enoch* 6-8 is surely to be found in *Ap. John,* probably in *Pistis Sophia,* and possibly in *Orig. World. 1 Enoch* 6-10 is surely utilized in the Manichaean *Kephalaia.* Thus, the Enochic 'Book of Watchers' can be seen to have enjoyed wide popularity in Gnostic circles.[93] In addition, the Manichaean *Book of Giants* was seen to be an elaboration of a previously-existing Enochic *Book of Giants.* Moreover the very probable use of *2 Enoch* in *Zost.* and *Poimandres,* and its possible use in *Orig. World,* is of great importance for the discussion of the date and provenience of that document.

Jewish and Jewish Gnostic Sources in Christian Gnostic Texts

We turn now to a consideration of some important Christian Gnostic texts, to see if we can detect in them the use of previously existing Jewish or Jewish Gnostic sources.

Behold, Zostrianos, you have heard all these things that the gods do not know and which are unattainable to the angels. (128, 15-18)

Not to my angels have I explained my secret and to you I explain it today. (ch. 11)

Her citations from *2 Enoch* are from Vaillant's edition, corresponding to *2 Enoch* 22:10 (B) and 24:3 (A) in Charles, *APOT.* Cf. also 40:2-3 (in *APOT*). Andersen's new translation (in Charlesworth, *Pseudepigrapha*) mainly follows Charles, *APOT* in its chapter-verse schema.

[88] Cf. also Perkins, *Gnostic Dialogue,* 80: Both *Zost.* and *Paraph. Shem* 'drew inspiration from the Enoch literature.'

[89] It was a key document in use among the Gnostics known to Plotinus. For further discussion see below.

[90] 'Apocalypse of Zostrianos,' 382.

[91] Pearson, *'Corpus Hermeticum* I,' 339-40.

[92] For additional discussion of *Poimandres* see below, p. 474f.

[93] We do not elaborate upon the oblique use of the myth of the fall of the angels in numerous Gnostic texts. On this see esp. Stroumsa, *Another Seed,* 43-111.

THE TESTIMONY OF TRUTH

This document is a Christian Gnostic tract with homiletical characteristics, which defends a rigorously encratic doctrine and praxis, and contends against doctrines and groups regarded by the author as 'heretical.'[94] What is of interest to us here is the apparent use of two 'midrashim' neither of which shows any Christian features. The first of these is a midrash on the serpent of Paradise,[95] who 'was wiser than all the animals that were in Paradise' (45, 30-46, 2; cf. Gen 3:1), and in typical midrashic fashion is associated with the 'serpent' traditions from Exod 4 and Num 21. The Paradise story is retold in such a way that the serpent is portrayed as the revealer of life and knowledge, whereas 'God' (i.e. the biblical Creator) is portrayed as a malevolent and ignorant demon. Despite the strong anti-Jewish tone of this piece, it is replete with specifically Jewish traditions of biblical interpretation, such as could hardly have been available to people not thoroughly acquainted with Jewish aggadah. It thus serves as a text-book example of a 'Jewish Gnosticism' in which traditional doctrines and values are turned upside-down in the interests of a higher *gnosis*.[96]

The other midrash occurs in *Testim. Truth* 69,32-70,24. The manuscript is quite fragmentary at that point, but the text has been restored. It concerns the association on the part of David and Solomon with demons. David, who 'laid the foundation of Jerusalem,' is said to have had demons dwelling with him, and Solomon is said to have built the temple with the aid of demons, which were afterwards imprisoned in jars. These details are derived from Jewish legends such as are reflected in rabbinic aggadah, and are elaborated in that curious apocryphon, the *Testament of Solomon*. The midrash contains nothing specifically Gnostic; it could easily be taken as a purely Jewish text.[97]

MELCHIZEDEK

It is most regrettable that this interesting and important tractate is so poorly preserved.[98] As it stands, it is a Christian text, in which both Jesus Christ and Melchizedek play central roles. It is also, apparently, a Gnostic text

---

[94] *NHC* IX, 29, 6-74, 30. See Pearson, *Nag Hammadi Codices IX and X*, 101-203. Cf. 'Anti-Heretical Warnings,' 150-4.

[95] The passage in question begins at 45,23, set off by the use of a *paragraphus* in the margin, and extends to 49,7.

[96] See further Pearson, 'Jewish Haggadic Traditions'; *id., Nag Hammadi Codices IX and X*, 106-7; 158-69. Cf. also Stone, *Scriptures*, 101-2; Nagel, 'Paradieserzählung,' 53; Koschorke, *Polemik der Gnostiker*, 148-51.

[97] For further discussion see Pearson, 'Gnostic Interpretation,' 315-17; *id., Nag Hammadi Codices IX and X*, 111-12; 191-5. Cf. n. 39, above. See also Duling in Charlesworth, *Pseudepigrapha*, 950.

[98] *NHC* IX, 1, 1-27, 10.

which can be identified as a product of Sethian Gnosticism.[99] What is of special interest to us here is the possibility that it is built up out of pre-Christian Jewish Melchizedek material. I have elsewhere[100] set forth the theory of a three-stage development of the document: 1) a Jewish substratum, presenting Melchizedek as a priest of primal history and recipient of visions of the future, and an eschatological warrior-high-priest-messiah; 2) an overlay of Christian materials, introducing the figure of Jesus Christ and equating him with Melchizedek; and 3) Sethian Gnostic additions.[101]

THE APOCRYPHON OF JOHN

This Sethian Gnostic document[102] is one of the most important of all the Gnostic texts known, and contains a comprehensive Gnostic myth which very probably served as the basis for that developed by the Christian Gnostic teacher Valentinus, and futher eleborated by his disciples.[103] The extant form of *Ap. John* is an apocalypse, containing a revelation given by the risen Christ to his disciple John.[104] Within the apocalyptic frame (evident at the beginning and at the end of the document) there are two main sections: a revelation discourse, and a commentary on Gen 1-6, roughly edited into a dialogue between Jesus and his interlocutor John. A number of sources seem to be reflected in the document, resulting in a good deal of confusion and even contradiction. The following outline of its content and main divisions is prepared on the basis of the version in Codex II, with the divisions in *BG* shown in parentheses:

Preamble and apocalyptic frame, 1,1-2,26 (19,6-22,17)
I. *Revelation discourse* A. *Theosophy* 1) negative theology; the unknown God, 2,26-4,10 (22,17-26,6); 2) the heavenly world, 4,10-9,24 (26,6-36,15). B. *Cosmogony* 1) Fall of Sophia, 9,25-10,23 (36,15-39,4); 2) the cosmic world of darkness, 10, 23-13,5 (39,4-44,9); 3) blasphemy of the Demiurge, 13,5–13 (44,9-18).

---

[99] Cf. n. 72, above.

[100] Pearson, *Nag Hammadi Codices IX and X,* 19-85.

[101] Schenke ('jüdische Melchisedek-Gestalt') also posits a Jewish substratum for *Melch.*, but argues that this material was re-edited in Sethian Gnostic circles and finally christanized. Schenke also argues that the christianization of *Melch.* involved at the same time a de-gnosticization.

[102] See n. 74, above, for reference to the standard editions. The document is extant in two basic recensions, a shorter one (*BG* and *NHC* III) and a longer one (*NHC* II and IV); there are also some minor differences to be observed among all four versions. Two of the extant versions are very fragmentary (III and IV); for our purposes they can safely be ignored. On the Sethian Gnostic system, see above n. 72.

[103] See esp. Quispel, 'Valentinian Gnosis'; Perkins, 'Ireneus,' 199-200, and *Gnostic Dialogue,* 79; Jonas, *Gnostic Religion,* 199.

[104] Cf. Kragerud, 'Formanalyse'; Fallon, Gnostic Apocalypses,' 130-1

II. *Dialogue: Soteriology* 1) repentance of Sophia, 13,13-14,13 (44,19-47,18); 2) anthropogony,[105] 14,13-21,16 (47,18-55,18); 3) Adam in Paradise, 21,16-24,8 (55,18-62,3); 4) seduction of Eve; Cain and Abel, 24,8-34 (62,3-63,12); 5) Seth and his seed, 24,35-25,16 (63,12-64,12); two spirits; classes of men, 25,16-27,30 (64,12-71,2); 7) production of *Heimarmene* (Fate), 27,31-28,32 (71,2-72,12); 8) Noah and the Flood, 28,32-29,15 (72,12-73,18); 9) the angels and the daughters of men, 29,16-30,11 (73,18-75,10); 10) the triple descent of Pronoia,[106] 30,11-31,25 (75,10-13). Apocalyptic frame and title, 31,25-32,9 (75,14-77,5).

There are obvious relationships between *Ap. John* and some other important Gnostic texts,[107] which in general can be accounted for by positing a basic Gnostic system which various groups and individual teachers have developed in different ways. The Sethian system posited by Schenke and others comes immediately to mind.[108]

A fragment from the second part in our outline (II, 9) was discussed above (pp. 453-5)9 It was shown that this section which deals with the angels and the daughters of men is based upon *1 Enoch* 6-8, a significant element being added: the material dealing with the Imitation Spirit. We turn now to another passage in *Ap. John* in which the Imitation Spirit is mentioned, this time in the context of a systematic treatment of the two spirits which govern mankind: II, 23,16-27,30 (*BG* 64,12-71,2), in our outline II, 6. This passage

---

[105] The longer version has a lengthy section devoted to the work of 365 angels: II, 15, 29-19, 2. Cf. *BG's* reference to 360 angels: 50, 8-51, 1.

[106] This hymnic passage is absent from *BG*, from which it seems to have been edited out.

[107] The material (referring to the outline) in I A, 2-3; B corresponds rather closely (but not exactly) to Irenaeus' report on the 'Barbelo-Gnostic'. Cf. Krause on *Ap. John* and Iren. *Adv. Haer.* 1:29 in Foerster, *Gnosis* 1, 100-103. Schenke, 'Das Literarische Problem', showed that Irenaeus did not use *Ap. John*, but one of its sources. Next, the negative theology of the unknown God (I A) is followed very closely in *Allogenes* (*NHC* XI), another Sethian Gnostic tractate, up to an almost verbatim agreement between *Allogenes* XI 62, 28-63, 23 and *Ap. John* II 3, 18-35. Cf. Turner, 'Gnostic Threefold Path,' 329. On the Sethian character of *Allogenes* see n. 72 above, and Pearson, 'The Figure of Seth,' p. 486, 495-6. There is a substantial relationship between the contents of I A-B and the body of *Eugnostos*. See *Eugnostos* III, 71, 14-90, 2. On *Eugnostos* and its relationship to *Soph. Jes. Chr.* see discussion below. There are clear relationship between the material in I A, 2; B, 2-3; II, 8 and the *Gospel of the Egyptians*. There are shared traditions evident, too, between *Ap. John* and the *Hypostasis of the Archons* and, to a lesser extent, the treatise *On the Origin of the World.* The *Ap. John* material in question involves particularly I B, 1-3; II, 2-5, 8. Further, the material involving the triple descent of Pronoia, II 10, seems to form the basis for the structure and content of the *Trimorphic Protennoia*. See e.g. Turner, 'Gnostic Threefold Path,' 326-8; and Janssens' recent edition, *La Protennoia Trimorphe*. Finally, the 'Blasphemy of the Demiurge' and its aftermath, I B, 3; II, 2, constitutes a basic Gnostic tradition found in a number of other sources, including *Hyp. Arch., Orig. World, Gos. Eg.,* and Irenaeus (1:29 and 30). See Dahl's important study, 'The Arrogant Archon.'

[108] See n. 72 above; cf. also Stroumsa, *Another Seed;* Pearson, 'Figure of Seth'. For strenuous objections raised against the attempts to define a Sethian system see esp. Wisse, 'Elusive Sethians.'

is a self-contained unit[109] which, in the present literary arrangement of *Ap. John,* is organized around six of the ten questions (questions 4-9) put to the Gnostic Revealer (Christ) by his interlocutor. It has been referred to as a catechism, in which the ultimate fate of the human soul is tied to the operation of two spirits: the Spirit of Life and the Imitation Spirit.[110] The two spirits are treated without any relation to the exegesis of Genesis, for the purpose of classifying mankind into two main groups, those who achieve salvation and those who do not:

> Those on whom the Spirit of life will descend and (with whom) he will be with the power, they will be saved and become perfect and be worthy of the greatnesses and be purified in that place from all wickedness and the involvements in evil ... When the Spirit of life increases and the power comes and strengthens that soul, no one can lead it astray with works of evil. But those on whom the opposing spirit descends are drawn by him and they go astray. (*NHC* II, 23-28; 26, 15-22)

The resemblance of this doctrine to that of the *Rule* scroll from Qumran (1QS 3:13ff) has been noted, and it has been argued that the entire passage must be understood from premises based not on Gnosticism but on sectarian Judaism.[111] In other words, the passage in question is not Gnostic at all.

It should be pointed out, however, that this passage does, in fact, reflect a gnosticizing tendency. A closer look reveals that the passage posits three classes of men:[112] the perfect, on whom the Spirit of Life has descended; 'those who have not known to whom they belong' (*NHC* II,26,33-34), and 'those who did know but have turned away' (II,27,22-23). The 'perfect' (= the Gnostics) are, of course, saved. Those in the second group are given another chance in another incarnation, and can thus be saved once they acquire *gnosis.* Those in the third group are 'punished with eternal punishment' (II,27,30). Moreover the entire passage has been placed by a redactor into the discussion of Seth and his race (II, 5 in our outline), as an anthropological excursus.[113] Thus it is the race of Seth which is seen to

---

[109] Kragerud sees it as an interpolation; see 'Formanalyse,' 31, 34-35.

[110] Hauschild, *Gottes Geist,* 225-35. In the preceding material in *Ap. John* (II, 2 and 3 in our outline), a 'helper' spirit also referred to as the 'Epinoia of Light' is sent by God to effect Adam's (i.e. man's) salvation. An 'Imitation Spirit' is created by the evil archons for the purpose of obstructing salvation. These entities are developed out of an exegesis of key texts in Gen 2 and 3, and also tied exegetically to the two trees of Paradise: the 'Thought of Light' = the Tree of Knowledge, and the 'Imitation Spirit' = the Tree of (counterfeit) Life. See *Ap. John* II, 21, 16-22, 5; *BG* 55, 18-57, 12. The *BG* version is clearer.

[111] Hauschild, *Gottes Geist,* 236; cf. 239-47.

[112] So also Schenke, 'Das literarische Problem,' 61.

[113] Cf. Kragerud, 'Formanalyse,' 35.

constitute the 'unmovable race' (*NHC* II,25,23) of perfected and perfectible Gnostics.[114]

Finally we must take up the issue whether, in fact, the basic mythology of the document, apart from its frame, should be regarded as a product of Jewish Gnosticism. In other words: can *Ap. John* be understood as a christianizing redaction of pre-existing non-Christian Gnostic material, similar to the classic examples represented by the *Sophia of Jesus Christ* and *Eugnostos*.[115] When one removes from *Ap. John* the apocalyptic framework at the beginning and the end, together with the dialogue features involving the ten questions put to 'Christ' by his interlocutor, one is left with material in which nothing basically 'Christian' remains, except for some easily-removed glosses. What is more, these vary in extent from one version to another.[116] The conclusion is that the 'Christian' elements are altogether secondary,[117] and that the basic material is a product of Jewish Gnosticism.

But why Jewish, if not Christian? Why not pagan? The answer to this is that the building-blocks of the mythological structure of *Ap. John* are the Jewish Bible and specifically Jewish traditions of interpretation thereof. The Jewish exegetical traditions appropriated in the Gnostic structure, moreover, derive not only from Greek-speaking diaspora Judaism, using the Septuagint as its text, but also from Aramaic-speaking Palestinian Judaism, using the Hebrew Bible as its text.

The theology of the 'unknown God' (I A, 1 in our outline) is developed out of a platonizing Jewish theology of divine transcendence, such as is richly documented in first-century diaspora Judaism. Philo of Alexandria

---

[114] On the concept of 'immovability' see Pearson, 'Jewish Elements in Gnosticism,' 157-8; Stroumsa, *Another Seed,* 190-1; Williams, 'Stability.'

[115] *Sophia of Jesus Christ III,* 90, 14-119, 18 and *BG* 3;*Eugnostos* III, 70, 1-90, 13. See esp. Krause, 'Literarische Verhältnis'; Parrott, 'Religious Syncretism'; Perkins, *Gnostic Dialogue,* 94-98. *Eugnostos* is an 'epistle' containing a discussion of the unknown God and the heavenly world, wherein one can easily detect a sophisticated Gnostic exegesis of key texts in Genesis. It shows no obvious Christian influences, and should be taken as a text of non-Christian (Jewish?) Gnosticism. *Soph. Jes. Chr.* is a composite document in which the text of *Eugnostos* has been utilized as a basis, and opened up into a revelation dialogue between Christ and his disciples.

[116] E.g., the heavenly aeon Autogenes ('self-begotten') is identified by means of glosses as the pre-existent 'Christ' in I A, 2 (in our outline); this identification is made initially in the *BG* version at 30, 14-17, but is absent from the parallel passage in II, 6, 23-25. Sophia (II, 9, 25) is called 'our sister Sophia' in the *BG* version (36, 16). On the other hand, whereas the *BG* version has Epinoia, a manifestation of Sophia, teach Adam and Eve knowledge from the forbidden tree (60, 16-61, 2), in the other version it is Christ who does this (II, 23, 26-28). Such examples could be multiplied. See esp. Arai, 'Christologie'; cf. Perkins, *Gnostic Dialogue,* 91-92. An analogy might be drawn between the 'christianizing' of *Ap. John,* as argued here, and the controversial problem of the origins and literary development of *Test. 12 Patr.,* on which see e.g. Becker, *Untersuchungen,* and the studies cited in Collins, 'Jewish Apocalypses,' 57-58.

[117] This is shown conclusively by Arai, 'Christologie.'

provides numerous examples,[118] but even Josephus is important in this connection, for he uses the term *agnōstos* (unknown) of God (*Ag. Ap.* 2, 167), a favourite designation for the supreme God in Gnosticism. What the Gnostics do, of course, is to split the transcendent God of the Bible into a supreme, ineffable Being (I A, 1), and a lower creator, responsible for the material world (I B). It is precisely this radical dualism which effectively removes the Gnostics out of the parameters of Judaism, even if we must posit a Jewish origin for much of the Gnostic mythology.

In *Ap. John* the heavenly world (outline, I A, 2) is made up of a number of emanations from the supreme God, chief among them being the 'Thought' (*ennoia*) of God, called 'Barbelo,' and her product *Autogenes* ('self-begotten'). Dependent upon the latter are the four 'luminaries' (Armozel, Oriel, Daveithai, and Eleleth). Heavenly prototypes of Adam and his son Seth are also given prominence. Indeed the supreme God himself is given the esoteric name 'Man.' Much of this is obviously based upon the theological speculations of contemporary philosophy,[119] but the key figures here have their origin in incipient Jewish mysticism. That God is 'Man' is read out of Gen 1:26f.,[120] and possibly Ezekiel 1:26 as well.[121] The esoteric name for the first divine emanation, 'Barbelo,' is probably to be seen as a word-play on the divine Tetragrammaton: *barba"elo*, 'in four, God'.[122] The four 'luminaries' are probably to be seen as counterparts to the four angelic beings beneath the throne of God in Ezekiel's vision (Ezek 1:4-21),[123] and/or perhaps to the four archangels of *1 Enoch* 9-10.[124] The divine counterparts of Adam and Seth are Platonic projections into the heavenly realm of the biblical patriarchs (Gen 5:1-3), and recall the platonizing exegesis of the double creation story in Gen 1 and 2 such as is found, for example, in Philo.[125] Adam and Seth, of course, play key roles in the development of Gnostic *Heilsgeschichte*.

The Gnostic figure of Sophia, whose fall, repentance, and subsequent

---

[118] E.g. *Quod Deus* 62; *Q.E.* 2:45; *Post.* 168-169; *Som.* 1:65-67. On the basis of such passages as these Jonas has argued that Philo is really a Gnostic! Cf. *Gnosis und spätantiker Geist* 2, 70-121. See my discussion in 'Philo and Gnosticism', 303-9. Cf. also Wilson, 'Philo and Gnosticism,' 216. It should be recalled in this connection that Norden, years ago, pointed out the *'unhellenisch'* nature of the concept of the ἄγνωστος God (*Agnostos Theos*, 83-87). As a Gnostic concept it derives, in my view, from early Jewish theology, rooted in biblical interpretation, with its concept of the transcendent Creator.

[119] See e.g. Whittaker, 'Self-Generating Principles.'

[120] See Schenke's ground-breaking study, *Der Gott 'Mensch'*.

[121] Cf. Quispel, 'Ezekiel 1:26.'

[122] This etymology of the name, first proposed by Harvey in his edition of Irenaeus (vol. 1, p. 221, n. 2) but not widely accepted, has been more convincingly stated by Scopello ('Youel et Barbélo,' esp. p. 378). For another solution see Stroumsa, *Another Seed*, 93-95 (based on Bousset, *Hauptprobleme*, 14, n. 3): a deformation of the word παρθένος.

[123] Cf. Böhlig, 'Jüdische Hintergrund,' 84.

[124] Stroumsa, *Another Seed.* 80.

[125] *Op.* 66-135. Cf. Pearson, *Philo and the Gnostics,* 3-8.

role in salvation-history (outline, I B, 1; II, 1-8, 10) loom so large in the Gnostic mythology, is clearly derived from the Wisdom theology of Judaism. What is said of her in the Gnostic sources cannot be understood apart from Sophia's pre-history in Jewish tradition, even if the Gnostics turn much of this tradition upside down.[126]

The myth of the origin of the Gnostic Demiurge (Yaldabaoth-Saklas-Samael) as an 'abortion' of Sophia (outline, I B, 1; II, 1: *houhe, BG* 46, 10) reflects a sophisticated reworking of the biblical traditions of the fall of Eve (Gen 3:4-6), the birth of Cain (4:1), and the fall of the 'sons of God' (Gen 6:1), together with traditional Jewish interpretations thereof. Even the use of the wordt 'abortion' reflects a Hebrew word-play (*nepīlīm*, 'fallen ones' — *nepalīm*, 'abortions') documented in rabbinic aggadah.[127]

The description of the world of darkness (outline, I B, 2), with its demonization of the seven planets and the twelve signs of the Zodiac, is based on contemporary astrological speculation, and reflects a heavy dose of specifically Jewish lore.[128]

The tradition of the 'Blasphemy of the Demiurge,' found in a number of Gnostic texts, reflects the Gnostic end-product of a discussion in Judaism concerning 'two powers in heaven,' in which a number of biblical texts appear both in the background and in the foreground. Here in *Ap. John* Exod 20:5 and Isa 46:9 are combined. This tradition is a succinct reflection of the 'revolution' on the part of Jewish Gnostics against the biblical Creator.[129]

The anthropogony which follows the blasphemy of the Demiurge and the repentance of Sophia (II, 1) is organized around several key texts in Genesis, 1:2; 1:26-27; 2:7; and 2:18. Moreover it is based upon Jewish traditions of exegesis, both Alexandrian and Palestinian. For example, one can see reflected in it both the Alexandrian Jewish tradition that God relegated the creation of man's mortal nature to the angels (e.g. Philo, *Fug.* 68-70; cf. Plato, *Timaeus* 41A-42B) and the Palestinian tradition that God created man initially as a *golem* (e.g. *Gen. Rabba* 14, 8).[130]

Finally, the role of Seth and his seed (II, 5) is developed out of Jewish traditions related to the birth and progeny of Seth. A number of recent studies have laid bare the essential points.[131]

Much of this material is found in other Gnostic texts, but it is clear that

---

[126] MacRae, 'Jewish Background'; Dahl, 'Arrogant Archon,' 706-12.

[127] Stroumsa, *Another Seed,* 101-8, esp. 106 (referring to *Gen. Rabba* 26,7). Cf. Dahl, 'Arrogant Archon,' 703, where the concept of the Demiurge as an 'abortion' is traced to Jewish interpretation of Isa 14:19. On the names Yaldabaoth, Saklas, and Samael see Pearson, 'Jewish Haggadic Traditions,' 466-8. Cf. also Barc, 'Samael-Saklas-Yaldabaoth.'

[128] Welburn, 'Identity of the Archons.'

[129] Dahl, 'Arrogant Archon.'

[130] See further Pearson, 'Biblical Exegesis'; *Philo and the Gnostics,* 9-15.

[131] Klijn, *Seth,* 81-117; Stroumsa, *Another Seed,* esp. 112-206; Pearson, 'The Figure of Seth.'

Ap. John is an exceedingly important document for the study of the Gnostic phenomenon and its history. The Jewish origins of its mythology are unquestionable, even if we cannot actually explain the Gnostic revolutionary hermeneutic as an organic development within Judaism.[132]

THE HYPOSTASIS OF THE ARCHONS

This tractate is also of prime importance for our consideration of Jewish Gnostic sources. It shares considerable material with *Ap. John*, and stands in an especially close relationship with *Orig. World,* though the latter is probably later, and represents a more advanced stage in the development of Gnostic religious syncretism.[133] In its present form *Hyp. Arch.* is a Christian text, but it can easily be argued that its Christian features are attributable to a secondary christianization of Jewish Gnostic material. They are primarily seen in the introduction, where the 'great apostle' (Paul) is quoted (Eph 6:12), and in the concluding passage, where a number of allusions to the Johannine literature of the New Testament are to be found.[134] Christian redaction is evident here and there in the body of the text as well. But before we proceed further with our discussion of this document, an outline of its content is in order:

Epistolary introduction (86, 20-27).
I. *Commentary on Gen 1-6.* A. *Introduction:* 1) blasphemy of Samael (86, 27-31); 2) rebuke of the Demiurge and ensuing cosmogony (86,31-87,11). B. *Anthropogony:* 1) appearance of the Image (87,11-23); 2) creation of man by the Archons (87,23-88,3); 3) vivification of man, naming the animals (88,3-24). C. *Adam in Paradise:* 1) Adam placed in Paradise; prohibition against eating of the Tree of Knowledge (88,24-89,3); 2) creation of woman (89,3-17); 3) the Archons' lust for Eve (89,17-31); 4) eating of the Tree, punishment by the Archons (89,31-91,11). D. *Eve's progeny: 1) Cain and Abel (91,11-30); 2) Seth and Norea (91,30-92,3).* E. *The Flood:* Noah and Norea (92, 3-18). F. *The Archons' lust* for Norea (92, 18-32).
II. *Apocalypse of Norea.* A. *Setting:* 1) Norea's cry for help (92,32-93,2); 2) appearance of Eleleth (93,2-17). B. *Revelation dialogue:* 1) inferiority of the Archons (93,18-32); 2) origin of the Archons: a) fall of Sophia (94,4-19), b) blasphemy and rebuke of Samael-Saklas (94,19-95,13), c) exaltation of Sabaoth (95,13-96,3), d) envy of Yaldabaoth and birth of his sons

---

[132] See the introductory section of this article, above. Cf. also Stroumsa, *Another Seed,* 300.
[133] *NHC* II, 86, 20-97, 23. Several editions of *Hyp. Arch.* have been published. The most recent are those of Layton and Barc. Böhlig's edition of *Orig. World (Schrift ohne Titel)* is still standard. For a perceptive study of biblical materials in *Orig. World* see Wintermute, 'Gnostic Exegesis.' See also Tardieu, *Trois mythes gnostiques.*
[134] See Bullard, *The Hypostasis of the Archons,* 113-4.

(96,3-14); 3) salvation of Norea's offspring: a) present salvation and promise (96,17-31), b) future salvation (96,31-97,21).

Title (97,22-23).

As this outline shows, *Hyp. Arch.* is made up of two main parts, with some evident duplication of material. Part I consists essentially of a commentary on Gen 1-6. Part II consists of a revelation given to Norea by the angel Eleleth (one of the four luminaries encountered in *Ap. John* and other Sethian texts), in which Norea begins to speak in the first person as the putative mediator of Eleleth's revelation (93,13). It is possible that the material in this second part of *Hyp. Arch.* is derived from a previously existing Apocalypse of Norea, which immediately reminds us of the references to books whose titles contain the name of this same figure, discussed above.[135] Indeed, a plurality of books featuring the Gnostic heroine Norea seem to have been circulating in antiquity.[136]

The redaction of such sources as were used in *Hyp. Arch.* is quite thoroughgoing, and it is difficult precisely to recover them, although some scholars have tried to do so.[137] For example, the transition from part I to part II is very skillfully done: the concluding narrative in the first part (I F) provides the occasion for the setting of the apocalypse in the second part. Moreover the main theme running through the entire work is the 'reality'[138] of the menacing Archons, from which the Gnostic is promised ultimate deliverance. Indeed the mythological deliverance of Norea is paradigmatic of the salvation of the Gnostic 'children of light,' her 'offspring' (97,13-14; 96,19).

There is widespread agreement that the material dealing with the exaltation of Sabaoth (II B, 2c in our outline) constitutes a distinct pericope within the larger revelation, and that this pericope and the parallel passage in *Orig. World* (*NHC* II,103,32-106,18) derive from a common source.[139]

---

[135] Pp. 446-8. Schenke suggests that an 'apocalypse of Norea' was a source used in common by *Orig. World* and *Hyp. Arch.;* see 'Gnostic Sethianism,' 596. However, there does not seem to be any specific correspondence between the material in *Hyp. Arch.* and the material said to be contained in the 'Book of Norea' in *Orig. World* (101, 26-102, 25). There are some features in common betyween the 'Book of Noria' described by Epiphanius (*Haer.* 26:1,3-9) and the *first* part of *Hyp. Arch.* (i.e. item I E in our outline), but also some differences between them. The 'apocalypse of Norea' in part II, on the other hand, does not seem to be reflected in Epiphanius' account.

[136] Cf. Bullard, *Hypostasis of the Archons,* 101; Fallon, *Enthronement of Sabaoth,* 15-16. *The Thought of Norea* (IX,2) is another 'Norea' book, and stands in close relationship with *Hyp. Arch.* Cf. *Hyp. Arch.* II, 92, 33-93, 2 and the opening passage of *Norea:* IX, 27, 11-24.

[137] The most complicated analysis is that of Barc, who posits three Jewish Gnostic sources and two redactions (one Jewish Gnostic and one Christian Gnostic). See *Hypostase des archontes,* 1-48.

[138] Layton's interpretation of the word *hypostasis;* see 'Hypostasis of the Archons' (1976), 44.

[139] See esp. Fallon, *Enthronement of Sabaoth.*

This passage constitutes, in fact, a piece of Gnostic 'Merkabah mysticism.'[140] It has the following structure: [141]

1. Repentance of Sabaoth, 95,13-18 (cf. *Orig. World* 103,32-104,6). 2. Ascent and enthronment of Sabaoth, 95,19-25 (cf. 104,6-31). 3. Creation of the throne-chariot of Sabaoth, 95,26-28 (cf. 104,31-105,16). 4. Creation of the ministering angele, 95,28-31 (cf. 105,*6-106,3)*. *5. Instruction of Sabaoth,* 95, 31-34 (cf. 104,26-31 + 106,3-11). 6. Sabaoth's right and left, 95, 34-96, 3 (cf. 106,11-19).

The entire pericope is built upon themes derived from various Jewish traditions, both Alexandrian and Palestinian. The figure of Sabaoth represents, of course, the Jewish God, who is partially rehabilitated by splitting the wicked and ignorant Creator into two: Yaldabaoth, banished to Tartaros, and his son, Sabaoth, now 'repentant,'[142] singing praises to Sophia, and installed in the seventh heaven.[143] Sabaoth's assumption into heaven places him in the role of the apocalyptic seer, such as Enoch,[144] and his enthronement reflects his ambiguous role, that of the apocalyptic seer (Enoch-Metatron is the best example)[145] and that of the Jewish God, YHWH Sabaoth. As part of his enthronement he is given the biblical name, 'God of the powers' (ϑεὸς τῶν δυνάμεων), which reflects the Hebrew etymology of the name 'Sabaoth' (צבאות).[146] The 'chariot of the Cherubim' is a designation found in the Greek Bible (ἄρμα τῶν χερουβιν, cf. 1 Chr 28:18; Sir 49:8),[147] but it also reflects, to some extent, the early stage of the Jewish Merkabah speculation based on Ezekiel's vision (Ezek 1).[148] The infinite multitude of ministering angels reflects a widespread apocalyptic tradition (e.g. *1 Enoch* 40:1),[149] while the placement of Zoe at

[140] Cf. Gruenwald, *Apocalyptic,* 112-118. In the immediately preceding context in *Hyp. Arch.* (II B, b) the Demiurge, Samael-Saklas-Yaldabatoh (all three names occur, cf. n. 127 above) claims to be the sole God, and is rebuked by a *bath qol* from heaven. (On the 'blasphemy of the Demiurge,' see my remarks on the relevant section of *Ap. John,* above, p. 463 and n. 129.) He then claims to be 'God of the All,' and is rebuked by Zoē (Eve, daughter of Sophia). She sends a fiery angel who binds him and throws him down to Tartaros, below the Abyss. The punishment of Yaldabaoth in this scene is reminiscent of the fate of the fallen angels in *1 Enoch* and other Jewish texts (e.g. *1 Enoch* 21:7-10; 88:1; etc. Cf. Fallon, *Enthronement of Sabaoth,* 28). Our pericope follows, in which the repentance of Sabaoth, son of Yaldabaoth, is featured, a scene which in effect replaces the pericope on the repentance of Sophia which is found, for example, in *Ap. John* II, 13, 13-14, 13.

[141] Cf. Fallon, *Enthronement of Sabaoth,* 10.

[142] Stroumsa compares the repentance of Shemhazai, one of the fallen angels in the *Midrash of Shemhazai and Azael;* see *Another Seed,* 81.

[143] His praise of Sophia seems to be derived from the Greek text of Prov 1:20 and 8:3 (ὑμνεῖται). See Fallon, *Enthronement of Sabaoth,* 37.

[144] *Ibid.,* 35; cf. Gruenwald, *Apocalyptic,* 115.

[145] Gruenwald, *Apocalyptic,* 115.

[146] Fallon, *Enthronement of Sabaoth,* 56.

[147] *Ibid.,* 57.

[148] This is even clearer in the parallel in *Orig. World.* Cf. Gruenwald, *Apocalyptic,* 114.

[149] Fallon, *Enthronement of Sabaoth,* 60.

Sabaoth's right hand and the 'Angel of Wrath' at his left[150] is reminiscent of Jewish throne visions such as that found in the *Testament of Abraham*,[151] and of traditions found in Philo.[152]

It is clear that Sabaoth, despite his exalted position on the cherubic throne-chariot, occupies an inferior role in the total picture. His throne is in the seventh heaven, just below the cosmic veil[153] which separates 'Above' from 'Below.' He needs to be instructed by Zoe about things that exist above him, in the 'Eighth.'[154] This is all quite consistent with Gnostic theology. Yet the Sabaoth pericope does represent a modification of the radical dualism characteristic, presumably, of the earliest stage of the Gnostic revolutionary hermeneutic.[155]

A most interesting feature of *Hyp. Arch.* is the role played in it by Norea.[156] She first appears in the text as the last of the four children born to Eve (Cain, Abel, Seth, Norea — I D in our outline), recalling the opening passage of the *Biblical Antiquities:* 'Adam begat three sons and one daughter: Cain, Naamah,[157] Abel, and Seth.' The name 'Naamah' is, in fact, Norea's original Hebrew name.[158] In Jewish tradition (perhaps reflected in the ordering of the names in the *Biblical Antiquities*) Naamah is frequently presented as a Cainite woman (cf. Gen 4:22), whose reputation for lewdness is extensively portrayed; in that connection her role in seducing the 'sons of God' (Gen 6:2) is an especially important detail for our purposes.[159] In *Hyp. Arch.*, however, she is associated closely with Seth,[160] and her exalted role is already made clear in the brief narrative of

---

[150] The parallel in *Orig. World* puts 'Israel, the man who sees God' (alias Jesus Christ), at Sabaoth's right. The (false) etymology of the Hebrew name Israel, i.e. 'man who sees God,' is attested in Philo (*Post.* 92; *Abr.* 57-59; etc.). Cf. Fallon, 106; Gruenwald, *Apocalyptic,* 115.

[151] See *Test. Abr.* A12, wherein 'angels of the right and of the left' record, respectively, righteous deeds and sins. See Fallon *ibid.,* 63.

[152] See *Abr.* 121: on either side of 'He who IS' (ὁ ὤν) are the two 'powers' (δυνάμεις), the creative (ποιητική) whose name is God (θεός) and the royal (βασιλική) whose name is Lord (κύριος). Barc, *Hypostase des Archontes,* 39-40. In *Cher.* 27-28 Philo says that the two powers symbolized by the Cherubim are called goodness (ἀγαθότης) and sovereignty (ἐξουσία).

[153] The *pargod* of Jewish mystical speculation. Cf. *Fallon, Enthronement of Sabaoth,* 55; Gruenwald, *Apocalyptic,* 147, 204, 210-11; Scholem, *Major Trends,* 72.

[154] Functionally, Zoe replaces the *angelus interpres* of apocalyptic speculation, but there is also probably a reflex here of the word play on the Semitic name for Zoe: חוה , Eve; חיה life; and חוא Aram., to instruct; Fallon, *Enthronement,* 61. Cf. Pearson, 'Jewish Haggadic Traditions,' 463-4.

[155] Cf. Fallon, *Enthronement,* 87.

[156] See Pearson, 'The Figure of Norea'; cf. now also Stroumsa, *Another Seed,* 78-91.

[157] The text reads *Noaba,* manifestly a corruption of Na'amah (Greek Νοεμα); cf. Pearson, 'The Figure of Norea,' 149.

[158] נעמה , meaning 'pleasing, lovely' in Greek is ὡραία. The name Norea is a hybrid construction from Noama and Horaia. Pearson, 'The Figure of Norea,' 150.

[159] See esp. *Pirke de R. Eliezer* 22; cf. Pearson, 'The Figure of Norea,' 150.

[160] Other Gnostic text specifically identify her as the wife-sister of Seth (e.g. Iren. *Adv. Haer.* 1:30, 9; Epiph. *Haer.* 39:5, 2), a detail found also in at least one Jewish source: *The Chronicles of Jerahmeel,* cf. Pearson, 'The Figure of Norea,' 149.

her birth: 'And Eve became pregnant, and she bore [Norea]. And she said, he has begotten on [me a] virgin as an assistance for many generations of mankind. She is the virgin whom the Forces did not defile' (91,34-92,3).

'He' in the text refers to the supreme Father, not Adam.[161] Seth, likewise, is said to have been born 'through God' (91, 33), in contrast to Cain, who is the product of the evil Archons (91,12).[162] Norea's destiny to be an 'assistance' for mankind (βοηθεία) recalls the role of Eve in Gen 2:18, 20-22.[163] Norea, indeed, emerges as a figure superior to Eve, not least in her chastity: a 'virgin whom the Forces did not defile.' The Gnostic portrayal of Norea thus stands in stark contrast to the reputation of Naamah in the Jewish haggadic traditions already referred to.

The story of Norea continues in the text in connection with the plan of the Archons to obliterate mankind in the Flood, and the command to Noah to build an ark (I E in our outline): 'Then Orea[164] came to him wanting to board the ark. And when he would not let her, she blew upon the ark and caused it to be consumed by fire. Again he made the ark, for a second time' (92, 14-18).

This story of the burning of the ark is reported by Epiphanius, where our heroine is called Noria (*Haer.* 26:1,4-9),[165] as a tradition current among the Nicolaitan Gnostics. According to this report Noria was Noah's wife, and it is worth noting, in this connection, that there are some Jewish haggadic traditions in which Noah's wife emerges as an evil woman, and tries to thwart the building of the ark.[166] To be sure, the Gnostics regard the opposition to Noah in a positive light, which is altogether consistent with the revolutionary thrust of their hermeneutic.

Norea's reputation as the 'undefiled virgin' is vindicated in the passage that follows (I F in our outline), wherein the Archons attempt to seduce the hapless Norea, as they claim they had done with her mother Eve:[167] 'You must render service to (i.e. sleep with)[168] us, [as did] also your mother Eve . . . (92, 30-31). The outcome of this encounter, not explicitly stated in

---

[161] Layton, 'Hypostasis', n. 96.

[162] Cf. Layton, 'Hypostasis', n. 84. This doctrine is derived from the Jewish (rabbinic) tradition that Cain was the son of Sammael; cf. *Targum Ps. Jonathan* on Gen 4:1.

[163] According to Barc, *Hypostase des Archontes,* 109, there is a play here on the traditional name of the wife of Seth, Azura (*Jub.* 4:11), i.e. 'she who assists.' The MT of Gen 2:18 has the word עזר , which the LXX translates with the word βοηθός; this may, in fact, be the origin of the name Azura for the wife of Seth in *Jubilees,* i.e. another Eve. In *Hyp. Arch.* Norea, also, is another Eve.

[164] Cf. n. 158 above.

[165] Cited above, p. 446.

[166] Pearson, 'The Figure of Norea'; cf. Stroumsa, *Another Seed,* 87-90.

[167] There is an ambiguity in the story of the rape of Eve: on the one hand she turns into a tree in their clutches, yet on the other hand leaves a shadowy reflection of herself (i.e. her body) which the Archons defile (89, 25-30). On Eve's becoming a tree cf. Pearson, 'She Became a Tree'; cf. also Stroumsa, *Another Seed,* 54-60.

[168] So Stroumsa, *Another Seed,* 60, n. 85.

our text, is that Norea is rescued from the clutches of the Archons by one (or all) of 'the four holy helpers,' about whom we read in the related text, the *Thought of Norea*.[169] Our text does represent one of these 'helpers,' the light-angel Eleleth, as coming down in response to her cry for help (outline II A, 1-2), and providing her with the revelation which constitutes the bulk of part II of *Hyp. Arch.*

In sum, the Gnostic myth of the encounter between Norea and the Archons is built upon Jewish traditions relating to the fall of the angels (Gen 6:1-3), the story of the Fall (Gen 3), and the birth and progeny of Cain (Gen 4:1).[170]

The salvation of Norea is paradigmatic of the salvation of all Gnostics, explicitly referred to in the text as her 'offspring' (96, 19). Norea is therefore presented in classic Gnostic fashion as a 'saved saviour,' akin to the figure of Sophia.[171] It is also to be observed that Norea has virtually displaced Seth in this text, even if she is initially presented in juxtaposition with him. The usual 'Sethian' Gnostic emphasis upon Seth as the progenitor of Gnostic mankind[172] has here been eclipsed by a 'feminist' perspective: Norea is progenetrix of Gnostic mankind. This, too, can be seen as an aspect of the Gnostic revolution.

While *Ap. John* and *Hyp. Arch.* are probably the most important examples of secondarily 'christianized' products of Jewish Gnosticism, a number of other examples can be cited. They include: the *Gospel of Mary* (*BG* 1), sometimes regarded as a composite of two non-Christian documents;[173] the *Trimorphic Protennoia* (*NHC* XIII,1) which is closely related to the longer version of *Ap. John*;[174] the *Gospel of the Egyptians* (*NHC* III, 2 and IV,2), which displays a number of features in common with the *Apocalypse of Adam* and other Sethian texts;[175] and the *Book of Thomas the Contender* (*NHC* II,7), which may be a Christian redaction of a Hellenistic Jewish

---

[169] *NHC* IX, 28, 27-30. Cf. Stroumsa, *Another Seed*, 80-82. Stroumsa compares the story of the rescue of Esterah in the *Midrash of Shemhazai and Azael*. Gero has recently called attention to the possibility that the story of Norea and her rescue is echoed in the Coptic *Book of the Installation of the Archangel Gabriel*, which refers to the rescue of Enoch's sister Sibyl from the hands of the devil by Gabriel. See 'Henoch und die Sibylle.'

[170] Cf. Pearson, 'Figure of Norea,' 151; Stroumsa, *Another Seed*, 78-91.

[171] Pearson, 'Figure of Norea,' 152. Cf my introduction to *Norea* (*NHC* IX,2) in *Nag Hammadi Codices IX and X*, 87-93.

[172] Cf. Pearson, 'Figure of Seth,' 489-91; Stroumsa, *Another Seed*, 112-206.

[173] Fallon, 'Gnostic Apocalypses,' 131; cf. Wilson, *Gnosis and the NT*, 101-2.

[174] Cf. above, p. 459 and n. 107. See esp. Schenke, *Die dreigestaltige Protennoia;* Colpe, 'Heidnische Überlieferung III,' 119-24; Robinson, 'Sethians and Johannine Thought.'

[175] *Gos. Eg.* displays only a thin Christian veneer, according to Schenke, 'Gnostic Sethianism,' 607. On its relationship with *Apoc. Adam* see e.g. Perkins, 'Apocalyptic Schematization'; MacRae's introduction in Parrott, *Nag Hammadi Codices V, 2-5 and VI*, p. 152. See esp. the Böhlig-Wisse edition, *Nag Hammadi Codices III,2 and IV,2*.

pseudepigraphic epistle of the patriarch Jacob.[176] Sources known from the church father Hippolytus might also be cited: the book *Baruch* (*Ref.* 5: 26, 1-27, 5);[177] the *Megalē Apophasis* associated with Simon Magus (*Ref.* 6:9, 4-18, 7),[178] and the 'Naassene Sermon' (*Ref.* 6:6, 3-9, 21).[179]

Jewish Gnostic Texts

We turn, finally, to a consideration of documents which, in their entirety, have been regarded as Jewish Gnostic documents.

THE APOCALYPSE OF ADAM

This is one of the most important of all the extant Gnostic texts for the question of the existence of Jewish Gnostic literature. Its first editor, Böhlig,[180] regards *Apoc. Adam* as a document of pre-Christian Sethian Gnosticism, with origins in a Jewish baptismal sect of the Syro-Palestinian area. Its most recent editor, MacRae, noting its close dependence upon Jewish apocalyptic traditions, suggests that it represents 'a transitional stage in an evolution from Jewish to gnostic apocalyptic.'[181] Formally, this document is both an apocalypse and a testament. It is an apocalypse in that it contains a revelation given by heavenly informants to Adam, who mediates the revelation to his son Seth. In general, it adheres closely to the apocalypse genre.[182] It is a testament, with close formal connections with the Jewish testamentary literature, in that it is presented as a speech given by Adam to his son just before his death, 'in the seven hundredth year' (64, 4).[183] Its lack of obvious Christian influence,[184] on the one hand, and its

---

[176] This work has heretofore been regarded as a purely Christian product of Syrian provenance; see Turner, *Thomas the Contender;* Perkins, *Gnostic Dialogue,* 100-107. However Schenke recently suggested that it is a Jewish pseudepigraph transformed into a dialogue between Christ and Judas Thomas. See Schenke, 'The Book of Thomas.'

[177] Foerster, *Gnosis* 1, 48-58. Greek text: Völker, *Quellen,* 27-33. On its Jewish character see e.g. Haenchen, 'Das Buch Baruch'; Grant, *Gnosticism,* 19-26; Kvideland, 'Elohims Himmelfahrt.'

[178] Foerster, *Gnosis* 1, 251-60. Greek text: Völker, *Quellen,* 3-11. For a survey of recent scholarship see Rudolph, 'Simon-Magus oder Gnosticus?' esp. 302-10.

[179] Foerster, *Gnosis* 1, 261-82. Greek text: Völker, *Quellen,* 11-26. See also Frickel, 'Naassener oder Valentinianer?'

[180] Böhlig, *Koptisch-Gnostische Apokalypsen,* esp. p. 95; cf. 'Jüdisches und Iranisches'.

[181] In Parrott, *Nag Hammadi Codices V,2-5 and VI,* 151-95, esp. 152. Cf. also MacRae, 'The Apocalypse of Adam Reconsidered,' and Hedrick, *Apocalypse of Adam,* whose edition and translation are organized according to a particular source theory. Cf. n. 187, below. See now MacRae's translation in Charlesworth, *Pseudepigrapha* 1, 707-19.

[182] See Fallon, 'Gnostic Apocalypses,' 126-7; Perkins, 'Apocalypse of Adam.' Indeed, it adheres more closely to the apocalypse *genre* than does *Adam and Eve,* with which it is closely related. Cf. Collins, *Apocalypse,* 1-59.

[183] MacRae, in Parrott, *Nag Hammadi Codices V, 2-5 and VI,* 152; cf. Perkins, 'Apocalypse of Adam,' 384-6.

[184] A disputed point; see below.

massive dependence upon Jewish traditions, on the other, make *Apoc. Adam* a primary test-case for the discussion of Jewish Gnosticism and Jewish Gnostic literature.

Its content can be outlined as follows:

Introduction (64, 1-5).
I. *Setting:* Adam's testamentary speech to Seth. A. Adam relates his and Eve's experiences with the Creator (64,5-65,23). B. Adam's dream vision: three heavenly men and their addresses to him (65,24-66,8). C. Adam's and Eve's experiences (cont.) (66,9-67,14). D. Adam's intention to reveal the heavenly revelation to Seth (67,14-21).
II. *The Revelation.* A. The end of Adam's generation (fragmentary material, 67,22-28 +). B. The Flood, first deliverance (69,2-73,29; p. 68 is blank). C. Destruction by fire, second deliverance (73,30-76,7). D. Third episode: end-time threat and redemption: 1) coming of the Illuminator (76,8-77,3); 2) the Powers' wrath against the Illuminator (77,4-18); 3) false and true views about the Illuminator: a) the Powers' *aporia* (77,18-27), b) the thirteen kingdoms (77,27-82,19), c) the generation without a king (82,19-83,4); 4) final struggle, repentance of the peoples (83,4-84,3); 5) condemnation of the peoples (84,4-28); 6) final salvation of the Gnostics (85,1-6). E. Revelations put on a high rock (85,7-18).
First conclusion (85, 19-22). Second conclusion (85, 22-31). Title (85, 32).

The close parallels between *Apoc. Adam* and the Jewish Adam literature, especially the *Life of Adam and Eve* and the *Apocalypse of Moses,* have often been noted.[185] These parallels are especially close in the first section, wherein Adam addresses Seth and gives him a biographical account of his and Eve's adventures after the creation. The 'slant,' of course, is different. In *Adam and Eve* the two protoplasts have been banished from Paradise for their sin, and are duly repentant. In *Apoc. Adam,* on the other hand, Adam and Eve are by nature 'higher than the god who had created us and the powers with him' (64, 16-18). The Creator acts against Adam and Eve out of jealous wrath, in a manner reminiscent of the devil in *Adam and Eve,* banished from heaven because of his refusal to worship the newly created Adam (chs. 12-17).

The parallels extend also into the second part, which narrates the future history of mankind, focusing on the Gnostic seed of Seth, and organized around the three-fold pattern of flood, fire, and end-time. In *Adam and Eve* (49:2-3) Eve reports what the archangel Michael had revealed to her and Adam concerning the coming flood and a subsequent judgment by fire. In

---

[185] Cf. e.g. Perkins, 'Apocalypse of Adam'; Pearson, 'Figure of Seth,' 492-4; Nickelsburg, 'Some Related Traditions.' The Armenian Adam books discussed by Stone ('Armenian Adam Books') should also be brought into the discussion.

Apoc. Adam the three angels' revelation of the destructions by flood and fire (Sodom and Gomorrah!), as well as the end-time struggle, are part of the Creator's attempt to destroy the Gnostic race. The reference at the end of *Apoc. Adam* to revelations written on rock (85,10-14) recalls the tradition found at the end of *Adam and Eve* (ch. 50-51) that the revelations given by Adam and Eve were to be preserved by Seth on stone and clay to survive the coming judgments of flood and fire.[186] These formal parallels, and others not treated here, lend a great deal of plausibility to the suggestion that *Apoc. Adam* and *Adam and Eve* share common sources.[187]

The essential point about *Apoc. Adam,* however, is that, from beginning to end, it is a Gnostic document in which numerous Jewish traditions, indeed the genre itself (apocalyptic testament), are thoroughly reinterpreted in the interests of a higher *gnosis*. With consummate irony the Gnostic author sets forth the 'real truth' concerning the heavenly origin of the spiritual 'seed of Seth' (the Gnostics) and the utter folly of servitude to the Creator.[188] It is a Jewish Gnostic document in the sense that its genre and its building-blocks are derived from Judaism. But in its intentionality it is anti-Jewish in the extreme, a product of the Gnostic revolt against the Jewish religion and the Jewish God.

Some scholars have found traces of Christian influence in *Apoc. Adam,* especially in the section dealing with the career of the saviour (II D, 1-2 in our outline. E.g.: 'Then they will punish the flesh of the man upon whom the holy spirit has come' (77, 16-18). It is alleged that this is a veiled reference to Christ.[189] But there is no need to see such a reference to Christ here, particularly in view of the fact that the entire context adheres to a

[186] Cf. Pearson, 'Figure of Seth,' 492-5, 502-3; Stroumsa, *Another Seed,* 157-87.

[187] See esp. Nickelsburg, 'Some Related Traditions,' 537: *Apoc. Adam* and *Adam and Eve* are dependent upon a previously existing apocalypse of Adam influenced by Enochic traditions. Hedrick has recently published an analysis (*The Apocalypse of Adam*) in which he isolates two main sources plus redaction. He dates the final redaction to the end of the first century C.E. The starting point for his source-analysis is the presence of what he takes to be two introductory sections at the beginning of the tractate (64, 6-67, 21), and two conclusions at the end (85, 19-31). These observations, in my mind, are ore cogent than his division of the body of the revelation proper into two sources (see p. 181), which in effect breaks up the triadic structure of the Gnostic history of salvation, based on the flood, fire, and end-time struggle, which is an essential feature of the revelation. I would, however, suggest that the n dealing with the 'false and true views about the Illuminator' (II D, 3 in out outline) is a redactional excursus. Böhling (*Koptisch-Gnostische Apokalypsen,* 87,91-83,109) regards 77,27-83,4 as an excursus; MacRae sees this passage as an interpolation (in his introduction in Parrott, *Nag Hammadi Codices V, 2-5 and VI,* 152). For a contrary view see Stroumsa, *Another Seed,* 123-57.

[188] Superbly treated by Perkins, 'Apocalypse of Adam.'

[189] See Beltz, *Adam-Apokalypse.* Beltz regards *Apoc. Adam* — even with all of its 'Jewish building blocks' — as a late (third century) product with clear Christian influences. Cf. also Yamauchi, *Pre-Christian Gnosticism,* 107-115 (esp. 110), 217-19; and most recently, Shellrude, 'Apocalypse of Adam.' It is noteworthy that Schenke, on the other hand, has retracted his earlier objection to Böhlig's view that *Apoc. Adam* is a pre-Christian document: 'Gnostic Sethianism,' 607.

pre-Christian Jewish literary pattern dealing with the earthly persecution and subsequent exaltation of the righteous man.[190] The conclusion drawn by Perkins in this connection is apposite: 'We see that from beginning to end *Apoc. Adam* invokes literary models developed in Jewish intertestamental writings. And it is equally clear that he uses them against their original intent: the God of Israel and those faithful to him are mocked; the Gnostics exalted.'[191]

The excursus on the various interpretations of the Illuminator's coming (outline, II D 3) has given rise to a number of interesting comments on the religious syncretism of *Apoc. Adam*.[192] Thirteen 'kingdoms' are listed, each with a different interpretation of the Illuminator, each of them ending with the clause, 'and thus he came to the water.' This passage has been utilized to prove the Christian provenance of the document.[193] However the phrase, 'he came to the water,' does not necessarily refer to baptism. Rather, it may be a reference to the saviour's descent.[194] The opposite line of argument is that the first twelve kingdoms, to whom the saviour comes in various disguises, represent the twelve tribes of Israel, while the thirteenth kingdom represents the Christian church, with its reference to the *logos* which is said to have 'received a mandate there' (82, 13-15). The Gnostic community, on the other hand, is represented by the 'generation without a king over it' (82, 19-20), of those who alone have true knowledge concerning the identity of the saviour, namely the heavenly Seth, and who alone constitute the 'seed' who 'receive his (i.e. the saviour's) name upon the water' (83, 4-6). *Apoc. Adam,* then, represents a strain of Sethian Gnosticism resistant and in reaction to the christianizing of Sethian *gnosis*.[195]

In conclusion, no certainty can be achieved on the question of the date of *Apoc. Adam*. Typologically it is a 'pre-Christian' text inasmuch as it ad-

---

[190] This pattern has been delineated by Nickelsburg (*Resurrection*, 48-111) with reference to Wis 1-6 and other ancient Jewish literature. In *Apoc. Adam* this pattern is fully represented:
1. *Earthly persecution:* signs and wonders of the Illuminator (77, 1-3); conspiracy against him (77, 4-15); punishment of the Illuminator (77, 16-18).
2. *Exaltation, judgment:* the peoples acknowledge their sin (83,4-84,3); condemnation of the peoples (84, 4-28); exaltation of the elect (85, 1-18).
Cf. Perkins, 'Apocalypse of Adam,' 390-1.

[191] *Ibid.,* 391.

[192] See esp. Böhlig, 'Jüdisches und Iranisches,' 154-61; Beltz, *Adam-Apokalypse,* esp. 135-75.

[193] Shellrude, 'Apocalypse of Adam,' 89-90, interprets the references to water to mean that the Gnostics' opponents lay claim to the same saviour as the Gnostic community, and that baptism is associated with their acceptance of him. The conclusion is that the Gnostics' opponents are orthodox Christians; the Gnostics themselves are Christian Gnostics opposed to water baptism.

[194] So MacRae, in Parrott, *Nag Hammadi Codices V, 2-5 and VI,* 179. This whole question turns on the interpretation of 83,4-85,18. See MacRae *ibid.,* 190-5, and esp. Stroumsa, *Another Seed,* 153-6.

[195] Stroumsa, *Another Seed,* 144-57. The *Gospel of the Egyptians,* with which *Apoc. Adam* shares much material (above, n. 175) represents that other side of Sethian *gnosis*.

heres to a very early type of Gnosticism, in which Jewish features are clearly displayed, and no positive Christian influence is clearly present. Nevertheless, it may be a comparatively late document (second or third century?) if the above interpretation of the 'thirteenth kingdom' is correct. Its possible relationships with Mandaean and Manichaean forms of the Gnostic religion deserve further investigation.[196]

POIMANDRES

At first glance it may seem strange to discuss this fundamental work of the Graeco-Egyptian Hermetic religion (*Corpus Hermeticum* I) as a 'Jewish Gnostic' document. To be sure, it is widely understood as a Gnostic document, one of a number of Hermetic tractates so designated.[197] Its title is the name given to the god who reveals himself in it, otherwise called 'The Mind of the Absolute' (ὁ τῆς αὐθεντίας νοῦς). The recipient of the revelation is unnamed but is traditionally identified as Hermes Trismegistus (cf. *C.H.* XIII, 15), the revealer-god *par excellence* in Graeco-Egyptian syncretism (the Egyptian Thoth).

In form, *Poimandres* is an apocalypse.[198] Its content can be outlined as follows:

    I. Introduction: Epiphany of Poimandres (ch. 1-3).

    II. The Revelation. A. Cosmogony (4-11). B. Anthropology: 1) anthropogony: the 'fall' of Man (12-19); 2) ethics and the nature of man (20-23). C. Eschatology: individual ascent to God (24-26).

    III. The prophet's mission (27-29).

    IV. Conclusion; hymns and prayers (30-32).

The structure of the document as a whole is very similar to that of *2 Enoch*.[199] Indeed, the parallels are so close that literary dependence of *Poimandres* upon *2 Enoch* could easily be argued.[200] The cosmogony and anthropogony are obviously dependent upon the Greek version of the book of Genesis, though of course they contain influences from disparate sources. *Poimandres'* use of the book of Genesis has been demonstrated in detail by Dodd,[201] who also notes numerous influences throughout this document from other portions of the Bible and calls attention to important resemblances to Philo of Alexandria and other Hellenistic-Jewish literature. To be sure, Dodd notes the heavy indebtedness of the document to

---

[196] See esp. Beltz, *Adam-Apokalypse,* and Böhlig, 'Jüdisches und Iranisches.'

[197] See e.g. Nilsson, *Geschichte* 2, 582-612, esp. 584.

[198] See Attridge, 'Greek and Latin Apocalypses,' 161. For the text see Nock-Festugière, *Corpus Hermeticum* 1. For English translation with brief introduction, see Foerster, *Gnosis* 1, 326-36.

[199] See Pearson, 'Jewish Element in *Corpus Hermeticum* I', 339-40.

[200] Cf. discussion above, p. 456.

[201] *The Bible and the Greeks,* 99-209.

contemporary Platonism and Stoicism (an indebtedness which is shared by Philo), and its (typically Gnostic) emphasis on *gnosis* as the basis of salvation. While he argues persuasively for its heavy indebtedness to Hellenistic Judaism, Dodd does not go so far as to call it a 'Jewish' document.

More recently this very step has been taken by Ludin Jansen, who argues that the Jewish emphasis in Poimandres is so pervasive that it must have been written by a Jew who had personally lived through the mystical experiences described in the 'autobiographical' sections of the text (I and III in our outline). His conclusion is that *Poimandres* is a Jewish Gnostic text.[202]

This judgment can easily be strengthened by the results of recent studies which have shown that the concluding chapters (IV in our outline) are fragments of Jewish liturgy, prayers and worship formulae actually utilized in the worship life of Hellenistic Jewish synagogues in the diaspora, including the *shema,* the *kedusha,* and the *amidah.*[203] It is therefore certain that the Hellenistic Jewish influences in the *Poimandres* are not only such as would be available to a pagan reader of the Septuagint and other Jewish literature; in addition, actual participation in Jewish worship is indicated.

Yet *Poimandres* cannot adequately be defined, simply, as just another Jewish apocalypse. For one thing, it is a Gnostic text, in that it posits a dualism of heavenly light versus a natural world of darkness, distinguishes between a higher God and a lower Demiurge (a second 'Mind', ch. 9), and equates knowledge of the self with knowledge of God (ch. 18, 21, 27-28), presenting this *gnosis* as the very basis of ultimate salvation and ascent to God. To be sure, its dualism is not expressed in such radical terms as that of some of the Gnostic texts we have already treated, in which the Creator is presented as a vengeful and ignorant demon.[204] In the final analysis, *Poimandres* represents a religious transition, from Judaism to a new religion: from the religion of Moses to that of Hermes the 'Thrice-Greatest.'[205]

OTHER GNOSTIC TEXTS WITH JEWISH INFLUENCE

In concluding this section reference must be made to other Gnostic texts in which no Christian influence is present but which contain indications of Jewish background or influence. They are noted here for the sake of a complete presentation of the evidence.

The *Paraphrase of Shem* (*NHC* VII, 1,1-49,9) is an apocalypse in which Shem is snatched up to heaven and receives a revelation from a heavenly

---

[202] 'Tendenz und Verfasserschaft.'

[203] Pearson, 'Jewish Elements in *Corpus Hermeticum* I,' esp. 342-5. Philonenko has independently arrived at similar conclusions in studies unknown to me at the time that I wrote that article. See 'Poimandrès et la liturgie' and 'Utilisation du Shema.'

[204] Cf. Segal, *Two Powers,* 245; and Foerster, *Gnosis* 1, 328.

[205] Pearson, 'Jewish Elements in *Corpus Hermeticum* I,' 347-8.

being called 'Derdekeas' (Aram. דרדקא, 'child') concerning the primary 'roots' of reality (Light, Darkness, Spirit) and the origin and fate of the world.[206] The document uses and reinterprets biblical material, especially Genesis, and also shows a number of features of possible Iranian origin.[207] It shows no traces of Christianity but a christianized version of the same basic Gnostic system is preserved by Hippolytus in his discussion of the 'Sethian' Gnostics (*Ref.* 5:19, 1-22, 1).[208]

Zostrianos (*NHC* VIII,1)[209] is an apocalypse in which the protagonist, Zostrianos, is guided on an otherworldly journey by an angelic informant and given knowledge concerning the various aeons of the heavenly world. Its possible dependence upon *2 Enoch* has already been mentioned.[210]

The Three Steles of Seth (*NHC* VII,5),[211] a 'revelation of Dositheos about the three steles of Seth' (118,10-12), consists of praises sent up to each member of the Sethian divine triad, 'Geradamas' (the Son), 'Barbelo' (the Mother), and the supreme Father.[212] Its Jewish features belong more to the traditional background than to the foreground, in which Platonic philosophical traditions predominate.

This last observation can be made with even greater emphasis regarding

---

[206] See esp. Fallon, 'Gnostic Apocalypses,' 136-7; Wisse, 'Redeemer Figure.' On 'Derdekeas' see Wisse, 133, n. 3; Stroumsa, *Another Seed,* 122.

[207] See esp. Colpe, 'Heidnische Überlieferung II,' 109-16.

[208] Hippolytus refers to a book called the *Paraphrase of Seth,* in which the whole Sethian system is said to be laid out (*Ref.* 5:22, 1). The question naturally arises as to the exact nature of the relationship between the *Paraphrase of Sem* and Hippolytus' *Paraphrase of Seth,* and whether or not the former should be regarded as a Sethian Gnostic document. Its character as a Jewish sectarian document remains to be defined with greater precision than has thus far been achieved. See e.g. Foerster, *Gnosis* 1, 299-305; Bertrand, 'Paraphrase de Sem'; Tröger, *Gnosis und N. T.,* 57-59. The phrase 'Jewish sectarian documents,' is used by Segal, *Two Powers,* 253.

[209] Cf. Fallon, 'Gnostic Apocalypses,' 137-8; Sieber, 'Introduction'; Scopello, 'Apocalypse of Zostrianos.'

[210] Above, p. 455f. The prophetic exhortation found at the end (Fr. VIII 130, 14-132, 4) resembles that found at the end of *Poimandres* (ch. 27-29). Its dependence upon Jewish traditions is evident, but how far in the Sethian Gnostic background these traditions lie, *i.e.* to what extent it may be termed a Jewish Gnostic document, remains to be determined. Its heavy indebtedness to Middle Platonism is an important ingredient in the discussion. We know that considerable effort was put forth in the school of Plotinus in Rome to combat its doctrines. Amelius wrote a 40-volume refutation of it, according to Porphyry, *Vit. Plot.* 16.

[211] See e.g. Fallon, 'Gnostic Apocalypses,' 146; Colpe, 'Heidnische Überlieferung II,' 123-5; Tardieu, 'Les trois stèles,' Robinson, 'The Three Steles.'

[212] On the name Geradamas (or Pigeradamas) see Jackson, 'Geradamas.' The praises are such as would be offered in an experience of intellectual ascent, but may also reflect actual (Sethian Gnostic) ritual practice. So Schenke, 'Gnostic Sethianism,' 601-2. The occurrence of the name 'Dositheos' in this text has given rise to speculations about a possible Samaritan connection. See e.g. Beltz, 'Samaritanertum und Gnosis,' esp. 94-5. Schenke, who had earlier subscribed to this view, has had second thoughts. See 'Gnostic Sethianism,' 592-3. On Dositheus and the Dositheans see Isser, *The Dositheans.*

Marsanes (*NHC* X),[213] a Sethian Gnostic apocalypse which reflects a situation of lively dialogue between Gnostics and Platonists such as is clearly represented in the school of Plotinus in third-century Rome. The putative author of the tractate, Marsanes, is mentioned by Epiphanius as one of the Gnostic prophets revered by the 'Archontic' (Sethian) Gnostics in Palestine (*Haer.* 40:7,6). He and Nicotheos[214] are also held in high honour by the author of the untitled tractate in the Bruce Codex, another document of Sethian Gnosticism.[215]

Allogenes (*NHC* XI,3)[216] is a Sethian Gnostic apocalypse featuring a revelation discourse in which 'Allogenes' (= Seth) records for his son 'Messos' the revelation he has received from a female heavenly being called 'Youel' (whose name is derived from esoteric Jewish sources).[217] Again, in the case of *Allogenes,* as also of the *Thought of Norea* (*NHC* IX,2), which has already been mentioned,[218] it can be said that Jewish features are part of the Gnostic tradition which is utilized.

Eugnostos has been mentioned above in connection with our discussion of *Ap. John.*[219] Its presentation of the unknown God and the heavenly world, based in large measure on speculative interpretations of Genesis, could easily belong to a 'Jewish Gnostic' document.

Hypsiphrone (*NHC* XI,4)[220] appears to be a Gnostic apocalypse, containing visions seen by a female figure called 'Hypsiphrone' ('high-minded'), but it is too badly preserved to allow any judgments on the question at issue here.

The Thunder, Perfect Mind (*NHC* VI,2)[221] is a revelation discourse presented by a female revealer in the first person, containing numerous self-predications of a deliberately paradoxical character (e.g.: 'I am the whore and the holy one; I am the wife and the virgin' —13, 18-20). Quispel, in an extensive study, regards *The Thunder* as a pre-Christian (3rd-1st cent. B.C.E.), pre-Gnostic Jewish document in which the revealer is the biblical

---

[213] See Pearson, *Nag Hammadi Codices IX and X,* 229-352.

[214] See n. 52, above.

[215] Cf. Schenke, 'Gnostic Sethianism,' 588.

[216] See e.g. Colpe, 'Heidnische Überlieferung III,' 113-115; Turner, 'The Gnostic Threefold Path'; Fallon, 'Gnostic Apocalypses,' 127; Scopello, 'Youel et Barbélo.'

[217] See esp. Scopello, 'Youel et Barbélo.' *Allogenes* stands in an especially close relationship with its occupation with *Marsanes, Zost.,* and *Steles Seth* in its occupation with philosophical (platonic) traditions. As noted above (p. 459, and n. 107) its 'negative theology' of the unknown God (61, 32-67, 20) is closely related to that of *Ap. John* (II, 3,17-4,1).

[218] Above, p. 469, in connection with our discussion of *Hyp. Arch.* See further Pearson, *Nag Hammadi Codices IX and X,* 87-99; Roberge, *Noréa.*

[219] Above, p. 461.

[220] See Fallon, 'Gnostic Apocalypses,' 134.

[221] See MacRae's edition, with introduction, in Parrott, *Nag Hammadi Codices V, 2-5 and VI, 231-55;* cf. also MacRae, 'The Thunder'; Fallon, 'Gnostic Apocalypses,' 143.

figure of Wisdom.[222] Another suggestion for the setting of this tractate has also been made, which does not necessarily negate the theory of a (sectarian) Jewish background: Simonian Gnosticism.[223]

With these observations I conclude this presentation of the evidence for Jewish Gnostic literature, but not without calling attention to a serious omission: the Mandaean material. The Jewish background of Mandaean Gnosticism is unquestionable,[224] and a thorough exploration of the Mandaean literature in our search for Jewish and Jewish Gnostic sources will surely turn up much of relevance to our study.[225] But I must leave this to scholars who are more competent in the Mandaean sources.

Conclusions

From the evidence considered above it can easily be seen that the Gnostics utilized and created a great number of books. In addition to the books of the Old Testament — Torah (especially Genesis), Prophets, and Writings, both in Greek and in Hebrew — a large number of apocryphal Jewish books were used by them. We have taken special notice of the popularity of the Enoch literature in Gnostic circles, but pseudepigraphical writings attributed to other Old Testament patriarchs, especially Adam and Seth, were also heavily used. Indeed it can be observed that Jewish apocryphal texts, especially those featuring midrashic reworking of biblical traditions, served as models for the Gnostics' own literary productions. *The Apocalypse of Adam* is an especially clear illustration of this. Even the Gnostic dialogue form, employed in a number of Christian Gnostic texts, can be regarded as a development of one feature of the Jewish apocalypse in which the recipient of the revelation questions an *angelus interpres* concerning aspects of his heavenly journey or vision.[226]

---

[222] Quispel, 'Jewish Gnosis', calls attention to the parallels between *Thunder* and a hymnic passage attributed to Eve in *Orig. World* (II, 114, 8-15) and similar parallels between *Thunder* and a Mandaean text from the 'Book of Dinanukht' in the *Right Ginza,* wherein 'Ewath, the Holy Spirit' is quoted in a similar vein (*ibid.,* p. 105; cf. Lidzbarski, *Ginza,* 207; MacRae, 'The Thunder,' esp. 1-6). This leads Quispel to extended comments on the Jewish origins of Mandaean Gnosticism. His views on the Jewish background of *Thunder* have much to commend them, even if one cannot subscribe to all of his arguments.

[223] Pearson, 'The Thunder.' The female revealer of *Thunder* is, in fact, remarkably reminiscent of the traditional portrayal of Simon's Helen. Cf. the table of parallels *ibid.,* 12-13. See further Rudolph, 'Simon,' 353-4, for discussion, with reference to other relevant literature. *The Exegesis on the Soul* (*NHC* II,6) has also been brought into connection with Simonian Gnosis; cf. Rudolph, 'Simon,' 354-9.

[224] Cf. Quispel's discussion in 'Jewish Gnosis.' See esp. Rudolph's numerous publications on Mandaeism, e.g. *Gnosis,* 344-66; and his translation of the texts, with introduction, in Foerster, *Gnosis* 2, 121-317.

[225] See e.g. Cohn-Sherbok, 'The Alphabet,' a discussion of the relationship between certain secret Mandaean texts and the Jewish *Sefer Yetsirah.*

[226] Perkins, *Gnostic Dialogue,* 19. Cf. also Koester's seminal discussion of Gnostic gospels in 'One Jesus,' 193-8, esp. 196-7.

It must also be stressed that much of the Jewish traditional material so radically reworked by the Gnostic writers must have circulated orally. Basic ingredients of the Gnostic cosmogonic and anthropogonic mythology are based upon Jewish haggadic traditions which eventually came to be recorded in writing in various rabbinic midrash collections or in the haggadic portions of the Talmud. Gnostic literary production represents, in effect, an aspect of the general transition observable not only in Judaism but in the wider context of the Hellenistic-Roman world from 'oral' to 'literary' religious expression.[227] What is especially interesting in this connection is that Gnostic texts frequently preserve exegetical traditions which are recorded only later within rabbinic Judaism in written form, sometimes much later.[228]

cf m. Jaffee on Rabb. lit.

To be sure, one can observe in the Gnostic sources the presence of Gnostic themes, patterns, lines of argument, etc., which seem to be the focus of on-going discussion and lively debate in Gnostic intellectual circles. For example, the Gnostic pattern featuring the 'blasphemy' or 'vain claim' of the Demiurge — itself based upon Jewish texts and exegetical traditions — occurs in a number of extant Gnostic texts. Yet the differences among them in details seem to preclude the literary dependence of one text upon another. What is found here is a common tradition, subject to refinement in this or that Gnostic book.[229]

Throughout our discussion of the Gnostic material we have noted the ambiguous relationship between the Gnostic texts and Judaism. Time and again we saw evidence of Jewish scriptures and traditions turned upside-down in a drastic reorientation of values and perceived religious truth. Indeed we began this essay with some general observations on the difficulty of appraising, historically, the actual relationship between the Gnostic religion and Judaism. But it must finally be borne in mind that 'Judaism' is not easy to define, at least not for the Second Temple period. To speak of any kind of 'normative' Judaism or Jewish 'orthodoxy' before the end of the first century C.E. is anachronistic and contrary to the evidence. The plethora of Jewish sects and religious movements in pre-70 Judaism is a well-established fact, and is becoming even clearer as a result of new discoveries and new research.[230] It is not, really, more difficult to conceive of groups of Jewish radicals, yes Jewish Gnostics, as a part of the religious maelstrom of Judaism, than it is to recognize the historical fact that the Christian religion itself originated as a Jewish messianic sect. As an illustration, we may with Gruenwald cite a saying of R. Yohanan (*P.T. San-*

---

[227] Cf. Perkins, *Gnostic Dialogue*, 7-9.
[228] This has been shown repeatedly by Stroumsa, in his groundbreaking book, *Another Seed*. See e.g. his remarks on p. 198.
[229] Cf. discussion, above, of *Ap. John;* and Dahl, 'Arrogant Archon,' esp. 692-5.
[230] Cf. Stone, *Scriptures*.

hedrin 10, 29c) to the effect that 'the people of Israel did not go into exile before they had become twenty-four sects of heretics.'[231]

The Gothic historian Jordanes calls the Scandinavian peninsula ('Scandza') a 'factory of peoples' and a 'womb of nations' (*officina gentium, vagina nationum* — *Getica* 4, 25), referring to the hordes of tribes and peoples who came out of the north and spread all over Europe in the Migration Period. In an analogous sense we can speak of Judaism as a *matrix religionum*, producing not only a plethora of ephemeral sects and parties but also major world religions. Christianity and Islam are obvious cases, but the Gnostic religion, which in its Manichaean form actually became a world religion,[232] can also be considered in this context.

Large gaps in our knowledge of the origin and early development of the Gnostic religion do remain, in the final analysis. Of the vast literary production of the ancient Gnostics, we have in our extant sources — now available as a result of chance discoveries — only the proverbial 'tip of the iceberg.'

BIBLIOGRAPHY

The standard bibliography on Gnosticism (except Manichaeism and Mandaeism), with special reference to the Coptic Gnostic materials, is SCHOLER, *Nag Hammadi Bibliography*. The best monographic treatments of Gnosticism are JONAS, *Gnostic Religion* (treated from a phenomenological perspective) and RUDOLPH, Die *Gnosis* (treated from a history-of-religions perspective). The latter contains basic discussions and bibliography on Mandaeism and Manichaeism, as well as other facets of Gnosticism. The most important of the older treatments of the relationship between Gnosticism and Judaism is FRIEDLÄNDER, *Der vorchristliche Gnosticismus*. A good survey of research done on Gnosticism up to 1970 is RUDOLPH, 'Forschungsbericht'; see esp. *TR* 36 (1971) 89-119, for a discussion of Gnosticism in relation to Judaism.

The Nag Hammadi texts are available in English translation in a single volume: Robinson, *The Nag Hammadi Library;* this volume also contains the tractates in the Berlin Gnostic Codex. A series of critical editions (Coptic text, English translation, introductions, notes) of all of the Coptic Gnostic texts ('The Coptic Gnostic Library') began to appear in 1975, as part of the *NHS* series. The standard anthology of other Gnostic materials in English translation, including patristic accounts as well as Mandaean texts, is FOERSTER, *Gnosis*. For the Manichaean material see now also *Gnosis* 3: 'Der Manichäismus'.

---

[231] 'Jewish-Gnostic Controversy,' 714.
[232] Rudolph, 'Gnosis-Weltreligion.'

A number of scholarly congresses have taken place at which papers beating upon the problems addressed in this article have been presented, and whose proceedings have been published. The most important of these are BIANCHI, *Le origini dello gnosticismo* (Messina, 1966), WIDENGREN, *Proceedings* (Stockholm, 1973), LAYTON, *Rediscovery* (Yale, 1978), and BARC, *Colloque International* (Quebec, 1978). Numerous other volumes of collected essays have appeared (including *Festschriften*), of which the two edited by TRÖGER should be mentioned here: *Gnosis und NT* and *Altes Testament*. Finally, the ground-breaking dissertation on Sethian Gnosticism by STROUMSA deserves special mention: *Another Seed.*

Chapter Twelve

Qumran Sectarian Literature

Devorah Dimant

The Site and the Community

In the spring of 1947, the accidental uncovering of scrolls hidden in a cave near Jericho led to one of the most spectacular discoveries of the century, namely that of the oldest Hebrew literary manuscripts, now known as the Dead Sea Scrolls. Between 1948 and 1956, eleven caves with manuscripts (designated as caves 1-11) were discovered near the site known as Khirbet Qumran, on the north corner of the western shore of the Dead Sea.[1] The findings aroused interest in the site of Qumran itself, and systematic excavations were conducted. At the same time an archaeological survey was made of the entire area between Qumran and Ein Feshkha, a site near a spring, three kilometers south of Qumran. Pottery and other remains found at Qumran, in the caves and near Ein Feshkha, point to the same period of settlement and to the same people.[2] The main periods of occupation at Qumran correspond to the dates of the scrolls. Qumran was inhabited mainly between 150 B.C.E. and 68 C.E.[3] The remains of a small Israelite settlement, dating from the 8th to the 6th centuries B.C.E.,[4] were resettled during the reign of Simon (142-134 B.C.E.).[5] During this first major occupation period, extensive building took place and the settlement acquired its definitive shape: a large enclosure with a network of cisterns and water channels, workshops, a warehouse and an assembly hall. This period terminates with a great fire and an earthquake, possibly the earthquake of 31

---

[1] The story of the discovery has been told many times. Cf. Milik, *Ten Years*, 11-19; Cross, *Library*, 3-20; Vermes, *Qumran in Perspective*, 9-24.

[2] Cf. De Vaux, *Archaeology*, 53-57, 91-109.

[3] Cf. the summary of De Vaux, *Archaeology*, the head of the excavations. Another, more recent resumée of the archaeological evidence was published by Laperrousaz, *Qoumrân*. He bases himself mainly on De Vaux's work, but supplements it and differs from it in the interpretation of a number of details. Carbon 14 tests of organic remains indicate a span of time around the beginning of the Era. Cf. De Vaux, *Archaeology*, 50, 101.

[4] Sometimes identified with the biblical City of Salt (Josh 15:61-62). Cf. Milik — Cross, 'Chronique,' 75; De Vaux, *Archaeology*, 922. Recently Bar-Adon suggested an identification with the biblical Sekākāh, while the City of Salt he identifies with Ein Aituraba, south of Ein Ghuweir. Both cities figure in the same list in Joshua 15; cf. Bar-Adon, 'Hasmonean Fortresses', 352.

[5] Cf. Milik, *Ten Years*, 51; De Vaux, *Archaeology*, 19; Cross, *Library*, 58, 122.

B.C.E.[6] The second building period started only at the beginning of Archelaus' reign in 4 B.C.E.,[7] and it ended in violent destruction, probably wrought by the Romans in 68 C.E. Of interest is the adjacent cemetery, belonging to the same periods. The graves contained skeletons of men, women and children, and are oriented with the head towards the south.[8] Later remains attest to the presence of a small Roman garrison until around 90 C.E. and a short sojourn of Bar-Kokhba fighters.

The majority of the manuscripts date from between the second century B.C.E. and the third quarter of the first century C.E.[9] Scrolls older than the beginning of the Qumran settlement must have been brought there from outside.[10] The close chronological correspondence between the archeology of the remains and the palaeography of the scrolls justifies the conclusion that the people who inhabited the site were identical with those who composed or copied the scrolls. Hence, data from the site and the scrolls were combined to reconstruct the life and history of the people involved.[11]

Two other settlements, probably connected with the inhabitants of Qumran, were discovered in the vicinity. One is an agricultural complex near the spring of Ein Feshkha, the other is at Ein el Ghuweir, fifteen kilometers south of Qumran.[12] In the small cemetery adjacent to Ein el Ghuweir, the same peculiar burial method was discovered, again contain-

---

[6] So De Vaux. On the earthquake in 31 B.C.E. see Josephus *Ant.* 15:121-122; *War* I: 370-380. Other scholars maintain that the two events should be kept apart: see Laperrousaz, *Qoumrân*, 40-41; Mazar, 'Ein Gedi,' 5 n. 16. Milik suggests that the fire was caused by events connected with the Parthian invasion of Eretz-Israel in 40 B.C.E.: see Milik, *Ten Years*, 52-53, 94.

[7] De Vaux thought that the site was abandoned for several years while Milik is of the opinion that some form of settlement might have continued. The rebuilding followed the previous lines of settlement. To this period belong fragments of a table and inkwells found among the debris. De Vaux, *Archaeology*, 29-32 suggested that they attest to the existence of a *scriptorium* at Qumran. Cf. also Cross, *Library*, 66-67.

[8] Both the careful ordering of the cemetery and the orientation of the graves are peculiar. The usual practice in Eretz-Israel was to orient graves from east to west. Cf. De Vaux, *Archaeology*, 45-48; Laperrousaz, *Qoumrân*, 19-25. De Vaux thought that there were three cemeteries, one major and two smaller; but now there is a tendency to see them as one cemetery. Yadin and Bar-Adon think that it served as a central cemetery for the entire area. See Yadin, *Temple Scroll* 1, 251, and Bar-Adon, 'Hasmonean Fortresses,' 351. As for the Qumran cemetery, cf. also Steckoll, 'Qumran Cemetery'; Haas — Nathan, 'Human Skeletal Remains.'

[9] The chronology of the palaeographic series is established by Cross, 'Jewish Scripts'. Cf. also the earlier study of Avigad, 'The Paleography.'

[10] This is the case, for instance, with manuscripts like 4QSam[b] (Cf. Cross, 'The Oldest Manuscripts') and 4QEnAstr[a] (cf. Milik, *Enoch*, 273).

[11] The Qumran discoveries led to intensive searches in the entire area of the Judaean Desert. These, in turn, brought a whole series of major discoveries in various locations in the area, the most important of which are Yadin's excavations at Masada and in Zealot caves. For a survey of the pertinent materials cf. Vermes, *Qumran in Perspective*, 14-21; Bietenhard, 'Handschriftenfunde', 761-74.

[12] Cf. Vaux, *Archaeology*, 58-87; Laperrousaz, *Qoumrân*, 65-89. In both places, pottery and coins similar to those of Qumran phases 1 and 2, were found.

ing skeletons of women and children. Consequently, the excavator concluded that the settlement belonged to the community of Qumran, i.e. to the Essenes.[13] The peculiar character of Qumran, namely that it lacks buildings suitable for living, led the archaeologists to conclude that it served as a centre for communal life; the installations suit communal activities, and Qumran is assumed to have served only for such purpose, while the members of the community lived in the surrounding area in huts or caves.[14]

With the absence of any self-designation in the scrolls, the first attempts to identify the community covered almost the whole range of Jewish sects known from classical sources.[15] The explanation which thus far accounts best for most of the data, identifies Qumran as the centre of the Essene movement.[16] The Essenes are well-known from a number of ancient accounts,[17] the most reliable of which are the observations of Pliny the Elder,[18] Philo[19] and Josephus.[20] The picture of the Essenes emerging from these sources is strikingly similar to what one gathers from the scrolls and the Qumran site:[21]

a) *Geographical information:* Pliny describes the Essene settlement as located north of Ein-Gedi (*infra hos Engada*). It suits the location of Qumran well.

b) *Social and religious practices.* Both sets of data speak of a community whose members share property, work and study, take meals together in a

[13] Cf. Bar-Adon, 'Another Settlement.' The identification of the settlement as Essene was cautiously accepted by De Vaux, *Archaeology,* 88-90, met with scepticism by Laperrousaz, *Qoumrân,* 110-114 and was endorsed by Yadin, *Temple Scroll* I, 251 n. 63.

[14] Cf. Vaux, *Archaeology,* 10, 86. Recent excavations in the entire region of Ein Gedi and the Araba, revealed additional sites and fortresses with remains similar to those of Qumran. They include a fortress in the mouth of Wadi en -Nar and Wadi Mazin, known as Qasr el-Jahud, and the fortress now being excavated on the Rujm el Bahr peninsula. Bar-Adon suggests that the networks of small fortresses, settlements and roads dating from the Hasmonaean Period formed part of John Hyrcanus' plan to fortify the area of Jericho and Ein-Gedi. In his opinion both agricultural and military settlements formed part of the system and in this capacity the communities of Qumran — Ein Feshkha and Ein el Ghuweir were first established. See Bar-Adon, 'The Hasmonean Fortresses.'

[15] The suggestions ranged from Pharisees (Rabin, *Qumran Studies*), Sadducees (North, 'The Qumran Sadducees'), Zealots (Roth, *The Historical Background*) and Judaeo-Christians (Teicher, 'Damascus Fragments'; *id.* 'Dead Sea Scrolls'; *id.* 'The Teaching') to Karaites (Zeitlin, *The Zadokite Fragments*).

[16] This identification was first suggested by Sukenik, *Dead Sea Scrolls,* 29 and argued in detail by Dupont-Sommer, *Aperçus,* 105-17.

[17] All the ancient testimonies on the Essenes were assembled and reproduced in Adam, *Antike Berichte.* Cf. also the summary of the evidence in Schürer, *History* 2, 562-74.

[18] *Naturalis historia* 5:73.

[19] *Prob.* 72-91; *Cont.* 1-90.

[20] *War* 2:119-161; *Ant.* 13:171-173; 15:371-379; 18:18-22.

[21] For early dissenting voices see Goshen-Gottstein, 'Anti-Essene Traits'; Roth, 'The Qumran Sect'; Driver, *The Judaean Scrolls,* 100-121.

ceremonial way and observe a strict state of ritual purity. Both have an elaborate procedure of admitting new members, and are strictly organized by ranks. They have a body of special teachings, most of which was kept secret. Religious ideas such as predestination, which Josephus ascribes to the Essenes, equally fit in with the ideology of the scrolls.[22]

c) *Historical setting*. Josephus introduced his account of the Essenes as one of the 'three Jewish philosophies', while discussing the reign of Jonathan (160-142 B.C.E.; *Ant.* 13:171). This corresponds to the beginning of the main period of occupation at Qumran and to the chronology established by the scrolls. Furthermore, most of the historical allusions contained in various sectarian works, fall within the Hasmonean Period.[23]

d) The *Temple Scroll*. Additional arguments in favour of identifying the Qumran community with the Essenes are provided by the *Temple Scroll*. The strict halakhic views of the scroll fit into our information about the Essenes. Specifically, the scroll prescribes the building of a sanitary installation outside the Temple-City, while Josephus tells of a similar installation serving the Essenes.[24] Furthermore, Josephus states that the Essenes considered oil as rendering impure, which may be reflected in the *Temple Scroll*.[25]

Two major difficulties are involved in the identification of the Qumran Community with the Essenes: the question of celibacy and the location. As for celibacy, all the classical accounts on the Essenes are unanimous in stating that the Essenes were celibates. This stands at variance with the presence of women's and children's remains in the cemeteries at Qumran and Ein Ghuweir. It also does not suit the mention of women and children in the sectarian writings.[26] As for the location, Pliny refers to one Essene centre in the desert, but from Philo and Josephus we learn that they lived in towns and villages in Judaea, which coincides with the indications of the *Damascus Covenant* that the sectaries lived in 'camps'.[27] However, the *Rule of the Community* does not mention these camps, but does include a *pesher* to Isa 40:3 on the preparation for the aproaching end in the desert (see

---

[22] Cf. Cross, *Library*, 70-106; Schürer, *History* 2, 583-90.

[23] Cf. below on the *Pesharim*, pp. 510-12.

[24] 11QTemp 46:13-16; Josephus *War* 2:147; 5:444 ff.; *Ant.* 15:373. Cf. below, p. 528. Cf. Yadin, *Temple Scroll* I, 228-35; 305; Pixner, 'Essene Quarter'.

[25] *War* 2:123, which Yadin (*Temple Scroll* 1, 92, 304-5) thinks is explained by the rule that one is permitted to oil oneself only once a year, 11QTemp 20:14-16. Cf. also CD 12:16 גאולי שמן , a reading proposed by Baumgarten, instead of גאילי שמו as read by Rabin; Cf. Baumgarten, 'The Essene Avoidance of Oil,' 88-89. The entire *Temple Scroll* is sectarian, as is proven, according to Yadin, by the fact that it adheres to the sectarian solar calendar. Cf. below pp. 528-9.

[26] E.g., CD 7:8, 12:1, 15:5, 16:10, 19:3.5; 1QM 7:3. The problem remains unsolved. Cf. Hübner, 'Zölibat'; Marx, 'Célibat'; Coppens, 'Célibat'.

[27] Cf. Philo, *Quod Omnis* 12, 75-76 and *Hypothetica* 11, 1; Josephus *War* 2:124; and CD 7:6, 12:23, 13:20, 14:3.9, 19:2.

1QS 8:13-16). These contradictions have often been resolved by suggesting either that the *Covenant* reflects a different phase of the sect, when its members were still in cities, or that it belongs to a group slightly different from the one portrayed by the *Rule*.[28] In light of Philo's and Josephus' attestations, of the evidence of the *Damascus Covenant,* and of the recent discovery of another possible Essene settlement, Qumran cannot be seen as the only Essene centre, as is the impression given by Pliny. It either served as a centre for other Essene settlements[29] or formed part of a more complex network of Essene settlements on the shores of the Dead Sea.[30]

In spite of the difficulties, the congruencies between the ancient descriptions of the Essenes and the information on the Qumran community are too numerous and comprehensive to be dismissed, while the difficulties are not insurmountable. The identification of the two is widely accepted.

The Qumran Library

The body of documents found at Qumran restores to us some of the lost literary riches produced in Eretz-Israel during the Second Commonwealth Era. The collection contains literary documents of a most varied nature, most of them of religious character. Apart from the oldest biblical manuscripts in our possession, many fragments come from works previously unknown,[31] while others yield the original Hebrew or Aramaic versions of apocryphal or pseudepigraphical works hitherto known only in translations.[32] Yet among this varied literary debris, a group of documents is discernable, distinctive in style and ideology, relating to the life and beliefs of a community identical to the one settled at Qumran. It is with this literature that the present chapter is concerned, a literature to be designated hereafter as 'the sectarian literature'.

The best-preserved and the most typical works in this category are the *Rule of the Community,* the *Damascus Covenant,* the *Thanksgiving Psalms*

---

[28] The second explanation points out that according to Josephus there existed another branch of the Essenes who married and lived in cities, *War* 2:160-161.

[29] Thus Cross, *Library,* 78-79.

[30] Cf. Sanders, 'The Dead Sea Scrolls,' 119. As De Vaux saw in Qumran the centre of the Essenes and also allowed the possibility of a smaller Essene settlement in Ein Ghuweir, he was forced to see in it 'no more than an annexe of very minor importance' (*Archaeology,* 135 n. 3). See also Bar Adon's opinion (above n. 14).

[31] These include, among others, many sectarian works, and various apocryphal and pseudepigraphic writings. For a description of some of them cf. Milik, 'Milkî-Ṣedeq'; 'Turfan et Qumran'; 'Écrits préesséniens'.

[32] E.g., *1 Enoch* and *Jubilees.*

(Hodayot), the *War of the Sons of Light against the Sons of Darkness (War Scroll)* and the biblical commentaries known as *Pesharim*.[33]

Practically all the sectarian writings published to date are written in Hebrew, while the Aramaic is reserved for Apocryphal and narrative works.[34] The Hebrew is a literary language, developed directly from later biblical Hebrew, but sharing many traits with the later Mishnaic Hebrew.[35] The Aramaic used in the non-sectarian compositions is a literary dialect belonging to the Middle Aramaic, current in Eretz-Israel and the vicinity between 200 B.C.E. and 200 C.E.[36] The languages spoken at Qumran were probably Mishnaic Hebrew[37] and Aramaic.

The scrolls were copied on papyrus or leather, but the leather proved more durable and has survived. The scrolls exhibit the scribal conventions and techniques generally prevalent in the Jewry of the Second Commonwealth.[38] The writing is in the square Hebrew script and occasionally in Palaeo-Hebrew. In some manuscripts Palaeo-Hebrew is employed to copy the Tetragrammaton YHWH.[39] Some biblical manuscripts, all of Palestinian origin, are written in this script throughout.[40]

Unlike medieval Hebrew manuscripts, the Qumran scrolls are not dated,

---

[33] In these works the sectarian traits are usually clear, but this is not always the case in other scolls. Thus there are some who doubt the sectarian provenance of the *Temple Scroll* (cf. n. 25 above). Recently it was claimed that the *Targum to Job* (11QtgJob) is a sectarian composition; see Caquot, 'Écrit sectaire'. However the features adduced are not sufficiently distinctive and can be explained otherwise. The present chapter includes all the clearly sectarian works but refers also to some borderline cases such as the *New Jerusalem.*

[34] Such are, for instance, compositions like the *Genesis Apocryphon* (1QGenApoc), *The Book of Giants* (4QGéants) and *The Visions of Amram* (4QVisAm). Cf. Fitzmyer, *Genesis Apocryphon* and Milik's publications referred to in n. 31.

[35] CF. Goshen-Gottstein, 'Linguistic Structure'; Rabin, 'The Historical Background'; Ben-Hayyim,'Traditions in the Hebrew Language'; Kutscher, 'The Language'; Qimron, *Grammar.*

[36] Typologically it reflects an intermediate phase between the Imperial Aramaic of the biblical Ezra and Daniel and the Jewish Aramaic of the Targumim. Cf. Fitzmyer, 'The Phases of the Aramaic'; 'Targum of Job'; Greenfield, 'Aramaic'; Sokoloff, 'Notes.'

[37] This is evident from the *Copper Scroll* from Cave 3 (cf. *DJD* 3, 201-302). It uses a colloquial Hebrew similar to the Mishnaic one. The same dialect of Hebrew is attested by the Bar-Kokhba letters, dated some seventy years after the destruction of Qumran. Cf. *DJD* 2, 124-65 and Yadin, 'Expedition D,' 40-52; 'The Cave of the Letters,' 248-57. Milik, *Ten Years,* 130 signals the existence of two works, written in Mishnaic Hebrew, of which several copies were found in cave 4. A letter from the sect's leader to his opponent, written in Mishnaic Hebrew, is being edited by John Strugnell.

[38] Cf. Talmon, 'Aspects,' 96.

[39] At times also other divine names. Cf. Siegel, 'The Employment of Palaeo-Hebrew'; Hanson, 'Paleo-Hebrew.'

[40] As, for instance, the manuscript 4QpaleoEx^m reproducing Exodus in a 'Samaritan' recension; cf. Skehan, 'Exodus.' Another peculiarity of the Hebrew manuscripts is their full orthography, both in biblical and in non-biblical manuscripts, from the Hasmonaean as well as the Herodian periods; Cf. Kutscher, 'The Language,' 5-8, 85-86, 126-86. Equally remarkable is the interchangeability of the gutturals, laryngeals and pharyngeals, which attests to their weakening in the current pronunciation (*ibid.* 505-10).

nor do they have colophons. Dating is, therefore, established on the basis of palaeographic typology. According to such dating, the entire body of Qumran manuscripts falls between the third century B.C.E. and the third quarter of the first century C.E. The majority of the manuscripts are assigned to 50 B.C.E. to 68 C.E.[41] No sectarian writing survived in a copy earlier than the last quarter of the second century B.C.E.

This could be interpreted to mean that the literary activity of the sect belonged to the second phase of its existence. But the picture is more complex. Significantly, within the sectarian literature itself two categories can be discerned. The first group consists of works surviving in more than one copy, of which at least one dates to the beginning of the first century B.C.E. All of these works are composite and seem to have had a literary history. They include: the *Rule of the Community,* the *Damascus Covenant,* the *War Scroll* and the *Thanksgiving Scroll.* The second group consists mainly of the *Pesharim.* All of them reached us in single copies dating between 50 B.C.E. and 68 C.E. Furthermore, some *Pesharim* contain references to Roman times and in this case it may be inferred that they are autographs and belong to the latter phase of the sectarian history, in contradistinction to the first group.[42]

Yet two considerations point to the possibility that the *Pesharim* in general originate from the early phase of the sect's history. First, some of them may exhibit traces of a literary history.[43] Secondly, their exegetical method and literary form are attested in older works. Furthermore, both the *Damascus Covenant* and the *Pesher on Habakkuk* attribute to the sect's leader, the Teacher of Righteousness, a special revelation and teaching of Scripture (CD 1:11-12; 1QpHab 2:7-10, 7:1-8). Hence, though the actual copies of the *Pesharim* are relatively late, the material they expound may go back to the beginnings of the sect. We must assume, then, either a literary or an oral transmission which is lost. Taking into account all these data, we must conclude that the *Pesharim* commit to writing exegetical traditions covering several generations, and that the dating of the manuscripts cannot be taken as their date of composition.[44]

Rules

The Library of Qumran yielded several examples of 'rules', i.e. collections of various rules, regulations and religious instructions. They are usually

[41] Cross, *Library,* 118-122.
[42] Cross, *ibid.*
[43] Horgan, *Peshar,* 2-3. She gives 1QpHab 2:5, 3:7 and 4QpIs^e 5:5a-5 as illustrations.
[44] Obviously, the manuscript dating only determines a *terminus ante quem,* the latest possible date of composition of a certain work, not the actual date. Therefore paleographical data are of limited value for the determination of the date of the sect's foundation and the chronology of its inner development.

indicated by the term *serekh* (סרך) meaning rule, order; and thus a *serekh* is a set of rules.[45] There are two examples of rules concerned with the actual life and organisation of the sectarian community: The *Rule of the Community* and the second part of the *Damascus Covenant*.[46] Two other examples deal with eschatological situations: the *War Scroll* lays down the rule for the final war, and the *Rule of the Congregation* discusses the future messianic banquet. Perhaps the work known as the *Benedictions* (1QS[b]) which contains eschateological blessings also formed a kind of rule.

By its very nature, a rule presents an ideal pattern of behaviour. Yet the prescriptions of rules such as the *Rule of the Community* and the *Damascus Covenant* show close resemblance to Josephus' and Philo's descriptions of Essene practice. We may assume, then, that the rules largely reflect the actual practice of the groups behind them.

The literary genre of rule is unknown in Jewish literature outside Qumran, but it resembles the regulations of various societies in the Hellenistic world.[47]

THE DAMASCUS COVENANT

The work currently known as the *Damascus Covenant* or the *Zadokite Documents* is the only sectarian document to have been known before the discoveries at Qumran. Found in the Geniza of the old Karaite synagogue at Cairo, it was published by Solomon Schechter as a Pharisaic sectarian document.[48] But with the first publications of scrolls from Qumran, the numerous affinities of style and terminology between the *Damascus Covenant* and the scrolls suggested that they belonged to the same group. This was confirmed by the discovery of fragments of the *Covenant* in several Qumran caves. A copy of it may have come into the hands of the Karaites through an ancient discovery of manuscripts and may have been copied, and eventually preserved in the Geniza.[49] Two important facts emerge from the state of the manuscripts: Manuscripts from cave 4 point to a different text, perhaps a different recension; although most of the copies are Herodian, the existence of one copy from 100-75 B.C.E. situates the composition of the work not later than 100 B.C.E.[50]

---

[45] 1QS 5:1, 6:8; 1QS[a] 1:1; 1QM 9:10. Cf. also the connotation of 'military unit'; e.g., 1QM 4:11, 5:4, 6:10, 13, 13:1.

[46] Note the term, *serekh* in CD 10:4, 12:19, 12:22, 13:7.

[47] Cf. Bardtke, 'Die Rechtsstellung'; Hengel, *Hellenism* I, 244; Weinfeld, 'Organizational Pattern'.

[48] Cf. Schechter, *Fragments.*

[49] For a convenient survey of possible contacts of the Karaites with sectarian manuscripts during the ninth and tenth centuries, cf. Rowley, *The Zadokite Fragments*, 22-29.

[50] The following MSS. are available: *Geniza MSS.:* MS. A (TS 10 K6), date: 10th century. Contents: pages 1-16. MS. B (TS 63 11), date: 12th century. Contents: pages 19-20; partly

The extant text from the Geniza falls into two distinct parts, each of a different character: a) leaves 1-8 (MS.A) and 19-20 (MS.B). Usually labelled as the Admonition, it contains admonitions, moral addresses and historical teachings; b) leaves 9-16 contain halakhic legal prescriptions and sectarian regulations, partly constituting a Rule proper. Although of a distinct nature, the two parts are closely interrelated in ideas and style. The opening of the admonition is especially instructive in this respect:

> And in the Epoch of Wrath, three hundred and ninety years (Ezek 4:5) after He had given them into the hand of Nebuchadnezzar King of Babylon (Jer 27:6), He visited them and He caused to grow forth from Israel and Aaron a root (Isa 60:21) of cultivation to possess his Land (Ps 37:29) and to wax fat in the goodness of His soil. And they considered their trespass and they knew that they were guilty men. But they were like blind and like them they grope (their) way (Isa 59:10) for twenty years. And God considered their works, for with a perfect heart (1 Chr 29:9) did they seek Him; and He raised for them a Teacher of Righteousness (Hos 10:12) to lead them in the way of His heart (CD 1:5-12).[51]

This passage takes up history from the point where God's punishment has lasted three hundred and ninety years. At the end of this period, God 'visited' Israel and caused a 'root of cultivation' to grow from Israel and Aaron. Thus the appearance of the group in question is described. Both 'visitation' and 'root' are biblical terms overlaid with eschatological significance. Hence, the entire event should be read in an eschatological

duplicating pages 7-8 of MS. A, but with important variants. The relationship between the two manuscripts is complex; on the whole A seems to reproduce a defective text (cf. 4:6). This impression is confirmed by a comparison with the 4Q fragments; see below, p. 495ff. Rabin, *Zadokite Documents*, was criticised for combining both MSS. into one text in his edition, otherwise the best available.

*Qumran MSS:*5Q12 — Date: first century c.e. Contents: CD 9:7-9. (Edited by Milik, *DJD* 3, 181.)

6Q15 — Date: first century c.e. Contents: CD 4:19-21; 5.13-14; 5:18-6:2; 6:20-7:1. Fragment 5 reproduces a legislative section not found in the Geniza text. Generally the text is that of the Geniza. (Edited by Baillet, *DJD* 3, 128-31.)

4QD*a-e* — still unpublished. Dates: 4QD*a* (formerly 4QD*b* = 4Q226) is the oldest, dated to the first third of the first century b.c.e. Cf. Milik, *Ten Years*, 58, 114, 117, 151-2. See also his 'Milki-Ṣedeq', 135 where he dates 4QD*e* (= 4Q270) to the Herodian period. Contents: substantially the same text as that of the Geniza, with important additions: a) an exhortation on God's saving plan in history and an introduction (according to Milik, to precede the present Geniza-text opening); b) various prescriptions (Milik: to be placed after CD 8:21 and followed by 19:35-20:34); c) a conclusion to the Legal Code (to follow CD 12:18); d) a liturgy for the Renewal of the Covenant (to follow CD 14:22), which Milik thinks took place at Pentecost. In this sense he understands the fragment 4QD*a* (= 4Q226) 3 X 16-20, published in 'Milki-Ṣedeq', 135.

[51] Translation: Rabin, *The Zadokite Documents*.

perspective. The initial impulse for the group's appearance is understood in the framework of the divine, foreordained plan for history. Yet the members of the sect have their own role to play; they recognize their sin and acknowledge it, thus actually going through confession and repentance. In a response, God raises the Teacher of Righteousness to instruct them. In an allusion to Hos 10:12, this leader's appellation, as well as the circumstances of his appearance, show him to be the divine Elect, inspired and sent to the sect to impart special teachings about 'God's way'.

Thus the sect's point of departure appears to have been a double awareness: on the one hand the recognition of their own sinfulness and the need to repent; on the other, the conviction that they possessed the true teaching and revelation through the Teacher of Righteousness. This explains why the sectaries call themselves both 'the Repenters of Israel'[52] and 'the comers into the New Covenant'[53]. In this context, the special teachings of the sectaries enable them to recognize the true way, and to practise true repentance in fidelity to the Torah of Moses. From the few allusions in the *Damascus Covenant* it seems that these teachings concerned a wide range of subjects, 'hidden things concerning which all of Israel err' (CD 3:14): the Sabbaths, the Appointed Times, His Will. The list may refer to the distinctive *halakhah* developed among the sectaries and perhaps also to the special exegetical method they elaborated to interpret the Torah and the prophets.[54] The allusion to the Appointed Times may refer to the solar calendar espoused by the sect, which set the festivals on dates different to the rest of Israel (cf. below pp. 528, 530).

All these teachings were divulged to the community in a divine revelation and thus render the community elect and just by its very nature. In order to preserve this character, a special way of life and thought was devised, consisting of strict segregation from the non-sectarian world. The members of the community were required '... to keep apart from the children of the Pit; to refrain from the unclean wealth of wickedness (acquired) by vowing and devoting ...' (CD 6:14-15). The outside world is considered impure and full of iniquity.

In order to preserve their own purity and righteous way, the members instituted a communal life described in the Rule of the second part (CD 12-16). The members live in camps organized in units of thousands, hundreds, fifties and tens (13:1-2, 20, 14:3), like the tribes of Israel in the desert (Exod 18:25).[55]

An official designated as the Overseer (מבקר) has special responsibilities: admitting new members, instructing them as well as the entire

---

[52] שבי ישראל — CD 4:2, 6:5, 8:16, 19:29.
[53] באי הברית — CD 6:19, 8:21, 19:33; cf. 2:2, 3:10, 6:11, 13:14, 15:5, 19:16, 20:25.
[54] CD 3:16-17; 6:2-11; 7:15-21.
[55] The same form of organization recurs in the eschatological war, cf. below, p. 516.

community, supervising income and expenses for the poor and performing judiciary functions.[56] The members of the community apparently work and have commercial contacts with non-sectaries, but these are strictly regulated by the Overseer (13:14-16, 14:12-13). They marry and have children 'according to the Law' (19:3). The general assembly of the members convenes according to a fixed order: first the Priests, followed by the Levites, the Israelites and the proselytes (14:3-7). All members take a solemn oath to adhere to the law of Moses (15:5-16:2). A considerable part of the time was apparently devoted to study, whether of the Torah or other sectarian books, for in each smallest unit of ten people the presence of a learned priest is obligatory (13:2).[57]

As was stressed above, at the very heart of the sectarian thought lay the belief that Israel at large is still living in sin and error, and is caught in 'the three nets of Belial' (4:15). This results in a total condemnation of non-sectarian Jews. Yet specific groups of adversaries are denounced; e.g., 'those who search slippery things,' led by 'the Spouter of Lies'.[58] In this connection too, the community's attitude to the Second Temple should be seen: it is considered impure, defiled by its priests, and therefore members were not allowed to bring sacrifices there.[59] But they were permitted to send them with offerings by someone else.[60]

The life and thought of the community described in the *Damascus Covenant* acquire a poignant intensity through their eschatological perspective. This is already implied in the description of the emergence of the sect (cf. above p. 491), and conforms to the pattern of the appearance of the Just and Elect at the dawn of the eschatological era, a pattern known from apocalyptic writings. It becomes clear that the just and perfect life to which the sect had converted formed part of the general divine plan of history. This is why the sect comes into being in 'the Last Generation' and in 'a Period of Wickedness' (1:12, 6:10, 14, 12:23, 15:7), both standing at the end of the historical sequence: the sect is destined to be the shoot from which the new eschatological world will spring. Hence the keen interest taken by the community in the historical circumstances surrounding its origins and existence. It accounts for the various interpretations of contemporary

---

[56] 9:19.22; 13:6-7, 13,16; 14:8, 11, 13, 20; 15:8, 11, 14.
[57] In this connection a sectarian work named *The Book of (the) Hago* (ספר ההגו) is mentioned (CD 10:6 13:2; cf. 1 QS[a] 1:7), which was subject to intensive study in the sect. Goshen-Gottstein, 'Puzzle,' suggested to read ספר ההגי; cf. 1QS[a] 1:7. Rabinowitz, 'SPR HHGU/Y', suggested that it was the Bible, while Yadin, *Temple Scroll* 1, 301 thought it refers to the *Temple Scroll* (below, p. 527). Cf. also Rabin, *The Zadokite Documents*, 50.
[58] 1:14, 18; 4:19, 20; 8:13; 19:25.
[59] 4:18; 5:6-11; 6:11-16; 11:17-20. A similar attitude to the Second Temple is attested by Mal 1:12, *1 Enoch* 89:73; *Test. Levi* 17; *Assump. Mosis* 5:4. Cf. *Psalms of Solomon* 2:3, 8:12.
[60] Yadin, *Temple Scroll* 1, 105 suggests that CD 11:17-18 concerns all sacrifices except those of the Shabbat proper.

events in light of the biblical text, according to the *pesher* method (see below). It also explains the presence of unique chronological indications concerning the initial phase of the sect. The most crucial one is the statement cited above (CD 1:5), that 390 years elapsed from the subjugation to Nebuchadnezzar to the appearance of the sect (on which see below, pp. 543-5).

Other historical allusions speak of a migration of the community from the Land of Judaea to the Land of Damascus.[61] While it is unclear exactly when this took place, it must belong to the early phase of the sect's history, apparently during the lifetime of the Teacher of Righteousness (20:12-14). This is certainly the case of the man named 'the Searcher of the Law (דורש התורה, 6:7) is the Teacher of Righteousness. He is described as responsible for devising new methods of interpreting the Torah (6:2-11). The combined internal and archaeological evidence shows that this migration did not take place during the main periods of occupation in Qumran,[62] and must precede them. Therefore it is unlikely that Damascus is a symbolic name for Qumran.[63] Nor is it convincing to interpret it as a designation for Babylon.[64] A growing number of scholars see in 'the Land of Damascus' a symbolic designation for exile, but not for a specific one. In any case, if it does point to a specific location, no satisfactory identification has yet been suggested.[65]

As for the literary structure of the *Damascus Covenant,* no clear agreement has yet emerged. The fact that the work consists of two parts of distinct

---

[61] CD 4:3, 6:5, 6:19, 8:21, 19:34, 20:12.

[62] As was suggested in the early years of research. Cf. e.g., Milik, *Ten Years,* 90. The main difficulty in this identification is the early date of the migration, as indicated by the data. Two considerations impose an early date: a) the oldest copy of CD, 4QDᵃ, dates to the first third of the first century B.C.E.; b) The work was written at least 40 years after the death of the Teacher of Righteousness (CD 20:13-15). The combined evidence of both data, together with the assumption that the migration took place in the Teacher's lifetime (CD, *ibid.*), impose the conclusion that the migration took place at least a generation before the earliest manuscript, i.e. during the second half of the second century B.C.E. Significantly, CD does not mention the Kittim, i.e. the Romans, but only 'the Kings of Greece' (8:10-12 מלכי יון), probably the Seleucids. Cf. Cross, *Library,* 81-82; De Vaux, *Archaeology,* 112-13.

[63] Cf. Rabinowitz, 'Reconsideration;' Jaubert, 'Damas'; Murphy-O'Connor, 'The Essenes', 219-23; Vermes, *Scripture,* 43-49; Milikowsky, 'Damascus'. Opting for a real migration to Damascus are e.g. Rowley, *The Zadokite Fragments,* 75; Iwry, 'Migration.'

[64] As proposed by Murphy-O'Connor, 'The Essenes,' 221. See below, p. 546 n. 294.

[65] Another chronological datum is the statement that forty years elapsed from the death of the Teacher of Righteousness to the extermination of the followers of the Man of Lies (20:13). Though it is obviously patterned after the period of Israel's wandering in the wilderness (Deut 2:14), there is no reason to doubt its historical value. It may also represent the span of a generation following the biblical view. The number is important for fixing the date of composition of the *Covenant,* or at least that of the passage in question well after the death of the Teacher of Righteousness. This lapse of time should be taken into account in all reconstructions of the sect's early history (cf. below, p. 545).

character led some scholars to conclude that they are separate works. [66] However there is no need to assume independent origin in order to account for distinct literary character, particularly when numerous affinities between the two parts can be discerned.[67] Moreover in the 4Q fragments the two sections are combined into one running text.[68]

Another literary problem is the considerable divergency between manuscripts A and B in their overlapping passages: 7-8 (A) parallels 19-20 (B). Some scholars concluded that the two manuscripts are 'faulty copies of one archetype';[69] others thought that MS.B is dependent on A and therefore must represent a later correction of A.[70] However, these theories rest on precarious bases. For there are also independent elements in MS. B which cannot be exlained by MS. A. Thus it is MS. B which mentions one Messiah, while MS. A contains a *pesher* on two Messiahs[71] (cf. below, p. 540). It should then be stressed that the relationship between the two MSS. is a complex one, and cannot be reduced to simple dependence. While it is reasonable to conclude that at least in the divergent passages two recensions are discernable, it is impossible to establish which one is earlier.[72]

With respect to the literary structure of the *Covenant,* the existence of various literary units led some scholars to the conclusion that it is a compilation of independent sources stemming from various periods and assembled by a later editor.[73] Methodologically one may well ask whether the distinct literary character of the units necessarily implies that they are

---

[66] Cf. Rabin, *The Zadokite Documents,* x.

[67] Cf. Murphy-O'Connor, 'Literary Analysis', 212-14.

[68] Cf. Milik, *Ten Years,* 39.

[69] See e.g. Rabin, *The Zadokite Documents,* viii.

[70] Cf. Carmignac, 'Comparaison entre les manuscripts', 66. Murphy-O'Connor, 'The Critique', 203-5, argues that MS. B must be the later one because the variants of a cannot be explained by it. Cf. also Jeremias, *Lehrer der Gerechtigkeit,* 112 n. 7. Iwry, 'Migration', 83 n. 10 sees in MS. B a later revised edition, because only in B the *Yahad* and the death of the Teacher are mentioned.

[71] In connection with the messianic teaching two recensions were discerned: A_1 (admonition) which mentions two Messiahs, and A_2 (law) — B (19-20) with one Messiah. See e.g. Huppenbauer, 'Zur Eschatologie'. Some scholars view MS. B as reflecting an earlier stage of the messianic teaching; cf. below p. 539.

[72] The most significant divergencies between the MSS. concern the *pesharim;* MS. A gives *pesharim* on Isa 7:17 and on Amos, referring to past events. MS. B gives *pesharim* on Zech 13:7 and on Ezekiel, alluding to eschatological events. In addition, MS. A includes a mention of Baruch and Gehazi (CD 8:20-21), while B refers to the Messiah. B tends to give biblical quotations more fully and gives more developed stylistic formulae.

[73] Denis, 'Evolution de Structures' and *Les Thèmes de Connaissance,* gives the following division: 1) the three admonitions; 1-4:6 + 7:13-8:3 and 20: 15-27, reflecting the beginnings of the new religious movement; 2) 4:6-7:4 + 20:27-34; these passages reflect a more developed eschatological movement in Damascus; 3) 7:4-8 (= 19-20); the initial movement became an organized sect; 4) the Large Code, leaves 9-16, contains many elements of diverse periods.

based on independent sources.[74] Even more questionable is the association of units of distinct literary character with specific historical situations.[75] The literary analysis itself is not always convincing,[76] nor are the historical reconstructions based on it.[77] Especially puzzling is the disregard for the literary information to be gained from the 4Q fragments. The following overall picture of the Geniza text with the 4Q fragments (in square brackets) clearly shows the unity of the work:[78]

[*Introduction* (4Q frg.)]
History: Historical introduction. The origin of the sect (1:1-2:1). The historical process and its laws (2:2-3:12).
The New Covenant: The sect, its significance and its contemporary role (3:12-4:12a).

---

[74] Murphy O'Connor, taking up the work of Denis and of Stegemann (*Die Entstehung*). See 'Missionary Document'; 'The Literary Analysis'; 'Analysis of CD XIX 33 ff.'; 'The Critique'; 'The Essenes'. He reconstructed the genesis of the *Covenant* as follows: 1) The Missionary Document (2:14-6:1) — designed to convert to the Essene reform. This is the oldest source. 2) The Memorandum (6:2-8:3) — devised to recall members of the community to a more faithful observance. 3) A criticism of the Rulers of Judaea (8:3-18). 4) A document aiming at meeting dissatisfaction (19:33-20:22b). See now also Davies, *Covenant*.

[75] This connection, assumed to exist between a typical literary form and a *Sitz im Leben* (a methodological assumption basic to form-criticism), has recently been criticized. Cf. Knierim, 'Form Criticism.'

[76] Thus the theory that 2:14-6:1 is a missionary document is explained by the suggestion that the community saw itself as the Israelites in Kadesh during the wilderness period, and therefore introduced the list of sinners in CD 2:14-3:12. Cf. Murphy-O'Connor, 'Missionary Document,' 205. This is far-fetched. The mention of Kadesh alludes to the sinful generation of the wilderness which was doomed to perish in the wilderness because of its sins. Cf. Deut 9:23, Ps 106:25 and CD 20:14-15 (B). Therefore it is very unlikely that it served as a typology for the sect itself. It is rather the patriarchs in this list who serve as archetypes. The mention of the wilderness generation occurs in the framework of a general list of sinners, which has a long literary history behind it (see e.g. Sir 16:7-10).

[77] Murphy-O'Connor's main contention is that the sect came into being as a priestly group in Babylon, and migrated to Judaea in the Maccabaean Revolt. The rest of the four stages are reconstructed from this point of departure. This contention is based on two questionable interpretations: a) The identification of the Land of Damascus as a symbolic designation of Babylon; b) The understanding of the sectaries' self-designation שבי ישראל (as 'those who returned from Exile'. Here, Murphy-O'Connor is greatly influenced by Iwry, 'Migration.' The evidence for such an understanding is null. Though from the linguistic point of view it is possible, nothing in the context suggests it. By contrast, Rabin's interpretation of שבי ישראל as 'those of Israel who repented' perfectly suits the general climate of sectarian ideas. It is probably based on the biblical expression שבי פשע (Isa 59:20), an appellation figuring in CD itself (CD 2:5 20:17). Expressions like 'returning to the Law of Moses' and 'repenting one's corrupted way' (CD 15:7) clearly point to the true background of the appellation. שבי ישראל thus forms another sectarian sobriquet, based on a *pesher* to a prophetic text. Cf. below, p. 505. The arguments of Davies, *Covenant* for a diaspora origin do not convince.

[78] The table is based on the reconstruction of Fitzmyer ('Prolegomenon', 18-19; *Tools* 90-92) who used all the available data on the 4Q fragments. For a detailed description of these fragments see above n. 50.

The Sins of Israel: The present rule of Belial over Israel: the sect's adversaries and their sins (4:12b-6:2a).
Repentance of the Sect: The sense and principles of the New Covenant (6:2b-7:9a).
Recompense of the Sinners and the Just: The fate of the faithful and the apostates (7:9b-8:21 and 19:35-20:34).

[*Various Laws* (4Q frg.)]
Practising the New Covenant: Rites and regulations of the sect (9:1-12:18). Organisation of the sect (12:19-14:19). The penal code (14:20-22). The entrance into the covenant and the law of oaths (15:1-16:12). Law of vows (16:13-20).[79]
[*Concluding Ceremony of Acceptance:* Liturgy for the feast of the renewal of the convenant (4Q frg.).[80] Conclusion (4Q frg.).]

The discernable structure is a complex one, embracing smaller units such as admonitions, history and law. In this respect, the framework manifests affinities to the structure of biblical covenant passages, such as Deut 26-27, 29-31; Neh 9-10, as well as a relationship with the *Rule of the Community.* Both the *Covenant* and the *Rule* illustrate the literary conventions of the Jewish post-biblical literature, especially of the apocalyptic works, in that they use complex forms, embracing various smaller forms, often modelled after biblical precedents.[81] Such works may and do use various sources of distinct forms and periods, but they work them out into one overall framework which expresses the intention of the author. Thus the exaggerated search for distinct literatyr sources and corresponding historical situations may often distort the original intentions of the work and obscure more fundamental historical considerations.

THE RULE OF THE COMMUNITY

A second example of a Rule is offered by the work known as the *Rule of the Community.* Preserved almost intact, and prescribing regulations for the community in the present, it also gives the fullest picture now existing of the actual functioning of the sect. The best preserved manuscript from cave 1, 1QS, was one of the first scrolls to be published. The fact that the work

---

[79] Form-critical considerations militate against Milik's suggestion to place the passage 15:1-17:12 at the beginning of the legal part of CD, unless there is evidence for it in the actual 4Q manuscripts. The passage in question fits well into its present context at the end of a list of laws. The same order of elements is attested by Deut 31:9-13.
[80] Milik proposes to place this section after the penal code, but comparison with various passages in Deuteronomy shows that the ceremony follows the detailed laws, according to the scheme of the covenant; cf. Deut 27: 31:9-13.
[81] Cf. the comment of Koch, *The Rediscovery,* 23-28; Collins, *Apocalypse,* 22.

exists in twelve copies ranging from 100 B.C.E. to the Herodian period, shows its popularity and importance in Qumran. The manuscript dating points to a composition during the second half of the second century B.C.E.[82]

As does the *Covenant,* the *Rule* also consists of distinct literary units of different character. A general introduction states the aims of the community (1:1-15). It is followed by a description of the 'Entrance into the Covenant' (1:16-3:12; see further below, p. 500). After a summary of the sect's main theological ideas, the 'Treatise of the Two Spirits' (3:13-4:26), there follows a loose combination of several sets of rules (5:1-6:23). It begins with another list of the sect's aims and obligations, followed by various rules and admonitions to the individual members, mainly to avoid all contact with outsiders and to obey one's superiors. More detailed rules are laid down in column 6. Next follows a penal code (6:24-7:25), a unit describing the ideal community (8:1-9:11), and finally a unit with instructions and guidance to the community (9:12-26). The extant work concludes with psalm-like hymns (10:1-11:22).

The community organisation which emerges from this collection of regulations aims at a separation from 'the men of iniquity' in order to repent, to practice the Law of Moses properly (5:8-10) and to prepare for the coming *eschaton* (8:12-16). The members live a communal life, sharing property and work, assembling to discuss matters of the community, studying together and probably also praying together:

> And this is the Rule for the members of the community who are willing to repent all evil and to hold fast to everything which He willed, to separate from the gathering of men of iniquity, to be a community (Yahad יחד) in the Torah and in property; and to submit to the authority of the Sons of Zadok, the priests who guard the covenant and according to the majority of the community members who adhere to the Covenant . . . (1QS 5:1-3).

---

[82] The following MSS. were recovered from Qumran caves:

1QS — Date: between 100 and 75 B.C.E. Contents: eleven leaves of almost the entire work. On the same manuscript, two other works were copied, 1QS^a and 1QS^b (cf. below). Cf. Milik and Barthélemy, *DJD* 1, 107-30. It was apparently copied from a defective copy, to judge from the blanks left and from the corrections by the scribe; cf. Cross, 'Introduction,' 4. Milik dates 1QS to the last quarter of the second century B.C.E. ('Milki-Ṣedeq,' 135). Photographs with transliterations were first published by John C. Trever, and were recently re-published.

5Q11 — Date: late writing. Contents: two fragments covering 1QS 2:4-7, 12-14. (Milik, *DJD* 3, 180).

4QS^{a-j} — Ten manuscripts from cave 4, still unpublished. Date: three copies dating from the first quarter of the first century B.C.E.; so Cross, *Library,* 119. According to Milik (*Ten Years,* 123-4), the oldest manuscript is 4QS^e, a papyrus copy. A list of variants from 4Q copies was published by Milik in 'Review', 411-16 and was incorporated into the Hebrew edition of Licht.

The priests are given precedence in all ceremonial matters. They lead the ceremony of the entry into the covenant (see below, p. 500), they bless first at the communal meal and they sit first in the council (1QS 6:5, 8). The same precedence is to be observed in the order of seating at the messianic banquet in 1QS^a (cf. below) as well as in the organisation of the eschatological war (1QM); a priest must also be present in a minimal group of ten (1QS 6:3-4).

While the priests, the Levites and the elders sit first in the 'Council of the Many' (6:8), it is the Overseer (6:12, 14) who is in charge of the practical management (cf. above, p. 494). A number of functions are allocated to the general assembly (the Council of the Many — מושב הרבים , 1QS 6:8, 11; 7:10, 13). Its role is to discuss various matters of the community; among other things, to admit new members. Strict rules of behaviour in the Council of the Many are prescribed: to talk in turn, not to interrupt each other's words, not to sleep and not to spit (1QS 6:10-11; 7:10, 13).

Special procedures were set for admitting new members into the sect: the candidate was first examined by the Overseer and after an oath of loyalty to the sect, he would study. Then he was brought for a first examination before the Many. If he was accepted, he lived in the community as a candidate for one year. He would not be permitted to participate in the communal meals and he would be allowed to keep his property. After a second examination by the Many, the candidate would give his property temporarily to the community, and live for another year in the community. If, at the end of the second year, he passed the third examination by the Many, he would become a full member of the community: he would give his property definitely to the community, he would participate in the Council of the Many and the communal meals, and he would be inscribed in the order of members (1QS 6:13-23).

The successive stages of admission are marked off by the purity rules of the sect.[83] The degree of purity of the candidate is raised after each examination. In the first year he is not allowed to touch the 'Purities of the Many' (6:16); in the second year the prohibition is restricted to the 'Drink of the Many' (6:20), and finally he is allowed to participate fully in the communal meals. In this respect the sect resembles the Pharisaic *Haburoth* (see below, p. 526), but unlike the latter it connected the maintenance of purity with the idea of repentance. True purity of the body became effective only when repentance takes place, i.e. by accepting the sectarian way of life. In this context, ritual purity is seen as only one facet of a more comprehensive idea of purity: purity from sin. Thus the strict practice of ritual purity forms an integral part of the sect's general outlook.

Interestingly, the property brought by new members also seems to be considered impure, for it is definitely accepted to the common treasury

---

[83] Cf. Licht, *The Rule Scroll,* 146-8; 294-303.

only when the candidate is a full member. This is connected with the community's withdrawal from the surrounding society: all money or property is considered 'property of iniquity' and should be shunned (1QS 9:8, 10:19; 1QH 10:22; CD 4:17, 6:15-16, 8:5, 12:7).

Another central ceremony in the sectarian life is the so-called Entry into the covenant. The ceremony is described in the opening section of the *Rule* and it took place every year, perhaps at Pentecost as celebrated by the sect, i.e. on the fifteenth of the third month. As often in the *Rule*, the ceremony and its liturgy are arranged in a chiastic structure, of which the confession of the Israelites, the blessings and the curses form the central part.[84] The ceremony itself was apparently modelled after the depiction of the Gerizim covenant (Deut 11:26-32; Josh 8:30-35). Two groups were arranged opposite to each other and some, perhaps the Priests and Levites, went through in procession. Likewise, liturgical elements were taken over from Deuteronomy, mainly the curses and blessings and the reiterated response of the participants (Amen, Amen; cf. Deut 27). Yet when comparing the biblical covenants (Lev 26:3-46; Deut 28; Josh 30-34) with the formulation of the *Rule,* the full measure of difference is apparent. While the biblical covenant implies a real choice and acceptance, and the curses and blessings function as threats and rewards, the covenant of the sectaries asserts and reinforces a situation predetermined by God from the beginning. The curses are addressed to the lot of Belial, the blessings to the lot of God. Therefore the real sanction is addressed not to the Sons of Darkness, who are damned in any case, but to those who did not persevere in the New Covenant. Not surprisingly, the language used is taken from the biblical threats to the Israelites betraying the covenant (Deut 29:19-20). As the ceremony in question contains a commitment to adhere to the New Covenant, it was identified with the oath taken by the members of the community and mentioned elsewhere. It is perhaps identical with 'the formidable oath' taken by the Essenes, according to Josephus.[85]

Among the literary units of the *Rule*, the section 3:13-4:26, called the

---

[84] On the hymns see below p. 569f. The chiasm is illustrated in the following table:
Instruction 'to enter into the covenant' (1:16-18)
    Priests and Levites bless God
    Participants' response: Amen (1:19-20)
        Priests recite God's deeds and pity, Levites recite Israel's sins
        Participants' response: confession (1:21-2:1)
        Priests bless God's lot, Levites curse Belial's lot
        Participants' response: Amen (2:1-10)
    Priests and Levites curse the one who betrays the New Covenant,
    i.e. a sectarian who betrayed (2:11-17)
    Participants' response: Amen (2:18)
The Ceremony of entering into the covenant:
Passing in a procession according to the fixed order (2:19-25).
[85] See *War* 2:141; and cf. 1QS 5:8; CD 8:15, 9:8, 9:12, 15:1.6.7, 16:7.

'Treatise of the Two Spirits', forms a special case.[86] Setting down the principles of the community's ideology, it displays the major belief of the sect in dualism and predestination.[87] Again it presents a unified chiastic structure, though consisting of distinct units.[88] We shall return to the contents of this treatise in the section on the religious thought of the sect (below, pp. 533-6).

Though the homogenous overall nature of the *Rule* was recognized early, it was also evident that it is a composite work, consisting of many sections of independent character. This, in addition to the fact that copies of cave 4 attest to different recension(s), prompted studies on the literary structure of the *Rule*. These studies make clear that the *Rule* is of composite character, but there is no agreement as to its precise nature. While some saw it as a unified work,[89] others regard it as a compilation of independent sources which they attribute to different historical periods.[90] Thus Murphy-O'Connor sees the passage 8:1-10:8 as the oldest nucleus, while the introduction, the Entrance Ceremony and the Two Spirits' Treatise (cols. 1-4), as well as the final hymns (10-11), are seen as the latest parts, and the legislation in cols. 5-6 as a later parallel to cols. 8-9.[91]

However, apparent doublets are not necessarily the result of an editorial process reflecting different life-situations. It may well be a literary characteristic of the *Rule*, unobserved up to the present. The unit 9:12-26 was usually attached to unit 8:1-9:11. However, 9:12 has a new opening addressed to the *Maskil*, and 9:12-26 appears to parallel 3:13-4:26. Once this is noticed, other parallelisms become clear. A close examination of the various literary parts of the *Rule* again reveals a chiastic pattern:

---

[86] Cf. Licht, 'The Treatise'; Becker, *Das Heil Gottes,* 83-103; Von der Osten-Sacken, *Gott und Belial,* 17-27, 165-184; Duhaime, 'L'instruction'. It was recently argued, unconvincingly, that the Treatise was composed by the Teacher of Righteousness: Allison, 'The Authorship'. The idea itself is an old one, cf. Carmignac, *Les Textes* I, 14-15.

[87] Cf. references below, n. 242.

[88] See the table presented by Licht, 'Treatise', 100.

[89] Cf. Gilbert, 'Le plan'; Licht, *The Rule.*

[90] Pouilly, *La Règle.* Leany, *The Rule,* 112-3, to a large extent follows Gilbert, and discerns the following sections: general introduction (1:1-15); entry into the community (1:16-3:12); doctrine of the community (3:13-4:26); purpose and way of life of the community (5:1-6:23); penal code (6:24-7:25); model of the pioneer community (8:1-9:26); closing hymn (10:1-11:22). The manifesto (8:1-9:26) would date back to 130 B.C.E., while the editing took place during the first century B.C.E.

[91] Murphy O'Connor, 'La genèse littéraire', gives the following scheme: Stage one, pre-Qumran: the manifesto (8:1-16a + 9:3 to 8a). Stage two, stage 1 a of Qumran: legislation (8:16b-19; 8:20-9:20). Stage three, stage 1 b of Qumran: reformulation of legislation and aim (5:1-13a; 5:15b-7:25). Stage four, a few years later: additions and interpolations (1-4; 10-11). His analysis is adopted with only slight changes by Pouilly, *La Règle.*

In the context of the chiasm, the parallelisms appear to have a literary-ideological significance. Thus the life of the community in 5:1-6:23, assigned to the third stage of rewriting in Murphy-O'Connor's theory, is matched to 8:1-9:11, the oldest part according to that theory.[92] The parallel study of both reveals and interesting interplay of style and terminology. The doublets may, then, function in this context, thus pointing to a definite unified plan of writing.[93]

THE RELATIONSHIP BETWEEN THE RULE AND THE COVENANT

The *Rule* and the *Covenant* are closely related both in themes and contents: they depict similar communities and ideologies. Yet differences of detail raised the question of the relationship between the two. Thus, e.g., the Overseer is mentioned in both documents, but in the *Covenant* he has greater responsibilities. For instance, the admitting of new members is the responsibility of the Many in the *Rule* (1QS 6:18-20), while in the *Covenant* it is the Overseer who takes this charge (CD 13:11-12; 15:7-11). Among his additional functions in the *Covenant* the Overseer is to instruct the congregation and the inexperienced priests and to allocate money to the needy (CD 13:5-6, 8-10; 14:12-16). Parallel to the increased responsibillities of the

---

[92] Murphy-O'Connor's suggestions are often questionable not only on the literary level but also from a historical point of view. For the literary aspect, cf. the criticisms levelled by Puech, 'Recension', on Pouilly, *La Règle,* which are valid also for Murphy-O'Connor. Puech rightly criticizes the attribution of a situation-in-life to a literary phenomenon. From the historical point of view, two general observations may be made. In Murphy-O'Connor's reconstruction, the *Rule* reflects four stages in the life of the community, which together lasted some fifty years. This seems too compressed a period for such a process. Secondly, part of the section alleged to be the oldest, i.e. 8:15-9:12, is omitted in the oldest manuscript of the *Rule,* 4QS^e. Cf. Milik, 'Review', 416. Murphy-O'Connor dismisses this too lightly as a scribal omission.

Milik points to various redactional differences between the 4Q manuscripts and 1QS. In his opinion the primitive form of the *Rule* consisted of 6:1-9:11 and was perhaps composed by the Teacher of Righteousness around 150-145 B.C.E. Shortly afterwards subsequent copyists amplified it with long additions. The passage describing the entrance into the covenant belongs, in his opinion, to this second recension. Cf. Milik, 'Milki-Sedeq', 135.

[93] Cf. Gilbert, 'Le Plan'; Licht, *The Rule,* 20-21; who both hold a similar view. Licht thought that the *Rule* was assembled and arranged according to a unified plan. Cf. also Leaney, *The Rule,* 112-13.

Overseer in the *Covenant,* there is an appreciable diminution of the role of the Many. While in the *Rule* they have various responsibilities, they are hardly mentioned in the *Covenant.* Now it was suggested that a transfer of authority from a community to a single person is more logical than the reverse, and that the *Rule* or its sources reflect an earlier stage in the history of the sect.[94]   Such a conclusion is at variance with other indications. Thus the *Covenant* mentions women and children, clearly indicating the existence of married couples in the sect. No such reference occurs in the *Rule.* The historical theories offered to reconcile this difference see the *Covenant* as reflecting an earlier stage of the sect when marriage was still practiced, while the *Rule* would envisage a celibate community which was installed at Qumran in a later stage.

Other important differences concern the Temple cult. While in the *Covenant* there are clear references to the participation of the sect in the Jerusalem Temple cult, none occur in the *Rule.* In fact, no mention is made in the *Rule* of the Temple. Again the question was asked how these data are related to each other. Does the *Covenant* indicate a stage when the sectaries still participated in the cult, in contrast to the *Rule?* An explanation which may be offered is that the omission by the *Rule* of the subjects in question is due to its choice of themes and literary character, and does not necessarily reflect a historical situation different from the one expressed by the *Covenant.*

Biblical Interpretation

The Qumran sect was no exception to contemporary Judaism at large in that it was centred around and drew upon the biblical tradition. In everyday life this was manifested by the strict observance of the Torah and the constant study and exposition of the Scriptures. It is this second aspect which will concern us now. The influence exercised by the biblical world on the sectarian literature may be discerned in three domains: the literary, the ideological and the exegetical.[95]   Literary influence is to be discerned in all those instances where use is made of biblical modes of expression, for literary purposes only, without implying a conscious exegetical attitude. Thus, there are numerous examples of borrowed biblical phraseology, style, literary forms and genres.[96] Another category included is the antho-

---

[94] Cf. Kruse, 'Community Functionaries'; Wernberg-Møller, 'Priests'.

[95] I am aware of the modern distinction made between exegesis and hermeneutic, but I am not convinced that it is helpful in the context of the present discussion. Cf. Patte, *Jewish Hermeneutic,* 2-3. Patte's own application of this distinction to the review of the scrolls does not make a real difference as compared with other discussions. Consequently I am using both terms in the current sense to indicate a conscious attitude of interpretation towards scriptures invested with divine authority.

[96] E.g., psalm style and form in the *Hodayot* (1QH), influence of biblical wisdom literature on the *Covenant,* and imitation of the Torah style in the *Temple Scroll.*

logical style, which makes use of biblical allusions, reminiscences and semi-citations as a literary feature. It should be distinguished from the anthological style with exegetical purpose.[97] Ideological influence of the Bible is to be seen in most of the sect's presentations of its religious ideas; it is expressed in terminology and formulations (see below, pp. 533ff.). The influence in the exegetical field differs from the previous ones in that it implies a conscious exegetical attitude and activity, and is crystallized in hermeneutic rules, exegetical devices and corresponding literary forms and genres.

LITERARY FORMS OF BIBLICAL EXEGESIS

In reviewing Qumran materials pertaining to biblical exegesis, too often the main stress was put on the continuous *pesharim*. But the sectarian literature offers a variety of forms which merits a comprehensive investigation. What is offered here is a tentative list, with the purpose of suggesting a general context for Qumran biblical exegesis.

The designation *pesharim* was given to a group of biblical interpretations of a peculiar type. They have a fixed literary structure: a biblical quotation to be expounded, followed by the commentary which is often introduced as such by the word *pesher*. It consists of an identification of certain nouns in the text with the aid of various exegetical methods, and further elaborations on one or two details.[98] Thus the term *pesher* designates the isolated unit of interpretation, the interpretation itself, its technique and its literary form.

There are three types of *Pesharim: a) Continuous Pesharim*. This term designates commentaries on entire biblical books, mostly the prophets.[99] *b) Thematic Pesharim*. These are characterized by the assembling of various biblical texts and their interpretations around certain themes. Typical of this type are the texts known as *4Q Florilegium* and the *Pesher on Melchizedek. c) Isolated Pesharim*. These consist of a citation of only one or two verses with an interpretation using *pesher* methods and terminology, interwoven into larger compositions of a different literary genre. Several examples of this type occur in the *Covenant* and the *Rule*. Thus, for

---

[97] The definition of the anthological style usually referred to is that of Robert, 'Attaches littéraires'; cf. also Bloch, 'Midrash'; both stressing the exegetical function of the anthological style. But Wright, *Midrash,* 121-31, rightly points out the existence of a non-midrashic anthological style, namely a style using the biblical phrases for literary aims.

[98] For the analysis of the *pesher* structure cf. Nizan, *Pesher Habakkuk,* 60-70; Horgan, *Pesharim,* 237-44; Brooke, 'Qumran Pesher', 497-502.

[99] This name, in contradistinction to the thematic *Pesharim,* was suggested by Carmignac, 'Melkisédeq', 360-3. Though most of the known *Pesharim* comment on one prophet, a *Pesher* like 4QpIsᶜ, which is interspersed with quotations from other prophets, should warn us from a hasty judgement that this is always the case (see p. 513f.).

instance, CD 19:5-13 has a *pesher* on Zech 13:7, and CD 7:14-19 contains a *pesher* on Amos 5:26-27. In 1QS 8:13-15 we find a *pesher* on Isa 40:3. Interestingly, the *Covenant* contains *pesharim* on Pentateuchal texts: CD 6:3-11 on Num 21:18, and CD 7:19-21 on Num 24:17.[100]

Apart from the *pesharim* three additional forms of biblical exegesis can be distinguished in the literature of the sect. *a*) The various *appellations* given to historical figures and groups should be considered as a special literary form. Each one actually constitutes a cryptogram for an entire *pesher*. This is obvious almost in all the extant examples: the designation 'The Teacher of Righteousness' stands for a *pesher* on Hos 10:12 and context; 'The Spouter of Lies' is a sobriquet based on Micah 2:11; while 'The Searchers of Slippery Things' is anchored in Isa 30:10 and context. The name 'Kittim' applied to the Romans is based on Num 24:24 and Dan 11:30. *b*) *Anthological style*. In this form the exegesis is not introduced explicitly by a conscious citation and interpretation, but is implied by the way the biblical text is interwoven into the general style.[101] *c*) *Halakhic exegesis* should be kept as a distinct category due to its special relation to the biblical text as a source of *halakhah,* in which specific literary forms and procedures are implied. The *Temple Scroll* now offers an interesting case of the rewritten Bible style, serving as a form of halakhic exegesis (see below, pp. 526-30).

THE CHARACTER OF THE PESHARIM

Hermeneutical principles and techniques play an important role in the *Pesharim* due to their specific purpose: to read historical and eschatological events into the biblical prophecies. Since there is a gap between the literal sense and the desired sense, a series of hermeneutical devices[102] were employed in order to extract the latter from the former.[103]

---

[100] The same verse is interpreted in a messianic sense also in 1QM 11:6 and 4QTest 9–13.

[101] For material and examples cf. Carmignac, 'Poèmes de serviteur'; 'Les citations dans la Guerre'; Elliger, *Studien,* 78-117; Fitzmyer, 'Quotations'. Recently Gabrion, 'L'interprétation' discussed some problems involved, but he does not attempt to attain a clear distinction between the various anthological styles.

[102] They may not, perhaps, be called hermeneutical rules in the precise sense, for they do not appear to have a definitive binding formulation, but hermeneutical principles undoubtedly were at work at Qumran.

[103] The main exegetical devices may be summarized as follows (cf. Horgan, *Pesharim,* 244-6):
  1. The use of synonyms for the words in the *lemma.* Cf. e.g., 1QHab 5:6-8 (רע / רשעה); 4QpNah 3-4 I 4-6 (כפיר / ארי); 3-4 II 3-6 (חרב / חנית).
  2. Use of the same roots as in the *lemma,* in the same or different grammatical form (very current).
  3. Play on words in the *lemma.* E.g.: 1QpHab 8:6-13 (משל); 4QpPs*a* 1-10 IV 13-16 (בקש).
  4. The use of a different textual tradition; e.g., 1QpHab 4:9-13. The Massoretic text for Hab 1:11 reads ואשם 'and a guilty one', the text cited by the *pesher* reads וישם 'and he makes,'

It is significant that many of the hermeneutical rules employed by the rabbinic *midrash* occur also in the *Pesharim*.[104] A particularly close similarity in structure and methods exists between the *pesher* and the rabbinical *midrash* of the *petira* type. The latter interprets a biblical verse with a general and undefined meaning by attributing specific motifs and circumstances to it.[105] The decisive difference between the *pesher* and the *petira* is in the contents: the *petira* always deals with moral lessons, while the subject of the *pesher* is historical-eschatological. In light of such an affinity between the *pesher* and rabbinic *midrashim*, it was rightly concluded that both drew upon a common Jewish heritage, each adapting it to its own purposes.[106]

Concurrently, it was noticed that the *pesher* shows affinities to another type of Jewish and non-Jewish interpretation, namely the interpretation of dreams. The same attitude is apparent in both: the dream, or the prophecy, is seen as a divinely-sent cryptogram, to be deciphered by applying a variety of exegetical methods. There is also a considerable resemblance between the methods themselves. Thus symbolism, atomization and *paronomasia* were widely used in the interpretation of dreams.[107] Hence the striking similarities between the *Pesharim* and the interpretation of dreams in the book of Daniel.[108]

The wide spectrum of elements converging in the *Pesharim* produced a lively debate as to their character and origin.[109] Some saw them as a *targum*,[110] others as a type of rabbinic *midrash*.[111] A third group of scholars

---

and the interpretation has (אשמ)תם) 'their guilt'.

5. Changing the order of the letters or words in the *lemma;* e.g., 1QpHab 1:5-6; 4QpHos[b] 2:2-3.

6. Referring back to an earlier *lemma* or anticipating a following *lemma*. (1QpHab 5:9-12 — בתוכחת מורה הצדק 'at the rebuke of the Teacher of Righteousness', probably referring to להוכיח 'to reprove', of Hab 1:12. Partially parallel lists of hermeneutical devices employed in the *pesharim* are offered also by Brownlee, 'Biblical Interpretation'; Fishbane, 'Qumran Pesher'; Solomovic, 'Exegesis'; Rabinowitz, 'Pesher/Pittāron'; Patte, *Jewish Hermeneutic*, 300-2; Brooke, *4QFlorilegium*.

[104] Thus, e.g., *Notarikon* and *Gematria* are used in CD 7:13-8:1; 1QpHab 1:5ff; 11:4-13; *Zekher Ledavar* and *Asmakhta* are used in CD 10:19-11:6 and 1QpHab 8:3-13. Cf. Solomovic, *ibid.;* Patte, *ibid.* Brooke, *4QFlorilegium*, 249-0, offers the following list of exegetical procedures: *Gezera Shawa;* deliberate editing of the biblical text; *Paronomasia; Binyan Av; Samakun* and double meaning. Cf. also Brooke, 'Amos-Numbers Midrash'.

[105] Silberman, 'The Riddle'.

[106] Cf. Vermes, *Post-Biblical Jewish Studies*, 37-49; Brownlee, 'The Background'.

[107] Cf. Finkel, 'Dreams;' Rabinowitz, 'Pesher/Pittāron'; Fishbane, 'Qumran-Pesher'.

[108] Cf. Elliger, *Studien*, 164; Szörényi, 'Das Buch Daniel'; Bruce, 'The Book of Daniel.' For affinities with Egyptian texts, cf. Daumas, 'Littérature prophétique'; Carmignac, 'Pistis-Sophia'.

[109] For the state of the question, cf. Horgan, *Pesharim*, 229-59.

[110] Cf. e.g., Wieder, 'The Habakkuk Scroll'.

[111] Cf. most recently Brooke, 'Qumran-Pesher,' 501-503. Unfortunately Brooke arrives at the conclusion that the *pesher* is a type of *midrash* by applying the too vague definition of *midrash*

considered them as a special literary genre peculiar to the sect.[112] The discussion on this issue suffers from a lack of precise terminology. In fact the term *pesher* not only designates the exegetical techniques and the literary form, but also the works themselves. Yet each of these elements involves a different complex of problems. Thus similar exegetical devices are shared by the interpretation of dreams, rabbinic *midrashim* and the *Pesharim.* Therefore they cannot be taken as characteristic features of the *Pesharim* but belong to a common Jewish and oriental heritage. The similarity of structure and technique between the *pesher* and the *petira midrash*[113] shows that these features, too, are not distinctive of the *Pesharim* and both should be seen as belonging to a broader common literary and exegetical tradition, applied in different contexts. The same may be said of the New Testament. It was claimed that the New Testament writers used *pesher* methods as a means of actualization[114] and biblical allusions to indicate additional sense.[115] But comparable methods are used in various Jewish literary works as well.

A definition of the *Pesharim,* therefore, ought to be based on a feature truly distinctive to it. Such is their subject matter, namely the special historical-eschatological exegesis of prophecy relating to the sect's own position in history, and rooted in its peculiar attitude to the biblical text. The traditional exegetical devices and literary forms are employed in the service of these particular ideas, and only in this respect can the *Pesharim* be defined as a special genre.

All the texts interpreted in the *Pesharim* are taken from authors writing under prophetic inspiration: Moses for the Torah, the prophets for prophecies and David for psalms.[116] As such, they have special significance for the sect, as is well explained by the *Habakkuk Pesher:* 'And as for that which He said for the sake of him who reads it (Hab 2:2), its interpretation *(pesher)* concerns the Righteous Teacher to whom God has made known all the mysteries of the words of His servants the Prophets' (1QpHab 7:3-5). This passage expresses the opinion that through the prophetic revelations God divulged the mysteries of the future, especially that of the last

offered by Bloch, 'Midrash'. Yet Horgan's contention (*Pesharim*, 252) that historically the *midrashim* are too late to be compared with the *pesharim* is no less erroneous; for it is well-known that the *midrashim* reflect forms and traditions much older than their date of redaction.

[112] Cf. e.g., Brownlee, *The Midrash-Pesher*, 23-36.

[113] On the acquaintance of the Sages with methods of interpreting dreams cf. Lieberman, *Hellenism*, 71-78.

[114] Stendahl, *School of St. Matthew*, 183-202, referring to the formula quotations in Matthew.

[115] Cf. Goldsmith, 'Acts 13, 33-37'; rightly criticized by Brooke, 'Qumran-Pesher', 483 for the loose definition of *pesher*.

[116] Both Moses and David, the authors of the Torah and the Psalms, were considered prophets. Moses is called such in Deut 34:10; David is described as a prophet in the *Psalms Scroll* 11QPs[a] 27:11. Cf. also Acts 2:30 and Fitzmyer, 'David'.

generation (cf. also 1QpHab 2:1-10). Elsewhere it is stated that 'the mysteries of God' are the secrets of the divine fore-ordained plan of history according to which all human events take place (cf., e.g., 1QS 3:23). Hence it is the mysteries of this plan which are imparted to the prophets. They include the significance of the entire sequence of history from the remote past to the *eschaton;* but believing that they lived on the verge of the *eschaton,* the sectaries were interested chiefly in the events of their own generations. As a result of this point of view, the study and exposition of the prophets acquired an utmost importance for the sectaries, for they contained the clue to their own situation. But as prophecies are enigmatic, just like the mysteries of God themselves, they can be understood only with the aid of a divinely inspired interpretation, i.e. by the Teacher of Righteousness. In this way, both the contents of the *Pesharim* and their exegetical methods acquire a status of a divinely inspired message, i.e. their authority is divine, just like the prophets' words themselves. This is a unique position in the Jewish post-biblical literature. Only pseudepigraphic writings may present a somewhat similar attitude. However, they claim divine inspiration by attributing their contents to a revered legendary personage in the past, not to a historical figure as do the *Pesharim.*[117]

As a concluding remark it may be said that although most of the *Pesharim* comment upon biblical texts, the form and methods of *pesher* may have had a wider application at Qumran. We possess a '*Pesher* on the Periods' (4Q180), which, though it is concerned with history and interpreting biblical texts, nevertheless expounds a subject, and not a particular text.[118]

In the following section we shall describe the major continuous *Pesharim.* The thematic *Pesharim,* 4QFlor and 4QMelch, will be discussed in the section on eschatological compositions (below, pp. 518-22).

THE PESHER ON HABAKKUK

This *Pesher* was one of the first scrolls to be published.[119] It is extant in a copy dated between 30 and 1 B.C.E. which preserved thirteen columns intact.[120] They contain a running commentary on the first two chapters of Habakkuk. The copy was written by two scribes; one wrote 1:1-12:13 and the other 12:13-13:14.

Through the commentary on the biblical text, a series of figures and

---

[117] The book of Daniel presents a special case: due to its subject matter and ideology it has special affinities with the *Pesharim.*
[118] Could it be another example of a thematic *pesher,* with the title preserved? It is difficult to tell. I have discussed this document in 'Pesher on the Periods'.
[119] For a convenient edition assembling all the continuous *Pesharim* see Horgan, *Pesharim.* See also Elliger, *Studien* and Brownlee, *Pesher Habakkuk.*
[120] Cf. Cross. 'Introduction,' 4-5.

events emerge. The central personality is that of the Teacher of Righteousness, the apparent leader of the sect (1:13; 2:2; 5:9-12; 7:4-5; 8:3; 9:9-12; 11:4-8) and known from the *Damascus Covenant* (CD 1:11; 20:1, 28, 32). He is the inspired interpreter of Scriptures. He has two adversaries: the Man of Lies and the Wicked Priest. The Man of Lies (2:1-2; 5:11) is probably identical with the Spouter of Lies (10:9-13 מטיף הכזב) and perhaps with the Man of Scorn in CD 1:14. This person is the leader of a group designated as the Traitors (2:1, 3, 5) who do not accept the inspired teachings of the Teacher of Righteousness and betray the covenant of God. As such he is usually identified with the religious opponent of the Teacher who heads 'the Searchers of Slippery Things' (דורשי החלקות 1 QH2:15, 32; CD 1:18; 4QpNah 3-4 II 2; 4QpIs^c 23 II 10).

That the Spouter of Lies was the leader of a rival congregation is implied by another passage, where he is accused of 'building through bloodshed his city of vanity and erecting through falsehood a congregation' (1QpHab 10:10). Undoubtedly we have here the typology of two opponents, heads of two congregations: the Man of Lies heads 'a congregation of falsehood,' while the Teacher of Righteousness leads 'the congregation of His elect' (1QpPs^{a}1-10 II 5; 1-10 III 5), symbolized by the eschatological Jerusalem (4 QpPs^d). Thus both congregations are symbolized by cities. It was also observed that the Teacher of Righteousness, as the inspired interpreter of the Prophets, may stand for the true prophet, while the Man of Lies is the opposite figure of the false prophet.[121]

It appears that the controversy between the Teacher of Righteousness and the Man of Lies concerns religious matters, perhaps different approaches to the interpretation of Scripture and *halakhah*. A different case is presented by the relationship between the Teacher of Righteousness and the other adversary, the Wicked Priest (הכהן הרשע , 8:8-13; 8:16-9:2; 11:4-8, 12-15; 12:2-6, 7-10). This person . . .

> . . . was called by the Name of Truth at the beginning of his rule; but while he ruled over Israel his heart became haughty and he abandoned God and became a traitor to the Laws because of wealth; and he robbed and amassed the wealth of the men of iniquity who had rebelled against God; and the wealth of the people he took, as to increase the guilt of transgression upon himself. And he committed abominable acts with every kind of defiling impurity. (1QpHab 8:8-13)

From this description emerges a ruler of Israel who at the beginning of his rule was probably acceptable for the sect, but in the course of time changed his ways and consequently was condemned by the community. In another context he is described as a persecutor of the Teacher of Righteousness.

---

[121] Cf. Betz, *Offenbarung*, 88-89.

The Wicked Priest came to the Teacher's 'house of exile' to disturb him during the Day of Atonement (11:4-8). The picture emerging from these details is of a political rivalry in which the archvillain is played by the Wicked Priest while the Teacher of Righteousness is the persecuted just and poor character.

Another major group figuring in the *Pesher* is designated by the name Kittim. It applies to a fearful warlike people coming from 'the islands of the Sea' to subjugate all the people cruelly (1QpHab 3-4, 6:1-12). They are used by God to punish 'the last priests of Jerusalem' (1QpHab 9:4-6).

The term Kittim itself is taken from the prophecy of Balaam in Num 24:24, where it designates the people which plays a decisive role in the eschatological era. Already in Dan 11:30 it is understood of the Greeks, but in the *Pesharim* it clearly applies to the Romans.[122] So also in our *Pesher* 'the Rulers of the Kittim' (1QpHab 4:5, 10) refers to the Roman governors, established in Eretz-Israel after the conquest by Pompey in 63 B.C.E.

Thus the events described in the *Pesher* seem to fall under the Hasmonaean rule and the beginning of the Roman rule. This span of time considerably limits the possibilities of identifying the main figures. The clearest and most convincing identification yet offered is the one suggested for the Wicked Priest.[123] The two possibilities which account best for most of the information offered on this figure are either Jonathan or Simon the Maccabees.[124] It is now widely agreed upon that Jonathan is the more suitable. For the time being, no satisfactory identification has been suggested for the Teacher of Righteousness.[125] In the light of the existing data and the texts published to date, none seems possible.[126]

---

[122] The *Pesharim* make a clear distinction between 'the kings of Greece', namely the Seleucids, and 'the Rulers of the Kittim' (4QpNah 3-4 I 3), namely the Roman governors.

[123] If, indeed, one and the same person is referred to by this name in all the texts. It was recently suggested that the Wicked Priest was a title applied to several high priests ruling in Jerusalem; see Van der Woude, 'Wicked Priest'.

[124] Cross, *Library*, 137-60, argues for identifying the Wicked Priest with Simon. Cf. also Nickelsburg, 'Simon'. Milik, *Ten Years*, 61-87 offers criticism to this option and argues for the identification with Jonathan. Thus also Vermes, 'The Essenes'; Stegemann, *Die Entstehung*, 204-207.

[125] If this title refers to one man. Starcky, 'Les Maîtres', suggested that there were at least two of them. Buchanan, 'The Priestly Teacher', and 'The Office', saw it as an office held by numerous men at different times.

[126] This is the estimation of Vermes, 'The Essenes', 27; and rightly so. In his opinion, it can further be assumed that the Teacher of Righteousness was 'a priest with Zadokite affiliation.' Even this is too much, considering the state of the evidence. Cf. below, p. 545. The assumption that the sect was led by Zadokite priests opposing the Hasmonaeans led to the proposition that the Teacher of Righteousness was the high priest serving between the death of Alkimos (159 B.C.E.) and the nomination of Jonathan (152 B.C.E., cf. *Ant.* 13:45-46; 20:238). Thus Stegemann, *Entstehung*, 198-252; Murphy-O'Connor, 'The Essenes'; Bunge, 'Geschichte'. This was convincingly refuted by Burgmann, 'Intersacerdotium'. Recently, Carmignac, 'Le Docteur de Justice' has reiterated his suggestion to identify the Teacher with Judah the Essene; cf. the criticism by Murphy-O'Connor, 'Judah the Essene'; Burgmann, 'Wer war der Lehrer', 554-7; and Carmignac, 'Précisions.'

THE PESHER ON NAHUM

Three columns of this pesher have survived in a manuscript dated to the end of the Hasmonaean or the beginning of the Herodian period.[127] Its special interest lies in the fact that it contains explicit historical references. It mentions two Greek kings: Antiochus and Demetrius (4QpNah 3-4 I 2-3). Of Demetrius it is stated: '[Deme]trius King of Greece, who sought to enter Jerusalem on the advice of the searchers of slippery things' (4QpNah *ib.*). Associated with Demetrius is the Lion of Wrath (כפיר החרון), 'who inflicted death on the searchers of slippery things and who will hang people alive' (4QpNah 3-4 I 7). Once Antiochus is identified as Antiochus IV Epiphanes (175-164 B.C.E.) and Demetrius as Demetrius III Eukairos (95-88 B.C.E.),[128] it becomes apparent that the events alluded to fall under the reign of Alexander Jannaeus (103-76 B.C.E.), who is identified as 'the Lion of Wrath'[129]. The references are best suited to the events surrounding the civil war which broke out between Jannaeus and a rebelling fraction supported by the Pharisees. The war continued for six years (93-98 B.C.E.), during which time the rebels first supported Demetrius Eukairos and then went over to Jannaeus. Jannaeus punished the rebels cruelly by crucifixion (Josephus *Ant.* 13:372-383; *War* 1: 90-98).[130]

The *Pesher* illuminates the internal situation in Israel in a particular way. From the above identification it is clear that 'the Searchers of Slippery Things' are the Pharisees. They are symbolized as Ephraim (cf. 4QpNah 3-4 II 2, 8; III 5), while the sectaries call themselves Israel or Judah (3-4 III 4; 1QpHab 8:1; 12:4). A third group is referred to as Manasseh (4QpNah 3-4 III 9-12; IV 1-6). The triple typology, of which one element corresponds

---

[127] Edited by Allegro, *DJD,* 5, 37-42. Cf. the corrections and additions by Strugnell, 'Notes en marge,' 163-276. Cf. Cross, *Library,* 121-127; Horgan, *Pesharim,* 158-91.

[128] Thus, e.g., Allegro, 'Further Light'; Amusin, 'Historical Events'. Rowley, '4Qp Nahum', more recently followed by Rabinowitz, 'Demetrius Passage,' argued for the identification with Demetrius I Soter (162-150 B.C.E.); see Cross, *Library,* 124-5 for arguments against this. Rabinowitz's view that 'the Searchers of Smooth Things' are the Hellenizers of the Maccabean period is not convincing. Stegemann, *Die Entstehung,* 126, 203 suggests that the reference to Antiochus is aimed at Antiochus VII Sidetes (138-129 B.C.E.).

[129] Cf. Allegro, 'Thrakidan'; Yadin, 'Pesher Nahum'; Amusin, 'Historical Events'; Milik, *Ten Years,* 73.

[130] The reference of 4QpNah 3-4 I 7 'who will hang men alive,' raises the question of exactly what type of hanging is implied. Does the episode in 4QpNah refer to a crucifixion and was crucifixion accepted by Jews as a form of execution? An affirmative answer to the latter question was given, e.g., by Yadin, 'Pesher Nahum'; *id., Temple Scroll* I, 289; Hengel, *Crucifixion,* 84-85; Fitzmyer, 'Crucifixion'. Others, like Baumgarten, *Studies,* 172-82, rejected this. Yadin, 'Pesher Nahum', and Halperin, 'Crucifixion,' suggest that the Talmud's rejection of crucifixion is a polemic against the approval of crucifixion by other Jewish sects, such as the Qumran sect (Cf. *T. Sanhedrin* 9:6; *B.T. Sanhedrin* 46b). Yadin goes on to interpret the statements of 4QpNah as an approval of Jannaeus' deeds, and not as their rejection, for the 'Searchers of Slippery Things' are to be considered as guilty of treason, and therefore merit the punishment. Cf. Yadin, 'Pesher Nahum'; *id. Temple Scroll* 1, 285-90.

511

to the Pharisees, is strinkingly reminiscent of the three Jewish parties described by Josephus: the Sadducees, the Pharisees and the Essenes. It was, therefore, inferred that the same three are alluded to by this typology: Judah is the sect, Ephraim the Pharisees and Manasseh the Sadducees.[131] Thus references to the government of 'the Searchers of Slippery Things' may refer to the reign of the last Hasmonaeans, Salome Alexandra (76-67 B.C.E.) and Hyrcanus II with Aristobulus II (67-63 B.C.E.). In all probability also the conquest of Pompey is referred to, from which the Sadducees are said to suffer heavily (4QpNah 3-4 IV 1-8).

One of the results of the safe identification of 'the Searchers of Smooth Things' is that the leader of this group, the Man of Lies, mentioned in the *Damascus Covenant* and the *Habakkuk Pesher,* cannot be identified as one of the Hasmonaean Kings, but should be seen as a Pharisaic leader.[132]

THE PESHER ON PSALMS

This *Pesher* is one of the two extant continuous *Pesharim* on a non-prophetic text. Its surviving fragments contain *pesharim* on Psalms 37, 45, 60.[133] They preserved the remains of four columns written in a 'semi-formal' hand.[134]

The *Pesher* under discussion is concerned with the same figures familiar from other *Pesharim:* the Teacher of Righteousness, the Wicked Priest and the Man of Lies. The Teacher of Righteousness is clearly called 'the Priest' (1-10 III 15; cf. II 18). He is also referred to as the 'Interpreter of Knowledge' (מליץ דעת , 1-10 I 27). The Wicked Priest is still persecuting the Teacher of Righteousness, actually seeking his death (1-10 IV 8). The Man of Lies figures again as an opponent of the Teacher who would not listen to his teaching but would 'lead many astray with deceitful words, for they chose empty words (קלות) and did not lis[ten] to the Interpreter of Knowledge' (1-10 I 27). The controversy between the Teacher of Righteousness and his followers, and the Man of Lies and his men, is read into the Psalm's dichotomy between the poor and just and the wicked and vain. The persecution of the community of the Teacher is effected by both 'Ephraim and Manasseh' (1-10 II 17-19), namely, by both the Pharisees and the Sadducees.

Other details concern the eschatological beliefs of the community. As in

---

[131] Cf. Amus, 'Ephraim et Manassé'; Flusser, 'Pharisäer'; Stegemann, *Die Entstehung,* 229-231.

[132] Flusser, *ibid.*

[133] The *siglum* for this *Pesher* is 4QpPs^a or 4Q171 (the other non-prophetic continuous *Pesher* is 4Q173). Text published by Allegro, *DJD* 5, 42-51. Cf. Strugnell, 'Notes en marge,' 211-18. Cf. further additions and corrections by Stegemann, 'Pesher Psalm 37'; *id.* 'Weitere Stücke'; Pardee, 'A Restudy'. Cf. Horgan, *Pesharim,* 192-226.

[134] Thus Strugnell, *ibid.* 211.

the *Damascus Covenant,* here too the number forty is employed for chronological purposes, but for future and not for past events. In interpreting Ps 37:10 the *Pesher* envisages that after forty years all the wicked adversaries of the sect will be condemned and evil will be annihilated. In the *War Scroll* the same number is used for the duration of the eschatological war (1QM 2:6-14, see below). Our *Pesher* may allude to this last event, for it goes on to describe the peace awaiting the Just thereafter (1-10 II 9-10). In this context the expression 'the Nets of Belial' (*ib.* 10-1), in which Israel is caught, recurs. These are the traps mentioned in CD 4:14-18 as consisting of fornication, riches and the defilement of the Temple.[135] They express the sway which Belial, the lord of the evil forces, has over Israel and the consequent sin and wickedness which rule Israel. As for the members of the community themselves, they are saved from these nets and will 'inherit the earth' (1-10 II 9-11). The Congregation of the Poor (עדת צאביונים *ib.* 10), namely the sect, is therefore waiting for the destruction of the Wicked and for the moment when it will rule Jerusalem. The *Pesher* implies that these events are near at hand.

OTHER CONTINUOUS PESHARIM

The rest of the extant *Pesharim* are relatively small; most of them are *Pesharim* on Isaiah.

4QpIs*ᵃ* (= 4Q161) covers Isa 10:21-22, 24-34; 11:1-5.[136] Fragments 5-6 interpret the Assyrian march described in Isa 10:28-32, which the *Pesher* applies to someone who is ascending from 'the Plain of Acre in order to fight with . . .' (2-6 II 27). It was suggested that this is an allusion to events connected with Acre-Ptolemais during the reign of Alexander Jannaeus (Jos. *Ant.* 13:324-364; *War* 1:86-87). More specifically, it is the march of Ptolemy Lathyrus from Acre to Judaea, which was stopped by his mother Cleopatra. Thus the halting of Ptolemy could have been seen as miraculous just as was the dispersion of the Assyrian army, referred to by Isaiah.[137]

4QpIs*ᶜ* (= 4Q163) covers scattered parts of Isaiah.[138] The interesting feature of this *Pesher* is that while commenting on its major text, Isaiah, it occasionally cites and interprets other prophets. Thus Zach 11:11 is quoted while commenting on Isa 30:1-5 (21 7-8) and Hos 6:9 is cited in 23 II 14. In this respect there is similarity to thematic *Pesharim.*[139] Several times the

[135] Cf. Kosmala, 'The Three Nets.'
[136] Text, Allegro in *DJD* 5, 11-15. Cf. Strugnell, 'Notes en marge,' 183-6; Horgan, *Pesharim,* 70-86.
[137] Cf. Amusin, '4Q161'; *id.,* 'Historical Events', 123-34.
[138] Isa 8:7-9; 9:11, 14-20; 10:12-13, 19-24; 14:8, 26-30; 19:9-12; 29:10-11, 15-32; 30:1-5, 15-18, 19-23; 31:1. Text Allegro, *DJD* 5, 17-27; Strugnell, 'Notes en marge', 188-95; Horgan, *Pesharim,* 94-124.
[139] Cf. Horgan, *Pesharim,* 95.

Pesher seems to skip verses; thus in 4,6-7 I 6-8, Isa 9:12 seems to have been omitted.

4QpIs*ᵈ* (= 4Q164), dating from the early Hasmonaean period, deals with Isa 54:11-12.[140] This *Pesher* is interesting in that it applies to the sect the description of the New Jerusalem in Isa 54, identifying the precious stones in the future city with various groups within the sect. This identification is a natural outgrowth of the sectarian beliefs. The sect saw itself as 'a holy house' and the opponent group of the 'Searchers of slippery things' as 'a city of iniquity'.[141] The *Pesher* also refers to a group of twelve, either the priests mentioned before, or the chiefs of Israel mentioned afterwards. Both groups, of twelve each, participate in the governing bodies of the sect.[142]

Apart from those on Isaiah, [143] fragmentary *Pesharim* have been found on Hosea,[144] Micah,[145] Zephaniah, [146] and Psalms.[147] One of the *Pesharim* on Hosea contains a mention of 'the Lion of Wrath' and of 'the last priest who will stretch out his hand to smite Ephraim' (4QpHos*ᵇ* 2:2-3).

Eschatological Compositions

Though few sectarian writings escaped the touch of eschatology, a distinction should be made between compositions entirely devoted to it, and

---

[140] Allegro, *DJD* 5, 27-28; Strugnell, 'Notes en marge,' 195-6; Horgan, *Pesharim,* 125-31. For commentaries cf. Allegro, 'More Isaiah Commentaries,' 220-1; Yadin, 'Some Notes'; Flusser, 'The Pesher of Isaiah.'

[141] 'Holy house': 1QS 5:6, 8:5, 8:9, 9:6, 11:8; CD 3:19, 20:10, 20:13. 'City of iniquity': 1QpHab 10:10. Cf. Flusser, 'The Pesher of Isaiah.' As we shall see below, the concept Temple-city probably contributed to the formulation of such an identification. The choice of Isa 54, then, takes up a symbol implied by other terms, in order to emphasize the eschatological aspect of the sect's existence.

[142] See 1QS 8:1-2; 1QM 2:1-3; 4QOrd 2-4:3-4 (= 4Q159). In 11QTemp 57:11-17 they figure in the council of the king. Cf. the section on 4QFlor, below, p. 519f. See Flusser, 'The Pesher of Isaiah'; Baumgarten, *Studies,* 145-71; Yadin, *Temple Scroll* 1, 268-70.

[143] To those mentioned should be added:

4QpIs*ᵇ*. Text Allegro, *DJD,* 5, 15-17; Strugnell, 'Notes en marge', 186-8; Horgan, *Pesharim,* 86-93.

4QpIs*ᵉ*. Allegro, *DJD* 5, 28-30; Strugnell, 'Notes en marge', 197-9; Horgan, *Pesharim,* 131-8.

[144] 4QpHos*ᵃ* (= 4Q 166) — on Hos 2:8-14. Allegro, *DJD* 5, 31-32; Strugnell, 'Notes en marge', 199-201; Horgan, Pesharim, 138-48.

4QpHos*ᵇ* (= 4Q167) — on Hos 5:13-15; 6:4, 7, 9-10; 8:6-14. Allegro, *DJD* 5, 32-36; Strugnell, 'Notes en marge', 201-203; Horgan, *Pesharim,* 148-158.

[145] 1QpMic (= 1Q14) — on Mic 1:2-9, 6:14-16, 7:8-9 (?). *DJD* 1, 77-80; Horgan, *Pesharim,* 55-63.

4QpMic (= 4Q168) — Mic 4:8-12. Allegro, *DJD* 5, 36; Strugnell, 'Notes en marge', 204.

[146] 1QpZep (= 1Q15) — on Zeph 1:18-2:2. Milik, *DJD* 1, 80; Horgan, *Pesharim,* 63-5.

[147] 4QpPs*ᵃ* (= 4Q171), cf. above; 4QpPs*ᵇ* (=4Q173) — on Ps 129:7-8. Allegro, *DJD,* 5 50-1; Strugnell, 'Notes en marge,' 219-20; Horgan, *Pesharim,* 226-8. The text should comprise only the fragments 1-4 of Allegro's edition. Cf. Strugnell, *ibid.*

other works dealing with it only in relationship to other subjects. Here we are concerned with the first category.

THE WAR SCROLL

This work, also known as the *War of the Sons of Light Against the Sons of Darkness*,[148] is extant in one better preserved manuscript from Cave 1 and six fragments from Cave 4; their dates of writing range from the first half of the first century B.C.E. to the beginning of the first century C.E.[149]

The *War Scroll* is a description of the final eschatological war between the forces of Light, commanded by the archangel Michael, and the forces of Darkness, headed by Belial. The camp of the forces of Light includes the sectarian community and a host of good angels, while in the opposite camp we find first of all the Kittim, the people ruling the world, and further some minor nations and those 'acting wickedly against the Covenant' (מרשיעי ברית), namely apostate Jews (1QM 1:2).[150] Such is the sectarian version of the final eschatological war as depicted in biblical prophecy.

The main purpose is apparently to supply the members of the sect with a detailed set of regulations for the day destined 'from of old for a battle of annihilation of the Sons of Darkness' (1:10). The result of this war is pre-ordained; God himself will intervene on the side of the Sons of Light. Yet this intervention will take place only after a series of real battles, in which the Sons of Darkness will alternately be defeated and victorious. The war will have to be fought according to all the rules of war practiced by the nations, but also in accordance with the Law of Moses. The fact that angels participate in the battle obliges the Sons of Light to observe all the biblical

---

[148] Edition: Yadin, *The Scroll of the War.*

[149] 1QM. Date: the second half of the first century B.C.E. Contents: though damaged, preserved most of the composition. The writing is an elegant early Herodian hand. Cf. Cross, 'Introduction', 4-5.

4Q MSS. (formerly 4QM*a-f*), now fully published by Baillet, *DJD* 7, 12-72:

4Q491 (4QM*a*). Date: Second half of the first century B.C.E. Contents: 2:1-6; 5:16-17; 7:3-7, 10-12; 9:17-18; 16:3-14; 17:10-15. Represents a different recension. For earlier discussions of this manuscript cf. Hunzinger, 'Fragmente'; Baillet, 'Les Manuscrits', 219-21.

4Q492 (4QM*b*). Date: middle of the first century B.C.E. Contents: 1-2:3.

4Q493 (4QM*c*). Date: first half of the first century B.C.E. It may be the most ancient MS. and may stem from a different recension. The contents do not correspond to any of the known sections of 1QM, but evidently are of the same work.

4Q494 (4QM*d*). Date: beginning of the first century C.E. Contents: 1:1-2:3.

4Q495 (4QM*e*). Date: middle of the first century B.C.E. Contents: 10:9-10; 13:9-12.

4Q496 (4QM*f*). Date: before 50 B.C.E. Contents: 1:4-9, 11-17; 2:5-6, 9-10, 13-14. 2-3:2; 3:6-7, 9-11, 11-15; 3-4:2. This is a papyrus of complex character. Cf. the detailed table in *DJD* 7, 57. Baillet publishes also 4Q499 which resembles 1QM but is not identical with it. Cf. also his evaluation, 'Le volume VII', 79-80.

[150] The appellation is taken from Dan 11:32. On the affinities between 1QM and Daniel cf. Carmignac, 'Les citations dans la Guerre'; Von der Osten-Sacken, *Gott und Belial*, 30-34.

laws of purity. This, and the general self-image of the sectarians, brought about an effort to model the whole army of the Sons of Light after the organization of Israel's camp during the wandering in the wilderness. Thus the men are organized by tribes, camps, families; thousands, hundreds, fifties and tens.[151]

In the first column of the scroll there is a description of how the community will become the divine instrument for establishing an ideal world. Column 2 specifies arrangements for the regular temple service at the time when most of the men will be fighting. Then follows a detailed depiction of the weapons and tactics. Column 7 deals with purity regulations, while columns 8-9 take up the description of tactics. In columns 10-19 we find various prayers, hymns and exhortations to be recited on various occasions. In column 13 there is a malediction of Belial and his lot, which states the dualistic theology of the sect. It is sharper than other statements in the sectarian writings, but lacks the radical determinism found in the Treatise of the Two Spirits.[151a]

The dating of the work is connected with its literary character. Early commentators were impressed by the unified plan of the work, and ascribed it to one author. In view of the military details the composition was seen as a military manual adapted from a similar Roman work, dating from the time of Herod the Great (37-4 B.C.E.).[152] This conclusion was later criticized and an earlier date was proposed, on the basis of historical considerations[153] and of linguistic affinities with the *Rule of the Community* and the *Thanksgiving Psalms.*[154] An early date is now imposed also by the oldest MS., 4Q493, and by the composite structure of the work which implies a literary history.[155] Today there is no generally accepted view on

---

[151] Cf. Exod 18. Compare CD 13:1-2, and above p. 492.

[151a] See pp. 533-4. On the peculiar apocalyptic character of the *War Scroll* see above, pp. 426-7.

[152] The theory was proposed by Yadin, *The Scroll of the War,* and was accepted by Milik, *Ten Years,* 39, 122; Dupont-Sommer, *Les Écrits,* 182-3.

[153] It was pointed out that knowledge of Roman tactics could have penetrated Eretz-Israel before the time of Herod. Segal suggested that the optimist and militarist atmosphere of the composition suits the period of John Hyrcanus (134-104 B.C.E.). Cf. Segal, 'The Qumran War Scroll'; Van der Ploeg, *Le Rouleau,* 19. Cf. also Atkinson, 'The Historical Setting,' showing that the military descriptions in 1QM are Hellenistic and not Roman.

[154] Carmignac, *La Règle,* xiii, also stressing the unity of the work. In his opinion the work was written by the Teacher of Righteousness around 110 B.C.E.

[155] Cf. Milik, *Ten Years,* 39; Hunzinger, 'Fragmente', 147-51. Baillet, 'Le volume VII', 79. All of them agree that some of the 4Q MSS, above all 4Q491 (=4QMᵃ), reflect a different recension of the work. But Hunzinger's judgement that it is older than the recension of 1QM is doubted by Baillet, *ibid.* and Carmignac, La *Règle,* 270-2. Among the additional passages found in 4Q491 and not in 1QM is a hymn placed in the mouth of the archangel Michael (4Q491 II 8-18). It shares elements with 1QM and a work designated as *Berakot-Milhama,* known in several copies from cave 4. The affinities with copy 4QS 1 86 are especially numerous. Cf. Baillet, 'Le volume VII', 79-80; *idem, DJD,* 7, 26-27.

the literary structure. Inner divergencies and duplications were noticed, among them the obvious parallel in the description of the eschatological war in 1:15-19 and 7:9-11:9.[156] These facts led to various literary explanations. It was proposed to see the *War Scroll* as a compilation of three distinct books.[157] According to another theory, a primitive work of the second half of the second century B.C.E. was considerably enlarged by a later redactor who turned it into a 'Rule'.[158] Finally, the theory is offered that two works of composite character were assembled together with independent additional material.[159]

Though not all the results of these analyses are agreed upon,[160] they establish with certainty that the *War Scroll* is a composite work. Considering the existence of an early copy, its composition should be assigned, along with the *Damascus Covenant* and the *Rule of the Community*, to the early phase of the sect's life, namely the second half of the second century B.C.E.

THE RULE OF THE CONGREGATION

Two smaller works of a 'rule'-type originally belonged to the 1QS scroll:[161] one (1QS^a) describes the eschatological community, while the other (1QS^b) is a collection of benedictions (see below, p. 524). The work under discussion, 1QS^a, gives eschatological legislation on two subjects. First, the duties of every citizen of the future Congregation of all Israel. These are graded by age, the main point being that at thirty, one must join the army for full service and undertake responsibilities of command. The second subject is the formal assembly of the leading elite in the messianic age. It shall be called together as needed, and include civil and military leaders, notables, as well as priests, who shall preside the sessions. The future festive banquet takes place according to a fixed order: the high priest is the first

---

[156] Von der Osten-Sacken, *Gott und Belial*, 42-115. Van der Ploeg, *Le Rouleau*, 11-25, noticed other inconsistencies. Thus, e.g., certain passages predict a swift victory over the Kittim in one day (1:6.9ff; 11:11; 14:4-14; 16:1; 18:1.11) while in col. 2 a war of forty years is predicted. There are also divergencies in the description of the trumpets (cols. 8, 9, 16, 17, 18).

[157] Rabin, 'The Literary Structure', proposing the following division: a) cols. 1-9, The Book of War; b) cols. 10-14, The Book of God's Time; c) col. 14:16 until the end, The Book of Victory.

[158] Van der Ploeg, *Le Rouleau*, 11-25. The original work would comprise cols. 1; 15:1-5,10-12; 15:6-16:1; 16:3-18.

[159] Davies, *1QM*, discerns two major documents: a) cols. 2-9:1, a compilation from the Hasmonaean period, consisting of traditions going back to the Maccabaean wars. b) cols. 15-19; an end-product of a long development from an originally Maccabaean war-rule. The final redaction is assigned by him to the period of Roman occupation of Eretz-Israel (50 B.C.E. onwards). c) Additional materials: Cols. 10-12 (hymns) and cols. 13, 14 (independent units).

[160] Cf. the sharp criticism levelled by Carmignac, 'Review', against Davies, *1QM*. He rejects both Davies' literary analysis and historical reconstruction.

[161] Cf. Milik, *DJD*, 1, 118-30.

and the most important, while 'the Messiah of Israel' is mentioned afterwards, in a position clearly less prominent. This indicates a doctrine of two Messiahs, one a priest and the other of the Davidic line (cf. below, pp. 539-41).

4Q TESTIMONIA

The work[162] was copied in a MS. dated to 100-75 B.C.E.[163] and was preserved almost intact. It contains a collection of scriptural texts pertaining to the messianic teachings of the sect,[164] and a quotation from the sectarian work the *Psalms of Joshua,* yet unpublished.[165] Though the citations are not accompanied by a commentary, the ideas behind the collection are implied in their selection and order. Thus it is evident that each quotation represents a messianic figure, in the following order: 1) 'a prophet like Moses'; 2) the Star of Jacob and the Sceptre of Israel, referring to the priestly and the Davidic Messiahs;[166] 3) a quotation concerning the priesthood, which may refer again to the priestly Messiah; 4) 'the son of Belial', presented by a quotation from the *Psalms of Joshua.* It is likely that this evil figure represents an early Jewish version of the idea of the Antichrist, i.e. the wicked opponent of the Messiah at the threshold of the End of Days.[167] In addition, this last figure seems to portray a historical figure, perhaps the Wicked Priest of the *Pesharim.*[168]

4Q FLORILEGIUM

Two fragmentary columns of this work have survived[169] in a manuscript copied by 'an old Herodian hand.'[170] The work gives a *pesher*-like inter-

---

[162] 4Q175. Text: Allegro, *DJD,* 5, 60; Strugnell, 'Notes en marge,' 225-9; cf. Cross, *Library,* 147-8; Milik, *Ten Years,* 61-64, 124-5.

[163] Cf. Cross, *Library,* 114; Milik, *Ten Years,* 124, dates it back to 100 B.C.E.

[164] Deut 5:28-29, 18:18-19; Num 24:15-17; Deut 33:8-11; Josh 6:26. Collections of proof-texts, *Testimonia,* are known also from New Testaments times. Cf. Milik, Ten Years, 125. For a review of the *Testimonia* question in relationship to 4QTest see Fitzmyer, '4QTestimonia'.

[165] Cf. Strugnell, 'Le Travail,' 65; Milik, *Ten Years,* 61-62.

[166] Thus Cross, *Library,* 147. 'The Star of Jacob' of Num 24:24 is interpreted as the priestly Messiah. Cf. CD 7:18-19 where it is understood of 'the Searcher of the Law', (the Teacher of Righteousness?); the sceptre is understood of the Messiah of Israel or David as is clear from 4QPatr 1-5. In CD 7:20-21 it is interpreted of 'the Prince of the congregation', who equals the Messiah of David in 1QS[a] 2:14, 20. Cf. also 4Q Flor 1:11.

[167] Cf. Milik, *Ten Years,* 125; on the idea of the Antichrist in Qumran sources cf. Flusser, 'The Hubris'.

[168] Thus Cross, *Library,* 147-52, who identifies him with Simon the Maccabee. Milik, *Ten Years,* 63-64 sees here a reference to Matthatias and his sons Jonathan and Simon. Both identifications depend on the authors' identifications of the Wicked Priest. Cf. above, on 1QpHab, p. 509f.

[169] Text, Allegro, *DJD* 5, 53-57; Strugnell, 'Notes en marge,' 220-5; cf. also restorations by Yadin, 'A Midrash'. Cf. Flusser, 'Two Notes'.

[170] Strugnell, 'Notes en marge,' 177, 220.

pretation of 2 Sam 7:10-14, Ps 2:1 and various other texts, with the aid of other verses. It was, therefore, often presented as a typical example of a thematic *pesher* (cf. above, p. 504).

The *Pesher* on 2 Sam 7:10-14 is divided into two parts: a citation of 2 Sam 7:10-11a, with interpretation (4QFlor 1:1-7); and second, a citation of 2 Sam 7:11b-14a, with interpretation (4QFlor 1:7-13). In each unit the author adduces additional citations to support and clarify his exposition.

The first section understands 2 Sam 7:10-11 as referring to three temples. The first one to be mentioned, the eschatological Temple inferred from 2 Sam 7:10a, is not preserved in the fragment, but is implied by the citing of Exod 15:17-18 which is the *locus classicus* for the eschatological Temple to be built by God himself.[171] Significantly, in the *Pesher* it is referred to as 'the House' (הבית , 1:2-3) and not as 'temple' (מקדש), thus playing on 'the House' in the biblical verse. This temple is further described by a citation of Deut 23:3-4, from which it is inferred that no Ammonite, Moabite and bastard could approach it.[172]

A second temple, named the 'Temple of Israel' (מקדש ישראל), is inferred from 2 Sam 7:10b. The text is understood as alluding to the Temple of Israel desolated[173] by foreigners[174] because of Israel's sins; it is an evident reference to the First Temple, the only one desolated by foreigners at the author's time.

A third temple is called a Temple of Men (מקדש אדם), obviously inferred from 2 Sam 7:11a.[175] This temple, then, should be understood as distinct from both the eschatological Temple of God and the Temple of Israel, destroyed in the past. It is a temple belonging to, or consisting of Men.[176] It is described as a temple in which instead of real offerings, Works

---

[171] The same verse from Exodus is interpreted as pertaining to the eschatological temple in 11QTemp 29:8-10. In the present *Pesher* the exegetical connection between 2 Sam 7:10 and Exod 15:17-18 is based on the similarity in wording in both passages (נטע).

[172] Deut 23:3-4 actually refers to 'the congregation of YHWH', not the sanctuary. This means that the *Pesher* identifies the congregation with the future Temple. Moreover, the Pesher excludes from the list foreigners and proselytes, who are not included in Deut 23 but inferred from Ezek 44:6-9, which depicts the future Temple. See Baumgarten, *Studies,* 77-78. But note Lam 1:10; Neh 13:1.

[173] Obviously the verb שמם means 'desolate' here, which would suit the context perfectly. Flusser's proposition to interpret it as 'desecrated' is against the common biblical usage and is influenced by his interpretation of this temple as the Second Temple. Cf. *idem,* 'Two Notes', 102 n. 9; cf. also Ben-Yashar, 'Miqdaš-Adam'.

[174] The *Pesher* is obviously interpreting בני עולה , probably in connection with Jer 51:51 which speaks of the First Temple.

[175] ולמן היום אשר צויתי שפטים על עמי ישראל ('From the day on which I have appointed judges on my people Israel'); possibly reading שפטים of the Massoretic text as the nominal form (מ)שפטים . Cf., e.g., Deut 7:11, 8:11. That this is the stretch commented upon is indicated by the *pesher* method of citation and structure. Therefore there is no basis for Schwartz's contention ('The Three Temples,' 83-91) that the Temple of Men was inferred from 2 Sam 7:13a.

[176] And not 'a sanctuary among men', as Yadin, *ibid.,* 96 and Flusser, *ibid.,* 102 would have it.

of Torah (מעשי תורה) are offered. [177] Now deeds or works of the Torah are part of the sectarians' ideals, who see themselves as 'the Doers of the Torah'.[178] Hence, the Temple of Israel being the Temple of Solomon, and the Second Temple of the Maccabees being defiled and not worth mentioning, the Temple of Men appears to be none other than the sect itself.[179]

This interpretation is supported by many other details of the sectarian ideology. We may refer to the designation of prayer as a sacrifice (CD 11:20-21; 1QS 9:4-5), indeed to the whole sectarian way of life as sacrificial (1QS *ibid.*). It also explains the symbols of 'the House' and 'Jerusalem' as applied to the sect, which both imply the Temple. Especially interesting is the self-designation of the sect as 'the New Jerusalem' (as in 4QpIs[d], cf. above, p. 514) which expresses the concept of the temple-city. This is especially significant in light of the *halakhah* of the *Temple Scroll* which considers all of Jerusalem as a temple-city and requires a corresponding state of purity.[180] In a sense, for the sect, the Temple and Jerusalem are one and the same.[181] Yet it should be emphasized that the sect's identity with a temple does not necessarily imply that it replaces the actual temple service. Rather, it may indicate the priestly life of the sectarians, like servants in the sanctuary.[182]

The second section of the *Florilegium* expounds 2 Sam 7:14 as referring to the Plant of David, a messianic figure in the eschatological age. This is undoubtedly the Davidic Messiah referred to as 'the Messiah of Justice, the Plant of David' in 4QPatr 3-4. He is mentioned together with 'the Searcher of the Torah' (4QFlor 1:11), who is referred to in CD 6:7 as a historical figure, but in CD 7:18-19 appears in an eschatological context. That means

---

[177] Both the terms אדם and תורה figure in 2 Sam 7:19 וזאת תורת האדם ('and this is the Torah of Men'). Thus Flusser, *ibid.;* Ben-Yashar, *ibid.* Therefore it is preferable to preserve this reading and not read תודה as suggested by Strugnell *ibid.* and adopted by Brooke, *4QFlor*, 138.

[178] עשי התורה, 1QpHab 7:11, 8:1; cf. CD 4:8, 6:14; 4QpPs[a] 1-10 II 15, 23; as observed by Baumgarten, *Studies*, 82-83; Klinzing, *Die Umdeutung des Kultus*, 83-4.

[179] As it is understood by many scholars. Thus, e.g., Gärtner, *The Temple*, 34-5; cf. also Klinzing, *Die Umdeutung des Kultus*, 83-4. Schwartz, *ibid.*, identifies it with the Temple of Solomon, but in the foregoing interpretation it is the Temple of Israel which is seen as referring to the Temple of Solomon. Ben Yashar *ibid.* sees the Temple of Men as the Second Temple. This is unacceptable because of the negative attitude of the sect towards that temple.

[180] Cf. Yadin, *Temple Scroll* 1, 215-63.

[181] In my contribution, 'Jerusalem and the Temple,' I have argued that the concept of the Temple-city in the halakhic interpretation of the sect can best account for the employment of one symbol, 'the House', for the Tabernacle, the historical Jerusalem and the eschatological Jerusalem, in the *Animal Apocalypse* (*1 Enoch* 85-90).

[182] Cf. The *Angelic Liturgy*, below pp. 524f. and 565f. Some passages show that the sectaries did not break with the Temple completely (cf. CD 6:11-16, 20) and hoped for a restoration of the Temple in the eschatological era (1QM 2:1-6; 11Q Temp 29:8-10).

he is to be identified with the priestly Messiah known from other sectarian writings.[183]

Consequently, the second part of the *Pesher* on 2 Sam 7 should be seem as a continuation of the first part. If the sect understood itself as the contemporary 'Temple of Men', it may well have understood its own future existence as 'the House', the designation of the eschatological Temple; or perhaps as 'the faithful House' (בית נאמן) of priests, mentioned in 1 Sam 2:35, which figures in CD 3:19.[184] Thus the author of the *Pesher* may have been playing with both senses of the term 'House' in the prophecy to David, seeing in it an allusion both to the eschatological temple and to the royal house, i.e. the Messiah of David.

THE PESHER ON MELCHIZEDEK

Thirteen fragments of one manuscript were preserved which contain the remains of three columns of an eschatological *Pesher*.[185] It dates to around the mid-first century B.C.E.[186] The manuscript is too fragmentary to give a precise idea of its nature, but the *pesher*-like interpretations and the citations from various biblical books designate it as a thematic *pesher*.[187] It depicts events which will take place in the tenth Jubilee when Melchizedek, the King-priest (Gen 14:18-19; Ps 110:4) will liberate 'those of his inheritance' and will effect expiation of their sin. In this respect he performs functions of a priest. But in addition he will also judge the Sons of Belial, effect vengeance on them and help the Sons of Light. The eschatological context, and the special significance of Melchizedek's role, led some scholars to conclude that he is a celestial being, perhaps even identical with the Archangel Michael.[188] It was further suggested that Melchizedek is identical with 'the Angel of His Truth' who helps the Sons of Light against Belial, according to 4Q177 12-13 1:7.[189]

[183] Cf. 1QS 9:11; CD 12:23, 14:19. 19:10, 20:1; also 1QS^a 2:12-21. Is it the Teacher of Righteousness who will return as Messiah? Cf. Cross, *Library*, 226-30.

[184] Cf. also the promise to Solomon 1Kgs 11:38. .

[185] 1QMelch edited by Van der Woude, 'Melchisedek'; improved edition: Van der Woude and De Jonge, 'Melchizedek and the New Testament', 302. For further improved editions cf. Fitzmyer, 'Further Light' 247-8; Kobelski, *Melchizedek*, 5-7 (freshly edited, from photographs). Milik, 'Milkî-ṣedeq', 97-99 argues that the present *pesher* and 4Q180 + 4Q181 form one work. In my 'Pesher on the Periods' I have attempted to show that this is unacceptable both on material and structural grounds.

[186] Van der Woude, 'Melchizedek', 357; Milik, 'Milkî-ṣedeq', 87; Kobelski, *Melkizedek*, 4 n. 4.

[187] Carmignac, 'Melkisédeq', 360-362. The *Pesher* is built around Lev 25, where the liberation taking place in the jubilee year is discussed. Also cited are Deut 15:2, Isa 52:7, 61:1, Ps 82:1-2, 7:8-9. Cf. Fitzmyer, 'Melchizedek,' 251; cf. Miller, 'Is 61:1-2'; Sanders, 'The Old Testament.'

[188] Milik, 'Milkî-ṣedeq', 141-144; Kobelski, *Melchizedek*, 71-74. Milik suggested that Melchizedek should be read as *Milki-Sedeq*, an angelic being opposed to the one known as *Milki-Resha* who figures in 4Q280 (= 4Q Amram^b) 22. Cf. Milik, *ibid.*, 127ff.

[189] Du Toit Laubscher, 'God's Angel'. Meyer proposed that we see the title of the Teacher of Righteousness as modelled after the name Melchizedek ('Melchisedek von Jerusalem').

Another point of interest is the chronological system implied in the *Pesher*. The mention of the tenth Jubilee, obviously the one destined for eschatological events, implies a system of ten Jubilees, which equals the seventy weeks' calculation ($49 \times 10 = 490 = 70 \times 7$), and therefore is another form of the system widely used in the Second Commonwealth era.[190]

The figure of Melchizedek as a supernatural redeemer and eschatological judge has striking affinities with the Epistle to the Hebrews (5:1-10; 6:20; 7:1-3), where Jesus is presented as a high priest 'in the order of Melchizedek.'[191] It is also suggested that the figure of Melchizedek influenced the title 'Son of Man' applied to Jesus in the New Testament.[192]

Poetic and Liturgical Works

Among the manuscripts of Qumran, the fragments of liturgical works form an important part. This may be explained by the prominent role assigned to prayer at Qumran. Being prevented from bringing sacrifices to the Second Temple, the sectaries may have developed 'offering of lips', namely prayer (1QS 9:4-5; CD 11:20-21). This situation would account for the variety of liturgical compositions.[193]

Yet it is not always possible to decide precisely which purpose such compositions served, whether for actual recitation in ceremonies, for private or public prayers, or for meditation. Nor is it always easy to conclude whether the work in question is sectarian or not. Some compositions, as the *Thanksgiving Psalms*, evince the characteristic sectarian features of style and thought, but this is not true of compositions like the apocryphal psalms contained in the *Psalms Scroll* ($11QPs^a$). Here, only strictly sectarian works will be discussed.

THE THANKSGIVING PSALMS

Collections of the sect's *Thanksgiving Psalms*, psalm-like hymns also called *Hodayot*, survived in one larger manuscript (1QH) and in several other

---

[190] The question is whether the period of ten jubilees covers all of history, or only part of it. In respect to the seventy weeks' calculation both variations are employed. According to Milik there exists another sectarian work, 4Q384-4Q390, designated as Pseudo-Ezekiel, which espouses the same chronological system. (Text to be edited by Strugnell.) Cf. Milik, 'Milkî-şedeq', 110; *Enoch*, 255.

[191] It is understood that the Epistle takes Melchizedek as an eternal priest, probably a priestly king chosen by God (cf. Ps 110:4). This *Pesher* points to a possibly Jewish background for such a view. Cf. Van der Woude and De Jonge, 'Melchizedek and the New Testament'; Horton, *Melchizedek*, 167-170; Kobelski, *Melchizedek*, 127-9. Kobelski (99-114) also suggests that the Melchizedek figure influenced the Johannine figure of the Paraclete. Cf. also Delcor, 'Melchizedek Figure'.

[192] Cf. Flusser, 'Melchizedek'; Kobelski, *Melchizedek*, 130-7. Cf. also above, pp. 408 and 457.

[193] Cf. Klinzing, *Die Umdeutung des Kultus*, 93-106.

manuscripts. Their dating ranges from 100 to 1 B.C.E.[194]

The first editors of the *Hodayot* were struck by their resemblance to the biblical Psalms, especially those of the type termed individual thanksgiving psalms.[195] But it was soon realized that the similarity is partial and does not apply to all the hymns. At the same time these hymns do contain elements taken from other biblical forms.[196] This eclecticism is typical of post-biblical literature in general. Hence the parallels to the *Hodayot* should be looked for in hymnic and psalmodic compositions found in the Apocrypha, Pseudepigrapha and the New Testament.[197] Some scholars are not even prepared to see real poetry in the *Hodayot* but call them 'rhythmic prose'.[198]

The *Hodayot* are divided into two groups: a type of hymn using the first person singular, and another using the first person plural. The first type of *Hodayot* are characterized by a strong personal tone and by many biographical details taken from the life of the speaker. Themes recurring in this connection are: the solitude of the speaker, his life in exile and persecution by his enemies, the grace of God in saving him and in electing him for a special knowledge, a knowledge that he transmits to a group of his followers. Similarities to what we know of the Teacher of Righteousness from other writings led to the attribution of these *Hodayot* to his own hand,[199] but this rests on hypothesis. It was assumed that the second type of *Hodayot* refer to the community as a whole.[200]

---

[194] 1QH. Date: 30-1 B.C.E. (cf. Cross, 'Jewish Script', 137). A badly preserved MS. Contents: originally it consisted of two scrolls, of which 18 columns have been reconstructed in the first edition (Sukenik, *Megillot*), leaving many fragments unlocated. Later, a better arrangement was made (Carmignac, *Les Textes*, 1, 129).
1Q 35 1-2. Two additional fragments of 1QH, edited by Milik, *DJD* 1, 136-8.
4QH[a-e]. Five MSS. on leather and one on papyrus (4QH[f]) from Cave 4, yet unpublished. Date: the oldest MS. is situated around 100 B.C.E. Cf. Starcky, 'Les quatre étapes', 483 n. 8. These MSS. complete 1QH in many places and show that the order of hymns was variable. Cf. Strugnell, 'Le travail', 64. A new edition, comprising both 1QH and the 4Q materials, is being prepared by Stegemann and Strugnell. Cf. Bardtke, 'Literaturbericht IX,' 213-14.
There exist another five MSS. resembling the *Hodayot* in style, but not corresponding to any known section in 1QH.
[195] Cf. Mowinckel, 'Some Remarks.' For a more comprehensive analysis of structure cf. Morawe, *Aufbau*. Recently a structural analysis was offered for some of the *Hodayot*. Cf. Kittel, *The Hymns*.
[196] Such as complaint motifs, and a *qinah* rythm. Cf. Silberman, 'Language', 96-98; Delcor, *Les Hymnes*, 19; Licht, *The Thanksgiving Scroll*, 17-21; Thiering, 'Suffering'; Dombkowski Hopkins, '1QHodayot', 329-31.
[197] Cf., e.g., Holm-Nielsen, 'Erwägungen'; *idem*, 'Religiöse Poesie', 165-172; Morawe, 'Vergleich'.
[198] Cf. Kraft, 'Poetic Structure'; Dombkowski Hopkins, '1QHodayot', 331.
[199] First suggested by Sukenik, *Megillot* 2, 32 and followed by many others. In a more comprehensive analysis Jeremias, *Der Lehrer*, 168-80, assigns the following sections to the Teacher of Righteousness: 1QH 2:1-19, 31-39; 3:1-18; 4:5-5:4; 5:5-19; 5:20-7:5; 7:6-25; 8:4-40. Becker, *Das Heil Gottes*, 53-54 assigns only the following to him: 5:5-19; 6:1-36; 7:6-25; 8:4-40.
[200] Becker, *Das Heil Gottes*, 54; Holm-Nielsen, 'Religiöse Poesie', 167-68; Dombkowski Hopkins, '1QHodayot', 355.

A related question concerns the *Sitz-im-Leben* in which the *Hodayot* came into being. Some suggested a liturgical function,[201] but others thought that they are more suited for edification and reflection.[202]

Though expressing themselves in a peculiar form of their own, the *Hodayot* produce a review of most of the sectarian ideas found in other works: dualism, predestination, election and grace, to mention a few.[203] Peculiar to the *Hodayot* is the view that man is constituted of a duality of flesh and spirit; the flesh is base by nature, for it is susceptible to sin, while the spirit is capable of purification and repentance. This teaching is placed in the context of the general dualism and predestination of the sect: God has created everything according to apre-ordained plan which divides the world into two camps, Good and Evil, so that repentance from sin is the lot only of those who belong to the camp Light. A special place is given to eschatological ideas. One *Hodaya* describes the future purification of the world in a great conflagration, and another describes the eschatological role of the sect as a small plant which will grow into a large tree.[204]

THE BENEDICTIONS

The fragments of this composition, 1QS^b, originally belong to the 1QS scroll.[205] They produced liturgical blessinns pronounced by the Instructor (*Maskil*) and are addressed to the Fearers of God, i.e. the entire community (1-2), to the Sons of Zadok, the Priests (3-4), and to the Prince of the Congregation (נשיא העדה 5:20-29). We do not know on what occasion these blessings were pronounced, but as the Prince of the Congregation appears in an eschatological context in the companion piece, the *Rule of the Congregation* (1QS^a), we may assume that the *Benedictions* were equally intended for an eschatological ceremony. Some blessings appear to be addressing the priestly Messiah. Likewise, the prominent function of Isa 11:1-5 in the blessing for the Prince of the Congregation suggests that the Messiah of Israel, i.e. of David, is intended. (See further below, pp. 539-41).

THE ANGELIC LITURGY

This work, 4QShirShabb, is extant in at least four manuscripts from cave 4, dating between 50 B.C.E. and 50 C.E. Linguistic peculiarities of the work define it as a sectarian composition. It has many affinities with prayers

---

[201] E.g., Reicke, 'Remarques'.
[202] E.g., Bardtke, 'Considération'; *idem*, 'Literaturbericht IX Teil'. Cf. also Flusser, below p. 566.
[203] For reviews of the religious ideas in *Hodayot* cf. Licht, 'The Doctrine'; Merill, *Qumran*.
[204] See below, pp. 537 and 539 and footnotes.
[205] Cf. Milik, *DJD* 1, 118-30.

found in the *War Scroll* and with a liturgical work yet unpublished, *4QBerakhot*. Only one fragment has been provisionally published.[206]

The work consists of liturgies composed by a *Maskil* for every Shabbat offering of the year, according to the Essene calendar. Perhaps these songs were connected with the sacrifices in the actual Temple. The participation of angels seems invoked, and in general the liturgy in the heavenly Temple corresponds to the liturgy on earth.

The work seems to reflect a conception of seven heavens, with seven chief princes of angels, seven princes of second rank, seven tongues and seven words. It has obvious affinities with the rabbinic Merkabah traditions, which are concerned with speculations about the heavens, angels, and the ascension of the visionary to see the Merkabah, i.e. the Throne of God.[207]

Interestingly, a copy of the same work was found in the excavation at Masada.[208] The presence of this specifically sectarian writing may indicate that sectarians were engaged in the defense of the Zealot fortress.[209]

Halakhah

As occurs in other groups of sectarian writings, the halakhic material also exhibits both affinities with Jewish literature outside the sect and a peculiar sectarian character of its own. While substantive parallels exist, e.g. with *halakhah* preserved in rabbinic tradition, the sectarian *halakhah* cannot be identified with it, nor with any other known halakhic tradition.

The debate on the origin of the sectarian *halakhah* dates from the publication of the *Damascus Covenant* (cf. above, p. 490), which on leaves 9-12 gives a varied collection of *halakhot*. Initially, these were identified either as Pharisaic or Sadducean.[210] But further research showed that the picture is more complex. Comparisons between the *Covenant* and Pharisaic traditions showed that different solutions are given to halakhic problems.[211] Comparative study of the sectarian *halakhah* and other halakhic

---

[206] 4QS¹39 1:16-26. Cf. Strugnell, 'The Angelic Liturgy' for the published fragment and the rest of the information. Cf. also Carmignac, 'Règle des chants'.

[207] See below, pp. 565-6. For the rabbinic traditions cf. Scholem, *Merkabah Mysticism;* Grünwald, *Apocalyptic;* Halperin, *Merkabah.*

[208] Cf. Yadin, 'The Excavation of Meṣada,' 105-8.

[209] A possibility of Zealot influence on the sect, especially in its last phase, was suggested by Milik, *Ten Years,* 94-98; Cross, *Library,* xv-xvi, 61-62 n. 16.

[210] A Pharisaic origin was argued by Ginzberg, *Unknown Jewish Sect.* 104-154. Much of his arguments and analysis are still valuable for the understanding of CD in general. A Sadducean background was advocated by Schechter, *Fragments.* For a general survey see Rosso-Ubigli, 'Il Documento di Damasco'.

[211] On the issue of testimony by two witnesses (CD 9:17-22) see Neusner, 'Testimony'; Rabinovitch, 'Damascus Documents IX 17-22'; Jackson, 'Dam. Doc. IX 16-23'.

traditions is necessary,[212] but it serves to emphasize the specific identity of the sect.[213]

An analysis of the sectarian *halakhah* in the *Covenant* and in the *Rule* recently indicated that the sect divided the biblical laws into two categories: *nigleh* (revealed) and *nistar* (hidden). The first type would consist of laws of which the interpretation is clear to everyone, while the other category is correctly understood only by the sectaries who derived it, according to this analysis, by means of a particular, divinely inspired exegesis.[214]

While the relationship between the *halakhah* of the Pharisees and the sectaries is complex, there are striking similarities between them. As we have seen above (p. 499) the graded process of admission to the sect was structured by the stratified system of purity rules. The three grades of admission correspond to three degrees of purity, the highest being that of the full members. A similar admission procedure is known of the Pharisaic *Haburoth,* fraternities for practising religious commandments such as the purity rules. There too, three grades of admission seem to have required corresponding, increasingly strict purity rules. In particular the distinction between the purity of food and that of liquids, the latter being more strictly guarded because it is more susceptible to contamination, sheds light on the sect's destinction between the 'Purities of the Many' and the 'Drink of the Many'.[215] As such, both communities attest to the wider usage of the Second Commonwealth era to practice purity rules in various degrees.[216] Yet there are also considerable differences, one of them being the very fact that the sect separated itself from the rest of Israel. We are then, dealing with similarities, perhaps springing from common sources, but not with identity.[217]

THE TEMPLE SCROLL

With the recent publication of the *Temple Scroll* (11QTemp), the halakhic material from Qumran has been considerably augmented. This is the longest sectarian work yet published, and it is entirely devoted to halakhic matters.

---

[212] Cf. Rabinovitch, *ibid.*

[213] Jackson, *Essays,* 21.

[214] Schiffman, *The Halakhah,* 75-76, who further suggests that the biblical text was the only source for the sectarian *halakhah.* See now also his *Sectarian Law,* 211-7.

[215] Cf. Lieberman, 'The Discipline'; Licht, *The Rule Scroll,* 294-303.

[216] Cf. Alon, *Jews, Judaism and the Classical World,* 190-234. Cf. also Josephus' testimony of the Essene purity rules, *Ant.* 18:19; *War* 2:129-143.

[217] As argued by Rabin, *Qumran Studies.* Cf. the criticism on the book by Baumgarten, *Studies,* 3-12.

The scroll, fully edited with commentary by Yadin,[218] is written on nineteen sheets of thin parchment, preserving sixty-seven columns. In its present state, the scroll measures 7.94 meters, but according to Yadin its original length was 8.75 meters. This is, then, the longest scroll yet known. It was copied by two scribes: one copied columns 1-5, the other, all the rest. The script of both is Herodian and Yadin assigns the manuscript to the first half of the first century C.E. But fragments of other copies of the work exist, according to Yadin, and one of them is assigned by him to the last quarter of the second century B.C.E.[219] Yadin, therefore, thinks that the work was composed in its essential parts during the reign of John Hyrcanus (135-104 B.C.E.), or at the beginning of the reign of Alexander Jannaeus (103-76 B.C.E.). Yadin sees some of the scroll's *halakhoth,* for instance the Law of the King and Temple regulations, as particularly suitable for the period in question.[220]

The language used by the scroll is the Hebrew literary style also found in the other scrolls,[221] though it lacks their distinctive religious vocabulary. Yet this may be due to the different purpose and contents of the present work; it ostensibly imitates biblical style. Nonetheless, the scroll unmistakably betrays its Second Commonwealth origin: there is the typical use of the composite verb, characteristic of Mishnaic Hebrew, the use of words rare in the Bible but current in Mishnaic Hebrew, and the use of technical terms known from rabbinic parlance.[222]

Yadin suggests that the scroll should be identified with the sectarian composition *Sefer Hahago,* mentioned in other works, which he asserts is identical with the *Book of the Torah* alluded to elsewhere.[223]

The scroll is written in the first person and the speaker is God himself, addressing Moses, as is indicated in 45:5, 'The Sons of Aaron your brother'. The opening of the work is lost, so we do not know how it was introduced, but the composition is evidently conceived as a Torah given to Moses by God. This is achieved not only by the literary setting (God addressing Moses), but also by a thoroughgoing rewriting of large passages from the Pentateuch.[224] While doing so, the author was undoubtedly convinced that

---

[218] Yadin, *Temple Scroll,* vols. 1-3. For corrections and new readings cf. Qimron, 'New Readings'; *idem,* 'The Language.'

[219] Fragment no. 43.366. Cf. Yadin,*Temple Scroll* 1, 14. Cf. also Flusser, 'The Temple Scroll'; Milgrom, 'The Temple Scroll'.

[220] Yadin, *Temple Scroll* I, 295-8.

[221] Cf. Qimron, 'The Language'.

[222] Yadin, *Temple Scroll* I, 29-34.

[223] Cf. Yadin, *Temple Scroll* I, 301-304. See above, n. 57. The *Book of Torah* is mentioned in CD 5:2; 4QpPs^a 1-10 iv 2, 8-9; 4Q177 1-4 13-14.

[224] Other methods employed include: *a)* altering the order of the biblical words; *b)* inserting additional sectarian *halakhot; c)* adding entire sections; *d)* interpreting the biblical text by emendations and glosses; *e)* conflating biblical laws of similar nature.

he was writing the truly divine Torah as revealed to him through tradition and divine inspiration.

The scroll contains the following subjects: the covenant between God and Israel, according to Exod 34:10-16 and Deut 7:1ff. (col. 2); the Temple, its structure, the sacrifices and offerings, the festivals (cols. 3-45); the Temple city and related purity regulations (cols. 45-52); the Law of the King (cols. 56-59); various prescriptions (cols. 53-56, 60-67). From this survey it is clear that the scroll's main preoccupations are with the Temple and its service, and with the King's Law.

In general the *halakhah* of the scroll is stricter than that of the Pharisees. Some of it is clearly polemical, such as the *halakhah* concerning the Temple and the Temple-city which stands in contrast to the practice in the contemporary Hasmonaean Temple as known from various sources. The scroll combines various biblical passages, among them Ezekiel 40-48, on the ideal Temple.[225]

The basic principle is that the Temple-city is equivalent to the camp of Israel in the wilderness, and correspondingly the biblical purity laws concerning the camp and the Tabernacle are strictly applied. In contradistinction to Pharisaic *halakhah,* the entire area of Jerusalem is considered as a Temple-city. Consequently, a three-day purification rite is required before admission, and all bearers of impurity are excluded from the city. Sexual intercourse is forbidden in the city (cf. CD 12:1), as is defecation; women were apparently not permitted to live in the city. All of this is reminiscent of the sanctity of the camp of the Sons of Light in the eschatological war described in the *War Scroll.* Indeed, the similarities to the camp rules of the *War Scroll* form another indication of the sectarian origin of the *Temple Scroll.*

Among the peculiar *halakhot* implied by the strict observance of levitical purity is the one prescribing a place for defecation outside Jerusalem, undoubtedly inspired by Deut 23:13-14.[226] In another *halakhah,* burial in Jerusalem or other cities is strictly forbidden and a central cemetery for each of four cities should be allocated (11QTemp 48:11-14).[227] Special attention was paid to food and drink brought into the city, wine and oil being mentioned in particular. Only pure food and drink is allowed in, to be carried only in skins of pure animals which were sacrificed in the Temple (11QTemp 47:7-18).

A prominent place in the scroll is allocated to the various festivals and their respective sacrifices. The peculiar feature of the festivals is that they are clearly reckoned according to the solar calendar of 364 days (cf.

---

[225] Cf. Flusser, 'Review', 273.

[226] Cf. Yadin, *Temple Scroll* I, 228-35; above p. 486.

[227] Such a halakhic prescription may explain the size of the Qumran cemetery, which may have served the entire area. Cf. above, p. 484.

below, p. 530). The sequence of festivals began with the waving of the *Omer* on the 26th day of the first month. On *Shavuot*, i.e. the 15th day of the third month, the offering of the New Wheat is celebrated. Two additional festivals are celebrated: the offering of the New Wine on the third day of the fifth month, and the New Oil festival on the 22nd of the sixth month. Each celebration is accompanied by a sacrificial meal in the Temple, where the corresponding first fruits are consumed.[228]

A section with many innovations is the one dealing with the king. In addition to a rewritten version of Deut 17:14-20, there are entirely new additions, as, for instance, the prescription that the king should consult an advisory council. The rules concerning the king's wife bear the widest applications. She cannot be a foreigner, but must be of the king's family. More strikingly, she is to be his only wife; he cannot remarry until she dies. In effect, polygamy and divorce are forbidden.[229] Interestingly, the king is absolutely subordinated to the high priest in all matters relating to optional war. Here the *halakhah* of the scroll again rallies itself to other sectarian scrolls where the future Messiah of Israel is clearly subordinate to the priestly Messiah (cf. p. 539f.).

The prominence of the king's law and its original additions led some scholars to suggest that it represents a Hebrew sectarian version of a tractate on kingship, a literary genre well-known in Hellenistic times, especially in Egypt.[230]

Another detail which intrigued scholars is the prescription for execution by hanging (11QTemp 64:6-13). The scroll changes the order of the words in the respective verse (Deut 21:22), indicating that death should occur by hanging, while the rabbinic *halakhah* prescribes that the convict be strangled before being hanged. This difference made Yadin suggest that the author of the *Pesher on Nahum* who describes the hanging of the Pharisees by Jannaeus is not criticizing him but, on the contrary, saw a justified punishment in it for the Pharisees' treachery (cf. p. 511).

In conclusion it may be reiterated that the *halakhah* of the sect as set

---

[228] The new data of the *Temple Scroll* shed light on various prescriptions for offerings of oil and wheat preserved in a fragmentary state in 4Qhalakhah[a] 5 (published by Baillet, *DJD*, 3, 300). Other related halakhic fragments named 'ordonnances': 4Q513, published by Baillet in *DJD* 7, 287-98; cf. also 4Q159 in *DJD* 5. In 4Q513 13 4, the expression ...מגו(אלים בשמן is mentioned, which is to be associated with גאולי שמן in CD 12:16 (cf. above n. 25). The *Temple Scroll* also confirms that a reference to the New Oil festival is included in a small fragment mentioned by Milik, 'Le travail'; cf. Baumgarten *Studies*, 131-42.

[229] Cf. Yadin, *Temple Scroll* I, 272-4; Vermes, *Post-Biblical Studies*, 52-56; Mueller, 'The Temple Scroll'. The verse adduced in support of this *halakhah* is Deut 17:17, the same verse used by CD 4:20-21 to forbid polygamy in general. Another matrimonial *halakhah* imposed on the king and shared by the *Covenant* is the prohibition to marry the daughter of one's brother or sister; 11QTemp 66:15-17 and CD 5:7-11. This prohibition was in force also among the Samaritans, Karaites, Falashas, Christians and Muslims, but not in rabbinic *halakhah*.

[230] Cf. Weinfeld, 'Temple Scroll'; Mendels, 'On Kingship.' Cf. also above, p. 268.

forth in the *Temple Scroll* is of a peculiar distinct character. The conception of Jerusalem as a Temple-city, the extreme purity rules involved in it, the deviating solar calendar and other details all confirm the close connection between the sect's exclusive character and its *halakhah*. This exclusiveness gains additional severity from the divine inspiration claimed by the author of the scroll.

THE SCROLLS AND JUBILEES

The book of *Jubilees* shows affinity both with the sect's severe *halakhah* and with its claim of divine inspiration (cf. above, p. 99-101). Therefore it is of particular interest to compare the *halakhah* of *Jubilees* with that of the *Temple Scroll* and the *Damascus Covenant*. Three main areas of affinity may be delineated: Sabbath, calendar and festivals, and general religious ideas.

As for Sabbath laws, both *Jubilees* and the *Damascus Covenant* permit only food prepared before the Sabbath to be eaten (CD 10:22-11:2; *Jub.* 2:29, 50:8), and both forbid fasting on the Sabbath (CD 11:4-5; *Jub.* 50:12).

Calendar and festivals: it was recognized long ago that the solar calendar advocated by *Jubilees* and *1 Enoch* must also have served the sectaries, but with the publication of the *Temple Scroll* many more details became evident. Thus the sacrifice of Passover is to be offered before the *Tamid* and in the Temple court, and not after the *Tamid* in the city, as the rabbinic *halakhah* ordains (11QTemp 17:6-9; *Jub.* 49:16-20). The festival of *Shavuot* is considered a festival of offering, and not only of new wheat (11QTemp 19:9; *Jub.* 6:21). Also, the second tithe is attached to the festival offerings (11QTemp 43:4-10; *Jub.* 32:10ff).

General religious climate: in this context the violent rejection by *Jubilees* of any sexual contact between Israelites and foreigners should be mentioned (*Jub.* 30:11). It coincides with the prohibition to the king to marry a foreign woman in 11QTemp 57:15-19. Further parallels are: the idea that God will build the eschatological Temple himself (11QTemp 29:8-10; cf. *Jub.* 1:15-17, 26-29, and *1 Enoch* 90:29) and the prominence of Levi reflected in the order of sacrifices in the *Temple Scroll* (11QTemp 23:10; cf. 1QM 1:2) and in the position of Levi as a priest in *Jubilees* (ch. 31).

In conclusion it may be said that though *Jubilees* and the Qumran scrolls share the same tradition in respect to many *halakhot*, yet they differ in various details and therefore cannot be simply identified. In consequence the question of the nature and the origin of the sect's *halakhah* remains open.

Varia

Up to this point the major compositions of distinctive sectarian character were reviewed. But there are many fragments of interest which do not fall into a specific category, nor is their sectarian character always evident. A few of them are reviewed now.

THE COPPER SCROLL

This document, 3Q15, consists of a list of real or imaginary treasures hidden in various locations. The list is engraved on copper plates found in Cave 3.[231] It describes some sixty-four caches of gold, silver, aromatics and manuscripts. The enormous amounts recorded led Milik to assume that they are imaginary. Others thought that the scroll may have referred to the sectarian treasures hidden during the Jewish Revolt.[232]

HOROSCOPES

This is a curious document (4Q186), written in Hebrew, but from left to right instead of the reverse. It is written in a mixture of archaic and square Hebrew letters and also Greek ones.[233] It appears to associate physical characteristics with specific psychological qualities, and to relate both to the position of the planets at the moment of one's birth. Of special interest is the allocation of portions of Light and Darkness to each person, which seems to decide on his place in the camp of Light or Darkness.[234]

THE NEW JERUSALEM

This name designates an Aramaic work found in several copies.[235] It seems to describe the New Jerusalem and the Temple along the line of Ezekiel 40-48, giving the general plan of the city, the gates and towers, the disposition of a house and the interior of a house.[236] Some fragments clearly

---

[231] Text: Milik, *DJD* 3, 211-302; Allegro, *The Treasure;* Lurie, *The Copper Scroll.*

[232] Cf. Jeremias and Milik, 'Remarques'; Ullendorff, 'The Greek Letters'; Lehmann, 'Identification'.

[233] Text: Allegro, *DJD* 5, 88-89; Strugnell, 'Notes en marge,' 274-6.

[234] Cf. Carmignac, 'Les horoscopes'; Dupont-Sommer, 'Deux Documents'; Gordis, 'A Document'; Delcor, 'Recherches'; Lehmann, 'New Light'. There exists another horoscope in Aramaic, 4QMess ar, which appears to depict a Messianic figure. Cf. Starcky, 'Un texte messianique'; Fitzmyer, *Essays,* 127-60.

[235] 1Q32 and 5Q15 were published by Milik, *DJD* 1, 134-5; 3, 184-93, with variants from the MSS of 4Q. Among others, Milik cites a sentence indicating that a seer, who describes Jerusalem, is accompanied by a divine messenger, just as in Ezekiel's description of the future Temple. 2Q24 was published by Baillet, *DJD* 3, 86-88, who dated it to the beginning of the first century C.E. A fragment of another MS., 11QJérNouv ar is being published by Jongeling. See his 'Publication provisoire'. The fragment shows many affinities with 2Q24. There are additional 4Q MSS. still unpublished, assigned to Strugnell and Milik. Cf. Jongeling, 'Note Additionelle'.

[236] Discussed in detail by Licht, 'An Ideal Town'.

refer to the altar and the priestly service. In some details this parallels the description of the *Temple Scroll*.[237]

The Religious Thought of the Sect

INTRODUCTION

The sect's literary corpus attests to an overall unity of thought, terminology and style. Yet it also manifests a variety of manners of exposition, and of nuances in detail and formulation. This situation led to two different evaluations. One saw the sectarian literary corpus as reflecting a unified system of thought. Consequently, the aim of the analysis was a synthesis of the thought expressed in the various writings.[238] More recently, scholars tend to detect various layers and stages of development in the sectarian literature, and the analysis aims at disentangling them.[239]

Yet two general considerations should be taken into account. The sectarian documents, while attesting to a variety of literary forms, genres and purposes, to a large extent employ a poetic, repetitive style. Therefore, nuances may be due to various literary conditions, and not necessarily reflect different concepts or ideas. Secondly, all the major sectarian writings, the *War Scroll,* the *Hodayot,* the *Rule,* the *Covenant* and the *Temple Scroll,* stem from a relatively short span of time, namely between 170 and 100 B.C.E.[240] This means that most of them were composed within the span of one or two generations. This seems to be too short a period to allows a far-reaching inner development of ideas, and even if divergencies exist, they should be seen as various components of basically one system which originated in a relatively short span of time (cf. p. 546 on the history of the sect). In light of these considerations it is preferable to pursue the first approach, and to see the sect's thought as one homogenous system, though variously reflected by the different documents.[241] The following survey outlines some central topics which are basic to the understanding of the documents.

---

[237] Yadin, *Temple Scroll,* I, 167-9 notes the similarity of 'the Houses of Steps' (בתי מעלות) mentioned in 5Q15 II 2 2-5 to the houses made to facilitate entry into the Temple mentioned in 11QTemp 42:7-8.

[238] E.g. Burrows, *More Light,* 277-362.

[239] See investigations such as those of Starcky, 'Les quatre étapes'; Von der Osten-Sacken, *Gott und Belial,* and Murphy-O'Connor (above, footnotes 74, 91).

[240] This, of course, is tenable only if the origins of the sect are dated to around 170 B.C.E. But it is possible that the origins are earlier (cf. below p. 545), which would give a larger span of time for composition and literary development.

[241] Literary analysis may reveal a subtle unity, not immediately apparent on the surface of the documents. Cf. Collins, 'Patterns of Eschatology', 352-3.

GOOD AND EVIL

The religious thought of the sect turns around two axes: a general view of man and the world and a conception of Israel in the context of its history. Usually these subjects are treated in separate contexts, but they converge into one consistent view of the world. The general world view of the sect is most thoroughly elaborated in the 'Treatise of the Two Spirits' (cf. above, p. 500):

> From the God of Knowledge comes all that is and was and before they came to be he prepared all their design; and when they come to be following their purposes according to the design of His glory, they will fulfill their function and cannot be changed . . .
> And He created man for dominion over the earth; and He set to him two spirits to conduct himself according to them until the time of His visitation. They are the Spirit of Truth and the Spirit of Perversity. (1QS 3:15-19)

The metaphysical outlook of the sect is anchored, as is all Jewish thought, in the biblical concept of one just God, the creator and sustainer of the world. However this outlook is here laid down in a series of concise, abstract statements, the earliest of this type in Jewish literature.[242]

The point of departure is a definition of the relationship between God and the world.[243] It has two aspects: the nature of every being, and its existence. The nature of everything is pre-determined in a divine plan, ordained by God before creation. Its existence is effected by the creative act. Creation, therefore, is a materialization of the divine plan which makes its laws into the laws of the existing world. In this way the act of creation not only brings the world into being, but establishes its total submission to God and his law. In other words, God's sovereignty over his creatures springs from the very fact of their being created by him. This, of course, is the biblical view, well expressed by the metaphor of the potter working clay (Isa 29:16, 45:9, 64:7).[244]

In such a conception of the world, there is no place for an 'evil world', or a supernatural evil power equal to God. It is, therefore, extremely interesting to see that into this system of strict predestination, powerful dualistic notions are introduced to form what is known as the 'double predestination'; for the system prescribes not only the predestination of events, but

---

[242] Intimations of such may be discerned in Ben Sira and Qohelet. See Hengel, *Hellenism* I, 219. The Treatise (1QS 3:13-4:26) may be compared with 1QH 1:5-38, 13:1-12; 1QM 10:11-16. See further Licht, 'the Treatise'; Wernberg-Møller, 'A Reconsideration;' Treves, 'The Two Spirits'; Charlesworth, *John and Qumran,* 176-103; Dombrowski, 'The Idea of God.'

[243] Cf. Licht, 'The Doctrine'; Merill, *Qumran and Predestination,* 24-32.

[244] The image is taken up by the *Hodayot* in respect to man, e.g. 1QH 3:23, 4:29, 7:13, 11:3, 12:26. Cf. in this connection Rom 9:19-23.

also their good or evil character.[245] Significantly these notions concern the human domain only; nature is governed by laws proper to it. Although both sets of laws, in nature and in humanity, bear the same mark of rigorous predestination, yet the laws governing humanity are of special character. They prescribe the existence of two spirits, the Spirit of Truth or Light, and the Spirit of Evil or Darkness. Each spirit stands for an entire domain, in outside reality as well as in man's heart:[246] there is a camp of truthful spirits and angels headed by the Angel of Light, and there is a camp of evil angels, commanded by Belial, the Angel of Evil.[247] Between the two camps lies eternal strife, which also divides humanity; all men are engaged in the struggle, either as 'Sons of Light' or as 'Sons of Darkness'.

In this context, there is a special significance in the term 'lot' or 'part' (גורל).[248] It is especially prominent in the *War Scroll,* where it signifies the 'part' of each spirit or angel. Thus, the lot of Belial includes the evil spirits but also the Sons of Darkness. Interestingly, the community is God's own lot, and not that of the Angel of Light (cf. 1QM 13:13, 15:1, 17:7; 1QS 2:2). This is a sectarian adaptation of the idea in Deut 32:8-9 that Israel is the part of God, while the nations are governed by angels.[249]

In this way the position of the governing angels acquires a special significance: it gives supernatural expression to the strife between the two camps. The dualistic idea that the camps of good and evil are headed by two corresponding angels, the Angel of Light and Belial, is probably of Iranian origin (see below, p. 546f.), but at the same time use was made of biblical ideas and terminology. The name Belial (בליעל) is used in biblical parlance as an adjective meaning 'base', 'wicked' (e.g., Deut 13:14; Prov 6:12). Later it is used as a proper name for the figure of Satan, who was meanwhile much more developed than the one known from the biblical texts (e.g., Zech 3:1; Job 1-2). A cosmic leader of the forces of Evil is known also in pseudepigraphic works such as *Jubilees,* the *Testaments of the Twelve Patriarchs,* and the *Ascension of Isaiah.* His opponent, the Angel of Light, shares many functions attributed to Michael, the Angel of Israel, as he is described in Daniel 10:21, 12:1, *1 Enoch* 20:5 and in rabbinic

---

[245] Cf. Isa 45:7. Shaked, 'Qumran and Iran', 433-4 warns that the common use of the phrase dualism is misleading, for it implies a rigid opposition of two equal forces of good and evil. He stresses that such equality does not exist in any of the religions, including Zoroastrianism. This is true also in Qumran. For a typology of dualism cf. Gammie, 'Spatial and Ethical Dualism.'
[246] Wernberg-Møller, 'A Reconsideration', and Treves, 'The Two Spirits,' interpret the entire Treatise as expression psychological dualism. See further below.
[247] For the Angel of Light see 1QS 3:20-22.24; 1QM 13:10; CD 5:17-19. For Belial see 1QS 1:18.24, 2:5.19; 1QM 1:1.5.13, 4:2, 11:8, 13:2; CD 4:13-15, 5:18, 8:2, 12:2, 19:14.
[248] Cf. Nötscher, *Zur theologischer Terminologie,* 169-173; Von der Osten-Sacken, *Gott und Belial,* 78-80.
[249] Deut 32:8-9 according to the Septuagint. Incidentally, a fragment of the *Vorlage* of the Greek text was found at Qumran (Deut 32:37-43). Cf. Skehan, 'A Fragment'; *idem,* 'The Qumran Manuscripts', 150 n. 1.

writings (cf. *B.T. Yoma* 77a). It was therefore concluded that the Angel of Light is identical with the Archangel Michael. From other documents such as the *Pesher of Melchizedek* and the 4Q *Visions of Amram*, it is clear that other angelic figures played important roles in the thought of the sect (cf. p. 521). In this respect, the sectarian doctrine is a faithful representation of Jewish thinking in the Persian and Hellenistic periods, which exhibits a developed angelology.

The fact that the two opposing camps are led by angels clearly implies a struggle taking place on the cosmic level and was, therefore, often labeled 'cosmic dualism'. At the same time another part of the Treatise of the Two Spirits (1QS 4:2-16, 23-26) describes the Spirits of Good and Evil as struggling 'in man's heart'. This was taken to indicate a psychological strife termed 'ethical' or 'psychological dualism' in contradistinction to the cosmic one. Further confirmation was found in the list of virtues and vices ascribed to the members of the respective camps,[250] as well as in the horoscopes discovered at Qumran (cf. above, p. 531). Yet there is no need to distinguish between a cosmic and a psychological dualism as distinct and different types.[251] They may be understood as aspects of the same basic cosmic dualism, which have a necessary counterpart on the moral and psychological level. This is not only possible but logically appropriate and consistent.[252] It is also well reflected in the terminology: the term 'Spirit' (רוח) which designates the two domains, at the same time denotes a cosmic entity, an angel, a manner of behaviour and a human quality.[253]

Thus the fundamental opposition between the two forces takes place on all levels, in the world at large and 'in man's heart'. Therefore it is further reflected in a series of other dualistic oppositions: between Israel and the nations, between Israel at large and the sect, and between the 'poor' and the wicked. The dichotomy of the spirit and the body as developed in the *Hodayot* may equally be associated with this basic dualism. Yet the struggle between the good and the evil is not one between equals, for God is not neutral in it. In the *eschaton* he will destroy evil, purify the world and man, and establish eternal peace and sovereignty for the just.

The sect's dualistic ideology is one of the most obvious areas of similarity with early Christianity. Both the Johannine and Pauline writings evince

---

[250] Cf. Winter, 'Ben Sira'; Flusser, 'Two Ways'.

[251] As implied e.g. by Gammie, 'Spatial and Ethical Dualism', who enumerates the different types of dualism. Often this is the same dualism reflected in different domains.

[252] Significantly, all the major components of Qumran dualism are found together in Zoroastrianism; cf. Shaked, 'Qumran and Iran'. So it is difficult to argue that Iranian influence operates on only one segment such as reflected in the Treatise of the Two Spirits, as claimed by von der Osten-Sacken, *Gott und Belial*, 239-40. He discerns three stages of Qumran dualism: *a*) the earliest, cosmic dualism as expressed in 1QM; *b*) a later ethical reinterpretation, as in 1QS, 1QH; *c*) the final, psychological dualism in the Two Spirits Treatise. Both from material and literary considerations, this reconstruction is questionable.

[253] Cf. Collins, 'Patterns of Eschatology,' 365.

dualistic conceptions and terminology very close to what is found in Qumran writings.[254]

PREDESTINATION AND ELECTION

It has already been stated that the dualism of the sect operates the so-called 'double predestination', i.e. the predetermination of man's life and of its good or evil character. How does it function? The sectarians solved this question by applying predestination both to human history and to personal biography.

As for history, the central idea effecting the belief in predestination is that of the periods (קצים) of history. It is well-known from the apocalyptic writings, but the few allusions in the scrolls suffice to conclude that the sectarians espoused the same teaching.[255] It conceives history as a sequence of 'periods', i.e. of units of time which are fixed in duration, in character and in their place in the sequence. The entire sequence and its components are preordained in the divine plan before creation. History is but the unfolding of this preordained sequence.

In addition, the sequence of periods is enigmatic and mysterious, and therefore is designated by the term 'the mysteries of God' (רזי אל).[256] Only the knowledge of these mysteries enables a true understanding of the historical process, its direction and its approaching End. The sectarians thought that this divine knowledge was divulged to the prophets, and that by true interpretation, equally inspired, the 'mysteries' of history could be revealed again. This was the function performed by the Teacher of Righteousness. The knowledge he imparted to the sect unveiled to its members the fact that they are living in the final generation, on the threshold of the Eschatological Era. Such a frame of mind clearly accounts for the utmost importance attributed by the sectarians to the proper understanding of the contemporary events and of the related biblical interpretation (cf. above, pp. 507-8). Though only referred to by allusions, undoubtedly the dualistic principle operated also in the sequence of the periods.[257]

What is the sense of the personal biography in such an ideology? Can

---

[254] Cf. John 14:16-17, 15:26, 16:13; 2 Cor 6:14-16; Eph 5:11-12; 1 Thess 5:21-22. See Flusser, 'Dead Sea Sect'; Charlesworth, 'Critical Comparison'.

[255] Cf. Licht, 'The Theory of Ages'. Unlike Licht, I think that the sect not only has a general teaching, but also entertained detailed elaborations concerning the various periods, as attested by 4Q180. See Dimant, 'Pesher on the Periods'.

[256] That the term 'the mysteries of God' refers to the divine plan is evident from passages like 1QS 3:23, 4:18; 1QM 3:9; 1QpHab 7:5, 8, 14. The term may have a wider application according to the various combinations of terms (cf. רזי פשע, רזי שכל, רזי פלא).

[257] Cf. the expression of 1QS 3:14-15: '... the visitation of their chastisements with their periods of their peace ...' Compare 1QH 1:16.

there be any place for freedom of choice, for moral responsibility? This presents a major difficulty for the understanding of the sectarian way of thought; especially so in light of the fact that the community did prescribe confession and repentance, did admit new members and consequently did allow for the possibility of a passage between the two camps. We have to go to other texts for an answer. The Treatise of the Two Spirits, usually taken as a paradigm of the sect's thought, is set forth from the perspective of the divine plan of creation and history. But other sections, chiefly in the *Hodayot*, take their point of departure in the human situation. The *Hodayot* depict man as weak and base by nature, inclined to sin and treachery and void of knowledge; he was made out of dust and water, and born out of a woman's womb (1QH1:21-22, 4:29-31). This situation is decreed by the eternal and just Creator. Human nature was created in another duality: that of flesh and spirit. The flesh is feeble and liable to sin, while the spirit is often that part which is capable of receiving God's grace (1QH 3:21). Undoubtedly this teaching draws on biblical formulations (e.g., 1Kgs 8:46; 2Chr 6:36; Job 15:14, 25:4), but it goes beyond the biblical tradition in its consequent distinction between spirit and flesh.

The total dependence of man on God, inherent in the fundamental laws of creation, implies that man's salvation, if possible, depends on God too. So it is expressed in the *Hodayot* and elsewhere. Yet such salvation demands a corresponding attitude of man. In fact, by truly repenting and by following God's true ways, i.e. the Law of Moses (1QH 10:30), man distinguishes himself as one who merits and is capable of receiving the divine grace.[258] At this point, the sect's doctrine of election comes in. Though the first initiative may come from God, it is the elect who has to show his willingness and merit. Only then is true purification effected by the Holy Spirit (1QH 16:12) from the impurity of sin (1QH 4:37 14:24), comparable to the effect of purifying water (1QS 4:21) on the body in ritual baptism (cf. above, p. 499). In this way the elect becomes an expression of the action of the Holy Spirit, thus bridging the gulf between the divine and the human.[259]

The string of ideas, sin — repentance — divine grace — salvation, is not exclusive to the *Hodayot*. It is also found in the *Damascus Covenant*, embedded in the history of Israel and the sect's beginnings, which indicates that this cluster of ideas formed a basic component of the sectarian thought from its earliest phase. In fact, it conforms with the dualistic character of the sectarian ideology in that it integrates the various dichotomies: Creator

---

[258] Cf. Garnet, *Salvation and Atonement*, 112-117.

[259] The close connection between election and divine grace is another area of close resemblance between Qumran and early Christianity. Compare e.g. 1QS 11:7; 1QH 9:29-31, 15:14-15 with Gal 1:15; Eph 1:11. The dependence of man on God is equally stressed by both communities: compare 1QS 11:16-17; 1QH 14:13, 16:12 with Rom 3:22-24, 11:5; Eph 2:8; 2 Tim 1:9.

and creatures; sin and purification; flesh and spirit. How, then, should this complex be reconciled with the double predestination? The answer must be that the elect too are part of the preordained plan of history, as stated in the *Covenant:*

> For God has not chosen them (i.e. the wicked) from the days of eternity, and before they were established He knew their works and abhorred the generations when they arose, and He hid His face from the land, from their arising until their being consumed . . . And in all of them (i.e. the epochs) He raised for Himself men called by name in order to leave a remnant for the land and to fill the face of the universe of their seed. (CD 2:7-12)

In this way, the predestination advocated in respect to individual lives, also operates in respect to general human history. Both the wicked and the elect are known by God 'of old', i.e. before the beginning of history; His divine predilection for the just as well as His hatred of the wicked are preordained.

The question remains what role is left for man. Man himself is incapable of deciphering that mystery, which embraces both his personal biography and history at large. His lot is to search all his life, by his own action, and by divine illuminating grace, in order to discover to which part he belongs, Light or Darkness. Thus, the emphasis is shifted from freedom of action to the mystery of knowledge. The freedom given to man is not to choose where to go but to discover where he is. This can be done only with the aid of divinely-inspired knowledge of the true meaning of the world, of man and of history. This is why the starting point of man is ignorance, while the final election is marked by a gift of knowledge.[260]

ESCHATOLOGY AND MESSIANISM

As it is, we do not possess a systematic presentation of the sect's eschatological teaching. It is expressed in various connections, and more fully in respect to some particular aspects. We do not know how all these elements fit into one picture and therefore the presentation remains fragmentary. However one of the fundamental characteristics of all of the sect's writings is the peculiar eschatological tension,[261] created by the special place in

---

[260] Cf. 1QH 1:21, 4:5, 30, 7:26, 10:29, 12:11-13, 15:12; 1QS 10:26-11:1, 5-7; CD 1:11-13, 3:13-14; 1QpHab 2:8-9, 7:4-5.

[261] The eschatology of Qumran was termed 'restorative' in that it sees the eschatological future as a return to an idealized past. Thus Talmon, 'Typen der Messiaserwartung', 582-583 and Collins, 'Patterns of Eschatology', 353-358, following a typology developed by Scholem, *The Messianic Idea*, 3-4. Yet in Qumran this terminology applies to an eschatological system not centered around a messianic figure, but around an eschatological community. Cf. Caquot, 'Messianisme Qumranien', 231. The peculiar structure of the sect's eschatology makes another distinction obsolete, i.e. between a historico-political messianism and an other-worldly,

history the sect ascribed to itself. The theoretical means by which this place is defined, is the teaching of the periods (cf. above, p. 536). Through it, the sect established its own special role on the threshold of the *eschaton,* which determines all its activities. The radical break with the past by repentance is at the same time a return to a purified, idealized past; the strict practice of the Law of Moses implies an uncompromising separation from the present wickedness and evil. Yet by these very elements, the sect announces the approaching End, and initiates the beginning of the eschatological process.[262]

This particular position of the sect is described with the image of a young, tender plant, which is hardly noticed in the present, but which in the future will grow into a large tree which will cover the earth (cf. Isa 60:21; Ezek 31). In sectarian parlance the plant refers to the group of the elect and the just, now few and hidden but destined to rule the world in the future.[263]

Not surprisingly, the decisive eschatological events and the appearance of the messianic protagonists take place within the community itself.[264] The role of these messianic figures is not always clear, and some of the texts, like the *Hodayot,* lack reference to the Messiah altogether, even though they contain eleborate eschatological depictions.[265]

Even in the case of explicit messianic references there is some uncertainty. The *Covenant* contains references to 'the Messiah of Aaron and (of) Israel' (CD 12:23, 14:19, 19:10 (B), 20:1(B)). Initially, it was concluded that the *Covenant* espoused one Messiah, of Aaron and Israel simultaneously: an idea not known from other sources. But already Ginzberg argued that linguistically the expression may be understood as referring to two Messiahs, one from Aaron and one from David, an idea which is well-known from other Jewish sources such as the *Testaments of the Twelve Patriarchs.*[266]When the *Rule* was first published, with its explicit reference to 'the Messiahs of Aaron and Israel' (1QS 9:11), this explanation gained much support. It was asserted that the expression משיח אהרון וישראל

---

supernaturally oriented one; cf., e.g., Mowinckel, *He That Cometh,* 282. Cf. Hultgård, *L'eschatologie* 1, 301. Cf. also Smith, 'Messianic figures'; Collins, 'Patterns of Eschatology', 353.

[262] A similar picture of history emerges from the *Animal Apocalypse* (*1 Enoch* 85-90). Cf. Dimant, 'History according to the Animal Apocalypse'.

[263] 1QS 8:5-6; CD1:7; 1QH 8:4-26; 4QpPs^a 1-10 II 2-11. Compare *1 Enoch* 10:16, 84:6, 93:5, 10; *Jub.* 1:16, 36:6; cf. Licht, 'The Plant Eternal.'

[264] As stressed by Huppenbauer, 'Zur Eschatologie'.

[265] The *Hodayot* (1QH3:7-18) describes the birth of 'a man' with terminology suggesting the Messiah of David (cf., e.g., 1QH 3:10 alluding to Isa 9:5). Cf. Van der Woude, *Die messianischen Vorstellungen,* 144-56. References to a future Davidic Messiah depicted in biblical terms are found also in a copy of the work knowns as 'The Words of the Luminaries', 4QDibHam^a (= 4Q504) 12 IV 5-8, dated to 150 B.C.E. There exist two other copies of this work, 4QDibHam^b (= 4Q505) and 4QDibHam^c (= 4Q506). Cf. Baillet in *DJD* 7, 137-75. See also below p. 567.

[266] Cf. Ginzberg, *Unknown Jewish Sect,* 222-53.

of the *Covenant* can be understood in the plural,[267] and consequently the *Rule* and the *Covenant* concur in the teaching of two Messiahs. Apart from the Pseudepigrapha this teaching is also found in other sectarian works.[268]

The role of the Messiahs is less clear. The references in CD and 1QS indicate that they will appear at the End of Days. In fact, they seem to inagurate the *eschaton* itself. The priestly Messiah plays a central role both in the great eschatological war and in the festive messianic banquet (cf. above, p. 517-8). By contrast, the role of the royal Messiah is less clear; he is hardly mentioned in the *War Scroll*, although in 1QS^b 5:27-28 it ⸱ is implied that he is to lead the battle against the nations.

The Balaam oracle (Num 24:17) served as a major prooftext for the teaching of the two Messiahs. The verse is cited in three different texts: CD 7:18-21 (A), 1QM 11:6-7 and 4QTest 9-13. The most explicit is the *Covenant*, which applies 'the Star' and 'the Scepter' mentioned in the verse to 'the Searcher of the Torah who came to Damascus' and to 'the Prince of the Congregation', respectively. In combination with other evidence it is clear that the *Covenant* interprets 'the Scepter' as referring to the Davidic Messiah.[269] The identification of 'the Star' with the priestly Messiah is less unequivocal. While 4Q *Testimonia* refers to the 'Searcher of the Torah' as an eschatological figure, the *Covenant* speaks of him as a historical person.[270]

As for the origin of the doctrine of the two Messiahs, one can point to the visions of Zechariah (4:14). Yet its central place in the scrolls and related

---

[267] Kuhn, 'The Two Messiahs'; and Liver, 'The Doctrine of the Two Messias', explained the singular form of the references in the *Covenant* (משיח אהרן וישראל) as a deliberate change by the medieval copyists. This solution is excluded by the Qumran MS. 4QD^e which confirms the reading in the singular. As it is, the expression can be explained as a singular *nomen regens* with two *nomina recta*, thus referring to two Messiahs. Cf. Ginzberg, *Unknown Jewish Sect*, 252-3; Van der Woude, *Die messianischen Vorstellungen*, 29; Deichgräber, 'Messiaserwartung.' This is the most plausible explanation yet offered. The sole real unsolved difficulty is presented by CD 14:19, which applies a verb in the singular (ויכפר) to the expression משיח אהרן וישראל . Ginzberg , *ibid.* , proposes to read ויכפר here, disconnecting it from the Messiahs. Another approach sees CD (one Messiah) as later and 1QS (two Messiahs) as an earlier stage in the development of the sect's ideas. See Starcky, 'Les quatre étapes'; Caquot, 'Messianisme Qumranien'; Laperrousaz, *L'Attente du Messie*. However, this is not a logical procecure. Historically, a late dating of CD (middle of the first century B.C.E.) is problematic; see above p. 490. Cf. the criticism of Starcky levelled by Brown, 'Starcky's Theory'; Fitzmyer, 'The Aramaic "Elect of God".' Moreover Starcky placed 1QM in the Roman times, while we know now that the work must go back to the second century B.C.E.
[268] Cf. the general presentations of Brown, 'The Messianism of Qumran'; Van der Woude, *Die messianischen Vorstellungen*; Liver, 'The Doctrine of the Two Messiahs'.
[269] Cf. 4QFlor 1:11-13 (above, p. 520-1). The same interpretation is given to the sceptre mentioned in Jacob's blessing to Judah (Gen 49:10; cf. 1QS^b 5:24, 27), in 4Q Patr bless 1-4. For the text see Allegro, 'Further Messianic References,' 174-6.
[270] It was suggested that this (the Teacher of Righteousness?) was a prefiguration of the priestly Messiah. Another uncertainty is involved in the way Num 24:17 is cited in 4QTest 9-13: between an allusion to the future prophet and another one to the priestly Messiah, possibly implying the royal Messiah as well.

works such as *Jubilees* and the *Testaments of the Twelve Patriarchs*,[271] shows that it was cherished by certain circles in particular. Perhaps this preference is due to the priestly tendencies of the sect and related documents. It may also reflect the criticism levelled by the sect against the contemporary temple priests, and its vision of a blameless priesthood.

Together with the figures of the two Messiahs, a third figure is sometimes mentioned, namely the eschatological prophet. In accordance with Mal 3:22-24, he is introduced before the other messianic figures, thus in fact announcing their coming; but his exact function remains unclear.[272]

As has been mentioned, both the Messiahs of Aaron and of Israel figure in the dramatic eschatological war. This war might be prompted by a large invasion of the Kittim as a measure of punishment,[273] and further consists of three periods in which Belial and his camp are victorious, another three round won by the Sons of Light, and a seventh period in which the war is decided in favour of the latter by God's own intervention. At this stage the sectaries themselves would come to rule in Jerusalem.

The relationship between these events and the various saviour figures and functions is not clear. Thus Melchizedek is attributed a role of executing vengeance on the Sons of Darkness and saving others from the hand of Belial (above, p. 521). His role may be connected with the final purification of the world by a great conflagration, an idea known from Persian sources,[274] and also may relate to the concept of the punishment of the wicked in eternal fire.[275]

For the sectarians the eschatological upheavals seem to culminate in a beatific state of eternal peace, length of days and sovereignty over the land,

[271] *Jub.* 31; *Test. Levi.* This is especially significant in light of the fact that copies of *Jubilees* and of documents related to the *Testaments* were found at Qumran (Milik, 'Ecrits préesséniens,' 95-102). On the general context of the two Messiah teaching, see Hultgård, *L'eschatologie* 1; cf. also Van der Woude, *Die messianischen Vorstellungen*, 190-216; Liver, 'The Doctrine of the Two Me siahs'; Laperrousaz, *L'Attente du Messie*, 138-48.

[272] See 1QS 9:11 and 4QTest 5-7. The role of the future prophet (cf. also Deut 18:18-19) is not unequivocal in other sources either. Cf. the pertinent rabbinic passages assembled by Ginzberg, *Unknown Jewish Sect*, 211-22, and cf. 1 Macc 4:46 and 14:41. The question whether this third figure found a prefiguration among the leaders of the sect is more difficult to answer. It might be the Teacher of Righteousness, corresponding to Moses in the wilderness. If Flusser is right in suggesting that *Ascensio Isaiae* reflects the early history of the sect (cf. *idem*, 'The Apocryphal Book of Ascensio Isaiae') the prophet Isaiah represents the Teacher of Righteousness.

[273] See 4QpIs[b] II-2; 1QpHab 9:4-7. Cf. Carmignac, 'La future intervention'. On the final war see also above p. 515-6.

[274] On the conflagration see 1QH 3:29-32, 6:17-19, 8:18-20; 1QS 4:13; 1QpHab 10:5, 12-13. Cf. Flusser, 'The Baptism', 97-112; Ringgren, 'Der Weltbrand'. On the Persian origin of the idea cf. Kuhn, 'Die Sektenschrift'; Winston, 'The Iranian Component'; Hultgård, 'Das Judentum,' 570-5. Kuhn and Winston see traces of Iranian influence in 1QH 3:19-36. The idea was also entertained by the Stoics (*ekpyrosis*). Stoic colouring is sometimes detectable in the use of this term in Jewish Hellenistic works, e.g. the Fourth *Sibylline Oracle*. Cf. Hengel, *Hellenism* 1, 191, 200-1, 236; vol. 2, 135 n. 607.

[275] 1QS 2:8, 4:13; 1QpHab 10:5, 13; CD 2:5. Cf. *1 Enoch* 18:12-13; 90:24-26.

while the wicked will be damned to eternal fire.[276] This final bliss is expected as an existence before God in the company of the angels, sharing angelic wisdom;[277] which again stresses the importance of divine knowledge for the sect.[278] It is not clear if this partnership with the angels will take place in a normal state of existence or after the resurrection, as might be expected. At least from one passage of the *Hodayot* (1QH 11:9-14) it seems that a passage from the sinful state of the flesh into a purified existence is implied.[279] Josephus states that the Essenes believed in the immortality of the soul, and Hippolytus adds that they believed in the resurrection.[280] However, nowhere in the scrolls is there a clear formulation of these beliefs, and some passages in 1QH (6:29-34, 11:12) interpreted to this effect may be otherwise explained.[281]

The History of the Sect

The history of the sect must be reconstructed on the basis of two sets of data: on the one hand the historical allusions in the scrolls, and on the other, the accounts of the Essenes, assuming their identity with the sect. The presentation is best served if we first start solely from the sectarian scrolls.[282]

According to the *Damascus Covenant*, the birth of the sect occurred '390 years' after the deliverance of Israel into the hands of Nebuchadnezzar' (cf. above, p. 491). A group of men, 'a root', sprung from 'Aaron and Israel' and searched for twenty years. Then they received a guide from God: the Teacher of Righteousness. A part of the congregation in question rebelled against the Teacher and followed the 'Spouter of Lies', who led the dissenters astray in matters of doctrine and morals. A violent conflict ensued. Perhaps in the wake of this conflict the Teacher and his followers went to 'the land of Damascus', where they established 'the New Covenant'. The

---

[276] 1QS 2:4, 4:7; 1QH 13:17, 15:16, 18:30; 1QS^{b}3:5.21; 1QM 1:9; 4QpPs^a 1-10 II 4-12. On the punishment of the wicked see preceding note.

[277] 1QS 4:22; 1QH 3:21-22, 6:13, 11:6-14; 4Q181 1:3-6. For 4Q181 cf. the text in *DJD* 5, 79-80 with the corrections and notes of Strugnell. In general see Kuhn, *Enderwartung*, 66-72; Lichtenberger, *Studien zum Menschenbild*, 224-7.

[278] Cf. above, p. 538. On knowledge at Qumran cf. Denis, *Les Thèmes de Connaissance;* Nötscher, *Theologische Terminologie*, 38-78; Romaniuk, 'Thème de la Sagesse.' For the partnership of the angels in the camp of the Sons of Light during the eschatological war see 1QM 7:6, 12:4, 8. Compare also 1QS^a 2:8 1QS^b 3:6 4:24-26. Note also the text 11QBer where a blessing is apparently addressed to the sect, and where it is stressed that the angels are participating. For text cf. Van der Woude, 'Segensspruche', 253.

[279] Cf. Brandenburger, *Fleisch und Geist*, 104-5.

[280] Josephus, *War* 2:157; Hippolytus, *Refutatio* 9:18-29.

[281] Cf. Kuhn, *Enderwartung*, 78-88; Nickelsburg, *Resurrection*, 146-56; Lichtenberger, *Studien zum Menschenbild*, 219-224.

[282] Cf. Cross, *Library*, 107-160; Milik, *Ten Years*, 44-98; Stegemann, *Die Entstehung;* Vermes, *Qumran in Perspective*, 137-162; *idem*, 'The Essenes and History'.

Teacher seems to have died there. The wicked continue to rule in Jerusalem. The *Pesher on Habakkuk* also describes these defections, but introduces the other opponent of the Teacher of Righteousness, the Wicked Priest,[283] who was first called by 'the Name of Truth', and later corrupted. He profaned Jerusalem and the Sanctuary, persecuted the Teacher and his followers, but was punished by God (cf. above, pp. 509-10). From the *Pesher on Psalm 37* we learn that the Teacher of Righteousness was a priest and that those who took revenge on the Wicked Priest are 'the violent of the nations', also called the Kittim, who seized the riches amassed by 'the last priests of Jerusalem'. In the *Pesher on Nahum* we hear of 'the Lion of Wrath', a Jewish ruler who attacked 'the Searchers of Slippery Things' because they invited 'Demetrius, King of Greece' to come to Jerusalem. The opponents of the sect are named as Ephraim and Manasseh (cf. above, p. 511-12). Finally, in a yet unpublished fragment, the names of Shelamzion (Alexandra), Hyrcanus (Hyrcanus II) and Emilius (M. Aemilius Scaurus, the first Roman governor of Syria), are mentioned.[284]

It is now agreed by most scholars that the Wicked Priest is to be identified with Jonathan the Maccabee and that the sect's opponents, Ephraim and Manasseh, should be identified with the Pharisees and the Sadducees. Most of the other events alluded to by the *Pesharim* fall into the Hasmonaean Period, from the reign of Alexander Jannaeus to the conquest of Jerusalem by Pompey (63 B.C.E.). Significantly, no later event is alluded to in the Qumran writings. Assuming the identity of the group in question with the inhabitants of Qumran, this means that most of the sectarian literature originated in the early period of the sect, between 150 and 50 B.C.E.

If we accept the identification of the sect with the Essenes, further references in Josephus to the Essenes provide information about the sect's later history. Thus Josephus states that the Essenes were favoured by Herod, who dispensed them from the obligatory oath of allegiance, because of the prophecy of the Essene Menachem foretelling that Herod would become king (*Ant.* 15:371-378). Essenes also participated in the Jewish Revolt and even supplied one of the commanders, John the Essene (*War* 2:567). The copy of a sectarian work found at Masada corroborates this evidence (cf. above, p. 525).

While the first active period of the sect is generally agreed to have fallen under the Hasmonaean rule, the issue of its origin is less clear. Most scholars agree upon the following elements. First, the number 390 in CD 1:5f. should be calculated from the destruction of the First Temple (586 B.C.E.), which together with the twenty years of searching yields the date 176 B.C.E. as the beginning of the sect. Assuming that the reckoning is

---

[283] The Wicked Priest is distinct from the Man of Lies, for they have different spheres of action and characterization. Cf. Stegemann, *Die Entstehung*, 106.

[284] Cf. Milik, *Ten Years*, 73.

symbolic and consequently schematic and imprecise, scholars inferred that it alludes to a date around 171-170 B.C.E., which marks the murder of Onias III and the beginning of the hellenization crisis. Therefore they saw the years 170-150 B.C.E. as the matrix for the sect's coming into existence. This, in turn, is associated with the alleged Zadokite origin of the Teacher of Righteousness and other leaders, and the sect is seen as schismatic group contesting the legitimacy of the Hasmonaean high priesthood.[285]

All these assumptions may be questioned. First, the chronological data of the *Covenant* may be differently interpreted. As the number 390 is probably connected with the reckoning of the seventy years' period (cf. Dan 9), the starting point for the calculation may be chosen at 605 B.C.E., the ascension of Nebuchadnezzar to the throne.[286] This yields the date 215 B.C.E. as the sect's beginning and 195 B.C.E. as the first appearance of the Teacher of Righteousness. According to this calculation the beginnings of the sect date back to a different historical context, namely the wars between the Seleucids and the Ptolemies on the control over Eretz-Israel.

Interestingly, such a dating is corroborated by a composition known as the *Animal Apocalypse* (*1 Enoch* 85-90) which was composed in the time of the Maccabean revolt. This composition is closely related to the sectarian literature in many respects and is, in my opinion, to be considered an early sectarian work.[287] The Apocalypse, too, calculates the last period of history in terms of seventy (year-)weeks, the end of which designates the beginning of the *eschaton*. The seventy weeks' period is further divided into four sections comprising twelve, twenty-three, twenty-three and twelve weeks; i.e. periods of eighty-four, 161, 161 and eighty-four years. The appearance of the group of elect, corresponding to the sect, takes place at the beginning of the fourth section. Taking this chronological scheme at face-value,[288] and here, too, starting the count in 605 B.C.E., i.e. before the destruction of the First Temple as is clear from *1 Enoch* 89:55-57,[289] the following dates

---

[285] Cross, *Library*, 132-134; Milik, *Ten Years*, 59; Stegemann, *Die Entstehung*, 210-220, 242. The beginning of the Teacher's office is associated with the hellenization crisis which was prompted by the ascension of Antiochus IV Epiphanes (175 B.C.E.) and the death of the high priest Onias III (171 B.C.E.).

[286] According to several sources, it is this date which serves as a starting point for the calculation of the seventy year period of Israel's 'subjugation to Nebuchadnezzar' (Jer 25:11-12, 29:10). Thus Ezra 1:1; 2 Chr 36:21-22; Dan 1:1, 10:3 and *1 Enoch* 89:59. The reckoning from the destruction of the First Temple is adopted by Zech 1:12.

[287] The affinity between the Apocalypse and the sectarian scrolls was noticed already by Smith, 'The Dead Sea Sect', 358. Beckwith, 'The Prehistory of the Pharisees', 6, 36, thinks that it is 'proto-Essenic'. For a discussion of the affinity between the apocalypse and the scrolls, see Dimant, 'Jerusalem and the Temple.'

[288] In my opinion, the various chronological schemes figuring in the apocalyptic writings cannot be lightly dismissed as inaccurate and symbolic, as is asserted concerning the 390 years in CD; cf., e.g., Milik, *Ten Years*, 58; Cross, *Library*, 133.

[289] Beckwith, 'The Significance of the Calendar', pushes the beginning of the seventy years' period to the ascension of Manasseh, i.e. 251 B.C.E. He arrives at this date by assuming,

emerge: 605, 521, 360 and 199 B.C.E. Each of these dates indicates a significant political event,[290] but here it will suffice to state that the year 199 B.C.E. coincides with the appearance of the group of just. The date marks major events in Eretz-Israel. Politically, Judaea passed from the hands of the Ptolemies into those of the Seleucids, after the victory of Antiochus III in the Battle of Panium (200 B.C.E.)[291] which ended the Fifth Syrian War. Internally, the year 200 B.C.E. saw the death of the high priest Simon II, the last of the prestigious Zadokite high priests. The office of his son Onias III is already marked by internal strife.

This evidence, when added to the calculation of the 390 years, may point to the same circumstances surrounding the passage of Eretz-Israel into the hands of the Seleucids as the crucial date for the sect's emergence. If we assume that the *Animal Apocalypse* refers to the appearance of the Teacher of Righteousness, this event can be assigned to a date between 199 and 195 B.C.E. This would allow nearly forty years of activity until 152 B.C.E., the appointment of Jonathan, the Hasmonean leader, as high priest. The events alluded to in the *Pesher on Habakkuk* (above, p. 509) would according to this argument, belong to the last days of the Teacher of Righteousness.

If these suggestions are correct, two important conclusions follow. First, the theory that the sect came into being in reaction to the Hasmoneans' rise to the high priesthood is invalidated; as is the view that the Teacher of Righteousness was himself of Zadokite lineage and had a claim to this office.[292] Secondly, it is unlikely that the hellenizing crisis presented the

wrongly, that the author of the *Apocalypse* places himself at the end of the period of the seventy weeks.

[290] 605 B.C.E., the ascensio of Nebuchadnezzar II; 522-521 B.C.E., the ascension of Darius I after revolts in his kingdom, a date which prompted the messianic expectation reflected in Zech 1; 360-359 B.C.E., the ascension of Philip II in Macedonia which marked the beginning of the Greek offensive against Persia; at the same time Artaxerxes III ascends to the throne amid unrest and revolts.

[291] Cf. Stern, *Greek and Latin Authors* 1, 110-116, commenting on Polybius, *Historiae* 16:38, 1.3.4 as cited by Josephus *Ant.* 12:135-136.

[292] The self-designation 'Sons of Zadok', recurring in sectarian literature (1QS 5:2.9, 9:14; 1QSa 1:2; 1QSb 3:22; CD 3:21; 4QFlor 1:17) is not necessarily to be taken as an indication of the Zadokite lineage of the leading core of the sect or of the Teacher of Righteousness himself; nor is it acceptable to present the contesting claim to the high priesthood as the *raison d'être* for the sect (see, e.g., Milik, *Ten Years*, 82f.; Cross, *Library*, 129-32; Vermes, *Qumran in Perspective* 138f., 152). The scarce historical evidence on the Zadokite family at least proves its obscure circumstances; cf. Beckwith, 'The Pre-History', 11-12. Furthermore, the complete absence in the scrolls, including the *Pesharim*, of any reference to the Zadokite lineage demonstrates its insignificance to the sect.
The name 'Sons of Zadok' may be a conceptual rather than a genealogical designation, as is indicated by the reference to Ezek 44:15 which describes the Sons of Zadok as model priests (CD 2:14, 3:21). It may also be a *pesher*-like appellation similar to the name of the Teacher of Righteousness himself (above, p. 505), stressing the element of 'Justice'; the variant reading בני הצדק in 4QSe for 1QS 9:24 בני צדוק may reflect this emphasis (cf. Baumgarten,

direct incentive to the emergence of the sect. Such a theory is not only problematic on internal grounds, since there are no real polemics against the hellenizers in the scrolls; it is also hard to be reconciled with the fact that certain pseudepigraphical works earlier than the sect's emergence contain ideas central to the sectarian ideology, as is the case with the 'Astronomical Book' (*1 Enoch* 72-82) which espouses the solar calendar.[293] This situation points to the early existence of circles cherishing ideas which were later adopted by the sect. It may also explain the various parallels between the sectarian literature and pseudepigraphical works such as *Jubilees* and the *Testaments of the Twelve Patriarchs*. Thus the sect should be viewed as the heir to a more ancient tradition. This would account for the fact that the sect's literature exhibits a well-developed system of thought which cannot have been created in the course of one generation, but rather must draw upon a tradition long established in Eretz-Israel.[294]

In this connection, the Iranian influence apparent in the sectarian literature is particularly interesting. This concerns the type of dualism, the concept of 'spirit' and the prominent role of knowledge.[295] There are no

---

'The Heavenly Tribunal, 233-6). This self-designation appears to be connected with the conception of the sect as a priestly body (cf. Exod 19:6), serving in the community like in the Temple; cf. above p. 520. This may be the sense of CD 3:19 which compares the sect to 'a sure house' (1 Sam 2:35 בית נאמן), i.e. the priestly house. Cf. Davies, 'The Ideology of the Temple', 288-91.

[293] According to its editor, Milik, the oldest copy of the work found at Qumran is to be assigned to the end of the third century B.C.E. or the beginning of the second century B.C.E. Thus, the composition should be assigned to the third century B.C.E. Cf. Milik, *Enoch,* 273. Only the *Astronomic Book* and the *Animal Apocalypse* contain elements later identifiable as sectarian, but this cannot be said of the other Enochic books. Therefore the attempt of Beckwith, 'The Pre-history' to see the Book of the Watchers (*1 Enoch* 1-36) or part of it as proto-Essene is unconvincing. By contrast, the Book of *Jubilees* may well represent a work closely connected to the sect.

[294] All indications are that it must be a Palestinian tradition; cf. the interrelationships of the *Pesharim* with rabbinic *midrashim;* of the sect's *halakhah* with Pharisaic traditions; and of the sectarian scrolls with 1 Enoch and *Jubilees*. These facts militate against Ourphy-O'Connor's theory of a Babylonian origin of the sect, as do also other arguments: a) the hypothesis that Damascus is a symbolic name for Babylon is unsubstantiated, cf. above p. 494; b) not less doubtful is the allegation that the so-called Missionary Document (CD 2:14-6:1) should have originated in a gentile environment; c) other alleged Babylonian traits of the sect (purification rites, interest in astrology, etc.), can be otherwise explained. Cf. the criticism by Knibb, 'Exile in the Damascus Document'. The theory is rejected as speculative by Charlesworth, 'The Origin,' 222 and Vermes, 'The Essenes and History', 28. Weinert, 'A Note' argued that 4Q159 is better explained in terms of the new theory, but it rests on an entirely speculative reconstruction. Davies, *The Damascus Covenant* further develops the theory of a diaspora origin of the Covenant, without fresh evidence.

[295] See Kuhn, 'Die Sektenschrift'; Winston, 'The Iranian Component', 200-210; Shaked, 'Qumran and Iran'; Frye, 'Qumran and Iran'; Hultgård, 'Das Judentum', 548-59. It was pointed out that the characteristic elements of Qumran dualism, in its combination with monotheism and predestination, are all found in the Zurvanite heterodoxy and not in Zoroastrianism. See Winston *ib.* 205; Michaud, 'Un mythe Zervanite'.

indications that this influence came through Hellenistic channels;[296] on the other hand it is historically plausible to assume direct contact of the Jews with the Persians during the Babylonian exile and the Persian rule.

If, then, the sectarian movement is a phenomenon proper to Judaea, in what context should it be understood? In the past it was usually associated with the Assidaeans mentioned in 1 Macc 2:42, 7:12-13. However our precise knowledge of that group is limited to those few verses.[297] It is here proposed to adopt a less restrictive frame of reference. The sectarian doctrine seems to have emerged from a wider trend existing in Judaism in at least the third and second centuries B.C.E. This trend is not directly connected with the hellenizing movement and the events which took place in Judaea between 170 and 150 B.C.E., but apparently has its roots in much earlier circumstances.[298] The one certain conclusion that follows from these considerations is that the problem of the origins of the sectarian doctrines should be separated from the question of the historical and political circumstances which led to the actual creation of the sect.

The problems involved in the later history of the sect, e.g. its influence on other groups, are no less complex than those of its beginnings. Especially striking are the numerous similarities between the Qumran community and that of the first Christians, who were active concurrently around the middle of the first century C.E. The main elements to be mentioned are the communal organization, baptism, the strong eschatological awareness, the conception of the community as sacral, and other theological concepts such as predestination, dualism in various aspects, election by grace, and the New Covenant; all of this underlined by a close similarity and sometimes identity of the characteristic vocabulary. Whether we should speak here of direct influence or of a more complex relationship remains to be discussed.[299]

---

[296] Thus Hengel, *Hellenism* 1, 230; Michaud, 'Un mythe Zervanite'. Hengel stresses in particular the Hellenistic influence on material circumstances (methods of construction, languages, etc.); cf. *idem*, 'Qumran und der Hellenismus', 359-60. However this influence does not necessarily imply influence in the religious domain.

[297] For criticism on the current theories about the *Hasidim*, cf. Davies, 'Hasidim'.

[298] For a general theory dating the origin of Jewish parties to the Restoration time, cf. Smith, *Palestine Politics*.

[299] Cf. above notes 254 and 259. For general surveys see Flusser, 'Dead Sea Sect'; Cross, *Library*, 197-243; La Sor, *Dead Sea Scrolls*, 142-264; Vermes, 'Impact of the Dead Sea Scrolls'. For discussion of particular details see Braun, *Qumran und das Neue Testament* 1-2; Stendahl ed., *The Scrolls and the New Testament;* Murphy-O'Connor, *Paul and Qumran;* Black ed., *The Scrolls and Christianity;* Charlesworth ed., *John and Qumran.* See also the bibliographies in Braun *ib.* and Fitzmyer, *Tools*, 124-30.

BIBLIOGRAPHY

Texts

After nearly a generation of publications and research, a considerable number of manuscripts are still unpublished, and consequently all discussions and text publications are partial and tentative. The volumes of *DJD* cover mainly the smaller fragments of Caves 1-3, 5-10 and some of cave 4. Other important publications include mainly the well-preserved scrolls from Cave 1: 1QS, 1QM, 1QH and 1QpHab. A list of all the known materials published to date, and those unpublished, is supplied by FITZMYER, *Tools*, 11-39.

The following texts from Cave 1 have been published in facsimile with transcription: BURROWS, *The Dead Sea Scrolls* (1QS, 1QpHab); SUKENIK, *Megillot* (1QH, 1QM) and YADIN, *The War* (1QM). New and better photographs of 1QIs^a, 1QS and 1QpHab were published in TREVER, *Scrolls from Qumran Cave I*.

Collections of the large major texts with some additional minor ones are offered by LOHSE, *Die Texte* and HABERMANN, *Megillot* (with a useful concordance); both have a vocalized text, but they assembled texts published until the sixties. A valuable handy edition of the *Pesharim* was recently offered by HORGAN.

The most reliable translation in English is VERMES, *The Dead Sea Scrolls in English;* in French, CARMIGNAC *et al.*, *Les textes;* in German, MAIER, *Die Texte*, 1. Especially important is the French collection, which contains important commentaries from the pen of CARMIGNAC (on 1QM, 1QH, 1QS^a, 1QpHab and minor texts). The commentaries of DUPONT-SOMMER, *Les Écrits Esséniens*, are also still of interest.

Commentaries

Due to the state of publication, major commentaries are available mainly for the larger scrolls:

1QS. GILBERT in CARMIGNAC *et al.*, *Les Textes*, I, 9-80; LEANEY, *The Rule of Qumran;* LICHT, ' *The Rule\ Scroll;* WERNBERG-MØLLER, *The Manual*. Especially rich are Leaney and Licht's commentaries.

1QM. The best commentary is still YADIN, *The War*. Also of interest are VAN DER PLOEG, *Le rouleau;* CARMIGNAC, *La Règle* and JONGELING, *Le rouleau*.

1QH. As a literary and conceptual analysis the commentary by LICHT, *The Thanksgiving Scroll*, offers the most. Also of interest is the commentary by CARMIGNAC in *id.* (*et al.*), *Les Textes*, I and DELCOR, *Les Hymnes*. Other commentaries include: MANSOOR, *The Thanksgiving Hymns* and DUPONT-SOMMER, *Le livre des hymnes*.

1QpHab. A comprehensive commentary was recently published by

BROWNLEE, *The Midrash-Pesher*. A resumée of the previous commentaries is offered also by HORGAN, *Pesharim*. Though not offering a verse by verse commentary, Elliger, *Studien*, written a few years after the publication, is the most detailed in many aspects. All the continuous *Pesharim* are commented upon by HORGAN, *Pesharim*.

CD. Though the integral text comes from the Genizah, the work is usually included in the collections of the Dead Sea Scrolls, translations as well as texts. The updating of the Qumran material in relation to the CD is incorporated in RABIN, *The Zadokite Document;* FITZMYER, 'Prolegomenon'; *idem, Tools*.

The *Temple Scroll* was translated into English (by YADIN) and into German (MAIER, *Tempelrolle*). The *editio princeps* is YADIN, *Temple Scroll*, Hebrew edition, with detailed introduction and commentary.

A special concordance for Qumran texts is KUHN, *Konkordanz*, with additions in *idem*, 'Nachträge'. It covers only publications up to 1965. The reader can consult the lists of Hebrew words provided by each of the *DJD* volumes. (*DJD* vol. 5 should be used together with STRUGNELL, 'Notes en marge', which amounts to a new edition. For a bibliography to this volume cf. FITZMYER, 'Bibliographic Aid'.)

Research

Though the number of publications in this domain is enormous, there are few overall up-to-date reviews. MILIK, *Ten Years* and CROSS, *Library* remain classical and readable presentations of the state of research in the sixties. They retain their value because both authors are working on the scrolls and draw on yet unlublished material, although later publications, especially of the *Temple Scoll*, have necessitated a new approach. Two more recent reviews should be noted. VERMES, *Qumran in Perspective* offers a concise, very clear introduction to the major issues involved, with a good selective bibliography. The recent fascicle of the *Supplément au Dictionnaire de la Bible*, dedicated to Qumran, represents some of the best French scholarship in the field, and offers a comprehensive review of the state of research. Especially valuable is the contribution of SKEHAN on the Bible at Qumran.

Other recent publications of interest are the collection edited by DELCOR, *Qumran, sa piété*, including numerous and varied contributions, and LICHTENBERGER, *Studien*. The latter book offers a useful review of the evidence and the state of research. Among the recent special studies dedicated to Qumran are the work of POUILLY on 1QS, DAVIES on 1QS and CD, MERILL on predestination (1QH). MURPHY-O'CONNOR's series of articles made a considerable impact on the research, especially of 1QS and CD. They concern mainly the literary structure of both documents and the reconstruction of the history of the sect.

Bibliographies

Several bibliographies exist which cover the subject more or less: BUCHARD, *Bibliographie,* 1-2, up to 1963; JONGELING, *A Classified Bibliography,* covering 1958-1968. FITZMYER, *Tools,* gives a selective introductory bibliography up to 1975, while VERMES, *Qumran in Perspective,* second edition, supplies an up to date bibliography. Qumran is regularly covered by the 'Elenchus bibliographicus' of *Biblica.* The review specialising in Qumran Studies, the *Revue de Qumran,* includes bibliography pertinent to the subject in each issue.

For the publications in Hebrew see YIZHAR, *Bibliography* for the years 1948-1964. Since 1969 the List of Articles in Judaic Studies, published in Jerusalem, covers the subject (*Reshimat Maamarim be-Madaei ha-Yahadut*).

Chapter Thirteen

Psalms, Hymns and Prayers

David Flusser

In the literary documents that are discussed in this volume, material of hymnic and liturgical nature is found scattered throughout. These psalms, hymns and prayers are the object of the present survey. The special interest they offer is that we can learn about various types of Jewish piety in the Second Temple period, including that of Hellenistic mystical circles, the Essenes and early synagogal liturgy.

The question, however, is to what extent these texts reflect actual liturgical practice. The majority are prayers put into the mouths of biblical persons who figure in these apocryphal works and it is clear that at least in their present form the primary purpose was not liturgical. Rather, such prayers and hymns were composed by the authors as parts of their literary output. Even in the case of purely hymnic compositions such as the *Thanksgiving Scroll* from Qumran, it is unlikely that they once formed part of a liturgy and they may rather have been written for studying. However in other cases, e.g. the apocryphal psalms from Qumran and Psalm 151 in the Septuagint, it is very probable that they were written for recitation before a congregation. There are also prayers in the Dead Sea scrolls with clear indications when they were to be said. Thus there is a basic difference between hymns and prayers contained in the Apocrypha and Pseudepigrapha and many prayers from Qumran. While the first are literary compositions, at least some of the prayers and psalms from Qumran were actual liturgical texts. Even so, merely 'literary' prayers or hymns may often serve as witnesses for liturgical forms in Judaism, because they may imitate current liturgical patterns.

We are thus confronted with a problem of presentation. When the emphasis is on certain types of prayer, we may collect material from the whole range of documents. However when we focus on the prayers and hymns as they are contained in the sources, we have to deal with a variety of genres in each document. Our method will shift between the two viewpoints, according to the interest of the material itself.

Magnificat and Benedictus

A good example of this complex situation is provided by the two hymns included in the Gospel of Luke, namely the *Magnificat* (Luke 1:46-55) and the *Benedictus* (Luke 1:68-79).[1] The *Magnificat* is a hymn recited by Mary, or according to other texts by Elisabeth the mother of John the Baptist, and the *Benedictus* is the song of Zechariah, the father of John te Baptist. Both became part of Christian liturgy. In the 'Nativity Gospel' (Luke chapters 1-2) other poetical passages are incorporated as well,[2] but many scholars believe that the *Magnificat* and the *Benedictus* are pre-Lucan and that their origin is to be found in circles attached to John the Baptist. They may originally have been written in Hebrew and only later translated into Greek; one opinion is that they are an elaboration of two Maccabean Hebrew psalms.[3] Indeed, even in their present form they are an expression of Jewish national feeling. In the *Magnificat* nothing is explicitly said about the birth of a child, and in the *Benedictus* only the second part (Luke 1:76-79) hints at John the Baptist as a prophet who will prepare the way of the Lord. There are scholars who assume that this second part was added, and that the first part (Luke 1:68-75) may simply be an ancient Jewish psalm of salvation. In any case the beginning of the *Benedictus* ('Blessed be the God of Israel') resembles the synagogal benedictions: it begins with the same word ברוך (Blessed). Moreover, there are important parallels in prayers from Qumran:[4] two prayers in the *War Scroll* (1QM 13:2 and 14:4) begin with the same word.[5] The first part of the *Benedictus* is an important witness for the development of the *Eighteen Benedictions*.

The Greek Additions to Esther and Daniel

While some of the psalms, hymns and prayers in the Apocrypha and Pseudepigrapha were originally written in Hebrew (or in Aramaic), others were composed in Greek. Such is the case with the Prayers of Mordecai and Esther in the additions to the Greek Book of Esther.[6] These prayers are a literary fiction. They were evidently composed, along with the other additions to the book, in order to form an integral part of the Greek version. One of their aims was apologetical: since in the Hebrew Book of Esther

---

[1] See especially Schürmann, *Lukasevangelium*, 70-80, 84-94; Schneider, *Lukas*, 54-56, 59-60.
[2] Luke 1:13-17, 30-33, 35, 46-55, 68-79; 2:14, 29-32. On the famous *Gloria* (Luke 2:14) see Flusser, 'Sanktus und Gloria', where I show that Luke 2:13-14 follows an exegetical tradition similar to the Aramaic Targum of Isa 6:3 and that the passage depends on an ancient *Kedusha*.
[3] See Winter, 'Magnificat and Benedictus'.
[4] See 1QS 11:15; 1QM 13:2; 14:4, 8; 18:6; 1QH 5:20; 10:14; 11:27, 29, 32; 16:8; and *DJD* 1, p. 153, 34 *bis* 2, 3; 3 I, 7.
[5] The beginning of the *Benedictus*, though very similar to 1 Sam 25:32, is not taken from there because there it is not a beginning of a prayer. See also Schürmann, *Lukasevangelium*, 86 n. 28. It seems to me that there are striking similarities between the content of the *Benedictus* and *Magnificat*, and 1QM 14:3-9 and 1QM 18:6-8. On the Qumran background of the *Magnificat* and *Benedictus* see Flusser, 'The Magnificat'.
[6] See especially Moore, *Daniel, Esther and Jeremiah*.

552

God is not directly mentioned, the Hellenistic Jewish author of the two prayers tried to correct this omission and had the two Jewish heroes of the book address God. Moreover, from the Hebrew text it is not clear why Mordecai declined to bow down before Haman, nor is it clear how Esther could marry a gentile or why Mordecai even forbade her to disclose her Jewishness to others. Thus in order to explain Mordecai's behaviour, the author of the Greek additions to Esther has Mordecai say: 'You know all things: you know, Lord that it was not because of insolence or arrogance or vanity that I did this; that I did not bow down before arrogant Haman; for I would have been quite willing to kiss the soles of his feet for Israel's sake. But I did it in order that I might not put the glory of a man above the glory of God, nor will I bow down to anyone except you who are Lord, nor will I do this out of arrogance.'[7]

Likewise Esther says in her apocryphal prayer that she loathes the bed of the uncircumcised and of all foreigners, and that she has not eaten forbidden meats nor drunk the wine of libations. 'From the day I arrived here until now, your maidservant has not delighted in anything except you, Lord, the God of Abraham.'[8] Thus the pious apologetical purpose of the two prayers is patent. At the same time they are an expression of a deep piety of Hellenistic Judaism. The exact time at which the prayers were written is not known.

One of the Greek additions to the Book of Daniel is 'The Prayer of Azariah and the Hymn of the Three Young Men'.[9] It contains the prayer and hymn uttered by Azariah and his two companions, Hananiah and Mishael, after they had been thrown into the fiery furnace for their refusal to worship a golden image set up by King Nebuchadnezzar. The first to quote these songs is Justin Martyr (d. 165 C.E.).[10] Their exact dating depends on whether they were compositions independent of the canonical Book of Daniel and whether the Greek texts are originals or translations or adaptations from a Hebrew original. The *terminus ad quem* of the songs seems to be c. 100 B.C.E.[11]

The main emphasis of the Prayer of Azariah is on the fact that God has acted justly in all he has brought upon the Jews, because they did not observe his commandments. As this emphasis does not fit the situation — the three martyrs did obey God's commandments — some scholars think that the prayer originally had nothing to do with the Book of Daniel and was inserted only later into the Greek translation of the book. As the main

---

[7] Addition C, 5-7. Translation Moore *ibid.,* p. 203.

[8] Addition C, 29.

[9] Cf. above, pp. 149-52; Moore, *Daniel, Esther and Jeremiah,* 39-76. The additions to Daniel are preserved in the Septuagint and in the Greek version ascribed to Theodotion.

[10] *Apologia* 1:46.

[11] The versions of the Septuagint and Theodotion are virtually identical; see Moore, *Daniel, Esther and Jeremiah,* 30-34.

motif of the prayer is very common in ancient Judaism, especially in 'apotropaic' prayers recited in a situation of danger, it could have been composed to be recited by Azariah. But even so, it is very probable that the prayer was once independent of the Book of Daniel. Danielic fragments from the Dead Sea scrolls show that our Book of Daniel was not the only book dealing with Daniel and his fellows (see below).

A similar situation is that of the Hymn of the Three Young Men, but here a somewhat free translation from a Hebrew original is far more probable. It seems that it is a single composition though it can be divided into two parts: an ode (verses 29-34) and a psalm (verses 35-68). Both parts are antiphonal and the refrains are very similar. A constant refrain appears also in Psalm 136; another refrain is repeated in the version of Psalm 145 in the *Psalms Scroll* from Qumran Cave 11 (columns 16-17). This refrain is added to each verse of 11QPs145, but does not appear in the Massoretic text and ancient versions and was probably added to the psalm for liturgical purposes. Thus the use of refrains in the Hymn of the Three Young Men is in accordance with the liturgical practice of the Second Temple period. Of particular importance for the history of Jewish liturgical poetry is the ode. So we read: 'Blessed is the holy name of your glory . . . forever . . . blessed are you in the temple of your sacred glory . . . forever . . . blessed are you on the throne of the glory of your kingship.'[12] This is an expansion of the doxology recited in the Temple of Jerusalem: 'Blessed be the name of the glory of his kinghip forever,' and the apocryphal prayer can serve as a kind of explanation of this famous Jewish doxology.[13] Though the place of the doxology was the Temple of Jerusalem, it seems that in the first part of the hymn the author referred to the heavenly temple where God is enthroned upon the cherubim. If so, the Hymn is evidently the oldest datable reference to the heavenly temple of God.

The Prayer of Nabonidus

A proof of the existence of 'Danielic' literature independent of and even anterior to the extant book of Daniel is a fragment from Qumran, the so-called 'Prayer of Nabonidus'.[14] The Qumran document, written in Aramaic, describes the healing of the last ruler of Babylon, Nabonidus (555-539 B.C.E.), by a Jewish exorcist. The name of the exorcist is not preserved, but it is probable that this was Daniel himself. The plot of the fragment is parallel to (but not identical with) the content of chapter 4 of

---

[12] Moore, *Daniel, Esther and Jeremiah*, 66. The words correspond verbally to כסאי כבוד מלכותו in 4Q403 25 I 3. See Newsom, *Angelic Liturgy*, 372.

[13] See Flusser, 'Sanktus und Gloria', 139 and n. 2 there.

[14] See above, pp. 35-7. The text was published by Milik, 'Prière de Nabonide', and Jongeling *et al.*, *Aramaic Texts*, 123-31. See Vermes, *Qumran in Perspective*, 72-73; Meyer, *Das Gebet des Nabonid*; Delcor, *Le livre de Daniel*, 120-4.

the Book of Daniel and thus it can be assumed that there the less famous Nabonidus was changed to Nebuchadnezzar. This also fits in with the compulsory worship of the image of gold on the plain of Dura mentioned in Daniel 3. It was the same Nabonidus, and not Nebuchadnezzar, who introduced a religious reform, abolishing the worship of Marduk and promoting the worship of Sin, the moongod. Thus it is probably that the legend reflected in chapter 3 of the Book of Daniel, also reflects events under Nabonidus. Consequently the fragment of the Prayer of Nabonidus elucidates a more ancient stage of some of the stories in the first part of the Book of Daniel and makes the historical element in Daniel more tangible. Unfortunately the prayer itself is no longer preserved and so the fragment from Qumran does not contribute to the history of Jewish prayers in the period of the Second Temple.

The Prayer of Manasseh

The 'Prayer of Manasseh' is an independent prayer, written to give an idea of the penitence of the wicked king Manasseh and it is most probably a Jewish and not a Christian composition.[15] According to 2 Chr 33:12-13 when Manasseh was in distress 'he humbled himself greatly before the God of his fathers. He prayed to him and God received his entreaty and heard his supplication . . .' The extant prayer is apocryphal; its task is to offer the wording of the prayer mentioned in 2 Chronicles. Its content is Manasseh's repentance and his request for God's mercy. A Syriac version is included in the Syriac *Didascalia*, a work of which the Greek text was probably written in Syria in the third century C.E.[16] The Greek text of the prayer is included in the *Apostolic Constitutions* 2:22, 12-14,[17] whence, probably, it entered some manuscripts of the Septuagint, among the Odes appended to the Book of Psalms. The Prayer of Manasseh was probably composed in Greek; if it was a translation from the Hebrew, the Greek translator approached the original in a free manner.

Prayers in the Book of Tobit

One of the most important sources for the history of Jewish prayer is the Book of Tobit.[19] The book is preserved in two Greek versions; it remains difficult to decide on the connection between these two translations, until the Aramaic and Hebrew fragments of this book found at Qumran are published. Then it will also be possible to decide whether the book of Tobit

[15] See Osswald, 'Gebet Manasses', 17-27.
[16] In the manuscript of the Latin translation only the last words of the prayer are preserved. See Tidner, *Didascalia Apostolorum*, 37-8.
[17] See Funk, *Didascalia*, 85-89.
[19] See above, p. 40-46; Flusser, 'Tuvia'; Grintz, *Chapters*, 49-66.

was originally written in Hebrew or in Aramaic. The date of the book is probably the fifth to fourth century B.C.E. One of the significant features is that the language of the Aramaic fragments largely resembles an Imperial Aramaic earlier than that of Daniel.[20] As the prayers in Tobit are ancient and more or less datable, they indicate how Jews prayed in a distant period for which such sure evidence is otherwise lacking.

Like most of the prayers in the Apocrypha and Pseudepigrapha, the prayers in the Book of Tobit are not independent compositions but serve to express the feelings of the personages of the book. The first two are the parallel prayers of the blind father Tobit (3:2-6) and of the unhappy Sarah, daughter of Raguel (3:11-15). As is common in such prayers, in both of them the captivity of Israel is mentioned. Typical are the words of Tobit's prayer about the sins committed by the previous generation:

> For they disobeyed thy commandments and thou gavest us under plunder, captivity and death; thou madest us a byword of reproach in all the nations among which we have been dispersed. And now thy many judgments are true in exacting penalty from me for my sins and for those of my fathers, because we did not keep thy commandments. For we did not walk in truth before thee (Tobit 3:3-5).

Tobias' prayer on his wedding night (8:5-8) throws light on the history of later Jewish nuptial liturgy, especially in the mention of Adam and Eve.[21] The prayer opens with standard phrases from Jewish liturgy: 'Blessed art thou, God of our fathers'.

The prayer in Tobit, chapter 13, is not particularly relevant to the Book of Tobit. It is the earliest witness of a special type of psalms which we shall now examine.

Eschatological Psalms

The eschatological psalms of the Second Temple period constitute a specific genre. They sprang from Israel's longing for deliverance from the foreign yoke and from the eschatological hopes connected with Jerusalem. The earliest evidence for this type of psalms is the hymn in Tobit 13, which according to one of the two Greek versions Tobit himself wrote. It contains numerous echoes of biblical passages. Its main content is an eschatological vision of the new Jerusalem. God will 'again show mercy and will gather us from all the nations among whom you have been scattered.' That Jerusalem will be built with precious stones is an echo of Isa 54:11-12 (cf. Rev 21:18-21). Tobit's hymn fits his views about the future given in the last chapter of the book (14:4-7).

The last part of the apocryphal Book of Baruch (4:5-5:9) contains a

[20] Grintz, *Chapters*, 66 n. 46.
[21] On this item see Flusser-Safrai, 'In His Image, After His Likeness'.

prayer which is near in spirit to Tobit's long prayer.[22] This psalm of encouragement is addressed first to the exiled children of Israel and then to their mother Jerusalem; it is probable that its original language was Hebrew. The captivity is seen as a punishment for Israel's sins, but God will deliver it from the power of its enemies and the sons of Jerusalem will be gathered there, rejoicing in God's glory. He will display his splendour to every nation. There is a clear connection between Baruch 4:36-5:9 and the eleventh of the *Psalms of Solomon* (composed in the middle of the first cent. B.C.E.); there is a possibility that both have a common source. If so, the prayer in the Book of Baruch was composed in Hebrew between the first half of the second and the first half of the first centuries B.C.E.[23]

Another representative of the genre of eschatological psalms is the eleventh of the *Psalms of Solomon* just mentioned.[24] Its author sees in spirit the future return of the dispersed Jews and the final grandeur of Jerusalem: 'Stand on the height, O Jerusalem, and behold thy children, from the East and the West, gathered together by the Lord; from the North they come in the gladness of their God, from the isles afar off God has gathered them . . . Put on, O Jerusalem, thy glorious garments, make ready thy holy robe . . .' (11:3-8).

An eschatological psalm is also to be found in the book of Ben Sira. The mention of God's future judgement and his vengeance on the wicked nation (35:17-20) induces the author of this Hebrew work to include a prayer for the deliverance and restoration of Israel (36:1-17).[25] May God cause the fear of him to come upon all the nations, 'and let them see thy might . . . and let them know thee, as we have known that there is no God but thee;' may God destroy the adversary and wipe out the enemy. Ben Sira prays that God's eschatological promises may be quickly fulfilled, and says: 'Gather all the tribes of Jacob and give them their inheritance as at the beginning . . . Have mercy on the city of thy holiness, Jerusalem, the place of thy rest. Fill Zion with thy splendour and thy temple with thy glory . . . and fulfill the prophecies spoken in thy name. Reward those who wait for thee and let thy prophets be found trustworthy . . . and all who are on the earth will know that thou art the eternal God' (36:1-17). Here, as in the other examples, we find the main motifs of the genre: the deliverance of Israel from their foes, the gathering of the dispersed and the future glory of Jerusalem and its Temple.

Our last example of the genre of eschatological prayers from the Second Temple period is found in the *Psalms Scroll* from Qumran, col. 22:1-15,

[22] See Moore, *Daniel, Ester and Jeremiah*, 258, 305-16.
[23] The book of Baruch also contains a prayer for the exiled community (2:6-3:8); see below, p. 571.
[24] See below, p. 573-4.
[25] Ben Sira likewise includes a prayer for selfcontrol (21:27-23:6). There is a similar prayer in *Pss. Sol.* 16:10-11.

where a prayer appears which its editor named 'Apostrophe to Zion' (11QPs^a Zion).[26] The Hebrew hymn is not to God but to Zion itself. The main statement is: 'Great is thy hope, O Zion: peace and thy longed-for salvation will come;' in other words, the well-known motifs of the genre appear. The hymn speaks of the generation of saints which will inhabit Jerusalem and walk in her splendid squares. All enemies of Zion will be cut off; violence will be purged from her midst; the hope of Zion will not perish. The poet even says in verse 17: 'Accept (i.e. Zion) the vision bespoken of thee and the dreams prophets sought for thee.' This is a clear reminiscence of Sir 36:14-15, especially in its Hebrew wording; thus the eschatological prayer in Ben Sira may be an ancestor of the 'Apostrophe to Zion'.

An interesting detail is that the group among whom the 'Apostrophe to Zion' was composed is characterized as 'those who yearn for the day of thy salvation' (verse 4); 'How much they have hoped for thy salvation, the pure ones have mourned for thee' (verse 9). These are evidently the same pious circles which we meet in Luke, chapter 2, including Simeon who 'was righteous and devout, looking for the consolation of Israel' (Luke 2:25) and the prophetess Anna who 'did not depart from the Temple worshipping with fasting and prayer night and day,' and when she saw the infant Jesus, 'spoke of him to all who were looking for the redemption of Jerusalem' (Luke 2:36-38).

The Qumran Psalms Scroll and the Syriac Psalms

The *Psalms Scroll* in its present form contains fourty-one biblical psalms and four apocryphal psalms which were already known from other sources.[27] In addition to these, three hitherto unknown hymnic compositions are found, which the editor of the scroll named the 'Apostrophe to Zion' (dealt with above), the 'Hymn to the Creator' (a sapiential hymn of which only nine verses have been preserved)[28] and the 'Plea for Deliverance' which we shall treat below. Finally, the *Psalms Scroll* contains a prose section known as 'David's Compositions.'[29] On palaeographical grounds the manuscript has to be assigned to the first half of the first century C.E. This date corresponds to the time when those circles lived in Jerusalem which appear to be attested in Luke and among whom the 'Apostrophe to Zion' was composed. However, this dating does not exclude the possibility that other non-biblical compositions contained in the scroll were composed in a far earlier time. The hymns seem to have originated in

---

[26] See Sanders, *Psalms Scroll*, 85-89.
[27] See Sanders, *Psalms Scroll;* Vermes, *Dead Sea Scrolls,* 58-61; Van der Woude, *Die fünf Syrischen Psalmen.* And see Yadin, 'Another Fragment,'
[28] Col. 26:9-15. The text speaks of God as creator of the world but does not address Him.
[29] 11 QPs^a 27:2-11. See above p. 138-40.

various circles. Some may have been composed within the broader movement in which Essenism crystallized. This impression is reinforced by the
sectarian calendar reflected in 'David's Compositions'.

One of the four apocryphal psalms was already known from Ben Sira
(51:13-30), both in the original Hebrew and in the Greek version. It is not a
prayer but a poem in which the author tells how he acquired wisdom and
sought to impart it to others. In the *Psalms Scroll* the poem is included as a
Davidic composition, which provides a definite proof that it was not part of
the original book of Ben Sira, which ended with chapter 50.[30] The other
additions to Ben Sira are not contained in the *Psalms Scroll.* Sir 51:1-12 is a
thanksgiving hymn which in the Greek version begins with 'I will give
thanks to thee' (Hebrew אודך), an opening known from most of the
Essene *Hodayot.*[31] The other addition is preserved only in Hebrew and has
the same structure as the biblical Psalm 136 ('The Great Hallel'). As this
hymn shows interesting affinities with Jewish synagogal prayers, especially
with the *Eighteen Benedictions,* it is a pity that the time of its composition is
unknown.

The three remaining apocryphal psalms were already known from a
Syriac translation and one of the three also from the Septuagint as Psalm
151. These three Syriac psalms appear together with two more psalms not
available in the *Psalms Scroll* as 'filler' material in a *Book of Discipline*
written by the Nestorian bishop Elijah of Al-Anbar (died c. 940).
Moreover, all five psalms are preserved in three Syriac biblical manuscripts.[32]

Syriac psalm I differs from the Qumran text and fits the Greek version
from which it apparently was translated, while the other four Syriac psalms
were evidently translated from the Hebrew. This evidence makes it probable that the Hebrew originals of all the five Syriac psalms stem from the
Qumran library, while Syriac psalm I which was already known from the
Greek Psalter, was translated into Syriac from there and not from its
Hebrew original. Interestingly, we learn from an ancient letter that around
the year 786, Hebrew manuscripts were discovered in the vicinity of Jericho

---

[30] 11QPs*a*Sirach. 'It is now quite clear that the canticle is totally independent of Sirach. If
Jesus, son of Sira, of Jerusalem, had penned the canticle it would hardly be found in 11QPs*a*,
which claims Davidic authorship' (Sanders, *Psalms Scroll,* 83).

[31] Cf. below p. 567. In the Geniza MS. the two parts of the first verse are interchanged.

[32] They have been given the following indications (see Van der Woude, pp. 31-32):
Syriac psalm I or Psalm 151 = Septuagint Psalm 151 = 11QPs*a* 28:3-14
Syriac psalm II or Psalm 154 = 11QPs*a* 18:1-16
Syriac psalm III or Psalm 155 = 11QPs*a* 24:3-17
Syriac psalm IV or Psalm 152
Syriac psalm V or Psalm 153.
See Sanders, *Psalms Scroll,* 53 and Van der Woude, *Syrischen Psalmen.* The last work contains
an introduction and a German translation of these five non-canonical psalms based upon a
new critical edition by Baars, 'Apocryphal Psalms'.

and among them were more than 200 Davidic psalms.[33] It is feasible to assume that the Hebrew originals of the Syriac psalms belonged to this find, although that does not necessarily mean that they were composed at Qumran. Syriac psalms I, III, IV and V will be discussed in the following sections as representing two specific literary genres which are also evidenced by other documents.

Syriac psalm II is a sort of sapiential hymn. It is surely not strictly Essene, as it speaks of the 'assembly of the pious' (line 12), a Hebrew designation which does occur in the biblical Ps 149:1,[34] but never in strictly Essene writings. The hymn was composed in this particular congregation and it praises Wisdom: 'From the gates of the righteous is heard her voice, and from the assembly of the pious her song. When they eat with satiety she is cited, and when they drink in community together, their meditation is the Law of the Most High.' We see that there was a more or less rigid and separatist community which studied the Torah at common meals and imparted wisdom to the simple folk who are far from its gates. The psalm may perhaps be called proto-Essene, or Hasidic.[35]

Apotropaic Prayers

Syriac psalm III represents a distinct type of prayer which still exists today. One scholar saw in this psalm an overall *individuelles Danklied* with a *Klagelied*,[36] but it is more precise to define its genre as an 'apotropaic' prayer.[37] Other texts in this genre are: a psalm in the *Psalms Scroll,* col. 19; a prayer from the Aramaic *Testament of Levi* which is put into the mouth of Levi the son of Jacob;[38] and four rabbinic prayers. The biblical Psalm 51 is a remote ancestor of this genre. It is natural that an apotropaic prayer, like other types of prayer, should not be exempt from other motifs; conversely, prayers of another kind can contain apotropaic sentences as well. The main objectives of this type of prayer are: understanding (Torah); protection against sin; forgiveness, purification, and removal from sin; salvation from troubles; resistance to temptation and deliverance from Satan.

Thus Syriac psalm III (*Psalms Scroll,* col. 24) is such an individual prayer for firgiveness, mercy and purity. It ends by saying that God fulfilled the psalmist's request. The most purely apotropaic passage is in lines 8-14. Of special interest is line 11b-12a: 'Do not bring me into difficulties insur-

---

[33] See Braun, 'Ein Brief des Katholikos Timotheos'.

[34] See also 1 Macc 2:42.

[35] See Sanders, *Psalms Scroll,* 70. Especially interesting are lines 10-11: 'A man who glorifies the Most High shall be condoned as one who brings a meal offering, as one who offers he-goats and bullocks, as one who fattens the altar with many burnt offerings, as a sweetsmelling fragrance from the hand of the righteous.' Sanders rightly compares these words with 1QS 9:4-5, but see also Sir 32(35):1-3.

[36] See Sanders, *Psalms Scroll,* 73.

[37] See Flusser, 'Apotropaic Prayers'.

[38] See Milik, 'Le Testament de Lévi en Araméen'.

mountable for me; kep me far from the sins of my youth.' This does not only resemble the rabbinic prayers of the apotropaic type, but also the last sentence of the Lord's prayer: 'And lead us not into temptation, but deliver us from evil' (Matt 6:13, cf. Luke 11:4 and see especially 1 Cor 10:13).

The other apotropaic prayer in the *Psalms Scroll* is what its editor called the 'Plea for Deliverance' (column 19:1-18). It is one of the three apocryphal psalms of the Scroll which are not preserved in any translation. Like the other apotropaic psalm, the 'Plea for Deliverance' is not typically Essene. We meet Satan and the evil inclination of rabbinic literature and prayer, rather than Belial and the spirit of wickedness of Qumran. The typically apotropaic passage which has parallels in similar texts is found in the lines 13-16. Of special importance are also lines 9-11: 'I belonged to death in (or: through) my sins and my iniquities had sold me to Hades,[39] but thou didst save me, O Lord.' In the Epistle to the Romans (6:23) Paul says that 'the wages of sin is death' and that man, being carnal, is 'sold under sin' (7:14), and he asks: 'Who will save me from this body of death?' (7:24). We see that Paul used specific Jewish concepts to serve his theology of the Law.

Autobiographical Poetry

As stated, the composition from the *Psalms Scroll* known as the Syriac psalm I is also contained in the Septuagint Psalter as Ps 151. The superscription reads: 'A Hallelujah of David the Son of Jesse.' However the composition itself is not a prayer to God or a hymn, but a poetical narrative; the speaker is David himself and the content is 1 Sam 16:1-13, his election and anointing by the prophet Samuel. David also mentions his skill as a musician: 'My hands have made an instrument and my fingers a lyre' (vs. 2). Verse 3 is preserved only in the Hebrew version and its interpretation is difficult. Some scholars think that the verse says with beauty and simplicity that mute nature appreciates David's masterful music in praise of God. If this interpretation is correct, then this is a very early description of David as a counterpart of the Greek musician Orpheus as we know him from Jewish and early Christian art.[40] The last two verses

[39] Sander's translation is incorrect. The wording is based upon Isa 50:1.
[40] See Sanders, *Psalms Scroll*, 61-63. If Van der Woude's interpretation of verse 3 of this apocryphal psalm is correct, it could be that the verse may be attacking an 'Orphic' interpretation of David. He translates: 'The mountains do not witness for me, nor the hills say (anything) about me, (nor) the trees my words, (nor) the flock my deeds.' I think that Van der Woude is basically right, but I propose the following interpretation of the whole passage (verses 2-4): 'My hands made an instrument and my fingers a lyre; and [so] I have rendered glory to the Lord. I thought within my soul: "The mountains cannot witness to him, nor the hills tell about him (read: עליו); the trees [cannot recount] his words, and the flock his deeds." For who can tell and who can bespeak and who can recount the deeds of the Lord? Everything has God seen, everything has he heard and he has heeded.'

561

of the Greek translation of Ps 151 speak of the Goliath episode, but they are in reality an epitome of another apocryphal psalm, in which David speaks of his clash with the Philistine. This psalm has a superscription which is naturally lacking in the Greek translation: 'The beginning of David's power after the prophet of God had anointed him.' Thus the Greek Psalm 151 is an amalgamation of the psalm mentioned earlier (called Ps 151A) which dealt only with David's musicianship and anointing, and the composition which follows (Ps 151B). Unfortunately only the beginning of this second composition is preserved, at the end of column 28 of the *Psalms Scroll*.[41]

As in Syriac psalm I (Psalm 151 A/B), the speaker in Syriac psalms IV and V is the young David, this time on the occasion of the events described in 1 Sam 17:34-37. There David himself tells how he watched the sheep for his father and killed a lion and a bear. In Syriac psalm IV, David, struggling with the lion and the bear, prays to God to rescue him from the danger and send a deliverer. Syriac psalm V is a thanksgiving psalm said by David after God sent an angel who shut the jaws of the two wild beasts and thus saved David's life. This legendary aspect goes beyond the biblical text, which states that David himself killed the animals.

Thus we know of four non-biblical, pseudo-Davidic psalms, all of them most probably written in Hebrew. All have events in the life of the young David as their theme. As we have observed, these psalms were probably once together in the library of Qumran. Thus it is not unlikely that these psalms were composed as parts of a pseudepigraphic autobiographical sequence. Liturgical purposes seem absent. As it is, we do not know whether this sequence contained more psalms, and whether it covered David's youth only or also the rest of his life. There is no doubt that the sequence was partly inspired by the secondary superscriptions of some of the biblical psalms.[42]   Thus we are able to recognize in ancient Judaism a special autobiographical poetical genre. The natural place of such autobiographical poetry is in a book which narrates the pertinent deeds and events. This is so in the Hebrew Bible, e.g. Moses' song at the Reed Sea; the song of Deborah; the song of Hannah, and other psalms in the Book of Samuel; so also in the Book of Tobit, in the additions to the Greek books of Esther and Daniel, in the prayer of Manasseh, in the Aramaic prayer of Nabonidus and in the psalm of encouragement in the apocryphal book of Baruch.

Another hymn which is related to this genre is the Greek prayer for wisdom in the Wisdom of Solomon (9:1-18; see 1 Kings 3:6-9).[43] Per-

---

[41] See Sanders, *Psalms Scroll*, 60-61.

[42] On this problem and related questions see now the important study of Bayer, 'The Titles of the Psalms'.

[43] See now especially Winston, *The Wisdom of Solomon*, 200-9, and Georgi, *Weisheit Salomos*, 433-6.

sonified Wisdom is defined here as the companion of God's throne and the petition for Divine Wisdom is the central theme of the prayer. Solomon prays for wisdom, because he needs it, being chosen by God as a king of his people: 'Send her (the Wisdom) forth from the holy heavens and dispatch her from your majestic throne, so she may labour at my side and I may learn your pleasure . . . So shall my works be acceptable, and I shall judge your people justly, and be worthy of my father's throne.' The end of the prayer (9:13-18) expresses the idea that man cannot know the counsel of God because his perishable body weighs down the soul. This concept of the body is Platonic; man is able to reach understanding only if God grants him wisdom and sends his holy spirit from on high. However the ideas expressed in this last part of the prayer are not only Platonic, but are also influenced by the Essene understanding of man.[44] The closest parallel to this passage is in the *Thanksgiving Scroll* (1QH 4:29-33).

Mystical Prayers

An important question is the role played in ancient Jewish liturgy by mysticism. A prominent witness is the Greek *Testament of Job*[45]; but the problem is that we do not know in what circles this book originated and what liturgical reality it may reflect. Music plays a prominent role in the book, as when Job says (chapter 14): 'And I used to have six harps and a ten-stringed lyre. And I would arise daily . . . and I would take the lyre and play for them (the servants) and they would chant. And by means of the harp I would remind them of God so that they may glorify the Lord. And if my maidservants ever began murmuring, I would take the harp . . . and I would make them stop murmuring in contempt.' Chapter 25 contains a poem with a refrain about the cruel lot of Job's wife, contrasting her prior wealth with her present misery. Parallel in content is Eliphas' 'royal lament' over Job's disaster (chapter 31:5-8 and chapter 32). This time the refrain is: 'Where is now the splendour of your throne?' As an answer to this mourning-song, Job utters a mystical hymn (chapter 33) and speaks about his throne and the splendour of its majesty among the holy ones, in a supra-terrestrial realm. Chapter 43 contains a song of condemnation of Elihu: Eliphas receives the spirit and recites the hymn in which Elihu is described as belonging to darkness and not to light, because 'he loved the beauty of the serpent and the scales of the dragon.' The *Testament of Job* mentions other prayers (40:14; 49:3; 50:3) which are not given in the book. It seems, however, that these indications are only literary fiction, as in the case of the mention of a great lamentation after Job's death in 53:1, which is followed only by a short poetical lament (53:2-4).

[44] See Flusser, 'Dead Sea Sect', 257-60.
[45] Above p. 349-54; Brock, *Testamentum Iobi;* Kraft, *The Testament of Job;* Schaller, *Das Testament Hiobs.*

563

The book contains interesting references to other mystical religious songs. After the happy ending to Job's suffering, his daughters receive wondrous sashes with which they gird themselves. Thereupon they are given a new heart, so that they no longer think of earthly things and are able to chant verses in the angelic language 'according to the hymnic style of the angels'; the author affirms that these hymns are recorded in other collections (chapters 48-57). Before he died, Job 'took a lyre and gave it to his daughter Hemera, and gave a censer to Kassia and gave a kettle-drum' to his third daughter, 'so that they might praise those who had come for his soul,' and indeed the daughters 'praised and glorified God in the exalted dialect' (53:3-7).

It is not very probable that the songs contained in the *Testament of Job* were actually used as liturgical poetry in the Jewish Hellenistic circles in which the book originated, although this possibility cannot be completely excluded. In any case, it is likely that the work in some way reflects the liturgy, including pneumatic songs, of a Jewish mystical group living probably in Egypt in the second century C.E.[46]

Another work, possibly written at the same period in similar circles, is the Greek legend of *Joseph and Asenath*.[47] The book tells the story of Joseph's marriage with the Egyptian Asenath, who is depicted as a prototype of the virtuous proselyte. As in the *Testament of Job*, the atmosphere is impregnated with the supernatural and miraculous. The book contains two poetical prayers; in the first (8:10-11) Joseph blesses Asenath. The second (chapters 12-13) is uttered by Asenath after she has repented, renounced her paganism and destroyed her idols. Both prayers begin with a praise of God as Creator. In the second prayer Asenath, after the praise of God, confesses that she has sinned as an idolatress and prays God for forgiveness and salvation. The content and structure of this prayer resemble the Prayer of Manasseh (above p. 555). These literary compositions may in some way reflect actual prayers of the Jewish Hellenistic group in which the book was written.

In the first prayer (8:10), it is said that God has called all things 'from darkness into light and from death into life' (cf. also 15:13). A parallel to these words exists in the *Easter Homily* of the Christian bishop Melito of Sardis (chapter 68).[48] In other parts of this sermon Melito is also dependent

---

[46] Schaller, *Das Testament Hiobs*, 309-11, suggested that the author belonged to the sect of the Therapeutae, without sufficient proof.

[47] See above, p. 65-71; Philonenko, *Joseph et Aséneth*.

[48] 'It is he that delivered us form slavery to liberty, from darkness to light, from death to life, from tyranny to eternal royalty'. This is parallel to the introduction to the *Hallel* in the Passover Haggadah. See Hall, 'Melito'. On Joseph and Asenath, Melito and the Passover Haggadah see Pines, 'From Darkness into Great Light'. On the same question see also Flusser, 'Some Notes on Easter'.

on the Jewish liturgy of the night of Passover. These complex connections pave the way for the assumption that the two prayers in *Joseph and Asenath* indirectly reflect some liturgical reality.

A further document reflecting ancient Jewish mysticism is the *Apocalypse of Abraham*,[49] a book which is preserved in a Slavonic translation from the Greek; it is probable that the original language of the book was Hebrew. It was evidently written in the same period as *Joseph and Asenath* and the Easter Homily, i.e. in the second century C.E. The traces of mysticism are even stronger than in the *Testament of Job;* there are clear affinities with the mystical school which is represented by the so-called *Hekhalot* literature.[50] The book even offers the song taught to Abraham by the angel who guides him on his way to heaven, and this song (17:8-18) is the very hymn sung by the angels who mount guard before the Throne. This hymn already has the numinous character of the later *Merkabah* hymns.[51]

Another important document contributing to the history of Jewish mystical liturgy is the *Angelic Liturgy*[52] in manuscripts from Qumran cave 4 which can be dated paleographically to the late Hasmonean or early Herodian period (c. 75-25 B.C.E.) It describes the Sabbath praise-offerings of the angels in the heavenly sanctuaries. The recitation of the *Angelic Liturgy* appears to have been a vehicle for the liturgical communion of the Qumran community with the angels. The songs of the angels are only referred to, but never quoted. These descriptions are clearly dependent upon the Book of Ezekiel. Although there is no direct genetic relationship between the *Angelic Liturgy* from Qumran and the *Hekhalot* hymns of later *Merkabah* mysticism, significant affinities of content and style are evident.[53] In the body of the composition very little if any characteristic sectarian terminology is used, but even if there was a prehistory of the *Angelic Liturgy* outside Qumran, the composition appears to have been used by the Qumran community. The liturgical *Sitz im Leben* of this composition is

[49] Above p. 415-8; see Philonenko-Sayar and Philonenko, *Die Apokalypse Abrahams*. This German translation is based upon a new study of the Slavonic manuscripts.

[50] See *id.*, 418-9. The possibility cannot be excluded that the *Apocalypse of Abraham* is an early Jewish-Christian book. At least 29:2b-11 is evidently Jewish-Christian; this can be seen even from the unclear Slavonic version. Is the man who is described there Jesus, or possibly Paul? I do not see any sufficient cause to exclude the passage as an interpolation. On the place of the *Apocalypse of Abraham* in the history of Jewish mysticism see Scholem, *Major Trends*.

[51] Scholem, *Major Trends*, 61 already saw that the attributes of God in this hymn are in some cases identical with those used in Greek and early Christian prayers. This (and other indications) makes it difficult to assume that the book was not composed in Greek, but in Hebrew. Philonenko, *Die Apokalypse Abrahams*, 417 saw this difficulty and therefore was prepared to consider the beginning of the hymn (17:8-10) as a later Greek interpolation.

[52] Above, p. 524-5; Strugnell, 'The Angelic Liturgy'. Meanwhile all the texts have been published, with introduction and commentary, by Newsom, *Angelic Liturgy*.

[53] Abstract from Newsom, *Angelic Liturgy*.

unclear, as the text does not contain actual liturgical prayers. It is possible that the text was recited on Sabbaths by the Instructor (*Maskil*), who is mentioned at the beginning of the various units.

Qumran Liturgical Texts

Our discussion of hymns of mystical quality brought us to the liturgy of the Qumran sect, and to a possible function in it of the *Maskil*.[54] We shall now deal with the other hymnic and liturgical texts from the Qumran caves, which in part document actual liturgical practices of a specific, socially well-defined group.[55]

The *Canticles of the Instructor* are an indication that the *Maskil* did have some liturgical function, although we can not define it precisely.[56] In this collection of canticles, which has been preserved in fragments from two copies, the Instructor speaks in the first person.[57] Like the *Angelic Liturgy*, these poems begin with the words 'To the Instructor, a song' (cf. Ps 45:1). Thus the canticles show an affinity with the *Angelic Liturgy*, an affinity also expressed in the angelology which figures prominently in both collections. But in content and wording they are sometimes closer to the *Thanksgiving Scroll*.

We now turn to the hymns in the *Thanksgiving Scroll*. As in the *Canticles of the Instructor,* their author speaks in the first person, and these hymns are markedly expressive of the religious and theological approach of a leader of the sect. This in itself makes it difficult to assume that such personal prayers could have been written for liturgical purposes, since that would require the speaker to be presented as a biblical person, as in the Davidic compositions from Qumran. Thus its seems probable that both the *Thanksgiving Scroll* and the *Canticles of the Instructor* were composed for study rather than for use as prayer. It is very unlikely that the two compositions were written by the same author: as far as we can judge from the fragments, the dualistic anthropology of flesh and spirit and the specific theology of election which are typical for the *Thanksgiving Scroll* and the concluding psalm of the *Manual of Discipline* are absent from the *Canticles of the Instructor*.[58]

Some of the hymns in the *Thanksgiving Scroll* open with the word 'Blessed be' (ברוך),[59] which opens many prayers from the period of the

---

[54] For other duties of this functionary, see 1QS 3:13, 9:12 (above, p. 501-2); CD 12:21.

[55] Most of the important liturgical fragments are now published by Baillet in *DJD* 7, but see also the other volumes of this series.

[56] See Newsom, *Angelic Liturgy*, 72-92.

[57] *DJD* 7, 215-62.

[58] On these concepts see Flusser, 'Dead Sea Sect', 252-63. See also Flusser, 'The Sect of the Judaean Desert'.

[59] The words 'Blessed be you God of Gods' appear in the *Canticles of the Instructor* (Baillet, *DJD* 7, 229).

Second Temple and many rabbinic prayers and benedictions. However, the regular opening of the thanksgiving hymns is 'I thank you' (אודך). This was also the opening of the thanksgiving hymn of Jesus (Matt 11:25-27; Luke 10:21-22).[60] Not only the opening of Jesus' hymn but also the free rhythm of the poem and its content show affinity with the Essene thanksgiving hymns. Furthermore, the high self-awareness expressed in Jesus' hymn resembles the Essene hymns; both Jesus and the author of the *Thanksgiving Scroll* proclaim that they reveal to the simple divine things hidden from others. Thus it seems evident that Jesus knew the Essene thanksgiving hymns and used their form in order to express his own place in the divine economy, though he introduced into his own hymn the motif of his divine sonship, which is naturally absent from the *Thanksgiving Scroll.*

In Cave 4 at Qumran, fragments of three copies of a collection of prayers were found of which the editor assumed that it was named *The Words of Luminaries.*[61] It is a work of great importance for the history of Jewish liturgy. The oldest manuscript dates from the early Hasmonean period (about 150 B.C.E.) and the collection itself is evidently pre-Essene. These hymns are not personal but community prayers to be recited on specific days of the week; Wednesday and Sabbath are indicated in the fragments.

The theme of these prayers is a plea for God's mercy on his people. Israel has sinned in the past and was rightly punished for its sins. 'Do not remember against us the sins of our forefathers!' God will also remember the election of Israel and his mighty deeds in its favour, and forgive them and gather the dispersed. Naturally, these prayers also contain reminiscences from biblical history, from the creation of Adam to the catastrophe at the end of the First Temple. An exception to this pattern is the prayer for the Sabbath, a day destined for joy; the pertinent fragment is a hymnic praise of God. With this exception, the prayers of this collection belong to the genre represented by biblical prayers such as Dan 9:3-19,[62] which can be termed *Tahanunim* (supplications) according to the word which appears in Dan 9:3, 17. The liturgical use of such supplications is convincingly proved by the evidence in the Qumran fragments showing that they were said on specific days of the week.[63]

There are more Qumran texts which carry indications as to their actual liturgical use. In Cave 1, fragments of another collection of liturgical

[60] See Flusser, *Die rabbinischen Gleichnisse,* 265-9.
[61] The fragments were published by Baillet, *DJD* 7, 137-75. It is doubtful whether the composition was really named 'The Words of Luminaries'. See also Baillet, 'Un recueil liturgique'.
[62] See below, p. 570-1.
[63] There are striking similarities to the actual *Tahanun* of the synagogue. See below.

prayers were discovered.[64] In the first of them, the beginning of what is named 'a prayer of the Day of Atonement' is preserved. It is very probable that two other fragments also belong to the liturgy of the Day of Atonement.[65] Especially interesting is the third fragment, which describes events from the creation of the luminaries until Moses.[66] It resembles the content of poetical introductions to the so-called *Avodah* which forms part of the synagogal liturgy of the Day of Atonement.[67]

As already said, most of the liturgical fragments are from Cave 4 of Qumran. Many are too small to allow conclusions to be drawn about the character of the scrolls they represent.[69] It was suggested by their editor that 4Q502 preserves fragments of the ritual of marriage, but that is by no means sure. The fragments of 4Q503 contain the remainder of short evening and morning benedictions for all the days of the month. They are introduced by indications as to when the community pronounces the pertinent benediction; the benedictions themselves are phrased in the plural; e.g. 'We, the sons of your covenant', or 'We, your holy people.' Introductory indications appear also in the fragments of 4Q512, in the so-called Ritual of Purification.[70] There the introductions specify the kinds of purification which call for specific prayers; these prayers are naturally phrased in the first person singular.

Another document deserves to be mentioned in this connection, although it was not discovered at Qumran. In the Cairo Geniza, four pages from a medieval manuscript were found which contain a fragment from a collection of non-biblical psalms, termed the *Songs of David*. Apparently these psalms were composed in the Second Temple period and probably were once brought from Qumran.[71]

The psalms are expressedly designed to be recited day after day and were consequently destined for actual liturgical use. This may be the collection mentioned in the prose list of 'David's Compositions' in the *Psalms Scroll*,

---

[64] Barthélemy-Milik, *DJD* 1, 152-5. Fragments of the same work were found in Qumran Cave 4 (4Q507, 4Q508, 4Q509). See Baillet, *DJD* 7, 175-215.

[65] See Grintz, *Chapters*, 155-8.

[66] The editor wrongly saw the fragment as being eschatological, speaking about the Dead Sea sect! In the last line of the fragment mention is made of רועה נאמן מ(שה אי)ש ענו (the faithful shepherd, Moses, a meek man). Moses is described as a meek man in Num 12:3 and 'the faithful shepherd' is a current attribute of Moses in rabbinic literature. Here it appears for the first time.

[67] See Elbogen, *Der jüdische Gottesdienst*, 216-7, 277-8.

[68] See *DJD* 7, 73-262.

[69] The language of the fragment of the lamentation in 4Q501 recalls the style of the *Thanksgiving Scroll*, while the content resembles the *Psalms of Solomon*.

[70] Baillet, *DJD* 7, 262-86.

[71] Flusser-Safrai, 'A Fragment'. Language and style of the fragment also point to a date of composition before 70 C.E.

where we read that David composed 'songs to sing before the altar every day, all the days of the year.'[72] As in the case of the non-biblical psalms from the *Psalms Scroll*, the *Songs of David* are attributed to David himself. Here he appears as a prophet, a universal messianic king who is to teach all the inhabitants of the earth, so that they may return to God's way, serve him truly and no longer adore the idols.[73] This combination of universalism and Jewish messianism is an important witness for the development of Jewish religious thought.

Specific expressions reveal a relationship to the Essene literature, but these Davidic psalms are not strictly sectarian. They were apparently composed in the same circles as the Davidic psalms from the *Psalms Scroll*, as is attested by similarities in terminology and phrasing.[74] More precisely, the *Songs of David* contain somewhat more sectarian terminology and concepts than the non-biblical psalms from the *Psalms Scroll* or the *Words of Luminaries*, and consequently seem nearer to the sect than the latter.

The importance of the *Songs of David* for the history of Jewish worship is undeniable. Not only do they attest actual liturgical practices of circles close to Essenism, they also contain liturgical phrases which reappear in rabbinic prayers.[75]

Some other liturgical texts may be mentioned, of a more formalized nature. The liturgy of the annual solemn renewal of the Essene covenant is described in the *Manual of Discipline* 1:16-2:18, although the full wording of the ceremony is not given.[76] Those who enter into the covenant make a confession (1QS 1:24-2:1) which has biblical roots and resembles the confession of the high priest on the Day of Atonement (*M. Yoma* 3:8) and the confession in the *Damascus Covenant* 20:27-30.[77] The benediction of the priests (1QS 2:2-4) is a poetical enlargement of the priestly blessing in Num 6:25 and in this respect resembles the blessings in 1QS[b]. Curses follow, against 'all the men of the lot of Belial', and against those who enter the covenant but in their heart resolve not to change their wicked ways (1QS 2:11-18). The latter curse owes its vocabulary to Deut 29:17ff., but enlarges it and deepens its meaning.[78] At the end of the *Manual of Disci-*

---

[72] Sanders, *Psalms Scroll*, 92.

[73] See the translation of one of the universalistic passages from the *Songs of David* (2:8-19) in Flusser, 'Paganism', 1097. It resembles so much to Tob 14:6 (Sinaiticus version) that dependence or a common source is probable. Another parallel is 1QH 6:11-13.

[74] Especially with Syriac psalm III (11QPs[a] 155); Sanders, *Psalms Scroll*, 70-71.

[75] E.g., the verses in leaves 2:20 and 4:11-12 are relevant for the history of the *Kaddish*.

[76] See above, p. 500; Licht, *The Rule Scroll*, 63-73 and Leany, *The Rule of Qumran*, 104-107, 123-36.

[77] Cf. also *Jubilees* 1:22.

[78] It is probable that the early Christian community used a similar curse against those who tried to join it dishonestly. This becomes evident from Peter's words to Simon Magus (Acts 8:21-23): 'You have neither part nor lot in this matter . . .' The words 'gall of bitterness' in Acts 8:23 are taken from Deut 29:17! See also Betz, *Offenbarung*, 170-6.

pline (10:1-11:15), we find religious poetry which in spirit is similar to the *Thanksgiving Scroll*, but is not a prayer properly speaking, because God is not addressed in it.

The scroll from Qumran Cave 1 containing the *Manual of Discipline* adds two more texts at the end. The second of them is a collection of blessings (1QS^b), to be pronounced by the Instructor on a specific solemn occasion, which cannot be precisely identified because of the fragmentary condition of the scroll.[79] We do know that it will occur in the eschatological future, because, for instance, one of these benedictions is in honour of the Prince, a title of the Essene Davidic Messiah.[80] The benedictions of this work are again another poetical elaboration of the priestly blessing in Num 6:25.

Of special interest are the prayers and other liturgical pieces contained in the *War Scroll* (1QM 9:17-16:1; 16:13-17:9; 18:6-19:8). When considering them, we must bear in mind that they are designed only for the eschatological war, not immediate use. Yet I venture to suggest that some of these liturgical pieces are not just the product of eschatological 'science fiction', but are based upon actual prayers and hymns which the author of the *War Scroll* adapted to the eschatological setting and to his own theology.[81] One of the significant features of these prayers is the frequent appeal to God's promises for the future as well as his mighty deeds in the past. God is asked to grant victory as in the days of Pharaoh (1QM 11:9-10); he has delivered Goliath into the hand of David (1QM 11:2-3); and he preserved for himself Eleazar and Ithamar for an eternal covenant (1QM 17:2-3). This return to the past is a constant motif in similar prayers for deliverance. Indeed, together with other features it constitutes another genre of Jewish prayers.

Prayers in Distress (Tahanunim)

Jews of all ages have said prayers in times of distress. The basic pattern is a combination of two elements: supplications for God's help and the remembrance of his saving deeds in the past. So, in *Mishnah Taanith* 2:4-5, a litany is quoted which was to be recited on fast days, and in which God is asked to help because it was he who answered Abraham in distress, Israel at the Red Sea, Joshua at Gilgal, Samuel, Elijah on Mount Carmel, Jonah, David and his son Solomon. The prayer for the deliverance and restoration of Israel in Ben Sira 36:1-17 asks God to fulfill the prophecies spoken in his name, and begins with the election of Israel. In the Book of Judith, the heroine prays God to help her (chapter 9) in the following words: 'O Lord

---

[79] See above, p. 524; *DJD* 1, 118-30 and Licht, *The Rule Scroll*, 273-89.

[80] It is also very probable that the blessing by which the high priest was to be blessed, was destined for the future priestly Messiah.

[81] For the characteristic patterns of the prayers in the Essene *War Scroll* see Flusser, 'The Magnificat'.

God of my father Simeon, to whom thou gavest a sword to take revenge on the strangers . . . O God, my God, hear me also, a widow.'[82]

This pattern becomes more specific when a third element is added: the repentance of the people and its prayer for forgiveness of sins. Such is the pattern we found in the 'Words of the Luminaries' (above p. 567). We may now be more explicit and term this a prototype of the later *Tahanun* prayer of the synagogue, which is said at the daily morning and afternoon service after the *Eighteen Benedictions*.[83] In the light of this evidence, the prehistory of this prayer of supplication appears in need of reconsideration.

The elements of supplication, repentance and remembrance of the past are already found together in the prayers of Nehemiah 9 and Daniel 9.[84] The combination is also present in the Greek additions to the Book of Esther (Esther's prayer speaks of the sins of Israel) and in the prayer of Azariah in the Greek additions to Daniel.

Another example is the prayer for the exiled community in the apocryphal book of Baruch (2:6-3:8). This prayer is highly reminiscent of the canonical book of Jeremiah; distinctive views and phraseology of Jeremiah occur in almost every verse.[85] It was originally composed in Hebrew and probably antedates the Hasmonean revolt of 168 B.C.E.

Two prayers of the same type were written by the author of the Third Book of Maccabees. The book has nothing to do with the Maccabean wars; its content is a legend, a miraculous story of deliverance which is said to have occurred in Alexandria and was celebrated every year by the Jews. It was written in Greek probably at the end of the first century B.C.E. by an Alexandrian Jew. The two prayers deserve close examination because of their importance for the history of Jewish prayers. The first is put into the mouth of the high priest Simeon (2:1-20), while the second (6:1-15) is said

---

[82] In Judith 16:1-17 there is also a song of praise which Judith and all the people sing after the victory. It is modelled on the pattern of Old Testament poetry. In its first part (Jdt 16:2-12) Judith speaks of herself in the third person, as Deborah did (Judg 5). The second part of Judith's song (16:13-17) is marked by a new beginning: 'I will sing to my God a new song.' It is a general hymn of praise: nothing can resist God; the foundations of the earth shall be shaken and in God's presence the rocks shall melt like wax, 'but to those who fear thee, thou wilt continue to show mercy.' Every sacrifice is for God a very little thing, 'but he who fears the Lord shall be great for ever.' At the end of the song Judith proclaims that the Lord Almighty will take vengeance on all enemies of Israel 'in the day of judgement'. Thus the song ends with an eschatological outlook (cf. *i.a.* Sir 35:18-20, a passage which precedes the prayer for deliverance of Israel). Grintz, *Sefer Yehudith*, rightly argues that the Book of Judith was written in the Persian period, as was the Book of Tobit; which indicates the antiquity of these prayers.
[83] On the *Tahanun* see Elbogen, *Der jüdische Gottesdienst*, 73-81; Ydit, 'Tahanun'.
[84] Neh 1:4-11, 9:6-37; Dan 9:3-19; cf. Ezra 9:6-15. On Dan 9:3-19 see Hartmann-Di Lella, *Daniel*. On pp. 245-6 and 248-9 these authors argue that this prayer is an insertion into the basic stratum of chap. 9 of Daniel. The assumption that the prayer is older than the chapter itself is strenghtened by the similarity with the Qumran Words of the Luminaries. See also Delcor, *Daniel*, 185-6.
[85] Cf. Jer 32:15-23. See Moore, *Daniel, Esther and Jeremiah*, 257-8, 283-94.

by a priest named Eleazar. Both contain the three motifs: the plea for God's help, the petition for forgiveness of Israel's sins and the enumeration of God's saving deeds in the past. We also find, as is usual in such prayers, an apostrophe to God as the Creator of the universe.

An important witness for Jewish prayers in distress in the Hasmonaean period is 1 and 2 Maccabees. In one of the prayers in the First Book of Maccabees[86] (7:40-42), Judas prays that God may crush Nicanor's army as once the angel struck down the army of the Assyrians in the time of Sennacherib. Another prayer of Judas Maccabaeus before a battle (1 Macc 4:30-33), which begins with the usual 'Blessed are you', also mentions mighty deeds of God in the past, namely those in the days of David. It is significant that in the same book (2:49-68) Matthatias in his last words asks his sons to remember the deeds of the fathers, mentioning Abraham, Joseph, 'Phineas our father', Joshua, Caleb, Elijah, Hananiah, Azariah and Mishael and Daniel. All this fits the genre of which we have spoken.

Of the prayers in the Second Book of the Maccabees,[87] two are found in the letters prefacing the book. In the first, from the year 124 B.C.E., written at Jerusalem to the Jews in Egypt, there is a prayer (2 Macc 1:2-5) which is reflected in a Jewish prayer still said today.[88] This is the oldest non-biblical Jewish prayer which can be dated precisely. The second opening letter was written by Judas Maccabaeus[89] to the Jews in Egypt before the purification of the Temple in the year 164 B.C.E. It contains an interesting prayer ascribed to the priests in the time of Nehemiah (2 Macc 1:24-29) and also a benediction connected with the death of Antiochus: 'Blessed for all things be our God who gave the impious doers for a prey.' This is a common form of Jewish benedictions.[90]

The Second Book of the Maccabees itself also gives prayers of the Maccabean warriors,[91] which reflect Jewish prayers of the time. This is an

---

[86] Others are: 1 Macc 3:50-53; 4:30-33; 7:36-38, 40-42.

[87] 2 Macc 1:2-6, 17, 24-29; 8:14-15, 18-20; 12:15; 14:35-36; 15:9, 22-24, 34.

[88] See Flusser, 'Sanktus und Gloria', 143. (The date of the letter is 124 B.C.E. and not 143 as indicated there.)

[89] I have shown elsewhere that this letter is authentic. See Flusser, 'Jerusalem', 277-80.

[90] Another benediction is pronounced by one of the heroes of the *Biblical Antiquities* (26:6) after seeing a miracle: 'Blessed be God who had done such great wonders (*virtutes,* גבורות for the sons of man.' This seems to have been a Jewish benediction said after a supernatural phenomenon had occurred. It is reflected in Matt 9:8 after the healing of a paralytic: 'When the crowds saw it, they were afraid, and they glorified God, who had given such authority to men.' The original wording of the benediction is changed here under the influence of Matt 9:6 and parallels. A very similar benediction is pronounced by Jews when they see a non-Jewish king: 'Blessed be you, o Lord our Lord, King of the universe, who has given of his glory to flesh and blood.' See *B.T. Berakhoth* 58a.

[91] 2 Macc 8:14-15, 18-20 (Judas' exhortation); 12:15; 14:35-36; 15:9 (Judas' encouragement); 15:21-24; 15:34.

additional indication that the book is not purely Hellenistic, but is also rooted in Palestinian Judaism. Most of these prayers are pleas for deliverance and, as befits the genre, include historical reminiscences. In 2 Macc 8:14-15, the Jews pray to be saved, 'if not for their own sake, yet for the sake of the covenants made with their fathers, and because he (God) had called upon them his holy and glorious name.' Then Judas Maccabaeus exhorts them not to fear the enemy and tells them of the times when help came to their ancestors (2 Macc 8:18-20). He also mentions the rescue in the time of Sennacherib, an event which is equally mentioned in Judas' prayer before the battle with Nicanor (15:21-24), beseeching God to send a good angel to save Israel (cf. 11:6). In another prayer (12:15) the fall of Jericho is recalled. According to 2 Macc 15:8-9, Judas exhorted his men to keep in mind the former times when help came from heaven, encouraging them from the Law and the prophets. In another prayer (14:34-36) the priests begged that the Temple that had recently been purified should remain undefiled for ever. And after the victory over Nicanor, the people 'blessed the Lord who had manifested himself, saying, "Blessed is he who has kept his own place undefiled"' (2 Macc 15:34). This is the language of Jewish benedictions.

Psalms of Solomon

This work was written in Jerusalem in the middle of the first century B.C.E. It was originally written in Hebrew, but only a Greek translation has been preserved.[92] Nothing but the title indicates the authorship of Solomon. The aim of the *Psalms of Solomon* is didactic, polemical and theological. It is difficult to assume that they were written for liturgical purposes or later became part of any liturgy. The eighteen psalms reflect the dramatic events of Jewish history in that period and criticize the various Jewish groups. A prominent theme is criticism of those who cause social evil. The author is influenced by the contemporary apocalyptic trend. This is surely the main reason why, after the manner of apocalyptics, he does not name persons and political parties. He apparently laments Pompey's conquest of Jerusalem in 63 B.C.E. (psalms 1, 2 and 8; and see psalm 17) and describes his violent death in Egypt (psalm 2), without naming him or the Romans. Some idea of the political and religious involvement of the author may be deduced from the way he speaks of those who love the assemblies of the pious who fled to the desert (psalm 17:18-20). This is the party of the Hasidim, which is already mentioned in 1 Macc 2:42 (cf. Ps 149:1); the author of the *Psalms of Solomon* was evidently one of the later adherents of this party. This explains why he denounces the Hasmonaean dynasty as illegal, and why his religious opinions resemble the teaching of the Pharisees, especially on the resurrection of the body and on the question of

---

92 See Holm-Nielsen, *Die Psalmen Salomos.*

free will. The *Psalms of Solomon* are important evidence for the Jewish eschatological hopes of the time.[93] The main substance of the seventeenth psalm and of part of the eighteenth is the coming of the Davidic Messiah, who is described as a mighty and righteous earthly king.

Prayers in Biblical Antiquities

The prayers in the *Book of Biblical Antiquities*[94] are mostly literary compositions integrated into the narrative, which presents the 'legends of the Jews' from the creation until Saul's death. The prayers in the book, like the speeches, often serve to express the religious position of its author and to bring in historical events omitted earlier in the narrative. This didactic purpose is evident for instance in Joshua's prayer (21:2-6), which begins by stressing God's prescience (21:2), then mentions the incident with Achan about which nothing has been said before, and for the rest consists of theology and prophecy. While the author does not mention the song at the Red Sea in Exod 15, the Song of Deborah in Judg 5 inspired him to give his own version (chapter 32): a historical retrospect, combined with other motifs, mostly didactic. A long passage in it is devoted to Abraham (32:2-4); among other things the author gives his own aggadic version of the sacrifice of Isaac, which he omitted before. Israel's history in retrospect ends at 32:11 and only then does the author return to the Song of Deborah, but even this part contains historical reminiscences, together with interesting religious information. After Deborah's death, the author gives a short poetical lament uttered by the people (33:6). This is his own composition, as is the lamentation of Jephthah's daughter (40:5-7). The latter is probably influenced (directly or indirectly) by Greek tragedy. The central motif of the lamentation is an identification of the virgin's violent death with her marriage which was never to occur.[95] In the case of Hannah's song (1 Sam 2:1-10), the paraphrase in the *Biblical Antiquities* (51:3-6)[96] is also a poetical song. But even here it is didactic: Hannah quotes what Asaph says about her son in Ps 99:6! Another poetical psalm is sung by David after being anointed by Samuel (59:4).[97] The theme of this psalm is the same as the apocryphal Psalm 151, of which we have spoken before, but there is no specific similarity between the two. Moreover, the mention of the sacrifice of Abel again shows the didactic purpose which is

---

[93] See above, p. 556-8.
[94] Above, pp. 107-10. The recent edition is Harrington *et al.*, *Pseudo-Philon*. See also the German translation by Dietzfelbinger, *Pseudo-Philo* and Feldman, 'Prolegomenon'. For a list of the prayers see Perrot-Bogaert, *Pseudo-Philon* 2, 50 n. 7.
[95] This motif appears also in Antigone's lamentation in Sophocles' tragedy (vv. 801ff, 891ff.) See also Philonenko, 'Iphigenie and Sheila'.
[96] See Philonenko, 'Une paraphrase'.
[97] See Strugnell, 'More Psalms'.

typical of most of the prayers in the *Biblical Antiquities*.

Only one poetical composition in this book seems important for the history of Jewish prayer, namely the other Davidic composition contained in the book (chapter 60). It is a psalm of David, supposedly said to bring about the departure of the evil spirit from Saul. It begins with the statement that 'there were darkness and silence before the world was', followed by an unusual description of creation in which God is not expressedly mentioned. The psalm ends this description by addressing the evil spirit of Saul: 'And after that was the tribe of your spirits created.' The unclear Latin wording of the beginning of verse 3 possibly hints at the concept that the spirits were created on the second day of creation. Therefore, all that is said about the creation is an aetiological preamble to the exorcism which follows. At the end of this exorcism, David evidently refers to his future son Solomon, who is to subdue the evil spirits; a very familiar item. One of the characteristics of the *Biblical Antiquities* is the importance of magic: the author betrays an ambivalent attitude to it and he evidently distinguishes, so to speak, between black[98] and white magic. Thus it is no wonder that David's song before Saul is built on the pattern of a real exorcism. There is a striking similarity in content with a Babylonian cosmological incantation against toothache,[99] which proceeds from the creation of the world to the creation of the worm which causes toothache, and then continues with the exorcism. Other Babylonian incantations likewise contain cosmological material, as do incantations from outside the ancient Near East.[100] From these observations we conclude that David's psalm before Saul reflects a type of ancient Jewish charm which is otherwise unknown to us. It is even possible that this kind of charm ultimately stems from non-Jewish circles. A further investigation might possibly show to what exent the supposed incantation against evil spirits was already Judaized before it was adapted to the biblical frame in the *Biblical Antiquities*.

Prayers in 4 Ezra and 2 Baruch

Prayers put into the mouths of the protagonists, as an organic part of the work, are also found in 4 Ezra and 2 Baruch. Between these non-epical,

---

[98] In rabbinic literature 'black magic' (which is prohibited) is named 'the ways of the Amorites'. See Urbach, *Sages* 1, 101. The author of the *Biblical Antiquities* understands this concept literally: black magic is performed by the Amorites.

[99] Prichard, *ANET*, 100-101. See also p. 671 (100d).

[100] Very like the psalm in *LAB* 60 and even more like the Babylonian incantation is the so-called *Wessobrunner Gebet*, from the beginning of the ninth century. Furthermore, two old German Merseburg charms in a manuscript from the tenth century begin with an aetiological mythological scene. See W. Braune-K. Helm, *Althochdeutsches Lesebuch*,16. Auflage bearbeitet von E. A. Ebbinghaus, Tübingen 1979, pp. 85-86, 89. For a translation see H. Mettke, *Aelteste deutsche Dichtung und Prosa*, Leipzig 1979, 84-6, 156-7.

apocalyptic works which were written in Hebrew around the year 100 C.E. there is a literary connection.[101] In the Syriac text of *2 Baruch* three such prayers bear the superscription 'Baruch's prayer' (21:1-26; 28:1-20; 54:1-14), but it is probable that these superscriptions are not original.[102] In 4 Ezra 5:20 only the Syriac translation bears such a superscription, while in 8:20 the superscription is 'The beginning of the words of Ezra's prayer before he was taken up,' which appears also in other translations. It is likely, however, that this superscription is secondary as well. The so-called confession of Ezra (8:20-36) which follows, was evidently used for Christian prayer in the *Apostolic Constitutions* 7:7,5-6.[104] The possibility cannot be excluded that the 'Confession of Ezra' stems from an originally independent Jewish prayer or that the Confession itself was once accepted in unknown Jewish circles, but this seems to me very improbable. The hymnic part of this prayer (8:20-25) much resembles the Prayer of Manasseh (verses 1-7).

The complaint of Ezra (3:4-36) contains in verses 4-27 a survey of history from Adam to the Babylonian exile. This survey has a similar structure to Stephen's speech in Acts 7:2-53. The main content of another prayer, namely 4 Ezra 6:38-59, is a poetic description of the days of creation. Similar descriptions appear also in other Jewish hymns from the time of the Second Temple, e.g. in the *Biblical Antiquities* chap. 60, in Ben Sira 42:15-43:15 and in the Qumran *Thanksgiving Scroll* 1:10-20.

Epilogue

In none of the Jewish writings from the Second Temple period do we find any quotations of the synagogal prayers transmitted by rabbinic tradition, with the single exception of the little prayer in 2 Macc 1:2-5. This is remarkable, because ancestors of other rabbinical prayers did exist at that time. Two of them, the *Tahanunim* and the apotropaic prayers, are clearly represented in the Apocrypha and Pseudepigrapha and the Dead Sea Scrolls. This situation cannot be fully explained by the fact that part of the sources are sectarian or at least not in the line of later rabbinic Judaism. It is not difficult to show that the Essene *Thanksgiving Scroll* betrays knowledge of the *Eighteen Benedictions*,[105] and it seems likely that while the

---

[101] See above, pp. 409-10, 414. Cf. also Myers, *I and II Esdras;* Schreiner, *Das 4. Buch Esra;* Bogaert, *Apocalypse de Baruch.*

[102] See Bogaert, *Apocalypse de Baruch* 2, 48.

[103] See Myers, *I and II Esdras,* 144.

[104] See Myers, *id.* 118, who also notes that Clement of Alexandria (*Stromata* 3:16) cites 2 Esdras 5:35. See also Schreiner, *Das 4. Buch Esra,* 294 n. 25.

[105] See Talmon, 'The Order of Prayer'. More material can be found, such as the psalm in Sir 51:12 already referred to, which contains material pertinent to the history of the *Eighteen Benedictions.*

Essenes knew the 'proto-rabbinic' liturgy, they rejected it because of their opposition to the Pharisees. However such a position is unthinkable for the circles in which *2 Baruch,* 4 Ezra and the *Biblical Antiquities* originated, since these were not far from the Pharisees and must have appreciated their prayers. We are left with the conclusion that the authors of such works did not find occasion to quote the common prayers. A factor which undoubtedly encouraged this reticence is that the synagogal prayers were oral,[106] and that it was considered forbidden to write them down.[107]

Meanwhile, the prayers and psalms contained in the Apocrypha and Pseudepigrapha, and in another way the actual Essene prayers, elucidate the religious life and thought of ancient Judaism. Especially important is the light they shed on the origin of the two types of informal rabbinic prayers we mentioned. Beyond the scope of this volume is the significance of these texts for the development of early synagogal poetry (*piyyut*). It is important to study the language and poetical style of these psalms, hymns and prayers, especially of those preserved in Hebrew, not only to enrich our knowledge of the various levels of post-biblical poetical Hebrew, but also to deepen our understanding of the various types of synagogal poetry and of private prayers.

BIBLIOGRAPHY

On the Magnificat and the Benedictus: SCHÜRMANN, *Lukasevangelium,* 70-80, 84-94; SCHNEIDER, *Lukas,* 54-56, 59-60; FLUSSER, 'Sanktus und Gloria'; *id.,* 'The Magnificat'; WINTER, 'Magnificat and Benedictus.'
On the Prayer of Nabonidus: MEYER, *Das Gebet des Nabonid.*
On the Prayer of Manasseh: OSSWALD, 'Gebet Manasses.'
On the Psalms Scroll and the Syriac Psalms: SANDERS, *Psalms Scroll;* VAN DER WOUDE, *Die fünf Syrischen Psalmen*; BAARS, 'Apocryphal Psalms'.
On Apotropaic Prayers: FLUSSER, 'Apotropaic Prayers.'
On Psalms of Solomon: HOLM-NIELSEN, *Die Psalmen Salomos.*
On Relationship to rabbinic Prayers: ELBOGEN, 'Der jüdische Gottesdienst'; HEINEMANN, *Prayer in the Talmud;* PINES, 'From Darkness into Great Light'; FLUSSER, 'Some Notes on Easter'; *id.,* 'Sanktus und Gloria'.
When prayers are parts of documents treated elsewhere in this volume, see the corresponding bibliographies.

---

[106] Cf. Heinemann, *Prayer*, index s.v. Oral composition.
[107] See the incident with R. Yishmael and the rule cited in connection with it, *T. Shabbath* 13:4; *P.T. Shabbath* 16, 15c; *B.T. Shabbath* 115b. The synagogal liturgical texts will be discussed in the volume on rabbinic literature.

Chapter Fourteen

Epistolary Literature

P. S. Alexander

The aim of the present study is to consider the form and function of the letter in the context of Jewish literary activity in the period c. 200 B.C.E. — c. 200 CÏE. Our first task is to collect all the surviving letters and to establish a corpus of texts o which to base our analysis.

The Corpus

The evidence may be conveniently surveyed as follows:

Manuscript Letters. Around 28 letters (some very fragmentary) in Hebrew, Aramaic and Greek were found at Murabbaat, Nahal Hever and Masada in the Judaean Desert. One letter is an ostracon, one is written on wood, the rest are on papyrus. The two Masada texts are pre-73 C.E., the others all belong to the period of the Bar Kokhba War (132-135 C.E.), and even include dispatches from Bar Kokhba himself.[1]

1 Maccabees quotes 11 letters. These fall into three rough groups: first,

---

[1] The Murabbaat texts were edited by Milik, in *DJD* 2. The letters, which are designated Mur 42-52, are all in Hebrew. Mur 49-52 are extremely fragmentary. For the Naḥal Ḥever letters see Yadin, 'Expedition D', 40-50; Lifshitz, 'Papyrus grecs', 240-58. Further, Kutscher, 'Language of Hebrew and Aramaic Letters'; Fitzmyer — Harrington, *Manual*, 158-162, 214-216. The sigla for the Naḥal Ḥever letters are as follows: 5/6 Ḥev 1 (Aramaic; on wood); 5/6 Ḥev 2 (Aramaic; a palimpsest); 5/6 Ḥev 3 (Greek; from Soumaios: edited by Lifshitz); 5/6 Ḥev 4 (Aramaic; a palimpsest); 5/6 Ḥev 5 (Hebrew); 5/6 Ḥev 6 (Greek; from Annanos: edited by Lifshitz); 5/6 Ḥev 7 (Hebrew); 5/6 Ḥev 8 (Aramaic); 5/6 Ḥev 9 (? Hebrew); 5/6 Ḥev 10 (Aramaic); 5/6 Ḥev 11 (Aramaic); 5/6 Ḥev 12 (Hebrew); 5/6 Ḥev 13 (? Hebrew); 5/6 Ḥev 14 (Aramaic); 5/6 Ḥev 15 (Aramaic). For the two Masada texts — papMas Ep gr and MasOstr (Aramaic) — see Yadin, 'Excavation of Masada', 110-111. For an unpublished Hebrew letter from Shimon b. Mattatyah to Shimon b. Kosibah (? discovered at Naḥal Ṣe'elim), see Milik, 'Travail d'Edition', 21. Fitzmyer, 'Aramaic Epistolography', 224, suggests that the fragmentary ostracon Mur 72 may be a letter, or a message of some kind, but this seems highly unlikely. Some of the numerous Greek papyrus letters from Egypt were presumably written by Jews, but they are hard to identify; see, however, Tcherikover — Fuks — Stern, *Corpus*, nos. 4, 5, 12, 13, 128, 141, 424, 469. The early letters from Elephantini (in Aramaic) and from Arad and Lachish (in Hebrew) lie outside our time limits. They are, however, very important for comparative purposes. On them see the bibliography, especially Fitzmyer, 'Aramaic Epistolography'; Pardee, 'Hebrew Epistolography'; *id., Handbook*.

letters sent by Jews either to other Jews or to Gentiles (e.g. 12:6-18, Jonathan's letter to the Spartans seeking an alliance); second, letters from various Seleucid kings to the Jews (e.g. 10:18-20, Alexander Balas' letter to Jonathan appointing him High Priest); third, letters from other foreign rulers to the Jews (e.g. 15:16-21, the encyclical of the Roman consul Lucius announcing a treaty of friendship between the Romans and the Jews).[2]

2 Maccabees contains 3 letters from Antiochus Epiphanes, one from Lysias, and one from the Roman ambassadors Quintus Memmius and Titus Manius. The work is prefaced by two important letters from the Jewish authorities in Jerusalem relating to the celebration of the festival of Hanukkah.[3]

3 Maccabees has 2 letters ascribed to Ptolemy IV Philopator (221-204 B.C.E.), both addressed to his generals.[4]

In his extensive writings *Josephus* cites some 37 letters both from Jews and non-Jews. 13 of these are derived from the Bible, or from texts already known to us (such as *Aristeas* and 1 Maccabees). These duplicates are not without interest since they provide us with evidence of how Josephus used his sources. The remaining letters are taken from literary works no longer extant, or from archives which Josephus explored for himself.[5]

A fragment of the Jewish historian *Eupolemus,* preserved in Eusebius' *Praeparatio Evangelica,* contains 4 letters which are supposed to have passed between Solomon, Hiram and Pharaoh.[6]

The *Epistle of Aristeas* quotes a letter from Ptolemy II Philadelphus (285-246 B.C.E.) to Eleazar the Jewish high priest, with Eleazar's reply.[7] Despite its title, *Aristeas* itself is not a letter: it is not in epistolary form, nor was it recognized as a letter by the earliest writers who refer to it.[8] The *Greek Esther* contains 2 decrees of Artaxerxes in epistolary form.[9] *Daniel*

---

[2] The following are the letters cited in 1 Maccabees: *Group 1:* 5:10-13; 12:6-18. *Group 2:* 10:18-20; 10:25-45; 11:30-37; 11:57; 13:36-40; 15:2-9. *Group 3:* 12:20-23; 14:20-22; 15:16-21.

[3] From Antiochus: 2 Macc 9:19-27; 11:23-26; 11:27-33. From Lysias: 2 Macc 11:17-21. From Quintus Memmius and Titus Manius: 2 Macc 11:34-38. The Hanukkah letters: 2 Macc 1:1-10; 1:10-2:18.

[4] 3 Macc 3:12-29; 7:1-9.

[5] Letters quoted in Josephus: *Ant.* 8:50-52; 8:53-54; 11:12-17; 11:22-25 (= 1 Esdr 2:16-24; Ezra 4:7-16); 11:104 (cf. 1 Esdr 6:34; Ezra 6:12); 11:118-119 (cf. 1 Esdr 6:27-31; 6:6-10); 11:123-130 (= 1 Esdr 8:9-24; Ezra 7:11-24); 11:273-283 (= Greek Esther Addition E); 12:36-39 (*Ep. Arist.* 28-32); 12:45-50 (*Ep. Arist.* 35-40); 12:51-56 (*Ep. Arist.* 41-46); 12:138-144; 12:148-152; 12:226-227 (= 1 Macc 12:20-23); 12:258-261; 12:262-263; 13:45 (= 1 Macc 10:18-20); 13:48-57 (= 1 Macc 10:25-45); 13:65-68; 13:70-71; 13:126-128 (= 1 Macc 11:30-37); 13:166-170 (= 1 Macc 12:6-18); 14:225-227; 14:241-243; 14:244-246; 17:134-135; 17:137; 17:139; 18:304; 20:10-14. *Life* 217-218; 226-227; 229; 235; 365; 366. *War* 1:643.

[6] Eusebius, *Praeparatio Evangelica* 9:31-34 (= Jacoby, *Fragmente* 723 F2).

[7] Ptolemy to Eleazar: *Ep. Arist.* 35-40; Eleazar's reply: *Ep. Arist.* 41-46.

[8] Josephus, *Ant.* 12:100 calls it a βιβλίον, Epiphanius, *De Mensuris et Ponderibus* 9, a σύνταγμα. Eusebius, *Praeparatio Evangelica* 9:38 gives it the title, Περὶ τῆς Ἑρμηνείας τοῦ τῶν Ἰουδαίων Νόμου. On the literary genre of *Aristeas* see further above, p. 78.

[9] Addition B 1-7 (= 3:13a-g), and Addition E 1-24 (= 8:12a-x). The Aramaic letter in *Targum*

quotes two Aramaic royal encyclicals, one attributed to Darius, the other to Nebuchadnezzar.[10]

The end of the *Syriac Apocalypse of Baruch* claims to give the text of a 'letter which Baruch son of Neriah sent to the nine and a half tribes which are across the river Euphrates.'[11]

The Greek *Paralipomena Ieremiae* contains a letter allegedly sent by Baruch to Jeremiah, along with Jeremiah's reply.[12]

Certain of the Pseudepigrapha were referred to as 'letters' in antiquity, though they are not in epistolary form. This was true of the Epistle of Jeremiah, 1 Baruch, and the 'Epistle of Enoch'.[13]

Rabbinic Texts. Several letters and fragments of letters have been preserved in rabbinic literature: 3 Aramaic letters attributed to Rabban Gamaliel;[14] 2 Hebrew letters supposedly sent jointly by Rabban Shimon b. Gamaliel and Yohanan b. Zakkai (both of whom flourished at the time of the First Jewish War against Rome, 66-74 C.E.);[15] a Hebrew letter from the Jews of Jerusalem to the Jews of Alexandria requesting the return of Judah b. Tabbai (first half of first century B.C.E.) to become Nasi;[16] the opening of

---

Sheni to Est 8:13 (Lagarde, p. 265, 30ff) has many similarities to Greek Addition E and is probably ultimately derived from it. For a late rendering of Addition E into Hebrew see Jellinek, *Beth haMidrasch* 5, 14-15.

[10] Nebuchadnezzar: Dan 3:31-4:33 (= English text 4:1-37); Darius: Dan 6:26-27.

[11] *2 Baruch* 78-87.

[12] Baruch to Jeremiah: *Paralipomena Ieremiae* 6:17-23; Jeremiah's reply: 7:23-29.

[13] The Epistle of Jeremiah opens: 'A copy of an epistle which Jeremiah sent to those who were to be led captives into Babylon.' 1 Baruch is entitled in certain text-witnesses: 'The Epistle of Baruch', or 'The Second Epistle of Baruch'. Certain Greek texts refer to *1 Enoch* 91-108 as 'The Epistle of Enoch' (cf. *1 Enoch* 100:6 in Greek); see Milik, *Books of Enoch*, 47. According to the colophon of the Greek Esther the whole of that book is a letter. We noted earlier the tradition that *Aristeas* is a letter, though it is not in letter form (see note 8 above). Note further the traditional New Testament classification of 'To the Hebrews' as a letter, though it does not have a normal epistolary opening; see Kümmel, *Introduction*, sect. 25.2.

[14] *P.T. Sanhedrin* 18d; *P.T. Maaser Sheni* 56c; *T. Sanhedrin* 2:6; *B.T. Sanhedrin* 11a. Cf. Dalman, *Aramäische Dialektproben*, 3. From the reference to his deposition in *B.T. Sanhedrin* 11a it appears that the Babli took Gamaliel here to be Gamaliel II who flourished 90-110 (cf. *B.T. Berakhoth* 27b-28a for the story of his deposition). However the accuracy of attribution of these letters must be in grave doubt. The first two of them are closely parallel to the two Hebrew letters attributed jointly to Shimon ben Gamaliel and Yohanan ben Zakkai in *Midrash Tannaim* (see note 15 below). The third is parallel to an Aramaic letter attributed to Shimon b. Gamaliel in *B.T. Sanhedrin* 11a. Whether or not the attributions are accurate, letters such as these were undoubtedly sent out by the religious authorities in Jerusalem, and it is very probable that the letters before us accurately reflect those letters' general formulae and style. Note further the reference in *P.T. Megillah* 71a, 6-9 to the two letters found by Mar Uqba.

[15] *Midrash Tannaim* to Deut 26:23 (2 p. 176). See n. 14 above.

[16] *P.T. Hagigah* 77d. The historical background and the text of this letter are very uncertain. *P.T. Sanhedrin* 23c tells more or less the same story as *P.T. Hagigah* 77d, but in *B.T. Sanhedrin* 107b (a passage cut by the censor), and in *B.T. Sotah* 47a, what appears to be the same letter is said to have been sent by Shimon ben Shetah to Joshua ben Perahiah (both contemporaries of Judah b. Tabbai).

a letter from Judah ha-Nasi (died c. 220 C.E.) to the Emperor Antoninus;[17] a reference to a letter from Judah ha-Nasi to R. Hananiah the nephew of R. Joshua which apparently began, 'To the holiness of Hananiah'.[18]

The *New Testament*. For the sake of completeness we should note here the New Testament letters, though they will not figure much in the ensuing discussion. These may be divided into three groups: the 14 letters by or attributed to Paul, the 7 so-called 'Catholic Epistles', the letters to the seven churches of Asia Minor contained in Revelation, and the two letters quoted in Acts.[19]

If we exclude the New Testament epistles and the duplicates in Josephus, then our corpus of texts numbers around 90 separate items. In no sense is it a unified body of material. It contains letters of diverse and often uncertain date, in very different languages — Hebrew, Aramaic and Greek. It includes both forged and genuine letters, letters written by Jews and by non-Jews, independent letters existing in manuscript and letters quoted in works of literature.

The existing manuscript letters are undoubtedly of primary importance for our purposes, but our analysis would be very thin if it were to be based solely on them: they are too few in number to admit of any substantial conclusions, and they are clearly not entirely representative of the uses to which Jews put letter-form at the turn of the eras. So we must bring in the other evidence as well, with all the problems it entails. Though some letters are almost certainly forgeries, or obviously pseudepigraphic, we have included them in our list, simply because it is not practicable at this stage to become involved in detailed decisions as to authenticity. Besides, even non-genuine letters, if properly handled, can be made to testify to the uses of letter-form, or to epistolary conventions. Reluctance to pre-empt the question of authenticity also dictates the inclusion of the letters by non-Jews. We must base our corpus on the broadest possible criteria. Some of these letters could be Jewish forgeries, and the simple fact that they are quoted in Jewish sources is sufficient to qualify them for admission to the body of evidence.

We must recognize that we face serious problems over using many of the letters which we have collected to illustrate the purely formal aspects of the letter. First, we must reckon with the fact that we do not always have the letters in their original languages. 2 Macc 1:1-10 was originally written in Hebrew or Aramaic, but only a Greek version survives. The Greek corre-

---

[17] *Genesis Rabba* 75, 5 (p. 883). MSS. Vatican 30 and 60 read: מן יהודה עבדך למרן למרן מלכא אנטונינוס, 'From Judah your servant, to our Lord, King Antoninus'. See further Kutscher in Rosenthal, *Aramaic Handbook* I/1, 64.

[18] *P.T. Sanhedrin* 19a; *P.T. Nedarim* 40a לקדושת חנניה . The parallel in *B.T. Berakhoth* 63a does not mention a letter.

[19] Letters to the Seven Churches in Asia: Rev 2-3. Letters in Acts: Acts 15:23-29; 23:25-30.

spondence of 1 Maccabees (assuming it is all genuine) has undergone a two-way process of translation — from Greek into Hebrew (when it was incorporated into the original 1 Maccabees), and then from Hebrew back into Greek (when the lost original of 1 Maccabees, was put into Greek). In this process of translation formulae can easily be replaced or distorted.[20] Second, in the case of letters quoted in narrative works, we cannot always be sure that the author has cited the text verbatim: he may only have given the gist of it, or the part relevant to his account, or he may have rewritten or interpolated it. Finally, it may be difficult to determine what was the opening of a quoted letter because all or part of the opening formula has been absorbed into the narrative framework. This is the case, for example, with the letters from Rabban Gamaliel quoted in *P.T. Sanhedrin* 18d (see below).

Types of Letters

The corpus of our letters falls into two groups which may be broadly termed literary and non-literary.[21] In literary letters epistolary form is used as a means of communicating moral, philosophical or religious ideas. No matter who are the named addressees, such letters are aimed at a wide readership. Non-literary letters, on the other hand, have a more specific, everyday purpose: they issue orders, make requests, assure friends of one's health and so on, and they are normally meant for a very limited and precise audience. The bulk of the non-literary letters in the corpus are official: they have been issued by people in various positions of authority — Bar Kokhba, Demetrius I and other Seleucid monarchs, Roman consuls and ambassadors. We can classify the first letter in 2 Macc 1:1-10 here, since it is an encyclical issued by the religious authorities in Jerusalem to remind Jews to celebrate the festival of Hanukkah. The authorities in Jerusalem attempted to maintain a spiritual hegemony over the diaspora by keeping firmly in their control the determination of the religious calendar. They may have issued letters like this regularly. The letters of Gamaliel were supposedly written in his capacity as Nasi.[22] We have also diplomatic correspondence between independent states (see e.g. 1 Macc

---

[20] Note how the Aramaic letter-opening in Ezra 5:7, לדריוש מלכא שלמא כלא, is rendered literally in 2 Esdr 5:7, Δαρείῳ τῷ βασιλεῖ εἰρήνη πᾶσα, but freely, using the Greek form of greeting, in 1 Esdr 6:7, Βασιλεῖ Δαρείῳ χαίρειν.

[21] Cf. Deissmann's famous distinction between a 'letter' (non-literary) and an 'epistle' (literary): *Light from the East*, 227-30. Deissmann's view has been much criticized: see Doty, 'Classification', 183-99; Doty, *Letters*, 24-27. However, for our comparatively undifferentiated corpus the simple distinction between literary and non-literary is adequate.

[22] The apostolic decree in Acts 15:23-29, which is in the form of a letter, should be read in the light of the Gamaliel letters and the Hanukkah letters in 2 Maccabees. It shows the Jerusalem Church playing a similar role to that of the Jewish religious authorities in Jerusalem.

14:20-22; 15:16-21). However, there are only a few examples of private or familiar letters in the corpus.[23]

The letter's original function was as a means of non-literary communication. How, then, did it become a vehicle for the exposition of religious ideas? The literary letter was an old, well-established genre in Greek,[24] so it is possible that there was Hellenistic influence on the development of literary letters among the Jews. On the other hand, the Jewish literary letter may have emerged as the result of an internal development within Jewish literary history. The literary letter could have grown out of the sermon: it may have been regarded as the written analogue of the sermon. That this was the case is strongly suggested by Baruch's letter in the *Syriac Apocalypse of Baruch*. This letter was basically conceived of as a sermon or exhortatory address. Note, among other features, how the author closes it with the injunction that it be read out publicly in the congregations of the exiles (86:1).[25] It was a substitute for an address by the author in person. A sermon, however, was fundamentally an oral means of communication, so when the author wished to put one into writing he was faced with the problem of the form in which to cast it. He found to hand in the letter a long-established mode of writing which allowed him to address his readers in the second person (78:5; 82:1; 83:4; 84:1; 86:1) and to use the hortatory 'we' (82:3-9; 83:4; 84:11), and which contained in its opening conventions a simple means for giving his work a setting. As an alternative the author could, perhaps, have employed the testament form, such as we find in the *Testaments of the Twelve Patriarchs*, which also allows direct address to the readers. It is interesting to note that Baruch's letter is, in fact, represented as his last will and testament (78:5; 84: 1).[26]

---

[23] See Josephus, *Life* 217-218; 226-227; 229; 235; 263.

[24] Note, e.g. the letters of Plato, Isocrates and Epicurus.

[25] New Testament letters such as Romans could be described fundamentally as sermons in the form of letters. Col 4:16 and 1 Thess 5:27 speak of reading letters to the assembled church. It is possible that the letters to the churches in Rev 2-3 were also intended for public reading.

[26] On the testament form see above, p. 325f. Like the letter of Baruch, the Epistle of Jeremiah has also certain sermonic characteristics. However, its literary form is much more problematic. The superscription speaks of a letter, yet the work is not in any obvious epistolary form. It is tempting to dismiss the superscription as simply mistaken, but two points should be borne in mind: (1) if the superscription is removed the work is bereft of any setting and becomes an incomplete fragment; (2) it is wrong to be too dogmatic as to what constitutes letter-form in a pseudepigraph. The superscription may, in fact, be intended as the opening of the letter; it is just possible that this is how the author thought Jeremiah would have written. Though Eupolemos was happy to have Solomon, Hiram and Pharaoh corresponding in the Greek conventions of his own day, other writers of pseudepigraphic letters apparently aimed at greater verisimilitude and a more antique style. Thus the letter of Baruch lifts a formula out of Jer 29:4 (*Syr. Apoc. Baruch* 78:2), and Jeremiah's letters to Baruch in *Paralipomena Ieremiae* 7:23-29 use the ancient didactic formula, 'My son'. Baruch's reply (6:17-23) begins, 'Baruch, the servant of God, writes to Jeremiah', while Artaxerxes' encyclical in Greek Esther Addition

The Problem of Authenticity

The papyrus letters from Judaea are unquestionably genuine. The Epistle of Jeremiah, the letters in the *Syriac Apocalypse of Baruch, Paralipomena Ieremiae,* and the Greek Additions to Esther, as well as the correspondence between Solomon, Hiram and Pharaoh in Eupolemos and Josephus (*Ant.* 8:50-54; cf. *Ag. Ap.* 1:111), are just as certainly fabrications. As to the authenticity of the remaining letters in the corpus, especially those in 1 and 2 Maccabees and Josephus, *Ant.* 12-14, the situation is far from clear. Some of them cause grave misgivings, but it seems well nigh impossible to produce an argument which will prove conclusively that any of them are not authentic.

Two tests of authenticity have been applied. First, the letters have been examined minutely for inappropriate epistolary formulae. The study of the large body of Greek papyri from Egypt indicates that the conventions of Greek letters changed over the years, and that certain formulae were in vogue only at certain periods of time. Thus the opening expression χαίρειν καὶ ἐρρῶσθαι apparently emerged first in the late Ptolemaic period: the earliest instances of it are dated to around 160 B.C.E. The opening formula χαίρειν καὶ ὑγιαίνειν comes into vogue about one hundred years later and is first attested in a papyrus of 57/56 B.C.E.[27] Now, it could be argued that the presence of χαίρειν καὶ ἐρρῶσθαι in the two letters of Ptolemy IV Philopator (221-204 B.C.E.) in 3 Macc 3:12 and 7:1, and even more so in the letter

B opens, 'The great king Artaxerxes to the princes ... these things writes'. Both these are unusual letter-openings, and may have been chosen to give the letters a stilted, antique ring. However, having given all these points their proper weight, it must be conceded in the end that letter-form does not enter deeply into the Epistle of Jeremiah: the work barely sustains even the second person address to the readers; after the opening verses (1-7) the second person is confined to the refrain, 'Whereby they are known not to be gods: therefore fear them not' (17, 23, 29, 65; cf. 69). So why was the term 'letter' used? It is possible that the author referred to his work as a letter not because of its literary form, but as a way of attaching it convincingly to the biblical tradition. He drew heavily on the denunciation of idols in Jer 10:1-6, and since Jeremiah was known to have corresponded with the exiles in Babylon (see Jer 29:1ff, where a letter from him — not on the subject of idolatry — is quoted), it occured to him to pass off his own composition as another letter of Jeremiah to the Babylonian Jews. It is interesting to note that *Targum Jonathan* contains a tradition that Jer 10:11 alludes to a letter from Jeremiah 'to the remnant of the captives of the Babylonian exile' in which he denounces idols. The verse runs in the Biblical text: 'Thus shall you (pl.) say to them: The gods who did not make the heavens and the earth shall perish from the earth and from under the heavens'. The Targumic tradition was meant to solve several problems posed by this verse: (1) Why is it in Aramaic, when the rest of the chapter is in Hebrew? (2) Who is addressed in the pronoun 'you'? It cannot be Jeremiah since the pronoun is plural. (3) Who is referred to by 'them'? The Targumic solution was ingenious and simple: the verse is a quotation from one of Jeremiah's letters. If this tradition is old, it might well have provided the inspiration for the Epistle of Jeremiah.

[27] For χαίρειν καὶ ἐρρῶσθαι, see Exler, *Form,* 32, 60, 64; for χαίρειν καὶ ὑγιαίνειν, see Exler, *Form,* 32, 46, with the correction of Chan-Hie Kim, *The Familiar Letter,* 15. Exler's cautious remarks (*Form,* 106-107) on the development of these two formulae should be carefully noted.

of Ptolemy II Philadelphus (285-246 B.C.E.) in *Ep. Arist.* 35-40, is decidedly suspicious. So, too, if χαίρειν καὶ ὑγιαίνειν first emerged in the mid-first century B.C.E., then its use in the letter of Antiochus Epiphanes in 2 Macc 9:19-27 might cast doubt on that letter's authenticity. However, this line of argument must lack the power of final conviction, simply because it is always at the mercy of some chance find which may upset the established chronology as to the currency of the formulae. Moreover, we must be especially careful in using this approach on translated letters. For example, it would clearly be dangerous to impugn the claim of the second Hanukkah letter (2 Macc 1:18) on the grounds that it contains the formula χαίρειν καὶ ὑγιαίνειν for if, as has been suggested, the extant Greek text is a translation of a lost Hebrew or Aramaic original, then the formula would only point to the date of the translation, not that of the original. As we noted earlier, epistolary conventions can become distorted in translation. Rather than render Semitic formulae literally, a translator may simply substitute the corresponding Greek formulae of his own day.[28]

Second, the letters can be examined for historical inaccuracy. The second Hanukkah letter once again illustrates this approach. It states (1:14-18) that Antiochus Epiphanes died *before* the rededication of the Temple. This agrees with the account in 2 Macc 9-10, but contradicts 1 Macc 4-6, which puts Antiochus' death *after* the rededication. Most scholars accept the chronology of 1 Maccabees at this point.[29] But it follows, then, that the letter is guilty of a gross historical error, which would be unlikely in an official document written so close to the events. This seems to be a convincing case. Nevertheless, we must still use caution. The categories 'genuine' and 'false' cannot be defined in any absolute way. We must allow for gradations between them. Thus it would be possible for an author to take a genuine document and rewrite it, or interpolate it, or adapt it in order to make it fit his purpose or his theme. It is also possible that a perfectly genuine document could have been corrupted accidently in copying. In either case the result would be a text containing both what is 'genuine' and what is 'false'. In view of the possibly mixed character of some of our letters it is premature to condemn a whole document as false on the basis of one false element detected in it.[30]

Given that some of the letters are not genuine, what could have been the motivation for forging them?[31] There are two rather different cases to be

---

[28] Cf. n. 20 above.

[29] See Schürer, *History* 1, 161 note 61.

[30] Normally scholars do not rely on a single argument to prove a document not genuine. The letters in *Aristeas* and 3 Maccabees would fall by the arguments which impugn the historical reliability of the works as a whole.

[31] The motives for forging letters are basically no different from those for forging other documents. In general see, Speyer, *Die literarische Fälschung,* and Brox, *Falsche Verfasserangaben.*

considered here: first, that of the single, independent forgery; and second, that of the forged letter incorporated into a narrative text. The second case naturally raises the further question of why narrative writers cited whole letters in their works. This question is important in its own right, whether or not the documents involved are genuine, but it has also a bearing on the question of authenticity, in that the motives for including whole documents could also be motives for forging them. An author may incorporate an entire document in his narrative for a variety of reasons. (1) He may be following a certain literary model, or source. The Chronicler (who was at work towards the end of the fourth century B.C.E.) took over intact from his Ezra-source a number of letters, and somewhat later Daniel and the Greek Esther also include letters. These early texts may have established a precedent. 1 and 2 Maccabees could be following this tradition. (2) Documents may be quoted to impart to a text 'the ring of truth', to persuade the reader that the account offered to him is reliable. 'Archaeologists' such as Josephus, Berossus and Manetho had a concern for documentation. This was partly due to the fact that they were interested in the distant past and so had to rely on written sources (rather than on eyewitness accounts),[32] and partly related to their apologetic aims. All were concerned with nationalistic propaganda and so strove to be persuasive. Josephus, for example, assembled the documents in *Ant.* 14 with the aim of making public 'all the honours given to our nation and the alliances made with them by the Romans and their emperors, in order that the other nations may not fail to recognize that both the kings of Asia and of Europe have held us in high esteem and admired our bravery and loyalty' (*Ant.* 14:186). (3) Finally, letters may be included in a text for purely literary reasons: like speeches and dialogue they can be used to vary the pace and texture of a narrative. In the Greek Esther the two letters from Artaxerxes serve to clarify the dramatic structure of the work by emphasizing the theme of the Jewish reversal of fortunes. The two letters from Ptolemy Philopator in 3 Maccabees are used to similar effect.

Among the independent forged letters we must include not only the Epistle of Jeremiah or the 'Letter of Baruch' (which, though now attached to the end of the *Syriac Apocalypse of Baruch,* was apparently meant to circulate separately: see 78:1 and 86:1-87:1), but also a number of the fabrications now contained in narrative texts, since it would be wrong to assume that every forgery which may be detected in, say, 1 Maccabees was invented by the author of that work. Some of the forgeries may have existed already as independent documents and may have been taken over in all good faith. It would be possible even for official archives to contain false documents. Among the letters which had, or may have had, an independent existence we can distinguish two main groups. First, there are

---

[32] See further Momigliano, *Historiography,* 211-217.

those like the Epistle of Jeremiah and *Syr. Apoc. Baruch* 78-87 which contain religious teaching and are attributed to important religious authorities in the distant past. The motive here is obvious: the author hopes to gain a readier ear for his ideas by putting them forward in the name of a respected sage, rather than in his own name. Second, there are letters ascribed to persons of political power (Seleucid kings, Roman consuls and so forth) in the more recent past. These texts normally grant privileges, make concessions, or express friendship to the recipients. It is not hard to imagine that such texts could have been fabricated with an eye to tangible, political advantage. At least some of the letters in favour of the Jews cited by Josephus in *Ant.* 12-14 belong to this category. As Josephus himself hints (*Ant.* 14:187), the authenticity of these documents had already been questioned in antiquity.

Analysis of the Bar-Kokhba and Masada Letters

The following three papyrus letters, all found in Judaea and dating to the period of the Bar Kokhba War (132-135), will serve to illustrate the general style of Jewish letters in the early second century C.E. They are in Hebrew, Aramaic and Greek, respectively.

> From the administrators of Beth Mashikho, from Yeshua and from Eleazar,/to Yeshua ben Galgula, Chief of the Camp, peace! Be it known/to you that the cow which Joseph ben Ariston took from Jacob/ben Judah, who dwells in Beth Mashikho, belongs to him by purchase. (5) Were it not for the fact that the Gentiles are close to us, I would have gone up/and satisfied you about this — lest you should say that it is out of contempt/that I have not come up to you. Peace be (to you) and to all the House of Israel!/Yeshua ben Eleazar has written it./Eleazar ben Joseph has written it. (10) Jacob ben Judah, for himself./Saul ben Eleazar, witness./Joseph bar Joseph, witness./Jacob ben Joseph testifies.[33]

> Shimon to Judah bar Manasseh, to Qiryat Arabayah. I have sent to you two asses, so that you may send/with them two men to Jonathan bar Baayan and Masabalah, that they may gather/and send to the camp, to you, palm-branches and citrons. And you, send others from

---

[33] Mur 42 (Hebrew). See Milik, *DJD* 2, 156, with plate XLV. Further, Yadin, *Bar Kokhba*, 134-6. The translation given above tries to reproduce faithfully the ambiguities of the original. The precise circumstances of the letter are far from clear. As Milik rightly notes, the document is, in fact, mixed in form: it is in part a certificate of purchase, and in part a letter. On the sense of כתבה in lines 8-9, see note 48 below.

your place/to bring you myrtles and willows. Prepare them and send them to the camp . . . (5) . . . Be well![34]

Sou[mai]os to Jonathes/(son of) Baianos and to Ma/[s]abala, greet-ing!/S[i]nce I have sent to (5) you A[g]rippa, make/h[ast]e to send me/s[ha]ft[s] and citrons,/and furnish th[em]/for the [C]itron-celebration of the (10) Jews: and do not do/otherwise. No[w] (this) has been writ/ten in Greek because/an [imp]ulse has not be[en]/found to w[ri]te (15) in Hebrew. Di[s]patch/him speedily/on accoun[t of t]he feast,/an[d do no]t do other/wise. (20) Soumaios./Farewell![35]

Out of our whole corpus only the Bar Kokhba and Masada letters provide first-rate evidence for the analysis of epistolary practice since they alone exist in their physically original form. Though they are in three languages these letters may be treated as a group, since they exhibit very much the same forms and conventions throughout. The typical letter falls into three parts: (a) an opening; (b) a body; and (c) a close. These are not simply convenient heads under which to discuss the various features of the letter; they indicate real structural elements. Ancient letter-writers recognized these divisions and employed various devices to demarcate them, and an analysis of the letter in terms of information theory also clearly indicates the existence of these three parts. The beginning and the ending of the letters are highly stereotyped: they are largely predictable and carry a light information load. The middle of the letter, on the other hand, is much less formalized: it contains the substance of the communication and is as varied as the messages people wish to convey.

The opening normally contains two elements occuring in the following order: (1) a parties' formula which states the names of the sender and of the recipient; and (2) a salutation. In the Aramaic and Greek letters the parties' formula is, 'X (the sender) to Y (the recipient)'.[36] In the Hebrew letters, on the other hand, it is 'From X to Y'.[37] It is striking that there should be this difference between the Aramaic and the Hebrew letters, given that both emanated from the same narrow circle at the same period of time. It could

[34] 5/6 Ḥev 15 (Aramaic). See Kutscher, 'Language of Hebrew and Aramaic Letters', 129-33. Further, Yadin, *Bar Kokhba*, 128-30. Yadin appears to read the difficult words at the end of line four and beginning of line five as: בדיל די אכלסה סגי , '(the request is made) since the army is big'.

[35] 5/6 Ḥev 3 (Greek). See Lifshitz, 'Papyrus grecs', 240-8. Further, Yadin, *Bar Kokhba*, 130. Lifshitz's restoration of line 13, τ[ὸ ὁρ]μᾶν, is very uncertain.

[36] E.g. 5/6 Ḥev 8: שמעון בר כוסבה ליהונתן בר בעין , 'Shimon bar Kosiba to Jonathan bar Baayan'; 5/6 Ḥev 3: Σου[μαῖ]ος Ἰωνάθηι Βαϊανου καὶ Μα[σ]άβαλα, 'Soumaios to Jonathes son of Baianos and to Masabala'.

[37] E. g. Mur 43: מן שמעון בר כוסבה לישע בן גלגלה , 'From Shimon ben Kosibah to Yeshua ben Galgulah'.

well reflect a genuine and strictly observed variation in epistolary practice. The parties' formula normally gives only the bare names of the sender and the recipient, but in the Aramaic letter 5/6 Ḥev 1 a title is attached to the name of the sender: 'Shimon bar Kosibah President over Israel, to Jonathan and Masabalah'; and in 5/6 Ḥev 6 (Greek) a defining epithet follows the name of the recipient: 'Annanos to Jonathes, the brother'.[38] The salutation is brief and mirrors the spoken greeting: in Aramaic it is שלם, in Hebrew שלום, and in Greek χαίρειν.[39] From the fact that Aramaic letters 5/6 Ḥev 8 and 15 do not have a salutation we may deduce that it was not regarded as obligatory. However, it is not clear under what circumstances it could be omitted. 5/6 Ḥev 4 (Aramaic) has a curious opening: 'A letter of Shimon bar Kosibah. Greetings to Jonathan bar Baayah'. 5/6 Ḥev 15 (Aramaic) introduces a third element into the opening, viz., an indication of the destination in the form of a prepositional phrase following the name of the recipient: 'Shimon to Judah bar Manasseh, to Qiryat Arabaya'.[39a]

Transition from the opening to the body of the letter is marked in several of the Aramaic texts by the particle ד / די . This is *di recitativum* and indicates the beginning of direct speech. The opening of the letter is implicitly in the third person, whereas the body is addressed directly to the recipient in the second. In two Hebrew letters the particle *she-* serves the same purpose.[40]

The close of the letter comprises two elements: (1) a wish for the wellbeing of the recipient (what is called the *formula valetudinis* in the analysis of Greek letters[41]), and (2) a signature. Some letters do not have a formal

---

[38] 'Brother' is used as address between social equals in the Aramaic letters of the Persian period: see e.g. Cowley, *Aramaic Papyri,* no 20 lines 1 and 11; further Fitzmyer, 'Padua Aramaic Papyrus Letters', 17. It seems, however, that the term means something more here: like the early Christians, the followers of Bar Kokhba were organised as a fellowship and called each other 'brother'; see Lifshitz, 'Greek Documents', 60-61; Lifshitz, 'Papyrus grecs', 256-8.

[39] שלם : 5/6 Ḥev 1 and 10; שלום : Mur 42, 43, 44, 46, 48; 5/6 Ḥev 12; χαίρειν: 5/6 Ḥev 3 and 6. On rabbinic spoken greetings see Billerbeck, *Kommentar,* I, 380-5. The short greeting שלם is found in Ezra 5:7, but normally in Aramaic correspondence of the Persian period a more fulsome salutation is favoured: see e.g. Kraeling, *Brooklyn Museum Aramaic Papyri,* no. 13, 1: [שלם מראי אלהיא ישאלו שגיא בכל עדן , 'The welfare of my lord may all the gods (seek) abundantly at all times'; Bresciani and Kamil, 'Le lettere aramaiche', no. 3, 5: שלם לך וחין שלחת , 'Peace and prosperity I send you': Driver, *Aramaic Documents,* no. 3, 1: שלם ושררת שגיא ושרת לך , 'Much peace and prosperity I send you'.

[39a] It is just possible, however, that לקרית ערביה is to be taken with the following שלחת לך , 'To Qiryat Arabaya I have sent to you . . .'.

[40] ד/די : 5/6 Ḥev 4, 8 and 10; ש' : Mur 42 and 44. For די *recitativum* see Dan 2:25; 5:7: 6:6; 6:14; 1QGenAp 19:20; 20:10; 20:27; 22:22. Cf. the use of ὅτι *recitativum* in Greek, e.g. Luke 1:25; John 1:20; Rom 3:8. See Blass-Debrunner, *Grammar,* sect. 470 (1) and Bauer, *Lexicon,* 593b. ש' introducing *oratio recta* is rare and may have developed by analogy with די *recitativum* in Aramaic. However, אשר is found before *oratio recta* in biblical Hebrew; see Gesenius-Kautzsch, *Hebrew Grammar,* sect. 157c; further Segal, *Mishnaic Hebrew,* sect. 431.

[41] Koskenniemi, *Idee und Phraseologie,* 130-9.

590

close, while some have only one of the elements.[42] When both elements occur together their order is flexible.[43] In several cases the distinction between the body and the close of the letter is indicated by the visual device of separating the elements of the close from the rest of the latter by a space.[44]

In Aramaic the concluding *formula valetudinis* is הוא שלם, and in Hebrew הוה שלום in both cases with an echo of the opening salutation.[45] Mur 42 (Hebrew) has the more elaborate formula, 'Peace be (to you) and to all the House of Israel'.[46] The Greek letters employ the verb ῥώννυμι in the concluding *formula valetudinis:* 5/6 Ḥev 3 has simply ἔρρωσο 'Be well', but 5/6 Ḥev 6, ἔρρωσο ἀδελφέ 'Be well, brother'. The signatures of the Greek letters are those of the senders, and they consist simply of their names.[47] At the end of the Hebrew and Aramaic letters we find the formula, 'So-and-so son of So-and-so כתבה '. It is not entirely clear whether this indicates the name of the scribe or of the sender.[48]

[42] No formal close: 5/6 Ḥev 1 (Aramaic); only a *formula valetudinis:* 5/6 Ḥev 4 (Aramaic); only a signature: 5/6 Ḥev 8 (Aramaic).

[43] In the Greek papyri (5/6 Ḥev 3 and 6) it is signature followed by *formula valetudinis;* so, too, in the Hebrew letter Mur 46; but in the Hebrew letters Mur 42 and 48 the order is reversed.

[44] This feature is clearest in the Greek letters 5/6 Ḥev 3 and 6, but see also Mur 46 (Hebrew).

[45] הוא שלם : 5/6 Ḥev 4, 11, 15; הוה שלום : Mur 46 and 48.

[46] אהוה שלום וכל בית ישראל . This recalls the expression שלום על ישראל , which occurs at the end of Pss 125 and 128, and is reminiscent of Paul's words towards the close of Galatians (6:16), 'Peace and mercy upon all who walk according to this rule, and upon the Israel of God'.

[47] For signatures in the Greek papyri from Egypt, see Turner, *Greek Papyri,* 82-83. Cf. Paul's 'signatures' in 1 Cor 16:21; Col 4:18; 2 Thess 3:17. In a letter written by a professional scribe the signature was a means of authentication. The use of an amanuensis did not necessarily mean that the sender of the letter was illiterate. Paul used an amanuensis (Rom 16:22), as did Rabban Gamaliel, Rabban Shimon b. Gamaliel, Yohanan b. Zakkai and Judah ha-Nasi — all of them well-educated men.

[48] It would be natural to translate the כתבה as, '(So-and-so) has written it (sc. the letter)' or 'was the scribe'. The signature would then be that of the amanuensis and not that of the sender. This interpretation certainly fits 5/6 Ḥev 8 (Aramaic), where the name in the signature is different from that of the parties' formula in the opening. However, it does not fit the Hebrew letters Mur 42 and 46. Two things are noteworthy in the two latter texts: (1) the names in the signatures are *the same* as the names of the senders; and (2) the handwriting of the signatures is *different* from that in the main body of the letter. So in these two cases כתבה cannot have its obvious sense: it must mean something like 'sent it', or 'issued it'. Cf. Milik's translation of כתבה in *DJD* 2, 158; 'l'a (fait) écrire', 'l'a dicté (à un scribe professionel)'. This meaning might be made to fit even in 5/6 Ḥev 8 if the person who signed the letter (Shimon bar Judah) was issuing an order in the name of Shimon bar Kosiba (who is mentioned as sender in the parties' formula). In this case Shimon bar Judah need not have written the letter himself, but may have dictated it to a professional scribe. The problem would obviously be resolved in favour of the latter view, if the signature were in a different hand from the rest of the letter, but we cannot tell this since photographs of the papyrus do not appear to have been published. It is interesting to note that a rather similar problem arises in the Arsham correspondence from the Persian period. Several letters state at the end, 'So-and-so was the scribe', but since a number of letters with the same scribe's name are in different hands, it seems that the scribe was not necessarily the man who penned the letter; see Driver, *Aramaic Documents,* 18-19.

It is interesting that the structure and conventions of the Bar Kohkba letters, whether they be in Hebrew, Aramaic or Greek, are so similar. Too much should not, perhaps, be made of this, since Semitic and Greek letters were in any case basically very similar, and the similarity is heightened in the present instance by the fact that all the letters are simple communications. However, it is not unlikely that in the narrow circle of the followers of Bar Kokhba a common letter-form would have emerged which would have been employed whatever the language of communication. The concluding *formula valetudinis*, 'Be well', in the Hebrew and Aramaic letters is instructive in this respect. There are no precise parallels to this closing imperative in earlier Hebrew-Aramaic epistolography:[49] it probably reflects the very common Greek ending ἔρρωσο/ἔρρωσθε (which we encountered in 5/6 Ḥev 3 and 6). If this is so, then it would appear that the convergence of letter-forms was towards Greek practice.

Analysis of the Remaining Letters

The analysis of the extant manuscript letters puts us in a good position to discuss the remaining letters in the corpus. As we noted earlier, there is a problem over how the Gamaliel letters in *P.T. Sanhedrin* 18d are supposed to open. They are introduced thus in the text: 'It happened once that Rabban Gamaliel and the Elders were sitting on a step on the Temple Mount, and Yohanan the scribe was sitting before them. Rabban Gamaliel said to him: Write to our brethren in the south ... may your peace be multiplied'. The question is, how are we to punctuate here? Dalman would make a break after 'write' and begin the quotation of the letter with, 'To our brethren is the south', but it is equally possible that verbatim quotation is not meant to begin until, 'May your peace be multipied'. If this is so, then, assuming the letter is genuine, the opening formula has been absorbed into the narrative and we cannot tell what it was.[50] Dalman seems under the impression that the letter — whether real or fictitious — could actually have opened, 'To our brethren in the south'. This is problematic on two counts: (1) it results in a defective letter-opening which fails to declare the name of the sender; and (2) none of the nearly contemporary Bar Kokhba letters begins in this way. The analogy of the Bar Kokhba texts

---

[49] Perhaps the nearest we get to it is the formula found in the Hermopolis papyri: לשלמכי שלחת ספרא זנה , 'For your peace/welfare (or, to greet you) I have sent this letter'; see Bresciani and Kamil,'Le lettere aramaiche', nos. 1, 12-13; 2, 17; 3, 13; 5, 9; 6, 10; 7, 4.

[50] A similar problem arises in Ezra 4:17 and 5:7. It is important to note that the issue here is how to punctuate the text of the Talmud. This is a problem whether or not the letters are genuine. Even if they are fictitious it is reasonable to assume that they reflect genuine contemporary epistolary conventions. On the problem of the authenticity of the Gamaliel letters see above note 14.

would suggest an opening, 'Gamaliel (? bar Shimon) . . . to our brethren in the south . . .' It is interesting that the parties' formula 'from X to Y', which we noted earlier as being confined to the Bar Kokhba letters in Hebrew, occurs also in the Hebrew letters from Shimon b. Gamaliel and Yohanan b. Zakkai, and from the Jews in Jerusalem to the Jews in Alexandria. The pattern is, however, broken by the occurrence of 'From X to Y' in the Aramaic letter from Judah ha-Nasi to Antoninus. In the Hebrew letters of Shimon b. Gamaliel and Yohanan b. Zakkai, we find the simple salutation שלום ; the Aramaic Gamaliel letters, however, have שלמכון יסגא 'may your peace be multiplied', probably in imitation of the use of this formula in the letters in Dan 3:31 and 6:20. On two occasions the verb ידע 'to know', serves to mark the transition from the opening to the body of the letter: thus we find in the Gamaliel letters, מהודענא לכון ד' 'I inform you that . . .', and in the letters of Shimon b. Gamaliel and Yohanan b. Zakkai, ידיע יהא לכם ש' 'be it known to you that . . .'. These phrases are stereotyped and largely redundant, but they can function as transition-markers to indicate the divisions of the letter.[51]

The original language of the letter of Baruch in *Syr. Apoc. Baruch* 78-87 was probably Hebrew or Aramaic. The exact wording of its opening and its close is in some doubt. According to one form of the text (Codex Ambrosianus) the opening runs: 'Thus says Baruch the son of Neriah to the brethren carried into captivity: mercy and peace be with you'. The other form of the text (found in all the other manuscripts) shortens the salutation simply to 'mercy and peace'.[52] The parties' formula, 'Thus says X to Y', is not common. It has probably been lifted straight out of the beginning of Jeremiah's letter to the exiles, Jer 29:4, 'Thus says the Lord of hosts, the God of Israel, to all the exiles whom I sent into exile from Jerusalem to Babylon'. The salutation 'Mercy and peace' ܪ̈ܚܡܐ ܘܫܠܡܐ (*raḥme' 'aph shelama'*) is also unusual. A similar expression occurs in Tobit 7:12, though in a non-epistolary context. It recalls the New Testament greeting, 'Grace to you and peace' (1 Thess 1:1; cf. also 1 Tim 1:2). There are two forms of the ending: Codex Ambrosianus, 'And bear me in mind by means of this letter, as I bear you in mind in it, and at all times'; the remaining manuscripts, 'And bear me in mind by means of this letter, as I bear you in mind in it. And at all times fare well'.[53] In the second reading the expression 'at all times' ܒܟܠܙܒܢ (*bekhulzebhan*) recalls the use of בכל עדן in salutations in the Aramaic letters of the Persian period: e.g., 'The welfare of

---

[51] For the use of phrases with ידע as transition-markers see also Mur 42; 5/6 Ḥev 14; Ezra 3:14; 4:12, 15; 5:8. For similar phenomenon in Greek letters see White, *Body of the Greek Letter*, 2-5.

[52] There may be more to this simple change than meets the eye; see Bogaert, *Apocalypse de Baruch*, I, 67-81.

[53] So Bogaert, but we might also translate: '. . . in it and at all times. Fare well.'

my lord may all the gods seek abundantly *at all times'*.[54]

It is reasonably certain that the first of the two Hanukkah letters in 2 Macc 1:1-10 had a Semitic original, though opinion is divided as to whether it was in Hebrew or Aramaic. The opening runs: 'To the brethren, the Jews in Egypt, greeting (χαίρειν). The brethren, the Jews in Jerusalem and in the country of Judaea, good peace (εἰρήνην ἀγάθην)'. The double greeting χαίρειν and εἰρήνην ἀγάθην is unusual: the χαίρειν may be eliminated as a secondary attempt by the translator to conform the letter to Greek usage. When it is removed a parties' formula of the 'To Y, X' type emerges.[55] The balance of epithets, 'brothers ... brothers' is a stylistic trick easily paralleled in Aramaic correspondence of the Persian period.[56] Torrey retroverts εἰρήνην ἀγάθην literally into Aramaic as שלם טב,[57] but such a greeting is unknown: perhaps the nearest we get to it is the שלמא כלא of Ezra 5:7. In the body of the letter we find twice the expression καὶ νῦν (verses 6 and 9); and now' (וכעת, וכען, וכענת) is a common transition-marker in Aramaic letters in the Persian period, and it is also found in Hebrew letter style.[58] The date in verse 10 is to be attached to the end of the first letter and not, as Torrey supposes, to the beginning of the second. In Aramaic letters of the Persian period a date is not common, but when it does occur it is usually at the end of the letter. In one text it was put on the outside of the letter along with the external address.[59]

On balance it is unlikely that the second Hanukkah letter in 2 Macc 1:10-2:28 had a Semitic original, though Torrey confidently offers a retroversion of it into Aramaic. Its parties' formula is of the 'X to Y' type, and its salutations is χαίρειν καὶ ὑγιαίνειν which is good Greek letter-style (see above).[60]

---

[54] See Kraeling, *Brooklyn Museum Aramaic Papyri*, no. 13,1 (note 38 above); Strasbourg Library Ostracon (= *Répertoire d'épigraphie sémitique* no. 1300): שלם אחי בכל עדן, 'Greetings, my brother, at all times'.

[55] This formula is attested e.g. in Cowley, *Aramaic Papyri*, no. 40,1: פלטי אחור אל אחי [ה] הושעי, 'To my brother Piltai, your brother Hoshai (ah)'; Bresciani and Kamil, 'Le lettere aramaiche', no. 3, 1: אל מראי פסמי עבדך מכבנת, 'To my lord Psami, your servant Makkibanit'.

[56] E.g. Bresciani and Kamil, 'Le lettere aramaiche', no. 1, 1: 'To my sister Rayah, from your brother Makkibanit'; see also Cowley, *Aramaic Papyri*, no. 40, 1 (quoted in note 55 above).

[57] Torrey, 'The Letters', 141.

[58] Cowley, *Aramaic Papyri*, nos. 37, 2; 41, 3; 32, 3; cf. Ezra 4:11; 7:12. Further, Fitzmyer, 'Aramaic Epistolography', 216. For 'and now' (ועתה) in a Hebrew letter see 2 Kings 10:2 (LXX καὶ νῦν).

[59] Date at the end of the letter: Cowley, *Aramaic Papyri*, nos. 30, 30; 42, 14; Kraeling, *Brooklyn Museum Aramaic Papyri*, no. 13, 8. Date on the outside: Cowley, *Aramaic Papyri*, no. 26, 28.

[60] Torrey's Aramaic version שלמא והנאה creates a formula unknown in Aramaic letters. If there was an Aramaic original we should perhaps think in terms of a variation of the formula found in one of the Elephantini papyri וחדה ושריר הוי בכל עדן, 'May you be happy and prosperous at all times'; see Cowley, *Aramaic Papyri*, no. 30, 3. Cf. Cowley, *Aramaic Papyri*, no 70, 2: חיא וחדה ושרירא ושריר מראי יהוי ית [יר, 'Living and prosperous may my lord be exceedingly'.

The vast majority of the quoted Greek letters in the corpus conform to the simple type we encountered in the Bar Kokhba Greek papyri (5/6 Ḥev 3 and 6). The opening is 'X to Y χαίρειν' (see e.g. 1 Macc 12:8-18; 13:36-40);[61] and several end with the *formula valetudinis* ἔρρωσο/ἔρρωσθε (see e.g. 2 Macc 11:21; 3 Macc 7:9; *Ep. Arist.* 40). There are, however, two new elements: (1) a number of the letters (all of them in 2 Maccabees; see 11:21, 33, 38) carry the date at the very end; and (2) several of them prolong the opening salutation to include a *formula valetudinis*. This takes the form of a wish for the good health of the recipient, and sometimes conjoined with it an assurance as to the well-being of the sender. The wish for the recipient's health is expressed in two ways: either (a) as an infinitive attached by καὶ to the opening salutation χαίρειν; or (b) as an independent sentence following directly after the χαίρειν. The well-being of the sender is always announced in a separate sentence. In both the wish for the recipient's welfare and the reassurance as to the well-being of the sender the verbs ῥώννυμι and ὑγιαίνω are used. As we noted earlier, this is standard Greek practice.[62]

BIBLIOGRAPHY

Modern study of epistolography began among classical scholars whose interest in the subject had been aroused by the great papyrus finds in Egypt, and it was the classicists who first outlined methods for the analysis of the ancient letter. For a survey of classical work in the field see DZIATZKO, 'Brief'; SYKUTRIS, 'Epistolographie'; and SCHNEIDER, 'Brief'. The two outstanding monographs are EXLER, *Form* and KOSKENNIEMI, *Idee und Phraseologie*.

DEISSMANN, *Light from the East* clearly demonstrated the importance of the papyrus letters for the study of the New Testament epistles, but New Testament scholars were rather slow to develop his insights. Until recently ROLLER's *Das Formular* was the only substantial monograph on the formal aspects of the New Testament letters. In the 1970's however, the situation changed with the publication of a number of dissertations in the United

---

[61] The most notable exception is the letter of Antiochus in 2 Macc 9:19. This opens with an expansion of the formula, 'To Y (= the recipient) χαίρειν, X (= the sender)'; see Chan-Hie Kim, *Familiar Letter*, 17.

[62] The following are examples of an opening *formula valetudinis* in the letters of our corpus:

(1) *Ep. Arist.* 35: χαίρειν καὶ ἐρρῶσθαι.

(2) 2 Macc 1:10: χαίρειν καὶ ὑγιαίνειν.

(3) 3 Macc 3:12-13: χαίρειν καὶ ἐρρῶσθαι · ἔρρωμαι δὲ καὶ αὐτὸς ἐγὼ καὶ τὰ πράγματα ἡμῶν.

(4) 2 Macc 11:27-28: χαίρειν. εἰ ἔρρωσθε, εἴη ἂν ὡς βουλόμεθα · καὶ αὐτοὶ δὲ ὑγιαίνομεν.

See also 2 Macc 9:19-20; 3 Macc 7:1; *Ep. Arist.* 41. See further note 27 above.

States. Particularly useful are CHAN-HIE KIM, *Familiar Letter;* WHITE, *Form and Structure;* and WHITE, *Body of the Greek Letter.* Also indicative of the new interest of New Testament scholars in letters are DOTY's article 'Classification', and his excellent survey of early Christian epistolography *Letters in Primitive Christianity.*

With attention focused on Greek letters, Semitic epistolography was largely neglected. Two pioneering studies of some merit were BEER, 'Briefliteratur', and MARTY, 'Contribution'. FITZMYER, 'Aramaic Epistolography', undoubtedly marked a turning-point. Since its publication in 1974 there has been a spate of articles on Hebrew and Aramaic letter-form. The following particularly deserve mention: ALEXANDER, 'Aramaic Epistolography'; PARDEE, 'Hebrew Epistolography'; *id.,* 'Letters from Tel Arad'; *id., Handbook;* PORTEN, 'Archive of Jedaniah'; DION, 'Les types épistolaires'. PORTEN, 'Aramaic Papyri and Parchments' offers a long-overdue re-examination of the purely physical aspects of ancient letter-writing, while COUROYER, 'BRK et les formules égyptiennes' provides a wealth of background material to the various *proskynesis* formulae.

Much has been written on the letters quoted in works such as 1 and 2 Macc and Josephus, *Ant.,* particularly on the question of their authenticity. The following will serve to introduce the subject: WILLRICH, *Urkundenfälschung;* MOMIGLIANO, *Prime Linee;* BICKERMANN, 'Ein jüdischer Festbrief'; TORREY, 'The Letters'.

Abbreviations

Abbreviations in source references in general follow the system of the Journal of Biblical Literature. For rabbinical literature see index of sources. For Philo, the abbreviations given in the Loeb edition, vol. 10 p. xxxv f. are used. Book, chapter and paragraph in classical sources are distinguished by semi-colon and comma.

References to modern literature in notes and bibliographies are by author and short title. Full bibliographical details are given in the accumulative bibliography below.

AJSL	American Journal of Semitic Languages and Literature (Formerly Hebraica) 1-12. Chicago 1884-96
AJSR	Association for Jewish Studies Review 1-5. Cambridge MA 1976-80
AFO	Archiv für Orientforschung. 1923ff.
AnBib	Analecta Biblica. 1952ff.
ANET	Ancient Near Eastern Texts (Pritchard)
ANRW	Aufstieg und Niedergang der Römischen Welt (Haase)
APOT	Apocrypha and Pseudepigrapha of the O.T. 1-2 (Charles)
ARW	Archiv für Religionswissenschaft 1-39. Leipzig 1898-1942
ASTI	Annual of the Swedish Theological Institute. 1962ff.
ASGW	Abhandlungen der kön. Sächsische Gesellschaft der Wiss. Theol.-Hist. Klasse
BA	Biblical Archaeologist. 1938ff.
Bar-Ilan	Annual of Bar-Ilan University. Ramat-Gan 1963ff.
BASOR	Bulletin of the American School of Oriental Research. 1919ff.
BG	Berlin Gnostic codex
BJPES	Bulletin of the Jewish Palestine Exploration Society. 1933ff.
BJRL	Bulletin of the John Rylands Library. 1914ff.
BR	Biblical Research. 1956ff.
BSAA, n.s.	Bulletin de la Sociéte Archéologique d'Alexandrie. 1898ff.
BSOAS	Bulletin of the School of Oriental (and African) Studies. 1917ff.

BTB   Biblical Theology Bulletin. Rome 1971ff.
BZAW   Beihefte zur Zeitschrift für die Alttestamentliche Wissen-
             schaft
CBQ   Catholic Biblical Quarterly. 1939ff.
Compendia   Compendia Rerum Iudaicarum ad Novum Testamentum.
             Section I: S. Safrai — M. Stern (eds.) The Jewish People in
             the First Century 1-2 (1974-76). Section II, see above p. II.
CRAI   Comptes Rendus de l'Académie des Inscriptions et Belles-
             Lettres. 1835ff.
CSEL   Corpus Scriptorum Ecclesiasticorum Latinorum 1-70.
             Vienna 1866-1942
CSCO   Corpus Scriptorum Christianorum Orientalium. Louvain
DJD   Discoveries in the Judaean Desert. Oxford 1955ff.
             Vol. 1 (1955) D. Barthélemy — J. T. Milik, Qumran Cave 1
             Vol. 2 (1961) P. Benoit et al., Les grottes de Murabbaat
             Vol. 3 (1962) M. Baillet et al., Les petites grottes
             Vol. 4 (1965) Sanders, Psalms Scroll
             Vol. 5 (1968) J. M. Allegro, Qumran Cave 4/I
             Vol. 6 (1972) J. T. Milik, Qumran grotte 4/II
             Vol. 7 (1982) M. Baillet, Qumran grotte 4/III
DBS   Supplément au Dictionnaire de la Bible. Paris 1928ff.
EJ   Encyclopedia Judaica 1-16. Jerusalem 1972ff.
EJ (Berlin) Encyclopaedia Judaica 1-10. Berlin 1928-34
ET   English Translation
ETL   Ephemerides Theologicae Lovanienses. Louvain 1929ff.
GCS   Die Griechischen Christlichen Schriftsteller der ersten drei
             Jahrhunderte. Leipzig-Berlin 1897ff.
GRBS   Greek, Roman and Byzantine Studies. Durham 1958ff.
HR   History of Religions. Chicago 1961ff.
HTR   Harvard Theological Review. 1908ff.
HUCA   Hebrew Union College Annual. Cincinnati 1924ff.
IDB   Interpreter's Dictionary of the Bible 1-4. Nashville 1962 and
             Supplement 1976
IEJ   Israel Exploration Journal. Jerusalem 1950ff.
Interpretation Interpretation. A Journal of Bible and Theology. Richmond
             1947ff.
JAC   Jahrbuch für Antike und Christentum. 1958ff.
JANESCU   Journal of the Ancient Near Eastern Society of Columbia
             University. 1970ff.
JAOS   Journal of the American Oriental Society. 1850ff.
JBL   Journal of Biblical Literature. 1881ff.
JBR   Journal of Bible and Religion (Later Journal of American
             Academy of Religion). 1933ff.
JE   Jewish Encyclopedia 1-12. New York 1901-05

JJS	Journal of Jewish Studies. London-Oxford 1948ff.
JNES	Journal of Near Eastern Studies. Chicago 1924ff.
JQR	The Jewish Quarterly Review. First Series 1-20, London 1889-1908. New Series, Philadelphia 1910ff.
JRS	Journal of Roman Studies. 1911ff.
JSHRZ	Jüdische Schriften aus Hellenistisch-Römischer Zeit I–V. Gütersloh 1973ff.
JSJ	Journal for the Study of Judaism. Leiden 1970ff.
JSNT	Journal of the Study of the New Testament, Sheffield 1978ff.
JSOT	Journal of the Study of the Old Testament, Sheffield 1976ff.
JSS	Journal of Semitic Studies. 1956ff.
JTC	Journal for Theology and the Church. New York 1965ff.
JTS	Journal of Theological Studies. Old Series 1-50. London 1899-1949. New Series. London 1950ff.
MGWJ	Monatschrift für Geschichte und Wissenschaft des Judentums 1-83. Breslau 1851-1939
n.F.	neue Folge
NHC	Nag Hammadi Codices
NHL	Nag Hammadi Library in English (Robinson)
NHS	Nag Hammadi Studies. Leiden 1971ff.
Nor TT	Norsk Teologisk Tidsskrift. 1900ff.
NRT	Nouvelle Revue Théologique 1-94. Louvain 1869-1972
n.s.	New Series
NT	Novum Testamentum. Leiden 1956ff.
NTS	New Testament Studies. London 1954ff.
NTT	Nederlands Theologisch Tijdschrift. 1946ff.
OLZ	Orientalische Literatur-Zeitung. 1898ff.
OTS	Oudtestamentische Studiën. Leiden 1924ff.
Peshitta	The Old Testament in Syriac according to the Peshitta Version. Parts I-IV, Leiden 1972ff.
PEQ	Palestine Exploration Quarterly. 1869ff.
PGM	Papyri graecae magicae (Preisendanz)
PG	Patrologia Graeca (Migne)
PL	Patrologia Latina (Migne)
PAAJR	Proceedings of the American Academy for Jewish Research. 1930ff.
PIASH	Proceedings of the Israel Acadamy of Sciences and Humanities. 1963ff.
PVTG	Pseudepigrapha Veteris Testamenti Graece. Leiden 1970ff.
PWRE	Paulys Real-Encyclopädie der classischen Altertumswissenschaft. New ed. by G. Wissowa et al. I/1-24; II/1-10; Suppl. 1-15. Stuttgart 1894-1978
RAC	Reallexikon für Antike und Christentum. 1950ff.

RB   Revue Biblique. Paris 1892ff.
REJ   Revue des Etudes Juives. 1880ff.
RGG   Religion in Geschichte und Gegenwart. 3rd rev. ed. 1-6.
                Tübingen 1957-65
RHPR   Revue d'Histoire et de Philosophie Religieuses. 1921ff.
RHR   Revue d'Histoire des Religions. 1880ff.
RQ   Revue de Qumran. Paris 1958ff.
RSPT   Revue des Sciences Philosophiques et Théologiques. 1907ff.
RSR   Revue des Sciences Religieuses. 1910ff.
SBFLA   Studii Biblici Franciscani, Liber Annuus. Jerusalem 1951ff.
SBLSP   Society of Biblical Literature Seminar Papers
SBLTT   Society of Biblical Literature. Texts and Translations
Scripta   Scripta Hierosolymitana. Jerusalem 1954ff.
SEA   Svensk Exegetisk Årsbok. Annual. Uppsala 1936ff.
Septuaginta   Septuaginta. Vetus Testamentum Graecum. Göttingen
                1931ff.
Shnaton   Shnaton. An Annual for Biblical and Ancient Near Eastern
                Studies. 1976ff.
SPA   Sitzungsberichte der Preuss. Akademie der Wissenschaften.
                Phil.-Hist. Klasse
ST   Studia Theologica. Lund 1974ff.
TAPA   Transactions and Proceedings of the American Philological
                Association. 1869/70ff.
TDNT   Theological Dictionary of the New Testament. (Reference
                may also be made to the original German edition,
                Theologisches Wörterbuch zum Neuen Testament)
Textus   Textus. Annual of the Hebrew University Bible Project.
                Jerusalem 1960ff.
TLZ   Theologische Literaturzeitung. Leipzig 1866ff.
TQ   Theologische Quartalschrift. Tübingen 1819ff.
TR   Theologische Rundschau. 1897ff.
TTZ   Trierer Theologische Zeitschrift. 1889ff.
TU   Texte und Untersuchungen zur Geschichte der altchristl.
                Literatur. Leipzig-Berlin 1882ff.
TZ   Theologische Zeitschrift. Basel 1945ff.
VC   Vigiliae Christianiae. 1947ff.
VT   Vetus Testamentum. Leiden 1951ff.
WHJP   World History of the Jewish People. Jerusalem-New
                Brunswick 1970ff. Vol. 6: The Hellenistic Age; Political
                History of Jewish Palestine from 332 to 67 B.C.E. ed. by A.
                Schalit (1972). Vol. 7: The Herodian Period, cd. by M.
                Avi-Yonah and Z. Baras (1975). Vol. 8: Society and
                Religion in the Second Temple Period, ed. by M. Avi-Yona
                and Z. Baras (1977)

YCS	Yale Classical Studies. 1928ff.
ZÄS	Zeitschrift für Ägyptische Sprache und Altertumskunde. 1863ff.
ZAW	Zeitschrift für die alttestamentliche Wissenschaft. Berlin 1881ff.
ZDMG	Zeitschrift der Deutschen Morgenländischen Gesellschaft. 1846ff.
ZNW	Zeitschrift für die neutestamentliche Wissenschaft. Berlin 1901ff.
ZPE	Zeitschrift für Papyrologie und Epigraphik. 1967ff.
ZRGG	Zeitschrift für Religions- und Geistesgeschichte. 1948ff.
ZTK	Zeitschrift für Theologie und Kirche. Tübingen 1891ff.

Accumulative Bibliography

AALEN, S. *Die Begriffe 'Licht' und 'Finsternis' im A.T., im Spätjudentum und im Rabbinismus.* Oslo 1951

ABEL, F.-M. *Géographie de la Palestine* 1-2. Paris 1933-38

— *Les livres des Maccabées.* Paris 1949

ABEL, F.-M. - STARCKY, J. *Les livres des Maccabées.* Paris 1961

ABRAHAMS, I. 'Recent Criticism of the Letter of Aristeas'. *JQR* 14 (1902) 321-42

ADAM, A. *Antike Berichte über die Essener.* Bearb. von Ch. Burchard. Berlin 1972

ADINOLFI, M. 'Il testamento di Mattatia e i suoi esempi etici (I Mac 2, 46-49). *SBFLA* 15 (1964/65) 74-97

ADLER, M. *Studien zu Philon von Alexandreia.* Breslau 1929

ALBECK, CH. *Das Buch der Jubiläen und die Halacha.* Berlin 1930

— *Shisha Sidrei Mishnah* 1-6. Jerusalem-Tel Aviv 1952-59

— *Introduction to the Mishnah.* Jerusalem 1959 (Hebrew)

ALBRIGHT, W. F. *From the Stone Age to Christianity.* 2nd ed. Garden City, N.Y. 1957

ALETTI, J.-N. *Colossiens 1, 15-20. Genre et exégèse du texte. Fonction de la thématique sapientielle.* Rome 1981

ALEXANDER, P. S. 'The Historical Setting of the Hebrew Book of Enoch'. *JJS* 28 (1977) 156-80

— 'Remarks on Aramaic Epistolography in the Persian Period'. *JSS* 23 (1978) 155-70

ALEXANDRE, C. N. *Oracula Sibyllina* 1-2. Paris 1841-56

ALEXANDRE, M. 'La culture profane chez Philon', in *Philon d'Alexandrie, Lyon Colloque.* Paris 1967, 105-29

ALLEGRO, J. M. 'Further Messianic References in Qumran Literature'. *JBL* 75 (1956) 174-87

— 'More Isaiah Commentaries from Qumran's Fourth Cave'. *BL* 77 (1958) 215-21

— 'Thrakidan, The "Lion of Wrath" and Alexander Jannaeus'. *PEQ* 91 (1959) 47-51

— *The Treasure of the Copper Scroll.* Garden City, N.Y. 1960

ALLISON, D. C. 'The Authorship of 1QS III,3-IV,14'. *RQ* 10 (1980) 257-68

ALON, G. 'The Halakhah in the Teaching of the Twelve Apostles', in *Studies in Jewish History in the Times of the Second Temple, the Mishnah and the Talmud* 1. Tel Aviv 1957, 274-94 (Hebrew)

— *Jews, Judaism and the Classical World.* Jerusalem 1977

— *The Jews in Their Land in the Talmudic Age* 1. Jerusalem 1980

ALONSO-SCHÖKEL, L. 'Narrative Structures in the Book of Judith', in *The Center for Hermeneutical Studies in Hellenistic and Modern Culture, Colloquy II.* Berkeley 1975, 1-20

ALONSO-SCHÖKEL, L. — SICRE DIAZ, J. L. *Sapienciales. Comentario 2: Job.* Madrid 1983

ALSTER, B. *The Instruction of Šuruppak A Sumerian Proverb Collection* (Mesopotamia 2) Copenhagen 1974.

ALTMANN, A. 'The Gnostic background of the Rabbinic Adam Legends'. *JQR* n.s. 35 (1944-45) 371-91

AMIR, Y. 'Philo Judaeus', in *EJ* 13, 409-15

— 'The Term Ioudaismos. A Study in Jewish-Hellenistic Self-Identification'. *Immanuel* 14 (1982) 34-41

603

AMSTUTZ, J. *Aplotes. Eine begriffsgeschichtliche Studie zum jüdisch-christlichen Griechisch.* Bonn 1968

AMUSIN, J. D. 'Ephraim et Manassé dans le pesher de Naum (4Qp Nahum)'. *RQ* 4 (1963/64) 389-96

— 'A propos de l'interprétation de 4Q161 (fragments 5-6 et 8)'. *RQ* 8 (1974) 381-92

— 'The Reflection of Historical Events of the First Century B.C.E. in Qumran Commentaries, (4Q 161; 169; 4Q 166)'. *HUCA* 48 (1977) 134-46

ANDREWS, H. T. 'The Letter of Aristeas', in *APOT* 2, 83-122

ANKLESARIA, B. T. *Zand-i Vohuman Yasn.* Bombay 1967

APELT, M. *De rationibus quibusdam quae Philoni Alexandriae cum Posidonio intercedunt.* Leipzig 1907

APPLEBAUM, S. 'The Legal Status of the Jewish Communities in the Diaspora', in *Compendia* I/1, 420-65

— 'The Zealots: the Case of Reevaluation'. *JRS* 61 (1971) 155-70

APTOWITZER, V. 'Asenath, The Wife of Joseph'. *HUCA* 1 (1924) 239-306

— 'Malkizedek: zu den Sagen der Agada'. *MGWJ* 70 (1926) 93-103

ARAI, S. 'Zur Christologie des Apokryphons des Johannes'. *NTS* 15 (1969) 302-18

ARENHOEVEL, D. 'Die Eschatologie der Makkabäerbücher'. *TTZ* 72 (1963) 257-69

— *Die Theokratie nach dem 1. und 2. Makkabäerbuch.* Mainz 1967

ARNALDEZ, R. *et al.* (eds.). *Les oeuvres de Philon d'Alexandrie* 1-35. Paris 1961ff.

ARNIM, H. VON. *Quellenstudien zu Philo von Alexandria.* Berlin 1888

— *Stoicorum veterum fragmenta* 1-4. 2nd ed. Stuttgart 1964

ASCHERMANN, P. H. *Die paränetischen Formen der 'Testamente der zwölf Patriarchen' und ihr Nachwirken in der frühchristlichen Mahnung.* Diss. Berlin, Humboldt-Universität 1955

ASSMANN, J. 'Königsdogma und Heilserwartung. Politische und kultische Chaosbeschreibungen in ägyptischen Texten', in Hellholm, *Apocalypticism*

ASMUSSEN, J. P. *Manichaean Literature: Representative Texts Chiefly from the Middle Persian and Parthian Writings.* New York 1975

ATKINSON, K. M. T. 'The Historical Setting of the War of the Sons of Light and the Sons of Darkness'. *BJRL* 40 (1958) 272-97

ATTRIDGE, H. W. 'The Ascension of Moses and the Heavenly Jerusalem', in Nickelsburg, *Studies on the Testament of Moses,* 122-5

— *The Interpretation of Biblical History in the Antiquitates Judaicae of Flavius Josephus.* Missoula 1976

— *First-Century Cynicism in the Epistles of Heraclitus.* Missoula 1976

— 'Greek and Latin Apocalypses', in Collins, *Apocalypse,* 159-86

— 'Gnosticism and Eschatology'. *Perkins Journal,* Spring 1980, 9-22

— 'Philo the Epic Poet', in Charlesworth, *Pseudepigrapha*

ATTRIDGE, H. W. — ODEN, R. A., JR. *Philo of Byblos: The Phoenician History.* Washington D.C. 1981

AUCHER, J. B. *Philonis Iudaei sermones tres inediti.* Venice 1822

— *Philonis Iudaei Paralipomena Armena nunc primum in Latinum fideliter translata.* Venice 1826

AUDET, J.-P. 'Affinités littéraires et doctrinales du Manuel de Discipline'. *RB* 59 (1952) 219-38; 60 (1953) 41-82

— *La Didachè. Instructions des âpotres.* Paris 1958

AVIGAD, N. 'The Paleography of the Dead Sea Scrolls and Related Documents', in *Scripta* 4 (1958) 56-87

AVIGAD, N. — YADIN, Y. *A Genesis Apocryphon.* Jerusalem 1956

AVI-YONAH, M. 'The Hasmoncan Revolt and Judah Maccabee's War against the Syrians', in *WHJP* 6, 147-64

— *The Jews of Palestine. A Political History from the Bar Kokhba War to the Arab Conquest.* Oxford 1976.

BAARS, W. 'Apocryphal Psalms', in *Peshitta* IV/6. Leiden 1972

BAARS, W. — ZUURMOND, R. 'The Project for a New Edition of the Ethiopic Book of Jubilees'. *JSS* 9 (1964) 67-74

BAER, R. A. *Philo's Use of the Categories Male and Female.* Leiden 1970

BAER, Y. 'Israel, the Christian Church and the Roman Empire', in *Scripta* 7 (1961) 79-149

BAILLET, M. 'Un recueil liturgique de Qumrân, Grotte 4: "Les paroles des luminaires"'. *RB* 68 (1961) 195-250

— 'Les Manuscrits de la Règle de la Guerre de la Grotte 4 de Qumran'. *RB* 79 (1972) 219-221

— 'Le volume VII de Discoveries in the Judaean Desert. Présentation,' in Delcor, *Qumran,* 75-89

BAILLET, M. *et al.* 'Le travail d'édition des fragments manuscrits de Qumrân'. *RB* 63 (1956) 49-67

BALL, C. J. 'The Epistle of Jeremy', in *APOT* 1, 526-611

BALTZER, K. *The Covenant Formulary.* Philadelphia 1971

BAMMEL, R. 'Zum Testimonium Flavianum', in *Josephus-Studien. Festschrift O. Michel.* Göttingen 1974, 9-22

BAR-ADON, P. 'Another Settlement of the Judean Desert Sect at Ein el-Ghuweir on the Dead Sea'. *Eretz Israel* 10 (1971) 72-89 (Hebrew); English: *BASOR* 227 (1977) 1-26

— 'The Hasmonean Fortresses and the Status of Khirbet Qumran'. *Eretz Israel* 15 (1981) 349-52

BARBER, E. A. 'Lycophron (2)', in *Oxford Classical Dictionary.* Oxford 1949, 520

BARC, B. *L'Hypostase des Archontes. Traité gnostique sur l'origine de l'homme, du monde et des archontes (NH II,4),* suivi de M. Roberge, *Noréa (NH IX, 2).* Quebec/Louvain 1980

BARC, B. (ed.) *Colloque International sur les textes de Nag Hammadi (Québec, 22-25 aout 1978).* Québec/Louvain 1981

BARDTKE, H. 'Considérations sur les cantiques de Qumrân'. *RB* 63 (1956) 220-33

— 'Die Rechtsstellung der Qumrân-Gemeinde'. *TLZ* 86 (1961) 93-104

— 'Qumran und seine Funde'. *TR* 29 (1963) 261-92; 30 (1963) 218-315

— 'Qumran und seine Probleme'. *TR* 33 (1968) 97-119; 185-236

— 'Literaturbericht über Qumran'. V.-IX. Teil. *TR* 35 (1970) 196-230; 37 (1972) 97-120; 193-319; 38 (1973) 257-91; 39 (1974) 189-221; 40 (1975) 210-26; 41 (1976) 97-140

BARDTKE, H. (ed.). *Qumran Probleme.* Leipzig 1963

BARISH, D. A. 'The Autobiography of Josephus and the Hypothesis of a Second Edition of his Antiquities'. *HTR* 71 (1978) 61-75

BARON, S. *A Social and Religious History of the Jews* 1-16, 2nd ed. New York 1952-76.

BARR, J. 'Jewish Apocalyptic in Recent Scholarly Study'. *BJRL* 58 (1975) 9-35

BARRETT, C. K. *The Gospel According to St. John.* 2nd ed. London 1978

BARTHÉLEMY, D. *Les devanciers d'Aquila.* Leiden 1963

BARTHÉLEMY, D. — RICKENBACHER, O. *Konkordanz zum hebräischen Sirach mit syrisch-hebräischem Index.* Göttingen 1973

BARTHELMUS, R. *Heroentum in Israel und seiner Umwelt.* Zürich 1979

BARUCQ, A. *Le livre des Proverbes.* Paris 1964

BATIFFOL, P. 'Le livre de la Prière d'Aseneth', in *Studia Patristica* 1-2. Paris 1889-90

BAUER, W. *A Greek-English Lexicon of the New Testament.* Trans. and adapted by W. P. Arndt and F. W. Gingrich. Cambridge 1957

— *Orthodoxy and Heresy in Earliest Christianity.* Engl. trans. ed. by R. A. Kraft and G. Krodel. Philadelphia 1971

BAUMGARTEN, J. M. 'Some Notes on the Ben Sira Scroll from Masada'. *JQR* 57 (1968) 323-7

— *Studies in Qumran Law.* Leiden 1977

BAUMGARTNER, W. 'Die literarischen Gattungen in der Weisheit des Jesus Sirach'. *ZAW* 34 (1914) 161-98

BAYER, B. 'Judith, Book of', in *EJ* 10, 460-1

BEARDSLEE, W. A. 'Uses of Proverbs in the Synoptic Gospels'. *Interpretation* 24 (1970) 61-73

BEAUCHAMP, P. 'Le salut corporel des justes et la conclusion du livre de la Sagesse'. *Biblica* 45 (1964) 491-526

— 'Epouser la Sagesse – ou n'épouser qu'elle? Une énigme du Livre de la Sagesse', in Gilbert, *La Sagesse de l'AT,* 347-69

BECKER, J. *Untersuchungen zur Entstehungsgeschichte der Testamente der zwölf Patriarchen.* Leiden 1970

— *Die Testamente der zwölf Patriarchen* (JSHRZ III/ 1) 2nd ed. Gütersloh 1980

BECKWITH, R. T. 'The Modern Attempt to reconcile the Qumran Calendar with the True Solar Year'. *RQ* 7 (1970) 379-96

— 'The Significance of the Calendar for Interpreting Essene Chronology and Eschatology'. *RQ* 10 (1980) 167-202

— 'The Earliest Enoch Literature and its Calendar: Marks of their Origin, Date and Motivation'. *RQ* 10 (1981) 365-403

— 'The Pre-History and Relationships of the Pharisees, Sadducees and Essenes: A Tentative Reconstruction'. *RQ* 11 (1982) 3-46

BEENTJES, P. C. 'Recent Publications on the Wisdom of Jesus Ben Sira (Ecclesiasticus)'. *Bijdragen* 43 (1982) 188-98

BEER, G. 'Zur israelitisch-jüdischen Briefliteratur', in *Alttestamentliche Studien Rudolf Kittel zum 60. Geburtstag dargebracht.* Leipzig 1913, 20-31

— 'Das Buch Henoch', in Kautzsch, *Die Pseudeprigraphen,* 217-310

BELKIN, S. *The Alexandrian Halakah in Apologetic Literature of the First Century* C.E. Philadelphia 1936

— *Philo and the Oral Law.* Cambridge (Mass.) 1940

BELL, A. A., JR. 'Josephus the Satirist? A Clue to the Original Form of the Testimonium Flavianum'. *JQR* n.s. 68 (1976) 16-22

BELL, H. I. *Juden und Griechen im römischen Alexandria.* Leipzig 1926

BELTZ, W. 'Samaritanertum und Gnosis', in Tröger, *Gnosis und N. T.,* 89-95

— *Die Adam-Apokalypse aus Codex V von Nag Hammadi. Jüdische Bausteine in gnostischen Systemen.* Habilitationschrift, Humboldt Universität Berlin 1970.

BEN-HAYYIM, Z. 'Traditions in the Hebrew Language, with Special Reference to the Dead Sea Scrolls', in *Scripta* 4, 200-14

BEN SIRA. *The Book of Ben Sira. Text, Concordance and an Analysis of the Vocabulary.* Jerusalem 1973

BENTWICH, N. *Philo Judaeus of Alexandria.* Philadelphia 1948

BENTZEN, A. *Daniel.* Tübingen 1952

BEN-SASSON, H. H. 'Galut', in *EJ* 7, 275-94

BEN-YASHAR, M. 'Noch zum Miqdaš Adam in Florilegium'. *RQ* 10 (1981) 587-8

BERGER, K. *Die Gesetzauslegung Jesu.* Neukirchen 1972

— *Die griechische Daniel-Diegese: eine altkirchliche Apokalypse.* Leiden 1976

BERNAYS, J. *Ueber das phokylideische Gedicht. Ein Beitrag zur hellenistischen Literatur.* Berlin 1856

BERTRAM, G. 'Hebräischer und griechischer Qohelet. Ein Beitrag zur Theologie der hellenistischen Bibel'. *ZA W* 64 (1952) 26-49

BERTRAND, D. A. 'Paraphrase de Sem et Paraphrase de Seth', in Ménard, *Nag Hammadi,* 146-57

BETZ, H. D. 'On the Problem of the Religio-Historical Understanding of Apocalypticism'. *JTC* 6 (1969) 134-56

BETZ, O. 'Geistliche Schönheit', in *Die Leibhaftigkeit des Wortes, Festschrift A. Köberle.* Hamburg 1958, 76-79

— *Offenbarung und Schriftforschung in der Qumransekte.* Tübingen 1960

— 'The Eschatological Interpretation of the Sinai Tradition in Qumran and in the New Testament'. *RQ* 6 (1967) 98-107

BETZ, O. *et al.* (eds.) *Josephus-Studien: Untersuchungen zu Josephus, dem antiken Judentum, und dem Neuen Testament, Otto Michel zum 70. Geburtstag gewidmet.* Göttingen 1974

BEZOLD, C. 'Das arabisch-äthiopische Testamentum Adami', in *Orientalische Studien Theodor Nöldeke zum siebzigsten Geburtstag*. Giessen 1906, vol. 2, 893-912

BIANCHI, U. (ed.) *Le origini dello gnosticismo. Colloquio di Messina 13-18 Aprile 1966*. Leiden 1967

BICKERMANN, E. 'Makkabäerbuch', in *PWRE* 14, 347-58
— 'Zur Datierung des Pseudo-Aristeas'. *ZNW* 29 (1930) 280-98
— 'Ein jüdischer Festbrief vom Jahre 124 v. Chr.' *ZNW* 32 (1933) 233-54; reprinted in *Studies* 2, 136-58
— 'La charte séleucide de Jérusalem'. *REJ* 100 (1935) 4-35
— *Der Gott der Makkabäer*. Berlin 1937
— 'The Colophon of the Greek Book of Esther'. *JBL* 63 (1944) 339-62; reprinted in *Studies* 1, 225-45
— 'Une proclamation séleucide relative au temple de Jérusalem'. *Syria* 25 (1946-8) 67-85
— 'The Date of the Testaments of the Twelve Patriarchs'. *JBL* 69 (1950) 245-60
— 'Notes on the Greek Book of Esther'. *PAAJR* 20 (1950) 101-33; reprinted in *Studies* 1, 246-74
— *Four Strange Books of the Bible*. New York 1967
— 'The Jewish Historian Demetrios', in *Christianity, Judaism and Other Greco-Roman Cults: Studies for Morton Smith at Sixty* 3. Leiden 1975, 72-84; reprinted in *Studies* 2, 347-58
— *Studies in Jewish and Christian History* 1-2. Leiden 1976-80
— *The God of the Maccabees: Studies on the Meaning and Origin of the Maccabean Revolt*. Leiden 1979

BIDAWID, R. J. (ed.) *Apocalypse of Baruch; 4. Esdras* (Peshitta IV, 3). Leiden 1973

BIDEZ, J. — CUMONT, F. *Les Mages Hellénisés*. Paris 1938

BIETENHARD, H. *Die himmlische Welt im Urchristentum und Spätjudentum*. Tübingen 1951
— 'Die Handschriftenfunde vom Toten Meer (Hirbet Qumran) und die Essenerfrage. Die Funde in der Wüste Juda (Eine Orientierung)', in *ANRW* II, 19/1, 704-78

BIGGS, R. D. 'More Babylonian Prophecies'. *Iraq* 29 (1967) 117-32

BILLERBECK, P. — STRACK, H. L. *Kommentar zum Neuen Testament aus Talmud und Midrasch* 1-4. München 1922-28

BLACK, M. 'The Account of the Essenes in Hyppolitus and Josephus', in *The Background of the New Testament and its Eschatology*, ed. by W. D. Davies and D. Daube. Cambridge 1956, 172-75
— *Apocalypsis Henochi Graece* (PVTG 3) Leiden 1970, 5-44

BLACK, M. (ed.). *The Scrolls and Christianity*. London 1969

BLASS, F. — DEBRUNNER, A. *A Greek Grammar of the New Testament*, transl. and rev. by R. W. Funk. Cambridge 1961

BLAU, L. 'Samael', in *JE* 10, 665-6

BLOCH, H. *Die Quellen des Flavius Josephus in seiner Archaeologie*. Leipzig 1879

BLOCH, J. *On the Apocalyptic in Judaism*. Philadelphia 1952

BLOCH, R. 'Midrash'. *DBS* 5 (1957) 1270-5

BLOCH, R. 'L'origine des Livres Sibyllines à Rome. Méthode de recherche et critique du récit des annalistes anciens', in *Neue Beiträge zur Geschichte der Alten Welt* 2. Berlin 1965, 281-92

BLOMMERDE, C. M. *Northwest Semitic Grammar and Job*. Rome 1964

BLUDAU, A. *Juden und Judenverfolgungen im alten Alexandrien*. Münster 1906

BÖCHER, O. 'Die heilige Stadt im Völkerkrieg. Wandlungen eines apokalyptischen Schemas', in Betz, *Josephus Studien*, 55-76

BÖHLIG, A. *Kephalia: Manichäische Handschriften der Staatlichen Museen Berlin*. Stuttgart 1940
— *Mysterion und Wahrheit: Gesammelte Beiträge zur spätantiken Religionsgeschichte*. Leiden 1968

BÖHLIG, A. - LABIB, P. *Die Koptisch-Gnostische Schrift ohne Titel aus Codex II von Nag Hammadi*. Berlin 1962

— *Koptisch-Gnostische Apokalypsen aus Codex V von Nag-Hammadi.* Halle-Wittenberg 1963
BÖHLIG, A. — WISSE, F. *Nag Hammadi Codices III, 2 and IV,2: The Gospel of the Egyptians (The Holy Book of the Great Invisible Spirit).* Leiden 1975
BOGAERT, P. M. 'Bulletin de la Bible Latine 5'. *Revue Bénédictine* 76 (1966) 73-112
— *Apocalypse de Baruch* (Sources Chrét.) Paris 1969
— 'Le nom de Baruch dans la littérature pseudépigraphique: l'apocalypse syriaque et le livre Deutéronomique', in *La littérature juive entre Tenach et Michna,* ed. by W. C. van Unnik. Leiden 1974, 56-62
BONNER, C. *The Last Chapters of Enoch in Greek.* London 1937
— *The Homily on the Passion by Melito Bishop of Sardis with some Fragments of the Apocryphal Ezekiel.* London 1940
BONWETSCH, G. N. *Die Apokalypse Abrahams.* Leipzig 1897
BORGEN, P. 'God's Agent in the Fourth Gospel', in *Religion in Antiquity. Essays in Memory of E.R. Goodenough.* Leiden 1968
— 'The Place of the O.T. in the Formation of N.T. Theology. Response'. *NTS* 23 (1976) 67-69
— *Religiøs pluralism i bibelsk tid og i Norge i dag.* Trondheim 1979
— 'Observations on the theme "Paul and Philo"', in S. Pedersen (ed.) *Die Paulinische Literatur und Theologie.* Århus 1980, 85-102
— *Bread from Heaven. An Exegetical Study of the Concept of Manna in the Gospel of John and the Writings of Philo.* Leiden 1960. Repr. with revisions 1981
— 'Paul preaches Circumcision and pleases Men', in *Paul and Paulinism. Essays in Honour of C.K. Barrett.* London 1982, 37-46
— 'Philo of Alexandria. A Critical and Synthetical Survey of Research since World War II', in *ANRW* II, 21/1, 98-154
— 'The Early Church and the Hellenistic Synagogue'. *ST* (forthcoming)
BORGEN, P. — SKARSTEN, R. *KWIC-Concordance to Philo of Alexandria.* Trondheim 1974
— 'Quaestiones et Solutiones: Some Observations on the Form of Philo's Exegesis'. *Studia Philonica* 4 (1976-7) 1-15
BOUSSET, W. 'Die Himmelsreise der Seele'. *ARW* 4 (1901) 229-73
— 'Die Beziehungen der ältesten jüdischen Sibylle zur Chaldäischen'. *ZNW* 3 (1902) 23-50
— 'Sibyllen und Sibyllinische Buecher', in *Real-Encyclopedia der Protestantischen Theologie und Kirche.* 3rd ed. vol. 18 (1906) 265-80
— *Hauptprobleme der Gnosis.* Göttingen 1907
— *Jüdisch-christlicher Schulbetrieb in Alexandria und Rom.* Göttingen 1915
— *Die Religion des Judentums im späthellenistischen Zeitalter.* Rev. by H. Gressmann, 3rd. ed. Tübingen 1926
BOX, G. H. *The Ezra-Apocalypse.* London 1912
— *The Apocalypse of Abraham,* with the assistance of J. Landsman. London 1918
— *The Testament of Abraham.* London 1927
— *Philonis Alexandrini: in Flaccum.* London 1939
BOYANCÉ, P. 'Les Muses et l'harmonie des sphères', in *Mélange F. Grat* 1. Paris 1946, 3-16
BOYARIN, D. 'Penitential Liturgy in 4 Ezra'. *JSJ* 3 (1972) 30-34
BOYSEN, C. *Flavii Josephi opera ex versione latina antiqua. Pars VI. De Judaeorum vetustate sive contra Apionem.* Prague 1898
BRANDENBURGER, E. *Adam und Christus.* Neukirchen 1962
— *Fleisch und Geist.* Neukirchen 1968
— *Himmelfahrt Mosis* (JSHRZ V/2) Gütersloh 1976
BRAUN, F.-M. 'Saint Jean, La Sagesse et l'histoire', in *Neotestamentica et Patristica. Festschrift O. Cullmann.* Leiden 1962, 122-33
— *Jean le Théologien* 2. Paris 1964
BRAUN, H. *Qumran und das Neue Testament* 1-2. Tübingen 1966.
BRAUN, M. *History and Romance in Graeco-Oriental Literature.* Oxford 1938
BRAUN, O. 'Ein Brief des Katholikos Timotheos über biblische Studien des 9. Jahrhunderts'. *Oriens Christianus* 1901, 138-52; 299-313

BRAUN, R. *Koheleth und die frühhellenistische Popularphilosophie* (BZAW Beihefte 130). Berlin 1973

BREECH, E. J. 'These Fragments I have Shored Against My Ruins: The Form and Function of 4 Ezra'. *JBL* 92 (1973) 267-74

— *Crucifixion as Ordeal: Tradition and Interpretation in Matthew.* Dissertation Harvard Univ. Cambridge, Mass. 1976

BRÉHIER, E. *Les idées philosophiques et religieuses de Philon d'Alexandrie.* Paris 1908

BREITENSTEIN, U. *Beobachtungen zu Sprache, Stil und Gedankengut des Vierten Makka-bäerbuchs.* Basel-Stuttgart 1976

BRESCIANI, E. — KAMIL, M. 'Le lettere aramaiche di Hermopoli', in *Atti della Accademia Nazionale dei Lincei.* Rome 1966, 357-428

BRETON, S. 'Qoheleth Studies'. *BTB* 3 (1973) 22-50

BRIESSMANN, A. *Tacitus und das flavische Geschichtsbild.* Wiesbaden 1955

BROCK, S. P. *Testamentum Iobi* (PVTG 2). Leiden 1967

— 'Abraham and the Ravens: A Syriac Counterpart to Jubilees 11-12 and its Implications'. *JSJ* 9 (1978) 135-52

BROEK, R. VAN DEN. *The Myth of the Phoenix According to Classical and Early Christian Traditions.* Leiden 1972

BROEK, R. VAN DEN. — VERMASEREN, M. J. (eds.). *Studies in Gnosticism and Hellenistic Religions presented to Gilles Quispel.* Leiden 1981

BROOKE, A. E. — MCLEAN, N. — THACKERAY, H. ST. J. (eds.) *The Old Testament in Greek 3: Esther, Judith, Tobit.* Cambridge 1940

BROOKE, G. J. *4Q Florilegium in the Context of Early Jewish Exegetical Method.* Dissertation Ann Arbor 1978

— 'Amos-Numbers Midrash and Messianic Expectation', *ZAW* 92 (1980) 397-404

— 'Qumran Pesher: Towards the Redefinition of a Genre'. *RQ* 10 (1981) 483-503

BROOKS, E. W. *Joseph and Aseneth.* London 1918

BROWN, R. E. 'The Messianism of Qumrân'. *CBQ* 19 (1957) 53-82

— 'J. Starcky's Theory of Qumran Messianic Development'. *CBQ* 28 (1966) 51-7

BROWNLEE, W. H. 'Biblical Interpretation among the Sectarians of the Dead Sea Scrolls'. *BA* 14 (1951) 54-76

— 'John the Baptist in the New Light of Ancient Scrolls', in Stendahl, *The Scrolls and the New Testament,* 33-53

— 'Le livre grec d'Esther et la royauté divine. Corrections orthodoxes au livre d'Esther'. *RB* 73 (1966) 161-85

— *The Midrash-Pesher Habakkuk.* Missoula 1977

— 'The Background of Biblical Interpretation at Qumran', in Delcor, *Qumran,* 183-93

BROX, N. *Falsche Verfasserangaben: Zur Erklärung der frühchristlichen Pseudepigraphie.* Stuttgart 1975

BRUCE, F. F. *Biblical Exegesis in the Qumran Texts.* Den Haag 1959

— 'The Book of Daniel and the Qumran Community', in *Neotestamentica et Semitica in Honour of M. Black,* ed. by E. Ellis and M. Wilcox. Edinburgh 1969, 221-35

BRYCE, G. *A Legacy of Wisdom.* London 1979

BUCCELLATI, G. 'Wisdom and Not: The Case of Mesopotamia'. *JAOS* 101 (1981) 34-47

BUCHANAN, G. W. 'The Priestly Teacher of Righteousness'. *RQ* 4 (1969) 553-58

— 'The Office of the Teacher of Righteousness'. *RQ* 9 (1977) 241-3

BUDGE, E. W. *The Book of the Cave of the Treasures.* London 1927

BÜCHLER, A. *Das Synedrion in Jerusalem und das grosse Beth-Din in der Quaderkammer des Jerusalemischen Tempels.* Vienna 1902

— 'Ben Sira's Conception of Sin and Atonement'. *JQR* n.s. 13 (1922-3) 303-35, 461-502; 14 (1923-4) 53-83

— *Studies in Sin and Atonement.* London 1928

BÜCKERS, H. *Die Unsterblichkeitslehre des Weisheitsbuches. Ihr Ursprung und ihre Bedeutung.* Münster 1938

BÜHLMANN, W. *Vom rechten Reden und Schweigen. Studien zu Proverbien 10-31.* Freiburg 1976
BULL, R. J. 'A Note on Theodotus' Description of Shechem'. *HTR* 60 (1967) 211-27
BULTMANN, R. *Die Geschichte der synoptischen Tradition.* 2nd ed. Göttingen 1931
— 'ἔλεος etc., in *TDNT* 2, 477-87
— 'Weissagung und Erfüllung', in *Glauben und Verstehen* 2. Tübingen 1965, 162-86
BUNGE, J.-G. 'Untersuchungen zum zweiten Makkabäerbuch'. Diss. Bonn 1971
— 'Zur Geschichte und Chronologie des Untergangs der Oniaden und des Aufstiegs der Hasmonäer'. *JSJ* 6 (1975) 1-46
BURCH, V. 'The Literary Unity of the Ascensio Isaiae'. *JTS* 20 (1919) 17-23
BURCHARD, C. *Bibliographie zu den Handschriften vom Toten Meer* (BZAW 76/89) Berlin 1957/65
— *Untersuchungen zu Joseph und Aseneth.* Tübingen 1965
— 'Zur armenischen Überlieferung der Testamente der zwölf Patriarchen', in Burchard-Jervell-Thomas, *Studien,* 1-29
— *Der dreizehnte Zeuge.* Göttingen 1970
— 'Joseph und Aseneth, Neugriechisch'. *NTS* 24 (1977-78) 68-84
— 'Joseph und Aseneth 25-29, Armenisch'. *JSJ* 10 (1980) 1-10
BURCHARD, CH. — JERVELL, J. — THOMAS, J. *Studien zu den Testamenten der Zwölf Patriarchen* (ZNW Beihefte 36). Berlin 1969
BURGMANN, H. 'Das umstrittene intersacerdotium in Jerusalem 159-152 v. Chr.' *JSJ* 11 (1980) 135-76
— 'Wer war der Lehrer der Gerechtigkeit?' *RQ* 10 (1981) 553-87
BURKE, D. G. *The Poetry of Baruch: A Reconstruction and Analysis of the Original Hebrew Text of Baruch 3:9-5:9.* Chico 1982
BURNEY, C. F. 'Christ as the APXH of Creation'. *JTS* 27 (1925s) 160-77
BURROWS, M. *The Dead Sea Scrolls.* New York 1955
— *More Light on the Dead Sea Scrolls.* New York 1958
BURROWS, M. (ed.) *The Dead Sea Scrolls of St. Mark's Monastery* 1-2. New Haven 1951
BURSTEIN, S. M. *The Babyloniaca of Berossus.* Malibu 1978
BUZY, D. *Introduction aux paraboles évangéliques.* Paris 1912
CAMERON, R. — DEWEY, A. J. *The Cologne Mani Codex (P. Colon. inv. nr. 4780): 'Concerning the Origin of His Body.'* (SBLTT 15) Missoula 1979
CANCIK, H. 'Libri Fatales', in Hellholm, *Apocalypticism,* 549-76
CAQUOT, A. 'Ben Sira et le Messianisme'. *Semitica* 16 (1966) 43-68
— 'Bref commentaire du Martyre d'Isaie'. *Semitica* 23 (1973) 65-93
— 'Un écrit sectaire de Qoumrân: le Targoum de Job.' *RHR* 185 (1974) 9-27
— 'Remarques sur les chapitres 70 et 71 du Livre éthiopien d'Henoch,' in *Apocalypses et Théologie de l'Espérance.* Paris 1977, 111-22
— 'Le Messianisme qumrânien', in Delcor, *Qumran,* 231-47
CARDAUNS, B. 'Juden und Spartaner'. *Hermes* 95 (1967) 317-24
CARMIGNAC, J. 'Les citations de l'Ancien Testament dans la guerre des fils de lumière contre les fils de ténèbres'. *RB* 63 (1965) 234-60; 375-90
— *La règle de la guerre des fils de lumière contre les fils de ténèbres.* Paris 1958
— 'Les citations de l'Ancien Testament et spécialement des Poémes du Serviteur dans les Hymnes de Qumrân'. *RQ* 2 (1959/60) 357-94
— 'Comparaison entre les Manuscrits 'A' et 'B' du document de Damas'. *RQ* 2 (1959/60) 53-67
— 'Le genre littéraire du Pesher dans le Pistis-Sophia'. *RQ* 4 (1963/64) 497-522
— 'Règle des chants pour l'holocouste du Sabbat'. *RQ* 4 (1964) 563-4
— 'Les horoscopes de Qumran'. *RQ* 5 (1965) 199-217
— 'Le document de Qumran sur Melkisédeq'. *RQ* 7 (1970) 343-78
— Review of Stegemann, Die Entstehung der Qumrangemeinde. *RQ* 8 (1973) 277-81
— Review of Davies, 1QM. *RQ* 9 (1978) 599-603
— 'La future intervention de Dieu selon la pensée de Qumrân', in Delcor, *Qumran,* 219-29
— 'Qu'est-ce que l'Apocalyptique? Son emploi à Qumran'. *RQ* 37 (1979) 3-33

– 'Qui était le Docteur de Justice'. *RQ* 10 (1980) 235-46
– 'Précision'. *RQ* 10 (1981) 585-6
CARMIGNAC, J. *et al.*, *Les textes de Qumran* 1-2. Paris 1961-63
CARROLL, R. P. 'Twilight of Prophecy or Dawn of Apocalyptic'. *JSOT* 14 (1979) 3-35
CARTLIDGE, D. R. — DUNGAN, D. L. *Documents for the Study of the Gospels*. Philadelphia 1980
CASEY, M. 'The Use of the term Son of Man in the Similitudes of Enoch'. *JSJ* 7 (1976) 11-29
CAZELLES, H. 'Sur les origines du calendrier des Jubilés. *Biblica* 43 (1962) 202-12
– 'Les nouvelles études sur Sumer (Alster) et Mari (Marzal) nous aident-elles à situer les origines de la sagesse israélite?' in Gilbert, *La Sagesse de l'A.T.,* 17-27
CERESKO, A. R. *Job 29-31 in the Light of Northwest Semitic*. Rome 1980
CERFAUX, L. *Le Christ dans la théologie de S. Paul*. Paris 1951
– 'Les sources scripturaires de Mt 11, 25-30'. *ETL* 30 (1954) 740-46; 31 (1955) 331-42
CHADWICK, H. *The Sentences of Sextus*. Cambridge 1959
– 'St. Paul and Philo of Alexandria'. *BJRL* 48 (1966) 286-307
– 'Philo and the Beginnings of Christian Thought', in *The Cambridge History of Later Greek and Early Medieval Philosophy*. London 1967, 137-92
CHAINE, J. *L'épître de saint Jacques*. Paris 1927
CHAN HIE KIM. *The Familiar Letter of Recommendation*. Missoula 1972
CHARLES, R. H. *The Ethiopic Version of the Hebrew Book of Jubilees*. Oxford 1895
– *The Apocalypse of Baruch*. London 1896
– *The Assumption of Moses*. London 1897
– *The Ascension of Isaiah*. London 1900
– *The Book of Jubilees*. Oxford 1902
– *The Ethiopic Version of the Book of Enoch*. Oxford 1906
– *The Greek Versions of the Testaments of the Twelve Patriarchs*. Oxford 1908
– *A Critical and Exegetical Commentary on the Book of Daniel*. Oxford 1929
CHARLES, R. H. (ed.) *Apocrypha and Pseudepigrapha of the Old Testament* (APOT) 1-2. Oxford 1913
CHARLESWORTH, J. H. 'The S.N.T.S. Pseudepigrapha Seminars at Tübingen and Paris on the Books of Enoch'. *NTS* 25 (1979) 315-23
– 'The Origin and Subsequent History of the Authors of the Dead Sea Scrolls: Four Transitional Phases among the Qumran Essenes'. *RQ* 10 (1980) 213-33
– *The Pseudepigrapha and Modern Research: with a Supplement*. Chico 1981
CHARLESWORTH, J. H. (ed.) *John and Qumran*. London 1972
– *The Old Testament Pseudepigrapha*. Garden City, N.Y. 1983.
CHRIST, F. *Jesus Sophia. Die Sophia-Christologie bei den Synoptikern*. Zürich 1970
CHRISTIANSEN, I. *Die Technik der allegorischen Auslegungswissenschaft bei Philon von Alexandrien*. Tübingen 1969
CLIFFORD, R. J. 'History and Myth in Daniel 10-12'. *BASOR* 220 (1975) 23-26
COHEN, S. J. D. *Josephus in Galilee and Rome: His Vita and Development as a Historian*. Leiden 1979
– 'Masada. Literary Tradition, Archaeological Remains and the Credibility of Josephus'. *JJS* 33 (1982) 385-405
COHN, L. *Einteilung und Chronologie der Schriften Philos* (Philologus Suppl. 7) Berlin 1899
– 'An Apocryphal Ascribed to Philo of Alexandria'. *JQR* 10 (1898) 227-332
– 'Zur Lehre vom Logos bei Philo', in *Judaica. Festschrift Hermann Cohen*. Berlin 1912
COHN, L. *et al. Die Werke Philos in deutscher Übersetzung* 1-7. Breslau 1919-64
COHN, L. — WENDLAND, P. (eds.) *Philonis Alexandrini opera quae supersunt. Editio Maior* 1-8. Berlin 1896-1930
COHN-SHERBOK, D. 'The Alphabet in Mandaean and Jewish Gnosticism'. *Religion* 11 (1981) 227-34
COLLINS, J. J. 'The Date and Provenance of the Testament of Moses', in Nickelsburg, *Studies on the Testament of Moses,* 15-32

611

— 'Some Remaining Traditio-Historical Problems in the Testament of Moses', in Nickelsburg, *Studies on the Testament of Moses,* 38-43
— 'Apocalyptic Eschatology as the Transcendence of Death'. *CBQ* 36 (1974) 21-43
— 'The Place of the Fourth Sibyl in the Development of the Jewish Sibyllina'. *JJS* 25 (1974) 365-80
— 'The Provenance and Date of the Third Sibylline Oracle'. *Bulletin of the Institute of Jewish Studies* 2 (1974) 1-18
— *The Sibylline Oracles of Egyptian Judaism.* Missoula 1974
— 'Structure and Meaning in the Testament of Job'. *SBLSP* 1 (1974) 35-52
— 'The Symbolism of Transcendence in Jewish Apocalyptic'. *BR* 19 (1974) 1-18
— 'The Court-Tales of Daniel and the Development of Apocalyptic'. *JBL* 94 (1975) 218-34
— 'Jewish Apocalyptic against its Hellenistic Near Eastern Environment'. *BASOR* 220 (1975) 27-36
— 'The Mythology of the Holy War in Daniel and the Qumran War Scroll: A Point of Transition in Jewish Apocalyptic'. *VT* 25 (1975) 496-612
— 'The Apocalyptic Technique: Setting and Function in the Book of Watchers'. *CBQ* 39 (1977) 91-111
— *The Apocalyptic Vision of the Book of Daniel.* Missoula 1977
— 'Cosmos and Salvation: Jewish Wisdom and Apocalyptic in the Hellenistic Age'. *HR* 17 (1977) 121-92
— 'Pseudonymity, Historical Reviews and the Genre of the Revelation of John'. *CBQ* 39 (1977) 329-43
— 'Methodological Issues in the Study of 1 Enoch: Reflections on the Articles of P. D. Hanson and G. W. Nickelsburg', *SBLSP* 5 (1978) 315-22
— 'The Epic of Theodotus and the Hellenism of the Hasmoneans'. *HTR* 73 (1980) 91-104
— 'The Heavenly Representative: The "Son of Man" in the Similitudes of Enoch', in Collins-Nickelsburg, *Ideal Figures,* 111-33
— 'Apocalyptic Genre and Mythical Allusions in Daniel'. *JSOT* 21 (1981) 83-100
— 'Patterns of Eschatology at Qumran', in *Traditions in Transformation,* ed. by B. Halpern and J. D. Levenson. Winona Lake, IN 1981, 351-75
— *Between Athens and Jerusalem. Jewish Identity in the Hellenistic Diaspora.* New York 1983
— 'The Genre Apocalypse in Hellenistic Judaism', in Hellholm, *Apocalypticism,* 531-48
— 'The Sibylline Oracles', in Charlesworth, *Pseudepigrapha*
COLLINS, J. J. (ed.) *Apocalypse. The Morphology of a Genre* (Semeia 14) Missoula 1979
COLLINS, J. J. — NICKELSBURG, G. W. (eds.) *Ideal Figures in Ancient Judaism: Profiles and Paradigms.* Chico 1980
COLOMBO, D. 'Pneuma Sophia eiusque actio in mundo in Libro Sapientiae'. *SBFLA* 1 (1950-1) 107-60
COLPE, C. 'Philo', in *RGG* 5, 341-6
— '"Die Himmelsreise der Seele" ausserhalb und innerhalb der Gnosis', in *Le origini dello gnosticismo,* ed. by U. Bianchi. Leiden 1969, 429-47
— 'Heidnische, jüdische und christliche Überlieferung in den Schriften aus Nag Hammadi II'. *JAC* 16 (1973) 106-26
— 'Heidnische, jüdische, und christliche Überlieferung aus Nag Hammadi III'. *JAC* 17 (1974) 109-24
COLSON, F. M. 'Philo on Education'. *JTS* 18 (1917)
— 'Philo's Quotations from the OT'. *JTS* 41 (1940) 237-51
COLSON, F. M. — WHITAKER, G. H. — MARCUS, R. *Philo Works, Greek Text and English Translation* 1-10 and Suppl. 1-2. (Loeb) London 1929-53
CONYBEARE, F. C. 'On the Apocalypse of Moses'. *JQR* 7 (1895) 216-35
— 'The Testament of Solomon'. *JQR* 11 (1898) 1-45
CONZELMANN, H. 'Die Mutter der Weisheit', in *Dankgabe an R. Bultmann.* Tübingen 1964, 225-34
— *1 Corinthians.* Philadelphia 1975

COOK, S. A. 'I Esdras', in *APOT* 1, 1-58

COPPENS, J. 'Le célibat essénien', in Delcor, *Qumran*, 295-303

CORNELY, R. *Commentarius in librum Sapientiae*, ed. by F. Zorell. Paris 1910

CORTÈS, E. *Los discursos de adiós de Gn 49 a Jn 13-17.* Barcelona 1976

COUROYER, B. 'BRK et les formules égyptiennes de salutation'. *RB* 85 (1978) 575-85

COWLEY, A. E. *Aramaic Papyri Discovered at Assuan.* London 1906

— *Aramaic Papyri of the Fifth Century B.C.* Oxford 1923

COWLEY, A. — NEUBAUER, A. *The Original Hebrew of a Portion of Ecclesiasticus.* Oxford 1897

CRAVEN, T. 'Artistry and Faith in the Book of Judith'. *Semeia* 8 (1977) 75-101

CRENSHAW, J. L. (ed.). *Studies in Ancient Israelite Wisdom.* New York 1976

CRENSHAW, J. L. 'The Contest of Darius' Guards', in *Images of Man and God: Old Testament Short Stories in Literary Focus,* ed. by O. Long. Sheffield 1981, 74-88; 119-20

CRÖNERT, G. 'Oraculorum Sibyllinorum Fragmentum Osloense'. *Symbolae Osloenses* 6 (1928) 57-59

CROSS, F. M. 'The Oldest Manusripts from Qumran'. *JBL* 74 (1955) 147-72

— *The Ancient Library of Qumran and Modern Biblical Studies,* rev. ed. Garden City, N.Y. 1961

— 'The Development of the Jewish Scripts', in *The Bible and the Ancient Near East. Essays in Honor of W. F. Albright,* ed. by G. E. Wright. New York 1961, 133-202

— 'Aspects of Samaritan and Jewish History in Late Persian and Hellenistic Times'. *HTR* 59 (1966) 201-11

— 'New Directions in the Study of Apocalyptic'. *JTC* 6 (1969) 157-65

— 'Introduction', in Trever, *Scrolls from Qumrân Cave 1,* 1-5

— *Canaanite Myth and Hebrew Epic.* Cambridge MA 1973

DAHL, N. A. *Das Volk Gottes.* Oslo 1941

— *Studies in Paul.* Minneapolis 1977

— 'The Arrogant Archon and the Lewd Sophia: Jewish Traditions in Gnostic Revolt', in Layton, *Rediscovery* 2, 599-712

DAHOOD, M. 'Canaanite-Phoenician Influence in Qoheleth'. *Biblica* 33 (1952) 30-52; 191-221

— *Proverbs and Northwest Semitic Philology.* Rome 1963

DALBERT, P. *Die Theologie der hellenistisch-jüdischen Missionsliteratur unter Ausschluss von Philo und Josephus.* Hamburg 1954

DALMAN, G. *Aramäische Dialektproben,* 2nd ed. Leipzig 1927

DAN, J. 'Allegory. In Talmudic and Medieval Literature', in *EJ* 1, 643

DAUBE, D. 'Typology in Josephus'. *JJS* 31 (1980) 18-36

DAUMAS, F. 'Littérature prophétique et exégétique égyptienne et commentaires esséniens', in *A la Rencontre de Dieu,* ed. by A. Barucq. Paris 1961, 203-21

DAVENPORT, G. L. *The Eschatology of the Book of Jubilees.* Leiden 1971

DAVIES, G. I. 'Apocalyptic and Historiography'. *JSOT* 5 (1978) 15-28

DAVIES, P. R. 'Hasidim in the Maccabean Period'. *JJS* 28 (1977) 127-40

— *1QM. The War Scroll from Qumran. Its Structure and History.* Rome 1977

— 'The Ideology of the Temple in the Damascus Document'. *JJS* 32 (1982) 287-301

— 'The Calendrical Change and Qumran Origins: An Assessment of VanderKam's Theory'. *CBQ* 45 (1983) 80-89

— *The Damascus Covenant.* Sheffield 1983

DAVIES, W. D. *Paul and Rabbinic Judaism.* London 1948

DEANE, W. J. *Sophia Salomon. The Book of Wisdom. The Greek Text, the Latin Vulgate and the Authorized English Version with an Introduction, Critical Apparatus and a Commentary.* Oxford 1881

DE BRUYNE, D. 'Etude sur le texte latin de l'Ecclésiastique'. *Revue Bénédictine* 40 (1928) 5-48

— 'Etude sur le texte latin de la Sagesse'. *Revue Bénédictine* 41 (1929) 101-33

DEBEVOISE, N. C. *A Political History of Parthia.* Chicago 1938

DECHENT, H· *Ueber das erste, zweite und elfte Buch der Sibyllinischen Weissagungen.* Diss. Jena 1873

DEHANDSCHUTTER, B. 'La rêve dans l'Apocryphe de la Genèse', in *La Littérature juive entre Tenach et Michna*, ed. by W. C. van Unnik. Leiden 1974, 48-55

DEICHGRABER, 'Zur Messiaserwartung der Damaskusschrift'. *ZAW* 78 (1966) 333-43

DEISSMANN, A. *Light from the Ancient East,* trans. by L.R.M. Strachan. New ed. London 1927

DELCOR, M. 'Contribution à l'étude de la législation des sectaires de Damas et de Qumran'. *RB* 61 (1954) 533-53; 62 (1955) 60-75

— 'L'immortalité de l'âme dans le livre de Sagesse et dans les documents de Qumrân'. *NRT* 77 (1955) 614-30

— *Les hymnes de Qumran (Hodayot).* Paris 1962

— 'Recherches sur un Horoscope en langue hébraïque provenant de Qumran'. *RQ* 5 (1966) 521-42

— 'Le texte hébreu du Cantique du Siracide LI, 13 et ss. et les versions anciennes'. *Textus* 6 (1968) 27-47

— 'Le Testament de Job, la prière de Nabonide et les traditions targoumiques', in *Bibel und Qumran,* ed. by S. Wagner. Berlin 1968, 57-74

— 'De l'origine de quelques traditions contenues dans le Testament d'Abraham', in *Proceedings of the Fifth World Congress of Jewish Studies* 1, Jerusalem 1969, 192-200

— *Le Livre de Daniel.* Paris 1971

— 'The Melchizedek Figure from Genesis to the Qumran Texts and the Epistle to the Hebrews'. *JSJ* 2 (1971) 115-35

— *Le Testament d'Abraham.* Leiden 1973

— 'Le mythe de la chute des anges et de l'origine des géants comme explication du mal dans le monde dans l'apocalyptique juive: Histoire des traditions'. *RHR* 190 (1976) 3-53

— 'Le Milieu d'origine et le développement de l'apocalyptique juive', in *La Littérature juive entre Tenach et Michna,* ed. by W. C. van Unnik. Leiden 1979, 101-17

DELCOR, M. (ed.) *Qumran, sa piété, sa théologie et son milieu.* Paris 1978

DELLING, G. 'Josephus und das Wunderbare'. *NT* 2 (1958) 291-309

— *Jüdische Lehre und Frömmigkeit in den Paralipomena Jeremiae* (BZAW 100) Berlin 1967

— 'Wunder-Allegorie-Mythus bei Philon von Alexandreia', in *Studien zum N.T. und zum hellen. Judentum.* Göttingen 1970, 72-129

— 'Die biblische Prophetie bei Josephus', in *Josephus-Studien. Festschrift O. Michel.* Göttingen 1974, 109-21

— 'Perspektiven der Erforschung des hellenistischen Judentums.' *HUCA* 45 (1974) 133-76

DELLING, G. — MASER, M. *Bibliographie zur jüdisch-hellenistischen und intertestamentarischen Literatur: 1900-1970,* 2nd ed. Berlin 1975

DENIS, A. M. 'Evolution des structures dans le secte de Qumran', in *Aux origins de l'Eglise* (Recherches Bibliques 7) Louvain 1965, 23-49

— *Les Thèmes de Connaissance dans le Document de Damas.* Louvain 1967

— *Fragmenta Pseudepigraphorum quae supersunt Graeca* (PVTG) Leiden 1970

— *Introduction aux pseudépigraphes grecs d'Ancient Testament.* Leiden 1970

— *Concordance Latine du Liber Jubilaeorum sive Parva Genesis.* Louvain 1973

DENIS, A. M. — JANSSENS, Y. *Concordance de l'Apocalypse grecque de Baruch.* Louvain 1970

DE VAUX, R. *Archaeology and the Dead Sea Scrolls.* Rev. ed. Oxford 1973

DESELAERS, P. *Das Buch Tobit. Studien zu seiner Entstehung, Komposition und Theologie.* Freiburg 1982

DEXINGER, F. *Henochs Zehnwochenapokalypse und offene Probleme der Apokalyptikforschung.* Leiden 1970

DHORME, P. *Le livre de Job.* Paris 1926

DIELS, H. *Sibyllinische Blätter.* Berlin 1890

DIETZFELBINGER, C. *Pseudo-Philo, Antiquitates Biblicae* (JSHRZ II/2) Gütersloh 1976

DI FONZO, L. *Ecclesiaste.* Torino-Roma 1967

DI LELLA, A. A. 'Qumran and the Geniza Fragments of Sirach'. *CBQ* 24 (1962) 245-67

— 'The Recently Identified Leaves of Sirach in Hebrew'. *Biblica* 45 (1964) 153-67

— *The Hebrew Text of Sirach. A Text-Critical and Historical Study.* London 1966

DILLMANN, A. *Lexicon Linguae Aethiopicae*. New York 1955
DILLON, J. 'The Transcendence of God in Philo: Some Possible Sources', in W. Wüellner (ed.), *Protocol of the 16th Colloquy. The Center for Hermeneutical Studies*. Berkeley 1975
— *The Middle Platonists*. London 1977
DIMANT, D. *The Fallen Angels in the Dead Sea Scrolls and in Apocryphal and Pseudepigraphic Books related to them*. Unpublished dissertation. Jerusalem, Hebrew University, 1974 (Hebrew)
— 'I Enoch 6-11: A Methodological Perspective'. *SBLSP* 5 (1978) 323-39
— 'Jerusalem and the Temple in the Animal Apocalypse (1 Enoch 85-90) in the light of the Dead Sea Scrolls Thought'. *Shnaton* 5-6 (1981/92) 177-83
— 'History according to the Animal Apolcalypse, *Jerusalem Studies in Jewish Thought* 2 (1982) 18-37 (Hebrew)
— 'The Pesher on the Periods (4Q180) and 4Q181'. *Israel Oriental Studies* 9
DION, P.-E. 'Les types épistolaires hébréo-araméens jusqu'au temps de Bar-Kokhba'. *RB* 86 (1979) 544-79
DODD, C. H. *The Bible and the Greeks*. London 1935
— *Interpretation of the Fourth Gospel*. Cambridge 1953
— *Historical Tradition in the Fourth Gospel*. Cambridge 1963
DODDS, E. R. *The Greeks and the Irrational*. Berkeley — Los Angeles 1963
DÖRRIE, H. (ed.) *Passio SS. Machabaeorum, die antike lateinische Uebersetzung des IV. Makkabäerbuches* (Abhandlungen der Gesellschaft der Wissenschaften zu Göttingen, Phil. Hist. Klasse 3, 22) Göttingen 1938
DÖRRIES, H. 'Erotopokriseis B', in *RAC* 6, 347-70
DOEVE, J. W. 'Lamechs achterdocht in 1Q Genesis Apokryphon'. *NTT* 15 (1960-61) 401-15
DOMBKOWSKI HOPKINS, D. 'The Qumran Community and the 1Q Hodayot: A Reassessment'. *RQ* 10 (1981) 324-31
DOMBROWSKI, B. W. 'The Idea of God in 1Q Serek'. *RQ* 7 (1971) 515-31
DORAN, R. '2 Maccabees and "Tragic History"'. *HUCA* 48 (1977) 107-14
— *Studies in the Style and Literary Character of 2 Maccabees*. Dissertation Harvard University 1977
— *Temple Propaganda: The Purpose and Character of 2 Maccabees*. Washington D.C. 1981
DORESSE, J. *The Secret Book of the Egyptian Gnostics*, trans. by P. Mairet. New York 1960
DOTY, W. G. 'Classification of Epistolary Literature'. *CBQ* 31 (1969) 183-99
— *Letters in Primitive Christianity*. Philadelphia 1973
DOWNING, F. G. 'Redaction Criticism: Josephus' Antiquities and the Synoptic Gospels'. *JSNT* 8 (1980) 46-65
DRIVER, G. R. *The Judaean Scrolls; The Problem and a Solution*. Oxford 1965
— *Aramaic Documents of the Fifth Century* B.C. Oxford 1965
DRIVER, S. R. — GRAY, G. B. *A Critical and Exegetical Commentary on the Book of Job together with a New Translation*. Edinburgh 1921
DUBARLE, A.-M. 'Une Source du Livre de la Sagesse?' *RSPT* 37 (1953) 425-43
— *Judith* 1-2. Rome 1966
— 'L'authenticité des textes hébreux de Judith'. *Biblica* 50 (1969) 187-211
— *La manifestation naturelle de Dieu d'après l'Ecriture*. Paris 1976
— 'Le témoignage de Josèphe sur Jésus d'après des publications récentes'. *RB* 94 (1977) 38-58
DUCHESNE-GUILLEMIN, J. *La religion de l'Iran ancien*. Paris 1962
DUESBERG, H. — FRANSEN, I. *Ecclesiastico*. Torino-Roma 1966
— *Les scribes inspirés. Introduction aux livres sapientiaux de la Bible*. Edition remaniée. Maredsous 1966
DUHAIME, J. L. 'L'Instruction sur les deux esprits et les interpolations dualistes à Qumran (1QS III, 13-IV, 26)'. *RB* 84 (1977) 566-94
— 'Remarque sur les dépôts d'ossements d'animaux à Qumran'. *RQ* 9 (1977) 245-51
DUNAND, F. 'L'Oracle du Potier et la formation de l'apocalyptique en Egypte', in *L'Apocalyptique*. Paris 1977, 39-67

DUPONT-SOMMER, A. *Le Quatrième livre des Machabées.* Paris 1939
— *Aperçus préliminaires sur les manuscripts de la Mer Morte.* Paris 1950
— *Nouveaux aperçus sur les manuscrits de la Mer Morte.* Paris 1953
— *Le Livre des Hymnes découvert près de la Mer Morte (1QH).* Semitica 7 (1957)
— *Les Ecrits Esséniens découverts près de la Mer Morte.* Paris 1960
— 'Deux Documents horoscopiques esséniens découverts à Qumran près de la Mer Morte'. *CRAI* (1965) 239-53
— *The Essene Writings from Qumran.* Gloucester MA 1973
DIJK, J. VAN. *La sagesse suméro-accadienne.* Leiden 1953
— 'Die Tontafelfunde der Kampagne 1959/60' *AFO* 20 (1963) 217-8
DZIATKO, K. 'Brief', in *PWRE* 3, 836-43
EARP, J. W. 'Index of Names', in Colson, *Philo* 10, 269-433
EBERHARTER, A. E. 'Die "Ekklesiasticuszitate" bei Klemens von Alexandrien. Gesammelt und mit LXX und Vulgata verglichen'. *TQ* 93 (1911) 1-22
— 'The Text of Ecclesiasticus in the Quotations of Clement of Alexandria and Saint Cyprian'. *Biblica* 7 (1926) 79-83
EDDY, S. K. *The King is Dead. Studies in the Near Eastern Resistance to Hellenism 334-31* B.C.E. Lincoln 1961
EDWARDS, R. *A Theology of Q. Eschatology, Prophecy and Wisdom.* Philadelphia 1976
EISSFELDT, O. *The Old Testament: An Introduction.* Oxford-New York 1965
EISSLER, R. *Jesous Basileus ou Basileusas.* Heidelberg 1929
ELBOGEN, I. *Der jüdische Gottesdienst in seiner geschichtlichen Entwicklung.* Frankfurt 1931 (repr. Hildesheim 1962)
ELLERMEIER, F. *Qohelet. I, 1. Untersuchungen zum Buche Qohelet.* Harz 1967
ELLIGER, K. *Studien zum Habakuk-Kommentar vom Toten Meer.* Tübingen 1953
EMERTON, J. A. — LANE, D. J. *Wisdom of Solomon* (Peshitta) Leiden 1979
EMMET, C. W. 'The Third Book of Maccabees', in *APOT* 2, 155-73
ENGLANDER, H. 'The Men of the Great Synagogne'. *HUCA* Jubilee Volume 1925, 145-69
ENSLIN, M. S. — ZEITLIN, S. *The Book of Judith.* Leiden 1972
EPPEL, R. *Le piétisme juif dans les Testaments des douze Patriarches.* Paris 1930
EPSTEIN, J. N. *Introduction to Tannaitic Literature.* Jerusalem 1957 (Hebrew)
EVEN-SHMUEL, Y. *Midreshei Geulah.* Tel Aviv 1943
EVERDING, H. E. *The Living God: A Study in the Function and Meaning of Biblical Terminology.* Harvard University Diss. 1968
EXLER, F. X. J. *The Form of the Ancient Greek Letter of the Epistolary Papyri.* Washington 1923
FABRICIUS, J. A. *Codex Pseudepigraphus Veteris Testamenti* 1-2. Hamburg 1713-23
FALLON, F. T. *The Enthronement of Sabaoth: Jewish Elements in Gnostic Creation Myths.* Leiden 1978
— 'The Gnostic Apocalypses', in Collins, *Apocalypse,* 123-58
— 'Theodotus', in Charlesworth, *Pseudepigrapha*
FARMER, W. R. *Maccabees, Zealots and Josephus.* New York 1956
— 'Judas, Simon and Athronges'. *NTS* 4 (1958) 147-55
FELDMAN, L. H. *Scholarship on Philo and Josephus (1937-1962).* New York 1962
— 'The Sources of Josephus' Antiquities, Book 19'. *Latomus* 21 (1962) 320-33
— *Josephus, Jewish Antiquities, XVIII-XX,* With an English Translation, in Thackeray, *Josephus* 9-10
— 'Abraham the Greek Philosopher in Josephus'. *TAPA* 99 (1968) 143-56
— 'Hellenizations in Josephus "Portrayal of Man's Decline"', in *Religions in Antiquity: Festschrift E.R. Goodenough.* Leiden 1968, 336-53
— 'Hellenizations in Josephus' Version of Esther (Ant. Jud. 11.185-295)'. *TAPA* 101 (1970) 143-70
— 'Prolegomenon', in M. R. James, *The Biblical Antiquities of Philo.* Repr. New York 1971, IX-CLXIX
— *Josephus and Modern Scholarship 1937-1980.* Berlin 1984

FENZ, A. K. 'Ein Drache in Babel'. *SEA* 35 (1970) 12 ff.

FESTUGIÈRE, A. J. *La révélation d'Hermès Trismégiste* 1-4. Paris 1944-54

FEUILLET, A. 'Jésus et la Sagesse divine d'après les Evangiles Synoptiques'. *RB* 62 (1955) 161-96
— *Le Christ Sagesse de Dieu d'après les épîtres pauliniennes.* Paris 1966
— 'Premiers-nés. Nouveau Testament'. *DBS* 8 (1972) 500-10

FIEBIG, P. *Altjüdische Gleichnisse und Gleichnisse Jesu.* Tübingen 1904

FINKEL, A. 'The Pesher of Dreams and Scriptures'. *RQ* 4 (193/64) 357-70

FINKELSTEIN, L. 'The Book of Jubilees and the Rabbinic Halaka'. *HTR* 16 (1923) 39-61
— *The Pharisees and the Men of the Great Synagogue.* New York 1950 (Hebrew)
— *The Pharisees.* 3rd ed. Philadelphia 1963

FISCHEL, H. A. 'Martyr and Prophet'. *JQR* 37 (1946-47) 265-80; 363-83

FISHBANE, M. 'The Qumran-Pesher and Traits of Ancients Hermeneutics', in *Proceedings of the Sixth World Congress of Jewish Studies* 6/1 (1977) 97-114

FISHBURNE, C. W. 'I Corinthians III, 10-15'. *NTS* 17 (1970-71) 109-15

FITZER, G. 'σφραγίς etc.', in *TDNT* 7, 939-53

FITZMYER, J. A. 'The Padua Aramaic Papyrus Letters'. *JNES* 21 (1962) 15-24
— 'Prolegomenon', in Schechter, *Fragments of a Zadokite work.* Repr. New York 1970, 9-37
— 'A Bibliographic Aid to the Study of Qumran Cave IV Texts 158-86'. *CBQ* 31 (1969) 59-71
— *Essays on the Semitic Background of the New Testament.* London 1971
— *The Genesis Apocryphon of Qumran Cave I,* 2nd ed. Rome 1971
— 'David, Being Therefore a Prophet . . ? (Acts 2:30)' *CBQ* 34 (1972) 332-9
— 'The Contribution of Qumran Aramaic to the Study of the New Testament'. *NTS* 20 (1974) 382-407
— 'Some Notes on Aramaic Epistolography'. *JBL* 93 (1974) 201-25
— *The Dead Sea Scrolls: Major Publications and Tools for Study.* Missoula 1977
— 'Crucifixion in Ancient Palestine, Qumran Literature and the New Testament'. *CBQ* 40 (1978) 493-513
— 'The First-Century Targum of Job from Qumran Cave XI', in *A Wandering Aramean.* Missoula 1979, 161-82
— 'The Phases of the Aramaic Language', in *A Wandering Aramean.* Missoula 1979, 57-84

FITZMYER, J. A. — HARRINGTON, D. J. *A Manual of Palestinian Aramaic Texts.* Rome 1978

FLEMING, J. — RADEMACHER, L. *Das Buch Henoch* (GCS) Leipzig 1901

FLEMMING, J. — DUENSING, M. 'The Ascension of Isaiah', in Hennecke-Schneemelcher, *New Testament Apocrypha* 2, 642-63

FLUSSER, D. 'The Apocryphal Book of Ascensio Isaiae and the Dead Sea Sect'. *IEJ* 3 (1953) 30-47
— 'The Sect of the Judean Desert and Its Opinions'. *Zion* 19 (1954) 89-103 (Hebrew)
— 'The Dead Sea Sect and Pre-Pauline Christianity', in *Scripta* 4, 215-66
— 'Sefer Tuvia', in *Encyclopaedia Biblica* 3, Jerusalem 1958, 367-75 (Hebrew)
— 'Two Notes on the Midrash on 2 Sam VII'. *IEJ* 9 (1959) 104-6
— 'Blessed are the Poor in Spirit'. *IEJ* 10 (1960) 1-13
— 'Sanktus und Gloria', in O. Betz *et al.* (eds.), *Abraham unser Vater. Festschrift für Otto Michel.* Leiden 1963, 129-52
— 'Melchizedek and the Son of Man'. *Christian News from Israel* 17 (1966) 23-9
— 'Qumran and Jewish "Apotropaic" Prayers'. *IEJ* 16 (1966) 194-205
— 'Martyrdom in the Second Temple Period and the Beginnings of Christianity', in *Holy War and Martyrology, Lectures Delivered at the Eleventh Convention of the Historical Society of Israel — March 1966.* Jerusalem 1967, 61-71 (Hebrew)
— 'A New Sensitivity in Judaism and the Christian Message'. *HTR* 61 (1968) 107-27
— '*Palaea Historica.* An Unknown Source of Biblical Legends', in *Scripta* 22, 48-79
— 'The Testaments of the Twelve Patriarchs', in *EJ* 13, 184-6
— 'Seventy Shepherds, Vision of', in *EJ* 14, 1198-99
— 'The Four Empires in the Fourth Sibyl and in the Book of Daniel'. *Israel Oriental Studies* 2 (1972) 148-75

617

— 'The Last Supper and the Essenes'. *Immanuel* 2 (1973) 23-7
— 'Jerusalem in the Literature of the Second Temple Period', in *We-im Bi-gvurot. A Tribute to Rubin and Hannah Mass.* Jerusalem 1974, 263-94 (Hebrew)
— 'Der lateinische Josephus and der hebräische Josippon', in *Josephus-Studien: Festschrift O. Michel.* Göttingen 1974, 122-32
— 'Some Notes on Easter and the Passover Haggadah'. *Immanuel* 7 (1977) 52-60
— *Sefer Josippon.* Ed. with Introduction. Commentary and Notes 1-2. Jerusalem 1978-81 (Hebrew)
— 'Paganism in Palestine', in *Compendia* I/2, 1065-1100
— Review of Yadin, The Temple Scroll. *Numen* 26 (1979) 271-4
— *Jewish Sources in Early Christianity. Studies and Essays.* Tel Aviv 1979 (Hebrew)
— 'The Temple Scroll from Qumran'. *Immanuel* 9 (1979) 49-52
— 'The Hubris of the Antichrist in a Fragment from Qumran'. *Immanuel* 10 (1980) 31-7
— 'Pharisäer, Sadduzäer und Essener im Pescher Nahum', in K. E. Gröziger *et al.* (eds.), *Qumran* (Wege der Forschung 410) Darmstadt 1981, 121-66
— *Die rabbinischen Gleichnisse und der Gleichniserzähler Jesus* 1. Bern 1981
— 'Hystaspes and John of Patmos', in *Irano-Judaica.* Jerusalem 1982, 12-75
FLUSSER, D. — SAFRAI, S. 'Who Sanctifies the Beloved in the Womb'. *Immanuel* 11 (1980) 46-55
— 'A Fragment of the Songs of David and Qumran', in *Bible Studies, Y. M. Grintz in Memoriam.* Tel Aviv 1982, 83-105 (Hebrew)
FOCKE, F. *Die Entstehung der Weisheit Salomos. Ein Beitrag zur Geschichte des jüdischen Hellenismus.* Göttingen 1913
FOERSTER, W. *Gnosis: A Selection of Gnostic Texts,* trans. by R. M. Wilson 1-2. Oxford 1972-74
FOHRER. G. *Das Buch Hiob.* Gütersloh 1963
FOX, M. V. 'Two Decades of Research in Egyptian Wisdom Literature'. *ZÄS* 107 (1980) 120-35
FRANKEL, Z. *Ueber den Einfluss der palästinischen Exegese auf die alexandrinische Hermeneutik.* Leipzig 1851
FRANXMAN, T. W. *Genesis and the 'Jewish Antiquities' of Flavius Josephus.* Rome 1979
FRASER, P. M. *Ptolemaic Alexandria* 1-2. Oxford 1972
FREEDMAN, H. — SIMON, M. *Midrash Rabbah 1-10.* London 1939
FREEDMAN, D. N. 'The Prayer of Nabonidus'. *BASOR* 145 (1957) 31-32
FREND, W. H. C. *Martyrdom and Persecution in the Early Church.* Oxford 1965
FREUDENTHAL, J. *Hellenistische Studien, 1-2, Alexander Polyhistor und die von ihm erhaltenen Reste jüdischer und samaritanischer Geschichtswerke.* Breslau 1875
FREY, J. B. 'Abraham (Apocalypse d')', in *DBS* 1, 28-33
—'Adam (Livres apocryphes sous son nom)', in *DBS* 1, 101-34
FREYNE, S. *Galilee from Alexander the Great to Hadrian, 323* B.C.E. *to 135* C.E. Wilmington-Notre Dame 1980
FRICKEL, J. 'Naassener oder Valentinianer?' in Krause, *Gnosis and Gnosticism,* 95-119
FRIEDLÄNDER, M. *Der vorchristliche jüdische Gnosticismus.* Göttingen 1898
FRITSCH, C. *The Anti-Anthropomorphisms of the Greek Pentateuch.* Princeton 1943
FROST, S. B. *Old Testament Apocalyptic: its Origins and Growth.* London 1952
FRÜCHTEL, H. *Die kosmologischen Vorstellungen bei Philo von Alexandrien.* Leiden 1968
FRYE, R. N. 'Qumran and Iran: The State of Studies', in *Christianity, Judaism and other Greco-Roman Cults. Studies for Morton Smith.* Leiden 1975, 107-73
FUCHS, C. 'Das Leben Adams und Evas', in Kautzsch, *Apokryphen,* 506-28
FUCHS, H. *Der geistige Widerstand gegen Rom in der antiken Welt.* Berlin 1938
FUNK, F. X. *Didascalia et Constitutiones Apostolorum.* Paderborn 1905
GABRION, H. L' interprétation de l'Ecriture dans la littérature de Qumran', in *ANRW* II, 19/1, 779-898
GÄRTNER, E. *Komposition und Wortwahl des Buches der Weisheit.* Berlin 1912
GAGER, J. 'Pseudo-Hecataeus Again'. *ZNW* 60 (1969) 130-39
— *Moses in Greco-Roman Paganism.* New York 1972
— 'Some Attempts to Label the Oracula Sibyllina, Book 7'. *HTR* 65 (1972) 91-97

GALILI, E. 'Raphia 217 B.C.E. Revisited'. *Scripta Classica Israelitica* 3 (1976-7) 52-126

GALL, A. F. VON. *Basileia tou Theou.* Heidelberg 1926

GAMBERONI, J. *Die Auslegung des Buches Tobias in der griechisch-lateinischen Kirche der Antike und der Christenheit des Westens bis 1600.* 1969

GAMMIE, J. G. 'Spatial and Ethical Dualism in Jewish Wisdom and Apocalyptic Literature'. *JBL* 93 (1974) 365-85

— (ed.) *Israelite Wisdom. Theological and Literary Essays in Honor of Samuel Terrien.* Missoula 1978

GASELEE, S. 'Appendix Containing a Translation of the Coptic Version of the Testaments of Isaac and Jacob', in Box, *Testament of Abraham,* 76-89

GARNET, P. *Salvation and Atonement in the Qumran Scrolls.* Tübingen 1977

GASTER, M. 'The Hebrew Text of One of the Testaments of the Twelve Patriarchs'. *Proceedings of the Society of Biblical Archaeology* (1893-94) 33-49; 109-17

— 'Das Buch Josua in hebräisch-samaritanischer Rezension'. *ZDMG* 62 (1906) 209-79; 494-549

GATZ, B. *Weltalter, goldene Zeit und sinnverwandte Vorstellungen.* Hildesheim 1967

GEFFCKEN, J. 'Die Babylonische Sibylle'. *Nachrichten der Königlichen Gesellschaft der Wissenschaften zu Göttingen* (1900) 88-102

— 'Römische Kaiser im Volksmunde der Provinz'. *Ibid.* (1901) 183-95

— *Komposition und Entstehungszeit der Oracula Sibyllina* (TU) Leipzig 1902

— *Die Oracula Sibyllina* (GCS) Leipzig 1902

GEMSER, B. *Sprüche Salomos.* 2nd ed. Tübingen 1963

GEOLTRAIN, P. *Le traité de la Vie Comtemplative de Philon d'Alexandrie* (Semitica 10) Paris 1960

GEOLTRAIN, P. — SCHMIDT, F. 'De l'apocalyptique juive aux apocalypses chrétiennes'. *Annuaire de l'Ecole des Hautes Etudes,* Sect. 5, 88 (1979-80) 337-9

GEORGI, D. *Weisheit Salomos* (JSHRZ 3) Gütersloh 1980.

GERHARDSSON, G. *Memory and Manuscript.* Uppsala 1961

GERLEMAN, G. 'The Septuagint Proverbs as a Hellenistic Document'. *OTS* 8 (1950) 15-27

— *Studies in the Septuaginta 3. Proverbs.* Lund 1956

GERO, S. 'Henoch und die Sibylle'. *ZWN* 73 (1982) 148-50

GESE, H. *Lehre und Wirklichkeit in der alten Weisheit.* Tübingen 1958

GESENIUS, W. — KAUTZSCH, E. *Hebrew Grammar.* Oxford 1960

GHIRSHMAN, R. *Iran. From the Earliest Times to the Islamic Conquest.* Harmondsworth 1965

GILBERT, M., 'La Structure de la Prière de Salomon (Sg 9)'. *Biblica* 51 (1970) 301-31

— 'Volonté de Dieu et don de la Sagesse (Sg 9, 17 s.)'. *NRT* 93 (1971) 145-66

— *La critique des dieux dans le Livre de la Sagesse* (Sg. 13-15). Rome 1973

— 'L'éloge de la Sagesse (Siracide 24)'. *Revue Théologique de Louvain* 5 (1974) 326-48

— 'La connaissance de Dieu selon le livre de la Sagesse', in *La Notion biblique de Dieu. Le Dieu de la Bible et le Dieu des philosophes.* ed. J. Coppens. Leuven-Gembloux 1976, 191-210

— 'La conjecture μετριότητι en Sg 12, 22a'. *Biblica* 57 (1976) 550-3

— 'Ben Sira et la femme'. *Revue Théologique de Louvain* 7 (1976) 426-42

— 'Bibliographie générale sur Sagesse', in Larcher, *Livre de la Sagesse*

GILBERT, M. (ed.) *La Sagesse de l'Ancien Testament.* Leuven-Gembloux 1979

GINSBURG, D. *Coheleth, Commonly Called The Book of Ecclesiastes.* London 1861

GINZBERG, L. 'Abraham, Apocalypse of', in *JE* 1, 91-92

— 'Baruch, Apocalypse of (Syriac)', in *JE* 2, 551

— *The Legends of the Jews* 1-7. Philadelphia 1910-38

— 'Some Observations on the Attitude of the Synagogue towards the Apocalyptic-eschatological Writings'. *JBL* 41 (1922) 115-36

GIVERSEN, S. *Apocryphon Johannis.* Copenhagen 1963

— 'The Apocryphon of John and Genesis'. *ST* 17 (1963) 60-76

GLASSON, T. F. *Greek Influence in Jewish Eschatology.* London 1961

GOLB, N. 'The Literary and Doctrinal Aspects of the Damascus Covenant in the Light of the Karaite Literature'. *JQR* 47 (1957) 354-74

– 'The Dietary Laws of the Damascus Covenant in Relation to those of the Karaites'. *JJS* 8 (1957) 51-69

GOLDSMITH, J. 'Acts 13-33-37: A Pesher on II Samuel 7'. *JBL* 87 (1968) 321-4

GOLDSTEIN, J. *I Maccabees* (Anchor Bible). New York 1976

– 'Tales of the Tobiads', in *Christianity, Judaism and Other Greco-Roman Cults: Studies for Morton Smith at Sixty* 3. Leiden 1976, 85-123

– 'The Apocryphal Book of 1 Baruch', in *American Academy for Jewish Research Jubilee Volume*, ed. by S. W. Baron and I. E. Barzilay. New York 1980, 179-99

GOODBLATT, D. 'The Origins of Roman Recognition of the Palestinian Patriarchate', in U. Rappaport ed., *Studies in the History of the Jewish People and the Land of Israel* 4. Haifa 1978, 89-102 (Hebrew)

GOODENOUGH, E. R. 'The Political Philosophy of Hellenistic Kingship'. *YCS* 1 (1928) 53-102

– *The Jewish Iurisprudence.* New Haven 1929

– 'A Neo-Pythagorean Source in Philo Judaeus'. *YCS* 3 (1932) 115-64

– 'Philo's Exposition of the Law and his De Vita Mosis'. *HTR* 26 (1933) 109-25

– *By Light, Light. The Mystic Gospel of Hellenistic Judaism.* New Haven 1935

– *The Politics of Philo Judaeus.* New Haven 1938

– *Jewish Symbols in the Greco-Roman Period* 1-13. New York 1953-68

– *An Introduction to Philo Judaeus.* 2nd ed. Oxford 1962

GOODING, D. W. 'Aristeas and Septuagint Origins'. *VT* 13 (1963) 357-79

GOODHART, H. I. – GOODENOUGH, E. R. 'A Bibliography of Philo', in Goodenough, *The Politics*, 130-321

GOODRICK, A. T. S. *The Book of Wisdom with Introduction and Notes.* London 1913

GORDIS, R. 'A Document in Code from Qumran'. *JSS* 11 (1966) 37-9

– *Koheleth – The Man and his World. A Study of Ecclesiastes.* 3rd ed. New York 1973

– *The Book of Job. Commentary, New Translation and Special Studies.* New York 1978

GOSHEN-GOTTSTEIN, M. 'Anti-Essene Traits in the Dead Sea Scrolls'. *VT* 4 (1954) 141-7

– 'Linguistic Structure and Tradition in the Qumran Documents', in *Scripta* 4, 101-37

– 'Sefer Hagu – The End of a Puzzle'. *VT* 8 (1958) 286-8

GRABBE, L. L. 'Aquila's Translation and Rabbinic Exegesis'. *JJS* 33 (1982) 527-36

GRAETZ, H. 'Die Abfassungszeit des Pseudo-Aristeas'. *MGWJ* 25 (1876) 289-308; 337-49

GRANT, R. M. *The Letter and the Spirit.* London 1957

– 'The Book of Wisdom at Alexandria. Reflections on the History of the Canon and Theology', in *Studia Patristica* 7 (TU 92). Berlin 1966, 462-72

– *Gnosticism and Early Christianity.* Rev. ed. Columbia 1966

GREENFIELD, J. C. 'Prolegomena', in H. Odeberg, *3 Enoch or the Hebrew Book of Enoch* (1928) new ed. New York 1973

– 'Aramaic and its Dialects', in H. H. Paper (ed.), *Jewish Languages*. Cambridge MA 1978, 29-43

– 'Ahiqar in the Book of Tobit', in *De la Torah au Messie. Mélanges Henri Cazelles*. Paris 1981, 329-36

GREENFIELD, J. C. – STONE, M. E. 'Ahikar', in *EJ* 2, 460-2

– 'The Enochic Pentateuch and the Date of the Similitudes'. *HTR* 70 (1977) 51-65

– 'The Books of Enoch and the Traditions of Enoch'. *Numen* 26 (1979) 89-103

– 'Remarks on the Aramaic Testament of Levi from the Cairo Geniza (Planches XIII-XIV)'. *RB* 86 (1979) 214-30

GRELOT, P. 'Notes sur le Testament Araméen de Lévi'. *RB* 63 (1956) 391-406

– 'La géographie mythique d'Henoch et ses sources orientales'. *RB* 65 (1958) 33-69

– 'La légende d'Henoch dans les Apocryphes et dans la Bible: origine et signification'. *RSR* 46 (1958) 5-26; 181-210

– 'Deux Tosephtas targoumiques inédites sur Isaïe 66'. *RB* 89 (1972) 511-43

– *Documents araméens d'Egypte. Introduction, traduction, présentation.* Paris 1972

– 'Hénoch et ses écritures'. *RB* 82 (1975) 481-500

GRIFFITHS, J. G. 'Apocalyptic in the Hellenistic Era', in Hellholm, *Apocalypticism*
GRIGORIAN, G. 'The Armenian Commentaries from Works of Philo of Alexandria'. *Banber Mantenadarani* 5 (1960) (in Armenian)
GRIMM, C. L. W. *Das Buch der Weisheit.* Leipzig 1860
GRINTZ, J. M. *Sefer Yehudith.* Jerusalem 1957 (Hebrew)
— *Chapters in the History of the Second Temple Times.* Jerusalem 1969 (Hebrew)
— 'Judith, Book of', in *EJ* 10, 451-9
— 'Baruch, Apocalypse of (Syriac)' in *EJ* 4, 270-2
— 'Baruch, Greek Apocalypse of', in *EJ* 4, 273-4
— 'Jubilees, Book of', in *EJ* 10, 324-6
GRUENWALD, I. *Apocalyptic and Merkavah Mysticism.* Unpublished dissertation. Jerusalem n.d. (Hebrew)
— The Mirror and the Technique of Prophetic and Apocalyptic Vision'. *Beth Miqra* 40 (1970) 95-97
— 'Jewish Esoteric Literature in the Time of the Mishnah and Talmud'. *Immanuel* 4 (1974) 37-46
— 'Jewish Apocalyptic Literature', in *ANRW* II, 19/1, 89-118
— *Apocalyptic and Merkavah Mysticism.* Leiden 1980
— 'Jewish Merkavah Mysticism and Gnosticism', in *Studies in Jewish Mysticism*, ed. by J. Dan and F. Talmage. Cambridge MA 1981, 41-55
— 'Aspects of the Jewish-Gnostic Controversy', in Layton, *Rediscovery* 2, 713-23
GRY, L. 'La Ruine du Temple par Titus: Quelques traditions juives plus anciennes et primitives à la base de Pesikta Rabbati 26'. *RB* 55 (1948) 215-26
GUNKEL, H. 'Das vierte Buch Esra', in Kautzsch, *Die Pseudepigraphen*, 331-401
GUTMAN, Y. 'Philo the Epic Poet'. *Scripta* 1 (1954) 36-63
— *The Beginnings of Jewish-Hellenistic Literature* 1-2. Jerusalem 1958-63 (Hebrew)
HAAG, E. *Studien zum Buch Judith.* Trier 1963
HAAS, N. — NATHAN, N. 'Anthropological Survey on the Human Skeletal Remains from Qumran'. *RQ* 6 (1968) 345-52
HAASE, W. (ed.) *Aufstieg und Niedergang der Römischen Welt. II, Principat. Vols. 19/1-2 Palästinensisches Judentum.* Berlin-New York 1979. Vol. 21/1 *Philon und Josephus.* Berlin-New York 1984
HABERMANN, A. M. *Megilloth Midbar Yehudah.* Tel Aviv 1959 (Hebrew)
HABICHT, C. *2. Makkabäerbuch* (JSHRZ I/2) Gütersloh 1976
HABICHT, C. 'Royal Documents in Maccabees II'. *Harvard Studies in Classical Philology* 80 (1976) 1-18
HADAS, M. *Aristeas to Philocrates.* New York 1951
— *The Third and Fourth Books of Maccabees.* New York 1953
— *Hellenistic Culture. Fusion and Diffusion.* New York 1959
HADOT, J. *Penchant mauvais et volonté libre dans la sagesse de Ben Sira (l'Ecclésiastique).* Bruxelles 1970
— 'Le problème de l'apocalypse syriaque de Baruch d'après un ouvrage récent'. *Semitica* 20 (1970) 59-76
HADOT, P. 'Être, Vie Pensée chez Plotin et avant Plotin', in *Les Sources de Plotin. Entretiens* 5. Genève 1960
HAENCHEN, E. 'Das Buch Baruch'. *ZTK* 50 (1953) 123-58
HAHN, I. 'Josephus und die Eschatologie von Qumran', in *Qumran Probleme.* Berlin 1963, 167-91
HALL, S. G. 'Melito in the Light of the Passover Haggadah'. *JTS* n.s.22 (1971) 29-46
HALLEWY, E. E. 'Biblical Midrash and Homeric Exegesis'. *Tarbiz* 31 (1961) 157-69 (Hebrew)
HALLO, W. 'Akkadian Apocalypses'. *IEJ* 16 (1966) 231-42
HALPERIN, D. N. *Merkabah and Maaseh Merkabah According to Rabbinic Sources.* Dissertation Ann Arbor 1977

— 'Crucifixion, the Nahum Pesher and the Penalty of Strangulation'. *JJS* 32 (1981) 32-46
HAMERTON-KELLY, R. G. The Temple and the Origins of Jewish Apocalyptic'. *VT* 20 (1970) 1-15
— 'Sources and Traditions in Philo Judaeus.' *Studia Philonica* 1 (1972)
HAMP, V. 'Zukunft und Jenseits im Buch Sirach', in *Alttestamentliche Studien. Festschrift F. Nötscher.* Bonn 1950, 86-97
HANHART, R. *Maccabaeorum liber II copiis usus quas reliquit Werner Kappler* (Septuaginta 9:2) Göttingen 1959
— *Maccabaeorum liber III* (Septuaginta 9:3) Göttingen 1960
— 'Zum Text des 2. und 3. Makkabäerbuches. Probleme der Überlieferung, der Auslegung und der Ausgabe'. *Nachrichten der Akademie der Wissenschaften in Göttingen.* Göttingen 1961, 427-86
— 'Zur Zeitrechnung des I und II Makkabäerbuches', in *Untersuchungen zur Israelitisch-jüdische Chronologie,* ed. by A. Jepsen and R. Hanhart (BZAW 88) Berlin 1964, 55-96
— *Esther* (Septuaginta 8:3) Göttingen 1966
— *Esdrae liber I* (Septuaginta 8:1) Göttingen 1974
HANSON, A. 'Philo's Etymologies'. *JTS* 18 (1967) 128-39
HANSON, P. D. 'Jewish Apocalyptic Against its Near Eastern Environment'. *RB* 78 (1971) 31-58
— 'Old Testament Apocalyptic Reexamined'. *Interpretation* 25 (1971) 454-79
— 'Zechariah 9 and the Recapitulation of an Ancient Ritual Pattern'. *JBL* 92 (1973) 37-59
— *The Dawn of Apocalyptic.* Philadelphia 1975
— 'Apocalypse, Genre', in *IDB Suppl.,* 27-28
— 'Apocalypticism', in *IDB Suppl.,* 28-34
— 'Prolegomena to the Study of Jewish Apocalyptic', in *Magnalia Dei: The Mighty Acts of God.* ed. by F. M. Cross, *et al.* New York 1976, 389-413
— 'Rebellion in Heaven, Azazel and Euhemeristic Heroes in I Enoch 6-11'. *JBL* 96 (1977) 195-233
— 'A Response to John Collins' Methodological Issues in the Study of 1 Enoch'. *SBLSP* 1978, 307-9
HANSON, R. P. C. *Allegory and Event.* Richmond 1959
HANSON, R. S. 'Paleo-Hebrew Scripts in the Hasmonean Age'. *BASOR* 175 (1964) 26-42
HARAN, M. 'Problems of the Canonisation of Scripture'. *Tarbiz* 25 (1955-6) 245-71 (Hebrew)
HARNISCH, W. *Verhängnis und Verheissung der Geschichte.* Göttingen 1969
HARRELSON, W. 'The Significance of "Last Words" for Intertestamental Ethics', in *Essays in Old Testament Ethics,* ed. by J. L. Crenshaw and J. T. Willis. New York 1974, 203-13
— 'Patient Love in the Testament of Joseph', in Nickelsburg, *Studies on the Testament of Joseph,* 29-35
HARRINGTON, D. J. 'Interpreting Israel's History: The Testament of Moses as a Rewriting of Deut. 31-34', in Nickelsburg, *Studies on the Testament of Moses,* 59-68
— *The Hebrew Fragments of Pseudo-Philo.* Missoula 1974
— 'Research on the Jewish Pseudepigrapha during the 1970's.' *CBQ* 42 (1980) 147-59
HARRINGTON, D. J. — CAZEAUX, J. *Pseudo-Philon: Les Antiquités Bibliques. 1: Introduction et texte critique. Traduction* (Sources Chrét.) Paris 1976 (See also Perrot-Bogaert)
HARRIS, J. R. *Fragments of Philo Judaeus.* Cambridge 1896
— *The Rest of the Words of Baruch.* London 1889
— *The Origin of the Prologue to St. John's Gospel.* Cambridge 1917
HARRIS, J. R. — LEWIS, A. S. — CONYBEARE, F. C. 'The Story of Ahikar', in *APOT* 2, 724-76
HART, J. H. A. *Ecclesiasticus. The Greek Text of Codex 248.* Cambridge 1909
HARTMAN, L. *Prophecy Interpreted.* Lund 1966
— 'The Functions of Some So-called Apocalyptic Time-tables'. *NTS* 22 (1975)1976) 1-14
— *Asking for a Meaning.* Lund 1979
HARTMANN, L. F. — DI LELLA, A. A. *The Book of Daniel* (Anchor Bible) New York 1978
HARVEY, W. W. (ed.). *Sancti Irenaei, libros quinque adversus haereses* 1-2. Cambridge 1857
HASPECKER, J. *Gottesfurcht bei Jesus Sirach. Ihre religiöse Struktur und ihre literarische und doktrinäre Bedeutung* (AnBib 30). Rome 1967

HATA, G. 'Is the Greek Version of Josephus' Jewish War a Translation or a Rewriting of the First Version? *JQR* n.s. 66 (1975) 89-108

HAUCK, F. 'κοινός κτλ', in *TDNT* 3, 799-803

HAUPT, D. *Das Testament Levi.* Diss. Halle 1969

HAUSCHILD, W.—D. *Studien zur frühchristlichen Pneumatologie.* München 1972

HAYMAN, A. P. 'The Problem of Pseudonymity in the Ezra-Apocalypse'. *JSJ* 6 (1975) 47-56

HECHT, R. D. 'Preliminary Issues in the Analysis of Philo's De specialibus legibus'. *Studia Philonica* (1978) 1-17

HEDRICK, C. W. *The Apocalypse of Adam.* Chico 1980

HEGSTAD, H. *Synagogen, sted for skriftlesning og utleggelse på sabbaten* (Typewritten dissert.) Trondheim 1977

HEINEMANN, I. 'Die Lehre vom ungeschriebenen Gesetz im jüdischen Schrifttum'. *HUCA* 4 (1927) 152-9

— 'Pseudo-Herakleitos', in *PWRE Suppl.* 5, 228-32

— *Philons griechische und jüdische Bildung.* Breslau 1932

— *Altjüdische Allegoristik.* Leipzig 1936

— 'Wer veranlasste den Glaubenszwang der Makkabäerzeit'. *MGWJ* 82 (1938) 145-72

— 'Josephus' Method in the Presentation of Jewish Antiquities'. *Zion* 5 (1939-40) 180-203 (Hebrew)

— *Darkei ha-Aggadah.* Jerusalem 1942

HEINEMANN, J. *Prayer in the Talmud: Forms and Patterns.* Berlin-New York 1977.

HEINISCH, P. *Der Einfluss Philos auf die älteste christliche Exegese.* Münster 1908

— *Die griechische Philosophie im Buche der Weisheit.* Münster 1908

— *Das Buch der Weisheit (Exegetisches Handbuch zum Alten Testament, XXIV).* Münster 1912

HELLHOLM, D. (ed.), *Apocalypticism in the Ancient Near East and the Hellenistic World.* Tübingen 1983

HELOT, J. 'La datation de l'Apocalypse syriaque de Baruch'. *Semitica* 15 (1965) 79-95

HENGEL, M. *Die Zeloten: Untersuchungen zur jüdischen Freiheitsbewegung in der Zeit von Herodes I bis 70 n. Chr.* Leiden 1961

— *Judaism and Hellenism: Studies in their Encounter in Palestine During the Early Hellenistic Period* 1-2. Philadelphia 1974

— 'Zeloten und Sikarier. Zur Frage der Einheit und Vielfalt der jüdischen Befreiungsbewegung 6-74 n. Chr.' in *Josephus-studien: Festschrift O. Michel.* Göttingen 1974, 175-96

— 'Der politische Messianismus in der jüdischen Diaspora Aegyptens', in Hellholm, *Apocalypticism*

— 'Qumran und der Hellenismus', in Delcor, *Qumran* 333-72

— *Crucifixion.* London 1977

HENNECKE, E. — SCHNEEMELCHER, W. *New Testament Apocrypha* 1-2. Philadelphia 1965

HENNING, W. B. 'Ein manichäisches Henochbuch'. *SPA* (1934) 27-35

— 'The Book of the Giants'. *BSOAS* 11 (1943-46) 52-74

HENRICHS, A. 'Literary Criticism of the Cologne Mani Codex', in Layton, *Rediscovery* 2, 724-33

HENRICHS, A. — KOENEN, L. 'Ein griechischer Mani-Codex'. *ZPE* 5 (1970) 97-216, plates 4-6

HERMANIUK, M. *La Parabole Evangélique. Enquête exégétique et critique.* Louvain 1947

HERMISSON, H. J. *Studien zur israelitischen Spruchweisheit* Neukirchen 1968

HERR, M. D. 'The Calendar', in *Compendia* I/2, 834-64

HERTZBERG, H. W. *Der Prediger.* Gütersloh 1963

HILGERT, E. 'A Bibliography of Philo Studies, 1963-70'. *Studia Philonica* 1 (1972) 57-71; 2 (1973) 55-73; 3 (1975) 117-25; 4 (1976-77) 79-85; 5 (1978) 113-120; 6 (1979-80) 197-200

— 'Bibliographia Philoniana 1935-1981', in *ANRW* II, 21/1, 47-97

HIMMELFARB, M. *Tours of Hell: The Development and Transmission of an Apocalyptic Form in Jewish and Christian Literature.* Unpublished dissertation. Princeton University 1980

HINDLEY, J. C. 'Towards a Date for the Similitudes of Enoch. An Historical Approach'. *NTS* 14 (1967-68) 551-65

HINNELS, J. R. 'The Zoroastrian Doctrine of Salvation in the Roman World: A Study of the Oracle of Hystaspes', in *Man and His Salvation: Studies in Memory of S.G.F. Brandon*, Manchester 1973, 125-48

HIRZEL, A. 'Agraphos Nomos'. *ASGW* 20, 1 (1900) 16-18

HOEHNER, H. W. *Herod Antipas*. Cambridge 1972

HÖLSCHER, G. 'Josephus', in *PWRE* 9, 1934-2000

HOFIUS, O. *Der Vorhang vor dem Thron Gottes*. Tübingen 1972

HOLLADAY, C. 'The Portrait of Moses in Ezekiel the Tragedian'. *SBLSP* 1976, 447-52

— *Theios Aner in Hellenistic Judaism: A Critique of the Use of This Category in New Testament Christology*. Missoula 1977

— *Fragments from Hellenistic Jewish Authors. Volume I: Historians* (SBLTT 20) Chico Cal. 1983

HOLLANDER, H. W. *Joseph as an Ethical Model in the Testaments of the Twelve Patriarchs*. Leiden 1981

HOLM-NIELSEN, S. *Hodayot, Psalms from Qumran*. Aarhus 1960

— 'Erwägungen zu dem Verhältnis zwischen den Hodayot und den Psalmen Salomos', in *Bibel und Qumran. Festschrift H. Bardtke*. Berlin 1968, 112-31

— 'On the Interpretation of Qoheleth in Early Christianity'. *VT* 24 (1974) 170-3

— *Die Psalmen Salomos* (JSHRZ 4, 2) Gütersloh 1977

— 'Religiöse Poesie des Spätjudentums', in *ANRW* II, 19/1, 152-86

HORGAN, P. M. *Pesharim: Qumran Interpretation of Biblical Books*. Washington 1979

HORSLEY, R. 'The Sicarii: Ancient Jewish Terrorists'. *Journal of Religion* 59 (1979) 435-58

HORST, P. W. VAN DER. *The Sentences of Pseudo-Phocylides*. With Introduction and Commentary. Leiden 1978

HOWARD, G. E. 'The "aberrant" Text of Philo's Quotations Reconsidered'. *HUCA* 44 (1973) 197-209

HÜBNER, H. 'Zölibat in Qumran?' *NTS* 17 (1971) 153-67

HUGHES, H. M. 'The Greek Apocalypse of Baruch (3 Baruch)', in *APOT* 2, 527-32

HULTGÅRD, A. *Croyances messianiques des Test. XII Patr.: critique textuelle et commentaire des passages messianiques*. Diss. Uppsala 1971

— *L'Eschatologie des Testaments des Douze Patriarches* 1-2. Uppsala 1977

— 'Das Judentum in der hellenistisch-römischen Zeit und die Iranische Religion', in *ANRW* II, 19/1, 512-59

— 'The Ideal "Levite", the Davidic Messiah and the Saviour Priest in the Testaments of the Twelve Patriarchs', in Collins-Nickelsburg, *Ideal Figures in Ancient Judaism*, 93-111

HUMBERT, P. '"Magna est veritas et praevalet" (3 Esra 4:35)'. *OLZ* 31 (1928) 148-50

— *Recherches sur les sources égyptiennes de la littérature sapientiennes d'Israel*. Neuchâtel 1929

HUMPHREYS, W. L. 'A Life-Style for Diaspora: A Study of the Tales of Esther and Daniel'. *JBL* 92 (1973) 217-23

HUNKIN, J. W. 'The Testaments of the Twelve Patriarchs'. *JTS* 16 (1914) 80-97

HUNZINGER, C. H. 'Fragmente einer älteren Fassung des Buches Milhama aus Höhle 4 von Qumrân'. *ZAW* 69 (1957) 131-51

HUPPENBAUER, H. W. 'Zur Eschatologie der Damaskusschrift'. *RQ* 4 (1964) 367-73

ILG, N. 'Überlegungen zum Verständnis von *Berith* in den Qumran-Texten', in Delcor, *Qumran*, 257-63

ISSAVERDENS, J. 'The Penitence of Adam', in *The Uncanonical Writings of the Old Testament*. Venice 1901

ISSER, S. J. *The Dositheans: A Samaritan Sect in Late Antiquity*. Leiden 1976

ISTRIN, V. *La prise de Jérusalem de Josèphe le Juif* 1-2. Paris 1934-38

IWRY, S. 'Was there a Migration to Damascus? The Problem of *Shavei Yisrael*'. *Eretz Israel* 9 (1969) 80-88

JACKSON, B. S. *Essays in Jewish and Comparative Legal History*. Leiden 1975

— 'Dam. Doc. IX 16-23 and Parallels'. *RQ* 9 (1978) 441-50

JACKSON, H. M. 'Geradamas, the Celestial Stranger'. *NTS* 27 (1981) 385-94

JACOB, E. 'Wisdom and Religion in Sirach', in Gammie, *Israelite Wisdom*, 247-60

JACOBS, I. 'Literary Motifs in the Testament of Job'. *JTS* 21 (1970) 1-10

JACOBS, L. 'Torah, Reading of, History', in *EJ* 15, 1246-55

JACOBY, F. *Die Fragmente der griechischen Historiker* 1-3. Berlin 1924ff. (repr. Leiden 1961-69)

JAEGER, W. *Nemesios von Emesa.* Berlin 1914

JAGIC, V. 'Slavische Beiträge zu biblischen Apocryphen I, Die Altkirchenslavischen Texte des Adambuches', in *Denkschriften der kaiserlichen Akademie der Wissenschaften.* Vienna 1893, 1-103

JAMES, M. R. *The Testament of Abraham*, with an appendix by W. E. Barnes. Cambridge 1892
— *Apocrypha Anecdota* 1-2. Cambridge 1893-97
— *The Biblical Antiquities of Philo.* London 1917 (repr. with 'Prolegomenon' by L. H. Feldman, New York 1971)
— *The Lost Apocrypha of the Old Testament.* London 1920

JANSEN, H. L. *Die Henochgestalt.* Oslo 1939

JANSEN, H. L. 'Die Frage nach Tendenz und Verfasserschaft im Poimandres', in Widengren, *Proceedings*, 157-63

JANSSEN, E. *Das Testament Abrahams* (JSHRZ III/2) Gütersloh 1975

JANSSENS, Y. *La Prôtennoia Trimorphe (NHC XIII, 1).* Québec 1978

JAUBERT, A. 'Le calendrier des Jubilés et de la secte de Qumrân'. *VT* 3 (1953) 250-64
— *La date de la Cène.* Paris 1957
— 'Le calendrier des Jubilés et les jours liturgiques de la semaine'. *VT* 7 (1957) 35-61
— 'Le Pays de Damas'. *RB* 65 (1958) 214-48
— 'Aperçus sur le calendrier de Qumrân', in *La Secte de Qumran et les origines du Christianisme*, ed. by J. van der Ploeg *et al.* Bruges 1959, 79-136

JELLICOE, S. 'The Occasion and Purpose of the Letter of Aristeas: A Re-examination'. *NTS* 12 (1966) 144-50
— *The Septuagint and Modern Study.* Oxford 1968

JELLINEK, A. *Bet ha-Midrasch* 1-6. 2nd ed. Jerusalem 1938

JEREMIAS, J. *Heiligengräber in Jesu Umwelt.* Göttingen 1958
— *Der Lehrer der Gerechtigkeit.* Göttingen 1963
— *Jerusalem in the Time of Jesus.* 1969

JEREMIAS, J. — MILIK, J. T. 'Remarques sur le Rouleau de Cuivre de Qumran'. *RB* 67 (1960) 220-33

JERVELL, J. *Imago Dei.* Göttingen 1960
— 'Ein Interpolator interpretiert. Zu der christlichen Bearbeitung der Testamente der zwölf Patriarchen', in Burchard-Jervell-Thomas, *Studien*, 30-61

JOHNSON, M. D. 'Reflections on a Wisdom Approach to Matthew's Christology'. *CBQ* 36 (1974) 44-64

JONAS, H. *Gnosis und spätantiker Geist* 1-2 and Ergänzungsheft. Göttingen 1934-64
— *The Gnostic Religion.* 2nd ed. Boston 1963
— *Philosophical Essays: From Ancient Creed to Technological Man.* Englewood Cliffs 1974

JONES, A. H. M. *The Herods of Judaea.* Oxford 1938

JONGE, H. J. DE 'Die Patriarchentestamente von Roger Bacon bis Richard Simon', in M. de Jonge, *Studies*, 3-42
— 'Die Textüberlieferung der Testamente der zwölf Patriarchen', *ibid.* 45-62

JONGE, M. DE. *The Testaments of the Twelve Patriarchs: A Study of Their Text, Composition and Origin.* Assen 1953
— 'Christelijke elementen in de Vitae Prophetarum'. *NTT* 16 (1961-62) 161-78
— *Testamenta XII Patriarcharum. Edited according to Cambridge University Library MS Ff 1.24 fol. 203a-261b with short notes* (PVTG) Leiden 1964, 1970
— 'Christian Interpolations in the Testaments of the Twelve Patriarchs'. *NT* 4 (1966) 182-235
— 'Recent Studies on the Testaments of the Twelve Patriarchs'. *SEA* 36 (1971) 77-96

— 'Josephus und die Zukunftserwartungen seines Volkes', in *Josephus-Studien: Festschrift O. Michel.* Göttingen 1974, 105-10
— (ed.) *Studies on the Testaments of the Twelve Patriarchs.* Leiden 1975
— *The Testaments of the Twelve Patriarchs. A Critical Edition of the Greek Text* (PVTG) Leiden 1978
JONGELING, B. *Le rouleau de la guerre des manuscrits de Qumrân.* Assen 1962
— 'Note Additionelle'. *JSJ* 1 (1970) 185-6
— 'Publication provisoire d'un fragment provenant de la grotte 11 de Qumran. 11Q Jér Nouv ar'. *JSJ* 1 (1970) 58-64
— *A Classified Bibliography of the Finds in the Desert of Judaea 1958-69.* Leiden 1971
JONGELING, B. — LABUSCHAGNE, C. J. — WOUDE, A. S. VAN DER. *Aramaic Texts from Qumran* 1. Leiden 1976
JOSIFOVIC, S. 'Lykophron', in *PWRE Suppl.*, 888-930
JUNG, C. G. *Answer to Job.* London 1954
JUSTUS, B. 'Zur Erzählkunst des Flavius Josephus'. *Theokratia* 2 (1973) 107-36
KABISCH, R. 'Die Entstehungszeit der Apokalypse Mose'. *ZNW* 6 (1905) 109-34
KÄSEMANN, E. *Das wandernde Gottesvolk.* Göttingen 1939
KAHANA, A. (ed.) *Ha-Sefarim ha-Hitsonim* 1-2. Tel Aviv 1941
KAISER, O. 'Die Begründung der Sittlichkeit im Buche Sirach'. *ZTK* 55 (1958) 51-63
KAMLAH, E. *Die Form der katalogischen Paränese im Neuen Testament.* Tübingen 1964
KAPELRUD, A. S. 'Der Bund in den Qumran-Schriften', in *Bibel und Qumran. Festschrift H. Bardtke.* Berlin 1968, 137-49
KAPPLER, W. *Maccabaeorum liber I* (Septuaginta 9:1) Göttingen 1936, 2nd ed. 1967
KATZ, P. *Philo's Bible.* Cambridge 1950
KAUFMANN, J. *Toledot ha-Emuna ha-Yisraelit* 1-8. Jerusalem 1948
KAUFMANN, J. 'Apokalyptik', in *EJ* (Berlin) 2, 1142-54
KAUTZSCH, E. *Die Apokryphen und Pseudepigraphen des A.T.* 1-2. Tübingen 1900
KAYARTZ, CH. *Studien zu Proverbien I-IX. Eine form-motivgeschichtliche Untersuchung unter Einbeziehung ägyptisches Vergleichmaterials.* Neukirchen 1966
KEARNS, C. 'Ecclesiasticus (The Wisdom of Jesus, the Son of Sirach)', in *A Catholic Commentary on Holy Scripture.* London 1953, 512-26
KEE, H. C. 'Satan, Magic and Salvation in the Testament of Job'. *SBLSP* 1974 (1) 53-76
— 'The Ethical Dimensions of the Testaments of the XII Patriarchs as a Clue to Provenance'. *NTS* 24 (1978) 259-70
— 'The Testaments of the 12 Patriarchs', in Charlesworth, *Pseudepigrapha*
KEULERS, J. *Die Eschatologische Lehre des vierten Esrabuches.* Freiburg 1922
KILPATRICK, G. C. D. 'Besprechung der Göttinger Septuaginta, 1-3 Makk und von Hanhart, "Zum Text"'. *Göttingische Gelehrte Anzeigen* (1963) 10-22
KIMELMAN, R. '*Birkat Ha-Minim* and the Lack of Evidence for an Anti-Christian Jewish Prayer in Late Antiquity', in Sanders, *Jewish and Christian Self-Definition* 2, 226-44
KIPPENBERG, H. G. *Garizim und Synagoge.* Berlin 1971
KITTEL, B. P. *The Hymns of Qumran.* Chico 1981
KLAUSER, T. 'Christlicher Märtyrerkult, heidnischer Heroenkult und spätjüdische Heiligenverehrung. Neue Einsichten und neue Probleme', in *Gesammelte Arbeiten zur Literaturgeschichte, Kirchengeschichte und christliche Archäologie*, ed. by E. Dassmann. Münster 1974, 221-29
KLEIN, F. N. *Die Lichtterminologie bei Philon von Alexandrien und in den Hermetischen Schriften.* Leiden 1962
KLEIN, R. W. *Studies in the Greek Texts of the Chronicler.* Harvard University Dissertation 1966
KLEIN, S. 'Al ha-Sefer *Vitae Prophetarum'*, in *Klausner Festschrift.* Tel Aviv 1937, 189-209 (Hebrew)
KLEINKNECHT, H. 'λεγω, B', in *TDNT* 4, 83-87
KLIJN, A, F. J. 'The Sources and the Redaction of the Syriac Apocalypse of Baruch'. *JSJ* 1 (1970) 65-76

— *Seth in Jewish, Christian and Gnostic Literature.* Leiden 1977
— 'From Creation to Noah in the Second Dream Vision of Ethiopic Henoch', in *Miscellanea Neotestamentica,* ed. by T. Baarda *et al.* Leiden 1978, 147-60
KLIJN, A. F. J. — REININK, G. J. *Patristic Evidence for Jewish Christian Sects.* Leiden 1973
KLINZING, G. *Die Umdeutung des Kultus in der Qumrangemeinde und im N.T.* Göttingen 1971
KNEUCKER, J. J. *Das Buch Baruch.* Leipzig 1879
KNIBB, M. A. 'The Ethiopic Version of the Lives of the Prophets: Ezekiel and Daniel'. *BSOAS* 40 (1978) 197-206
— *The Ethiopic Book of Enoch* 1-2. Oxford 1978
— 'The Date of the Parables of Enoch: A Critical Review'. *NTS* 25 (1979) 345-59
— 'Exile in the Damascus Document'. *JSOT* 25 (1983) 99-117
KNIERIM, R. 'Old Testament Form Cristicism Reconsidered'. *Interpretation* 27 (1973) 435-68
KNOX, W. L. 'A Note on Philo's use of the Old Testament'. *JTS* 41 (1940) 30-34
KOBELSKI, P. J. *Melchizedek and Melchiresa.* Washington 1981
KOCH, K. *The Rediscovery of Apocalyptic.* Naperville 1972
— 'Die mysteriösen Zahlen der Judäischen Könige und die apokalyptischen Jahrwochen'. *VT* 28 (1978) 433-41
KOCSIS, E. 'Der Ost-West Gegensatz in den jüdischen Sibyllinen'. *NT* 5 (1962) 105-10
KOENEN, L. 'Die Prophezeiungen des "Töpfers"'. *ZPE* 2 (1968) 178-209
— 'The Prophecies of the Potter: A Prophecy of World Renewal becomes an Apocalypse', in *Proceedings of the Twelfth International Congress of Papyrology.* Ann Arbor 1970, 249-54
KOESTER, H. 'One Jesus and Four Primitive Gospels', in Robinson — Koester, *Trajectories,* 158-204
KOHLER, K. 'The Testament of Job, An Essene Midrash on the Book of Job', in *Semitic Studies in Memory of A. Kohut.* Berlin 1897, 264-338
KOLENKOW, A. B. 'The Assumption of Moses as a Testament', in Nickelsburg, *Studies on the Testament of Moses,* 71-77
— 'What is the Role of Testament in the Testament of Abraham?' *HTR* 67 (1974) 182-84
— 'The Narratives of the TJ and the Organization of the Testaments of the XII Patriarchs', in Nickelsburg, *Studies on the Testament of Joseph,* 37-46
— 'The Genre Testament and Forecasts of the Future in the Hellenistic Jewish Milieu'. *JSJ* (1975) 51-71
— 'The Genre Testament and the Testament of Abraham', in Nickelsburg, *Studies on the Testament of Abraham,* 139-52
KOMLOSH, Y. 'PSHAT and DRASH in Targum Kohelet'. *Bar-Ilan* 3 (1963) 46-55 (Hebrew)
KONINGSVELDT, R. VAN. 'An Arabic Manuscript of the Apocalypse of Baruch'. *JSJ* 6 (1975) 205-06
KORTEWEG, TH. 'The Meaning of Naphtali's Visions', in M. de Jonge, *Studies,* 261-82
KOSCHORKE, K. *Die Polemik der Gnostiker gegen das kirchliche Christentum.* Leiden 1978
KOSKENNIEMI, H. *Studien zur Idee und Phraseologie des griechischen Briefes bis 400 n. Chr.* Helsinki 1956
KOSMALA, H. 'The Three Nets of Belial', in *Studies, Essays and Reviews* 2. Leiden 1978, 115-37
KRAELING, E. G. *The Brooklyn Museum Aramaic Papyri.* New Haven 1954
KRAFT, C. F. 'Poetical Structure in the Qumran Thanksgiving Psalm'. *Biblical Research* 2 (1957) 1-8
KRAFT, R. A. *The Testament of Job* (SBLTT) Missoula 1974
— 'Reassessing the "Recensional Problem" in Testament of Abraham', in Nickelsburg, *Studies on the Testament of Abraham,* 121-37
KRAFT, R. A. — PURINTUN, A. E. *Paraleipomena Jeremiou* (SBLTT) Missoula 1972
KRAGERUD, A. 'Apocryphon Johannis: En formanalyse'. *NorTT* 66 (1965) 15-38
KRALL, J. 'Vom König Bökchoris,' in *Festgaben zu Ehren Max Budingers.* Innsbruck 1898, 1-11
KRAUS, H.—J. *Die Psalmen.* Neukirchen 1961
KRAUS, S. 'The Great Synod'. *JQR* 10 (1981) 347-77

KRAUSE, M. 'Das literarische Verhältnis des Eugnostosbriefes zur Sophia Jesu Christi', in *Mullus. Festschrift für Theodor Klausner.* Münster 1964, 215-23

KRAUSE, M. (ed.) *Gnosis and Gnosticism. Papers Read at the Seventh International Conference on Patristic Studies (Oxford, September 8th-15th. 1975).* Leiden 1977

— *Gnosis and Gnosticism. Papers read at the Eighth International Conference on Patristic Studies (Oxford, September 3rd-8th 1979).* Leiden 1981

KRAUSE, M. — LABIB, P. *Die Drei Versionen des Apokryphon des Johannes im koptischen Museum zu Alt-Kairo.* Wiesbaden 1962

KRUSE, C. G. 'Community Functionaries in the Rule of the Community and the Damascus Document: A Test of Chronological Relationships'. *RQ* 10 (1981) 543-51

KÜCHLER, M. *Frühjüdische Weisheitstraditionen. Zum Fortgang weisheitlichen Denkens im Bereich des früh-jüdischen Jahweglaubens.* Freiburg 1979

KÜMMEL, W. G. *Introduction to the New Testament.* London 1956

KUHL, C. *Die drei Männer im Feuer* (BZAW 55) Giessen 1930

KUHN, H.—W. *Enderwartung und Gegenwärtiges Heil.* Göttingen 1966

KUHN, K. G. ' Die Sektenschrift und die iranische Religion'. *ZTK* 49 (1952) 296-316

— 'Die beiden Messias Aarons und Israels'. *NTS* 1 (1955) 168-79

— 'The Sahidic Version of the Testament of Isaac'. *JTS* 8 (1957) 225-39

— *Konkordanz zu den Qumran-Texten.* Göttingen 1960

— 'Nachträge zur Konkordanz zu den Qumrantexten'. *RQ* 4 (1963) 163-234

— 'An English Translation of the Sahidic Version of the Testament of Isaac'. *JTS* 18 (1967) 325-36

— 'The Lord's Supper and the Communal Meal at Qumran' in Stendahl, *The Scrolls and the New Testament,* 65-93

— 'The Two Messiahs of Aaron and Israel', *ibid.* 54-64

KUIPER, K. 'Le poète juif Ezechiel'. *REJ* 46 (1903) 48-73; 161-77

KURFESS, A. 'Das Mahngedicht des sogenannten Phokylides im zweiten Buch der Oracula Sibyllina'. *ZNW* 38 (1939) 171-81

— 'Oracula Sibyllina I-II'. *ZNW* 40 (1941) 151-65

— *Sibyllinische Weissagungen.* Berlin 1951

— 'Oracula Sibyllina XI (IX) — XIV (XII), nicht christlich sondern jüdisch'. *ZRGG* 7 (1955) 270-2

— 'Christian Sibyllines', in Hennecke-Schneemelcher, *New Testament Apocrypha* 2, 703-45

KUTSCH, E. 'Der Kalendar des Jubiläenbuches und das Alte und das Neue Testament'. *VT* 11 (1961) 39-47

— 'Die Solstitien im Kalendar des Jubiläenbuches und in äth. Henoch 72'. *VT* 12 (1962) 205-07

KUTSCHER, E. Y. *The Language and the Linguistic Background of the Isaiah Scroll.* Jerusalem 1959 (Hebrew)

— 'The Language of the Hebrew and Aramaic Letters of Bar-Koseva and his Contemporaries'. *Leshonenu* 25 (1960-61) 117-33; 26 (1961-62) 7-23 (Hebrew)

KVIDELAND, K. 'Elohims Himmelfahrt', in *Temenos* 10 (1974) 68-78

LACOCQUE, A. *The Book of Daniel.* Atlanta 1979

LAGARDE, P. A. *Libri Veteris Testamentti apocryphi syriace.* Leipzig 1861

LAKE, K. 'The Date of Slavonic Enoch'. *HTR* 16 (1923) 397-99

LAMBERT, G. 'Les manuscrits du désert de Juda. Tient-on un nouveau chapître de l'histoire de la grotte?' *NRT* 72 (1950) 199-202

— 'Mon joug est aisé et mon fardeau léger'. *NRT* 77 (1955) 963-9

LAMBERT, W. G. *Babylonian Wisdom Literature.* Oxford 1960

— 'History and the Gods: A Review Article'. *Orientalia* n.s. 39 (1970) 170-77

— *The Background of Jewish Apocalyptic.* London 1978

LANCHESTER, H. 'The Sibylline Oracles', in *APOT* 2, 368-406

LANCZKOWSKY, G. *Altägyptischer Prophetismus.* Wiesbaden 1960

LANG, B. *Die weisheitliche Lehrrede. Eine Untersuchung von Sprüche I-VII.* Stuttgart 1972

— *Frau Weisheit. Deutung einer biblischen Gestalt.* Düsseldorf 1975
LAPP, P. W. 'The Second and Third Campaigns at Araq al-Emîr'. *BASOR* 165 (1962) 16-34
LAPERROUZAS, E. M. *Le Testament de Moïse* (Semitica 19) Paris 1970
— *Qoumrân. L'Etablissement Essénien des Bords de la Mer Morte.* Paris 1976
— 'A propos des dépôts d'ossements d'animaux trouvés à Qoumrân'. *RQ* 9 (1978) 569-73
— *L'Attente du Messie en Palestine.* Paris 1982
LAQUEUR, R. 'Ephoros'. *Hermes* 46 (1911) 161-206
LAQUEUR, T. *Der jüdische Historiker Flavius Josephus.* Giessen 1920, repr. Darmstadt 1970
LARCHER, C. *Etudes sur le Livre de la Sagesse.* Paris 1969
— *Le Livre de la Sagesse.* Paris 1983
LA SOR, W. *The Dead Sea Scrolls and the New Testament.* Grand Rapids 1972
LATTEY, C. 'The Messianic Expectation in the Assumption of Moses'. *CBQ* 4 (1952) 9-21
LAUBSCHER, F. DU TOIT. 'God's Angel of Truth and Melchizedek'. *JSJ* 3 (1972) 46-51
LAUHA, A. *Kohelet.* Neukirchen 1978
LAURIN, R. B. 'The Problem of Two Messiahs in the Qumran Scrolls'. *RQ* 4 (1963) 39-52
LAUTERBACH, J. Z. 'Ancient Jewish Allegorists'. *JQR* n.s. 1 (1910) 129-36
LAYTON, B. 'The Hypostasis of the Archons, or The Reality of the Rulers'. *HTR* 67 (1974) 351-425; 69 (1976) 31-101
— (ed.) *The Rediscovery of Gnosticism. Proceedings of the International Conference on Gnosticism at Yale, 1978* 1-2. Leiden 1981-82
LEACH, E. R. 'A Possible Method of Intercalation for the Calendar of the Book of Jubilees'. *VT* 7 (1957) 391-97
LEANY, A. R. C. *The Rule of Qumran and its Meaning.* London 1966
LEBRAM, J. 'Die Weltreiche in der jüdischen Apokalyptik: Bemerkungen zu Tobit 14:4-7'. *ZAW* 76 (1964) 329-31
— 'Zur Chronologie in den Makkabäerbüchern', in *Das Institutum Judaicum der Universität Tübingen 1968-70.* Tübingen 1970, 63-70
— 'Tobit', in *Peshitta* IV/6. Leiden 1972
— 'Der Idealstaat der Juden', in *Josephus-Studien: Festschrift O. Michel.* Göttingen 1974, 233-53
— 'The Piety of the Jewish Apocalyptists', in Hellholm, *Apocalypticism*
LECLANT, L. 'Documents nouveaux et points de vue récents sur les sagesses de l'Egypte ancienne', in *Les sagesses du Proche-Orient ancien.* Paris 1963, 5-26
— 'Les sagesses de l'Egypte pharaonique. Etat de la bibliographie récente', in *Sagesse et Religion.* Paris 1979, 7-19
LEEUW, G. VAN DER. 'Anthropomorphismus', in *RAC* 1, 446-50
LEHMANN, M. R. 'Identification of the Copper Scroll Based on its Technical Terms'. *RQ* 5 (1964) 97-105
— 'New Light on Astrology in Qumran and the Talmud'. *RQ* 8 (1975) 599-602
— 'The Temple Scroll as a Source of Sectarian Halakha'. *RQ* 9 (1978) 579-87
LEISEGANG, H. *Der heilige Geist. Das Wesen und Werden der mystisch-intuitiven Erkenntnis in der Philosophie und Religion der Griechen.* Leipzig-Berlin 1919
— 'Philo', in *PWRE* 20, 1-50
— 'Sophis', in *PWRE* 3 A, 1, 1019-39
LEPAPE, A. 'Préfet d'Alexandrie et Egypte'. *BSAA* n.s. 8 (1934) 331-41
LESLAU, W. *Falasha Anthology.* New York 1969
LÉVÊQUE, J. *Job et son Dieu. Essai d'exégèse et de théologie biblique.* Paris 1970
LEVI, I. *L'Ecclesiastique édité et commenté.* Paris 1898-1901
— *The Hebrew Text of the Book of Ecclesiasticus*(Semitic Studies Series 3) 2nd ed. Leiden 1951
— 'Les deux livres des Maccabés et le livre hébraïque des Hasmonéens'. *Semitica* 5 (1955) 15-36
LEVINE, L. I. 'The Jewish-Greek Conflict in First Century Caesarea'. *JJS* 25 (1974) 381-97
— *Caesarea Under Roman Rule.* Leiden 1975
— 'On the Political Involvement of the Pharisees under Herod and the Procurators'. *Cathedra* 8 (1978) 12-28 (Hebrew)

— 'The Political Struggle Between Pharisees and Sadducees in the Hasmonean Period', in *Jerusalem in the Second Temple Period. Abraham Schalit Memorial Volume.* Jerusalem 1980, 61-83

LEWIS, J. P. *A Study of the Interpretation of Noah and the Flood in Jewish and Christian Literature.* Leiden 198

LEWY, H. *Sobria Ebrietas.* Giessen 1929

— *The Pseudo-Philonic De Iona.* London 1936

LICHT, J. 'The Doctrine of the Thanksgiving Scroll'. *IEJ* 6 (1956) 1-13; 89-101

— *The Thanksgiving Scroll.* Jerusalem 1957 (Hebrew)

— 'An Analysis of the Treatise of the Two Spiritis in the DSD'. *Scripta* 4, 88-100

— 'Taxo, or the Apocalyptic Doctrine of Vengeance'. *JJS* 12 (1961) 95-103

— 'The Plant Eternal and the People of Divine Deliverance', in *Essays on the Dead Scrolls in Memory of E. L. Sukenik,* ed. by C. Rabin and Y. Yadin. Jerusalem 1961, 49-75 (Hebrew)

— 'Time and Eschatology in Apocalyptic Literature and in Qumran'. *JJS* 16 (1965) 177-82

— *The Rule Scroll.* Jerusalem 1965 (Hebrew)

— 'The Theory of Ages of the Judean Desert Sect and of other Calculators of Periods'. *Eretz Israel* 8 (1967) 63-70 (Hebrew)

— 'Abraham: Apocalypse of', in *EJ* 2, 126-27

— 'An Ideal Town Plan from Qumran. The Description of the New Jerusalem'. *IEJ* 29 (1979) 45-59

LICHTENBERGER, H. *Studien zum Menschenbild in Texten der Qumrangemeinde.* Göttingen 1980

LICHTENSTEIN, H. 'Die Fastenrolle'. *HUCA* 8-9 (1931-32) 257-351

LICHTHEIM, M. *Ancient Egyptian Literature. A Book of Reading* 1-3. Berkeley 1975-80

LIDDELL, H. G. — SCOTT, R. A Greek-English Lexicon. New ed. rev. by H. S. Jones. Oxford 1940. Repr. 1966

LIDZBARSKI, M. (ed.). *Ginza: Der Schatz, oder Das Grosse Buch der Mandäer.* Göttingen / Leipzig 1925

LIEBERMAN, S. *Greek in Jewish Palestine.* New York 1942

— 'The Discipline in the So-called Dead Sea Manual of Discipline'. *JBL* 71 (1952) 199-206

— *Hellenism in Jewish Palestine.* 2nd improved ed. New York 1962

LIFSHITZ, B. 'The Greek Documents from Nahal Seelim and Nahal Mishmar'. *IEJ* 11 (1961) 60-61

— 'Papyrus grecs du désert de Juda'. *Aegyptus* 42 (1962) 240-58

LIMBECK, M. *Die Ordnung des Heils.* Düsseldorf 1971

LINDER, H. *Die Geschichtsauffassung des Flavius Josephus im Bellum Judaicum.* Leiden 1972

LIVER, J. 'The Doctrine of the Two Messiahs in Sectarian Literature in the Time of the Second Commonwealth'. *HTR* 52 (1959) 149-85

— 'The "Sons of Zadok the Priests" in the Dead Sea Sect'. *RQ* 6 (1967) 3-30

LÖFGREN, O. 'An Arabic Recension of the Vitae Prophetarum'. *Orientalia Suecana* 25-26 (1976-77) 77-105

LOEWENSTAMM, S. 'The Testament of Abraham and the Texts Concerning the Death of Moses', in Nickelsburg, *Studies on the Testament of Abraham,* 219-25

LOFTUS, F. 'The Anti-Roman Revolts of the Jews and the Galileans'. *JQR* 68 (1977) 78-98

LOHFINK, N. *Kohelet.* Würzburg 1978

LOHMEYER, E. *Diatheke.* Leipzig 1913

LOHSE, E. *Die Texte aus Qumran: hebräisch und deutsch.* Darmstadt 1971

— 'Σολομών'. *TDNT* 7, 459-65

LORETZ, O. *Qohelet und der alte Orient.* Freiburg 1964

LÜDTKE, W. 'Georgische Adam-Bücher'. *ZAW* 38 (1919) 155-68

LURIE, B. Z. *The Copper Scroll.* Jerusalem 1963 (Hebrew)

LUTHER, M. 'Prefaces to the Apocrypha'. *Luther's Works,* ed. and trans. by E. T. Bachmann. Philadelphia 1960, 337-54

LUYTEN, J. 'Psalm 73 and Wisdom', in Gilbert, *La Sagesse de l'A.T.,* 59-81

LYS, D. *L'Ecclésiaste ou Que vaut la vie? Traduction, introduction générale, commentaire de 1/1 à 4/3.* Paris 1977

MACDONALD, J. *The Theology of the Samaritans.* London-Philadelphia 1964
— *The Samaritan Chronicle No. 11 (or: Sepher Ha-Yamim) From Joshua to Nebuchadnezzar* (BZAW 107) Berlin 1969

MACK, B. L. 'Imitatio Mosis'. *Studia Philonica* 1 (1972) 27-55
— *Logos und Sophia. Untersuchungen zur Weisheitstheologie im hellenistischen Judentum.* Göttingen 1973

MACRAE, G. W. 'Miracle in the Antiquities of Josephus', in *Miracles, Cambridge Studies in their Philosophy and History,* ed. by C. F. D. Moule. London 1965, 126-47
— 'The Jewish Background of the Gnostic Sophia Myth'. *NT* 12 (1970) 86-101
— 'The Apocalypse of Adam Reconsidered', in *The Society of Biblical Literature One Hundred Eighth Annual Meeting, Proceedings* 2, ed. by L. McGaughy. Missoula 1972, 573-77
— *The Thunder: Perfect Mind. Protocol of the Fifth Colloguy of the Center for Hermeneutical Studies in Hellenistic and Modern Culture, 11: March 1973,* ed. by W. Wuellner. Berkeley 1973
— 'Apocalyptic Eschatology in Gnosticism', in Hellholm, *Apocalypticism*

MACRAE, G. W. — PARROTT, D. M. 'The Apocalypse of Adam', in Robinson, *The Nag Hammadi Library,* 256-64

MACKENZIE, R. A. F. 'Ben Sira as Historian', in *Trinification of the World. Festschrift F. E. Crowe.* Toronto 1978, 312-27

MAIER, J. *Die Texte vom Toten Meer* 1-2. Basel 1960
— 'Zum Begriff *Jachad* in den Texten von Qumran'. *ZAW* 72 (1960) 148-66
— *Vom Kultus zur Gnosis.* Salzburg 1964
— *Die Tempelrolle vom Toten Meer.* Basel 1982
— 'Jüdische Faktoren bei der Entstehung der Gnosis?, in Tröger, *Altes Testament,* 239-58

MALHERBE, A. J. *The Cynic Epistles.* Missoula 1977

MANTEL, H. *Studies in the History of the Sanhedrin.* Cambridge MA 1961
— 'The Nature of the Great Synagogue'. *HTR* 60 (1967) 69ff.

MANSOOR, M. *The Thanksgiving Hymns.* Leiden 1961
— 'Sadducees', in *EJ* 14, 620-2

MARBÖCK, J. *Weisheit im Wandel. Untersuchungen zur Weisheitstheologie bei Ben Sira.* Bonn 1971
— 'Das Gebet um die Rettung Zions, Sir 36,1. 22 (Gr. 33,1-13a; 36,16b-22) im Zusammenhang der Geschichtsschau Ben Siras', in *Memoria Jerusalem. Festschrift Sauer.* Graz 1977, 93-115
— 'Sir. 38,24-39,11: Der schriftgelehrte Weise. Ein Beitrag zu Gestalt und Werk Ben Siras', in Gilbert, *La Sagesse de l'A.T.,*293-316

MARCUS, R. 'Recent Literature on Philo (1924-34)', in *Jewish Studies in Memory of G. A. Kohut.* New York 1935
— 'Alexander the Great and the Jews', in Thackeray, *Josephus* 6, 512-32
— *Josephus, Antiquities IX-XVII,* With an English Translation, in Thackeray, *Josephus* 6-8
— 'The Pharisees in the Light of Modern Scholarship'. *Journal of Religion* 32 (1952) 153-64
— *Philo, Supplement. Questions on Genesis and Exodus* 1-2, in Colson, *Philo Works*

MARGALIOTH, M. (ed.). *Sefer ha-Razim. A Newly Recovered Book of Magic from the Talmudic Period.* Jerusalem 1966

MARTIN, R. A. 'Some Syntactical Criteria of Translation Greek'. *VT* 10 (1960) 295-310
— 'Syntactical Evidence for a Semitic *Vorlage* of the Testament of Joseph', in Nickelsburg, *Studies on the Testament of Joseph,* 105-23
— 'Syntax Criticism of the Testament of Abraham', in Nickelsburg, *Studies on the Testament of Abraham,* 95-120

MARTY, J. 'Contribution à l'étude de fragments épistolaires antiques conservés principalement dans la Bible hébraïque: Les formules de salutation', in *Mélanges syriens offerts à M. René Dussaud.* Paris 1939, 22-24

MARX, A. 'Les racines du célibat essénien'. *RQ* 7 (1970) 323-42

MARZAL, A. *La enseñanza de Amenemope*. Madrid 1965

MAYBAUM, S. *Die Anthropomorphien und Anthropathien bei Onkelos und den späteren Targumen*. Breslau 1870

MAYER, G. *Index Philoneus*. Berlin 1975

MAYOR, J. B. *The epistle of St. James*. London 1897

MAZAR, B. 'The Tobiads'. *IEJ* 7 (1957) 137-45; 229-38

MAZAR, B. *et al. Ein Gedi. The First and Second Seasons of Excavations 1961-62* (Atiqot 5) Jerusalem 1966

MCCOWN, C. C. *The Testament of Solomon*. Leipzig 1922

— 'Hebrew and Egyptian Apocalyptic Literature'. *HTR* 18 (1925) 357-411

— 'The Araq el Emir and the Tobiads'. *BA* 20 (1957) 63-76

MCGINN, B. *Visions of the End. Apocalyptic Traditions in the Middle Ages*. New York 1979

MCKANE, W. *Prophets and Wise Men*. London 1965

— *Proverbs. A New Approach*. London 1970

MCMULLEN, R. *Enemies of the Roman Order*. Cambridge 1966

MEARNS, C. L. 'The Parables of Enoch — Origin and Date'. *Expository Times* 89 (1978) 118-19

MEECHAM, H. G. *The Oldest Version of the Bible: Aristeas on its Traditional Origin*. London 1932

— *The Letter of Aristeas*. Manchester 1935

MEEKS, W. A. *The Prophet-King: Moses Traditions and the Johannine Christology*. Leiden 1967

MÉNARD, J.-É. *Les Textes de Nag Hammadi. Colloque du Centre d'Histoire des Religions (Strasbourg, 23-25 Octobre 1974)*. Leiden 1975

MENDELS, D. 'On Kingship in the Temple Scroll and the Ideological Vorlage of the Seven Banquets in the Letter of Aristeas'. *Aegyptus* 59 (1979) 126-36

— 'A Note on the Tradition of Antiochus IV's Death'. *IEJ* 31 (1981) 53-56

MENDELSON, A. *Secular Education in Philo of Alexandria*. Cincinnati 1982

MERILL, E. H. *Qumran and Predestination*. Leiden 1975

MESHCHERSKII, N. A. *Istoriga iudeskoig voiny Josifa Flaviga*. Moscow-Leningrad 1958

METZGER, B. M. 'Literary Forgeries and Canonical Pseudepigrapha'. *JBL* 91 (1972) 3-24

MEYER, R. *Hellenistisches in der rabbinischen Anthropologie*. Stuttgart 1937

— *Das Gebet des Nabonid* (Sitzungsberichte der Sächsischen Akademie der Wissenschaften zu Leipzig 104/3) Berlin 1962

— 'Melchisedek von Jerusalem und Moresedek von Qumran'. *VT Suppl.* 15 (1965) 228-39

— 'Prophecy and Prophets in the Judaism of the hellenistic Period', in *TDNT* 6, 812-28

MEYER, W. 'Vitae Adae et Evae', in *Abhandlungen der königlichen Bayerischen Akademie der Wissenschaft*. Munich 1879, 187-250

MEZZAGASA, G. *Il libro dei Proverbi di Salomone. Studio critico sulle aggiunte greco-alessandrine*. Rome 1913

MICHAELIS, W. 'ὁδός', in *TDNT* 5, 42-96

MICHAUD, H. 'Un mythe Zervanite dans un des manuscrits de Qumran'. *VT* 15 (1965) 137-47

MICHEL, H. J. *Die Abschiedsrede des Paulus an die Kirche*. München 1973

MICHEL, O. 'Spätjüdisches Prophetentum', in *Neutestamentliche Studien für Rudolf Bultmann*. Berlin 1954, 60-66

— 'Ich komme (Jos. Bell. III.400)'. *TZ* 24 (1968) 123-24

— 'Studien zu Josephus; apokalyptische Heilsansagen im Bericht des Josephus (BJ 6,290f., 293-95); ihre Umdeutung bei Josephus', in *Neutestamentica et Semitica: Festschrift M. Black*. Edinburgh 1969, 240-44

— 'Zur Arbeit an den Textzeugnissen des Josephus'. *ZAW* 83 (1971) 101-2

MICHEL, O. — BAUERNFEIND, O. *Flavius Josephus: De Bello Judaico. Der jüdische Krieg 1-3*. Darmstadt 1959-69

— 'Die beide Eleazarreden in Jos. Bell. 7,323-336; 7,341-388'. *ZNW* 58 (1967) 267-72

MIDDENDORP, TH. *Die Stellung Jesu Ben Siras zwischen Judentum und Hellenismus*. Leiden 1973

MILGROM, J. 'Studies in the Temple Scroll'. *JBL* 97 (1978) 501-23
— 'The Temple Scroll'. *BA* 41 (1978) 105-20
MILIK, J. T. 'Le Testament de Lévi en araméen: Fragment de la grotte 4 de Qumran'. *RB* 62 (1955) 398-406
— 'Testament de Lévi (Pl. XVII)', in *DJD* 1, 87-91
— 'Prière de Nabonide et autres écrits d'un cycle de Daniel'. *RB* 63 (1956) 407-15
— 'Le Travail d'édition des manuscrits du Désert de Juda'. *VT Suppl.* 4 (1957) 17-26
— *Ten Years of Discovery in the Wilderness of Judea,* trans. J. Strugnell. London 1958
— Review of Wernberg-Møller, The Manual of Discipline. *RB* 67 (1960) 410-16
— 'Textes hébreux et araméens', in *DJD* 2, 67-208
— 'Un fragment mal placé dans l'édition du Siracide de Masada'. *Biblica* 47 (1966) 425-6
— 'La Patrie de Tobie'. *RB* 73 (1966) 522-30
— 'Fragments grecs du livre d'Henoch'. *Chronique d'Egypte* 47 (1971) 821-43
— 'Recherches sur la version grecque du livre des Jubilés'. *RB* 78 (1971) 545-57
— 'Problèmes de la littérature hénochite à la lumière des fragments araméens de Qumrân'. *HTR* 64 (1971) 333-78
— 'Turfan et Qumran: Livre des Géants juif et manichéen', in *Tradition und Glaube. Festgabe K. G. Kuhn.* Göttingen 1971, 117-27
— 'Milkî-Sedeq et Milkî-Reša dans les anciens écrits juifs et chrétiens'. *JJS* 23 (1972) 95-144
— '4Q Visions de Amran et une citation d'Origène'. *RB* 79 (1972) 77-97
— *The Books of Enoch: Aramaic Fragments of Qumran Cave 4.* Oxford 1976
— 'Ecrits préesséniens de Qumrân', in Delcor, *Qumran,* 97-102
MILIK, J. T. — CROSS, F. M. 'Chronique archéologique'. *RB* 63 (1956) 74-76
MILIKOWSKY, CH. 'Again: *Damascus* in the Damascus Covenant and in Rabbinic Literature'. *RQ* 41 (1982) 97-106
MILLAR, F. The Background to the Maccabean Revolution. Reflections on Martin Hengel's Judaism and Hellenism'. *JJS* 29 (1978) 1-21
MILLER, M. P. 'Isa 61:1-2 in 11Q Melchizedek'. *JBL* 88 (1969) 467-9
MOEHRING, H. 'The Acta pro Judaeis in the Antiquities of Flavius Josephus', in *Christianity, Judaism and Other Greco-Roman Cults. Studies for Morton Smith at Sixty.* 3. Leiden 1975, 124-58
— *Novelistic Elements in the Writings of Josephus.* Diss. Chicago 1957
MOMIGLIANO, A. *Prime linee di storia della tradizione maccabaica.* Rome 1930 (repr. with a bibliographical appendix, Amsterdam 1968)
— *Studies in Historiography.* Oxford 1966
— 'La Portata Storica dei Vaticini sul Settimo Re nel Terzo Libro degli Oracoli Sibyllini', in *Forma Futuri: Studi in onore del Cardinale Michele Pellegrino.* Torino 1975, 1077-84
— *Alien Wisdom: The Limits of Hellenization.* Cambridge 1975
— 'The Second Book of Maccabees'. *Classical Philology* 70 (1975) 81-88
MONTGOMERY, J. A. *A Critical and Exegetical Commentary on the Book of Daniel.* Edinburgh 1927
MOORE, C. A. *Daniel, Esther and Jeremiah: The Additions* (Anchor Bible) Garden City 1977
MOORE, G. F. 'Christian Writers on Judaism', *HTR* 14 (1921) 197-254
— 'Fate and Free Will in the Jewish Philosophies according to Josephus'. *HTR* 22 (1929) 371-89
— *Judaism* 1-3. Cambridge MA 1929 (repr. in 2 vols. New York 1971)
MORAWE, G. *Aufbau und Abgrenzung der Loblieder von Qumran.* Berlin 1961
— 'Vergleich des Aufbaus der Danklieder und hymnischen Bekenntnislieder (1QH) von Qumran mit dem Aufbau der Psalmen im Alten Testament und im Spätjudentum'. *RQ* 4 (1963) 323-56
MORFILL, W. R. — CHARLES, R. H. *The Book of the Secrets of Enoch.* Oxford 1896
MORTON, S. 'The Dead Sea Sect in Relation to Ancient Judaism'. *NTS* 7 (1960/61) 347-60
— *Palestinian Parties and Politics that shaped the Old Testament.* London 1971
MOTZO, B. 'Il rifacimento Greco di Ester e il III Mac.', in *Saggi de storia e letteratura Guideo-Ellenistica.* Florence 1934, 272-90

MOWINCKEL, S. 'The Hebrew Equivalent of Taxo in Ass. Mos. IX', in *Congress Volume Copenhagen 1953* (VT Suppl. 1) Leiden 1953, 88-96
— 'Die Metrik bei Jesus Sirach'. *ST* 9 (1955) 137-65
— *He That Cometh.* Oxford 1956
— 'Some Remarks on the Hodayoth XXXIX 5-20'. *JBL* 75 (1956) 265-76
MOZLEY, J. H. 'Documents: The Vita Adae'. *JTS* 20 (1929) 121-49
MRAS, K. *Eusebius Werke 8:1 Praeparatio Evangelica* (GCS 43/1) Berlin 1954
— 'Die Hegesippus-Frage', in *Anzeiger der Oesterreichischen Akademie der Wissenschaften.* Vienna 1958, 143-53
MÜHLENBERG, E. 'Das Problem der Offenbarung in Philo von Alexandrien'. *ZNW* 64 (1973) 1-18
MUELLER, J. B. 'The Temple Scroll and the Gospel Divorce Texts'. *RQ* 10 (1980) 247-56
MÜLLER, H. P. *Ursprünge und Strukturen alttestamentlicher Eschatologie* (BZAW 109) Berlin 1969
MUILENBURG, J. 'A Qoheleth Scroll from Qumran'. *BASOR* 135 (1954) 20-8
MUNCK, 'Discourses d'adieu dans le Nouveau Testament et dans la littérature biblique', in *Aux Sources de la tradition chrétienne. Mélanges M. Goguel.* Paris 1950, 155-70
MURPHY, R. E. 'Hebrew Wisdom'. *JAOS* 101 (1981) 21-34
MURPHY-O'CONNOR, J. *Paul and Qumran.* London 1968
— 'La genèse littéraire de la Règle de la Communauté'. *RB* 76 (1969) 528-49
— 'An Essene Missionary Document CD II, 14-VI, 1'. *RB* 77 (1970) 201-29
— 'A Literary Analysis of Damascus Document VI, 2-VIII, 3'. *RB* 78 (1971) 210-32
— 'The Original Text of CD 7:9—8:2 = 19:5—14'. *HTR* 64 (1971) 379-86
— 'A Literary Analysis of Damascus Document XIX, 33-XX, 34'. *RQ* 79 (1972) 544-64
— 'The Critique of the Princes of Judah CD VIII 3-19'. *RB* 79 (1972) 200-16
— 'The Essenes and their History'. *RB* 81 (1974) 215-44
— 'Judah the Essene and the Teacher of Righteousness'. *RQ* 10 (1981) 579-85
MYERS, M. *Ezra-Nehemia* (Anchor Bible) Garden City, N.Y. 1965
— *I and II Esdras* (Anchor Bible) Garden City, N.Y. 1974
NABER, S. *Flavii Josephi Opera Omnia* 1-6. Leipzig 1888-96
NAGEL, M. *La Vie grecque d'Adam et d'Eve: Apocalypse de Moïse.* Dissertation Strassbourg 1972
NAGEL, P. 'Die Auslegung der Paradieserzählung in der Gnosis', in Tröger, *Altes Testament,* 49-70
NAUMANN, W. *Untersuchungen über den apokryphen Jeremiasbrief* (BZAW 25) Giessen 1913
NAZZARO, A. V. *Recenti Studi Filoniani* (1963-70) Napoli 1973
NEMO, PH. *Job et l'excès du mal.* Paris 1978
NESTLE, E. 'Die dem Epiphanus zugeschriebenen Vitae Prophetarum in doppelter griechischer Rezension', in *Marginalien und Materialien.* Tübingen 1893, 1-64
NEUHAUS, G. O. 'Quellen im 1.Makkabäerbuch? Eine Entgegnung auf die Analyse von K.-D. Schunk'. *JSJ* 5 (1973) 162-75
— *Studien zu den poetischen Stücken im 1.Makkabäerbuch.* Würzburg 1974
NEUSNER, J. *A Life of Yohanan ben Zakkai, ca. 1-80* C.E. 2nd ed. Leiden 1970.
— *The Rabbinic Traditions about the Pharisees* 1-3. Leiden 1971
— 'By the Testimonies of Two Witnesses in Damascus Document IX, 17-22 and in Pharisaic-Rabbinic Law'. *RQ* 8 (1973) 197-217
— *From Politics to Piety: The Emergence of Pharisaic Judaism.* Entlewood Cliffs, N.J. 1973
— *Early Rabbinic Judaism.* Leiden 1975
NEWSOM, C. A. 'The Development of 1 Enoch 6-19: Cosmology and Judgement'. *CBQ* 42 (1980) 310-29
— *4Q Serek Shirot Olat Hasshabat (The Qumran Angelic Liturgy)* Diss. Harvard, Cambridge MA 1982
NICHOLLS, P. H. *The Structure and Purpose of the Testament of Job.* Unpublished diss. Hebrew University, Jerusalem 1982

NICKELSBURG, G. W. E. *Resurrection, Immortality and Eternal Life in Intertestamental Judaism.* Cambridge MA 1972
— 'Narrative Traditions in the Paraleipomena of Jeremiah and 2 Baruch'. *CBQ* 35 (1973) 60-68
— 'Simon, A Priest with Reputation for Faithfulness'. *BASOR* 223 (1976) 67-8
— 'Apocalyptic and Myth in I Enoch 6-11'. *JBL* 96 (1977) 383-405
— 'Reflections upon Reflections: A Response to John Collins' Methodological Issues in the Study of 1 Enoch'. *SBLSP* 1978 (1) 311-14
— 'Enoch 97-104: A Study of the Greek and Ethiopic Texts', in *Armenian and Biblical Studies,* ed. by M. E. Stone. Jerusalem 1976, 90-156
— 'The Apocalyptic Message of 1 Enoch 92-105'. *CBQ* 39 (1977) 309-28
— 'Good and Bad Leaders in Pseudo-Philo's *Liber Antiquitatum Biblicarum*', in Collins-Nickelsburg, *Ideal Figures,* 49-65
— 'The Epistle of Enoch and the Qumran Literature'. *JJS* (forthcoming)
— 'The Genre and Function of the Markan Passion Narrative'. *HTR* 73(1980) 153-84
— 'The Book of Enoch in Recent Research'. *RSR* 7 (1981) 210-217
— *Jewish Literature Between the Bible and the Mishnah.* Philadelphia 1981
— 'Enoch, Levi and Peter: Recipients of Revelation in Upper Galilee'. *JBL* 100 (1981) 575-600
— 'Social Aspects of Palestinian Jewish Apocalypticism', in Hellholm, *Apocalypticism*
— 'Some Related Traditions in the Apocalypse of Adam, the Books of Adam and Eve and 1 Enoch', in Layton, *Redisovery,* 515-39
NICKELSBURG, G. W. E. (ed.) *Studies on the Testament of Moses.* Cambridge MA 1973
— *Studies on the Testament of Joseph.* Missoula 1975
— *Studies on the Testament of Abraham.* Missoula 1976
NIDITCH, S. — DORAN, R. 'The Success Story of the Wise Courtier'. *JBL* 96 (1977) 179-93
NIESE, B. *Flavii Josephi Opera* 1-7. Berlin 1885-95
— 'Der jüdische Historiker Josephus'. *Historische Zeitschrift* 76 (1896) 193-237
— 'Josephus', in *Hastings Encyclopedia of Religion and Ethics* 7 (1914) 569-79
NIKIPROWETZKY, V. *La troisième Sibylle.* Paris 1970
— 'Réflexions sur quelques problèmes du Quatrième et du Cinquième Livre des Oracles Sibyllins'. *HUCA* 43 (1972) 29-76
— *Le commentaire de l'Ecriture chez Philon d'Alexandrie.* Leiden 1977
NILSSON, M. P. *Geschichte der griechischen Religion 2: Die Hellenistische und römische Zeit.* München 1961
NIZAN, B. *Pesher Habakkuk.* M. A. Thesis Tel Aviv-University 1976 (Hebrew)
NOACK, B. 'Der hervorragende Mann und der Beste der Hebräer (Or Sib V, 256-59)'. *ASTI* 3 (1964) 122-46
— 'Are the Essenes referred to in the Sibylline Oracles'. *ST* 17 (1963) 92-102
NOCK, A. D. 'Posidonius'. *Journal of Roman Studies* 49 (1959) 1-15 (repr. in *Essays on Religion and the Ancient World* 2. Ed. Z. Stewart. Cambridge 1972, 853-76)
NOCK, A. D. — FESTUGIERE, A.-J. (eds.) *Corpus Hermeticum* 1. 2nd ed. Paris 1960
NOLLAND, J. 'Sib Or III. 265-94. An Early Maccabean Messianic Oracle'. *JTS* 30 (1979) 158-67
NÖTSCHER, F. *Zur theologischen Terminologie der Qumran-Texte.* Bonn 1956
NORDEN, E. *Agnostos Theos. Untersuchungen zur Formengeschichte religiöser Rede.* Repr. Darmstadt 1956
NORDHEIM, E. VON. *Die Lehre der Alten.* 1. *Das Testament als Gliedgattung im Judentum der Hellenistisch-Römischen Zeit.* Leiden 1980
— *Die Lehre der Alten* 2 (forthcoming)
NORTH, R. 'The Qumran Sadducees'. *CBQ* 17 (1955) 164-88
— 'From Prophecy to Apocalyptic via Zechariah'. *VT Suppl.* 22 (1972) 47-71
NOTH, M. — WINTON THOMAS, D. (eds.). *Wisdom in Israel and in the Ancient Near East.* Leiden 1955
NOUGAYROL, J. 'Les sagesses babyloniennes. Etudes récentes et textes inédits', in *Les sagesses du Proche-Orient ancien.* Paris 1963, pp. 40-51

ODEBERG, G. *Third Enoch or the Hebrew Book of Enoch.* Cambridge 1928

OFFERHAUS, U. *Komposition und Intention der Sapientia Salomonis.* Bonn 1981

OEPKE, A. 'Βίβλιοι ἀπόκρυφοι in Christianity', in *TDNT* 3, 994

OPPENHEIM, A. L. 'Nabonidus'. *IDB* 3, 493-5

OPPENHEIMER, A. 'The Bar Kokhba Revolt', in *Eretz Israel from the Destruction of the Second Temple to the Muslim Conquest,* ed. Z. Baras *et al.,* Jerusalem 1982 (in Hebrew)

ORLINSKY, H, M. 'The Septuagint as Holy Writ and the Philosophy of the Translators'. *HUCA* 46 (1975) 89-114

OSSWALD, E. *Das Gebet Manasses* (JSHRZ IV/1) Gütersloh 1974

OSTEN-SACKEN, P. VON DER. *Die Apokalyptik in ihrem Verhältnis zu Prophetie und Weisheit.* München 1969

— *Gott und Belial.* Göttingen 1969

OTTE, K. *Das Sprachverständnis bei Philon von Alexandrien.* Tübingen 1968

OTZEN, B. 'Die neugefundenen hebräischen Sektenschriften und die Testamente der zwölf Patriarchen'. *ST* 7 (1953) 125-57

PARDEE, A. 'A Restudy of the Commentary on Psalm 37 from Qumran Cave 4 (DJD 5, n. 171)'. *RQ* 8 (1973) 163-94

— 'Letters from Tel Arad'. *Ugarit-Forschungen* 10 (1978) 289-336

— 'An Overiew of Ancient Hebrew Epistolography'. *JBL* 97 (1978) 321-46

— *Handbook of Ancient Hebrew Letters* (SBL Sources for Biblical Study 15) Chico CA 1982

PARROTT, D.M. (ed.) *Nag Hammadi Codices V, 2-5 and VI, with Papyrus Berolinensis 8502, 1 and 4.* Leiden 1979

PASCHER, J. *Der Köningsweg zu Wiedergebuhrt und Vergöttung bei Philon van Alexandrien.* Paderborn 1931

PATTE, D. *Early Jewish Hermeneutic in Palestine.* Missoula 1975

PAUTREL, R. 'Les canons du mashal rabbinique'. *RSR* 26 (1936) 5-45; 28 (1938) 264-81

— 'Ben Sira et le stoïcisme'. *RSR* 51 (1963) 535-49

PEARSON, B. A. 'Jewish Haggadic Traditions in The Testimony of Truth from Nag Hammadi (CG IX 3)', in *Ex Orbe Religionum; Studia G. Widengren* 1. Leiden 1972, 456-70

— 'Friedländer Revisited. Alexandrian Judaism and Gnostic Origins'. *Studia Philonica* 2 (1973) 23-39

— 'The Pierpont Morgan Fragments of a Coptic Enoch Apocryphon', in Nickelsburg, *Studies on the Testament of Abraham,* 227-83

— 'Anti-Heretical Warnings in Codex IX from Nag Hammadi', in M. Krause (ed.) *Essays on the Nag Hammadi Texts in Honour of Pahor Labib.* Leiden 1075, 145-54

— 'Biblical Exegesis in Gnostic Literature', in M. Stone (ed.) *Armenian and Biblical Studies.* Jerusalem 1976, 70-80

— 'The Figure of Norea in Gnostic Literature', in Widengren, *Proceedings,* 143-52

— 'The Figure of Seth in Gnostic Literature', in Layton, *Rediscovery* 2, 472-504

— 'She Became a Tree- A Note to CG II,4: 89, 25-26'. *HTR* 69 (1976) 413-5

— 'Philo and the Gnostics on Man and Salvation', in W. Wüellner (ed.) *Protocol on the 29th Colloquy. The Center for Hermeneutical Studies.* Berkeley 1977

— 'Gnostic Interpretation of the Old Testament in the Testimony of Truth (NHC IX, 3)'. *HTR* 73 (1980) 311-19

— 'Jewish Elements in Corpus Hermeticum I (Poimandres)', in Van den Broek — Vermaseren, *Studies in Gnosticism,* 336-48

— 'Jewish Elements in Gnosticism and the Development of Gnostic Self-Definition', in Sanders, *Jewish and Christian Self-Definition* 1, 151-60

— 'The Thunder, Prefect Mind: Some Observations', in MacRae, *The Thunder,* 10-14

— 'Introduction to IX, 1: Melchizedek', in *Nag Hammadi Codices IX and X,* 19-40

— 'Philo and Gnosticism', in *ANRW* II, 21/1, 295-342

PEARSON, B. A. (ed.). *Nag Hammadi Codices IX and X.* Leiden 1981

PEEL, M. L. — ZANDEE, J. 'The Teachings of Silvanus from the Library of Nag Hammadi (CG VII: 84,15-118,7)'. *NT* 14 (1972) 294-311
— The Teachings of Sylvanus (VII,4)', in Robinson, *Nag Hammadi Library*, 346-61 (translation)
PELLETIER, A. *Flavius Josèphe, Autobiographie.* Paris 1959
— *Flavius Josèphe adaptateur de la Lettre d'Aristée: une réaction atticisante contre la Koine.* Paris 1962
— *Lettre d'Aristée à Philocrate* (Sources Chrét.) Paris 1962
— *Philo Judaeus, In Flaccum.* Paris 1967
— *Philo Judaeus, Legatio ad Gaium.* Paris 1972
PERDUE, L. G. *Wisdom and Cult. A Critical Analysis of the Views of Cult in the Wisdom Literatures of Israel and the Ancient Near East.* Missoula 1977
PERETTI, A. *La Sibilla Babilonese nella propaganda Ellenistica.* Firenze 1943
— 'Echi di dottrine esseniche negli Oraculi Sibillini Giudaici'. *La Parola del Passato* 17 (1962) 247-95
PERKINS, P. 'Apocalyptic Schematization in the Apocalypse of Adam and the Gospel of the Egyptians', in *The Society of Biblical Literature One Hundred Eight Annual Meeting, Proceedings* 2, ed. L. McGaughy. Missoula 1972, 591-9
— 'Ireneus and the Gnostics: Rhetoric and Composition in Adversus Haereses Book One'. *VC* 30 (1976) 193-200
— 'Apocalypse of Adam: The Genre and Function of a Gnostic Apocalypse'. *CBQ* 39 (1977) 382-95
— *The Gnostic Dialogue: The Early Church and the Crisis of Gnosticism.* New York 1980
PERRENCHIO, F. 'Struttura e analisi letteraria di Sapienzia 1,1-15 nel quadro del suo contesto letterario immediato'. *Salesianum* 37 (1975) 289-325
— 'Struttura e analisi letteraria di Sapienzia 1,16-2,24 e 5,1-23'. *Salesianum* 43 (1981) 3-43
PERROT, C. — BOGAERT, P.-M. *Pseudo-Philon. Les Antiquités Bibliques* 2: Introduction littéraire, commentaire et index (Sources Chrét.) Paris 1976 (See also Harrington-Cazeaux)
PERVO, R. I. 'The Testament of Joseph and Greek Romance', in Nickelsburg, *Studies on the Testament of Joseph,* 15-28
— 'Joseph and Asenath and the Greek Novel'. *SBLSP* 1976, 171-81
PETERS, N. *Das Buch Jesus Sirach oder Ecclesiasticus.* Münster 1913
PFEIFFER, R. H. *History of New Testament Times with an Introduction to the Apocrypha.* New York 1949
PFITZNER, V. *Paul and the Agon Motif.* Leiden 1967
PHILONENKO, M. 'Le Testament de Job et les Thérapeutes'. *Semitica* 8 (1958) 41-53
— *Les interpolations chrétiennes des Testaments des Douze Patriarches et les manuscrits de Qoumrân.* Paris 1960
— 'Une paraphrase du Cantique d'Anne'. *RHPR* 42 (1962) 43-54
— 'Le Martyre d'Esaïe et l'histoire de la secte de Qoumrân'. *Cahiers de la RHPR* 41 (1967) 1-10
— *Joseph et Aséneth.* Leiden 1968
— 'La cosmogonie du Livre des Secrets d'Hénoch', in *Religions en Egypte hellénistique et romaine. Colloque de Strasbourg 16-18 mai 1967.* Paris 1969, 109-116
— 'Le Testament de Job'. *Semitica* 18 (1969) 9-24
— 'Iphigénie and Sheila', in *Syncrétisme dans les réligions grecques et romaines.* Paris 1973, 165-77
— 'Le Poimandrès et la liturgie juive', in *Les syncrétismes dans les religions de l'antiquité: Colloque de Besançon (22-23 octobre 1973),* ed. by F. Dunand and P. Lévêque. Leiden 1975, 204-11
— 'Une utilisation du Shema dans le Poimandrès'. *RHPR* 59 (1979) 369-72
PHILONENKO-SAYAR, B. — PHILONENKO, M. *Die Apokalypse Abrahams* (JSHRZ V/5) Gütersloh 1982

PICARD, J.-C. *Apocalypsis Baruchi graece* (PVTG 2) Leiden 1967
— 'Observations sur l'Apocalypse grecque de Baruch'. *Semitica* 20 (1970) 77-103
PIETERSMA, A. — COMSTOCK, S. — ATTRIDGE, H. (eds.) *The Apocalypse of Elijah* (SBLTT 19) Missoula 1979
PINES, S. 'Eschatology and the Concept of Time in the Slavonic Book of Enoch', in *Types of Redemption*, ed. by R. J. Z. Werblowsky and C. J. Bleeker. Leiden 1970, 72-87
— *An Arabic Version of the Testimonium Flavianum and Its Implications (PIASH)*. Jerusalem 1971
— 'From Darkness into Great Light'. *Immanuel* 4 (1974) 47-51
PIXNER, B. 'An Essene Quarter on Mount Zion', in *Studia Hierosolymitana*. Jerusalem 1976, 245-84
PLOEG, J. P. M. VAN DER. *Le Rouleau de la Guerre*. Leiden 1959
— 'Un petit rouleau de psaumes apocrypes (11QPsApᵃ)', in *Tradition und Glaube. Das frühe Christentum in seiner Umwelt. Festgabe für K. G. Kuhn*. Göttingen 1971, 128-39
PLOEG, J. P. M. VAN DER — WOUDE, A. S. VAN DER. *Le Targum de Job de la grotte XI de Qumran*. Edité et traduit avec la collaboration de B. Jongeling. Leiden 1971
PLÖGER, O. *Das Buch Daniel*. Gütersloh 1965
PODECHARD, E. *L'Ecclésiaste*. Paris 1912
PÖTSCHER, W. 'Josephus Flavius. Antiquities 18.63f. Sprachliche Form und thematischer Inhalt'. *Eranos* 73 (1975) 26-42
POHLMANN, K.-F. *Studien zum dritten Esra. Ein Beitrag zur Frage nach dem ursprünglichen Schluss des chronistischen Geschichtswerks*. Göttingen 1970
— *3. Esra-Buch* (JSHRZ I/5) Gütersloh 1980
POLOTSKY, H. J. *Manichäische Homilien. Manichäische Handschriften der Sammlung A. Chester Beatty* 1. Stuttgart 1934
POPE, M. H. *Song of Songs* (Anchor Bible) Garden City, N.Y. 1977
PORTEN, B. 'The Archive of Jedaniah son of Gemariah of Elephantine — The Structure and Style of the Letters (1)'. *Eretz Israel* 14 (1978) 165-77
— 'Aramaic Papyri and Parchments: A New Look'. *BA* 42 (1979) 74-104
PORTER, F. C. 'The Yeçer Hara', in *Yale Centennial Publications*. New York 1902, 146-52
POUILLY, J. *La Règle de la Communauté de Qumran*. Paris 1976
PRATO, G. L. *Il problema della teodicea in Ben Sira. Composizione dei contrari e richiamo alle origini* (AnBib). Roma 1975
— 'La lumière interprète de la sagesse dans la tradition textuelle de Ben Sira', in Gilbert, *La sagesse de l'A.T.*, 317-46
PREUSCHEN, E. 'Die Apocryphen gnostischen Adamschriften, aus dem Armenischen übersetzt und untersucht', in *Festgruss B. Stade*. Giessen 1900, 163-252
PREISENDANZ, K. *Papyri graecae magicae* 1-2. Leipzig 1928-31
PRIESSNING, A. 'Die literarische Form der Patriarchenbiographien des Philon von Alexandrien'. *MGWJ* 73 (1929) 143-55
PRIEST, J. 'Some Reflections on the Assumption of Moses'. *Perspectives in Religious Studies* 4 (1977) 92-111
— 'The Assumption of Moses', in Charlesworth, *Pseudepigrapha*
PRIGENT, P. — KRAFT, R. A. *Epître de Barnabé* (Sources Chrét.) Paris 1971
PRITCHARD, J. B. *Ancient Near Eastern Texts Relating to the O.T.* 2nd rev. ed. Princeton 1955
PUECH, H.-C. 'Fragments retrouvés de l'Apocalypse d'Allogène', in *Enquête de la Gnose* 1. Paris 1978, 271-300
— Recension of Pouilly, La Règle. *RQ* 10 (1979) 103-16
— 'Remarques sur l'écriture de 1QS VII-VIII'. *RQ* (1979) 35-43
PURINTON, C. E. 'Translation Greek in the Wisdom of Salomon'. *JBL* 47 (1928) 276-304
QIMRON, E. *A Grammar of the Hebrew Language of the Dead Sea Scrolls*. Dissertation Hebrew University. Jerusalem 1976 (Hebrew)
— 'New Readings in the Temple Scroll.' *IEJ* 28 (1978) 161-72

— 'The Language of the Temple Scroll'. *Leshonenu* 42 (1978) 83-98 (Hebrew)
— 'Qumran'. *DBS* 9 (1979) 737-1011
QUINN, E. C. *The Quest of Seth for the Oil of Life.* Chicago 1962
QUISPEL, G. 'Jewish Gnosis and Mandaean Gnosticism: Some Reflections on the Writing *Bronte',* in Ménard, *Les Textes de Nag Hammadi,* 82-122
— 'The Origins of the Gnostic Demiurge', in Quispel, *Gnostic Studies* 1. Istanbul 1974, 213-20
— 'Valentinian Gnosis and the Apocryphon of John', in Layton, *Rediscovery* 1, 118-27
RABIN, CH. 'Alexander Jannaeus and the Pharisees'. *JJS* 7 (1956) 3-21
— *Qumran Studies.* Oxford 1957
— 'The Historical Background of Qumran Hebrew', in *Scripta* 4, 144-61
— *The Zadokite Documents.* Oxford 1958
— 'The Literary Structure of the War Scroll', in *Essays on the Dead Sea Scrolls in Memory of E. L. Sukenik,* ed. Ch. Rabin and Y. Yadin. Jerusalem 1961, 31-48 (Hebrew)
RABINOVITCH, N. L. 'Damascus Document IX, 17-22 and Rabbinic Parallels'. *RQ* 9 (1977) 113-6
RABINOWITZ, I. 'A Reconsideration of Damascus and 390 Years in the Damascus (Zadokite) Fragment'. *JBL* 73 (1954) 11-35
— 'The Qumran Authors' SPR HHGW/Y'. *JNES* 20 (1961) 109-14
— 'The Qumran Hebrew Original of Ben Sira's Concluding Acrostic on Wisdom'. *HUCA* 42 (1971) 173-84
— 'Pesher/Pittaron. Its Biblical Meaning and its Significance in the Qumran Literature'. *RQ* 8 (1973) 219-32
— 'The Demetrius-Passage of the Qumran Nahum-Pesher'. *JAOS* 98 (1978) 394-9
RAD, G. VON. 'Die Vorgeschichte der Gattung vom 1 Kor. 13:4-7', in *Geschichte und Altes Testament. Albrecht Alt zum siebzigsten Geburtstag.* Tübingen 1953, 153-68
— *Gesammelte Studien zum Alten Testament.* München 1958
— 'The Origin of the Concept of the Day of Yahweh.' *JSS* 4 (1959) 97-108
— *Theologie des Alten Testaments.* München 1965
— *Weisheit in Israel.* Neukirchen 1970
— *Wisdom in Israel.* Nashville 1972
RAHNENFÜHRER, D. 'Das Testament Hiobs und das NT'. *ZNW* 62 (1971) 68-93
RAJAK, T. 'Justus of Tiberias'. *Classical Quarterly* 23 (1973) 345-68
— 'Moses in Ethiopia: Legend and Literature'. *JJS* 29 (1978) 111-22
RAMPOLLA DEL TINDARO, M. 'Martyre et sépulture des Machabées'. *Revue de l'art chrétien* (1899) 295 ff.
RAPPAPORT, U. 'The Emergence of Hasmonean Coinage'. *AJSR* 1 (1976) 171-86
— 'The Relations between Jews and Non-Jews and the Great War against Rome'. *Tarbiz* 47 (1978) 1-14 (Hebrew)
— 'John of Gischala', in *Josephus Flavius. Historian of Eretz Israel.* 1982, 203-15
— 'John of Gischala. From Galilee to Jerusalem'. *JJS* 33 (1982) 479-93
RAPPAPORT, S. *Agada und Exegese bei Flavius Josephus.* Vienna 1930
REESE, J. M. 'Plan and Structure in the Book of Wisdom'. *CBQ* 27 (1965) 391-9
— *Hellenistic Influence on the Book of Wisdom and its Consequences.* Rome 1970
REICKE, B. 'Remarques sur l'histoire de la forme (Formgeschichte) des textes de Qumran', in *Les Manuscrits de la Mer Morte. Colloque de Strasbourg 1955.* Paris 1957, 38-44
— 'Da'at and Gnosis in Intertestamental Literature', in *Neotestamentica et Semitica,* ed. by E. E. Ellis and M. Wilcox. Edinburgh 1969, 245-55
REINACH, T. — BLUM, L. *Flavius Josèphe, Contre Apion.* Paris 1930
REITERER, F. V. *'Urtext' und Uebersetzungen. Sprachstudie über Sir 44,16-45,25 als Beitrag zur Siraforschung.* St. Ottilien 1980
REITZENSTEIN, R. *Poimandres: Studien zur griechisch-ägyptischen und frühchristlichen Literatur.* Leipzig 1904 (repr. Darmstadt 1966)
— *Die hellenistischen Mysterienreligionen.* 3rd ed. Leipzig 1927
RELAND, H. *Palaestina ex Monumentibus Veteribus Illustrata.* Utrecht 1714

RENGSTORFF, K. H. *A Complete Concordance to Flavius Josephus.* Leiden 1968 ff.
— 'Herkunft und Sinn der Patriarchenreden in den Testamenten der zwölf Patriarchen', in *La Littérature juive entre Tenach et Mischna,* ed. by W. C. van Unnik. Leiden 1974
RHOADS, D. M. 'The Assumption of Moses and Jewish History: 4 B.C.-A.D. 48', in Nickelsburg *Studies on the Testament of Moses,* 53-58
— *Israel in Revolution 6-74 C.E.: A Political History Based on the Writings of Josephus.* Philadelphia 1976
RICHARDS, G. C. — SHUTT, R. J. H. 'The Composition of Josephus' Antiquities'. *Classical Quarterly* 33 (1939) 36-40
RICHTER, W. *Recht und Ethos. Versuch einer Ortung des Weisheitlichen Mahnspruches.* München 1966
RICKENBACHER, O. *Weisheitsperikopen bei Ben Sira.* Freiburg 1973
RIESSLER, P. *Altjüdisches Schrifttum ausserhalb der Bibel.* Augsburg 1928
RINGGREN, H. *Word and Wisdom. Studies in the Hypostatization of Divine Qualities and Functions in the Ancient Near East.* Lund 1947
— 'Der Weltbrand in den Hodayoth', in *Bibel und Qumran. Festschrift H. Bardtke.* Berlin 1968, 177-82
RITTER, B. *Philo und die Halacha.* Leipzig 1879
ROBERGE, M. *Noréa.* See Barc, *L'Hypostase*
ROBERT, A. 'Les attaches littéraires bibliques de Prov I-IX'. *RB* 43 (1934) 42-68; 172-204; 374-84; 44 (1935) 344-65; 502-25
— 'Littéraires (Genres)' in *DBS* 5 (1957) 411-8
ROBERTSON, J. 'Ezekiel the Tragedian', in Charlesworth, *Pseudepigrapha.*
ROBINSON, J. M. *The Problem of History in Mark.* 1957
— 'Logoi Sophou. Zur Gattung der Spruchquelle Q', in *Zeit und Geschichte. Festschrift R. Bultmann.* Tübingen 1964, 77-96
— 'Three Steles of Seth and the Gnostics of Plotinus', in Widengren, *Proceedings,* pp. 132-42
— 'Sethians and Johannine Thought: The *Trimorphic Protennoia* and the Prologue of the Gospel of John', in Layton, *Rediscovery* 2, pp. 643-62
ROBINSON, J. M. (ed.). *The Facsimile Edition of the Nag Hammadi Codices.* Codices I-XIII, Leiden 1972-79
ROBINSON, J. M. — KOESTER, H. *Trajectories Through Early Christianity.* Philadelphia 1971
ROBINSON, J. M. — MEYER, M., (eds.) *The Nag Hammadi Library in English.* Leiden/San Francisco 1977
ROBINSON, E. *The Testament of Abraham. An Examination of the Syriac and Greek Traditions.* Chico 1982
ROLLER, O. *Das Formular der paulinischen Briefe: Ein Beitrag zur Lehre vom antiken Briefe.* Stuttgart 1933
ROMANIUK, J. 'Le thème de la sagesse dans les documents de Qumran'. *RQ* 9 (1978) 429-35
ROON, A. VAN. 'The Relation between Christ and the Wisdom of God according to Paul'. *NT* 16 (1974) 207-39
RORDORF, W. — TUILIER, A. *La doctrine des douze apôtres (Didachè)* (Sources Chrét.) Paris 1978
ROSENSTIEHL, J. M. *L'Apocalypse d'Elie.* Paris 1972
ROSENTHAL, F. *An Aramaic Handbook* 1-4. Wiesbaden 1967
ROSSO-UBIGLI, I. 'Il Documento di Damasco e la Halakhah settaria'. *RQ* 9 (1978) 357-99
ROTH, C. 'Why the Qumran Sect cannot have been Essenes'. *RQ* 1 (1959) 417-22
ROTH, W. 'On the Gnomic- Discursive Wisdom of Jesus ben Sirach'. *Semeia* 17 (1980) 59-79
ROTH, W. M. W. 'For Life, He Appeals to Death (Wis 13:18). A Study of Old Testament Idol Parodies'. *CBQ* 37 (1975) 21-47
ROST, L. *Einleitung in die alttest. Apokryphen und Pseudepigraphen einschliesslich der grossen Qumranhandschriften.* Heidelberg 1971
ROWLAND, C. 'The Visions of God in Apocalyptic Literature'. *JSJ* 10 (1979) 137-54

ROWLEY, H. H. 'The Interpretation and Date of the Sibylline Oracles III,388-400'. *ZAW* 44 (1926) 324-27
— *The Zadokite Fragments and the Dead Sea Scrolls.* Oxford 1952
— '4QpNahum and the Teacher of Righteousness'. *JBL* 75 (1956) 188-93
— *The Relevance of Apocalyptic.* 3rd ed. London 1963
RUBINKIEWICZ, R. 'Un fragment grec du IVe livre d'Esdras (chapitres xi et xii)'. *Le Muséon* 89 (1976) 75-87
RUBINSTEIN, A. 'Hebraisms in Slavonic Apocalypse of Abraham'. *JJS* 4 (1953) 108-15; 5 (1954) 132-35
— 'Observations on the Old Russian Version of Josephus' Wars'. *JSS* 2 (1957) 329-48
— 'A Problematic Passage in the Apocalypse of Abraham'. *JJS* 8 (1957) 45-50
— 'Observations on the Slavonic Book of Enoch'. *JJS* 13 (1967) 1-21
RUDOLPH, K. 'Gnosis und Gnostizismus, ein Forschungsbericht'. *TR* 34 (1969) 121-75; 181-231; 358-61; 36 (1971) 1-61; 89-124
— *Die Gnosis: Wesen und Geschichte einer spätantiken Religion.* Göttingen 1977 (E.T.: *Gnosis. The Nature and History of Gnosticism.* Ed. by R. McL. Wilson. Edinburgh-New York 1983)
— 'Simon. Magus oder Gnosticus? Zum Stand der Debatte'. *TR* 42 (1977) 279-359
— 'Gnosis. Weltreligion oder Sekte'. *Kairos* 21 (1979) 255-63
RUDOLPH, K. (ed.) *Gnosis und Gnostizismus* (Wege der Forschung 262). Darmstadt 1975
RUDOLF, W. 'Der Wettstreit der Leibwächter des Darius, 3 Esr. 3,1-5,6'. *ZAW* 61 (1945-48) 176-90
RÜGER, H. P. *Text und Textform im hebräischen Sirach* (BZAW 112). Berlin 1970
RUNIA, D. T. *Philo of Alexandria and the Timaeus of Plato* 1-2. Amsterdam 1983
RUSCH, A. 'Phoinix: Der Wundervogel', in *PWRE* 20, 414-23 (first ed.)
RUSSELL, D. S. *The Method and Message of Jewish Apocalyptic.* London 1964
RYLE, H. E. — JAMES, M. R. *Psalms of the Pharisees.* Cambridge 1891
RZACH, A. *Oracula Sibyllina.* Leipzig 1891
— *Metrische Studien zu den Sibyllinischen Orakel.* Wien 1892
— 'Sibyllinische Orakel', in *PWRE* 2A, 2073-83
SACCHI, P. 'Il 'Libro de Vigilanti e l'apocalittica'. *Henoch* 1 (1979) 42-98
SÄNGER, D. *Antikes Judentum und die Mysterien. Religionsgeschichtliche Untersuchungen zu Joseph und Aseneth.* Tübingen 1980
SAFRAI, S. 'The Teaching of Pietists in the Mishnaic Literature'. *JJS* 16 (1965) 15-33
— 'New Research concerning the Status and Actions of Rabban Yohanan ben Zakkai', in *G. Alon Memorial Volume.* Jerusalem 1970, 203-26 (Hebrew)
— 'Jewish Self-Government', in *Compendia* I/1, 377-419
— 'Relations between the Diaspora and the Land of Israel', in *Compendia* I/1, 184-215
— 'The Temple', in *Compendia* I/2, 865-907
— 'The Decision according to the School of Hillel in Yavneh', in *Proceedings of the Seventh World Congress of Jewish Studies. Studies in the Talmud, Halacha and Midrash.* Jerusalem 1981, 21-44 (Hebrew)
— 'Restoration of the Jewish Community in the Yavneh Generation', in *Eretz Israel from the Destruction of the Second Temple to the Muslim Conquest,* ed. Z. Baras *et al.* Jerusalem 1982 (Hebrew)
— 'Halakhic Literature', in *Compendia* II/3 (forthcoming)
SALDARINI, A. J. 'Apocalyptic and Rabbinic Literature'. *CBQ* 37 (1975) 348-58
— 'Last Words and Deathbed Scenes in Rabbinic Literature'. *JQR* n.s. (1977) 28-45
— 'Apocalypses and Apocalyptic in Rabbinic Literature and Mysticism', in Collins, *Apocalypse,* 187-206
SANDERS, E. P. *Paul and Palestinian Judaism.* Philadelphia 1977
— 'The Testament of Abraham', in Charlesworth, *Pseudepigrapha*
SANDERS, E. P. (ed.) *Jewish and Christian Self-Definition* 1-2. London-Philadelphia 1980-81

SANDERS, J. A. *The Psalms Scroll of Qumran Cave 11 (11QPsᵃ)* (DJD 4) Oxford 1965
— *The Dead Sea Psalms Scroll.* Ithaca, N.Y. 1967
— 'Palestinian Manuscripts 1947-67'. *JBL* 86 (1967) 431-40
— 'Palestinian Manuscripts 1947-1972'. *JJS* 24 (1973) 74-83
— 'The Old Testament in 11Q Melchizedek'. *JANESCU* 5 (1973) 373-82
SANDMEL, S. 'Philo's Environment and Philo's Exegesis'. *JBR* 22 (1954)
— *Philo's Place in Judaism.* New edition. New York 1971
— *Philo of Alexandria. An Introduction.* New York 1979
SATRAN, D. 'Daniel: Seer, Philosopher, Holy Man', in Collins-Nickelsburg, *Ideal Figures in Ancient Judaism,* 33-48
SAUER, G. *Die Sprüche Agurs. Untersuchungen zur Herkunft, Verbreitung und Bedeutung einer biblischen Stilform unter bes. Berücksichtigung von Prov. 30.* Stuttgart 1963
SCALIGER, J. J. 'Animadversiones in Chronologica Eusebii', in *Thesaurus Temporum.* Leiden 1606
SCHÄUBLIN, C. *Untersuchungen zu Methode und Herkunft der antiochenischen Exegese.* Köln 1974
SCHALIT, A. 'Josephus und Justus: Studien zur Vita des Josephus'. *Klio* 26 (1933) 67-95
— 'The Date and Place of the Story about the Three Bodyguards of the King in the Apocryphal Book of Ezra'. *BJPES* 13 (1947) 119-28
— *Flavius Josephus, Qadmoniot ha-Yehudim.* 2nd ed. Jerusalem 1967
— *König Herodes.* Berlin 1969
— 'Alexander Lysimachus', in *EJ* 2, 581
SCHALLER, B. 'Hekataios von Abdera über die Juden. Zur Frage der Echtheit und der Datierung'. *ZNW* 54 (1963) 15-31
— *Das Testament Hiobs* (JSHRZ III/3) Gütersloh 1979
— 'Das Testament Hiobs und die Septuaginta-übersetzung des Buches Hiobs'. *Biblica* 61 (1980) 377-406
SCHAUMBERGER, J. B. 'Die neue Seleukidenliste BM 45603 und die makkabäische Chronologie'. *Biblica* 36 (1955) 423-55
SCHECHTER, S. 'The Quotations from Ecclesiasticus in Rabbinic Literature'. *JQR* 3 (1891) 682-706
— *Fragments of a Zadokite Work. Documents of Jewish Sectaries* 1. Cambridge 1910. Reprinted with prolegomenon by J. A. Fitzmyer. New York 1970
SCHENKE, H.-M. *Der Gott 'Mensch' in der Gnosis.* Göttingen 1962
— 'Nag Hammadi Studien I: Das literarische Problem des Apokryphon Johannis'. *ZRGG* 14 (1962) 57-63
— *Die dreigestaltige Protennoia (Nag Hammadi-Codex XIII),* herausgegeben und kommentiert. Diss. Rostock 1977 (typewritten)
— 'Die jüdische Melchisedek-Gestalt als Thema der Gnosis', in Tröger, *Altes Testament,* 111-36
— 'The Phenomenon and Significance of Gnostic Sethianism', Layton, *Rediscovery* 2, 588-616
— 'The Book of Thomas (NHC II, 7): A Revision of a Pseupigraphical Letter of Jacob the Contender', in A. H. B. Logan — A. J. M. Wedderburn (eds.) *The New Testament and Gnosis. Essays in Honour of R. McL. Wilson.* Edinburgh 1983, 213-28
SCHERMANN, T. *Prophetarum vitae fabulosae. Indices apostolorum discipulorumque Domini.* Leipzig 1907
— *Propheten- und Apostellegenden nebst Jungerkatalogen des Dorotheus und verwandter Texte* (TU 31, 3) Leipzig 1907
SCHIFFMAN, L. H. *The Halakhah at Qumran.* Leiden 1975
— 'Communal Meals at Qumran'. *RQ* 10 (1979) 45-56
— *Sectarian Law in the Dead Sea Scrolls.* Chico 1983
SCHILDENBERGER, J. *Die altlateinischen Texte des Proverbienbuches.* Beuron 1941
SCHLATTER, A. *Zur Topographie und Geschichte Palästinas.* Stuttgart 1893
— *Das neugefundene hebräische Stück des Sirach. Der Glossator des griechischen Sirach und seine Stellung in der Geschichte der jüdischen Theologie.* Gütersloh 1897

— *Geschichte Israels von Alexander dem Grossen bis Hadrian.* 3rd ed. Stuttgart 1925

— *Die Theologie des Judentums nach dem Bericht des Josefus.* Gütersloh 1932

— *Wie Sprach Josephus von Gott.* Gütersloh 1910, reprinted in *Kleinere Schriften zu Flavius Josephus,* ed. by K. Rengstorf. Darmstadt 1970

SCHLÜSSLER-FIORENZA, E. 'Wisdom Mythology and Christological Hymns of the New Testament', in *Aspects of Wisdom in Judaism and Early Christianity,* ed. by R. L. Wilken. Notre Dame 1975, 17-41

SCHMID, H. H. *Wesen und Geschichte der Weisheit. Eine Untersuchung zur altorientalischen und israelitischen Weisheitsliteratur* (BZAW 101) Berlin 1966

SCHMID, W. — STÄHLIN, O. *Geschichte der griechischen Literatur* 2,1. *Die nachklassische Periode von 320 v. Chr. bis 100 n. Chr.* (Handbuch der Altertumswiss. VII) 6th ed. München 1920

SCHMIDT, C. (ed.) — MACDERMOT, V. (tr.) *The Books of Jeu and the Untitled Text in the Bruce Codex.* Leiden 1978

— *Pistis Sophia.* Leiden 1978

SCHMIDT, F. *Le testament d'Abraham* 1-2. Diss. Strasbourg 1971

SCHMIDT, J. M. *Die jüdische Apokalyptik.* Neukirchen 1969

SCHMITHALS, W. *The Apocalyptic Movement.* Nashville 1975

SCHMITT, J. 'Le milieu baptiste de Jean le Précurseur', in *Exégèse biblique et Judaisme.* Strasbourg 1973

— 'Qumran et la première génération judéo-chrétienne', in Delcor, *Qumran,* 387-402

SCHNABEL, P. *Berossos und die babylonisch-hellenistische Literatur.* Leipzig 1923

SCHNAPP, F. *Die Testamente der zwölf Patriarchen untersucht.* Halle 1884

SCHNEIDER, G. *Das Evangelium nach Lukas* 1. Gütersloh 1977

SCHNEIDER, J. 'Brief', in *RAC* 2 (1952) 564-85

SCHOEPS, H.-J. 'Die jüdischen Prophetenmorde', in *Aus frühchristlicher Zeit.* Tübingen 1950, 127-43 (originally publ. in *Symbolae Biblicae Uppsalienses* 1943)

SCHOLEM, G. *Major Trends in Jewish Mysticism.* New York 1941 (3rd ed. 1954)

— *Jewish Gnosticism, Merkabah Mysticism, and Talmudic Tradition.* New York 1960

— *Ursprung und Anfänge der Kabbala.* Berlin 1962

— *The Messianic Idea in Judaism and other Essays on Jewish Spirituality.* New York 1971

— *Kabbalah.* Jerusalem 1974

SCHOLER, D. *Nag Hammadi Bibliography 1948-1969.* Leiden 1971

— 'Bibliographia Gnostica, Supplementa'. *NT* 13 (1971) 322-36; 14 (1972) 312-31; 15 (1973) 327-45; 16 (1974) 316-36; 17 (1975) 305-36; 19 (1977) 293-336; 20 (1978) 300-31; 21 (1979) 357-82; 22 (1980) 352-84; 23 (1981) 361-80

SCHRECKENBERG, H. *Bibliographie zu Flavius Josephus.* And: *Supplementband mit Gesamtregister.* 2 vols. Leiden 1968-79

— *Die Flavius-Josephus Tradition in Antike und Mittelalter.* Leiden 1972

— *Rezeptionsgeschichtliche und textkritische Untersuchungen zu Flavius Josephus.* Leiden 1977

SCHREINER, J. *Das 4. Buch Esra* (JSHRZ V/4) Gütersloh 1981

SCHROYER, M. J. 'Alexandrian Jewish Literalists'. *JBL* 55 (1936) 267-71

SCHUBERT, K. 'The Sermon on the Mount and the Qumran Texts', in Stendahl, *The Scrolls and the New Testament,* 118-28

SCHÜTZ, R. *Les idées eschatologiques du Livre de la Sagesse.* Paris-Strasbourg 1935

SCHÜLLER, S. 'Some Problems Connected with the Supposed Common Ancestry of Jews and Spartans and their Relations during the Last Three Centuries B.C.E.' *JSS* 1 (1956) 257-68

SCHÜRER *Geschichte des jüdischen Volkes im Zeitalter Jesu Christi* 1-3. 4th ed. Leipzig 1901-11

— *The History of the Jewish People in the Age of Jesus Christ* 1-2. Ed. by G. Vermes and F. Millar, Edinburgh 1973-79

SCHÜRMANN, H. *Das Lukasevangelium* 1. Freiburg 1969

SCHUNK, K.-D. *Die Quellen des I. und II. Makkabäerbuches.* Halle 1954

— *1. Makkabäerbuch* (JSHRZ 1/4) Gütersloh 1980

SCHWARTZ, D. R. 'The Three Temples of 4Q Florilegium'. *RQ* 10 (1979) 83-91

— 'The Tribes of As. Mos. 4:7-9'. *JBL* 99 (1980) 217-23

SCHWARTZ, J. 'Note sur la famille de Philon d'Alexandrie'. *Annuaire de l'Institut de Philologie et d'Hist. Orient. et Slaves* 13 (1953) 591-602

— 'L'Egypte de Philon', in *Philon d'Alexandrie. Colloque Lyon*. Paris 1967, 35-44

— 'Sur la date de IV Esdras', in *Mélanges André Neher*. Paris 1975, 191-6

SCOPELLO, M. 'The Apocalypse of Zostrianos (Nag Hammadi VIII, 1) and the Book of the Secrets of Enoch'. *VC* 34 (1980) 376-85

— 'Youel et Barbélo dans le traité de l'Allogène', in Barc, *Colloque International,* 374-82

SCOTT, W. 'The Last Sibylline Oracle of Alexandria'. *Classical Quarterly* 9 (1915) 144-46, 207-28; 10 (1916 7-16

— (ed.-tr.) *Hermetica* 1-4. Oxford 1924-36. Repr. London 1968

SEGAL, A. *Two Powers in Heaven: Early Rabbinic Reports about Christianity and Gnosticism.* Leiden 1977

SEGAL, M. H. *Grammar of Mishnaic Hebrew.* Oxford 1927

— 'Evolution of the Hebrew Text of Ben Sira' *JQR* n.s. 25 (1934) 91-149

— *Sefer Ben Sira haShalem.* 2nd ed. Jerusalem 1958

— 'Ben Sira in Qumran'. *Tarbiz* 33 (1964) 243-6 (Hebrew)

SHAKED, S. 'The Notions of *menog* and *gētig* in the Pahlavi Texts and their Relations to Eschatology'. *Acta Orientalia* 33 (1971) 59-107

— 'Qumran and Iran: Further Considerations'. *Israel Oriental Studies* 2 (1972) 433-46

SHARPE, J. L. 'The Second Adam in the Apocalypse of Moses'. *CBQ* 35 (1973) 35-46

SHELLRUDE, G. M. 'The Apocalypse of Adam: Evidence for a Christian-Gnostic Provenance', in Krause, *Gnosis and Gnosticism* (1981) 82-91

SHUTT, R. J. H. *Studies in Josephus.* London 1961

SIEBER, J. H. 'An Introduction to the Tractate Zostrianos from Nag Hammadi'. *NT* 15 (1973) 233-40

SIEGEL, J. P. 'The Employment of Paleo-Hebrew Characters in the Light of Tannaitic Sources'. *HUCA* 42 (1971) 159-72

SIEGERT, F. *Drei Hellenistisch-Jüdische Predigte.* Tübingen 1980

SIEGRIED, C. *Philo von Alexandria als Ausleger des Alten Testaments.* Jena 1875

SILBERMAN, L. H. 'Unriddling the Riddle: A Study in the Structure and Language of the Habakkuk Pesher 1QpHab'. *RQ* 3 (1961) 323-64

SIMON, M. 'Les Saints d'Israël dans la devotion de l'Eglise ancienne'. *RHPR* 34 (1954) 98-127

— Eléments gnostiques chez Philon', in Bianchi, *Le origine dello gnosticismo,* 359-76

— *Jewish Sects at the Time of Jesus.* Philadelphia 1967

SIMONSEN, D. 'Ein Midrasch im IV Buch Esra', in *Festschrift zu Israel Lewy's 70. Geburtstag.* Breslau 1911, 270-8

SIMPSON, D. C. 'The Book of Tobit', in *APOT* 2, 174-241

SJÖBERG, E. *Der Menschensohn im äthiopischen Henochbuch.* Lund 1946

SKEHAN, P. W. 'A Fragment of the Song of Moses (Deut 32) from Qumran'. *BASOR* 136 (1954) 12-15

— 'Exodus in the Samaritan Recension from Qumran'. *JBL* 74 (1955) 182-7

— 'The Qumran Manuscripts and Textual Criticism'. *VT Suppl.* 4 (1957) 148-60

— 'The Date of the Last Supper'. *CBQ* 20 (1958) 192-9

— 'Didache 1, 6 and Sirach 12,1'. *Biblica* 44 (1963) 533-6

— *Studies in Israelite Poetry and Wisdom.* Washington D.C. 1971

— 'The Acrostic Poem in Sirach 51:13-20'. *HTR* 64 (1971) 387-400

— Review of Rüger, Text und Textform. *Biblica* 52 (1971) 273-5

SLINGERLAND, H. DIXON. *The Testaments of the Twelve Patriarchs. A Critical History of Research.* Missoula 1977

— 'The Testament of Joseph: A Redaction-Critical Study'. *JBL* 96 (1977) 507-16

SMALLWOOD, E. M. 'High Priests and Politics in Roman Palestine'. *JTS* 13 (1962) 14-34

— *Philonis Alexandrini Legatio ad Gaium.* 2nd ed. Leiden 1970

— *The Jews under Roman Rule.* 2nd ed. Leiden 1981

SMEND. R. *Die Weisheit des Jesus Sirach erklärt*. Berlin 1906

SMITH, E. W. J. JR. *Joseph and Aseneth and Early Christian Literature: A Contribution to the Corpus Hellenisticum Novi Testamenti*. Diss. Claremont Graduate School 1974

SMITH, J. Z. 'Wisdom and Apocalyptic', in *Religious Syncretism in Antiquity*, ed. by B. A. Pearson. Missoula 1975, 131-70

SMITH, M. 'The Common Theology of the Ancient Near East'. *JBL* 71 (1952) 135-47

— 'Palestinian Judaism in the First Century', in *Israel: Its Role in Civilization*, ed. by M. Davis. New York 1956, 67-81

— 'The Description of the Essenes in Josephus and the Philosophoumena'. *HUCA* 29 (1958) 273-313

— 'What is implied by the Variety of Messianic Figures'. *JBL* 78 (1959) 66-72

— 'The Dead Sea Sect in Relation to Ancient Judaism'. *NTS* 7 (1960/61) 347-60

— 'Zealots and Sicarii: Their Origin and Relation'. *HTR* 64 (1971) 1-19

— *Palestinian Parties and Politics that shaped the Old Testament*. London 1971

— *Clement of Alexandria and a Secret Gospel of Mark*. Cambridge MA 1974

SNAITH, N. *The Book of Job*. London 1968

SNELL, B. 'Ezechiels Moses-Drama'. *Antike und Abendland* 13 (1967) 150-64

SOKOLOFF, M. *The Targum to Job from Qumran Cave XI*. Ramat-Gan 1974

— 'Notes on the Aramaic Fragments of Enoch from Qumran Cave 4', in *Maarav* 1-2 (1978-79) 187-224

SOLOMOVIC, E. 'Towards an Understanding of the Exegesis of the Dead Sea Scrolls'. *RQ* 7 (1970) 3-15

SOWERS, S. G. *The Hermeneutics of Philo and Hebrews*. Richmond 1965

SPEYER, W. *Die literarische Fälschung im heidnischen und christlichen Altertum*. München 1971

SPICQ, C. 'Le Siracide et la structure littéraire du Prologue de Saint Jean', in *Mémorial Lagrange*. Paris 1940, 183-95

SPITTA, F. *Zur Geschichte und Literatur des Urchristentums III/2*. Göttingen 1907

SPITTLER, R. *The Testament of Job. Introduction, Translation and Notes*. Diss. Harvard 1971

SPRÖDOWSKY, H. *Die Hellenisierung der Geschichte von Joseph in Aegypten bei Flavius Josephus*. Greifswald 1937

STADELMANN, H. *Ben Sira als Schriftgelehrter*. Tübingen 1980

STAEHLE, K. *Die Zahlenmystik bei Philo von Alexandria*. Leipzig 1931

STÄHLIN, G. 'Das Schicksal im Neuen Testament und bei Josephus', in *Josephus-Studien: Festschrift O. Michel*. Göttingen 1974, 319-43

STÄHLIN, O. *Clemens Alexandrinus* 3 (GCS 17) Leipzig 1909

STARCKY, J. 'Les Maitres de Justice et la chronologie de Qumran', in Delcor, *Qumran*, 249-56

— Les quatre étapes du messianisme à Qumran'. *RB* 70 (1963) 481-501

— 'Un texte messianique de la grotte 4 de Qumran', in *Memorial de cinqantenaire 1914-1964 de l'Ecôle des Langues Orientales de l'Institut Catholique de Paris*. Paris 1964, 51-66

STAROBINSKI-SAFRAN, E. 'Un poète judéo-hellénistique: Ezechiel le tragique'. *Museum Helveticum* 31 (1974) 216-24

STAUFFER, E. 'Abschiedsreden', in *RAC* 1, 29-35

STECK, O. H. *Israel und das gewaltsame Geschick der Propheten*. Neukirchen 1967

— 'Die Aufnahme von Genesis 1 in Jubiläen 2 and 4. Ezra 6'. *JSJ* 8 (1977) 154-82

STECKOLL, S. H. 'Preliminary Excavation Report on the Qumran Cemetery'. *RQ* 6 (1968) 323-36

STEGEMANN, H. 'Der Pešer Psalm 37 aus Höhle 4 von Qumran (4QpPs37)'. *RQ* 4 (1963-64) 235-70

— 'Weitere Stücke von 4QpPsalm 37'. *RQ* 6 (1967-69) 193-210

— 'Ein Handschrift aus Höhle 4Q mit Exzerpten aus dem Deuteronomium'. *RQ* 6 (1967) 193-227

— *Die Entstehung der Qumrangemeinde* (privately published). Bonn 1971

STEIN, E. *Die allegorische Exegese des Philo aus Alexandria* (BZAW 51) Giessen 1929

— *Philo und der Midrasch* (BZAW 57) Giessen 1931

STENDAHL, K. *The School of St. Matthew and its Use of the O.T.* Uppsala 1954
— (ed.) *The Scrolls and the New Testament.* New York 1957
STERN, M. 'The Relations between Judaea and Rome during the Rule of John Hyrcanus'. *Zion* 26 (1961) 1-22 (Hebrew)
— 'Notes on the Story of Joseph the Tobiad'. *Tarbiz* 32 (1962) 35-47 (Hebrew)
—, 'The Hasmonean Revolt and its Place in the History of Jewish Society and Religion', in H. H. Ben-Sasson — S. Ettinger (eds.) *Jewish Society through the Ages.* New York 1971, 92-106
— 'Nicolaus of Damascus as a Source of Jewish History in the Herodian and Hasmonean Age', in *Studies in Bible and Jewish History Dedicated to the Memory of Jacob Liver.* Jerusalem 1971, 375 ff. (Hebrew)
— 'Zealots', in *EJ* Yearbook 1973, 135-52
— *The Documents Relating to the Hasmonean War.* 2nd ed. Jerusalem 1973 (Hebrew)
— 'The Jewish Diaspora', in *Compendia* I/1, 117-83
— 'Philo of Alexandria', in *Compendia* I/1, 18-19
— 'The Province of Judaea', in Compendia I/1, 308-76
— 'The Reign of Herod and the Herodian Dynasty', in *Compendia* I/1, 216-307
— *Greek and Latin Authors on Jews and Judaism* 1-2. Jerusalem 1974-80
— 'Aspects of Jewish Society: the Prieshood and Other Classes', in *Compendia* I/2, 561-630
— 'The Jews in Greek and Latin Literature', in *Compendia* I/2, 1101-59
— 'Sicarii and Zealots', in *WHJP* 8, 263-71
— 'Judaea and Her Neighbours in the Days of Alexander Jannaeus'. *Cathedra* 1 (1981) 22-46 (Hebrew)
— 'The Roman Administration in Provincia Judaea from the Destruction of the Second Temple to the Bar Kokhba Uprising', in *Eretz Israel from the Destruction of the Second Temple to the Muslim Conquest,* ed. Z. Baras *et al.* Jerusalem 1982, 1-17 (Hebrew)
— 'The Suicide of Eleazar ben Yair and his Men at Masada and the Fourth Philosophy'. *Zion* 47 (1982) 367-97 (Hebrew)
— 'Social and Political Realignments in Herodian Judaea'. *Cathedra* 2 (1982) 46-62 (Hebrew)
STONE, M. E. *Features of the Eschatology of IV Ezra.* Unpublished dissertation Cambridge MA 1965
— 'The Death of Adam — An Armenian Book'. *HTR* 59 (1966) 283-91
— 'Paradise in 4 Ezra iv:8 and vii:36, viii:52'. *JJS* 17 (1966) 85-88
— 'Some Remarks on the Textual Criticism of iv Ezra'. *HTR* 60 (1967) 107-15
— 'The Concept of the Messiah in IV Ezra', in *Religions in Antiquity. Essays in Memory of E.R. Goodenough.* Leiden 1968, 295-312
— 'The Testament of Jacob'. *Revue des études arméniennes* 5 (1968) 261-70
— 'Two additional notes on the Testament of Jacob', *ibid.* 6 (1969) 103-04
— *The Testament of Levi. A First Study of the Armenian MSS. of the Testaments of the Twelve Patriarchs in the Convent of St. James, Jerusalem.* Jerusalem 1969
— 'Baruch, Rest of the Words of', in *EJ* 4, 276-7
— 'Ezekiel, Apocryphal Books of', in *EJ* 6, 1099
— 'Ezra, Apocalypse of', in *EJ* 6, 1108-09
— 'Isaiah, Martyrdom of', in *EJ* 9, 71-72
— 'Noah, Books of', in *EJ* 12, 1198
— 'Prophets, Lives of', in *EJ* 13, 1149-50
— 'The Testament of Jacob', in *EJ* 9, 1213
— *The Testament of Abraham.* Missoula 1972
— 'Judaism at the Time of Christ'. *American School of Oriental Research. Newsletter* 1 (1973-74) 4-5
— 'Some Observations on the Armenian Version of the Paralipomena of Jeremiah'. *CBQ* 35 (1973) 47-59
— 'Apocalyptic, Vision or Hallucination?, *Milla wa-Milla* 14 (1974) 47-56

646

— *The Armenian Version of the Testament of Joseph: Introduction, Critical Edition and Translation.* Missoula 1975
— 'Lists of Revealed Things in Apocalyptic Literature', in *Magnalia Dei. The Mighty Acts of God,* ed. by F. M. Cross *et al.* Garden City, N.Y. 1976, 414-52
— 'A New Manuscript of the Syro-Arabic Version of the Fourth Book of Ezra'. *JSJ* 8 (1977) 183-4
— 'New Evidence for the Armenian Version of the Testaments of the Twelve Patriarchs'. *RB* 84 (1977) 94-107
— 'The Book of Enoch and Judaism in the Third Century B.C.E.' *CBQ* 40 (1978) 479-92
— 'Report on Seth Traditions in the Armenian Adam Books', in Layton, *Rediscovery* 2, 459-71
— *The Armenian Version of IV Ezra.* Missoula 1979
— *Scriptures, Sects and Visions: A Profile of Judaism from Ezra to the Jewish Revolts.* Philadelphia 1980
— *The Armenian Apocrypha Related to Patriarchs and Prophets.* Jerusalem 1982
— 'Reactions to Destructions of the Second Temple'. *JSJ* 12 (1982) 195-204
— 'The Metamorphosis of Ezra: Jewish Apocalypse and Mediaeval Vision'. *JTS* n.s. 33 (1982) 1-18
STONE, M. E. (ed.). *The Penitence of Adam* 1-2 (CSCO 429-30) Leuven 1981
STONE, M. E. — STRUGNELL, J. (eds.) *The Books of Elijah, Parts 1-2.* Index by L. Lipscomb (SBLTT) Missoula 1979
STROBEL, A. 'Der Termin des Todes Jesu'. *ZNW* 51 (1960) 88-94
— 'Zur Funktionsfähigkeit des essenischen Kalenders'. *RQ* 3 (1961-62)
STROUMSA, G. *Another Seed. Studies in Sethian Gnosticism.* Diss. Harvard 1978 (typewritten)
STRUGNELL, J. 'The Angelic Liturgy at Qumran, 4Q Serek Sirot Olat Hassabbat'. *VT Supp.* 7 (1960) 318-45
— 'More Psalms of David'. *CBQ* 27 (1965) 207-16
— 'Notes on the Text and Metre of Ezekiel the Tragedian's Exagoge'. *HTR* 60 (1967) 449-57
— 'Notes and Queries on The Ben Sira Scroll from Masada'. *Eretz-Israel* 9 (1969) 109-19
— 'Philo (Pseudo) or Liber Antiquitatum Biblicarum', in *EJ* 13, 408-9
SUGGS, M. J. 'Wisdom of Solomon 2,10-5. A Homily Based on the Fourth Servant Song'. *JBL* 76 (1957) 26-33
— *Wisdom, Christology and Law in Matthew's Gospel.* Cambridge MA 1970
SUKENIK, E. L. *The Dead Sea Scrolls of the Hebrew University.* Jerusalem 1956
SUNDBERG, A. C. *The Old Testament of the Early Church.* Cambridge, MA 1964
SURKAU, H.-W. *Martyrien in jüdischer und früchristlicher Zeit.* Göttingen 1938
SUTER, D. W. *Tradition and Composition in the Parables of Enoch.* Missoula 1979
— 'Fallen Angel, Fallen Priest: The Problem of Family Purity in 1 Enoch 6-16'. *HUCA* 50 (1979) 115-35
SWAIN, J. W. 'The Theory of the Four Monarchies — Opposition History under the Roman Empire'. *Classical Philology* 25 (1940) 1-21
SWETE, H. B. *An Introduction to the Old Testament in Greek.* Cambridge 1902
SYKRUTIS, 'Epistolographie', in *PWRE* Suppl. 5, 185-220
SYLBURG, F. *Epicae elegiacaeque minorum poetarum gnomae.* Frankfurt 1591
SZÖRNEY, A. 'Das Buch Daniel, ein kanonisierter Pescher?' *VT Suppl.* 15 (1966) 278-94
TALBERT, C. H. 'The Myth of a Descending-Ascending Redeemer in Mediterranean Antiquity'. *NTS* 22 (1976) 418-40
TALMON, S. 'The Calendar Reckoning of the Sect from the Judaean Desert', in *Scripta* 4, 162-99
— 'Aspects of the Textual Transmission of the Bible in the Light of Qumran Manuscripts', in *Textus* 4 (1964) 95-132
— 'The Order of Prayer in the Sect from the Judean Desert'. *Tarbiz* 29 (1959-60) 1-20 (Hebrew)
— 'Typen der Messiaserwartung und die Zeitenwende', in *Probleme Biblischer Theologie. Festschrift G. von Rad,* ed. by H. W. Wolff. München 1971, 571-88
TARDIEU, M. 'Les trois stèles de Seth: un écrit gnostique retrouvé a Nag Hammadi'. *RSPT* 57 (1973) 545-75

— *Trois mythes gnostiques: Adam, Eros et les animaux d'Egypte dans un écrit de Nag Hammadi (II, 5)*. Paris 1974
— 'Les livres mis sous le nom de Seth et les Séthiens de l'hérésiologie', in Krause, *Gnosis and Gnosticism* (1977) 204-10
TARN, W. W. 'Alexander Helios and the Golden Age'. *JRS* 22 (1932) 135-59
TARN, W. W. — GRIFFITH, G. T. *Hellenistic Civilization*. 3rd ed. London 1952
TAYLOR, R. J. 'The Eschatological Meaning of Life and Death in the Book of Wisdom I-V'. *ETL* 42 (1966) 72-137
TCHERIKOVER, V. A. 'Palestine in the Light of the Zenon Papyri'. *Tarbiz* 4 (1933) 226-47, 354-65; 5 (1934) 37-44 (Hebrew)
— 'Palestine under the Ptolemies'. *Mizraim* 4-5 (1937) 9ff. (Hebrew)
— 'The Ideology of the Letter of Aristeas'. *HTR* 51 (1958) 59-85
— 'The Third Book of Maccabees as a Historical Source', in *Scripta* 7, 1-26
— *Hellenistic Civilization and the Jews*. Philadelphia 1966
TCHERIKOVER, V. A. — FUKS, A. — STERN, M. *Corpus Papyrorum Judaicorum* 1-3. Cambridge MA — Jerusalem 1957-64
TEICHER, J. L. 'The Dead Sea Scrolls — Documents of the Jewish Christian Ebionites'. *JJS* 2 (1950-51) 67-99
— 'The Damascus Fragments and the Origin of the Jewish Christian Sect'. *Ibid.* 115-43
— 'The Teaching of the Pre-Pauline Church in the Dead Sea Scrolls'. *JJS* 3 (1952) 111-18, 139-50; 4 (1953) 1-18, 49-58, 93-103, 139-53
TERIAN, A. *Philonis Alexandrini De Animalibus. The Armenian Text with an Introduction, Translation and Commentary*. Chico 1981
TESTUZ, M. *Les idées réligieuses du Livre des Jubilés*. Genève 1960
THACKERAY, H. ST. J. 'The Letter of Aristeas'. Appendix to H. B. Swete, *Introduction to the Old Testament in Greek*. Cambridge 1902
— *Josephus, the Man and the Historian*. Repr. with an introd. by S. Sandmel. New York 1967
THACKERAY, H. ST. J. et al. *Josephus. With an English Translation* (Loeb Class. Library) 1-10. Cambridge MA — London 1926-65
THEILER, W. *Forschungen zum Neuplatonismus*. Berlin 1965
— 'Philo von Alexandria und der Beginn des Kaiserzeitlichen Platonismus', in *Parusia. Festschrift für J. Hirschberger*. Frankfurt 1965, 199-217
— 'Philo von Alexandria und der hellenistisierte Timaeus', in *Philomathes. Studies and Essays in the Memory of Philip Merlan*. The Hague 1971, 25-35
THEISOHN, J. *Der auserwählte Richter*. Göttingen 1975
THIELE, W. (ed.) *Sapientia Salomonis* (Vetus Latina) Freiburg 1977
THIERING, B. 'Suffering and Ascetism at Qumran, as illustrated in the Hodayot'. *RQ* 8 (1974) 393-405
— '*Mebaqqer* and *Episkopos* in the Light of the Temple Scroll'. *JBL* 100 (1981) 59-74
THOMA, C. 'Die Weltanschauung des Flavius Josephus dargestellt an Hand seiner Schilderung des jüdischen Aufstandes gegen Rom (66-73 n. Chr.)'. *Kairos* 11 (1969) 39-52
THOMAS, J. *Le Mouvement Baptiste en Palestine et Syrie*. Gembloux 1938
THOMAS, J. 'Aktuelles im Zeugnis der zwölf Väter,' in Burchard, *Studien*, 62-150
THOMAS, J. D. 'The Greek Text of Tobit'. *JBL* 91 (1972) 463-71
THOMPSON, A. L. *Responsibility for Evil in the Theology of IV Ezra*. Missoula 1977
THORNDIKE, J. P. 'The Apocalypse of Weeks and the Qumran Sect'. *RQ* 3 (1961) 163-84
THYEN, H. *Der Stil der Jüdisch-Hellenistischen Homilie*. Göttingen 1955
TIDNER, E. *Didascalia apostolorum canonum ecclesiasticorum, traditionis apostolicae versiones Latinae*. Berlin 1963
TIEDE, D. L. *The Charismatic Figure as Miracle Worker*. Missoula 1972
TIMPE, D. 'Der römische Vertrag mit den Juden von 161 v. Chr.' *Chiron* 4 (1974) 133-52
TIGERSTEDT, E. N. *The Legend of Sparta in Classical Antiquity* 1-2. Stockholm 1965-74
TILL, W. C. — SCHENKE, H.-M. (eds.) *Die gnostischen Schriften des koptischen Papyrus Berolinensis 8502*. 2nd ed. Berlin 1972

TISCHENDORF, K. VON. *Apocalypses Apocryphae.* Leipzig 1866

TISSERANT, E. *Ascension d'Isaie.* Paris 1909

TORREY, C. C. 'The Story of the Three Youths'. *AJSL* 23 (1907) 177-201

— *Ezra Studies.* Chicago 1910

— 'The Letters Prefixed to Second Maccabees'. *JAOS* 60 (1940) 119-50

— *The Apocryphal Literature.* New Haven 1945

— *The Lives of the Prophets. Greek Text and Translation.* Philadelphia 1946

TOV, E. *The Book of Baruch* (SBLTT) Missoula 1975

— *The Septuagint Translation of Jeremiah and Baruch: A Discussion of an Early Revision of the LXX of Jeremiah 29-52 and Baruch 1:1-3:8.* Missoula 1976

TOY, C. H. *A Critical and Exegetical Commentary on the Book of Proverbs.* Edinburgh 1899

TRACY, S. 'III Maccabees and Pseudo-Aristeas'. 1 (1928) 241-52

TREVER, J. C. (ed.) *Scrolls from Qumran Cave 1. The Great Isaiah Scroll; The Order of the Community; The Pesher to Habakkuk.* From Photographs. Jerusalem 1972

TREVES, M. 'The Two Spirits in the Rule of the Community'. *RQ* 3 (1961-62) 449-52

TRÖGER, K.-W. *Gnosis und Neues Testament. Studien aus Religionswissenschaft und Theologie.* Berlin 1973

— 'Spekulativ-Esoterische Ansätze (Frühjudentum und Gnosis)', in *Literatur und Religion des Frühjudentums,* ed. by J. Maier and J. Schreiner. Würzburg 1973, 310-19

— 'The Attitude of the Gnostic Religion towards Judaism as Viewed by a Variety of Perspectives', in Barc, *Colloque International,* 96-98

— (ed.). *Altes Testament — Fruhjudentum — Gnosis: Neue Studien zu Gnosis und Bibel.* Berlin 1980

TURDEANU, E. *Apocryphes slaves et roumains de l'Ancien Testament.* Leiden 1981

TURNER, E. G. 'Tiberius Iulius Alexander'. *JRS* 44 (1954) 54-64

— *Greek Papyri: An Introduction.* Oxford 1968

TURNER, J. *The Book of Thomas the Contender* (SBLDS 23) Missoula 1975

TURNER, J. D. 'The Gnostic Threefold Path to Enlightenment. The Ascent of Mind and the Descent of Wisdom'. *NT* 22 (1980) 324-51

TURNER, N. *The Testament of Abraham: A Study of its Origin, Date and Language.* Diss. University of London 1953

UFFENHEIMER, B. *The Vision of Zechariah: From Prophecy to Apocalyptic.* Jerusalem 1961 (Hebrew)

ULLENDORFF, E. 'The Greek Letters of the Copper Scroll'. *VT* 11 (1961) 227-8

ULRICH, C. U. JR. *The Qumran Text of Samuel and Josephus.* Missoula 1978

UNNIK, W. C. VAN 'Die jüdischen Komponente in der Entstehung der Gnosis', in Rudolph, *Gnosis und Gnostizismus,* 476-94

— 'An Attack on the Epicureans by Flavius Josephus', in *Romanitas et Christianitas: Festschrift H. Waszink.* Amsterdam 1973, 349-50

— 'Josephus' Account of the Story of Israel's Sin with Alien Women', in *Travels in the World of the Old Testament. Studies presented to M. A. Beek on the Occasion of his 65th Birthday.* Assen 1974, 241-61

— *Flavius Josephus als historischer Schriftsteller.* Heidelberg 1978

URBACH, E. E. 'The Jews in their Land in the Age of the Tannaim'. *Behinot* 4 (1953) 61-72 (Hebrew)

— 'Class Status and Leadership in the World of the Palestinian Sages'. *PIASH* 2 (1968) 48-74

— *The Sages: Their Concepts and Beliefs* 1-2. Jerusalem 1975

USSANI, V. *Hegesippi qui dicitur historiae libri quinque* 1-2 (CSEL 66,2) Vienna 1932-60

VACCARI, A. 'Dove sta scritto che Dio "Strangola i propri figli"?', in *Scritti di Erudizione e di Filologia* 2. Roma 1958, 7-11

VAILLANT, A. *Le Livre des Sécrets d'Hénoch.* Paris 1952

VANDERKAM, J. 'The Theophany of Enoch I, 37-7, 9'. *VT* 23 (1973) 129-50

— *Textual and Historical Studies in the Book of Jubilees.* Missoula 1977

— 'Enoch Traditions in Jubilees and other Second Century Sources', in *SBLSP* 1978, 229-51
— 'The Textual Affinities of the Biblical Citations in the Genesis Apocryphon'. *JBL* 97 (1978) 45-55
— 'The Origin, Character and Early History of the 364-Day Calendar: A Reassessment of Jaubert's Hypotheses'. 41 (1970) 390-411
— '2 Maccabees 6, 7a and Calendrial Change in Jerusalem'. *JSJ* 12 (1981) 52-74
— 'The Putative Author of the Book of Jubilees'. *JSS* 26 (1981) 209-17
— 'Some Major Issues in the Contemporary Study of 1 Enoch: Reflections on J. T. Milik's The Books of Enoch: Aramaic Fragments of Qumran Cave 4'. *Maarav* 3 (1982) 85-97
VATTIONI, F. *Ecclesiastico. Testo ebraico con apparato e versioni greca, latina e siriaca.* Napoli 1968
— 'Studi sul libro dei Proverbi', in *Augustinianum* 12 (1972) 121-68
VERMES, G. *Scripture and Tradition in Judaism.* Leiden 1961
— *The Dead Sea Scrolls in English.* 2nd ed. Harmondsworth 1975
— *Post-Biblical Jewish Studies.* Leiden 1975
— 'The Impact of the Dead Sea Scrolls on the Study of the New Testament'. *JJS* 27 (1976) 107-16
— *The Dead Sea Scrolls. Qumran in Perspective.* London 1977 (new ed. 1981)
— 'The Present State of the Son of Man Debate'. *JJS* 29 (1978) 123-34
— 'The Essenes and History'. *JJS* 32 (1981) 18-31
VIELHAUER, P. 'Apocalyptic', in Hennecke-Schneemelcher, *New Testament Apocrypha* 2, 581-607
VIOLET, B. *Die Esra-Apokalypse, I. Die Überlieferung* (GCS 18) Leipzig 1910
— *Die Apocalypsen des Esra und des Baruch in deutscher Gestalt* (GCS 32) Leipzig 1924
VÖGTLE, A. *Die Tugend- und Lasterkataloge im Neuen Testament.* Münster 1936
VÖLKER, W. *Quellen zur Geschichte der christlichen Gnosis.* Tübingen 1932
— *Fortschritt und Vollendung bei Philo von Alexandrien.* Leipzig 1938
VOGT, E. 'Fragmentum Qohelet ex Qumran'. *Biblica* 36 (1955) 265-6
VOLZ, P. *Der Geist Gottes.* Tübingen 1910
WACHOLDER, B.-Z. *Nicolaus of Damascus.* Berkeley 1962
— 'Pseudo-Eupolemus' Two Greek Fragments on the Life of Abraham'. *HUCA* 34 (1963) 83-113
— 'Philo (The Elder)' in *EJ* 13, 407-8
— *Eupolemus: A Study of Judeo-Greek Literature.* Cincinnati 1974
— 'The Letter from Judah Maccabee to Aristobulus: Is 2 Maccabees 1:10b-2:18 Authentic? *HUCA* 49 (1978) 89-133
WÄCHTER, L. 'Die unterschiedliche Haltung der Pharisäer, Sadduzäer und Essener zur Heimarmene nach dem Bericht des Josephus'. *ZRGG* 21 (1969) 97-114
WALTER, N. 'Anfänge alexandrisch-jüdischer Bibelauslegung bei Aristobulus'. *Helikon* 3 (1963) 353-72
— *Der Thoraausleger Aristobulos* (TU 86) Berlin 1964
— 'Nur Überlieferung einiger Reste früher jüdisch-hellenistischer Literatur bei Josephus, Clemens und Euseb'. (Studia Patristica 7, TU 92), Berlin 1966, 314-20
— *Fragmente jüdisch-hellenistischer Historiker* (JSHRZ I/2) Gütersloh 1976
— *Fragmente jüdisch-hellenistischer Exegeten: Aristobulos, Demetrios, Aristeas* (JSHRZ III/2) 2nd ed. Gütersloh 1980
WAMBACQ, B. N. 'Les prières de Baruch (1,15-2,19) et de Daniel (9,5-19)'. *Biblica* 40 (1959) 463-75
— 'L'unité du livre de Baruch'. *Biblica* 47 (1966) 574-76
WEBER, W. *Josephus und Vespasian: Untersuchungen zu dem jüdischen Krieg des Flavius Josephus.* Berlin 1921
WEIDEN, W. A. VAN DER. *Le livre des Proverbes. Notes philologiques.* Rome 1970
WEINFELD, M. 'Organizational Patterns and Penal Law of the Qumran Sect'. *Shnaton* 2 (1977) 60-81 (Hebrew)

— 'Temple Scroll or King's Law'. *Shnaton* 3 (1978/79) 214-37 (Hebrew)

WEINERT, F. D. 'A Note on 4Q159 and a New Theory of Essene Origins'. *RQ* 9 (1977/78) 223-30

WEISENGOFF, J. P. 'The Impious in Wisdom 2'. *CBQ* 11 (1949) 40-65

WELLBURN, A. J. 'The Identity of the Archons in the Apocryphon Johannis'. *VC* 32 (1978) 241-54

WELLS, L. S. A. 'The Books of Adam and Eve', in *APOT* 2, 123-54

WENDLAND, P. 'Aristobulus', in A. Elter, *De Gnomologiorum Graecorum Historia atque Origine Commentatio* (1-9. Bonn 1893-5) Vol. 9, 229-34

— *Philo und die Kynisch-Stoische Diatribe.* Berlin 1895

— 'Eine doxographische Quelle Philos'. *SPA* 2 (1897) 1074-9

— *Die hellenistisch-römische Kultur in ihren Beziehungen zu Judentum und Christentum* (Handbuch zum N.T.) 3rd ed. Tübingen 1912

WERBLOWSKY, R. J. Z. 'Anthropomorphism', in *EJ* 3, 50-6

— 'Mysticism and Messianism. The Case of Hasidism' in *Man and his Salvation. S.G.F. Brandon Memorial.* Manchester 1973, 305-14

WERNBERG-MØLLER, P. *The Manual of Discipline.* Leiden 1957

— 'A Reconsideration of the Two Spirits in the Rule of the Community 1Q Serek III, 13-IV, 26'. *RQ* 3 (1961) 413-41

— 'Priests and Laity in the Yahad of the Manual of Discipline', in *Studies Offered to Meir Wallenstein on the Occasion of his Seventy-fifth Birthday.* Jerusalem 1979, 72-83

WESTERMANN, C. *Der Aufbau des Buches Hiob.* Tübingen 1956

WEVERS, J. W. *Genesis.* Göttingen 1974

WHITE, J. L. *The Form and Function of the Body of the Greek Letter.* Missoula 1972

— *The Form and Structure of the Official Petition.* Missoula 1972

WHITEHOUSE, O. C. 'The Book of Baruch', in *APOT* 1, 569-95

WHITTAKER, J. 'Self-Generating Principles in Second-Century Gnostic Systems', in Layton, *Rediscovery* 1, 176-89

— *God-Time-Being in Philo of Alexandria.* Oslo 1971

WHYBRAY, R. N. *Wisdom in Proverbs. The Concept of Wisdom in Prov.* 1-4. London 1965

— *The Intellectual Tradition in the Old Testament* (BZAW 135) Berlin 1974

WIBBING, S. *Die Tugend- und Lasterkataloge im Neuen Testament.* Berlin 1959

WIDENGREN, G. *Mani and Manichaeism.* London-New York 1965

— 'Iran and Israel in Parthian Times'. *Temenos* 2 (1966) 139-77

— (ed.) *Proceedings of the International Colloquium on Gnosticism Stockholm August 20-25, 1973.* Stockholm 1977

WIEDER, N. 'The Habakkuk Scroll and the Targum'. *JJS* 4 (1953) 14-18

— *The Judaean Scrolls and Karaism.* London 1962

WIENEKE, J. *Ezechielis Judaei poetae Alexandrini fabulae quae inscribitur Exagoge fragmenta.* Dissertation Münster 1931

WIESENBERG, E. 'The Jubilee of Jubilees'. *RQ* 9 (1961) 3-40

WILCKEN, U. *Zum Alexandrinischen Antisemitismus.* Leipzig 1909

WILCKENS, U. 'Σοφία', in *TDNT* 7, 465-75; 497-529

WIKGREN, A. 'Tobit, Book of', in *IDB* 4, 658-62

WILLIAMS, M. A. 'Stability as a Soteriological Theme in Gnosticism', in Layton, *Rediscovery* 2, 819-29

WILLIAMS, R. J. 'The Sages of Ancient Egypt in the Light of Recent Scholarship'. *JAOS* 101 (1981) 1-20

WILLIAMSON, R. *Philo and the Epistle to the Hebrews.* Leiden 1970

WILLRICH, H. *Urkundenfälschung in der hellenistisch-jüdischen Literatur.* Göttingen 1924

WILSON, R. M. *Gnosis and the New Testament: Gnosticism and Newly Discovered Gnostic Writings in Relation to the New Testament.* Philadelphia/Oxford 1968

— 'Philo of Alexandria and Gnosticism'. *Kairos* 14 (1972) 213-9

— 'The Gnostics and the Old Testament', in Widengren, *Proceedings*, 164-8

WINDISCH, H. *Die Frömmigkeit Philos.* Leipzig 1909
— 'Die göttliche Weisheit der Juden und die paulinische Christologie', in *Neutestamentliche Studien. Festschrift G. Heinrici.* Leipzig 1914, 220-34
— *Die Orakel des Hystaspes.* Amsterdam 1929
WINSTON, D. 'The Iranian Component in the Bible, Apocrypha and Qumran: A Review of the Evidence'. *HR* 5 (1966) 183-216
— *The Wisdom of Solomon* (Anchor Bible) New York 1979
WINSTON, D. — DILLON, D. *Two Treatises of Philo of Alexandria. A Commentary on De Gigantibus and Quod Deus Sit Immutabilis* (Brown Judaic Studies 25) Chico 1983
WINTER, D. 'Ben Sira and the Teaching of the Two Ways'. *VT* 5 (55) 315-8
WINTER, M. M. *A Concordance to the Peshitta Version of Ben Sira.* Leiden 1976
WINTER, P. 'Judith, Book of', in *IDB* 2, 1023-6
— 'Magnificat and Benedictus'. *BJRL* 37 (1954) 328-43
WINTERMUTE, O. 'A Study of Gnostic Exegesis of the Old testament', in *The Use of the Old Testament in the New and Other Essays: Studies in Honor of William Franklin Stinespring,* ed. by J. Efird. Durham N.C. 1972, 241-70
WIRGIN, W. *The Book of Jubilees and the Maccabean Era of Shmittah Cycles.* Leeds 1964
WISSE, F. 'The Redeemer Figure in the Paraphrase of Shem'. *NT* 12 (1970) 130-40
— 'Stalking Those Elusive Sethians', in Layton, *Rediscovery* 2, 563-76
WOLFF, C. *Jeremia im Frühjudentum und Urchristentum* (TU 118) Berlin 1976
WOLFF, M. J. 'Sibyllen und Sibyllinen'. *Archiv für Kulturgeschichte* 24 (1934) 312-25
WOLFSON, H. A. *Philo. Foundations of Religious Philosophy in Judaism, Christianity and Islam* 1-2. Cambridge MA 1948 (3rd rev. ed. 1962)
WOUDE, A. S. VAN DER. *Die messianischen Vorstellungen der Gemeinde von Qumran.* Assen 1957
— 'Melchisedek als himmlische Erlösergestalt in den neugefundenen eschatologischen Midraschim aus Qumran Höhle XI'. *OTS* 14 (1965) 354-73
— 'Ein neuer Segensspruch aus Qumran (11QBer)', in *Bibel und Qumran. Festschrift H. Bardtke.* Berlin 1968, 253-8
— *Die fünf syrischen Psalmen* (JSHRZ IV/1) Gütersloh 1974
— 'Wicked Priest or Wicked Priests'. *JJS* 33 (1982) 349-59
WOUDE, A. S. VAN DER — JONGE, M. DE. '11Q Melchizedek and the New Testament'. *NTS* 12 (1966) 301-26
WRIGHT, A. G. *The Literary Genre Midrash.* Staten Island 1967
— 'The Structure of the book of Wisdom'. *Biblica* 48 (1967) 165-84
WÜNSCHE, A. *Der Midrasch Kohelet.* Leipzig 1880
YADIN, Y. 'The Dead Sea Scrolls and the Epistle to the Hebrews', in *Scripta* 4, 36-55
— 'A Midrash on 2 Sam VII and Ps I-II (4Q Florilegium)'. *IEJ* 9 (1959) 95-8
— 'Some Notes on the Newly Published Pesharim of Isaiah'. *IEJ* 9 (1959) 39-42
— 'Expedition D'. (The Expedition to the Judaean Desert) *IEJ* 11 (1961) 36-52
— *The Scroll of the War of the Sons of Light against the Sons of Darkness.* English ed. Oxford 1962
— 'Expedition D'. (The Cave of the Letters) *IEJ* 12 (1962) 227-57
— 'The Excavation of Masada — 1963/64: Preliminary Report'. *IEJ* 15 (1965) 1-20
— *The Ben Sira Scroll from Masada.* Jerusalem 1965
— 'Another Fragment (E) of the Psalms Scroll from Qumran Case 11 (11QPsᵃ)'. *Textus* 5 (1966) 1-10
— *Bar-Kokhba: The Rediscovery of the Legendary Hero of the Second Jewish Revolt against Rome.* London 1971
— 'Pesher Nahum (4QpNahum) Reconsidered'. *IEJ* 21 (1971) 1-12
— *The Temple Scroll* 1-3. Hebrew ed. Jerusalem 1977; English ed. Jerusalem 1983
YAMAUCHI, E. M. 'Jewish Gnosticism? The Prologue of John, Mandaean Parallels, and the Trimorphic Protennoia', in Van den Broek — Vermaseren, *Studies in Gnosticism,* 467-97
— *Pre-Christian Gnosticism: A Survey of the Proposed Evidences.* Grand Rapids 1973 (2nd ed. 1983)

– 'Pre-Christian Gnosticism in the Nag Hammadi Texts?' *Church History* 48 (1979) 129-41
YARBRO COLLINS, A. *The Combat Myth in the Book of Revelation.* Missoula 1976
– 'Composition and Redaction of the Testament of Moses 10'. *HTR* 69 (1976) 179-86
– 'The Early Christian Apocalypses', in Collins, *Apocalypse,* 61-122
YAVETZ, Z. 'Reflections on Titus and Josephus'. *GRBS* 16 (1975) 411-32
YDIT, M. 'Tahanun', in *EJ* 15, 702-3
YIZHAR, M. *Bibliography of Hebrew Publications on the Dead Sea Scrolls 1958-1964.* Cambridge 1967
YOUNG, D. *Theognis, Ps.-Pythagoras, Ps.-Phocylides, Chares, Anonymi Aulalia, fragmentum teleiambicum.* Leipzig 1961
ZAMBELLI, M. 'La composizione del secundo libro dei Maccabei e la nuova chronologia di Antioco IV Epifane', in *Miscellanea Greca e Romana.* Rome 1965, 195-300
ZANDEE, J. 'La morale des Enseignements de Silvain', in *Orientalia Lovaniensia Periodica* (1975-76) 615-30
ZEITLIN, S. 'The Book of Jubilees, its Character and its Significance'. *JQR* 30 (1939-40) 1-31
– *The Zadokite Fragments.* Philadelphia 1952
– 'The Judaean Calendar During the Second Commonwealth and the Scrolls'. *JQR* 57 (1966) 28-45
– 'Josephus Flavius: A Biographical Essay', in *The Rise and Fall of the Judean State* 3. Philadelphia 1978, 385-417
ZEITLIN, S. – TEDESCHE, S. *The First Book of Maccabees.* New York 1950
ZENGER, E. *Historische und legendarische Erzählungen: Das Buch Judit* (JSHRZ I/6) Gütersloh 1981, 428-534
ZERAFA, P. P. *The Wisdom of God in the Book of Job.* Rome 1977
ZIEGLER, J. *Susanna, Daniel, Bel et Draco* (Septuaginta) Göttingen 1954, 80-91; 215-23
– *Ieremias, Baruch, Threni, Epistula Ieremiae* (Septuaginta) Göttingen 1957
– 'Die hexaplarische Bearbeitung des griech. Sirach.' *BZ* n. F. 4 (1960) 174-85
– *Sapientia Salomonis* (Septuaginta) Göttingen 1962
– 'Zu ἐνεθυσίωσεν und *iugulavit* im Sirach-Zitat 4, 11 (12) bei Clemens von Alexandrien und Tertullian'. *BZ* n.F. 8 (1964) 277-80
– *Sapientia Iesu filii Sirach* (Septuaginta) Göttingen 1965
ZIEGLER, K. 'Lykophron (8)'. *PWRE* 13, 2316-81
ZIENER, G. *Die theologische Begriffssprache im Buche der Weisheit.* Bonn 1956
– 'Weisheitsbuch und Johannesevangelium'. *Biblica* 38 (1957) 396-418; 39 (1958) 37-60
ZIMMERLI, W. *Das Buch des Predigers Salomo.* Göttingen 1962
– *Ezechiel* 1-2. Neukirchen 1969
ZIMMERMANN, F. 'Aids for the Recovery of the Hebrew Original of Judith'. *JBL* 57 (1938) 67-74
– *The Book of Tobit.* New York 1958
– 'The Story of the Three Guardsmen'. *JQR* 54 (1963/64) 179-200
– 'The Book of Wisdom: Its Language and Character'. *JQR* 57 (1966) 1-27, 101-35
ZUNTZ, G. 'Aristeas Studies II: Aristeas on the Translation of the Torah'. *JSS* 4 (1959) 109-26

Index of Sources

Division: 1. Hebrew Bible 2. Septuagint 3. Targum 4. New Testament 5. Mishnah 6. Tosefta 7. Palestinian Talmud 8. Babylonian Talmud 9. Midrash and Related Works 10. Early Christian Writings 11. Greek and Latin Authors 12. Varia

Works treated in this volume are not included in the index of sources. Substantial references to these works appear in the subject index.

1. HEBREW BIBLE

2. SEPTUAGINT

3. TARGUM

1 Peter			*Revelation*	
1:6-7	313		2-3	582, 584
			2:14	71
2 Peter			2:20	71
3:6-7	378		18	75
			21:1f.	70
Jude			21:9-27	387
			21:18-21	556
9	345		22:10	383
14b-15	397			

<h3 style="text-align:center">5. MISHNAH</h3>

Shekalim			*Eduyoth*	
8:5	435		5:6	31
Yoma			*Aboth*	
3:8	569		1-2	319
			1:1	23, 101
Rosh ha-Shanah			3-4	319
			5	319
2:8-9	31		5:1	236
4:1-4	29		5:2	364
			5:4	99
Taanith				
2:4-5	570		*Hullin*	
4:6	204		5:1	28

<h3 style="text-align:center">6. TOSEFTA</h3>

Berakhoth			8:7-9	242, 259
2:21	286		9:6	511
Shabbat			*Eduyoth*	
13:4	577		1:1	30
Sukkah			*Hullin*	
4:6	257		2:17	286
Hagigah			*Menahot*	
· 2:9	23		13:21	19
			13:22	197
Sotah				
15:11-15	29		*Yadaim*	
			2:13	300
Sanhedrin			2:14	287
2:6	581			
7:1	23			

667

9. MIDRASH AND RELATED WORKS

10. EARLY CHRISTIAN WRITINGS

12. VARIA

Index of Names and Subjects

677

Jesus, the priest; speech of 195, 207; death of 204
Jeu, Book of (Gnostic)   449, 455
Jewish sects (philosophical schools)   186f., 193, 214-5, 226, 486, 512
Job   39, 63, 99, 168, 285-6, 326, 349-53, 563-4; polemic against idolatry 63; Job and Satan 349; Job's soul taken up to heaven on a chariot 350; Job = Iobab 168, 350; conversion of 350, 353; Job's suffering 350, 564; death of 286, 563
Job, Book of   41, 98, 141, 168, *285-6*, 287, 310, 321, 349
Job, Targum to (Qumran)   286, 321, 488
Job, Testament of   63, 99, 168, 286, 321, 326, 330, *349-54*, 355, 563, 565
Joel, Book of   386
Joel, Life of   56, 57, 59
Johanan ben Torta, Rabbi   197
John, Apocryphon of (Gnostic)   118, 447, *453-5*, 456, *458-64*, 465-6, 469, 477, 479,
John, Gospel of   280, 300, 320, 324, 353; Johannine writings 464, 522, 535
John the Baptist   55, 216, 222, 362, 364, 552
John the Essene   543
John of Gischala   27, 188-9, 198-9, 202-4, 207
Jonah   57, 59, 246, 570
Jonathan (the Hasmonean)   10-11, 13, 102, 172-4, 486, 510, 543, 545, 580; first Hasmonean high priest 11, 545, 580
Joseph   34, 36, 38, 65-71, 99, 105, 119-20, 127, 172, 239, 283, 333-6, 338, 344, 353, 572; the patriarch Joseph 65, 119; marriage with Aseneth 65, 68, 335, 564; chastity of 317, 333, 336; wisdom of 283, 310; dreams of 245; ten trials of 99; death 236; Son of God 66-7, 69, 71; type of Christ 334, 341
Joseph and Aseneth   *65-71*, 86, 130, 353, 564-5
Joseph, Prayer of   428
Joseph, Testament of   326, 333, 344, 353
Josephus, Flavius   XX, XXII, 4, 6, 13, 15-18, 22-7, 81, 106, 115-6, 120, 124, 133, 157-64, 168-72, 183, 185ff., 232, 277, 288, 318-9, 357, 360, 462, 485-7, 490, 500, 512, 526, 542-3, 580, 582, 585, 587-8; *The Antiquities*   3, 109, 157, 164, *210-27*, 596; *The Jewish War* 157, *192-210*; *Against Apion* 164, 170, 185-92, *227-31*; *Life* 185-92; On Customs and Causes 212; genealogy 185f.; relations wit the Flavians 186-7; marriages 187; leadership in Galilee 187f., 194; brought before Vespasian 188; prophecy of 188, 205; speeches of 195, 199, 202; lament of 208. *See also* John of Gischala, Jotapata, siege of
Joshua   74, 108, 172, 234, 325, 345, 347, 570, 572; testament of 329
Joshua, Book of   74, 107-8, 247
Joshua, Book of (Samaritan)   231
Joshua, Psalms of (Qumran)   518
Joshua, Rabbi   582
Joshua ben Hananiah, Rabbi   30
Joshua ben Perahiah, Rabbi   581
Josippon   231
Jotapata, Siege of   187-90, 192, 194-5, 200-1, 206-7, 209
Juba II of Mauretania; court chronicles of   169
Jubilees, Book of   48, 89, *97-104*, 105-6, 110, 139, 152-3, 212, 234, 238, 248, 277, 329, 340, 353, 395, 398, 401, 403, 415, 425, 468, 487, *530*, 534, 541, 546. *See also* Chronology, Eschatology, Halakhah
Judah, Testament of   332-4, 337-41
Judah ben Tabbai, Rabbi   581
Judah the Essene   510
Judah the Galilean   21, 26, 215, 222, 348. *See* Fourth Philosophy
Judah ha-Nasi, Rabbi   286, 519, 582, 593
Judas Maccabaeus   9-12, 15, 49-51, 54, 75, 163-4, 172-9, 181-2, 348, 404; battles of 50, 101, 172,

3 Maccabees   33, *80-4*, 87, 121, 130, 135-7, 155, 183, 250, 571, 587; letters in 580, 586
4 Maccabees   XXII, 183, 277, *316-9*, 323
5 Maccabees   231
Magic   68, 327, 448, 454, 455, 575; leukanomancy 430; theurgical literature 408; Magical
        Papyri 289
Magnificat. See Luke, Gospel of
Malachi (prophet)   59
Manasseh   52-5, 58, 544, 555
Manasseh, Prayer of   427, *555*, 562, 564, 576-7
Manetho   163, 165, 228, 587
Manichaeism   96, 152, 397, 449-53, 474, 480; Mani 450-52; Manichaean literature 397, 450;
        Cologne Mani Codex 445-6, 450-1
Manna, Heavenly   68, 259f., *266-7*, 304-5, 310, 312
Manual of Discipline. See Rule of the Community
Mar Uqba   581
Marcosians   445
Marcus Agrippa   213, 226
Marcus Aurelius   371
Mark, Gospel of   38, 54
Mark Anthony   19, 225
Marsanes (Gnostic)   453, *477*
Martyrdom   58-9, 62, 316-9, 347-8, 420, 533; seven brothers and their mother 48, 180, 316-8;
        the old man Eleazar 180, 316-7, 346; Razes, an old man 180; Taxo and his seven sons
        420; Maccabean martyrs 183
Mary, Gospel of (Gnostic)   469
Masada, fall of   26, 194-5, 200, 209, 290-1, 300, 322, 484, 525, 543; Masada texts 291, 579;
        Masada Letters *588-92*
Mattathias   9, 12, 48, 54, 172, 174, 329, 348, 572
Matthew, Gospel of   38, 94, 507; Sermon on the Mount 319
Megalē Apophasis (Gnostic)   470
Megillath Antiochus   231
Megillath Taanith   10, 231
Megillath Yuhasin   57
Meir, Rabbi   286
Mekhilta de-Rabbi Ishmael   243, 278
Melchizedek   94, 106, 326, 402, 405-8, 453, 457; miraculous birth of 94, 405-8; assumption to
        heaven 407; priest-king 165, 458, 521; eschatological judge 541; Milki-Sedeq 521;
        Melchi-ra, Melchi-resha, *see* Demons; Melchizedek texts 439, 458
Melchizedek (Gnostic)   *457-8*
Melchizedek (Qumran)   364, 390, 402, 408, 508
Melito of Sardes   287, 301; *Easter Homily* 564-5
Menahem (Manaemus) the Essene   223, 543
Menahem the Galilean   26
Menander, Wisdom of   314
Menelaus   8-9, 179
Menippus of Gadara   *Nekyia,* epistles   329
Merkabah mysticism   268, 353, 273, 417, 466, 565; rabbinic merkabah traditions 525; Gnostic
        merkabah 466; Merkabah mystical books 114, 417-8, 430, 433, 436
Messiah   298, 335, 337-9, 341, 366-7, 495, 538-41; Davidic Messiah 366, 402, 413-4, 518, 520-1,
        524, 539-40, 570, 574; Plant of David 520; priestly Messiah 338, 518, 521, 524, 529, 540,
        570; dual messiahship 339-41, 344, 495, 518, 540; Messiah from Judah 341; Messiah of
        Aaron and Israel 339-40, 539; Messiah of Aaron 541; Messiah of Israel 518, 524, 529,
        541

689

Narrative literature   XX, XXI, 1, 33, 54, 64, 80, 89, 98, 110, 118, 121, 123, 130, 140, 143, 149,
    157, 194, 239, 326-30, 346, 349, 415, 420; narrative framework 326-8, 393, 583; narrative
    sections in Test. 12 Patr. 333-4; *narratio* 183; *see* Fiction, Historiography
Nathan, Rabbi   286
Nebuchadnezzar   36, 37, 46-8, 50, 55, 57, 75, 140, 145-6, 491, 494, 542, 544-5, 553, 555;
    conquest of Jerusalem 72, 74; royal encyclical of 581
Neferrohu, Visions of (Egyptian)   361-2
Nehemiah   2, 75, 158-60, 297; legend of Nehemiah's fire 182; speech of 219
Nero   27, 178, 186-7, 194, 200, 205, 216; legend of Nero's return 362, 364, 371-2, 377; Poppaea,
    Nero's consort 186; death of 27
Nerva   228
New Jerusalem, Description of (Qumran)   385, 387, 395, 425, 488, *531-2*
Nicanor (general of Demetrius I)   10, 51, 102, 176-81, 572-3
Nicephorus   *Stichometry*   345, 419
Nicodemus, Gospel of   117
Nicolaus of Damascus   16, 170, 193, 212-5, 219-20, 227, 262
Nikotheos   450, 447; apocalypses of 450
Noah   89-95, 152, 237-8, 240, 243, 306, 377-8, 402-8, 412, 431, 446, 459, 464, 468; Noachic
    traditions 89, 110, 406; Noachic stories 95, 96; conception, birth and naming of 93, 104,
    106, 234, 405; wisdom guided Noah 310; burning of the Ark 468; Noah's brother Nir
    407-8. *See also* Norea
Noah, Book of (Qumran)   94, 398, 402, 405-6, 425
Norea   446, 448, 464, 465; birth of 468; the Archons' lust for Norea 464, 469
Norea, Apocalypse of. See Archons, Hypostasis of
Norea, Book of (Gnostic)   446, 448, 465. *See also* Origin of the World, On the
Norea, Thought of (Gnostic)   448, 465, 467, 469, 477
Novel   6, 76, 105, 166, 235
Numa   230
Numbers   107, 239, 241

Obadiah (prophet)   59
Ocellus   256
Octavian   19
Oniads   214, 372, 376; Oniad Temple 160, 367
Onias II   6
Onias III   7, 179, 181, 544-5
Onias IV   183, 367
Oracle   25, 122, 124, *357-81*, 421f., 439; oracular literature 25, 408; The False Oracle 55
Oracle of the Lamb to Bocchoris   362, 422
Oral Tradition   60, 64, 95, 101, 115, 212, 226, 257-8, 332, 479, 489; Oral Law 23-4, 258
Origen   30, 171, 274, 280, 285, 313, 345-6, 410, 421
Origin of the World, On the (Gnostic)   446, 448-9, 455-6, 459, 464-7, 478
Orpheus   165, 561; Orphic works 275-6, 370
Orpheus, Testament of   329

Pacorus   353
Palaea (Greek)   345
Panaetius   256
Panegyric   120, 235, 238
Parable   48, 70, 283, 319, 323; parable of Nathan 283
Paradise   90, 115, 260, 294, 338, 449
Parchor, Expositions of the Prophet (Gnostic)   447
Parenesis   41, 44, 60, 102, 285, 342, 344, 419; two ways parenesis 41; testamentary parenesis 41